FOURTH CANADIAN EDITION

Cost Accounting

A MANAGERIAL EMPHASIS

FOURTH CANADIAN EDITION

Cost Accounting

A MANAGERIAL EMPHASIS

Charles T. Horngren
Stanford University

George Foster
Stanford University

Srikant M. Datar
Stanford University

Howard D. Teall
Wilfrid Laurier University

Maureen P. Gowing
University of Windsor

PEARSON
Prentice
Hall

Toronto

Library and Archives Canada Cataloguing in Publication

Cost accounting (Scarborough, Ont.)
    Cost accounting: a managerial approach / Charles T. Horngren . . . [et al.]. —
Canadian ed.

Issues called 2nd ed.– have subtitle: a managerial emphasis.
Triennial.
1st ed.–
ISSN: 1491-8773
ISBN-13: 978-0-13-197190-5 (4th edition)
ISBN-10: 0-13-197190-5 (4th edition)

1. Cost accounting.   2. Costs, Industrial.   I. Horngren, Charles T., 1926–   II. Title.

HF5686.C8C67   657'.42   C99-304569-3

ISBN-10: 0-13-197190-5
ISBN-13: 978-0-13-197190-5

Editor-in-Chief, Business & Economics: Gary Bennett
Executive Acquisitions Editor: Samantha Scully
Executive Marketing Manager: Cas Shields
Senior Developmental Editor: Madhu Ranadive
Production Editor: Jen Handel
Copy Editor: Shirley Corriveau
Proofreader: Valerie Adams
Production Coordinator: Andrea Falkenberg
Page Layout: Integra
Permissions and Photo Research: Amanda McCormick
Art Director: Julia Hall
Interior Design: Miguel Acevedo
Cover Design: David Cheung
Cover Image: Getty Images

  2 3 4 5   11 10 09 08 07

Printed and bound in the United States of America.

This book is dedicated to the memory
of Howard Teall—a great teacher, author, and friend.

Brief Contents

Contents

3

COST-VOLUME-PROFIT ANALYSIS   69

4

JOB COSTING   111

9

INCOME EFFECTS OF ALTERNATIVE INVENTORY COSTING METHODS   323

PART THREE

COST INFORMATION FOR DECISIONS

10

DETERMINING HOW COSTS BEHAVE   365

13

STRATEGY, BALANCED SCORECARD, AND STRATEGIC PROFITABILITY ANALYSIS 513

PART FOUR
COST ALLOCATION AND REVENUES

14

COST ALLOCATION 553

15

COST ALLOCATION: JOINT PRODUCTS AND BYPRODUCTS   592

16

REVENUES, SALES VARIANCES, AND CUSTOMER PROFITABILITY ANALYSIS   625

17
PROCESS COSTING   667

PART FIVE
QUALITY AND JIT

18
SPOILAGE, REWORK, AND SCRAP   709

PART SEVEN
MANAGEMENT CONTROL SYSTEMS

23

MANAGEMENT CONTROL SYSTEMS, TRANSFER PRICING, AND MULTINATIONAL CONSIDERATIONS   882

24

PERFORMANCE MEASUREMENT, COMPENSATION, AND MULTINATIONAL CONSIDERATIONS   918

Preface

In the for-profit domain, business managers must accept responsibility for making important, ethical decisions that respect social values and maximize profit. Reasonable estimates of quantitative financial and non-financial data are an elegant, effective, and efficient way to communicate information about any business process. Quantitative reports are the language of business. This information is vital to the survival of companies whether they compete in a regulated (e.g., milk production and sale) or free (e.g., automobile production and sale) market. Each phase of management from planning product and service design through to delivery and customer service, requires quantitative data used to organize, monitor, and control actions. The goal is to improve the probability that actual social and business results met or exceed expectations.

Students face several learning challenges as they develop the skills required to more accurately estimate costs, profitable prices, inventory valuation, and return on investments in long-term projects. By surmounting these challenges, they will be able both to produce more accurate estimates, and to understand that these estimates are often used as future performance thresholds to which managers are held accountable. This text will support instructors as students learn how to apply their understanding of these estimation techniques to explain the causes of performance shortfalls. Students will also grasp how the choice of costing techniques affects amounts reported on the income statement, cash flow, and balance sheet.

Similar to financial accounting, there are different techniques of estimation appropriate to different costing, pricing, and valuation situations and this is the central theme of the text. The difference from financial accounting is that no formal standards constrain managers' choices; however, ultimately, financial failure will claim those who make inappropriate choices and consistently act on inappropriate estimates. The text presents a comprehensive set of techniques but emphasizes that students should never lose sight of the objective, which is to provide the most accurate information possible upon which to make ethical, profitable, and socially responsible management decisions.

HALLMARK FEATURES

The first thirteen chapters are the basis of a one-semester course that follows immediately after an introductory course in financial accounting. There is ample material in the remaining chapters to sustain either a two-term course or another one-term advanced topics course. Reviewers continue to praise the hallmark features of this text:

◆ Balanced emphasis on both the preparation and use of cost information through extensive use of real-world examples
◆ Excellent integration of modern methods of data collection and analysis
◆ Clarity in the logic used to teach different cost estimation techniques
◆ Flexibility in sequencing the order of topics taught
◆ Excellent quantity, quality, and scope of assignment material

This text organizes the presentation of topics in a modular way that gives instructors the independence to teach the topics in a *sequence customized to their students' needs*. For example, Exhibit 2-7 of Chapter 2 presents the heart of the explanation of how choosing different cost allocation methods in different manufacturing contexts affects the income statement and balance sheet. Once students understand this content, instructors can move on to a simple application where there is only one cost pool, the material in Chapter 17 on process costing. The format of Exhibit 2-7 is used again in Chapter 17 to link cost allocation in the context of process costing with its objectives—the estimate of cost of goods sold on the income statement, and the valuation of inventory on the balance sheet. Instructors could decide to follow Chapter 2 with an exploration of improved accuracy of cost estimation and pricing arrived at by changing from one cost object to another and delve into the contrast of job-order and activity-based costing (Chapters 4 and 5). Others may prefer teaching in the order presented in the text. The framework of Exhibit 2–7 is also an excellent template to introduce line-by-line budgeting (Chapter 6), variance analyses (Chapters 7, 8 and 16), and inventory valuation (Chapters 6–9).

MAJOR CHANGES IN CONTENT

Throughout production of the fourth Canadian edition, knowledgeable critics scrutinized the content of each chapter, which contributed to the excellence of this text. Material has been added to broaden the scope of qualitative and regulatory considerations and strengthen the coverage of how important these factors are to improving ethical, profitable management decisions. Major changes include the following:

◆ New Focus on Values and Behaviours feature highlights the importance of ethics in the selection of an appropriate estimation method.

◆ New Canadian examples illustrate that costing techniques can be applied appropriately in both regulated and free markets.

◆ New expanded discussions of current Canadian tax regulations and their effects on selecting an appropriate estimation method illustrate how important it is for managers of national and multinational companies to comply.

◆ New opening vignettes illustrate the relevance of each chapter's content in a real-life Canadian company or multinational subsidiary, e.g., Bombardier, DaimlerChrysler, Gildan Activewear, and Magna International Inc.

◆ New extended and revised material for Chapter 10 clarifies how statistical techniques such as time-series and linear regression analyses provide managers with powerful tools to select appropriate estimation and valuation methods.

◆ New spreadsheet format and revised content for numerical examples clarify concise step-by step explanations of estimation techniques.

◆ New and revised content for all assignment material and solutions engage students in practical applications of the chapter's content.

ASSIGNMENT MATERIAL

The fourth Canadian edition tightly links new chapter content to assignment material, a precedent set in previous editions. Assignment material presents increasing levels of difficulty from less difficult questions and exercises to more difficult problems and collaborative learning problems. *Questions* test how well students understand key terms and content, while *Exercises* are short, structured calculations to test the development of basic skills. *Problems* present students with a more difficult challenge to develop their ability to assess alternatives and make the most appropriate choice among techniques of estimation. The *Collaborative Learning Problem* ending each chapter's assignment material requires students to gather information and critically reflect on a specific issue or situation. Each chapter's assignment material also contains a relevant question related to either ethics, social responsibility, or both.

Content that Motivates: Real Business Examples

Real-world vignettes report how companies apply techniques and deal with challenges presented in each chapter to engage students actively with the material. Each chapter begins with vignette about a familiar North-American company, which, when coupled with the other pedagogical features, encourages critical reflection on actual practices. Companies that are the source of vignettes include:

Canadian companies:

Buckland & Taylor Ltd. Independent Engineers	Chapter 4
Inco.	Chapter 8
Bombardier	Chapter 10
Gildan Activewear	Chapter 11
IPSCO Inc.	Chapter 12
Bell Canada	Chapter 14
Highliner Foods	Chapter 17
Magna International Inc.	Chapter 18
Stantec Engineering	Chapter 21
Intrawest Corporation	Chapter 22
Canadian oil and gas exploration consortium: Hibernia	Chapter 15

Canadian subsidiaries of multinational companies:

GlaxoSmithKline	Chapter 1
DaimlerChrysler	Chapter 2
Ford	Chapter 3

As well as familiar US companies:

Dell Computer	Chapter 5
Fairmont Hotels and Resorts, Chateau Lake Louise	Chapter 6
McDonald's	Chapter 13
Imperial Oil	Chapter 9
Challenger Freight	Chapter 20
Sheraton Hotels	Chapter 24

Focus on Values and Behaviours Feature. Managers face difficult ethical and behavioural challenges throughout the decision-making process. This new pedagogical content, based on real examples, explores behavioural and ethical issues by presenting the consequences of both appropriate and inappropriate management decisions. This material responds to the public's increased expectations of managers to make ethical, socially responsible decisions and avoid more high-profile scandals like those endured by Xerox Corp., Livent, Cinar, and YBM Magnex. Topics include the following:

Topic	Company	Page
Working in cross-functional teams as business partners of managers	Johnson & Johnson	258
	Toyota	481
Promoting fact-based analysis and making tough-minded critical judgments without being adversarial	Cisco Systems	443
	Nortel	521
	Fidelity Investments	644
	Bridgestone/Firestone	747
Communicating clearly, openly and candidly	Starbucks	258
	Boeing	378
	Petro-Canada	605
	El Paso Corp	791
	Motorola	903

(Continued)

Note: Many other chapters address behavioural issues such as building a culture for learning and support and tradeoffs between setting attainable versus ideal standards (Chapter 7), effect of joint-cost allocations on performance measurement and managerial behaviour (Chapter 15), effect of management control and transfer pricing on manager's behaviour (Chapter 23) and the role of organization culture, values and intrinsic motivation (Chapter 24).

Concepts in Action Feature. Found in most chapters, this pedagogical content reinforces the user balance of this text. By covering diverse industries and topics ranging from how to debottleneck an Internet process to target pricing at IKEA, students will see how estimation techniques are applied in practice. Topics and management issues include the following:

Global Surveys of Company Practice Feature.   Again, this feature informs students about how widespread is the managerial use of cost estimation, pricing, and inventory valuation practices. Examples of multinational companies in industries including electronics, retailing, financial services, and manufacturing give students ample evidence that what they are learning is widely practiced across the globe. Examples include the following:

Topic		Chapter
Purposes of distinguishing between variable and fixed costs	US book retailing industry	2
Cost -allocation bases for manufacturing overhead	UK and US defense industry	4
Varying interest in activity-based costing	Canadian financial services ATM delivery	5
Budget practices around the globe	Australia, Holland, Japan, UK, US	6
The widespread use of standard costs	Ireland, Japan, Sweden, UK, and US	7
Company use of variable costing	Australia, Canada, Japan, Sweden, UK, and US	9
Differences in pricing practices and cost management methods	Australia, Ireland, Japan, UK and US	12
Allocation of support department costs	Australia, Japan, and UK	14
Cost allocation methods	Australia, Japan, and UK	15
Customer profitability analysis attracts increasing attention	Australia, Japan, and US	16
International comparison of capital budgeting methods	Australia, Canada, Ireland, Japan, Poland, Scotland, South Korea, UK and US	21
Risk adjustment methods in capital budgeting	Australia, Canada, Poland, Taiwan, UK, and US	22
Domestic and Multinational transfer-pricing practices	Australia, Canada, India, Japan, New Zealand, UK, and US	23
Nonfinancial measures of performance	Australia, Ireland, Japan, UK, and US	24

TEACHING AND LEARNING SUPPORT

Supplements available to students include the following:

◆ *Student Solutions Manual.* Designed to enable students to monitor their progress, this supplement contains fully worked-out solutions for all of the even-numbered questions, exercises, and problems in the textbook. This supplement may be purchased with the instructor's permission. 0-13-197224-3

◆ *Companion Website.* Both instructors and students will be sure to benefit from the unparalleled Internet support offered by Pearson Education Canada's accounting websites. Our online study guide offers students the perfect platform for quick review and study. Multiple choice, true/false, and matching questions are offered for each chapter, along with instant feedback and page references to the text to facilitate further review. Every chapter also contains one exercise (with suggested answer) that covers a key concept from that chapter. The Companion Website also includes Destinations (based on the chapter-specific Weblinks in the margins of the textbook). Go to www.pearsoned.ca/horngren and explore!

Supplements available to instructors include the following:

◆ *Instructor's Resource CD-ROM.* This CD-ROM contains the Pearson TestGen and PowerPoint Lecture slides. Also included on the CD are electronic versions of the *Instructor's Solutions Manual* and *Instructor's Resource Manual* in Word and PDF format. This makes it extremely easy for faculty to customize supplements, access supplements on computer, and transport a large supplement package from home, to class, to office. 0-13-239019-1

  ❐ *Instructor's Solutions Manual:* In addition to fully worked-out solutions for every question, exercise, and problem in the text, the *Instructor's Solutions*

Manual also provides suggested alternative chapter sequences and categorization of assignment material. The solutions will be available in both PDF and Word formats.

❒ *Pearson TestGen:* Utilizing our new TestGen program, the computerized test bank for *Cost Accounting*, Fourth Canadian Edition, offers a comprehensive suite of tools for testing and assessment. TestGen allows educators to easily create and distribute tests for their courses, either by printing and distributing through traditional methods or by online delivery via a Local Area Network (LAN) server. Once you have opened TestGen, you'll advance effortlessly through a series of folders allowing you to quickly access all available areas of the program. Also downloadable for instructors from a special password-protected site on the Pearson Canada online catalogue.

❒ *PowerPoint® Lecture Slides:* For each chapter of the text approximately 20 slides have been prepared in PowerPoint. The interactive presentation offers helpful graphics that illustrate key figures and concepts from the text, chapter outlines, and additional examples. These are also downloadable for instructors from a special password-protected site on the Pearson Canada online catalogue.

❒ *Instructor's Resource Manual with Cases* provides a chapter overview, outline, additional examples, alternative means of presenting topics, chapter quiz/ demonstration exercises with solutions, and suggested readings. The IRM will be available in both PDF and Word formats.

In addition to the support that continues to be provided to instructors and students, new Excel Labs have been added.

◆ *Instructors*—Instructors now can benefit from the key tables and exhibits reproduced from the content of each chapter in Excel format. These worksheets contain the logic used to produce each key table. Instructors can use the worksheets as a pedagogical resource to explain cost estimation, pricing, and valuation techniques and by changing key inputs can instantly illustrate their effects. These worksheets have proven their value as a way to present examination material, solutions, and marking keys in standardized format for large classes.

◆ *Students*—Excel templates for selected end-of-chapter exercises and problems are available on the Companion Website. Students may use these templates to hone their Excel skills should they choose to do so.

ACKNOWLEDGMENTS TO THE FOURTH CANADIAN EDITION

I would like to acknowledge the excellent assistance I have received from many people. This fourth Canadian edition is based upon the twelfth US edition by Charles T. Horngren, George Foster, and Srikant M. Datar. I thank them for their willingness to share their work with me. Their knowledge and experience have significantly contributed to this book.

I also extend my sincere appreciation to my colleagues at Pearson Education Canada who have supported me throughout the production of this book—To Samantha Scully, the Acquisitions Editor; Madhu Ranadive, the Developmental Editor; Jennifer Handel, the Production Editor; Shirley Corriveau, the Copy Editor; and Valerie Adams, the Proofreader. And a special thanks to Jeff Power, Lawrence Tenenbaum, and Michelle Hodgson for their careful technical reviews.

I am grateful to the Odette School of Business at the University of Windsor for providing an environment that supports the development of teaching materials.

My appreciation goes as well to the Certified Management Accountants Association of Canada and, in particular, to Deborah Clarke, the Southwestern Ontario Regional Director of Marketing and Communication. I express my appreciation as well to the Certified General Accountants Association of Canada and many other individuals, publishers, and companies for their generous permission to quote from their publications. A special thanks to Thomas Haddrath for his invaluable guidance on how to improve the presentation of tax issues in Chapter 22. Problems from the Certified Management Accountant examination are designated (CMA); problems from the Certified General Accountants Association examination are designated (CGA). These problems have been adapted to highlight specific points. I am also grateful to professors and individuals in the industry who contributed both chapter content and assignment material for this edition. I thank the reviewers for their patient, timely, and meticulous reviews that provided me with valuable insights and suggestions, especially:

Barbara Katz	Kwantlen University College
Audra Ong	University of Windsor
Andrews Oppong	Dalhousie University
John Parkinson	York University
Jeff Power	St. Mary's University
Randolph Robinson	British Columbia Institute of Technology
Harry Soltermann	Northern Alberta Institute of Technology
Lawrence Tenenbaum	McGill University
Oleg Tyan	Southern Alberta Institute of Technology

Most importantly, I would like to recognize the support of my husband, David, who also produced the revised assignment material and all the revised solutions. I dedicate this textbook to him.

Comments are most welcome.

Maureen P. Gowing

About the Authors

Charles T. Horngren is the Edmund W. Littlefield Professor of Accounting, Emeritus, at Stanford University. A Graduate of Marquette University, he received his MBA from Harvard University and his Ph.D. from the University of Chicago. He is also the recipient of honorary doctorates from Marquette University and DePaul University.

A Certified Public Accountant, Horngren served on the Accounting Principles Board for six years, the Financial Accounting Standards Board Advisory Council for five years, and the Council of the American Institute of Certified Public Accountants for three years. For six years, he served as a trustee of the Financial Accounting Foundation, which oversees the Financial Accounting Standards Board and the Government Accounting Standards Board.

Horngren is a member of the Accounting Hall of Fame.

A member of the American Accounting Association, he has been its President and its Director of Research. He received its first annual Outstanding Accounting Educator Award.

The California Certified Public Accounts Foundation gave Horngren its Faculty Excellence Award and its Distinguished Professor Award. He is the first person to have received both awards.

The American Institute of Certified Public Accountants presented its first Outstanding Educator Award to Horngren.

Horngren was named Accountant of the Year, Education, by the national professional accounting fraternity, Beta Alpha Psi.

Professor Horngren is also a member of the Institute of Management Accountants, from whom he received its Distinguished Service Award. He was also a member of the Institutes' Board of Regents, which administers the Certified Management Accountant examinations.

Horngren is the author of other accounting books published by Prentice Hall: *Introduction to Management Accounting*, 13th ed. (2005, with Sundem and Stratton); *Introduction to Financial Accounting*, 9th ed. (2005, with Sundem and Elliott); *Accounting*, 5th ed. (2005, with Harrison and Bamber); and *Financial Accounting*, 6th ed. (2005, with Harrison).

Horngren is the Consulting Editor for the Charles T. Horngren Series in Accounting.

George Foster is the Paul L. and Phyllis Wattis Professor of Management at Stanford University. He graduated with a university medal from the University of Sydney and has a Ph.D. from Stanford University. He has been awarded honorary doctorates from the University of Ghent, Belgium, and from the University of Vaasa, Finland. He has received the Outstanding Educator Award from the American Accounting Association.

Foster has received the Distinguished Teaching Award at Stanford University and the Faculty Excellence Award from the California Society of Certified Public Accountants. He has been a Visiting Professor to Mexico for the American Accounting Association.

Research awards Foster has received include the Competitive Manuscript Competition Award of the American Accounting Association, the Notable Contribution to Accounting Literature Award of the American Institute of Certified Public Accountants, and the Citation for Meritorious Contribution to Accounting Literature Award of the Australian Society of Accountants.

He is the author of *Financial Statement Analysis*, published by Prentice Hall. He is co-author of *Activity-Based Management Consortium Study (APQC and CAM-I)* and *Marketing, Cost Management and Management Accounting (CAM-I)*. He is also co-author of two monographs published by the American Accounting Association: *Security Analyst Multi-Year Earnings Forecasts and The Capital Market and Market Microstructure* and *Capital Market Information Content Research*. Journals publishing his articles include *Abacus, The Accounting Review, Harvard Business Review, Journal of Accounting and Economics, Journal of Accounting Research, Journal of Cost Management, Journal of Management Accounting Research, Management Accounting*, and *Review of Accounting Studies*.

Foster works actively with many companies, including Apple Computer, ARCO, BHP, Digital Equipment Corp., Exxon, Frito-Lay Corp., Hewlett-Packard, McDonalds Corp., Octel Communications, PepsiCo, Santa Fe Corp., and Wells Fargo. He also has worked closely with Computer Aided Manufacturing-International (CAM-I) in the development of a framework for modern cost management practices. Foster has presented seminars on new developments in cost accounting in North and South America, Asia, Australia, and Europe.

Srikant M. Datar is the Arthur Lowes Dickinson Professor of Business Administration at Harvard University. A graduate with distinction from the University of Bombay, he received gold medals upon graduation from the Indian Institute of Management, Ahmedabad, and the Institute of Cost and Works Accountants of India. A Chartered Accountant, he holds two masters degrees and a Ph.D. from Stanford University.

Cited by his students as a dedicated and innovative teacher, Datar received the George Leland Bach Award for Excellence in the Classroom at Carnegie Mellon University and the Distinguished Teaching Award at Stanford University.

Datar has published his research in various journals, including *The Accounting Review, Contemporary Accounting Research, Journal of Accounting, Auditing and Finance, Journal of Accounting and Economics, Journal of Accounting Research*, and *Management Science*. He has also served on the editorial board of several journals and presented his research to corporate executives and academic audiences in North America, South America, Asia, Africa, and Europe.

Datar is a member of the Board of Directors of Novartis A. G. and has worked with many organizations, including Apple Computer, AT&T, Boeing, British Columbia Telecommunications, The Cooperative Bank, Du Pont, Ford, General Motors, Hewlett-Packard, Kodak, Mellon Bank, PepsiCo, Solectron, Store 24, Stryker, TRW, Visa, and the World Bank. He is a member of the American Accounting Association and the Institute of Management Accountants.

Howard D. Teall was a Professor in the School of Business and Economics at Wilfrid Laurier University, where he previously held the positions of Acting Dean, Associate Dean of Business, and Accounting Area Head. He received HBA, MBA, and Ph.D. degrees from the Ivey School of Business Administration at the University of Western Ontario. He obtained a CA designation while employed with Price Waterhouse and was awarded an FCA by the Institute of Chartered Accountants of Ontario.

Previous university positions were held at the Graduate School of Business Marseille France, the Helsinki School of Economics and Business Administration, INSEAD (The European Institute of Business Administration), The International University of Japan, and the University of Western Ontario.

Professor Teall published articles in both financial and managerial fields of accounting. He co-authored, with Charles Horngren, Gary Sundem, and William Stratton, *Management Accounting*, Fourth Canadian Edition; with Charles Horngren, George Foster, and Srikant Datar, *Cost Accounting: A Managerial Emphasis*, Third Canadian Edition; and with Charles Horngren, Gary Sundem, and John Elliott, *Introduction to Financial Accounting*, Third Canadian Edition.

Professor Teall provided management training programs and consulting for IBM Canada Ltd., Bayer Inc., Equifax Canada, Rockwell Automation Canada Ltd., Tiger Brand Knitting Factory Co., Woodbridge Limited, Lear Corporation Canada Ltd., Centra Gas Corporation, Challenger Motor Freight Inc., Ontario Hydro,

B.F. Goodrich Canada Limited, Petro-Canada, General Motors of Canada Limited, General Motors Corporation, the Federal Business Development Bank, the Canadian Department of Industry, Science and Technology Canada, The Liquor Control Board of Ontario, The Banff Centre for Management, Polysar Rubber Corporation, Royal Bank of Trinidad and Tobago, and professional qualification programs for PricewaterhouseCoopers, Deloitte & Touche, the Chartered Accountants Students' Association of Ontario, the Institute of Chartered Accountants of Ontario, the Atlantic Provinces Association of Chartered Accountants, and CMA Canada. Professor Howard Teall passed away on May 13, 2004.

Maureen P. Gowing is an Assistant Professor in the Odette School of Business at the University of Windsor. Prior to being appointed at Odette, she worked as an assistant professor at the John Molson School of Business at Concordia University. She received her BA (psychology) from Carleton University, her MBA from the University of Toronto, and her Ph.D. from Queen's University. Dr. Gowing received the Award of Excellence from the Administrative Sciences Association of Canada for her doctoral dissertation.

She has co-authored many journal articles and published in the *Journal of Business Ethics* and the *Canadian Journal of Higher Education*, among others. In addition to co-authoring, with Charles Horngren, George Foster, Srikant Datar, and Howard Teal, *Cost Accounting: A Managerial Emphasis*, Fourth Canadian Edition, Dr. Gowing has also co-authored an introductory financial accounting textbook with Dr. George Kanaan.

Dr. Gowing obtained both her BA and MBA while working full time. She has worked as a financial analyst with an upstream oil exploration and development company that was controlled by Noranda, and a boutique Canadian investment banker, Pemberton Securities Ltd., now part of the Royal Bank. Her research portfolio of companies newly listed on the Toronto Stock Exchange included Westar, Ballard Technologies, and QLT Pharmaceuticals. She has also consulted for Discovery Foundation of British Columbia, and just prior to her return to university to obtain her Ph.D, she did forensic analysis for the Vancouver Stock Exchange.

A Great Way to Learn and Instruct Online

The Pearson Education Canada Companion Website is easy to navigate and is organized to correspond to the chapters in this textbook. Whether you are a student in the classroom or a distance learner you will discover helpful resources for in-depth study and research that empower you in your quest for greater knowledge and maximize your potential for success in the course.

Companion Website

[www.pearsoned.ca/horngren]

PEARSON Prentice Hall

Jump to...   http://www.pearsoned.ca/horngren | Home | Search | Help | Profile   Companion Website

Home >

Cost Accounting: A Managerial Emphasis, Fourth Canadian Edition, by Horngren, Foster, Datar, Teall, and Gowing

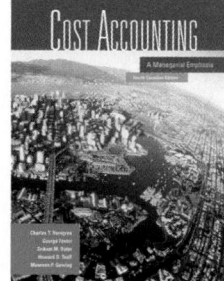

Student Resources

The modules in this section provide students with tools for learning course material. These modules include:

- Learning Objectives
- Chapter Overviews
- Self-Test Quizzes, including Multiple-Choice, True and False, and Matching questions
- Exercises
- Case Studies
- Glossary

In the quiz modules students can send answers to the grader and receive instant feedback on their progress through the Results Reporter. Coaching comments and references to the textbook may be available to ensure that students take advantage of all available resources to enhance their learning experience.

Instructor Resources

A link to this book on the Pearson Education Canada online catalogue (vig.pearsoned.ca) provides instructors with additional teaching tools. Downloadable PowerPoint Presentations and an Instructor's Manual are just some of the materials that may be available. The catalogue is password protected. To get a password, simply contact your Pearson Education Canada Representative or contact Faculty Sales and Services at 1-800-850-5813.

In today's complex business environment, management accountants play a key role as part of the organization's management team. With an ability to make business decisions that focus on long-term profitability, the management accountant is well suited for senior management roles.

As the vice-president at GlaxoSmithKline (GSK), Diane Daniel (CMA) oversees five challenging functions. Not only is she responsible for the fiscal management of the business but also for ensuring the supply of products from GSK's manufacturers reaches retail customers, at a competitive price.

LEARNING OBJECTIVES

After studying this chapter, you should be able to

1. Describe how cost accounting supports management accounting and financial accounting
2. Understand how management accountants affect strategic decisions
3. Describe the set of business functions in the value chain
4. Identify the dimensions of performance that customers are expecting of companies
5. Distinguish between the planning and control decisions of managers
6. Distinguish among the problem-solving, scorekeeping, and attention-directing roles of management accountants
7. Describe three guidelines management accountants follow in supporting managers
8. Understand how management accounting fits into an organization's structure
9. Understand what professional ethics mean to management accountants

CHAPTER 1

The Accountant's Role in the Organization

Modern management accounting serves business managers needing information to make good decisions that result in growth and success for their companies. Students of management accounting gain insight into what management accountants do for an organization. Large domestic and multinational companies in Canada such as GlaxoSmithKline, Noranda Aluminum Inc., Rogers Communications Inc., Hewlett Packard (Canada) Co., and Kraft Foods employ senior executives who are professional CMAs.

This book focuses on the challenges of producing timely, relevant financial and nonfinancial information to assist managers as they make business decisions. These decisions are most difficult when little is known with certainty about future consequences. By applying appropriate techniques, management accountants produce information that helps clarify the nature of the problem and the scope of potential actions most likely to improve the situation. This information assists managers through all stages of product or service design, marketing, delivery, and customer service. Chapter 1 describes the role of management accountants in the process of management decision making.

MANAGEMENT ACCOUNTING, FINANCIAL ACCOUNTING, AND COST ACCOUNTING

OBJECTIVE 1

Describe how cost accounting supports management accounting and financial accounting

Accounting systems take economic events and business transactions that have occurred and process these data into information helpful to users such as sales representatives, production supervisors, and senior managers. Processing any economic transaction entails collecting, categorizing, summarizing, and analyzing data for a specified time period. For example, costs are collected by cost categories (materials, labour, and shipping); summarized to determine total costs by month, quarter, or one year; and analyzed to evaluate how costs have changed relative to revenues, say, from one period to the next. Accounting systems provide information such as financial statements (the income statement, balance sheet, and statement of cash flows) and performance reports (such as the cost of operating a plant or providing a service). Managers use accounting information (a) to administer each of the activity or functional areas for which they are responsible and (b) to coordinate those activities or functions within the framework of the organization as a whole. This book focuses on the management accountant's role in these tasks.

Managers often require the information from an accounting system to be presented or reported differently because the decisions they must make vary. Consider, for example, sales order information. A sales manager needs the total dollar amount of sales to determine the commissions to be paid. A distribution manager needs the sales order quantities by geographic region and customer-requested delivery dates to ensure timely deliveries. A manufacturing manager needs the quantities of various products and their desired delivery dates to schedule production. An ideal database—sometimes called a data warehouse or infobarn—consists of detailed bits of information that can be used for multiple purposes. For example, the sales order database will contain detailed information about product, quantity ordered, selling price, and delivery (place and date) for each sales order. The data warehouse stores information in a way that allows managers to access exactly what they need. Many companies are building their own Enterprise Resource Planning (ERP) systems, single databases to collect data and feed it into applications that support each business activity, such as purchasing, production, distribution, sales, and customer service.

Management accounting and financial accounting have different goals. **Management accounting** focuses on reporting to internal parties. It measures and reports financial and nonfinancial information in a format that is most useful for managers to make decisions which achieve specified goals of an organization. Managers use this information to choose, communicate, and implement strategy. They also use management accounting information to coordinate product design, production, and marketing decisions.

Financial accounting focuses on reporting to external parties in a standardized format. It measures and records business transactions to provide financial statements that are based on generally accepted accounting principles (GAAP). Managers are responsible for the financial statements issued to investors, government regulators, and other parties outside the organization. Executive compensation is often directly affected by the net income reported in these financial statements. It is easy to see that managers are interested in both management accounting and financial accounting. Exhibit 1-1 summarizes the major differences between management accounting and financial accounting.

Cost accounting measures and reports financial and nonfinancial information relating to the cost of either acquiring or utilizing resources in an organization. It provides information useful for both management and financial accounting. For example, calculating the cost of a product is a cost accounting function that responds to financial accounting's inventory-valuation needs and management accounting's decision-making needs such as choosing the most profitable products to offer. Modern cost accounting takes the perspective that collecting cost information is a function of the management decisions being made. Thus, the distinction between management accounting and cost accounting is not so clear-cut, and we often use these terms interchangeably in the book.

Management accounting. Measures and reports financial information and other types of information to assist managers in fulfilling the goals of the organization.

Financial accounting. Focuses on external reporting that is guided by generally accepted accounting principles.

Cost accounting. Measures and reports financial and other information related to the organization's acquisition or consumption of resources; it provides information for both management accounting and financial accounting.

In financial accounting courses, the product costs used to calculate cost of goods sold (COGS) are given. Students of cost and management accounting learn and apply different techniques to estimate these product costs.

EXHIBIT 1-1
Major Differences Between Management Accounting and Financial Accounting

	Management Accounting	Financial Accounting
Purpose of information	Help managers make decisions to fulfill an organization's goals	Communicate organization's financial position to investors, banks, regulators, and other outside parties
Primary users	Managers of the organization	External users such as investors, banks, regulators, and suppliers
Focus and emphasis	Future-oriented (budget for 2008 prepared in 2007)	Past-oriented (reports on 2007 performance prepared in 2008)
Rules of measurement and reporting	Internal measures and reports do not have to follow GAAP but are based on cost-benefit analysis	Financial statements must be prepared in accordance with GAAP and be certified by external, independent auditors
Time span and type of reports	Varies from hourly information to 15 to 20 years, with financial and nonfinancial reports on products, departments, territories, and strategies	Annual and quarterly financial reports, primarily on the company as a whole, and presented as consolidated financial statements
Behavioural implications	Designed to influence the behaviour of managers and other employees	Primarily reports economic events but also influences behaviour because manager's compensation is often based on reported financial results

Unfortunately the term *cost management* has no uniform definition. We use **cost management** to describe the approaches and activities of managers who undertake both short and long-run planning and control decisions that lower the costs of products and services and increase value for customers. Examples include decisions regarding the amounts and kinds of materials being used, changes in plant processes, and changes in product designs. Information from accounting systems helps managers to manage costs, but the information and the accounting systems themselves are not cost management.

Cost management has a broad focus. It includes but is not confined to the continuous reduction of costs because the planning and control of costs is usually inextricably linked with revenue and profit planning. For example, to enhance revenues and profits, managers can decide to increase costs for advertising and product modifications. Other examples include programs that enhance customer satisfaction and quality, as well as programs that promote "blockbuster" new-product development. The examples illustrate that cost management is not practised in isolation. It's an integral part of general management strategies and their implementation.

Cost management. Actions undertaken by managers to satisfy customers while continually reducing and controlling costs.

STRATEGIC DECISIONS AND THE MANAGEMENT ACCOUNTANT

A company earns profit by attracting customers willing to pay more for the goods and services it offers than the costs to design and deliver them. A company succeeds by both creating value for customers and differentiating itself from its competitors. This is what strategy is all about. But a great strategy can be defeated by ineffective implementation. Management accountants provide input to aid in both developing and implementing strategy, as well as building resources and capabilities. To understand the management accountant's role, we must first understand the manager's tasks.

Strategy specifies how an organization accomplishes its objectives by matching its own capabilities with the opportunities in the marketplace. Strategy describes how a company will compete and the opportunities its employees should seek and pursue. Companies follow one of two broad strategies. Some companies, such as WestJet and Costco, compete on the basis of providing quality products or services at low prices. Others, such as RIM (developer of the BlackBerry wireless communicator) and QLT Inc. (a biopharmaceutical company), compete on their ability to offer unique, new products or services that are often priced higher than the products or services of competitors.

OBJECTIVE 2

Understand how management accountants affect strategic decisions

Strategy. Describes one of two ways organizations choose to compete in the long term. Managers may match the appropriate quality of goods or services to the price customers are willing to pay; or, managers may choose to innovate and produce unique products for which customers will pay a higher price.

Deciding between these strategies is a big part of what managers do. Management accountants work closely with managers in formulating strategy by providing information about the sources of competitive advantage. Examples include information about cost, productivity, or efficiency advantages of their company relative to competitors and the premium prices a company can charge relative to the costs of adding features that make its products or services distinctive. Management accountants also help formulate a strategy by answering questions such as:

◆ Who are our most important customers and how do we deliver value to them to retain their loyalty (CRM or customer relationship management)? How sensitive are their purchases to price, quality, and service?

◆ Who are our most important suppliers and how do we ensure timely access to appropriate quality and cost (SCM or supply-chain management)?

◆ What substitute products exist in the marketplace, and how do they differ from our product in terms of price and quality?

◆ What is our most critical resource—technology, production, or marketing? What demands will be made on this critical resource by the new strategic initiatives?

◆ Will adequate cash be available to fund the strategy, or will additional funds need to be raised?

Strategic management. Requires that managers coordinate cost reduction throughout the organization in order to provide the appropriate goods, with appropriate features, at the appropriate price to ensure the long-run profitability of the organization.

Strategic management often describes cost management that focuses on strategic issues such as these. Successful companies design strategies to respond to the opportunities and threats in the marketplace with appropriate resources and capabilities. Sometimes companies see opportunities and threats that require them to build capabilities. For example, after Amazon.com's success in selling books online, Chapters also developed capabilities to sell online.

At other times, companies use their existing capabilities to create new opportunities. For example in Toyota's computer-integrated manufacturing (CIM) plants, computers instruct robotic equipment directly to set up and complete tasks. Manufacturing labour in CIM plants is largely computer programming, engineering support, and machine maintenance. CIM technology enables plants to quickly make major design modifications, such as switching from manufacturing a two-door to a four-door car. In CIM plants, computers also monitor and directly control the manufacturing process to achieve high-quality output. Continuous monitoring and control enables reports of real-time information about process parameters (such as temperature and pressure), units produced, defects, and product costs. The best-designed strategies and the best-developed capabilities are useless, however, unless they are effectively executed.

THE MANAGEMENT ACCOUNTANT'S ROLE IN IMPLEMENTING STRATEGY

OBJECTIVE 3

Describe the set of business functions in the value chain

Managers implement strategy by translating it into action. As they build action plans, managers seek input from customers and evaluate and assess how competitors will react. They answer questions such as: Are the right executives in place to execute the plans? Do the executives have the necessary cash and human and physical resources to implement the plans? Should the company sell more products to existing customers or find new customers? What can go wrong? What contingency plans does the company have if things do go wrong? Questions such as these must be freely debated if managers are to create a good strategic plan and implement it effectively to create value for customers. Value is the usefulness a customer gains from a company's product or service. We now discuss how a company goes about creating this value.

Value and Supply-Chain Analysis

Value chain. The sequence of business functions in which customer usefulness is added to the products or services.

Value chain refers to the sequence of business functions in which customer usefulness is added to products or services. Exhibit 1-2 shows six business functions: research and development (R&D), design, production, marketing, distribution, and customer service. We illustrate these business functions using SONY Corporation's

EXHIBIT 1-2
The Value Chain of Business Functions

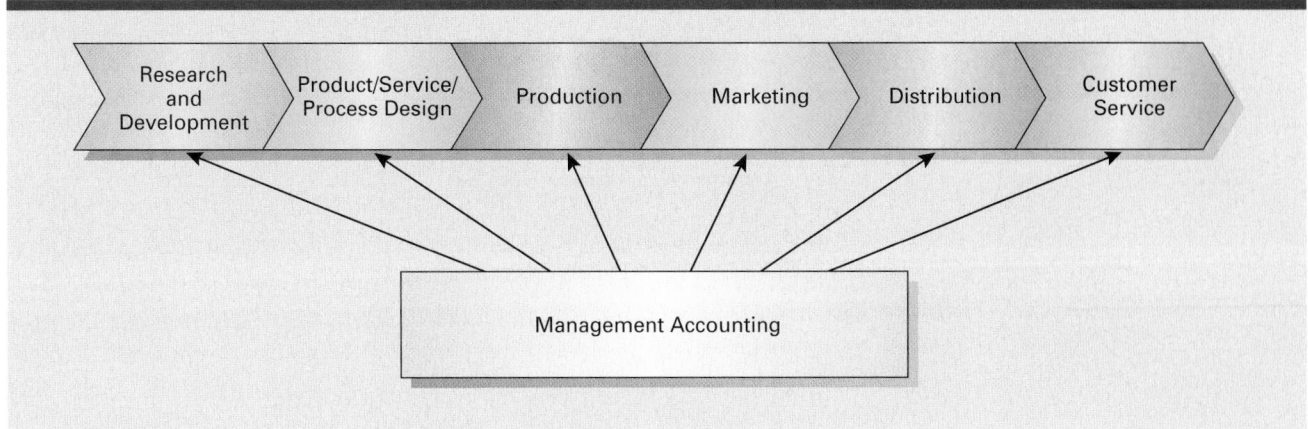

television division. Management accountants provide information managers need to make decisions in each of these six business functions:

- **Research and development**—Generating and experimenting with ideas related to new products, services, or processes. At SONY, this function includes research on alternative ways of television signal transmission (analogue, digital, high definition) and on the clarity of different shapes and portability of television screens.

- **Design of products, services, or processes**—Detailed planning and engineering of products, services, or processes. Design at SONY includes determining the number of component parts in a television set and the effect of alternative product designs on quality and manufacturing costs.

- **Production**—Acquiring, coordinating, and assembling resources to produce a product or deliver a service. Production of a SONY television set includes the acquisition and assembly of the electronic parts, the cabinet, and the packaging used for shipping.

- **Marketing**—Promoting and selling products or services to customers or prospective customers. SONY markets its televisions through trade shows, advertisements in newspapers and magazines, and on the Internet.

- **Distribution**—Delivering products or services to customers. Distribution for SONY includes shipping to retail outlets, catalogue vendors, direct sales via the Internet, and other channels through which customers purchase televisions.

- **Customer service**—Providing after-sale support to customers. SONY provides customer service on its televisions in the form of customer-help telephone lines, support on the Internet, and warranty repair work.

Each function in the value chain sequence is essential if SONY is to satisfy its customers and keep them satisfied (and loyal) over time. Customer relationship management (CRM) describes a strategy that integrates people and technology in all business functions to enhance relationships with customers, partners, and distributors. CRM initiatives use technology to coordinate research, design, and production activities necessary to put the product or service in the customer's hands as well as all customer-facing activities (marketing, sales calls, distribution, and customer support).

Exhibit 1-2 depicts the usual order in which different business-function activities physically occur. But it is inefficient and ineffective if managers always plan and manage activities by proceeding step-by-step through the value chain. Companies accelerate the development of new products if two or more individuals from different business functions of the value chain work concurrently as a team. For example, when production, marketing, distribution, and customer service managers discuss product design together they have the opportunity to make design choices that reduce total costs to the company instead of to only one business function.

> Understand the distinctions between research and design. Research is investigation and idea generation. Design turns research and ideas into reality. It encompasses prototype development and specifications of the manufacturing process.

> The value chain in Exhibit 1-2 could be expanded to highlight costs implicitly included in each business function. Examples include administrative costs and future cash outlays for environmental cleanup costs associated with actions of the current period.

> Accounting helps managers coordinate the business functions of the value chain—for example, by analyzing whether more money spent on R&D and design will reduce subsequent production and customer-service costs.

> Some companies subcontract one or more of the six business functions. For example, Nike subcontracts its production (manufacturing) function. Even with subcontracting, the challenge of coordinating all of the business functions remains.

EXHIBIT 1-3
Supply Chain for a Cola Bottling Company

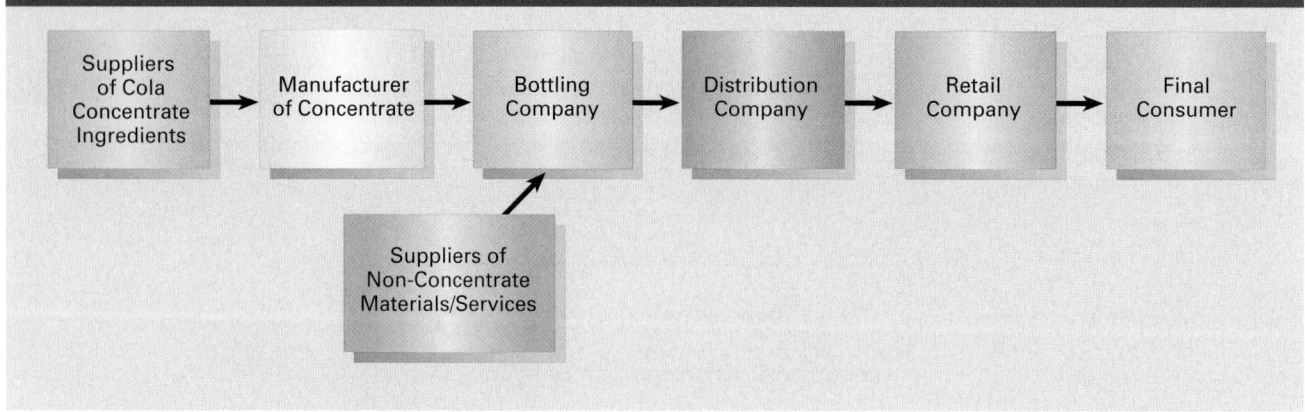

Supply-Chain Management (SCM)

Companies can also implement strategy, cut costs, and create value by improving the management of their supply chain.

The supply chain describes the flow of goods, services, and information from the initial sources of materials and services to the delivery of products to consumers regardless of whether those activities occur in the same organization or in other organizations. Consider the soft drinks Coke and Pepsi. Many companies play a role in bringing these products to consumers. Exhibit 1-3 presents an overview of the supply chain. Supply-chain management (SCM) emphasizes integrating and coordinating activities across all companies in the supply chain, as well as across each business function in an individual company's value chain to reduce costs and improve reliability. For example, both Coca-Cola Company and Pepsi Bottling Group contract with their suppliers (such as glass and can companies and sugar refiners) to frequently deliver small quantities of materials directly to the production floor to reduce materials-handling costs. To reduce inventory levels in the supply chain, Wal-Mart is asking its suppliers such as Coca-Cola to be responsible for and to manage inventory at both the Coca-Cola warehouse and Wal-Mart.

Key Success Factors

OBJECTIVE 4

Identify the dimensions of performance that customers are expecting of companies

Customers are demanding that companies use the value chain and supply chain to deliver ever-improving levels of performance regarding several (or even all) of the following:

- ◆ **Cost and efficiency**—Companies face continuous pressure to reduce the cost of the products or services they sell. Understanding the tasks or activities (such as setting up machines or distributing products) that cause costs is useful for calculating and managing the cost of products. To set cost-reduction targets, managers start by scanning the market to discover prices that customers are willing to pay for products or services. From this "target price," managers subtract the operating income they want to earn to arrive at the target cost. Managers strive to achieve the target cost by eliminating some activities (such as rework) and by reducing the costs of performing activities. They do so across all value-chain functions and over the entire life cycle of the product—from its initial R&D to customer support including products that are no longer offered. The pace of global competition has placed increasing pressure on companies to lower costs. North American companies now outsource not only their manufacturing labour but also customer service and computer technical support as well as software development to Taiwan, Mexico, and India.

- ◆ **Quality**—Customers expect high levels of quality management. Total quality management (TQM) is a management process undertaken to improve operations throughout the value chain to produce and deliver products and services that exceed the customers' expectations with zero or minimal defects and waste.

Toyota often "loans" its engineers to suppliers to help suppliers streamline their production processes. In return, Toyota expects to receive cost savings in the form of reduced prices.

Outsourcing production and service support to other countries and the accelerating pace of international trade agreements has led to the increasing importance of consistent quality and safety standards. The International Organization for Standardization (ISO) develops not only technical but also environmental and social standards. Companies worldwide can become accredited as ISO compliant to inform their customers and suppliers that the company meets global standards of quality. Management accountants evaluate the costs and revenue benefits of TQM initiatives, including ISO compliance.

◆ **Time**—Time has many components. *New-product development time* is the time to develop and bring new products to market. The increasing pace of technological innovation has led to shorter product life cycles and the need for companies to bring new products to market more rapidly.

    Customer-response time describes the speed at which an organization responds to customer requests. To increase customer satisfaction, organizations must complete activities faster and meet promised delivery dates reliably. Delays or bottlenecks occur when the work to be performed exceeds the available capacity. To increase output, managers need to increase the capacity of the bottleneck operation. The management accountant's role is to quantify the cost and benefits of relieving the bottleneck constraints.

◆ **Innovation**—A constant flow of innovative products or services is the basis for ongoing company success. Management accountants help managers evaluate alternative investment decisions and R&D decisions.

Management accountants help managers track performance of key success factors relative to the performance of competitors on the same factors. Tracking improvements competitors are making and implementing those which are appropriate leads to continuous improvement in the key business functions of the value chain. The best practice in industry is the benchmark. Benchmarking is the process of measuring the company's performance of the key success factors against the best levels of performance found in competing companies. These key factors differ across industries. For example, WestJet seeks improvement in the percentage of flights arriving and departing on time while Sympatico seeks to reduce Internet service interruptions and increase security.

At times, a company may have to make more-fundamental changes in its operations and restructure, often referred to as reengineering its processes to improve cost, quality, timeliness, or service. Management accountants provide the financial and nonfinancial information that helps managers make decisions about reengineering and continuous improvement. The Concepts in Action box on p. 8 describes how companies choose their e-business strategies to reduce costs, improve quality, innovate, and grow. However, successful strategy implementation requires more than value-chain and supply-chain analysis and execution of key success factors. Companies must also look to planning and control systems to help them to fully integrate, develop, and implement their strategies.

Budget. The quantitative expression of a plan of action and an aid to the coordination and implementation of the plan.

PLANNING AND CONTROL SYSTEMS

Is Magna's management control system better than Linamar's? Is Sleeman's better than Brick Brewing Company's? This section provides an overview of management control systems, illustrating the role of management accounting information.

There are countless definitions of planning and control. We define **planning** as choosing goals, predicting results under various ways of achieving those goals, deciding how to attain the desired goals, and then communicating the goals and how to achieve them throughout the organization. The most important planning tool is a budget. Why? Because a budget is a benchmark against which actual performance can be compared.

A **budget** is the quantitative expression of a proposed plan of action by management. The budgeting process aids coordination of what needs to be done to implement that plan. The information used to project budgeted amounts includes past financial and nonfinancial information routinely recorded in accounting systems. The budget expresses the strategy by describing the sales goals; the production, distribution, and customer-service costs that would be needed to achieve sales goals; the anticipated cash flows; and the potential financing needs. Because the

OBJECTIVE 5

Distinguish between the planning and control decisions of managers

Planning. Choosing goals, predicting results under various ways of achieving those goals, and then deciding how to attain the desired goals.

E-Business Strategies and the Management Accountant

How should a company choose its e-business strategy? Should it focus on initiatives that reduce costs, make the company more responsive to customers, or integrate the value chain and the supply chain? One way to think about strategic choices is the E-Business Value Matrix, which is organized into four quadrants along the dimensions of business criticality and practice innovation.

New Fundamentals include such e-business applications as creating an employee directory or putting information about employee benefits on a company's internal Web site so that employees can access information easily. These applications are not critical to the success of the business nor do they create new markets. But they will probably reduce costs and require only a small investment.

Rational Experimentation refers to strategies such as those pursued by pharmaceutical companies, including Pfizer and QLT Inc., to provide information and literature about their products to doctors and insurers. Such practices are innovative but not critical to business success because the companies' sales representatives can also provide the doctors with this information. Such initiatives can be justified on the basis of their revenue potential and lower costs.

Federal Express also uses rational experimentation by offering customers a wide range of shipping information (including options and package tracking), account management tools, and sales and promotional opportunities on its Web site. Like the pharmaceutical companies, this information is available elsewhere, but the Internet allows for greater customer control and operating efficiency.

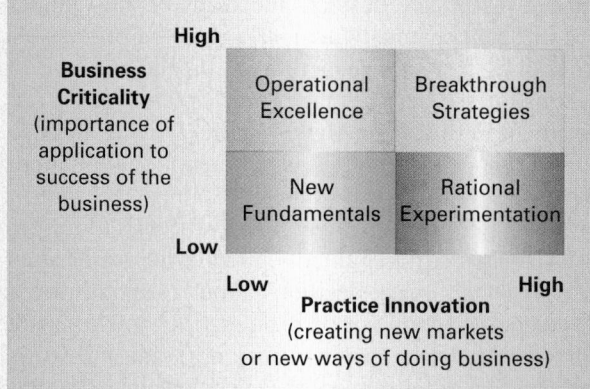

Breakthrough Strategies are strategies like those pursued by eBay, the auction site that enables individuals to buy and sell goods online, or Google, which uses complex algorithms to provide the most accurate online content searches. These strategies are innovative, critical, and risky and are motivated by opportunities for rapid revenue growth.

Operational Excellence includes strategies pursued by companies such as Dell Computer. Dell uses the Internet to sell computers directly to customers and to efficiently acquire materials and components from suppliers. Managing customer relationships and the supply chain is critical to Dell's business, and the use of the Internet is now standard practice at Dell. Dell's operational excellence leads to lower costs and, consequently, more sales, and is central to sustaining competitive advantage.

Most successful companies have tried to populate all four quadrants with their e-business initiatives. Management accountants have helped identify the costs and benefits of these alternative investment strategies. As a broad generalization, the benefits of e-business initiatives on the left side of the matrix have emphasized cost reductions; the benefits on the right side have emphasized revenue growth from distinctive product offerings.

Source: Hartman, A., J. Sifonis, and J. Kador, *Net Ready* (New York: McGraw Hill, 2000). Copyright © 2000. Reprinted by permission of The McGraw-Hill Companies; Google, Inc. April 29, 2004, S-1: Registration Statement. Mountain View, CA: Google, Inc., 2004, and various company financial reports.

EXHIBIT 1-4
How Accounting Facilitates Planning and Control

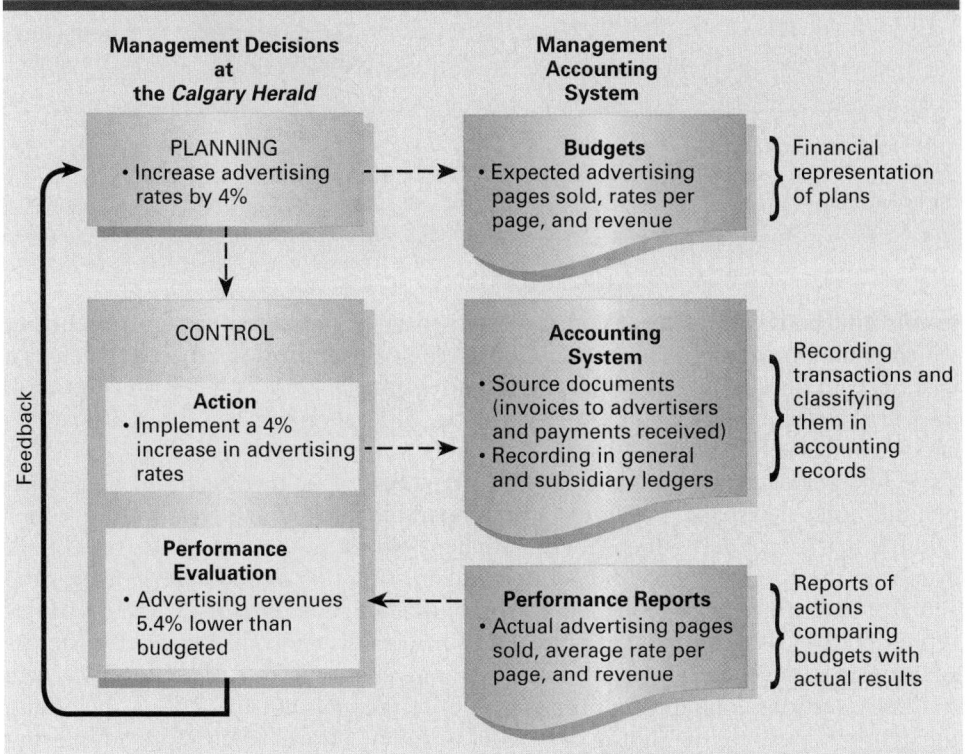

process of preparing a budget crosses business functions in the value chain, it forces coordination and communication throughout the company, as well as with the company's suppliers and customers. Management accountants play a valuable role in the budgeting process because they have an overview of the organization as a whole and understand the financial consequences of different actions.

Study the left side of Exhibit 1-4, which uses planning and control at the *Calgary Herald* as an illustration. For example, one goal of the *Calgary Herald* may be to increase operating income. Three main alternatives are considered to achieve this goal:

1. Change the price per newspaper

2. Change the rate per page charged to advertisers

3. Reduce labour costs by increasing automation of the printing process

Analyzing the effects of choosing alternative 2, assume that the publisher increases advertising budgeted rates by 4% to $5,200 per page for the month. Total budgeted advertising revenue is the product of the expected pages sold and the budgeted rate per page, which equals $4,160,000 ($5,200 × 800).

Control (the bottom box in Exhibit 1-4) covers both the action that implements the planning decision and the performance evaluation of the personnel and operations. Control requires that companies take coordinated action to implement their planning decisions, evaluate actual against expected performance, and provide timely feedback on current results. With our example, the action would include communicating the new advertising rate schedule to marketing sales representatives and advertisers.

During the month, the *Calgary Herald* sells advertising, sends out invoices, and receives payments. These invoices and receipts are recorded in the accounting system. Exhibit 1-5 shows the advertising revenue performance report for the *Calgary Herald*. This report indicates that 760 pages of advertising (40 pages fewer than the budgeted 800 pages) were sold in the month. The average rate per page was $5,080, compared with the budgeted $5,200 rate, yielding actual advertising revenue in the month of $3,860,800. The actual advertising revenue is $299,200 less than the budgeted $4,160,000. Understanding the reasons for any difference between actual

Control. Covers both the action that implements the planning decision and the performance evaluation of the personnel and operations.

EXHIBIT 1-5
Advertising Revenue Performance Report at the *Calgary Herald*

	Actual Results (1)	Variance (difference) (1) – (3)	Budgeted Amounts (3)
Advertising pages sold	760	(40) U	800
Average rate per page	$5,080	$ (120) U	$ 5,200
Advertising revenue	$3,860,800	$(299,200) U	$4,160,000

Management by exception. The practice of concentrating on areas that are not operating as expected and placing less attention on areas operating as expected.

Variance. Difference between an actual result and a budgeted amount when that budgeted amount is a financial variable reported by the accounting system.

results and budgeted results is an important part of **management by exception**, which is the practice of concentrating on areas not operating as expected (such as a cost overrun on a project) and placing less attention on areas operating as expected. The term **variance** in Exhibit 1-5 refers to the difference between the actual results and the budgeted amounts.

The performance report in Exhibit 1-5 should spur investigation. For example, did other newspapers experience a comparable decline in advertising revenue? Did the marketing department make sufficient efforts to convince advertisers that, even with the new rate of $5,200 per page, advertising was a good buy? Why was the actual average rate per page $5,080 instead of the budgeted rate of $5,200? Did sales representatives offer discounted rates? Did a major advertiser threaten to transfer its advertising to another newspaper unless it was given a large rate reduction? Answers to these questions could prompt the publisher to take subsequent actions, including, for example, pushing marketing personnel to renew efforts to promote advertising by existing and potential advertisers.

A well-conceived plan includes enough flexibility so that managers can seize opportunities unforeseen at the time the plan is formulated. A plan is made as a possible response to anticipated events but never as a necessary response. If actual events differ from those anticipated (fewer advertising pages were sold), then the plan should change. The best actual response will provide the best profitability for the company.

Planning and control are so strongly intertwined that managers do not spend time drawing artificially rigid distinctions between them. Unless otherwise stated, we use control in its broadest sense to denote the entire management process of both planning and control. For example, instead of referring to a management planning and control system, we will refer to a management control system. Similarly, we will often refer to the control purpose of accounting instead of the awkward planning and control purpose of accounting.

Feedback: Linking Planning and Control

Exhibit 1-4 shows a feedback loop from control back to planning. Feedback involves managers examining past performance and systematically exploring alternative ways to improve future performance. It can lead to a variety of responses, including the following:

Air Canada
www.aircanada.ca

DaimlerChrysler Canada Inc.
www.daimlerchrysler.ca/en/index.html

Bell Canada
www.bell.ca

USE OF FEEDBACK	EXAMPLE
◆ Changing goals	◆ Air Canada increases emphasis on cash flow rather than income, after emerging from bankruptcy protection.
◆ Changing how decision alternatives are identified	◆ DaimlerChrysler adopts a team-based new-product development process with input from both manufacturing and marketing.
◆ Changing the range of information collected in order to make predictions	◆ Bell Canada incorporates average inflation forecasts for wages when predicting future labour costs.
◆ Changing how the company operates	◆ Wal-Mart Canada Corp. has Coca-Cola store and deliver the product as needed instead of building its own warehouse.

- Changing reward systems

- Changing managers

- Research In Motion (RIM) considers basing its marketing bonuses on the profitability of sales rather than on the dollar amount of sales.

- Royal Dutch/Shell dismisses its chairman Sir Philip Watts after a huge writedown in the value of oil reserves.

Wal-Mart Canada Corp.
www.walmartcanada.ca

Research In Motion (RIM)
www.rim.net

Problem-Solving, Scorekeeping, and Attention-Directing Functions

Management accountants contribute to the company's decisions about strategy, planning, and control by problem solving, scorekeeping, and attention directing.

- **Problem solving:** Comparative analysis serves to reduce the scope of and identify the best available alternatives to achieve the company's goals. The *Calgary Herald*, for example, could compare the expected additional revenues and costs of outsourcing the production of an online version of the newspaper.
- **Scorekeeping:** Accumulating data and reporting reliable results to all levels of management. An example, Exhibit 1-5, illustrates the importance of comparing actual to expected performance in order for the *Calgary Herald* to clarify the causes for its failure.
- **Attention directing:** Clarifying and sorting out situations requiring management attention from those which do not. For example, the *Calgary Herald* could report daily the number of unsold newspapers compared to the printing press costs. Establishing an acceptable threshold of costs per returned newspaper would then direct attention to exceptions requiring some remedy. Attention directing should also focus on all opportunities to add value to an organization and not just on cost-reduction opportunities.

OBJECTIVE 6

Distinguish among the problem-solving functions, scorekeeping, and attention-directing roles of management accountants

Problem solving. Management accountant's function that involves comparative analysis to identify the best alternatives in relation to the organization's goals.

Scorekeeping. Management accountant's function that involves accumulating data and reporting reliable results to all levels of management.

Attention directing. Management accountant's function that involves clarifying and sorting out situations requiring management attention from those which do not.

Different decisions place different emphases on these three roles. For strategic decisions and planning decisions, the problem-solving role is most prominent. Consider the *Calgary Herald*'s strategic decision to try to increase revenues by increasing advertising rates per page (Exhibit 1-5). The newspaper's management accountants serve as problem-solvers to help make this strategic decision. They provide information about past increases or decreases in advertising rates and the subsequent changes in advertising revenue. They also collect and analyze information about past increases or decreases in advertising rates charged by competing media outlets (including other newspapers). The manager works with the management accountant to make the best decision about whether to increase the advertising rate per page and by how much to increase the rate.

For control decisions at the *Calgary Herald* (which include both actions to implement planning decisions and decisions about performance evaluation), the management accountant's scorekeeping and attention-directing roles are most prominent because they provide feedback to managers. For example, recording the details of advertising revenues and writing up a summary in the monthly income statement show how scorekeeping aids control. An example of control via attention directing would be a report highlighting the reduced year-to-date advertising revenues, with details of the specific advertisers that cut back or stopped advertising after the rate increase went into effect. This feedback helps managers decide which advertisers to target for intensive follow-up by sales representatives.

Feedback from scorekeeping and attention directing often leads managers to revise planning decisions and sometimes to make new strategic decisions. Information that prompts a planning decision is frequently reanalyzed and supplemented by the management accountant in the problem-solving and business-partner roles. The ongoing interaction among strategic decisions, planning decisions, and control decisions means that management accountants often are simultaneously doing problem-solving, scorekeeping, and attention-directing activities. The Global Surveys of Company Practice box (p. 12) indicates the increasingly important roles management accountants are playing in helping managers develop and implement strategy.

Today's Management Accountant

What do management accountants do? The following table, based on a survey of U.S. certified management accountants,[a] shows the percentage of respondents who named a particular work activity in their top five work activities (out of 29 activities identified to them) in terms of time devoted to the activity.

Accounting systems and financial reporting	62%
Managing the accounting/finance function	42%
Internal consulting	42%
Short-term budgeting	37%
Long-term strategic planning	25%
Financial and economic analysis	24%
Computer systems and operations	21%
Process improvement	20%
Performance evaluation	17%
Tax compliance	14%
Accounting policy	13%
Consolidations	11%

But to what end are management accountants using their time and skills? In recent years, management accounting has reached a critical juncture. Shifts in perceptions have caused management accountants to be increasingly seen as business partners focusing more and more on key strategic issues, well beyond the boundaries of the traditional finance functions. A recent survey of 2,000 Institute of Management Accountants members identified the following seven priorities facing today's management accountants:[b]

1. Generating cost information
2. Cost reduction
3. Improving processes
4. Contributing to core strategy
5. Setting standards
6. Reducing risk
7. Automating processes

Similar changes are also occurring globally within the profession. One survey of United Kingdom accounting professionals predicted the following tasks would be the most vital to the management accountant's job in the next five years: [c]

1. Business performance evaluation
2. Cost/financial control
3. Interpreting/presenting management accounts
4. Profit improvement
5. Planning/managing budgets
6. Strategic planning and decision making
7. Implementing business strategy

Another survey of Irish accountants noted several trends within management accounting practice.[d] Among these were management reliance on traditional accounting techniques (with only supplemental use of new methods) and movement toward accountants as business partners. Similarly, U.S. respondents identified the demand for "actionable" cost information and continued use of traditional management accounting tools.

[a]Siegel, G., and J. Sorensen, "The Practice Analysis of Management Accounting, *Management Accounting* (1999)."
[b]Ernst & Young, *2003 Survey of Management Accounting* (New York: Ernst & Young, March 2003).
[c]Burns, J., and H. Yazdifar, "Tricks or Treats?" *Financial Management* (2001).
[d]Pierce, B., "Management Accounting Without Accountants?" *Accountancy Ireland* (2001).

Many organizations now have management accountants who concentrate solely on the attention-directing or problem-solving function. The titles of these individuals differ. For instance, Clorox has special staff positions for "cost systems and financial reporting," "planning and analysis," "forecasting," and "manufacturing analysis and support." The Yoplait Company, a French yogurt company, has staff positions for "operations analysis," "budget analysis and reporting," and "marketing and sales analysis," while Siemens VDO has "senior cost price analysts."

KEY MANAGEMENT ACCOUNTING GUIDELINES

Three important guidelines help management accountants provide the most value in performing their problem-solving, scorekeeping, and attention-directing functions: (1) employ a cost-benefit approach, (2) give full recognition to behavioural as well as technical considerations, and (3) adopt the different-costs-for-different-purposes theme.

Cost-Benefit Approach

Management accountants continually face resource-allocation decisions, such as whether to purchase a new software package or whether to employ a new associate. A **cost-benefit approach** should be used in these decisions—resources should be spent if they promote decision making that better attains organization goals in relation to the costs of those resources. The perceived net benefits from spending those resources should exceed their perceived expected costs. The expected benefits and costs may not be easy to quantify, and although the benefits may take many forms they can be summarized as the collective set of decisions that will better attain the organization's goals.

Consider the installation of a company's first budgeting system. Previously, the company had probably been using some historical record keeping and little formal planning. A major benefit of installing the budgeting system is that it compels managers to plan more formally. They can make a different, more profitable set of decisions than they would have made using only a historical system. Thus, the expected benefits exceed the expected costs of the new budgeting system. These costs include investments in physical assets, in training people, and in ongoing operating costs of the system.

Behavioural and Technical Considerations

The cost-benefit test is the overarching criterion that assists managers in deciding whether, say, to install a proposed budgeting system instead of using an existing historical system. Note the human side of why budgeting is used. As was just mentioned, budgets induce a different set of collective decisions because of compelled collaborative planning. A management accounting system should have two simultaneous missions for providing information: (1) to help managers make wise economic decisions and (2) to help motivate managers and other employees to aim and strive for the goals of the organization. In other words, the technical information by itself might guide managers to wise economic decisions, but it is worthless if managers fail to understand and use it.

Do not underestimate the role of individuals and groups in management planning and control systems. Both accountants and managers should always remember that management systems are not confined exclusively to technical matters such as the type of computer software systems used and the frequency with which reports are prepared. Management is primarily a human activity that should focus on how to help individuals do their jobs better. For example, it is often better for managers to speak personally with underperforming workers about how to improve performance than to send those workers a report highlighting their underperformance.

Different Costs for Different Purposes

This book discusses alternative ways to estimate costs. That is because there are different costs for different purposes. This is the management accountant's version of the "one size does not fit all" notion. A cost concept used for external reporting may not be

OBJECTIVE 7

Describe three guidelines management accountants follow in supporting managers

Cost-benefit approach. Primary criterion for choosing among alternative accounting systems, which is how each system achieves organizational goals relative to the cost of those systems.

Although it is difficult to quantify all the costs and benefits of a budgeting system, the question is: Will costs and benefits be considered implicitly ("gut feeling") or examined explicitly (estimated dollar value)? The best situation is to be able to make dollar estimates but when uncertainty is high (for example, the benefit of increased communication), using gut feeling cannot be avoided.

the appropriate concept for internal reporting to managers. Consider the advertising costs associated with launching a major new Microsoft product. The product is expected to have a useful life of two years or more. For external reporting to shareholders, advertising costs are fully expensed in the income statement in the year in which they are incurred. This immediate expensing is a requirement of GAAP governing external reporting to shareholders. In contrast, for evaluating management performance (an example of the internal routine reporting purpose), the advertising costs could be capitalized and then written off as expenses over several years. Microsoft could capitalize these advertising costs if it believed this treatment would better represent the performance of the managers launching the new product. In short, immediate-period expensing of advertising costs for external reporting does not imply it is always the "ideal" cost treatment for other purposes of an accounting system.

A management accountant following these guidelines operates within a given organization structure. We now discuss how organization structure affects the reporting responsibilities of a management accountant.

ORGANIZATION STRUCTURE AND THE MANAGEMENT ACCOUNTANT

OBJECTIVE 8

Understand how management accounting fits into an organization's structure

Line management. Managers directly responsible for attaining the objectives of the organization.

Staff management. Managers who provide advice and assistance to line management.

Chief financial officer (CFO), finance director. The senior officer responsible for oversight of the financial operations of an organization.

Controller. The financial executive primarily responsible for both management and financial accounting.

We focus first on broad management functions and then examine the accounting and finance functions in more detail.

Line and Staff Relationships

Most organizations distinguish between line and staff management. **Line management** is directly responsible for attaining the objectives of the organization. For example, managers of manufacturing divisions may have objectives for a specified amount of operating income plus targets for product quality, safety, and compliance with environmental laws. **Staff management**, such as management accountants, exist to provide advice and assistance to line management. Increasingly, however, organizations such as DaimlerChrysler Canada Inc. and GlaxoSmithKline use teams to achieve their objectives. These teams include both line and staff management so that all inputs into a decision are available simultaneously. As a result, the traditional distinctions between line and staff have become less clear-cut than they were a decade ago. Line management and staff management designations are best viewed as different ends of a spectrum.

The Chief Financial Officer and the Controller

The **chief financial officer (CFO)**—also called the **finance director**—is the senior officer empowered with overseeing the financial operations of an organization. The responsibilities of the CFO vary among organizations, but they almost always encompass the following four areas:

- ◆ **Controllership** includes providing financial information for both internal reports to managers and external reports to investors as well as overseeing the overall operations of the accounting system.
- ◆ **Treasury** includes short-term and long-term financing and investments, banking, and cash, foreign exchange, and derivatives management.
- ◆ **Tax** includes income taxes, sales taxes, and domestic and international tax planning.
- ◆ **Investor relations** includes responding to and interacting with shareholders.

In some organizations, the CFO also has responsibility for information systems. In other organizations, an officer of equivalent rank to the CFO, who is called *chief information officer*, or CIO, has responsibility for information systems.

The **controller** is the financial executive primarily responsible for both management accounting and financial accounting. This book focuses on the management accounting function of the controller. The modern controller does not do any controlling in terms of line authority except over his or her own department. Yet the modern concept of controllership maintains that the controller does control in a special sense. That is, by reporting and interpreting relevant data, the controller

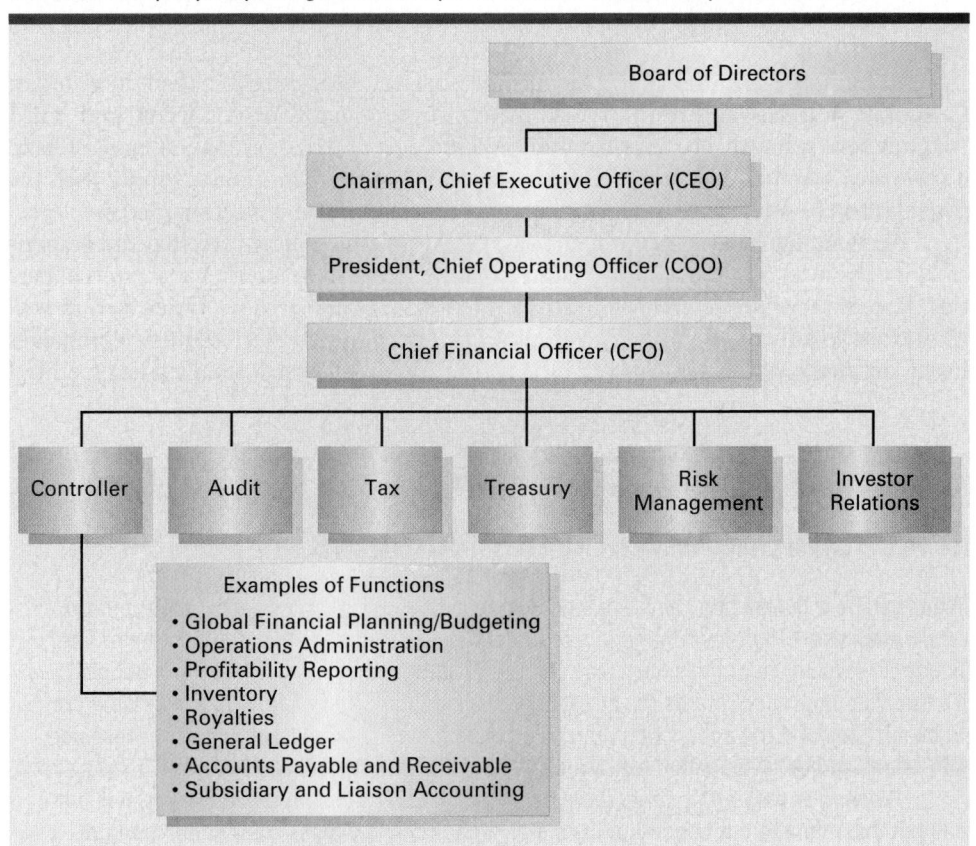

exerts a force or influence that impels management toward making better-informed decisions.

Exhibit 1-6 presents an organization chart depicting the reporting relationships for the CFO and the corporate controller at Nike, a leading footwear and apparel company. The CFO is a staff management function that reports to the most senior line managers (who in turn report to the board of directors). As in most organizations, the corporate controller at Nike reports to the CFO. Organization charts, like that in Exhibit 1-6, show formal reporting relationships. In most organizations, informal relationships also exist that must be understood when managers attempt to implement their decisions. Examples of informal relationships are friendships among managers (of a professional or personal kind) and the personal preferences of senior managers for the type of managers they choose to rely on in decision making.

The CFO at Nike is one of 13 corporate officers. These include the chief executive officer (CEO), the president and chief operating officer (COO), the treasurer, and ten vice-presidents (such as for its geographic regions in the United States, Asia Pacific, and Europe; for its products of apparel and footwear; for its brand management; for its global human resources; and a chief legal counsel). Exhibit 1-6 provides examples of the functions undertaken in the controller's group. Each of Nike's major geographic groups (United States, Asia Pacific, and Europe) has its own group controller. Many individual countries within each geographic group also have a country controller.

You may not be aware of the variety of jobs available to accountants. Exhibit 1-6 illustrates the diverse areas that report to the CFO. An understanding of accounting is essential in many of those areas.

PROFESSIONAL ETHICS

Ponder what managers do to design and implement strategies and the organization structures within which they operate. Reflect on the management accountant's and controller's roles. Clearly, successful management accountants possess both technical and analytical competence *as well as* behavioural and interpersonal skills. The Focus on Values and Behaviours box below lists some desirable values and behaviours. We will elaborate on these values and behaviours as we discuss different topics in subsequent chapters of this book.

At no time has the focus on ethical conduct been sharper than it is today. Corporate scandals at Enron, WorldCom, Bre-X, Cinar Corp., Livent, and YBM Magnex have seriously eroded the public's confidence in corporations. All employees in a company, whether in line management or staff management, must comply with the organization's—and, more broadly, society's—expectations of ethical standards.

Accountants have special obligations regarding ethics, given that they are responsible for the integrity of the financial information provided to internal and external parties. Recent securities legislation in the United States, the Sarbanes Oxley Act, as well as international and Canadian counterparts (e.g., MIS2-109), require companies listed on stock exchanges to create, enforce, and publish a formal code of ethical

FOCUS ON VALUES AND BEHAVIOURS

Management Accounting Beyond the Numbers

When you hear the job title "accountant," what comes to mind? The CA who does your tax return each year? High-level managers at Rogers Communications Inc. or GlaxoSmithKline? To people outside the profession, it may seem like accountants are just "numbers people." It's true that most accountants are adept financial managers, yet their skills don't stop there. To be successful in the accounting profession, management accountants must possess certain values and behaviours that reach well beyond basic analytical abilities.

Working in cross-functional teams and as a business partner of managers. It is not enough that management accountants simply be technically competent about management accounting. They need to be able to work in teams, to learn about business issues, to understand the motivations of different individuals, to respect the views of their colleagues, and to show empathy and trust.

Promoting fact-based analysis and making tough-minded, critical judgments without being adversarial. Management accountants must raise tough questions for managers to consider, especially when preparing budgets. They must do so thoughtfully and with the intent of improving plans and decisions. For example, in Enron's energy services division, executives were compensated based on internal estimates of company worth, motivating them to inflate contract values even though no actual cash flow was generated. The company's leaders then used reporting methods to hide its decline in economic worth. Upon accurate restatement this decline totalled almost US$600 million, causing Enron to file for bankruptcy, share price to plummet, and many people to lose both their jobs and retirement savings.

Leading and motivating people to change and be innovative. Implementing good new ideas is seldom easy. When Kanthal, the Swedish manufacturer of heating elements, introduced its innovative product-costing system, the controller and his team of management accountants made sure that both the vision for the change was well understood and managers were well trained in the new methods. Managers achieving short-term successes became champions for the new system.

Communicating clearly, openly, and candidly. Communicating information is a large part of what management accountants do. Many techniques used to estimate improved revenue or reduced costs are communicated in a formal manner, such as budgets, project profitability statements, and special reports on proposed changes. These reports have in common a heavy reliance on excellent quantitative estimates of the effect of proposed changes provided by management accountants, as well as careful analysis of relevant qualitative factors.

Having a strong sense of integrity and of doing the right things. Management accountants must never succumb to pressure from managers to manipulate financial information. Their primary commitment is to the organization and its shareholders, not its managers.

Source: Andy Serwer, "The Hole Story," *Fortune*, July 7, 2003; Mark Green, Jeannine Garrity, Andrea Gumbus, and Bridget Lyons, "Pitney Bowes Calls for New Metrics," *Strategic Finance*, May 2002.

and business conduct. Clauses in the new legislation focus on improving internal control, corporate governance, monitoring of managers, and disclosure practices of public corporations. These regulations legislate tough ethical standards and provide a process for employees to report wrongdoing, both illegal and unethical acts.

Ethical Guidelines

Professional accounting organizations representing management accountants exist in many countries. Appendix C discusses professional organizations in Canada, the United States, Australia, Japan, and the United Kingdom. Each of these organizations provides certification programs. For example, the **Society of Management Accountants of Canada (SMAC)**—the largest association of management accountants in Canada—provides a program leading to the **Certified Management Accountant (CMA)** certificate. This certificate signals that the holder has passed the admission criteria and demonstrated the competency of technical knowledge and skills required by the SMAC.

Professional accounting organizations play an important role in promoting a high standard of ethics. The SMAC has issued a Code of Professional Ethics (see Exhibit 1-7). As you can see, the first duty of management accountants is to act in the public interest, then in the interests of the profession, clients, and employers.

It is important to understand what a profession is to understand why professional ethics are important. A profession is distinguished by certain characteristics:

◆ Mastery of a specific intellectual skill acquired by education and training
◆ Acceptance of duties to society (i.e., protection of the public) as a whole in addition to duties to the employer or client
◆ An outlook that is essentially objective
◆ A high standard in the conduct and performance of personal service

A professional provides a service (e.g., advice regarding legal, financial, or medical issues) rather than producing a specific product (e.g., furniture, vehicles). Thus it is difficult, if not impossible, for the public (i.e., a layperson) to assess the quality of a professional service, because the public lacks the specialized knowlege and skills that are necessary to assess that quality. This lack of skills is what sends the public to the professional in the first place, but it leaves the public vulnerable to those professionals. Because of this vulnerability, the public must be protected by standards established by those who have the appropriate knowledge and skills.

Such protection is achieved when provincial governments pass legislation that establishes professional organizations and sets out governance criteria. These criteria require, among other things, that members of the profession set standards for the knowledge and skills necessary for entry into the profession, for continuing competency, and for discipline. Because the members establish the standards and then monitor other members for adherence to those standards, this is considered "self-governance."

An important component of a profession's self-governance is that it is responsible for disciplining its members found guilty of "unprofessional conduct." By setting out what constitutes "unprofessional conduct" the profession ensures that the public will be protected by acceptable minimum standards and disciplinary processes. For example, for CMAs in Alberta, "unprofessional conduct" would include

(a) conduct that is detrimental to the best interest of the public or harms the integrity of the accounting profession;
(b) conduct that contravenes this Act, the regulations, or the bylaws;
(c) conduct that contravenes the rules of professional conduct or practice standards;
(d) conduct that displays a lack of competence.[1]

[1]*Source:* Excerpt from Section 91(1) of the Regulated Accounting Profession Act, Alberta

Society of Management
Accountants of Canada
www.cma-canada.org

Society of Management Accountants of Canada (SMAC). The largest association of management accountants in Canada.

Certified Management Accountant (CMA). The professional designation for management accountants in Canada.

All Members shall adhere to the following "Code of Professional Ethics" of the Society:

(a) A Member shall act at all times with
   (i) responsibility for and fidelity to public needs;
   (ii) fairness and loyalty to his associates, clients, and employers; and
   (iii) competence through devotion to high ideals of personal honour and professional integrity;

(b) A Member shall
   (i) maintain at all times independence of thought and action;
   (ii) not express his opinion on financial statements without first assessing his relationship with his client to determine whether he might expect his opinion to be considered independent, objective, and unbiased by one who has knowledge of all the facts; and
   (iii) when preparing financial statements or expressing an opinion on financial statements which are intended to inform management only, disclose all material facts known to him in order not to make such financial statements misleading, acquire sufficient information to warrant an expression of opinion, and report all material misstatements or departures from generally accepted accounting principles;

(c) A Member shall
   (i) not disclose or use any confidential information concerning the affairs of his employer or client unless acting in the course of his duties or except when such information is required to be disclosed in the course of any defence of himself or any associate or employee in any lawsuit or other legal proceeding or against alleged professional misconduct by order of lawful authority of the Board or any committee of the Society in the proper exercise of their duties but only to the extent necessary for such purpose;
   (ii) inform his employer or client of any business connections or interests of which his employer or client would reasonably expect to be informed;
   (iii) not, in the course of exercising his duties on behalf of his employer or client, hold, receive, bargain for, or acquire any fee, remuneration, or benefit without his employer's or client's knowledge and consent; and
   (iv) take all reasonable steps, in arranging any engagement as a consultant, to establish a clear understanding of the scope and objectives of the work before it is commenced and shall furnish the client with an estimate of cost, preferably before the engagement is commenced, but in any event as soon as possible thereafter.

(d) A Member shall
   (i) conduct himself toward other Members with courtesy and good faith;
   (ii) not commit an act discreditable to the profession;
   (iii) not engage in or counsel any business or occupation which, in the opinion of the Society, is incompatible with the professional ethics of a management accountant;
   (iv) not accept any engagement to review the work of another Member for the same employer except with the knowledge of that Member, or except where the connection of that Member with the work has been terminated, unless the Member reviews the work of others as a normal part of his responsibilities;
   (v) not attempt to gain an advantage over other Members by paying or accepting a commission in securing management accounting work;
   (vi) uphold the principle of adequate compensation for management accounting work; and
   (vii) not act maliciously or in any other way which may adversely reflect on the public or professional reputation or business of another Member.

(Continued)

(e) A Member shall

   (i) at all times maintain the standards of competence expressed by the academic and experience requirements for admission to the Society and for continuation as a Member;

   (ii) disseminate the knowledge upon which the profession of management accounting is based to others within the profession and generally promote the advancement of the profession;

   (iii) undertake only such work as he is competent to perform by virtue of his training and experience and shall, where it would be in the best interests of an employer or client, engage, or advise the employer or client to engage, other specialists;

   (iv) expose before the proper tribunals of the Society any incompetent, unethical, illegal, or unfair conduct or practice of a Member which involves the reputation, dignity, or honour of the Society; and

   (v) endeavour to ensure that a professional partnership or company with which he is associated as a partner, principal, director, or officer abides by the Code of Professional Ethics and the rules of professional conduct established by the Society.

Source: Management Accounting Handbook: Bylaw 20 (The Society of Management Accountants of Ontario). Reproduced with permission of The Society of Management Accountants of Ontario.

Typical Ethical Challenges

Ethical issues can confront management accountants in many ways. The following examples are illustrative.

◆ **Case A** A management accountant, knowing that reporting a loss for a software division will result in yet another "rightsizing initiative" (a euphemism for layoffs), has concerns about the commercial viability of software for which development costs are currently being capitalized. The division manager argues vehemently that the new product will be a "winner" but has no credible evidence to support the opinion. The last two products from this division have not been successful in the market. The management accountant has friends in the division and wants to avoid a personal confrontation with the division manager. Should the management accountant require the development to be expensed immediately because of the lack of evidence as to its commercial viability?

◆ **Case B** A packaging supplier, bidding for a new contract, offers the management accountant of its customer an all-expenses-paid weekend to the Grey Cup. The supplier does not mention the new contract when making the invitation. The accountant is not a personal friend of the supplier. He knows operating cost issues are critical in approving the new contract and is concerned that the supplier will ask for details about bids by competing packaging companies.

In each case the management accountant is faced with an ethical challenge. Case A involves competence, objectivity, and integrity, whereas case B involves confidentiality and integrity. Ethical issues are not always black and white. For example, the supplier in case B may have no intention of raising issues associated with the bid. However, the appearance of a conflict of interest in case B is sufficient for many companies to prohibit employees from accepting free "favours" from suppliers.

Most professional accounting organizations around the globe issue statements about professional ethics. Although these statements include many of the same issues discussed by the Society of Management Accountants of Ontario outlined in Exhibit 1-7, differences do exist in their content. For example, the Chartered Institute of Management Accountants (CIMA) in the United Kingdom identifies four fundamental principles of competency, confidentiality, integrity, and objectivity. A statement by the Institute of Management Accountants in the United States goes further by providing guidance on the resolution of ethical conflict.

(Try to solve this problem before examining the solution that follows.)

PROBLEM

The Campbell Soup Company incurs the following costs:

a. Purchase of tomatoes by canning plant for Campbell's tomato soup products.

b. Materials purchased for redesigning Mr. Christie biscuit containers to make biscuits stay fresh longer.

c. Payment to Bates, the advertising agency for the Healthy Request line of soup products.

d. Salaries of food technologists researching feasibility of a Prego pizza sauce that has zero calories.

e. Payment to Safeway for shelf space to display Campbell's food products.

f. Cost of a toll-free telephone line used for customer inquiries about possible taste problems with Campbell's soups.

g. Cost of gloves used by line operators on the Swanson Fiesta breakfast food production line.

h. Cost of hand-held computers used by Maple Leaf Foods delivery staff serving major supermarket accounts.

REQUIRED

Classify each cost item (a) to (h) into a component of the value chain shown in Exhibit 1-2 (p. 5).

SOLUTION

a. Production

b. Design of products, services, or processes

c. Marketing

d. Research and development

e. Marketing

f. Customer service

g. Production

h. Distribution

DECISION POINTS   SUMMARY

The following decision guidelines use a question-and-answer format to summarize the chapter's main points. Each decision presents a key question. The guideline is the answer to that question.

DECISIONS	GUIDELINES
1. What information does cost accounting provide?	Cost accounting measures, analyzes, and reports financial and nonfinancial information related to the cost of acquiring or using resources in an organization. Cost accounting provides information for both management accounting and financial accounting.
2. How do management accountants support strategic decisions?	Management accountants contribute to strategic decisions by providing information about the sources of competive advantage.
3. How do companies add value?	Companies add value through research and development (R&D); design of products, services, or processes; production; marketing; distribution; and customer service. Managers in all business functions of the value chain are customers of management accounting information.
4. What are the dimensions of performance that customers are expecting of companies?	Customers are expecting companies to deliver performance through cost, efficiency, quality, timeliness, and innovation.
5. How do managers implement strategy?	Managers implement strategy by making planning and control decisions. Planning decisions include deciding on organization goals, predicting results under various alternative ways of achieving those goals, and then deciding how to attain the desired goals. Control decisions include taking actions to implement the planning decisions and deciding on performance evaluation and feedback that will help future decision making.

6. What roles do management accountants perform?	In most organizations, management accountants perform multiple roles to implement strategies: problem solving (comparative analyses for decision making), scorekeeping (accumulating data and reporting reliable results), and attention directing (helping managers properly focus their attention).
7. What guidelines do management accountants use?	Three guidelines that help management accountants increase their value to managers are (a) employ a cost-benefit approach, (b) recognize behavioural as well as technical considerations, and (c) identify different costs for different purposes.
8. Where does the management accounting function fit into an organization's structure?	Management accounting is an integral part of the controller's function in an organization. In most organizations, the controller reports to the chief financial officer, who is a key member of the top management team.
9. What are the ethical responsibilities of management accountants?	Management accountants have ethical responsibilities that are related to competence, confidentiality, integrity, and objectivity.

▼ TERMS TO LEARN

Each chapter will include this section. Like all technical subjects, accounting contains many terms with precise meanings. Pin down the definitions of new terms when you initially encounter them. The meaning of each of the following terms is explained in this chapter.

attention directing (p. 11)
budget (p. 7)
Certified Management Accountant (CMA) (p. 17)
chief financial officer (CFO) (p. 14)
control (p. 9)
controller (p. 14)
cost accounting (p. 2)
cost-benefit approach (p. 13)
cost management (p. 3)
customer service (p. 5)
design of products, services, or processes (p. 5)
distribution (p. 5)
finance director (p. 14)
financial accounting (p. 2)

line management (p. 14)
management accounting (p. 2)
management by exception (p. 10)
marketing (p. 5)
planning (p. 7)
problem solving (p. 11)
production (p. 5)
research and development (R&D) (p. 5)
scorekeeping (p. 11)
Society of Management Accountants of Canada (SMAC) (p. 17)
staff management (p. 14)
strategic management (p. 4)
strategy (p. 3)
value chain (p. 4)
variance (p. 10)

▼ ASSIGNMENT MATERIAL

QUESTIONS

1-1 How does management accounting differ from financial accounting?

1-2 "Management accounting should not fit the straitjacket of financial accounting." Explain and give an example.

1-3 How can a management accountant help formulate a strategy?

1-4 Describe the business functions in the value chain.

1-5 Explain the term "supply chain" and its importance to cost management.

1-6 "Management accounting deals only with costs." Do you agree? Explain.

1-7 How can management accountants help improve quality and achieve timely product deliveries?

1-8 Distinguish planning decisions from control decisions.

1-9 What are the three roles management accountants perform?

1-10 What three guidelines help management accountants provide the most value to managers?

1-11 "Knowledge of technical issues such as computer technology is necessary but not sufficient to becoming a successful accountant." Do you agree? Why?

1-12 As a new controller, reply to this comment by a plant manager: "As I see it, our accountants may be needed to keep records for shareholders and Canada Revenue Agency—but I don't want them sticking their noses in my day-to-day operations. I do the best I know how. No pencil-pushing bean counter knows enough about my responsibilities to be of any use to me."

1-13 As used in accounting, what do "SMAC" and "CMA" stand for?

1-14 Name the four areas in which standards of ethical conduct exist for management accountants in Canada. What organization sets forth these standards?

1-15 What steps should a management accountant take if established written policies provide insufficient guidance on how to handle an ethical conflict?

EXERCISES

1-16 Value chain and customer relationship management. A recent annual report of Ford Motor Company included the following comments:

> "Delivering great value to our customers. That's our passion . . .
> Throughout Ford Motor Company, we're focused on improving the quality and value of our products and speeding delivery to market."

1. Who are the customers of management accounting?
2. How may the value of management accounting systems to the customers of management accounting be enhanced?

1-17 Value chain, supply chain, and key success factors. A survey on the ways organizations are changing their management accounting systems reported the following:
  a. Company A now prepares a value-chain income statement for each brand it sells.
  b. Company B now presents in a single report all costs related to achieving high quality levels in its products.
  c. Company C now presents in its performance reports estimates of the manufacturing costs of its two most important competitors, in addition to its own manufacturing costs.
  d. Company D now contracts with its suppliers to frequently deliver small quantities of materials directly to the production floor.
  e. Company E now reports the percentage of times it fails to meet delivery dates that it has promised to customers.

REQUIRED
Link each of these changes to value-chain or supply-chain analysis or to the key success factors that are important to managers.

1-18 Value chain and classification of costs, pharmaceutical company. QLT Inc., a Canadian biopharmaceutical company, incurs the following costs:
  a. Cost of redesigning blister packs to make drug containers more tamperproof
  b. Cost of videos sent to doctors to promote sales of a new drug
  c. Cost of a toll-free telephone line used for customer inquiries about usage, side-effects of drugs, and so on
  d. Equipment purchased by a scientist to conduct experiments on drugs awaiting approval by the government
  e. Payment to actors on infomercial to be shown on television promoting Visudyne®, a new treatment for age-related progressive blindness
  f. Labour costs of workers in the packaging area of a production facility
  g. Bonus paid to a salesperson for exceeding monthly sales quota
  h. Cost of the Purolator courier service to deliver drugs to hospitals

REQUIRED
Classify each cost item in parts (a) to (h) as belonging to a component of the value chain shown in Exhibit 1-2 (p. 5).

1-19 Value chain and classification of costs, computer company. Apple Computer incurs the following costs:
  a. Electricity costs for the plant assembling the Macintosh computer line of products
  b. Transportation costs for shipping Macintosh software to a retail chain
  c. Payment to David Kelley Designs for design of the Powerbook carrying case
  d. Salary of a computer scientist working on the next generation of laptops
  e. Cost of Apple employees' visit to a major customer who has purchased an Apple product to illustrate Apple's ability to interconnect with other computers

f. Purchase of competitors' products for testing against potential future Apple products

g. Payment to a television station for running Apple advertisements

h. Cost of cables purchased from an outside supplier to be used with the Macintosh printer

REQUIRED

Classify each cost item in parts (a) to (h) as belonging to a component of the value chain shown in Exhibit 1-2 (p. 5).

1-20 Problem solving, scorekeeping, and attention directing. For each of the following activities, identify the major function (problem solving, scorekeeping, and attention directing) the accountant is performing.

a. Preparing a monthly statement of Australian sales for the IBM marketing vice-president

b. Interpreting differences between actual results and budgeted amounts on a performance report for the customer warranty department of General Electric

c. Preparing a schedule of amortization[2] for forklift trucks in the receiving department of a Hewlett Packard plant in Scotland

d. Analyzing, for a Mitsubishi international manufacturing manager, the desirability of buying some auto parts made in Korea

e. Interpreting why a Birmingham distribution centre did not adhere to its delivery costs budget

f. Explaining a Xerox shipping department's performance report

g. Preparing, for the manager of production control of a U.S. steel plant, a cost comparison of two computerized manufacturing control systems

h. Preparing a scrap report for the finishing department of a Toyota parts plant

i. Preparing the budget for the maintenance department of Mount Sinai Hospital

j. Analyzing, for a General Motors product designer, the impact on product costs of some new headlight lamps

REQUIRED

Identify each activity in parts (a) to (j) as a problem-solving, scorekeeping, or attention-directing function.

1-21 Problem solving, scorekeeping, and attention directing. Each of the following activities are functions accountants perform.

a. Interpreting differences between actual results and budgeted amounts on a shipping manager's performance report at a Daewoo distribution centre

b. Preparing a report showing the benefits of leasing motor vehicles versus owning them

c. Preparing adjusting journal entries for amortization on the personnel manager's office equipment at the Bank of Montreal

d. Preparing a customer's monthly statement for a Sears store

e. Processing the weekly payroll for the University of Alberta maintenance department

f. Explaining the product design manager's performance report at a DaimlerChrysler division

g. Analyzing the costs of several different ways to blend materials in the foundry of a General Electric plant

h. Tallying sales, by branches, for the sales vice-president of Unilever

i. Analyzing, for the president of CorelDraw, the impact of a contemplated new product on net income

j. Interpreting why an IBM sales district did not meet its sales quota

REQUIRED

Identify each of the activities in parts (a) to (j) as a problem-solving, scorekeeping, or attention-directing function.

1-22 Problem solving, scorekeeping, and attention directing. The International Sports Management Group (ISMG) manages and promotes sporting events and sporting personalities. Its managers are currently examining the following reports and accounting statements:

a. Five-year projections for expanding into managing sports television networks for cable television

b. Income statement to be included in a six-month interim report to be sent to investors and filed with the securities regulators

c. Profitability comparison of golf tournaments directed by different managers, each of whom receives a percentage of that tournament's profits

d. Monthly reports of office costs for each of the 14 ISMG offices worldwide

e. Statement showing the revenues ISMG earns from different types of sporting events (for example, golf, motor racing, and tennis)

---

[2]The term *amortization* is used in this book to be consistent with the *CICA Handbook*. It is synonymous with depreciation and depletion.

Identify each of the activities in parts (a) to (e) as a problem-solving, scorekeeping, or attention-directing function.

1-23 Professional ethics and reporting divisional performance. Marcia Miller is division controller and Tom Maloney is division manager of the Sports Shoe Company. Miller has line responsibility to Maloney, but she also has staff responsibility to the company controller.

Maloney is under severe pressure to achieve budgeted division income for the year. He has asked Miller to book $240,000 of sales on December 31. The customers' orders are firm, but the shoes are still in the production process. They will be shipped on or about January 4. Maloney said to Miller, "The key event is getting the sales order, not shipping of the shoes. You should support me, not obstruct my reaching division goals."

REQUIRED
1. Describe Miller's ethical responsibilities.
2. What should Miller do if Maloney gives her a direct order to book the sales?

PROBLEMS

1-24 Planning and control decisions. Indigo is a book retailing company. The majority of its sales are made at its own stores. These stores are often located in shopping malls or in the downtown central business districts of cities. A small but increasing percentage of sales are made via its Internet shopping division.

The following five reports were recently prepared by the management accounting group at Indigo:
1. Annual financial statements included in the annual report sent to its shareholders
2. Weekly report to the vice-president of operations for each Indigo store—includes revenue, gross margin, and operating costs
3. Study for vice-president of new business development of the expected revenue and expected costs of the Indigo Internet Division selling music products (CDs, cassettes, etc.) as well as books
4. Weekly report to book publishers and trade magazines on the sales of the top-ten fiction and nonfiction books at both its own stores and in the Internet Division
5. Report to insurance company on losses Indigo suffered at its three Toronto stores resulting from a storm.

REQUIRED
1. For each report, identify both a planning-decision and a control-decision use by a manager (either at Indigo or another company).

1-25 Planning and control, feedback. In April 2007, Naomi Campbell, editor of *The Daily Sporting News* (DSN), decides to reduce the price per newspaper from $0.84 to $0.60, starting May 1, 2007. Actual paid circulation in April is 7.5 million (250,000 per day × 30 days). Campbell estimates that the $0.24 price reduction will increase paid circulation in May to 12.4 million (400,000 × 31 days). The actual May circulation turns out to be 13,640,000 (440,000 × 31 days). Assume that one goal of DSN is to increase operating income. The budgeted increase in circulation would enable DSN to charge higher advertising rates in later months of 2007 if those budgeted gains actually occur. The actual price paid in May 2007 was the budgeted $0.60 per newspaper.

REQUIRED
1. Distinguish between planning and control at DSN, giving an example of each.
2. Prepare a newspaper revenue performance report for DSN for May 2007 showing the actual results, budgeted amounts, and the variance.
3. Give two types of action Campbell might take based on feedback on the May 2007 circulation revenue.

1-26 Planning and control decisions: Internet company. WebNews.com offers its subscribers several services, such as an annotated TV guide and local-area information on weather, restaurants, and movie theatres. Its main revenue sources are fees for banner advertisements and fees from subscribers. Recent data are:

Month/Year	Advertising Revenues	Actual Number of Subscribers	Monthly Fee per Subscriber
June 2006	$ 481,186	28,642	$17.94
December 2006	999,790	54,813	23.94
June 2007	1,033,241	58,178	23.94
December 2007	1,773,686	86,437	23.94
June 2008	$3,500,354	146,581	23.94

The following decisions were made from June through October 2008:

a. June 2008: Raised subscription fee to $29.94 per month from July 2008 onward. The budgeted number of subscribers for this monthly fee is shown in the table below.

b. June 2008: Informed existing subscribers that from July onward, monthly fee would be $29.94.

c. July 2008: Offered e-mail service to subscribers and upgraded other online services.

d. October 2008: Dismissed the vice-president of marketing after significant slowdown in subscribers and subscription revenues, based on July through September 2008 data in table.

e. October 2008: Reduced subscription fee to $26.34 per month from November 2008 onward. Results for July–September 2008 are:

Month/Year	Budgeted Number of Subscribers	Actual Number of Subscribers	Monthly Fee per Subscriber
July 2008	140,000	128,933	$29.94
August 2008	150,000	139,419	29.94
September 2008	160,000	143,131	29.94

REQUIRED

1. Classify each of the decisions (a) to (e) as either a planning or a control decision

2. Give two examples of other planning decisions and two examples of other control decisions that may be made at WebNews.com

1-27 Problem solving, scorekeeping, attention directing, and feedback, Internet company (continuation of 1-26). Consider the five decisions made in Problem 1-26.

1. For each of the five decisions (a–e), provide an example of pertinent information that an accountant could provide, and indicate whether the accountant would be acting in a problem-solving, scorekeeping, or attention-directing role.

2. Identify one decision that WebNews.com made as a result of feedback from the control system.

3. What further action might WebNews.com take based on the feedback from the July through September 2008 subscriber information?

1-28 Management accounting guidelines. For each of the following items, identify which of the management guidelines applies—cost-benefit approach, behavioural and technical considerations, or different costs for different purposes.

1. Analyzing whether to keep the billing function within the organization or outsourcing it

2. Deciding to give bonuses for superior performance to the employees in a Japanese subsidiary and extra vacation time to the employees in a Swedish subsidiary

3. Including costs of all the value-chain functions before deciding to launch a new product but including only its manufacturing costs in determining its inventory valuation

4. Considering the desirability of hiring one more salesperson

5. Giving each salesperson the compensation option if choosing either from a low salary and high-percentage sales commission or a high salary and a low-percentage sales commission

6. Selecting the costlier computer system after considering two systems

7. Installing a participatory budgeting system in which managers set their own performance targets, instead of top management imposing performance targets on them

8. Recording research costs as an expense for financial reporting purposes but capitalizing and expensing them over a longer period for management performance-evaluation purposes

9. Introducing a profit-sharing plan for employees

1-29 Responsibility for analysis of performance. Karen Phillipson is the new corporate controller of a multinational company that has just overhauled its organizational structure. The company is now decentralized. Each division is under an operating vice-president who, within wide limits, has responsibility and authority to run the division like a separate company.

Phillipson has a number of bright staff members. One of them, Bob Garrett, is in charge of a newly created performance analysis staff. Garrett and staff members prepare monthly division performance reports for the company president. These reports are division income statements, showing budgeted performance and actual results, and they are accompanied by detailed written explanations and appraisals of variances. In the past, each of Garrett's staff members was responsible for analyzing one division; each consulted with division line and staff executives and became generally acquainted with the division's operations.

After a few months, Bill Whisler, vice-president in charge of Division C, stormed into the controller's office. The gist of his complaint follows:

"Your staff is trying to take over part of my responsibility. They come in, snoop around, ask hundreds of questions, and take up plenty of our time. It's up to me, not you and your detectives, to analyze and explain my division's performance to central headquarters. If you don't stop trying to grab my responsibility, I'll raise the whole issue with the president."

REQUIRED

1. What events or relationships may have led to Whisler's outburst?
2. As Phillipson, how would you answer Whisler's contentions?
3. What alternative actions can Phillipson take to improve future relationships?

1-30 The chief financial officer and the controller. Juan Rodriguez used to be the controller of Alliance Electronics and has just been promoted to the position of chief financial officer (CFO) of the company.

REQUIRED

1. Describe Rodriguez's major responsibilities in his former position as a controller.
2. As CFO, what is the scope of Rodriguez's new responsibilities?

1-31 Software procurement decision, ethics. Jorge Michaels is the Winnipeg-based controller of Mexa Foods, a rapidly growing manufacturer and marketer of Mexican food products. Michaels is currently considering the purchase of a new cost management package for use by each of its six manufacturing plants and its many marketing personnel. Four major competing products are being considered by Michaels.

Horizon 1-2-3 is an aggressive software developer. It views Mexa as a target of opportunity. Every six months Horizon has a three-day users conference in a Caribbean location. Each conference has substantial time left aside for "rest and recreation." Horizon offers Michaels an all-expenses-paid visit to the upcoming conference in Cancun, Mexico. Michaels accepts the offer, believing that it will be very useful to talk to other users of Horizon software. He is especially looking forward to the visit as he has close relatives in the Cancun area.

Before leaving, Michaels receives a visit from the president of Mexa. She shows him an anonymous letter sent to her. It argues that Horizon is receiving unfair favourable treatment in the Mexa software decision-making process. The letter specifically mentions Michaels's upcoming "all-expenses-paid trip to Cancun during Winnipeg's deep winter." Michaels is deeply offended. He says he has made no decision and believes he is very capable of making a software choice on the merits of each product. Mexa currently does not have a formal written code of ethics.

REQUIRED

1. Do you think Michaels faces an ethical problem as regards his forthcoming visit to the Horizon users' group meeting? Refer to Exhibit 1-7 (pp. 18–19). Explain.
2. Should Mexa allow executives to attend users' meetings while negotiating with other vendors about a purchase decision? Explain. If yes, what conditions on attending should apply?
3. Would you recommend Mexa develop its own code of ethics to handle situations such as this one? What are the pros and cons of having such a written code?

1-32 Professional ethics and end-of-year games. Janet Taylor is the new division controller of the snack foods division of National Foods. National Foods has reported a minimum 15% growth in annual earnings for each of the past five years. The snack foods division has reported annual earnings growth of more than 20% each year in this same period. During the current year, the economy went into a recession. The corporate controller estimates a 10% annual earnings growth rate for National Foods in this year. One month before the December 31 fiscal year-end of the current year, Taylor estimates the snack foods division will report an annual earnings growth of only 8%. Warren Ryan, the snack foods division president, is less than happy, but he says with a wry smile, "Let the end-of-year games begin."

Taylor makes some inquiries and is able to compile the following list of end-of-year games that were more or less accepted by the prior division controller:

a. Deferring routine monthly maintenance in December on packaging equipment by an independent contractor until January of next year
b. Extending the close of the current fiscal year beyond December 31 so that some sales of next year are included in the current year
c. Altering dates of shipping documents of next January's sales to record them as sales in December of the current year
d. Giving salespeople a double bonus to exceed December sales targets
e. Deferring the current period's advertising by reducing the number of television spots run in December and running more than planned in January of next year
f. Deferring the current period's reported advertising costs by having National Foods' outside advertising agency delay billing December advertisements until January of next year or having the agency alter invoices to conceal the December date
g. Persuading carriers to accept merchandise for shipment in December of the current year although they normally would not have done so

1. Why might the snack foods division president want to play the end-of-year games described here?
2. The division controller is deeply troubled and reads the Code of Professional Ethics in Exhibit 1-7 (pp. 18–19). Classify each of the end-of-year games as (i) acceptable or (ii) unacceptable according to that document.
3. What should Taylor do if Ryan suggests that end-of-year games are played in every division of National Foods and that she would greatly harm the snack foods division if she did not play along and paint the rosiest picture possible of the division's results?

COLLABORATIVE LEARNING PROBLEMS

1-33 Responding to allegations of fraud. You are the controller of Broad Street Finance (BSF). BSF is an investment banking company that has recently encountered severe financial difficulties and has had to lay off more than 200 employees. The only bright spot in this picture is BSF's bond trading division, but you have just received the following anonymous letter:

Dear Sir,

Last year's reported earnings for the bond trading division are fictitious. The top three managers of the division recently received bonuses of more than $12 million, based on their share of last year's reported earnings. The head of bond trading has been inventing bond trades that are supposed to be highly profitable. They are not. The division profits are like a house of cards about to collapse. The head of bond trading cares only about "how much you reportedly made" and nothing about how you made it. The auditors don't understand the complexity of today's bond trading operations. This problem will blow up in your face unless handled quickly and carefully. I am sending a copy of this letter to the Ontario Securities Commission, the *Financial Post*, *Canadian Business*, *The Globe and Mail*, and all members of Broad Street's board of directors.

Sincerely,
Concerned Ex-employee

INSTRUCTIONS

Form groups of three or more students. One will be the chief financial officer, one the president, and one the chairperson of the board of directors. Other members are on the board of directors.

REQUIRED

Develop a group consensus on how you should respond to this letter. Like many firms in the financial services industry, BSF has no formal code of ethics. Should BSF formalize a code of ethics statement?

1-34 Global company, ethical challenges with bribery. Shell Oil Company operates in many parts of the globe. These operations include oil exploration, production, transportation, refining, and marketing. One challenge faced by Shell is how to handle requests for "bribes" and "facilitating payments." The chair of Shell's operations recently gave an address where he "claimed that Shell loses valuable business because it refuses to pay bribes."

One form of bribe is a payment to a private bank account that is portrayed as a charitable donation. Shell's chair noted that "on occasion it has been suggested to me that Shell's cause would be much helped by a donation to a national cultural or humanitarian fund—which just happens to have a bank account in Switzerland." Another form of a bribe is a payment to an "intermediary" in which a company pays a third party for a "go-between" role that could be more efficiently handled without the third party. The "intermediary" handles the bribery payment plus takes an extra facilitating payment.

The Shell chair concluded the address as follows: "We do not bribe. We do not sanction any type of illegal payment of any kind anywhere, directly or indirectly, and any employee who is found to have done so will be dismissed and, if possible, prosecuted. The principle employees have to follow is simple: 'Just say no.'"

REQUIRED

1. Suppose you are a shareholder of Shell. Would you prefer Shell to pay bribes if it meant "gaining valuable business"?
2. Suppose you are the CFO of Shell. You suspect that one of your overseas subsidiaries is making payments to a local law firm for being an "intermediary" as well as for legal services. This subsidiary also makes payments to several Swiss-based "humanitarian funds" of questionable nature. How would you examine whether bribery is occurring? If you discovered it was, what actions would you take?

3. Suppose again you are the CFO of Shell. A major oil discovery by Shell occurs in a country whose political regime is run by a dictator. His extended family has vast business dealings with oil companies. Shell's market capitalization increases by $2 billion when news of the discovery is released. Shell owns the oil leases and is negotiating with the government for construction of an oil refining plant. You are told by the dictator's key advisor that one of the dictator's sons has a company that will have 10% equity in the oil refinery (with no payment) and be actively involved at the director and operating level of the local refining subsidiary. You contact two other oil companies with prior dealings in this country and hear stories about "facilitating payments" and other questionable expenditures. One company called it an "auditor's nightmare." The board of directors of Shell has asked you (as CFO) to make a presentation on all financial aspects of the oil refinery project. What ethical issues (with proposed solutions) would you raise in your presentation?

1-35 Global company, ethical challenges with bribery. In June, the government of Safistan invited bids for construction of two hydroelectric plants. Norris Energy Company obtained the necessary information and specifications. Because Norris was eager to enter the market in the region where Safistan is located, the company's bid was prepared very carefully with an expected profit margin only one-half of the normal profit on similar projects. The bid was submitted before the deadline. After two weeks, Norris received an acknowledgment from Safistan's Ministry of Water and Electricity that its bid had been received. Several weeks went by without any further communication. After waiting what Norris thought was a reasonable period, Stan Cheng, vice-president of global operations, wrote letters to the appropriate government officials of Safistan but received no response. He talked by telephone to several officials at the ministry but they were not helpful. Finally, Cheng sought assistance from the government's commercial attaché in Safistan. The commercial attaché advised Cheng to visit Safistan because: "In this culture they only deal with business people they know personally." Cheng immediately left for Safistan. The commercial attaché was able to arrange a meeting for Cheng with the minister of water and electricity. Cheng made himself thoroughly familiar with the project specifications and the bid in preparation for the meeting with the deputy minister. He was anxious for the meeting to go well because it was a multi-million-dollar project.

Cheng went to the deputy minister's office and from there was escorted to the meeting room. Soon the deputy minister arrived with his second-in-command, Sufi Gharib. After introductions and exchanging pleasantries, the deputy minister asked Cheng a few questions about Norris Energy's bid. After listening to Cheng's responses, the deputy minister said, "I am favourably inclined toward your bid, but a few details need to be worked out. I have to go to another meeting, but Mr. Gharib is authorized to negotiate with you."

After the departure of the deputy minister, Gharib said to Cheng, "I can guarantee that your bid will be accepted if you pay a $1-million commission." It was clear to Cheng that "commission" was nothing more than a bribe. He told Gharib that it would be impossible for his company to make such a payment due to government laws and corporate policy. Gharib stood up, shook Cheng's hand, and wished him a pleasant trip home.

REQUIRED
1. As a shareholder of the company, would you prefer that Norris Energy make the payment?
2. Cheng shared his experience in Safistan with Charlie Short, who is manager of global operations in another company. Charlie told him that his "personal philosophy" is to make such payments if such a practice is part of the local culture. Do you think that Charlie's comment has some merit?
3. Why would Norris Energy have a corporate policy against such payments?

CHAPTER 2

An Introduction to Cost Terms and Purposes

Successful business managers understand not only the costs of a business but also how costs will change when a new course of action is undertaken. For example, at the auto show in Detroit in 2005, DaimlerChrysler introduced its production vehicle, the Dodge Charger (top), and in 2006 its concept car, the Dodge Challenger (bottom). To make decisions regarding pricing, capital acquisitions, and expansion that result in growth and improved profitability, managers must distinguish among cost objects, direct costs, indirect costs, fixed costs, and variable costs. The introduction of new vehicles by DaimlerChrysler has produced both higher sales revenue and increased market share—a successful decision.

LEARNING OBJECTIVES

After studying this chapter, you should be able to

1. Define and illustrate a cost object
2. Distinguish between direct costs and indirect costs
3. Explain cost drivers, variable costs, and fixed costs
4. Interpret unit costs cautiously
5. Distinguish among merchandising companies, manufacturing companies, and service-sector companies
6. Describe the three categories of inventories commonly found in manufacturing-sector companies
7. Distinguish inventoriable costs from period costs
8. Explain why product costs are computed in different ways for different purposes
9. Describe a framework for cost accounting and cost management

Accounting reports contain a variety of cost concepts and terms representing a lot of information. Managers who understand these concepts and terms are able to best use the information provided, as well as to avoid misuse of that information. A common understanding of the meaning of cost concepts and terms facilitates communication among managers and management accountants. This chapter discusses cost concepts and terms expressed in accounting information used for internal and external reporting.

COSTS AND COST TERMINOLOGY

OBJECTIVE 1

Define and illustrate
a cost object

Cost. Resource sacrificed or forgone to achieve a specific objective.

Actual costs. Costs incurred (historical costs), as distinguished from budgeted or forecasted costs.

Budgeted costs. Costs that are a management estimate of probable future costs in contrast to actual costs that have already been incurred (historical).

An understanding of this chapter's cost terms and concepts provides the foundation for the remaining chapters.

In the definition of *cost,* "sacrificed" refers to a resource that is consumed—for example, a company paying $3,000 to lease a warehouse. "Forgone" refers to giving up an opportunity to use a resource—for example, after spending the $3,000 to lease a warehouse, the company could not use it for another purpose.

Cost object. Anything for which a separate measurement of costs is desired.

Cost accumulation. The collection of cost data in some organized way through an accounting system.

Cost assignment. General term that encompasses both (1) tracing accumulated costs to a cost object and (2) allocating accumulated costs to a cost object.

Accountants usually define **cost** as a resource sacrificed or forgone to achieve a specific objective. A cost (such as direct materials or advertising) is usually measured as the monetary amount that must be paid to acquire goods or services. An **actual cost** is the cost incurred (a historical or past cost), as distinguished from a **budgeted cost**, which is a predicted or forecasted cost (a future cost).

To guide their decisions, managers want to know how much a particular thing (such as a product, machine, service, or process) costs. We call this thing a **cost object**, which is anything for which a measurement of costs is desired. Exhibit 2-1 provides examples of several different types of cost objects.

Cost Accumulation and Cost Assignment

A costing system typically accounts for costs in two basic stages:

◆ **Stage 1.** It *accumulates* costs by some "natural" (often self-descriptive) classification such as materials, labour, fuel, advertising, or shipping.
◆ **Stage 2.** It *assigns* these costs to cost objects.

Cost accumulation is the collection of cost data in some organized way through an accounting system. For example, a publishing company that purchases rolls of paper for printing magazines collects (accumulates) the costs of individual rolls used in any one month to obtain the total monthly cost of paper. **Cost assignment** is a general term that encompasses both (1) tracing accumulated costs to a cost object and (2) allocating accumulated costs to a cost object. Costs that are traced to a cost object are direct costs, and costs that are allocated to a cost object are indirect costs. Management accountants help managers to assign costs to designated cost objects (such as each magazine the company publishes) to help managers make strategic decisions (such as the pricing of different magazines and which magazines to emphasize). Managers also assign costs to cost objects to implement strategy. For example, costs assigned to a department aid in decision making about department efficiency. Costs may also be assigned to a product or a customer to facilitate product or customer profitability analysis and help managers decide how to profitably allocate resources to support different customers.

EXHIBIT 2-1
Examples of Cost Objects

Cost Object	Illustration
Product	A ten-speed bicycle
Service	An airline flight from Toronto to Marseilles
Project	An airplane assembled by Boeing for Singapore Airlines
Customer	All products purchased by Loblaws (the customer) from General Foods
Brand category	All soft drinks sold by a Pepsi-Cola bottling company with "Pepsi" in their name
Activity	A test to determine the quality level of a television set
Department	A department within a government environmental agency that studies air emissions standards
Program	A university's athletic program

Cost Tracing and Cost Allocation

A major question concerning costs is whether they have a direct or an indirect relationship to a particular cost object.

◆ **Direct costs of a cost object** are costs that are related to the particular cost object and can be *traced* to it in an economically feasible (cost-effective) way. For example, the cost of wood used to make hockey sticks and baseball bats is a direct cost. Why? Because the type and amount of wood used can be easily traced to each stick or bat.

Direct costs of a cost object. Costs that are related to the particular cost object and can be traced to it in an economically feasible way.

◆ **Indirect costs of a cost object** are costs that are related to the particular cost object but cannot be traced to it in an economically feasible (cost-effective) way. Indirect costs are *allocated* to the cost object using a cost allocation method. For example, the cost of leasing the factory where the sticks and bats are manufactured is an indirect cost of each product. Why? Because, although the building is necessary to house the materials, machinery, and workers as they make the sticks and bats, it is not cost-effective to try to determine exactly how much of the monthly lease cost was used during the production of a specific stick or a specific bat.

Indirect costs of a cost object. Costs that are related to the particular cost object but cannot be traced to it in an economically feasible way.

The relationship between these terms is shown below:

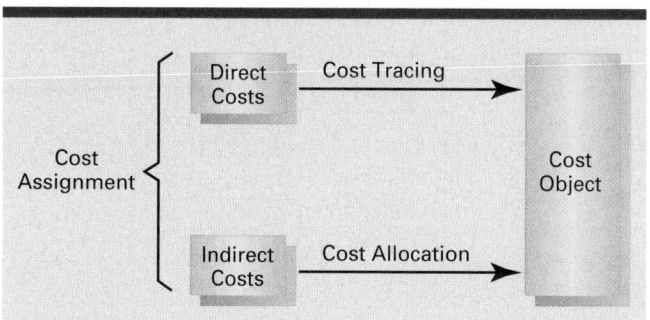

Cost tracing is the assigning of direct costs to the chosen cost object. **Cost allocation** is the assigning of indirect costs to the chosen cost object. *Cost assignment* encompasses both cost tracing and cost allocation.

Cost tracing. The assigning of direct costs to the chosen cost object.

Managers want to assign costs accurately to cost objects. Inaccurate product costs will mislead managers about the profitability of different products; as a result, managers might unknowingly promote unprofitable products while not promoting profitable products. Generally, managers are more confident about the accuracy of direct costs of cost objects, such as the cost of wood for a hockey stick.

Cost allocation. The assigning of indirect costs to the chosen cost object.

Indirect costs pose more problems. Consider the lease. Allocating the cost of the lease on the basis of the total floor space occupied by the workers of each type of product makes sense. This approach measures the building resources used by each product (stick or bat) reasonably accurately. The more square metres of floor space a manufacturing line occupies, the more lease costs that should be assigned to it. This allocation assumes that the quality of the space (such as the layout and the number of windows offering good lighting) used by the product lines is similar. Accurately allocating other indirect costs, such as the cost of heating, is more difficult. Should these costs be allocated on the basis of the number of workers, the square metres heated, the number of sticks or bats sold? Some other measure? It is not so clear how to measure the share of heating costs used to manufacture each product. The Focus on Values and Behaviours feature (p. 32) describes some additional issues managers might face when allocating costs.

Overcharging the Government

Distinguishing direct costs from indirect costs and deciding how to allocate indirect costs to products requires management accountants to work closely with managers. Sometimes, however, managers may have a personal financial incentive to propose a cost allocation method that will allocate fewer costs to some products and higher costs to others. For example, General Electric (GE), a top Fortune 500 company with multi-million-dollar government aerospace contracts, was found to have overcharged employee direct labour hours on projects. Top management responded by developing the company's ethics and integrity policy, which all employees must now sign when hired. In addition, the company posts its policy publicly on the Web and includes a section urging employees to be on the lookout for improper, incomplete, or unauthorized cost charging on contracts.

Consider another example. The U.S. Department of Defense (DoD) has contracts with private companies such as Lockheed Martin, General Dynamics, and Boeing to supply military equipment such as fighter jets, submarines, and tanks. Through its own internal Defense Contract Audit Agency (DCAA), the DoD discovered that some of its equipment suppliers had overallocated indirect costs to the DoD products and underallocated indirect costs to their other commercial products. The reason: the DoD paid suppliers on the basis of a cost-plus profit margin. The higher the costs the supplier allocated to the DoD business, the higher the revenues the supplier earned. In a recent case, the DCAA, through its normal audit process, found that Halliburton KBR overcharged the U.S. government as much as US$61 million for fuel sold to Iraq as part of the government's rebuilding contract.

Management accountants must always make careful and professional judgments when choosing among alternative cost-allocation methods. The failure of the defence contractors' management accountants to properly allocate costs to the DoD led to severe penalties and fines for their companies and, in some cases, criminal prosecution.

Sources: For Halliburton and DCAA; Lawrence DiRita, Acting ASD (Public Affairs) Thursday, December 11, 2003; www.defenselink.mil/transcripts/2003/ tr20031211-0985.html.

Factors Affecting Direct/Indirect Cost Classifications

Several factors will affect the classification of a cost as direct or indirect:

1. **The materiality of the cost in question.** The higher the cost in question, the more likely it is economically feasible to trace it as a direct cost to a particular cost object. Consider a mail-order catalogue company. It would probably be economically feasible to trace the courier charges for delivering a package directly to each customer. But the cost of the invoice paper included in the package sent to the customer is likely to be classified as an indirect cost, because it is not economically feasible to trace the cost of this paper to each customer. The benefits of knowing the exact number of (say) $0.05 worth of paper included in each package does not justify the costs of money and time to trace it to each package.

2. **Information-gathering technology.** Improvements, such as bar codes, allow many manufacturing plants to reclassify certain materials previously classified as indirect costs as direct costs of products. Bar codes can be read simultaneously into both the inventory and product manufacturing cost

file by waving a handheld scanner or "wand" in the same quick and efficient way supermarkets now enter the cost of many items purchased by their customers.

3. **Design of operations.** Facility design can affect cost classification. For example, classifying a cost as direct is helpful if an organization's facility (or part thereof) is dedicated exclusively for a specific cost object such as a product or particular customer.

This book examines different ways to assign costs to cost objects. What complicates matters further is that a specific cost may be a direct cost of one cost object and an indirect cost of another cost object. *That is, the direct/indirect classification depends on the choice of the cost object.* For example, the salary of an Assembly Department supervisor at DaimlerChrysler is a direct cost if the cost object is the Assembly Department, but it is an indirect cost if the cost object is a product such as the company's Dodge Charger because the Assembly Department assembles many different models. In general, the broader the definition of the cost object—an entire department rather than a single product—the higher direct costs are as a proportion of total costs and the more confidence management has in the accuracy of the resulting cost amounts.

COST DRIVERS AND COST MANAGEMENT

The continuous cost reduction efforts of competitors create a never-ending need for organizations to reduce their own costs. Cost reduction efforts frequently focus on two key areas:

OBJECTIVE 3

Explain cost drivers, variable costs, and fixed costs

1. Doing only **value-added activities**, that is, those activities that customers perceive as adding value to the products or services they purchase

2. Efficiently managing the use of the cost drivers in those value-added activities

A **cost driver** (*cost generator* or *cost determinant*) is any factor that causes costs to change for a specified cost object. For example, if the cost of product design activity increases when the quantity of parts for the product increases, then the quantity of parts in the product is a cost driver of product design costs.

Exhibit 2-2 presents examples of cost drivers in each business function in the value chain. Some cost drivers are financial measures found in accounting systems (such as direct manufacturing labour costs and sales dollars), while others are non-financial variables (such as the number of parts per product and the number of service calls).

Cost management is the set of actions that managers take to satisfy customers while continuously reducing and controlling costs. Successful managers, however, understand that changes in a particular cost driver do not automatically lead to the same changes in overall costs. Consider the situation where the cost driver for labour distribution costs is measured as quantity of items distributed. Assume managers reduce the quantity of items distributed by 25%. This reduction will not automatically translate to a 25% reduction in labour distribution costs. If some types of items take more time to distribute than others and if the items eliminated took little time, then the reduction in labour costs will not equal the reduction in quantity of items distributed. To reduce labour distribution costs, perhaps managers must shift workers out of distribution into other business functions, employ workers with lower seniority and therefore lower wages, or lay off some distribution employees. We now discuss the role of cost drivers in describing cost behaviour.

Value-added activities. Activities that customers perceive as adding value to the products or services they purchase.

Cost driver. Any factor that affects total costs. That is, a change in the level of the cost driver will cause a change in the level of the total cost of a related cost object.

Business Function	Cost Driver
Research and development	Number of research projects
	Personnel hours on a project
	Technical complexity of projects
Design of products, services, and processes	Number of products in design
	Number of parts per product
	Number of engineering hours
Production	Number of units produced
	Direct manufacturing labour costs
	Number of setups
	Number of engineering change orders
Marketing	Number of advertisements run
	Number of sales personnel
	Sales dollars
Distribution	Number of items distributed
	Number of customers
	Weight of items distributed
Customer service	Number of service calls
	Number of products serviced
	Hours spent servicing products

COST BEHAVIOUR PATTERNS: VARIABLE COSTS AND FIXED COSTS

Variable cost. Cost that changes in total in proportion to changes in a cost driver.

Fixed cost. Cost that does not change in total despite changes in a cost driver.

The distinction between variable costs and fixed costs is necessary to address key questions. For example, how much would manufacturing costs change if the output level increased by 5%?

Management accounting systems record the cost of resources acquired and track their subsequent use. By tracing these costs, managers can observe how these costs behave. Let us now consider two basic types of cost behaviour patterns found in many of these systems: variable costs and fixed costs. A **variable cost** is a cost that changes in total in proportion to changes in a cost driver. A **fixed cost** is a cost that does not change in total despite changes in a cost driver.

◆ **Variable costs.** If DaimlerChrysler buys a steering wheel at $60 for each of its Dodge Charger automobiles, then the total cost of steering wheels should be $60 times the number of cars assembled. This is an example of a variable cost, a cost that changes *in total* in proportion to changes in the cost driver (number of cars). The variable cost per car does not change with the number of cars assembled.

Number of Cars Produced (1)	Variable Cost per Steering Wheel (2)	Total Variable Cost of Steering Wheels (3) = (1) × (2)
1	$60	$ 60
1,000	60	60,000
3,000	60	180,000

Exhibit 2-3 (panel A) illustrates this variable cost. A second example of a variable cost is a sales commission of 5% of each sales dollar. Exhibit 2-3 (panel B) shows this variable-cost example.

◆ **Fixed costs.** DaimlerChrysler may incur $20 million in a given year for the leasing and insurance of its plant in Windsor. Assume the plant has the capacity to produce up to 50,000 cars. Both are examples of fixed costs, costs that are unchanged in total over a designated range of the cost driver during a

EXHIBIT 2-3
Examples of Variable Costs

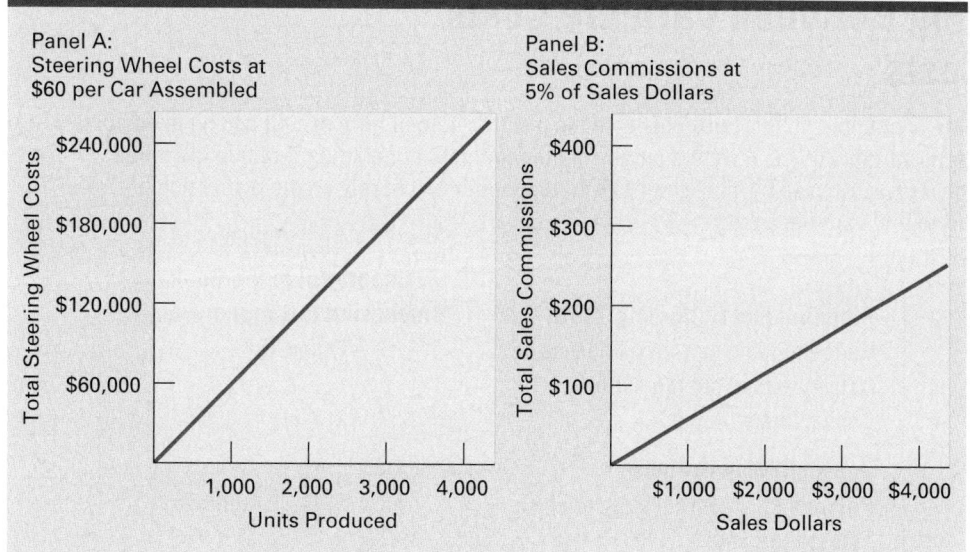

Panel A:
Steering Wheel Costs at
$60 per Car Assembled

Panel B:
Sales Commissions at
5% of Sales Dollars

given time span. Fixed costs become progressively smaller on a per-unit basis as the cost driver increases. For example, if DaimlerChrysler assembles 10,000 cars at this plant in a year, the fixed cost for leasing and insurance per vehicle is $2,000 ($20 million ÷ 10,000). In contrast, if 25,000 or 50,000 vehicles are assembled, the fixed cost per vehicle becomes $800 and $400 respectively.

Annual Total Fixed Leasing Costs (1)	Number of Cars Produced (2)	Fixed Leasing Cost per Car (3) = (1) ÷ (2)
$20,000,000	10,000	$2,000
20,000,000	25,000	800
20,000,000	50,000	400

Notice that the total leasing costs remain fixed. When this total is divided by the number of cars produced, the result is an average cost per unit. The average cost per vehicle changes because the denominator changes. Remember, however, that whether one or 50,000 vehicles are produced at the plant, the leasing cost will not change. Do not be misled by the change in average cost per unit. You must focus on the total cost, which remains unchanged despite significant changes in production output.

Some costs are fixed in the short run and therefore have no cost driver, but in the long run these same costs may vary. For example, the costs of testing colour printers at Hewlett-Packard are primarily the salary costs of unionized workers who run the testing equipment. These costs cannot be easily changed in the short run to match the volume of printers that must be tested. In the long run, however, if either a reduction or increase in volume of printers is permanent, then the company can plan either an orderly reduction or increase in levels of the equipment and labour that match the new volume. In the short run volume of printers is not a cost driver, but in the long run it is a cost driver of testing.

Do not assume that specific costs are inherently variable or fixed (see Global Surveys of Company Practice on p. 36). Consider labour costs. An example of purely variable labour costs occurs when workers are paid on a piece-unit basis. Some textile workers are paid on a per-shirt-sewn basis. In contrast, labour costs are appropriately classified as fixed when lifetime employment exists or where union conditions severely restrict an organization's flexibility to assign workers to any area that has extra labour requirements.

Example: Suppose you make belts using leather that costs $5/belt (a variable cost) in a workshop rented for $450/month (a fixed cost). Calculate total costs and per unit costs for 1 belt and 10 belts:

	1 Belt		10 Belts	
	Total	Per Unit	Total	Per Unit
Leather	$ 5	$ 5	$ 50	$ 5
Rent	450	450	450	45
Total	$455	$455	$500	$50

Total VC vary with the number of belts produced (from $5 to $50 as volume increases from 1 to 10 belts), but *per unit VC are constant* at $5/belt (for both 1 and 10 belts). *Total FC are constant* at $450 (for both 1 and 10 belts), but *per unit FC vary* with the number of belts produced (from $450 to $45 as volume increases from 1 to 10 belts). Therefore, total cost per belt depends on the number of belts produced.

DaimlerChrysler Canada Inc.
www.daimlerchrysler.ca/en/
index.html

Understanding Costs and Outputs
www.nps.navy.mil/drmi/
uccostout.htm

Distinguishing Between Variable Costs and Fixed Costs

Many chapters in this book illustrate the insights gained from distinguishing fixed costs from variable costs. A recent survey of management accounting practice identified several tools used by more than 40% of respondents that rely on the distinction between fixed and variable costs.[a]

Planning and Budgeting Tools	Chapter(s) in the Book Discussing the Tool in Detail
Budgeting and variance analysis	6, 7, 8, and 16
Activity-based management	5
Capital budgeting	21, 22
Decision-Support Tools	
Profitability and breakeven analysis	3, 4, 5, 11, 12, and 13
Transfer pricing	23
Product-Costing Analysis Tools	
Traditional costing	4
Overhead allocations	14, 15, and 16

Global surveys of company practice provide additional evidence that a large percentage of firms use systems that distinguish fixed costs from variable costs.

New Zealand[b] = 84%
United Kingdom[b] = 90%
Estonia[c] = 80%

When companies were asked to describe how they identify fixed and variable costs, "classification on a subjective basis based on managerial experience" and "treating all overheads as fixed and all direct costs as variable" were selected as the two most popular methods used in the United Kingdom and New Zealand.

[a]Garg, A., D. Ghosh, J. Hudick, and C. Nowacki, "Roles and Practices in Management Accounting Today: Results from the 2003 IMA–E & Y Survey," *Strategic Finance* (2003).

[b]Guilding, C., D. Lamminmaki, and C. Drury, "Budgeting and Standard Costing Practices in New Zealand and the United Kingdom," *The International Journal of Accounting* (1998).

[c]Haldma, T., and K. Lääts, "Contingencies Influencing the Management Accounting Practices of Estonian Manufacturing Companies," *Management Accounting Research* (2002).

Major Assumptions

The definitions of variable costs and fixed costs have five important underlying assumptions:

1. Costs are defined as variable or fixed with respect to a specific cost object.

2. The time span must be specified. Consider the $20 million rent and insurance DaimlerChrysler pays for its Windsor plant. This amount may be fixed for one year. Beyond that time, the rent and insurance may be renegotiated to be, say, $22 million for a subsequent year.

3. Total costs are linear. That is, when plotted on ordinary graph paper, a total variable-cost or fixed-cost relationship to the cost driver will appear as an unbroken straight line.

4. There is only one cost driver. The influences of other possible cost drivers on total costs are held constant or deemed insignificant.

5. Variations in the level of the cost driver are within a relevant range (which we discuss in the next section).

Variable costs and fixed costs are the two most frequently recognized cost behaviour patterns in existing management accounting systems. Additional cost behaviour patterns are discussed in subsequent chapters.

Relevant Range

A **relevant range** is the range of the cost driver in which a specific relationship between cost and driver is valid. A fixed cost is fixed only in relation to a given relevant range (usually wide) of the cost driver and a given time span (usually a particular budget period). Consider the Thomas Transport Company (TTC), which operates two refrigerated trucks that carry agricultural produce to market. Each truck has an annual fixed cost of $40,000 (including an annual insurance cost and registration fee) and a variable cost of $1.20 per kilometre of hauling. TTC has chosen kilometres of hauling to be the cost driver. The maximum annual usage of each truck is 120,000 kilometres. In the current year, the predicted combined total hauling of the two trucks is 170,000 kilometres.

Exhibit 2-4 shows how annual fixed costs behave at different levels of kilometres of hauling. Up to 120,000 kilometres, TTC can operate with one truck; from 120,001 to 240,000 kilometres, it can operate with two trucks; and from 240,001 to 360,000, it can operate with three trucks. This pattern would continue as TTC added trucks to its fleet. The bracketed section from 120,001 to 240,000 is the range at which TTC expects the $80,000 to be valid given the predicted 170,000-kilometre usage for the year.

Fixed costs may change from one year to the next. For example, if the annual registration fee for refrigerated trucks is increased, the total level of fixed costs will increase (unless offset by a reduction in other fixed items).

Relevant range. Range of the cost driver in which a specific relationship between cost and driver is valid.

Relationships of Types of Costs

We have introduced two major classifications of costs: direct/indirect and variable/fixed. Costs may simultaneously be

◆ Direct and variable
◆ Direct and fixed
◆ Indirect and variable
◆ Indirect and fixed

EXHIBIT 2-4
Fixed-Cost Behaviour at Thomas Transport Company

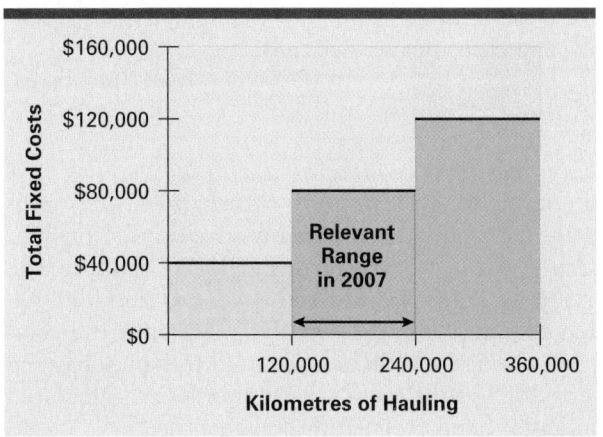

EXHIBIT 2-5
Examples of Simultaneous Direct/Indirect-Cost and Variable/Fixed-Cost Classifications

		Assignment of Costs to Cost Object	
		Direct Cost	**Indirect Cost**
Cost Behaviour Pattern	**Variable Cost**	*Cost object*: Assembled automobile *Example*: Tires used in assembly of automobile	*Cost object*: Assembled automobile *Example*: Power costs where power usage is metered only to the plant
	Fixed Cost	*Cost object*: Marketing department *Example*: Annual leasing cost of cars used by sales force representatives	*Cost object*: Marketing department *Example*: Monthly charge by corporate computer centre for marketing's share of corporate computer costs

Exhibit 2-5 presents examples of simultaneous cost classifications with each of the four cost types.

TOTAL COSTS AND UNIT COSTS

OBJECTIVE 4

Interpret unit costs cautiously

Unit cost (average cost).
Computed by dividing some total cost (the numerator) by some number of units (the denominator).

The preceding section concentrated on the behaviour patterns of total costs in relation to activity or volume levels. We now consider unit costs.

Meaning of Unit Costs

Accounting systems typically report both total-cost and unit-cost numbers. A **unit cost** (also called an **average cost**) is computed by dividing some total cost by some number of units. Suppose that $980,000 of manufacturing costs were incurred to produce 10,000 units of a finished good. Then the unit cost would be $98:

$$\frac{\text{Total Manufacturing Costs}}{\text{Quantity of Units Produced}} = \frac{\$980,000}{10,000} = \$98 \text{ per unit}$$

If 8,000 units are sold and 2,000 units remain in ending inventory, the unit-cost concept helps in the assignment of total costs for the income statement and balance sheet:

Cost of Goods Sold in the income statement	$784,000	(8,000 × $98)
Ending inventory of finished goods on the balance sheet	196,000	
Total manufacturing costs of 10,000 units	$980,000	

Unit costs are found in all areas of the value chain—for example, there are unit costs for product design, sales calls, and customer service calls.

Use Unit Costs Cautiously

Unit costs are averages. As we will see, they must be interpreted with caution. For decision making, it is best to think in terms of total costs rather than unit costs. Nevertheless, unit-cost numbers are frequently used in many situations. Consider the manager of the manufacturing plant of Western Products. Assume the $40,000,000 costs in 2007 consist of $10,000,000 of fixed costs and $30,000,000 of variable costs (at $60 variable costs per phone assembled). Suppose the total fixed costs and the variable cost per phone in 2008 are expected to be unchanged from 2007. The budgeted costs for 2008 at different production levels calculated on the basis of total variable costs, total fixed costs, and total costs are:

For many decisions, managers should use total costs rather than unit costs because fixed cost per unit changes when the related level of total volume changes. Consequently, unit costs should be interpreted with caution when they include a fixed-cost component.

Units Produced	Variable Cost per Unit	Total Variable Costs	Total Fixed Costs	Total Costs	Unit Cost
100,000	$60	$ 6,000,000	$10,000,000	$16,000,000	$160.00
200,000	60	12,000,000	10,000,000	22,000,000	110.00
500,000	60	30,000,000	10,000,000	40,000,000	80.00
800,000	60	48,000,000	10,000,000	58,000,000	72.50
1,000,000	60	60,000,000	10,000,000	70,000,000	70.00

A plant manager who uses the 2007 unit or average cost of $80 per unit would underestimate actual total costs if 2008 output is below the 2007 level of 500,000 units. If actual volume is 200,000 units due to, say, the presence of a new competitor, actual costs would be $22,000,000. Using the unit cost of $80 times 200,000 units predicts $16,000,000, which underestimates the actual total costs by $6,000,000 ($22,000,000 − $16,000,000). *The unit cost of $80 only applies when 500,000 units are produced.* An overreliance on unit cost in this situation could lead to insufficient cash being available to pay costs if volume declines to 200,000 units. As the preceding table indicates, for decision making, managers should think in terms of total variable costs, total fixed costs, and total costs rather than unit cost.

We now discuss cost concepts used in different sectors of the economy.

MERCHANDISING-, MANUFACTURING-, AND SERVICE-SECTOR COMPANIES

We first define three different sectors and provide examples of companies in each sector.

◆ **Merchandising-sector companies** purchase and then sell tangible products without changing their basic form. This sector includes companies engaged in retailing (such as bookstores or department stores), distribution, or wholesaling.

◆ **Manufacturing-sector companies** purchase materials and components and convert them into various finished goods. Examples are automotive companies, food-processing companies, and textile companies.

◆ **Service-sector companies** provide services or intangible products—for example, legal advice or audits—to their customers. Examples are law firms, accounting firms, banks, insurance companies, transportation companies, advertising agencies, radio and television stations, and Internet-based companies.

OBJECTIVE 5

Distinguish among merchandising companies, manufacturing companies, and service-sector companies

Service-sector company. A company that provides services or intangible products to their customers—for example, legal advice or an audit.

FINANCIAL STATEMENTS, INVENTORIABLE COSTS, AND PERIOD COSTS

The distinction between *inventoriable costs* and *period costs* is necessary for financial reporting in both the manufacturing and merchandising sectors of the economy. The deliverable of a service-sector company is intangible. Therefore service companies cannot maintain inventories. This is why concepts of inventoriable and period costs do not apply to service-sector companies. As background, we will first look at the different types of inventory that companies hold and some commonly used classifications of manufacturing costs.

OBJECTIVE 6

Describe the three categories of inventories commonly found in manufacturing-sector companies

Types of Inventory

Manufacturing-sector companies purchase materials and components and convert them into finished goods. These companies typically have one or more of the following three types of inventory:

1. **Direct materials inventory (DM).** Direct materials in stock and awaiting use in the manufacturing process (for example, the computer chips and components needed to manufacture cellular phones).

2. **Work-in-process inventory (WIP).** Goods partially worked on but not yet fully completed (for example, cellular phones at various stages of completion in the manufacturing process). Also called work-in-progress inventory.

Direct materials inventory (DM). Direct materials in stock and awaiting use in the manufacturing process.

Work-in-process inventory (work-in-progress inventory, WIP). Goods partially worked on but not yet fully completed.

Finished-goods inventory (FG).
Goods fully completed but not yet sold.

3. **Finished-goods inventory (FG).** Goods (for example, cellular phones) fully completed but not yet sold.

Merchandising-sector companies purchase tangible products and then sell them without changing their basic form. They hold only one type of inventory, which is products in their original purchased form called *merchandising inventory*. Service-sector companies provide only services or intangible products; they do not hold inventories.

Commonly Used Classifications of Manufacturing Costs

Three terms commonly used when describing manufacturing costs are direct materials costs, direct manufacturing labour costs, and indirect manufacturing costs.

Direct materials (DM) costs. The acquisition costs of all materials that eventually become part of the cost object (units finished or in process) and that can be traced to that cost object in an economically feasible way.

1. **Direct materials (DM) costs** are the acquisition costs of all materials that eventually become part of the cost object ("work in process" or "finished goods") and that can be exclusively and unambiguously linked to the cost object in an economically feasible way. Acquisition costs of direct materials include freight-in (inward delivery) charges, sales taxes, and custom duties. Examples include the bottles and cans used at Pepsi-Co, the paper used to print the *Calgary Herald*, and the wood used to manufacture hockey sticks and baseball bats.

Direct manufacturing labour (DL) costs. Compensation of all manufacturing labour specifically identified with the cost object (units finished or in process) and that can be traced to the cost object in an economically feasible way. This text uses the term direct manufacturing labour because labour used in other business functions of the value chain can also be traced directly to cost objects. For example, if the salaries of salespeople can be traced to specific customers, then these salaries will be direct costs and they can be termed direct marketing labour.

2. **Direct manufacturing labour (DL) costs** include the compensation of all manufacturing labour that can be exclusively and unambiguously linked to the cost object in an economically feasible way. Examples include wages and fringe benefits paid to machine operators and assembly-line workers.

Indirect manufacturing costs (manufacturing overhead costs, factory overhead costs). All manufacturing costs considered part of the cost object (units finished or in process) but cannot traced to that cost object in an economically feasible way.

3. **Indirect manufacturing costs** are all manufacturing costs considered part of the cost object, units finished or in process, but that cannot be exclusively and unambiguously linked to that cost object in an economically feasible way. Examples include heating, power, supplies, indirect materials (equipment lubricants), indirect manufacturing labour (custodial labour), plant rent or lease costs, plant insurance, property taxes, and amortization, as well as the compensation of plant managers. Other terms for this cost category include **manufacturing overhead costs** and **factory overhead costs.** We use *indirect manufacturing costs* and *manufacturing overhead costs* interchangeably in this book.

We next describe the important distinction between inventoriable and period costs.

Inventoriable Costs

OBJECTIVE 7

Distinguish inventoriable costs from period costs

Inventoriable costs. All costs of a product that are regarded as an inventory asset when they are incurred and then become a cost of goods sold when the product is sold. These are assets and have value as long as the company owns them. When product is sold from finished goods inventory, its cost is transferred from the balance sheet to the income statement as cost of goods sold (COGS).

Inventoriable costs are all costs of a product that are regarded as assets when they are incurred and then become cost of goods sold when the product is sold. For manufacturing-sector companies, all manufacturing costs are inventoriable costs. Costs of direct materials issued to production from direct materials inventory, direct manufacturing labour costs, and indirect manufacturing costs create new assets, beginning as work in process and becoming finished goods. Hence, manufacturing costs are included in work-in-process inventory and in finished-goods inventory (they are "inventoried") to accumulate the costs of creating these assets. When finished goods are sold, the cost of manufacturing the goods sold is matched against the revenues from the sale. The **cost of goods sold (COGS)** includes all manufacturing costs (direct materials, direct manufacturing labour, and indirect manufacturing costs) incurred to produce the goods sold. Finished goods may be sold during a different accounting period than the period in which the goods were manufactured. Thus, inventorying manufacturing costs during the period when they were manufactured and expensing the manufacturing costs of goods sold later when revenues are recognized achieves matching of revenues and expenses.

Cost of goods sold (COGS). Includes all manufacturing costs incurred to produce the goods sold.

For merchandising-sector companies such as Sears Canada Inc., inventoriable costs are the costs of purchasing the goods that are resold in their same form. These costs are the costs of the goods themselves and any incoming freight, insurance, and handling costs for those goods. For service-sector companies, the absence of inventories means there are no inventoriable costs.

Period Costs

Period costs (also called **operating costs**[1]) are all the costs on an income statement other than cost of goods sold. These costs are treated as expenses because they are presumed not to benefit future periods (or because there is insufficient evidence to conclude that such benefit exists). Expensing these costs in the period they are incurred matches expenses to revenues.

For manufacturing-sector companies, period costs include all nonmanufacturing costs, for example, research and development costs and distribution costs. For merchandising-sector companies, period costs include all costs not related to the cost of goods purchased for resale in their same form, for example, labour cost of shop floor personnel and marketing costs.

Merchandising-Sector Example

Panel A of Exhibit 2-6 (p. 42) presents the income statement of Prestige Bathrooms, a merchandiser of bathroom fixtures and furnishings (showers, sinks, fixtures, and so on). A merchandiser's cost of goods sold consists of the cost of goods purchased for resale adjusted for changes in the level of merchandise inventory:

$$\begin{array}{c}\text{Beginning} \\ \text{merchandise} \\ \text{inventory}\end{array} + \begin{array}{c}\text{Purchases of} \\ \text{merchandise}\end{array} - \begin{array}{c}\text{Ending} \\ \text{merchandise} \\ \text{inventory}\end{array} = \text{Cost of goods sold}$$

For Prestige Bathrooms in 2007, the corresponding amounts in Exhibit 2-6 (panel A) are

$$\$95,000 + \$1,100,000 - \$130,000 = \$1,065,000$$

The $315,000 operating costs of Prestige in panel A include amortization of noninventory assets as well as costs expensed to the period as incurred (such as the salaries of checkout staff and monthly cost of electricity). Examples of Prestige's operating costs include the costs of designing the showroom, sales personnel, and advertising.

Exhibit 2-6 (panel B) shows the relationship between inventoriable and period costs for merchandising companies. Merchandise purchased for resale is first shown as an asset; its cost is a capitalized inventoriable cost. As the merchandise is sold, its cost becomes an expense of that period in the form of cost of goods sold, sometimes termed cost of sales. Capitalized noninventoriable costs (such as the costs of fixtures and computers) are shown on the balance sheet as assets and then become operating cost line items in the form of amortization (and other forms of asset write-downs) over the useful life of the asset.

Subsequent chapters examine merchandising-sector costs in detail. These costs include cost of goods sold, period expensing of capitalized noninventoriable costs, and costs expensed as incurred (noncapitalized costs).

Manufacturing-Sector Example

The manufacturing sector differs from the merchandising sector in that the products sold to customers are converted to a different form from that of the products purchased from suppliers.

The income statement of a manufacturer, Cellular Products, is shown in Exhibit 2-7 (panel A, p. 43). This company manufactures telephone systems for large organizations.

The revenues of Cellular Products are (in thousands) $210,000. **Revenues** are inflows of assets (usually cash or accounts receivable) received for products or services provided to customers. Cost of goods sold in a manufacturing company is computed as follows:

$$\begin{array}{c}\text{Beginning} \\ \text{finished goods} \\ \text{inventory}\end{array} + \begin{array}{c}\text{Cost of} \\ \text{goods} \\ \text{manufactured}\end{array} - \begin{array}{c}\text{Ending} \\ \text{finished goods} \\ \text{inventory}\end{array} = \text{Cost of goods sold}$$

---

[1]The term *operating costs* is used by some companies to include cost of goods sold. In this book, we do not include cost of goods sold in operating costs.

EXHIBIT 2-6
Merchandising-Sector Income Statement

PANEL A: PRESTIGE BATHROOMS—INCOME STATEMENT FOR THE YEAR ENDED DECEMBER 31, 2007

Revenues		$1,500,000
Cost of goods sold:		
Beginning merchandise inventory, January 1, 2007	$ 95,000	
Purchases of merchandise	1,100,000	
Cost of goods available for sale	1,195,000	
Ending merchandise inventory, December 31, 2007	130,000	1,065,000
Gross margin (or gross profit)		435,000
Operating costs		315,000
Operating income		$ 120,000

PANEL B: MERCHANDISING COMPANY (RETAILER OR WHOLESALER)

Note that the term *cost of goods manufactured* refers to the cost of goods brought to completion (finished) during the year, whether they were started before or during the current year. Some of the manufacturing costs incurred during the year are held back as costs of the ending work-in-process inventory; similarly, the costs of the beginning work-in-process inventory become part of the cost of goods manufactured for the year.

Costs of goods manufactured (COGM). All costs incurred to produce finished goods during a specified accounting period, irrespective of the time period when production began.

For Cellular Products in 2007, the cost of goods sold and gross margin (refer to Panel A of Exhibit 2-7) are:

Revenue	$210,000
Beginning inventory of finished goods January 1, 2007	$ 22,000
+ Cost of goods manufactured in 2007	104,000
− Ending inventory of finished goods, December 31, 2007	(18,000)
= Cost of goods sold in 2007	$108,000
Gross margin = Revenues − Cost of goods sold = $210,000 − $108,000 =	$102,000

Cost of goods manufactured refers to the cost of goods brought to completion, whether they were started before or during the current accounting period. Cellular Products calculates the cost of goods manufactured in three steps (see Exhibit 2-7, Panel B).

Beginning work-in-process inventory January 1, 2007	$ 6,000
+ Total manufacturing costs incurred in 2007	105,000
= Total manufacturing costs to be accounted for	111,000
− Ending work-in-process inventory	(7,000)
= Cost of goods manufactured in 2007	$104,000

EXHIBIT 2-7

Income Statement and Schedule of Cost of Goods Manufactured of a Manufacturing-Sector Company, Cellular Products

	A	B	C
1	**PANEL A: INCOME STATEMENT**		
2	**Cellular Products**		
3	**Income Statement**		
4	**For the Year Ended December 31, 2007 (in thousands)**		
5	Revenues		$210,000
6	Cost of goods sold		
7	Beginning finished goods, January 1, 2007	$ 22,000	
8	Cost of goods manufactured (see Panel B)	104,000 ◀	
9	Cost of goods available for sale	126,000	
10	Ending finished goods, December 31, 2007	(18,000)	
11	Cost of goods sold		108,000
12	Gross margin (or gross profit)		102,000
13	Operating costs		
14	Marketing, distribution, and customer-service costs	70,000	
15	Total operating costs		70,000
16	Operating Income		$ 32,000
17			
18	**PANEL B: COST OF GOODS MANUFACTURED**		
19	**Cellular Products**		
20	**Schedule of Cost of Goods Manufactured[a]**		
21	**For the Year Ended December 31, 2007 (in thousands)**		
22	Direct Materials		
23	Beginning inventory of direct materials, January 1, 2007	$ 11,000	
24	Purchases of direct materials in 2007	73,000	
25	Cost of direct materials available for use	84,000	
26	Ending inventory of direct materials, December 31, 2007	(8,000)	
27	Direct materials used in 2007		76,000
28	Direct manufacturing labour		9,000
29	Indirect manufacturing costs:		
30	Indirect manufacturing labour	7,000	
31	Supplies	2,000	
32	Heat, light, and power	5,000	
33	Amortization—plant building	2,000	
34	Amortization—plant equipment	3,000	
35	Miscellaneous	1,000	
36	Total indirect manufacturing costs (manufacturing overhead)		20,000
37	Manufacturing costs incurred during 2007		105,000
38	Beginning work-in-process inventory, January 1, 2007		6,000
39	Total manufacturing costs to account for		111,000
40	Ending work-in-process inventory, December 31, 2007		(7,000)
41	Cost of goods manufactured (to Income Statement)		$104,000 ─
42			
43	[a]Note that this schedule can become a Schedule of Cost of Goods Manufactured and sold simply by including the beginning and ending finished goods inventory figures in the supporting schedule rather than in the body of the income statement.		

◆ **Step 1:** *Cost of direct materials used*

Beginning inventory of direct materials January 1, 2007	$ 11,000
+ Purchases of direct materials in 2007	73,000
− Ending inventory of direct materials, December 31, 2007	(8,000)
= Direct materials used in 2007	$ 76,000

◆ **Step 2:** *Total manufacturing costs incurred in 2007*

The manufacturing costs incurred during 2007 ($105,000) is a line item in panel B. This item refers to the "new" direct manufacturing costs and the "new" manufacturing overhead costs that were incurred during 2007 for all goods worked on during 2007, regardless of whether all those goods were fully completed during this year.

(i) Direct materials used in 2007 (shaded light green)	$ 76,000
(ii) Direct manufacturing labour in 2007 (shaded dark blue)	$ 9,000
(iii) Manufacturing overhead costs (shaded green)	$ 20,000
Total manufacturing costs incurred in 2007	$105,000

◆ **Step 3:** *Cost of goods manufactured in 2007*

The cost of goods manufactured during 2007 includes the cost of beginning work in process and costs incurred during the year. Also note that some of the manufacturing costs incurred during 2007 are held back as the cost of the ending work-in-process inventory. The cost of goods manufactured in 2007 is calculated as (shaded in a different colour from the items above in Panel B):

Beginning work-in-process inventory January 1, 2007	$ 6,000
+ Total manufacturing costs incurred in 2007	105,000
= Total manufacturing costs to be accounted for	111,000
− Ending work-in-process inventory	(7,000)
= Cost of goods manufactured in 2007	$104,000

Exhibit 2-8 shows related general-ledger T-accounts for Cellular Products' manufacturing cost flow. Note how the cost of goods manufactured ($104,000) is the cost of all goods completed during the accounting period. These costs are all inventoriable costs. Goods completed during the period are transferred to finished goods inventory. These costs become cost of goods sold in the accounting period when the goods are sold. Also note that the direct materials, direct manufacturing labour, and manufacturing overhead costs of the units in work-in-process inventory ($7,000) and finished goods inventory ($18,000) as of December 31, 2007, will appear as an asset on the balance sheet. These costs will become expenses next year, when these units are sold.

The $70,000 comprising marketing costs, distribution costs, and customer-service costs are period costs of Cellular Products. These period costs include operating cost items in the income statement in panel A of Exhibit 2-7 (1) the expensing of capitalized noninventoriable costs (such as amortization on a fleet of delivery vehicles or amortization on computers purchased for marketing personnel) and (2) the cost of items recorded

EXHIBIT 2-8
General-Ledger T-Accounts for Cellular Products' Manufacturing Cost Flow

Work-in-Process Inventory		Finished Goods Inventory		Cost of Goods Sold
Bal. Jan. 1, 2007 6,000	Cost of goods	Bal. Jan. 1, 2007 22,000	Cost of goods sold 108,000 →	108,000
Direct materials used 76,000	manufactured 104,000 →	104,000		
Direct manuf. labour 9,000		Bal. Dec. 31, 2007 18,000		
Manuf. overhead costs 20,000				
Bal. Dec. 31, 2007 7,000				

as an expense as incurred (such as the salaries of customer service representatives). Operating income of Cellular Products is $32,000. **Operating income** is total revenues from operations minus cost of goods sold and period costs (excluding interest expense and income taxes).

> **Operating income.** Operating income is the total revenues from operations minus total costs from operations (excluding interest expense and income taxes) including costs of goods sold.

Newcomers to cost accounting frequently assume that indirect costs such as rent, telephone, and amortization are always costs of the period in which they are incurred and are not associated with inventories. When these costs are incurred in marketing or in corporate headquarters, they are period costs. However, when these costs are incurred in manufacturing, they are manufacturing overhead costs and are inventoriable.

Recap of Inventoriable Costs and Period Costs

Exhibit 2-9 highlights the differences between inventoriable costs and period costs.

Panel A uses the merchandising sector and Panel B the manufacturing sector to illustrate these differences. First study Panel A. The merchandising costs of goods available for sale are simply the costs of purchasing these goods. The purchase costs are the only inventoriable costs, which become cost of goods sold when the inventory is sold. In Panel B the manufacturing costs of finished goods include direct materials, other direct manufacturing costs such as direct manufacturing labour, and manufacturing overhead costs such as supervision, production control, and machine maintenance. All these costs are inventoriable. They are assigned to work-in-process inventory until the goods are completed and then to finished goods inventory until the goods are sold. All nonmanufacturing costs, such as R&D, design, and distribution costs, are period costs.

Prime Costs and Conversion Costs

Two terms used in manufacturing cost systems are *prime costs* and *conversion costs*. **Prime costs** are all direct manufacturing costs. For Cellular Products,

> **Prime costs.** All direct manufacturing costs.

$$\text{Prime costs} = \text{Direct material costs} + \text{Direct manufacturing labour costs}$$
$$= \$76,000 + \$9,000 = \$85,000$$

EXHIBIT 2-9
Relationships of Inventoriable Costs and Period Costs

PANEL A: MERCHANDISING COMPANY (RETAILER OR WHOLESALER)

BALANCE SHEET   INCOME STATEMENT

Inventoriable Costs { Merchandise Purchases → Merchandise Inventory — when sales occur → Cost of Goods Sold (an expense)

Revenues
deduct

Equals Gross Margin
deduct

Design Costs
Purchasing Dept. Costs
Marketing Costs
Distribution Costs
Customer-Service Costs
Administration Costs[a] } Period Costs

[a] Examples include labour costs of accounting, legal, and information technology support as well as insurance and amortization on non-manufacturing equipment.

Equals Operating Income

EXHIBIT 2-9
Continued

PANEL B: MANUFACTURING COMPANY

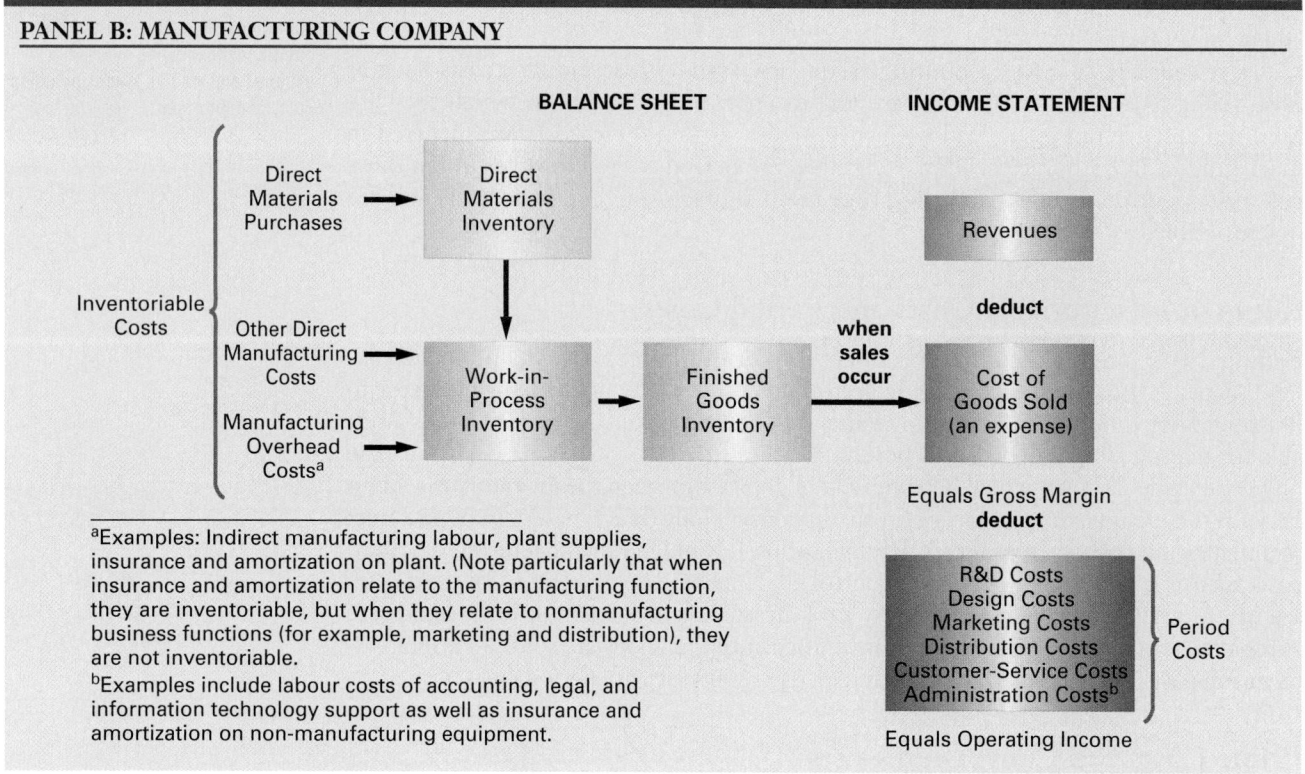

BALANCE SHEET   INCOME STATEMENT

ᵃExamples: Indirect manufacturing labour, plant supplies, insurance and amortization on plant. (Note particularly that when insurance and amortization relate to the manufacturing function, they are inventoriable, but when they relate to nonmanufacturing business functions (for example, marketing and distribution), they are not inventoriable.

ᵇExamples include labour costs of accounting, legal, and information technology support as well as insurance and amortization on non-manufacturing equipment.

Conversion costs. All manufacturing costs other than direct materials costs.

Question: Do prime costs + conversion costs = total manufacturing costs?
Answer: Only under the two-part classification: prime costs = direct material costs, and conversion costs = manufacturing overhead costs (which include direct manufacturing labour). Under the three-part classification, direct manufacturing labour is both a prime cost and a conversion cost, so the equation in the question would double-count direct manufacturing labour.

We have already noted that the higher the proportion of prime costs in a company's cost structure, the more confident managers can be about the accuracy of their product costs. As information-gathering technology improves, companies have the capability to create additional direct cost categories. For example, power costs might be metered in specific areas of a plant that are dedicated totally to the assembly of separate products. In this case, prime costs would include direct materials, direct manufacturing labour, and direct metered power. Furthermore, if a production line was dedicated to the manufacture of a specific product, the amortization on the production equipment could be traced as a direct manufacturing cost and would be included in the prime costs. Computer software companies often have a "purchased technology" direct manufacturing cost item. This item, which covers payments to third parties who develop software algorithms included in a product, would also be included in prime costs.

Conversion costs are all manufacturing costs other than direct materials costs. These represent all manufacturing costs incurred to convert direct materials into finished goods. For Cellular Products,

Conversion costs = Direct manufacturing labour costs + Manufacturing overhead costs
= $9,000 + $20,000 = $29,000

Note that direct manufacturing labour costs can be a part of both prime costs and conversion costs.

Some manufacturing operations such as computer-integrated manufacturing (CIM) plants have very few workers. The workers' roles are to monitor the manufacturing process and to maintain the equipment that produces multiple products. Costing systems in CIM plants do not have a direct manufacturing labour cost category because direct manufacturing labour cost is relatively small and because it is difficult to trace this cost to products. In CIM plants, the only prime cost is direct materials costs, and conversion costs consist only of manufacturing overhead costs.

The components of prime costs and conversion costs for the three-part and two-part classifications can be summarized as follows:

	Three-Part Classification	Two-Part Classification
Prime costs	Direct materials costs	Direct materials costs
Conversion costs	Direct manufacturing labour costs Indirect manufacturing costs	All remaining manufacturing costs

MEASURING COSTS REQUIRES JUDGMENT

Since differences can exist in the way accounting terms are defined, judgment is frequently required when measuring costs. Care should be taken to define and understand the way costs are measured in an organization or situation in which costs are an issue. We first illustrate this point with respect to labour cost measurement.

Measuring Labour Costs

Manufacturing labour-cost classifications vary among companies, but the following distinctions are generally found:

Direct labour (already defined)

Manufacturing overhead (examples of prominent labour components of this manufacturing overhead follow):

    Indirect labour (compensation)
        Forklift truck operators (internal handling of materials)
        Janitors (custodial)
        Plant guards (security)
        Maintenance
        Rework labour (time spent by direct labourers redoing defective work)
        Overtime premium paid to *all* plant workers
        Idle time

    Managers' salaries

    Payroll fringe costs (for example, health care premiums, pension costs)

All manufacturing labour compensation, other than that for direct labour and managers' salaries, is usually classified as *indirect labour costs*, a major component of manufacturing overhead. The term *indirect labour* is usually divided into many sub-classifications. The wages of forklift truck operators are generally not combined with janitors' wages, for example, although both are regarded as indirect labour.

Managers' salaries are usually not classified as part of indirect labour. Instead, the compensation of supervisors, department heads, and all others who are regarded as part of manufacturing management is placed in a separate classification of manufacturing overhead labelled Miscellaneous in Panel B of Exhibit 2-7 (p. 43).

Overtime Premium

Costs are classified in a detailed fashion mainly to associate an individual cost with its specific cause or reason for incurrence. Two classes of indirect labour need special mention. **Overtime premium** consists of wages paid to all workers (for both direct labour and indirect labour) in *excess* of their straight-time wage rates. Overtime premium is usually considered a part of overhead. Consider an example from the service sector. George Flexner does home service calls for Sears Appliance Services. He gets $20 per hour for straight-time and gets time-and-a-half for overtime. His *premium* would be $10 per overtime hour. If he works 44 hours, including four overtime hours, in one week, his gross earnings would be classified as follows:

Overtime premium. Wages paid to all workers in excess of their straight-time wage rates.

Direct service labour: 44 hours × $20 per hour	$880
Overtime premium: 4 hours × $10 per hour	40
Total compensation for 44 hours	$920

Why is overtime premium of direct labour usually considered an indirect rather than a direct cost? After all, it can usually be traced to specific batches of work. It is generally not considered a direct charge because the scheduling of repair jobs is generally either random or in accordance with overall minimizing of travel times. For example, assume that jobs 1 through 5 are scheduled for a specific workday of ten hours, including two overtime hours. Each service call (job) requires two hours. Should the job scheduled during hours nine and ten be assigned the overtime premium? Or should the premium be prorated over all the jobs? The latter approach does not "penalize"—add to the cost of—a particular batch of work solely because it happened to be worked on during the overtime hours. *Instead, the overtime premium is considered attributable to the heavy overall volume of work. Its cost is thus regarded as part of service overhead, which is borne by all repair jobs.*

Sometimes overtime is not random. For example, a special or rush job may clearly be the sole source of the overtime. In such instances, the overtime premium is regarded as a direct cost of the service on that job.

Another subclassification of indirect labour is the idle time of both direct and indirect manufacturing or service labour. This **idle time** typically represents wages paid for unproductive time caused by lack of orders, machine breakdowns, material shortages, poor scheduling, and the like. For example, if the Sears repair truck broke down for three hours, earnings would be classified as follows:

Idle time. Unproductive time caused by lack of orders, machine breakdowns, material shortages, poor scheduling, and so on.

Direct service labour: 41 hours × $20 per hour	$820
Idle time (service overhead): 3 hours × $20 per hour	60
Overtime premium: 4 hours × $10 per hour	40
Total compensation for 44 hours	$920

Clearly, the idle time is not related to a particular job, nor, as we have already discussed, is the overtime premium. Both overtime premium and idle time are considered overhead costs.

Benefits of Defining Accounting Terms

We cannot overemphasize the value of obtaining a thorough understanding of the classifications and cost terms introduced in this chapter and later in this book. Managers, accountants, suppliers, and other people will avoid many misunderstandings if they use the same meanings for technical terms.

Consider the classification of manufacturing labour *payroll fringe costs* (for example, employer contributions to employee benefits such as employment insurance, life insurance, health insurance, and pensions). Some companies classify these costs as manufacturing overhead. In other companies, however, the fringe benefits related to direct labour are charged as an additional direct labour cost.

Consider a direct labourer, such as a lathe operator or an assembly-line worker, who earns gross wages computed on the basis of a regular wage rate of $20 per hour. This person receives employee fringe benefits (employer contributions to the employee's pension plan, life insurance, health insurance, and so on) totalling $8 per hour. Some companies classify the $20 as direct manufacturing labour cost and the $8 as manufacturing overhead cost. Other companies classify the entire $28 as direct manufacturing labour cost. The latter approach is conceptually preferable, because these payroll fringe benefit costs are a fundamental part of acquiring manufacturing labour services. The magnitude of fringe benefits makes this issue important. Recently, the automotive industry in the United States compared the per vehicle costs of fringe benefits such as medical care coverage and payments incurred in the United States and Canada. The cost in the United States of these fringe benefits was approximately three times higher per vehicle than the Canadian cost.

The problem here is pinpointing what direct manufacturing labour includes and excludes in a particular situation. Achieving clarity may avoid disputes regarding cost reimbursement contracts, income tax provisions, and labour union matters. For example, some countries offer substantial income tax savings to companies that locate manufacturing plants there. To qualify, the "direct manufacturing labour" costs of these companies must meet a specified minimum percentage of the total manufacturing costs of their products produced in that country. What incentive does such an income tax provision give managers to classify fringe benefit costs as direct manufacturing labour or manufacturing overhead? Classifying payroll fringe benefit costs as direct manufacturing labour will increase the percentage of direct manufacturing labour costs, thereby making it easier to qualify for the income tax savings. Consider a company with $8 million of payroll fringe benefit costs (dollar amounts are in millions):

	Method A			**Method B**	
	Costs	Percentage		Costs	Percentage
Direct materials	$ 40	40%	Direct materials	$ 40	40%
Direct manufacturing labour	20	20	Direct manufacturing labour	28	28
Manufacturing overhead	40	40	Manufacturing overhead	32	32
Total manufacturing costs	$100	100%	Total manufacturing costs	$100	100%

Method A classifies payroll fringe benefit costs of $8 per hour as part of manufacturing overhead. In contrast, method B classifies payroll fringe benefit costs as part of direct manufacturing labour. If a country sets the minimum percentage of direct manufacturing labour costs at 28%, the company would receive a tax savings using method B but not using method A. In addition to payroll fringe benefits, other items subject to different possible classifications include compensation for training time, idle time, vacations, sick leave, and extra compensation for overtime. To prevent disputes, contracts and laws should be as specific as feasible regarding definitions and measurements of accounting terms.

DIFFERENT MEANINGS OF PRODUCT COSTS

An important theme of this book is "different costs for different purposes." This theme can be illustrated with respect to product costing. A **product cost** is the sum of the costs assigned to a product for a specific purpose. Exhibit 2-10 illustrates three different purposes:

1. **Product pricing and product emphasis.** For this purpose, the costs of all those areas of the value chain required to bring a product to a customer should be included.

EXHIBIT 2-10
Different Product Costs for Different Purposes

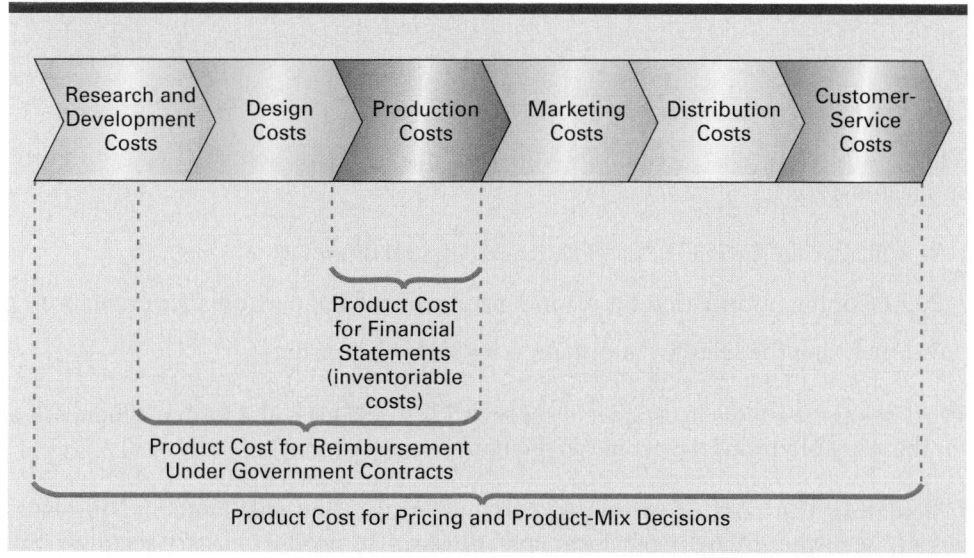

EXHIBIT 2-11
Alternative Classifications of Costs

1. Business function
   a. Research and development
   b. Design of products, services, or processes
   c. Production
   d. Marketing
   e. Distribution
   f. Customer service
2. Assignment to a cost object
   a. Direct costs
   b. Indirect costs
3. Behaviour pattern in relation to changes in the level of activity or volume
   a. Variable costs
   b. Fixed costs
4. Aggregate or average
   a. Total costs
   b. Unit costs
5. Assets or expenses
   a. Inventoriable costs
   b. Period costs

2. **Contracting with government agencies.** Government agencies frequently provide detailed guidelines on the allowable and nonallowable items in a product cost amount. For example, some government agencies explicitly exclude marketing costs from reimbursement to contractors and may reimburse only a part of R&D costs. Hence, the bracket in Exhibit 2-10 shows that a specific contract may provide for recovering all design and production costs and part of R&D costs.

3. **Financial statements.** The focus here is on inventoriable costs. For example, under GAAP, in manufacturing companies, only manufacturing costs are assigned to products reported in the financial statements. For purposes of calculating inventory costs, product costs include only inventoriable (manufacturing) costs.

Generally, *inventoriable costs* are called *product costs* in financial accounting courses.

Example: Numbers help illustrate the concepts in Exhibit 2-10. Using assumed numbers, the inventoriable cost of a testing device is $100 per unit, the device's cost for reimbursement under a government contract is $180, and the device's cost from throughout the value chain for a pricing decision is $300 per unit.

Exhibit 2-10 illustrates how product cost ranges from a narrow set of costs for financial statements (only inventoriable costs) to a broad set for reimbursement under product and product-mix decisions.

This section focused on how different purposes require the inclusion of different cost items of the value chain of business functions when calculating product costs. This is why it is important to be clear and precise about the classifications introduced in this chapter. Exhibit 2-11 summarizes the key cost classifications.

The next section describes how the basic concepts introduced in this chapter lead to a framework for understanding cost accounting and cost management that can then be applied to the study of many topics, such as strategy evaluation, quality, and investment decisions.

A FRAMEWORK FOR COST MANAGEMENT

OBJECTIVE 9

Describe a framework for cost accounting and cost management

Three features of cost accounting and cost management across a wide range of applications are:

1. Calculating the cost of products, services, and other cost objects

2. Obtaining information for planning and control and performance evaluation

3. Analyzing the relevant information for making decisions

We develop these ideas in Chapters 3 through 12. These ideas also form the foundation for the study of various topics later in the book.

Calculating the cost of products, services, and other cost objects We have already seen the different purposes and measures of product costs. Whatever the purpose, the costing system traces direct costs and allocates indirect costs to products. Chapters 4, 5, and 17 describe basic systems used to calculate total and unit costs of products and services and how managers use this information for pricing, product mix, and cost management decisions.

Obtaining information for planning and control and performance evaluation
Budgeting is the most commonly used tool for planning and control. A budget forces managers to look ahead, to translate strategy into plans, to coordinate and communicate within the organization, and to provide a benchmark for evaluating performance. Chapter 6 describes budgeting systems.

At the end of a reporting period, managers compare actual results to planned performance. The manager's task is to understand why differences between actual and planned performance (called variances) arise and to use the information provided by these variances as feedback to promote learning and future improvement. Managers also use variances as well as nonfinancial measures, such as defect rates and customer satisfaction ratings, to control and evaluate the performance of various departments, divisions, and managers. Chapters 7, 8, and 16 discuss variance analysis. Chapter 9 describes the planning and control and inventory costing issues relating to capacity. Chapters 6 through 9 focus on the management accountant's role in implementing strategy.

Analyzing the relevant information for making decisions When making decisions, managers must understand which revenues and costs to consider and which ones to ignore. Management accountants help managers identify what information is relevant and what information can be ignored because it is irrelevant. Consider a decision about whether to buy a product from an outside vendor or to make it in-house. The costing system indicates that it costs $25 per unit to make the product in-house. A vendor offers the product for $22 per unit. At first glance, it seems it will cost less for the company to buy the product than to make it. However, suppose that, of the $25 to make it in-house, $5 consists of plant lease payments that the company will have to make whether the product is made or is bought. Under this condition, it will cost less to make the product than to buy it. Why? Because making the product only costs an additional $20 per unit ($25 – $5), compared with an additional $22 per unit if it is bought. The $5 per unit of lease payments is irrelevant to the decision because it will be incurred whether the product is made or bought. Analyzing relevant information is a key aspect of making decisions.

When making strategic decisions about what products to produce, managers need to know how revenues and costs vary with changes in output levels. For this purpose, managers need to distinguish between which costs are fixed and which costs are variable. Chapter 3 analyzes how operating income changes with changes in output levels and how managers use this information to make decisions such as how much to advertise. Chapter 10 describes methods to estimate fixed and variable components of costs. Chapter 11 applies the concept of relevance to making decisions in many different situations. Chapter 12 describes how management accountants help managers determine prices and manage costs across the value chain and over a product's life.

Later chapters in the book discuss topics such as strategy evaluation, customer profitability, quality, just-in-time (JIT) systems, investment decisions, transfer pricing, and performance evaluation. Each of these topics invariably has product costing, planning and control, and decision-making perspectives. A command of the first 12 chapters is helpful to master these topics. For example, Chapter 13 on strategy describes a set of financial and nonfinancial measures, commonly known as the balanced scorecard, used to implement strategy that builds on the planning and control functions. The section on strategic analysis of operating income builds on ideas of product costing and variance analysis. The section on downsizing and managing capacity builds on ideas of relevant revenues and relevant costs.

(Try to solve this problem before examining the solution that follows.)

PROBLEM
Foxwood Company is a metal- and wood-cutting manufacturer selling products to the home construction market. Consider the following data for the year 2007:

Sandpaper	$ 2,000
Materials-handling costs	70,000
Lubricants and coolants	5,000
Miscellaneous indirect manufacturing labour	40,000
Direct manufacturing labour	300,000
Direct materials, January 1, 2007	40,000
Direct materials, December 31, 2007	50,000
Finished goods January 1, 2007	100,000
Finished goods December 31, 2007	150,000
Work in process, January 1, 2007	10,000
Work in process, December 31, 2007	14,000
Plant leasing costs	54,000
Amortization—plant equipment	36,000
Property taxes on plant equipment	4,000
Fire and casualty insurance on plant equipment	3,000
Direct materials purchased in 2007	460,000
Revenue	1,360,000
Marketing and promotion	60,000
Marketing salaries	100,000
Shipping costs	70,000
Customer service costs	100,000

FOXWOOD COMPANY

Income Statement for the Year Ended December 31, 2007

Revenues		
Cost of goods sold		1,360,000
Beginning finished goods, January 1, 2007	$ 100,000	
Cost of goods manufactured (see below)	960,000	
Cost of goods available for sale	1,060,000	
Ending finished goods, December 31, 2007	(150,000)	
Cost of goods sold		910,000
Gross margin (or gross profit)		450,000
Operating costs		
Marketing and promotion	60,000	
Marketing salaries	100,000	
Shipping costs	70,000	
Customer service costs	100,000	
Total operating costs		330,000
Operating Income		$120,000

REQUIRED
1. Prepare an income statement with a separate supporting schedule of cost of goods manufactured. For all manufacturing items, indicate by V or F whether each is basically a variable cost or a fixed cost (where the cost

object is a product unit). If in doubt, decide on the basis of whether the total cost will change substantially over a wide range of production output.

2. Suppose that both the direct materials and plant leasing costs are tied to the production of 900,000 units. What is the unit cost for the direct materials assigned to each unit produced? What is the unit cost of the plant leasing costs? Assume that the plant leasing costs are a fixed cost.

3. Repeat the computation in requirement 2 for direct materials and plant leasing costs assuming that the costs are being predicted for the manufacturing of 1 million units next year. Assume that the implied cost behaviour patterns persist.

4. As a management consultant, explain concisely to the president why the unit costs for direct materials did not change in requirements 2 and 3 but the unit costs for plant leasing costs did.

SOLUTION

1.

FOXWOOD COMPANY

Schedule of Cost of Goods Manufactured
for the Year Ended December 31, 2007

Direct Materials		
Beginning inventory of direct materials January 1, 2007	$ 40,000	
Purchases of direct materials in 2007	460,000	
Cost of direct materials available for use	500,000	
Ending inventory of direct materials, December 31, 2007	(50,000)	
Direct materials used in 2007	450,000	(V)
Direct manufacturing labour	300,000	(V)

Indirect manufacturing costs:			
Supplies	$ 2,000(V)		
Materials-handling costs	70,000(V)		
Lubricants and coolants	5,000(V)		
Miscellaneous indirect manufacturing labour	40,000(V)		
Plant leasing costs	54,000(F)		
Amortization—plant equipment	36,000(F)		
Property taxes on plant equipment	4,000(F)		
Fire and casualty insurance on plant equipment	3,000(F)	214,000	
Manufacturing costs incurred during 2007		964,000	
Add: Beginning work-in-process inventory January 1, 2007		10,000	
Total manufacturing costs to account for		974,000	
Deduct: Ending work-in-process inventory December 31, 2007		(14,000)	
Cost of goods manufactured (to Income Statement)		$960,000	

2. Direct materials unit cost = Direct materials used ÷ Units produced
$$= \$450,000 \div 900,000 = \$0.50$$
Plant leasing unit cost = Plant leasing costs ÷ Units produced
$$= \$54,000 \div 900,000 = \$0.06$$

3. The direct materials costs are variable, so they would increase in total from $450,000 to $500,000 (1,000,000 × $0.50). However, their unit costs would be unaffected: $500,000 ÷ 1,000,000 units = $0.50.

In contrast, the plant leasing costs of $54,000 are fixed, so they would not increase in total. However, if the plant leasing costs were assigned to units produced, the unit costs would decline from $0.060 to $0.054: $54,000 ÷ 1,000,000 = $0.054.

4. The explanation would begin with the answer to requirement 3. As a consultant, you should stress that the unitizing (averaging) of costs that have different behaviour patterns can be misleading. A common error is to assume that a total unit cost, which is often a sum of variable unit costs and fixed unit costs, is an indicator that total costs change in a wholly variable way as the level of production output changes. The next chapter demonstrates the necessity for distinguishing between cost behaviour patterns. You must be especially wary about unit fixed costs. Too often, unit fixed costs are erroneously regarded as being indistinguishable from unit variable costs.

DECISION POINTS   SUMMARY

The following decision guidelines use a question-and-answer format to summarize the chapter's main points. Each decision presents a key question. The guideline is the answer to that question.

DECISIONS	GUIDELINES
1. How do managers choose a cost object?	A cost object is anything for which a separate measurement of costs is needed. Examples include product, service, project, customer, brand category, activity, and department.
2. How do managers decide whether a cost is a direct or an indirect cost?	An indirect cost is any cost that is related to a particular cost object but cannot be traced to it in an economically feasible way. A direct *cost* can be traced to the cost object in an economically feasible way. The same cost can be direct for one cost object and indirect for other cost objects. This book uses *cost tracing* to describe the assignment of direct cost to a cost object and *cost allocation* to describe the assignment of indirect costs to a cost object.
3. How do managers decide whether a cost is a variable or a fixed cost?	A variable cost changes *in total* in proportion to changes in the related level of total activity or volume. A fixed cost remains unchanged in total for a given time period despite wide changes in the related level of total activity or volume.
4. How should costs be estimated?	In general, focus on total costs, not unit costs. When making total cost estimates, think of variable costs as an amount per unit and fixed costs as a total amount. The unit cost of a cost object should be interpreted cautiously when it includes a fixed-cost component.
5. How do you distinguish among manufacturing, merchandising, and service companies?	Manufacturing-sector companies purchase materials and components and convert them into finished goods. Merchandising-sector companies purchase and then sell tangible products without changing their basic form. Service-sector companies provide services or intangible products to their customers.
6. How do manufacturing companies classify inventories?	The three classifications of inventories found in many manufacturing companies depict stages in the conversion process: direct materials, work in process, and finished goods.
7. Which costs are initially treated as assets for external reporting, and which costs are expensed as they are incurred?	Inventoriable costs are all costs of a product that are regarded as an asset when they are incurred and then become a cost of goods sold when the product is sold. Period costs are expensed in the period in which they are incurred and include all costs in an income statement except cost of goods sold.
8. How do managers assign costs to cost objects?	Managers can assign different costs to the same cost object depending on the purpose. For example, for the external reporting purpose in a manufacturing company, the inventoriable cost of a product includes only manufacturing costs. In contrast, costs from all business functions of the value chain are assigned to a product for pricing and product-mix decisions.
9. What are the features of cost accounting and cost management systems?	Three features of cost accounting and cost management are (1) calculating the cost of products, services, and other cost objects, (2) obtaining information for planning, control, and performance evaluation, and (3) analyzing the relevant information for making decisions.

This chapter contains more basic terms than any other in this book. Do not proceed before you check your understanding of the following terms. You will find definitions of these terms in this chapter.

actual costs (p. 30)
average cost (p. 38)
budgeted costs (p. 30)
conversion costs (p. 46)
cost (p. 30)
cost accumulation (p. 30)
cost allocation (p. 31)
cost assignment (p. 30)
cost driver (p. 33)
cost object (p. 30)
cost of goods manufactured (p. 42)
cost of goods sold (p. 40)
cost tracing (p. 31)
direct costs of a cost object (p. 31)
direct manufacturing labour costs (p. 40)
direct materials costs (p. 40)
direct materials inventory (p. 39)
factory overhead costs (p. 40)
finished goods inventory (p. 40)
fixed cost (p. 34)
idle time (p. 48)

indirect costs of a cost object (p. 31)
indirect manufacturing costs (p. 40)
inventoriable costs (p. 40)
manufacturing overhead costs (p. 40)
manufacturing-sector company (p. 39)
merchandising-sector company (p. 39)
operating costs (p. 41)
operating income (p. 45)
overtime premium (p. 47)
period costs (p. 41)
prime costs (p. 45)
product cost (p.49)
relevant range (p. 37)
revenues (p. 41)
service-sector company (p. 39)
unit cost (p. 38)
value-added activities (p. 33)
variable cost (p. 34)
work-in-process inventory (p. 39)
work-in-progress inventory (p. 39)

▼ **ASSIGNMENT MATERIAL**

QUESTIONS

2-1 Define *cost object* and give three examples.

2-2 Define *cost assignment*, *cost tracing*, and *cost allocation*. How are these terms related?

2-3 Define *direct costs* and *indirect costs*. How are these terms related?

2-4 Why do managers consider direct costs to be more accurate than indirect costs?

2-5 Name three factors that affect the classification of a cost as direct or indirect.

2-6 Describe two areas that cost reduction efforts frequently focus on.

2-7 What is a *cost driver?* Give one example for each area in the value chain.

2-8 Define *variable cost* and *fixed cost*. Give an example of each.

2-9 What is the *relevant range?* What role does the relevant-range concept play in explaining how costs behave?

2-10 Explain why *unit costs* must often be interpreted with caution.

2-11 Describe how service-, merchandising-, and manufacturing-sector companies differ from each other.

2-12 Do service-sector companies have inventoriable costs? Explain.

2-13 What are the three major categories of the inventoriable costs of a manufactured product?

2-14 Define the following: *direct materials costs, direct manufacturing labour costs, indirect manufacturing costs, prime costs,* and *conversion costs.*

2-15 Define *product costs.* Describe three different purposes for computing product costs.

EXERCISES

2-16 **Total costs and unit costs.** A student association has hired a musical group for a graduation party. The cost will be a fixed amount of $4,800.

1. Suppose 500 people attend the party. What will be the total cost of the musical group? the unit cost per person?
2. Suppose 2,000 people attend. What will be the total cost of the musical group? the unit cost per person?
3. For prediction of total costs, should the manager of the party use the unit cost in requirement 1? the unit cost in requirement 2? What is the major lesson of this problem?

2-17 **Cost drivers and the value chain.** A Toyota analyst is preparing a presentation on cost drivers. Unfortunately, both the list of its business function areas and the accompanying list of representative cost drivers are accidentally randomized. The two lists now on the computer screen are as follows:

BUSINESS FUNCTION AREA	REPRESENTATIVE COST DRIVER
A. Design of products/processes	1. Number of cars recalled for defective parts
B. Customer service	2. Number of machine assembly hours
C. Marketing	3. Number of research scientists
D. Research and development	4. Hours of computer-aided design (CAD) work
E. Distribution	5. Number of sales personnel
F. Production	6. Weight of cars shipped

REQUIRED

1. Rearrange the business functions into a logical value-chain sequence then match each business function area with its representative cost driver.
2. Give a second example of a cost driver for each of Toyota's business function areas.

2-18 **Computing and interpreting unit manufacturing costs.** Finnish Forest Products (FFP) produces three different paper products at its Vaasa lumber plant—supreme, deluxe, and regular. Each product has its own dedicated production line at the plant. FFP currently uses the following three-part classification for its manufacturing costs: direct materials, direct manufacturing labour, and indirect manufacturing costs. Indirect manufacturing costs are allocated to each product line on the basis of direct manufacturing labour costs on each line. Summary data for the most recent month (July 2007) are (in millions):

	Supreme	Deluxe	Regular
Direct materials cost	$100.80	$ 64.80	$ 74.40
Direct manufacturing labour costs	16.80	33.60	9.60
Indirect manufacturing costs	50.40	100.80	28.80
Kilograms produced	80	120	100

REQUIRED

1. Compute the unit manufacturing cost per kilogram for each product produced in July 2007.
2. Suppose that, in August 2007, production was 120 kilograms of Supreme, 160 kilograms of Deluxe, and 180 kilograms of Regular. Why might the July 2007 unit manufacturing cost information be misleading when predicting total manufacturing costs in August 2007?

2-19 **Direct and indirect costs, effect of changing the classification of a cost item (continuation of 2-18).** Finnish Forest Products (FFP) employs a consultant to help reduce energy costs at its Vaasa plant. Currently, FFP does not trace energy costs to each product line. The energy consultant notes that each production line at the Vaasa plant has multiple energy meters and that tracing of energy costs to each line is possible. Of the $180 million of indirect manufacturing costs in July 2007, $108 million is for energy costs traceable to individual production lines and $24 million is fixed cost. Using this information, FFP's cost analyst reports the following revised numbers for July 2007 (in millions):

	Supreme	Deluxe	Regular
Direct materials cost	$100.80	$ 64.80	$ 74.40
Direct manufacturing labour cost	16.80	33.60	9.60
Direct energy costs	47.76	24.84	35.40
Indirect manufacturing costs	20.16	40.32	11.52
Kilograms produced	80	120	100

1. What is the difference between a direct cost and an indirect cost?
2. Why might FFP's managers prefer energy costs to be traced as a direct cost rather than included as part of indirect manufacturing costs?
3. Compute the revised unit manufacturing cost per kilogram for each product produced in July 2007. Compare these costs with those computed in requirement 1 of Exercise 2-18. Comment on any differences in the unit cost numbers.

2-20 Cost drivers and the value chain. A Johnson & Johnson analyst is preparing a presentation on cost drivers at its pharmaceutical drug subsidiary. Unfortunately, both the list of its business function areas and the accompanying list of representative cost drivers are accidentally randomized. The two lists now on the computer screen are as follows:

BUSINESS FUNCTION AREA	REPRESENTATIVE COST DRIVER
A. Production	1. Minutes of television advertising time
B. Research and development	2. Number of calls to toll-free customer phone line
C. Marketing	3. Hours Tylenol packing line in operation
D. Distribution	4. Number of packages shipped
E. Design of products/processes	5. Hours spent designing tamper-proof bottles
F. Customer service	6. Number of patents filed with government agency

REQUIRED

1. Arrange the business functions into a logical value-chain sequence and then match each business function area with its representative cost driver.
2. Give a second example of a cost driver for each of the business functions of Johnson & Johnson's pharmaceutical drug subsidiary.

2-21 Total costs and unit costs. Susan Wang is a well-known software engineer. Her speciality is writing software code used in maintaining the security of credit card information. Wang is approached by the Electronic Commerce Group (ECG). They offer to pay her $120,000 for the right to use her code under licence in their e-procurement software package. Wang rejects this offer because it provides her with no additional benefits if the e-procurement package is a runaway success. Both parties eventually agree to a contract in which ECG pays Wang a flat fee of $120,000 for the right to use her code in up to 10,000 packages. If e-procurement sells more than 10,000 packages, Wang receives $9.60 for each package sold beyond the 10,000 level.

REQUIRED

1. What is the unit cost of ECG for Wang's software code included in its e-procurement package if it sells (a) 2,000, (b) 6,000, (c) 10,000, and (d) 20,000 packages? Comment on the results.
2. For prediction of ECG's total cost of using Wang's software code in e-procurement, which unit cost (if any) of (a) to (d) in requirement 1 would you recommend ECG use? Explain.

2-22 Variable costs and fixed costs. Consolidated Minerals (CM) owns the rights to extract minerals from beach sands on Fraser Island. CM has costs in three areas:

a. Payment to a mining subcontractor who charges $96 per tonne of beach sand mined and returned to the beach (after being processed on the mainland to extract three minerals: ilmenite, rutile, and zircon).
b. Payment of a government mining and environmental tax of $60 per tonne of beach sand mined.
c. Payment to a barge operator. This operator charges $180,000 per month to transport batches of beach sand—up to 100 tonnes per batch per day to the mainland and then return to Fraser Island (i.e., 0–100 tonnes per day = $180,000 per month; 101–200 tonnes = $360,000, and so on). Each barge operates 25 days per month. The $180,000 monthly charge must be paid even if fewer than 100 tonnes are transported on any day and even if Consolidated Minerals requires fewer than 25 days of barge transportation in that month.

CM is currently mining 180 tonnes of beach sand per day for 25 days per month.

REQUIRED

1. What is the variable cost per tonne of beach sand mined? What is the fixed cost to CM per month?
2. Plot one graph of the variable costs and another graph of the fixed costs of CM. Your plots should be similar to Exhibits 2-3 and 2-4 (pp. 35 and 37). Is the concept of relevant range applicable to your plots?

3. What is the unit cost per tonne of beach sand mined (a) if 180 tonnes are mined each day and (b) if 220 tonnes are mined each day? Explain the difference in the unit-cost figures.

2-23 Classification of costs, manufacturing sector. The Fremont, California, plant of NUMMI (New United Motor Manufacturing, Inc.), a joint venture of General Motors and Toyota, assembles two types of cars (Corollas and Geo Prisms). A separate assembly line is used for each type of car.

REQUIRED
Classify each of the following cost items as
a. Direct or indirect (D or I) costs with respect to the type of car assembled (Corolla or Geo Prism).
b. Variable or fixed (V or F) costs with respect to how the total costs of the plant change as the number of cars assembled changes. (If in doubt, select the cost type based on whether the total costs will change substantially if a large number of cars are assembled.)

You will have two answers (D or I, and V or F) for each of the following items:

Cost Item	D or I	V or F
A. Cost of tires used on Geo Prisms		
B. Salary of public relations manager for NUMMI plant		
C. Annual awards dinner for Corolla suppliers		
D. Salary of engineer who monitors design changes on Geo Prism		
E. Freight costs of Corolla engines shipped from Toyota City, Japan, to Fremont, California		
F. Electricity costs for NUMMI plant (single bill covers entire plant)		
G. Wages paid to temporary assembly-line workers hired in periods of high production (paid on an hourly basis)		
H. Annual fire insurance policy cost for NUMMI plant		

2-24 Inventoriable costs versus period costs. Each of the following cost items pertains to one of the following companies: General Electric (a manufacturing-sector company), Loblaws (a merchandising-sector company), and Excite (a service-sector company):
a. Perrier mineral water purchased by Loblaws for sale to its customers
b. Electricity used to provide lighting for assembly-line workers at a General Electric refrigerator assembly plant
c. Amortization on computer equipment at Excite used to update Web site directories.
d. Electricity used to provide lighting for Loblaws store aisles
e. Amortization on computer equipment at General Electric used for quality testing of refrigerator components during the assembly process
f. Salaries of Loblaws' marketing personnel planning local newspaper advertising campaigns
g. Perrier mineral water purchased by Excite for consumption by its software engineers
h. Salaries of Excite marketing personnel selling banner advertising

REQUIRED
1. Distinguish among manufacturing-sector, merchandising-sector, and service-sector companies. Which of these have inventories of goods for sale?
2. Distinguish between inventoriable costs and period costs.
3. Classify each of the (a) to (h) cost items as an inventoriable cost or a period cost. Explain your answers.

2-25 Classification of costs, service sector. Consumer Focus is a marketing research firm that organizes focus groups for consumer-product companies. Each focus group has eight individuals who are paid $50 per session to provide comments on new products. These focus groups meet in hotels and are led by a trained independent marketing specialist hired by Consumer Focus. Each specialist is paid a fixed retainer to conduct a minimum number of sessions at a per-session fee of $2,000. A Consumer Focus staff member attends each session to ensure that all the logistical aspects run smoothly.

REQUIRED

Classify each of the following cost items as:

a. Direct or indirect (D or I) costs with respect to each individual focus group.

b. Variable or fixed (V or F) costs with respect to how the total costs of Consumer Focus change as the number of focus groups changes. (If in doubt, select the cost type based on whether the total costs will change substantially if a large number of groups are conducted.)

You will have two answers (D or I, and V or F) for each of the following items:

Cost Item	D or I	V or F
A. Payment to individuals in each focus group to provide comments on new products		
B. Annual subscription of Consumer Focus to *Consumer Reports* magazine		
C. Phone calls made by Consumer Focus staff member to confirm individuals will attend a focus group session (records of individual calls are not kept)		
D. Retainer paid to focus group leader to conduct 20 focus groups per year on new medical products		
E. Hotel meals provided to participants in each focus group		
F. Lease payment by Consumer Focus for corporate office		
G. Cost of tapes used to record comments made by individuals in a focus group session (these tapes are sent to the company whose products are being tested)		
H. Gasoline costs of Consumer Focus staff for company-owned vehicles (staff members submit monthly bills with no breakdowns)		

2-26 Classification of costs, merchandising sector. Home Entertainment Centre (HEC) operates a large store in Halifax. The store has both a video section and a musical section (compact discs, records, and tapes). HEC reports revenues for the video section separately from the musical section.

REQUIRED

Classify each of the following cost items as

a. Direct or indirect (D or I) costs with respect to the video section.

b. Variable or fixed (V or F) costs with respect to how the total costs of the video section change as the number of videos sold changes. (If in doubt, select the cost type based on whether the total costs will change substantially if a large number of videos are sold.)

You will have two answers (D or I; V or F) for each of the following items:

Cost Item	D or I	V or F
A. Annual retainer paid to a video distributor		
B. Electricity costs of HEC store (single bill covers entire store)		
C. Costs of videos purchased for sale to customers		
D. Subscription to *Video Trends* magazine		
E. Leasing of computer software used for financial budgeting at HEC store		
F. Cost of popcorn provided free to all HEC customers		
G. Fire insurance policy for HEC store		
H. Freight-in costs of videos purchased by HEC		

2-27 Computing cost of goods manufactured and cost of goods sold. The following are account balances relating to 2007 (in thousands):

Property tax on plant building	$ 3,600
Marketing, distribution, and customer service costs	44,400
Finished goods inventory, January 1, 2007	32,400
Plant utilities	20,400

Work-in-process inventory, December 31, 2007	31,200
Amortization of plant building	10,800
General and administrative costs (nonplant)	51,600
Direct materials used	104,400
Finished goods inventory, December 31, 2007	40,800
Amortization of plant equipment	13,200
Plant repairs and maintenance	19,200
Work-in-process inventory, January 1, 2007	24,000
Direct manufacturing labour	40,800
Indirect manufacturing labour	27,600
Indirect materials used	13,200
Miscellaneous plant overhead	4,800

REQUIRED

Compute cost of goods manufactured and cost of goods sold.

2-28 Computing cost of goods purchased and cost of goods sold. The data below are for Marvin Department Store. The account balances (in thousands) are for 2007.

Marketing, distribution, and customer-service costs	$ 44,400
Merchandise inventory, January 1, 2007	32,400
Utilities	20,400
General and administrative costs	51,600
Merchandise inventory, December 31, 2007	40,800
Purchases	186,000
Miscellaneous costs	4,800
Transportation-in	8,400
Purchase returns and allowances	4,800
Purchase discounts	7,200

REQUIRED

Compute (a) cost of goods purchased and (b) cost of goods sold.

PROBLEMS

2-29 Cost of goods manufactured. Consider the following account balances (in thousands) for the Canseco Company:

	Beginning of 2007	End of 2007
Direct materials inventory	$26,400	$ 31,200
Work-in-process inventory	25,200	24,000
Finished goods inventory	21,600	27,600
Purchases of direct materials		90,000
Direct manufacturing labour		30,000
Indirect manufacturing labour		18,000
Plant insurance		10,800
Amortization—plant building and equipment		13,200
Repairs and maintenance—plant		4,800
Marketing, distribution, and customer service costs		111,600
General and administrative costs		34,800

REQUIRED

1. Prepare a schedule of cost of goods manufactured for 2007.

2. Revenues in 2007 were $360 million. Prepare the 2007 income statement.

Excel Application For students who wish to practise their spreadsheet skills, the following is a step-by-step approach to creating an Excel spreadsheet to work this problem.

Step-by-Step

1. In a new spreadsheet, create an income statement and a schedule of cost of goods manufactured in the same format as Exhibit 2-7 on page 43. Your categories of indirect manufacturing costs will differ from those in Exhibit 2-7 and should be the following: indirect manufacturing labour, plant insurance, amortization, and repairs and maintenance.

2. In your schedule of cost of goods manufactured, enter the amounts for beginning direct materials inventory, purchases of direct materials, ending direct materials inventory, direct manufacturing labour, indirect manufacturing labour, plant insurance, amortization, repairs and maintenance, beginning work-in-process inventory, and ending work-in-process inventory. Follow the format in Panel B of Exhibit 2-7. (Program your spreadsheet to perform all necessary calculations. Do not "hard-code" any amounts, such as gross margin or operating income, requiring addition or subtraction operations.)

3. In your schedule of cost of goods manufactured, enter calculations for (a) cost of direct materials available for use and (b) direct materials used.

4. In your schedule of cost of goods manufactured, enter calculations for (a) total indirect manufacturing costs, (b) manufacturing costs incurred during the period, (c) total manufacturing costs to account for, and (d) cost of goods manufactured.

5. In your income statement, enter the calculation that sets the amount of cost of goods manufactured equal to the amount in the cell where you calculated cost of goods manufactured in step 4.

6. To complete the income statement: enter revenues, and enter the amounts for marketing, distribution, and customer-service costs, general and administrative costs, beginning finished goods inventory, and ending finished goods inventory. Enter a calculation for cost of goods available for sale. Finally, enter calculations for gross margin, operating costs, and operating income.

7. *Verify the accuracy of your spreadsheet.* Go to your schedule of cost of goods manufactured and change direct manufacturing labour from $30,000 to $42,000. If your spreadsheet is programmed correctly, cost of goods manufactured should change to $175,200, and operating income should change to $44,400.

2-30 Income statement and schedule of cost of goods manufactured. The Howell Corporation has the following account balances (in millions):

For Specific Date		For Year 2007	
Direct materials, January 1, 2007	$ 18	Purchases of direct materials	$390
Work in process, January 1, 2007	12	Direct manufacturing labour	120
Finished goods, January 1, 2007	84	Amortization—plant building	
Direct materials, December 31, 2007	24	and equipment	96
Work in process, December 31, 2007	6	Plant supervisory salaries	6
Finished goods, December 31, 2007	66	Miscellaneous plant overhead	42
Revenues	1,140		
Marketing, distribution, and customer service costs	288		
Plant supplies used	12		
Plant utilities	36		
Indirect manufacturing labour	72		

REQUIRED

Prepare an income statement and a supporting schedule of cost of goods manufactured for the year ended December 31, 2007. (For additional questions regarding these facts, see the next problem.)

2-31 Interpretation of statements (continuation of 2-30). Refer to the preceding problem.

REQUIRED

1. How would the answer to the preceding problem be modified if you were asked for a schedule of cost of goods manufactured and sold instead of a schedule of cost of goods manufactured? Be specific.

2. Would the sales manager's salary (included in marketing, distribution, and customer service costs) be accounted for differently if the Howell Corporation were a merchandising company instead of a manufacturing company? Using the flow of costs outlined in Exhibit 2-10 (p. 49), describe how the wages of an assembler in the plant would be accounted for in this manufacturing company.

3. Plant supervisory salaries are usually regarded as indirect manufacturing costs. Under what conditions might some of these costs be regarded as direct manufacturing costs? Give an example.
4. Suppose that both the direct materials used and the plant amortization were related to the manufacture of 1 million units of product. What is the unit cost for the direct materials assigned to those units? What is the unit cost for plant building and equipment amortization? Assume that yearly plant amortization is computed on a straight-line basis.
5. Assume that the implied cost behaviour patterns in requirement 4 persist—that is, direct materials costs behave as a variable cost and amortization behaves as a fixed cost. Repeat the computations in requirement 4, assuming that the costs are being predicted for the manufacture of 1.2 million units of product. How would the total costs be affected?
6. As a management accountant, explain concisely to the president why the unit costs differed in requirements 4 and 5.

2-32 Income statement and schedule of cost of goods manufactured. The following items (in millions) pertain to the Chan Corporation:

For Specific Date		For Year 2007	
Work in process, January 1, 2007	$12.00	Plant utilities	$ 6.00
Direct materials, December 31, 2007	6.00	Indirect manufacturing labour	24.00
Finished goods, December 31, 2007	14.40	Amortization—plant, building, and equipment	10.80
Accounts payable, December 31, 2007	24.00	Revenues	420.00
Accounts receivable, January 1, 2007	60.00	Miscellaneous manufacturing overhead	12.00
Work in process, December 31, 2007	2.40	Marketing, distribution, and customer service costs	108.00
Finished goods, January 1, 2007	48.00	Purchases of direct materials	96.00
Accounts receivable, December 31, 2007	36.00	Direct manufacturing labour	48.00
Accounts payable, January 1, 2007	48.00	Plant supplies used	7.20
Direct materials, January 1, 2007	36.00	Property taxes on plant	1.20

Chan's manufacturing cost system uses a three-part classification of manufacturing costs: direct materials, direct manufacturing labour, and indirect manufacturing costs.

REQUIRED
Prepare an income statement and a supporting schedule of cost of goods manufactured. (For additional questions regarding these facts, see the next problem.)

2-33 Interpretation of statements (continuation of 2-32). Refer to the preceding problem.

REQUIRED
1. How would the answer to the preceding problem be modified if you were asked for a schedule of cost of goods manufactured and sold instead of a schedule of cost of goods manufactured? Be specific.
2. Would the sales manager's salary (included in marketing, distribution, and customer service costs) be accounted for any differently if the Chan Corporation were a merchandising company instead of a manufacturing company? Using the flow of costs outlined in Exhibit 2-10 (p. 49), describe how the wages of an assembler in the plant would be accounted for in this manufacturing company.
3. Plant supervisory salaries are usually regarded as indirect manufacturing costs. Under what conditions might some of these costs be regarded as direct manufacturing costs? Give an example.
4. Suppose that both the direct materials used and the plant amortization were related to the manufacture of 1 million units of product. What is the unit cost for the direct materials assigned to those units? What is the unit cost for plant building and equipment amortization? Assume that yearly amortization is computed on a straight-line basis.
5. Assume that the implied cost behaviour patterns in requirement 4 persist. That is, direct materials costs behave as a variable cost and plant amortization behaves as a fixed cost. Repeat the computations in requirement 4, assuming that the costs are being predicted for the manufacture of 1.5 million units of product. How would the total costs be affected?
6. As a management accountant, explain concisely to the president why the unit costs differed in requirements 4 and 5.

2-34 Overtime premium, defining accounting terms. Gwen Benson, Ian Blacklaw, and Eduardo Cabrera are sales representatives for Electronic Manufacturing Inc. (EMI). EMI specializes in low-volume production orders for the research groups of major companies. Each sales representative receives a base salary plus a bonus based on 20% of the actual profit of each order they sell. Before this year, the bonus was 5% of the revenues of each order they sold. Actual profit in the revised system was defined as actual revenue minus actual manufacturing cost. EMI uses a three-part classification of manufacturing costs—direct materials, direct manufacturing labour, and indirect manufacturing costs. Indirect manufacturing costs are determined as 200% of actual direct manufacturing labour cost.

Benson receives a report on an EMI job for BBC Inc. She is dismayed by the low profit on the BBC job. She prided herself on not discounting the price BBC would pay by convincing them of the quality of EMI's work. Benson discussed the issue with Blacklaw and Cabrera. They share with her details of their most recent jobs. Summary data are as follows:

Customer Sales Representative	Westec Blacklaw	La Electricidad Cabrera	BBC Benson
Revenues	$504	$984	$576
Direct materials	300	492	324
Direct manuf. labour	48	120	72
Indirect manufacturing	96	240	144
Direct labour hours	2 hours	5 hours	2 hours

Benson asks Hans Brunner, EMI's manufacturing manager, to explain the different labour costs charged on the Westec and BBC jobs, given both used two direct labour hours. She was told the BBC job was done in overtime and that the actual overtime rate ($36) was 50% higher than the $24 per hour straight-time rate. Benson noted that she brought the BBC order to EMI one week ago and that there was no rush-order on the job. In contrast, the Westec order was a "hot-hot" one with a request it be done by noon the day after the order was received. Brunner said that the "actual cost" he charged to the BBC job was actually paid to the workers on that job.

REQUIRED

1. Using both the actual straight-time and overtime rates paid for direct labour, what is the actual profit EMI would report on each of the three jobs?
2. Assume that EMI charges each job for direct labour at the $24 straight-time rate (and that the indirect-manufacturing rate of 200% includes an overtime premium). What would be the revised profit EMI would report on each of the three jobs? Comment on any differences from requirement 1.
3. Discuss the pros and cons of charging the BBC job the $36 labour rate per hour.
4. Why might EMI adopt the 20% profit incentive instead of the prior 5% of revenue incentive? How might EMI define "profit" to reduce possible disagreements with its sales representatives?

2-35 Finding unknown balances. An auditor for Canada Revenue Agency is trying to reconstruct some partially destroyed records of two taxpayers. For each case in the accompanying list, find the unknowns designated by capital letters (figures are in thousands).

	Case 1	Case 2
Accounts receivable, December 31, 2007	$ 7,200	$ 2,520
Cost of goods sold	A	24,000
Accounts payable, January 1, 2007	3,600	2,040
Accounts payable, December 31, 2007	2,160	1,800
Finished goods inventory, December 31, 2007	B	6,360
Gross margin	13,560	C
Work in process, January 1, 2007	0	960
Work in process, December 31, 2007	0	3,600
Finished goods inventory, January 1, 2007	4,800	4,800
Direct materials used	9,600	14,400
Direct manufacturing labour	3,600	6,000
Indirect manufacturing costs	8,400	D
Purchases of direct material	10,800	8,400
Revenues	38,400	38,160
Accounts receivable, January 1, 2007	2,400	1,680

2-36 Fire loss, computing inventory costs. A distraught employee, Guy Arson, put a torch to a manufacturing plant on a blustery February 26. The resulting blaze completely destroyed the plant and its contents. Fortunately, certain accounting records were kept in another building. They revealed the following for the period from January 1, 2007, to February 26, 2007:

Direct materials purchased	$192,000
Work in process, January 1, 2007	$ 40,800
Direct materials, January 1, 2007	$ 19,200
Finished goods, January 1, 2007	$ 36,000
Indirect manufacturing costs	40% of conversion costs
Revenues	$600,000
Direct manufacturing labour	$216,000
Prime costs	$352,800
Gross margin percentage based on sales	20%
Cost of goods available for sale	$540,000

The loss was fully covered by insurance. The insurance company wants to know the historical cost of the inventories when negotiating a settlement.

REQUIRED
Calculate the cost of
1. Finished goods inventory, February 26, 2007
2. Work-in-process inventory, February 26, 2007
3. Direct materials inventory, February 26, 2007

2-37 Comprehensive problem on unit costs, product costs. Regina Office Equipment manufactures and sells metal shelving. It began operations on January 1, 2007. Costs incurred for 2007 are as follows (V stands for variable; F stands for fixed):

Direct materials used costs	$168,000 V
Direct manufacturing labour costs	36,000 V
Plant energy costs	6,000 V
Indirect manufacturing labour costs	12,000 V
Indirect manufacturing labour costs	19,200 F
Other indirect manufacturing costs	9,600 V
Other indirect manufacturing costs	28,800 F
Marketing, distribution, and customer service costs	147,420 V
Marketing, distribution, and customer service costs	48,000 F
Administrative costs	60,000 F

Variable manufacturing costs are variable with respect to units produced. Variable marketing, distribution, and customer service costs are variable with respect to units sold.
Inventory data are as follows:

	Beginning, January 1, 2007	Ending, December 31, 2007
Direct materials	0 kilograms	2,000 kilograms
Work in process	0 units	0 units
Finished goods	0 units	? units

Production in 2007 was 100,000 units. Two kilograms of direct materials are used to make one unit of finished product.

Revenues in 2007 were $524,160. The selling price per unit and the purchase price per kilogram of direct materials were stable throughout the year. The company's ending inventory of finished goods is carried at the average unit manufacturing costs for 2007. Finished goods inventory, at December 31, 2007, was $25,164.

1. Direct materials inventory, total cost, December 31, 2007
2. Finished goods inventory, total units, December 31, 2007
3. Selling price per unit, 2007
4. Operating income, 2007 (show your computations)

2-38 Budgeted income statement (continuation of 2-37). Assume management predicts that the selling price per unit and variable cost per unit will be the same in 2008 as in 2007. Fixed manufacturing costs and marketing, distribution, and customer service costs in 2008 are also predicted to be the same as in 2007. Sales in 2008 are forecast to be 122,000 units. The desired ending inventory of finished goods, December 31, 2008, is 12,000 units. Assume zero ending inventories of both direct materials and work in process. The company's ending inventory of finished goods is carried at the average unit manufacturing costs for 2008. The company uses the first-in, first-out inventory method. Management has asked that you prepare a budgeted income statement for 2008. December 31, 2007, Finished Goods Inventory is 9,000 units.

REQUIRED

1. Units of finished goods produced in 2008
2. Budgeted income statement for 2008

2-39 Revenue and cost recording and classifications, ethics. Canadian Outfitters (C.O.) designs and markets jeans to many retailers and distributors around the globe. Its corporate headquarters are in Montreal, Quebec. Manufacturing is done by a subcontractor (Jeans West) on the island state of Caribe. The Caribe government grants locally owned companies a 20% income tax rebate if the ratio of their domestic labour costs to total costs exceeds 25%. Domestic labour costs are defined as the employment costs of all employees who are citizens of Caribe. Nicola Roberts, the newly appointed controller of C.O., has recently been examining payments made to Jeans West. She observes that Jeans West purchases denim from C.O. ($3.60 million in 2007). C.O. paid Jeans West $14.40 million for the jeans manufactured in Caribe in 2007. Based on her industry experience, the $14.40-million amount is very low. She was told it was "a great deal" for C.O. There is also a sizable payment by C.O. to the Swiss subsidiary of Jeans West ($5.76 million in 2007). Roberts is told by the Jeans West president that this payment is for fabric design work that Jeans West does with C.O. C.O. has included the $5.76-million payment in its own product design cost. The director of product design at C.O. told Roberts it is an "off-statement" item that historically he has no responsibility for and no say about. To his knowledge, Jeans West uses only C.O. designs with either zero or minimal changes.

Jeans West's domestic labour costs in 2007 were $4.32 million, while its total costs were $12 million. Included in this $4.32 million was $1.56 million for labour fringe benefits (for health insurance, etc.). A component of this $1.56 million is $720,000 for life insurance for Jeans West's executives. C.O. helped arrange this life insurance policy. It negotiated with the insurance company managing its own executive life insurance plans to include the Jeans West executives at rates much more favourable than those available in Caribe.

REQUIRED

1. What concerns should Roberts have about the revenue and cost numbers in C.O.'s financial reports?
2. Which (if any) of the concerns in requirement 1 raise ethical issues for Roberts? Explain.
3. What steps should Roberts take to address the ethical issues you identified in requirement 2?

2-40 Missing data. Shaheen Plastics, Inc.'s selected data for the month of August 2007 are presented below (in millions):

Work-in-process inventory 8/1/2007	$240
Direct materials inventory 8/1/2007	108
Direct materials purchased	432
Direct materials used	450
Variable manufacturing overhead	300
Total manufacturing overhead	576

Total manufacturing costs	1,920
Cost of goods manufactured	1,980
Cost of goods sold	2,040
Finished goods inventory 8/1/2007	150

REQUIRED

Calculate the following costs:

1. Direct materials inventory 8/31/2007
2. Fixed manufacturing overhead costs for August
3. Direct manufacturing labour costs for August
4. Work-in-process inventory 8/31/2007
5. Goods available for sale in August
6. Finished goods inventory 8/31/2007

COLLABORATIVE LEARNING PROBLEMS

2-41 Cost analysis, litigation risk, ethics. Sam Nash is the head of new-product development of Forever Young (FY). Nash is currently considering Enhance, which would be FY's next major product in its beauty/cosmetics line and its estimated unit cost is currently $144. Enhance represents a new direction for FY. All FY's current products are cosmetics applied to the skin by the consumer. In contrast, Enhance is inserted via needle into the skin by a nurse after an initial meeting with a doctor. FY planned to sell Enhance at cost plus 20% to physicians. FY used an estimated treatment cost to patients of $432 to provide a financial incentive to physicians. Each treatment will last three months. Enhance is an animal-based product that fills out the skin so that fewer wrinkles are observable.

Nash, however, questions the economics of this product because FY has failed to budget for any litigation costs, which Nash estimated as $132 per unit. At present, the costs recognized are research and development, manufacturing by a third party, marketing, distribution, and a small amount for customer support. Nash's main concern is with recognizing in the current costing proposal potential future litigation costs (such as the costs of lawyers and expert witnesses in defending lawsuits against Enhance). He points to the litigation with breast implants and notes that a settlement of more than $4.80 billion is being discussed in the press. He also notes the tobacco company litigation and those proposed billion-dollar settlements. Elisabeth Savage, the CEO and president of the company, disagrees with Nash. She maintains that she has total confidence in her medical research team and directs Nash not to include any dollar amount for potential litigation cost in his upcoming presentation to the board of directors on the economics and pricing of the Enhance product. Nash was previously controller of FY and has a strong background in finance. His current job represents his first nonfinance position, and he views himself as potential CEO material.

REQUIRED

1. What reasons might Savage have for not wanting Nash to record potential future litigation costs on the product in a presentation on Enhance's economics and pricing?
2. Suppose Savage asks Nash to give her an "off-the-record" presentation on the possible magnitude of the potential litigation costs of Enhance. What is the new unit cost including the estimated litigation costs? What should the new selling price to physicians be to maintain the triple-the-cost target? What is the percentage decrease in the margin physicians could expect per unit assuming the cost to the patient cannot be changed?
3. After hearing Nash's presentation (see requirement 2), Savage directs Nash to drop any further discussion of the litigation issue. He is to focus on making Enhance the block-buster product that field research has suggested it will be. Nash is uneasy with this directive. He tells Savage it is an "ostrich approach" (head-in-the-sand) to a real problem that could potentially bankrupt the company. Savage tells Nash to go and think about her directive. What should Nash do next?

2-42 Movie profit sharing, defining terms. Brad Fittler, first-time author of *The Sporting Life*, has just had a meeting with Bill Harrigan, a senior executive of Golden Ventures (GV). GV is a major movie studio with many successes. *The Sporting Life* is a best-selling novel about the personal and professional career of Allan Langer, a recently retired

Golden Venture Report on
Bill Goldberg Superstar
Cumulative Distribution Statement (in $ thousands)
From: July 1, 2006
To: March 31, 2007

1. Gross receipts (a)	$192,354
2. Less distribution fee (b)	67,324
3. Gross after distribution fees	125,030
4. Less distribution expenses (c)	66,076
5. Balance	58,954
6. Less gross participation fees of directors, screen stars, and so on (d)	38,471
7. Balance	20,483
8. Less negative cost (e)	(82,104)
9. Balance	(61,621)
10. Less interest on negative cost (f)	12,943
11. Net profit	$(74,564)

(a) The studio's revenues from the film to date. All North American theatre screen and television revenues are included. Only 50% of non–North American revenues are included. Only 20% of the gross is included for home video sales. The film's video distributor, Golden Ventures Home Video (100% owned by GV), kept 80% because it was treated as a separate company. Revenues from nontheatre, nonvideo, and nontelevision sources are not included.
(b) Distribution fees. Covers overhead costs of running a studio and is a flat percentage 35% of revenues.
(c) Distribution expenses. The actual costs of putting the movie in theatres, including advertising, printing copies of the film, and transportation.
(d) Gross participation fees of directors, screen stars. The major "talent" on the movie receive 20% of the gross receipts for the first $240 million and 25% thereafter.
(e) Negative cost is the cost of producing everything that is seen onscreen, from film and sets to up-front fees paid to cast and crew.
(f) Interest on negative cost. The studio views the cost of financing a film as a loan and charges 125% of the prime rate for any negative balance in line 9 as long as the movie "remains in the red."

football superstar. Harrigan bubbled with excitement during the meeting. He said the book was the "best thing he had seen in many years" and would make *"Titanic* look like a minor movie." Fittler felt great about a luminary such as Harrigan being so full of praise for a film based on a book that many publishers initially rejected as "not meeting their commercial criteria."

After the meeting, Fittler called Penny Carr, a friend for many years. Carr showed Fittler some extracts from an exposé on "Accounting, Hollywood Style"—see the exhibit above for this problem. Fittler was dismayed by the Cumulative Distribution Statement. He thought *Bill Goldberg Superstar* was a box-office success and yet it still was more than $74 million "in the red."

REQUIRED
You are asked to give advice to Brad Fittler. You should
   a. identify the weaknesses in the Golden Ventures Cumulative Distribution Statement for an author whose payment is 5% of net profits
   b. propose ways to reduce (or even eliminate) the weaknesses you identify in (a) for a contract for Fittler.

2-43 **Defining cost terms.** You are the controller of the Heinz potato processing subsidiary in Ireland. This subsidiary processes potatoes for frozen dinners, fast food restaurants, and other large institutional buyers. Assume that companies setting up manufacturing facilities in Ireland receive an income tax rebate equivalent to the ratio of employment costs of Irish citizens to total manufacturing costs in Ireland. Thus, if the Irish subsidiary has a "pre-rebate" tax bill of $12 million and the ratio of employment costs to total manufacturing costs is 22%, its actual tax bill will be reduced by $2.64 million to $9.36 million.

INSTRUCTIONS

Form groups of two or more students to complete the following requirement.

REQUIRED

Develop guidelines as to how Heinz should define costs at its Irish subsidiary. Assume one aim is to minimize the income taxes that Heinz is legitimately required to pay to the Irish government.

CHAPTER 3

Cost-Volume-Profit Analysis

Breakeven analysis incorporates the integral relationship among selling prices, costs, volume of sales, and profits. Breakeven analysis is a technique to produce extremely useful information for planning. From running a university concert to operating an automobile company, the fundamental issues are the same. Ford has determined that some of its plants will need to be closed in order to reduce its costs to achieve a breakeven volume plus a targeted profit. As a result, Ford had to make difficult decisions to restructure operations at its Oakville assembly plants.

LEARNING OBJECTIVES

After studying this chapter, you should be able to

1. Understand basic cost-volume-profit (CVP) assumptions

2. Explain essential features of CVP analysis

3. Determine the breakeven point and target operating income using the equation, contribution margin, and graph methods

4. Incorporate income tax considerations into CVP analysis

5. Explain the use of CVP analysis in decision making, and explain how sensitivity analysis can help managers cope with uncertainty

6. Use CVP analysis to plan costs

7. Apply CVP analysis to a multiproduct company

8. Adapt CVP analysis to multiple cost driver situations

9. Distinguish between contribution margin and gross margin

This chapter examines one of the most basic planning tools available to managers: cost-volume-profit analysis. **Cost-volume-profit (CVP)** analysis examines the behaviour of total revenues, total costs, and operating income as changes occur in the output level, selling price, variable costs per unit, or fixed costs. Managers commonly use CVP as a tool to help them answer such questions as: How will revenues and costs be affected if we sell 1,000 more units? If we raise or lower our selling prices? If we expand business into overseas markets? These questions have a common "what if" theme. CVP is built on simplifying assumptions about revenue and cost behaviour patterns. By examining various possibilities and alternatives, CVP analysis illustrates various decision outcomes and this serves as a valuable aid in the planning process.

As you read this chapter, you will begin to understand the difficulties faced by capital-intensive companies that have high fixed costs. Many of the companies, such as Global Crossing and WorldCom in the telecommunications industry, are in bankruptcy. Air Canada only recently emerged from bankruptcy protection. As sales declined at these companies during 2001 and 2002, high fixed costs led to substantial losses. CVP analysis is one way management accountants can alert managers to the risks and rewards of the decisions they make.

COST-VOLUME-PROFIT ANALYSIS (CVP) ASSUMPTIONS

Cost-volume-profit (CVP). Examines the behaviour of total revenues, total costs, and operating income as changes occur in the output level, selling price, variable costs per unit, or fixed costs; a single revenue driver and a single cost driver are used in this analysis.

Global surveys show that more than 50% of responding companies use some form of CVP analysis.

Revenue driver. Any factor that affects revenues.

Be aware that a short-run decision can have long-run consequences. To illustrate, assume WestJet accepts last-minute passengers at reduced fares because the contribution margin from these passengers is positive. This decision could have long-run consequences because future passengers might come to expect reduced fares at the last minute.

The CVP analysis is based on the following six assumptions:

1. Changes in the level of revenues and costs arise only because of changes in the number of product (or service) units produced or sold—for example, the number of televisions produced or sold by SONY Corporation. Since we assume production equals sales, the number of units is the only *revenue* and *cost driver*. Just as a cost driver is any factor that affects costs, a **revenue driver** is any factor that affects revenues.

2. Total costs can be divided into a fixed component and a component that is variable with respect to the level of output. Furthermore, you know from Chapter 2 (Exhibit 2-5, p. 38) that variable costs include both direct variable costs and indirect variable costs of a product. Similarly, fixed costs include both direct fixed costs and indirect fixed costs of a product. (We discuss details of determining fixed and variable components of costs in Chapter 10.)

3. The behaviour of total revenues and total costs is linear (straight-line) in relation to output units within the relevant range.[1]

4. The unit selling price, unit variable costs, and total fixed costs are known. (This assumption is discussed later in the chapter and in the appendix to this chapter.)

5. The analysis either covers a single product or assumes that a given revenue mix of products will remain constant as the level of total units sold changes. (This assumption is also discussed later in the chapter.)

6. All revenues and costs can be added and compared without taking into account the time value of money. (Chapters 21 and 22 relax this assumption.)

As you will learn, CVP relationship, although simple, provide powerful assistance to companies in all industries when managers make both strategic and short-run decisions about product features and pricing. CVP analyses aid decisions made in all business functions of the value chain. For example, WestJet needed to decide if it would switch its primary Ontario airport from Hamilton to Toronto. This strategic decision will affect the company for a long period of time. Because landing fees at Toronto are far higher for each flight, the number of paying passengers per flight must increase to not only cover the additional costs, but also produce a target profit. In contrast in the short run, when a British Airways' flight from Toronto to London has empty seats and passengers with transferable tickets from a competitor arrive shortly before takeoff, British Airways' managers must decide what additional money they require to cover the variable cost of flying one more passenger. In this situation the cost object is the flight and once it is scheduled the costs are fixed. The only additional cost to the company may be the in-flight meal, which is about $10 per passenger. In this case, once the flight is scheduled, the number of passengers will only cause the cost of meals to vary and boarding one more passenger will cause an almost negligible change in the cost of the flight.

The six simplifying assumptions, however, do not always hold in practice when, for example, there are multiple revenue (e.g., number of sales visits and number of advertisements) and cost drivers (e.g., number of batches, engineering hours of labour). While more difficult analysis could represent these complex relationships more faithfully, management accountants weigh the benefit of so doing against the costs. They may find that applying simplified CVP relationships generates sufficiently accurate predictions of how total revenues and total costs behave. Managers generally use a complicated approach only if doing so will significantly improve their decisions.

[1] For example, assumption 3 describes well the following situation: prices and productivity and costs of production are constant within the relevant range. Assumption 3 does not describe situations where either reductions in the selling price are necessary to spur sales at higher levels of output or variable costs per unit decline when output increases as employees learn to handle the process more efficiently. The learning curve is discussed in Chapter 10.

Before explaining the basics of CVP analysis, we must first clarify some terms. As described in Chapter 2,

Operating income. Total revenues from operations minus total costs from operations (excluding interest and income tax expenses) including cost of goods sold.

$$\text{Operating income} = \text{Total revenues from operations} - \text{Cost of goods sold and operating expenses (excluding interest and income tax expenses)}$$

Net income is **operating income** plus nonoperating revenues (such as interest revenue) minus nonoperating costs (such as interest cost) minus income taxes. For simplicity, throughout this chapter we assume nonoperating revenues and nonoperating costs to be zero. Thus, net income will be computed as

Net income. Operating income plus nonoperating revenues (such as interest revenue) minus nonoperating costs (such as interest cost) minus income taxes.

$$\text{Net income} = \text{Operating income} - \text{Income taxes}$$

ESSENTIALS OF COST-VOLUME-PROFIT (CVP) ANALYSIS

To see how CVP analysis works, consider the following example.

> **Example:** Madhu Frost plans to sell Do-All Software, a home-office software package, at a heavily attended two-day computer convention in Montreal. Madhu can purchase this software from a computer software wholesaler at $120 per package with the privilege of returning all unsold units and receiving a full $120 refund per package. The units (packages) will be sold at $200 each. She has already paid $2,000 to Computer Conventions Inc. for the booth rental for the two-day convention. Assume there are no other costs. What profits will Madhu make for different quantities of units sold?

OBJECTIVE 2

Explain essential features of CVP analysis

In the Do-All Software example, the privilege of returning unsold packages means that cost of goods sold is variable with respect to the number of units sold.

Cost-Volume-Profit Analysis
www.toolkit.cch.com/text/
P06_7500.asp

The booth rental costs of $2,000 are fixed costs because they will not change no matter how many units Madhu sells. The costs of the package are variable costs because these costs increase in proportion to the number of units sold. For each unit that Madhu sells, she incurs a cost of $120 to purchase it. If Madhu sells 10 packages, the variable purchase costs are $1,200 ($120 × 10).

Madhu can use CVP analysis to examine changes in operating income as a result of selling different quantities of software packages. If Madhu sells 5 software packages:

	Madhu Sells 5 Packages		**Madhu Sells 40 Packages**	
Revenues at	$ 1,000	($200 per package × 5 packages)	$8,000	($200 per package × 40 packages)
Variable Costs at	600	($120 per package × 5 packages)	4,800	($120 per package × 40 packages)
Fixed Costs	2,000		2,000	
Operating Income	$(1,600)		$1,200	

Note that the only numbers that change from selling different quantities of packages are *total revenues* and *total variable costs*. The difference between total revenues and total variable costs is called **contribution margin**. Contribution margin is an effective summary of the reasons that operating income changes as the number of units sold changes. The contribution margin when Madhu sells two packages is $160 (total revenues, $400, minus total variable costs, $240), and the contribution margin when Madhu sells 40 packages is $3,200 (total revenues, $8,000, minus total variable costs, $4,800). Note that contribution margin calculations subtract all variable costs. For instance, if Madhu had hired a salesperson to sell Do-All Software at the convention based on a sales commission on each unit sold, variable costs would include the cost of the package plus the sales commission.

Contribution margin. Revenues minus all costs of the output (a product or service) that vary with respect to the number of output units.

Contribution margin per unit is a useful tool for calculating contribution margins. The contribution margin per unit is the difference between the *selling price* and the *variable cost per unit*. In the Do-All Software example, the contribution margin per unit = $200 − $120 = $80. Contribution margin can then be calculated as

$$\text{Contribution margin} = \text{Contribution margin per unit} \times \text{Number of packages sold}$$

Contribution income statement. Income statement that groups line items by cost-behaviour pattern to highlight the contribution margin.

Contribution margin percentage (contribution margin ratio). Contribution margin per unit divided by selling price, or total contribution margin divided by total revenues.

The variable cost percentage (VC%) is the result of dividing the variable cost by revenue. Note that the CM% + VC% must equal 100% of revenue and therefore VC% = 100% − CM%. In our example the VC% = 100% − 40% = 60%.

For example, when 40 packages are sold, contribution margin = $80 × 40 = $3,200.

Contribution margin is a key concept in CVP analysis. It represents the amount of revenues remaining, after earning back variable costs, that contribute to reimbursing fixed costs. Once fixed costs are fully recovered, the contribution margin contributes to earning operating income. Exhibit 3-1 calculates the contribution margins for different quantities of packages sold and shows how contribution margin recovers fixed costs and generates operating income. The income statement presentation in Exhibit 3-1 is called a **contribution income statement** because it groups line items by cost-behaviour pattern to highlight the contribution margin. Note that each additional unit sold from 0 to 1 to 2 increases contribution margin by $80, covering more of the fixed costs and reducing the operating loss. If Madhu sells 25 packages, the contribution margin equals $2,000 ($80 × 25), exactly reimbursing the fixed costs and resulting in zero operating income. Each package sold beyond 25 packages generates an additional per-unit contribution margin of $80, which adds directly to operating income because fixed costs of $2,000 have already been recovered. For example, if Madhu sells 40 units, 15 units more than the breakeven point of 25 units, the contribution margin increases by $1,200 ($80 × 15), all of which becomes operating income. Note that, as you move across Exhibit 3-1 from left to right, the increase in contribution margin exactly equals the increase in operating income (or the decrease in operating loss).

Instead of expressing the contribution margin as a per-unit amount, we can also express it as a percentage. **Contribution margin percentage** or **contribution margin ratio** is the contribution margin per unit divided by the selling price. In our example,

$$\text{Contribution margin percentage} = \frac{\$80}{\$200} = 40\%$$

The contribution margin percentage is the contribution margin achieved per dollar of sales. It indicates that 40% of every dollar of sales (40 cents) will go toward the contribution margin.[2] This $0.40 per unit dollar of sales is what remains to the company to pay all its fixed costs plus achieve a specified profit per unit sold.

Madhu can calculate the total contribution margin for different sales levels by multiplying the contribution margin percentage and the total revenue dollars shown in Exhibit 3-1, line 1. For example, if Madhu sells 25 packages, revenues would be $5,000, and the contribution margin would equal 40% × $5,000 = $2,000, exactly offsetting fixed costs.[3] Madhu breaks even by selling 25 packages worth $5,000.

EXHIBIT 3-1

Contribution Income Statement for Different Quantities of Do-All Software Packages Sold

	A	B	C	D	E	F	G	H
1					**Number of Packages Sold**			
2				0	1	5	25	40
3	Revenues at	$ 200	per package	$ –	$ 200	$ 1,000	$5,000	$8,000
4	Variable Costs at	120	per package	–	120	600	3,000	4,800
5	Contribution Margin at	80	per package	$ –	$ 80	$ 400	$2,000	$3,200
6	Fixed Costs	2,000		2,000	2,000	2,000	2,000	2,000
7	Operating Income			$(2,000)	$(1,920)	$(1,600)	$ –	$1,200

[2]Sometimes the contribution margin is expressed as a percentage of variable costs. Suppose this percentage is 25%. We would then have

Variable costs per unit	$100
Add contribution margin per unit	25
Selling price	$125

By definition, contribution margin percentage, as a term, is always expressed as a percentage of selling price. In our example, it equals $25 ÷ $125 or 20%.

[3]Note from Exhibit 3-1 that, given a contribution income statement, contribution margin percentage can also be calculated as total contribution margin divided by total revenues. For example, if 40 packages are sold, contribution margin percentage = $3,200 ÷ $8,000 = 40%.

The **breakeven point** is that quantity of output at which total revenues equal total costs—that is, where the operating income is zero. Why would managers be interested in the breakeven point? Mainly because they want to avoid operating losses, and the breakeven point tells them what level of sales they must generate to avoid a loss.

This section will continue to use the Do-All Software information to examine three methods for determining the breakeven point: the equation method, the contribution margin method, and the graph method.

The following abbreviations are useful in the subsequent analysis:

- ◆ USP = unit selling price
- ◆ UVC = unit variable costs
- ◆ UCM = unit contribution margin (USP – UVC)
- ◆ CM% = contribution margin percentage (UCM ÷ USP)
- ◆ FC = fixed costs
- ◆ Q = quantity of output units sold (or manufactured)
- ◆ OI = operating income
- ◆ TOI = target operating income
- ◆ TNI = target net income

Breakeven point. Quantity of output at which total revenues and total costs are equal; that is, where the operating income is zero.

Equation Method

The first approach for computing the breakeven point is the equation method. Using the terminology in this chapter, the income statement can be expressed in equation form as follows:

$$\text{Revenues} - \text{Variable costs} - \text{Fixed costs} = \text{Operating income}$$
$$(USP \times Q) - (UVC \times Q) - FC = OI \tag{1}$$

Just remember the format of the contribution income statement and you can reconstruct this equation.

This equation provides the most general and easy-to-remember approach to any CVP situation. Setting operating income equal to zero in the preceding equation, we obtain:

$$\$200Q - \$120Q - \$2,000 = \$0$$
$$\$80Q = \$2,000$$
$$Q = \$2,000 \div \$80 = 25 \text{ units}$$

If Madhu sells fewer than 25 units, she will have a loss; if she sells 25 units, she will break even; and if she sells more than 25 units she will make a profit. This breakeven point is expressed in units. It can also be expressed in sales dollars: 25 units × $200 selling price = $5,000.

Contribution Margin Method

A second approach for computing the breakeven point is the contribution margin method, which is simply an algebraic manipulation of the equation method. Contribution margin is equal to revenues minus all costs of the output (a product or service) that vary with respect to the units of output. This method uses the fact that

Breakeven Analysis
www.toolkit.cch.com/text/
p06_7530.asp

$$(USP \times Q) - (UVC \times Q) - FC = OI$$
$$(USP - UVC) \times Q = FC + OI$$
$$UCM \times Q = FC + OI$$
$$Q = \frac{FC + OI}{UCM} \tag{2}$$

At the breakeven point, operating income is, by definition, zero. Setting OI = 0, we obtain

$$\frac{\text{Breakeven}}{\text{number of units}} = \frac{\text{Fixed costs}}{\text{Unit contribution margin}}$$
$$= \frac{FC}{UCM} \tag{3}$$

The calculations in the equation method and the contribution margin method appear similar because one is a restatement of the other. In our example, fixed costs are $2,000 and the unit contribution margin is $80 ($200 − $120). Therefore,

$$\text{Breakeven number of units} = \$2,000 \div \$80 = 25 \text{ units}$$

We can also algebraically manipulate equation (3) to calculate breakeven in revenue dollars using the contribution margin percentage. Multiplying both sides of equation (3) by the USP gives

$$\text{Breakeven in revenue dollars} = \text{Breakeven number of units} \times \text{USP} = \frac{\text{FC} \times \text{USP}}{\text{UCM}}$$

$$= \frac{\frac{\text{FC}}{\text{UCM}}}{\text{USP}} \quad \text{(By dividing both numerator and denominator by USP)}$$

$$= \frac{\text{FC}}{\text{CM\%}} \quad \text{(because contribution margin percentage, CM\%, equals unit contribution margin, UCM, divided by unit selling price, USP)} \qquad (4)$$

In the Do-All Software sample,

$$\text{CM\%} = \frac{\text{UCM}}{\text{USP}} = \frac{\$80}{\$200} = 40\%$$

$$\text{Breakeven in revenue dollars} = \frac{\text{FC}}{\text{CM\%}} = \frac{\$2000}{40\%} = \$5,000$$

A contribution income statement groups line items by cost-behaviour pattern to highlight the contribution margin. The following statement confirms the preceding breakeven calculations:

Revenues at	$5,000	($200 × 25 packages)
Variable Costs at	$3,000	($120 per package × 25 packages)
Contribution Margin at	$2,000	($80 per package × 25 packages)
Fixed Costs	$2,000	
Operating Income	$ 0	

Graph Method

In common use we refer to three methods for CVP analysis. These are, however, simple variations on the equation for the contribution income statement.

In the graph method, we plot the total costs line and the total revenues line. Their point of intersection is the breakeven point. Exhibit 3-2 illustrates this method for our Do-All example. We need only two points to plot each line if each is assumed to be linear:

1. **Total costs line.** This line is the sum of the fixed costs and the variable costs. Fixed costs are $2,000 at all output levels within the relevant range. To plot fixed costs, measure $2,000 on the vertical axis (point A) and extend a line horizontally. Variable costs are $120 per unit. To plot the total costs line, use as one point the $2,000 fixed costs at 0 output units (point A). Select a second point by choosing any other convenient output level (say, 40 units) and determining the corresponding total costs. The total variable costs at this output level are $4,800 (40 × $120). Fixed costs are $2,000 at all output levels within the relevant range. Hence, total costs at 40 units of output are $6,800, which is point B in Exhibit 3-2. The total costs line is the straight line from point A passing through point B.

2. **Total revenues line.** One convenient starting point is zero revenues at the zero output level, which is point C in Exhibit 3-2. Select a second point by choosing any other convenient output level and determining its total revenues. At 40 units of output, total revenues are $8,000 (40 × $200), which is point D in Exhibit 3-2. The total revenues line is the straight line from point C passing through point D.

The breakeven point is where the total revenues line and the total costs line intersect. At this point, total revenues equal total costs. But Exhibit 3-2 shows the profit or loss outlook for a wide range of output levels. Many people describe the topics covered in this chapter as *breakeven analysis*. We prefer to use the phrase *cost-volume-profit analysis* to avoid overemphasizing the single point where total revenues

EXHIBIT 3-2
Cost-Volume-Profit Graph

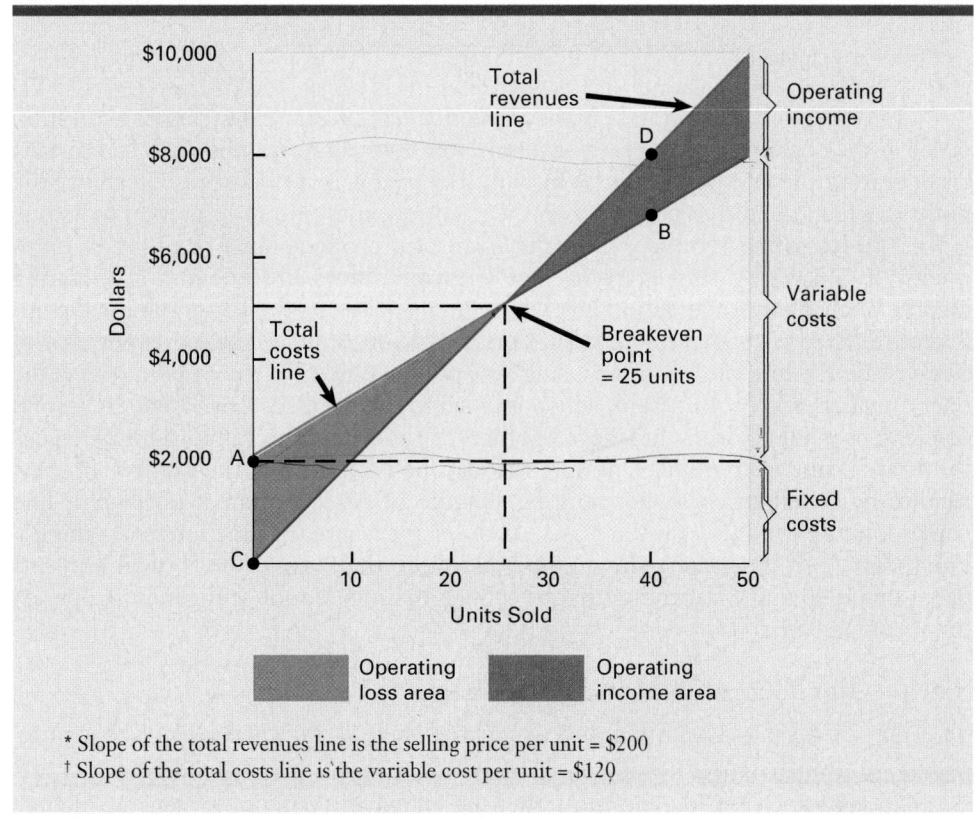

* Slope of the total revenues line is the selling price per unit = $200
† Slope of the total costs line is the variable cost per unit = $120

equal total costs. Managers want to know how operating income differs at many different output levels.

Target Operating Income

Let us introduce a profit element by asking how many units must be sold to earn an operating income of $1,200? The equation method provides a straightforward way to answer this question:

Let Q = Number of units sold to earn target operating income

Revenues − Variable costs − Fixed costs = Target operating income

$$\$200Q - \$120Q - \$2,000 = \$1,200$$
$$\$80Q = \$2,000 + \$1,200$$
$$\$80Q = \$3,200$$
$$Q = \$3,200 \div \$80 = 40 \text{ units}$$

Alternatively, we could use the contribution margin method. The numerator now consists of fixed costs plus target operating income:

$$Q = \frac{\text{Fixed costs} + \text{Target operating income}}{\text{Unit contribution margin}} = \frac{\text{FC} + \text{TOI}}{\text{UCM}}$$

$$Q = \frac{\$2,000 + \$1,200}{\$80}$$

$$\$80Q = \$3,200$$

$$Q = \$3,200 \div \$80 = 40 \text{ units}$$

Proof:		
	Revenues, $200 × 40	$8,000
	Variable costs, $120 × 40	4,800
	Contribution margin, $80 × 40	3,200
	Fixed costs	2,000
	Operating income	$1,200

The revenue in dollars to earn an operating income of $1,200 can also be calculated directly using the approach of equation 4:

$$\frac{\text{Revenue}}{\text{in dollars}} = \frac{\text{FC} + \text{TOI}}{\text{CM\%}} = \frac{\$2,000 + \$1,200}{0.40} = \frac{\$3,200}{0.40} = \$8,000$$

The graph in Exhibit 3-2, however, is not helpful for answering the question posed at the beginning of this section about how many units Madhu must sell to earn an operating income of $1,200. Why not? Because it is not easy to determine the point at which the difference between the total revenues line and the total costs line is $1,200. Recasting Exhibit 3-2 in the form of a profit-volume (PV) graph helps greatly in answering this question. A **PV graph** shows the impact on operating income of changes in the output level. Exhibit 3-3 presents the PV graph for Do-All Software (fixed costs of $2,000, selling price of $200, and variable costs per unit of $120). The PV line can be drawn using two points. One convenient point (X) is the operating loss at zero units sold, which is equal to the fixed costs of $2,000. A second convenient point (Y) is the breakeven point—25 units in our example. The PV line is the straight line from point X passing through point Y. To find the number of units Madhu must sell to earn an operating income of $1,200, draw a horizontal line corresponding to $1,200 on the y-axis. At the point where this line intersects the PV line (point A on the graph), draw a vertical line to the x-axis. The vertical line cuts the x-axis at 40 units, indicating that by selling 40 units Madhu will generate operating income of $1,200.

PV graph. Shows the impact on operating income of changes in the output level.

Target Net Income and Income Taxes

OBJECTIVE 4

Incorporate income tax considerations into CVP analysis

Thus far, we have ignored the effect of income taxes in our CVP analysis. At times, managers want to know the effect of their decision on income after taxes. CVP calculations for target income must then be stated in terms of target net income instead of target operating income. Net income is operating income minus income taxes. For example, Madhu may be interested in knowing the number of units of Do-All Software she must sell to earn a net income of $1,200, assuming an income tax rate of 40%. We modify the target operating income calculations of the previous section to allow for income taxes. Using the equation method,

Revenues − Variable costs − Fixed costs = Target operating income

EXHIBIT 3-3
The Profit-Volume Graph

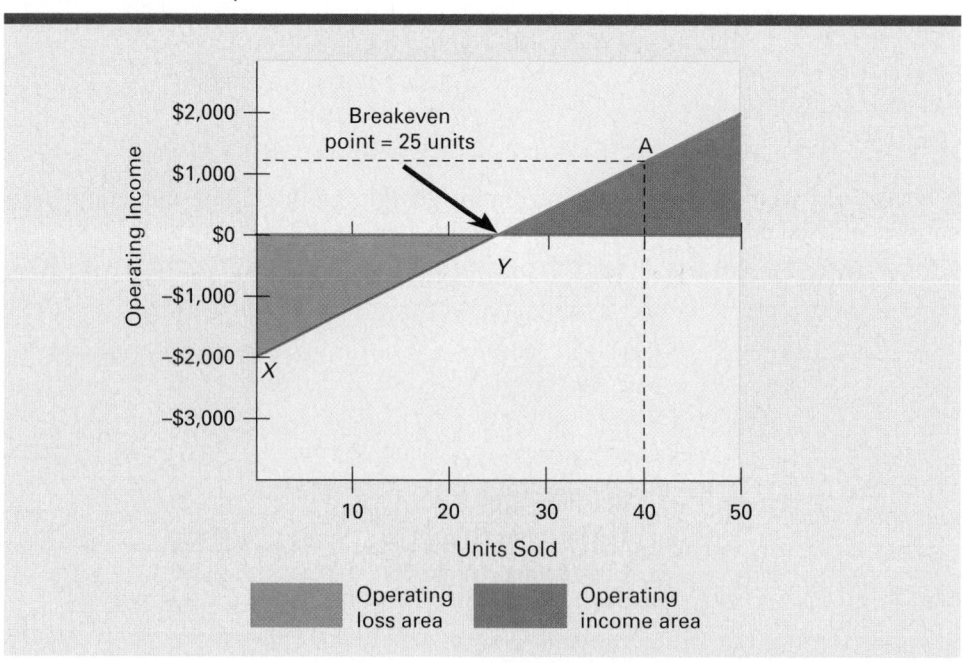

Furthermore,

$$\text{Target net income} = (\text{Target operating income}) - [(\text{Target operating income}) \times (\text{Tax rate})]$$

$$\text{Target net income} = (\text{Target operating income})(1 - \text{Tax rate})$$

$$\text{Target operating income} = \frac{\text{Target net income}}{(1 - \text{Tax rate})}$$

Substituting for target operating income, we have

$$\text{Revenues} - \text{Variable costs} - \text{Fixed costs} = \frac{\text{Target net income}}{(1 - \text{Tax rate})}$$

Substituting numbers from our Do-All Software example, we have

$$\$200Q - \$120Q - \$2,000 = \frac{\$1,200}{(1 - 0.40)}$$

$$\$200Q - \$120Q - \$2,000 = \$2,000$$

$$\$80Q = \$4,000$$

$$Q = \$4,000 \div \$80 \text{ per unit} = 50 \text{ units}$$

Alternatively, we could use the method of equation 2 and substitute

$$\text{Target operating income} = \frac{\text{Target net income}}{(1 - \text{Tax rate})}, \text{ that is}$$

$$Q = \frac{\text{Fixed costs} + \dfrac{\text{Target net income}}{(1 - \text{Tax rate})}}{\text{Unit contribution margin}} = \frac{\text{FC} + \dfrac{\text{TNI}}{(1 - \text{Tax rate})}}{\text{UCM}}$$

$$Q = \frac{\$2,000 + \dfrac{\$1,200}{(1 - 0.40)}}{\$80} = \frac{\$2,000 + \$2,000}{\$80 \text{ per unit}} = 50 \text{ units}$$

Proof:

Revenues at	$10,000	($200 × 50 packages)
Variable costs at	$ 6,000	($120 per package × 50 packages)
Contribution margin at	$ 4,000	($80 per package × 50 packages)
Fixed costs	$ 2,000	
Operating income	$ 2,000	
Income taxes	$ 800	($2,000 × 40%)
Net income	$ 1,200	

Focusing the analysis on target net income instead of on target operating income will not change the breakeven point. Why? Because, by definition, operating income at the breakeven point is zero, and thus no income taxes will arise.[4]

Madhu can also use the PV graph in Exhibit 3-3. For a target net income of $1,200, $\text{Target operating income} = \frac{\text{Target net income}}{(1 - \text{Tax rate})} = \frac{\$1,200}{(1 - 0.40)} = \$2,000$. From Exhibit 3-3, to earn operating income of $2,000, Madhu will need to sell 50 packages.

USING CVP ANALYSIS IN PLANNING AND DECISION MAKING

We have seen how CVP analysis is useful for determining breakeven quantities and the quantities for achieving targeted operating and net incomes. Managers also use CVP analysis to guide other decisions.

Decision to Advertise

Consider again the Do-All Software example. Suppose Madhu Frost anticipates selling 40 packages. Exhibit 3-3 indicates that Madhu's operating income would be $1,200. Madhu is considering placing an advertisement describing the product and its features in the convention brochure. The advertisement will cost $500. This will be a fixed cost

OBJECTIVE 5

Explain the use of CVP analysis in decision making, and explain how sensitivity analysis can help managers cope with uncertainty

[4]Other types of taxes may affect the breakeven point. For example, a sales tax collected by the seller that is a fixed percentage of revenues can be treated as a variable cost and hence will increase the breakeven point.

because this cost will stay the same regardless of the number of units Madhu sells. She anticipates that advertising will increase sales to 45 packages. Should Madhu advertise? The following table presents the CVP analysis.

	40 Packages Sold with No Advertising	45 Packages Sold with Advertising	Difference
	(1)	(2)	(3) = (2) − (1)
Contribution margin ($80 × 40; 45)	$3,200	$3,600	$ 400
Fixed costs	(2,000)	(2,500)	(500)
Operating income	$1,200	$1,100	$(100)

Operating income decreases by $100, so Madhu should not advertise. Note that Madhu could focus only on the incremental changes and come to the same conclusion. If Madhu advertises, contribution margin will increase by $400 ($80 per unit × 5 additional units), and fixed costs will increase by $500, resulting in a $100 decrease in operating income.

Decision to Reduce Selling Price

Having decided not to advertise, Madhu is contemplating whether to reduce the selling price of Do-All Software to $175. At this price, she thinks sales will be 50 units. At this quantity, the software wholesaler who supplies Do-All Software will sell the packages to Madhu for $115 per package instead of $120. Should Madhu reduce the selling price? No, as the following CVP analysis shows:

Expected contribution margin from lowering price to $175, ($175 − $115) × 50 units	$3,000
Expected contribution margin from maintaining price at $200, ($200 − $120) × 40 units	3,200
Increase/(decrease) in contribution margin from lowering price	$(200)

Because the fixed costs of $2,000 do not change, decreasing the price will lead to a lower contribution margin and a lower operating income.

Madhu can examine other alternatives to increase operating income such as simultaneously increasing advertising costs and lowering prices. In each case, Madhu compares the changes in contribution margin (through the effect on selling price, variable costs, and output volume) to the changes in fixed costs and chooses the alternative that gives the highest operating income.

SENSITIVITY ANALYSIS AND UNCERTAINTY

Sensitivity analysis. A what-if technique that examines how a result will change if the original predicted data are not achieved or if an underlying assumption changes.

When revenue, costs, or taxes are not known with certainty, they must be estimated. Estimation requires judgment and reasonable managers can disagree among themselves on their estimates of unit revenue and unit cost. When management accountants apply the technique of sensitivity analysis they can help managers understand whether their different estimates significantly affect the outcome of CVP analyses. Only significant differences will be relevant to the decisions managers make.

Margin of safety. Excess of budgeted revenues over the breakeven revenues.

Sensitivity analysis is a what-if technique that examines how a result will change if the original predicted data are not achieved or if an underlying assumption changes. In the context of CVP, sensitivity analysis answers such questions as what will operating income be if the output level decreases by 5% from the original prediction? What will operating income be if variable costs per unit increase by 10%? The sensitivity to various possible outcomes broadens managers' perspectives as to what might actually occur despite their well-laid plans.

The widespread use of electronic spreadsheets has promoted the use of CVP analysis in many organizations. Using spreadsheets, managers can easily conduct CVP-based sensitivity analyses to examine the effect and interaction of changes in selling prices, unit variable costs, fixed costs, and target operating incomes. Exhibit 3-4 displays a spreadsheet for our Do-All example.[5] Madhu can immediately see the revenues that need to be generated to reach particular operating income levels, given alternative levels of fixed costs and variable costs per unit. For example, revenues of $6,000 (30 units at $200 per unit) are required to earn an operating income of $1,000 if fixed costs are $2,000 and variable costs per unit are $100. Madhu can also use Exhibit 3-4 to assess whether she wants to sell at the Montreal computer convention if, for example, the booth rental is raised to $3,000 (thus increasing fixed costs to $3,000) or the software supplier raises its price to $140 per unit (thus increasing variable costs to $140 per unit).

One aspect of sensitivity analysis is the **margin of safety**, which is the excess of budgeted revenues over the breakeven revenues. The margin of safety is the answer

[5]Spreadsheet packages such as Excel facilitate sensitivity analyses.

EXHIBIT 3-4
Spreadsheet Analysis of CVP Relationships for Do-All Software

	A	B	C	D	E	F
1			Revenue Dollars Required at $200			
2			Selling Price to Earn Operating Income of			
3		Variable Costs				
4	Fixed Costs	per Unit	$0	$1,000	$1,500	$2,000
5	$2,000	$100	$ 4,000	$ 6,000	$ 7,000	$ 8,000
6		120	5,000	7,500	8,750	10,000
7		140	6,667	10,000	11,667	13,333
8	$2,500	$100	$ 5,000	$ 7,000	$ 8,000	$ 9,000
9		120	6,250	8,750	10,000	11,250
10		140	8,333	11,667	13,333	15,000
11	$3,000	$100	$ 6,000	$ 8,000	$ 9,000	$10,000
12		120	7,500	10,000	11,250	12,500
13		140	10,000	13,333	15,000	16,667

to the what-if question: If budgeted revenues are above breakeven and drop, how far can they fall below budget before the breakeven point is reached? Such a fall could be due to a competitor having a better product, poorly executed marketing, and so on. Assume that Madhu Frost has fixed costs of $3,000, a selling price of $200, and variable costs per unit of $140. For 75 units sold, the budgeted revenues are $15,000 and the budgeted operating income is $1,500. The breakeven point for this set of assumptions is 50 units ($3,000 ÷ $60) or $10,000 ($200 × 50). Hence, the margin of safety is $5,000 ($15,000 – $10,000) or 25 units.

Sensitivity analysis is one approach to recognizing **uncertainty**, which is defined here as the possibility that an actual amount will deviate from an expected amount. Another approach is to compute expected values using probability distributions. The appendix to this chapter (p. 89) illustrates this approach.

Uncertainty. The probability (p) that the actual future outcome will equal the estimated, predicted outcome. If managers are certain, then the probability is 100% or (p) = 1 that the actual future outcome will equal the estimated future outcome. If they are not certain, then the probability is less than 100% or (p) < 1. A simple technique to represent this situation is to multiply all the estimates about which managers are uncertain by the value of p(x). The effect is to lower the dollar value of the estimated amounts. For example, if managers were only 80% certain that the future price would be $200, then they would use 0.8 × $200 = $160 in their sensitivity analyses. This could apply to both variable and fixed costs as well.

COST PLANNING AND CVP

Alternative Fixed-Cost/Variable-Cost Structures

Sensitivity analysis highlights the risks that an existing cost structure poses for an organization. This may lead managers to consider alternative cost structures. CVP helps managers in this task. Consider again Madhu and her booth rental agreement with Computer Conventions, Inc. Our original example has Madhu paying a $2,000 booth rental fee. Suppose, however, Computer Conventions offers Madhu three rental alternatives:

◆ **Option 1:** $2,000 fixed fee
◆ **Option 2:** $1,400 fixed fee plus 5% of the convention revenues from Do-All sales
◆ **Option 3:** 20% of the convention revenues from Do-All sales with no fixed fee

Madhu is interested in how her choice of a rental agreement will affect the risks she faces. Exhibit 3-5 presents these options in the CVP format.

◆ **Option 1** exposes her to fixed costs of $2,000 and a breakeven point of 25 units. This option brings $80 additional operating income for each unit sold above 25 units.

◆ **Option 2** exposes her to lower fixed costs of $1,400 and a lower breakeven point of 20 units. There is, however, only $70 in additional operating income for each unit sold above 20 units.

◆ **Option 3** has no fixed costs. Madhu makes $40 in additional operating income for each unit sold. This $40 addition to operating income starts from the first unit sold. This option enables Madhu to break even if no units are sold.

EXHIBIT 3-5
CVP Graphs for Alternative Rental Schedules for Do-All Software

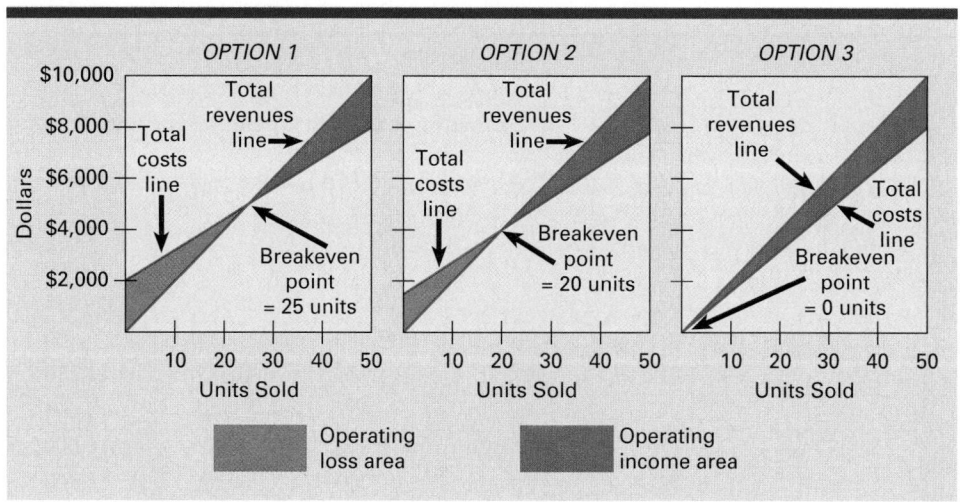

CVP analysis highlights the different risks and different returns associated with each option. For example, although option 1 has the most downside risk (a $2,000 fixed up-front payment), it also has the highest contribution margin per unit. This $80 contribution margin per unit translates to high upside potential if Madhu is able to generate sales above 25 units. By moving from option 1 to option 2, Madhu faces less risk (lowers her fixed costs) if demand is low, but she must accept less upside potential (because of the higher variable costs) if demand is high. The choice between options 1, 2, and 3 will be influenced by her confidence in the level of demand for Do-All Software and her willingness to risk money. The table below illustrates the degree of operating leverage at the sales level of 40 units for the three alternative rental options.

	Option 1	Option 2	Option 3
Contribution margin per unit	$ 80	$ 70	$ 40
Contribution margin (row 1 × 40 units)	$3,200	$2,800	$1,600
Operating income (from Exhibit 3-5)	$1,200	$1,400	$1,600
Degree of operating leverage (row 2 ÷ row 3)	2.67	2.00	1.00

Operating leverage. Describes the effects that fixed costs have on changes in operating income as changes occur in units sold and hence in contribution margin.

Degree of operating leverage. Contribution margin divided by operating income.

Degree of operating leverage (DOL) is specific to a given level of sales as the starting point. If the starting point, volume of sales, changes, then the DOL will change. For example, if the starting point was sales of 50 units, the DOL for option 1 would be:

$$\frac{\text{CM}}{\text{CM} - \text{FC}} = \frac{\$80 \times 50}{(\$80 \times 50) - \$2,000} = 2.00$$

The risk-return tradeoff across alternative cost structures is usefully summarized in a measure called *operating leverage*. **Operating leverage** describes the effects that fixed costs have on changes in operating income as changes occur in units sold and hence in contribution margin. Organizations with a high proportion of fixed costs in their cost structures, as in the case under option 1 in our example, have high operating leverage. As a result, small changes in sales lead to large changes in operating incomes. Consequently, if sales increase, operating incomes increase even more, yielding large returns. If sales decrease, however, operating incomes decline substantially, leading to a greater risk of losses. At any given level of sales, **degree of operating leverage** equals contribution margin divided by operating income.

These numbers indicate that, when sales are 40 units, a percentage change in sales and contribution margin will result in 2.67 times that percentage change in operating income for option 1, but the same percentage change in operating income (as before the change in sales) for option 3. Consider, for example, a sales increase of 50% from 40 units to 60 units. Contribution margin also increases by 50% under each option. Operating income, however, increases by 2.67 × 50% = 133% from $1,200 to $2,800 in option 1 but only by 1 × 50% = 50% from $1,600 to $2,400 in option 3. Knowing the degree of operating leverage at a given level of sales helps managers to calculate quickly the effect of changes in sales on operating incomes.

Managers must carefully monitor operating leverage because increasing the level of fixed costs poses a threat to profitability when the expected level of sales decreases. Companies such as Air Canada, WorldCom, and Global Crossing had high operating leverage and all suffered when demand for their services decreased

WorldCom: Simply a Matter of Poor Planning?

A major benefit of CVP analysis is accurate planning. Conscientious planning requires management to make realistic assumptions about the future of the company by answering critical questions such as: How much will revenues be? What are the risks if revenues are lower than planned? What will costs be? Could costs be higher than expected? Realistic planning is particularly important in companies with large commitments of fixed costs, such as plant costs, loan and interest payments, and maintenance expenses, because lower-than-expected sales result in heavy losses. WorldCom, formerly North America's second-largest telecommunications company, acquired companies and ramped up its investment in telecommunications infrastructure and equipment over a short period of time. When demand for its services fell, it began to face significant financial pressures. So what did the company do? It improperly booked billions of dollars of routine business costs as capital expenditures, overstating income by more than US$11 billion by early 2002. The company also had loaned its then–chief executive officer, Bernard Ebbers, more than US$400 million to cover personal stock trading losses.

Could WorldCom have avoided these problems if the assumptions underlying its financial projections had been realistic? Could CVP analysis have revealed to management that the company would face severe problems if its investment plans did not materialize? Yes, but reports in the financial press suggest that WorldCom's managers did not plan well. Even worse, they chose to manipulate financial statements to conceal the company's disastrous performance. The chief financial officer and finance executives failed in their responsibilities to be realistic, ask tough-minded, critical questions, and communicate results with integrity.

On June 25, 2002, WorldCom finally revealed its improper accounting practices. This led to a halt in the trading of its stock on the NASDAQ stock exchange and, just a few weeks later, Chapter 11 bankruptcy. To prevent bankruptcy, under Chapter 11, companies receive relief from existing debt payment schedules to renegotiate new terms of repayment. They continue their normal business operations throughout Chapter 11 protection. On March 2, 2004, WorldCom's former chief financial officer, Scott Sullivan, finally admitted that, "as CFO at WorldCom, I participated with other members of WorldCom to conspire to paint a false and misleading picture of WorldCom's financial results." Bernard Ebbers, the former CEO, was indicted on charges of fraud, conspiracy, and making false statements in the US$11-billion accounting scandal. He has been convicted and sentenced to 25 years in prison.

Sources: "WorldCom Chief Turns Himself In to FBI," March 3, 2004, Reuters.com newswire; S. N. Mehta, "Is MCI Being Good Enough?" *Fortune*, October 27, 2003; B. Klayman, "MCI Reduces Earnings by $74.4 Billion," March 12, 2004, Reuters.com.

(see the Focus on Values and Behaviours box above). Anticipating accelerating demand growth for their services, each company borrowed money to increase their capacity by acquiring fixed assets. The result was high fixed costs and when demand diminished these companies could not generate sales sufficient to meet their cash needs to pay total variable and fixed cost of operation (for example, employees' salaries, contributions to pension plans, and health plan contributions).

Today, with increased cross-border trade and access to worldwide pools of labour, managers can reduce fixed costs of plant and equipment for Canadian manufacturing companies, such as Gildan Activewear, by moving these facilities to Mexico or offshore to Haiti, Honduras, and the Dominican Republic. They can also substitute fixed with variable costs by, for example, purchasing the right to use software from an applications software provider (ASP) and paying only for the applications and time instead of incurring the costs of in-house development. The rapid change in technology makes this a wise decision for growing companies. A prominent example is the cost undertaken by large airline companies to create their own computer reservation systems, a service for which passengers paid each time they booked a flight. With the advent of the Internet and development of appropriate software, these in-house systems were made obsolete along with the revenue they produced because people could book flights at their convenience on their own efficiently and without charge. Many service industries such

Influencing Cost Structures to Manage the Risk-Return Tradeoff at Amazon.com

Building up too many fixed costs can be hazardous to a company's health. Because fixed costs, unlike variable costs, do not automatically decrease as volume declines. Companies with too many fixed costs can lose a considerable amount of money during lean times. Amazon.com, the Internet retailer, understood this concept well. Amazon began business using a "virtual" business model. When Amazon received a customer order for a book on its Web site, it immediately turned around and placed an order with a book wholesaler, which shipped the book directly to the customer. The "virtual" in Amazon's business model referred to the fact that Amazon was able to sell books from its Web site without having to invest in

warehouses or inventory. Amazon only incurred the cost of acquiring books on an as-needed basis after it had received a confirmed order from a customer. Amazon essentially had a variable-cost structure—costs were high when sales were strong, and costs were low when sales were weak. Without warehousing and inventory costs, Amazon avoided being stuck with costs if business was slow. But this low-risk strategy came at a price—purchasing books from wholesalers costs significantly more than purchasing books directly from publishers.

The competitive disadvantage from the higher cost of books became apparent in 1997 when Barnes & Noble, the largest U.S. bricks-and-mortar book retailer, opened an online store. It already had a large distribution centre to supply books to its stores. It planned to use the same warehouse facility to fill the orders it received from online customers. Moreover, Barnes & Noble paid less for its books than Amazon because its distribution-centre capacity enabled it to order books in the minimum-order quantities required by publishers. When it opened its online store, Barnes & Noble claimed it would offer "the lowest everyday prices of any online bookseller," as well as better service, because it controlled the product, rather than having to rely on wholesalers to supply it. Barnes & Noble had higher fixed costs but lower variable costs than Amazon. At high volume levels, Barnes & Noble's costs would be less than Amazon's costs.

In response to Barnes & Noble's threat, Amazon decided to build and acquire distribution centres of its own. Doing so increased Amazon's fixed costs, operating leverage, and risk but decreased its variable costs. Amazon was counting on a rapid and dramatic expansion in sales. How rapid? At the beginning of 2000, stock analysts estimated that Amazon's warehouse capacity was three to five times more than it needed. In early 2001, Amazon acknowledged that sales in 2000 had fallen short of expectations, projected even lower sales growth in 2001, and announced the closing of two of its distribution facilities. As sales decreased, Amazon had to cut its fixed costs to increase its chances of breaking even.

Amazon.com
www.amazon.com

Barnes & Noble
www.bn.com

Source: Amazon.com financial statements, stock-analyst reports, and conversations with company management.

as telecommunications and airlines also outsource their customer service and technical support call centres to countries such as India, where labour costs are far lower (see the Concepts in Action box above).

EFFECT OF TIME HORIZON

A critical assumption of CVP analysis is that costs can be classified as either variable or fixed. This classification can be affected by the time period being considered. The shorter the time horizon we consider, the higher the percentage of total costs we may view as fixed. Suppose an Air Canada plane will depart from its gate in 30 minutes and there are 20 empty seats. A potential passenger arrives bearing a transferable ticket from a competing airline. What are the variable costs to British Airways of placing one more passenger in an otherwise empty seat? Variable costs (such as one more meal) would be negligible. Virtually all the costs in that decision situation are fixed.

In contrast, suppose British Airways must decide whether to include another city in its routes. This decision may have a one-year planning horizon. Many more costs would be regarded as variable and fewer as fixed in this decision.

This example underscores the importance of how the time horizon of a decision affects the analysis of cost behaviour. In brief, whether costs are really fixed depends heavily on the relevant range, the length of the time horizon in question, and the specific decision situation.

EFFECTS OF REVENUE MIX ON INCOME

Revenue mix (also called **sales mix**) is the relative contribution of quantities of products or services that constitutes total revenues. If the mix changes, overall revenue targets may still be achieved. However, the effects on operating income depend on how the original proportions of lower or higher contribution margin products have shifted.

Revenue mix (sales mix). The relative contribution of quantities of products or services that constitutes total revenues.

Suppose Madhu in our computer convention example is now budgeting for the next convention. She plans to sell two software products—Do-All and Superword—and budgets the following:

	Do-All	Superword	Total
Units sold	60	30	90
Revenues, $200 and $130 per unit	$12,000	$3,900	$15,900
Variable costs $120 and $90 per unit	7,200	2,700	9,900
Contribution margin, $80 and $40 per unit	$ 4,800	$1,200	$ 6,000
Fixed costs			2,000
Operating income			$ 4,000

What is the breakeven point? Unlike the single product (or service) situation, there is not a unique number of units for a multiple-product situation. This number instead depends on the revenue mix. The following approach can be used when it is assumed that the budgeted revenue mix (two units of Do-All sold for each unit of Superword sold) will not change at different levels of total revenue

$$\text{Let } S = \text{Number of units of Superword to break even}$$
$$2S = \text{Number of units of Do-All to break even}$$
$$\text{Revenues} - \text{Variable costs} - \text{Fixed costs} = \text{Operating income}$$
$$[\$200(2S) + \$130S] - [\$120(2S) + \$90S] - \$2,000 = 0$$
$$\$530S - \$330S = \$2,000$$
$$\$200S = \$2,000$$
$$S = 10$$
$$2S = 20$$

The breakeven point is 30 units when the revenue mix is 20 units of Do-All and 10 units of Superword. The total contribution margin of $2,000 (Do-All $80 × 20 = $1,600 plus Superword $40 × 10 = $400) equals the fixed costs of $2,000 at this mix.

Alternative revenue mixes (in units) that have a contribution margin of $2,000 and thus result in breakeven operations include the following:

	1	2	3	4	5	6
Do-All	25	20	15	10	5	0
Superword	0	10	20	30	40	50
Total	25	30	35	40	45	50

Other things being equal, for any given total quantity of units sold, if the mix shifts toward units with higher contribution margins, operating income will be higher. Thus, if the mix shifts toward Do-All (say, to 70% Do-All from 60% Do-All) with a contribution margin of twice that of Superword, Madhu's operating income will increase.

CVP ANALYSIS IN SERVICE AND NONPROFIT ORGANIZATIONS

Thus far, our examination of CVP analysis has focused on merchandising companies seeking to make a profit. CVP can be applied readily to decisions by service and nonprofit organizations. The key to applying CVP analysis to these organizations is measuring their output. Examples of output measures in various service and nonprofit industries follow.

Industry	Measure of Output
Airlines	Revenue passenger-miles
Hotels/motels	Room-nights occupied
Hospitals	Patient-days
Universities	Student course credits

Suppose a social welfare agency has a government budget appropriation (revenue) for 2007 of $900,000. This nonprofit agency's major purpose is to assist people with disabilities who are seeking employment. On average, the agency supplements each person's income by $5,000 annually. The agency's fixed costs are $270,000. There are no other costs. The agency manager wants to know how many people could be assisted in 2007. We can use CVP analysis here by assuming zero operating income. Let Q be the number of people to be assisted:

$$\text{Revenue} - \text{Variable costs} - \text{Fixed costs} = \$0$$
$$\$900,000 - \$5,000Q - \$270,000 = \$0$$
$$\$5,000Q = \$900,000 - \$270,000$$
$$Q = \$630,000 \div \$5,000 = 126 \text{ people}$$

Suppose the manager is concerned that the total budget appropriation for 2007 will be reduced by 15% to a new amount of $(1 - 0.15) \times \$900,000 = \$765,000$. The manager wants to know how many people with disabilities will be assisted. Assume the same amount of monetary assistance per person:

$$\$765,000 - \$5,000Q - \$270,000 = \$0$$
$$\$5,000Q = \$765,000 - \$270,000$$
$$Q = \$495,000 \div \$5,000 = 99 \text{ people}$$

Note the following two characteristics of the CVP relationships in this non-profit situation:

1. The percentage drop in service, $(126 - 99) \div 126$, or 21.4%, is more than the 15% reduction in the budget appropriation. Why? Because the existence of $270,000 in fixed costs means that the percentage drop in service exceeds the percentage drop in budget appropriation.

2. If the relationships were graphed, the budget appropriation (revenue) amount would be a straight horizontal line of $765,000. The manager could adjust operations to stay within the reduced appropriation in one or more of three major ways: (a) reduce the number of people assisted, (b) reduce the variable costs (the assistance per person), or (c) reduce the total fixed costs.

MULTIPLE COST DRIVERS

OBJECTIVE 8

Adapt CVP analysis to multiple cost driver situations

Throughout this chapter we have assumed that the number of units sold is the only revenue and cost driver. In this section, we relax this important assumption and describe how some aspects of CVP analysis can be adapted to the more general case of multiple cost drivers.

Consider again the Do-All Software example. Suppose that Madhu will incur a cost of $10 for preparing documents and invoices associated with the sale of Do-All Software. These documents and invoices must be prepared for each customer that buys Do-All Software; that is, the cost driver of document-and-invoice-preparation costs is the number of different customers that buy Do-All Software. Madhu's operating income can then be expressed as

$$\begin{array}{l}\text{Operating} \\ \text{income}\end{array} = \text{Revenue} - \left(\begin{array}{c}\text{Costs of each} \\ \text{Do-All Software} \\ \text{package}\end{array} \times \begin{array}{c}\text{Number of} \\ \text{packages sold}\end{array} - \begin{array}{c}\text{Costs of preparing} \\ \text{each document} \\ \text{and invoice}\end{array} \times \begin{array}{c}\text{Number of} \\ \text{documents} \\ \text{and invoices}\end{array}\right) - \begin{array}{c}\text{Fixed} \\ \text{costs}\end{array}$$

Assuming that Madhu sells 40 packages to 15 customers, then

$$\begin{aligned}
\text{Operating income} &= (\$200 \times 40) - (\$120 \times 40) - (\$10 \times 15) - \$2,000 \\
&= \$8,000 - \$4,800 - \$150 - \$2,000 \\
&= \$1,050
\end{aligned}$$

If, instead, Madhu sold 40 packages to 40 customers, then

$$\begin{aligned}
\text{Operating income} &= (\$200 \times 40) - (\$120 \times 40) - (\$10 \times 40) - \$2,000 \\
&= \$8,000 - \$4,800 - \$400 - \$2,000 \\
&= \$800
\end{aligned}$$

Note that the number of packages sold is not the only determinant of Madhu's operating income. For a given number of packages sold, Madhu's operating income will be lower if she sells Do-All Software to more customers. Madhu's cost structure depends on the interaction of two cost drivers: the number of packages sold and the number of customers.

Just as in the case of multiple products, there is no unique breakeven point when there are multiple cost drivers. For example, Madhu will break even if she sells 26 packages to 8 customers or 27 packages to 16 customers:

$$(\$200 \times 26) - (\$120 \times 26) - (\$10 \times 8) - \$2,000 = \$5,200 - \$3,120 - \$80 - \$2,000 = \$0$$
$$(\$200 \times 27) - (\$120 \times 27) - (\$10 \times 16) - \$2,000 = \$5,400 - \$3,240 - \$160 - \$2,000 = \$0$$

This example illustrates that CVP-type analysis can be adapted to multiple cost driver situations. However, in cases involving multiple cost drivers, the various simple formulas described earlier in the chapter can no longer be used.

CONTRIBUTION MARGIN AND GROSS MARGIN

Contribution margin is a key concept in this chapter. We now consider how it is related to the gross margin concept discussed in Chapter 2. First some definitions:

$$\text{Contribution margin} = \text{Revenues} - \begin{array}{c}\text{All costs that vary with respect} \\ \text{to number of output units}\end{array}$$
$$\text{Gross margin} = \text{Revenues} - \text{Cost of goods sold}$$

OBJECTIVE 9

Distinguish between contribution margin and gross margin

"All costs that vary" refers to variable costs in each business function of the value chain. Cost of goods sold in the merchandising sector is made up of goods purchased for resale. Cost of goods sold in the manufacturing sector consists entirely of manufacturing costs (including fixed manufacturing costs).

Service-sector companies can compute a contribution margin figure but not a **gross margin** figure. Service-sector companies do not have a cost of goods sold line item in their income statement.

Gross margin. Revenues minus cost of goods sold.

Merchandising Sector

The two areas of difference between contribution margin and gross margin for companies in the merchandising sector are fixed cost of goods sold (such as a fixed annual payment to a supplier to guarantee an exclusive option to purchase merchandise) and variable non-cost-of-goods-sold items (such as a salesperson's commission that is a percentage of sales dollars). Contribution margin is computed after all variable costs have been deducted, whereas gross margin is computed by deducting only cost of goods sold from revenues. The following example (figures are in thousands) illustrates this difference:

Contribution Margin Format			Gross Margin Format	
Revenues		$200	Revenues	$200
Variable cost of goods sold	$120		Cost of goods sold ($120 + $5)	125
Other variable costs	43	163	Gross margin	75
Contribution margin		37	Operating costs ($43 + $19)	62
Fixed cost of goods sold	5		Operating income	$ 13
Other fixed costs	19	24		
Operating income		$ 13		

Fixed cost of goods sold for a merchandiser includes only fixed costs directly related to the purchase of merchandise. The preceding example is a fixed annual payment to a supplier of merchandise. It would not include fixed costs (such as fixed salaries) of the purchasing department. These costs would be included in other fixed costs in the contribution margin format.

Manufacturing Sector

The two areas of difference between contribution margin and gross margin for companies in the manufacturing sector are fixed manufacturing costs and variable nonmanufacturing costs. The following example (figures are in thousands) illustrates this difference:

Contribution Margin Format			Gross Margin Format	
Revenues		$1,000	Revenues	$1,000
Variable manufacturing costs	$250		Cost of goods sold ($250 + $160)	410
Variable nonmanufacturing costs	270	520	Gross margin	590
Contribution margin		480	Nonmanufacturing costs ($270 + $138)	408
Fixed manufacturing costs	160		Operating income	$ 182
Fixed nonmanufacturing costs	138	298		
Operating income		$ 182		

Fixed manufacturing costs are not deducted from revenues when computing contribution margin but are deducted when computing gross margin. Cost of goods sold in a manufacturing company includes all and only manufacturing costs. Variable nonmanufacturing costs are deducted from revenues when computing contribution margins but are not deducted when computing gross margins.

Variable-cost percentage. Total variable costs (with respect to units of output) divided by revenues.

Gross margin percentage. Gross margin divided by revenues.

Both the contribution margin and the gross margin can be expressed as totals, as amounts per unit, or as percentages. The contribution margin percentage is the total contribution margin divided by revenues. The **variable-cost percentage** is the total variable costs (with respect to units of output) divided by revenues. The contribution margin percentage in our manufacturing-sector example is 48% ($480 ÷ $1,000), while the variable-cost percentage is 52% ($520 ÷ $1,000). The **gross margin percentage** is the gross margin divided by revenues—59% ($590 ÷ $1,000) in our manufacturing-sector example.

Wembley Travel is a travel agency specializing in Atlantic cruises from Halifax to Marseilles and other ports in Europe. It books passengers on Euro-Cruise, which charges passengers $3,000 per round-trip ticket. Until last month, Euro-Cruise paid Wembley a commission of 10% of the ticket price paid by each passenger. This was Wembley's only source of revenues. Wembley's fixed costs are $35,000 per month (for salaries, rent, etc.), and its variable costs are $40 per ticket purchased for a passenger. This $40 includes a $15 per ticket delivery fee paid to Federal Express. (To keep the analysis simple, we assume each round-trip ticket purchased is delivered in a separate package; thus the $15 delivery fee applies to every ticket.)

Euro-Cruise has just announced a revised payment schedule for travel agents. It will now pay travel agents a 10% commission per ticket up to a maximum of $200. Any ticket costing more than $2,000 receives only a $200 commission, irrespective of the ticket price.

REQUIRED

1. Under the old 10% commission structure, how many round-trip tickets must Wembley sell each month to (a) break even and (b) earn an operating income of $30,000 per month?
2. How does Euro-Cruise's revised payment schedule affect your answers to (a) and (b) in requirement 1?
3. Wembley is approached by DHL Express, who offers to charge $10 per ticket delivered. How would accepting this offer affect your answers to (a) and (b) in requirement 2? (Assume the maximum commission is $200 per ticket.) DHL Express offers next-day service, with reliability comparable to Federal Express.

SOLUTION

1. a. Wembly receives a 10% commission

$$USP = \$300$$
$$UVC = \$40$$
$$UCM = \$300 - \$40 = \$260$$
$$FC = \$35,000 \text{ per month}$$
$$Q = \$35,000 \div \$260 = 135 \text{ tickets per month}$$

b. When target operating income (TOI) = $30,000 per month,

$$USP = \$300$$
$$UVC = \$40$$
$$UCM = \$300 - \$40 = \$260$$
$$FC + TOI = \$65,000 \text{ per month}$$
$$Q = \$(35,000 + 30,000) \div \$260 = 250 \text{ tickets per month}$$

2. a. Maximum commission set at $200

$$USP = \$200$$
$$UVC = \$40$$
$$UCM = \$200 - \$40 = \$160$$
$$FC = \$35,000 \text{ per month}$$
$$Q = \$35,000 \div \$160 = 219 \text{ tickets per month}$$

b. When target operating income (TOI) = $30,000 per month,

$$USP = \$200$$
$$UVC = \$40$$
$$UCM = \$200 - \$40 = \$160$$
$$FC + TOI = \$65,000 \text{ per month}$$
$$Q = \$(35,000 + 30,000) \div \$160 = 406 \text{ tickets per month}$$

3. a. Use DHL Express to reduce UVC

$$USP = \$200$$
$$UVC = \$35$$
$$UCM = \$200 - \$35 = \$165$$
$$FC = \$35,000 \text{ per month}$$
$$Q = \$35,000 \div \$165 = 212 \text{ tickets per month}$$

b. When target operating income (TOI) = $30,000 per month,

$$USP = \$200$$
$$UVC = \$35$$
$$UCM = \$200 - \$35 = \$165$$
$$FC + TOI = \$65,000 \text{ per month}$$
$$Q = \$(35,000 + 30,000) \div \$165 = 394 \text{ tickets per month}$$

Notice that the cap of $200 on the commission paid per ticket causes the breakeven point to increase from 219 to 406 tickets. When the required operating income is $35,000, the total amount almost doubles from 219 to 406. Of course, this travel agency would be very displeased with Euro-Cruise's new commissions policy.

When the reduction in unit variable cost is included, the increase in contribution margin changes the outcome very little. The breakeven point under the new commissions policy decreases slightly from 219 to 212 tickets, and with a target operating income of $30,000, the breakeven point decreases from 406 to 394 tickets. If Wembley cannot increase the volume of tickets it sells, it will have to reduce its costs. The effect of a 30% reduction in delivery costs from $15 to $10 scarcely changes the breakeven volume. Wembley must either reduce its other variable costs substantially, reduce its fixed costs, or reduce its target operating income.

DECISION POINTS   SUMMARY

The following decision guidelines use a question-and-answer format to summarize the chapter's main points. Each decision presents a key question. The guideline is the answer to that question.

DECISIONS	GUIDELINES
1. What assumptions must hold to apply CVP analysis?	CVP analysis requires simplifying assumptions, such as costs are either fixed or variable with respect to the number of output units (units produced and sold) and the relationship between total revenues and total costs is linear.
2. How can CVP analysis assist managers?	CVP analysis assists managers in understanding the behaviour of a product's total costs, total revenues, and operating income as changes occur in that product's output level, selling price, variable costs, or fixed costs.
3. How do companies determine the breakeven point or the output needed to achieve a target operating income?	The breakeven point is the quantity of output at which total revenues equal total costs. The three methods for computing the breakeven point and the quantity of output to achieve target operating income are the equation method, the contribution margin method, and the graph method. Each method is merely a restatement of the others. Managers often select the method they find easiest to use in their specific situation.
4. How should companies incorporate income taxes into CVP analysis?	Income taxes can be incorporated into CVP analysis by using target net income rather than target operating income. The breakeven point is unaffected by the presence of income taxes because no income taxes are paid if there is no operating income.
5. How should companies cope with uncertainty or changes in underlying assumptions?	Sensitivity analysis, a "what if" technique, examines how a result will change if the original predicted data are not achieved or if an underlying assumption changes. When making decisions, managers use CVP analysis to compare contribution margins and fixed costs under different assumptions.

6. How should companies choose among different variable-cost/fixed-cost structures?	CVP analysis highlights the risk of losses when revenues are low and the upside return when revenues are high for different proportions of variable and fixed costs in a company's cost structure.
7. Can CVP analysis be applied to a company producing multiple products?	CVP analysis can be applied to a company producing multiple products by assuming the sales mix of products sold remains constant as the total quantity of units sold changes. There is no unique breakeven number of units for a company producing multiple products.
8. Can CVP analysis be applied to a product that has multiple cost drivers?	The basic concepts of CVP analysis can be applied to multiple cost-driver situations, but the simple formulas of the single cost-driver case, for example, to calculate the breakeven point, cannot be used.
9. Can contribution margin and gross margin be used interchangeably?	No. Contribution margin is revenues minus all variable costs (throughout the value chain); gross margin is revenues minus cost of goods sold.

APPENDIX: DECISION MODELS AND UNCERTAINTY

Managers make predictions and decisions in a world of uncertainty. This appendix explores the characteristics of uncertainty and describes an approach managers can use to cope with it. We also illustrate the additional insights gained when uncertainty is recognized in CVP analysis using data from the Do-All Software example on p. 71.

Coping with Uncertainty[6]

Role of a Decision Model Uncertainty is the possibility that an actual amount will deviate from an expected amount. For example, Madhu Frost might forecast sales at 40 units but actual sales may turn out to be 30 units or 60 units. A **decision model** helps managers deal with uncertainty. It is a formal method for making a choice that often involves both quantitative and qualitative analyses. The quantitative analysis usually has the following steps:

1. A **choice criterion**, which is an objective that can be quantified. This objective can take many forms. Most often the choice criterion is expressed as a maximization of income or a minimization of cost. The choice criterion provides a basis for choosing the best alternative action.

2. A set of the alternative actions being considered.

3. A set of all the relevant **events** that may occur, where an event is a possible occurrence. This set of events should be mutually exclusive and collectively exhaustive. Events are mutually exclusive if they cannot occur at the same time. Events are collectively exhaustive if, taken together, they make up the entire set of possible occurrences (and no other event can occur). Examples are growth or no growth in industry demand, and increase, decrease, or no change in interest rates. Only one event in a set of mutually exclusive and collectively exhaustive events will actually occur.

4. A set of probabilities, where a **probability** is the likelihood or chance of occurrence of an event.

5. A set of possible **outcomes** that measure, in terms of the choice criterion, the predicted consequences of the various possible combinations of actions and events.

It is important to distinguish actions from events. Actions are choices made by management—for example, the prices it should charge for the company's products. Events are occurrences that management cannot control—for example, a growing or

Decision model. Formal model for making a choice under uncertainty, frequently involving both quantitative and qualitative analysis.

Choice criterion. Objective that can be quantified in a decision model.

Events. Possible occurrences in a decision model.

Probability. Likelihood or chance of occurrence of an event.

Outcomes. Predicted consequences of the various possible combinations of actions and events in a decision model.

[6]The presentations here draw (in part) from teaching notes prepared by R. Williamson.

EXHIBIT 3-6
A Decision Model and Its Link to Performance Evaluation

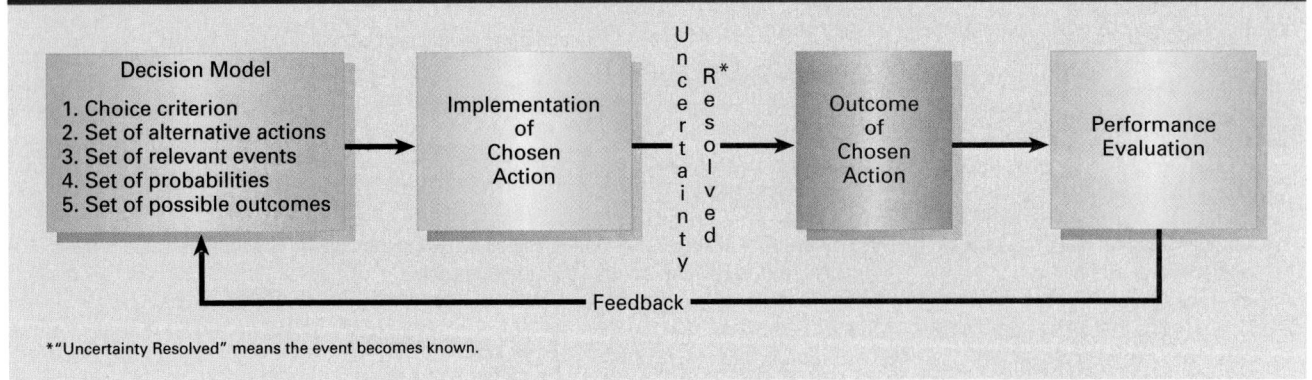

declining economy. The outcome is the operating income the company makes, which depends both on the action management selects (pricing strategy) and the event that occurs (how the economy performs). Exhibit 3-6 presents an overview of a decision model, the implementation of the chosen action, its outcome, and subsequent performance evaluation.

Probabilities Assigning probabilities is a key aspect of the decision model approach to coping with uncertainty. A **probability distribution** describes the likelihood (or probability) of each of the mutually exclusive and collectively exhaustive sets of events. The probabilities of these events will add to 1.00, because they are collectively exhaustive. In some cases, there will be much evidence to guide the assignment of probabilities. For example, the probability of obtaining a head in the toss of a fair coin is 1/2; that of drawing a particular playing card from a standard, well-shuffled deck is 1/52. In business, the probability of having a specified percentage of defective units may be assigned with great confidence, on the basis of production experience with thousands of units. In other cases, little evidence will support estimated probabilities. For example, how many units of a new pharmaceutical product will be sold next year?

The concept of uncertainty can be illustrated by a decision situation facing a book editor. The editor is deciding between publishing a spy novel and publishing a historical novel. Both book proposals require a $200,000 investment at the beginning of the year. (For simplicity here, we ignore the time value of money, which is covered in Chapters 21 and 22.) On the basis of experience, the editor believes that the following probability distribution (assume that the sales life of each book is one year) describes the relative likelihood of cash inflows for the next year:

Probability distribution. Describes the likelihood (or probability) of each of the mutually exclusive and collectively exhaustive sets of events.

Proposal A: Spy Novel		Proposal B: Historical Novel	
Probability	Cash Inflows	Probability	Cash Inflows
0.10	$300,000	0.10	$200,000
0.20	350,000	0.25	300,000
0.40	400,000	0.30	400,000
0.20	450,000	0.25	500,000
0.10	500,000	0.10	800,000
1.00		1.00	

Exhibit 3-7 compares the probability distributions graphically.

Expected Value An **expected value** is a weighted average of the outcomes with the probability of each outcome serving as the weight. Where the outcomes are

EXHIBIT 3-7
Decisions under Uncertainty: Comparison of Probability Distributions

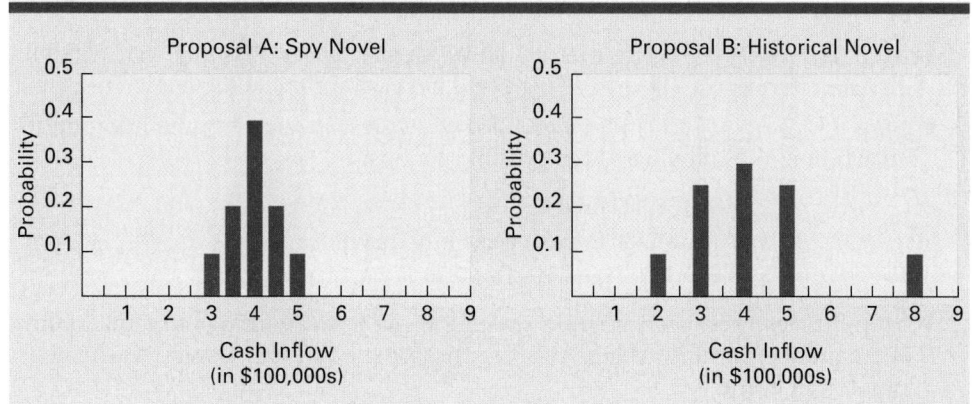

measured in monetary terms, *expected value* is often called **expected monetary value**. The expected monetary value of the cash inflows from the spy novel—denoted $E(a_1)$—is $400,000:

$$E(a_1) = 0.1(\$300{,}000) + 0.2(\$350{,}000) + 0.4(\$400{,}000) + 0.2(\$450{,}000) + 0.1(\$500{,}000)$$

$$= \$400{,}000$$

The expected monetary value of the cash inflows from the historical novel—denoted $E(a_2)$—is $420,000:

$$E(a_2) = 0.1(\$200{,}000) + 0.25(\$300{,}000) + 0.3(\$400{,}000) + 0.25(\$500{,}000) + 0.1(\$800{,}000)$$

$$= \$420{,}000$$

Expected value (expected monetary value). Weighted average of the outcomes of a decision with the probability of each outcome serving as the weight.

Expected monetary value is widely used as a decision criterion. For a book editor wanting to maximize the expected monetary value, the historical novel is preferable to the spy novel.

To interpret expected value, imagine that the company publishes many historical novels, each with a probability distribution of cash inflows given in proposal B. The expected value of $420,000 is the average cash inflow per novel that the publisher will receive when averaged across all novels. For a specific novel, the cash inflows will be either $200,000, $300,000, $400,000, $500,000, or $800,000. But if the company publishes 100 such novels, it will expect to receive $42 million in total cash inflows, for an average of $420,000 per novel.

Many statisticians and accountants favour presenting the entire probability distribution to the decision maker. Others present information in three categories: optimistic, most likely, and pessimistic. Either presentation reminds the user that uncertainty exists in the decision at hand.

Illustrative Problem

Reconsider Madhu and the booth rental alternatives offered by Computer Conventions, Inc., to sell Do-All Software (p. 80):

◆ **Option 1:** $2,000 fixed fee

◆ **Option 2:** $1,400 fixed fee plus 5% of the convention revenues from Do-All sales

◆ **Option 3:** 20% of the convention revenues from Do-All sales (but no fixed fee)

Madhu estimates a 0.60 probability that sales will be 40 units and a 0.40 probability that sales will be 70 units. Each Do-All software package will be sold for $200. Madhu will purchase the package from a computer software wholesaler at $120 per unit with the privilege of returning all unsold units. Which booth rental alternative should Madhu choose?

General Approach to Uncertainty The construction of a decision model consists of five steps that are keyed to the five characteristics described at the beginning of this appendix.[7]

- ◆ **Step 1:** *Identify the choice criterion of the decision maker.* Assume that Madhu's choice criterion is to maximize expected net cash inflow at the convention.

- ◆ **Step 2:** *Identify the set of alternative actions under consideration.* The notation for an action is a. Madhu has three possible actions:

$$a_1 = \text{Pay \$2,000 fixed fee.}$$
$$a_2 = \text{Pay \$1,400 fixed fee plus 5\% of convention revenues.}$$
$$a_3 = \text{Pay 20\% of convention revenues (but no fixed fee).}$$

- ◆ **Step 3:** *Identify the set of relevant events that can occur.* Madhu's only uncertainty is the number of units of Do-All software that she can sell. Using x as the notation for an event:

$$x_1 = 40 \text{ units}$$
$$x_2 = 70 \text{ units}$$

- ◆ **Step 4:** *Assign the set of probabilities for the events that can occur.* Madhu assesses a 60% chance that she will sell 40 units and a 40% chance that she will sell 70 units. Using $P(x)$ as the notation for the probability of an event, the probabilities are:

$$P(x_1) = 0.60$$
$$P(x_2) = 0.40$$

- ◆ **Step 5:** *Identify the set of possible outcomes that are dependent on specific actions and events.* The outcomes in this example take the form of six possible net cash flows that are displayed in a decision table in Exhibit 3-8. A **decision table** is a summary of the contemplated actions, events, outcomes, and probabilities of events.

Decision table. Summary of the contemplated actions, events, outcomes, and probabilities of events in a decision.

Madhu can now use the information in Exhibit 3-8 to compute the expected net cash inflow of each action as follows:

EXHIBIT 3-8
Decision Table for Do-All Software

	A	B	C
1		**Probability of Events**	
2		$x_1 = 40$ **units sold**	$x_2 = 70$ **units sold**
3	**Actions**	$P(x_1) = 0.60$	$P(x_2) = 0.40$
4	a_1: Pay \$2,000 fixed fee	\$1,200[l]	\$3,600[m]
5	a_2: Pay \$1,400 fixed fee plus 5% of convention revenues	\$1,400[n]	\$3,500[p]
6	a_3: Pay 20% of convention revenues (but no fixed fee)	\$1,600[q]	\$2,800[r]
7			
8	[l]Net cash flows = (\$200 − \$120)(40) − \$2,000	= \$1,200	
9	[m]Net cash flows = (\$200 − \$120)(70) − \$2,000	= \$3,600	
10	[n]Net cash flows = (\$200 − \$120 − \$10*)(40) − \$1,400	= \$1,400	
11	[p]Net cash flows = (\$200 − \$120 − \$10*)(70) − \$1,400	= \$3,500	
12	[q]Net cash flows = (\$200 − \$120 − \$40**)(40)	= \$1,600	
13	* \$10 = 5% of selling price of \$200		
14	**\$40 = 20% of selling price of \$200		

[7]For more formal approaches, refer to Eppen, G., F. Gould, and C. Schmidt, *Introductory Management Science*, 4th Edition (Upper Saddle River, NJ: Prentice Hall, [1993]).

Pay \$2,000 fixed fee: $\quad\quad\quad\quad\quad\quad$ $E(a_1) = 0.60(\$1,200) + 0.40(\$3,600) = \$2,160$

Pay \$1,400 fixed fee plus 5% of revenues: $E(a_2) = 0.60(\$1,400) + 0.40(\$3,500) = \$2,240$

Pay 20% of revenues (but no fixed fee): $\quad E(a_3) = 0.60(\$1,600) + 0.40(\$2,800) = \$2,080$

To maximize expected net cash inflows, Madhu should select action a_2—that is, contracting to pay Computer Conventions a \$1,400 fixed fee plus 5% of convention revenues.

Consider the effect of uncertainty on the preferred action choice. If Madhu were certain that she would sell only 40 units of Do-All Software (i.e., $P(x_1) = 1$), she would prefer alternative a_3—pay 20% of revenues and no fixed fee. To follow this reasoning, examine Exhibit 3-8. When 40 units are sold, alternative a_3 yields the maximum net cash inflows of \$1,600. Because fixed costs are zero, booth rental costs are low when sales are low.

However, if Madhu were certain that she would sell 70 units of Do-All Software (i.e., $P(x_2) = 1$), she would prefer alternative a_1—pay a \$2,000 fixed fee. Exhibit 3-8 indicates that when 70 units are sold, alternative a_1 yields the maximum net cash inflows of \$3,600. Rental payments under a_2 and a_3 increase with units sold but are fixed under a_1.

Good Decisions and Good Outcomes Always distinguish between a good decision and a good outcome. One can exist without the other. By definition, uncertainty rules out guaranteeing, after the fact, that the best outcome will always be obtained. It is possible that bad luck will produce unfavourable consequences even when good decisions have been made.

Suppose you are offered a one-time-only gamble tossing a fair coin. You will win \$20 if the event is heads, but you will lose \$1 if the event is tails. As a decision maker, you proceed through the logical phases: gathering information, assessing outcomes, and making a choice. You accept the bet. Why? Because the expected value is \$9.50 $[0.5(\$20) + 0.5(-\$1)]$. The coin is tossed and the event is tails. You lose. From your viewpoint, this was a good decision but a bad outcome.

A decision can be made only on the basis of information available at the time of the decision. Hindsight is flawless, but a bad outcome does not necessarily mean that a bad decision was made. Making a good decision is our best protection against a bad outcome.

▼ TERMS TO LEARN

This chapter contains definitions of the following important terms:

breakeven point (p. 73)	margin of safety (p. 78)
choice criterion (p. 89)	net income (p. 71)
contribution income statement (p. 72)	operating income (p. 71)
contribution margin (p. 71)	operating leverage (p. 80)
contribution margin percentage (p. 72)	outcomes (p. 89)
contribution margin ratio (p. 72)	probability (p. 89)
cost-volume-profit (CVP) (p. 69, 70)	probability distribution (p. 90)
decision model (p. 89)	PV graph (p. 76)
decision table (p. 92)	revenue driver (p. 70)
degree of operating leverage (p. 80)	revenue mix (p. 83)
events (p. 89)	sales mix (p. 83)
expected monetary value (p. 91)	sensitivity analysis (p. 78)
expected value (p. 91)	uncertainty (p. 79)
gross margin (p. 85)	variable-cost percentage (p. 86)
gross margin percentage (p. 86)	

QUESTIONS

Note: To underscore the basic CVP relationships, the assignment material ignores income taxes unless stated otherwise.

3-1 Define *cost-volume-profit analysis.*

3-2 Describe the assumptions underlying CVP analysis.

3-3 Distinguish between operating income and net income.

3-4 Define *contribution margin, gross margin, contribution margin percentage, variable-cost percentage,* and *margin of safety.*

3-5 Describe three methods that can be used to calculate the breakeven point.

3-6 Why is it more accurate to describe the subject matter of this chapter as CVP analysis rather than as breakeven analysis?

3-7 "CVP is both simple and simplistic. If you want realistic analysis to underpin your decisions, look beyond CVP." Do you agree? Explain.

3-8 How does an increase in the income tax rate affect the breakeven point?

3-9 Describe sensitivity analysis. How has spreadsheet software affected its use?

3-10 Give an example of how a manager can decrease variable costs while increasing fixed costs.

3-11 Give an example of how a manager can increase variable costs while decreasing fixed costs.

3-12 What is operating leverage? How is knowing the degree of operating leverage helpful to managers?

3-13 "There is no such thing as a fixed cost. All costs can be 'unfixed' given sufficient time." Do you agree? What is the implication of your answer for CVP analysis?

3-14 How can a company with multiple products compute its breakeven point?

3-15 "Gross margin is a less useful concept than contribution margin in CVP analysis." Do you agree? Explain.

EXERCISES

3-16 CVP analysis computations. In the following data, fill in the blanks for each of the four independent cases.

Case	Revenues	Variable Costs	Fixed Costs	Total Costs	Operating Income	Contribution Margin Percentage	Contribution Margin
a	$ —	$600	$—	$ 960	$1,440	—	1,800
b	2,400	—	360	—	240	—	600
c	1,200	840	—	1,200	—	—	360
d	1,800	—	360	1,440	—	40%	—

3-17 CVP analysis computations. Fill in the blanks for each of the following independent cases.

Case	Selling Price	Variable Costs per Unit	Total Units Sold	Total Contribution Margin	Total Fixed Costs	Operating Income
a	$36	$24	70,000	$ —	$ —	($18,000)
b	30	—	180,000	1,080,000	960,000	—
c	—	12	150,000	360,000	264,000	—
d	24	16.80	—	144,000	—	14,000

3-18 CVP analysis, changing revenues and costs. Sunshine Tours is a travel agency specializing in cruises between Toronto and Jamaica. It books passengers on Carib Cruises. Carib Cruises charges passengers $1,200 per round-trip ticket. Sunshine receives a commission of 8% of the ticket price paid by the passenger. Sunshine's fixed costs are $26,400 per month. Its variable costs are $42 per ticket, including a $21.60 delivery fee by Emory Express. (Assume each ticket purchased is delivered in a separate package; thus the delivery fee applies to every individual ticket.)

REQUIRED

1. What is the number of tickets Sunshine must sell each month to (a) break even and (b) make a target operating income of $12,000?
2. Assume Emory Express offers to charge Sunshine only $14.40 per ticket delivered. How would accepting this offer affect your answers to (a) and (b) in requirement 1?

3-19 CVP analysis, changing revenues and costs (continuation of 3-18). Carib Cruises changes its commission structure for travel agents. Up to a ticket price of $720, the 8% commission applies. For tickets costing $720 or more, there is a fixed commission of $57.60. Assume Sunshine Tours has fixed costs of $26,400 per month and variable costs of $34.80 per ticket (including a $14.40 delivery fee by Emory).

REQUIRED

1. What is the number of Toronto-to-Jamaica round-trip tickets Sunshine must sell each month to (a) break even and (b) make a target operating income of $12,000? Comment on the results.
2. Sunshine tours decides to charge its customers a delivery fee of $6 per ticket. How would this change affect your answers to (a) and (b) in requirement 1? Comment on the results.

3-20 CVP exercises. The Super Doughnut owns and operates six doughnut outlets in and around Quebec City. You are given the following corporate budget data for next year:

Revenues	$12,000,000
Fixed costs	2,040,000
Variable costs	9,840,000

Variable costs change with respect to the number of doughnuts sold.

REQUIRED

Compute the budgeted operating income for each of the following deviations from the original budget data. (Consider each case independently.)

1. A 10% increase in contribution margin, holding revenues constant
2. A 10% decrease in contribution margin, holding revenues constant
3. A 5% increase in fixed costs
4. A 5% decrease in fixed costs
5. An 8% increase in units sold
6. An 8% decrease in units sold
7. A 10% increase in fixed costs and 10% increase in units sold
8. A 5% increase in fixed costs and 5% decrease in variable costs

3-21 CVP exercises. The Doral Company manufactures and sells pens. Present sales output is 5,000,000 units per year at a selling price of $0.60 per unit. Fixed costs are $1,080,000 per year. Variable costs are $0.36 per unit.

REQUIRED

(Consider each case separately.)

1. a. What is the present operating income for a year?
   b. What is the present breakeven point in revenues?

Compute the new operating income for each of the following changes:

2. A $0.048 per unit increase in variable costs
3. A 10% increase in fixed costs and a 10% increase in units sold
4. A 20% decrease in fixed costs, a 20% decrease in selling price, a 10% decrease in variable costs per unit, and a 40% increase in units sold

Compute the new breakeven point in units for each of the following changes:

5. A 10% increase in fixed costs
6. A 10% increase in selling price and a $24,000 increase in fixed costs

3-22 CVP, income taxes. The Bratz Company has fixed costs of $360,000 and a variable-cost percentage of 80%. The company earns net income of $100,800 in 2007. The income tax rate is 40%.

REQUIRED

Compute (1) operating income, (2) contribution margin, (3) total revenues, and (4) breakeven revenues.

3-23 CVP, income taxes. The Rapid Meal has two restaurants that are open 24 hours a day. Fixed costs for the two restaurants together total $540,000 per year. Service varies from a cup of coffee to full meals. The average sales cheque for each customer is $9.60.

The average cost of food and other variable costs for each customer is $3.84. The income tax rate is 30%. Target net income is $126,000.

REQUIRED
1. Compute the revenues needed to obtain the target net income.
2. How many sales cheques are needed to earn net income of $126,000? To break even?
3. Compute net income if the number of sales cheques is 150,000.

3-24 CVP, margin of safety. Suppose Lattin Corp's breakeven point is revenues of $1,200,000. Fixed costs are $480,000.

REQUIRED
1. Compute the contribution margin percentage.
2. Compute the selling price if variable costs are $14.40 per unit.
3. Suppose 80,000 units are sold. Compute the margin of safety.

3-25 CVP computations. Patel Manufacturing sold 180,000 units of its product for $30 per unit in 2007. Variable cost per unit is $24 and total fixed costs are $960,000.

REQUIRED
1. Calculate (a) contribution margin and (b) operating income.
2. Patel's current manufacturing process is labour intensive. Kate Schoenen, Patel's production manager, has proposed investing in state-of-the-art manufacturing equipment, which will increase the annual fixed costs to $3,000,000. The variable costs are expected to decrease to $12 per unit. Patel expects to maintain the same sales volume and selling price next year. How would acceptance of Ms. Schoenen's proposal affect your answers to (a) and (b) in requirement 1?
3. Should Patel accept Schoenen's proposal? Explain.

3-26 Gross margin and contribution margin, making decisions. Schmidt Men's Clothing's revenues and cost data for 2007 appears below.

Revenues		$600,000
Cost of goods sold (40% of sales)		240,000
Gross margin		360,000
Operating costs:		
Salaries and wages	$180,000	
Sales commissions (10% of sales)	60,000	
Amortization of equipment and fixtures	14,400	
Store rent ($4,800 per month)	57,600	
Other operating costs	60,000	372,000
Operating income (loss)		$ (12,000)

Mr. Schmidt, the owner of the store, is unhappy with the operating results. An analysis of other operating costs reveals that it includes $48,000 variable costs, which vary with sales volume, and $12,000 fixed costs.

REQUIRED:
1. Compute the contribution margin of Schmidt Men's Clothing.
2. Compute the contribution margin percentage.
3. Mr. Schmidt estimates he can increase revenues by 20% by incurring additional advertising costs of $12,000. Calculate the impact on operating income of this action.

3-27 Operating leverage. Colour Rugs is holding a 2-week carpet sale at Jerry's Club, a local warehouse store. Colour Rugs plans to sell carpets for $600 each. Colour Rugs will purchase the carpets from a local distributor for $420 each with the privilege of returning any unsold units for a full refund. Jerry's Club has offered Colour Rugs two payment alternatives for the use of space.

◆ Option 1: A fixed payment of $6,000.
◆ Option 2: 10% of the total revenues earned during the sale period. Assume Colour Rugs will incur no other costs.

REQUIRED
1. Calculate the breakeven point in units for (a) option 1 and (b) option 2.
2. At what level of sales revenue will Colour Rugs earn the same operating income under either option?

3.
  a. For what range of unit sales will Colour Rugs prefer option 1?
  b. For what range of unit sales will Colour Rugs prefer option 2?
4. Calculate the degree of operating leverage at sales of 100 units for the two alternative rental options.
5. Briefly explain and interpret your answer in requirement 4.

3-28 CVP, sensitivity analysis. Hoot Washington is the newly elected charismatic leader of the Western Party. He is the darling of the right-wing media. His "take no prisoners" attitude has left many an opponent on a talk show feeling run over by a Mack truck.

Media Publishers is negotiating to publish *Hoot's Manifesto*, a new book that promises to be an instant bestseller. The fixed costs of producing and marketing the book will be $600,000. The variable costs of producing and marketing will be $4.80 per book. These costs are before any payments to Hoot. Hoot negotiates an up-front payment of $3.60 million plus a 15% royalty rate on the net sales price of each book. The net sales price is the listed book store price of $36 minus the margin paid to the book store to sell the book. The normal book store margin of 30% of the listed book store price is expected to apply.

REQUIRED
1. Present a PV graph for Media Publishers.
2. How many copies must Media Publishers sell to (a) break even and (b) earn a target operating profit of $2.4 million?
3. Examine the sensitivity of the breakeven point to the following changes:
  a. Decreasing the normal bookstore margin to 20% of the listed book store price of $36
  b. Increasing the listed book store price to $48 while keeping the book store margin at 30%
  Comment on the results.

3-29 CVP, international cost structure differences. Knitwear, Inc., is considering three countries for the sole manufacturing site of its new sweater: Singapore, Thailand, and Canada. All sweaters are to be sold to retail outlets in Canada at $38.40 per unit. These retail outlets add their own markup when selling to final customers. The three countries differ in their fixed costs and variable costs per sweater.

	Annual Fixed Costs	Variable Manufacturing Costs per Sweater	Variable Marketing and Distribution Costs per Sweater
Singapore	$ 7.8 million	$ 9.60	$13.20
Thailand	5.4 million	6.60	13.80
Canada	14.4 million	15.60	10.80

REQUIRED
1. Compute the breakeven point of Knitwear, Inc., in both (a) units sold and (b) revenues for each of the three countries considered for manufacturing the sweaters.
2. If Knitwear, Inc., sells 800,000 sweaters in 2008, what is the budgeted operating income for each of the three countries considered for manufacturing the sweaters? Comment on the results.

3-30 Revenue mix, new and upgrade customers. Zapo 1-2-3 is a top-selling spreadsheet product. Zapo is about to release Version 5.0. It groups its customers into two groups: new customers and upgrade customers (those who previously purchased Zapo 1-2-3 Version 4.0 or earlier). Although the same physical product is provided to each customer group, sizable differences exist in their selling prices and variable marketing costs:

	New Customers		Upgrade Customers	
Selling price		$252		$144
Variable cost:				
Manufacturing	$30		$30	
Marketing	78	108	18	48

The fixed costs of Zapo 5.0 are $16,800,000.

The planned revenue mix in units is 60% new customers and 40% upgrade customers.

1. What is the Zapo 1-2-3 Version 5.0 breakeven point in units, assuming that the planned 60/40 mix is maintained?
2. If the mix is maintained, what is the operating income when 200,000 units are sold?
3. Show how the breakeven point in units changes with the following customer mixes:
   a. New 50%/upgrade 50%
   b. New 90%/upgrade 10%
   Comment on the results.

3-31 Athletic scholarships, CVP analysis. West University has an annual budget of $6,000,000 for athletic scholarships. Students who receive athletic scholarships do not have to pay tuition, which equals $24,000 per year. Fixed costs of the athletic scholarship program are $1,200,000.

REQUIRED

1. How many athletic scholarships can West University offer each year?
2. Suppose the total budget for the following year is reduced by 20%. Fixed costs are to remain the same. Calculate the number of athletic scholarships that West can offer in the following year.
3. As in requirement 2, assume a budget reduction of 20%. Fixed costs are to remain the same. If West wanted to offer the same number of athletic scholarships as it did in requirement 1, how much reduction in tuition would it be able to offer to each student who receives a scholarship?

3-32 Gross margin and contribution margin. (R. Lambert, adapted) Operating income for Foreman Fork Inc. for the year 2007 on production and sales of 200,000 units was as follows:

Sales	$3,120,000
Cost of goods sold	1,920,000
Gross margin	1,200,000
Marketing and distribution costs	1,380,000
Operating income (loss)	$ (180,000)

Foreman's fixed manufacturing costs were $600,000, and variable marketing and distribution costs were $6 per unit.

REQUIRED

1. Calculate Foreman's variable manufacturing costs per unit in 2007.
2. Calculate Foreman's fixed marketing and distribution costs in 2007.
3. Because Foreman's gross margin per unit is $6 ($1,200,000 ÷ 200,000 units), Sam Hogan, Foreman's president, believes that if Foreman had produced and sold 230,000 units, it would have covered the $1,380,000 of marketing and distribution costs ($1,380,000 ÷ $6 = $230,000) and enabled Foreman to break even for the year. Calculate Foreman's operating income if production and sales equal 230,000 units. Explain briefly why Sam Hogan is wrong.
4. Calculate the breakeven point for the year 2007 in units and dollars.

3-33 CVP analysis, multiple cost drivers. Susan Wong is a distributor of brass picture frames. During 2008, she plans to purchase frames for $36 each and sell them for $54 each. Susan's fixed costs for 2008 are expected to be $288,000. Susan's only other costs will be variable costs of $72 per shipment for preparing the invoice and delivery documents, organizing the delivery, and collecting cash. The $72 cost will be incurred each time Susan ships an order of picture frames, regardless of the number of picture frames in the order.

REQUIRED

1. Suppose Susan sells 40,000 picture frames in 1,000 shipments in 2008. Calculate Susan's 2008 operating income.
2. Suppose Susan sells 40,000 picture frames in 800 shipments in 2008. Calculate Susan's 2008 operating income.
3. Suppose Susan anticipates making 500 shipments in 2008. How many picture frames must Susan sell to break even in 2008?
4. Calculate another breakeven point for 2008, different from the one described in requirement 3. Explain briefly why Susan has multiple breakeven points.

3-34 Appendix, uncertainty, CVP. Angela King is the Las Vegas promoter for Mike Foreman. King is promoting a new world championship fight for Foreman. The key area of uncertainty is the size of the cable pay-per-view TV market. King will pay Foreman a fixed fee of $2.4 million and 25% of net cable pay-per-view revenue. Every cable TV home receiving the event pays $35.94, of which King receives $19.20. King pays Foreman $4.80, 25% of the $19.20.

King estimates the following probability distribution for homes purchasing the pay-per-view event:

Demand	Probability
100,000	0.05
200,000	0.10
300,000	0.30
400,000	0.35
500,000	0.15
1,000,000	0.05

REQUIRED

1. What is the expected value of the payment King will make to Foreman?
2. Assume the only uncertainty is over cable TV demand for the fight. King wants to know the breakeven point given her own fixed costs of $1.2 million and her own variable costs of $2.40 per home. (Also include King's payments to Foreman in your answer.)

PROBLEMS

3-35 **CVP, executive teaching compensation**. Brian Smith is an internationally known Canadian professor specializing in consumer marketing. In 2007, Smith and the United Kingdom Business School (UKBS) agreed to conduct a one-day seminar at UKBS for marketing executives. Each executive would pay £312 to attend. The non–speaker-related fixed costs for UKBS conducting the seminar would be

Advertising in magazines	£4,800
Mailing of brochures	3,600
Administrative labour at UKBS	2,400
Charge for UKBS lecture auditorium	1,200

The variable costs to UKBS for each participant attending the seminar would be

Meals and drinks	£30
Binders and photocopying	42

The dean at UKBS initially offered Smith its regular compensation package of (a) business-class airfare and accommodation (£3,600 maximum) and (b) a £2,400 lecture fee. Smith views the £2,400 lecture fee as providing him no upside potential (that is, no sharing in the potential additional operating income that arises if the seminar is highly attended). He suggests instead that he receive 50% of the operating income to UKBS (if positive) from the one-day seminar and no other payments. The dean of UKBS quickly agrees to Smith's proposal after confirming that Smith is willing to pay his own airfare and accommodation and deliver the seminar irrespective of the number of executives signed up to attend.

REQUIRED

1. What is UKBS's breakeven point (in number of executives attending) if
   a. Smith accepts the regular compensation package of £3,600 expenses and a £2,400 lecture fee.
   b. Smith receives 50% of the operating income to UKBS (if positive) from the one-day seminar and no other payments.
   Comment on the results for (a) and (b).
2. Smith gave the one-day seminar at UKBS in 2005 (60 attended), 2006 (90 attended), and 2007 (180 attended). How much was Smith paid by UKBS for the one-day seminar under the 50% of UKBS's operating income compensation plan in (a) 2005, (b) 2006, and (c) 2007? (Assume that the £312 charge per executive attending and UKBS's fixed and variable costs are the same each year.)
3. After the 2007 seminar, the dean at UKBS suggested to Smith that the 50%–50% profit-sharing plan was resulting in Smith getting excessive compensation in 2007 and that a more equitable arrangement to UKBS be used in 2008. How should Smith respond to this suggestion?

3-36 CVP analysis, service firm. Wildlife Escapes generates average revenue of $4,800 per person on its five-day package tours to wildlife parks in Kenya. The variable costs per person are

Airfare	$1,800
Hotel accommodations	1,200
Meals	360
Ground transportation	720
Park tickets and other costs	240
Total	$4,320

Annual fixed costs total $576,000.

1. Calculate the number of package tours that must be sold to break even.
2. Calculate the revenue needed to earn a target operating income of $120,000.
3. If fixed costs increase by $28,800, what decrease in variable costs must be achieved to maintain the breakeven point calculated in requirement 1?

3-37 CVP, target income, service firm. Teddy Bear Daycare provides daycare for children Mondays through Fridays. Its monthly variable costs per child are

Lunch and snacks	$120
Educational supplies	90
Other supplies (paper products, toiletries, etc.)	30
Total	$240

Monthly fixed costs consist of

Rent	$2,400
Utilities	360
Insurance	360
Salaries	3,000
Miscellaneous	600
	$6,720

Teddy Bear charges each parent $720 per child

1. Calculate the breakeven point.
2. Teddy Bear's target operating income is $12,480 per month. Compute the number of children that must be enrolled to achieve the target operating income.
3. Teddy Bear lost its lease and had to move to another building. Monthly rent for the new building is $3,600. At the suggestion of parents, Teddy Bear plans to take children on field trips. Monthly costs of the field trips are $1,200. By how much should Teddy Bear increase fees per child to meet the target operating income of $12,480 per month, assuming the same number of children as in requirement 2?

3-38 CVP analysis. (CMA, adapted) Galaxy Disk's projected operating income for 2008 is $240,000, based on a sales volume of 200,000 units. Galaxy sells disks for $19.20 each. Variable costs consist of the $12 purchase price and a $2.40 shipping and handling cost. Galaxy's annual fixed costs are $720,000.

REQUIRED
1. Calculate Galaxy's breakeven point in units.
2. Calculate the company's operating income in 2008 if there is a 10% increase in projected unit sales.
3. For 2009, management expects that the unit purchase price of the disks will increase by 30%. Calculate the sales revenue Galaxy must generate in 2009 to maintain the current year's operating income if the selling price remains unchanged.

3-39 CVP, shoe stores. The Walk Rite Shoe Company operates a chain of shoe stores. The stores sell ten different styles of inexpensive men's shoes with identical unit costs and selling prices. A unit is defined as a pair of shoes. Each store has a store manager who is paid a fixed salary. Individual salespeople receive a fixed salary and a sales commission. Walk Rite is trying to determine the desirability of opening another store, which is expected to have the following revenue and cost relationships:

Selling price	$36.00
Unit variable cost per pair:	
Cost of shoes	$23.40
Sales commissions	1.80
Total variable costs	$25.20
Annual fixed costs:	
Rent	$ 72,000
Salaries	240,000
Advertising	96,000
Other fixed costs	24,000
Total fixed costs	$432,000

REQUIRED

(Consider each question independently.)

1. What is the annual breakeven point in (a) units sold and (b) revenues?
2. If 35,000 units are sold, what will be the store's operating income (loss)?
3. If sales commissions were discontinued for individual salespeople in favour of a $97,200 increase in fixed salaries, what would be the annual breakeven point in (a) units sold and (b) revenues?
4. Refer to the original data. If the store manager were paid $0.36 per unit sold in addition to his current fixed salary, what would be the annual breakeven point in (a) units sold and (b) revenues?
5. Refer to the original data. If the store manager were paid $0.36 per unit commission on each unit sold in excess of the breakeven point, what would be the store's operating income if 50,000 units were sold? (This $0.36 is in addition to both the commission paid to the sales staff and the store manager's fixed salary.)

Excel Application For students who wish to practise their spreadsheet skills, the following is a step-by-step approach to creating an Excel spreadsheet to work this problem.

Step-by-Step

1. At the top of a new spreadsheet, create an "Original Data" section for the data provided by Walk Rite. Create rows for the unit variable data and annual fixed cost data in the same format as shown for Walk Rite above.

(Program your spreadsheet to perform all necessary calculations. Do not "hard-code" any amounts, such as breakeven quantities or revenues, requiring addition, subtraction, multiplication, or division operations.)

2. Skip down rows. Create a new section labelled "Problem 1." Create rows for "Contribution margin per unit," "a. Breakeven units," and "b. Breakeven revenues." Use the data in the "Original Data" section and enter calculations for contribution margin, breakeven units, and breakeven revenues in rows (a) and (b).
3. Skip two rows and create a new section labelled "Problem 2." Create rows for revenues, cost of shoes, sales commissions, total variable costs, contribution margin, total fixed costs, and operating income. The format should be similar to the contribution income statement in the "Merchandising Sector" section on page 86. Enter calculations for cost of shoes and sales commissions, total revenues, total variable costs, contribution margin, total fixed costs, and operating income.
4. Skip two rows. Create a new section labelled "Problem 3" using the same format created for "Problem 1." Enter calculations for contribution margin, breakeven units, and breakeven revenues that reflect the discontinuance of sales commissions and increase in fixed salaries.
5. Skip two rows. Create a new section labelled "Problem 4" using the same format as steps 2 and 4. Enter calculations for contribution margin, breakeven units, and breakeven revenues that reflect the new fixed-salary plus commission structure.
6. Skip two rows. Create a new section labelled "Problem 5." Create a contribution income statement using the same format as created for "Problem 2." Enter the same calculations as in step 3, reflecting the new salary plus commission structure and the 50,000 units sold.
7. *Verify the accuracy of your spreadsheet.* Go to your "Original Data" section and change the cost of shoes from $23.40 to $24.00. If your spreadsheet is programmed correctly, breakeven revenues in Problem 1 should change to $1,524,708 and operating income in Problem 5 should change to $74,400.

3-40 CVP, shoe stores (continuation of 3-39). Refer to requirement 3 of 3-39.

REQUIRED

1. Calculate the number of units sold where the operating income under (a) a fixed salary plan and (b) a lower fixed salary and commission plan (for salespeople only) would be equal. Above that number of units sold, one plan would be more profitable than the other; below that number of units sold, the reverse would occur.
2. Compute the operating income or loss under each plan in requirement 1 at sales levels of (a) 50,000 units and (b) 60,000 units.
3. Suppose the target operating income is $201,600. How many units must be sold to reach the target under (a) the fixed salary plan and (b) the lower fixed salary and commission plan?

3-41 Sensitivity and inflation (continuation of 3-39). As president of Walk Rite, you are concerned that inflation may squeeze your profitability. Specifically, you feel committed to the $36 selling price and fear that diluting the quality of the shoes in the face of rising costs would be an unwise marketing move. You expect the cost of shoes to rise by 10% during the coming year. You are tempted to avoid the cost increase by placing a noncancellable order with a large supplier that would provide 50,000 units of the specified quality for each store at $23.40 per unit. (To simplify this analysis, assume that all stores will face identical demands.) These shoes could be acquired and paid for as delivered throughout the year. However, all shoes must be delivered to the stores by the end of the year.

As a shrewd merchandiser, you foresee some risks. If sales are less than 50,000 units, you feel that markdowns of the unsold merchandise will be necessary to sell the goods. You predict that the average selling price of the leftover units will be $21.60. The regular commission of 5% of revenues would be paid to salespeople.

REQUIRED

1. Suppose that actual sales at $36 for the year are 48,000 units and that you contracted for 50,000 units. What is the operating income for the store?
2. If you had perfect forecasting ability, you would have contracted for 48,000 units rather than 50,000 units. What would the operating income have been if you had ordered 48,000 units?
3. Given actual sales of 48,000 units, by how much would the average cost per unit have had to rise before you would have been indifferent between having the contract for 50,000 units and not having the contract?

3-42 CVP analysis, income taxes, sensitivity. (CMA, adapted) Almo Company manufactures and sells adjustable canopies that attach to motor homes and trailers. For its year 2008 business plan, Almo estimated the following:

Selling price	$480
Variable cost per canopy	$240
Annual fixed costs	$120,000
Net (after-tax) income	$288,000
Tax rate	40%

The May financial statements reported that sales were not meeting expectations. For the first five months of the year, only 350 units had been sold at the established price, with variable costs as planned, and it was clear that the 2008 after-tax profit projection would not be reached unless some action were taken. A management committee presented the following mutually exclusive alternatives to the president.

1. Reduce the selling price by $48. The sales organization forecasts that, with the significantly reduced selling price, 2,700 units can be sold during the remainder of the year. Total fixed and variable unit costs will stay as budgeted.
2. Lower variable costs per unit by $12 through the use of less expensive direct materials and slightly modified manufacturing techniques. The selling price will also be reduced by $36, and sales of 2,200 units for the remainder of the year are forecast.
3. Cut fixed costs by $12,000 and lower the selling price by 5%. Variable costs per unit will be unchanged. Sales of 2,000 units are expected for the remainder of the year.

REQUIRED

1. If no changes are made to the selling price or cost structure, determine the number of units that Almo Company must sell (a) to break even and (b) to achieve its net income objective.
2. Determine which alternative Almo should select to achieve its net income objective. Show all calculations.

3-43 CVP, movie production. Royal Rumble Productions has just finished production of *Feature Creatures*, the latest action film directed by Tony Savage and starring Ralph Michaels and Sally Martel. The total production cost to Royal Rumble was $6 million. All the production personnel and actors on *Feature Creatures* received a fixed salary (included in the $6 million) and will have no "residual" (equity interest) in the revenues or operating income from the movie. Media Productions will handle the marketing of *Feature Creatures*. Media agrees to invest a minimum $3.6 million of its own money in marketing the movie and will be paid 20% of the revenues Royal Rumble itself receives from the box office receipts. Royal Rumble receives 62.5% of the total box office receipts (out of which comes the 20% payment to Media Productions).

REQUIRED

1. What is the breakeven point to Royal Rumble for *Feature Creatures* expressed in terms of (a) revenues received by Royal Rumble and (b) total box office receipts?
2. Assume that, in its first year of release, the box office receipts for *Feature Creatures* total $360 million. What is the operating income to Royal Rumble from the movie in its first year?

3-44 CVP, cost structure differences, movie production (continuation of 3-43). Royal Rumble is negotiating for *Feature Creatures 2*, a sequel to its mega-blockbuster *Feature Creatures*. This negotiation is proving more difficult than for the original movie. The budgeted production cost (excluding payments to the director Savage and the stars Michaels and Martel) for *Feature Creatures 2* is $25.2 million. The agent negotiating for Savage, Michaels, and Martel proposes either of two contracts:

◆ **Contract A.** Fixed salary component of $18 million for Savage, Michaels, and Martel (combined) with no residual interest in the revenues from *Feature Creatures 2*.

◆ **Contract B.** Fixed salary component of $3.6 million for Savage, Michaels, and Martel (combined) plus a residual of 15% of the revenues Royal Rumble receives from *Feature Creatures 2*.

Media Productions will market *Feature Creatures 2*. It agrees to invest a minimum of $12 million of its own money. Because of its major role in the success of *Feature Creatures*, Media Productions will now be paid 25% of the revenues Royal Rumble receives from the total box office receipts. Royal Rumble receives 62.5% of the total box office receipts (out of which comes the 25% payment to Media Productions).

REQUIRED

1. What is the breakeven point for Royal Rumble expressed in terms of (a) Revenues received by that company and (b) total box office receipts for *Feature Creatures 2* for contracts A and B? Explain the difference between the breakeven points for contracts A and B.
2. Assume *Feature Creatures 2* achieves the same $360 million in box office revenues as *Feature Creatures*. What is the operating income to Royal Rumble from *Feature Creatures 2* if it accepts contract B? Comment on the difference in operating income between the two films.

3-45 Choosing between compensation plans, operating leverage. (CMA, adapted) Marston Corporation manufactures pharmaceutical products that are sold through a network of sales agents. The agents are paid a commission of 18% of sales. The income statement for the year ending December 31, 2007, is as follows:

Marston Corporation
Income Statement for the Year Ending December 31, 2007

Sales		$31,200,000
Cost of goods sold		
Variable	$14,040,000	
Fixed	3,444,000	17,484,000
Gross margin		13,716,000
Selling and marketing expenses		
Commissions	$ 5,616,000	
Fixed costs	4,104,000	9,720,000
Operating income		$ 3,996,000

Marston is considering hiring its own sales staff to replace the network of agents. Marston will pay its salespeople a commission of 10% and incur fixed costs of $2,496,000.

REQUIRED

1. Calculate Marston Corporation's breakeven point in sales dollars for the year 2007.
2. Calculate Marston Corporation's breakeven point in sales dollars for the year 2007 if the company hires its own sales force in 2007 to replace the network of agents.

3. Calculate the degree of operating leverage at sales of $31,200,000 if (a) Marston uses sales agents and (b) Marston employs its own staff. Describe the advantages and disadvantages of each alternative.

4. If Marston increases the commission paid to its sales staff to 15%, keeping all other costs the same, how much revenue (in dollars) would Marston have to generate to earn the same operating income it did in 2007?

3-46 Revenue mix, two products. The Goldman Company retails two products, a standard and a deluxe version of a luggage carrier. The budgeted income statement is as follows:

	Standard Carrier	Deluxe Carrier	Total
Units sold	150,000	50,000	200,000
Revenues @ $24 and $36 per unit	$3,600,000	$1,800,000	$5,400,000
Variable costs @ $16.80 and $21.60 per unit	2,520,000	1,080,000	3,600,000
Contribution margins @ $7.20 and $14.40 per unit	$1,080,000	$ 720,000	1,800,000
Fixed costs			1,440,000
Operating income			$ 360,000

REQUIRED
1. Compute the breakeven point in units, assuming that the planned revenue mix is maintained.
2. Compute the breakeven point in units (a) if only standard carriers are sold and (b) if only deluxe carriers are sold.
3. Suppose 200,000 units are sold, but only 20,000 are deluxe. Compute the operating income. Compute the breakeven point if these relationships persist in the next period. Compare your answers with the original plans and the answer in requirement 1. What is the major lesson of this problem?

3-47 CVP analysis, decision making. (M. Rajan, adapted) Tocchet Company manufactures CB1, a citizens' band radio that is sold mainly to truck drivers. The company's plant in Camden has an annual capacity of 50,000 units. Tocchet currently sells 40,000 units at a selling price of $126. It has the following cost structure:

Variable manufacturing costs per unit	$ 54
Fixed manufacturing costs	$960,000
Variable marketing and distribution costs per unit	$ 12
Fixed marketing and distribution costs	$720,000

REQUIRED
(Consider each question separately.)
1. Calculate the breakeven volume in units and in dollars.
2. The marketing department indicates that decreasing the selling price to $118.80 would stimulate sales to 50,000 units. This strategy will require Tocchet to increase its fixed costs, although variable costs per unit will remain the same as before. What is the *maximum* increase in fixed costs for which Tocchet will find it worthwhile to reduce the selling price?
3. The manufacturing department proposes changes in the manufacturing process to add new features to the CB1 product. These changes will increase fixed manufacturing costs by $120,000 and variable manufacturing costs per unit by $2.40. At its current sales quantity of 40,000 units, what is the *minimum* selling price above which Tocchet will find it worthwhile to add these new features?

3-48 Revenue mix, three products. The Ronowski Company has three product lines of belts, A, B, and C, with contribution margins of $3.60, $2.40, and $1.20 respectively. The president forecasts sales of 200,000 units in the coming period, consisting of 20,000 units of A, 100,000 units of B, and 80,000 units of C. The company's fixed costs for the period are $306,000.

REQUIRED
1. What is the company breakeven point in units, assuming that the given revenue mix is maintained?
2. If the mix is maintained, what is the total contribution margin when 200,000 units are sold? What is the operating income?

3. What would operating income become if 20,000 units of A, 80,000 units of B, and 100,000 units of C were sold? What is the new breakeven point in units if these relationships persist in the next period?

3-49 Nonprofit institution. The City of Edmonton, Alberta, makes a $480,000 lump sum budget appropriation to an agency to conduct a counselling program for drug addicts for a year. All the appropriation is to be spent. The variable costs for drug prescriptions average $480 per patient per year. Fixed costs are $180,000.

REQUIRED

1. Compute the number of patients that could be served in a year.
2. Suppose the total budget for the following year is reduced by 10%. Fixed costs are to remain the same. The same level of service to each patient will be maintained. Compute the number of patients that could be served in a year.
3. As in requirement 2, assume a budget reduction of 10%. Fixed costs are to remain the same. The drug counsellor has discretion as to how much in drug prescriptions to give to each patient. She does not want to reduce the number of patients served. On the average, what is the cost of drugs that can be given to each patient? Compute the percentage decline in the annual average cost of drugs per patient.

3-50 CVP, nonprofit event planning. The American-Canadian Chamber of Commerce is planning its July 4 gala ball. There are two possible plans:

a. Toronto Country Golf Club, which has a fixed rental cost of $2,400 plus a charge of $96 per person to cater meals and serve the drinks and hors d'oeuvres.
b. Toronto Town Hall, which has a fixed rental cost of $7,920. The Chamber of Commerce can hire a caterer and waitstaff to serve drinks and hors d'oeuvres at $72 per person.

The Chamber of Commerce budgets $4,200 for administration and marketing. The band will cost a fixed amount of $3,000. Tickets to this prestigious event will be $144 per person. All the drinks served and the prizes given away at the ball will be paid for by corporate sponsors.

REQUIRED

1. Compute the breakeven point for each plan in terms of tickets sold.
2. For each plan, compute the operating income of the ball (a) if 150 people attend and (b) if 300 people attend. Comment on your results.
3. At what level of tickets sold will the two plans have the same operating income?

3-51 Multi-product breakeven, decision making. Evenkeel Corporation manufactures and sells one product, an infant car seat called Evenflo at a price of $60 per car seat. Variable costs equal $24 per car seat. Fixed costs are $594,000. Evenkeel manufactures Evenflo only after it gets firm orders from its customers. In 2007, it sold 30,000 units of Evenflo. One of Evenkeel's customers, Plaston Corporation, has asked if in 2008 Evenkeel will manufacture a different style of car seat called Ridex. Plaston will pay $30 for each unit of Ridex. The variable costs for Ridex are estimated to be $18 per seat. Fortunately, Evenkeel has enough capacity to manufacture all the units of Evenflo it can sell and the units of Ridex that Plaston wants and thus will incur no additional fixed costs. Evenkeel estimates it will sell 30,000 units of Evenflo and 20,000 units of Ridex in 2008.

As Andy Minton, the president of Evenkeel, checked the impact of accepting Plaston's offer on the breakeven sales revenues for 2008, he was surprised to find that the dollar sales revenues required to break even using the sales mix for 2008 appeared to increase. He was not sure that his numbers were correct, but if they were, Andy felt inclined to reject Plaston's offer. In any event, he thought it best to seek your advice.

REQUIRED

1. Calculate the breakeven point in units and sales dollars for 2007.
2. Calculate the breakeven point in units and sales dollars for 2008 at the expected sales mix.
3. Explain why the breakeven points in sales dollars calculated in requirements 1 and 2 are different.
4. What would you advise Andy Minton to do? Provide Andy with the support underlying your reasoning.

3-52 CVP, income taxes. (CMA) R. A. Ro and Company, a manufacturer of quality handmade walnut bowls, has experienced a steady growth in sales for the past five years. However, increased competition has led Mr. Ro, the president, to believe that an aggressive marketing campaign will be necessary next year to maintain the company's present growth.

To prepare for next year's marketing campaign, the company's controller has prepared and presented Mr. Ro with the following data for the current year, 2008:

Variable costs (per bowl):	
Direct manufacturing labour	$ 9.60
Direct materials	3.90
Variable overhead (manufacturing, marketing distribution, customer service, and administration)	3.00
Total variable costs	$ 16.50
Fixed costs:	
Manufacturing	$ 30,000
Marketing, distribution, and customer service	48,000
Administrative	84,000
Total fixed costs	$162,000
Selling price per bowl	$ 30.00
Expected revenues, 2008 (20,000 units)	$600,000
Income tax rate	40%

REQUIRED

1. What is the projected net income for 2008?
2. What is the breakeven point in units for 2008?
3. Mr. Ro has set the revenue target for 2009 at a level of $660,000 (or 22,000 bowls). He believes an additional marketing cost of $13,500 for advertising in 2009, with all other costs remaining constant, will be necessary to attain the revenue target. What will be the net income for 2009 if the additional $13,500 is spent and the revenue target is met?
4. What will be the breakeven point in revenues for 2009 if the additional $13,500 is spent for advertising?
5. If the additional $13,500 is spent for advertising in 2009, what is the required 2009 revenue for 2009's net income to equal 2008's net income?
6. At a sales level of 22,000 units, what maximum amount can be spent on advertising if a 2009 net income of $72,000 is desired?

3-53 Review of Chapters 2 and 3. For each of the following independent cases, find the unknowns designated by the capital letters.

	Case 1	Case 2
Direct materials used	$H	$48,000
Direct manufacturing labour	36,000	18,000
Variable marketing, distribution, customer service, and administrative costs	K	T
Fixed manufacturing overhead	I	24,000
Fixed marketing, distribution, customer service, and administrative costs	J	12,000
Gross margin	30,000	24,000
Finished goods inventory, January 1, 2007	0	6,000
Finished goods inventory, December 31, 2007	0	6,000
Contribution margin (dollars)	36,000	V
Revenues	120,000	120,000
Direct materials inventory, January 1, 2007	14,400	24,000
Direct materials inventory, December 31, 2007	6,000	W
Variable manufacturing overhead	6,000	X
Work in process, January 1, 2007	0	10,800
Work in process, December 31, 2007	0	10,800
Purchases of direct materials	18,000	60,000
Breakeven point (in dollars)	80,000	Y
Cost of goods manufactured	G	U
Operating income (loss)	L	(6,000)

3-54 Appendix, CVP under uncertainty. (J. Patell) In your new position as supervisor of product introduction, you have to decide on a pricing strategy for a talking doll specialty product with the following cost structure:

Variable costs per unit	$ 60
Fixed costs	$240,000

The dolls are manufactured upon receipt of orders, so the inventory levels are insignificant. Your market research assistant is very enthusiastic about probability models and has presented the results of his price analysis in the following form:

a. If you set the selling price at $120 per unit, the probability distribution of revenues is uniform between $360,000 and $720,000. Under this distribution, there is a 0.50 probability of equalling or exceeding revenues of $540,000.

b. If you lower the selling price to $84 per unit, the distribution remains uniform, but it shifts up to the $720,000–$1,080,000 range. Under this distribution, there is a 0.50 probability of equalling or exceeding revenues of $900,000.

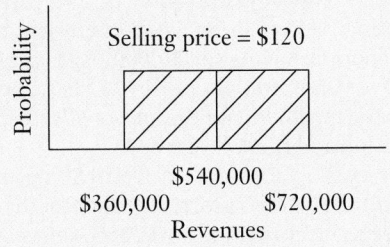

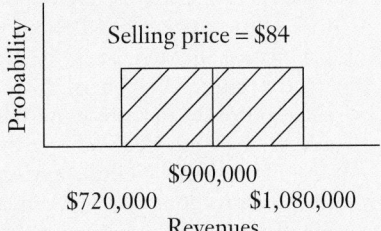

REQUIRED

1. This is your first big contract and, above all, you want to show an operating income. You decide to select the strategy that maximizes the probability of breaking even or earning a positive operating income.
   a. What is the probability of at least breaking even with a selling price of $120 per unit?
   b. What is the probability of at least breaking even with a selling price of $84 per unit?

2. Your assistant suggests that maximum expected operating income might be a better objective to pursue. Which pricing strategy would result in the higher expected operating income? (Use the expected revenues under each pricing strategy when making expected operating income computations.)

3-55 Appendix, CVP under uncertainty. (R. Jaedicke and A. Robichek, adapted) The Jaro Company is considering two new colours for their umbrella products—emerald green and shocking pink. Either can be produced using present facilities. Each product requires an increase in annual fixed costs of $480,000. The products have the same selling price ($12) and the same variable costs per unit ($9.60).

Management, after studying past experience with similar products, has prepared the following probability distribution:

	Probability for	
Event **(Units Demanded)**	**Emerald Green** **Umbrella**	**Shocking Pink** **Umbrella**
50,000	0.0	0.1
100,000	0.1	0.1
200,000	0.2	0.1
300,000	0.4	0.2
400,000	0.2	0.4
500,000	0.1	0.1
	1.0	1.0

REQUIRED

1. What is the breakeven point for each product?
2. Which product should be chosen, assuming that the objective is to maximize expected operating income? Why? Show your computations.

3. Suppose management is absolutely certain that 300,000 units of shocking pink will be sold, but it still faces the same uncertainty about the demand for emerald green as outlined in the problem. Which product should be chosen? Why? What benefits are available to management from having the complete probability distribution instead of just an expected value?

3-56 Ethics, CVP, cost analysis. Ahmed Diba is the controller of the Body Products Division of World Wide Drugs (WWD). It is located in Winnipeg, which is also the headquarters of WWD. Diba is helping develop a proposal for a new product to be called Vital Hair. This product is a cream to be rubbed on the scalp to restore hair growth. Cheryl Kelly, president of the division, and Diba are scheduled to make a presentation to the WWD executive committee on the expected profitability of Vital Hair. The fixed costs associated with the development, production, and marketing of Vital Hair are $24,000,000. Each customer will pay a doctor $96 per monthly treatment, of which $66 is paid to WWD. Diba estimates WWD's variable costs per treatment to be $26.40. Included in this $26.40 is $9.60 for potential product litigation costs. Kelly is livid at Diba for including the $9.60 estimate. She argues that it is imperative to get the R&D funds approved (and quickly) and that any number that increases the breakeven point reduces the likelihood of the Vital Hair project being approved. She notes that WWD has had few successful lawsuits against it, in contrast to some recent "horrendous" experiences of competitors with breast implant products. Moreover, she is furious that Diba put the $9.60 amount in writing. "How do we know there will be any litigation problem?" She suggests Diba redo the report excluding the $9.60 litigation risk cost estimate. "Put it on the chalkboard in the executive committee room, if you insist, but don't put it in the report sent to the committee before the meeting. You can personally raise the issue at the executive committee meeting and have a full and frank discussion."

Diba takes Kelly's "advice." He reports a variable cost of $16.80 per treatment in the proposal. Although he feels uneasy about this, he is comforted by the fact that he will flag the $9.60 amount to the executive committee in his forthcoming oral presentation.

One month later, Kelly walks into Diba's office. She is in a buoyant mood and announces she has just come back from an executive committee meeting that approved the Vital Hair proposal. Diba asks why he was not invited to the meeting. Kelly says the meeting was held in Toronto, and she decided to save the division money by going alone. She then says to Diba that it "was now time to get behind the new venture and help make it the success the committee and her team members believe it will be."

REQUIRED

1. What is the breakeven point (in units of monthly treatments) when WWD's variable costs (a) include the $9.60 estimate and (b) exclude the $9.60 estimate for potential product litigation costs?

2. Should Diba have excluded the $9.60 estimate in his report to the executive committee of WWD? Explain your answer.

3. What should Diba do in response to Kelly's decision to make the Vital Hair presentation on her own?

3-57 Ethics, CVP analysis. Allen Corporation produces a moulded plastic casing LX201, for desktop computers. Summary data from its year 2007 income statement are as follows:

Revenues	$6,000,000
Variable costs	3,600,000
Fixed costs	2,592,000
Operating income	$ (192,000)

Jane Woodall, Allen's president, is very concerned about Allen's poor profitability. She asks Max Lemond, production manager, and Lester Bush, controller, to see if there are ways to reduce costs.

After two weeks, Max returns with a proposal to reduce variable costs to 52% of revenues by reducing the expenses Allen currently incurs for safe disposal of wasted plastic. Lester is concerned that this would expose the company to potential environmental liabilities. He tells Max, "We would need to estimate some of these potential future costs and include them in our analysis." "You can't do that," Max replied. "We are not violating any laws. There is some possibility that we may have to incur costs in the future, but if we bring it up now, this proposal will not go through because our senior management always assumes these costs to be larger than they are. The market is very tough and we are in danger of shutting down the company. We don't want all our colleagues to lose their jobs. The only reason our competitors are making money is because they are doing exactly what I am proposing."

1. Calculate Allen's breakeven revenues for the year 2007.
2. Calculate Allen's breakeven revenues if variable costs are 52% of revenues.
3. Calculate Allen's operating income in 2007 if variable costs had been 52% of sales.
4. Given Max Lemond's comments, what should Lester Bush do?

COLLABORATIVE LEARNING PROBLEMS

3-58 Deciding where to produce. (CMA, adapted) The PTO Division of the Galva Manufacturing Company produces the same power take-off units for the farm equipment business in two plants, a newly renovated, automated plant in Peoria, and an older, less automated plant in Moline. The PTO Division expects to produce and sell 192,000 power take-off units during the coming year. The following data are available for the two plants:

	Peoria	Moline
Selling price	$180.00	$180.00
Variable manufacturing cost per unit	$86.40	$105.60
Fixed manufacturing cost per unit	36.00	18.00
Sales commission (5% of sales)	9.00	9.00
Variable marketing and distribution cost per unit	7.80	7.80
Fixed marketing and distribution cost per unit	22.80	17.40
Total cost per unit	162.00	157.80
Operating income per unit	$ 18.00	$ 22.20
Production rate per day	400 units	320 units

All unit fixed costs are calculated based on a normal year of 240 working days. When the number of working days exceeds 240, variable manufacturing costs increase by $3.60 per unit in Peoria and $9.60 per unit in Moline. Capacity for each plant is 300 working days.

Wanting to maximize the higher unit profit at Moline, PTO's production manager has decided to manufacture 96,000 units at each plant. This production plan results in Moline operating at capacity (320 units per day × 300 days) and Peoria operating at its normal volume (400 units per day × 240 days). Galva's corporate controller is not happy with this plan as he does not believe it represents optimal usage of PTO's plants.

INSTRUCTIONS
Form pairs to complete the following requirements.

REQUIRED
1. Determine the breakeven point for the Peoria and Moline plants in units.
2. Calculate the operating income that would result from the division production manager's plan to produce 96,000 units at each plant.
3. Determine how the production of the 192,000 units should be allocated between Peoria and Moline to maximize operating income for the PTO division. What is the maximum operating income that the PTO division can earn? Show all calculations.

3-59 CVP, theatre planning. *The Globe and Mail* has just published a stinging criticism of the inflation in theatre ticket prices. The article was titled, "The $90 Price Gouge: Is $120 Next?" This article has increased the concerns of a group planning Toronto's future productions. It had been planning for a $90 price for all of its seats. The up-front fixed costs to open are $9.60 million. Production and operating costs are $480,000 per week. The theatre has capacity for 2,000 seats with six performances per week planned. Approximately 100 seats per night are held as complimentary house seats.

INSTRUCTIONS
Form groups of two or more students to complete the following requirements.

REQUIRED
Your group is charged with exploring ways of improving the profitability of the venture and of reducing its breakeven point. Areas you should explore (but are not restricted to) include the following:

a. Increase the number of shows per week. The cast is under contract for up to eight shows a week for a fixed amount that is included in the $480,000.

b. Provide the two star performers with a $30,000 weekly salary and a percentage of revenues or operating income instead of the fixed $60,000 per week each is budgeted to receive.

c. Change the single $90 pricing policy. Whereas all seats in the 2,000-person auditorium have unobstructed views, a recent theatre reviewer referred to the back rows of the balcony section as "binocular land" (e.g., 400 seats at $108; 500 seats at $84; and 1,000 seats at $60—the policy is your choice).

d. The assumptions about sales quantity changes and so on.

CHAPTER 4

Job Costing

On major construction projects, it is essential to understand the costs of each project. Job costing is used to accumulate the costs of each job, in order that the profitability of projects can be assessed and the pricing of future projects improved.

Buckland & Taylor Ltd., Independent Engineers, was responsible for the calculation of the costs of constructing the Confederation Bridge, which connects Prince Edward Island to the mainland. Job costing techniques would have been essential to them in these important calculations.

LEARNING OBJECTIVES

After studying this chapter, you should be able to

1. Describe the building-block concept of costing systems
2. Distinguish between job costing and process costing
3. Outline a seven-step approach to job costing
4. Distinguish between actual costing and normal costing
5. Track the flow of costs in a job-costing system
6. Account for end-of-period under- or overallocated indirect costs using alternative methods
7. Apply variation of normal costing

How much does it cost Ernst & Young to audit Magna International Inc.? How much does it cost Loblaws to sell a six-pack of Pepsi-Cola? How much does it cost the DaimlerChrysler Company to manufacture and sell a Dodge Charger automobile to a dealer? Managers ask these questions for many purposes, including formulating overall strategies, product and service emphasis and pricing, cost control, and meeting external reporting obligations. Chapters 4 and 5 present concepts and techniques that guide the responses to such questions. Chapter 4 presents basic concepts of job costing. Chapter 5 describes applications of activity-based costing.

Before we explore the details of costing systems, four points are worth noting:

1. The cost-benefit approach we discussed in Chapter 1 is essential in designing and choosing costing systems. The costs of elaborate systems, including the costs of educating managers and other personnel, can be quite high. Managers should install a more sophisticated system only if they believe that its benefits will outweigh its costs.

2. Systems should be tailored to the underlying operations, and not vice versa. Any significant change in underlying operations is likely to justify a corresponding change in the accompanying costing systems. The best system design begins with a careful study of how operations are conducted and a resulting determination of which information

to gather and report. The worst systems are those that operating managers perceive as misleading or useless.

3. Costing systems accumulate costs to facilitate decisions. Because the types of specific decisions that might need to be made cannot always be foreseen, costing systems are designed to fulfill several general desires that are common among most managers. In this chapter, we will focus on decisions regarding *product costing*. Therefore, we will pay most attention to the part of the costing system that aims to report cost estimates that indicate the manner in which particular cost objects—such as products or services—use the resources of an organization. Managers use product costing information for cost management, planning and control, and inventory valuation.

4. Costing systems are only one source of information for managers. When making decisions, managers combine information on costs with other noncost information. These include personal observation of operations and nonfinancial performance measures such as setup times, absentee rates, and number of customer complaints.

BUILDING-BLOCK CONCEPT OF COSTING SYSTEMS

We will now review some terms introduced in Chapter 2 that we will use in discussing costing systems:

- ◆ **Cost object.** Anything for which a separate measurement of costs is desired.
- ◆ **Direct costs of a cost object.** Costs that are related to the particular cost object and can be traced to it in an economically feasible (cost-effective) way.
- ◆ **Indirect costs of a cost object.** Costs that are related to the particular cost object but cannot be traced to it in an economically feasible (cost-effective) way. Indirect costs are allocated to the cost object using a cost-allocation method.

The relationships among these three concepts are as shown here:

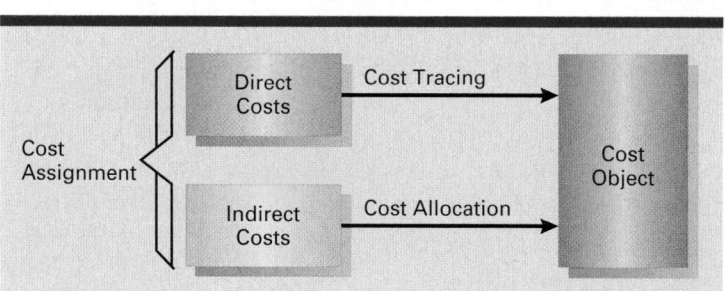

▲ These two cost objects— departments and products — represent two purposes of management accounting: providing information for (1) planning and control and (2) determining the cost of products. To illustrate, when manufacturing custom furniture, the cost of lumber and workers' wages are assigned to (1) the Production Department for control and performance evaluation (for example, did workers cut lumber and assemble furniture efficiently?) and (2) the finished pieces of furniture for inventory valuation. Estimating the cost of a piece of furniture *before* manufacturing occurs is often the basis of a pricing decision.

Cost pool. A grouping of individual costs.

Recall from Chapter 2 that *cost tracing* is the method to assign direct costs to a cost object, whereas *cost allocation* is the method to assign indirect costs to a cost object. Throughout this chapter, assigned costs include both *variable* and *fixed* costs. How costs are estimated and assigned affects not only strategic decisions about changes to the design of products and services, but also shorter-run decisions on how to respond to a competitor's price change. In the long run more costs can be escaped and managed than in the short run; moreover, all businesses survive only if they cover both their variable and fixed costs, irrespective of how these costs are assigned.

Two concepts not previously defined are also important when discussing costing systems:

- ◆ **Cost pool.** A grouping of individual cost items. Cost pools can range from the very broad (such as a companywide total-cost pool for telephones and fax machines) to the very narrow (such as the costs of operating a car used by a travelling salesperson).

- **Cost-allocation base.** A factor that is the common denominator for systematically linking either an indirect cost or an indirect cost pool to a cost object. A cost-allocation base can be financial (such as direct labour costs) or nonfinancial (such as the number of kilometres travelled). When the cost object is a specific client, product, or job, the cost allocation base is called a **cost application base.** Companies often seek to use the cost driver of the indirect costs as the cost-allocation base. For example, the number of kilometres travelled may be used as the base for allocating motor vehicle operating costs among different sales districts.

These terms constitute the building blocks that we will use to design the costing systems described later in this chapter. Management accountants have the expertise to identify cost objects and assign costs to best inform the managers making decisions. This means management accountants work closely with managers to design a relevant and cost-effective information set (see Concepts in Action on p. 120). Be aware that supervision, engineering, and quality control costs, which are considered direct costs when the cost object is the Manufacturing Department, will be considered indirect or overhead costs when the cost object is an individual job or product. The reason is that these costs are difficult to trace in an economically feasible way to individual jobs or products, but they are easily identified with and traced to the department itself.

JOB-COSTING AND PROCESS-COSTING SYSTEMS

Companies frequently adopt one of two basic types of costing systems to assign costs to products or services:

- **Job-costing system.** In this system, costs are assigned to a distinct unit, or set of units of a product or service called a job. A job is a task for which resources are expended in bringing a distinct product or service to market. The product or service is often custom-made, such as an audit by an accounting firm.
- **Process-costing system.** In this system, the output comprises a large quantity of identical unit products or services. The total cost of a product or service is often estimated for a specific time period. It is obtained by using broad averages to assign costs to masses of similar units. Frequently, identical items (such as iPods or roofing nails) are mass-produced for general sale and not for any specific customer.

Exhibit 4-1 presents examples of job and process costing in the service, merchandising, and manufacturing sectors.

These two types of costing systems are best viewed as ends of a continuum:

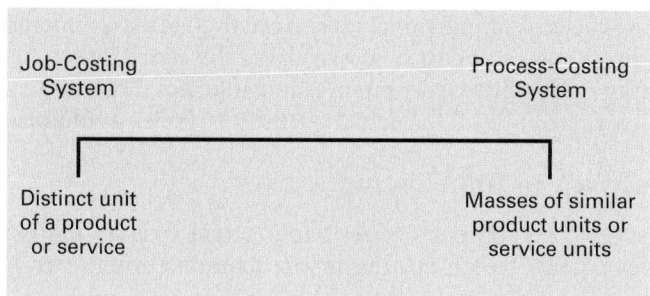

Job-Costing System — Process-Costing System

Distinct unit of a product or service — Masses of similar product units or service units

Most companies have costing systems that are neither pure job costing nor pure process costing. Rather, they combine elements of both job costing and process costing. In this chapter we focus on pure job-costing systems. Chapters 17 and 18 discuss process-costing systems.

EXHIBIT 4-1
Examples of Job Costing and Process Costing in the Service, Merchandising, and Manufacturing Sectors

	Service Sector	Merchandising Sector	Manufacturing Sector
Job Costing Used	◆ Audit engagements done by Price-WaterhouseCoopers ◆ Consulting engagements done by Angus Reid ◆ Advertising-agency campaign run by Ogilvy ◆ Individual legal cases argued by Torys LLP ◆ Computer-repair jobs done by CompUSA ◆ Movies produced by Alliance Atlantis	◆ L. L. Bean sending individual items by mail order ◆ Special promotion of new products by Canadian Tire	◆ Assembly of individual aircrafts at Bombardier ◆ Construction of ships at Litton Industries
Process Costing Used	◆ Bank cheque clearing at INTRIA ◆ Postal delivery (standard items) by Canada Post	◆ Grain handling by JRI ◆ Lumber dealing by BC Lumber Sales	◆ Oil refining by Nova Corp. ◆ Coal transport by Teck Cominco Inc.

JOB COSTING IN MANUFACTURING

We illustrate job costing using the example of Robinson Company, which manufactures and installs specialized machinery for the paper-making industry at its Vancouver, British Columbia, plant. For those of you interested in the process of paper-making, take a look at Howe Sound Pulp and Paper Limited Partnership. In its job-costing system, Robinson accumulates costs incurred on a job in all parts of the value chain: R&D, design, manufacturing, marketing, distribution, and customer service. For simplicity, we focus on Robinson's manufacturing area. To make a machine, Robinson procures some of the components from outside suppliers and makes others itself. Key to each of Robinson's jobs is assembling and installing the machine at customer sites, integrating it with the customer's other machines and processes, and ensuring its effective functioning.

The specific job we will focus on is the manufacture and installation of a small pulp machine for Western Pulp and Paper Company in the year 2007 for a price of $15,000. A key issue for Robinson in determining this price is the cost of doing the job. Knowledge about its own costs helps Robinson to price jobs to make a profit and to make informed estimates of the costs of future jobs.

Consider Robinson's *actual-costing* system, a job-costing system that uses *actual costs* to determine the cost of individual jobs. **Actual costing** is a method of job costing that traces direct costs to a cost object by using the actual direct-cost rate(s) times the actual quantity of the direct-cost input(s) and allocates indirect costs based on the actual indirect-cost rate(s) times the actual quantity of the cost-allocation base.

General Approach to Job Costing

We present a seven-step approach to assigning actual costs to individual jobs. The approach applies equally to job costing in the manufacturing, merchandising, and service sectors.

◆ **Step 1:** *Identify the chosen cost object(s).* The cost object in this case is the job of manufacturing a pulp machine for the Western Pulp and Paper Company in the year 2007.

◆ **Step 2:** *Identify the direct costs for the cost object(s).* Robinson identifies two direct manufacturing cost categories: direct materials and direct manufacturing

Cost-Allocation Bases Used for Manufacturing Overhead

How do companies around the world allocate manufacturing overhead costs to products? The percentages in the following table indicate how frequently particular cost-allocation bases are used in costing systems in six countries. If the reported percentages for a country exceed 100%, that's because many companies surveyed use more than one cost-allocation base.

	United States[a]	Australia[b]	Ireland[c]	Japan[b]	New Zealand[d]	United Kingdom[b]
Direct labour	62%	73%	52%	68%	84%	78%
Machine-hours	12	17	22	27	53	60
Units of production	4	17	28	32	47	55
Direct material cost	5	14	7	36	44	40
Other	17	—	22	—	10	15

As the survey data identifies, a growing global trend is the use of multiple allocation bases for manufacturing overhead. Surveys also indicate that as companies begin to identify activity drivers of manufacturing overhead costs, such as setup hours and inspection hours, more of the manufacturing overhead costs are allocated to products using measures other than direct labour and machine-hours.[e]

[a] Cohen, J., and L. Paquette, "Management Accounting Practices: Perceptions of Controllers," *Journal of Cost Management* (1991).

[b] Wijewardena, H., and A. De Zoysa, "A Comparative Analysis of Management Accounting Practices in Australia and Japan: An Empirical Investigation," *International Journal of Accounting* (1999).

[c] Clarke, P., "Management Accounting Practices in Large Irish Manufacturing Firms," *Irish Journal of Management* (1997).

[d] Lamminmaki, D., and C. Drury, "A Comparison of New Zealand and British Product-Costing Practices," *International Journal of Accounting* (2001).

[e] Groot, T., "Activity Based Costing in U.S. and Dutch Food Companies," *Advances in Management Accounting* (1999).

labour. Direct materials costs for the Western Pulp and Paper Company job are $4,606, while direct manufacturing labour costs are $1,579.

◆ **Step 3:** *Select cost-allocation bases to use in allocating indirect costs to the cost object(s).* Indirect manufacturing costs are costs that are not identified individually or directly with specific jobs. Yet completing various jobs would be impossible without incurring indirect costs such as supervision, manufacturing engineering, utilities, and repairs. These costs must be allocated to jobs. Different jobs require different quantities of indirect resources. The objective of allocating indirect costs is to measure the underlying usage of indirect resources by individual jobs.

Companies often use multiple cost-allocation bases to allocate indirect costs (see Global Surveys of Company Practice) because different indirect costs have different cost drivers. For example, some indirect costs such as amortization and repairs of machines are more closely related to machine-hours. Other indirect costs such as supervision and production support are more closely related to direct manufacturing labour-hours.

Robinson, however, chooses direct manufacturing labour-hours as the sole allocation base for linking all indirect manufacturing costs to jobs. That is because, in its labour-intensive environment, Robinson believes that the number of direct manufacturing labour-hours is a good measure of how individual jobs use all the manufacturing overhead resources, such as salaries paid to supervisors, engineers, production support staff, and quality management staff. There is a strong cause-and-effect relationship between the direct manufacturing labour-hours required by an individual job—that's the cause—and the indirect manufacturing resources demanded by that job—that's the effect. In the year 2007, Robinson records 27,000 actual direct manufacturing labour-hours.

◆ **Step 4:** *Identify the indirect costs associated with each cost-allocation base.* Because Robinson believes that a single cost-allocation base, direct manufacturing labour hours, is appropriate to allocate indirect manufacturing costs to products, it creates a single cost pool called *manufacturing overhead costs.* This pool represents the indirect costs of the Vancouver Manufacturing Department that are difficult to trace directly to individual jobs. *Actual indirect costs* are often known only at the end of the year. In 2007, actual indirect manufacturing costs total $1,215,000.

As we saw in steps 3 and 4, managers first identify cost-allocation bases and then identify the costs related to each cost-allocation base, not the other way around. That's because managers must first understand the cost driver, the reasons why costs are being incurred (for example, for setting up machines, moving materials, or designing jobs), before they can determine the costs associated with each cost driver. The reason for not doing step 4 before step 3 is that there is nothing to guide the creation of the cost pools. As a result, the cost pools created may not have cost-allocation bases that are cost drivers of the costs in the cost pool.

◆ **Step 5:** *Compute the rate per unit of each cost-allocation base used to allocate indirect costs to the cost object(s).* For each cost pool, the *indirect-cost rate* is calculated by dividing total overhead costs in the pool (determined in step 4) by the total quantity of the cost-allocation base (determined in step 3). Robinson calculates the allocation rate for its single manufacturing overhead cost pool as follows:

$$\text{Actual indirect-cost rate} = \frac{\text{Actual total costs in indirect-cost pool}}{\text{Actual total quantity of cost-allocation base}}$$

$$= \frac{\$1,215,000}{27,000 \text{ direct manufacturing labour-hours}}$$

$$= \$45 \text{ per direct manufacturing labour-hour}$$

◆ **Step 6:** *Compute the indirect costs allocated to the cost object(s).* The indirect costs of a job are computed by multiplying the actual quantities of the different allocation bases (one for each pool) used to complete a job by their respective indirect cost rates (computed in step 5). To make the pulp machine, Robinson uses 88 direct manufacturing labour-hours, the cost-allocation base for its only indirect-cost pool (out of the 27,000 total direct manufacturing labour-hours for the year 2007). Indirect costs allocated to the pulp machine job equal $3,960 (88 hours × $45 per direct manufacturing labour-hour).

◆ **Step 7:** *Determine the costs of the cost object(s) by adding all direct and indirect costs assigned to it.* The cost of the pulp machine job for Western Pulp is $10,145.

Direct manufacturing costs		
Direct materials	$4,606	
Direct manufacturing labour	1,579	$6,185
Indirect manufacturing costs		
Manufacturing overhead costs		
($45 × 88 direct manufacturing labour-hours)		3,960
Total manufacturing costs of job		$10,145

Recall that Robinson was paid $15,000 for the job. Thus the actual-costing system shows a gross margin of $4,855 ($15,000 − $10,145) or a gross margin percentage of 32.37% ($4,855 ÷ $15,000).

Robinson can use the gross margin and gross margin percentage calculations to compare profitability across various jobs and identify the most profitable types of jobs for its sales force to target. At the same time, Robinson can examine the reasons that some jobs show low profitability. Have direct materials been wasted? Is direct manufacturing labour too high? Are there ways to improve the efficiency with which these jobs are done? Or were these jobs simply mispriced? Job cost analysis provides crucial

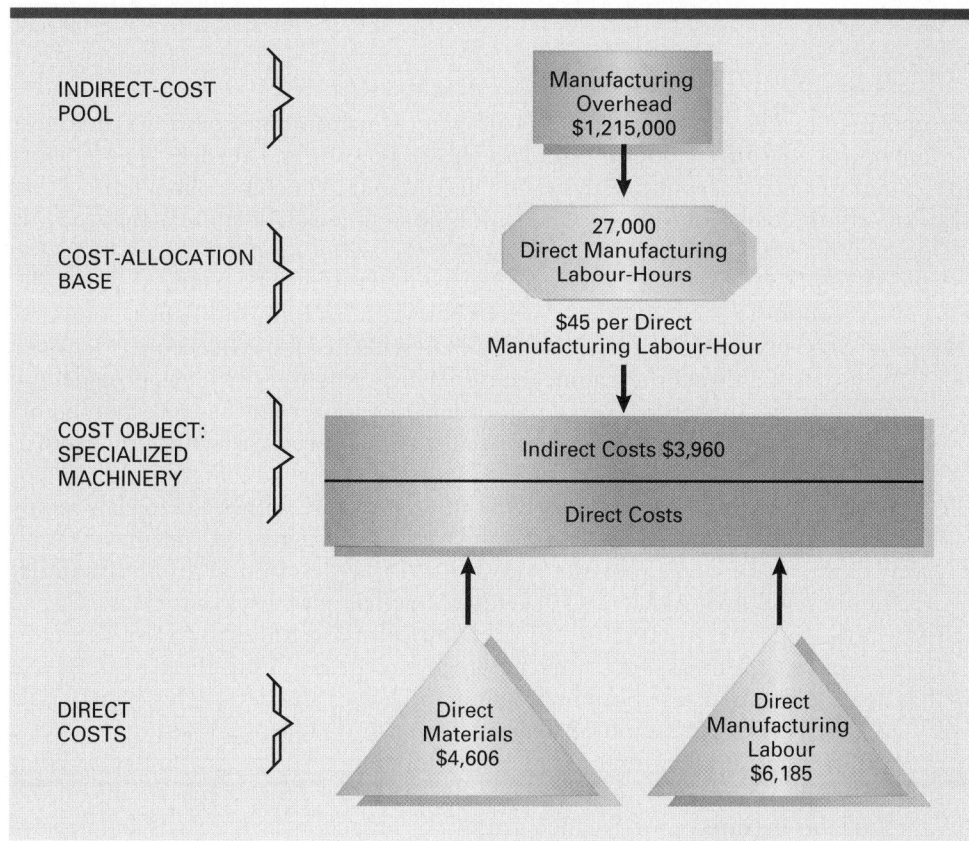

information for judging performance and making future improvements (see the Concepts in Action box on p. 120).

Exhibit 4-2 presents an overview of the Robinson Company job-costing system. This exhibit includes the five building blocks of this chapter—*cost object, cost pool, direct costs of a cost object, indirect costs of a cost object*, and *cost-allocation base*. Costing-system overviews like Exhibit 4-2 are important learning tools. We urge you to sketch one when you need to understand a costing system in manufacturing, service, or merchandising settings. The symbols in Exhibit 4-2 are used consistently in the costing-system overviews presented in this book. For example, a triangle always identifies a direct cost and long rectangles identify indirect costs. Octagons identify cost-allocation bases and small rectangles the indirect cost pools. Note also that the colours are consistent throughout the text. Note the correspondence between the exhibit diagram and the cost of the pulp-machine job described in steps 5 and 7. Exhibit 4-2 shows two direct-cost categories (direct materials and direct manufacturing labour) and one indirect-cost pool (manufacturing overhead) used to allocate costs. The costs in step 7 also have three dollar amounts that correspond to the two direct- and one indirect-cost categories.

Exhibit 4-2 presents concepts that appear throughout this book in a similar format. In the Robinson Company example, the cost object (a pulping machine) has two direct costs (direct materials and direct manufacturing labour) and one indirect cost (manufacturing overhead) allocated on the basis of direct manufacturing labour-hours.

Two Major Cost Objects: Products and Departments

One important cost object of any accounting system is the output, either *products or services*. Another major cost object is **responsibility centres**, which are subunits of an organization whose managers are accountable for specified activities. Examples of responsibility centres are departments or groups of departments (such as operations and sales at eBay), divisions (such as Cadillac and Buick at General Motors), and geographic territories (such as North America, Europe, and Asia Pacific at Nike).

The most common responsibility centre is a department that performs a specified function. Identifying department costs helps managers control the costs for which they are responsible. It also enables senior managers to evaluate the performance of their subordinates and the performance of subunits as economic investments.

Responsibility centre. A part, segment, or subunit of an organization whose manager is accountable for a specified set of activities.

In manufacturing companies, the direct costs that can be traced to the Manufacturing Department include all costs of materials, manufacturing labour, supervision, engineering, production, and quality control.

Source Documents

Source documents. The original records that support journal entries in an accounting system.

Robinson's managers and accountants gather information that goes into their cost systems through **source documents**, which are the original records that support journal entries in an accounting system. The key source document in a job-costing system is a **job cost record** (also called a **job cost sheet**), a document that records and accumulates all the costs assigned to a specific job. The job cost record is started as soon as work begins on a particular job. Exhibit 4-3, panel A, shows the job cost record for the pulp machine ordered by Western Pulp and Paper Company.

Job cost record (job cost sheet). Source document that records and accumulates all the costs assigned to a specific job.

Source documents also exist for individual items in a job cost record. Consider direct materials. Based on the engineering specifications and drawings provided by Western Pulp, a manufacturing engineer orders material from the storeroom. This is done using a basic source document called a **materials requisition record**, which is a form used to charge job cost records and departments for the cost of direct materials used on specific jobs. Exhibit 4-3, panel B, shows a materials requisition record for the Robinson Company. Note how the record specifies the job for which the material is requested (WPP 298), a description of the material (Part Number MB 468–A, Metal brackets), the actual quantity (8), the actual price ($14), and the actual total cost ($112). The cost of $112 for Part Number MB 468–A also appears as a cost on the job cost record. Adding the cost of all the materials requisitioned for the pulp machine job gives the actual direct materials cost of $4,606 shown on the job cost sheet.

Materials requisition record. Form used to charge departments and job cost records for the cost of the materials used on a specific job.

The accounting for direct manufacturing labour is very similar to that described for direct materials. The basic source document for direct manufacturing labour is a **labour time record**, which is used to charge job cost records and departments for labour time used on specific jobs. Exhibit 4-3, panel C, shows a typical weekly labour time record for a particular employee. Each day the employee records the time spent on individual jobs (in this case WPP 298 and JL 256) as well as the time spent on another task such as maintenance of machines or cleaning that is not related to a specific job.

Labour time record. Record used to charge departments and job cost records for labour time used on a specific job.

The 25 hours that the employee spends on Job WPP 298 appears on the job cost record in panel A at a cost of $450 (25 hours × hourly rate of $18 per hour). Similarly, the job cost record for job JL 256 will carry a cost of $216 (12 hours × $18 per hour). The three hours of time spent on maintenance and cleaning at $18 per hour, equal to $54, are indirect manufacturing costs because these costs are not traceable to any particular job. These indirect costs are included as part of the manufacturing overhead cost pool that is allocated to jobs using direct manufacturing labour-hours. The total direct manufacturing labour costs of $1,579 for the pulp machine that appear on the job cost record in panel A are the sum of all the direct manufacturing labour costs charged to this job by different employees.

The reliability of job cost records depends on the reliability of the inputs. Problems occurring in this area include materials recorded on one job being "borrowed" and used on other jobs and erroneous job numbers being assigned to material or labour inputs.

In many costing systems, the source documents exist only in the form of computer records. Bar coding and other forms of online information recording enable the materials and labour time used on jobs to be recorded without human intervention.

The Role of Technology

To improve the efficiency of their operations, managers use product-costing information to control materials, labour, and overhead costs. Modern information technology provides managers with quick and accurate product-cost information that makes it easier to manage and control jobs.

PANEL A:

JOB COST RECORD

JOB NO:	WPP 298		CUSTOMER:	Western Pulp and Paper
Date Started:	Feb. 7, 2007		Date Completed:	March 1, 2007

DIRECT MATERIALS

Date Received	Materials Requisition No.	Part No.	Quantity Used	Unit Cost	Total Costs
Feb. 7, 2007	2007: 198	MB 468–A	8	$14	$112
Feb. 7, 2007	2007: 199	TB 267–F	12	63	756
					•
					•
					•
Total					$4,606

DIRECT MANUFACTURING LABOUR

Period Covered	Labour Time Record No.	Employee No.	Hours Used	Hourly Rate	Total Costs
Feb. 7–13, 2007	LT 232	551-87-3076	25	$18	$450
Feb. 7–13, 2007	LT 247	287-31-4671	5	19	95
					•
					•
					•
Total					$1,579

MANUFACTURING OVERHEAD*

Date	Cost Pool Category	Allocation Base Dir Manuf.	Allocation Base Units Used	Allocation Base Rate	Total Costs
Dec. 31, 2007	Manufacturing	Labour-Hours	88 Hours	$45	$3,960
					•
					•
					•
Total					$3,960
TOTAL JOB COST					$10,145

PANEL B:

MATERIALS REQUISITION RECORD

Materials Requisition Record No:				2007:198

Job No:	WPP 298	Date:	Feb. 7, 2007

Part No.	Part Description	Quantity	Unit Cost	Total Cost
MB 468-A	Metal Brackets	8	$14	$112

Issued By:	B. Clyde	Date: Feb. 7, 2007
Received By:	L. Daley	Date: Feb. 7, 2007

PANEL C:

LABOUR TIME RECORD

Labour Time Record No:		LT 232

Employee Name:	G.L. Cook	Employee No:	551-87-3076

Employee Classification Code: Grade 3 Machinist

Hourly Rate: $18

Week Start:		Feb. 7, 2007		Week End:		Feb. 13, 2007	

Job. No.	M	T	W	Th	F	S	Su	Total
WPP 298	4	8	3	6	4	0	0	25
JL 256	3	0	4	2	3	0	0	12
Maintenance	1	0	1	0	1	0	0	3
Total	8	8	8	8	8	0	0	40

Supervisor:	R. Stuart	Date:	Feb. 14, 2007

*The Robinson Company uses a single manufacturing overhead cost pool. The use of multiple overhead cost pools would mean multiple entries in the "Manufacturing Overhead" section of its job cost record.

Consider, for example, direct materials charged to jobs for product-costing purposes. Managers control these costs well before the materials are used. Through technologies such as electronic data interchange (EDI), companies like Robinson can order materials from their suppliers by clicking a few keys on a computer keyboard. EDI, an electronic computer link between a company and its suppliers, ensures that the order is transmitted quickly and accurately with minimum paper work and costs. A bar code scanner records the receipt of incoming materials. The computer matches the receipt with the order, prints out a cheque to the supplier, and records the material received. When an operator on the production floor transmits

Job Costing on the Joint Strike Fighter Project

Northrop Grumman, Inc., is a leading provider of systems and technologies for the U.S. Department of Defense. Competitive bidding processes and increased public and congressional oversight make understanding costs critical in pricing decisions as well as in winning and retaining government contracts. Each job must be estimated individually because the unique end products demand different amounts of Northrop Grumman's resources.

In 2001, the team of Northrop Grumman, Lockheed Martin, and BAE Systems was awarded the System Design and Demonstration contract for the Joint Strike Fighter (JSF) project. This project, worth US$200 billion over seven years, will create a family of supersonic, multirole fighter airplanes designed for the U.S. Air Force, Navy, and Marine Corps, as well as the United Kingdom's Royal Air Force and Royal Navy. This project has five primary stages: (1) conceptualization, (2) design and review, (3) manufacturing, (4) assembly, and (5) testing and delivery. In the conceptualization phase, detailed plans for each aircraft model are created. Technologies for these plans are researched, developed, and approved during the design and review phase. Subsequently, thousands of components, created by the primary contractors and various subcontractors, are manufactured, assembled in multiple locations, and tested prior to delivery to the purchasing organizations. If they do not meet required specifications during testing, the fighter jets are reworked before delivery.

To ensure proper allocation and accounting of resources, JSF project managers use a job-costing system. The system first calculates the budgeted cost of direct materials and direct-labour hours for the project. It then allocates all overhead costs (supervisory salaries, rent, amortization, materials handling, and so on) to jobs using budgeted direct material costs and direct-labour hours as allocation bases. Northrop Grumman's job-costing system allows managers to assign costs to processes and projects. Northrop Grumman continually estimates the profitability of these projects based on the percentage of work completed and the related revenue earned. Managers use the job-costing system to actively manage costs, while program representatives from the Department of Defense and members of Congress have access to clear, concise, and transparent costing data. Therefore, Northrop Grumman's job-costing system improves cost identification and management for all Department of Defense projects.

Source: Conversations with Stephen Bryant, Northrop Grumman, Inc., in October and November 2003.

a request for materials via a computer terminal, the computer prepares a materials-requisition record, instantly recording the issue of materials in the materials and job-cost records. Each day, the computer sums the materials-requisition records charged to a particular job or manufacturing department. A performance report is then prepared comparing budgeted costs versus actual costs of direct materials. Direct materials usage might be reported hourly—if there is an economic payoff for such frequent reporting.

Similarly, information about manufacturing labour is obtained as employees log into computer terminals and punch in the job numbers, their employee numbers, and start and end times of their work on different jobs. The computer automatically prints the labour-time record and, using hourly rates stored for each employee, calculates the labour costs of individual jobs. Information technology also provides managers with instantaneous feedback to control manufacturing overhead, jobs in process, jobs completed, and jobs shipped and installed at customer sites.

Robinson Company computes indirect-cost rates in step 5 based on an annual period. Why must Robinson wait until the end of the year to calculate indirect-cost rates? Why can't Robinson calculate indirect-cost rates each week or each month? If it could do so, Robinson would be able to calculate actual costs of jobs much earlier and not have to wait until the end of the year. There are two important reasons for using longer time periods to calculate indirect-cost rates.

1. *The numerator reason* (indirect costs). The shorter the period, the greater the influence of seasonal patterns on the level of costs. For example, if indirect-cost rates were calculated each month, costs of heating (included in the numerator) would be charged only to winter production. The use of an annual period incorporates the effects of all four seasons into a single indirect-cost rate.

   Levels of total indirect costs are also affected by nonseasonal erratic costs. Examples include costs incurred in a particular month that benefit operations during future months: repairs and maintenance of equipment, and vacation and holiday pay outlays. If monthly indirect-cost rates were calculated, jobs done in a month with high nonseasonal erratic costs would be loaded with these costs. Pooling all indirect costs together over the course of a full year and calculating a single annual indirect-cost rate helps to smooth out some of the erratic and period-specific bumps.

2. *The denominator reason* (quantity of the allocation base). Another rationale for longer periods is the need to spread monthly fixed indirect costs over fluctuating levels of output. Some indirect costs (for example, supplies) may be variable with respect to the cost-allocation base, whereas other indirect costs are fixed (for example, property taxes and rent).

Suppose a company schedules its production to correspond with a highly seasonal sales pattern. Assume the following mix of variable indirect costs (such as supplies, repairs, and indirect manufacturing labour) and fixed indirect costs (plant amortization and engineering support):

	Indirect Costs			Direct Manufacturing Labour-Hours	Allocation Rate per Direct Manufacturing Labour-Hour
	Variable	Fixed	Total		
	(1)	(2)	(3) = (1) + (2)	(4)	(5) = (3) ÷ (4)
High-output month	$40,000	$60,000	$100,000	3,200	$31.25
Low-output month	10,000	60,000	70,000	800	87.50

Note that variable indirect costs change in proportion to changes in direct manufacturing labour-hours. As a result, the variable indirect-cost rate is the same in both the high-output and the low-output month ($40,000 ÷ 3,200 = $10,000 ÷ 800 = $12.50). Because of the fixed costs of $60,000, monthly total indirect-cost rates vary sizably—from $31.25 per hour to $87.50 per hour. Few managers believe that identical jobs done in different months should be allocated indirect-cost charges per hour that differ so significantly ($87.50 ÷ $31.25 = 280%). In our example, management has committed itself to a specific level of capacity far beyond a mere 30 days per month. An average, annualized rate based on the relationship of total annual indirect costs to the total annual level of output will smooth out the effect of monthly variations in output levels.

The nonuniform design of the calendar also affects the calculation of monthly indirect-cost rates. The number of Monday-to-Friday workdays in a month varies from 20 to 23 during a year. If separate rates are computed each month, jobs undertaken in February, the shortest month, would bear a greater share of indirect costs (such as amortization and property taxes) than would jobs undertaken in March. Many managers believe such results to be unreasonable. Use of an annual budget period reduces the effect that the number of working days per month has on unit costs.

In this example, the change in the indirect cost-allocation rate arises solely because of fixed costs. Variable cost per unit = $12.50 at both 3,200 and 800 hours. The average fixed cost per unit, however, = $31.25 at 3,200 hours and $87.50 at 800 hours. This is an example where unit fixed costs must be cautiously used. If the cost object were the department there would be no unit or average fixed cost allocated, but rather the focus would have been on the total value of this monthly cost.

NORMAL COSTING

OBJECTIVE 4

Distinguish between actual costing and normal costing

Normal costing. A costing method that traces direct costs to a cost object by using the actual direct-cost rate(s) times the actual quantity of the direct-cost input and allocates indirect costs based on the budgeted indirect-cost rate(s) times the actual quantity of the cost-allocation base.

The difficulty of calculating actual indirect-cost rates weekly or monthly means that managers cannot calculate the actual costs of jobs as the jobs are completed. Managers often want a close approximation of the manufacturing costs of various jobs on a timely basis, not just at the end of the year. Managers need these costs (often together with other costs such as marketing costs) for various ongoing uses, including choosing which job to emphasize or deemphasize, pricing jobs, managing costs, and preparing interim financial statements. Because management benefits from immediate access to costs of jobs, few companies wait until the *actual* manufacturing overhead is finally known (at year-end) before allocating overhead costs in computing the costs of jobs. Instead, a *predetermined* or *budgeted* indirect-cost rate is calculated for each cost pool at the beginning of a fiscal year and overhead costs are allocated to jobs as work progresses. For the numerator and denominator reasons described in the preceding section, the *budgeted indirect-cost rate* is computed for each cost pool using the budgeted *annual* indirect cost and the budgeted *annual* quantity of the cost-allocation base. The use of budgeted indirect-cost rates gives rise to normal costing.

Normal costing is a costing method that traces direct costs to a cost object by using the actual direct-cost rate(s) times the actual quantity of the direct-cost input(s) and allocates indirect costs based on the budgeted indirect-cost rate(s) times the actual quantity of the cost-allocation base(s). Note that both actual costing and normal costing trace direct costs to jobs in the same way. The actual quantities and actual rates of direct materials and direct manufacturing labour used on a job are known from the service records as the work is done. The only difference between actual costing and normal costing is that actual costing uses an *actual* indirect-cost rate whereas normal costing uses a *budgeted* indirect-cost rate to cost jobs. Exhibit 4-4 summarizes the differences between the actual costing and normal costing methods.

We illustrate normal costing with the Robinson Company example using the seven-step procedure described earlier in the chapter. The following budgeted data for the year 2007 pertain to the manufacturing operations of Robinson Company:

	Budget
Total manufacturing overhead costs	$1,280,000
Total direct manufacturing labour-hours	32,000

Steps 1 and 2 are exactly as before. Actual direct materials costs total $4,606, and actual direct manufacturing labour costs equal $1,579. Recall from step 3 that Robinson uses a single cost-allocation base, direct manufacturing labour-hours, to allocate all manufacturing overhead costs to jobs. The budgeted quantity of direct manufacturing labour-hours for the year 2007 is 32,000 hours. In step 4, Robinson groups all the indirect manufacturing costs into a single manufacturing overhead cost pool. The budgeted amount of manufacturing overhead costs in the year 2007 is

EXHIBIT 4-4
Actual Costing and Normal Costing Systems

	Actual Costing	**Normal Costing**
Direct Costs	*Actual direct-cost rates* × actual quantities of direct-cost inputs	*Actual direct-cost rates* × actual quantities of direct-cost inputs
Indirect Costs	*Actual indirect-cost rates* × actual quantities of cost-allocation bases	*Budgeted indirect-cost rates* × actual quantities of cost-allocation bases

$1,280,000. The budgeted indirect-cost rate for 2007 (step 5) is $40 per direct manufacturing labour-hour:

$$\text{Budgeted indirect-cost rate} = \frac{\text{Budgeted total costs in indirect-cost pool}}{\text{Budgeted total quantity of cost-allocation base}}$$

$$= \frac{\$1,280,000}{32,000 \text{ direct manufacturing labour-hours}}$$

$$= \$40 \text{ per direct manufacturing labour-hour}$$

Indirect costs allocated to the Western Pulp and Paper Company's pulp machine order (step 6) are calculated as the *actual* quantity of direct manufacturing labour-hours used on the job, 88 × budgeted indirect-cost rate, $40 = $3,520. The cost of the machine job under normal costing (step 7) is $9,705, calculated as follows:

Direct manufacturing costs		
Direct materials	$4,606	
Direct manufacturing labour	1,579	$6,185
Indirect manufacturing costs		
Manufacturing overhead costs		
($40 × 88 actual direct manufacturing labour-hours)		3,520
Total manufacturing costs of job		$9,705

The manufacturing cost of the Western Pulp job is lower by $440 under normal costing ($9,705) than it is under actual costing ($10,145) because the budgeted indirect-cost rate is $40 per hour, whereas the actual indirect-cost rate is $45 per hour.

AN ILLUSTRATION OF A JOB-COSTING SYSTEM IN MANUFACTURING

We continue the Robinson Company example to illustrate how a normal job-costing system operates in manufacturing. The following example considers events that occurred in February 2007.

General Ledger and Subsidiary Ledgers

As we have noted, a job-costing system has a separate job cost record for each job. This record is typically found in a subsidiary ledger. The general ledger combines these separate job cost records in the Work-in-Process Control account, which pertains to all jobs undertaken.

Think of subsidiary ledger accounts as the "little" T-accounts that support the general ledger control T-account; for example, individual job-cost records are the support for Work-in-Process Control.

Exhibit 4-5 shows T-account relationships for the Robinson Company's general ledger and illustrative records in the subsidiary ledgers. Panel A shows the general ledger section that gives a "bird's-eye view" of the costing system; the amounts are based on the detailed transaction analysis, which begins near the bottom of page 124. Panel B shows the subsidiary ledgers and the basic source documents that contain the underlying details—the "worm's-eye view." General ledger accounts with the word *Control* in their titles (such as Materials Control and Accounts Payable Control) are supported by underlying subsidiary ledgers.

Software programs guide the processing of transactions in most accounting systems. Some programs make general ledger entries simultaneously with entries in the subsidiary ledger accounts. Other software programs make general ledger entries at, say, weekly or monthly intervals, with entries made in the subsidiary ledger accounts more frequently. The Robinson Company makes entries in its subsidiary ledger when transactions occur and then makes entries in its general ledger on a monthly basis.

A general ledger should be viewed as only one of many tools that assist management in planning and control. To control operations, managers not only use the source documents in the subsidiary ledgers, but also study nonfinancial variables such as the percentage of jobs requiring rework.

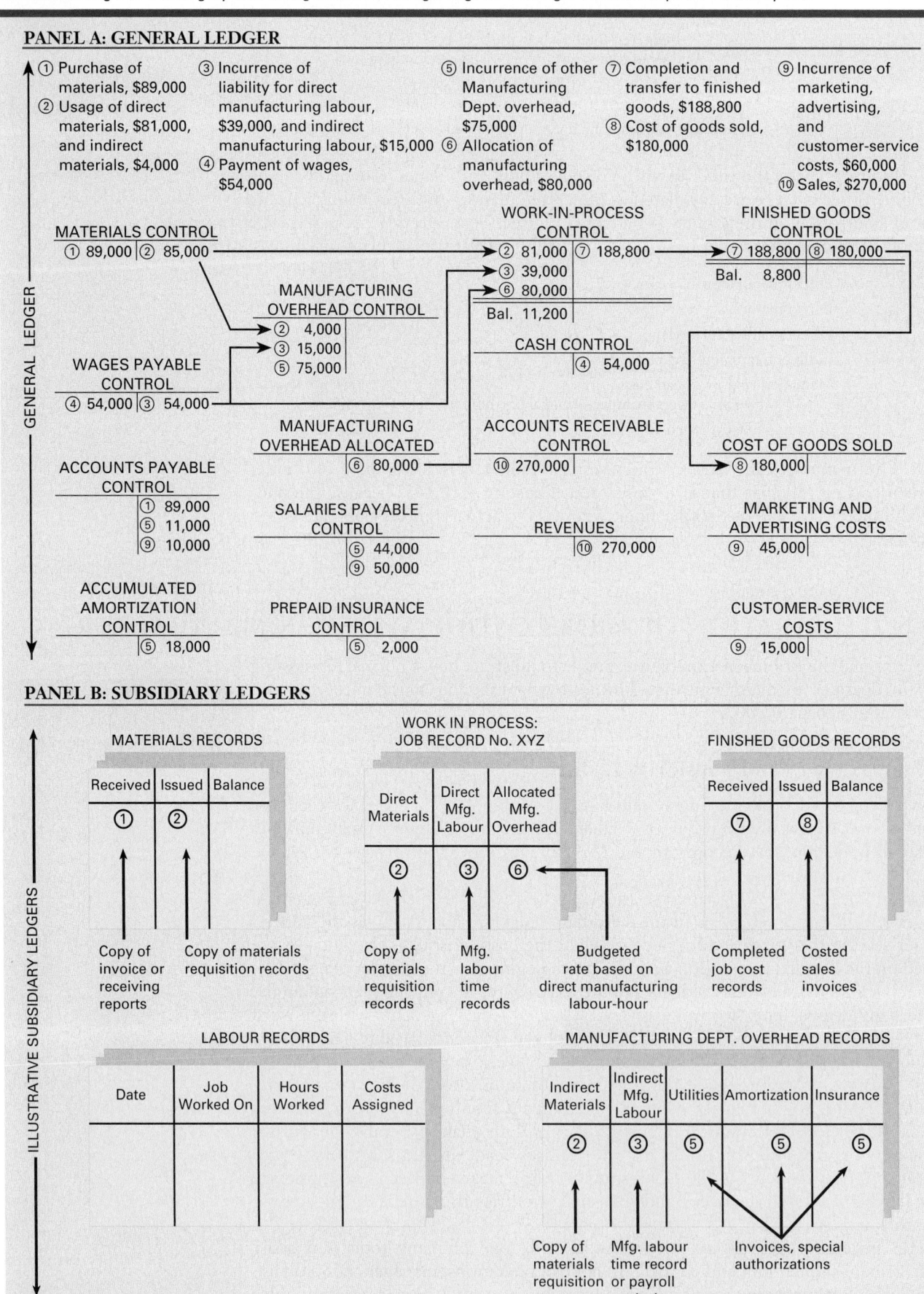

Explanations of Transactions

The transaction-by-transaction summary analysis below explains how a job-costing system serves the twin goals of (1) department responsibility and control and (2) product costing. These transactions track stages (a) through (d):

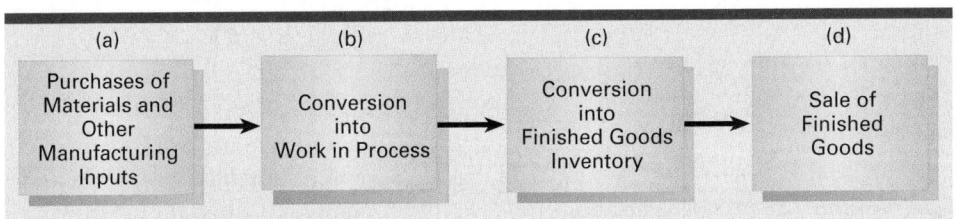

The graphic, showing the *physical flow of product* through a manufacturing process, clarifies the economic transactions occurring. To more easily understand the first 8 journal entries that follow, link the discussion of each entry to the graphic. For example transaction 1 illustrates stage (a).

1. **Transaction.** Purchase of materials (direct and indirect), $89,000 on account.

   Analysis. The asset Materials Control is increased. The liability Accounts Payable Control is increased. Both accounts have the word *Control* in their title in the general ledger because they are supported by records in the subsidiary ledger. The subsidiary records for materials at the Robinson Company—called *Materials Records*—maintain a continuous record of additions to, and reductions from, inventory. At a minimum, these records would contain columns for quantity received, issuance to jobs, and balance (see panel B of Exhibit 4-5, page 124). There is a separate subsidiary materials record for each type of material in the subsidiary ledger. The following journal entry summarizes all the February 2007 entries in the materials subsidiary ledgers:

Journal Entry:	Materials Control	89,000	
	Accounts Payable Control		89,000

   Post to General Ledger:

Materials Control		Accounts Payable Control	
① 89,000			① 89,000

   Materials Control includes all material purchases, whether the items are classified as direct or indirect costs of products.

2. **Transaction.** Materials sent to manufacturing plant floor: direct materials, $81,000, and indirect materials, $4,000.

   Analysis. The accounts Work-in-Process Control and Manufacturing Overhead Control are increased. The account Materials Control is decreased. The assumption is that costs incurred on the work in process "attach" to the work in process, thereby making it a more valuable asset. Responsibility is fixed by using *materials requisitions records* as a basis for charging departments for the materials issued to them. Requisitions are accumulated and posted monthly to the general ledger at the Robinson Company. As direct materials are used, they are charged to individual job records, which are the subsidiary ledger accounts for the Work-in-Process Control account in the general ledger. Indirect materials are charged to individual Manufacturing Department overhead cost records, which make up the subsidiary ledger for Manufacturing Overhead Control at the Robinson Company. The cost of these indirect materials is allocated to individual jobs as a part of the Manufacturing Overhead. The Manufacturing Overhead Control account is the record of the *actual costs* in all the individual overhead categories.

   Each indirect-cost pool in a job-costing system will have its own account in the general ledger. Robinson has only one indirect-cost pool—manufacturing overhead.

Journal Entry:	Work-in-Process Control	81,000	
	Manufacturing Overhead Control	4,000	
	Materials Control		85,000

Post to General Ledger:

Materials Control				Work-in-Process Control	
①	89,000	②	85,000	②	81,000

Manufacturing Overhead Control	
②	4,000

3. **Transaction.** Manufacturing labour wages liability incurred, direct ($39,000) and indirect ($15,000).

Analysis. The accounts Work-in-Process Control and Manufacturing Overhead Control are increased. Wages Payable Control is also increased. Labour time records are used to trace direct manufacturing labour to Work-in-Process Control (see panel B of Exhibit 4-5, p. 124) and to accumulate the indirect manufacturing labour in Manufacturing Overhead Control. The indirect manufacturing labour is, by definition, not being traced to the individual job. Department managers are responsible for making efficient use of available labour.

Journal Entry:	Work-in-Process Control	39,000	
	Manufacturing Overhead Control	15,000	
	Wages Payable Control		54,000

Post to General Ledger:

Wages Payable Control				Work-in-Process Control		
		③	54,000	②	81,000	
				③	39,000	

Manufacturing Overhead Control		
②	4,000	
③	15,000	

4. **Transaction.** Payment of total manufacturing payroll for the month, $54,000. (For simplicity, payroll withholdings from employees are ignored in this example.)

Analysis. The liability Wages Payable Control is decreased. The asset Cash Control is decreased.

Journal Entry:	Wages Payable Control	54,000	
	Cash Control		54,000

Post to General Ledger:

Wages Payable Control				Cash Control		
④	54,000	③	54,000		④	54,000

For convenience here, wages payable for the month are assumed to be completely paid at month-end.

Utilities, amortization, and insurance are debited to Manufacturing Overhead Control only if they are related to *producing the products,* and they are considered to be inventoriable costs (assets) until the products are sold. In contrast, utilities for a sales office, amortization on executives' automobiles, and insurance on those automobiles are period costs and therefore are not part of manufacturing overhead.

5. **Transaction.** Additional manufacturing overhead costs incurred during the month, $75,000. These costs consist of salaries, $44,000; payables, $11,000; insurance expired, $2,000; and amortization on equipment, $18,000.

Analysis. The indirect cost account of Manufacturing Overhead Control is increased. The liability Accounts Payable Control is increased, the asset Prepaid Insurance Control is decreased, and the asset Equipment is decreased by means of a related contra asset account Accumulated Amortization Control. The detail of these costs is entered in the appropriate columns of the individual manufacturing overhead cost records that make up the subsidiary ledger for Manufacturing Overhead Control. The source documents for these distributions include invoices (for example, a utility bill) and special schedules (for example, an amortization schedule) from the responsible accounting officer.

Journal Entry:

Manufacturing Overhead Control	75,000	
Salaries Payable Control		44,000
Accounts Payable Control		11,000
Accumulated Amortization Control		18,000
Prepaid Insurance Control		2,000

Post to General Ledger:

Salaries Payable Control

	⑤	44,000

Accounts Payable Control

	①	89,000
	⑤	11,000

Manufacturing Overhead Control

②	4,000	
③	15,000	
⑤	75,000	

Accumulated Amortization Control

	⑤	18,000

Prepaid Insurance Control

	⑤	2,000

6. **Transaction.** Allocation of manufacturing overhead to products, $80,000.

Analysis: The asset Work-in-Process Control is increased. The indirect cost account of Manufacturing Overhead Control is, in effect, decreased by means of its contra account, called Manufacturing Overhead Allocated. **Manufacturing overhead allocated** is the record of manufacturing overhead allocated to individual jobs based on the budgeted rate multiplied by actual units used of the allocation base. It comprises all manufacturing costs that are assigned to a product (or service) using a cost-allocation base because they cannot be traced to it in an economically feasible way. The 2007 budgeted overhead rate used by Robinson is $40 per direct manufacturing labour-hour. The overhead cost allocated to each job depends on the direct manufacturing labour-hours used on that job. The job record for each individual job in the subsidiary ledger will include a debit item for manufacturing overhead allocated. For example, the job cost record for WPP 298 shows Manufacturing Overhead Allocated of $3,520 (88 actual direct manufacturing labour-hours used × budgeted rate of $40). It is assumed that 2,000 machine-hours were used for all jobs, resulting in a total manufacturing overhead allocation of 2,000 × $40 = $80,000.

Note that a subsidiary entry is made for Manufacturing Overhead Allocated when machine-hours are used on a job. These entries are made to the individual job records in the subsidiary ledger. In contrast, subsidiary entries are made for Manufacturing Overhead Control when actual transactions occur during the period.

> **Manufacturing overhead allocated.** All manufacturing costs that are assigned to a product (or service) using a cost-allocation base because they cannot be traced to a product (or service) in an economically feasible way.

> Actual manufacturing overhead (MOH) is debited to MOH Control as incurred; the total actual MOH is unknown until the end of the accounting period. Allocated MOH is the budgeted MOH rate (known at the *beginning* of the period) multiplied by the actual quantity of the MOH allocation base recorded upon completion of the jobs (or the *end* of the period) — when usage of the allocation base is known.

Journal Entry:

Work-in-Process Control	80,000	
Manufacturing Overhead Allocated		80,000

Post to General Ledger:

Manufacturing Overhead Allocated

	⑥	80,000

Work-in-Process Control

②	81,000	
③	39,000	
⑥	80,000	

Keep in mind that transactions 5 and 6 are distinct and different. In transaction 5, actual overhead costs incurred throughout the month are debited to Manufacturing Overhead Control, and the subsidiary manufacturing overhead records are *not* debited to Work-in-Process Control and the individual job cost records. Manufacturing overhead costs are added (debited) to Work-in-Process Control and individual job cost records *only when* manufacturing overhead costs are allocated in transaction 6. At this time, Manufacturing Overhead Control is, in effect, decreased (credited). Under the normal costing system described in our illustration, the budgeted indirect cost rate of $40 per direct manufacturing labour-hour is calculated at the beginning of the year based on predictions of annual manufacturing overhead costs and predictions of the annual quantity of the cost-allocation base. Almost certainly, the actual amounts will differ from the predictions.

7. **Transaction.** Completion and transfer to finished goods of 12 individual jobs, $188,800.

   Analysis. The asset Finished Goods Control is increased and the asset Work-in-Process Control is decreased to signify the completion of jobs. The Work-in-Process records in the subsidiary ledger indicate that the costs of the 12 individual jobs completed in February 2007 equal $188,800.

   Journal Entry: Finished Goods Control   188,800
           Work-in-Process Control   188,800

   Post to General Ledger:

Work-in-Process Control				Finished Goods Control	
②	81,000	⑦	188,800	⑦	188,800
③	39,000				
⑥	80,000				
	11,200				

In transaction 7, the completed goods are moved out of the manufacturing area and into the finished goods area, stage (c) in the graphic. The $188,800 cost of completed goods is the "cost of goods manufactured." A *schedule* of cost of goods manufactured for a different company was presented in Exhibit 2-7 (p. 43).

The debit balance of $11,200 in the Work-in-Process Control account represents the total costs of all job cost records (in the subsidiary ledger) that have not been completed.

8. **Transaction.** Cost of Goods Sold, $180,000.

   Analysis. The $180,000 amount represents the cost of goods sold in sales transactions with customers during February 2007. The account Cost of Goods Sold is increased. The asset Finished Goods Control is decreased.

   Journal Entry: Cost of Goods Sold   180,000
           Finished Goods Control   180,000

   Post to General Ledger:

Finished Goods Control				Cost of Goods Sold	
⑦	188,800	⑧	180,000	⑧	180,000
	8,800				

The debit balance of $8,800 in the Finished Goods Control account represents the costs of all jobs that have been completed and are part of the finished goods records but that have not yet been sold to customers.

Accounting for Nonmanufacturing Costs

We have so far concentrated on job costing in the manufacturing function. Manufacturing companies such as Robinson also incur costs in other parts of the value chain—R&D, design, marketing, distribution, and customer service. Robinson Company, for example, incurs costs in the marketing and customer-service areas.

9. **Transaction.** Liabilities incurred for the following:

Marketing and Administration Department salaries	$35,000
Advertising costs	10,000
Customer-Service Department salaries	15,000

Analysis. As described in Chapter 2, for financial accounting these costs are non-inventoriable. They should be charged directly as period expenses for February 2007 to be matched against revenues. Unlike manufacturing costs, these costs are not added to work-in-process assets because they do not transform or change a physical product. Robinson would record the following entries.

Journal Entries:	Marketing, Advertising, and Admin. Expense	45,000	
	Customer Service Expense	15,000	
	Salaries Payable Control		50,000
	Accounts Payable Control		10,000

Post to General Ledger:

Marketing, Advertising, and Administration Expense		Salaries Payable Control	
⑨ 45,000			⑨ 50,000

Customer-Service Expense		Accounts Payable Control	
⑨ 15,000			⑨ 10,000

10. **Transaction.** Sales, all on accounts, are $270,000.

Analysis. The $270,000 represents amounts due from customers for sales made in February 2007.

Journal entry:	Accounts Receivable Control	270,000	
	Revenues		270,000

Post to General Ledger:

Accounts Receivable Control		Revenues	
⑩ 270,000			⑩ 270,000

At this point, please pause and review all 10 entries in the illustration. Be sure to trace each journal entry, step by step, to the general ledger accounts in the general ledger section in panel A of Exhibit 4-5 on page 124.

Nonmanufacturing Costs and Job Costing

Chapter 2 pointed out that companies use product costs for different purposes. The product costs reported as inventoriable costs to shareholders may differ from those reported to tax authorities. Both sets of costs may further differ from those reported to managers for guiding pricing and product-mix decisions. We emphasize this even though, as described previously, marketing and customer-service costs are expensed for financial accounting purposes. Companies often trace or allocate these costs to individual jobs for pricing, product mix, and cost management decisions.

To identify marketing and customer-service costs of individual jobs, Robinson can use the same basic approach to job costing described earlier in the chapter in the context of jobs. Robinson can then calculate a budgeted indirect-cost rate by dividing budgeted indirect marketing and customer-service costs by the budgeted quantity of the cost-allocation base, say, revenues. Robinson can use this rate to allocate indirect costs to jobs. For example, if this rate were $0.15 per dollar of revenue, Robinson would allocate $2,250 to the WPP 298 job (0.15 × $15,000, the revenue from the WPP 298 job). By assigning both manufacturing and nonmanufacturing costs to jobs, Robinson can compare all the resources demanded by different jobs against the revenues earned from them.

BUDGETED INDIRECT COSTS AND END-OF-PERIOD ADJUSTMENTS

Underallocated indirect costs (underapplied indirect costs, underabsorbed indirect costs). These occur when the allocated amount of indirect costs in an accounting period is less than the actual (incurred) amount in that period.

Overallocated indirect costs (overapplied indirect costs, overabsorbed indirect costs). These occur when the allocated amount of indirect costs in an accounting period is greater than the actual (incurred) amount in that period.

Budgeted indirect-cost rates have the advantage of being more timely than actual indirect-cost rates. With budgeted rates, indirect costs can be assigned to individual jobs on an ongoing basis rather than waiting until the end of the accounting period when actual costs are known. However, the disadvantage of budgeted rates is that they likely will be inaccurate, having been calculated up to 12 months before actual costs are incurred. We now consider adjustments made when the indirect costs allocated differ from the actual indirect costs incurred.

Underallocated indirect costs occur when the allocated amount of indirect costs in an accounting period is less than the actual (incurred) amount in that period. **Overallocated indirect costs** occur when the allocated amount of indirect costs in an accounting period exceeds the actual (incurred) amount in that period.

$$\begin{array}{c} \text{Under- or overallocated} \\ \text{indirect costs} \end{array} = \begin{array}{c} \text{Indirect costs} \\ \text{incurred} \end{array} - \begin{array}{c} \text{Indirect costs} \\ \text{allocated} \end{array}$$

Equivalent terms are **underapplied** (or **overapplied**) **indirect costs** and **underabsorbed** (or **overabsorbed**) **indirect costs**.

The Robinson Company has a single indirect-cost pool (Manufacturing Overhead) in its job-costing system. There are two indirect-cost accounts in its general ledger that pertain to manufacturing overhead:

◆ **Manufacturing Overhead Control,** which is the record of the *actual* costs in all the individual overhead categories (such as indirect materials, indirect manufacturing labour, power, and rent)

◆ **Manufacturing Overhead Allocated,** which is the record of the manufacturing overhead allocated to individual jobs based on the budgeted rate multiplied by actual machine-hours

Assume the following annual data for the Robinson Company:

Manufacturing Overhead Control		Manufacturing Overhead Allocated	
Bal. Dec. 31, 2007 1,215,000			Bal. Dec. 31, 2007 1,080,000

The $1,080,000 credit balance in Manufacturing Overhead Allocated results from multiplying the 27,000 actual direct manufacturing labour-hours worked on all the jobs in year 2007 by the budgeted rate of $40 per hour.

The $135,000 difference (a net debit) is an underallocated amount because actual manufacturing overhead costs are greater than the allocated amount. This difference arises from two reasons related to the calculation of the $40 budgeted hourly rate:

1. *Numerator reason (indirect costs).* Actual manufacturing overhead costs of $1,215,000 are lower than the budgeted amount of $1,280,000.

2. *Denominator reason (quantity of allocation base).* Actual direct manufacturing labour-hours of 27,000 are lower than the budgeted amount of 32,000 hours.

There are three main approaches to disposing of this $135,000 underallocation of manufacturing overhead caused by Robinson's overestimating indirect costs and the quantity of the cost-allocation base. These approaches are (1) the adjusted allocation rate, (2) the prorated, and (3) the immediate write-off to cost of goods sold.

Adjusted Allocation Rate Approach

The **adjusted allocation rate approach,** in effect, restates all entries in the general ledger by using actual cost rates rather than budgeted cost rates. First, the actual indirect-cost rate is computed at the end of each period. Then, every job to which indirect costs were allocated during the period has its amount recomputed using the actual indirect-cost rate (rather than the budgeted indirect-cost rate). Finally, end-of-period closing entries are made. The result is that every single job cost record—as well as the ending inventory and cost of goods sold accounts—accurately represents actual indirect costs incurred.

The widespread adoption of computerized accounting systems has greatly reduced the cost of using the adjusted allocation rate approach. Consider the Robinson Company example. The actual manufacturing overhead ($1,215,000) exceeds the manufacturing overhead allocated ($1,080,000) by 12.5% [($1,215,000 − $1,080,000) ÷ $1,080,000]. The actual 2007 manufacturing overhead rate is $45 per direct manufacturing labour-hour ($1,215,000 ÷ 27,000) rather than the budgeted $40 per direct manufacturing labour-hour. At year-end, Robinson could increase the year 2007 manufacturing overhead allocated to each job in that year by 12.5% using a single software directive. The directive would affect both the subsidiary ledger and the general ledger.

For example, consider the Western Pulp Machine Job WPP 298. Under normal costing, the manufacturing overhead allocated to the job is $3,520 (88 direct manufacturing labour-hours × the budgeted rate of $40 per hour). Increasing the manufacturing overhead allocated by 12.5% or $440 ($3,520 × 12.5%) means that the new manufacturing overhead allocated to Job WPP 298 equals $3,960 ($3,520 + $440). Recall that under actual costing, manufacturing overhead allocated is also $3,960 (88 manufacturing labour-hours × the actual rate of $45 per hour). Making this adjustment for each job on the subsidiary ledger ensures that all $1,215,000 of manufacturing overhead is allocated to jobs.

This approach yields the benefits of both the timeliness of convenience of normal costing and the accuracy of actual costing. Each individual product cost amount and the end-of-year account balances for inventories and cost of goods sold are at actual costs. After-the-fact analysis of actual individual product profitability provides managers with useful insights for future decisions about product pricing and about which products to emphasize. These decisions are improved by having the more accurate actual product-profitability numbers on prior jobs.

Proration Approach

Proration is the spreading of under- or overallocated overhead among ending inventories and cost of goods sold. Consider the Robinson Company, where manufacturing overhead is allocated based on machine-hours. Materials are not allocated any overhead costs. It is not until materials are put into work in process that machining of them commences. Only the ending work-in-process and finished goods inventories will have an allocated manufacturing overhead component. Hence, in our Robinson example, it is only these two ending inventory accounts (and Cost of Goods Sold) for which end-of-period proration is an issue. Assume the following actual results for Robinson Company in 2007:

Adjusted allocation rate approach. The adjusted allocation rate approach "corrects" all manufacturing overhead (MOH) entries in the general and subsidiary ledgers to what they would have been if accountants had had a crystal ball and perfectly forecasted actual MOH costs and the actual quantity of the allocation base used. The feasibility of implementing the adjusted allocation rate approach increases as technology decreases information processing costs.

Proration. The spreading of under-allocated or overallocated overhead over ending inventories and cost of goods sold.

BG–PBRAS Proration Based Revenue Accounting system www.bg-aerosoft.com/pbras.htm

	A	B	C
1			**Manufacturing Overhead**
2			**Allocated Component of**
3		**End-of-Year Balances**	**Year-End Balances**
4		**(before Proration)**	**(before Proration)**
5	Work in Process	$ 50,000	$ 16,200
6	Finished Goods	75,000	31,320
7	Cost of Goods Sold	2,375,000	1,032,480
8		$2,500,000	$1,080,000

How should Robinson prorate all the underallocated $135,000 of manufacturing overhead at the end of year 2007?

Robinson should prorate under- or overallocated amounts from each cost pool based on the total amount of manufacturing overhead allocated (before proration) from the cost pool to the ending balances of Work-in-Process Control, Finished Goods Control, and Cost of Goods Sold. In our Robinson Company example, the $135,000 underallocated overhead is prorated over the three pertinent accounts in proportion to their total amount of manufacturing overhead allocated (before proration) in column 2 in the following table, resulting in the ending balances (after proration) in column 5 at actual costs.

	A	B	C	D	E	F
1				Allocated		
2			Manufacturing	Manufacturing		
3			Overhead	Overhead	Proration of	
4		End-of-Year	Allocated	Included	$135,000	Account
5		Balances	Component of	in Each Account	of Underallocated	Balance
6		(before	Year-End Balances	Balance	Manufacturing	(after
7		Proration)	(before Proration)	Percent of Total	Overhead	Proration)
8		(1)	(2)	(3) = (2) ÷ $1,080,000	(4) = (3) × $135,000	(5) = (1) + (4)
9	Work in Process	$ 50,000	$ 16,200	1.5%	$ 2,025	$ 52,025
10	Finished Goods	75,000	31,320	2.9%	3,915	78,915
11	Cost of Goods Sold	2,375,000	1,032,480	95.6%	129,060	2,504,060
12		$2,500,000	$1,080,000	100.0%	$135,000	$2,635,000

Recall that the actual manufacturing overhead ($1,215,000) exceeds the manufacturing overhead allocated ($1,080,000) by 12.5%. The proration amounts in column 4 can also be derived by multiplying the balances in column 2 by 12.5%. For example, the $3,915 proration to Finished Goods is 12.5% × $31,320.

The journal entry to record this proration would be:

Work-in-Process Control	2,025	
Finished Goods Control	3,915	
Cost of Goods Sold	129,060	
Manufacturing Overhead Allocated	1,080,000	
Manufacturing Overhead Control		1,215,000

Note that if manufacturing overhead had been overallocated, the Work-in-Process, Finished Goods, and Cost of Goods Sold accounts would be decreased (credited) instead of increased (debited).

This journal entry restates the year 2007 ending balances for Work-in-Process, Finished Goods, and Cost of Goods Sold to what they would have been had actual cost rates rather than budgeted cost rates been used. The proration approach reports the same 2007 ending balances in the general ledger as does the adjusted allocation rate approach.

Some companies use the proration approach but base it on column 1 of the preceding table—that is, the ending balances in Work-in-Process, Finished Goods, and Cost of Goods Sold before proration. It gives the same results as the proration approach only if the proportions of direct costs of manufacturing based on column 2 are constant in the Work-in-Process, Finished Goods, and Cost of Goods Sold accounts. Why? Because, if this were the case, prorating based on total costs is the same as prorating based on allocated overhead costs. It is likely, however, that prorations based on column 1 will not be the same as the more accurate prorations based on column 2. This is true in our example. For instance, work in process is 2% ($50,000 ÷ $2,500,000) of the total of column 1 but 1.5% using the calculation method shown in column 3. If column 1 were used for proration, work in process would be allocated 2% of $135,000 = $2,700 instead of the $2,025 allocated to it using column 2. Similarly, finished goods would be allocated 3% ($75,000 ÷ $2,500,000) of $135,000 = $4,050, and cost of goods sold would be allocated 95% ($2,375,000 ÷ $2,500,000) of $135,000 = $128,250, instead of $3,915 and

$129,060 allocated to these accounts, respectively, using the calculation method shown in column 3. Proration based on ending balances is frequently justified as being a lower-cost way of approximating the more accurate results based on indirect costs allocated.

Write-off to Cost of Goods Sold Approach

In this case, the total under- or overallocated overhead is included in this year's Cost of Goods Sold. In our Robinson Company example, the journal entry would be

Cost of Goods Sold	135,000	
Manufacturing Overhead Allocated	1,080,000	
Manufacturing Overhead Control		1,215,000

Robinson's two Manufacturing Overhead accounts are closed out with all the difference between them now included in cost of goods sold. The Cost of Goods Sold account after write-off to cost of goods sold equals $2,510,000, the balance before proration of $2,375,000 plus the underallocated overhead amount of $135,000.

No matter which approach is used, the underallocated overhead is not carried in the overhead accounts beyond the end of the year. That is, the ending balances in Manufacturing Overhead Control and Manufacturing Overhead Allocated are closed to Work-in-Process Control, Finished Goods, or Cost of Goods Sold, and consequently become zero at the end of each year.

Choice among Approaches

In choosing among the approaches, managers should be guided by how the resultant information is to be used. If managers desire to develop the most accurate record of individual job costs for profitability analysis, the adjusted allocation rate approach is preferred. The proration approach does not make any adjustment to individual job cost records. If the purpose is confined to reporting the most accurate inventory and cost of goods sold figures, proration based on the indirect cost allocated component of ending balances should be used because it adjusts the balances to what they would have been under actual costing but does not adjust individual job cost records.

The write-off to Cost of Goods Sold is the simplest approach for dealing with under- or overallocated overhead. If the amount of underallocated (or overallocated) overhead is small—in comparison to total operating income or some other measure of materiality—the approach yields a good approximation to more accurate but more complex approaches. Modern companies are also becoming increasingly conscious of inventory control; thus, inventories are lower than they were in earlier years, and Cost of Goods Sold tends to be higher in relation to inventories of Work-in-Process and Finished Goods. Also, the inventory balances of job-costing companies are usually relatively small because goods are often made in response to specific sales orders. Consequently, as is true in our Robinson example, writing off underallocated or overallocated overhead instead of prorating it is unlikely to cause significant distortions in financial statements. For all these reasons, the cost-benefit test would favour the simplest method—immediate write-off to Cost of Goods Sold method—because the more costly attempts at accuracy represented by the other approaches do not appear to provide additional useful information.

MULTIPLE OVERHEAD COST POOLS

The Robinson Company illustration assumed that a single manufacturing overhead cost pool with direct manufacturing labour-hours as the cost-allocation base was appropriate for allocating indirect manufacturing costs to jobs. Robinson could have used multiple cost-allocation bases, say, direct manufacturing labour-hours and machine-hours, to allocate indirect costs to jobs. It would do so if Robinson's managers believed that the benefits of the information generated by adding more pools (more accurate costing and pricing of jobs and better ability to manage costs) exceeded the costs of implementing a more complex system. We discuss these issues in more detail in Chapter 5.

To implement a normal costing system with multiple overhead cost pools, Robinson would determine the budgeted total direct manufacturing labour-hours and the budgeted total machine-hours for the year 2007, and identify the associated budgeted indirect total costs for each cost pool. It would then calculate two indirect-cost rates, one based on direct manufacturing labour-hours and one based on machine-hours used by various jobs. The General Ledger would contain Overhead Control and Overhead Allocated amounts for each cost pool. End-of-period adjustments for under- or overallocated indirect costs would then need to be made separately for each cost pool.

VARIATION OF NORMAL COSTING: A SERVICE INDUSTRY EXAMPLE

OBJECTIVE 7

Apply variation of normal costing

As we discussed at the start of this chapter, job costing is very useful in service industries such as accounting and consulting firms, advertising agencies, auto repair shops, and hospitals. In an accounting firm, each audit is a job. The costs of the audit are accumulated on a job cost record, much like the document used by Robinson Company, using the seven-step approach described earlier in the chapter. Based on labour time records, direct labour costs of audit partners, audit managers, and audit staff are traced to individual jobs. Other direct costs such as travel, out-of-town meals and lodging, telephone, fax, and copying are also traced to jobs. The costs of secretarial support, head office staff, rent, and amortization of furniture and equipment are indirect costs because these costs cannot be identified with jobs in an economically feasible way. Indirect costs are allocated to jobs, for example, using a cost-allocation base such as professional labour-hours.

In some service, merchandising, and manufacturing organizations, a variation of normal costing is helpful because actual direct-labour costs (the largest component of total cost) are difficult to trace to jobs as they are completed. For example, in our audit illustration, the actual direct-labour costs may include bonuses that are known only at the end of the year (a numerator reason). Also, the hours worked each period might vary significantly, depending on the number of working days each month and the demand from clients (a denominator reason). In these situations, to obtain timely information as a job is completed rather than wait until the end of the year, an organization may choose to use budgeted rates for some direct costs in addition to using budgeted rates for indirect costs. All budgeted rates used are calculated at the start of the accounting period. Recall that normal costing uses actual cost rates for all direct costs, and budgeted cost rates only for indirect costs.

The mechanics of using budgeted rates for direct costs are similar to the methods employed when using budgeted rates for indirect costs in normal costing. We illustrate using Lindsay and Associates, a public accounting firm. At the start of the year 2007, Lindsay budgets total direct labour costs of $14,400,000, total indirect costs of $12,960,000, and total direct (professional) labour-hours of 288,000 for the year. In this case,

$$\begin{aligned} \text{Budgeted direct} \\ \text{labour cost rate} \end{aligned} = \frac{\text{Budgeted total direct labour costs}}{\text{Budgeted total direct labour-hours}}$$

$$= \frac{\$14,400,000}{288,000 \text{ hours}} \qquad = \$50 \text{ per direct labour-hour}$$

Assuming only one indirect-cost pool and total direct labour-hours as the cost allocation base,

$$\begin{aligned} \text{Budgeted indirect-} \\ \text{cost rate} \end{aligned} = \frac{\text{Budgeted total costs in indirect-cost pool}}{\text{Budgeted total quantity of cost-allocation base}}$$

$$= \frac{\$12,960,000}{288,000 \text{ hours}} \qquad = \$45 \text{ per direct labour-hour}$$

Suppose an audit of Tracy Transport, a client of Lindsay, completed in March 2007, uses 800 direct labour-hours. Lindsay calculates the direct costs of the Tracy Transport audit by multiplying the budgeted direct-cost rate by the actual quantity of the direct-cost input. It allocates indirect costs to the Tracy Transport audit by multiplying the budgeted indirect-cost rate by the actual quantity of the cost-allocation base. Assuming no other direct costs for travel, outsourcing, computer work, and so on, the cost of the Tracy Transport audit is

Direct labour costs, $50 × 800	$40,000
Indirect costs allocated, $45 × 800	36,000
Total	$76,000

At the end of the year, the direct costs traced to jobs using budgeted rates will generally not equal the actual direct costs because the actual and budgeted rates are developed at different points in time using different information. End-of-period adjustments for under- or overallocated direct costs would need to be made in the same way that adjustments were made for under- or overallocated indirect costs.

The Lindsay and Associates example illustrates that all costing systems do not map neatly onto either the actual costing or normal costing system described earlier in the chapter. As another example, engineering consulting firms often have some actual direct costs (cost of making blueprints or fees paid to outside experts), other direct costs traced to jobs using a budgeted rate (professional labour costs), and indirect costs allocated to jobs using a budgeted rate (engineering and office support costs).

MANAGEMENT CONTROL AND TECHNOLOGY

Managers use product-costing information to improve the efficiency of their operations by managing and controlling the materials, labour, and overhead costs used to complete jobs. Modern technology provides the manager with quick and accurate product-cost information that facilitates the management and control of jobs.

Data Interchange Standards Association
www.disa.org

We have already introduced the technology of EDI, which simply inputs direct materials and costs, and reports variances. This electronic support assists managers who are responsible for controlling job costs. Other systems are also being used to manage resource planning for the entire enterprise.

Enterprise resource planning (ERP) systems are increasingly being used to integrate an organization's systems to maximize efficiency and effectiveness. An ERP provides managers with the information to make decisions regardless of their function within the company. For example, the sales department can use an ERP system to monitor customer requests and respond quickly to them by being able to verify that sufficient inventory exists and that the shipping department can meet the delivery time. The purchasing department manager can use the ERP system to monitor inventory levels with customer orders and keep track of the logistical requirements to ensure that everything arrives as needed. A production supervisor can use the ERP system to reassign the production schedule to meet changes in customer orders while ensuring that costs remain within budget.

Customer relationship management (CRM) systems provide information to maximize the value delivered to customers. The systems focus on all the processes a company uses to market, sell, and supply its products and services to customers. For example, a CRM system can enhance the level of communication between a company and its customers. The system can also automate the processes to ensure that goods are delivered on time and that any follow-up concerns are monitored and addressed. In addition, a CRM system will gather information essential to the strategic position of a company and its products.

Technology, the Internet, and the extensive use of Web pages have provided enhanced capability for systems such as EDI, ERP, and CRM in today's world. These systems are now highly integrated with the management accounting systems in organizations.

Re-examine the Exhibit 4-5 illustration of a job-costing system on page 124. Then try to solve the following problem, which requires consideration of many of this chapter's important points in a service-sector company.

PROBLEM

You are asked to bring the following incomplete accounts of Endeavour Printing, Inc., up to date through January 31, 2008. Consider the data that appear in the T-accounts as well as the following information in items (a) through (i).

Endeavour's job-costing system, which uses normal costing, has two direct-cost categories (direct materials and direct manufacturing labour) and one indirect-cost pool (manufacturing overhead, which is allocated using direct manufacturing labour costs).

Materials Control		Wages Payable Control	
12-31-2007 Bal. 15,000			1-31-2008 Bal. 3,000

Work-in-Process Control		Manufacturing Overhead Control	
		1-31-2008 Bal. 57,000	

		Manufacturing Overhead Allocated	

Finished Goods Control		Cost of Goods Sold	
12-31-2007 Bal. 20,000			

ADDITIONAL INFORMATION

a. Manufacturing overhead is allocated using a budgeted rate set every December. Management forecasts next year's manufacturing overhead and next year's direct manufacturing labour costs. The budget for 2008 is $400,000 of direct manufacturing labour and $600,000 of manufacturing overhead.

b. The only job unfinished on January 31, 2008, is No. 419, on which direct manufacturing labour costs are $2,000 (125 direct manufacturing labour-hours) and direct materials costs are $8,000.

c. Total materials placed into production during January are $90,000.

d. Cost of goods completed during January is $180,000.

e. Materials inventory as of January 31, 2008, is $20,000.

f. Finished goods inventory as of January 31, 2008, is $15,000.

g. All plant workers earn the same wage rate. Direct manufacturing labour-hours used for January total 2,500. Other labour and supervision labour total $10,000.

h. The gross plant payroll paid in January equals $52,000. Ignore withholdings.

i. All "actual" Manufacturing Department overhead incurred during January has already been posted.

REQUIRED

Calculate the following:

1. Materials purchased during January
2. Cost of Goods Sold during January
3. Direct Manufacturing Labour Costs incurred during January
4. Manufacturing Overhead Allocated during January
5. Balance of Wages Payable Control, December 31, 2007
6. Balance of Work-in-Process Control, January 31, 2008
7. Balance of Work-in-Process Control, December 31, 2007
8. Manufacturing Overhead under- or overallocated for January 2008

SOLUTION

Amounts from the T-accounts are labelled "(T)".

1. From Materials Control T-account, Materials purchased: $90,000 (c) + $20,000 (e) − $15,000 (T) = $95,000

2. From Finished Goods Control T-account, Cost of Goods Sold: $20,000 (T) + $180,000 (d) − $15,000 (f) = $185,000

3. Direct manufacturing wage rate: $2,000 (b) ÷ 125 direct manufacturing labour-hours (b) = $16 per direct manufacturing labour-hour.
   Direct manufacturing labour costs: 2,500 direct manufacturing labour-hours (g) × $16 = $40,000

4. Manufacturing overhead rate: $600,000 (a) ÷ $400,000 (a) = 150%
   Manufacturing Overhead Allocated: 150% of $40,000 (see 3) = $60,000

5. From Wages Payable Control T-account, Wages Payable Control, December 31, 2007: $52,000 (h) + $3,000 (T) − $40,000 (see 3) − $10,000 (g) = $5,000

6. Work-in-Process Control, January 31, 2008: $8,000 (b) + $2,000 (b) + 150% of $2,000 (b) = $13,000 (This answer is used in item 7.)

7. From Work-in-Process Control T-account, Work-in-Process Control, December 31, 2007: $180,000 (d) + $13,000 (see 6) − $90,000 (c) − $40,000 (see 3) − $60,000 (see 4) = $3,000

8. Manufacturing overhead overallocated: $60,000 (see 4) − $57,000 (T) = $3,000

Entries in T-accounts are lettered in accordance with the preceding additional information and are numbered in accordance with the requirements above.

Materials Control

December 31, 2007 Bal.	(given)	15,000			
	(1)	95,000*	(c)		90,000
January 31, 2008 Bal.	(e)	20,000			

Work-in-Process Control

December 31, 2007 Bal.	(7)	3,000	(d)		180,000
Direct materials	(c)	90,000			
Direct manufacturing labour	(b) (g) (3)	40,000			
Manufacturing overhead allocated	(g) (a) (4)	60,000			
January 31, 2008	Bal. (b) (6)	13,000			

Finished Goods Control

December 31, 2007 Bal.	(given)	20,000	(2)		185,000
	(d)	180,000			
January 31, 2008 Bal.	(f)	15,000			

Wages Payable Control

	(h)	52,000	December 31, 2007	(5)	5,000
				(g), (3)	40,000
				(g)	10,000
			January 31, 2008	(given)	3,000

Manufacturing Overhead Control

Total January charges (given) 57,000		

Manufacturing Overhead Allocated

		(g) (a) (4)	60,000

Cost of Goods Sold

(f) (2)	185,000	

*Can be computed only after all other postings in the account have been found.

The following decision guidelines use a question-and-answer format to summarize the chapter's main points. Each decision presents a key question. The guideline is the answer to that question.

DECISIONS	GUIDELINES
1. What are the building-block concepts of costing systems?	The building-block concepts of a costing system are cost object, direct costs of a cost object, indirect costs of a cost object, cost pool, and cost-allocation base. Costing-system overview diagrams represent these concepts in a systematic way. Costing systems aim to report cost numbers that reflect the way chosen cost objects (such as products or services) use the resources of an organization.
2. How do you distinguish job costing from process costing?	Job-costing systems assign costs to distinct units of a product or service. Process-costing systems assign costs to masses of identical or similar units and compute unit costs on an average basis. These two costing systems represent opposite ends of a continuum. The costing systems of many companies combine some elements of both job costing and process costing.
3. How do you implement a job-costing system?	A general approach to job costing requires identifying (a) the job, (b) the direct-cost categories, (c) the cost-allocation bases, (d) the indirect-cost categories, (e) the cost-allocation rates, (f) the allocated indirect costs of a job, and (g) the total direct and indirect costs of a job.
4. How do you distinguish actual costing from normal costing?	Actual costing and normal costing differ in the way each uses actual or budgeted indirect-cost rates:

	Actual Costing	**Normal Costing**
Direct-cost rates	Actual rates	Actual rates
Indirect-cost rates	Actual rates	Budgeted rates

	Both methods use actual quantities of inputs for tracing direct costs and actual quantities of the allocation bases for allocating indirect costs.
5. What are the stages for recording transactions in a job-costing system?	The transactions in a job-costing system in manufacturing track (a) the acquisition of materials and other manufacturing inputs; (b) their conversion into Work-in-Process; (c) their eventual conversion into finished goods; and (d) the sale of finished goods. Each of the (a) to (d) stages in the manufacture/sale cycle are represented by journal entries in the costing system.
6. How should you account for underallocated or overallocated manufacturing overhead costs?	The two theoretically correct approaches to disposing of underallocated or overallocated manufacturing overhead costs are to adjust the allocation rate and to prorate based on the total amount of the allocated manufacturing overhead cost in the ending balances of Work-in-Process Control, Finished Goods Control, and Cost of Goods Sold. Many companies simply write off amounts of underallocated or overallocated manufacturing overhead to Cost of Goods Sold on the basis of practicality.
7. What variations from normal costing can be used?	In some variations from normal costing, organizations use budgeted rates to assign direct costs, as well as indirect costs, to jobs.

TERMS TO LEARN

This chapter contains definitions of the following important terms:

actual costing (p. 114)
adjusted allocation rate approach (p. 131)
cost-allocation base (p. 113)
cost application base (p. 113)
cost pool (p. 112)
job cost record (p. 118)
job cost sheet (p. 118)
job-costing system (p. 113)
labour time record (p. 118)
manufacturing overhead allocated (p. 127)
materials requisition record (p. 118)

normal costing (p. 122)
overabsorbed indirect costs (p. 130)
overallocated indirect costs (p. 130)
overapplied indirect costs (p. 130)
process-costing system (p. 113)
proration (p. 131)
responsibility centre (p. 117)
source documents (p. 118)
underabsorbed indirect costs (p. 130)
underallocated indirect costs (p. 130)
underapplied indirect costs (p. 130)

QUESTIONS

4-1 Define *cost pool, cost tracing, cost allocation,* and *cost-allocation base.*

4-2 How does a job-costing system differ from a process-costing system?

4-3 Why might an advertising agency use job costing for an advertising campaign for Pepsi while a bank uses process costing for the cost of chequing account withdrawals?

4-4 Describe the seven steps in job costing.

4-5 What are the two major cost objects that managers focus on?

4-6 Describe three major source documents used in job-costing systems.

4-7 What is the main concern about source documents of job cost records?

4-8 Give two reasons why most organizations use a six-month or annual period rather than a weekly or monthly period to compute budgeted indirect-cost rates.

4-9 Distinguish between actual costing and normal costing.

4-10 Describe two ways in which an accounting firm may use job cost information.

4-11 Comment on the following statement: "In a normal costing system, the amounts in Manufacturing Overhead Control account will always equal the amounts in Manufacturing Overhead Allocated account."

4-12 Describe three different debit entries in the Work-in-Process Control general ledger T-account.

4-13 Describe three alternative ways to dispose of under- or overallocated indirect costs.

4-14 When might a company use budgeted costs rather than actual costs to compute direct labour rates?

4-15 Describe briefly why modern technology such as electronic data interchange (EDI) is helpful to managers.

EXERCISES

4-16 Actual costing, normal costing, manufacturing overhead. Destin Products uses a job-costing system with two direct-cost categories (direct materials and direct manufacturing labour) and one manufacturing overhead cost poll. Destin allocates manufacturing overhead costs using direct manufacturing labour costs. Destin provides the following information:

	Budget for Year 2007	Actuals for Year 2007
Direct manufacturing labour costs	$1,200,000	$1,176,000
Direct manufacturing overhead costs	$2,100,000	$2,234,400
Direct materials costs	$1,800,000	$1,740,000

REQUIRED

1. Compute the actual and budgeted manufacturing overhead rates for 2007.

2. During March, the cost record for Job 626 contained the following:

Direct materials used	$48,000
Direct manufacturing labour costs	$36,000

Compute the cost of Job 626 using (a) an actual-costing system and (b) a normal-costing system.

3. At the end of 2007, compute the under- or overallocated manufacturing overhead under Destin's normal costing system. Why is there no under- or overallocated overhead under Destin's actual-costing system?

4. Comment briefly on the advantages and disadvantages of actual-costing and normal-costing systems.

4-17 Job costing, normal and actual costing. Anderson Construction assembles residential homes. It uses a job-costing system with two direct-cost categories (direct materials and direct labour) and one indirect-cost pool (assembly support). Direct labour-hours is the allocation base for assembly support costs. In December 2007, Anderson budgets 2007 assembly support costs to be $9,600,000 and 2007 direct labour-hours to be 160,000.

At the end of 2007, Anderson is comparing the costs of several jobs that were started and completed in 2007.

Construction Period	Laguna Model February–June 2007	Mission Model May–October 2007
Direct materials	$127,740	$153,125
Direct labour	$43,531	$49,692
Direct labour-hours	900	1,010

Direct materials and direct labour are paid for on a contract basis. The costs of each are known when direct materials are used or direct labour-hours are worked. The 2007 actual assembly support costs were $8,265,000, while the actual direct labour-hours were 164,000.

REQUIRED

1. Compute the (a) budgeted and (b) actual indirect cost rate. Why do they differ?
2. What is the job cost of the Laguna Model and the Mission Model using (a) normal costing and (b) actual costing?
3. Why might Anderson Construction prefer normal costing over actual costing?

4-18 Job costing, accounting for manufacturing overhead, budgeted rates. The Lynn Company uses a job-costing system at its Mississauga plant. The plant has a Machining Department and an Assembly Department. Its job-costing system has two direct-cost categories (direct materials and direct manufacturing labour) and two manufacturing overhead cost pools (the Machining Department, allocated using actual machine-hours, and the Assembly Department, allocated using actual direct manufacturing labour cost). The 2007 budget for the plant is as follows:

	Machining Department	Assembly Department
Manufacturing overhead	$2,160,000	$4,320,000
Direct manufacturing labour cost	$1,680,000	$2,400,000
Direct manufacturing labour-hours	120,000	240,000
Machine-hours	60,000	240,000

The company uses a budgeted overhead rate for allocating overhead to production orders on a machine-hour basis in Machining and on a direct manufacturing labour cost basis in Assembly.

REQUIRED

1. Present an overview diagram of Lynn's job-costing system. Compute the budgeted manufacturing overhead rate for each department.
2. During February, the cost record for Job 494 contained the following:

	Machining Department	Assembly Department
Direct materials used	$54,000	$84,000
Direct manufacturing labour cost	$16,800	$18,000
Direct manufacturing labour-hours	1,200	1,800
Machine-hours	2,400	1,200

Compute the total manufacturing overhead costs of Job 494.

3. At the end of 2007, the actual manufacturing overhead costs were $2,520,000 in Machining and $4,440,000 in Assembly. Assume that 66,000 actual machine-hours were used in Machining and that actual direct manufacturing labour costs in Assembly were $2,640,000. Compute the over- or underallocated manufacturing overhead for each department.

4-19 Job costing, consulting firm. Taylor & Partners, a consulting firm, has the following condensed budget for 2008:

Revenues		$24,000,000
Total costs:		
Direct costs: Professional labour	$ 6,000,000	
Indirect costs: Client support	15,600,000	21,600,000
Operating income		$ 2,400,000

Taylor has a single direct-cost category (professional labour) and a single indirect-cost pool (client support). Indirect costs are allocated to jobs based on professional labour costs.

REQUIRED

1. Present an overview diagram of the job-costing system. Compute the 2008 budgeted indirect-cost rate for Taylor & Partners.
2. The markup rate for pricing jobs is intended to produce a 10% operating-income-to-revenue margin. Compute the markup rate as a percentage of professional labour costs.
3. Taylor is bidding on a consulting job for Red Rooster, a fast-food chain specializing in poultry meats. The budgeted breakdown of professional labour on the job is as follows:

Professional Labour Category	Budgeted Rate per Hour	Budgeted Hours
Director	$240	3
Partner	120	16
Manager	60	40
Assistant	36	160

Compute the budgeted cost of the Red Rooster job. How much will Taylor bid for the job if it is to earn its target operating-income-to-revenue margin of 10%?

4-20 Computing indirect cost rates, job costing. Mike Rotundo, the president of Tax Assist, is examining alternative ways to compute indirect cost rates. He collects the following information from the budget for 2008:

◆ Budgeted variable indirect costs: $12 per hour of professional labour time
◆ Budgeted fixed indirect costs: $60,000 per quarter

The budgeted billable professional labour-hours per quarter are:

January–March	24,000 hours
April–June	12,000 hours
July–September	4,800 hours
October–December	7,200 hours

Rotundo pays all tax professionals employed by Tax Assist on an hourly basis ($36 per hour, including all fringe benefits).

Tax Assist's job-costing system has a single direct-cost category (professional labour at $36 per hour) and a single indirect-cost pool (office support that is allocated using professional labour-hours).

Tax Assist charges clients $78 per professional labour-hour.

REQUIRED

1. Compute budgeted indirect cost rates per professional labour-hour using
   a. Quarterly budgeted billable hours as the denominator
   b. Annual budgeted billable hours as the denominator
2. Compute the operating income for the following four customers using
   a. Quarterly based indirect-cost rates
   b. An annual indirect-cost rate
      ◆ Stan Hansen: 10 hours in February
      ◆ Lelani Kai: 6 hours in March and 4 hours in April
      ◆ Ken Patera: 4 hours in June and 6 hours in August
      ◆ Evelyn Stevens: 5 hours in January, 2 hours in September, and 3 hours in November
3. Comment on your results in requirement 2.

4-21 Job costing, journal entries. The University of Toronto Press is wholly owned by the university. It performs the bulk of its work for other university departments, which pay as though the Press were an outside business enterprise. The Press also publishes and maintains a stock of books for general sale. A job-costing system is used to cost each job. There are two direct-cost categories (direct materials and direct manufacturing labour) and one indirect-cost pool (manufacturing overhead, allocated based on direct labour costs).

The following data (in thousands) pertain to 2007:

Direct materials and supplies purchased on account	$ 960
Direct materials used	852
Indirect materials issued to various production departments	120
Direct manufacturing labour	1,560
Indirect manufacturing labour incurred by various departments	1,080
Amortization on building and manufacturing equipment	480
Miscellaneous manufacturing overhead* incurred by various departments (ordinarily would be detailed as repairs, photocopying, utilities, etc.)	660
Manufacturing overhead allocated at 160% of direct manufacturing labour costs	?
Cost of goods manufactured	4,944
Revenues	9,600
Cost of goods sold	4,824
Inventories, December 31, 2006:	
Materials control	120
Work-in-process control	72
Finished goods control	600

*The term *manufacturing overhead* is not used uniformly. Other terms that are often encountered in printing companies include *job overhead* and *shop overhead*.

REQUIRED

1. Present an overview diagram of the job-costing system at the University of Toronto Press.
2. Prepare general journal entries to summarize 2007 transactions. As your final entry, dispose of the year-end over- or underallocated manufacturing overhead as a direct write-off to Cost of Goods Sold. Number your entries. Explanations for each entry may be omitted.
3. Show posted T-accounts for all inventories, Cost of Goods Sold, Manufacturing Overhead Control, and Manufacturing Overhead Allocated.

4-22 Job costing, journal entries, and source documents (continuation of 4-21). For each journal entry in your answer to Exercise 4-21, (a) indicate the source document that would most likely authorize the entry and (b) give a description of the entry in the subsidiary ledgers, if any entry needs to be made there.

4-23 Job costing, journal entries. Donnell Transport assembles prestige mobile homes. Its job-costing system has two direct-cost categories (direct materials and direct manufacturing labour) and one indirect-cost pool (manufacturing overhead allocated at a budgeted $36 per machine-hour in 2007). The following data (in millions) pertain to operations for the year 2007:

Materials control (beginning balance), December 31, 2006	$14.40
Work-in-process control (beginning balance), December 31, 2006	2.40
Finished goods control (beginning balance), December 31, 2006	7.20
Materials and supplies purchased on account	180
Direct materials used	174
Indirect materials (supplies) issued to various production departments	12
Direct manufacturing labour	108
Indirect manufacturing labour incurred by various departments	36
Amortization on plant and manufacturing equipment	23
Miscellaneous manufacturing overhead incurred (credit Various Liabilities; ordinarily would be detailed as repairs, utilities, etc.)	11
Manufacturing overhead allocated, 2,520,000 actual machine-hours	?
Cost of goods manufactured	353
Revenues	480
Cost of goods sold	350

REQUIRED

1. Present an overview diagram of Donnell Transport's job-costing system.
2. Prepare general journal entries. Number your entries. Post to T-accounts. What is the ending balance of Work-in-Process Control?
3. Show the journal entry for disposing of over- or underallocated manufacturing overhead directly as a year-end write-off to Cost of Goods Sold. Post the entry to T-accounts.

4-24 Accounting for manufacturing overhead. Consider the following selected cost data for the Hamilton Forging Company for 2007.

Budgeted manufacturing overhead	$8,400,000
Budgeted machine-hours	200,000
Actual manufacturing overhead ending balance	$8,160,000
Actual machine-hours	195,000

Hamilton's job-costing system has a single manufacturing overhead cost pool (allocated using a budgeted rate based on actual machine-hours). Any amount of under- or overallocation is immediately written off to cost of goods sold.

REQUIRED
1. Compute the budgeted manufacturing overhead rate.
2. Journalize the allocation of manufacturing overhead.
3. Compute the amount of under- or overallocation of manufacturing overhead. Is the amount significant? Journalize the disposition of this amount based on the ending balances in the relevant accounts.

4-25 Disposition of overhead under/overallocated. (Z. Iqbal, adapted) The Zaf Radiator Company uses a single manufacturing overhead cost pool in its job-costing system. It uses a normal-costing system with actual machine-hours as the allocation base. The following data are for 2007:

Budgeted manufacturing overhead	$5,760,000
Overhead allocation base	Machine-hours
Budgeted machine-hours	80,000
Manufacturing overhead incurred	$5,880,000
Actual machine-hours	75,000

Machine-hours data and the ending balances (before proration of underallocated or overallocated overhead) are as follows:

	Actual Machine-Hours	2007 End-of-Year Balance
Cost of Goods Sold	60,000	$9,600,000
Finished Goods	11,000	1,500,000
Work in Process	4,000	900,000

REQUIRED
1. Compute the budgeted manufacturing overhead rate for 2007.
2. Compute the under- or overallocated manufacturing overhead of Zaf Radiator in 2007. Dispose of this under- or overallocated amount using
   a. Immediate write-off to Cost of Goods Sold
   b. Proration based on ending balances (before proration) in Work-in-Process, Finished Goods, and Cost of Goods Sold
   c. Proration based on the allocated overhead amount (before proration) in the ending balances of Work in Process, Finished Goods, and Cost of Goods Sold
3. Which disposition method do you prefer in requirement 3? Explain.

4-26 Job order costing, process costing. In each of the following situations, determine whether job costing or process costing would be more appropriate.

a.	A CA firm	l.	A landscaping company
b.	An oil refinery	m.	A cola-drink-concentrate producer
c.	A custom furniture manufacturer	n.	A movie studio
d.	A tire manufacturer	o.	A law firm
e.	A textbook publisher	p.	A commercial aircraft manufacturer
f.	A pharmaceutical company	q.	A management consulting firm
g.	An advertising agency	r.	A breakfast-cereal company
h.	An apparel manufacturing factory	s.	A catering service
i.	A flour mill	t.	A paper mill
j.	A paint manufacturer	u.	An auto repair garage
k.	A medical care facility		

4-27 Budgeted manufacturing overhead rate, allocated manufacturing overhead. Waheed Company uses a normal costing system. It allocates manufacturing overhead costs using a budgeted rate per machine-hour and actual machine-hours. The following data are available for 2007:

Budgeted manufacturing overhead costs	$3,420,000
Budgeted machine-hours	190,000
Actual manufacturing overhead costs	3,492,000
Actual machine-hours	195,000

REQUIRED
1. Calculate the budgeted manufacturing overhead rate.
2. Compute the manufacturing overhead allocated during 2007.
3. Calculate the amount of underallocated or overallocated manufacturing overhead.

4-28 Job costing, unit cost, ending work in process. Raymond Company worked on only two jobs during May. Information on the jobs is given below:

	Job M1	Job M2
Direct materials	$90,000	$60,000
Direct labour	324,000	252,000
Direct labour-hours	6,000	5,000

Manufacturing overhead costs are allocated at the budgeted rate of $36 per direct-labour hour. Job M1 was completed in May.

REQUIRED
1. Compute the total cost of Job M1.
2. Calculate per unit cost for Job M1 assuming it has 15,000 units.
3. Make this journal entry transferring Job M1 to Finished Goods.
4. Determine the ending balance in the Work-in-Process account.

4-29 Job costing; actual, normal, and variation of normal costing. Chirac & Partners is an Ontario-based public accounting partnership specializing in audit services. Its job-costing system has a single direct-cost category (professional labour) and a single indirect-cost pool (audit support, which contains all the costs in the Audit Support Department). Audit support costs are allocated to individual jobs using actual professional labour-hours. Chirac & Partners employs ten professionals who are involved in their auditing services.

Budgeted and actual amounts for 2007 are as follows:

Budget for 2007	
Professional labour compensation	$1,152,000
Audit support department costs	$ 864,000
Professional labour-hours billed to clients	16,000 hours
Actual results for 2007	
Audit support department costs	$ 892,800
Professional labour-hours billed to clients	15,500 hours
Actual professional labour-cost rate is $69.60 per hour.	

REQUIRED
1. Identify the direct-cost rate per professional labour-hour and the indirect-cost rate per professional labour-hour for 2007 under (a) actual costing, (b) normal costing, and (c) variation of normal costing that uses budgeted rates for direct costs.
2. The audit of the Toronto Blue Jays done in 2007 was budgeted to take 110 hours of professional labour time. The actual professional labour time on the audit was 120 hours. Compute the 2007 job cost using (a) actual costing, (b) normal costing, and (c) variation of normal costing that uses budgeted rates for direct costs. Explain any differences.

Excel Application For students who wish to practise their spreadsheet skills, the following is a step-by-step approach to creating an Excel spreadsheet to work this problem.

Step-by Step
1. At the top of a new spreadsheet, create an "Original Data" section for the data provided by Chirac & Partners.

(Program your spreadsheet to perform all necessary calculations. Do not "hard-code" any amounts, such as direct and indirect cost rates, requiring addition, subtraction, multiplication, or division operations.)

2. Skip two rows. Create a "Cost Rates" section. Set up rows for direct-cost rate and indirect-cost rate. Set up columns "Actual costing," "Normal costing," and "Variation of normal costing." Use data in the "Original Data" section to compute the direct and indirect cost rates under actual costing, normal costing, and variation of normal costing that uses budgeted rates for direct costs.

3. Skip two rows and create a separate "Job Cost for Toronto Blue Jays Audit" section, with rows for direct costs, indirect costs, and total job costs, and columns for "Actual Costing," "Normal Costing," and "Variation of Normal Costing." Use the direct and indirect cost rates in your "Cost Rates" section to calculate direct costs, indirect costs, and total job cost for the Toronto Blue Jays audit under actual costing, normal costing, and variation of normal costing that uses budgeted rates for direct costs.

4. *Verify the accuracy of your spreadsheet.* Go to your "Original Data" section and change the budgeted professional labour-hours billed from 16,000 to 17,000. If your spreadsheet is programmed correctly, the indirect cost rate under normal costing should change to $50.82, and total job cost for the Toronto Blue Jays audit under normal costing should change to $14,451.

4-30 **Job costing; actual, normal, and variation of normal costing.** Vista Group provides architectural services for residential and business clients. It employs 25 professionals. Its job-costing system has a single direct-cost category (professional labour) and a single indirect-cost pool (client support, which contains all the costs in the Client Support Department). Client support costs are allocated to individual jobs using actual professional labour-hours.

Budgeted and actual amounts for 2007 are as follows:

Budget for 2007

Professional labour compensation	$4,800,000
Client Support Department costs	$3,120,000
Professional labour-hours billed to clients	40,000 hours

Actual Results for 2007

Client Support Department costs	$2,923,200
Professional labour-hours billed to clients	42,000 hours

Actual professional labour-cost rate is $132 per hour.

REQUIRED

1. Identify the direct-cost rate per professional labour-hour and the indirect-cost rate per professional labour-hour for 2007 under (a) actual costing, (b) normal costing, and (c) variation normal costing that uses budgeted rates for direct costs.

2. In 2007, the Vista Group designed a new retirement village in Victoria, British Columbia, for Carefree Years, Inc. Vista budgeted to spend 1,500 professional labour-hours on the project. Actual professional labour-hours spent were 1,720. Compute the job cost of the Carefree Years project using (a) actual costing, (b) normal costing, and (c) variation of normal costing that uses budgeted rates for direct costs. Explain any differences.

PROBLEMS

4-31 **Overview of general-ledger relationships.** The Blakely Company is a small machine shop that uses highly skilled labour and a job-costing system (using normal costing). The total debits and credits in certain accounts just before year-end are as follows:

	December 30, 2007	
	Total Debits	**Total Credits**
Materials Control	$120,000	$ 84,000
Work-in-Process Control	384,000	366,000
Manufacturing Department Overhead Control	102,000	—
Finished Goods Control	390,000	360,000
Cost of Goods Sold	360,000	—
Manufacturing Overhead Allocated	—	108,000

All materials purchased are for direct materials. Note that "total debits" in the inventory accounts would include beginning inventory balances, if any.

The preceding accounts *do not* include the following:

a. The manufacturing labour costs recapitulation for the December 31 working day: direct manufacturing labour, $6,000, and indirect manufacturing labour, $1,200.

b. Miscellaneous manufacturing overhead incurred on December 30 and December 31: $1,200.

ADDITIONAL INFORMATION

◆ Manufacturing overhead has been allocated as a percentage of direct manufacturing labour costs through December 30.

◆ Direct materials purchased during 2007 were $102,000.

◆ There were no returns to suppliers.

◆ Direct manufacturing labour costs during 2007 totalled $180,000, not including the December 31 working day described previously.

REQUIRED

1. Compute the inventories (December 31, 2007) of materials control, work-in-process control, and finished goods control. Show T-accounts.

2. Prepare all adjusting and closing journal entries for the preceding accounts. Assume that all under- or overallocated manufacturing overhead is closed directly to Cost of Goods Sold.

4-32 Job costing, law firm. Keating & Partners is a law firm specializing in labour relations and employee-related work. It employs 25 professionals (5 partners and 20 managers) who work directly with its clients. The average budgeted total compensation per professional for 2007 is $124,800. Each professional is budgeted to have 1,600 billable hours to clients in 2007. Keating is a highly respected firm, and all professionals work for clients to their maximum 1,600 billable hours available. All professional labour costs are included in a single direct-cost category and are traced to jobs on a per-hour basis.

All costs of Keating & Partners other than professional labour costs are included in a single indirect-cost pool (legal support) and are allocated to jobs using professional labour-hours as the allocation base. The budgeted level of indirect costs in 2007 is $2.64 million.

REQUIRED

1. Present an overview diagram of Keating's job-costing system.

2. Compute the 2007 budgeted professional labour-hour direct-cost rate.

3. Compute the 2007 budgeted indirect-cost rate per hour of professional labour.

4. Keating & Partners is considering bidding on two jobs:

    a. Litigation work for Richardson, Inc., that requires 100 budgeted hours of professional labour

    b. Labour contract work for Punch, Inc., that requires 150 budgeted hours of professional labour

    Prepare a cost estimate for each job.

4-33 Job costing with two direct- and two indirect-cost categories, law firm (continuation of 4-32). Keating has just completed a review of its job-costing system. This review included a detailed analysis of how past jobs used the firm's resources and interviews with personnel about what factors drive the level of indirect costs. Management concluded that a system with two direct-cost categories (professional partner labour and professional manager labour) and two indirect-cost categories (general support and secretarial support) would yield more accurate job costs. Budgeted information for 2007 related to the two direct-cost categories is as follows:

	Professional Partner Labour	Professional Manager Labour
Number of professionals	5	20
Hours of billable time per professional	1,600 per year	1,600 per year
Total compensation (average per professional)	$240,000	$96,000

Budgeted information for 2007 relating to the two indirect-cost categories is

	General Support	Secretarial Support
Total costs	$2,160,000	$480,000
Cost allocation base	Professional labour-hours 40,000 hours	Partner labour-hours 8,000 hours

The budgeted total number of days out of town for all professionals in 2007 is 2,000 days.

REQUIRED

1. Compute the 2007 budgeted direct-cost rates for (a) professional partners and (b) professional managers.
2. Compute the 2007 budgeted indirect-cost rates for (a) general support and (b) secretarial support.
3. Compute the budgeted job costs for the Richardson and Punch jobs, given the following information:

	Richardson, Inc.	Punch, Inc.
Professional partners	60 hours	30 hours
Professional managers	40 hours	120 hours

4. Comment on the results in requirement 3. Why are the job costs different from those computed in Problem 4-32?

4-34 **Normal costing, overhead allocation, working backwards.** Gibson Company uses a normal-costing system with two direct-cost categories—direct materials and direct manufacturing labour—and one indirect-cost category—manufacturing overhead. The following information is obtained from the company's records for 2007:

◆ Total manufacturing costs $9,600,000
◆ Cost of goods manufactured   9,504,000
◆ Manufacturing overhead allocated $4,320,000
◆ Manufacturing overhead was allocated to production at a rate of 200% of direct manufacturing labour cost
◆ The dollar amount of work-in-process inventory on January 1, 2007, was $384,000

REQUIRED

1. What was the total direct labour cost in 2007?
2. What was the total cost of direct materials used in 2007?
3. What was the dollar amount of work-in-process inventory on December 31, 2007?

4-35 **Job costing, accounting for manufacturing overhead, budgeted rates.** The Solomon Company uses a job-costing system at its Dover plant. The plant has a Machining Department and a Finishing Department. Its job-costing system has two direct-cost categories (direct materials and direct manufacturing labour) and two manufacturing overhead cost pools (the Machining Department, allocated using actual machine-hours, and the Finishing Department, allocated using actual labour cost). The 2007 budget for the plant is as follows:

	Machining Department	Finishing Department
Manufacturing overhead	$12,000,000	$9,600,000
Direct manufacturing labour cost	$ 1,080,000	$4,800,000
Direct manufacturing labour-hours	30,000	160,000
Machine-hours	200,000	33,000

REQUIRED

1. Present an overview diagram of Solomon's job-costing system.
2. What is the budgeted overhead rate that should be used in the Machining Department? in the Finishing Department?
3. During the month of January, the cost record for Job 431 shows the following:

	Machining Department	Finishing Department
Direct material used	$16,800	$3,600
Direct manufacturing labour cost	$ 720	$1,500
Direct manufacturing labour-hours	30	50
Machine-hours	130	10

What is the total manufacturing overhead allocated to Job 431?

4. Assuming that Job 431 consisted of 200 units of product, what is the unit product cost of Job 431?

5. Balances at the end of 2007 are as follows:

	Machining Department	Finishing Department
Manufacturing overhead incurred	$13,440,000	$9,480,000
Direct manufacturing labour cost	$ 1,140,000	$4,920,000
Machine-hours	220,000	32,000

Compute the under- or overallocated manufacturing overhead for each department and for the Dover plant as a whole.

6. Why might Solomon use two different manufacturing overhead cost pools in its job-costing system?

4-36 Disposition of overhead over/underallocation, two indirect-cost pools. The Glavine Corporation manufactures precision equipment made to order for the semiconductor industry. Glavine uses two manufacturing overhead cost pools—one for the overhead costs incurred in its highly automated Machining Department and another for overhead costs incurred in its labour-paced Assembly Department. Glavine uses a normal costing system. It allocates Machining Department overhead costs to jobs based on actual machine hours using a budgeted machine-hour overhead rate. It allocates Assembly Department overhead costs to jobs based on actual direct manufacturing labour-hours using a budgeted direct manufacturing labour-hour rate.

The following data are for the year 2007:

	Machining Department	Assembly Department
Budgeted overhead	$7,200,000	$6,000,000
Budgeted machine hours	100,000	0
Budgeted direct manufacturing labour-hours	0	125,000
Actual manufacturing overhead costs	$7,440,000	$5,640,000

Machine-hours and direct manufacturing labour-hours and the ending balances (before proration of underallocated overhead) are as follows:

	Actual Machine-Hours	Actual Direct Manufacturing Labour-Hours	Balance before Proration, December 31, 2007
Cost of Goods Sold	67,500	90,000	$19,200,000
Finished Goods	4,500	4,800	900,000
Work in Process	18,000	25,200	3,900,000

REQUIRED

1. Compute the budgeted overhead rates for the year 2007 in the Machining and Assembly Departments.
2. Compute the under- or overallocated overhead in *each* department in 2007. Dispose of the under- or overallocated amount in *each* department using:
   a. Immediate write-off to Cost of Goods Sold.
   b. Proration based on ending balances (before proration) in Cost of Goods Sold, Finished Goods, and Work in Process.
   c. Proration based on the allocated overhead amount (before proration) in the ending balances of Cost of Goods Sold, Finished Goods, and Work in Process.
3. Which disposition method do you prefer in requirement 2? Explain.

4-37 Allocation of manufacturing overhead and disposition of over/underallocation. (SMA, heavily adapted) Nicole Limited is a company that produces machinery to customer order. Its job-costing system (using normal costing) has two direct-cost categories (direct materials and direct manufacturing labour) and one indirect-cost pool (manufacturing overhead, allocated using a budgeted rate based on direct manufacturing labour costs). The budget for 2007 was:

Direct manufacturing labour	$504,000
Manufacturing overhead	$302,400

At the end of 2007, two jobs were incomplete: No. 1768B (total direct manufacturing labour costs were $13,200) and No. 1819C (total direct manufacturing labour costs were $46,800). Machine time totalled 287 hours for No. 1768B and 647 hours for No. 1819C. Direct materials issued to No. 1768B amounted to $26,400. Direct material for No. 1819C came to $50,400.

Total charges to the Manufacturing Overhead Control account for the year were $223,200. Direct manufacturing labour charges made to all jobs were $480,000, representing 20,000 direct manufacturing labour-hours.

There were no beginning inventories. In addition to the ending work in process, the ending finished goods showed a balance of $187,200 (including a direct manufacturing labour cost component of $48,000). Sales for 2007 totalled $3,240,816, cost of goods sold was $1,920,000, and marketing costs were $1,029,444.

Nicole prices on a cost-plus basis. It currently uses a guideline of cost plus 40% of cost.

REQUIRED

1. Prepare a detailed schedule showing the ending balances in the inventories and cost of goods sold (before considering any under- or overallocated manufacturing overhead). Show also the manufacturing overhead allocated to these ending balances.
2. Compute the under- or overallocated manufacturing overhead for 2007.
3. Prorate the amount computed in requirement 2 on the basis of:
   a. The ending balances (before proration) of work in process, finished goods, and cost of goods sold
   b. The allocated overhead amount (before proration) in the ending balances of work in process, finished goods, and cost of goods sold
4. Assume that Nicole decides to immediately write off to Cost of Goods Sold any under- or overallocated manufacturing overhead. Will operating income be higher or lower than the operating income that would have resulted from the proration in requirements 3(a) and 3(b)?
5. Calculate the cost of job No. 1819C if Nicole Limited had used the adjusted allocation-rate approach to disposing of under- or overallocated manufacturing overhead in 2007.

4-38 Job costing, contracting, ethics. Jack Halpern is the owner and CEO of Aerospace Comfort, a firm specializing in the manufacture of seats for air transport. He has just received a copy of a letter written to the Auditor General of the Canadian government. He believes it is from an ex-employee of Aerospace.

Dear Sir,

Aerospace Comfort in 2007 manufactured 100 X7 seats for the Canadian Forces. You may be interested to know the following:

1. Direct materials cost billed for the 100 X7 seats was $30,000.
2. Direct manufacturing labour cost billed for 100 X7 seats was $7,200. This cost includes 16 hours of setup labour at $30 per hour, an amount included in the manufacturing overhead cost pool as well. The $7,200 also includes 12 hours of design time at $60 an hour. Design time was explicitly identified as a cost the Canadian Forces was not to reimburse.
3. Manufacturing overhead cost billed for 100 X7 seats was $10,800 (150% of direct manufacturing labour costs). This amount includes the 16 hours of setup labour at $30 per hour that is incorrectly included as part of direct manufacturing labour costs.

You may also want to know that over 40% of the direct materials is purchased from Frontier Technology, a company that is 51% owned by Jack Halpern's brother.

For obvious reasons, this letter will not be signed.

c.c.: *The Globe and Mail*
     Jack Halpern, CEO of Aerospace Comfort

Aerospace Comfort's contract states that the Canadian Forces reimburses Aerospace at 130% of manufacturing costs.

REQUIRED

Assume that the facts in the letter are correct as you answer the following questions.

1. What is the cost amount per X7 seat that Aerospace Comfort billed the Canadian Forces? Assume that the actual direct materials costs are $30,000.
2. What is the amount per X7 seat that Aerospace Comfort should have billed the Canadian Forces? Assume that the actual direct materials costs are $30,000.
3. Based on the problems highlighted in the letter, what should the Canadian Forces do to tighten its procurement procedures to reduce the likelihood of such situations recurring?

4-39 General ledger relationships, under- and overallocation, service industry. John Brody and Co. is an engineering consulting firm. Brody uses a variation of a normal-costing system. It charges jobs for blueprints made and fees paid to outside experts at actual costs, professional direct-labour costs at a budgeted direct-labour rate, and engineering support overhead costs (for engineering and office support) at a budgeted indirect-cost rate.

Brody maintains a Jobs-in-Process Control account in its general ledger that accumulates all costs of jobs. As a job is completed, Brody immediately bills the client and transfers the costs of the completed job to the Cost of Jobs Billed account to be matched against the revenues billed to the client. Consequently, unlike manufacturing companies, Brody has no accounts that correspond to Materials Control and Finished Goods Control accounts.

The following data pertain to the year 2007:

Cost of jobs in process on 1–1–2007	$240,000
Direct costs of fees and blueprints (all cash)	$180,000
Actual direct professional labour costs (all cash)	$1,800,000
Direct professional labour allocated at $60 per direct professional labour-hour	?
Actual direct professional labour-hours	29,000
Actual engineering support overhead costs (all cash)	$1,416,000
Engineering support overhead allocated at $0.80 per direct professional labour dollar	?
Cost of jobs billed	$3,000,000
Revenues	$3,360,000

Brody incurs no marketing and business development costs.

REQUIRED

1. Summarize the year 2007 transactions by preparing T-accounts for Jobs-in-Process Control, Cost of Jobs Billed, Direct Professional Labour Control, Direct Professional Labour Allocated, Engineering Support Overhead Control, Engineering Support Overhead Allocated, and Cash Control. As your final entry, dispose of the year-end under- or overallocated account balances as a direct write-off to Cost of Goods Sold.
2. Calculate Brody's operating income for the year 2007.

4-40 General ledger relationships, under- and overallocation. (S. Sridhar, adapted) Partially completed T-accounts and additional information for the Needham Company for the year 2007 are presented below. Needham uses a normal costing system.

Materials Control		
1-1-2007	480,000	456,000
	36,000	

Work-in-Process Control		
1-1-2007	24,000	
Dir. manuf. labour	432,000	

Finished Goods Control		
1-1-2007	12,000	1,080,000
	1,128,000	

Manufacturing Overhead Control	
648,000	

Manufacturing Overhead Allocated	

Cost of Goods Sold	

ADDITIONAL INFORMATION

1. Direct manufacturing labour wage rate was $18 per hour.
2. Manufacturing overhead is allocated at $24 per direct manufacturing labour hour.
3. During the year, sales revenues were $1,308,000, and marketing and distribution expenses were $168,000.

REQUIRED

1. What was the amount of direct materials issued to manufacturing during 2007?
2. What was the amount of manufacturing overhead allocated to jobs during 2007?
3. What was the cost of jobs completed during 2007?
4. What was the balance in work-in-process inventory on December 31, 2007?
5. What was the cost of goods sold before any proration or under- or overallocated overhead?
6. What was the under- or overallocated manufacturing overhead in 2007?
7. Dispose of the under- or overallocated manufacturing overhead using

   a. Immediate write-off to Cost of Goods Sold
   b. Proration based on ending balances (before proration) in Work-in-Process, Finished Goods, and Cost of Goods Sold.

8. Using each of the disposition methods in requirement 7, calculate Needham's operating income for the year 2007.
9. Which disposition method in requirement 7 do you recommend Needham use? Explain your answer briefly.

COLLABORATIVE LEARNING PROBLEM

4-41 Job costing, accounting for overhead costs, budgeted rates. Jefferson Company is a painting contractor for office and factory buildings. Jefferson uses a normal-costing system to cost each job. Jefferson's normal-costing system has two direct-cost categories (direct materials and direct labour) and one indirect-cost pool called *overhead costs*. Jefferson uses a budgeted overhead rate for allocating overhead costs to jobs on the basis of direct labour costs.

Jefferson provides the following additional information:

1. Budgeted overhead costs for the year 2007 $1,440,000
   Budgeted direct labour costs for the year 2007 $1,800,000
2. As of January 31, Job 101 was the only job in process, with direct materials costs of $36,000 and direct labour costs of $60,000.
3. Jobs 102, 103, and 104 were started during February.
4. Direct materials used during February equal $180,000.
5. Direct labour costs for February are $144,000.
6. Actual overhead costs for February are $122,400.
7. The only job still in process at February 28, 2007 was job 104, with direct materials costs of $24,000 and direct labour costs of $48,000.

Jefferson maintains a Jobs in Process Control account in its general ledger. As a job is completed, Jefferson immediately bills the client and transfers the cost of the completed job to the Cost of Jobs Billed account to be matched against the revenues billed to the client. Consequently, unlike manufacturing companies, Jefferson does not have an account that corresponds to Finished Goods Control. Each month, Jefferson closes any under- or overallocated overhead to Cost of Jobs Billed.

INSTRUCTION

Form pairs to complete the following requirements.

REQUIRED

1. Calculate the budgeted overhead rate for allocating overhead costs in 2007.
2. Calculate the manufacturing overhead allocated to Job 101 as of January 31, 2007, and the manufacturing overhead allocated to Job 104 as of February 28, 2007.
3. Calculate the under- or overallocated overhead for February 2007.
4. Calculate the Cost of Jobs Billed by Jefferson in February 2007.

CHAPTER **5**

Activity-Based Costing and Activity-Based Management

LEARNING OBJECTIVES

After studying this chapter, you should be able to

1. Explain undercosting and overcosting of products or services

2. Present three guidelines for refining a costing system

3. Distinguish between the traditional and the activity-based costing (ABC) approaches to designing a costing system

4. Describe a four-part cost hierarchy

5. Assign costs to products or services using activity-based costing (ABC)

6. Use ABC systems for activity-based management (ABM)

7. Compare ABC and department overhead rate systems

8. Evaluate the costs and benefits of implementing ABC systems

Chapter 4 describes a basic job-costing system. In particular, it uses a single cost pool and a single indirect-cost rate to allocate indirect costs to jobs. An important question is "Does using a single indirect-cost rate provide misleading job cost numbers?" The answer depends on whether different jobs, products, and services are relatively alike (identical or at least similar) in the way they consume the indirect costs of an organization. If they are alike, as was the case in Chapter 4, then a simple costing system will suffice for job-costing purposes. If they are not alike, a simple costing system will yield inaccurate cost numbers for jobs, products, and services.

As their variety increases, organizations are finding that different products and services place varying demands on resources. The need to measure more accurately how different products and services use organization resources has led companies to refine their costing systems. Companies worldwide have implemented activity-based costing (ABC) to refine their costing systems. ABC is the focus of this chapter. We describe how ABC systems improve information managers use to make better pricing and product mix decisions. We also describe how activity-based management (ABM) improves cost management decisions by improving processes and product designs.

BROAD AVERAGING VIA TRADITIONAL OR PEANUT BUTTER COSTING APPROACHES

Companies may use a broad average (for example, a single cost pool) to allocate (or assign) indirect costs to products. This approach is appropriate when indirect costs are a relatively small percentage of total costs and products or services are relatively uniform. The phrases **traditional costing, cost smoothing,** or **peanut butter costing** describe this simple costing approach to uniformly assign (smooth or spread out) the indirect cost of resources to cost objects. But with diverse products and services and the increasing percentage of total costs contributed by indirect costs, traditional costing is inappropriate if individual products, services, or customers in fact use those resources in a nonuniform way.

Undercosting and Overcosting

Use of broad averages via traditional or peanut butter costing may lead to undercosting or overcosting of products (services, customers, and so on):

◆ **Product undercosting.** A product consumes a relatively high level of resources but is reported to have a relatively low total cost.

◆ **Product overcosting.** A product consumes a relatively low level of resources but is reported to have a relatively high total cost.

Companies that undercost products may actually make sales that result in losses under the erroneous impression that these sales are profitable. That is, these sales bring in less revenue than the cost of the resources they use. Companies that overcost products run the risk of losing market share to existing or new competitors. Because these products actually cost less than what is reported to management, the company could cut selling prices to maintain or enhance market share and still make a profit on each sale.

Product Cost Cross-Subsidization

Product cost cross-subsidization means that at least one miscosted product is resulting in the miscosting of other products in the organization. A classic example arises when a cost is uniformly spread (broad-averaged or "peanut-buttered") across multiple users without recognition of their different resource demands. Consider the costing of a restaurant bill for four colleagues who meet once a month to discuss business developments. Each diner orders separate entrées, desserts, and drinks. The restaurant bill for the most recent meeting is as follows:

	Entrée	Dessert	Drinks	Total
Emma	$11	$ 0	$ 4	$ 15
James	20	8	14	42
Beatta	15	4	8	27
Matthew	14	4	6	24
Total	$60	$16	$32	$108
Average	$15	$ 4	$ 8	$ 27

The $108 total restaurant bill produces a $27 average cost per dinner. This broad-average costing approach treats each diner the same. Emma would probably object to paying $27, because her actual cost is only $15. Indeed, she ordered the lowest-cost entrée, had no dessert, and had the lowest drink bill. When costs are averaged across all four diners, both Emma and Matthew are overcosted, James is undercosted, and Beatta is accurately costed.

The restaurant example is both simple and intuitive. The amount of cost cross-subsidization of each diner can be readily computed given that all cost items can be traced as direct costs to each diner. More complex costing issues arise, however, when there are indirect costs. Then resources are used by two or more individual

OBJECTIVE 1

Explain undercosting and overcosting of products or services

Traditional costing, cost smoothing (peanut butter costing). A simple costing approach that uses broad averages to assign (spread or smooth out) uniformly the cost of resources to cost objects (such as products, services, or customers) when the individual products, services, or customers in fact use those resources in a nonuniform way.

Product undercosting. Occurs when a product consumes a relatively high level of resources but is reported to have a relatively low total cost.

Product overcosting. Occurs when a product consumes a relatively low level of resources but is reported to have a relatively high total cost.

Product cost cross-subsidization. Costing outcome wherein at least one miscosted product results in the miscosting of other products in the organization.

Activity-Based Costing (ABC) Economic Value Added Internet Website Guide
www.pitt.edu/~roztocki/abc/abc.htm

SAS Activity-Based Management
www.sas.com/solutions/abm/index.html

It's relatively easy to determine "accurate" costs of products (or services) when a company has only a few products. Companies turn to activity-based costing when they expand their product offerings and the products use different amounts of resources (such as supervision and quality control), which makes it more difficult to determine accurate costs.

diners. By definition, indirect costs require allocation—for example, the cost of a bottle of wine shared by two or more diners.

We now examine how costing systems can be refined to reduce the miscosting of jobs, products, or customers.

COSTING SYSTEM AT PLASTIM CORPORATION

Plastim Corporation manufactures lenses for rear (tail) lamps of automobiles. The lens, made from black, red, orange, or white plastic, is the part of the lamp visible from the outside. Lenses are made using injection moulding. The moulding operation consists of injecting molten plastic into a mould to give the lamp its desired shape. The mould is cooled to allow the molten plastic to solidify, and the part is ejected.

Under its contract with Giovanni Motors, a major automobile manufacturer, Plastim makes two types of lenses—a complex lens, CL5, and a simple lens, S3. The complex lens is a large lens with special features such as multicolour moulding (where more than one colour is injected into the mould) and complex shapes that wrap around the side of the car. Manufacturing these lenses is more complex because various parts in the mould must align and fit accurately and precisely. The simple lens is smaller and has few special features.

Design, Production, and Distribution Processes

The sequence of steps to design, produce, and distribute lenses, whether simple or complex, is as follows.

1. *Design of products and processes.* Each year Giovanni Motors specifies some modifications to the simple and complex lenses. Plastim's Design Department designs the moulds from which the lenses will be made and defines the processes needed (details of the manufacturing operations).

2. *Manufacturing operations.* The lenses are moulded, as described earlier, finished, cleaned, and inspected.

3. *Shipping and distribution.* Finished lenses are packed and sent to Giovanni Motors.

Plastim is operating at capacity and incurs very low marketing costs. Because of its high-quality products, Plastim has minimal customer-service costs. Plastim's business environment is very competitive with respect to simple lenses. At a recent meeting, Giovanni's purchasing manager indicated that a new competitor, who makes only simple lenses, was offering to supply the S3 lens to Giovanni at a price of around $53, well below Plastim's price of $63. Unless Plastim lowered its selling price, it would be in jeopardy of losing the Giovanni business for the simple lens, similar to S3, for the upcoming model year. Plastim's management was very concerned about this development. The same competitive pressures did not exist for the complex lens, which Plastim currently sells to Giovanni at a price of $137 per lens.

Plastim's management had various alternatives open to it. Plastim could give up the Giovanni business in simple lenses if it were going to be very unprofitable. It could reduce the price on the simple lens and either accept a lower margin or aggressively seek to reduce costs. But first management needed to understand what it costs to make and sell the S3 and CL5 lenses. To guide its pricing and cost management decisions, Plastim's managers assign all costs, both manufacturing and nonmanufacturing, to the S3 and CL5 lenses. Had the focus been on inventory costing, Plastim would have assigned only manufacturing costs to the lenses.

Existing Single Indirect-Cost Pool System

To cost products, Plastim currently uses a single indirect-cost pool job-costing system, similar to the system described in Chapter 4. The steps are as follows.

◆ **Step 1:** *Identify the chosen cost objects.* The items (jobs) to be costed are the *total* costs of manufacturing and distributing 60,000 simple S3 lenses and 15,000 complex CL5 lenses. Plastim determines unit costs of each lens by dividing total costs of each model by 60,000 for S3 and 15,000 for CL5.

◆ **Step 2:** *Identify the direct costs of the cost objects.* Plastim identifies the direct costs of the lenses—direct materials and direct manufacturing labour—as follows:

	60,000 Simple Lenses (S3)		15,000 Complex Lenses (CL5)		
	Total (1)	Per Unit (2) = (1) ÷ 60,000	Total (3)	Per Unit (4) = (3) ÷ 15,000	Total (5) = (1) + (3)
Direct materials	$1,125,000	$18.75	$675,000	$45.00	$1,800,000
Direct manufacturing labour	600,000	10.00	195,000	13.00	795,000
Total direct costs	$1,725,000	$28.75	$870,000	$58.00	$2,595,000

◆ **Step 3:** *Select the cost-allocation bases to use in allocating indirect costs to the cost object(s).* Plastim uses direct manufacturing labour-hours as the only allocation base to allocate all indirect costs to S3 and CL5. Most of the indirect costs consist of salaries paid to supervisors, engineers, production support, and maintenance staff that support direct manufacturing labour. In the current year, 2007, Plastim used 39,750 actual direct manufacturing labour-hours.

◆ **Step 4:** *Identify the indirect costs associated with each cost-allocation base.* Plastim groups all indirect costs totalling $2,385,000 into a single overhead cost pool.

◆ **Step 5:** *Compute the rate per unit of each cost-allocation base used to allocate indirect costs to the cost object(s).*

$$\text{Actual indirect-cost rate} = \frac{\text{Actual total costs in indirect-cost pool}}{\text{Actual total quantity of cost-allocation base}}$$

$$= \frac{\$2,385,000}{39,750 \text{ hours}} = \$60 \text{ per direct manufacturing labour-hour.}$$

> Accountants need to reevaluate the costing system if it yields numbers that don't agree with what operating and marketing managers intuitively expect or if costs/prices appear to be out of line with competitors' costs/prices.

Exhibit 5-1, panel A, shows an overview of Plastim's existing costing system.

◆ **Step 6:** *Compute the indirect costs allocated to the cost object(s).* Plastim uses 30,000 total direct manufacturing labour-hours to make the simple S3 lenses and 9,750 direct manufacturing labour-hours to make the complex CL5 lenses. Exhibit 5-1, panel B, shows indirect costs of $1,800,000 ($60 per direct manufacturing labour-hour × 30,000) allocated to the simple lens and $585,000 ($60 per direct manufacturing labour-hour × 9,750) allocated to the complex lens.

◆ **Step 7:** *Determine the cost of the cost objects by adding all direct and indirect costs assigned to them.* Exhibit 5-1, panel B, presents the product costs for the simple and complex lenses. The direct costs are calculated in step 2 and the indirect costs in step 6. Note the correspondence between the costing system overview diagram (Exhibit 5-1, panel A) and the costs calculated in step 7. Panel A shows two direct-cost categories and one indirect-cost pool. Hence, the cost of each type of lens in step 7 (panel B) has three line items, two for direct costs and one for allocated indirect costs.

Plastim's management begins investigating why the S3 lens costs $58.75, well above the $53 price quoted by Plastim's competitor. Are Plastim's technology and processes inefficient in producing and distributing the simple S3 lens? Further analysis indicates that this is not the reason. Plastim has years of experience in manufacturing and distributing lenses like S3. Because Plastim often makes process improvements, management is confident that Plastim's technology and processes for making simple lenses are not inferior to those of its competitors. However, management is less certain about Plastim's capabilities in manufacturing and distributing the complex lens. Indeed, Plastim has only recently started making these types of lenses. Management is pleasantly surprised to learn that Giovanni Motors considers the prices of CL5 lenses to be very competitive. Even more puzzling is that, even at these prices, Plastim earns very large margins on the CL5 lenses:

> Allocating indirect costs to both products at the $60 rate per direct manufacturing labour-hour is the traditional or peanut butter costing approach.

| | 60,000 Simple Lenses (S3) | | 15,000 Complex Lenses (CL5) | | Total |
	Total (1)	Per Unit (2) = (1) ÷ 60,000	Total (3)	Per Unit (4) = (3) ÷ 15,000	Total (5) = (1) + (3)
Revenues	$3,780,000	$63.00	$2,055,000	$137.00	$5,835,000
Costs	3,525,000	58.75	1,455,000	97.00	4,980,000
Operating income	$ 255,000	$ 4.25	$ 600,000	$ 40.00	$ 855,000
Operating income ÷ Revenues	6.75%		29.20%		

EXHIBIT 5-1
Product Costs at Plastim Inc. with Existing Single Overhead-Cost Pool

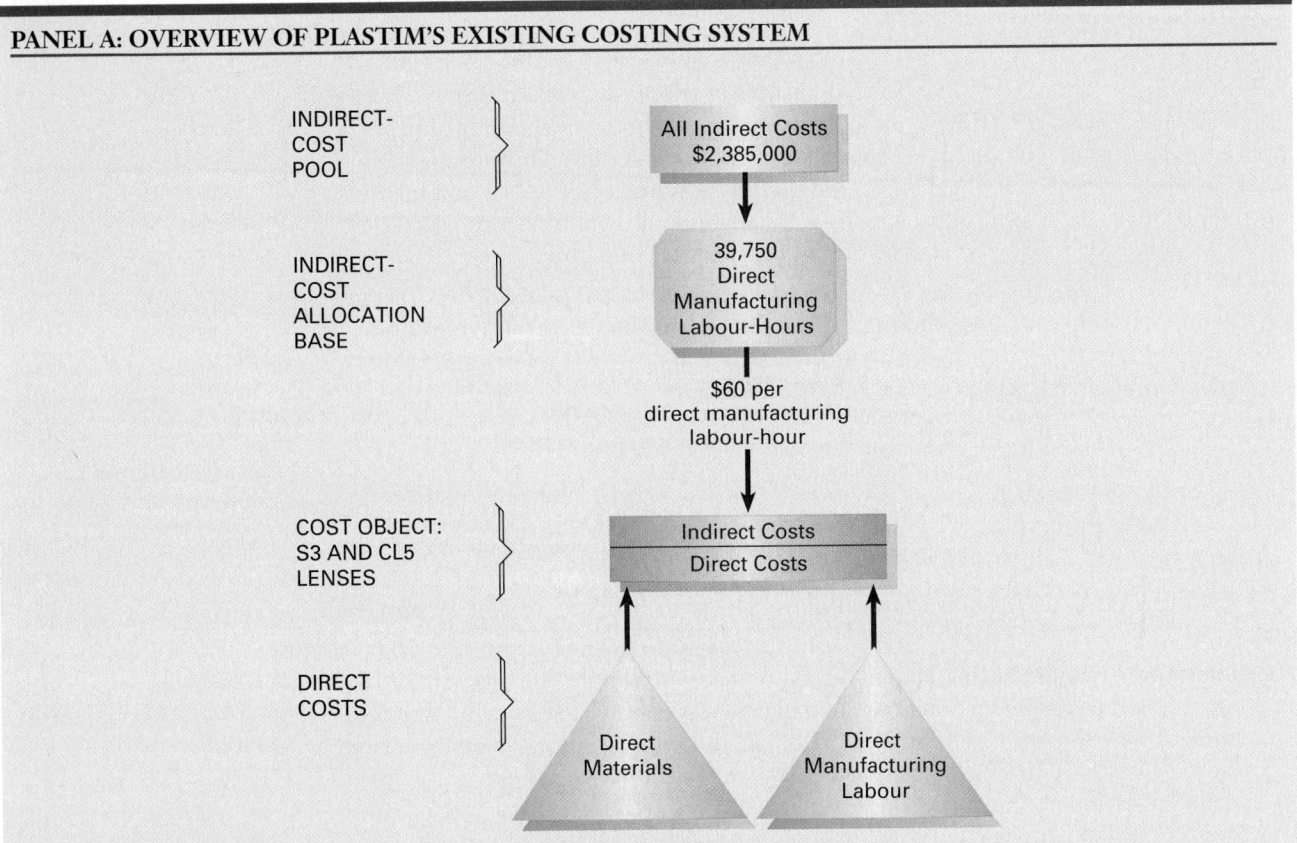

PANEL A: OVERVIEW OF PLASTIM'S EXISTING COSTING SYSTEM

INDIRECT-COST POOL — All Indirect Costs $2,385,000

INDIRECT-COST ALLOCATION BASE — 39,750 Direct Manufacturing Labour-Hours

$60 per direct manufacturing labour-hour

COST OBJECT: S3 AND CL5 LENSES — Indirect Costs / Direct Costs

DIRECT COSTS — Direct Materials / Direct Manufacturing Labour

PANEL B: PRODUCT COST USING THE EXISTING COSTING SYSTEM

	A	B	C	D	E	F
1		60,000		15,000		
2		Simple Lenses (S3)		Complex Lenses (CL5)		
3		Total	Per Unit	Total	Per Unit	Total
4		(1)	(2) = (1)÷60,000	(3)	(4) = (3)÷15,000	(5) = (1) + (3)
5	Direct materials	$1,125,000	$18.75	$ 675,000	$45.00	$1,800,000
6	Direct manufacturing labour	600,000	10.00	195,000	13.00	795,000
7	Total direct costs (Step 2)	$1,725,000	28.75	870,000	58.00	2,595,000
8	Indirect costs allocated (Step 6)	1,800,000	30.00	585,000	39.00	2,385,000
9	Total costs (Step 7)	$3,525,000	$58.75	$1,455,000	$97.00	$4,980,000

Plastim's managers are surprised that the margins are low on the S3 product where it has strong capabilities, while the margins are quite high on the newer, less-established CL5 product. Since they were not deliberately charging a low price for the S3, they wonder if the cost system overcosts the simple S3 lens (assigning excessive costs to it) and undercosts the complex CL5 lens (assigning too little costs to it).

Plastim's management is quite confident about the direct materials and direct manufacturing labour costs of the lenses. Why? Because these costs can be traced to the lenses in an economically feasible way. It is less certain that the costing system effectively measures the overhead resources demanded by each type of lens. The key question, then, is how the system of allocating overhead costs to lenses might be refined.

REFINING A COSTING SYSTEM

A **refined costing system** results in a better measure of the nonuniformity in the use of an organization's resources by jobs, products, and customers. Increased competition and advances in information technology have accelerated these refinements.

What has caused companies in such diverse industries, operating in different parts of the world, to do so? There are four principal reasons.

Present three guidelines for refining a costing system

Refined costing system. Costing system that results in a better measure of the nonuniformity in the use of resources by jobs, products, and customers.

1. **Increase in product diversity.** Customers are demanding more customized products and companies respond by adopting strategies to differentiate their product offerings from competitors. Companies are producing and selling many more products than in the past. Banks are offering many different types of accounts and services: special passbook accounts, ATMs, credit cards, electronic payments, and investment and insurance services. These different products make different demands on the resources needed to produce them because of differences in volume, process, and complexity. The resources demanded by these different products cannot be measured by a simple costing system that allocates indirect costs on the basis of, say, direct manufacturing labour-hours. Using such a simple costing system will result in inaccurate and misleading product costs.

2. **Increase in indirect costs.** Advances in product and process technology have led to increases in indirect costs and decreases in direct costs, particularly direct manufacturing labour costs. Plant automation, such as computer-integrated manufacturing (CIM) and flexible manufacturing systems (FMS), has significantly reduced the direct manufacturing labour costs of products. Computers on the manufacturing floor give instructions to set up and run equipment quickly and automatically. The computers accurately measure hundreds of production parameters, directly control the manufacturing processes, and achieve high-quality output. Managing more-complex technology and producing very diverse products requires committing an increasing amount of resources for various support functions, such as production scheduling and product and process design and engineering. Direct manufacturing labour is not a cost driver of these support costs. Therefore, allocating indirect costs on the basis of direct manufacturing labour does not accurately measure how resources are being used by different products.

3. **Advances in information technology.** Costing system refinements require more data gathering and more analysis and make the costing system more detailed. Improvements in information technology and the accompanying decline in the costs of tracking data make it more cost-effective to implement refinements in costing systems. It is more practical now to create systems that have multiple pools of indirect costs for allocating costs to products.

4. **Competition in product markets.** As markets have become more competitive, managers have felt the need to obtain more-accurate cost information to help them make important strategic decisions, such as how to price products and which products to sell. Making correct pricing and product mix decisions is critical in competitive markets because competitors quickly capitalize on a company's mistakes.

Three guidelines for refining a costing system are as follows:

1. *Direct-cost tracing.* Classify as direct costs as many of the total costs as is economically feasible. This guideline reduces the amount of costs classified as indirect.

ACTIVITY-BASED COSTING AND ACTIVITY-BASED MANAGEMENT **157**

2. *Indirect-cost pools.* Expand the number of indirect-cost pools until each of these pools is homogeneous. In a *homogeneous cost pool*, all costs in the cost pool have the same or a similar cause-and-effect or benefits-received relationship with the cost-allocation base.

3. *Cost-allocation bases.* Identify the preferred cost-allocation base for each indirect-cost pool. In this chapter we focus on the cause-and-effect criterion when choosing allocation bases.

ACTIVITY-BASED COSTING SYSTEMS

O B J E C T I V E 3

Distinguish between the traditional and the activity-based costing (ABC) approaches to designing a costing system

Activity-based costing (ABC). Approach to costing that focuses on activities as the fundamental cost objects. It uses the cost of these activities as the basis for assigning costs to other cost objects such as products, services, or customers.

Activity. An event, task, or unit of work with a specified purpose.

One of the best tools for refining a cost system is *activity-based costing*. **Activity-based costing (ABC)** systems refine costing systems by focusing on individual activities as the fundamental cost objects. An **activity** is an event, task, or unit of work with a specified purpose. Some examples are designing products, setting up machines, operating machines, and distributing products. ABC systems calculate the costs of individual activities and assign costs to cost objects such as products and services based on the activities undertaken for each product or service:

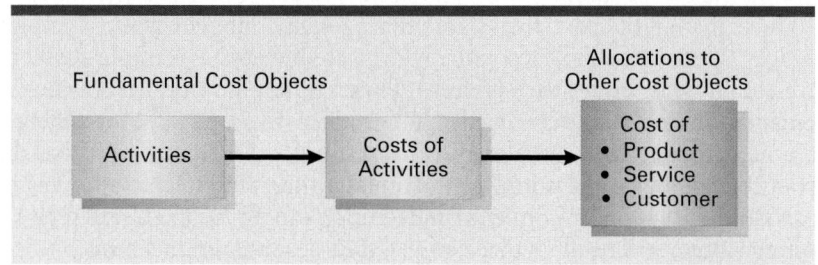

We describe key ideas of an ABC system in the context of our Plastim example. To define activities, Plastim organizes a cross-functional team from design, manufacturing, distribution, accounting, and administration. The team identifies key activities using a flow chart of all the steps and processes needed to design, produce, and distribute lenses.

Plastim's team identifies seven major activities:

1. Design products and processes

2. Set up moulding machine to ensure mould is properly held in place and parts are properly aligned before manufacturing starts

3. Operate machines to manufacture lenses

4. Maintain and clean the mould after lenses are manufactured

5. Set up batches of finished lenses for shipment

6. Distribute lenses to customer sites

7. Administer and manage all processes at Plastim

Activities consume resources (for example, workers are paid to pack and ship finished goods to customers). Then, products that consume the activities (packing and shipping) are allocated the costs of those activities.

By defining activities and identifying the costs of performing each activity, ABC systems seek a greater level of detail in understanding how an organization uses its resources. As we describe ABC systems, keep in mind three features:

1. *Direct-cost tracing.* A feature of ABC systems is aiming to identify some costs or cost pools that can be reclassified as direct costs instead of indirect costs. ABC systems do this by subdividing existing cost pools. Costs in some new pools may qualify as direct costs. In the Plastim example, the cleaning and maintenance activity consists of salaries and wages paid to workers responsible for cleaning the mould. These costs can be traced directly to the specific mould used to produce the lens. Direct tracing of costs improves cost accuracy and is simple because, unlike for indirect costs, cost pools and cost-allocation bases do not have to be identified.

2. *Indirect-cost pools.* ABC systems create smaller cost pools (numerators) comprising costs of smaller groups of associated activities. Plastim subdivides its original single

overhead cost pool into one direct activity-cost pool and six indirect activity-related cost pools, each pool corresponding to one of the seven activities described earlier.

The single overhead cost pool is not homogeneous because the costs of activities comprising the cost pool have a weak cause-and-effect relationship with direct manufacturing labour-hours. This means that changes in the dollar value of the cost pool will not necessarily be accompanied by changes in quantity in the cost-allocation base. For example, changes in the costs of activities undertaken to distribute products will not arise because of a change in direct manufacturing labour-hours. At Plastim, the cost of distribution activities for each product is caused by (varies with) the cubic metres of lenses shipped. The appropriate homogeneous cost pool is the costs of distribution activities, not total manufacturing overhead. The appropriate cost driver or cause of distribution activity-costs is total cubic metres shipped. The appropriate activity-cost rate is dollars per cubic metre shipped, not dollars per direct manufacturing labour-hour. The appropriate assigned costs result from multiplying the activity-cost rate by the cubic metres shipped for each product.

Using the traditional method, distribution activities costs are lumped into a single inappropriate cost allocation rate. Managers have no choice but to assign this set of costs to each product by multiplying the traditional cost-allocation rate by the quantity of direct manufacturing labour-hours consumed when producing each product. They obtain an inaccurate cost of each product.

Each of the eight new activity-related cost pools is homogeneous. Why? Because each activity cost pool includes only a narrow and focused set of costs (for example, setup or distribution). Over time, the costs in each activity-cost pool have a cause-and-effect relationship with the cost-allocation base (denominator) for that activity (for example, setup-hours in the case of setup costs and cubic metres of packages moved in the case of distribution costs).

3. *Cost-allocation bases.* For each activity-cost pool, a measure of the activity performed serves as the cost-allocation base. For example, Plastim identifies and separately measures hours of labour incurred to set up the machines (setup hours) each time it switches from manufacturing S3 to CL5 lenses. Setup hours is the cost driver of the activity, setup, and becomes the cost-allocation base for this homogeneous setup cost pool. Plastim identifies cubic metres of packages moved (the measure of distribution activity) as the cost-allocation base for distribution costs.

The logic of ABC systems produces more accurate cost allocation rates based on smaller, homogeneous activity-cost pools (numerators) accompanied by appropriate measures of activities — the cost-allocation bases (denominators) — that drive or cause the total costs to vary. The result is a more accurate cost of activities. It becomes a simple matter to assign more accurate product costs by multiplying the new rates per activity cost-driver by the total quantity of cost driver each product consumes. When the cause-and-effect relationship between overhead costs and the cost-allocation base(s) is weak, Plastim assigns costs of all activities including setup and distribution using direct manufacturing labour-hours. The result is an inaccurate estimate of the product costs of the S3 and the CL5.

A numerical example beginning with setup activity illustrates how product costs change when the company switches to an ABC system. After producing each batch of CL5 lenses the moulds must be cleaned, and during this time the machines are set up to produce S3 lenses. The quantity of CL5 lenses per batch is lower than for S3 lenses because the mould is more complex and must be cleaned more frequently. Each setup requires time for activities such as trial runs of product to ensure the calibration of the machines produces unscratched lenses and correct shapes and colours. If the total quantity of output units for S3 and CL5 lenses is identical then it will require more batches and therefore more setups of CL5 than S3 to achieve the same total output.

We illustrate the effect of allocating all overhead costs to products using direct manufacturing labour-hours, versus an ABC system with its emphasis on individual activities, by focusing on the setup activity. Setups frequently entail trial runs, fine tuning, and adjustments. Improper setups cause quality problems, such as scratches on the surface of the lens. The resources needed to set up the machines depend on the complexity of the manufacturing operation. Complex lenses require more setup resources than do simple lenses. Furthermore, complex lenses can be produced only in small batches because the mould needs to be cleaned more often. Relative to simple lenses, complex lenses not only use more resources per setup, but also need more frequent setups.

Setup data for the simple S3 lens and the complex CL5 lens are as follows:

		Simple S3 Lens	Complex CL5 Lens	Total
1	Quantity of lenses produced	60,000	15,000	
2	Number of lenses produced per batch	240	50	
3 = (1) ÷ (2)	Number of batches	250	300	
4	Setup time per batch	2 hours	5 hours	
5 = (3) × (4)	Total setup-hours	500 hours	1,500 hours	2,000 hours

Plastim identifies the total costs of setups (consisting mainly of allocated costs of process engineers, supervisors, and setup equipment) as $300,000. The actual quantity of direct labour-hours of 39,750 was provided in step 3. The following table shows how setup costs are allocated to the simple and complex lenses using direct manufacturing labour-hours and setup-hours, respectively, as the allocation bases. Assuming that the total setup costs for the year are $300,000, the setup cost per direct manufacturing labour-hour equals $7.54717 ($300,000 ÷ 39,750). The setup cost per setup-hour equals $150 ($300,000 ÷ 2,000 setup-hours).

	Simple S3 Lens	Complex CL5 Lens	Total
Cost allocated using direct manufacturing labour-hours			
$7.54717 × 30,000; 9,750	$226,415	$ 73,585	$300,000
Cost allocated using setup-hours			
$150 × 500; $150 × 1,500	$ 75,000	$225,000	$300,000

Which allocation base should Plastim use? Plastim should allocate setup costs based on setup-hours. Why? Because, following guidelines 2 and 3, there is a strong cause-and-effect relationship between setup-related overhead costs and setup-hours. There is almost no relationship between setup-related overhead costs and direct manufacturing labour-hours. Setup costs depend on the number of batches and the complexity of the setups; hence, setup-hours drive setup costs. The simple S3 lens attracts more of the setup costs when costs are allocated based on direct manufacturing labour-hours. This occurs because more direct manufacturing labour-hours are needed to produce S3 lenses. However, direct manufacturing-labour time required by the S3 and CL5 lenses bears no relationship to the setup-hours demanded by the S3 and CL5 lenses. If direct manufacturing labour-hours (rather than setup-hours) were the cost allocation base to assign setup costs, the simple S3 lens would be overcosted. The S3 lens uses a larger proportion of direct manufacturing labour-hours (30,000 ÷ 39,750 = 75.47%) compared to the proportion of setup-hours (500 ÷ 2,000 = 25%).

Note that setup hours are related to batches (groups) of lenses made, not individual lenses.

An important feature of activity-based costing is its emphasis on highlighting the different levels of activities. For example, managers differentiate the two cost objects, individual units of output from batches of output, when identifying cause-and-effect relationships. As our discussion of setups illustrates, limiting the drivers of costs to only units of output (or cost-allocation bases related to units of output such as direct manufacturing labour-hours) will weaken the cause-and-effect relationship between costs in a cost pool and the cost-allocation base (denominator). The *cost hierarchy* distinguishes costs by whether the cost driver is a unit of output (or variables such as machine-hours or direct labour-hours that are a function of units of output), or a *group* of units of a product (such as a batch in the case of setup costs), or the *product itself* (such as the complexity of the model in the case of design costs).

Cost Hierarchies

A **cost hierarchy** is a categorization of costs into different cost pools based on the different types of cost drivers (or cost-allocation bases) or different degrees of difficulty in determining cause-and-effect (or benefits-received) relationships.

ABC systems commonly use a four-part cost hierarchy—output unit-level costs, batch-level costs, product-sustaining costs, and facility-sustaining costs—to identify cost-allocation bases that are identified as cost drivers of costs in activity-cost pools.

Output unit-level costs are for resources sacrificed on activities performed on each individual unit of product or service. Manufacturing operations costs (such as energy, machine amortization, and repair) that support Plastim's automated moulding machines are output unit-level costs. Why? Because the cost of this activity increases with each additional unit of output produced (or machine-hour run).

Suppose that, in our Plastim example, each S3 lens requires 0.15 hours of moulding machine time. Then S3 lenses require a total of 9,000 hours of moulding machine time (0.15 hours × 60,000 lenses). Similarly, suppose CL5 lenses require 0.25 hours of moulding machine time. Then the CL5 lens requires 3,750 moulding machine-hours (0.25 hours × 15,000 lenses). The *total* moulding machine costs allocated to S3 and CL5 depend on the number of each type of lens produced, regardless of the number of batches in which the lenses are made. Plastim's ABC system uses machine-hours, an output unit-level cost-allocation base, to allocate manufacturing operations costs to products.

Batch-level costs are resources sacrificed on activities that are related to a group of units of product(s) or service(s) rather than to each individual unit of product or service. In the Plastim example, setup costs are batch-level costs. Setup resources are used each time moulding machines are set up to produce a batch of lenses. The S3 lens requires 500 setup-hours (2 hours per setup × 250 batches). The CL5 lens requires 1,500 setup-hours (5 hours per setup × 300 batches). The setup costs per batch vary first because the setup-hours for the CL5 are higher than for the S3. The number of setups also differs and is higher for the CL5 than for the S3 product. Therefore, there are two causes for why the *total* setup cost assigned for the CL5 will be higher than for the S3. Plastim's ABC system uses setup-hours, a batch-level cost-allocation base to allocate setup costs to products.

In companies that purchase many different types of direct materials (Plastim purchases mainly plastic pellets), procurement costs can be significant. Procurement (purchasing) costs include the costs of placing purchase orders, receiving materials, and paying suppliers. These costs are batch-level costs because they are related to the number of purchase orders placed rather than to the quantity or value of materials purchased.

Product-sustaining (or **service-sustaining**) **costs** are resources sacrificed on activities undertaken to support individual products or services. In the Plastim example, design costs are product-sustaining costs. Design costs for each type of lens depend largely on the time spent by designers on designing and modifying the product, mould, and process. These costs are a function of the complexity of the mould, measured by the number of parts in the mould multiplied by the square metre area over which the molten plastic must flow (say, 30 parts × square metre area for the S3 lens, and 70 parts × square metre area for the CL5 lens). The *total* design costs allocated to S3 and CL5 depend on the complexity of the mould, regardless of the number of units or batches in which the units are produced. Design costs cannot be linked in any cause-and-effect way to individual units of products or to individual batches of products. Plastim's ABC system uses parts times square-metre area, a product-sustaining cost-allocation base, to allocate design costs to products. Another example of product-sustaining costs is engineering costs incurred to change product designs, although such changes are infrequent at Plastim.

Facility-sustaining costs are resources sacrificed on activities that cannot be traced to individual products or services but support the organization as a whole. In the Plastim example, the general administration costs (including rent costs and cost of hiring building security) are facility-sustaining costs. It is usually difficult to find good cause-and-effect relationships between these costs and a cost-allocation base. In the absence of a clear cause-and-effect relationship, some companies deduct these costs directly from operating income as period costs rather than include them in product costs. Other companies, such as Plastim, allocate facility-sustaining costs to products on some basis, for example direct

Cost hierarchy. Categorization of costs into different cost pools based on different classes of cost drivers or different degrees of difficulty in determining cause-and-effect (or benefits-received) relationships.

Output unit-level costs. The costs of resources sacrificed on activities performed on each individual unit of product or service.

Batch-level costs. The costs of resources sacrificed on activities that are related to a group of units of products or services rather than to each individual unit of product or service.

Product-sustaining costs (service-sustaining costs). The costs of resources sacrificed on activities undertaken to support specific products (or services).

A major reason low-volume products are often undercosted is that low-volume products' *batch-level* costs and *product-sustaining* costs should be spread over the relatively few units of low-volume products rather than spread over all products using *output-unit-level cost-allocation bases*.

Facility-sustaining costs. The costs of resources sacrificed on activities that cannot be traced to specific products or services but support the organization as a whole.

manufacturing labour-hours, because management believes all costs should be allocated to products. Allocating all costs becomes particularly important when management wants to set prices based on a cost number that includes all costs.

IMPLEMENTING ACTIVITY-BASED COSTING AT PLASTIM CORPORATION

OBJECTIVE 5

Assign costs to products or services using activity-based costing (ABC)

Now that we understand the basic concepts of ABC, we use it to refine Plastim's existing costing system. We again follow the seven-step approach to costing presented at the start of the chapter and the three guidelines for refining costing systems (increasing direct-cost tracing, creating homogeneous indirect-cost pools, and identifying cost-allocation bases that have a cause-and-effect relationship with costs in the cost pool).

◆ **Step 1:** *Identify the chosen cost objects.* The cost objects are the S3 and CL5 lenses. The objective is to calculate the *total* costs of designing, manufacturing, and distributing the S3 and CL5 lenses.

◆ **Step 2:** *Identify the direct costs of the cost objects.* Plastim identifies direct materials costs, direct manufacturing labour costs, and mould cleaning and maintenance costs as direct costs of the lenses. In its traditional cost system, Plastim had classified mould cleaning and maintenance costs as indirect costs that were allocated to products using direct manufacturing labour-hours. However, these costs can be traced directly to a lens because each type of lens can be produced only from a specific mould. Mould cleaning and maintenance costs, however, consist of wages paid to workers for cleaning moulds after each batch of lenses is run. Therefore, the cost object for cleaning and maintenance costs is a batch. The costs can be traced and therefore are direct costs. Batches of complex lenses incur more cleaning and maintenance costs than simple lenses because the moulds of complex lenses are harder to clean. Direct manufacturing labour-hours do not capture the larger cost per batch incurred to clean and maintain the complex moulds in contrast to the simple lens moulds.

Plastim's direct costs are as follows:

	Cost Hierarchy Category	60,000 Simple Lenses (S3)		15,000 Complex Lenses (CL5)		Total
		Total (1)	Per Unit (2) = (1) ÷ 60,000	Total (3)	Per Unit (4) = (3) ÷ 15,000	(5) = (1) + (3)
Direct materials	Unit-level	$1,125,000	$18.75	$ 675,000	$45.00	$1,800,000
Direct manufacturing labour	Unit-level	600,000	10.00	195,000	13.00	795,000
Mould cleaning & maintenance	Batch-level	120,000	2.00	150,000	10.00	270,000
Total costs		$1,845,000	$30.75	$1,020,000	$68.00	$2,865,000

◆ **Step 3:** *Select the cost-allocation bases to use in allocating indirect costs to the cost object(s).* Plastim identifies six activities—design, moulding-machine setups, manufacturing operations, shipment setup, distribution, and administration— for allocating indirect costs to products. Exhibit 5-2, column 4, shows the cost-allocation base and the quantity of the cost-allocation base for each activity.

The cost-allocation base is pivotal in defining the number of activity pools in an ABC system. For example, rather than define the design activities of product design, process design, and prototyping as separate activities, Plastim defines all these activities as part of a larger design activity. Why? Because the complexity of the mould is an appropriate cost driver for costs incurred in all three design subactivities.

A second consideration in choosing a cost-allocation base is the availability of reliable data and measures. Consider, for example, the problem of choosing a cost-allocation base for the design activity. The driver of design cost, a product-sustaining cost, is the complexity of the mould. More complex moulds take more time to design. In its ABC system, Plastim measures complexity in terms of the number of parts in the mould and the surface area of the mould. If these data were difficult to obtain, or if measurement

EXHIBIT 5-2
Activity Cost Rates for Indirect-Cost Pools

	A	B	C	D	E	F
1			(Step 4)	(Step 3)	(Step 5)	
2	Activity	Cost Hierarchy Category	Total Indirect Costs	Cost Allocation Base Quantity	Overhead Activity Cost Allocation Rate	Cause-and-Effect Relationship between Allocation Base and Activity Cost
3	(1)	(2)	(3)	(4)	(5) = (3)÷(4)	(6)
4	Design	Product	$450,000	100 parts per sq metre	$4,500.00 per part per sq metre	Design dept. indirect costs increase with more complex moulds
5	Setup of moulding machines	Batch	$300,000	2,000 setup-hours	$150.00 per setup-hour	Indirect setup costs increase with setup-hours
6	Manufacturing operations	Unit	$637,500	12,750 moulding machine-hours	$50.00 per moulding machine-hour	Indirect moulding machine operation costs increase with machine-hours
7	Shipment	Batch	$81,000	200 shipments	$405.00 per shipment	Costs to prepare batches for shipment increase with number of shipments
8	Distribution	Unit	$391,500	67,500 cubic metres delivered	$5.80 per cubic metre delivered	Distribution costs increase with number of cubic metres delivered
9	Administration	Facility	$255,000	39,750 direct mfg. labour-hours	$6.415 per direct mfg. labour-hour	Demand for administration increases with direct mfg. labour-hours

errors were large, Plastim could be forced to use some other measure of complexity, such as the amount of material flowing through the mould. The problem then is that the quantity of material flow may not adequately represent the complexity of the design activity.

◆ **Step 4:** *Identify the indirect costs associated with each cost-allocation base.* In this step, overhead costs incurred by Plastim are assigned to activities based on a cause-and-effect relationship between the costs of an activity and the cost-allocation base for the activity. For example, costs in the distribution-cost pool have a cause-and-effect relationship to cubic metres of packages moved.

Some costs can be directly identified with a particular activity. For example, salaries paid to design engineers are directly identified with the design activity. Other costs need to be allocated across activities. For example, based on interviews or time records, manufacturing engineers and supervisors identify the time spent on design activities, moulding machine setup activity, and manufacturing operations. The time spent on these activities serves as a basis for allocating manufacturing engineers' and supervisors' salary costs to various activities. Similarly, other costs are allocated to activity-cost pools using allocation bases that best describe the costs incurred for the different activities. For example, space costs are allocated based on square-metre area used for different activities. However, the allocation base chosen may sometimes be constrained by the availability of reliable data.

The key point here is that all costs do not fit nicely into activity categories. Often, costs may need to be first allocated to activities before the costs of the activities can be allocated to products.

◆ **Step 5:** *Compute the rate per unit of each cost-allocation base used to allocate indirect costs to the cost object(s).* Exhibit 5-2 summarizes the calculation of the activity-cost rates using the cost-allocation bases selected in step 3 and the indirect costs of each activity calculated in step 4. Exhibit 5-3, panel A, presents an overview of the ABC system.

◆ **Step 6:** *Compute the indirect costs allocated to the cost object(s).* Exhibit 5-3, panel B, shows indirect costs of $1,153,953 allocated to the simple lens and $961,047 allocated to the complex lens. To calculate indirect costs of each lens, the total quantity of the cost-allocation base used for each activity by each type of lens

Companies that have successfully implemented ABC usually limit the number of activities considered per department to between 5 and 10, at least in the initial implementation. More activities can be added if the additional complexity improves the quality of information and produces improved decisions. Many implementations of ABC fail because initially too many activities were identified.

EXHIBIT 5-3
Product Costs at Plastim Inc. Using Activity-Based Costing

PANEL A: AN OVERVIEW OF PLASTIM'S ACTIVITY-BASED COSTING SYSTEM

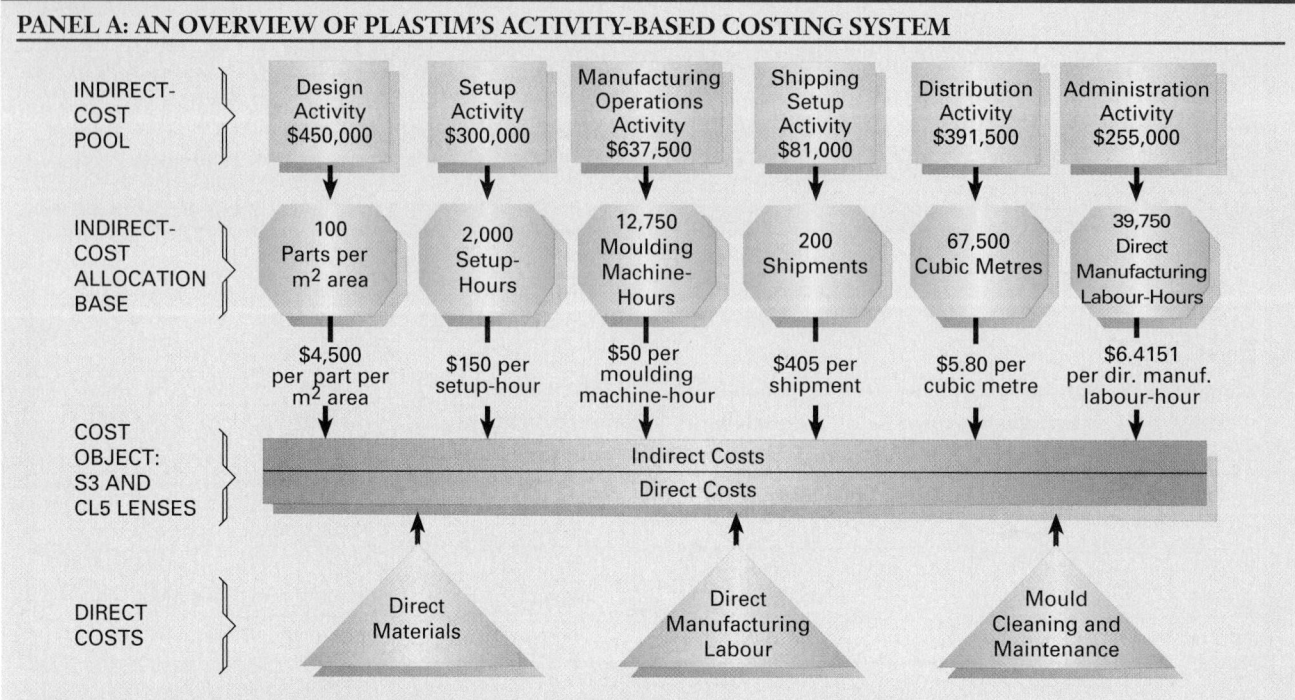

PANEL B: PRODUCT COSTS USING THE ACTIVITY-BASED COST SYSTEM

	A	B	C	D	E	F
1		**60,000**		**15,000**		
2		**Simple Lenses (S3)**		**Complex Lenses (CL5)**		
3		Total	Per Unit	Total	Per Unit	Total
4		(1)	(2) = (1) ÷ 60,000	(3)	(4) = (3) ÷ 15,000	(5) = (1) + (3)
5	Direct materials	$1,125,000	$18.75	$ 675,000	$ 45.00	$1,800,000
6	Direct manufacturing labour	600,000	10.00	195,000	13.00	795,000
7	Mould cleaning & maintenance	120,000	2.00	150,000	10.00	270,000
8	Total costs	$1,845,000	$30.75	$1,020,000	$ 68.00	$2,865,000
9	Indirect costs					
10	Design activity costs					
11	S3: 30 parts per metre² × $4,500	135,000	2.25			450,000
12	CL5: 70 parts per metre² × $4,500			315,000	21.00	
13	Setup activity costs					
14	S3: 500 setup-hours × $150	75,000	1.25			300,000
15	CL5: 1,500 setup-hours × $150			225,000	15.00	
16	Mfg. operations activity costs					
17	S3: 9,000 moulding machine-hours × $50	450,000	7.50			637,500
18	CL5: 3,750 moulding machine-hours × $50			187,500	12.50	
19	Shipping setup activity					
20	S3: 100 shipments × $405	40,500	0.68			81,000
21	CL5: 100 shipments × $405			40,500	2.70	
22	Distribution activity					
23	S3: 45,000 metres³ × $5.80	261,000	4.35			391,500
24	CL5: 22,500 metres³ × $5.80			130,500	8.70	
25	Administration activity					
26	S3: 30,000 dir. mfg. labour-hours × $6.4151	192,453	3.21			255,000
27	CL5: 9,750 dir. mfg. labour-hours × $6.4151	–	–	62,547	4.17	–
28	Total indirect costs	1,153,953	19.23	961,047	64.07	2,115,000
29	Total costs	$2,998,953	$49.98	$1,981,047	$132.07	$4,980,000

(the data for which are provided by Plastim's operations personnel) is multiplied by the cost-allocation rate calculated in step 5 (see Exhibit 5-2, column 5). For example, of the 2,000 hours of the setup activity (Exhibit 5-2, column 4), the S3 lens uses 500 setup-hours and the CL5 lens uses 1,500 setup-hours. Hence, the total costs of the setup activity allocated to the S3 lens is $75,000 (500 setup-hours × $150, the setup rate calculated in Exhibit 5-2, column 5) and to the CL5 lens is $225,000 (1,500 setup-hours × $150). The setup cost per unit can then be calculated for the S3 lens as $1.25 ($75,000 ÷ 60,000 units) and for the CL5 lens as $15 ($225,000 ÷ 15,000 units).

◆ **Step 7:** *Determine the costs of the cost objects by adding all direct and indirect costs assigned to them.* Exhibit 5-3, panel B, presents the product costs for the simple and complex lenses. The direct costs are calculated in step 2 and the indirect costs in step 6. The activity-based cost system overview in Exhibit 5-3, panel A, shows three direct-cost categories and six indirect-cost pools. Hence, the cost of each type of lens in Exhibit 5-3, panel B, has nine line items, three for direct costs and six for allocated indirect costs. The differences in the ABC product costs of S3 and CL5 calculated in Exhibit 5-3, panel B, highlight how these products use different amounts of direct costs and different amounts of resources in each activity area.

We emphasize two key features of ABC systems. First, these systems identify all costs used by products, whether the costs are variable or fixed in the short run. Why? Because the focus of ABC systems is on longer-run decisions when more of the costs can be managed and fewer costs are regarded as fixed and given. Hence, ABC systems identify all resources used by products regardless of how individual costs behave in the short run. Second, as we have already described, recognizing the hierarchy of costs is critical when allocating costs to products. It is easiest to use the cost hierarchy to calculate *total* costs. For this reason, we recommend calculating total costs first. The per unit costs are easily calculated by dividing total costs by the number of units produced.

COMPARING ALTERNATIVE COSTING SYSTEMS

Exhibit 5-4 compares key features of and differences between Plastim's existing single indirect-cost pool system (Exhibit 5-1, p. 156) and the ABC system (Exhibit 5-3). We emphasize three points in Exhibit 5-4: (1) ABC systems trace more costs as direct costs; (2) ABC systems create more cost pools linked to different activities; and (3) for each activity-cost pool, ABC systems seek a cost-allocation base that has a cause-and-effect relationship with costs in the cost pool.

The homogeneous cost pools and the choice of cost-allocation bases, tied to the cost hierarchy, gives Plastim's managers greater confidence in the activity and product cost numbers from the ABC system. Allocating costs to lenses using only an output unit-level allocation base, direct manufacturing labour-hours, as in the existing single indirect-cost pool system overcosts the simple S3 lens and undercosts the complex CL5 lens. The CL5 (S3) lens uses a disproportionately larger (smaller) amount of output unit-level, batch-level, and product-sustaining costs than is represented by the direct manufacturing labour-hour cost-allocation base.

The benefits of ABC systems arise from using ABC information for making better decisions. But these benefits must be traded off against the measurement and implementation costs of these systems. We focus on these issues next.

USING ABC SYSTEMS FOR COST MANAGEMENT AND PROFITABILITY IMPROVEMENT

The emphasis of this chapter so far has been on the role of ABC systems in obtaining better activity and product costs. But companies use ABC information for both pricing and cost management decisions. **Activity-based management (ABM)** describes management decisions that use activity-based costing information to improve operations and processes, satisfy customers, and generate profits. In this section, we focus on ABM, including performing activities more efficiently, eliminating activities that do not add value, and improving product design.

This chapter's ABC calculations have been done in Excel and illustrate how technology eases the implementation of ABC. The basic database is Exhibit 5-4, where activity cost rates are calculated for homogeneous indirect cost pools. The Excel worksheet for Exhibit 5-5 draws on Exhibit 5-4 to calculate product costs. Companies use specifically designed ABC software that has this same type of architecture to connect resources, activities, and cost objects.

OBJECTIVE 6

Use ABC systems for activity-based management (ABM)

EXHIBIT 5-4
Comparing Alternative Costing Systems

	Existing Single Indirect-Cost Pool System (1)	ABC System (2)	Difference (3) = (2) − (1)
Direct-cost categories	2	3	+ 1
	Direct materials	Direct materials	
	Direct manufacturing labour	Direct manufacturing labour	
		Direct cleaning and maintenance labour	
Total direct costs	$2,595,000	$2,865,000	+$270,000
Indirect-cost pools	1	6	+ 5
	Single indirect-cost pool allocated using direct manufacturing labour-hours	Design cost pool allocated using parts per square-metre area	
		Moulding machine setup cost pool allocated using setup-hours	
		Manufacturing operations cost pool allocated using moulding machine-hours	
		Shipment setup cost pool allocated using number of shipments	
		Distribution cost pool allocated using cubic metres of packages shipped	
		Administration cost pool allocated using direct manufacturing labour-hours	
Total indirect costs	$2,385,000	$2,115,000	−$270,000
Total costs assigned to simple (S3) lens	$3,525,000	$2,998,953	−$526,047
Cost per unit of simple (S3) lens	$58.75	$49.98	−$8.77
Total costs assigned to complex (CL5) lens	$1,455,000	$1,981,047	+$526,047
Cost per unit of complex (CL5) lens	$97.00	$132.07	+$35.07

Activity-based management (ABM). Describes management decisions that use activity-based costing information to improve operations and processes, satisfy customers, and generate profits.

The heart of the ABC approach is the analysis of activities. Activities consume resources; products consume activities. When Plastim analyzes its activity—setups of moulding machines—the managers have the opportunity to find ways of reducing setup time and therefore the labour cost of setups (the cost-management benefit of ABC). Managers also will improve their estimates of the total setup cost per unit of product (the product-costing benefit of ABC).

Product and pricing decisions. The ABC system gives insight into the cost management structures for making and selling diverse products. As a result, management can make better product and pricing decisions. For example, the ABC system indicates that Plastim can reduce the price of S3 to the $53 range and still make a profit, because the ABC cost of S3 is $49.98. Without the ABC information, Plastim management may have erroneously concluded that it would incur an operating loss on the S3 lens at the $53 price. This incorrect conclusion may have caused Plastim to reduce its business in simple lenses and focus instead on complex lenses, where its existing single indirect-cost pool system indicates it is very profitable.

Focusing on complex lenses would be a mistake. The ABC system indicates that the cost of making the complex lens is much higher ($132.07 versus $97 under Plastim's existing direct manufacturing labour-based costing system). As Plastim's operations staff had thought all along, Plastim has no comparative advantage in making CL5 lenses. At a price of $137 per lens for CL5, the margins look very small. As Plastim reduces prices on simple lenses, it will probably have to negotiate a higher price for the complex lenses.

Cost-reduction decisions. Manufacturing and distribution personnel use ABC systems to focus cost-reduction efforts. Managers set cost-reduction targets in terms of reducing the cost per unit of the cost-allocation base in different activity areas. For example, the supervisor of the distribution activity area at Plastim could have a performance target of decreasing the distribution cost per cubic metre from $5.80 to $5.40 by reducing distribution labour and warehouse rental costs.

Process decisions. Creating a map of the cost of important activities (activity cost pools) and the factors that cause these costs to be incurred (cost drivers and cost-allocation bases) opens many opportunities for improving efficiency. Management can evaluate whether particular activities can be reduced or eliminated by improving processes. Each indirect cost-allocation base in the ABC system is a nonfinancial variable (number of hours of setup time, cubic metres shipped, and so on). Controlling physical items such as setup hours or cubic metres shipped is often the most fundamental way that operating personnel manage costs. For example, Plastim can reduce distribution costs by packing the lenses in a way that reduces the bulkiness of the shipment.

The following table shows the reduction in distribution costs of the S3 and CL5 lenses as a result of process and efficiency improvements that lower the cost per cubic metre (from \$5.80 to \$5.40) and the total cubic metres of shipments (from 45,000 to 40,000 for S3 and 22,500 to 20,000 for CL5).

	60,000 Simple Lenses (S3)		15,000 Complex Lenses (CL5)	
	Total (1)	Per Unit (2) = (1) ÷ 60,000	Total (3)	Per Unit (4) = (3) ÷ 15,000
Distribution activity				
S3: 45,000 metres^3 × \$5.80	\$261,000	\$4.35		
CL5: 22,500 metres^3 × \$5.80			\$130,500	\$8.70
Distribution costs after process improvements				
S3: 40,000 metres^3 × \$5.40	\$216,000	\$3.60		
CL5: 20,000 metres^3 × \$5.40			\$108,000	\$7.20
Distribution cost savings after improvements	\$ 45,000	\$0.75	\$ 22,500	\$1.50

Clearly, in the long-term or strategic view of ABC systems, the planned reduction in total distribution costs will be \$67,500 as Plastim managers reach their reduced volumes of lenses shipped and the unit cost per cubic metre (m^3). In the short to medium run, distribution costs may be primarily fixed costs. For example, costs of renting distribution space will be fixed in the short run, according to the terms of the lease agreement.

To encourage timely process improvements that will realize long-run cost reductions, management accountants designing ABC systems distinguish *costs incurred* from *resources used* when allocating costs to products. The costs incurred in the short and medium run will remain \$391,500 but the resources used in the improved distribution process will decrease to \$324,000. The lesser amount is allocated to each product—for S3, \$216,000 and for CL5, \$108,000. The difference of \$67,500 is the cost of available but unused distribution capacity.

$$\text{Costs incurred} = \text{Resources used} + \text{Costs of unused capacity}$$
$$= \$324,000 + \$67,500 = \$391,500$$

Efficiency improvements will cause long-term cost reductions and the unused capacity can be calculated as follows:

$$\text{Number of m}^3 \text{ of lenses that can be delivered after efficiency improvements} = \frac{\$391,500}{\$5.40 \text{ per m}^3} = 72,500 \text{ m}^3$$

$$\text{Number of m}^3 \text{ required to deliver 60,000 S3 and 15,000 CL5 lenses} = 40,000 + 20,000 = 60,000 \text{ m}^3$$

$$\text{Unused distribution capacity} = 12,500 \text{ m}^3$$

$$\text{Cost of unused capacity} = 12,500 \text{ m}^3 \times \$5.40 \text{ per m}^3 = \$67,500$$

This example highlights an important advantage of ABC systems, which is that they do not allocate the costs of unused capacity to products but rather report them as a separate line item. Unused capacity costs are not incurred to support the product and therefore the product remains unburdened by this cost. This improves the presentation of the cause-and-effect link between the resources consumed in the improved distribution process and the volume of product actually shipped. For managers who receive bonuses for reducing the costs of existing processes, this approach provides a financial incentive to seek and implement appropriate process improvements in a timely way.

Often, more opportunities to reduce costs exist at the design stage of the value chain than the production stage.

Design decisions. Management can identify and evaluate new designs to improve performance by evaluating how product and process designs affect activities and costs. Companies can then work with their customers to evaluate the costs and prices of alternative design choices. For example, creative design decisions that decrease the complexity of the mould reduce costs of design, materials, labour, setups, moulding machine operations, and mould cleaning and maintenance.

If Plastim used its existing direct manufacturing labour-hour-based system to choose among alternative designs, which design choices would Plastim favour? Those designs that reduce direct manufacturing labour-hours the most. Why? Because the cost system sends an erroneous signal that reducing direct manufacturing labour-hours reduces overhead costs. In fact, the cause-and-effect relationship between direct manufacturing labour-hours and Plastim's overhead costs is very weak. Therefore, reducing direct manufacturing labour-hours would have little effect on Plastim's indirect costs.

Planning and managing activities. Most companies implementing ABC systems for the first time analyze actual costs to identify activity-cost pools and activity-cost rates. Many then use ABC systems for planning and managing activities. They specify budgeted cost rates for activities, then, using a variation on normal costing for direct costs and normal costing for indirect costs, multiply these rates by actual quantity of activities. At year-end, actual costs are compared to budgeted costs, providing feedback on how well activities were managed. Adjustments are also made for under- or overallocated indirect costs for each activity area, using the methods described in Chapter 4 (writeoff, proration, or adjusted allocation rate).

Our objective is to introduce activity-based management (ABM), wherein managers use ABC information to improve their decisions on pricing, design, process improvement, and cost reduction. Many variables causing cost are nonfinancial, such as complexity of a mould, and ABC provides the way to link nonfinancial causes to financial effects. By dividing large processes into smaller sets of activities, ABC also improves the ability of managers to identify cost-reduction opportunities by changing either the quantity of activity undertaken or the resources consumed by a product. Our application of ABM techniques is described in Chapter 6, where we discuss activity-based budgeting; in Chapter 11, where we discuss outsourcing and adding or dropping business segments; and in Chapter 12, where we evaluate alternative design choices to improve efficiency and reduce nonvalue-added costs. Our discussion continues in Chapter 13, where we cover reengineering and downsizing, and in Chapter 14, where we explore managing customer profitability. We also present how to apply ABM techniques in Chapter 19, where we explain quality improvements, and in Chapter 20, where we describe how to evaluate suppliers.

ACTIVITY-BASED COSTING AND DEPARTMENT INDIRECT-COSTS RATES

OBJECTIVE 7

Compare ABC and department overhead rate systems

Companies often use costing systems that have features of ABC systems—such as multiple cost pools and multiple cost-allocation bases—but that do not emphasize individual activities. Many companies calculate separate indirect-cost rates for each department (for example, design, manufacturing, distribution, and so on) or subdepartment (for example, machining and assembly departments within manufacturing) using a cost-allocation base that best represents the usage of resources in that department or subdepartment. Using the same logic that we described for ABC systems, companies prefer using department indirect-cost rates rather than a single company-wide indirect-cost rate when the drivers of costs in each department differ. In this section, we compare ABC systems and department rate costing systems.

Consider again our Plastim illustration. The indirect-cost rate for the design activity is, in fact, a design department indirect-cost rate. Plastim calculates the design activity rate by dividing total design department costs by a measure of the complexity of the mould (the driver of design department costs). Plastim does not find it worthwhile to calculate separate activity rates within the design department. Why? Because the complexity of the mould is an appropriate cost-allocation base for costs incurred for all design activities—the design department costs are homogeneous.

In contrast, in the manufacturing (as also in the distribution) department, Plastim identifies two activity-cost pools—setup-cost pool and a manufacturing operations-cost pool—rather than use a single manufacturing department indirect-cost pool. Why? For two reasons. First, each of these activities within manufacturing incurs significant costs and has very different cost drivers. Second, the S3 and CL5 lenses do not use resources from these two activity areas in the same proportion. For example, CL5 uses 75% (1,500 ÷ 2,000) of the setup-hours but only 29.4% (3,750 ÷ 12,750) of the machine hours. Using only machine-hours, say, to allocate all manufacturing department costs at Plastim would result in CL5 being undercosted because it would not be charged for the significant setup resources it actually uses.

The preceding discussion suggests that using department indirect-cost rates to allocate costs to products would result in the same product costs as activity-cost rates would if (1) a single activity, for example, machining in a manufacturing department, accounts for a sizable fraction of the department's costs or (2) significant costs are incurred on different activities within a department but each activity has the same cost-allocation base or (3) significant costs are incurred on different activities with different cost-allocation bases within a department but different products use resources from the different activity areas in the same proportions.

In many companies, where any of these three conditions hold, a department indirect-cost rate system is often adequate. In companies where these conditions do not hold, department indirect-cost rate systems can be refined using ABC. Emphasizing activities leads to more focused and homogeneous cost pools, and aids in identifying activity-cost-allocation bases that have a better cause-and-effect relationship with the costs in activity-cost pools. But the benefits of an ABC system must be balanced against its costs and limitations.

IMPLEMENTING ABC SYSTEMS

Managers choose the level of detail in their costing systems by evaluating the costs of the system against the benefits that accrue from using these systems to make better decisions. Are there "telltale" signs that indicate when ABC systems are likely to provide the most benefits? We list six signals below:

OBJECTIVE 8

Evaluate the costs and benefits of implementing ABC systems

1. Significant amounts of indirect costs are allocated using only one or two cost pools.

2. All or most costs are identified as output unit-level costs (that is, few costs are described as batch, product-sustaining, or facility-sustaining costs).

3. Products make diverse demands on resources because of differences in volume, process steps, batch size, or complexity.

4. Products that a company is well suited to make and sell show small profits, while products that a company is less suited to produce and sell show large profits.

5. Complex products appear to be very profitable and simple products appear to be losing money.

6. Operations staff have significant disagreements with the accounting staff about the costs of manufacturing and marketing products and services.

Even if a company decides to implement ABC, it must make important choices about the level of detail. Should it choose many finely specified activities, cost drivers, and cost pools, or would a few suffice? For example, Plastim could define a different moulding machine-hour rate for each different type of moulding machine. In making such choices, managers consider the costs and limitations of refining costing systems.

The main costs and limitations of ABC are the measurements necessary to implement the systems. ABC systems require management to estimate costs of activity pools and to identify and measure cost drivers for these pools to serve as cost-allocation bases. Even basic ABC systems require many calculations to determine costs of products and services. These measurements are costly. Activity-cost rates also need to be updated regularly. Very detailed ABC systems are costly to operate and difficult to understand.

Varying Interest in Activity-Based Costing

A number of companies around the world are investigating and implementing activity-based costing. However, ABC applications vary from organization to organization. Some companies use ABC as their basic, ongoing cost accounting system. Other organizations are more selective, so perhaps only a single business division uses ABC before it becomes a companywide initiative.

One study of 162 U.S.-based companies (including 29 service-sector companies) reported the following ranking of the primary applications for which ABC is used: (1) product/service costing, (2) cost reduction, and (3) process improvement.[a] Areas in which ABC-based information produced "significant" or "very significant" changes in decisions ranked as follows: (1) pricing strategy, (2) processes, and (3) product mix. Another recent survey of U.S. manufacturers reported that only 30 out of 145 respondents, or 20.6%, currently use ABC.[b] Unfortunately, the survey does not indicate why respondents are not using ABC. Some of these companies may already have information similar to the information developed by ABC systems. For other manufacturers, ABC may not be relevant or useful or the costs of implementing ABC may exceed the benefits.

Among United Kingdom companies, one survey indicates that 17.5% of businesses have implemented ABC and another 20.3% are considering using it.[c] For what applications are these firms using ABC?

Cost reduction	90.3%
Product/service pricing	68.9
Performance measurement/improvement	74.2
Cost modelling	64.5
Budgeting	54.8

A New Zealand survey found that 20.3% of respondents use ABC.[d] Other studies found that 20% of respondents from India and 11% of respondents from Singapore had implemented ABC systems.[e,f]

A survey of Irish manufacturing companies that have implemented ABC reported the following percentages for the benefits experienced: (1) more-accurate cost information for product costing and pricing (71%), (2) improved cost control and management (66%), (3) improved insight into cost drivers (58%), (4) better performance measures (46%), and (5) more-accurate customer profitability analysis (25%).[g] A survey of Irish service-sector companies reports similar percentages for the benefits experienced.[h]

The Irish survey also reported that the three most common implementation problems were assigning costs to activities, identifying and selecting cost drivers, and inadequate computer software. A survey of Dutch companies in the food and beverage industry cited problems of other priorities and lack of time, as well as the difficulty and cost of collecting data.[i]

---

[a]APQC/CAM-1, *Activity Based Management Consortium Study* (American Productivity and Quality Center/ CAM-1, 1995).

[b]Sharman, P., "The Case for Management Accounting," *Strategic Finance* (2003).

[c]Innes, J., F. Mitchell, and D. Sinclair, "Activity-Based Costing in the U.K.'s Largest Companies: A Comparison of 1994 and 1999 Survey Results," *Management Accounting Research* (2000).

[d]Cotton, W., S. Jackman, and R. Brown, "Note on a New Zealand Replication of the Innes et al. UK Activity-Based Costing Survey," *Management Accounting Research* (2003).

[e]Anderson, S., and W. Lanen, "Economic Transition, Strategy and the Evolution of Management Accounting Practices: The Case of India," *Accounting, Organizations and Society* (1999).

[f]Ghosh, B., and Y. Chan, "Management Accounting in Singapore—Well in Place?" *Managerial Auditing Journal* (1997).

[g]Clarke, P., N. Hill, and K. Stevens, "Activity-Based Costing in Ireland: Barrier to, and Opportunities for, Change," *Critical Perspectives on Accounting* (1999).

[h]Clarke, P., and T. Mullins, "Activity-Based Costing in the Non-Manufacturing Sector in Ireland: A Preliminary Investigation," *Irish Journal of Management* (2001).

[i]Groot, T., "Activity Based Costing in U.S. and Dutch Food Companies," *Advances in Management Accounting* (1999).

In very detailed ABC systems, the allocations necessary to calculate activity costs often result in activity-cost pools being measured with error. At times, companies are also forced to use substitute allocation bases for which data are readily available rather than preferred allocation bases. For example, a company might be forced to use the number of loads moved instead of the complexity and distance of different loads moved as the allocation base for material handling costs because the former is easier to track. When measurement errors are large, activity-cost information can be misleading. For example, if the cost per load moved decreases, a company may conclude that it has become more efficient in its material handling operations. In fact, the lower cost per move may have resulted solely from moving lighter loads over shorter distances.

Managers always trade off the benefits of designing a more detailed and accurate ABC system against the measurement and implementation costs of the system. Improvements in information technology and accompanying declines in technology costs have enabled ABC to be a practical costing system in many organizations. As such trends continue, ABC systems should be better able to meet the cost-benefit test.

The Global Surveys of Company Practice box indicates that ABC implementation varies among companies. What is important is that it is an alternative against which managers can assess the usefulness of the information provided by their simple, traditional costing approach. Managers considering refinement to these simple systems can use ABC as a framework to guide change. The Focus on Values and Behaviours box describes some issues to which management accountants must be sensitive as they face the challenge of changing how managers in organizations think about costing systems.

Successfully Championing ABC

Successfully implementing ABC systems requires more than an understanding of the technical details. ABC implementation often represents a significant change in the costing system and, as the chapter indicates, it requires managers to make major choices with respect to the definition of activities and the level of detail. What then are some of the behavioural issues that the management accountant must be sensitive to?

1. **Gaining support of top management and creating a sense of urgency for the ABC effort.** This requires management accountants to lay out the vision for the ABC project and to clearly communicate its strategic benefits (for example, the resulting improvements in product and process design). It also requires selling the idea to end users, working with members of other departments and as business partners of the managers in the various areas affected by the ABC project. For example, project managers must demonstrate how the information gained from ABC would provide insights into the efficiency of operations that were previously unavailable. The ABC project will require that the finance area communicate regularly with operations about new reports and proposed changes to the financial reporting package that managers receive.

2. **Creating a guiding coalition of managers throughout the value chain for the ABC effort.** ABC systems measure how the resources of an organization are used. Managers responsible for these resources have the best knowledge about activities and cost drivers. Getting managers to cooperate and take the initiative for implementing ABC is essential for gaining the required expertise, the proper credibility, and the necessary leadership. There are several other benefits to gaining wide participation among managers. First, implementing ABC requires a significant time commitment. If managers feel more involved in the process, they are more likely to be willing to commit their time to the ABC effort. Second, there inevitably will be some managers who may be, or may perceive themselves to be, negatively affected by the ABC information. In our Plastim example, the managers of the complex CL5 lens may feel that ABC disadvantages them because it assigns more costs to the CL5 lens. Involving managers who are skeptical of the ABC process and giving them an opportunity to express their concerns reduces the

(Continued)

likelihood of these managers obstructing change. Finally, engaging managers throughout the value chain creates greater opportunities for coordination and cooperation across the different functions. For example, an ABC analysis might reveal that a company is incurring high manufacturing costs because of quality problems in its plant. The best way to reduce costs may be to redesign the product. This requires that the design department and the manufacturing department work closely together.

3. **Educating and training employees in ABC as a basis for employee empowerment.** Disseminating information about ABC throughout all facets of an organization allows workers in all areas of a business to use their knowledge of ABC to make improvements. For example, WS Industries, an Indian manufacturer of insulators, not only shared ABC information with its workers but also established an incentive plan that gave employees a percentage of the cost savings. The results were dramatic because employees were empowered and motivated to implement numerous cost-saving projects.

4. **Seeking small short-run successes as proof that the ABC implementation is yielding results.** Too often, managers and management accountants seek big results and major changes far too quickly. In many situations, achieving a significant change overnight is difficult. However, showing how ABC information has helped improve a process and save costs, even if only in small ways, motivates the team to stay on course and build momentum. The credibility gained from small victories leads to additional and bigger improvements involving larger numbers of people and different parts of the organization. Eventually ABC and ABM will be rooted in the culture of the organization. Sharing short-run successes may also help motivate employees to be innovative. Managers can create a "process improvement" mailbox to facilitate the sharing of process improvement ideas.

5. **Recognizing that ABC information is not perfect because it balances the need for better information against the costs of creating a complex system that managers and employees may not understand.** The management accountant must help managers recognize both the value and the limitations of ABC and not oversell it. Open and honest communication about ABC ensures that managers use ABC thoughtfully to make good decisions. Critical judgments can then be made without being adversarial, and tough questions can be answered to help drive better decisions about the system.

ACTIVITY-BASED COSTING IN MERCHANDISING AND SERVICE COMPANIES

Although many of the early examples of ABC originated in manufacturing, it has many applications in the merchandising and service areas. Companies in merchandising such as Chapters and Amazon.com, which resell products without changing them, also have implemented ABC and ABM. Many retail and wholesale companies are working with ABC systems. Costs of activities are grouped into homogeneous cost pools and classified as output unit-level, batch-level, product- or service-sustaining, and facility-sustaining costs. The cost pools correspond to key activities. Costs are allocated to products or customers using activity drivers or cost-allocation bases that have a cause-and-effect relationship with the costs in the cost pool.

The general approach to ABC in service and even not-for profit organizations is very similar to the approach described in this chapter. Service and not-for-profit organizations also have to confront the problems of measuring activity-cost pools and identifying and measuring allocation bases. Companies in banking, insurance, accounting, and consulting industries have implemented ABC systems to define profitable product mixes, improve efficiency, and satisfy customers. Similarly, some of the Canadian government's service providers (for example, Environment Canada, the Departments of the Auditor General of Canada, National Defence Maritime Command, the Meteorological Service, and Citizenship and Immigration) have implemented ABC and ABM.

The Co-operative Bank in the United Kingdom followed this approach when it implemented ABC in its retail bank. It calculated the costs of various activities, such as making ATM transactions, opening and closing accounts, administering mortgages, and processing VISA transactions. It then used the activity-cost rates to calculate costs of various products, such as chequing account, mortgage, and VISA card. ABC information

AimCorp
www.aimamc.com/staci/
selected_projects.htm

The Co-operative Bank
www.co-operativebank.co.uk

Analyzing and Managing Multichannel Banking with Activity-Based Costing

Activity-based costing (ABC) can help banks, such as the Bank of Montreal, with strategic analysis, measurement, and management of their service delivery. This support is critical because banks offer consumers multiple service channels for transactions, including traditional branches, ATMs, and Internet banking. Because the costs for each channel are different, ABC can help answer questions such as: What costs are associated with branch transactions versus online transactions? Which channels help reduce overall costs? How much does it cost to get a new customer to use online banking? To answer these questions, ABC systems identify and measure the costs of activities aimed at servicing the customer.

Banking cost drivers are unique because the costs associated with each cost driver are different depending on whether customers use branch tellers, automated phone systems, or the Internet. Examples of these cost drivers include:

Activity	Cost Driver
1. Transaction processing—the costs associated with executing deposits, withdrawals, transfers, and other banking business	Number of transactions per channel
2. Product/service offerings—selecting service offerings, creating and developing new services, supporting existing offerings	Number of products/services per channel
3. Customer service—helping customers with problems and answering questions about service offerings	Number of inquiries per channel
4. Customer acquisition and retention—acquiring new customers and structuring programs to retain existing customers	Number of targeted customers per channel
5. Technology services—information technology support, including ATM maintenance, performance upgrades, and online banking service development	Number of support hours per channel

The activity costs are used to identify costs of different services within the different channels on the basis of the activities needed to support different service offerings. According to one recent report, ATM transactions are nine times cheaper and online banking fifteen times cheaper than traditional branch transactions. With such drastic cost differences, banks use ABC information to evaluate (1) the profits earned on customers that extensively use different transaction channels, (2) the profitability of placing new ATMs in high-traffic areas, and (3) the effectiveness of advertising that encourages existing customers to use online banking more.

Based on this cost information alone, it may appear that it is more profitable for banks to have all their customers rely exclusively on ATM and online banking. Not so fast! Research has shown that customers using online banking conduct many more transactions than other types of customers and use other channels of banking as well. The result: Conversion to online banking alone won't necessarily reduce banking costs, at least in the short run.

Sources: R. Brett, et al., "The Business Case for Right Channeling," *The TechStrategy Report* (June 2003); Conversations with Dr. Dennis Campbell, Harvard Business School (February 19, 2004, and February 26, 2004).

helped the bank to improve its processes and to identify profitable products and customer segments. The Concepts in Action box on p. 173 provides an example of how ABC can improve the information used in banks to make management decisions.

The Problem for Self-Study provides one example of an application of ABC in the merchandising sector.

PROBLEM

Family Supermarkets (FS) has decided to increase the size of its St. John's store. It wants information about the profitability of individual product lines: soft drinks, fresh produce, and packaged food.

Operating personnel at FS provide the following data for each product line:

	Soft Drinks	Fresh Produce	Packaged Food
Revenue	$317,400	$840,240	$483,960
Cost of goods sold	$240,000	$600,000	$360,000
Cost of bottles returned	$ 4,800	$ 0	$ 0
Number of purchase orders placed	144	336	144
Number of deliveries received	120	876	264
Hours of shelf-stocking time	216	2,160	1,080
Items sold	50,400	441,600	122,400

FS also provides the following information for the year 2007:

Activity (1)	Description of Activity (2)	Total Costs (3)	Cost-Allocation Base (4)
Bottle returns	Returning empty bottles to store	$ 4,800	Direct tracing to soft-drink line
Ordering	Placing orders for purchases	$ 62,400	purchase orders = 624
Delivery	Physical delivery and receiving of merchandise	$100,800	deliveries = 1,260
Shelf-stocking	Stocking and restocking merchandise	$ 69,120	hours stocking = 3,456
Customer support	Assistance provided for customers	$122,880	items sold = 614,400
Total		$360,000	

REQUIRED

1. Family Supermarkets currently allocates store support costs (all costs other than cost of goods sold) to product lines based on cost of goods sold of each product line. Calculate the operating income and operating income as a percentage of revenues for each product line.
2. If Family Supermarkets allocates store support costs (all costs other than cost of goods sold) to product lines using an activity-based costing (ABC) system, calculate the operating income and operating income as a percentage of revenues for each product line.
3. Comment on your answers to requirements 1 and 2.

SOLUTION

1. The following table shows the operating income and operating income as a percentage of revenues. All store support costs (that is, costs other than cost of goods sold) are allocated to product lines using cost of goods sold of each product line as the cost-allocation base. Total store support costs equal $360,000 (cost of bottles returned, $4,800 + cost of purchase orders, $62,400 + cost of deliveries, $100,800 + cost of shelf-stocking, $69,120 + cost of customer

support, $122,880). If cost of goods sold is the cost-allocation base, the allocation rate for store support costs = $360,000 ÷ $1,200,000 = $0.30 per dollar of cost of goods sold. To allocate support costs to each product line, FS multiplies the cost of goods sold of each product line by 0.30. Operating income for each product line is as follows:

	Soft Drinks	Fresh Produce	Packaged Food	Total
Revenue	$317,400	$840,240	$483,960	$1,641,600
Cost of goods sold	240,000	600,000	360,000	1,200,000
Store support cost ($240,000; $600,000; $360,000 × 0.30)	72,000	180,000	108,000	360,000
Total costs	312,000	780,000	468,000	1,560,000
Operating income	$ 5,400	$ 60,240	$ 15,960	$ 81,600
Operating margin (Operating income ÷ Revenue)	1.70%	7.17%	3.30%	4.97%

2. Under an ABC system, FS identifies bottle return costs as a direct cost since these costs can be traced easily to the soft drink product line. FS then calculates cost-allocation rates for each activity area (as in step 5 described in the chapter). The activity rates are as follows:

Activity (1)	Cost Hierarchy (2)	Total Costs (3)	Quantity of Cost-Allocation Base (4)	Overhead Allocation-Rate (5) = (3) ÷ (4)
Ordering	Batch-level	$ 62,400	624 purchase orders	$ 100 per purchase order
Delivery	Batch-level	$100,800	1,260 deliveries	$ 80 per delivery
Shelf-stocking	Unit level	$ 69,120	3,456 hours stocking	$ 20 per hour stocking
Customer support	Unit level	$122,880	614,400 items sold	$0.20 per item sold

Store support costs for each product line by activity are obtained by multiplying the total quantity of the cost-allocation base for each product line by the activity-cost rate. Operating income for each product line is as follows:

	Soft Drinks	Fresh Produce	Packaged Food	Total
Revenue	$317,400	$840,240	$483,960	$1,641,600
Cost of goods sold	240,000	600,000	360,000	1,200,000
Bottle-return costs	4,800	–	–	4,800
Ordering costs (144; 336; 144) p.o. × $100	14,400	33,600	14,400	62,400
Delivery costs (120; 876; 264) del. × $80	9,600	70,080	21,120	100,800
Shelf-stocking costs (216; 2,160; 1,080) hr. × $20	4,320	43,200	21,600	69,120
Customer support costs (50,400; 441,600; 122,400) items × $0.20	10,080	88,320	24,480	122,880
Total costs	283,200	835,200	441,600	1,560,000
Operating income	$ 34,200	$ 5,040	$ 42,360	$ 81,600
Operating margin (Operating income ÷ Revenue)	10.78%	0.60%	8.75%	4.97%

3. Managers believe the ABC system is more credible than the previous costing system. It distinguishes the different types of activities at FS more precisely. It also tracks more accurately how individual product lines use their resources. Rankings of relative profitability (the percentage of operating income to revenues) of the

three product lines under the previous costing system and under the ABC system are as follows:

Simple Costing System		ABC System	
1. Fresh produce	7.17%	1. Soft drinks	10.78%
2. Packaged food	3.30%	2. Packaged food	8.75%
3. Soft drinks	1.70%	3. Fresh produce	0.60%

The percentage of revenues, cost of goods sold, and activity costs for each product line are as follows:

	Soft Drinks	Fresh Produce	Packaged Food
Revenue	19.335%	51.184%	29.481%
Cost of goods sold	20.000%	50.000%	30.000%
Bottle-return costs	100.000%	0.000%	0.000%
Ordering costs	23.077%	53.846%	23.077%
Delivery costs	9.524%	69.524%	20.952%
Shelf-stocking costs	6.250%	62.500%	31.250%
Customer support costs	8.203%	71.875%	19.922%

Soft drinks consume less of all resources. Soft drinks have fewer deliveries and require less shelf-stocking than does either fresh produce or packaged food. Most major soft-drink suppliers deliver merchandise to the store shelves and stock the shelves themselves. In contrast, the fresh produce area has the most deliveries and consumes a large percentage of shelf-stocking time. It also has the highest number of individual sales items. The previous costing system assumed that each product line used the resources in each activity area in the same ratio as their respective individual cost of goods sold to total cost of goods sold ratio. Clearly, this assumption was inappropriate. The previous costing system was a classic example of broad averaging via cost smoothing.

FS managers can use the ABC information to guide decisions on how to allocate the planned increase in floor space. An increase in the percentage of space allocated to soft drinks is warranted. Note, however, that ABC information should be but one input into decisions about shelf space allocation. FS may have minimum limits on the shelf space allocated to fresh produce because of shoppers' expectations that supermarkets will carry merchandise from this product line.

Pricing decisions can also be made in a more informed way with the ABC information. For example, suppose a competitor announces a 5% reduction in soft-drink prices. Given the 10.78% margin FS currently earns on its soft-drink product line, it has flexibility to reduce prices and still make a profit on this product line. In contrast, the previous costing system erroneously implied that soft drinks only had a 1.70% margin, leaving little room to counter a competitor's pricing initiatives.

DECISION POINTS   SUMMARY

The following decision guidelines use a question-and-answer format to summarize the chapter's main points. Each decision presents a key question. The guideline is the answer to that question.

DECISIONS	GUIDELINES
1. When does product undercosting or product overcosting occur?	Product undercosting (overcosting) occurs when a product or service consumes a high (low) level of resource but is reported to have a low (high) cost. Cost smoothing, or peanut butter costing, a common cause of undercosting or overcosting, is the result of using broad

averages that uniformly assign, or spread, the cost of resources to products when the individual products use those resources in a nonuniform way. Product cost cross-subsidization exists when one undercosted (overcosted) product results in at least one other product being overcosted (undercosted).

2. How do you refine a costing system?

Refining a costing system means making changes that result in cost numbers that better measure the way different cost objects, such as products, use different amounts of company resources. These changes can require additional direct-cost tracing, the choice of more homogeneous indirect-cost pools, or the use of different cost-allocation bases.

3. What is the difference between the traditional approach and the activity-based costing (ABC) approach to designing costing systems?

The ABC approach differs from the traditional approach by its fundamental focus on activities. The ABC approach typically results in more homogeneous indirect-cost pools than the traditional approach and more cost drivers used as cost-allocation bases.

4. What is a cost hierarchy?

A cost hierarchy categorizes costs into different cost pools based on the different types of cost-allocation bases or different degrees of difficulty in determining cause-and-effect (or benefits-received) relationships. A four-part cost hierarchy consists of output unit-level costs, batch-level costs, product-sustaining or service-sustaining costs, and facility-sustaining costs.

5. How do you cost products or services using ABC systems?

In ABC, costs of activities are used to assign costs to other cost objects such as products or services, based on the activities the products or services consume.

6. How do you use ABC systems to manage better?

Activity-based management (ABM) describes management decisions that use ABC information to satisfy customers and improve profits. ABC systems are used for such management decisions as pricing, product-mix, cost reduction, process improvement, product and process redesign, and planning and managing activities.

7. When can you use department costing systems instead of ABC systems?

Cost information in department-costing systems approximates cost information in ABC systems only when each department has a single activity, or a single cost-allocation base for different activities, or when different products use the different activities of the department in the same proportions.

8. When should you use ABC systems?

ABC systems are likely to yield the most benefits when indirect costs are a high percentage of total costs or products and services make diverse demands on indirect resources. The main costs of ABC systems are the measurements necessary to implement and update the systems.

TERMS TO LEARN

This chapter contains definitions of the following important terms:

ABC (p. 158)
ABM (p. 166)
activity (p. 158)
activity-based costing (p. 158)
activity-based management (p. 166)
batch-level costs (p. 161)
cost hierarchy (p. 161)
cost smoothing (p. 153)
facility-sustaining cost (p. 161)

output unit-level costs (p. 161)
peanut butter costing (p. 153)
product cost cross-subsidization (p. 153)
product overcosting (p. 153)
product-sustaining costs (p. 161)
product undercosting (p. 153)
refined costing system (p. 157)
service-sustaining costs (p. 161)
traditional costing (p. 153)

ASSIGNMENT MATERIAL

QUESTIONS

5-1 Define *cost smoothing*, and explain how managers can determine whether it occurs with their costing system.

5-2 Why should managers worry about product over- or undercosting?

5-3 What is costing system refinement? Describe three guidelines for such refinement.

5-4 What is an activity-based approach to designing a costing system?

5-5 Describe four levels of a manufacturing cost hierarchy.

5-6 "The existence of non-output-unit-level costs means that managers should not compute unit product costs based on total manufacturing costs in all levels of the cost hierarchy." Do you agree? Explain.

5-7 What are the key reasons for product cost differences between traditional costing systems and ABC systems?

5-8 Describe four decisions for which ABC information is useful.

5-9 "Department indirect-cost rates are never activity-cost rates." Do you agree? Explain.

5-10 Describe four ways that help indicate when ABC systems are likely to provide the most benefits.

5-11 What are the main costs and limitations of implementing ABC systems?

5-12 "ABC systems apply only to manufacturing companies." Do you agree? Explain.

5-13 "Activity-based costing is the wave of the present and the future. All companies should adopt it." Do you agree? Explain.

5-14 "Increasing the number of indirect-cost pools is guaranteed to sizably increase the accuracy of product or service costs." Do you agree? Why?

5-15 The controller of a retailer has just had a $50,000 request to implement an ABC system quickly turned down. A senior vice-president involved in rejecting the request noted, "Given a choice, I will always prefer a $50,000 investment in improving things a customer sees or experiences, such as our shelves or our store layout. How does a customer benefit by our spending $50,000 on a supposedly better accounting system?" How should the controller respond?

EXERCISES

5-16 **Cost smoothing or peanut butter costing, cross-subsidization.** For many years, five former classmates—Steve Armstrong, Lola Gonzales, Rex King, Elizabeth Poffo, and Gary Young— have had a reunion dinner at the annual meeting of the Canadian Academic Accounting Association. The bill for the most recent dinner at a Montreal restaurant was broken down as follows:

Diner	Entrée	Dessert	Drinks	Total
Armstrong	$32	$10	$29	$71
Gonzales	29	4	0	33
King	25	7	16	48
Poffo	37	7	14	58
Young	18	5	7	30

For at least the last ten dinners, King has put the total restaurant bill on his Visa card. He then mailed the other four a bill for the average cost. They shared the gratuity at the restaurant by paying cash. King continued this practice for the Montreal dinner. However, just before he sent the bill to the other diners, Young phoned him to complain. He was livid at Poffo for ordering the steak and lobster entrée ("She always does that!") and at Armstrong for having three glasses of imported champagne ("What's wrong with domestic beer?").

REQUIRED
1. Why is the average cost approach in the context of the reunion dinner an example of peanut butter costing?
2. Compute the average cost to each of the five diners. Who is undercharged and who is overcharged under the average cost approach? Is Young's complaint justified?
3. Give an example of a dining situation where King would find it more difficult to compute the amount of under- or overcosting. How might the behaviour of the diners be affected if each person paid his or her own bill instead of continuing with the average cost approach?

5-17 **Cost hierarchy.** Telecom Inc. manufactures boom boxes (music systems with radio, cassette, and compact disc players) for different well-known companies. The boom boxes differ significantly in their complexity and the batch sizes in which they are manufactured. The following costs were incurred in 2007:
   a. Designing processes, drawing process charts, making engineering process changes for products, $960,000
   b. Procurement costs of placing purchase orders, receiving materials, and paying suppliers that are related to the number of purchase orders placed, $600,000
   c. Direct materials costs, $7,200,000

d. Costs incurred to set up machines each time a different product needs to be manufactured, $720,000

e. Direct manufacturing labour costs, $1,200,000

f. Machine-related overhead costs such as amortization, maintenance, production engineering, $1,320,000. These resources are related to the activity of running the machines.

g. Plant management, plant rent, and insurance, $1,080,000

REQUIRED

1. Classify each of the preceding costs as output unit level, batch level, product sustaining, or facility sustaining. Explain your answers.

2. Consider two boom boxes made by Telecom Inc. One boom box is complex to make and is made in many batches. The other boom box is simple to make and is made in few batches. Suppose that Telecom needs the same number of machine-hours to make either boom box. If Telecom allocated all overhead costs using machine-hours as the only allocation base, how, if at all, would the boom boxes be miscosted? Briefly explain why.

3. How is the cost hierarchy helpful to Telecom in managing its business?

5-18 Cost hierarchy, ABC, distribution. Niagara Winery makes two different grades of wine— regular wines and specialty wines. Recently, Niagara has shown small profits on its regular wines and large profits on its specialty wines. As a result, management is considering getting out of the regular wine business and concentrating on specialty wines. This is a difficult decision because Niagara had been very profitable in regular wines, its original business. In fact, the profitability of regular wines dipped substantially only after Niagara got into the specialty wine business. Before making a decision, Niagara wants to be sure that it understands what it costs to make and sell the regular and specialty wines. This question focuses on costs in the distribution area.

Niagara distributes the regular wines and the specialty wines through completely different distribution channels. It distributes 120,000 cases of the regular wines through 10 provincial distributors and 80,000 cases of the specialty wines through 30 specialty distributors. Niagara incurs $2,556,000 in distribution costs. Under its existing costing system Niagara allocates distribution costs to products based on cases shipped.

To understand better the demands on its resources in the distribution area, Niagara identifies three activities and related activity costs:

1. Promotional activity including advertising and point-of-sales material at each distributor. Niagara estimates it incurs $9,600 per distributor.

2. Order handling costs including costs to confirm and input the order into the order-entry system, set aside the correct number of cases, organize shipment and delivery, verify order packing, ensure delivery, send invoices, and follow up for payments. Niagara estimates costs of $360 for performing all the activities pertaining to each order. Niagara's records show that distributors of regular wine placed an average of 10 orders per year, while distributors of specialty wine placed an average of 20 orders per year.

3. Distribution costs of $10 per case for freight.

REQUIRED

1. Calculate the total distribution costs and distribution cost per case for the regular wine and the specialty wine using Niagara's existing costing system.

2. a. For each activity, classify the cost of the activity as an output unit-level, batch-level, product- or service-sustaining, or facility-sustaining cost. Explain your answers.

   b. Calculate the total distribution costs and distribution cost per case for the regular wine and the specialty wine using Niagara's activity-based costing system.

3. Explain the cost differences and the accuracy of the product costs calculated using the existing and the ABC systems. How might Niagara's management use the information from the ABC system to manage its business better?

5-19 ABC, cost hierarchy, service. Halifax Test Laboratories does heat testing (HT) and stress testing (ST) on materials. Under its current costing system, Halifax aggregates all operating costs of $1,440,000 into a single overhead cost pool. Halifax calculates a rate per test hour of $18 ($1,440,000 ÷ 80,000 total test-hours). HT uses 50,000 test-hours and ST uses 30,000 test-hours. Gary Celeste, Halifax's controller, believes that there is enough variation in test procedures and cost structures to establish separate costing and billing rates. The market for test services is very competitive, and without this information, any miscosting and mispricing could cause Halifax to lose business. Celeste breaks down Halifax's costs into four activity-cost categories.

1. Direct labour costs, $288,000. These costs can be directly traced to HT, $216,000, and ST, $72,000.

2. Equipment-related costs (rent, maintenance, energy, and so on), $480,000. These costs are allocated to HT and ST based on test-hours.

3. Setup costs, $420,000. These costs are allocated to HT and ST based on the number of setup-hours required. HT requires 13,500 setup-hours and ST requires 4,000 setup-hours.
4. Costs of designing tests, $252,000. These costs are allocated to HT and ST based on the time required to design the tests. HT requires 2,800 hours and ST requires 1,400 hours.

REQUIRED

1. Classify each of the activity costs as output unit level, batch level, product or service sustaining, or facility sustaining. Explain your answer.
2. Calculate the cost per test-hour for HT and ST. Explain briefly the reasons why these numbers differ from the $18 per test-hour that Halifax had calculated using its existing costing system.
3. Explain the cost differences and the accuracy of the product costs calculated using the existing and the ABC systems. How might Halifax's management use the cost hierarchy and ABC information to manage its business better?

5-20 Alternative allocation bases for a professional services firm. The Wolfson Group (WG) provides tax advice to multinational firms. WG charges clients for (a) direct professional time (at an hourly rate), and (b) support services (at 30% of the direct professional costs billed). The three professionals in WG and their rates per professional hour are as follows:

Professional	Billing Rate per Hour
Myron Wolfson	$600
Naomi Ku	144
John Anderson	96

WG has just prepared the May 2007 bills for two clients. The hours of professional time spent on each client are as follows:

	Hours per Client	
Professional	Winnipeg Dominion	Tokyo Enterprises
Wolfson	15	2
Ku	3	8
Anderson	22	30
Total	40	40

REQUIRED

1. What amounts did WG bill to Winnipeg Dominion and Tokyo Enterprises for May 2007?
2. Suppose support services were billed at $60 per professional labour-hour (instead of 30% of professional labour costs). How would this change affect the amounts WG billed to the two clients for May 2007? Comment on the differences between the amounts billed in requirements 1 and 2.
3. How would you determine whether professional labour costs or professional labour-hours is the more appropriate allocation base for WG's support services?

5-21 Plantwide indirect-cost rates. Automotive Products (AP) designs, manufactures, and sells automotive parts. It has three main operating departments: design, engineering, and production.

◆ There were no returns to suppliers.
◆ *Design*—the design of parts, using state of the art, computer-aided design (CAD) equipment
◆ *Engineering*—the prototyping of parts and testing of their specifications
◆ *Production*—the manufacture of parts

For many years, AP has had long-term contracts with major automobile assembly companies. These contracts have large production runs. AP's costing system allocates variable manufacturing overhead based on machine-hours. Actual variable manufacturing overhead costs for 2007 were $370,320. AP had three contracts in 2007, and its machine-hours used in 2007 were assigned as follows:

United Motors	120
Holden Motors	2,800
Leland Vehicle	1,080
Total	4,000

1. Compute the plantwide variable manufacturing overhead rate for 2007.
2. Compute the variable manufacturing overhead allocated to each contract in 2007.
3. What conditions must hold for machine-hours to provide an accurate estimate of the variable manufacturing overhead incurred on each individual contract at AP in 2007?

5-22 Department indirect-cost rates as activity rates (continuation of 5-21). The controller of Automotive Parts (AP) decides to interview key managers of the design, engineering, and production departments. Each manager is to indicate the consensus choice among department personnel as to the cost driver of variable manufacturing overhead costs in that department. Summary data are:

	2007 Variable Manufacturing Overhead	Cost Driver
Design	$ 46,800	CAD design-hours
Engineering	35,520	Engineering-hours
Production	288,000	Machine-hours
	$370,320	

Details pertaining to usage of these cost drivers for each of the three 2007 contracts are:

Operating Areas	Cost Driver	United Motors	Holden Motors	Leland Vehicle
Design	CAD design-hours	110	200	80
Engineering	Engineering-hours	70	60	240
Production	Machine-hours	120	2,800	1,080

REQUIRED

1. What is the variable manufacturing overhead rate for each department in 2007?
2. What is the variable manufacturing overhead allocated to each contract in 2007 using department variable manufacturing overhead rates?
3. Compare your answer in requirement 2 to that in requirement 2 of Exercise 5-21. Comment on the results.

5-23 ABC, process costing. Huey Parker produces mathematical and financial calculators. Data related to the two products is presented below.

	Mathematical	Financial
Annual production in units	50,000	100,000
Direct materials costs	$180,000	$360,000
Direct manufacturing labour costs	$ 60,000	$120,000
Direct manufacturing labour-hours	2,500	5,000
Machine-hours	25,000	50,000
Number of production runs	50	50
Inspection hours	1,000	500

Both products pass through Department 1 and Department 2. The departments' combined manufacturing overhead costs are:

	Total
Machining costs	$450,000
Setup costs	144,000
Inspection costs	126,000

REQUIRED

1. Compute the manufacturing overhead cost for each product.
2. Compute the manufacturing cost for each product.

5-24 ABC, wholesale, customer profitability. Villeagas Wholesalers sells furniture items to four department-store chains. Mr. Villeagas commented, "We apply ABC to determine profit line profitability. The same ideas apply to customer profitability, and we should find out our customer profitability as well." Villeagas Wholesalers sends catalogues to the corporate purchasing departments on a monthly basis. The customers are entitled to return unsold merchandise within a six-month period from the purchase date and receive a full purchase price refund. The following data were collected from last year's operations:

	Chain			
	1	**2**	**3**	**4**
Gross sales	$60,000	$36,000	$120,000	$84,000
Sales returns:				
Number of items	100	26	60	40
Amount	$12,000	$ 6,000	$ 8,400	$ 7,200
Number of orders:				
Regular	40	150	50	70
Rush	10	50	10	30

Villeagas has calculated the following activity rates:

Activity	Cost Driver Rate
Regular order processing	$24 per regular order
Rush order processing	$120 per rush order
Returned items processing	$12 per item
Catalogues and customer support	$1,200 per chain

Customers pay the freight costs. The cost of goods sold averages 80% of sales.

REQUIRED
Determine the contribution to profit from each chain last year. Comment on your solution.

5-25 ABC, retail product line profitability. Family Supermarkets (FS) found that its ABC analysis (see p. 174) provided important insights. FS extends the analysis to cover three more product lines: baked goods, milk and fruit juice, and frozen products. It identifies four activities and activity-cost rates for each activity as:

Ordering	$120 per purchase order
Delivery and receipt of merchandise	$96 per delivery
Shelf-stocking	$24 per hour
Customer support and assistance	$0.24 per item sold

The revenues, cost of goods sold, store support costs, and activity area usage of the three product lines are as follows:

	Baked Goods	Milk and Fruit Juice	Frozen Products
Financial data:			
Revenues	$68,400	$75,600	$62,400
Cost of goods sold	45,600	56,400	42,000
Store support	13,680	16,920	12,600
Activity area usage (cost driver):			
Ordering (purchase orders)	30	25	13
Delivery (deliveries)	98	36	28
Shelf-stocking (hours)	183	166	24
Customer support (items sold)	15,500	20,500	7,900

There are no bottle returns for any of these three product lines.

REQUIRED
1. Use the previous costing system (support costs allocated to products at the rate of 30% of cost of goods sold) to compute a product line profitability report for FS.
2. Use the ABC system (ordering at $120 per purchase order, delivery at $96 per delivery, shelf-stocking at $24 per hour, and customer support at $0.24 per item sold) to compute a product line profitability report for FS.
3. What new insights does the ABC system in requirement 2 provide to FS managers?

5-26 ABC, product costing at banks, cross-subsidization. First International Bank (FIB) is examining the profitability of its Premier Account, a combined savings and chequing account. Depositors receive a 7% annual interest rate on their average deposit. FIB earns an interest rate spread of 3% (the difference between the rate at which it lends money and the rate it pays depositors) by lending money for residential home loan purposes at 10%. Thus, FIB would gain $72 on the interest spread if a depositor has an average Premier Account balance of $2,400 in 2007 ($2,400 × 3% = $72).

The Premier Account allows depositors unlimited use of services such as deposits, withdrawals, chequing account, and foreign currency drafts. Depositors with Premier Account balances of $1,200 or more receive unlimited free use of services. Depositors with minimum balances of less than $1,200 pay a $24 monthly service fee for their Premier Account.

FIB recently conducted an activity-based costing study of its services. It assessed the following costs for six individual services. The use of these services in 2007 by three customers is as follows:

	ABC-Based Cost per Transaction	Account Usage		
		Robinson	Skerrett	Farrel
Deposit/withdrawal with teller	$ 3.00	40	50	5
Deposit/withdrawal with automatic teller machine	0.96	10	20	16
Deposit/withdrawal prearranged monthly	0.60	0	12	60
Bank cheques written	9.60	9	3	2
Foreign currency drafts	14.40	4	1	6
Inquiries about account balance	1.80	10	18	9
Average Premier Account balance for 2007		$1,320	$960	$30,000

Assume Robinson and Farrel always maintain a balance above $1,200 while Skerrett always has a balance below $1,200 in 2007.

REQUIRED

1. Compute the 2007 profitability of the Robinson, Skerrett, and Farrell Premier Accounts at FIB.
2. What evidence is there of cross-subsidization across Premier Accounts? Why might FIB worry about this cross-subsidization if the Premier Account product offering is profitable as a whole?
3. What changes at FIB would you recommend for its Premier Account?

5-27 ABC, product cost cross-subsidization. PEI Potatoes processes potatoes into potato cuts at its highly automated plant. For many years, it processed potatoes for only the retail consumer market where it had a superb reputation for quality. Recently, it started selling potato cuts to the institutional market, which includes hospitals, cafeterias, and university dormitories. Its penetration into the institutional market has been slower than predicted.

PEI's existing costing system has a single direct-cost category (direct materials, which are the raw potatoes) and a single indirect-cost pool (production support). Support costs are allocated on the basis of kilograms of potato cuts processed. Support costs include packaging material. The 2007 total actual costs for producing 1,000,000 kilograms of potato cuts (900,000 for the retail market and 100,000 for the institutional market) are:

Direct materials used	$ 180,000
Production support	1,179,600

The existing costing system does not distinguish between potato cuts produced for the retail or the institutional markets.

At the end of 2007, PEI unsuccessfully bid for a large institutional contract. Its bid was reported to be 30% above the winning bid. This came as a shock, as PEI included only a minimum profit margin on its bid. Moreover, the PEI plant was widely acknowledged as the most efficient in the industry.

As part of its lost contract bid review process, PEI decided to explore several ways of refining its costing system. First, it identified that $225,600 of the $1,179,600 pertains to packaging materials that could be traced to individual jobs ($216,000 for retail and $9,600 for institutional). These will now be classified as a direct material. The $180,000 of direct materials used were classified as $162,000 for retail and $18,000 for institutional. Second, it used activity-based costing (ABC) to examine how the two products (retail potato cuts and institutional potato cuts) used the support area differently. The finding was that three activity areas could be distinguished and that different usage occurred in two of these three areas. The indirect cost per kilogram of finished product at each activity area is as follows:

Activity Area	Retail Potato Cuts	Institutional Potato Cuts
Cleaning	$0.144	$0.144
Cutting	0.288	0.180
Packaging labour	0.576	0.144

There was no beginning or ending amount of any inventory (materials, work in process, or finished goods).

REQUIRED

1. Using the current costing system, what is the cost per kilogram of potato cuts produced by PEI?
2. Using the refined costing system, what is the cost per kilogram of (a) retail market potato cuts, and (b) institutional market potato cuts?
3. Comment on the cost differences shown between the two costing systems in requirements 1 and 2. How might PEI use the information in requirement 2 to make better decisions?

PROBLEMS

5-28 Activity-based job-costing system. The Calgary Company manufactures and sells packaging machines. It recently used an activity-based approach to refine the job costing system at its Calgary plant. The resulting job-costing system has one direct cost category (direct materials) and four indirect manufacturing cost pools. These four indirect-cost pools and their allocation bases were chosen by a team of product designers, manufacturing personnel, and marketing personnel:

Indirect-Manufacturing Cost Pool	Cost-Allocation Base	Budgeted Cost-Allocation Rate
1. Materials-handling	Component parts	$ 9.60 per part
2. Machining	Machine-hours	$ 81.60 per hour
3. Assembly	Assembly-line-hours	$ 90.00 per hour
4. Inspection	Inspection-hours	$124.80 per hour

Cola Supreme recently purchased 50 can-packaging machines from the Calgary Company. Each machine has direct materials costs of $3,600, and requires 50 component parts, 12 machine-hours, 15 assembly line-hours, and 4 inspection-hours.

Calgary's prior costing system had one direct-cost category (direct materials) and one indirect-cost category (manufacturing overhead, allocated using assembly-line-hours).

REQUIRED

1. Present overview diagrams of the prior job-costing system and the refined activity-based job-costing system.
2. Compute the unit manufacturing costs (using ABC) of each machine and the total manufacturing cost of the Cola Supreme job.
3. The activity-based job-costing system of Calgary has only one manufacturing direct-cost category—direct materials. A competitor of the Calgary Company has two direct-cost categories at its manufacturing plant—direct materials and direct manufacturing labour. Why might Calgary not have a direct manufacturing labour costs category in its job-costing system? Where are the manufacturing labour costs included in the Calgary costing system?
4. What information might members of the team that refined the prior costing system find useful in the activity-based job-costing system?

5-29 Activity-based costing, job-costing system. The Hewlett-Packard (HP) plant in Roseville, California, assembles and tests printed circuit (PC) boards. The job-costing system at this plant has two direct-cost categories (direct materials and direct manufacturing labour) and seven indirect-cost pools. These indirect-cost pools represent the seven activity areas that operating personnel at the plant determined were sufficiently different (in terms of cost behaviour patterns or in terms of individual products being assembled) to warrant separate cost pools. The cost-allocation base chosen for each activity area is the cost driver at that activity area.

Debbie Berlant, a newly appointed marketing manager at HP, attends a training session that describes how an activity-based costing approach has been used to design the Roseville plant's job-costing system. Berlant is provided with the following incomplete information for a specific job (an order for a single PC board, No. A82):

Direct materials	$90	
Direct manufacturing labour	18	$108
Manufacturing overhead (see below)		?
Total manufacturing costs		$?

Manufacturing Overhead Cost Pool	Cost-Allocation Base	Cost-Allocation Rate	Units of Base Used on Job No. A82	Manufacturing Overhead Allocated to Job
1. Axial insertion	Axial insertions	0.096	45	?
2. Dip insertion	Dip insertions	0.30	?	7.20
3. Manual insertion	Manual insertions	?	11	6.60
4. Wave solder	Boards soldered	4.20	?	4.20
5. Backload	Backload insertions	?	6	5.04
6. Test	Budgeted time board is in test activity	108.00	0.25	?
7. Defect analysis	Budgeted time for defect analysis and repair	?	0.10	9.60

REQUIRED

1. Present an overview exhibit of the activity-based job-costing system at the Roseville plant.
2. Fill in the blanks (signalled by a question mark) in the cost information provided to Berlant for Job No. A82.
3. Why might manufacturing managers and marketing managers favour this ABC job-costing system over the prior costing system, which had the same two direct-cost categories but only a single indirect-cost pool (manufacturing overhead allocated using direct labour cost)?

5-30 Job costing with single direct-cost category, single indirect-cost pool, law firm. Wigan Partners is a recently formed law partnership. Ellery Hanley, the managing partner of Wigan Partners, has just finished a tense phone call with Martin Offiah, president of Widnes Coal. Offiah complained about the price Wigan charged for some conveyancing (drawing up property documents) legal work done for Widnes Coal. He requested a breakdown of the charges. He also indicated to Hanley that a competing law firm, Hull & Kingston, was seeking more business with Widnes Coal and that he was going to ask them to bid for a conveyancing job next month. Offiah ended the phone call by saying that if Wigan bid a price similar to the one charged last month, Wigan would not be hired for next month's job.

Hanley is dismayed by the phone call. He is also puzzled because he believes that conveyancing is an area where Wigan Partners has much expertise and is highly efficient. The Widnes Coal phone call is the bad news of the week. The good news is that yesterday Hanley received a phone call from its only other client (St. Helen's Glass) saying it was very pleased with both the quality of the work (primarily litigation) and the price charged on its most recent case.

Hanley decides to collect data on the Widnes Coal and St. Helen's Glass cases. Wigan Partners uses a cost-based approach to pricing (billing) each legal case. Currently it uses a single direct-cost category (for professional labour time) and a single indirect-cost pool (general support). Indirect costs are allocated to cases on the basis of professional labour-hours per case. The case files show the following:

	Widnes Coal	St. Helen's Glass
Professional labour time	104 hours	96 hours

Professional labour costs at Wigan Partners are $84 an hour. Indirect costs are allocated to cases at $126 an hour. Total indirect costs in the most recent period were $25,200.

1. Why is it important for Wigan Partners to understand the costs associated with individual cases?
2. Present an overview diagram of the existing job-costing system.
3. Compute the costs of the Widnes Coal and St. Helen's Glass cases.

5-31 Job costing with multiple direct-cost categories, single indirect-cost pool, law firm (continuation of 5-30). Hanley speaks to the other partners about the pricing of the two cases. Several believe that the relative prices charged seem out of line with their intuition. One partner observes that a useful approach to obtaining more accurate job costs is to increase direct-cost tracing.

Hanley asks his assistant to collect details on those costs included in the $25,200 indirect-cost pool that can be traced to each individual case. After further analysis, Wigan is able to reclassify $16,800 of the $25,200 as direct costs:

Other Direct Costs	Widnes Coal	St. Helen's Glass
Research support labour	$1,920	$ 4,080
Computer time	600	1,560
Travel and allowances	720	5,280
Telephone/faxes	240	1,200
Photocopying	300	900
Total	$3,780	$13,020

Hanley decides to calculate the costs of each case had Wigan used six direct-cost pools and a single indirect-cost pool. The single indirect-cost pool would have $8,400 of costs and would be allocated to each case using the professional labour-hours base.

REQUIRED
1. Present an overview diagram of the refined job-costing system with its multiple direct-cost categories.
2. What is the revised indirect cost-allocation rate per professional labour-hour for Wigan Partners when total indirect costs are $7,000?
3. Compute the costs of the Widnes and St. Helen's cases if Wigan Partners had used its refined costing system with multiple direct-cost categories and one indirect-cost pool.
4. Compare the costs of the Widnes and St. Helen's cases in requirement 3 with those in requirement 3 of Problem 5-30. Comment on the results.

5-32 Job costing with multiple direct-cost categories, multiple indirect-cost pools, law firm (continuation of 5-30 and 5-31). Hanley examines the job-costing approaches in Problems 5-30 and 5-31. He questions the use of a single cost rate for all professional labour of Wigan Partners. Wigan has two classifications of professional staff—partners and managers. Hanley asks his assistant to examine the relative use of partners and managers on the recent Widnes Coal and St. Helen's cases. The Widnes case used 24 partner-hours and 80 manager-hours. The St. Helen's case used 56 partner-hours and 40 manager-hours.

Hanley decides to examine how the use of separate direct- and indirect-cost pools for partners and managers would have affected the costs of the Widnes and St. Helen's cases. Indirect costs in each cost pool would be allocated based on total hours of that category of professional labour.

The rates per category of professional labour are as follows:

Category of Professional Labour	Direct Cost per Hour	Indirect Cost per Hour
Partner	$120.00	$69.00
Manager	60.00	24.00

These indirect-cost rates are based on a total indirect-cost pool of $8,400; $5,520 of this $8,400 is attributable to the activities of partners, and $2,880 is attributable to the activities of managers. (The indirect cost per hour of $69 is calculated by dividing $5,520 by 80 partner-hours; the indirect-cost rate of $24 is calculated by dividing $2,880 by 120 manager-hours.)

REQUIRED
1. Present an overview diagram of the refined job-costing system with its multiple direct-cost categories and its multiple indirect-cost pools.

2. Compute the costs of the Widnes and St. Helen's cases with Wigan Partners' further refined system, with multiple direct-cost categories and multiple indirect-cost pools.
3. For what decisions might Wigan Partners find it more useful to use this job-costing approach rather than the approach in Problems 5-30 or 5-31?

5-33 **Activity-based job costing, unit cost comparisons.** The Tracy Corporation has a machining facility specializing in jobs for the aircraft components market. The prior job-costing system had two direct-cost categories (direct materials and direct manufacturing labour) and a single indirect-cost pool (manufacturing overhead, allocated using direct labour-hours). The indirect-cost allocation rate of the prior system for 2007 would have been $138 per direct manufacturing labour-hour.

Recently, a team with members from product design, manufacturing, and accounting used an activity-based approach to refine its job-costing system. The two direct-cost categories were retained. The team decided to replace the single indirect-cost pool with five indirect-cost pools. These five cost pools represent five activity areas at the facility, each with its own supervisor and budget responsibility. Pertinent data are as follows:

Activity Area	Cost Driver Used as Allocation Base	Cost Allocation Rate
Materials handling	Parts	$ 0.48
Lathe work	Turns	0.24
Milling	Machine-hours	24.00
Grinding	Parts	0.96
Testing	Units tested	18.00

Information-gathering technology has advanced to the point where all the data necessary for budgeting in these five activity areas are automatically collected.

Two representative jobs processed under the new system at the facility in the most recent period had the following characteristics:

	Job 410	Job 411
Direct materials cost per job	$11,640	$71,880
Direct manufacturing labour cost per job	$ 900	$13,500
Direct manufacturing labour-hours per job	25	375
Parts per job	500	2,000
Turns per job	20,000	60,000
Machine-hours per job	150	1,050
Units per job (all units are tested)	10	200

REQUIRED
1. Compute the per unit manufacturing costs of each job under the prior job-costing system.
2. Compute the per unit manufacturing costs of each job under the activity-based job-costing system.
3. Compare the per-unit cost figures for Jobs 410 and 411 computed in requirements 1 and 2. Why do the prior and the activity-based costing systems differ in their job-cost estimates for each job? Why might these differences be important to the Tracy Corporation?

5-34 **Activity-based job costing.** The Schramka Company manufactures a variety of prestige boardroom chairs. Its job-costing system was designed using an activity-based approach. There are two direct-cost categories (direct materials and direct manufacturing labour) and three indirect-cost pools. The three cost pools represent three activity areas at the plant:

Manufacturing Activity Area	Budgeted Costs for 2007	Cost Driver Used as Allocation Base	Cost-Allocation Rate
Materials handling	$ 240,000	Parts	$ 0.30
Cutting	2,592,000	Parts	3.00
Assembly	2,400,000	Direct manufacturing labour-hours	30.00

Two styles of chairs were produced in March, the executive chair and the chairperson chair. Their quantities, direct material costs, and other data for March 2007 are as follows:

	Units Produced	Direct Material Costs	Number of Parts	Direct Manufacturing Labour-Hours
Executive chair	5,000	$720,000	100,000	7,500
Chairperson chair	100	30,000	3,500	500

The direct manufacturing labour rate is $24 per hour. Assume no beginning or ending inventory.

REQUIRED

1. Compute the March 2007 total manufacturing costs and unit costs of the executive chair and the chairperson chair.
2. Suppose that the upstream activities to manufacturing (R&D and design) and the downstream activities (marketing, distribution, and customer service) were analyzed. The unit costs in 2007 were budgeted as follows:

	Upstream Activities	Downstream Activities
Executive chair	$ 72.00	$132.00
Chairperson chair	175.20	283.20

Compute the full product costs per unit of each line of chairs. (Full product costs are the sum of the costs in all business function areas.)

5-35 **Activity-based costing, product cost cross-subsidization.** Baker's Delight (BD) has been in the food-processing business three years. For its first two years (2005 and 2006), its sole product was raisin cake. All cakes were manufactured and packaged in one-kilogram units. A normal-costing system was used by BD. The two direct-cost categories were direct materials and direct manufacturing labour. The sole indirect manufacturing cost category—manufacturing overhead—was allocated to products using a units-of-production allocation base. BD prices on a cost-plus basis. It currently uses a "cost plus 40% of cost" guideline.

In its third year (2007), BD added a second product—layered carrot cake—that was packaged in one-kilogram units. This product differs from raisin cake in several ways:

◆ More expensive ingredients are used.

◆ More direct manufacturing labour time is required.

◆ More complex manufacturing is required.

In 2007, BD continued to use its existing costing system where a unit of production of either cake was weighted the same.

Direct materials costs in 2007 were $0.72 per kilogram of raisin cake and $1.08 per kilogram of layered carrot cake. Direct manufacturing labour cost in 2007 was $0.168 per kilogram of raisin cake and $0.24 per kilogram of layered carrot cake.

During 2007, BD salespeople reported greater-than-expected sales of layered carrot cake and less-than-expected sales of raisin cake. The budgeted and actual sales volume for 2007 were as follows:

	Budgeted	Actual
Raisin cake	160,000 kilograms	120,000 kilograms
Layered carrot cake	40,000 kilograms	80,000 kilograms

The budgeted manufacturing overhead for 2007 was $252,960.

At the end of 2007, Jonathan Davis, the controller of BD, decided to investigate how the use of an activity-based costing system would affect the product cost numbers. After consultation with operating personnel, the single manufacturing overhead cost pool was subdivided into five activity areas. These activity areas, their driver, their 2007 budgeted rate, and the driver units used per kilogram of each cake are as follows:

Activity	Driver	Budgeted 2007 Cost per Driver Unit	Driver Units per Kilogram of Raisin Cake	Driver Units per Kilogram of Layered Carrot Cake
1. Mixing	Labour time	$0.048	5	8
2. Cooking	Oven time	$0.168	2	3
3. Cooling	Cool room time	$0.024	3	5
4. Creaming/icing	Machine time	$0.30	0	3
5. Packaging	Machine time	$0.096	3	7

REQUIRED

1. Compute the 2007 unit product cost of raisin cake and of layered carrot cake with the normal costing system used in the 2005 to 2007 period.
2. Compute the 2007 unit product cost per cake under the activity-based normal costing system.
3. Explain the differences in unit product costs computed in requirements 1 and 2.
4. Describe three uses Baker's Delight might make of the activity-based cost numbers.

5-36 **ABC, health care.** Uppervale Health Centre runs four programs: (1) alcoholic rehabilitation, (2) drug-addict rehabilitation, (3) children's services, and (4) after-care (counselling and support of patients after release from a psychiatric hospital).

The centre's budget for 2007 follows:

Professional salaries:
6 physicians at $120,000	$ 720,000	
19 psychologists at $60,000	1,140,000	
23 nurses at $30,000	690,000	$2,550,000
Medical supplies		360,000
General overhead (administrative salaries, rent, utilities, etc.)		1,530,000
		$4,440,000

Mrs. Muriel Clayton, the director of the Centre, is keen on determining the cost of each program. She has limited funds and feels that this information will help her to budget better and allocate resources more effectively. For example, Clayton needs to decide whether to allocate funds to alcoholic rehabilitation or to drug-addict rehabilitation. Her decision rule is that if the cost to treat a drug-addict patient for a year is more than 15% higher than the cost to treat an alcoholic patient for a year, the alcohol program would receive additional funds.

As a first step, Mrs. Clayton, who had earned uniformly high respect from the professional staff, asked the staff to fill out a form indicating the time devoted to each of the four programs. She then allocated costs of medical supplies based on physician-hours spent in each program and general overhead based on direct-labour cost (where direct labour is defined to include the time of doctors, psychologists, and nurses multiplied by the salary rate of each). Clayton compiled the following data describing employee allocations to individual programs:

	Alcohol	Drug	Children	After-Care	Total Employees
Physicians		2	4		6
Psychologists	6	4		9	19
Nurses	4	6	4	9	23

Eighty patients are in residence in the alcohol program, each staying about a half-year. Thus, the clinic provided 40 patient-years of service in the alcohol program. Similarly, 100 patients were involved in the drug program for about a half-year each. Thus the clinic provided 50 patient-years of service in the drug program.

Clayton has recently become aware of activity-based costing as a method to refine cost systems. She asks her accountant, Huey Deluth, how she should apply this new technique. Deluth obtains the following information:

1. Consumption of medical supplies depends on the number of patients in each department and the length of their stays (that is, patient-years).

2. General overhead costs consist of

Rent and clinic maintenance	$ 240,000
Administrative costs to manage patient charts, food, laundry	960,000
Laboratory services	330,000
Total	$1,530,000

3. Other information about individual departments is

	Alcohol	Drug	Children	After-Care	Total
Square metres of space occupied by each program	9,000	9,000	10,000	12,000	40,000
Patient-years of service	40	50	50	60	200
Number of patients	80	100	200	120	500
Number of laboratory tests	400	1,400	3,000	700	5,500

REQUIRED

1. a. Compute indirect-cost rates for medical supplies and general overhead under Clayton's existing costing system.

  b. What is the cost of each program and the cost per patient-year of the alcohol and drug programs, using Clayton's existing costing system?

  c. Using the existing costing system, would Clayton allocate additional funds to the drug program or to the alcohol program?

2. a. Calculate the indirect-cost rates for medical supplies, rent and clinic maintenance, administrative cost rate for patient charts, food, and laundry, and laboratory services, selecting cost-allocation bases that you believe are the most appropriate for allocating indirect costs to programs.

  b. What is the cost of each program and the cost per patient-year of the alcohol and drug programs, using an activity-based costing approach to cost analysis?

  c. Using the ABC system, would Clayton allocate additional funds to the drug program or to the alcohol program?

3. Explain the cost differences and the accuracy of program costs calculated using the existing and the ABC system. What other benefits can Uppervale Health Centre obtain by implementing the ABC system?

4. What factors, other than cost, do you think Uppervale Health Centre should consider in allocating resources to its programs?

5-37 Plantwide versus department overhead cost rates. (CMA) The MumsDay Corporation manufactures a complete line of fibreglass attaché cases and suitcases. MumsDay has three manufacturing departments (moulding, component, and assembly) and two support departments (maintenance and power).

The sides of the cases are manufactured in the moulding department. The frames, hinges, locks, and so on are manufactured in the component department. The cases are completed in the assembly department. Varying amounts of materials, time, and effort are required for each of the various cases. The maintenance and power departments provide services to the three manufacturing departments.

MumsDay has always used a plantwide manufacturing overhead rate. Direct manufacturing labour-hours are used to allocate the overhead to each product. The budgeted rate is calculated by dividing the company's total budgeted manufacturing overhead cost by the total budgeted direct labour-hours to be worked in the three manufacturing departments.

Whit Portlock, manager of Cost Accounting, has recommended that MumsDay use department overhead rates. Portlock has projected operating costs and production levels for the coming year. They are presented (in thousands) by department in the following tables:

	Manufacturing Department		
	Moulding	**Component**	**Assembly**
Department operating data			
Direct manufacturing labour-hours	500	2,000	1,500
Machine-hours	875	125	–
Department costs			
Direct manufacturing materials	$14,880	$36,000	$ 1,500
Direct manufacturing labour	4,200	24,000	14,400
Manufacturing overhead	25,200	19,440	27,120
Total departmental costs	$44,280	$79,440	$43,020

Use of support departments

Estimated usage of maintenance resources in labour-hours for coming year	90	25	10
Estimated usage of power (in kilowatt-hours) for coming year	360	320	120

Estimated costs of the maintenance department are $4,800 and of the power department are $22,080.

REQUIRED

1. Calculate the plantwide overhead rate for the MumsDay Corporation for the coming year using the same method as used in the past.
2. Whit Portlock has been asked to develop department overhead rates for comparison with the plantwide rate. Follow these steps in developing the department rates:
   a. Allocate the maintenance department and power department costs to the three manufacturing departments.
   b. Calculate department overhead rates for the three manufacturing departments using a machine-hour allocation base for the moulding department and a direct manufacturing labour-hour allocation base for the component and assembly departments.
3. Should the MumsDay Corporation use a plantwide rate or department rates to allocate overhead to its products? Explain your answer.

5-38 Plantwide, department, and activity cost rates. (CGA, adapted) The Sayther Company manufactures and sells two products, A and B. The manufacturing activity is organized in two departments. Manufacturing overhead costs at its Calgary plant are allocated to each product using a plantwide rate of $20.40 per direct manufacturing labour-hour. This rate is based on budgeted manufacturing overhead of $408,000 and 20,000 budgeted direct manufacturing labour-hours:

Manufacturing Department	Budget Manufacturing Overhead	Budgeted Direct Manufacturing Labour-Hours
1	$288,000	10,000
2	120,000	10,000
Total	$408,000	20,000

The number of direct manufacturing labour-hours required to manufacture each product is:

Manufacturing Department	Product A	Product B
1	4	1
2	1	4
Total	5	5

Per unit costs for the two categories of direct manufacturing costs are:

Direct Manufacturing Costs	Product A	Product B
Direct materials costs	$144	$180
Direct manufacturing labour costs	96	96

At the end of the year, there was no work in process. There were 200 finished units of product A and 600 finished units of product B on hand. Assume that the budgeted production level of the Calgary plant was exactly attained.

Sayther sets the listed selling price of each product by adding 120% to its unit manufacturing costs; that is, if the unit manufacturing costs are $100, the listed selling price is $220 ($100 + $120). This 120% markup is designed to cover costs upstream to manufacturing (for example, product design) and costs downstream from manufacturing (for example, marketing and customer service) as well as to provide an operating income.

REQUIRED

1. What is the manufacturing cost included in the inventory of products A and B if Sayther uses (a) a plantwide overhead rate and (b) department overhead rates?
2. What difference would result in the per unit selling prices of product A and product B from using a plantwide overhead rate instead of department overhead rates?
3. Should Sayther Company prefer plantwide or department manufacturing overhead rates?

4. Under what conditions should Sayther Company further subdivide the department cost pools into activity-cost pools?

5-39 Activity-based costing, merchandising. Figure Four, Inc., specializes in the distribution of pharmaceutical products. Figure Four buys from pharmaceutical companies and resells to each of three different markets:

a. General supermarket chains

b. Drugstore chains

c. "Mom and Pop" single-store pharmacies

Rick Flair, the new controller of Figure Four, reported the following data for August 2007:

	General Supermarket Chains	Drugstore Chains	"Mom and Pop" Single Stores
Average revenue per delivery	$37,080	$12,600	$2,376
Average cost of goods sold per delivery	$36,000	$12,000	$2,160
Number of deliveries	120	300	1,000

For many years, Figure Four has used gross margin percentage [(Revenue − Cost of goods sold) ÷ Revenue] to evaluate the relative profitability of its different groupings of customers (distribution outlets).

Flair recently attended a seminar on activity-based costing and decides to consider using it at Figure Four. Flair meets with all the key managers and many staff members. People generally agree that there are five key activity areas at Figure Four:

Activity Area	Cost Driver
1. Customer purchase order processing	Purchase orders by customers
2. Line item ordering	Line items per purchase order
3. Store delivery	Store deliveries
4. Cartons shipped to stores	Cartons shipped to a store per delivery
5. Shelf-stocking at customer stores	Hours of shelf-stocking

Each customer purchase order consists of one or more line items. A line item represents a single product (such as Extra-Strength Tylenol tablets). Each store delivery entails delivery of one or more cartons of products to a customer. Each product is delivered in one or more separate cartons. Figure Four staff stack cartons directly onto display shelves in a store. Currently, there is no charge for this service, and not all customers use Figure Four for this activity.

The August 2007 operating costs (other than cost of goods sold) of Figure Four are $361,296. These operating costs are assigned to the five activity areas. The costs in each area and the amount of the cost driver units used in that area for August 2007 are as follows:

Activity Area	Total Costs in August 2007	Total Units of Cost Driver Used in August 2007	
1. Customer purchase order processing	$ 96,000	2,000	orders
2. Line item ordering	76,608	21,280	line items
3. Store delivery	85,200	1,420	store deliveries
4. Cartons shipped to stores	91,200	76,000	cartons
5. Shelf-stocking at customer stores	12,288	640	hours
	$361,296		

Other data for August 2007 include the following:

	General Supermarket Chains	Drugstore Chains	"Mom and Pop" Single Stores
Total number of orders	140	360	1,500
Average number of line items per order	14	12	10
Total number of store deliveries	120	300	1,000
Average number of cartons shipped per store delivery	300	80	16
Average number of hours of shelf-stocking per store delivery	3.0	0.6	0.1

1. Compute the August 2007 gross margin percentage for each of Figure Four's three distribution markets. What is the operating income of Figure Four? What are the overall gross and operating income margins from Figure Four?
2. Compute the August 2007 per unit cost driver rate for each of the five activity areas.
3. Compute the operating income of each distribution market in August 2007 using the activity-based costing information. Comment on the results. What new insights are available with the activity-based information?
4. Describe four challenges Flair would face in assigning the total August 2007 operating costs of $361,296 to the five activity areas.

Excel Application For students who wish to practise their spreadsheet skills, the following is a step-by-step approach to creating an Excel spreadsheet to work this problem.

Step-by Step
1. In a new spreadsheet, create a "Financial Data" section for the financial data provided by Rick Flair, with rows for average revenue per delivery, average cost of goods sold per delivery, and number of deliveries, and columns for "General Supermarket Chains," "Drugstore Chains," and "Mom and Pop Single Stores." When you are finished, this section should look just like the table provided by Rick Flair on page 192.
2. Skip two rows. Create a "Cost-Allocation Data" section with columns labelled "Activity Area," "Total Costs as of August 2007," and "Total Units of Cost-Allocation Base Used in August 2007." Next, set up a column beside the "Total Units of Cost-Allocation Base Used in August 2007" column and call the new column "Rate per Unit of Cost-Allocation Base." Enter the five activity area data in the next five rows.
3. Skip down two rows and create an "Activity Data" section. Set up columns for "General Supermarket Chains," "Drugstore Chains," and "Mom and Pop Single Stores." Set up separate rows for each activity area. Enter the quantity of each activity used by each market during the period.
4. Skip two rows. Create a "Profitability Analysis" section; columns for "General Supermarket Chains," "Drugstore Chains," "Mom and Pop Single Stores," and "Figure Four, Inc."; rows for total revenues, total cost of goods sold, gross margin percentage, each of the five activity areas, total operating costs, operating income, and operating margin percentage.
5. In the "Profitability Analysis" section, enter calculations for total revenues, total cost of goods sold, and gross margin percentage for each market. Next calculate operating income for Figure Four, Inc., as a whole and enter this number in the operating income row of the "Figure Four, Inc." column.
6. Go to the "Cost Allocation Data" section, enter calculations for the rate per unit of the cost-allocation base for each of the five activity areas in the "Rate per Unit of Cost-Allocation Base" column.
7. Enter calculations for the total cost of each activity in each of the different markets in your "Profitability Analysis" section.
8. Compute operating income for each market by entering the appropriate calculation in the operating income row of the "Profitability Analysis" section.
9. *Verify the accuracy of your spreadsheet.* Go to your "Cost-Allocation Data" section and change total order processing costs from $96,000 to $120,000. If you programmed your spreadsheet correctly, operating income for Figure Four, Inc., should change to $140,304.

5-40 **ABC, implementation, ethics.** (CMA, adapted) Applewood Electronics, a division of Elgin Corporation, manufactures two large-screen television models: the Monarch, which has been produced since 2000 and sells for $1,080, and the Regal, a new model introduced in early 2003, which sells for $1,368. Based on the following income statement for the year ended November 30, 2007, senior management at Elgin have decided to concentrate Applewood's marketing resources on the Regal model and begin to phase out the Monarch model.

Applewood Electronics
Income Statement
for the Fiscal Year Ended November 30, 2007

	Monarch	Regal	Total
Sales	$23,760,000	$5,472,000	$29,232,000
Cost of goods sold	15,048,000	3,830,400	18,878,400
Gross margin	8,712,000	1,641,600	10,353,600
Selling and administrative expense	6,996,000	1,173,600	8,169,600
Operating income	$ 1,716,000	$ 468,000	$ 2,184,000
Units produced and sold	22,000	4,000	
Net income per unit sold	$78.00	$117.00	

Unit costs for the Monarch and Regal are as follows:

	Monarch	Regal
Direct manufacturing materials	$249.60	$700.80
Direct labour		
Monarch (1.5 hours × $14.40)	21.60	
Regal (3.5 hours × $14.40)		50.40
Machine costs*		
Monarch (8 hours × $21.60)	172.80	
Regal (4 hours × $21.60)		86.40
Manufacturing overhead other than machine costs†	240.00	120.00
Total cost	$684.00	$957.60

*Machine costs include lease costs of the machine, repairs, and maintenance.
†Manufacturing overhead was allocated to machine hours at the rate of $30 per hour.

Applewood's controller, Susan Benzo, is advocating the use of activity-based costing and activity-based management and has gathered the following information about the company's manufacturing overhead costs for the year ended November 30, 2007.

Activity Centre (Cost-Allocation Base)	Total Activity Costs	Units of the Cost-Allocation Base		
		Monarch	Regal	Total
Soldering (number of solder points)	$1,130,400	1,185,000	385,000	1,570,000
Shipments (number of shipments)	1,032,000	16,200	3,800	20,000
Quality control (number of inspections)	1,488,000	56,200	21,300	77,500
Purchase orders (number of orders)	1,140,480	80,100	109,980	190,080
Machine power (machine hours)	69,120	176,000	16,000	192,000
Machine setups (number of setups)	900,000	16,000	14,000	30,000
Total manufacturing overhead	$5,760,000			

After completing her analysis, Benzo showed the results to Filipe Figueira, the Applewood Division President. Figueira did not like what he saw. "If you show headquarters this analysis, they are going to ask us to phase out the Regal line, which we have just introduced. This whole costing thing has been a major problem for us. First Monarch was not profitable and now Regal.

"Looking at the ABC analysis, I see two problems. We do many more activities than the ones you have listed. If you had included all activities, maybe your conclusions would have been different. Second, you used number of setups and number of inspections as allocation bases. The numbers would have been different had you used setup-hours and inspection-hours instead. I know that measurement problems precluded you from using these other cost-allocation bases, but at least you ought to make some adjustments to our current numbers to compensate for these issues. I know you can do better. We can't afford to phase out either product."

Benzo knew her numbers were fairly accurate. On a limited sample, she had calculated the profitability of Regal and Monarch using different allocation bases. The set of activities and activity rates she had chosen resulted in numbers that approximated closely those based on more detailed analyses. She was confident that headquarters, knowing that Regal was introduced only recently, would not ask Applewood to phase it out. She was also aware that a sizable portion of Figueira's bonus was based on division sales. Phasing out either product would adversely affect the bonus. Still, she felt some pressure from Figueira to do something.

REQUIRED
1. Using activity-based costing, calculate the profitability of the Regal and Monarch models.
2. Explain briefly why these numbers differ from the profitability of the Regal and Monarch models calculated using Applewood's existing costing system.
3. Comment on Figueira's concerns about the accuracy and limitations of ABC.
4. How might Applewood find the ABC information helpful in managing its business?
5. What should Susan Benzo do?

COLLABORATIVE LEARNING PROBLEM

5-41 **Activity-based costing, cost hierarchy.** (CMA, adapted) Coffee Bean, Inc. (CBI) is a distributor and processor of a variety of different blends of coffee. The company buys coffee beans from around the world and roasts, blends, and packages them for resale. CBI currently offers 15 different coffees to gourmet shops in one-kilogram bags. The major cost is raw materials;

however, there is a substantial amount of manufacturing overhead in the predominantly automated roasting and packing process. The company uses relatively little direct labour.

Some of the coffees are very popular and sell in large volumes, while a few of the newer blends have very low volumes. CBI prices its coffee at budgeted cost, including allocated overhead, plus a markup of 30%. If prices for certain coffees are significantly higher than market, the prices are lowered. The company competes primarily on the quality of its products, but customers are price-conscious as well.

Data for the 2007 budget include manufacturing overhead of $3.6 million, which has been allocated in the existing costing system based on each product's budgeted direct labour cost. The budgeted direct labour cost for 2007 totals $720,000. Purchases and use of materials (mostly coffee beans) are budgeted to total $7.2 million.

The budgeted direct costs for one-kilogram bags of two of the company's products are:

	Mona Loa	Malaysian
Direct materials	$5.04	$3.84
Direct labour	0.36	0.36

CBI's controller believes the traditional costing system may be providing misleading cost information. She has developed an activity-based analysis of the 2007 budgeted manufacturing overhead costs shown in the following table:

Activity	Cost Allocation	Budgeted Activity	Budgeted Cost
Purchasing	Purchase orders	1,158	$ 694,800
Materials handling	Setups	1,800	864,000
Quality control	Batches	600	172,800
Roasting	Roasting-hours	96,100	1,153,200
Blending	Blending-hours	33,600	403,200
Packaging	Packaging-hours	26,000	312,000
Total manufacturing overhead cost			$3,600,000

Data regarding the 2007 production of Mona Loa and Malaysian coffee are presented here. There will be no beginning or ending materials inventory for either of these coffees.

	Mona Loa	Malaysian
Expected sales	100,000 kilograms	2,000 kilograms
Batch size	10,000 kilograms	500 kilograms
Setups	3 per batch	3 per batch
Purchase order size	25,000 kilograms	500 kilograms
Roasting time	1 hour/100 kilograms	1 hour/100 kilograms
Blending time	0.5 hour/100 kilograms	0.5 hour/100 kilograms
Packaging time	0.1 hour/100 kilograms	0.1 hour/100 kilograms

INSTRUCTIONS

Form groups of two or more students to complete the following requirements.

REQUIRED

1. Using Coffee Bean, Inc.'s existing costing approach,
   a. Determine the company's 2007 budgeted manufacturing overhead rate using direct-labour cost as the single allocation base.
   b. Determine the 2007 budgeted costs and selling prices of one kilogram of Mona Loa coffee and one kilogram of Malaysian coffee.
2. Use the controller's activity-based approach to estimate the 2007 budgeted cost for one kilogram of
   a. Mona Loa coffee
   b. Malaysian coffee
   Allocate all costs to the 100,000 kilograms of Mona Loa and the 2,000 kilograms of Malaysian. Compare the results with those in requirement 1.
3. Discuss how CBI could use a cost hierarchy approach to better understand its cost structure.
4. Examine the implications of your answers to requirements 2 and 3 for CBI's pricing and product emphasis strategy.

Sound budgeting practices are important to ensure that companies can remain profitable despite changes in their business, economic, and seasonal environments. Management of the Chateau Lake Louise, which is part of the Fairmont Hotels and Resorts chain, must make decisions given changes in the economy and weather. A budget is useful to assess whether these decisions will be profitable and whether any plans for the future need to be updated.

CHAPTER 6

Master Budget and Responsibility Accounting

LEARNING OBJECTIVES

After studying this chapter, you should be able to

1. Define *master budget* and explain its major benefits to an organization

2. Describe the advantages of budgets

3. Prepare the operating budget and its supporting budget schedules

4. Describe the uses of computer-based financial planning models

5. Explain kaizen budgeting and its importance for cost management

6. Prepare an activity-based budget

7. Describe responsibility centres and responsibility accounting

8. Explain how controllability relates to responsibility accounting

Budgets are one of the most widely used tools for planning and controlling organizations. Surveys show an almost universal use of budgets by medium and large companies in many parts of the world. Budgeting systems turn managers' perspectives forward. A forward-looking perspective enables managers to be in a better position to exploit opportunities. It also enables them to anticipate problems and take steps to eliminate or reduce their severity. As one observer said, "Few businesses plan to fail, but many of those that flop failed to plan."

This chapter examines budgeting as a planning and coordinating device. Topics covered in prior chapters are widely used in this discussion. Chapter 1 described some newly evolving management themes that affect management accounting. Budgets give financial expression to many of these themes. For example, budgets can quantify the planned financial effects of activities aimed at continuous improvement and cost reduction. By understanding cost behaviour (covered in Chapters 2 and 3), managers can better predict how total budgeted costs are affected by different projected output levels. By understanding cost tracing and cost allocation (covered in Chapters 4 and 5), managers can show how different projected revenue and cost amounts will affect the budgeted income statement and balance sheet. The material covered in this chapter is also integral to subsequent chapters. For example, Chapters 7 and 8 examine how the numbers used in budgets assist in evaluating the performance of managers or the business areas where they have responsibility.

Definition and Role of Budgets

A *budget* is a quantitative expression for a set time period of a proposed future plan of action by management. It can cover both financial and nonfinancial aspects of the plan and acts as a blueprint for the company to follow in the upcoming period. Budgets covering financial aspects quantify management's expectations regarding future income, cash flows, and financial position. Just as individual financial statements are prepared covering past periods, so they can be prepared covering future periods—for example, a budgeted income statement, a budgeted cash flow statement, and a budgeted balance sheet.

Well-managed organizations usually have the following budgeting cycle:

1. Planning the performance of the organization as a whole as well as of its subunits. The entire management team agrees as to what is expected.

2. Providing a frame of reference, a set of specific expectations against which actual results can be compared.

3. Investigating variations from plans. If necessary, corrective action follows investigation.

4. Planning again, considering feedback and changed conditions.

The **master budget** coordinates all the financial projections in the organization's individual budgets in a single, organizationwide set of budgets for a set time period. It embraces the impact of both *operating* decisions and *financing* decisions. Operating decisions centre on the acquisition and use of scarce resources. Financing decisions centre on how to get the funds to acquire resources. This book concentrates on how accounting helps managers make operating decisions, and we emphasize operating budgets in this chapter.

The term *master* in *master budget* refers to its being a comprehensive, organizationwide set of budgets. Consider Bombardier Inc. Each of its individual product lines, either aerospace or ground transportation, has a separate budgeted income statement, a separate budgeted cash flow statement, and so on. The master budgeted income statement for Bombardier is a single income statement that combines information from all these many individual budgeted income statements. Similarly, the master budgeted cash flow statement is a single cash flow statement that combines information from all these many individual budgeted cash flow statements.

Terminology

The terminology used to describe budgets varies among organizations. For example, budgeted financial statements are sometimes called **pro forma statements**. The budgeted financial statements of many companies include the budgeted income statement, the budgeted balance sheet, and the budgeted statement of cash flows. Some organizations, such as Hewlett-Packard, refer to budgeting as *targeting*. Indeed, to give a more positive thrust to budgeting, many organizations—for example, Nissan Canada and Bombardier—describe the budget as a *profit plan*.

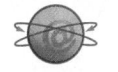
Budgets are a major feature of most management control systems. When administered intelligently, budgets (1) compel planning, including the implementation of plans, (2) provide performance criteria, and (3) promote communication and coordination within the organization.

Strategy and Plans

Budgeting is most useful when done as an integral part of an organization's strategic analysis.[1] **Strategic analysis** considers how an organization best combines its own capabilities with the opportunities in the marketplace to accomplish its overall objectives.

It includes consideration of such questions as

1. What are the overall objectives of the organization?

2. Are the markets for its product local, regional, national, or global? What trends will affect its markets? How is the organization affected by the economy, its industry, and its competitors?

3. What forms of organizational and financial structures serve the organization best?

4. What are the risks of alternative strategies, and what are the organization's contingency plans if its preferred plan fails?

Malaspina University-College
www.mala.ca/gap/index.asp

Planning is setting goals and developing strategies to achieve those goals. Budgets show how resources will be deployed to implement strategy. The master budget helps managers implement their strategies.

Consider the diagram in Exhibit 6-1. Strategic analysis underlies both long-run and short-run planning. In turn, these plans lead to the formulation of budgets. The arrows in the diagram are pointing in two directions. Why? Because strategy, plans, and budgets are interrelated and affect one another. Malaspina University-College in Nanaimo, British Columbia, has published details outlining this process, ranking its nine strategic objectives and evaluating the organization's achievements. Budgets provide feedback to managers about the likely effects of their strategic plans. Managers then use this feedback to revise their strategic plans. DaimlerChrysler's strategic decision to reduce the selling prices of its Dodge Durango illustrates the interrelation between strategic analysis and budgets. By reducing its prices, DaimlerChrysler expected to increase the demand for the Durango. The budget, however, indicated that, even at the predicted higher sales quantities, the company would be unable to meet its financial targets. For the strategy to succeed, the company would need to reduce operating costs by streamlining operations and moving facilities to lower-cost areas. DaimlerChrysler then used cross-functional teams with members from different parts of the value chain to seek major cost reductions.

A Framework for Judging Performance

Budgeted performance measures can overcome two key limitations of using past performance as a basis for judging actual results. One limitation is that past results incorporate past miscues and substandard performance. Consider a cellular telephone company examining the 2007 performance of its sales force. Suppose the past performance in 2006 incorporates the efforts of many departed salespeople who left because they did not have an understanding of the marketplace. Using the sales record of those departed employees would set the performance bar for new salespeople way too low.

A second limitation of past performance is that the future may be expected to be very different from the past. Consider again our cellular telephone company.

EXHIBIT 6-1
Strategic Analysis in the Formulation of Long-Run and Short-Run Budgets

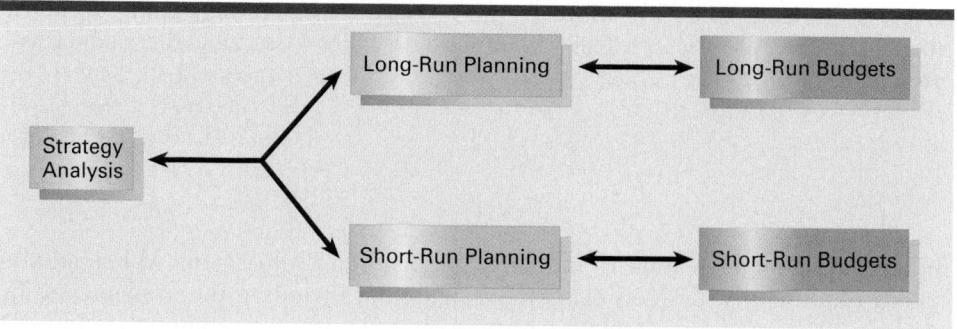

[1] See J. Hope and R. Fraser, *Beyond Budgeting* (Boston, MA: Harvard Business School Press, 2003) for several examples.

Suppose the company had a 20% revenue increase in 2007, compared with a 10% increase in 2006. Does this indicate stellar sales performance? Before saying yes, consider two additional facts. Fact one is that, in November 2006, an industry trade association forecast that the 2007 growth rate in industry revenues would be 40%. Fact two is that, in 2006, the actual growth rate in industry revenues was 50%. The 20% actual revenue gain in 2007, although it exceeds the 2006 actual growth rate of 10%, remains below the actual industry gain of 50%. Use of the 40% figure as the budgeted rate provides a better way to evaluate the 2007 sales performance than does use of the 2006 actual rate of 10%.

A company's internal budget is not the only threshold of year-to-year accomplishment that can be used to evaluate performance. Companies must also consider their own performance relative to their peers in the industry and relative to the overall industry's annual performance. When companies evaluate accomplishment exclusively on their internal performance the situation is ripe for "gaming," whereby managers set easily achieved targets,[2] but those to whom they report know this game. In turn, they set more challenging targets and negotiating begins among the levels of the company's managers to decide upon what the budget will be. General Electric's former CEO Jack Welch maintained that demanding but achievable goals created anxiety for managers but improved corporate performance. He perceived "stretch" goals as a way to motivate creative change and progress in existing processes comprising each business function.

Coordination and Communication

Coordination is the meshing and balancing of all factors of production or service and of all the departments and business functions so that the company can meet its objectives. *Communication* is getting those objectives understood and accepted by all employees.

Coordination forces executives to think of relationships among individual operations, departments, and the company as a whole. Coordination implies, for example, that purchasing officers make material purchase plans based on production requirements. Also, production managers plan personnel and machinery needs to produce the number of products necessary to meet revenue forecasts. How does a budget lead to coordination? Consider Snapple Beverage. Production managers who are evaluated on maximizing output while keeping unit costs per bottle low would prefer long production runs with very few changeovers of flavours. But if the output cannot be sold, Snapple may find itself awash in a costly inventory buildup of Mango Madness. The budget achieves coordination by constraining production managers to produce only what marketing is forecasting it can sell. This may entail doing a changeover from Mango Madness to Lemonade partway into a production shift.

For coordination to succeed, communication is essential. The production manager must know the sales plan. The purchasing manager must know the production plan, and so on. Having a formal document such as the budget is an effective way to communicate a consistent set of plans to the organization as a whole.

Challenges in Budget Administration

Budgeting consumes a lot of time at all levels of an organization. Those employees on the front lines possess hands-on experience with day-to-day production and their managers possess specialized knowledge of how to control these processes. Communication from the bottom up that is reflected in the budget creates greater commitment and accountability towards its achievement among all levels. But ultimately, top management bears responsibility for producing and achieving the budget targets for the companies they lead. *Management at all levels, however, should understand and support the budget and all aspects of the management control system.*

The prevalence of budgets in companies of all sizes is evidence that the benefits of budgeting processes outweigh their costs (see Global Surveys of Company Practice on the next page). Top management support is especially critical for obtaining active line participation in the formulation of budgets and for successful administration of

The master budget helps coordinate business functions in the value chain. Management accountants provide the information required to coordinate the budgeting process.

Snapple Beverage
www.snapple.com

Studies of large companies report about 5% of total staff positions are dedicated to the budgeting process.

---

[2]For a more detailed discussion, see R. Varnick, G. Wu, and C. Heath, "Raising the Bar on Goals," Graduate School of Business Publication, University of Chicago, Spring, 1999.

Budget Practices Around the Globe

Surveys of financial officers of large companies throughout the United States, Europe, Asia, and Oceania indicate some interesting similarities and differences in budgeting practices. The use of master budgets is widespread; however, differences arise with respect to other dimensions of budgeting. U.S. controllers and managers, for example, favour participation by division managers and regard return on investment as the most important budget goal.[a] Similarly all of the Greek budget directors surveyed report that division managers participate in completing the master budget.[b] In contrast, fewer division managers in New Zealand and the United Kingdom participated in the budget committee process even though most executives in these countries place average to vital importance on adherence to budgets when evaluating managers.[c] Japanese companies have the smallest amount of participation by division managers in the budgeting process (relative to other countries surveyed) and regard sales revenue as the most important budget goal. A survey of Australian managers reported that budgeting is the management accounting practice that they benefit from the most.[d]

1. Percentage of companies that prepare a complete master budget:

United States	Australia	Finland[e]	Greece	India[f]	Japan[a]	New Zealand	Singapore[g]	Sweden[h]	U.K.
91%	100%	92%	93%	91%	93%	98%	97%	89%	95%

2. Percentage of companies reporting division-manager participation in budget committee discussions:

United States	Greece	India	Japan	New Zealand	U.K.
78%	93%	84%	67%	70%	71%

3. Ranking of the most important budget goals for division managers (1 is most important):

	United States	Japan
Return on investment	1	4
Operating income	2	2
Sales revenue	3	1
Production costs	4	3

4. Percentage of executives who place importance on the budget when appraising management performance:

	New Zealand	United Kingdom
Not important	0%	1%
Below average importance	7	4
Average importance	22	14
Above average importance	45	39
Vital importance	26	28

What reduces the effectiveness of the planning and budgeting processes of companies? A survey of chief financial officers (CFOs) in the United States reported the following four factors in order of importance.[i]

1. Lack of a well-defined strategy
2. Lack of a clear linkage of strategy to operating plans
3. Lack of individual accountability for results
4. Lack of meaningful performance measures

(Continued)

Two planning methodologies viewed as "significant to extremely valuable" by more than 60% of CFOs surveyed were activity-based budgeting and rolling budget forecasts.

[a]Asada, T., J. Bailes, and M. Amano, "An Empirical Study of Japanese and American Budget Planning and Control Systems," (Working Paper, Tsukuba University and Oregon State University, 1989).

[b]Ballas, A., and G. Venieris, "A Survey of Management Accounting Practice in Greek Firms," in Bhimani, A. (ed.) *Management Accounting: European Perspectives* (Oxford: Oxford University Press, 1996).

[c]Guilding, C., D. Lamminmaki, and C. Drury, "Budgeting and Standard Costing Practices in New Zealand and the United Kingdom," *The International Journal of Accounting* (1998).

[d]Crenhall, R., and K. Smith, "Adoption and Benefits of Management Accounting Practices: An Australian Study," *Management Accounting Research* (1998).

[e]Ekholm, B., and J. Wallin, "Is the Annual Budget Really Dead?" *The European Accounting Review* (2000).

[f]Joshi, P., "The International Diffusion of New Management Accounting Practices: The Case of India," *Journal of International Accounting Auditing & Taxation* (2001).

[g]Ghosh, B., and Y. Chan, "Management Accounting in Singapore—Well in Place?" *Managerial Auditing Journal* (1997).

[h]Glader, M., "Ekonomistyrning i Svenska Börsföretag," Rapport från Sektionen för Redovisning och Finansiering," (Stockholm: Stockholm School of Economics, 1996).

[i]Lazere, C., "All Together Now," *CFO* (February 1998).

the budget. If line managers feel that top management does not "believe" in the budget, these managers are unlikely to be active participants in the budgeting process. Similarly, a top manager that always mechanically institutes "across the board" cost reductions (say, a 10% reduction in all areas) in the face of revenue reductions is unlikely to have line managers willing to communicate honestly.

Budgets should not be administered rigidly. Changing conditions call for changes in plans. A manager may commit to the budget, but a situation might develop where some special repairs or a special advertising program would better serve the interests of the organization. The manager should not defer the repairs or the advertising in order to meet the budget if such actions will hurt the organization in the long run. Attaining the budget should not be an end in itself.

TYPES OF BUDGETS

Time Coverage

The purpose(s) for budgeting should guide the time period chosen for the budget. Consider budgeting for a new Harley-Davidson 500-cc motorcycle. If the purpose is to budget for the total profitability of this new model, a five-year period (or more) may be appropriate (covering design, manufacture, sales, and after-sales support). In contrast, consider budgeting for a Christmas play. If the purpose is to estimate all cash outlays, a six-month period from the planning to staging of the play may be adequate.

The most frequently used budget period is one year. The annual budget is often subdivided by months for the first quarter and by quarters for the remainder of the year. The budgeted data for a year are frequently revised as the year unfolds. For example, at the end of the first quarter, the budget for the next three quarters is changed in light of new information.

Businesses are increasingly using *rolling budgets*. A **rolling budget** is a budget or plan that is always available for a specified future period by adding a month, quarter, or year in the future as the month, quarter, or year just ended is dropped. Thus, a 12-month rolling budget for the March 2006 to February 2007 period becomes a 12-month rolling budget for the April 2006 to March 2007 period the next month, and so on. There is always a 12-month budget in place. Rolling budgets constantly force management to think concretely about the forthcoming 12 months, regardless of the month at hand. The NEC Corporation of Japan has a one-year operating budget that is updated each month. Companies also frequently use rolling budgets when developing five-year budgets for long-run planning. For example, the NEC Corporation also has a five-year budget that is updated each year.

Rolling budget. Budget or plan that is always available for a specified future period by adding a month, quarter, or year in the future as the month, quarter, or year just ended is dropped.

NEC Corporation
www.nec.com

Steps in Developing an Operating Budget

A good way to explain the budgeting process is to walk through the development of an actual budget. We shall use a master budget, because it provides a comprehensive picture of the entire budgeting process at Halifax Engineering, a manufacturer of aircraft replacement parts. Its job-costing system for manufacturing costs has two direct-cost categories (direct materials and direct manufacturing labour) and one indirect-cost pool (manufacturing overhead). Manufacturing overhead (both variable and fixed) is allocated to products using direct manufacturing labour-hours as the allocation base.

Exhibit 6-2 shows a simplified diagram of the various parts of the master budget for Halifax Engineering. The master budget summarizes the financial projections of all the organization's individual budgets. The master budget results in a set of related financial statements for a set time period, usually a year. The bulk of Exhibit 6-2 presents a set of budgets that together is often called the **operating budget**, which includes the budgeted income statement and its supporting budget schedules. The supporting budget schedules cut across different categories of the value chain from R&D to customer service. The **financial budget** is that part of the master budget that comprises the capital budget, cash budget, budgeted balance sheet, and budgeted statement of cash flows. It focuses on the impact of operations and planned capital outlays on cash.

The final master budget is often the result of several iterations. Each draft involves interaction across the various business functions of the value chain.

Basic Data and Requirements

Halifax Engineering is a machine shop that uses skilled labour and metal alloys to manufacture two types of aircraft replacement parts—Regular and Heavy-Duty. Halifax managers are ready to prepare a master budget for the year 2007. To keep our illustration manageable for clarifying basic relationships, we make the following assumptions:

1. The only source of revenues is sales of the two parts. Non-sales-related revenue, such as interest income, is assumed to be zero.

2. Work-in-process inventory is negligible and is ignored.

3. Direct materials inventory and finished goods inventory are costed using the first-in, first-out (FIFO) method.

4. Unit costs of direct materials purchased and finished goods sold remain unchanged throughout the budget year (2007).

5. Variable production costs are variable with respect to direct manufacturing labour-hours. Variable nonproduction costs are variable with respect to revenues. Both assumptions are simplifying ones made to keep our example relatively straightforward.

6. For computing inventoriable costs, all manufacturing costs (fixed and variable) are allocated using a single allocation base—direct manufacturing labour-hours.

After carefully examining all relevant factors, the executives of Halifax Engineering forecast the following figures for 2007:

	A	B	C
1	Direct materials:		
2	Material 111 alloy	$ 7	per kilogram
3	Material 112 alloy	$10	per kilogram
4	Direct manufacturing labour	$20	per hour
5			
6	**Content of Each Product Unit**	**Regular**	**Heavy-Duty**
7	Direct materials 111 alloy—kilograms	12	12
8	Direct materials 112 alloy—kilograms	6	8
9	Direct manufacturing labour-hours (DLH)	4	6

Operating budget. The budgeted income statement and its supporting schedules.

Financial budget. That part of the master budget that comprises the capital budget, cash budget, budgeted balance sheet, and budgeted statement of cash flows.

EXHIBIT 6-2
Overview of the Master Budget for Halifax Engineering

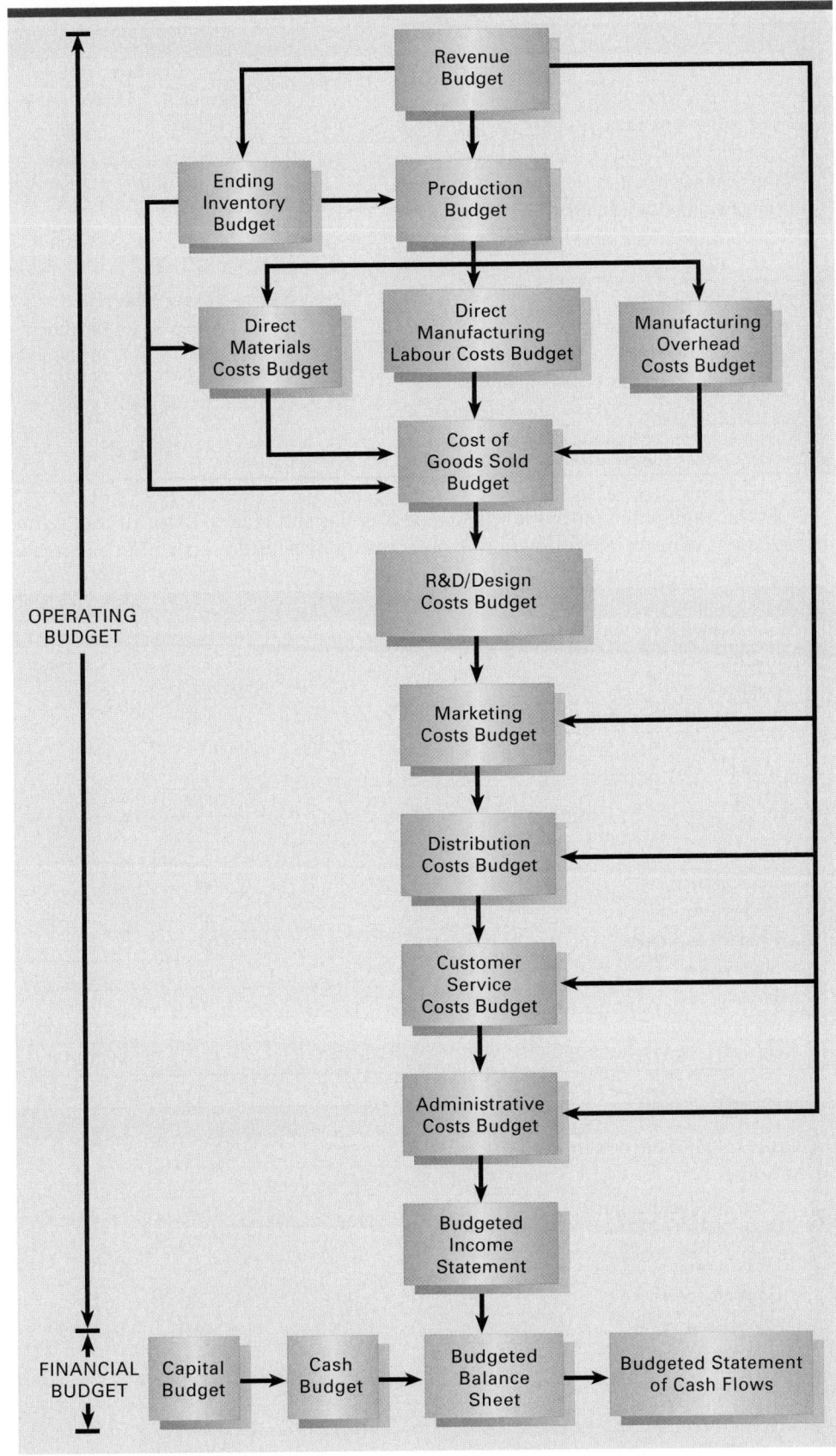

All direct manufacturing costs are variable with respect to the units of output produced. Additional information regarding the year 2007 is as follows:

	A	B	C
		Product	
1		Regular	Heavy-Duty
2			
3	Expected sales in units	5,000	1,000
4	Selling price per unit	$ 600	$ 800
5	Target ending inventory in units*	1,100	50
6	Beginning inventory in units	100	50
7	Beginning inventory value in dollars	$38,400	$26,200
8			
9		Direct Materials	
10		111 Alloy	112 Alloy
11	Beginning inventory in kilograms	7,000	6,000
12	Target ending inventory in kilograms*	8,000	2,000
13			
14	*Target inventories depend on expected sales, expected variation in demand for products, and management philosophies such as just-in-time (JIT) inventory management.		

At the anticipated output levels for the Regular and Heavy-Duty aircraft parts, management believes the following manufacturing overhead costs will be incurred:

	A	B	C
1	**Manufacturing Overhead Costs**		
2	Variable:		
3	Supplies	$ 90,000	
4	Indirect manufacturing labour	210,000	
5	Direct and indirect manufacturing labour fringe costs	300,000	
6	Power	120,000	
7	Maintenance	60,000	$ 780,000
8	Fixed:		
9	Amortization	220,000	
10	Property taxes	50,000	
11	Property insurance	10,000	
12	Supervision	100,000	
13	Power	22,000	
14	Maintenance	18,000	420,000
15	Total		$1,200,000

	A	B	C
1	**Other (Nonproduction or Period) Costs**		
2	Variable:		
3	R&D/product design	$ 76,000	
4	Marketing	133,000	
5	Distribution	66,500	
6	Customer Service	47,500	
7	Administrative	152,000	$475,000
8	Fixed:		
9	R&D/product design	60,000	
10	Marketing	67,000	
11	Distribution	33,500	
12	Customer Service	12,500	
13	Administrative	222,000	395,000
14	Total		$870,000

Our task at hand is to prepare a budgeted income statement for the year 2007. As shown in Exhibit 6-2 (p. 203), this is one component of Halifax's master budget. Other components of the master budget—the budgeted balance sheet and the cash budget—are discussed in the appendix to this chapter (p. 220).

The following supporting budget schedules will be prepared when developing Halifax's budgeted income statement:

1. Revenue budget

2. Production budget (in units)

3. Direct materials usage budget and direct materials purchases budget

4. Direct manufacturing labour budget

5. Manufacturing overhead budget

6. Ending inventory budget

7. Cost of goods sold budget

8. Other (nonproduction) costs budget

Most organizations have a budget manual, which contains instructions and relevant information for preparing budgets. Although the details differ between organizations, the following basic steps are common for developing a budgeted income statement. Beginning with the revenue budget, each budget follows step by step in logical fashion. In most cases, computer software speeds the budget computations.

Steps in Preparing an Operating Budget

◆ **Step 1:** *Revenue budget.* The revenue budget (schedule 1) is the usual starting point for budgeting. Why? Because production (and hence costs) and inventory levels generally depend on the forecasted level of revenue. See the Concepts in Action box on p. 210 to illustrate this application.

	A	B	C	D
1		**Schedule 1: Revenue Budget**		
2		**for the Year Ended December 31, 2007**		
3			**Selling**	**Total**
4		**Units**	**Price**	**Revenues**
5	Regular	5,000	$600	$3,000,000
6	Heavy-Duty	1,000	800	800,000
7	Total			$3,800,000

The $3.8 million is the amount of revenues in the budgeted income statement. The revenue budget is often the outcome of elaborate information-gathering and discussions among sales managers and field sales representatives.

Pressures can exist for budgeted revenues to be either over- or underestimates of the expected amounts. Some firms set "stretch" or "challenge" targets for revenues. These targets are actually overestimates of expected revenues intended to motivate employees to put in extra effort and achieve higher performance.

Pressure for employees to underestimate budgeted revenues can occur when a company uses the difference between actual and budget amounts to evaluate managers. These managers may respond by giving highly conservative forecasts. **Padding** the budget or introducing **budgetary slack** refers to the practice of underestimating budgeted revenues (or overestimating budgeted costs) to make budgeted targets more easily achievable. Introducing budgetary slack makes it more likely that actual revenues will exceed budgeted amounts. From the marketing manager's standpoint, budgetary slack hedges against unexpected adverse circumstances.

Occasionally, revenues are limited by available production capacity. For example, unusually heavy market demand, shortages of personnel or materials, or strikes may cause a company to exhaust its finished goods inventory completely.

Padding (budgetary slack). The practice of underestimating budgeted revenues (or overestimating budgeted costs) to make budgeted targets more easily achievable.

Additional sales cannot be made because no stock of the product is available. In such cases, the production capacity—the factor that limits revenue—is the starting point for preparing the revenue budget.

◆ **Step 2:** *Production budget (in units).* After revenues are budgeted, the production budget (schedule 2) can be prepared. The total finished goods units to be produced depends on planned sales and expected changes in inventory levels:

$$\begin{array}{c} \text{Budgeted} \\ \text{production} = \\ \text{(units)} \end{array} \begin{array}{c} \text{Budgeted} \\ \text{sales} \\ \text{(units)} \end{array} + \begin{array}{c} \text{Target ending} \\ \text{finished goods} \\ \text{inventory} \\ \text{(units)} \end{array} - \begin{array}{c} \text{Beginning} \\ \text{finished goods} \\ \text{inventory} \\ \text{(units)} \end{array}$$

	A	B	C
1	Schedule 2: Production Budget		
2	for the Year Ended December 31, 2007		
3		Product	
4		Regular	Heavy-Duty
5	Budgeted sales (schedule 1)	5,000	1,000
6	Add: Target ending finished goods inventory	1,100	50
7	Total requirements	6,100	1,050
8	Deduct: Beginning finished goods inventory	(100)	(50)
9	Units to be produced	6,000	1,000

When unit sales are not stable throughout the year, managers must decide whether (1) to adjust production levels periodically to minimize inventory held or (2) to maintain constant production levels and let inventory rise and fall. Increasingly, managers are choosing to adjust production.

◆ **Step 3:** *Direct materials usage budget and direct materials purchases budget.* The decision on the number of units to be produced (schedule 2) is the key to computing the usage of direct materials in quantities and in dollars (schedule 3A).

	A	B	C	D	E
1	Schedule 3A: Direct Materials Usage Budget in Kilograms and Dollars				
2	for the Year Ended December 31, 2007				
3		Materials			
4		111 Alloy	112 Alloy	Total	
5	Direct materials to be used in production of Regular parts (6,000 units) × 12 and 6 kilograms	72,000	36,000		see schedule 2
6	Direct materials to be used in production of Heavy-Duty (1,000 units) × 12 and 8 kilograms	12,000	8,000		
7	Total direct materials to be used (in kilograms)	84,000	44,000		see schedule 2
8	Direct materials to be used from beginning inventory (assume FIFO cost flow)	7,000	6,000		
9	Multiply by: Cost per kilogram of beginning inventory	$ 7	$ 10		
10	Cost of direct materials to be used from beginning inventory	$ 49,000	$ 60,000	$ 109,000	(a)
11	Direct materials to be used from purchases (84,000 − 7,000; 44,000 − 6,000)	77,000	38,000		
12	Multiply by: Cost per kilogram of purchased materials	$ 7	$ 10		
13	Cost of direct materials to be used from purchases	$539,000	$380,000	$ 919,000	(b)
14	Total costs of direct materials to be used (a) + (b)	$588,000	$440,000	$1,028,000	

Schedule 3B computes the budget for direct materials purchases, which depends on the budgeted direct materials to be used, the beginning inventory of direct materials, and the target ending inventory of direct materials:

$$
\begin{array}{ccc}
\text{Purchases} & \text{Usage} & \text{Target ending} & \text{Beginning} \\
\text{of direct} = \text{of direct} + & \text{inventory} & - & \text{inventory} \\
\text{materials} & \text{materials} & \text{of direct} & \text{of direct} \\
& & \text{materials} & \text{materials}
\end{array}
$$

	A	B	C	D
1	Schedule 3B: Direct Materials Usage Budget in Kilograms and Dollars			
2	for the Year Ended December 31, 2007			
3		Materials		
4		111 Alloy	112 Alloy	Total
5	Direct materials to be used in production (in kilogram)	84,000	44,000	
6	Add: Target ending direct materials inventory	8,000	2,000	
7	Total requirements (in kilograms)	92,000	46,000	
8	Deduct: Beginning direct materials inventory	(7,000)	(6,000)	
9	Direct materials to be purchased (in kilograms)	85,000	40,000	
10	Multiply by: Cost per kilogram of purchased materials	$ 7	$ 10	
11	Total direct materials purchase costs	$595,000	$400,000	$995,000

◆ **Step 4:** *Direct manufacturing labour budget.* These costs depend on wage rates, production methods, and hiring plans. The computations of budgeted direct manufacturing labour costs appear in schedule 4.

	A	B	C	D	E	F
1	Schedule 4: Direct Manufacturing Labour Budget					
2	for the Year Ended December 31, 2007					
3		Output	Direct			
4		Units	Manufacturing		Hourly	
5		Produced	Labour-Hours	Total	Wage	
6		(Schedule 2)	per Unit	Hours	Rate	Total
7	Regular	6,000	4	24,000	$20	$480,000
8	Heavy-Duty	1,000	6	6,000	$20	120,000
9	Total			30,000		$600,000

◆ **Step 5:** *Manufacturing overhead budget.* The total of these costs depends on how individual overhead costs vary with the assumed cost driver, direct manufacturing labour-hours. The calculations of budgeted manufacturing overhead costs appear in schedule 5.

	A	B	C	D
1	Schedule 5: Manufacturing Overhead Budget*			
2	for the Year Ended December 31, 2007			
3		At Budgeted Level of 30,000 Direct		
4		Manufacturing Labour-Hours		
5	Variable manufacturing overhead costs:			
6	Supplies	$ 90,000		
7	Indirect manufacturing labour	210,000		
8	Direct and indirect manufacturing labour fringe costs	300,000		
9	Power	120,000		
10	Maintenance	60,000	$ 780,000	

11	Fixed:				
12	Amortization		220,000		
13	Property taxes		50,000		
14	Property insurance		10,000		
15	Supervision		100,000		
16	Power		22,000		
17	Maintenance		18,000	420,000	
18	Total			$1,200,000	
19					
20	NOTE: The annual amortization expense becomes part of Cost of Goods Sold (schedule 7)				
21	*Data are from p. 204.				

Halifax treats both variable and fixed manufacturing overhead as inventoriable costs.[3] It inventories manufacturing overhead at the budgeted rate of $40 per direct manufacturing labour-hour—total manufacturing overhead, $1,200,000 ÷ 30,000 budgeted direct manufacturing labour-hours. It does not use separate variable and fixed manufacturing overhead rates.

◆ **Step 6:** *Ending inventory budget.* Schedule 6A shows the computation of unit costs for the two products. These unit costs are used to calculate the costs of target ending inventories of direct materials and finished goods in schedule 6B.

	A	B	C	D	E	F
1	**Schedule 6A: Computation of Units Costs of Manufacturing**					
2				**Product**		
3			**Regular**		**Heavy-Duty**	
4		**Cost per Unit**				
5		**of Input***	**Inputs***	**Amount**	**Inputs***	**Amount**
6	Material 111 alloy	$ 7	12	$ 84	12	$ 84
7	Material 112 alloy	$10	6	60	8	80
8	Direct manufacturing labour	$20[†]	4	80	6	120
9	Manufacturing overhead	$40[‡]	4	160	6	240
10	Total			$384		$524
11						
12	*In kilograms or hours					
13	†Data are from p. 207.					
14	‡Direct manufacturing labour-hours is the sole allocation base for manufacturing overhead (both variable and fixed). The budgeted manufacturing overhead rate per direct manufacturing labour-hour of $40 was calculated in step 5.					

	A	B	C	D	E
1	**Schedule 6B: Ending Inventory Budget for the Year**				
2	**Ended December 31, 2007**				
3			**Cost per**		
4		**Kilograms**	**Kilogram**		**Total**
5	Direct materials				
6	111 alloy	8,000*	$ 7	$ 56,000	
7	112 alloy	2,000*	$10	20,000	$ 76,000
8			**Cost per**		
9		**Units**	**Unit**		
10	Finished goods				
11	Regular	1,100[†]	$384[‡]	$422,400	
12	Heavy-Duty	50[†]	$524[‡]	26,200	$448,600
13	Total Ending Inventory				$524,600
14					
15	*Data are from p. 204.				
16	†Data are from p. 204.				
17	‡From schedule 6A: this is based on 2007 costs of manufacturing finished goods because, under the FIFO costing method, the units in finished goods ending inventory consist of units that are produced during 2007.				

[3] This inventory costing method is termed *absorption costing* (see Chapter 9).

◆ **Step 7:** *Cost of goods sold budget.* The information from schedules 3 to 6 leads to schedule 7:

	A	B	C	D
1	**Schedule 7: Cost of Goods Sold Budget**			
2	**for the Year Ended December 31, 2007**			
3		From Schedule		Total
4	Beginning finished goods inventory, January 1, 2007	Given*		$ 64,600
5	Direct materials used	3A	$1,028,000	
6	Direct manufacturing labour	4	600,000	
7	Manufacturing overhead	5	1,200,000	
8	Cost of goods manufactured			2,828,000
9	Cost of goods available for sale			2,892,600
10	Deduct: Ending finished goods inventory			
11	December 31, 2007	6B		(448,600)
12	Cost of goods sold			$2,444,000
13				
14	NOTE: The annual amortization expense has been included in manufacturing overhead and therefore is part of Cost of goods sold.			
15	*Given in the description of basic data and requirements (Regular $38,400, Heavy-Duty $26,200) on p. 204.			

Note that the following holds:

$$\text{Cost of goods sold} = \text{Beginning finished goods inventory} + \text{Cost of goods manufactured} - \text{Ending finished goods inventory}$$

◆ **Step 8:** *Other (nonproduction) costs budget.* Schedules 2 to 7 cover budgeting for Halifax's production area of the value chain. For brevity, other areas of the value chain are combined into a single schedule.

	A	B	C	D	E
1	**Schedule 8: Other (Nonproduction) Costs**				
2	**Budget for the Year Ended December 31, 2007**				
3					
4	Variable costs:				
5	R&D product design	$ 76,000			
6	Marketing	133,000			
7	Distribution	66,500			
8	Customer service	47,500			
9	General and administrative	152,000	475,000*		
10	Fixed costs:				
11	R&D product design	60,000			
12	Marketing	67,000			
13	Distribution	33,500			
14	Customer service	12,500			
15	General and administrative	222,000	395,000		
16	Total costs		$870,000		
17					
18	Total variable cost for schedule 8 is $0.125 per revenue dollar or $475,000 ÷ $3,800,000.				

◆ **Step 9:** *Budgeted income statement.* Schedules 1, 7, and 8 provide the necessary information to complete the budgeted income statement, shown in Exhibit 6-3 on p. 211. Of course, more details could be included in the income statement and then fewer supporting schedules would be prepared.

Web-Enabled Budgeting and Hendrick Motorsports

In recent years, many companies have implemented comprehensive software packages that manage budgeting and forecasting functions across the organization. One such option available is FRx® Software Corporation's Forecaster package. Forecaster is specifically designed for mid-market and corporate businesses wishing to gain control over their budgeting and forecasting process within a fully integrated, Web-based environment.

Among the many companies implementing Forecaster is Hendrick Motorsports. Featuring renowned drivers including Jeff Gordon, Hendrick is the premier NASCAR Nextel Cup stock car racing organization. Headquartered near Charlotte, North Carolina, Hendrick operates four full-time teams within the Nextel Cup series, which runs annually from early February through late November and features 36 races at 23 speedways across the United States. The Hendrick organization has over 400 employees, with tasks ranging from accounting and marketing to engine building and racecar driving. Such an environment features multiple functional areas and units, varied worksites, and ever-changing circumstances. Patrick Perkins, director of marketing, noted, "Racing is a fast business. It's just as fast off the track as it is on. With the work that we put into the development of our teams and technologies, and having to respond to change as well as anticipate change, I like to think of us in this business as change experts."

FRx Forecaster has allowed Hendrick's financial managers to seamlessly manage the planning and budgeting process. Authorized users from each functional area or team sign on to the application through the corporate intranet. Security on the system is tight: Access is limited to only the accounts that a manager is authorized to budget. Forecaster also allows users at the racetracks to access the application remotely, which allows managers to receive or update real time "actuals" from the system. This way, team managers know their allotted expenses for each race. Forecaster also provides users with additional features, including simplified functionality, human resource (labour) budgeting and planning data, seamless links with general ledger accounts, and the option to perform various what-if (sensitivity) analyses. Scott Lampe, chief financial officer, said, "Forecaster allows us to change our forecasts to respond to changes, either rules changes (such as changes in the Nextel Cup series' points system) or technology changes (such as the addition of restrictor plates), throughout the racing season."

FRx Forecaster and other similar packages are available from application service providers (ASPs). With this setup, companies like Hendrick Motorsports can rent the application over the Internet rather than buy it, which can provide significant cost savings. Moreover, companies renting from an application service provider do not have to maintain or upgrade the software, because the ASP does all such work.

Web-enabled budgeting frees the finance department so it can focus on strategy, analysis, and decision making. It increases service levels to employees, reduces costs, accelerates the planning and budgeting cycles, and improves the value from budgeting. Patrick Perkins of Hendrick Motorsports agrees: "In racing, the team that wins is not only the team with the fastest car, but the team that is the most disciplined and prepared week in and week out. Forecaster allows us to respond to that changing landscape."

Sources: T. Powell, "Software Tends," *Journal of Cost Management* (January/February 1999), pp. 36–37; PR Newswire, "FRx Software Announces Availability of Forecaster 6.7," PR Newswire Web site http://www.prnewswire.com (July 31, 2003); FRx Software, "Hendrick Motorsports (Internet video)," FRx Software Web site http://www.frxsoftware.com (February 17, 2004); and Hendrick Motorsports, "About Hendrick Motorsports," Hendrick Motorsports Web site http://www.hendrickmotorsports.com (February 17, 2004).

EXHIBIT 6-3
Budgeted Income Statement for Halifax Engineering for the Year Ended December 31, 2007

	A	B	C	D
1	**Budgeted Income Statement for Halifax Engineering**			
2	**for the Year Ended December 31, 2007**			
3	Revenues	Schedule 1		$3,800,000
4	Costs:			
5	Cost of goods sold	Schedule 7		2,444,000
6	Gross margin			1,356,000
7	Operating (period) costs			
8	R&D/product design costs	Schedule 8	$136,000	
9	Marketing costs	Schedule 8	200,000	
10	Distribution costs	Schedule 8	100,000	
11	Customer service costs	Schedule 8	60,000	
12	General and administrative costs	Schedule 8	374,000	870,000
13	Operating income			$ 486,000
14				
15	NOTE: Unlike financial accounting, this budgeted income statement contains the noncash annual amortization expense in Cost of goods sold (see schedule 5 and schedule 7).			

Top management's strategies for achieving revenue and operating income goals influence the costs planned for the different business functions of the value chain. As strategies change, the budget allocations for different elements of the value chain will also change. For example, a shift in strategy toward emphasizing product development and customer service will result in increased resources being allocated to these parts of the master budget. The actual data resulting from this strategy will be compared to budgeted results. Management can then evaluate whether the focus on product development and customer service has been successful. This feedback is an important input in subsequent plans.

COMPUTER-BASED FINANCIAL PLANNING MODELS

Exhibit 6-1 (p. 198) illustrated the interrelationship among strategic analysis, planning, and budgeting. The value of budgets to managers in their strategic analysis and planning is enhanced by conducting sensitivity analysis. Sensitivity analysis is a what-if technique that examines how a result will change if the original predicted data are not achieved or if an underlying assumption changes. Although a hand-held calculator would suffice to do the calculations, commercial software packages are now available for more complex tasks, such as sensitivity analysis for the financial statements found in a master budget. These packages do the calculations for **financial planning models**, which are mathematical representations of the relationships across operating activities, financial activities, and financial statements.

Consider Halifax Engineering. Their financial planning model assumes the following:

◆ Direct materials and direct manufacturing labour costs vary proportionately with the quantities of Regular and Heavy-Duty parts produced.

◆ Variable manufacturing overhead costs vary with direct manufacturing labour-hours.

◆ Variable nonmanufacturing costs vary with revenue dollars.

◆ Target ending inventories remain unchanged.

Exhibit 6-4 presents the budgeted operating income for three what-if scenarios for Halifax Engineering:

◆ **Scenario 1.**   A 3% decrease in the selling price of the Regular part and a 3% decrease in the selling price of the Heavy-Duty part.

OBJECTIVE 4

Describe the uses of computer-based financial planning models

Financial planning models.
Mathematical representations of the relationships among all operating activities, financial activities, and financial statements.

EXHIBIT 6-4
Effect of Changes in Budget Assumptions on Budgeted Income for Halifax Engineering

| What-if Scenario | Key Assumptions | | | | | | Budgeted Operating Income | |
| | Units Sold | | Selling Price | | Direct Materials Cost* | | | |
	Regular	Heavy-Duty	Regular	Heavy-Duty	111 Alloy	112 Alloy	Dollars	Change from Master Budget
Master budget	5,000	1,000	$600	$800	$7.00	$10.00	$486,000	—
Scenario 1	5,000	1,000	582	776	7.00	10.00	386,250	20.52% decrease
Scenario 2	4,800	960	600	800	7.00	10.00	438,562	9.82% decrease
Scenario 3	5,000	1,000	600	800	7.35	10.50	448,380	7.74% decrease

*Per kilogram.

◆ **Scenario 2.** A 4% decrease in units sold of the Regular part and a 4% decrease in units sold of the Heavy-Duty part.
◆ **Scenario 3.** A 5% increase in the price per kilogram of 111 alloy and a 5% increase in the price per kilogram of 112 alloy.

Exhibit 6-4 indicates that, relative to the master budget, budgeted operating income decreases by 21% under scenario 1, by 10% under scenario 2, and by 8% under scenario 3. Managers can use this information to plan actions that they may need to take if faced with these scenarios.

KAIZEN BUDGETING

Kaizen budgeting. Budgetary approach that explicitly incorporates continuous improvement during the budget period into the resultant budget numbers.

Chapter 1 noted how continuous improvement is one of the key issues facing management today. The Japanese use the term *kaizen* for continuous improvement. **Kaizen budgeting** is a budgetary approach that explicitly incorporates continuous improvement during the budget period into the resultant budget numbers.[4]

Consider our Halifax Engineering example in schedule 4. The 2007 budget assumes that it will take 4.0 and 6.0 manufacturing labour-hours respectively for each Regular and Heavy-Duty aircraft part. A kaizen budgeting approach would incorporate continual reduction in these manufacturing labour-hour requirements during 2007. Assume Halifax budgets the following labour-hour amounts:

| | Budgeted Amounts (Labour-Hours) | |
	Regular	Heavy-Duty
January–March 2007	4.00	6.00
April–June 2007	3.90	5.85
July–September 2007	3.80	5.70
October–December 2007	3.70	5.55

Much of the cost reduction associated with kaizen budgeting arises from many small improvements rather than "quantum leaps." A significant aspect of kaizen budgeting is the quantity and quality of employees' suggestions.

Unless Halifax meets these continuous improvement goals, unfavourable variances will be reported. Note that, in the Halifax budget, the implications of these direct labour-hour reductions would extend to reductions in variable manufacturing overhead costs, given that direct manufacturing labour-hours is the driver of these costs.

ACTIVITY-BASED BUDGETING

Chapters 4 and 5 explained how activity-based costing systems can lead to improved decision making. Activity-based costing principles extend to budgeting. **Activity-based budgeting** focuses on the cost of activities necessary to produce

[4]For an overview of Japanese management accounting, see Cooper, R., "Japanese Cost Management Practices," *CMA Magazine*, October 1994.

and sell products and services. It separates indirect costs into separate homogeneous activity cost pools. Management uses the cause-and-effect criterion to identify the cost drivers for each of these indirect cost pools.

Four key steps in activity-based budgeting are as follows:

1. Determine the budgeted costs of performing each unit of activity for each activity area.

2. Determine the demand for each individual activity based on budgeted, production, new-product development, and so on.

3. Compute the costs of performing each activity.

4. Describe the budget as costs of performing various activities (rather than budgeted costs of functional or conventional value-chain spending categories).

An activity-based budgeting approach is facilitated by adopting activity-based costing as described in Chapter 5.

Consider activity-based budgeting for the R&D/product design parts of the value chain at Bradford Aerospace. Four activity areas and their cost drivers have been identified. The budgeted 2007 rates for the costs in each activity area are as follows:

Activity	Cost Driver/Budgeted Cost Rate
Computer aided design (CAD)—using computer software to design aircraft parts	CAD hours, $80 per hour
Manual design—manually designing aircraft parts	Manual design hours, $50 per hour
Prototype development—building actual versions of aircraft parts	Prototyping hours, $60 per hour
Testing—examining how new aircraft parts "perform" in different operating conditions	Testing hours, $40 per hour
Procurement—purchasing supplies and component parts	Purchase orders, $25 per purchase order

Exhibit 6-5 presents the activity-based budget for January to December 2007. Bradford budgets usage of the cost driver in each activity area based on budgeted production and new-product development. This budgeted usage of the cost driver for each activity is multiplied by the respective budgeted costs rates per activity to obtain the budgeted activity costs. The budgeted total costs for R&D/product design is the sum of the budgeted costs of the individual activities in that part of the value chain.

The activity-based budget in Exhibit 6-5 is for one part of Bradford's value chain. In many cases, the same activity will appear in more than one part of the value chain. For example, procurement activities such as purchase ordering and supplier payment are found in most areas of the value chain. Companies using activity-based budgeting may choose to present their budgets at either the individual value-chain level or at some more basic activity level such as procurement by combining budgeted procurement costs from different parts of the value chain.

A survey of U.K. managers reported the following ranking of the benefits from activity-based budgeting: (1) ability to set more realistic budgets, (2) better

EXHIBIT 6-5
Activity-Based Budget for R&D/Product Design Costs of Bradford Aerospace:
January to December 2007

Activity Area	Budgeted Usage of Driver	Budgeted Rate per Cost Driver	Budgeted Costs
Computer-aided design	200 hours	$80	$16,000
Manual design	70 hours	50	3,500
Prototype development	80 hours	60	4,800
Testing	280 hours	40	11,200
Procurement	120 purchase orders	25	3,000
Total			$38,500

identification of resource needs, (3) linking of costs to outputs, (4) clearer linking of costs with staff responsibilities, and (5) identification of budgetary slack[5] (see the Focus on Values and Behaviours box on p. 215).

BUDGETING AND RESPONSIBILITY ACCOUNTING

Organizational Structure and Responsibility

OBJECTIVE 7

Describe responsibility centres and responsibility accounting

Organizational structure. The arrangement of lines of responsibility within the entity.

Surveys indicate that companies generally establish budgetary reporting by responsibility centre.

Responsibility accounting. System that measures the plans (by budgets) and actions (by actual results) of each responsibility centre.

Cost centre. A responsibility centre in which a manager is accountable for costs only.

Revenue centre. A responsibility centre in which a manager is accountable for revenues only.

Profit centre. A responsibility centre in which a manager is accountable for revenues and costs.

Investment centre. A responsibility centre in which a manager is accountable for investments, revenues, and costs.

Organizational structure is an arrangement of lines of responsibility within the entity. A company such as Petro-Canada may be organized primarily by business function: exploration, refining, and marketing.

Another company such as Procter & Gamble, a household products giant, may be organized by product or brand line. The managers of the individual divisions (toothpaste, soap, and so on) would each have decision-making authority concerning all the business functions (manufacturing, marketing, and so on) within that division.

To attain the goals described in the master budget, an organization must coordinate the efforts of all its employees—from the top executive through all levels of management to every supervised worker. Coordinating the organization's efforts means assigning responsibility to managers who are accountable for their actions in planning and controlling human and physical resources. Management is essentially a human activity. Budgets exist not for their own sake, but to help managers.

Each manager, regardless of level, is in charge of a responsibility centre. A *responsibility centre* is a part, segment, or subunit of an organization whose manager is accountable for a specified set of activities. The higher the manager's level, the broader the responsibility centre he or she manages and, generally, the larger the number of subordinates who report to him or her. **Responsibility accounting** is a system that measures the plans (by budgets) and actions (by actual results) of each responsibility centre. Four major types of responsibility centres are

1. **Cost centre.** Manager accountable for costs only

2. **Revenue centre.** Manager accountable for revenues only

3. **Profit centre.** Manager accountable for revenues and costs

4. **Investment centre.** Manager accountable for investments, revenues, and costs

The maintenance department of a Delta hotel could be a cost centre if the maintenance manager is responsible only for costs. Hence, the budget would emphasize costs. The sales department of the hotel could be a revenue centre if the sales manager is responsible only for revenues. Here the budget would emphasize revenues. The hotel manager could be in charge of a profit centre if the hotel manager is accountable for both revenues and costs. Here the budget would emphasize both revenues and costs. The regional manager responsible for investments in new hotel projects and for revenues and costs could be in charge of an investment centre; revenues, costs, and the investment base would be emphasized in the budget for this manager.

Responsibility accounting affects behaviour. Consider the following incident:

The Sales Department requests a rush production run. The plant scheduler argues that it will disrupt his production and will cost a substantial though not clearly determined amount of money. The answer coming from sales is, "Do you want to take the responsibility of losing the X Company as a customer?" Of course, the production scheduler does not want to take such a responsibility and he gives up, but not before a heavy exchange of arguments and the accumulation of a substantial backlog of ill feeling. The controller proposes an innovative solution. He analyzes the payroll in the Assembly Department to determine the costs involved in getting out rush orders. This information eliminates the cause for argument. Henceforth, any rush order is accepted by the production scheduler, "no questions asked." The extra costs are duly recorded and charged to the Sales Department.

---

[5]Innes, J., and F. Mitchell, "A Survey of Activity-Based Costing in the U.K.'s Largest Companies," *Management Accounting Research*, Vol. 6, pp. 137–53.

As a result, the tension created by rush orders disappears, and, somehow, the number of rush orders requested by the Sales Department is progressively reduced to an insignificant level.[6]

The responsibility accounting approach traces costs to either (1) the individual who has the best knowledge about why the costs arose or (2) the activity that caused the costs. In this incident, the cause was the sales activity, and the resulting costs were charged to the sales department. If rush orders occur regularly, the sales department might have a budget for such costs, and the department's actual performance would then be compared against the budget.

Feedback

Budgets coupled with responsibility accounting provide feedback to top management about the performance relative to the budget of different responsibility-centre managers.

Differences between actual results and budgeted amounts—also called *variances*—if properly used, can be helpful in three ways:

1. *Early warning.* Variances alert managers early to events not easily nor immediately evident. Managers can then take corrective actions or exploit the available opportunities. For example, is a small decline in sales this period an indication of an even steeper decline to follow later in the year?

2. *Performance evaluation.* Variances inform managers about how well the company has performed in implementing its strategies. Were materials and labour used efficiently? Was R&D spending increased as planned? Did product warranty costs decrease as planned?

3. *Evaluating strategy.* Variances sometimes signal to managers that their strategies are ineffective. For example, a company seeking to compete by reducing cost and improving quality may find that it is achieving these goals but having little effect on sales and profits. Top management may then want to reevaluate the strategy.

FOCUS ON VALUES AND BEHAVIOURS

Management Accountants: The Heart of the Budgeting Process

An accurate budget is essential to a company's success. Billion-dollar companies—such as Intel, Amgen, and Microsoft—will spend as many as 25,000 person-days per year compiling and finalizing their budgets. Budgeting is a cross-functional activity that requires the knowledge and expertise of managers from all areas of an organization, including management accountants, who are central to the budgeting process. If a company is going to benefit from its budget, its management accountants must possess several skills. They need to be able to communicate well and to establish themselves as trusted partners of the management team. They must be able to simplify the budgeting process by adeptly sharing complex financial information with each business function without getting lost in technical details. Consider the following quote from a financial director at Boeing:

In wing manufacturing, [the staff focuses] on particular parts of the process in building the airplane. The demand for financial support is insatiable. [The staff] want to know and they need to know: What is the consequence of doing this? If we streamline this, how does it impact us financially? What does that do to us? Does it impact the value stream?

Only management accountants can help the staff answer these critical questions.

(Continued)

---

[6]Villers, R. "Control and Freedom in a Decentralized Company," *Harvard Business Review*, Vol. 32, No. 2, p. 95.

Consider the Facilities & Operations Business Office of the Battelle Pacific Northwest National Laboratory. In 2000, budget managers worked with the company's management accountants to build a Web-based budget and planning system that streamlined the budget process. The system, which is still used throughout the company today, provides a single point of contact for overhead planning and budgeting and includes real-time data and standard analysis reporting. The results: higher quality and greater accuracy in the budgeting process, at a fraction of the time formerly spent on the process.

In addition to simplifying the budgeting process, management accountants work to ensure that managers' ideas and their resulting budgets are realistic. Management accountants must challenge faulty assumptions and incorrect logic ("let's assume a 10% increase in sales even though the overall market for the product is expected to decline") and probe for alternative approaches ("a 5% increase in sales is possible but this will require more resources to be devoted to marketing").

When it comes time to discuss the budget, some managers approach the negotiation process with an eye toward protecting their own interests. If managers make their budgets—or, better, improve on them—financial rewards will come their way. So managers may intentionally ask for budget amounts that will help them achieve their targets but that will not maximize the company's overall profits. Addressing this issue of budgetary slack may be the most difficult role for management accountants because they must be able to deal with conflict and argue persuasively for more realistic targets.

Sources: P. Smith, C. Goranson, and M. Astley, "Intranet Budgeting Does the Trick," *Strategic Finance*, May 2003; L. Gray, "Why Budgeting Kills Your Company," *Working Knowledge*, Harvard Business School, August 11, 2003; G. Siegal, J. Sorenson, and S. Richtermeyer, "Are You a Business Partner?" *Strategic Finance*, September 2003.

RESPONSIBILITY AND CONTROLLABILITY

Definition of Controllability

OBJECTIVE 8

Explain how controllability relates to responsibility accounting

Controllability. The degree of influence that a specific manager has over costs, revenues, or other items in question.

Controllable cost. Any cost that is primarily subject to the influence of a given manager of a given responsibility centre for a given time span.

If the purchasing manager forgets to order a direct-material item and must then place a rush order, the cost of the rush order is controllable by the purchasing manager. If, however, suppliers increase their prices, the purchasing manager has no control. The purchasing manager is, however, responsible because he is in the best position to explain the price increase. Purchasing managers who establish good supplier relationships can often influence prices through bargaining.

Controllability is the degree of influence that a specific manager has over costs, revenues, or other items in question. A **controllable cost** is any cost that is primarily subject to the influence of a given manager of a given responsibility centre for a given time span. A responsibility accounting system could either exclude all uncontrollable costs from a manager's performance report or segregate such costs from the controllable costs. For example, a machining supervisor's performance report might be confined to quantities (not costs) of direct materials, direct manufacturing labour, power, and supplies.

In practice, controllability is difficult to pinpoint:

1. Few costs are clearly under the sole influence of one manager. For example, costs of direct materials may be influenced by a purchasing manager, but such costs also depend on market conditions beyond the manager's control. Quantities used may be influenced by a production manager, but quantities used also depend on the quality of materials purchased. Moreover, managers often work in teams. How can individual responsibility be evaluated in a team decision?

2. With a long enough time span, all costs will come under somebody's control. However, most performance reports focus on periods of a year or less. A current manager may have inherited problems and inefficiencies from his or her predecessor. For example, present managers may have to work under undesirable contracts with suppliers or labour unions that were negotiated by their predecessors. How can we separate what the current manager actually controls from the results of decisions made by others? Exactly what is the current manager accountable for? Answers to such questions may not be clear-cut.

Senior managers differ in how they embrace the controllability notion when evaluating those reporting to them. For example, a newly appointed president took his management team on a cruise and commented, "I expect everybody to meet their budget targets no matter what happens, and those who don't should stand a little closer to the railing." Other presidents believe that a more risk-sharing approach with managers is preferable where noncontrollable factors are taken into account when making judgments about the performance of managers who miss their budgets.

Emphasis on Information and Behaviour

Managers should avoid overemphasizing controllability. Responsibility accounting is more far-reaching. It focuses on *information* and *knowledge*, not control. The key question is, who is the best informed? To put it another way: Who is the person who can tell us the most about the specific item in question, regardless of that person's ability to exert personal control? For instance, purchasing managers may be held accountable for total purchase costs, not because of their ability to affect market prices, but because of their ability to predict uncontrollable prices and explain uncontrollable price changes. Similarly, managers at a Tim Hortons store may be held responsible for operating income of their units, even though they do not fully control selling prices or the costs for many food items, and have minimal flexibility as to items to sell or their ingredients. Why? Because unit managers are in the best position to explain variances between their actual operating income and their budgeted operating income.

Performance reports for responsibility centres may also include uncontrollable items because this approach could change behaviour in the directions top management desires. For example, some companies have changed the accountability of a cost centre to a profit centre. Why? Because the manager will probably behave differently. A cost centre manager may emphasize production efficiency and deemphasize the pleas of sales personnel for faster service and rush orders. In a profit centre, the manager is responsible for both costs and revenues. Thus, even though the manager still has no control over sales personnel, the manager will now more likely weigh the impact of his or her decisions on costs and revenues, rather than solely on costs.

HUMAN ASPECTS OF BUDGETING

Why did we cover two major topics, master budgets and responsibility accounting, in the same chapter? Primarily to emphasize that human factors are crucial parts of budgeting. Too often, students study budgeting as though it were a mechanical tool.

The budgeting techniques themselves are free of emotion; however, their administration requires education, persuasion, and intelligent interpretation. To be effective, budgeting requires "honest" communication about the business from subordinates and lower-level managers to their bosses. But subordinates may try to build in budgetary slack. Budgetary slack provides managers with a hedge against unexpected adverse circumstances. But budgetary slack also misleads top management about the true profit potential of the company.

What can top management do to obtain accurate budget forecasts from lower-level managers? There are several options.

To explain one approach, let's consider the plant manager of a beverage bottler who is suspected by top management of understating the productivity potential of the bottling lines in his forecasts for the coming year. His presumed motivation is to increase the likelihood of meeting next year's production bonus targets. Suppose top management could purchase a consulting firm's study that reports productivity levels—such as the number of bottles filled per hour—at a number of comparable plants owned by other bottling companies. This report shows that their own plant manager's productivity forecasts are well below actual productivity levels being achieved at other comparable plants.

Top management could share this independent information source with their plant manager and ask him to explain why his productivity differs from that at other comparable plants. They could also base part of the plant manager's compensation on his plant's productivity vis-à-vis other "benchmark" plants rather than on the forecasts he provided. Using external benchmark performance measures reduces a manager's ability to set budget levels that are easy to achieve.[7]

Another approach to reducing budgetary slack is for managers to involve themselves regularly in understanding what their subordinates are doing. Such involvement should not result in managers dictating the decisions and actions of subordinates. Rather, a manager's involvement should take the form of providing support, challenging in a motivational way the assumptions subordinates make, and enhancing mutual learning about the operations. Regular interaction with subordinates allows managers to become knowledgeable about the operations and diminishes the ability of subordinates to create slack in their budgets.

Part of top management's responsibility is to improve organization commitment to a set of core values and norms. The values and norms describe what constitutes acceptable and unacceptable behaviour. Companies such as General Electric and Johnson & Johnson have developed values and a culture that discourage budgetary slack.

Some companies, such as IBM and Kodak, have designed innovative performance evaluation measures that reward managers based on the subsequent accuracy of the forecasts used in preparing budgets. For example, the *higher and more accurate* the budgeted profit forecasts of division managers, the higher their incentive bonuses.

Many of the best performing companies set "stretch" or "challenge" targets. *Stretch targets* are actually overestimates of expected performance, intended to motivate employees to exert effort and attain better performance.

Many managers regard budgets negatively. To them, the word *budget* is about as popular as, say, *downsizing*, *layoff*, or *strike*. Top managers must convince their subordinates that the budget is a tool designed to help them set and reach goals. But budgets are not remedies for weak management talent, faulty organization, or a poor accounting system.

The management style of executives is a factor in how budgets are perceived in companies. Some CEOs argue that "numbers always tell the story." An executive once noted that "you can miss your plan once, but you wouldn't want to miss it twice." Other CEOs believe "too much focus on making the numbers in a budget" can lead to poor decision making.

In multinational companies management accountants must also help managers budget in foreign currencies as well as anticipate changes in foreign exchange rates. Exchange rates fluctuate daily; however, mathematically complex models have been applied to guide managers as they invest in derivatives contracts. Derivatives are one way to limit losses should exchange rate changes be unfavourable. This is only one way in which managers can deal with the uncertainty of the future change in factors over which they have no control, including commodity prices, interest rates, inflation rates, regulatory change, and political change.

BUDGETING: A DISCIPLINE IN TRANSITION

Many areas of management accounting are subject to ongoing debate. Budgeting is no exception. Advocates of new proposals invariably include criticisms of so-called "traditional budgeting." These criticisms are often exaggerations of "current worst practice." Exhibit 6-6 summarizes six proposals designed to improve traditional budgeting systems. Few of the negative features cited in the left-hand column are new; they have long been singled out for criticism. Indeed, prior sections of this chapter have mentioned the importance of avoiding many of these problems. Nonetheless, major changes that address these problems are currently being examined by managers.

---

[7]For an excellent discussion of these issues, see Chapter 14 ("Formal Models in Budgeting and Incentive Contracts") of R. S. Kaplan and A. A. Atkinson, *Advanced Management Accounting*, 3rd ed. (Upper Saddle River, NJ: Prentice Hall, 1998).

EXHIBIT 6-6
Criticisms of Traditional Budgeting and Proposals for Change

Criticism of Traditional Budgeting	Proposal for Change
Excessive reliance on extrapolating past trends	Link budgeting explicitly to strategy.
Making across-the-board fixed percentage cuts when early iterations of a budget provide "unacceptable results"	Use activity-based budgeting to identify areas for cost reduction.
Examining individual functional areas as if they are independent (so-called silos, to use a farming analogy)	Explicitly adopt a cross-functional approach where interdependencies across business function areas of the value chain are recognized.
Myopically overemphasizing a fixed time horizon such as a year. Viewing annual cost targets as a key task to be accomplished	Tailor the budget cycle to the purpose of budgeting. Events beyond current period are recognized as important when evaluating current actions. Value creation is given paramount importance.
Being preoccupied with financial aspects of events in the budget period	Balance financial aspects with nonfinancial (such as quality and time) aspects.
Not using budgets to evaluate performance until end of budget period	Signal to all employees the need for continuous improvement of performance (such as revenue enhancement and cost reduction) within the budget period.

Source: Adapted from "*Advanced Budgeting Study Group Report* for CAM-I," *Management Accounting* (U.K.).

PROBLEM FOR SELF-STUDY

Before trying to solve the following problem, review the illustration of the master budget, page 203.

PROBLEM

Prepare a budgeted income statement, including all necessary detailed supporting budget schedules. Use the data given in the illustration of the master budget to prepare your own budget schedules. (See the "Basic Data and Requirements" section on p. 202.)

DECISION POINTS   SUMMARY

The following decision guidelines use a question-and-answer format to summarize the chapter's main points. Each decision presents a key question. The guideline is the answer to that question.

DECISIONS	GUIDELINES
1. What is a master budget and why is it useful?	The master budget summarizes the financial projections of all the company's budgets and plans. It expresses management's operating and financing plans—the formalized outline of the company's financial objectives and how they will be attained. Budgets are tools that, by themselves, are neither good nor bad. Budgets are useful when administered skillfully.
2. When should a company prepare budgets? What are the advantages?	Budgets should be prepared when their expected benefits exceed their expected costs.The advantages of budgets include (a) they compel strategy analysis and planning, (b) they provide a framework for judging performance, (c) they motivate managers and employees, and (d) they promote coordination and communication among subunits of the company.

DECISIONS	GUIDELINES
3. What is an operating budget and why is it useful?	The starting point for the operating budget is generally the revenues budget. The following supporting schedules are derived from the revenues budget: production budget, direct materials usage budget, direct materials purchases budget, direct manufacturing labour budget, manufacturing overhead costs budget, ending inventory budget, cost of goods sold budget, R&D/design budget, marketing budget, distribution budget, and customer-service budget. The operating budget results in the budgeted income statement that measures the profits a company expects to make.
4. How should managers consider what might happen if the assumptions underlying the budget change?	Managers should use computer-based financial planning models—mathematical statements of the relationships among operating activities, financing activities, and other factors that affect the budget. These models make it possible for management to conduct what-if (sensitivity) analysis of the effects on the master budget of changes in the original predicted data or changes in underlying assumptions and to develop plans to respond to changed conditions.
5. How can budgets include the effects of future improvements?	Kaizen budgeting is based on the idea that it is possible to continually reduce costs over time. Costs in kaizen budgeting are based on improvements that are yet to be implemented rather than on current practices or methods.
6. How can a company prepare a budget based on costs of different activities?	Activity-based budgeting focuses on the budgeted costs of activities needed to produce and sell products and services. It is linked to activity-based costing but differs in its emphasis on future costs and future use of activity areas.
7. How do companies use responsibility centres and responsibility accounting?	A responsibility centre is a part, segment, or subunit of an organization, whose manager is accountable for a specified set of activities. Four types of responsibility centres are cost centres, revenue centres, profit centres, and investment centres. Responsibility accounting systems are useful because they measure the plans by budgets, and actions by actual results, of each responsibility centre.
8. Should performance reports of responsibility-centre managers only include costs the manager can control?	Controllable costs are costs primarily subject to the influence of a given manager of a given responsibility centre for a given time span. Performance reports of responsibility centre managers often include costs, revenues, and investments that the managers cannot control. Responsibility accounting associates financial items with managers based on which manager has the most knowledge and information about the specific items, regardless of the manager's ability to exercise full control.

APPENDIX: THE CASH BUDGET

If you have studied the statement of cash flows in a financial accounting course, be aware that the direct method of determining cash flows corresponds to the approach used in preparing the cash budget.

The major illustration in this chapter features the operating budget. The other major part of the master budget is the financial budget, which includes the capital budget, cash budget, budgeted balance sheet, and budgeted statement of cash flows. This appendix focuses on the cash budget and the budgeted balance sheet. Capital budgeting is covered in Chapters 21 and 22; coverage of the budgeted statement of cash flows is beyond the scope of this book.

Suppose Halifax Engineering in our chapter illustration had the balance sheet for the year ended December 31, 2006, shown in Exhibit 6-7. The budgeted cash flows for 2007 are as follows:

	A	B	C	D	E
1		Quarters			
2		(1)	(2)	(3)	(4)
3	Collections from customers	$913,700	$975,600	$976,500	$918,400
4	Disbursements:				
5	Direct materials	314,360	283,700	227,880	213,800
6	Payroll	557,520	432,080	409,680	410,720
7	Income taxes	50,000	47,912	47,912	47,912
8	Other costs	184,000	156,000	151,000	149,000
9	Machinery purchase	—	—	—	35,080

EXHIBIT 6-7
Balance Sheet for Halifax Engineering for the Year Ended December 31, 2006

	A	B	C
1	**Assets**		
2	Current Assets		
3	Cash	$ 30,000	
4	Accounts receivable	400,000	
5	Direct materials	109,000	
6	Finished goods	64,600	$ 603,600
7	Property, plant, and equipment		
8	Land	200,000	
9	Building and equipment	2,200,000	
10	Accumulated amortization	(685,000)	1,715,000
11	Total Assets		$2,318,600
12			
13	**Liabilities and Shareholders' Equity**		
14	Current Liabilities		
15	Accounts payable	150,000	
16	Income taxes payable	50,000	200,000
17	Shareholders' equity:		
18	Common shares, no par value 25,000 issued and outstanding	350,000	
19	Retained earnings	1,768,600	2,118,600
20	Total Liabilities and Shareholders' Equity		$2,318,600

The quarterly data are based on the cash effects of the operations formulated in schedules 1 to 8 in the chapter, but the details of that formulation are not shown here in order to keep the illustration relatively brief and focused.

The company wants to maintain a $35,000 minimum cash balance at the end of each quarter of their budgeted year. The company can borrow or repay exactly the amount required at an annual interest rate of 6%. The company will repay total interest owed and as much of the principal outstanding as possible, leaving the required cash balance at the end of the quarter. Interest each quarter is on an annualized rate of 0.05% per month. Assume that borrowing and repayment occur at the end of the quarters in question. Interest is calculated to the nearest dollar. Tax expense has been rounded to the nearest dollar, using a 40% tax rate.

Suppose an accountant at Halifax Engineering is given the preceding data and the other data contained in the budgets in the chapter. He is instructed as follows:

1. Prepare a cash budget; that is, prepare a statement of cash receipts and disbursements by quarters, including details of borrowing, repayment, and interest expense.

2. Prepare a budgeted balance sheet.

3. Prepare a budgeted income statement, including the effects of interest expense and income taxes. Assume that income taxes for 2007 (at a tax rate of 40%) are $191,650.

Preparation of Budgets

1. The **cash budget** (Exhibit 6-8) is a schedule of expected cash receipts and disbursements. It predicts the effects on the cash position at the given level of operations. Exhibit 6-8 presents the cash budget by quarters to show the impact of cash flow timing on bank loans and their repayment. In practice, monthly—and sometimes weekly—cash budgets are very helpful for cash planning and control. Cash budgets help avoid unnecessary idle cash and unexpected cash

Cash budget. Schedule of expected cash receipts and disbursements.

EXHIBIT 6-8
Cash Budget for Halifax Engineering for the Year Ended December 31, 2007

	A	B	C	D	E	F
1		Quarters				Year as
2		(1)	(2)	(3)	(4)	as a Whole
3	Cash balance, beginning	$ 30,000	$ 35,000	$ 35,000	$ 35,000	$ 30,000
4	Add: Receipts:					
5	Collections from customers	913,700	975,600	976,500	918,400	3,784,200
6	Total cash available for needs: (a)	943,700	1,010,600	1,011,500	953,400	3,814,200
7	Deduct: Disbursements					
8	Direct materials	314,360	283,700	227,880	213,800	1,039,740
9	Payroll	557,520	432,080	409,680	410,720	1,810,000
10	Income taxes	50,000	47,912	47,912	47,912	193,736
11	Other costs	184,000	156,000	151,000	149,000	640,000
12	Machinery purchase	—	—	—	35,080	35,080
13	Total disbursements (b)	1,105,880	919,692	836,472	856,512	3,718,556
14	Cash balance before borrowing (a) − (b)	(162,180)	90,908*	175,028	96,888	95,644
15	Minimum cash balance desired (c)	35,000	35,000	35,000	35,000	35,000
16	Additional cash needed	197,180	—	—	—	197,180
17	Loan repayment including interest 6% per year	—	55,908	140,028	6,461	202,397
18	Cash balance end of quarter (after borrowing)	$ 35,000	$ 35,000	$ 35,000	$ 90,427	$ 90,427
19	Financing					
20	Borrowing (at end of each quarter)	$ 197,180**	$ —	$ —	$ —	$ 197,180
21	Repayment (at end of next quarter)	—	(52,950)	(137,865)	(6,365)	(197,180)
22	Interest (at 6% per year or 0.50% per month)	—	(2,958)***	(2,163)	(96)	(5,217)
23	Total effects of financing	$ 197,180	$ (55,908)	$ (140,028)	$ (6,461)	$ (5,217)
24	Cash balance end of quarter (after repayments)†	$ 35,000†	$ 35,000	$ 35,000	$ 90,427	$ 90,427
25						
26	*Excess of total cash available over total cash needed before current financing.					
27	**Note that the interest payments pertain only to the principal balance outstanding at the end of the quarter after the borrowing has occurred. For simplicity assume the company pays its loan as quickly as possible.					
28	***Note that the interest is charged at an annualized rate of 0.50% per month for 3 months on the principal outstanding after the loan repayment is made at the end of the quarter = $197,180 × 0.005 × 3 months = $2,958.					
29	†Note: Amortization expense is noncash and excluded from the cash budget.					

Keep in mind three important points about cash budgets. (1) The ending balance (EB) of cash in one quarter is the beginning balance (BB) of cash in the next quarter. (2) In the "Year as a Whole" column, receipts and disbursements are totalled for the four quarters. The BB in that column, however, is the BB for quarter 1 and the EB is the EB for quarter 4. (3) Amortization is not a cash disbursement.

deficiencies. Cash balances are kept in line with needs. Ordinarily, the cash budget has the following main sections:

a. The beginning cash balance plus cash receipts equals the total cash available before financing. Cash receipts depend on collections of accounts receivable, cash sales, and miscellaneous recurring sources such as rental or royalty receipts. Information on the prospective collectibility of accounts receivable is needed for accurate predictions. Key factors include bad debt (uncollectible accounts) experience and average time lag between sales and collections.

b. Cash disbursements include the following items:
   i. *Direct materials purchases.* Depends on credit terms extended by suppliers and bill-paying patterns of the buyer.
   ii. *Direct labour and other wage and salary outlays.* Depends on payroll dates.
   iii. *Other costs.* Depends on timing and credit terms. *Be sure to note that amortization does not require a cash outlay.*
   iv. *Other disbursements.* Outlays for property, plant, and equipment, and for long-term investments.

c. Financing requirements depend on how the cash balance before borrowing, keyed as (a) − (b) in Exhibit 6-8, compares with the minimum cash balance desired, keyed as (c). The financing plans will depend on the relationship between the cash balance before borrowing and the minimum cash balance desired. If there is excess cash, loans may be repaid or temporary investments made. The outlays for interest expense are usually shown in this section of the cash budget.

d. The ending cash balance. The total effect of the financing decisions on the cash budget. When the amount is negative as at the end of the first quarter $(162,180), the company must borrow enough to cover this shortfall plus $35,000 to achieve its desired ending balance for the quarter.

The cash budget in Exhibit 6-8 shows the pattern of short-term "self-liquidating cash loans." Seasonal peaks of production or sales often result in heavy cash disbursements for purchases, payroll, and other operating outlays as the products are produced and sold. Cash receipts from customers typically lag behind sales. The loan is *self-liquidating* in the sense that the borrowed money is used to acquire resources that are combined for sale, and the proceeds from sales are used to repay the loan. This **self-liquidating cycle**—sometimes called the **working capital cycle, cash cycle,** or **operating cycle**—is the movement of cash to inventories to receivables and back to cash.

Self-liquidating cycle (cash cycle, operating cycle, working capital cycle). The movement of cash to inventories to receivables and back to cash.

2. The budgeted balance sheet is presented in Exhibit 6-9. Each item is projected in the light of the details of the business plan as expressed in all the previous budget schedules. For example, the ending balance of accounts receivable of $415,800 is computed by adding the budgeted revenues of $3,800,000 (from

EXHIBIT 6-9

Halifax Engineering: Budgeted Balance Sheet for the Year Ended December 31, 2007

	A	B	C	D
1	**Assets**			
2	Current Assets			
3	Cash (from Exhibit 6-8)	$ 90,427		
4	Accounts receivable (1)	415,800		
5	Direct materials (2)	76,000		
6	Finished goods (2)	448,600		$1,030,827
7	Property, plant, and equipment			
8	Land (3)		200,000	
9	Building and equipment (4)	2,235,080		
10	Accumulated amortization (5)	906,754	1,328,326	1,528,326
11	Total Assets			$2,559,155
12				
13	**Liabilities and Shareholders' Equity**			
14	Current Liabilities			
15	Accounts payable (6)		$ 105,260	
16	Income taxes payable (7)		47,876	$ 153,136
17	Shareholders' equity:			
18	Common shares, no par value 25,000 issued and outstanding (8)		350,000	
19	Retained earnings (9)		2,056,017	2,406,017
20	Total Liabilities and Shareholders' Equity			$2,559,153
21				
22	*Notes:*			
23	Beginning balances from Exhibit 6-7 are used as the starting point for most of the following computations:			
24	(1) $400,000 + $3,800,000 revenues − $3,784,200 receipts (Exhibit 6-8) = $415,800.			
25	(2) From schedule 6B, p. 208.			
26	(3) From beginning balance sheet (Exhibit 6-7)			
27	(4) $2,200,000 + $35,080 purchases = $2,235,080.			
28	(5) $685,000 + $220,000 (schedule 5, p. 207) plus incremental amortization of $1,754 Exhibit 6-10.			
29	(6) $150,000 + $995,000 (schedule 3B, p. 207) − $1,039,740 (Exhibit 6-8) = $105,260.			
30	(7) $50,000 + $191,612 current year (Exhibit 6-10) − $193,736 payment (Exhibit 6-8) = $47,876.			
31	(8) From beginning balance sheet (Exhibit 6-7)			
32	(9) $1,768,600 + $287,417 net income (Exhibit 6-10) = $2,056,017.			

EXHIBIT 6-10
Budgeted Income Statement for Halifax Engineering for the Year Ended December 31, 2007

	A	B	C	D
1	Revenues	Schedule 1		$3,800,000
2	Costs:			
3	Cost of goods sold	Schedule 7		2,444,000
4	Gross margin			1,356,000
5	Period costs			
6	R&D and product design costs	Schedule 8	$136,000	
7	Marketing costs	Schedule 8	200,000	
8	Distribution	Schedule 8	100,000	
9	Customer service	Schedule 8	60,000	
10	Administration costs	Schedule 8	374,000	
11	Amortization on new purchase*		1,754	871,754
12	Operating income			484,246
13	Interest expense			(5,217)
14	Income before tax			479,029
15	Income tax at 40%			191,612
16	Net income			$ 287,417
17				
18	*Amortization on the new purchase was excluded from the initial estimate of manufacturing overhead and cost of goods sold. Incremental expense has been calculated by applying a tax rule, the half-year rule, assuming a useful life of 10 years and no residual value.			

schedule 1) to the beginning balance of $400,000 (given) and subtracting cash receipts of $3,784,200 (given in Exhibit 6-8).

3. The budgeted income statement is presented in Exhibit 6-10. It is merely the budgeted operating income statement in Exhibit 6-3 (p. 211) expanded to include interest expense and income taxes.

For simplicity, the cash receipts and disbursements were given explicitly in this illustration. Frequently, there are lags between the items reported on the accrual basis of accounting in an income statement and their related cash receipts and disbursements. In the Halifax Engineering example, collections from customers are derived under two assumptions: (1) In any month, 10% of sales are cash sales and 90% of sales are on credit, and (2) half the total credit sales are collected in each of the two months subsequent to the sale, as illustrated for the third quarter in the following table:

	A	B	C	D	E	F	G
1							**Cash Collections**
2							**in 3rd Quarter**
3		May	June	July	August	September	**as a Whole**
4	Monthly revenue budget for Halifax (given)						
5	Credit sales, 90%	$307,800	$307,800	$280,800	$280,800	$280,800	
6	Cash sales, 10%	34,200	34,200	31,200	31,200	31,200	
7	Total revenues	$342,000	$342,000	$312,000	$312,000	$312,000	
8	Cash collections from:						
9	Cash sales this month			$ 31,200	$ 31,200	$ 31,200	
10	Credit sales last month			153,900*	140,400‡	140,400§	
11	Credit sales two months ago			153,900†	153,900*	140,400‡	
12	Total collection			$339,000	$325,500	$312,000	$976,500
13							
14	*0.50 × $307,800 (June sales) = $153,900.						
15	†0.50 × $307,800 (May sales) = $153,900.						
16	‡0.50 × $280,800 (July sales) = $140,400.						
17	§0.50 × $280,800 (August sales) = $140,400.						

Of course, such schedules of cash collections depend on credit terms, collection histories, and expected bad debts. Similar schedules can be prepared for operating costs and their related cash disbursements.

The chapter contains definitions of the following important terms:

activity-based budgeting (p. 213)
budgetary slack (p. 205)
cash budget (p. 221)
cash cycle (p. 223)
controllability (p. 216)
controllable cost (p. 216)
cost centre (p. 214)
financial budget (p. 202)
financial planning models (p. 211)
investment centre (p. 214)
kaizen budgeting (p. 212)
master budget (p. 197)

operating budget (p. 202)
operating cycle (p. 223)
organizational structure (p. 214)
padding (p. 205)
pro forma statements (p. 197)
profit centre (p. 214)
responsibility accounting (p. 214)
revenue centre (p. 214)
rolling budget (p. 201)
self-liquidating cycle (p. 223)
strategic analysis (p. 198)
working capital cycle (p. 223)

▼ ASSIGNMENT MATERIAL

QUESTIONS

6-1 Define *master budget*.

6-2 What are the elements of the budgeting cycle?

6-3 "Strategy, plans, and budgets are unrelated to one another." Do you agree? Explain.

6-4 "Budgeted performance is a better criterion than past performance for judging managers." Do you agree? Explain.

6-5 "Production and marketing are like oil and water. They just don't mix." How can a budget assist in reducing traditional battles between these two areas?

6-6 How might a company benefit by sharing its own internal budget information with other companies?

6-7 "Budgets meet the cost-benefit test. They force managers to act differently." Do you agree? Explain.

6-8 Define *rolling budget*. Give an example.

6-9 Outline the steps in preparing an operating budget.

6-10 "The revenue budget is the cornerstone for budgeting." Why?

6-11 How can the use of sensitivity analysis increase the benefits of budgeting?

6-12 What factors reduce the effectiveness of companies' budgeting?

6-13 Define *kaizen budgeting*.

6-14 Describe how non-output-based cost drivers can be incorporated into budgeting.

6-15 Explain how the choice of the responsibility centre type (cost, revenue, profit, or investment) affects budgeting.

EXERCISES

6-16 Production budget (in units), fill in the missing numbers. The following (in units) is taken from the production budget for three models of fax machines in October 2007:

	Model 101	Model 201	Model 301
1. Beginning finished goods inventory	13	10	?
2. Target ending finished goods inventory	?	7	40
3. Budgeted production	?	?	1,026
4. Budgeted sales	216	?	1,040
5. Total required units (2 + 4)	233	240	?

REQUIRED
Fill in the missing numbers.

6-17 Sales and production budget. The Mendez Company expects 2008 sales of 120,000 units of serving trays. Mendez's beginning inventory for 2008 is 8,400 trays; target ending inventory, 13,200 trays.

REQUIRED
Compute the number of trays budgeted for production in 2008.

6-18 Direct materials budget. The London Wines Company produces wine. The company expects to produce 1.8 million three-litre bottles of Chablis in 2008. London purchases empty glass bottles from an outside vendor. Its target ending inventory of such bottles is 60,000; its beginning inventory is 24,000. For simplicity, ignore breakage.

REQUIRED
Compute the number of bottles to be purchased in 2008.

6-19 Budgeting material purchases. The Mahoney Company has prepared a sales budget of 50,400 finished units for a three-month period. The company has an inventory of 26,400 units of finished goods on hand at December 31 and has a target finished goods inventory of 28,800 units at the end of the succeeding quarter.

It takes three litres of direct materials to make one unit of finished product. The company has an inventory of 108,000 litres of direct materials at December 31 and has a target ending inventory of 132,000 litres.

REQUIRED
How many litres of direct materials should be purchased during the three months ending March 31?

6-20 Sales and production budget. Purity, Inc., bottles and distributes mineral water from the company's natural springs in Northern Ontario. Purity markets its product in 1-litre disposable plastic bottles and in 16-litre reusable plastic containers.

REQUIRED
1. For the year 2008, Purity marketing managers project monthly sales of 480,000 1-litre and 120,000 16-litre units. Average selling prices are estimated at $0.30 per 1-litre unit and $1.80 per 16-litre unit. Prepare a revenue budget for Purity, Inc., for the year ending December 31, 2008.
2. Purity begins 2008 with 1,080,000 1-litre units in inventory (that is, beginning inventory). The VP of Operations requests that 1-litre ending inventory on December 31, 2008, be no fewer than 720,000 units. Based on sales projections as budgeted above, what is the minimum number of 1-litre units Purity must produce during 2008?
3. The VP of Operations requests that ending inventory of 16-litre units on December 31, 2008, be 240,000 units. If the production budget calls for Purity to produce 1,560,000 16-litre units during 2008, what is the beginning inventory of 16-litre units on January 1, 2008?

6-21 Budgeting revenue, cost of goods sold, and gross margin. Janet Grossman operates the Centrum Gift Shop. She expects cash sales of $12,000 for October, $13,200 for November, and $19,200 for December. Grossman expects credit card sales of $8,400 during October and $9,600 and $14,400, respectively, during November and December. Sales returns and allowances can be ignored. Credit card companies such as VISA and MasterCard charge 4% on credit card sales, so Centrum's net sales will be 96%. Cost of goods sold averages 40% of net sales.

Grossman asks you to prepare a schedule of budgeted revenue, cost of goods sold, and gross margin for each month of the last quarter. She also wants you to show totals for the quarter.

6-22 Revenue, production, and purchases budget. The Suzuki Company in Japan has a division that manufactures two-wheel motorcycles. Its budgeted sales for Model G in 2008 is 960,000 units. Suzuki's target ending inventory is 120,000 units, and its beginning inventory is 144,000 units. The company's budgeted selling price to its distributors and dealers is 480,000 yen (¥) per motorcycle.

Suzuki buys all its wheels from an outside supplier. No defective wheels are accepted. (Suzuki's needs for extra wheels for replacement parts are ordered by a separate division of the company.) The company's target ending inventory is 36,000 wheels, and its beginning inventory is 24,000 wheels. The budgeted purchase price is ¥19,200 per wheel.

REQUIRED
1. Compute the budgeted revenue in yen.
2. Compute the number of motorcycles to be produced.
3. Compute the budgeted purchases of wheels in units and in yen.

6-23 Budget for production and direct manufacturing labour. (CMA, adapted) The Roletter Company makes and sells artistic frames for pictures of weddings, graduations, and other special events. Bob Anderson, controller, is responsible for preparing Roletter's master budget and has accumulated the following information for 2007:

| | 2007 | | | | |
	January	February	March	April	May
Estimated sales in units	12,000	14,400	9,600	10,800	10,800
Selling price	$64.80	$61.80	$61.80	$61.80	$61.80
Direct manufacturing labour-hours per unit	2.0	2.0	1.5	1.5	1.5
Wage per direct manufacturing labour-hour	$12.00	$12.00	$12.00	$13.20	$13.20

Besides wages, direct manufacturing labour-related costs include pension contributions of $0.60 per hour, workers' compensation insurance of $0.18 per hour, employee medical insurance of $0.48 per hour, and employment insurance. Assume that as of January 1, 2007, the employment insurance rates are 7.5% of wages for employers and 7.5% of wages for employees. The cost of employee benefits paid by Roletter for its employees is treated as a direct manufacturing labour cost.

Roletter has a labour contract that calls for a wage increase to $13.20 per hour on April 1, 2007. New labour-saving machinery has been installed and will be fully operational by March 1, 2007.

Roletter expects to have 19,200 frames on hand on December 31, 2006, and has a policy of carrying an end-of-month inventory of 100% of the following month's sales plus 50% of the second following month's sales.

REQUIRED
Prepare a production budget and a direct manufacturing labour budget for the Roletter Company by month and for the first quarter of 2007. Both budgets may be combined in one schedule. The direct manufacturing labour budget should include labour-hours and show the detail for each labour cost category.

6-24 Activity-based budgeting. Family Supermarkets (FS) is preparing its activity-based budget for January 2008 for its operating costs (that is, its costs for goods other than those purchased for resale). Its current concern is with its four activity areas (which are also indirect-cost categories in its product profitability reporting system):

a. **Ordering**. Covers purchasing activities. The cost driver is the number of purchase orders.

b. **Delivery**. Covers the physical delivery and receipt of merchandise. The cost driver is the number of deliveries.

c. **Shelf-stocking**. Covers the stocking of merchandise on store shelves and the ongoing restocking before sale. The cost driver is hours of stocking time.

d. **Customer support**. Covers assistance provided to customers, including checkout and bagging. The cost driver is the number of units sold.

Assume FS has only three product areas—soft drinks, fresh produce, and packaged food. The budgeted usage of each cost driver in these three areas of the store and the January 2008 budgeted cost driver rates are as follows:

	Cost Driver Rates		January 2008 Budgeted Amount of Driver Used		
Activity Area and Driver	2007 Actual Rate	January 2008 Budgeted Rate	Soft Drinks	Fresh Produce	Packaged Food
Ordering (per purchase order)	$120	$108	14	24	14
Delivery (per delivery)	$ 96	$ 98	12	62	19
Shelf-stocking (per hour)	$ 24	$ 25	16	172	94
Customer support (per item sold)	$ 0.24	$ 0.22	4,600	34,200	10,750

REQUIRED
1. What is the total budgeted cost for each activity area in January 2008?
2. What advantages might FS gain by using an activity-based budgeting approach rather than an approach for budgeting operating costs based on a budgeted percentage of the budgeted cost of goods sold?

6-25 **Kaizen approach to activity-based budgeting (continuation of 6-24).** Family Supermarkets (FS) has a kaizen (continuous improvement) approach to budgeting monthly activity area costs for each month of 2008. February's budgeted cost driver rate is 0.998 times the budgeted January 2008 rate. March's budgeted cost driver rate is 0.998 times the budgeted February 2008 rate, and so on. Assume that March 2008 has the same budgeted amount of cost drivers used as did January 2008.

REQUIRED
1. What is the total budgeted cost for each activity area in March 2008?
2. What are the benefits for FS in adopting a kaizen budgeting approach? What are the limitations?

6-26 **Budgeting and behaviour.** (CMA, adapted) Many managers claim that budgets are impractical because companies experience so many uncertainties. However, it is very probable that a firm's competitors are using budgets as indispensable management tools. A major objective of budgeting is to substitute deliberate, well-conceived business judgment for accidental success or failure in enterprise management. Implicit in this objective is the confidence that a competent management team can plan for, manage, and control in large measure the relevant variables that dominate the life of a business. Managers must grapple with uncertainties, regardless of whether they have a budget.

REQUIRED
1. Describe at least three benefits, other than improved cost control, that an organization can expect to realize from the implementation of budgeting.
2. Because a reliable prediction of sales is critical to the planning process, describe at least two factors that should be considered when preparing sales forecasts.

6-27 **Responsibility and controllability.** Consider each of the following independent situations:
1. A purchasing agent forgot to order a part. A rush order had to be placed for the part, resulting in extra costs.
2. A supplier has increased prices of the materials ordered by a purchasing agent, resulting in higher costs of the materials purchased.
3. A higher-than-budgeted quantity of direct materials was used for the output. The supervisor of the production department correctly pointed out that it was due to the substandard quality of materials purchased by the purchasing department.
4. A higher-than-budgeted quantity of direct materials was used for the output. The cause was traced to abnormal spoilage resulting from a faulty machine setting by the machine operator.
5. A higher-than-budgeted quantity of direct materials was used for the output. This happened because of the spoilage occurring from the machine breakdown. The machine was to undergo regular maintenance last month. However, maintenance was not

performed because the maintenance department is behind schedule due to heavy labour turnover.

6. A newly appointed division manager has high labour costs as a result of the unfavourable terms of a labour contract negotiated by her predecessor. Her predecessor, who was retiring, according to one observer, "gave the store away during labour contract negotiations."

7. A production department operated only at 80% of its capacity during a month. This was done at the instructions of the plant superintendent, who commented that increasing the department output will only build up inventory in the next production department, which is a bottleneck department.

REQUIRED

Determine for each situation where (a) responsibility and (b) controllability lie.

6-28 **Appendix, cash flow analysis.** (CMA, adapted) TabComp Inc. is a retail distributor for MZB-33 computer hardware and related software and support services. TabComp prepares annual sales forecasts, of which the first six months for 2008 are presented as follows:

TabComp Inc.
Sales Forecast
Six Months—2008

| | Hardware Sales | | Software | Total |
	Units	Dollars	Sales and Support	Sales
January	130	$ 468,000	$ 192,000	$ 660,000
February	120	432,000	168,000	600,000
March	110	396,000	180,000	576,000
April	90	324,000	156,000	480,000
May	100	360,000	150,000	510,000
June	125	450,000	270,000	720,000
Total	675	$2,430,000	$1,116,000	$3,546,000

Cash sales account for 25% of TabComp's total sales, 30% of the total sales are paid by bank credit card, and the remaining 45% are on open account (TabComp's own charge accounts). The cash and bank credit card sales are received in the month of the sale. Bank credit card sales are subject to a 4% discount deducted at the time of the daily deposit. The cash receipts for sales on open account are 70% in the month following the sales, 28% in the second month following the sale, and the remaining are estimated to be uncollectible.

TabComp's month-end inventory requirements for computer hardware units are 30% of the next month's sales. A one-month lead time is required for delivery from the manufacturer. Thus, orders for computer hardware units are placed on the 25th of each month to ensure that they will be in the store by the first day of the month needed. The computer hardware units are purchased under terms of n/45, measured from the time the units are delivered to TabComp. TabComp's purchase price for the computer units is 60% of the selling price.

REQUIRED

1. Calculate the cash that TabComp can expect to collect during April 2008. Be sure to show all your calculations.

2. TabComp is determining the MZB-33 computer hardware units that will be ordered on January 25, 2008.

   a. Determine the projected number of computer hardware units that will be ordered.
   b. Calculate the dollar value of the order that TabComp will place for these computer hardware units.
   c. In which month will TabComp pay for these computer hardware units?

3. As part of the annual budget process, TabComp prepares a cash budget by month for the entire year. Explain why a company such as TabComp prepares a cash budget by month for the entire year.

PROBLEMS

6-29 Budget schedules for manufacturer. Sierra Furniture is an elite desk manufacturer. It manufactures two products:

- **Executive desks.** 0.91 m × 1.5 m oak desks = 1.365 m²
- **Chairperson desks.** 1.8 m × 1.2 m red oak desks = 2.16 m²

The budgeted direct-cost inputs for each product in 2008 are as follows:

	Executive Line	Chairperson Line
Direct materials:		
Oak top	1.5 square metres	—
Red oak top	—	2.3 square metres
Oak legs	4 legs	—
Red oak legs	—	4 legs
Direct manufacturing labour	3 hours	5 hours

Unit data pertaining to the direct materials for March 2008 are as follows:

Actual Beginning Direct Materials Inventory (March 1, 2008)

	Product	
	Executive Line	Chairperson Line
Oak top	29.8 square metres	—
Red oak top	—	13.9 square metres
Oak legs	100 legs	—
Red oak legs	—	40 legs

Target Ending Direct Materials Inventory (March 31, 2008)

	Product	
	Executive Line	Chairperson Line
Oak top	17.9 square metres	—
Red oak top	—	18.6 square metres
Oak legs	80 legs	—
Red oak legs	—	44 legs

Unit cost data for direct-cost inputs pertaining to February 2008 and March 2008 are

	February 2008 (Actual)	March 2008 (Budgeted)
Oak top (per square metre)	$21.60	$24.00
Red oak top (per square metre)	27.60	30.00
Oak legs (per leg)	13.20	14.40
Red oak legs (per leg)	20.40	21.60
Manufacturing labour cost per hour	36.00	36.00

Manufacturing overhead (both variable and fixed) is allocated to each desk based on budgeted direct manufacturing labour-hours per desk. The budgeted variable manufacturing overhead rate for March 2008 is $42 per direct manufacturing labour-hour. The budgeted fixed manufacturing overhead for March 2008 is $51,000. Both variable and fixed manufacturing overhead costs are allocated to each unit of finished goods.

Data relating to finished goods inventory for March 2008 are

	Executive Line	Chairperson Line
Beginning inventory	20 units	5 units
Beginning inventory in dollars (cost)	$12,576	$5,820
Budgeted ending inventory	30 units	15 units

Budgeted sales for March 2008 are 740 units of the Executive Line and 390 units of the Chairperson Line. The budgeted selling prices per unit in March 2008 are $1,224 for an Executive Line desk and $1,920 for a Chairperson Line desk.

Assume the following in your answer:

a. Work-in-process inventories are negligible and ignored.
b. Direct materials inventory and finished goods inventory are costed using the FIFO method.
c. Unit costs of direct materials purchased and finished goods are constant in March 2008.
d. Budgeted beginning finished goods inventory: Executive Line = 20; Chairperson Line = 5.
e. Budgeted ending finished goods inventory: Executive Line = 30; Chairperson Line = 15.

REQUIRED

Prepare the following budgets for March 2008:

1. Revenue budget
2. Production budget in units
3. Direct materials usage budget and direct materials purchases budget
4. Direct manufacturing labour budget
5. Manufacturing overhead budget
6. Ending inventory budget
7. Cost of goods sold budget and gross margin calculation

6-30 **Continuous improvement, budgeting (continuation of 6-29).** Sierra Furniture decides to incorporate continuous improvement into its budgeting process. Describe four areas where Sierra could incorporate continuous improvement into the budget schedules in Problem 6-29, Parts 3 to 5. Be explicit as to how the incorporation would occur.

6-31 **Sensitivity analysis, changing budget assumptions, and kaizen approach.** Choco Chips produces two brands of chocolate chip cookies: Chippo and Choco. Choco Chips's cookies are produced from two ingredients: chocolate chips and cookie dough. Chippo is 50% chips and 50% dough, whereas Choco is 25% chips and 75% dough.

Packages of either brand weigh 1 kilogram. Choco Chips's master budget projects sales of 600,000 packages of each product in 2008. According to the master budget, estimated selling prices are $3.60 per package for each product. Forecasted 2008 ingredients costs are as follows: 1 kilogram of chocolate will cost $2.40, and 1 kilogram of cookie dough will cost $1.20. A total of 6,000 direct manufacturing labour-hours—2,400 hours for Chippo and 3,600 hours for Choco—are budgeted at the hourly rate of $24 per hour. Indirect manufacturing costs are expected to be $192,000. The indirect manufacturing costs are allocated equally between Chippo and Choco on the basis of packages produced in 2008.

1. Use the preceding information to calculate Choco Chips's budgeted gross margins for 2008.
2. By working with suppliers, Choco Chips was able to reduce the purchase cost of ingredients by 3%. Calculate Choco Chips's revised gross margin for 2008.
3. Assume that in addition to the 3% reduction in the purchase cost of ingredients mentioned in requirement 2, Choco Chips plans a 1% cost reduction in direct manufacturing labour-hours and a 2% cost reduction in the indirect manufacturing costs from the original data. These revisions to the original budget resulted from an analysis of all activities by a cross-functional team as a part of Choco Chips's efforts toward continuous improvement. Compute Choco Chips's revised gross margin for 2008 under these assumptions.

Excel Application For students who wish to practise their spreadsheet skills, the following is a step-by-step approach to creating an Excel spreadsheet to work this problem.

Step-by-Step

1. At the top of a new spreadsheet, create an "Original Data" section with columns for "Chippo" and "Choco" and rows for "% chips," "% dough," "Projected sales," "Estimated selling price per package," "Cost of chocolate ($/kg)," "Cost of cookie dough ($/kg)," "Budgeted direct manuf. labour hours," "Direct manuf. labour rate ($/hr)," and "Indirect manufacturing costs." Enter the data provided for Problem 6-31 in this section.

   (Program your spreadsheet to perform all necessary calculations. Do not "hard-code" any amounts, such as total revenue or gross margin, requiring addition or subtraction operations.)

2. Skip two rows, and create a section "Problem 1." Create rows for revenues and each of the categories of cost of goods sold, including chocolate chips, cookie dough, direct manuf. labour, and indirect manufacturing costs. Next, create rows for total cost of goods sold and gross margin. Create columns labelled "Chippo," "Choco," and "Total." Format as necessary.

3. Use the data from the original data section to calculate budgeted revenues for the Chippo product line, the Choco product line, and total revenues from both product lines.

4. Use the data from the original data section to calculate the cost of chocolate chips, cost of cookie dough, direct manuf. labour costs, and indirect manufacturing costs for

each of the Chippo and Choco product lines, and total costs for each of these categories respectively. Use the data to calculate cost of goods sold for each product line and total cost of goods sold. Finally, calculate gross margins for each product line and total gross margins.

5. Skip two rows, and create a section "Problem 2." Follow steps 2 through 4, but make the appropriate adjustments to the cost of chocolate chips and cookie dough.

6. Skip down two rows, and create a section "Problem 3." Again, follow steps 2 through 4, but make the appropriate adjustments to direct manuf. labour and indirect manufacturing costs.

7. *Verify the accuracy of your spreadsheet.* Go to your original data section and change the cost of cookie dough from $1.20/kg to $1.40/kg. If you programmed your spreadsheet correctly, gross margin for the Chippo product line, Choco product line, and total gross margins should change to $901,896; $1,018,884; and $1,920,780 respectively.

6-32 **Revenue and production budgets.** (CPA, adapted) The Scarborough Corporation manufactures and sells two products, Thingone and Thingtwo. In July 2007, Scarborough's Budget Department gathered the following data in order to prepare budgets for 2008:

2008 Projected Sales

Product	Units	Price
Thingone	60,000	$198
Thingtwo	40,000	$300

2008 Inventories in Units

Product	Expected January 1, 2008	Target December 31, 2008
Thingone	22,000	27,000
Thingtwo	10,000	11,000

To produce one unit of Thingone and Thingtwo, the following direct materials are used:

Direct Material	Unit	Amount Used per Unit Thingone	Thingtwo
A	Kilograms	4	5
B	Kilograms	2	3
C	Each	0	1

Projected data for 2008 with respect to direct materials are as follows:

Direct Material	Anticipated Purchase Price	Expected Inventories January 1, 2008	Target Inventories December 31, 2008
A	$14	32,000 kilograms	36,000 kilograms
B	$ 7	29,000 kilograms	32,000 kilograms
C	$ 5	6,000 units	7,000 units

Projected direct manufacturing labour requirements and rates for 2008 are as follows:

Product	Hours per Unit	Rate per Hour
Thingone	2	$15
Thingtwo	3	$19

Manufacturing overhead is allocated at the rate of $24 per direct manufacturing labour-hour.

REQUIRED

Based on the preceding projections and budget requirements for Thingone and Thingtwo, prepare the following budgets for 2008:

1. Revenue budget (in dollars)
2. Production budget (in units)
3. Direct materials purchases budget (in quantities)
4. Direct materials purchases budget (in dollars)
5. Direct manufacturing labour budget (in dollars)
6. Budgeted finished goods inventory at December 31, 2008 (in dollars)

6-33 Budgeted income statement. (CMA, adapted) The Easecom Company is a manufacturer of videoconferencing products. Regular units are manufactured to meet marketing projections, and specialized units are made after an order is received. Maintaining the videoconferencing equipment is an important area of customer satisfaction. With the recent downturn in the computer industry, the videoconferencing equipment segment has suffered, leading to a decline in Easecom's financial performance. The following income statement shows results for the year 2007:

Income Statement for the Easecom Company
for the Year Ended December 31, 2007 (in thousands)

Revenues:		
Equipment	$7,200	
Maintenance contracts	2,160	
Total revenues		$9,360
Cost of goods sold		5,520
Gross margin		3,840
Operating costs:		
Marketing	720	
Distribution	180	
Customer maintenance	1,200	
Administration	1,080	
Total operating costs		3,180
Operating income		$ 660

Easecom's management team is in the process of preparing the 2008 budget and is studying the following information:

a. Selling prices of equipment are expected to increase by 10% as the economic recovery begins. The selling price of each maintenance contract is unchanged from 2007.

b. Equipment sales in units are expected to increase by 6%, with a corresponding 6% growth in units of maintenance contracts.

c. The cost of each unit sold is expected to increase by 3% to pay for the necessary technology and quality improvements.

d. Marketing costs are expected to increase by $300,000, but administration costs are expected to be held at 2007 levels.

e. Distribution costs vary in proportion to the number of units of equipment sold.

f. Two maintenance technicians are to be added at a total cost of $150,000, which covers wages and related travel costs. The objective is to improve customer service and shorten response time.

g. There is no beginning or ending inventory of equipment.

REQUIRED

Prepare a budgeted income statement for 2008.

6-34 Operating budget. Slopes Inc. manufactures and sells snowboards. Slopes manufactures a single model, the Pipex. In the summer of 2007, Slopes's accountant gathered the following data to prepare budgets for 2008. These units are standard in the lumber industry. Wage rate = $25/hr.

Materials and labour requirements

Direct materials	
Wood	5 board-feet per snowboard
Fibreglass	6 yards per snowboard
Direct labour	5 hours per snowboard

Slopes's CEO expects to sell 1,200 snowboards during 2008 at an estimated retail price of $540 per board. Further, she expects 2008 beginning inventory to be 100 boards and would like to end 2008 with 200 snowboards in stock. The company follows FIFO for inventory flow.

Direct material inventories

	Beginning Inventory January 1, 2008	Ending Inventory December 31, 2008
Wood	2,000	1,500
Fibreglass	1,000	2,000

The beginning inventory of wood was purchased at $34 per board foot and fibreglass was purchased at $5.80 per yard. Prices have now risen to $36 per board foot of wood and $6 per yard of fibreglass. Variable manufacturing overhead is allocated at the rate of $8.40 per direct manufacturing labour-hour. Fixed manufacturing overhead costs are budgeted at $78,000 for 2008. Variable marketing costs are allocated at the rate of $300 per sales visit, and the marketing plan calls for 36 sales visits during 2008. Finally, fixed nonmanufacturing costs are budgeted at $36,000 for 2008.

REQUIRED

Based on the data and projections supplied by Slopes's managers,

1. Prepare the 2008 revenue budget (in dollars).
2. Prepare the 2008 production budget (in units).
3. Prepare direct materials usage and purchases budgets for 2008.
4. Prepare a direct manufacturing labour budget for 2008.
5. Prepare a manufacturing overhead budget for 2008.
6. What is the budgeted manufacturing overhead rate?
7. What is the budgeted manufacturing overhead cost per output unit?
8. Calculate the cost of a snowboard in finished goods inventory at the end of 2008.
9. Prepare an ending inventory budget for 2008.
10. Prepare a cost-of-goods-sold budget for 2008. (Opening finished goods inventory is $44,976.)
11. Prepare the budgeted income statement for Slopes Inc. for 2008.

6-35 **Cash budgeting.** Retail outlets purchase snowboards from Slopes, Inc., throughout the year. However, in anticipation of late summer and early fall purchases, outlets ramp up inventories from May through August. Outlets are billed when boards are ordered. Invoices are payable within 60 days. From past experience, Slopes's accountant projects 20% of invoices are paid in the month invoiced, 50% are paid in the following month, and 30% of invoices are paid two months past the month of invoice. The average selling price per snowboard is $540.

To meet demand, Slopes increases production from April through July. The snowboards are produced a month before their projected sale. Materials are purchased in the month of production and paid for during the following month (terms are invoice date plus 30 days). During this period there is no production to inventory, and no materials are purchased for inventory.

Direct labour and manufacturing overhead are paid monthly. Variable manufacturing overhead is incurred at the rate of $8.40 per direct manufacturing labour-hour. Variable marketing costs are driven by the number of sales visits. However, there are no sales visits during the months studied. Slopes, Inc., also incurs fixed manufacturing overhead costs of $6,600 per month and fixed nonmanufacturing overhead costs of $3,000 per month.

Projected Sales

May	96 units
June	144 units
July	240 units
August	120 units
September	72 units
October	48 units

Materials and Labour Utilization and Cost

	Units per Board	Price per Unit	Unit
Wood	5	$36	Board feet
Fibreglass	6	6	Yard
Direct labour	5	25	Hour

On September 1, 2007, Slopes had a cash crunch and borrowed $36,000 on a 6% 1-year note with interest payable monthly. The note is due October 1, 2008. Using the preceding information, determine whether Slopes will be in a position to pay off this short-term debt on October 1, 2008.

REQUIRED

1. Prepare a cash budget for July through September 2008, assuming an opening cash balance of zero. Show supporting schedules for the calculation of receivables and payables.

2. Will Slopes be in a position to pay off the $36,000 1-year note on October 1, 2008? If not, what actions would you recommend to Slopes's management?

3. Suppose Slopes is interested in maintaining a minimum cash balance of $12,000. Does the company manage to maintain such a balance during all three months analyzed? If not, suggest a suitable cash management strategy.

6-36 Responsibility of purchasing agent. (Adapted from a description by R. Villers) Marc Richards is the purchasing agent for the Hart Manufacturing Company. Kent Sampson is head of the production planning and control department. Every six months, Sampson gives Richards a general purchasing program. Richards gets specifications from the engineering department. He then selects suppliers and negotiates prices. When he took this job, Richards was informed very clearly that he bore responsibility for meeting the general purchasing program once he accepted it from Sampson.

During week 24, Richards was advised that Part No. 1234—a critical part—would be needed for assembly on Tuesday morning of week 32. He found that the regular supplier could not deliver. He called everywhere and finally found a supplier in the West and accepted the commitment.

He followed up by mail. Yes, the supplier assured him, the part would be ready. The matter was so important that on Thursday of week 31, Richards checked by phone. Yes, the shipment had left on time. Richards was reassured and did not check further. But on Tuesday of week 32, the part had not arrived. Inquiry revealed that the shipment had been misdirected by the railroad and was stuck in Winnipeg.

REQUIRED

What department should bear the costs of time lost in the plant? Why? As purchasing agent, do you think it fair that such costs be charged to your department?

6-37 Fixing responsibility. (Adapted from a description by H. Bierman, Jr.) The city of Mountainvale hired its first city manager four years ago. She favoured a "management by objectives" philosophy and accordingly set up many profit responsibility centres, including a sanitation department, a utility department, and a repair shop.

For many months, the sanitation manager had been complaining to the utility manager about wires being too low at one point in the road. There was barely clearance for large sanitation trucks. The sanitation manager asked the repair shop to make changes in the clearance. The repair shop manager asked, "Should I charge the sanitation or the utility department for the $2,400 cost of making the adjustment?" Both departments refused to accept the charge, so the repair department refused to do the work.

Late one day, the top of a sanitation truck caught the wires and ripped them down. The repair department made an emergency repair at a cost of $3,120. Moreover, the city lost $1,200 of utility revenues (net of variable costs) because of the disruption of service.

Investigation disclosed that the sanitation truck had failed to clamp down its top properly. The extra two inches of height caused the wire to be caught.

Both the sanitation manager and the utility manager argued strenuously about who should bear the $3,120 cost. Moreover, the utility manager demanded reimbursement from the sanitation department of the $1,200 of lost utility income.

REQUIRED

As the city controller in charge of the responsibility accounting system, how would you favour accounting for these costs? Specifically, what would you do next? What is the proper role of responsibility accounting in assigning cost in this situation?

6-38 Traditional budgeting and its critics. Critics of traditional budgeting often make their points in a colourful way. Consider the following comments by the CEO of a multinational with revenues of more than $36 billion and more than 200,000 employees:

> We set "stretch" goals for our people. Stretch means that we try for huge gains while having no idea how to get there—but our people figure out ways to get there. To reach these stretch goals, it takes an atmosphere where a goal doesn't become part of the old-fashioned budget. The budget is the bane of the corporate world. It never should have existed. A budget is this: If you make it, you generally get a pat on the back and a few bucks. If you miss it, you get a stick in the eye—or worse.
>
> Making a budget is an exercise in minimization. You're always trying to get the lowest out of people, because everyone is negotiating to get a lower number.
>
> If I worked for you, you would come charging into the boardroom and say, "I need four! We'd haggle all day, me making presentations, with 50 charts, saying the right number is two. In the end we'd settle on three. We'd go home and tell our families that we had a helluva day at the office. And what did we do? We ended

up minimizing our activity. We weren't dreaming, reaching. I was trying to get the lowest budget number I could sell you. It's all backward.

REQUIRED

1. Do you agree that "The budget is the bane of the corporate world. It never should have existed"? Explain.
2. Assume you are the CEO of a television station. Your marketing manager shows you the preceding extract and suggests that you "dispense with the annual budget ritual." How would you respond?

6-39 Comprehensive review of budgeting. British Beverages bottles two soft drinks under licence to Cadbury Schweppes at its Manchester plant. Bottling at this plant is a highly repetitive, automated process. Empty bottles are removed from their carton, placed on a conveyor, and sterilized, rinsed, dried, filled, capped, and heated (to reduce condensation). All inventory is in direct materials and finished goods at the end of each working day. There is no work-in-process inventory.

The two soft drinks bottled by British Beverages are lemonade and diet lemonade. The syrup for both soft drinks is purchased from Cadbury Schweppes. Syrup for the regular brand contains a higher sugar content than the syrup for the diet brand.

British Beverages uses a lot size of 1,000 cases as the unit of analysis in its budgeting. (Each case contains 24 bottles.) Direct materials are expressed in terms of lots, where one lot of direct materials is the input necessary to yield one lot (1,000 cases) of beverage. In 2008, the following purchase prices are forecast for direct materials:

	Lemonade	Diet Lemonade
Syrup	$1,440 per lot	$1,320 per lot
Containers (bottles, caps, etc.)	$1,200 per lot	$1,200 per lot
Packaging	$ 960 per lot	$ 960 per lot

The two soft drinks are bottled using the same equipment. The equipment is sanitized daily, but it is only rinsed when a switch is made during the day between diet lemonade and lemonade. Diet lemonade is always bottled first each day to reduce the risk of sugar contamination. The only difference in the bottling process for the two soft drinks is the syrup.

Summary data used in developing budgets for 2008 are as follows:

a. Sales
   ◆ Lemonade, 1,296 lots at $10,800 selling price per lot
   ◆ Diet lemonade, 648 lots at $10,200 selling price per lot
b. Beginning (January 1, 2008) inventory of direct materials
   ◆ Syrup for lemonade, 80 lots at $1,320 purchase price per lot
   ◆ Syrup for diet lemonade, 70 lots at $1,200 purchase price per lot
   ◆ Containers, 200 lots at $1,140 purchase price per lot
   ◆ Packaging, 400 lots at $1,080 purchase price per lot
c. Beginning (January 1, 2008) inventory of finished goods
   ◆ Lemonade, 100 lots at $6,360 per lot
   ◆ Diet lemonade, 50 lots at $6,240 per lot
d. Target ending (December 31, 2008) inventory of direct materials
   ◆ Syrup for lemonade, 30 lots
   ◆ Syrup for diet lemonade, 20 lots
   ◆ Containers, 100 lots
   ◆ Packaging, 200 lots
e. Target ending (December 31, 2008) inventory of finished goods
   ◆ Lemonade, 20 lots
   ◆ Diet lemonade, 10 lots
f. Each lot requires 20 direct manufacturing labour-hours at the 2008 budgeted rate of $30 per hour. Indirect manufacturing labour costs are included in the manufacturing overhead forecast.
g. Variable manufacturing overhead is forecast to be $720 per hour of bottling time; bottling time is the time the filling equipment is in operation. It takes two hours to bottle one lot of lemonade and two hours to bottle one lot of diet lemonade.
   Fixed manufacturing overhead is forecast to be $1,440,000 for 2008.
h. Hours of budgeted bottling time is the sole allocation base for all fixed manufacturing overhead.

i. Administration costs are forecast to be 10% of the cost of goods manufactured for 2008. Marketing costs are forecast to be 12% of dollar sales for 2008. Distribution costs are forecast to be 8% of dollar sales for 2008.

REQUIRED

Assume British Beverages uses the first-in, first-out method for costing all inventories. Based on the preceding data, prepare the following budgets for 2008:

1. Revenue budget (in dollars)
2. Production budget (in units)
3. Direct materials usage budget (in units and dollars)
4. Direct materials purchases budget (in units and dollars)
5. Direct manufacturing labour budget
6. Manufacturing overhead costs budget
7. Ending inventory budget (direct materials and finished goods)
8. Cost of goods sold budget
9. Marketing costs budget
10. Distribution costs budget
11. Administration costs budget
12. Budgeted income statement

6-40 **Appendix, cash budgeting for distributor.** (CMA) Alpha-Tech, a rapidly growing distributor of electronic components, is formulating its plans for 2008. Carol Jones, the firm's marketing director, has completed the revenue budget presented here:

Alpha-Tech
2008 Budgeted Revenues
(in thousands)

Month	Revenues	Month	Revenues
January	$10,800	July	$18,000
February	12,000	August	18,000
March	10,800	September	19,200
April	13,800	October	19,200
May	15,000	November	18,000
June	16,800	December	20,400

Phillip Singh, an accountant in the planning and budgeting department, is responsible for preparing the cash flow projection. The following information will be used in preparing the cash flow projection:

a. Alpha-Tech's excellent record in accounts receivable collection is expected to continue: 60% of billings are collected the month after the sale and the remaining 40% two months after.

b. The purchase of electronic components is Alpha-Tech's largest expenditure and is estimated to be 40% of revenues. Alpha-Tech receives 70% of the parts one month before sale and 30% during the month of sale.

c. Historically, 75% of accounts payable have been paid one month after receipt of the purchased components and the remaining 25% paid two months after receipt.

d. Hourly wages and fringe benefits, estimated to be 30% of the current month's revenues, are paid in the month incurred.

e. General and administrative expenses are projected to be $18,744,000 for the year. The breakdown of these expenses is as follows:

2008 Budgeted General and Administrative Costs
(in thousands)

Salaries and fringe benefits	$ 3,840
Promotion	4,560
Property taxes	1,632
Insurance	2,400
Utilities	2,160
Amortization	4,152
Total	$18,744

All expenditures are paid uniformly throughout the year, except the property taxes, which are paid at the end of each quarter in four equal instalments.

f. Income tax payments are made at the beginning of each calendar quarter based on the income of the prior quarter. Alpha-Tech is subject to an effective income tax rate of 40%. Alpha-Tech's operating income for the first quarter of 2008 is projected to be $3,840,000. The company pays 100% of the estimated tax payment.

g. Alpha-Tech maintains a minimum cash balance of $600,000. If the cash balance is less than $600,000 at the end of each month, the company borrows amounts necessary to maintain this balance. All amounts borrowed are repaid out of subsequent positive cash flow. The projected April 1, 2008, opening balance is $600,000.

h. Alpha-Tech has no short-term debt as of April 1, 2008.

i. Alpha-Tech uses a calendar year for both financial reporting and tax purposes.

REQUIRED

1. Prepare a cash budget for Alpha-Tech by month for the second quarter of 2008. Ignore any interest expense associated with borrowing.
2. Discuss why cash budgeting is important for Alpha-Tech.

6-41 **Cash budgeting.** On December 1, 2007, the Itami Wholesale Company is attempting to project cash receipts and disbursements through January 31, 2008. On this latter date, a note will be payable in the amount of $120,000. This amount was borrowed in September to carry the company through the seasonal peak in November and December.

The trial balance on December 1 shows in part the following information:

Cash	$ 12,000	
Accounts receivable	336,000	
Allowance for bad debts		$ 18,960
Inventory	105,000	
Accounts payable		110,400

Sales terms call for a 2% discount if payment is made within the first ten days of the month after purchase; after that, the full amount is due by the end of the month after purchase. Experience has shown that 70% of the billings will be collected within the discount period, 20% by the end of the month after purchase, 8% in the following month, and 2% will be uncollectible. There are no cash sales.

The average selling price of the company's products is $120 per unit. Actual and projected sales are as follows:

October actual	$ 216,000
November actual	300,000
December estimated	360,000
January estimated	180,000
February estimated	144,000
Total estimated for year ended June 30, 2008	1,800,000

All purchases are payable within 15 days. Thus, approximately 50% of the purchases in a month are due and payable in the next month. The average unit purchase cost is $84. Target ending inventories are 500 units plus 25% of the next month's unit sales.

Total budgeted marketing, distribution, and customer service costs for the year are $480,000. Of this amount, $180,000 is considered fixed (and includes amortization of $36,000). The remainder varies with sales. Both fixed and variable marketing, distribution, and customer service costs are paid as incurred.

REQUIRED

Prepare a cash budget for December and January. Supply supporting schedules for collections of receivables, payments for merchandise, and marketing, distribution, and customer service costs. Will there be enough cash available on January 31, 2008 to repay the $120,000 note?

6-42 **Activity-based budgeting.** Anderson Manufacturing, Inc., uses activity-based costing and activity-based budgeting. Budgetary information for selected activities for 2008 is as follows:

Activity	Cost Driver	Items in Cost Pool (fixed cost + cost per unit of cost driver)
Machining	Machine hours	Indirect materials $0 + $12 per hour Indirect labour $24,000 + $18 per hour Utilities $0 + $6 per hour
Setups and quality assurance	Production runs	Indirect materials $0 + $1,200 per run Indirect labour $0 + $1,440 per run Inspection $96,000 + $2,400 per run
Procurement	Purchase orders	Indirect materials $0 + $4.80 per order Indirect labour $54,000 + $0 per order
Design	Design hours	Engineering $90,000 + $60 per hour
Material handling	Square feet of material handled	Indirect materials $0 + $2.40 per sq metre handling Indirect labour $36,000 + $0 per sq metre

Additional budget data for 2008:

Activity	Cost driver budgeted volume
a. Machining	10,000 machine hours
b. Setups and quality assurance	40 production runs
c. Procurement	15,000 purchase orders
d. Design	100 engineering hours
e. Material handling	100,000 square metres

Calculate the budgeted amount for each activity in 2008.

6-43 Comprehensive budget, fill in schedules. The following information is for the Newport Stationery Store.

Balance Sheet Information as of September 30

Current assets:	
Cash	$14,400
Accounts receivable	12,000
Inventory	76,320
Equipment, net	120,000
Liabilities as of September 30	None

Recent and Anticipated Sales

September	$48,000
October	57,600
November	72,000
December	96,000
January	43,200

◆ **Credit sales.** Sales are 75% for cash and 25% on credit. Assume that credit accounts are all collected within 30 days from sale. The accounts receivable on September 30 are the result of the credit sales for September (25% of $48,000). Gross margin averages 30% of sales. Newport treats cash discounts on purchases in the income statement as "other income."

◆ **Operating costs.** Salaries and wages average 15% of monthly sales; rent, 5%; other operating costs, excluding amortization, 4%. Assume that these costs are disbursed each month. Amortization is $1,200 per month.

◆ **Purchases.** Newport keeps a minimum inventory of $36,000. The policy is to purchase additional inventory each month in the amount necessary to provide for the following month's sales. Terms on purchases are 2/10, n/30: a 2% discount is available if the payment is made within ten days after purchase; no discount is available if payment is made beyond ten days after purchase; and the full amount is due within thirty days. Assume that payments are made in the month of purchase and that all discounts are taken.

◆ **Light fixtures.** The expenditures for light fixtures are $720 in October and $480 in November. These amounts are to be capitalized.

Assume that a minimum cash balance of $9,600 must be maintained. Assume also that all borrowing is effective at the beginning of the month and all repayments are made at the end of the month of repayment. Loans are repaid when sufficient cash is available. Interest is paid only at the time of repaying principal. The interest rate is 18% per year. Management does not want to borrow any more cash than is necessary and wants to repay as soon as cash is available.

REQUIRED

1. Based on the preceding facts, complete schedule A.
2. Complete schedule B. Note that purchases are 70% of next month's sales.
3. Complete schedule C.
4. Complete schedule D.
5. Complete schedule E.
6. Complete schedule F (assume that borrowings must be made in multiples of $1,000).
7. What do you think is the most logical type of loan needed by Newport? Explain your reasoning.
8. Prepare a budgeted income statement for the fourth quarter and a budgeted balance sheet as of December 31. Ignore income taxes.
9. Some simplifications have been introduced in this problem. What complicating factors would be met in a typical business situation?

Schedule A
Budgeted Monthly Cash Receipts

Item	September	October	November	December
Total sales	$48,000	$57,600	$72,000	$96,000
Credit sales	12,000	14,400		
Cash sales				
Receipts:				
Cash sales		$43,200		
Collections on accounts receivable		12,000		
Total		$55,200		

Schedule B
Budgeted Monthly Cash Disbursements for Purchases

Item	October	November	December	4th Quarter
Purchases	$50,400			
Deduct: 2% cash discount	1,008			
Disbursements	$49,392			

Schedule C
Budgeted Monthly Cash Disbursements for Operating Costs

Item	October	November	December	4th Quarter
Salaries and wages	$ 8,640			
Rent	2,880			
Other cash operating costs	2,304			
Total	$13,824			

Schedule D
Budgeted Total Monthly Cash Disbursements

Item	October	November	December	4th Quarter
Purchases	$49,392			
Cash operating costs	13,824			
Light fixtures	720			
Total	$63,936			

Schedule E
Budgeted Cash Receipts and Disbursements

Item	October	November	December	4th Quarter
Receipts	$55,200			
Disbursements	63,936			
Net cash increase (decrease)	$(8,736)			

Schedule F
Financing Required

Item	October	November	December	Total
Beginning cash balance	$14,400			
Net cash increase				
Net cash decrease	8,736			
Cash position before borrowing	5,664			
Minimum cash balance required	9,600			
Excess/deficiency	(3,936)			
Borrowing required	4,000			
Interest payments				
Borrowing repaid				
Ending cash balance	$9,664			

6-44 Budgetary slack and ethics. (CMA) Marge Atkins, the budget manager at the Norton Company, a manufacturer of infant furniture and carriages, is working on the 2008 annual budget. In discussions with Scott Ford, the sales manager, Atkins discovers that Ford's sales projections are lower than what Ford believes is actually achievable. When Atkins asked Ford about this, Ford said, "Well, we don't want to fall short of the sales projections, so we generally give ourselves a little breathing room by lowering the sales projections anywhere from 5 to 10%." Atkins also finds that Pete Granger, the production manager, makes similar adjustments. He pads budgeted costs, adding 10% to estimated costs.

REQUIRED

As a management accountant, should Marge Atkins take the position that the behaviour described by Scott Ford and Pete Granger is unethical? Refer to the Code of Professional Ethics described in Chapter 1.

COLLABORATIVE LEARNING PROBLEM

6-45 Athletics department of a university, budget revision options. Gary Connolly is the athletics director of Pacific University (PU). He has been director for more than ten years. PU is a men's football and basketball powerhouse. The women's athletics program, however, has had less success. Last year, the women's basketball team finally had more wins than losses.

Connolly has just had a meeting with Laura Reddy, the newly appointed president of PU. It did not go well. Reddy and Connolly discussed what she called "Draft I" of the 2008 athletics department budget. He had believed it was the final draft. Reddy expressed four grave concerns about Draft I in particular and about the PU athletics program in general:

◆ **Concern 1.** The athletics department was budgeting a loss of more than $3.6 million in 2008. Given the tight fiscal position of the university, this was unacceptable. A budgeted loss of $1.2 million was the most she would tolerate for 2008. Draft II of the 2008 budget was due in two weeks' time. By 2009, the athletics department had to operate with a balanced budget. She told Connolly this was nonnegotiable.

◆ **Concern 2.** The low allocation of money to the women's athletics program. *Frontline*, a tabloid television show, recently ran a program titled "It's a Man's World at the Pacific University Athletics Program." Reddy said Connolly was treating woman athletes as "third-class citizens."

◆ **Concern 3.** The low academic performance of the men's football athletes, many of whom had full scholarships. Reddy noted that the local TV news recently ran an interview with three football-team students, none of whom "exemplified the high academic credentials she wanted Pacific to showcase to the world." She called one student "incoherent" and another "incapable of stringing sentences together."

◆ **Concern 4.** The outrageous salary paid to Bill Madden, the football coach. Reddy noted it was twice that of the highest-paid academic on campus, a Nobel Prize winner! Moreover, Madden received other payments from his "Football the Pacific Way" summer program for high-school students.

Exhibit 6-11 is a summary of the Draft I athletics department budget for 2008.

INSTRUCTIONS
Form groups of two or more students to complete the following requirement.

REQUIRED
Your group is to prepare Draft II of the athletics department's 2008 budget. This draft will form the basis of a half-day meeting Connolly will have with key officials of the athletics department.

EXHIBIT 6-11
Pacific University 2008 Athletics Department Budget (in Millions)

Revenues:		
Men's athletics programs	$12.420	
Women's athletics programs	0.936	
Other (endowment income, gifts)	4.080	$ 17.436
Costs:		
Men's athletics programs	$13.248	
Women's athletics programs	3.360	
Other (not assigned to programs)	4.440	21.048
Operating income		$ (3.612)

Men's Athletics Programs

	Football	Basketball	Swimming	Other	Total
Revenues	$10.320	$1.800	$0.120	$0.180	$12.420
Costs	8.880	3.240	0.360	0.768	13.248
Full student scholarships	37	21	6	4	68

Women's Athletic Programs

	Basketball	Swimming	Other	Total
Revenues	$0.720	$0.096	$0.120	$0.936
Costs	2.160	0.240	0.960	3.360
Full student scholarships	11	4	2	17

At McDonald's, when they ask, "Would you like fries with that?" it's part of a technique called "upselling." More often than not, diners respond "yes," making more contributions to the restaurant's budgeted sales targets and profitability.

Managers track these sales, as well as the costs associated with them. Standard food costs and labour costs are budgeted, and actual restaurant performance is compared against planned performance based on those budgeted costs. Any significant variances from the budget must be explained and addressed.

CHAPTER 7

Flexible Budgets, Variances, and Management Control: I

LEARNING OBJECTIVES

After studying this chapter, you should be able to

1. Distinguish between a static budget and a flexible budget

2. Develop flexible budgets and compute flexible-budget and sales-volume variances

3. Explain why standard costs are often used in variance analysis

4. Compute the price and efficiency variances for direct cost categories

5. Understand how managers use variance analyses

6. Perform variance analysis in activity-based costing systems

7. Describe benchmarking and how it can be used by managers in cost management

We have learned that managers quantify their plans in the form of budgets. In particular, we focused on a budgeted operating income statement. A budgeted operating income statement is a one-year or short-term month-by-month commitment to achieving specified financial targets. This chapter focuses on how flexible budgets and variances can play a key role by providing feedback that compares the actual results with the planned performance. From Chapter 6 you learned how budgets help in the planning function. Feedback in the form of a variance report is one control function that focuses managers' attention not only on potential operations problems but also on how to remedy them. A manager's careful analysis of the differences between the actual and budgeted (or expected, or planned) performance—the *variance*—helps him or her gain insights into why the actual results differ from the planned performance. It is this insight into "why" that makes variance analyses of both the quantities and unit prices of inputs important management accounting techniques.

Each *variance* we compute is the difference between an actual result and a budgeted amount. The budgeted amount is a point of reference from which comparisons may be made. Companies choose various points of reference, including

1. Financial variables reported in a company's own accounting system (such as Subaru's manufacturing cost for a Legacy wagon)

2. Financial variables not reported in a company's own accounting system (such as when GM uses the estimated cost of a Subaru Legacy wagon as the benchmark for evaluating the cost competitiveness of its Legacy product line)

3. Nonfinancial variables (such as Subaru's assembly line defect rate)

This chapter emphasizes financial points of reference reported in a company's own accounting system. Points of reference related to items 2 and 3 above are covered in less detail.

Organizations differ widely in how they compute and label the budgeted amounts they report in their own accounting system. Some organizations rely heavily on historical results while others conduct and rely on current engineering or time-and-motion studies to develop budgeted amounts. The term **standard** is frequently used when current engineering studies are the basis for budgeted amounts. Standard amounts are usually expressed on a per-unit basis. In practice, the difference in the meaning of these two terms *budgeted amount* and *standard amount* is imprecise. We use *budgeted amount* as the more general term, because some budgeted amounts may not be based on current engineering studies. However, all the variances we discuss can be computed using either standard amounts or budgeted amounts.

Standard. Carefully predetermined amount; usually expressed on a per-unit basis.

STATIC BUDGETS AND FLEXIBLE BUDGETS

OBJECTIVE 1

Distinguish between a static budget and a flexible budget

Static budget. Budget that is based on one level of output; when variances are computed at the end of the period, no adjustment is made to the budgeted amounts.

Flexible budget. A budget developed using budgeted revenues or cost amounts; when variances are computed, the budgeted amounts are adjusted (flexed) to recognize the actual level of output and the actual quantities of the revenue and cost drivers.

Favourable variance. Variance that increases operating income relative to the budgeted amount. Denoted "F."

Unfavourable variance. Variance that decreases operating income relative to the budgeted amount. Denoted "U."

This chapter illustrates both static budgets and flexible budgets. A **static budget**, or master budget, is a budget that is based on one level of output; it is not adjusted or altered after it is set, regardless of ensuing changes in actual output (or actual revenue and cost drivers). A **flexible budget** is adjusted in accordance with ensuing changes in actual output (or actual revenue and cost drivers). As we will see, a flexible budget enables managers to compute a richer set of variances than does a static budget. A **favourable variance**—denoted F in the exhibits—is a variance that increases operating income relative to the budgeted amount. An **unfavourable variance**—denoted U—is a variance that decreases operating income relative to the budgeted amount.

Budgets, both static and flexible, can differ in their level of detail. Increasingly, organizations are developing approaches to budgeting that report summary figures with the capability to display more detailed breakdowns of these figures on a computer screen. In this book, the term *Level* followed by a number denotes the amount of detail indicated by the variance(s) isolated. Level 0 reports the least detail, Level 1 offers more information, and so on.

Accounting System at Webb

The example of the Webb Company illustrates static budgets and flexible budgets. Webb manufactures and sells a single product, a distinctive jacket that requires many materials, tailoring, and hand operations. Sales are made to independent clothing stores and retail chains. Webb sets budgeted revenues (budgeted selling price × budgeted units sold) based on input from its marketing personnel and an analysis of general and industry economic conditions.

The costing system at Webb includes both manufacturing costs and marketing costs. There are direct and indirect costs in each category:

	Direct Costs	**Indirect Costs**
Manufacturing	Direct materials Direct manufacturing labour	Variable manufacturing overhead Fixed manufacturing overhead
Marketing	Direct marketing labour	Variable marketing overhead Fixed marketing overhead

Webb's manufacturing costs include direct materials (all variable), direct manufacturing labour (all variable), and manufacturing overhead (both variable and fixed). Its marketing costs (which include distribution and customer service costs as well as advertising costs) are made up of direct marketing labour (primarily distribution personnel, which are all variable) and marketing overhead (both variable and fixed). The cost driver for direct materials, direct manufacturing labour, and variable manufacturing overhead is the *number of units manufactured*. The cost driver for direct marketing labour and variable marketing overhead is the *number of units sold*. The revenue driver is the *number of units sold*. The relevant range for the $180 selling price per jacket and for the cost drivers in both manufacturing and marketing is from 8,000 to 16,000 units. All costs at Webb are either driven by output units or are fixed. We make this simplifying assumption to highlight the basic approach to flexible budgeting.

STATIC-BUDGET VARIANCES

The actual results and the static-budget amounts of Webb for April 2007 are as follows:

	Actual Results	Static Budget Amounts
Units sold	10,000	12,000
Revenues	$1,850,000	$2,160,000
Variable costs	1,120,000	1,188,000
Fixed costs	705,000	710,000
Operating income	$ 25,000	$ 262,000

Exhibit 7-1 presents the Level 0 and Level 1 variance analyses for April 2007. Level 0 gives the least detailed comparison of the actual and budgeted operating

EXHIBIT 7-1
Static-Budget-Based Variance Analysis for the Webb Company for April 2007

LEVEL 0 ANALYSIS

Actual operating income	$ 25,000 F*
Budgeted operating income	262,000 F
Static-budget variance of operating income	$237,000 U

LEVEL 1 ANALYSIS

	A	B	C	D
		Actual	Static-Budget	Static
		Results	Variances	Budget
		(1)	(2)	(3)
4	Units sold	10,000	2,000 U	12,000
5	Revenues	$1,850,000	$310,000 U	$2,160,000
6	Variable costs	1,120,000	$ (68,000) F	1,188,000
7	Contribution margin	730,000	242,000 U	972,000
8	Fixed costs	705,000	(5,000) F	710,000
9	Operating income	$ 25,000	$237,000 U	$ 262,000
10				
11			$237,000 U	
12			Total static-budget variance	
13				
14	*F = favourable effect on operating income; U = unfavourable effect on operating income.			

income. The unfavourable variance of $237,000 is simply the result of subtracting the budgeted operating income of $262,000 from the actual operating income of $25,000:

$$\begin{array}{c}\text{Static budget variance}\\\text{of operating income}\end{array} = \begin{array}{c}\text{Actual}\\\text{results}\end{array} - \begin{array}{c}\text{Static budget}\\\text{amount}\end{array}$$

$$= \$25,000 - \$262,000$$

$$= \$237,000\ \text{U}$$

This variance is often called a *static-budget variance* because the number used for the budgeted amount ($262,000) is taken from a static budget.

Level 1 analysis in Exhibit 7-1 provides managers with more detailed information on the static-budget variance of operating income of $237,000 U. The additional information added in Level 1 pertains to revenues, variable costs, and fixed costs. The budgeted contribution margin percentage of 45.0% ($972,000 ÷ $2,160,000) decreases to 39.5% ($730,000 ÷ $1,850,000) for the actual results.

Although Level 1 contains more information than Level 0, additional insights into the causes of variances can be gained by incorporating a flexible budget into the computation of variances.

STEPS IN DEVELOPING A FLEXIBLE BUDGET

OBJECTIVE 2

Develop flexible budgets and compute flexible-budget and sales-volume variances

Webb's five-step approach to developing a flexible budget is relatively straightforward, given the assumption that all costs are either variable with respect to output units or fixed. The five steps are as follows:

◆ **Step 1:** *Determine the budgeted selling price per unit, the budgeted variable costs per unit, and the budgeted fixed costs.* Each output unit (a jacket) has a budgeted selling price of $180. The budgeted variable cost is $99 per jacket. Column 2 of Exhibit 7-2 has a breakdown of this $99 amount. The budgeted fixed costs total $710,000 ($276,000 manufacturing and $434,000 marketing).

EXHIBIT 7-2
Flexible-Budget Data for the Webb Company for April 2007

	A	B	C	D	E	F
		Budgeted	Flexible Budget Amounts for			Actual Results
2		Cost Amount	Alternative Levels of Output Units Sold			Results for
3	Line Item	Per Unit	10,000	12,000	15,000	10,000 units
4	(1)	(2)	(3)	(4)	(5)	(6)
5						
6	Revenue	$ 180	$1,800,000	$2,160,000	$2,700,000	$1,850,000
7	Variable cost					
8	Direct materials	60	600,000	720,000	900,000	688,200
9	Direct manufacturing labour	16	160,000	192,000	240,000	198,000
10	Direct marketing labour	6	60,000	72,000	90,000	57,600
11	Variable manufacturing overhead	12	120,000	144,000	180,000	130,500
12	Variable marketing overhead	5	50,000	60,000	75,000	45,700
13	Total variable costs	99	990,000	1,188,000	1,485,000	1,120,000
14	Contribution margin	$ 81	$ 810,000	$ 972,000	$1,215,000	$ 730,000
15	Fixed costs					
16	Manufacturing overhead		276,000	276,000	276,000	285,000
17	Marketing overhead		434,000	434,000	434,000	420,000
18	Total fixed costs		710,000	710,000	710,000	705,000
19	Total costs		1,700,000	1,898,000	2,195,000	1,825,000
20	Operating Income		$ 100,000	$ 262,000	$ 505,000	$ 25,000

- **Step 2:** *Determine the actual quantity of the revenue driver.* Webb's revenue driver is the number of units sold. In April 2007, Webb sold 10,000 jackets.
- **Step 3:** *Determine the flexible budget for revenue based on budgeted unit revenue and the actual quantity of the revenue driver.*

$$\text{Flexible budget revenues} = \$180 \times 10,000$$
$$= \$1,800,000$$

- **Step 4:** *Determine the actual quantity of the cost driver(s).* Webb's cost driver for manufacturing costs is units produced. The cost driver for marketing costs is units sold. In April 2007, Webb produced and sold 10,000 jackets.
- **Step 5:** *Determine the flexible budget for costs based on the budgeted unit variable costs and fixed costs and the actual quantity of the cost driver(s).*

Flexible-budget variable costs:
$$\text{Manufacturing} = \$88 \times 10,000 = \$880,000$$
$$\text{Marketing} = \$11 \times 10,000 = \underline{110,000}$$
$$\$990,000$$

These five steps enable Webb to move to a Level 2 variance analysis, which helps them better explore reasons for the $237,000 unfavourable static budget variance of operating income. Exhibit 7-2 shows the flexible budget for 10,000 units (column 3) as well as for 12,000 and 15,000 units (columns 4 and 5).

FLEXIBLE-BUDGET VARIANCES AND SALES-VOLUME VARIANCES

Exhibit 7-3 presents the Level 2 flexible-budget-based variance analysis for Webb. Note that the $237,000 unfavourable static-budget variance of operating income is now split into two categories—a flexible-budget variance and a sales-volume variance. The **flexible-budget variance** is the difference between the actual results and the flexible-budget amount for the actual levels of the revenue and cost drivers. The **sales-volume variance** is the difference between the flexible-budget amount and the static-budget amount; unit selling prices, unit variable costs, and fixed costs

Flexible-budget variance. Difference between the actual result and the flexible-budget amount for the actual output achieved.

Sales-volume variance. Difference between the flexible-budget amount and the static-budget amount sold; unit selling prices, unit variable costs, and fixed costs are held constant.

EXHIBIT 7-3
Flexible-Budget-Based Variance Analysis for the Webb Company for April 2007

LEVEL 2 ANALYSIS					
A	**B**	**C**	**D**	**E**	**F**
	Actual	**Flexible-Budget**	**Flexible**	**Sales-Volume**	**Static**
	Results	**Variances**	**Budget**	**Variances**	**Budget**
	(1)	(2) = (1) − (3)	(3)	(4) = (3) − (5)	(5)
Units sold	10,000	–	10,000	2,000 U	12,000
Revenue	$1,850,000	$ 50,000 F	$1,800,000	$(360,000) U	$2,160,000
Variable costs	1,120,000	$130,000 U	990,000	(198,000) F	1,188,000
Contribution margin	730,000	(80,000) U	$ 810,000	(162,000) U	972,000
Fixed costs	705,000	(5,000) F	710,000	–	710,000
Operating income	$ 25,000	$ (75,000) U	$ 100,000	$(162,000) U	$ 262,000
		$ (75,000) U		$(162,000) U	
		Total flexible-budget variance		Total sales volume variance	
			$(237,000) U		
			Total static budget variance		

are held constant. Knowing these variances helps managers better explain the static-budget variance of $237,000 U.

Flexible-Budget Variances

The first three columns of Exhibit 7-3 compare the actual results with the flexible-budget amounts. Flexible-budget variances are reported in column 2 for four line items in the income statement:

Flexible-budget variance = Actual results − Flexible-budget amount

For the operating income line item, the flexible-budget variance is $75,000 U ($25,000 − $100,000). This variance arises because the actual selling price, unit variable costs, and fixed costs differ from the budgeted amounts. The actual and budgeted unit amounts for the selling price and variable costs are as follows:

	Actual Unit Amount	Budgeted Unit Amount
Selling price	$185	$180
Variable cost	112	99

From Exhibit 7-3, the actual total fixed cost of $705,000 is $5,000 less than the budgeted total fixed cost of $710,000. This is a favourable change from what was expected. Refer back to Exhibit 7-2 and it is clear that the total fixed cost variance is the net result of adding the variance from fixed manufacturing overhead of $9,000 unfavourable, and fixed marketing overhead of $14,000 favourable. Exhibit 7-2 also reveals a total variable manufacturing overhead variance of $10,500 unfavourable because the actual exceeded budgeted costs as well as a variable marketing overhead variance of $4,300 favourable to result in a net variable overhead variance of $6,200 unfavourable, but this is not all that is included in the total variable cost variance. As Exhibit 7-2 indicates, the direct materials and total direct labour costs also comprise total variable costs. The direct materials variance is $88,200 unfavourable while the total direct labour variance is $35,600 unfavourable. The direct labour variance is the net of both the direct manufacturing labour variance of $38,000 unfavourable and the direct marketing labour variance of $2,400 favourable. When you add the direct materials, total direct labour and marketing, and total variable manufacturing and marketing overhead variances, you obtain the total variable cost variance of $130,000 unfavourable.

Selling-price variance. Flexible budget variance that pertains to revenues; arises solely from differences between the actual selling price and the budgeted selling price.

The flexible-budget variance pertaining to revenues is often called a **selling-price variance**, because it arises solely from differences between the actual selling price and the budgeted selling price:

$$\begin{align} \text{Selling-price} \atop \text{variance} &= \left(\begin{matrix} \text{Actual selling} \\ \text{price} \end{matrix} - \begin{matrix} \text{Budgeted} \\ \text{selling price} \end{matrix} \right) \times \begin{matrix} \text{Actual units} \\ \text{sold} \end{matrix} \\ &= (\$185 - \$180) \times 10,000 \\ &= \$50,000 \text{ F} \end{align}$$

Webb has a favourable selling-price variance because the actual selling price exceeds the budgeted amount (by $5). Marketing managers typically are best-informed as to why this selling price difference arose.

The flexible-budget variance for variable costs is unfavourable for the actual output of 10,000 jackets. It's unfavourable because either (a) Webb used more quantities of inputs (such as direct manufacturing labour-hours) relative to the budgeted quantities of inputs, or (b) Webb incurred higher prices per unit for the inputs (such as the wage rate per direct manufacturing labour-hour) relative to the budgeted prices per unit for the inputs, or (c) both (a) and (b). Higher input quantities relative to the budget and/or higher input prices relative to the budget could be the result of Webb deciding to produce a superior product to what was planned in the budget, or the result of inefficiencies in Webb's manufacturing and purchasing, or both. *You should always think of variance analysis as providing suggestions for further investigation rather than as establishing conclusive evidence of good or bad performance.*

Sales-Volume Variances

The flexible-budget amounts in column 3 of Exhibit 7-3 and the static-budget amount in column 5 are both computed using the budgeted selling prices and budgeted costs. This variance is labelled the "sales-volume variance," because in many contexts the number of units sold is both the revenue driver and the cost driver. For the operating income line item,

$$\text{Sales-volume variance} = \text{Flexible-budget amount} - \text{Static-budget amount}$$
$$= \$100,000 - \$262,000$$
$$= \$162,000 \text{ U}$$

In our Webb example, this sales-volume variance in operating income arises solely because Webb sold 10,000 units, which was 2,000 less than the budgeted 12,000 units.

Webb's unfavourable sales-volume variance could be due to one or more of the following:

1. The overall demand for jackets is not growing at the rates that were anticipated.

2. Competitors are taking away share from Webb.

3. Webb did not adapt quickly to changes in customer preferences and tastes.

4. Quality problems developed that led to customer dissatisfaction with Webb's jackets.

5. Budgeted sales targets were set without careful analysis of market conditions.

How Webb responds to the unfavourable sales-volume variance will be influenced by what is presumed to be the cause of the variance. For example, if Webb believes the variance was caused by market-related reasons (reasons 1 or 2), the sales manager would be in the best position to explain what happened and to suggest corrective actions, such as sales promotions, that may be needed. If, however, the unfavourable variance was caused by quality problems, the manufacturing manager would be in the best position to analyze the causes and to suggest strategies for improvement, such as changes in the manufacturing process or investments in new machines.

Price variance (input-price variance, rate variance). The difference between actual price and budgeted price multiplied by the actual quantity of input in question.

Efficiency variance (input-efficiency variance, usage variance). The difference between the actual quantity of input used (such as square metres of materials) and the budgeted quantity of input that should have been used, multiplied by the budgeted price.

PRICE VARIANCES AND EFFICIENCY VARIANCES FOR INPUTS

The flexible-budget variance (Level 2) captures the difference between the actual results and the flexible budget. The sources of this variance (as regards costs) are the individual differences between actual and budgeted prices or quantities for inputs. The next two variances we discuss—price variances and efficiency variances for inputs—analyze such differences. This information helps managers to better understand past performance and to plan for future performance. We call this a Level 3 analysis, as it takes a more detailed analysis of the Level 2 variances.

A **price variance** is the difference between the actual price and the budgeted price multiplied by the actual quantity of input in question (such as direct materials purchased or used). *Price variances* are sometimes called **input-price variances** or **rate variances** (especially when those variances are for direct labour). An **efficiency variance** is the difference between the actual quantity of input used (such as metres of cloth in direct materials) and the budgeted quantity of input that should have been used, multiplied by the budgeted price. *Efficiency variances* are sometimes called **input-efficiency variances** or **usage variances**.

Managers generally have more control over efficiency variances than price variances. This is because the quantity of inputs used is primarily affected by factors managers can control but prices change largely due to factors beyond the control of a company's managers.

The relationship of these two variances to those we have already discussed for Webb is shown here:

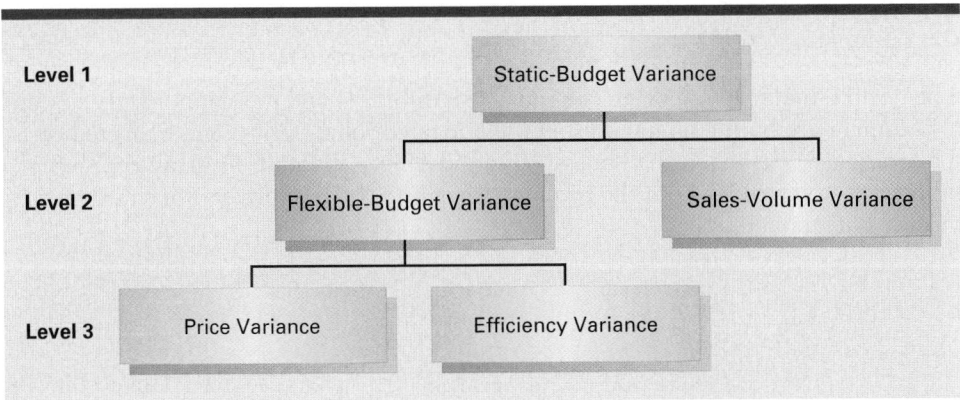

Obtaining Budgeted Input Prices and Input Quantities

Webb's two main sources of information about budgeted input prices and budgeted input quantities are

1. *Actual input data from past periods.* Most companies have past data on actual input prices and actual input quantities. These past amounts could be used for the budgeted amounts in a flexible budget. Past data are typically available at a relatively low cost. The limitations of using this source are (a) past data include past inefficiencies and (b) past data do not incorporate any expected changes planned to occur in the budget period.

2. *Standards developed by Webb.* A standard is a carefully predetermined amount; it is usually expressed on a per-unit basis. Webb uses time-and-motion and engineering studies to determine its standard amounts. For example, it conducts a detailed breakdown of the steps in making a jacket. Each step is then assigned a standard time based on work by a skilled operator using equipment operating in an efficient manner. The advantages of using standard amounts are that (a) they can exclude past inefficiencies and (b) they can take into account expected changes in the budget period. An example of (a) is a supplier making dramatic improvements in its ability to consistently meet Webb's demanding quality requirements for the cloth used to make jackets. An example of (b) is the acquisition of new loom machines that operate at a faster speed and that enable work to be done with lower reject rates.

Standard input. Carefully predetermined quantity of inputs (such as kilograms of materials or hours of labour time) required for one unit of output.

Standard cost. Carefully predetermined cost. Standard costs can relate to units of inputs or units of outputs.

Webb has developed standard inputs and standard costs for each of its variable-cost items. A **standard input** is a carefully predetermined quantity of inputs (such as kilograms of materials or hours of labour time) required for one unit of output. A **standard cost** is a carefully predetermined cost. Standard costs can relate to units of inputs or units of outputs. Webb's budgeted cost for each variable cost item is computed using the following formula:

$$\text{Standard inputs allowed for one output unit} \times \text{Standard cost per input unit}$$

And the variable cost items are

◆ **Direct materials:** 2 square metres of cloth input allowed per output unit (jacket) manufactured, at $30 standard cost per square metre:

$$\text{Standard cost} = 2 \times \$30 = \$60 \text{ per output unit manufactured}$$

◆ **Direct manufacturing labour:** 0.80 manufacturing labour-hours of input allowed per output unit manufactured, at $20 standard cost per hour:

$$\text{Standard cost} = 0.80 \times \$20 = \$16 \text{ per output unit manufactured}$$

◆ **Direct marketing labour:** 0.25 marketing labour-hours of input allowed per output unit sold, at $24 standard cost per hour:

Standard cost = 0.25 × $24 = $6 per output unit sold

◆ **Variable manufacturing overhead:** Allocated based on 1.20 machine-hours per output unit manufactured, at $10 standard cost per machine-hour:

Standard cost = 1.20 × $10 = $12 per output unit manufactured

◆ **Variable marketing overhead:** Allocated based on 0.125 direct marketing labour-hours per output unit sold, at $40 standard cost per hour:

Standard cost = 0.125 × $40 = $5 per output unit sold

These standard cost computations explain how Webb developed the numbers in column 2 of Exhibit 7-2 on p. 246 (see also Global Surveys of Company Practice box on p. 252).

The breakdown of the flexible-budget variance into its price and efficiency components is important when evaluating individual managers. At Webb, the production manager is responsible for the efficiency variance, while the purchasing manager is responsible for the price variance. This separate computation of the price variance enables the efficiency variance to be computed using budgeted input prices. Thus, judgments about efficiency (the quantity of inputs used to produce a given level of output) are not affected by whether actual input prices differ from budgeted input prices. A word of caution, however, is appropriate. As will be discussed next, the causes of price and efficiency variances can be interrelated. For this reason, do not interpret these variances in isolation from each other.

OBJECTIVE 4

Compute the price and efficiency variances for direct cost categories

An Illustration of Price and Efficiency Variances for Inputs

Consider Webb's three direct-cost categories. The actual cost for each of these three categories is as follows:

	Actual Results	Budgeted Inputs	Standard Inputs/ Unit Output
Direct materials purchased and used			
Direct materials total cost	$688,200		
Square metres of cloth purchased and used	22,200	–	2.00 sq metres
Actual price per square metre	$ 31.00	$30.00	$60.00 per output unit
Direct manufacturing labour			
Direct manufacturing labour total costs	$198,000		
Direct manufacturing total labour-hours of input consumed	9,000	–	0.80 DLH
Actual price per direct manufacturing labour-hour	$ 22.00	$20.00	$16.00 per output unit
Direct marketing labour			
Direct marketing labour total costs	$ 57,600		
Direct marketing total labour-hours of input consumed	2,304	–	0.25 marketing LH
Actual price per direct marketing labour-hour	$ 25.00	$24.00	$6.00 per output unit

For simplicity, we assume here that direct materials used is equal to direct materials purchased. The reason is that we do not want to complicate the variance analyses with questions of inventory valuation. If you refer back to Chapter 2, Exhibit 2-7 (page 43), you will see in Panel B a calculation for cost of goods manufactured where there are dollar values for beginning and ending inventories of direct materials. As a result the cost of direct materials purchased is incremental to the beginning inventory value to provide us with a cost of direct materials available for use from which the ending inventory of direct materials is subtracted to give us the cost of direct materials used. By assuming the beginning and ending inventories of direct materials are zero, the calculations in Panel B collapse into a simple equivalence that direct materials purchased equals direct materials used. This makes both the calculation and interpretation of direct materials variances much more straightforward.

The Widespread Use of Standard Costs

Surveys from around the world report widespread use of standard costs by manufacturers. The following data are representative of surveys conducted in nine countries:

	Percentage of Respondents Using Standard Costs in Their Accounting System
United States[a]	76%
Ireland[b]	87%
China[c]	87%
United Kingdom[d]	76%
New Zealand[d]	73%
India[e]	68%
Singapore[f]	56%
Australia[g]	92%
Japan[g]	90%

What explains the popularity of standard costs? A survey of Australian and Japanese companies reports the following purposes for using standard costs (1, most important; 7, least important):[g]

	Australia	Japan
Product costing	1	4
Budgeting	2	1
Inventory valuation	3	6
Management control	4	3
Cost control	5	2
Cost reduction	6	5
Simplification of bookkeeping	7	7

[a] Ernst & Young, *2003 Survey of Management Accounting* (New York: Ernst & Young, March 2003).

[b] Clarke, P., "Management Accounting Practices in Large Irish Manufacturing Firms," *Irish Journal of Management* (1997).

[c] Firth, M., "The Diffusion of Managerial Accounting Procedures in the People's Republic of China and the Influence of Foreign Partnered Joint Ventures," *Accounting, Organizations and Society* (1996).

[d] Lamminmaki, D., and C. Drury, "A Comparison of New Zealand and British Product-Costing Practices," *International Journal of Accounting* (2001).

[e] Anderson, S., and W. Lanen, "Economic Transition, Strategy and the Evolution of Management Accounting Practices: The Case of India," *Accounting, Organizations and Society* (1999).

[f] Ghosh, B., and Y. Chan, "Management Accounting in Singapore—Well in Place?" *Managerial Auditing Journal* (1997).

[g] Wijewardena, H., and A. De Zoysa, "A Comparative Analysis of Management Accounting Practices in Australia and Japan: An Empirical Investigation," *International Journal of Accounting* (1999).

The actual results and the flexible-budget amounts for each category of direct costs of inputs consumed to produce the 10,000 actual output units in April 2007 are as follows:

	Actual Results	Flexible Budget Variances	Flexible Budget
	(1)	(2) = (1) − (3)	(3)
Direct materials (22,200 × $31)	$688,200	$ 88,200 U	$600,000 (20,000 × $30)
Direct manufacturing labour (9,000 × $22)	198,000	38,000 U	160,000 (8,000 × $20)
Direct marketing labour (2,304 × $25)	57,600	(2,400) F	60,000 (2,500 × $24)
Total	$943,800	$123,800 U	$820,000

We now use this Webb Company data to illustrate the input price and input-efficiency variances. Consider first the input-price variances.

The materials price and efficiency variances discussed in this chapter illustrate the use of standard costs in promoting cost management.

Price Variances

The formula for computing a price variance is

$$\begin{array}{c}\text{Price}\\\text{variance}\end{array} = \left(\begin{array}{c}\text{Actual price}\\\text{of input}\end{array} - \begin{array}{c}\text{Budgeted price}\\\text{of input}\end{array}\right) \times \begin{array}{c}\text{Actual quantity}\\\text{of input}\\\text{purchased}\end{array}$$

Price variances for each of Webb's three direct cost categories are

	Actual – Budgeted Price per Input Unit	Actual Quantity of Input Units Purchased	=	Input Price Variance
	(1)	(2)	=	(1) × (2)
Direct materials ($31 − $30) × 22,200 m²	$1.00	22,200	=	$22,200 U
Direct manufacturing labour ($22 − $20) × 9,000 direct labour-hours	$2.00	9,000	=	18,000 U
Direct marketing labour ($25 − $24) × 2,304 direct marketing labour-hours	$1.00	2,304	=	2,304 U
				$42,504 U

All three price variances are unfavourable (they reduce operating income) because the actual price of each direct-cost input exceeds the budgeted price; that is, Webb incurred more cost per input unit than was budgeted.

Always consider a broad range of possible causes for price variances. For example, Webb's unfavourable direct materials price variance could be due to one or more of the following reasons:

◆ Webb's purchasing manager negotiated less skillfully than was assumed in the budget.

◆ Webb's purchasing manager bought in smaller lot sizes than budgeted, even though quantity discounts were available for the larger lot sizes.

◆ Materials prices unexpectedly increased because of unanticipated increases in market demand or unanticipated increases in costs of transportation from the supplier to Webb.

◆ Quality of materials purchased exceeded the production specifications leading to higher prices

◆ The specified quality of materials required was discontinued by suppliers.

◆ Budgeted purchase prices for Webb's materials were set without careful analysis of the market.

Webb's first response to a materials price variance will be to ascertain the cause, then controlling the unfavourable variance will be affected by the reason for the variance. Assume Webb discovers an unfavourable variance is due to poor negotiating by its purchasing officer. Webb may decide to invest more in training this officer in negotiations, or it may decide to hire a more skillful purchasing officer.

When interpreting materials price variances, Webb's managers should consider any change in the relationship with the company's suppliers. For example, assume that Webb can negotiate fixed prices for future shipments of direct materials with its suppliers. It is likely that price variances will be minimal because they have been fixed according to a new contract.

Efficiency Variances

Consider now the efficiency variance. Computation of efficiency variances requires measurement of inputs for a given level of output. For any actual level of output, the efficiency variance is the difference between the input that was actually used and the input that should have been used to achieve that actual output, holding input price constant:

$$\text{Efficiency variance} = \left(\begin{array}{c} \text{Actual quantity} \\ \text{of input used} \end{array} - \begin{array}{c} \text{Budgeted quantity of input allowed} \\ \text{for actual output units achieved} \end{array} \right) \times \begin{array}{c} \text{Budgeted price} \\ \text{of input} \end{array}$$

The idea here is that an organization is inefficient if it uses more inputs than budgeted for the actual output units achieved, and it is efficient if it uses fewer inputs than budgeted for the actual output units achieved.

The efficiency variances for each of Webb's direct-cost categories are as follows:

Direct-Cost Category	(Actual Quantity of Input Used	− Budgeted Quantity of Input Allowed for Actual Output Units Achieved)	× Budgeted Price of Input	(1)	(2)		= Efficiency Variance (3)
Direct materials	[22,200 m²	− (10,000 units of output × 2 m²) ×	$30]	2,200	$30.00	=	$66,000 U
Direct manufacturing labour	[9,000	− (10,000 units of output × 0.80) ×	$20]	1,000	$20.00	=	$20,000 U
Direct marketing labour	[2,304	− (10,000 units of output × 0.25) ×	$24]	(196)	$24.00	=	$ (4,704) F
Total						=	$81,296 U

The flexible budget for inputs is based on the *budgeted quantity of inputs allowed for the actual output level (BQIA)*. To understand BQIA in the Webb example, distinguish *inputs* (square metres of cloth, direct manufacturing labour-hours) from *output* (jackets). BQIA is calculated by multiplying the actual quantity of output produced by how much of each input should have been used per output unit.

The two manufacturing-efficiency variances (direct materials and direct manufacturing labour) are both unfavourable because more input was used than was budgeted, resulting in a decrease in operating income. The marketing-efficiency variance is favourable because less input was used than was budgeted, resulting in an increase in operating income (see the Concepts in Action box on p. 255).

As with price variances, Webb's managers need to consider a broad range of possible reasons for efficiency variances. For example, Webb's unfavourable direct manufacturing labour variance could be due to one or more of the following reasons:

♦ Webb's personnel manager hired underskilled workers or their training was inadequate.

♦ Webb's production process is being reorganized or a new machine has been installed, creating additional direct manufacturing labour time per jacket as workers learn the new process.

♦ Webb's production scheduler inefficiently scheduled work, resulting in more direct manufacturing labour time per jacket.

♦ Webb's marketing department promised early deliveries to clients, which created too many rush order interruptions that led to overtime.

♦ Webb's maintenance department did not properly maintain machines, resulting in additional direct manufacturing labour time per jacket to avoid damage done by the machines.

♦ Webb's jacket design became obsolete, leading to a new, more complicated design, requiring more direct manufacturing labour time.

♦ Budgeted time standards were set without careful analysis of the operating conditions and the employees' skills.

Suppose Webb determines that the unfavourable variance is due to poor machine maintenance. One reasonable response is to create a team consisting of plant machine engineers and machine operators who will develop a new maintenance schedule so that, in the future, jackets can be sewn in shorter times.

Comparing Efficiency Variances and Yield Improvements at Analog Devices

Analog Devices, Inc. (ADI), produces integrated circuits and systems used in computer disc drives, medical instruments, and customer electronics. To be successful, ADI must deliver high-quality products to its customers on time and at low cost. To control cost, ADI must improve yield—the quantity of good die produced on a silicon wafer divided by the total number of die that could be printed and produced on the wafer.

ADI's cost system tracks costs by major production cost centres. Each production cost centre classifies costs into direct materials, direct labour, and fixed indirect costs. ADI uses a standard-costing system and has standard costs for each of the products it produces. Each month, ADI calculates price and efficiency variances for materials, and efficiency and rate variances for labour. Preparing a flexible budget is key to isolating these variances.

Most operating managers at ADI pay more attention to physical yields than the direct materials efficiency computations. They believe that a higher yield is a more direct measure of their performance and that if they improve yield, efficiency gains will follow. Indeed, in most periods, higher yields are associated with favourable direct materials efficiency variances.

In one period, however, a puzzling thing happened—yields increased, suggesting performance improvement, but the accounting system reported an unfavourable direct materials efficiency variance. The flexible budget was key to resolving these conflicting signals!

In the period in question, ADI had begun producing high-volume standardized products in place of the low-volume, nonstandardized products it previously produced. Standardized products are easier to manufacture and have higher yields than nonstandardized products, so it's not surprising that yields improved, but did performance improve? To find out, ADI looked at the actual quantity of wafers started and compared it to the flexible budget—the budgeted quantity of wafers allowed for the actual quantity of standardized product produced. ADI discovered that it actually started more wafers than the flexible-budget amount, resulting in the unfavourable direct materials efficiency variance. Performance was weak because, although yield increased, it did not increase as much as it should have for the actual quantity and type of output produced.

Source: Analog Devices: The Half-Life System, Harvard Business School case number 9–190–061, and discussions with company management.

Presentation of Price and Efficiency Variances for Inputs

Note how the sum of the price variance and the efficiency variance equals the flexible budget variance:

	Input Price Variances	Input Efficiency Variances	Flexible Budget Variance
Direct materials	$22,200 U	$66,000 U	$ 88,200 U
Direct manufacturing labour	$18,000 U	$20,000 U	$ 38,000 U
Direct marketing labour	$ 2,304 U	$ (4,704) F	$ (2,400) F
Total	$42,504 U	$81,296 U	$123,800 U

Exhibit 7-4 on the next page illustrates a convenient way to integrate the actual and budgeted input information used to compute the price and efficiency variances for direct materials. This exhibit assumes that materials purchased equals materials used.

EXHIBIT 7-4
Columnar Presentation of Variance Analysis: Direct Materials Costs for the Webb Company for April 2007

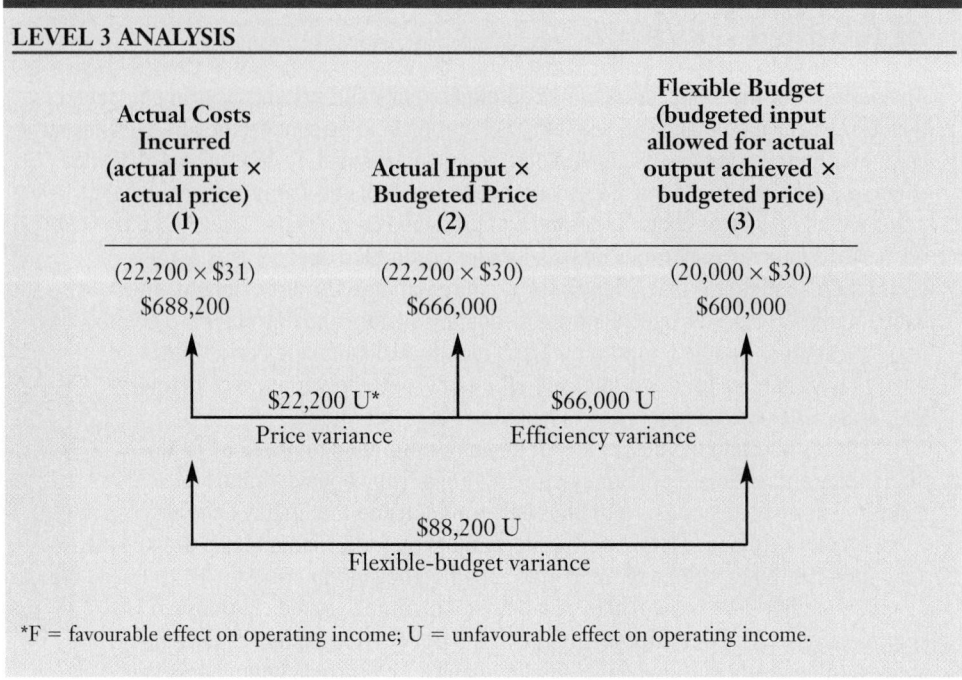

LEVEL 3 ANALYSIS

Actual Costs Incurred (actual input × actual price) (1)	Actual Input × Budgeted Price (2)	Flexible Budget (budgeted input allowed for actual output achieved × budgeted price) (3)
(22,200 × $31) $688,200	(22,200 × $30) $666,000	(20,000 × $30) $600,000

$22,200 U* → Price variance

$66,000 U → Efficiency variance

$88,200 U → Flexible-budget variance

*F = favourable effect on operating income; U = unfavourable effect on operating income.

Overview of Variance Analysis

Exhibit 7-5 presents a comprehensive road map of where we have been. The Level 1 analysis depicts the analysis in Exhibit 7-1. Level 2 relies on data presented in Exhibits 7-2 and 7-3. We have just discussed price and efficiency variances, which are Level 3.

Some managers refer to proceeding through successively more detailed data as "drilling-down" (or "peeling the onion"). The growing use of online data collection is increasing the number of databases that have this drill-down capability.

A key use of variance analysis is in performance evaluation. Two attributes of performance are commonly measured:

◆ **Effectiveness.** The degree to which a predetermined objective or target is met
◆ **Efficiency.** The relative amount of inputs used to achieve a given level of output

Be careful to understand the cause(s) of a variance before using it as a performance measure. Assume that a Webb purchasing manager has just negotiated a deal that results in a favourable price variance for materials. The deal could have achieved a favourable variance for any or all of three reasons:

1. The purchasing manager bargained effectively with suppliers.

2. The purchasing manager accepted lower-quality materials at a lower price.

3. The purchasing manager secured a discount for buying in bulk. However, he or she bought higher quantities than necessary for the short run, which resulted in excessive inventories.

If the purchasing manager's performance is evaluated solely on materials price variances, then only reason 1 will be considered acceptable, and the evaluation will be positive. Reasons 2 and 3 will be considered unacceptable and will likely cause the company to incur additional costs, such as higher inventory storage costs, higher

EXHIBIT 7-5
Performance Measurement Using Variances

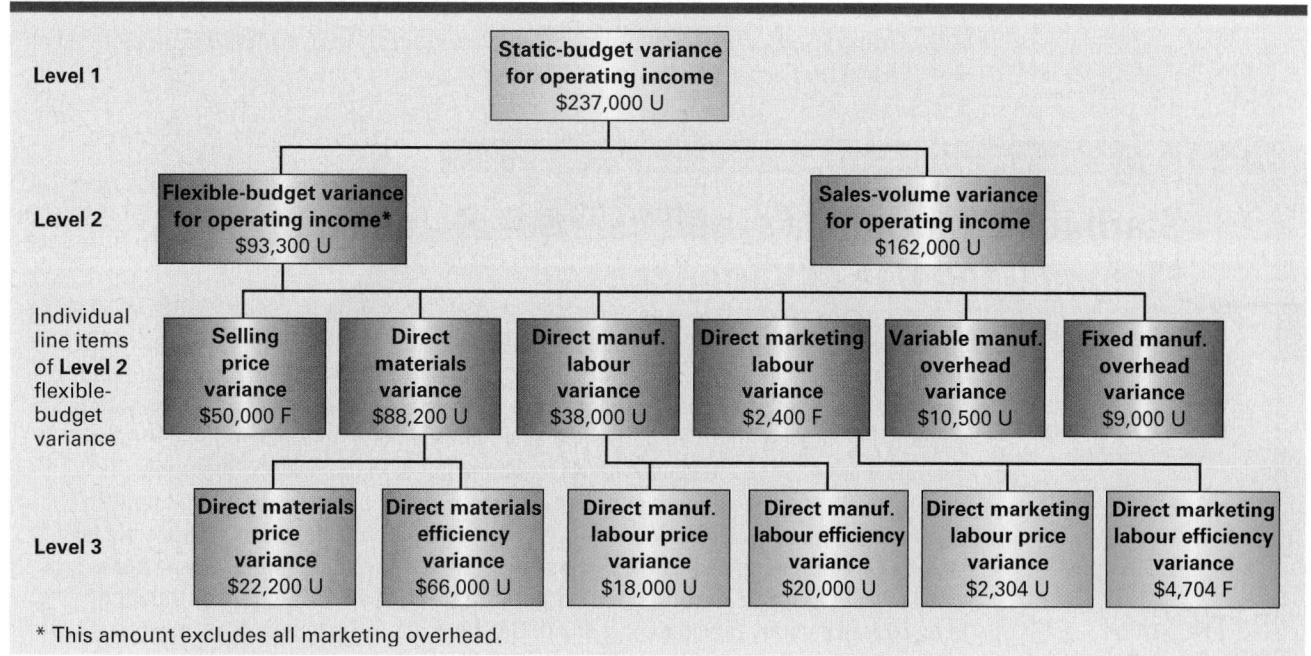

* This amount excludes all marketing overhead.

quality inspection costs, higher costs to repair or replace defects, and higher materials scrap costs. *Managers should not automatically interpret a favourable variance as "good" news.*

Performance measures should focus the managers' attention on reducing the total costs incurred by the entire company. Such a focus is central to the total value-chain analysis theme in the new management approach. In the purchasing manager example, the company may ultimately lose more money because of reasons 2 and 3 than it gains from reason 1. Conversely, manufacturing costs may be deliberately increased (for example, because higher costs are paid for better materials or more direct manufacturing labour time) to obtain better product quality. In turn, the costs of the better product quality may be more than offset by reductions in customer-service costs.

If any single performance measure (for example, a labour efficiency cost variance or a consumer rating report) receives excessive emphasis, managers tend to make decisions that will maximize their own reported performance in terms of that single performance measure. Such actions may conflict with the organization's overall goals. This faulty perspective on performance arises because top management has designed a performance measurement and reward system that does not adequately emphasize total organization objectives (see the Focus on Values and Behaviours box on the next page).

Multiple Causes of Variances

Often the causes of variances are interrelated. For example, an unfavourable materials-efficiency variance can be related to a favourable materials price variance because a purchasing officer purchased lower-priced, lower-quality materials. It is always best to consider possible interdependencies among variances and not to interpret variances in isolation from each other. In some cases, the causes of variances are in different parts of the value chain in one organization or in other organizations. Consider an unfavourable materials-efficiency variance in the production area of Webb. Possible causes of this variance across the value chain of the organization are

1. Poor design of products or processes
2. Poor work in the manufacturing area

3. Inadequate training of the labour force

4. Inappropriate assignment of labour or machines to specific jobs

5. Congestion due to scheduling a large number of rush orders required by Webb marketing representatives

Starbucks, McDonald's, and Johnson & Johnson: Making Good Use of Variances

There aren't many accounting processes that generate as much interest and anxiety among managers as analyzing reports comparing actual performance with budgeted performance. That's because managers are accountable for achieving their negotiated budgets and don't want to be perceived as a failure among their colleagues. But the main goal of variance analysis is not to fix blame but to learn, and it's ultimately the responsibility of top managers and management accountants to set the right tone so improvements can be made. Managers at Starbucks, for example, are responsible for making sure that each new store's sales meet or exceed expectations. This is not a small task. In March 2004, projected corporate sales growth was 12%, contributing to an overall monthly revenue increase of US$494 million. Starbucks currently has 8,000 stores globally and plans to grow to around 25,000 locations worldwide, approaching McDonald's in its number of retail outlets. Management accountants at the company are intimately involved in establishing budgeted performance and monitoring actual performance for each of the company's stores.

Whether it's Starbucks, McDonald's, or any other major corporation, management accountants must be able to provide managers with clear and precise explanations for variances. They must do so in a thoughtful, constructive, and helpful way. Instead of simply pointing out problems, they need to understand the reasons for the variances and help develop solutions and action plans for tackling the issues. Rather than focusing only on negative performance, management accountants should also discuss the positive outcomes. Ideally, variances should be addressed by teams so that there is shared responsibility and accumulation of ideas from all areas of the organization. McDonald's, for example, established a systemwide response to upgrading its coffee offerings due to increased competition from Starbucks.

Another organization in which management accountants take a learning approach to variance analysis is Johnson & Johnson, the giant pharmaceutical and consumer products company. Johnson & Johnson conducts business via hundreds of subsidiary companies within a highly decentralized structure. Management accountants in these subsidiary companies use variances to help managers discover and correct problems. This is often done in meetings that bring together the entire senior management team of the subsidiary company. A Johnson & Johnson executive remarked that "managers are forced to review their businesses in depth for costs, trends, manufacturing efficiency, marketing plans, and their competitive situation. Program and action plans result. . . . These meetings force us to think about how we should respond and to look at both the upside and downside of changes in the business. They really get our creative juices flowing."

Variance analyses are critical to an organization's success. Management accountants must never waver from accurately presenting the numbers and from persuading managers to be realistic about performance. Learning from past mistakes and implementing corrective action plans quickly can happen only when management accountants are successful in their roles as motivators, communicators, and team players.

Sources: Allison Linn, "Starbucks Lays Out Aggressive Growth Plans," *Seattle Post-Intelligence,* March 30, 2004; "Schaeffer's Market Observation Features Starbucks: SBUX," Businesswire.com, April 1, 2004; Andy Serwer, "Starbucks to Go," Fortune, January 26, 2004; R. Simons, Codman and Shurtleff Inc.: Planning and Control System, Harvard Business School case number 9–187–081.

6. Webb's suppliers do not manufacture cloth materials of uniformly high quality

An even broader perspective is to consider actions taken in the supply chain of an organization. A *supply chain* is the flow of goods, services, and information from cradle to grave (womb to tomb) of a product or service. The supply chain of Webb (the manufacturer) includes

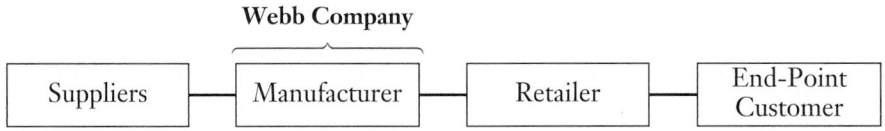

Webb Company

| Suppliers | — | Manufacturer | — | Retailer | — | End-Point Customer |

For example, actions taken by Webb's suppliers could cause unfavourable material-efficiency variances at Webb (see point 6 above).

This list of six possible causes is far from exhaustive. However, it does indicate that the cause of a variance in one part of the value chain (production in our example) can be due to actions taken in other parts of the value chain (for example, product design, or marketing) and in other organizations. Note how improvements in early stages of the supply chain or value chain can sizably reduce the magnitudes of variances in subsequent stages.

The most important task in variance analysis is to understand why variances arise and then to use that knowledge to promote learning and continuous improvement. For instance, in our list of examples on pages 257–258, we may seek improvements in product design, in the commitment of the manufacturing labour force to do the job right the first time, in the activities undertaken by suppliers to provide high-quality materials, and so on. Variance analysis should not be a tool to "play the blame game" (that is, for every unfavourable variance a person is sought to blame or even punish); rather, it should be an essential ingredient that helps promote learning in the organization.

Top management should recognize that this learning/continuous improvement use of variance analysis can be undermined if it places excessive (or obsessive) emphasis on meeting individual variance targets. For example, managers may engage in padding of the standard input quantities or input prices so that their targets are more easily attained. Padded numbers in a budget, however, mean that management underperformance potentially is rewarded and less learning and less improvement potentially occur.

When to Investigate Variances

When should variances be investigated? Frequently, managers base their answer on thresholds they set using either subjective judgments or rules of thumb. For critical items, a small variance may prompt follow-up. For other items, a minimum dollar variance or a certain percentage of variance from budget may prompt investigations. Of course, a 4% variance in direct materials costs of $1 million may deserve more attention than a 20% variance in repair costs of $10,000. Therefore, rules such as "investigate all variances exceeding $5,000 or 25% of budgeted cost, whichever is lower" are common. Variance analysis is subject to the same cost-benefit test as all other phases of a management control system.

Management accounting systems have traditionally implied that a standard is a single acceptable measure. Practically, managers realize that the standard is a band or range of possible acceptable outcomes. Consequently, they expect actual outcomes to vary from budgeted or expected outcomes within some normal limits. A variance within this band is deemed to be from an in-control process and calls for no corrective action by managers.

Investigating variances entails activities ranging from phone calls and e-mails to engineering analyses of the production processes, which can be expensive. Detailed investigation is warranted only when the expected benefits (for example, reduced costs or improved management decisions from more accurate data) exceed the expected costs of the investigation.

Continuous Improvement

There is a trade-off between pushing for too much continuous improvement and the motivational problems associated with judging performance that workers perceive to be unattainable. Managers need to recognize that the rate of improvement will probably decrease over time after those most identifiable with the largest effects have been achieved.

Continuous improvement budgeted costs. Budgeted cost that is successfully reduced over succeeding time periods.

Continuous improvement is one of the evolving management themes highlighted in this book (see Exhibit 1-6, p. 15, and the discussion of kaizen budgeting in Chapter 6). Using **continuous improvement budgeted costs** is yet another way to control variances. This is a budgeted cost that is successively reduced over succeeding time periods. The budgeted direct materials cost for each jacket that Webb Company manufactured in April 2007 is $60 per unit. The budgeted cost used in variance analysis for subsequent periods could be based on a targeted 1% reduction each period:

Month	Prior Month's Budgeted Amount	Reduction in Budgeted Amount	Revised Budgeted Amount
April 2007	–	–	$60.00
May 2007	$60.00	$0.600 (0.01 × $60.00)	59.40
June 2007	59.40	0.594 (0.01 × $59.40)	58.81
July 2007	58.81	0.588 (0.01 × $58.81)	58.22

The source of the 1% reduction in budgeted direct materials costs could be efficiency improvements or price reductions. By using continuous improvement budgeted costs, an organization signals the importance of constantly seeking ways to reduce total costs. For example, managers could avoid unfavourable materials efficiency variances by continuously reducing materials waste.

Products in the initial months of their production may have higher budgeted improvement rates than those that have been in production for, say, three years. Improvement opportunities may be much easier to identify when products have just started in production. Once the easy opportunities have been identified ("the low-hanging fruit picked"), much more ingenuity may be required to identify successive improvement opportunities. The improvements in production that arise as people learn new processes are expanded upon in Chapter 10.

Financial and Nonfinancial Performance Measures

To control the process, the supervisor cannot wait for an accounting report with variances reported in dollars. Instead supervisors use personal observations and timely nonfinancial performance measures. For example, a Nissan plant compiles data such as defect rates and production-schedule attainment and broadcasts them in ticker-tape fashion on screens throughout the plant.

Even though lower-level control depends primarily on nonfinancial performance measures, there are two reasons why these results need to be reported in dollars: (1) to compare different variances for performance evaluation and strategic planning and (2) to decide which variances to investigate.

Almost all organizations use a combination of financial and nonfinancial performance measures rather than relying exclusively on either type. Consider our Webb Company illustration. In its cutting room, fabric is laid out and cut into pieces, which are then matched together and assembled. Control is often exercised at the cutting room level by focusing on nonfinancial measures such as the number of square metres of cloth used to produce 1,000 jackets or the percentage of jackets started and completed without requiring any rework. Production managers at Webb also will likely use financial measures to evaluate the overall cost efficiency with which operations are being run and to help guide decisions about, say, changing the mix of inputs used in manufacturing jackets. Financial measures are often critical in an organization because they summarize the economic impact of diverse physical activities in a way managers readily understand. Moreover, managers are often evaluated on results compared with financial measures.

IMPACT OF INVENTORIES

Our Webb Company illustration assumed the following:

1. All units are manufactured and sold in the same accounting period. There are no work-in-process or finished goods inventories at either the beginning or the end of the accounting period.

2. All direct materials are purchased and used in the same accounting period. There is no direct materials inventory at either the beginning or the end of the period.

Both assumptions can be relaxed without changing the key concepts introduced in this chapter. However, changes in the computation or interpretation of variances would be required when beginning or ending inventories exist.

Suppose direct materials are purchased some time before their use and that direct materials inventories exist at the beginning or end of the accounting period. Managers typically want to pinpoint variances at the earliest possible time so that their decisions can be best informed by the variances. For direct materials price variances, the purchase date will almost always be the earliest possible time to isolate them. As a result, many organizations compute direct materials price variances using the quantities purchased in an accounting period. The Problem for Self-Study (p. 267) illustrates how to use two different times (purchase time and use time) to pinpoint direct materials variances.

AN ILLUSTRATION OF JOURNAL ENTRIES USING STANDARD COSTS

Control Feature of Standard Costs

We will now illustrate journal entries when standard costs are used. For illustrative purposes, we will focus on direct materials and direct manufacturing labour.

We will continue with the data in the Webb Company illustration with one exception. Assume that during April 2007 Webb purchases 25,000 square metres (m²) of materials. Recall that the actual quantity used is 22,200 m² and that the standard quantity allowed for the actual output achieved is 20,000 m². The actual purchase price was $31 per m², while the standard price was $30 m².

Note that in each of the following entries, unfavourable cost variances are always debits and favourable cost variances are always credits.

◆ **Entry 1(a).** Isolate the direct materials price variance at the time of purchase by debiting Materials Control at standard prices. This is the earliest date possible to isolate this variance.

1. a. Materials Control
   $(25,000 \text{ m}^2 \times \$30/\text{m}^2)$ $750,000

   Direct Materials Price Variance
   $(25,000 \text{ m}^2 \times \$1/\text{m}^2)$ 25,000

        Accounts Payable Control
        $(25,000 \text{ m}^2 \times \$31/\text{m}^2)$ 775,000

   To record direct materials purchased.

◆ **Entry 1(b).** Isolate the direct materials efficiency variance at the time of usage by debiting Work-in-Process Control at standard input quantities allowed for actual output units achieved at standard input prices.

1. b. Work-in-Process Control
   $(20,000 \text{ m}^2 \times \$30/\text{m}^2)$ $600,000

   Direct Materials Efficiency Variance
   $(2,200 \text{ m}^2 \times \$30/\text{m}^2)$ 66,000

        Materials Control
        $(22,200 \text{ m}^2 \times \$30/\text{m}^2)$ 666,000

   To record direct materials used.

◆ **Entry 2.** Isolate the direct manufacturing labour price and efficiency variances at the time this labour is used by debiting Work-in-Process Control at standard quantities allowed for actual output units achieved at standard input prices. Note that Wages Payable Control measures the payroll liability and hence is always at actual wage rates.

> Unfavourable variances reduce operating income so they're recorded as debits, like expenses. Favourable variances increase operating income, so they're recorded as credits, like either contra expenses or revenues.

> Unlike materials, labour cannot be stored for future use, so there is only one journal entry for both the purchase and use of direct manufacturing labour.

2. Work-in-Process Control
   (8,000 hours × $20/hr) $160,000

   Direct Manufacturing Labour Price Variance
   (9,000 hours × $2/hr)   18,000

   Direct Manufacturing Labour Efficiency Variance
   (1,000 hours × $20/hr)   20,000

       Wages Payable Control
       (9,000 hours × $22/hr)   198,000

To record liability for direct manufacturing labour costs.

A major advantage of this standard costing system is its emphasis on the control feature of standard costs. All variances are isolated at the earliest possible time, when managers can make informed decisions based on those variances.

End-of-Period Adjustments

Chapter 4 discussed two main approaches to recognizing the under- or overallocated manufacturing overhead at the end of a period:

◆ The adjusted allocation rate approach, which adjusts every job cost record for the difference between the allocated and actual indirect cost amounts

◆ The proration approach, which makes adjustments to one or more of the following end-of-period account balances: materials, work in process, finished goods, and cost of goods sold

Price and efficiency variances can also be disposed of using these same two approaches.

Standard Costing and Information Technology

Modern information technology greatly facilitates the use of standard costing systems for product costing and control. A company's standard prices and standard quantities are stored in its computer systems. A bar code scanner records the receipt of materials, immediately costing each material using its stored standard price. The receipt of materials is matched with the purchase order to record Accounts Payable and to isolate the direct materials price variance.

As output is completed, the standard quantity of direct materials that should have been used is computed and compared with the computerized request for direct materials submitted by an operator on the production floor. This difference multiplied by the standard direct material price is the direct materials efficiency variance. Labour variances are calculated as employees log into production floor terminals and punch in their employee numbers, start and end times, and the quantity of the product they helped produce. Managers use this instantaneous feedback on variances to initiate immediate corrective action, as needed.

Wide Applicability of Standard Costing Systems

Companies that have implemented just-in-time systems, total quality management (TQM), and computer integrated manufacturing (CIM) systems, as well as companies in the service sector, find standard costing to be a useful tool. It provides valuable information for the management and control of materials, labour, and other activities related to production. Companies implementing total quality management programs use standard costing to control materials costs. Service-sector companies are labour intensive and use standard costs to control labour costs. Companies implementing CIM use flexible budgeting and standard costing to manage activities such as materials handling and setups.

FLEXIBLE BUDGETING AND ACTIVITY-BASED COSTING

Activity-based costing (ABC) systems focus on individual activities as the fundamental cost objects. ABC systems classify the costs of various activities into a cost hierarchy—output unit-level costs, batch-level costs, product-sustaining costs, and facility-sustaining costs. Webb's two direct-cost categories—direct material costs and direct manufacturing labour costs—are examples of output unit-level costs. In this section, we show how the basic principles and concepts of flexible budgets and variance analysis can be applied to other levels of the cost hierarchy. We focus on batch-level costs. Batch-level costs are the costs of activities related to a group of units of products or services rather than to each individual unit of product or service.

Relating Batch Costs to Product Output

Consider Lyco Brass Works, which manufactures Jacutaps, a line of decorative brass faucets for home spas. Lyco produces Jacutaps in batches. For each product line, Lyco dedicates material-handling labour to bring materials to the manufacturing area, transport work in process from one work centre to the next, and take the finished product to the shipping area. Hence, material-handling labour costs for Jacutaps are direct costs of Jacutaps. Because the materials for a batch are moved together, material-handling labour costs vary with the number of batches rather than with the number of units in a batch. Material-handling labour costs are variable direct batch-level costs.

Information regarding Jacutaps for 2007 follows:

	Static-Budget Amounts	Actual Amounts
1. Units of Jacutaps produced and sold	180,000	151,200.00
2. Batch size (units per batch)	150	140.00
3. Number of batches (Line 1 ÷ Line 2)	1,200	1,080.00
4. Material-handling labour-hours per batch	5	5.25
5. Total material-handling labour-hours (Line 3 × Line 4)	6,000	5,670.00
6. Cost per material-handling labour-hour	$ 14	$ 14.50
7. Total material-handling labour costs (Line 5 × Line 6)	$ 84,000	$ 82,215.00

To prepare the flexible budget for material-handling labour costs, Lyco starts with the actual units of output produced, 151,200 units, and proceeds in the following steps:

◆ **Step 1:** *Using budgeted batch size, calculate the number of batches that should have been used to produce the actual output.* At the budgeted batch size of 150 units per batch, Lyco should have produced the 151,200 units of output in 1,008 batches (151,200 units ÷ 150 units per batch).

◆ **Step 2:** *Using budgeted material-handling labour-hours per batch, calculate the number of material-handling labour-hours that should have been used.* At the budgeted quantity of 5 hours per batch, 1,008 batches should have required 5,040 material-handling labour-hours (1,008 batches × 5 hours per batch).

◆ **Step 3:** *Using budgeted cost per material-handling labour-hour, calculate the flexible-budget amount for material-handling labour-hours.* The flexible-budget amount is 5,040 material-handling labour-hours × $14 budgeted cost per material-handling labour-hour = $70,560.

Note how the flexible-budget calculations for material-handling costs focus on batch-level quantities (material-handling labour-hours) rather than on output unit-level amounts (such as material-handling labour-hours per unit of output). The flexible-budget variance for material-handling costs can then be calculated as:

$$\text{Flexible-budget variance} = \text{Actual costs} - \text{Flexible-budget costs}$$
$$= (5{,}670 \text{ hours} \times \$14.50 \text{ per hour}) - (5{,}040 \text{ hours} \times \$14 \text{ per hour})$$
$$= \$82{,}215 - \$70{,}560$$
$$= \$11{,}655, \text{ or } \$1{,}655 \text{ U}$$

The unfavourable variance indicates that material-handling labour costs were $11,655 higher than the flexible-budget target.

Price and Efficiency Variances

We can get some insight into the possible reasons for this $11,655 unfavourable variance by examining the price and efficiency components of the flexible-budget variance:

$$\begin{aligned}\text{Price variance} &= \left(\begin{array}{c}\text{Actual price} \\ \text{of input}\end{array} - \begin{array}{c}\text{Budgeted price} \\ \text{of input}\end{array}\right) \times \begin{array}{c}\text{Actual quantity} \\ \text{of input}\end{array} \\ &= (\$14.50 \text{ per hour} - \$14 \text{ per hour}) \times 5{,}670 \text{ hours} \\ &= \$0.50 \text{ per hour} \times 5{,}670 \text{ hours} \\ &= \$2{,}835, \text{ or } \$2{,}835 \text{ U}\end{aligned}$$

The unfavourable price variance for material-handling labour indicates that the $14.50 actual cost per material-handling labour-hour exceeds the $14.00 budgeted cost per material-handling labour-hour. This variance could be due, for example, to (1) Lyco's human resources manager negotiating less skillfully than was planned in the budget and (2) wage rates increasing unexpectedly due to scarcity of labour.

$$\begin{aligned}\text{Efficiency variance} &= \left(\begin{array}{c}\text{Actual quantity} \\ \text{of input used}\end{array} - \begin{array}{c}\text{Budgeted quantity of input} \\ \text{allowed for actual output}\end{array}\right) \times \begin{array}{c}\text{Budgeted price} \\ \text{of input.}\end{array} \\ &= (5{,}670 \text{ hours} - 5{,}040 \text{ hours}) \times \$14 \text{ per hour} \\ &= 630 \text{ hours} \times \$14 \text{ per hour} \\ &= \$8{,}820, \text{ or } \$8{,}820 \text{ U}\end{aligned}$$

The unfavourable efficiency variance indicates that the 5,670 actual material-handling labour-hours exceeded the 5,040 material-handling labour-hours that Lyco should have used for the number of units it produced. Two reasons for the unfavourable efficiency variance are (1) smaller actual batch sizes of 140 units, instead of the budgeted batch sizes of 150 units, resulting in Lyco producing the 151,200 units in 1,080 batches instead of 1,008 (151,200 ÷ 150) batches; and (2) higher actual material-handling labour-hours per batch of 5.25 hours instead of budgeted material-handling labour-hours of 5 hours.

Reasons for smaller than budgeted batch sizes could include (1) quality problems, if batch sizes exceed 140 faucets, and (2) high costs of carrying inventory.

Reasons for larger actual material-handling labour-hours per batch could include (1) inefficient layout of the Jacutap production line relative to the layout proposed in the budget; (2) material-handling labour having to wait at work centres before picking up or delivering materials; (3) unmotivated, inexperienced, and underskilled employees; and (4) too tight standards for material-handling time.

Identifying the reasons for the efficiency variance helps Lyco's managers develop a plan for improving material-handling labour efficiency.

Focus on Hierarchy

The idea is to focus the flexible-budget quantity computations at the appropriate level of the cost hierarchy. For example, because material handling is a batch-level cost, the flexible-budget quantity calculations are made at the batch level—the quantity of material-handling labour-hours that Lyco should have used based on the number of batches it should have taken to produce the actual quantity of

151,200 units. If a cost had been a product-sustaining cost—such as product design cost—the flexible-budget quantity computations would focus at the product-sustaining level, for example, by evaluating the actual complexity of product design relative to the budget.

BENCHMARKING AND VARIANCE ANALYSIS

The budgeted amounts in the variance formulas discussed in this chapter are baseline points of reference from which comparisons can be made. The term **benchmarking** is often used to refer to the continual process of measuring products, services, and activities against the best levels of performance achieved by any company undertaking similar activities in each function of the value chain. Many consulting firms now offer benchmarking services. Here we discuss information provided by one such service and then note how the variance computations discussed in this chapter can incorporate this information.

HayGroup is a global human resources consulting organization. HayGroup, among other things, collects and analyzes cost information submitted by hospitals to provincial and federal governments to comply with financial and non-financial reporting regulations. From this and other data HayGroup collects privately, the firm can prepare benchmark reports. These reports show how costs to treat case-mix groups (CMG) in a target hospital differ from those of other comparable hospitals. CMG refers to a set of related medical diagnoses, for example stroke, respiratory disorders, etc. Standard lengths of stay per CMG have been calculated and from this standard costs have been estimated. A standard cost, however, is not a benchmark. A benchmark is the lowest-cost for treatment of a particular CMG. If a hospital's actual costs per CMG are higher than an average for comparable hospitals, they will most certainly be higher than the benchmark cost per CMG in that same group of hospitals.

Exhibit 7-6 on the next page illustrates a typical report for a client hospital. Panel A reports the target hospital's cost per CMG is 10% above the average for comparable hospitals. Note that the benchmark hospital is Hospital E and the target hospital's costs are 31% higher than this benchmark. Panel B reports costs for four specific CMGs. Focus on the costs per CMG for stroke. The problem for the target hospital is that the government that funds treatment of patients in this CMG will only pay the average amount. If the target hospital cannot reduce its costs it will show an operating deficit. The government has the power to replace managers of the hospital with others appointed by the government. It may be true that higher CMG costs can be justified because those admitted are more seriously ill than at other hospitals, or the treatment provided is superior, but this is rare. Moreover the costs per CMG are adjusted for severity levels and hospitals must report these severity levels in the normal course of complying with government reporting requirements.

While those managing hospitals are responsible for prudent fiscal management, their overriding concern is for the safety of their patients. That is why the managers of the target hospital must exercise caution when they change their treatment processes to become more cost-efficient. Safe treatment of patients is made more complex because many patients are not admitted until they are very close to death. Simply changing one or two activities may reduce the costs of activities but not treatment processes. Costs saved by changing one set of activities can easily drive up the costs of a second interlinked and more expensive set of activities. The result may be higher rather than lower overall costs per CMG. It is also the case that hospitals are funded to provide effective and safe medical treatment, not to develop sophisticated and reliable costing systems. This means the input used to calculate costs per CMG may not be accurate. Despite these potential shortcomings, benchmarking does give managers the opportunity to investigate different, equally safe treatment processes that also reduce costs.

PANEL A: COST COMPARISONS AT HOSPITAL LEVEL

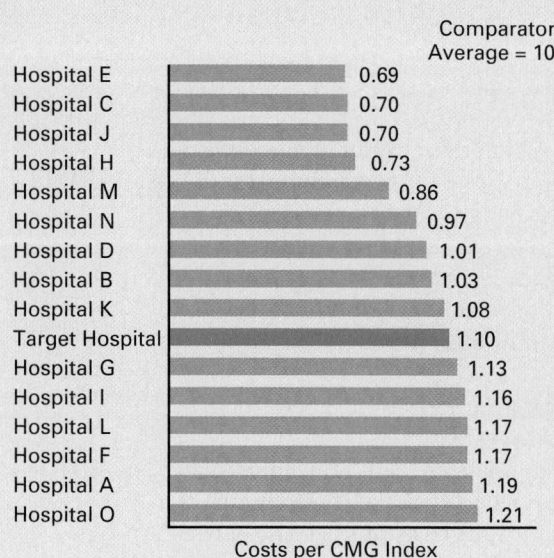

Comparator Average = 100

Hospital	Costs per CMG Index
Hospital E	0.69
Hospital C	0.70
Hospital J	0.70
Hospital H	0.73
Hospital M	0.86
Hospital N	0.97
Hospital D	1.01
Hospital B	1.03
Hospital K	1.08
Target Hospital	1.10
Hospital G	1.13
Hospital I	1.16
Hospital L	1.17
Hospital F	1.17
Hospital A	1.19
Hospital O	1.21

Costs per CMG Index

HOW TO READ THIS CHART:

This chart shows the target hospital's relative-case costs performance versus that of comparable hospitals. The target hospital is benchmarked with the average-case costs of its peers at the CMG level for funding purposes.

EXAMPLE:

On an overall costs per case basis, after adjusting for case mix, the target hospital's cost is 10% higher than the comparable group average. There are nine hospitals that have lower overall case costs than the target hospital.

PANEL B: COST COMPARISONS AT DIAGNOSTIC GROUP LEVEL

Case-Mix Group	Target Hospital	Group Average	25th Percentile	Average of Lowest Cost Quartile (0–25th)
Stroke	$33,700	$31,300	$21,900	$20,500
Respiratory disorders	66,800	53,700	44,400	38,400
Simple pneumonia	37,100	29,500	23,300	22,000

Source: Market Insights (San Francisco, California).

The Benchmarking Network, Inc.
www.benchmarkingnetwork.com

Cost reports like Exhibit 7-6 provide an external benchmark that forces the administrator to ask *why* cost levels differ between hospitals and *how* best practices can be transferred from the more efficient to the less efficient hospitals.

Evaluating the overall performance of a hospital or hospital personnel requires analyzing other factors in addition to costs. These factors include the perceived quality of service to patients; the success rate of operations (for example, how many patients with strokes survive?); and the morale of the doctors, nurses, and other staff. In many cases, however, cost factors have been given too little weighting in the past, in part because of the lack of reliable information on cost relationships in this sector of the economy.

Benchmark reports based on the costs of other companies can be developed for many activities and products. For example, the Webb Company could estimate (possibly with the aid of consultants) the materials cost of the jackets manufactured by its competitors. The materials cost estimate of the lowest-cost competitor could be used as the budgeted amounts in its variance computations. An unfavourable materials-efficiency variance would signal that Webb has a higher materials cost than "best cost practice" in its industry. The magnitude of the cost difference would be of great interest to Webb. It could prompt Webb to do an extensive search into how to bring its own cost structure in line with that of the lowest in the industry.

PROBLEM

The O'Shea Company manufactures ceramic vases. It uses its standard costing system when developing its flexible budget amounts. In April 2007, 2,000 finished units were produced. The following information is related to its two direct manufacturing cost categories of direct materials and direct manufacturing labour.

Direct materials used were 4,400 kilograms. The standard direct materials input allowed for one output unit is 2 kilograms at $15 per kilogram, and 5,000 kilograms of materials were purchased at $16.50 per kilogram, a total of $82,500.

Actual direct manufacturing labour-hours were 3,250 at a total cost of $66,300. Standard manufacturing labour time allowed is 1.5 hours per output unit, and the standard direct manufacturing labour cost is $20 per hour.

REQUIRED

1. Calculate the direct materials price and efficiency variances and the direct manufacturing labour price and efficiency variances. The direct materials price variance will be based on a flexible budget for actual quantities purchased, but the efficiency variance will be based on a flexible budget for actual quantities used.
2. Prepare journal entries for a standard-costing system that isolates variances as early as feasible.

SOLUTION

1. Exhibit 7-7 shows how the columnar presentation of variances introduced in Exhibit 7-5 can be adjusted for the difference in timing between the purchase and use of materials. In particular, note the two sets of computations in column 2 for direct materials. The $75,000 pertains to the direct materials purchased; the $66,000 pertains to the direct materials used.

2.
Materials Control		
(5,000 kilograms × $15/kg)	$75,000	
Direct Materials Price Variance		
(5,000 kilograms × $1.50/kg)	$ 7,500	
Accounts Payable Control		
(5,000 kilograms × $16.50/kg)		$82,500
Work-in-Process Control		
(2,000 units × 2 kg/unit × $15/kg)	$60,000	
Direct Materials Efficiency Variance		
(400 kilograms × $15/kg)	$ 6,000	
Materials Control		
(4,400 kilograms × $15/kg)		$66,000
Work-in-Process Control		
(2,000 units × 1.5 hrs/unit × $20/hr)	$60,000	
Direct Manufacturing Labour Price Variance		
(3,250 hours × $0.40/hr)	$ 1,300	
Direct Manufacturing Labour Efficiency Variance		
(250 hours × $20/hr)	$ 5,000	
Wages Payable Control		
(3,250 hours × $20.40/hr)		$66,300

EXHIBIT 7-7
Columnar Presentation of Variance Analysis: Direct Materials and Direct Manufacturing Labour*

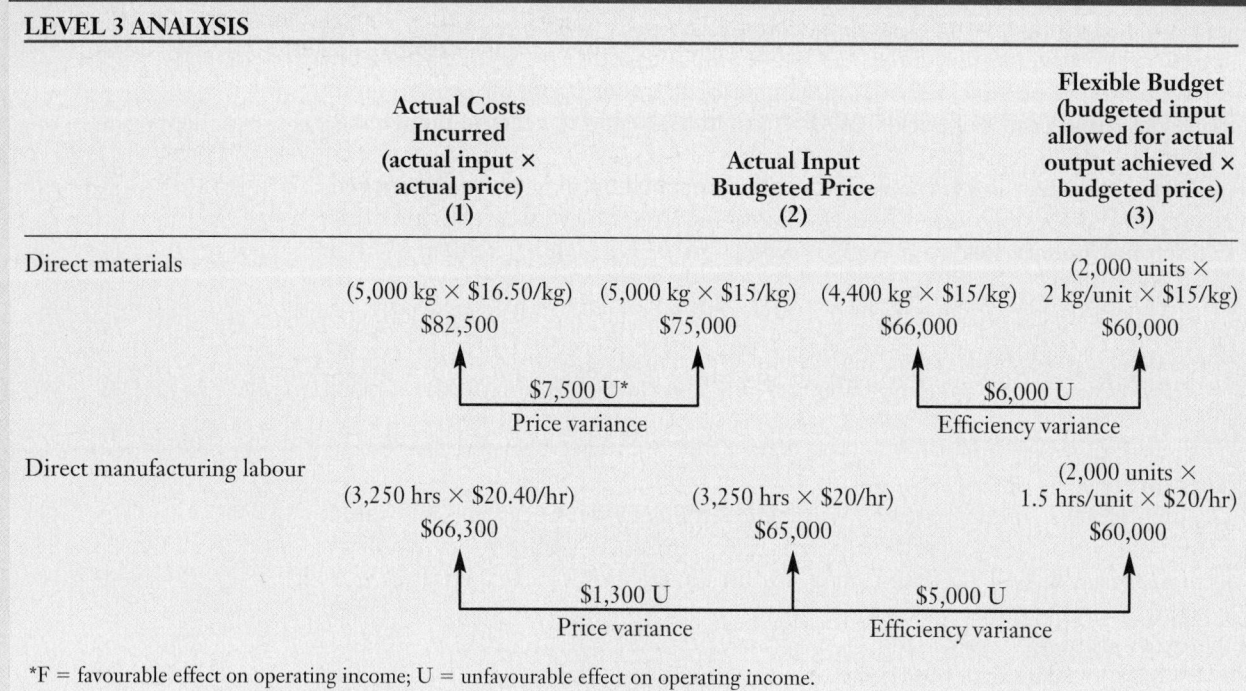

LEVEL 3 ANALYSIS

	Actual Costs Incurred (actual input × actual price) (1)		Actual Input Budgeted Price (2)	Flexible Budget (budgeted input allowed for actual output achieved × budgeted price) (3)
Direct materials	(5,000 kg × $16.50/kg) $82,500	(5,000 kg × $15/kg) $75,000	(4,400 kg × $15/kg) $66,000	(2,000 units × 2 kg/unit × $15/kg) $60,000
	↑ $7,500 U* Price variance ↑		↑ $6,000 U Efficiency variance ↑	
Direct manufacturing labour	(3,250 hrs × $20.40/hr) $66,300		(3,250 hrs × $20/hr) $65,000	(2,000 units × 1.5 hrs/unit × $20/hr) $60,000
	↑ $1,300 U Price variance ↑		↑ $5,000 U Efficiency variance ↑	

*F = favourable effect on operating income; U = unfavourable effect on operating income.

The following decision guidelines use a question-and-answer format to summarize the chapter's main points. Each decision presents a key question. The guideline is the answer to that question.

DECISIONS	GUIDELINES
1. How do flexible budgets differ from static budgets, and why should companies use flexible budgets?	A static budget is based on the level of output planned at the start of the budget period. A flexible budget is adjusted (flexed) to recognize the actual output level of the budget period. Flexible budgets help managers gain more insight into the causes of variances than is available from static budgets.
2. How can you develop a flexible budget and compute the flexible-budget variance and the sales-volume variance?	Use a three-step procedure to develop a flexible budget. When all costs are either variable with respect to output units or fixed, these three steps require only information about budgeted selling price, budgeted variable cost per output unit, budgeted fixed costs, and the actual quantity of output units. The static-budget variance can be subdivided into a flexible-budget variance (the difference between an actual result and the corresponding flexible-budget amount) and a sales-volume variance (the difference between the flexible-budget amount and the corresponding static-budget amount).
3. What is a standard cost, and why should a company use standard costs?	A standard cost is a carefully determined cost based on efficient operations. Standard costs aim to exclude past inefficiencies and to take into account changes expected to occur in the budget period.
4. Why should a company calculate price variances and efficiency variances?	The computation of price variances and efficiency variances helps managers gain insight into two different—but not independent—aspects of performance. The price variance focuses on the difference between the actual input price and the budgeted input price. The efficiency variance focuses on the difference between the actual quantity of input and the budgeted quantity of input allowed for the actual output.

5. Should a purchasing manager's performance be evaluated only based on the price variance?	The price variance captures only one aspect of a purchasing manager's performance. Other aspects include the quality of the inputs the manager purchases and his or her ability to get suppliers to deliver on time.
6. Can variance analysis be used with an activity-based costing system?	Variance analysis can be applied to activity costs (such as setup costs) to gain insight into why actual activity costs differ from activity costs in the static budget or in the flexible budget. Interpreting cost variances for different activities requires understanding whether the costs are output unit-level, batch-level, product-sustaining, or facility-sustaining costs.
7. What is benchmarking and why is it useful?	Benchmarking is the continuous process of comparing the level of performance in producing products and services and executing activities against the best levels of performance. Benchmarking measures how well a company and its managers are doing.

▼ TERMS TO LEARN

This chapter contains definitions of the following important terms:

benchmarking (p. 265)
continuous improvement budgeted
   costs (p. 260)
effectiveness (p. 256)
efficiency (p. 256)
efficiency variance (p. 249)
favourable variance (p. 244)
flexible budget (p. 244)
flexible-budget variance (p. 247)
input-efficiency variance (p. 249)
input-price variance (p. 249)

price variance (p. 249)
rate variance (p. 249)
sales-volume variance (p. 247)
selling-price variance (p. 248)
standard (p. 244)
standard cost (p. 250)
standard input (p. 250)
static budget (p. 244)
unfavourable variance (p. 244)
usage variance (p. 249)

▼ ASSIGNMENT MATERIAL

QUESTIONS

7-1 What is the relationship between *management by exception* and *variance analysis*?

7-2 What are two possible sources of information a company might use to compute the *budgeted amount* in variance analysis?

7-3 Distinguish between a *favourable variance* and an *unfavourable variance*.

7-4 What is the key difference between a *static budget* and a *flexible budget*?

7-5 Why might managers find a Level 2 flexible-budget analysis more informative than a Level 1 static-budget analysis?

7-6 Describe the steps in developing a flexible budget.

7-7 List four reasons for using standard costs.

7-8 How might a manager gain insight into the causes of a flexible-budget variance for direct materials?

7-9 List three causes of a favourable materials-price variance.

7-10 Describe why direct materials price variance and direct materials efficiency variance may be computed with reference to different points in time.

7-11 How might the continuous improvement theme be incorporated into the process of setting budgeted costs?

7-12 Why might an analyst examining variances in the production area look beyond that business function for explanations of those variances?

7-13 Comment on the following statement made by a plant supervisor: "Meetings with my plant accountant are frustrating. All he wants to do is pin the blame for the many variances he reports."

7-14 How can variances be used to analyze costs in individual activity areas?

7-15 "Benchmarking against other companies enables a company to identify the lowest-cost producer, which should become the performance measure for the next year." Do you agree?

EXERCISES

7-16 Flexible budget. Brabham Enterprises manufactures tires for the Formula I motor racing circuit. For August 2007, Brabham budgeted to manufacture and sell 3,000 tires at a variable cost of $88 per tire and a total fixed cost of $64,800. The budgeted selling price was $132 per tire. Actual results in August 2007 were 2,800 tires manufactured and sold at a selling price of $134 per tire. The actual total variable costs were $275,520, and the actual total fixed costs were $60,000.

REQUIRED
1. Prepare a performance report (akin to Exhibit 7-3, p. 247) that uses a flexible budget and a static budget.
2. Comment on the results in requirement 1.

7-17 Flexible budget. The budgeted prices for direct materials, direct manufacturing labour, and direct marketing (distribution) labour per attaché case are $48, $9.60, and $14.40 respectively. The president is pleased with the following performance report:

	Actual Costs	Static Budget	Variance
Direct materials	$436,800	$480,000	$43,200 F
Direct manufacturing labour	93,600	96,000	2,400 F
Direct marketing (distribution) labour	132,000	144,000	12,000 F

REQUIRED
Actual output was 8,800 attaché cases. Is the president's pleasure justified? Prepare a revised performance report that uses a flexible budget and a static budget. Assume all three direct-cost items are variable costs.

7-18 Flexible budget. The Virtual Candy Company sells sweets in bulk over the Internet. Virtual Candy's budgeted operating income for the year ended December 31, 2007, was $3,780,000. As a result of continued explosive growth on the Internet, actual operating income totalled $7,867,200.

REQUIRED
1. Calculate the total static-budget variances.
2. Flexible-budget operating income was $8,316,000. Calculate the total flexible-budget and total sales-volume variance.
3. Comment on the total flexible-budget variance in the light of Virtual Candy's explosive growth.

7-19 Price and efficiency variances. Peterson Foods manufactures pumpkin scones. For January 2007, it budgeted to purchase and use 15,000 kilograms of pumpkin at $1.07 a kilogram; budgeted output was 60,000 scones. Actual purchase and use for January 2007 was 16,000 kilograms at $0.98 a kilogram; actual output was 60,800 scones.

REQUIRED
1. Compute the flexible-budget variance.
2. Compute the price and efficiency variances.
3. Comment on the results in requirements 1 and 2.

7-20 Materials and manufacturing-labour variances. Consider the following data collected for Great Homes, Inc.:

	Direct Materials	Direct Manufacturing Labour
Costs incurred: Actual inputs × actual prices	$240,000	$108,000
Actual inputs × standard prices	256,800	103,200
Standard inputs allowed for actual outputs × standard prices	270,000	96,000

REQUIRED

Compute the price, efficiency, and flexible-budget variances for direct materials and direct manufacturing labour.

Excel Application

For students who wish to practise their spreadsheet skills, the following is a step-by-step approach to creating an Excel spreadsheet to work this problem.

Step-by-Step

1. At the top of a new spreadsheet, create an "Original Data" section for the data provided by Great Homes, Inc., in exactly the same format as shown above, with rows labelled "Cost Incurred: Actual Inputs × Actual Prices," "Actual Inputs × Standard Prices," and "Standard Inputs Allowed for Actual Outputs × Standard Prices," and columns labelled "Direct Materials" and "Direct Manufacturing Labour."

2. Skip two rows, and create a section, "Variance Calculations." Create rows for "Price Variance," "Efficiency Variance," and "Flexible-Budget Variance." Create columns for "Direct Materials" and "Direct Manufacturing Labour."

(Program your spreadsheet to perform all necessary calculations. Do not "hard-code" any of your variance calculations.)

3. Use the data in the Original Data section to calculate price variance, efficiency variance, and flexible-budget variance for direct materials and direct manufacturing labour. For example, to calculate direct materials price variance, in the cell corresponding to the "Price Variance" row and the "Direct Materials" column, enter a formula to subtract cost incurred from actual inputs times standard prices.

4. Unfavourable variances will show up as negative numbers. If you want to remain consistent with the format for calculating variances presented throughout this chapter, when calculating variances, take the absolute value of any differences you calculate in step 3 and label favourable variances with an "F" and unfavourable variances with a "U."

5. *Verify the accuracy of your spreadsheet.* Go to your Original Data section and change costs incurred for direct manufacturing labour from $108,000 to $120,000. If you programmed your spreadsheet correctly, the flexible-budget variance for direct manufacturing labour should change to $24,000 (unfavourable).

7-21 Price and efficiency variances. CellOne, a cellular phone service reseller, contracts with major cellular operators for airtime in bulk and then resells service to retail customers. CellOne budgeted to sell 7,800,000 minutes in the month ended March 31, 2007. Actual minutes sold totalled only 7,500,000. Because of fluctuations in hourly usage, CellOne "overbuys" airtime from cellular operators. CellOne plans to buy 10% more airtime than they plan to sell—for example, CellOne's budgets called for the purchase of 8,580,000 minutes (the actual purchased amount as well) based on the plan to sell 7,800,000 minutes. We refer to purchased airtime as direct materials. Use 8,250,000 (7,500,000 × 1.1) minutes in the flexible budget.

CellOne budgeted purchased airtime to cost 5.4 cents per minute. Actual purchased airtime in 2007 averaged 6.0 cents per minute. CellOne incurs direct labour costs from the employment of technicians. One hour of technical support is required for every 5,000 minutes of airtime sold. In practice, only 1,600 hours of technical support were used. Technical support was planned at $72 per hour. Actual technical support costs averaged $74.40 per hour.

REQUIRED

1. Calculate the flexible-budget variance for direct materials and direct labour costs.
2. Calculate the price and efficiency variances for materials and labour.

7-22 Comprehensive variance analysis. Pacific Furniture is an elite desk manufacturer. At the start of May 2007, the following budgeted unit amounts (based on a standard costing system) related to its manufacture of executive desks (made out of oak):

- ◆ Direct materials:
  1.6 square metres of oak per desk
  $24 per square metre
- ◆ Direct manufacturing labour:
  3 hours per desk
  $36 per direct manufacturing labour-hour

Budgeted production for May 2007 was 700 executive desks. There were no beginning inventories of direct materials or finished goods on May 1, 2007. Work in process is minimal.

Actual results for May 2007 are as follows:

◆ Direct materials purchased (1,264 square metres) $31,094
◆ Direct materials used (1,185 square metres)   ?
◆ Direct manufacturing labour (2,325 hours at $37 per hour)   ?

Actual production in May 2007 is 750 executive desk units. A constant purchase price for oak wood existed in May 2007.

REQUIRED

1. Prepare a detailed flexible-budget variance analysis for May 2007 covering direct materials and direct manufacturing labour.
2. Give two explanations for each of the variances you compute in requirement 1.

7-23 **Flexible budgets, variance analysis.** You have been hired as a consultant by Mary Flanagan, the president of a small manufacturing company that makes automobile parts. Flanagan is an excellent engineer, but she has been frustrated by working with inadequate cost data.

You helped install flexible budgeting and standard costs for Flanagan's company. She has now asked you to consider the following data for May and recommend how variances might be computed and presented in performance reports:

Static budget in output units	20,000
Actual output units produced and sold	23,000
Budgeted selling price per output unit	$ 48
Budgeted variable costs per output unit	$ 30
Budgeted total fixed costs per month	$ 240,000
Actual revenue	$1,048,800
Actual variable costs	$ 756,000
Favourable variance in fixed costs	$ 6,000

Flanagan is disappointed in the May data. Although output units sold exceeded expectations, operating income did not. Assume that there was no beginning or ending inventory.

REQUIRED

1. You decide to present Flanagan with alternative ways to analyze variances so that she can decide what level of detail she prefers. The reporting system can then be designed accordingly. Prepare an analysis similar to Levels 1 and 2 in Exhibit 7-5 (p. 257).
2. What are some likely causes for the variances you report in requirement 1?

7-24 **Flexible-budget preparation and analysis.** Bank Management Printers, Inc., produces luxury chequebooks with three cheques and stubs per page. Each chequebook is designed for an individual customer and is ordered through the customer's bank. The company's operating budget for September 2007 included these data:

Number of chequebooks	15,000
Selling price per book	$ 24
Variable costs per book	$ 9.60
Total fixed costs for the month	$174,000

The actual results for September 2007 were

Number of chequebooks produced and sold	12,000
Average selling price per book	$ 25.20
Variable costs per book	$ 8.40
Total fixed costs for the month	$180,000

The executive vice-president of the company observed that the operating income for September was much less than anticipated, despite a higher-than-budgeted selling price and a lower-than-budgeted variable cost per unit. You have been asked to provide explanations for the disappointing September results.

Bank Management develops its flexible-budget-based budgeted revenue per output unit and variable costs per output unit without a detailed analysis of budgeted inputs.

REQUIRED

1. Prepare a Level 1 analysis of the September performance.
2. Prepare a Level 2 analysis of the September performance.
3. Why might Bank Management find the Level 2 analysis more informative than the Level 1 analysis? Explain your answer.

7-25 Flexible budget, working backward. The Specialty Balls Company designs and manufactures ball bearings for extreme performance machinery. The following table is a partially completed variance analysis of Specialty Balls budgeted and actual results from sales of platinum balls for the year ended December 31, 2007.

Variance Analysis for Specialty Balls for 2007, Incomplete

	Actual Results (1)	Flexible-Budget Variances (2) = (1) − (3)	Flexible Budget (3)	Sales-Volume Variances (4) = (3) − (5)	Static Budget (5)
Units sold	650,000				600,000
Revenues (sales)	$4,290,000				$2,520,000
Variable costs	3,090,000				1,440,000
Contribution margin	1,200,000				1,080,000
Fixed costs	840,000				720,000
Operating income	$ 360,000				$ 360,000

Total flexible-budget variance   Total sales-volume variance

Total static-budget variance

REQUIRED

1. Complete the variance analysis. Calculate all the required variances. If your work is accurate, you will find that the total static-budget variance is $0 (zero).
2. What are the actual and budgeted prices per unit? What are the actual and budgeted costs per unit?
3. Specialty Balls's CEO was delighted with the lack of a static-budget variance. Was his reaction appropriate? Review the variances you have calculated and discuss possible causes and potential problems.

7-26 Activity-based costing, flexible-budget variances for finance function activities. Josh Sanchez is the chief financial officer of Bouquets.com, an Internet company that enables customers to order deliveries of flowers by accessing its Web site. Sanchez is concerned with the efficiency and effectiveness of the finance function. He collects the following information for three activities in 2007:

			Rate per Unit of Cost Driver	
Activity	Activity Level	Cost Driver	Static Budget	Actual
Receivables	Output unit	Remittances	$0.767	$0.90
Payables	Batch	Invoices	3.480	3.36
Travel expenses	Batch	Travel claims	9.120	8.88

The output measure is the number of deliveries, which is the same as the number of remittances. The following is additional information.

	Static-Budget Amounts	Actual Amounts
Number of deliveries	1,000,000	948,000
Batch size in terms of deliveries:		
Payables	5	4.46801
Travel expenses	500	501.587

1. Calculate the flexible-budget variance for each activity in 2007.

2. Calculate the price and efficiency variances for each activity in 2007.

7-27 Finance function activities, benchmarking (continuation of 7-26). Josh Sanchez, CFO of Bouquets.com, engages The Hackett Group, a consulting firm specializing in benchmarking. He asks Hackett to provide benchmark data of the finance function at "world-class" retail companies (both traditional retail and Internet-based retail). Hackett's cost benchmarks for Bouquet.com's three finance activities are

Finance Activity	"World-Class" Cost Performance
Receivables	$0.12 per remittance
Payables	$0.85 per invoice
Travel expenses	$1.90 per travel claim

REQUIRED

1. What new insights might arise with the Hackett benchmark data using the amounts in Exercise 7-26?

2. Assume you are in charge of travel-claim processing. What concerns might you have with Sanchez using the Hackett benchmark of $1.90 per travel claim as the key to evaluate your performance next period?

7-28 Flexible budget, direct materials and direct manufacturing labour variances. Tuscany Statuary manufactures bust statues of famous historical figures. All statues are the same size. Each unit requires the same amount of resources. The following information is from the static budget for 2007:

Expected production and sales	5,000 units
Direct materials	50,000 kg
Direct manufacturing labour	20,000 hours
Direct fixed costs	$1,200,000

Standard quantities, standard prices, and standard unit costs follow for direct materials and direct manufacturing labour.

	Standard Quantity	Standard Price	Standard Unit Cost
Direct materials	10 kilograms	$12 per kilogram	$120
Direct manufacturing labour	4 hours	$48 hour	$192

During 2007, actual number of units produced and sold was 6,000. Actual cost of direct materials used was $792,000, based on 60,000 kilograms purchased and used at $13.20 per kilogram.

Direct manufacturing labour-hours actually used were 25,000, at the rate of $45 per hour. This resulted in actual direct manufacturing labour cost of $1,125,000. Actual fixed costs were $1,206,000. There were no beginning or ending inventories.

REQUIRED

1. Calculate sales volume variance and flexible-budget variance. Level 2.

2. Compute price and efficiency variances for direct materials and direct manufacturing labour. Level 3.

7-29 Price and efficiency variances, journal entries. Chemical, Inc., has set up the following standards per finished output unit for direct materials and direct manufacturing labour:

◆ Direct materials: 10 kilograms at $3.60 per kilogram $36
◆ Direct manufacturing labour: 0.5 hour at $24 per hour   12

The number of finished units budgeted for March 2007 was 10,000; 9,810 units were actually produced.

    Actual results in March 2007 were:
      Direct materials: 98,073 kilograms used
      Direct manufacturing labour: 4,900 hours $123,480

Assume that there was no beginning inventory of either direct materials or finished units.

    During the month, materials purchases amounted to 100,000 kilograms, at a total cost of $372,000. Price variances are isolated upon purchase. Efficiency variances are isolated at the time of usage.

REQUIRED

1. Compute the March 2007 price and efficiency variances of direct materials and direct manufacturing labour. Comment on these variances.
2. Prepare journal entries to record the variances in requirement 1.
3. Why might Chemical, Inc., calculate materials-price variances and materials-efficiency variances with reference to different points in time?

7-30 Continuous improvement (continuation of 7-29). Chemical, Inc., adopts a continuous improvement approach to setting monthly standards costs. Assume the direct materials standard quantity input of ten kilograms per output unit and the direct manufacturing labour quantity input of 0.5 hours per output unit pertain to January 2007. The standard amounts for February 2007 are 0.997 of the January standard amount. The standard amounts for March 2007 are 0.997 of the February standard amount. Assume the same information for March 2007 as in Exercise 7-29 except for these revised standard amounts.

REQUIRED

1. Compute the March 2007 standard quantity input amounts per output unit for direct materials and direct manufacturing labour.
2. Compute the March 2007 price and efficiency variances of direct materials and direct manufacturing labour.

7-31 Materials and manufacturing labour variances, standard costs. Consider the following selected data regarding the manufacture of a line of upholstered chairs:

	Standards per Chair
Direct materials	2 square metres of input at $12 per square metre
Direct manufacturing labour	0.5 hour of input at $24 per hour

The following data were compiled regarding actual performance: actual output units (chairs) produced, 20,000; square metres of input purchased and used, 37,000; price per square metre, $12.24; direct manufacturing labour costs, $211,680; actual hours of input, 9,000; labour price per hour, $23.52.

REQUIRED

1. Show your computations on the price and efficiency variances for direct materials and for direct manufacturing labour. Give a plausible explanation of why the variances occurred.
2. Suppose 60,000 square metres of materials were purchased (at $12.24 per square metre) even though only 37,000 square metres were used. Suppose further that variances are identified with their most likely control point; accordingly, direct materials price variances are isolated and traced to the purchasing department rather than to the production department. Compute the price and efficiency variances under this approach.

7-32 Journal entries and T-accounts (continuation of 7-31). Prepare journal entries and post them to T-accounts for all transactions in Exercise 7-31, including requirement 2. Summarize in three sentences how these journal entries differ from the normal costing entries described in Chapter 5.

7-33 Flexible budget (continuation of 7-31 and 7-32). Suppose the static budget was for 24,000 units of output. The general manager is thrilled about the following report:

	Actual Results	Static Budget	Variance
Direct materials	$452,880	$576,000	$123,120 F
Direct manufacturing labour	211,680	288,000	76,320 F

REQUIRED

Is the manager's glee warranted? Prepare a report that provides a more detailed explanation of why the static budget was not achieved. Actual output was 20,000 units.

PROBLEMS

7-34 Flexible budget preparation, service sector. Meridian Finance helps prospective homeowners of substantial means to find low-cost financing and assists existing homeowners in refinancing their current loans at lower interest rates. Meridian works only for customers with excellent borrowing capacity. Hence, Meridian is able to obtain a loan for every customer with whom it decides to work.

Meridian charges clients 1/2% of the loan amount it arranges. In 2005, the average loan amount per customer was $238,800. In 2006, the average loan amount was $240,252. In its 2007 flexible budgeting system, Meridian assumes the average loan amount will be $240,000. Budgeted cost data per loan application for 2007 are

◆ Professional labour: 6 budgeted hours at a budgeted rate of $48 per hour
◆ Loan filing fees: budgeted at $120 per loan application
◆ Creditworthiness checks: budgeted at $144 per loan application
◆ Courier mailings: budgeted at $60 per loan application

Office support (the costs of leases, secretarial workers, and others) is budgeted to be $37,200 per month. Meridian Finance views this amount as a fixed cost.

REQUIRED

1. Prepare a static budget for November 2007 assuming 90 loan applications.
2. Actual loan applications in November 2007 were 120. Other actual data for November 2007 were

◆ Professional labour: 7.2 hours per loan application at $50.40 per hour
◆ Loan filing fees: $120 per loan application
◆ Creditworthiness checks: $150 per loan application
◆ Courier mailings: $64.80 per loan application

Office support costs for November 2007 were $40,200. The average loan amount for November 2007 was $268,800. Meridian received its 1/2% fee on all loans. Prepare a Level 2 variance analysis of Meridian Finance for November 2007. Meridian's output measure in its flexible budgeting system is the number of loan applications.

7-35 Professional labour efficiency and effectiveness (continuation of 7-34). Meridian Finance is analyzing the efficiency and effectiveness of its professional labour staff.

REQUIRED

1. Compute professional labour price and efficiency variances for November 2007. (Compute labour price on a per-hour basis.)
2. What factors would you consider in evaluating the effectiveness of professional labour in November 2007?

7-36 Direct-materials variances, long-term agreement with supplier. Yamazaki Mazak manufactures large-scale machining systems that are sold to other industrial companies. Each machining system has a sizable direct materials cost, consisting primarily of the purchase price for a metal compound. For its Montreal, Quebec, manufacturing facility, Mazak has a long-term contract with Fuji Metals. Fuji will supply to Mazak up to 2,400 kilograms of metal per month at a fixed purchase price of $144 per kilogram for each month in 2006. For purchases above 2,400 kilograms in any month, Mazak renegotiates the price for the additional amount with Fuji Metals (or another supplier). The standard price per kilogram is $144 for each month in the January to December 2006 period.

Production data, direct materials actual usage in dollars, and direct materials actual price per kilogram for the January to May 2006 period, are

	Number of Machining Systems Produced	Total Actual Direct Materials Usage	Average Actual Direct Materials Purchase Price per Kilogram of Metal
January	10	$290,880	$144.00
February	12	343,872	144.00
March	18	530,712	151.20
April	16	474,317	153.60
May	11	304,128	144.00

The average actual direct materials purchase price is for all units purchased in that month. Assume that (a) the direct materials purchased in each month are all used in that month and (b) each machining system is started and completed in the same month.

The Montreal facility is one of three plants that Mazak operates to manufacture large-scale machining systems. The other plants are in Worcester, U.K., and Tokyo, Japan.

1. Assume that Mazak's standard materials input per machining system is 198 kilograms of metal. Compute the direct materials price variance and direct materials efficiency variance for each month of the January to May 2006 period.
2. How does the signing of a long-term agreement with a supplier—an agreement that includes a fixed-purchase-price clause—affect the interpretation of a materials price variance?

7-37 Flexible and static budgets, service company. Avanti Transportation Company executives have had trouble interpreting operating performance for several years. The company has used a budget based on detailed expectations for the forthcoming quarter. For example, the condensed performance report for a Western branch for the most recent quarter was as follows:

	Actual Result	Budget	Variance
Revenue	$11,400,000	$12,000,000	$600,000 U*
Variable costs:			
Fuel	1,183,200	1,200,000	16,800 F
Repairs and maintenance	117,600	120,000	2,400 F
Supplies and miscellaneous	235,200	240,000	4,800 F
Variable labour payroll	6,600,000	6,840,000	240,000 F
Total variable costs†	8,136,000	8,400,000	264,000 F
Fixed costs:			
Supervision	240,000	240,000	0
Rent	240,000	240,000	0
Amortization	1,920,000	1,920,000	0
Other fixed costs	240,000	240,000	0
Total fixed costs	2,640,000	2,640,000	0
Total costs	10,776,000	11,040,000	264,000 F
Operating income	$ 624,000	$ 960,000	$336,000 U

*U = unfavourable; F = favourable.

†For purposes of this analysis, assume that all these variable costs are purely variable (in relation to revenue dollars). Also assume that the prices and mix of services sold remain unchanged.

Although the branch manager was upset about the unfavourable revenue variance, he was happy that his cost performance was favourable; otherwise his operating income would have been even lower. His immediate superior, the vice-president for operations, was totally unhappy and remarked:

> I can see some merit in comparing actual performance with budgeted performance, because we can see whether actual revenue coincided with our best guess for budget purposes. But I can't see how this performance report helps us evaluate the cost control performance of the branch manager.

REQUIRED

1. Prepare a columnar flexible budget for Avanti at revenue levels of $10.8 million, $12 million, and $13.2 million. Use the format of Exhibit 7-2 (p. 246). Assume that the prices and mix of products sold are equal to the budgeted prices and mix.
2. Express the flexible budget for costs in formula form.
3. Prepare a condensed contribution format income statement showing the static-budget, sales-volume, and flexible-budget variances. Use the format of Exhibit 7-3 (p. 247).

7-38 Direct materials and manufacturing labour variances, solving unknowns. (CPA, adapted) On May 1, 2007, the Bovar Company began the manufacture of a new Internet paging device known as Dandy. The company installed a standard costing system to account for manufacturing costs. The standard costs for a unit of Dandy are as follows:

Direct materials (3 kilograms at $6 per kilogram)	$18.00
Direct manufacturing labour (0.5 hour at $24 per hour)	12.00
Manufacturing overhead (75% of direct manufacturing labour costs)	9.00
	$39.00

The following data were obtained from Bovar's records for the month of May:

	Debit	Credit
Revenues		$150,000
Accounts payable control (for May's purchases of direct materials)		81,900
Direct materials price variance	$3,900 U	
Direct materials efficiency variance	3,000 U	
Direct manufacturing labour price variance	2,280 U	
Direct manufacturing labour efficiency variance		2,400 F

Actual production in May was 4,000 units of Dandy, and actual sales in May were 2,500 units. The amount shown for direct materials price variance applies to materials purchased during May. There was no beginning inventory of materials on May 1, 2007.

REQUIRED
Compute each of the following items for Bovar for the month of May. Show your computations.
1. Standard direct manufacturing labour-hours allowed for actual output achieved
2. Actual direct manufacturing labour-hours worked
3. Actual direct manufacturing labour wage rate
4. Standard quantity of direct materials allowed (in kilograms)
5. Actual quantity of direct materials used (in kilograms)
6. Actual quantity of direct materials purchased (in kilograms)
7. Actual direct materials price per kilogram

7-39 Activity-based costing variance analysis. Toymaster, Inc., produces a special kind of plastic toy car, TGC, for various manufacturers. Toymaster produces TGC in batches. After each batch of TGC is run, the moulds are cleaned. The labour costs of cleaning the moulds can be traced directly to TGC because TGC can only be produced from a specific mould. Cleaning labour is paid on an hourly basis. The following information pertains to June 2007:

	Static-Budget Amounts	Actual Amounts
Units of TGC produced and sold	30,000	22,500
Batch size (number of units per batch)	250	225
Cleaning labour-hours per batch	3	3.5
Cleaning labour cost per hour	$16.80	$15.00

REQUIRED
1. Calculate the flexible-budget variance for total cleaning labour costs in June 2007.
2. Calculate the price and efficiency variances for total cleaning labour costs in June 2007. Comment on the results.

7-40 Activity-based costs, variance analysis. King Taste is a manufacturer of fruit cakes. One of its plants produces five different cake products. Each cake product differs in terms of material inputs (different fruits, flour, and liquor). They are identical in terms of both the cooking and the setup processes.

King Taste prefers to make long production runs of each cake product. A major benefit is that fewer changeovers are made. A changeover is the process of switching the production line from the manufacture of one product to another product. The costs of a changeover are a batch cost. They comprise the labour cost of the workers who clean the mixing equipment so that the contents of each different product are not mixed together. The following information pertains to March 2007.

	Static-Budget Amounts	Actual Amounts
Units of cakes produced and sold	240,000	330,000
Average number of cakes per production run	6,000	10,000
Changeover labour-hours per production run	20 hours	24 hours
Changeover labour cost per hour	$24	$25

1. Compute the flexible-budget variance for total changeover labour costs in March 2007. Comment on the results.
2. Compute the price and efficiency variance for total changeover labour costs in March 2007. Comment on the results.
3. Provide two explanations for each of the price and efficiency variances in requirement 2.

7-41 Benchmarking, hospital cost comparisons. Julie Leung is the newly appointed president of Provincial University. Provincial University Hospital (PUH) is a major problem for her, because it is running large deficits. While it is not-for-profit, the province will reduce funding if hospitals fail to meet their budgets. Sam Horn, the chairman of the hospital, tells Leung that he and his staff have cut costs to the bare bone. Any further cost cutting, he argues, would destroy the culture of the hospital. He also argues that the use of detailed cost studies is totally inappropriate for a medical institution because of (a) the inability to have well-defined relationships between inputs and outputs and (b) the problem of defining what a good output for a hospital is. He notes that he is "fed up with people equating continuous improvement at PUH with continued cost reduction. This is only a cost accountant's view of the world. Our top priority is to help doctors save lives and to help people recover their health."

Leung hears about a new benchmark cost analysis service offered by Market Insights. She asks Horn to hire Market Insights to provide a benchmark cost report that pertains to PUH. Horn is not enthusiastic about doing so, but he complies with her request. The report includes the following:

a. **Aggregate Hospital Cost Comparison**
(average = 1.00)

Hospital E	0.69
Hospital C	0.70
Hospital J	0.70
.	.
.	.
.	.
Hospital A	1.19
Provincial University Hospital	1.20
Hospital O	1.21

b. **Diagnostic Group Cost Comparison**

Diagnostic Group	Provincial University Hospital	Market Average	25th Percentile	Average of Best Quartile (0–25th)
Angina, chest pain	$27,600	$24,600	$20,760	$18,360
Asthma, bronchitis	18,480	15,720	12,480	10,800
Skin disorders, cellulitis	11,520	11,040	7,800	6,960
Renal failure and dialysis	9,120	6,600	5,040	4,320
Diabetes	8,040	6,120	4,440	3,720
Gastroenteritis	14,400	22,200	19,200	15,360

REQUIRED

1. Do you agree with Horn that the use of detailed cost studies at PUH is totally inappropriate? Explain your answer and comment on Horn's reasoning.
2. What inferences do you draw from the MI benchmark cost report on PUH?
3. What use might Leung make of the MI benchmark cost report?
4. What criticisms might you anticipate Horn would make of the MI benchmark cost report?
5. What factors other than cost might Leung consider in evaluating Horn's performance and that of PUH?

7-42 Comprehensive variance analysis. (CMA, adapted) Aunt Molly's Old Fashioned Cookies bakes cookies for a chain of U.K. retail stores. The company's best-selling cookie is chocolate nut supreme, which is marketed as a gourmet cookie and regularly sells for $9.60 per kilogram. The standard input cost per kilogram of chocolate nut supreme, based on Aunt Molly's normal monthly production of 400,000 kilograms, is calculated as follows:

Cost Item	Standard Quantity		Unit Costs	Total Cost
Direct materials:				
Cookie mix	625	grams	$0.384 per kg	$0.24
Milk chocolate	312.5	grams	$ 2.88 per kg	0.90
Almonds	62.5	grams	$ 9.60 per kg	0.60
1,000 g = 1 kg				$1.74
Direct labour:*				
Mixing	1 minute		$17.28 per hour	$0.288
Baking	2 minutes		21.60 per hour	0.720
				$1.008

*Direct labour rates include employee benefits.

Aunt Molly's management accountant, Karen Blair, prepares monthly budget reports based on these standard costs. Presented here is April's report, which compares budgeted and actual performance.

Performance Report
April 2007

	Budget	Actual	Variance
Units (in kilograms)*	400,000	450,000	50,000 F
Revenue	$3,840,000	$4,266,000	$426,000 F
Direct material	$ 696,000	$1,017,365	$321,365 U
Direct labour	$ 403,200	$ 453,600	$ 50,400 F

*Units produced and sold

Usage Report
April 2007

Cost Item	Quantity	Actual Cost
Direct materials:		
Cookie mix	290,000 kilograms	$111,360
Milk chocolate	161,720 kilograms	$621,005
Almonds	29,688 kilograms	$285,000
$1,017,365 total DM		
Direct labour:		
Mixing	450,000 minutes	129,600
Baking	800,000 minutes	288,000

REQUIRED

1. Compute the following variances:
   a. Selling-price variance
   b. Material-price variance
   c. Material-efficiency variance
   d. Labour-price variance
   e. Labour-efficiency variance

2. What explanations might exist for the variances in requirement 1?

7-43 Comprehensive variance analysis responsibility issues. (CMA, adapted) Horizons Unlimited manufactures a full line of well-known sunglass frames and lenses. Horizons uses a standard cost system to set attainable standards for direct materials, labour, and overhead costs. Standards have been reviewed and revised annually, as necessary. Departmental managers, whose evaluations and bonuses are affected by their department's performance, have been held responsible to explain variances in their departmental performance reports.

Recently, the manufacturing variances in the Visionaire prestige line of sunglasses have caused some concern. For no apparent reason, unfavourable material and labour variances have increased. At the monthly staff meeting, Jim Denton, manager of the Visionaire line, will be expected to explain his variances and suggest ways of improving performance. The performance report for 2007 that Denton will be asked to explain is presented below.

	Actual Results	Static Budget Amounts
Units sold	4,850	5,000
Revenues	$477,240	$480,000
Variable manufacturing costs	281,572	259,200
Fixed manufacturing costs	86,718	90,000
Gross margin	108,950	130,800

Denton collected the following information:

a. The standard variable manufacturing costs in 2007 comprise three items:

Direct materials: Frames. Static budgeted cost of $39,600. The standard input (in grams) for 2007 is 3.00 grams per unit.

Direct materials: Lenses. Static budgeted costs of $111,600. The standard input (in grams) for 2007 is 6.00 grams per unit.

Direct manufacturing labour. Static budgeted costs of $108,000. The standard input (in hours) for 2007 is 1.20 hours per unit.

Assume there are no indirect manufacturing costs.

b. The actual variable manufacturing costs in 2007 were

Direct materials: Frames. Actual costs of $44,698. Actual grams used per frame was 3.20 grams per unit.

Direct materials: Lenses. Actual costs of $120,590. Actual grams used per frame was 7.00 grams per unit.

Direct manufacturing labour. Actual costs of $116,284. The actual labour rate was $17.76 per hour.

REQUIRED

1. Prepare a manufacturing performance analysis report that includes
   a. Selling-price variance
   b. Sales-volume variance and flexible-budget variance for
      ◆ revenues
      ◆ variable manufacturing costs
      ◆ fixed manufacturing costs
      ◆ gross margin
   c. Price and efficiency variances for
      ◆ total direct materials
      ◆ direct materials: lenses
      ◆ direct manufacturing labour
2. Give three possible explanations for each of the three price and efficiency variances at Horizons in requirement 1(c).

7-44 Continuous improvement (continuation of 7-43). Horizons receives a suggestion that continuous improvement standard costs be used and updated monthly. Consider monthly revisions in 2007 for the three variable manufacturing cost items.

REQUIRED

1. Assume the data in Problem 7-43 is the December 2006 standard. The January 2007 standard is 0.995 times the December 2006 standard. The February 2007 standard is 0.995 times the January 2007 standard. Using the data from Problem 7-43, what is the standard for the direct materials usage for each variable cost item in January and February 2007?
2. What are the pros and cons of using the approach in (a) as the primary approach to drive the cost competitiveness of Horizon?

7-45 Variance analysis, solve for unknowns. Homerun Headgear manufactures and distributes baseball caps to ballparks and other sports venues. Homerun's budget for 2007 forecasts sales of 600,000 caps. However, only 500,000 caps were sold. Based on the data provided in the table below, calculate the missing numbers and complete the analysis.

Variance Analysis for Homerun Headgear for 2007, Incomplete

	Actual Results (1)	Flexible-Budget Variances (2) = (1) − (3)	Flexible Budget (3)	Sales-Volume Variances (4) = (3) − (5)	Static Budget (5)
Units sold	500,000				600,000
Revenues (sales)	$6,000,000				$5,760,000
Variable costs	1,680,000				2,160,000
Contribution margin		1,320,000 F		600,000 U	
Fixed costs	1,380,000		1,200,000		1,200,000
Operating income					

Total flexible-budget variance   Total sales-volume variance

Total static-budget variance

REQUIRED

1. Calculate the budgeted and actual unit sales price.
2. Assuming that the driver for variable costs is units sold, what are the budgeted and actual variable costs per unit?
3. What is Homerun's 2007 flexible-budget operating income?
4. What is the total flexible-budget variance?
5. What is the total sales-volume variance?
6. What is the total static-budget variance?

7-46 Procurement costs, variance analysis, ethics. Rashid Daley is the manager of the athletic shoe division of Raider Products. Raider is a European-based company that has just purchased Fastfoot, a leading European shoe company. Fastfoot has long-term production contracts with suppliers in two East European countries, Hergovia and Tanistan. Daley receives a request from Kevin Neal, president of Raider Products. Daley and his controller, Brooke Mullins, are to make a presentation to the next board of directors' meeting on the cost competitiveness of its Fastfoot subsidiary. This should include budgeted and actual procurement costs for 2007 at its Hergovia and Tanistan supply sources.

Mullins decides to visit the two supply operations. The budgeted average procurement cost for 2007 was $14 per pair of shoes. This includes payments to the shoe manufacturer and all other payments to conduct business in each country. Mullins reports the following to Daley:

◆ **Hergovia.** Total 2007 procurement costs for 250,000 pairs of shoes were $3,900,000. Payment to the shoe manufacturer was $3,108,000. Very few receipts exist for the remaining $792,000. Kickback payments are viewed as common in Hergovia.

◆ **Tanistan.** Total 2007 procurement costs for 900,000 pairs of shoes were $12,300,000. Payment to the shoe manufacturer was $10,136,000. Receipts exist for $827,000 of the other costs, but Mullins is skeptical of their validity. Kickback payments are a "way of business" in Tanistan.

At both the Hergovia and Tanistan plants, Mullins is disturbed by the employment of young children (many of them under 15 years). She is told that all major shoe-producing companies have similar low-cost employment practices in both countries.

Daley is uncomfortable about the upcoming presentation to the board of directors. He was a leading advocate of the acquisition. A recent business magazine reported that the Fastfoot acquisition would make Raider Products the global low-cost producer in its market lines. The stock price of Raider Products jumped 21% the day the Fastfoot acquisition was announced. Mullins likewise is widely identified as a proponent of the acquisition. She is seen as a rising star due for promotion to a division management post in the near future.

1. What summary procurement cost variances could be reported to the board of directors of Raider Shoes?
2. What ethical issues do (a) Daley and (b) Mullins face when preparing and making a report to the board of directors?
3. How should Mullins address the issues you identify in requirement 2?

7-47 Comprehensive variance analysis review. FlexMem, Inc., manufactures 120 Mb diskettes that are compatible with a popular portable storage device. FlexMem sells diskettes wholesale to computer retail chains and direct marketing organizations that resell the diskettes as a house brand. The diskettes retail for an average of $9.60 per unit, and compete with well-known brands that retail for between $12.00 and $14.40 per diskette.

FlexMem's CFO has provided you with the following budgeted standards for the month of February 2007:

Budgeted average wholesale selling price per unit	$	4.80
Total direct material standard cost per diskette	$	1.02
Direct manufacturing labour		
Direct manufacturing labour standard cost per hour	$	18.00
Average labour productivity rate (diskettes per hour)		300
Direct marketing cost per unit	$	0.36
Total fixed overhead	$1,080,000	

The VP of Marketing forecasts sales of 1,500,000 units for the month.

On March 7, the VP of Planning and Control meets with the executive committee to discuss February results. He reports as follows:

◆ Unit sales totalled 80% of plan. (1,200,000 units)
◆ Actual average selling price declined to $4.44.
◆ Productivity dropped to 250 diskettes/hour; however, because of favourable market conditions, the actual price per unit dropped to $0.96.
◆ Fixed costs came in $36,000 below plan.
◆ All other costs were incurred at their standard rates.

REQUIRED

As the senior financial analyst, you are asked to calculate the following:

1. Static-budget and actual operating income
2. Total static-budget variance
3. Flexible-budget operating income
4. Total flexible-budget variance
5. Total sales-volume variance
6. Price and efficiency variances
7. What is the material-price variance? labour-price variance?
8. What is the material-efficiency variance? labour-efficiency variance?

COLLABORATIVE LEARNING PROBLEM

7-48 Price and efficiency variances, problems in standard-setting, benchmarking. NorthWest Fashions manufactures shirts for retail chains. Jorge Rivera, the controller, is becoming increasingly disenchanted with NorthWest's six-month-old standard costing system. The budgeted amounts for both its direct materials and direct manufacturing labour are drawn from its standard costing system. The budgeted and actual amounts for July 2007 were

	Budgeted	Actual
Shirts manufactured	4,000	4,488
Direct materials cost	$24,000	$24,235
Direct materials units used (rolls of cloth)	400	408
Direct manufacturing labour costs	$21,600	$22,154
Direct manufacturing labour-hours	1,000	1,020

There was no beginning or ending inventory of materials.

Rivera observes that in the past six months he has rarely seen an unfavourable variance of any magnitude. The standard costing system is based on a study of the operations conducted by an independent consultant. Rivera decides to play detective and makes some unobtrusive observations of the workforce at the plant. He notes that, even at their current output levels, the workers seem to have a lot of time to discuss baseball, sitcoms, and the local hot fishing spots.

At a recent industry conference on "Benchmarking and Competitiveness," Mary Blanchard, the controller of Winston Fabrics, told Rivera that Winston had employed the same independent consultant to design a standard costing system. However, the company dismissed him after two weeks, because Winston employees quickly became aware of the consultant observing their work.

At the industry conference, Rivera participated in seminars on "benchmarking for the fabric industry." A consultant for the Benchmarking Clearing House showed how she could develop six-month benchmark reports on the estimated costs of NorthWest's major competitors. She indicated that she was already examining the estimated cost of shirts manufactured by the four largest importers into Canada. These importers had taken much business from NorthWest in recent years. This information would soon be available by subscribing to the Benchmarking Clearing House monthly service.

INSTRUCTIONS
Form groups of two or more students to complete the following requirements.

REQUIRED
1. Compute the price and efficiency variances of NorthWest Fashions for direct materials and direct manufacturing labour in July 2007.
2. Describe the types of actions the employees at Winston Fabrics may have taken to reduce the accuracy of the standards set by the independent consultant. Why would employees take those actions? Is this behaviour ethical?
3. Describe how NorthWest might use information from the Benchmarking Clearing House when computing the variances in requirement 1.
4. Discuss the pros and cons of NorthWest using the Benchmarking Clearing House information to increase its cost-competitiveness.

In mature industries, the need to be cost competitive is very significant. For organizations where substantial portions of their costs are in overheads, it is especially important to monitor costs and their impact on budgeted versus actual production.

Inco in Sudbury, Ontario, must manage its costs within an industry that is heavily influenced by world demand and supply for nickel. Changes in production volumes have an impact on the costs of nickel mined and therefore the profitability of Inco's operations.

CHAPTER **8**

Flexible Budgets, Variances, and Management Control: II

Overhead or indirect costs are a major cost area for many organizations. Chemical, paper, steel, and telecommunications companies, for example, incur sizable costs to construct and maintain their physical plant and equipment and other aspects of their infrastructure. For service companies such as airlines, up to 50% of their total costs are indirect, passenger-related costs such as ticketing, security, and landing fees. Indirect costs are allocated to the individual products or services companies produce and sell. This chapter presents methods to plan and control overhead costs, to analyze overhead variances, and to allocate these indirect costs to products.

Please proceed slowly as you study this chapter. Trace each level of analysis by systematically referring to the specific data provided in examples. In particular, note how fixed manufacturing overhead is accounted for in one way for the purpose of planning and control but in a different way for the purpose of inventory costing.

LEARNING OBJECTIVES

After studying this chapter, you should be able to

1. Explain the similarities and differences in planning both variable overhead costs and fixed overhead costs

2. Identify and understand the features of a standard-costing system

3. Contrast static (Level 1) and flexible budget (Level 2) approaches when analyzing overhead variable cost variance

4. Calculate, analyze, and explain the sources of flexible budget variance (Level 3), which consist of the variable overhead efficiency variance and the variable overhead spending variance

5. Calculate the budgeted fixed overhead rate and fixed overhead cost variance; explain the source of variance

6. Explain why the production-volume variance may not be a good measure of the economic cost of unused capacity

7. Explain how variance analysis can provide an integrated overview of overhead-cost variances

8. Illustrate how the flexible-budget variance approach can be used in activity-based costing

PLANNING THE VARIABLE AND FIXED OVERHEAD COSTS

A Primer on Job Costing—
Walker Mowers
www.walkermowers.com/
index.htm1?section=walkertalk10

It is not unusual for more than 50% of a company's total product costs throughout the value chain to be classified as overhead. Increased automation, more-complex production and distribution processes, and product proliferation increase overhead costs.

Value-added cost. A cost that, if eliminated, would reduce the value customers obtain from using the product or service.

Non-value-added cost. A cost that, if eliminated, would not reduce the value customers obtain from using the product or service.

The two ways of managing variable overhead costs are (1) eliminate non-value-added costs (for example, consume less electricity by using more energy-efficient equipment) and (2) reduce consumption of the cost-allocation bases (for example, redesign products to require fewer machine-hours of processing time).

We continue the analysis of Webb Company begun in Chapter 7, which illustrated how a static-budget variance can be divided into a flexible-budget variance and a sales-volume variance. This chapter focuses on understanding flexible-budget variances for overhead costs and their causes.

Webb's cost structure illustrates why planning of overhead costs is important. The following percentages of total static-budget costs (see column 4 of Exhibit 7-2, p. 246) are based on Webb's budget for 12,000 output units for April 2007:

	Variable Overhead Costs	Fixed Overhead Costs	Total Overhead Costs
Manufacturing[1]	7.59%	14.54%	22.13%
Marketing	3.16	22.87	26.03
Total	10.75%	37.41%	48.16%

Total overhead costs amount to almost half (48.16%) of Webb's total budgeted costs at 12,000 output units for April 2007. Clearly, Webb would greatly improve its profitability through more effective planning of both variable and fixed overhead costs.

Planning Variable Overhead Costs

Among Webb's variable manufacturing overhead costs are energy, machine maintenance, engineering support, indirect materials, and indirect manufacturing labour. Effective planning of variable overhead costs involves reducing or eliminating activities that fail to add value to a product or service. Webb must focus on undertaking only value-added variable overhead activities and then managing the cost drivers of those activities in the most efficient way. A **value-added cost** is one that, if eliminated, would reduce the value customers obtain from using the product or service. For example, Webb's customers expect the jackets to last; therefore, managers consider sewing an essential value-added activity, and the costs of supplies such as sewing needles and maintenance of the sewing machines are considered value-added overhead costs. A **non-value-added cost** is one that, if eliminated, would not reduce the value customers obtain from using the product or service. For example, to offset problems that arise if suppliers fail to meet their delivery schedule, Webb also undertakes the activity of storing rolls of cloth in its warehouse. To the customer, a jacket sewn from cloth stored in a warehouse is no different from a jacket sewn from cloth delivered by a supplier directly to the production floor. Therefore, the activity of storing cloth is non-value-added for the customer, and managers view the costs associated with warehousing as non-value-added costs. There is a continuum between value-added costs and non-value-added costs. Many overhead cost items are in a grey, uncertain area between value-adding and non-value-adding costs.

Planning Fixed Overhead Costs

Effective planning of fixed overhead costs includes undertaking only value-added fixed overhead activities and then determining the appropriate level for those activities. Webb examples in manufacturing include either amortization on assets owned by the company or leasing costs on plant and equipment, some administrative costs (for example, the plant manager's salary), and property taxes. Frequently, the most critical issue is how much plant and equipment to acquire. Consider Webb's leasing

---

[1]Manufacturing variable overhead as a percentage of total costs is $144,000 ÷ $1,898,000 = 7.59% and manufacturing fixed overhead is $276,000 ÷ 1,898,000 = 14.54%. Total manufacturing overhead is $420,000 ÷ $1,898,000 = 22.13%. Similar calculations will result in the percentages shown for marketing overhead costs. The total variable marketing and manufacturing overhead costs as a percentage of total costs is ($144,000 + $60,000) ÷ $1,898,000 = 10.75% and similar calculations can be made for the fixed manufacturing and marketing overhead as a percentage of total costs.

of sewing machines, each of which has a fixed cost per year. Failure to lease sufficient machine capacity will result in an inability to meet demand and thus in lost sales of jackets. In contrast, if Webb greatly overestimates demand, it will lease too many machines and incur additional fixed leasing costs on machines that are not fully utilized during the year. At the start of a budget period, management will have made most of the decisions that determine the level of fixed overhead costs to be incurred. But, it's the day-to-day, ongoing operating decisions that primarily determine the level of variable overhead costs incurred in that period.

> The two ways of managing fixed overhead costs are (1) eliminate non-value-added costs (for example, arrange to have vendors deliver direct materials to the production floor just when needed, to enable termination of a warehouse lease) and (2) plan for appropriate capacity levels.

STANDARD COSTING AT WEBB COMPANY

Webb uses standard costing. The development of standards for Webb's direct-cost categories was described in Chapter 7. This chapter discusses Webb's indirect-cost categories. Standard costing is a costing method that (a) traces direct costs to output produced by multiplying the standard prices or rates by the standard quantities of inputs allowed for actual outputs produced and (b) allocates indirect costs on the basis of the standard indirect rates multiplied by the standard quantities of the allocation bases allowed for the actual outputs produced.

With a standard-costing system, the standard costs of every product or service budgeted as output during the period can be computed at the start of that period. This feature of standard costing makes the recording system a simple one. To calculate the cost of products or services, no record needs to be kept of the actual costs of items used nor of the actual quantities of the cost-allocation bases used on individual products or services worked on during the period. In addition to the standard direct costs, what is required is the standard indirect cost rates for variable and fixed overhead. This can be calculated because the standard quantities in the allocation bases are known and the total fixed and total variable costs have been budgeted. Once standards have been set, the costs of operating a standard-costing system can be low relative to the costs of operating an actual or a normal-costing system.

The Webb Company summary information for April 2007 that we will use in this chapter is as follows:

Overhead Category	Actual Results	Flexible Budget Amount (for 10,000 Output Units)	Static Budget Amount (for 12,000 Output Units)
Variable manufacturing overhead	$130,500	$120,000	$144,000
Fixed manufacturing overhead	285,000	276,000	276,000
Variable marketing overhead	45,700	50,000	60,000
Fixed marketing overhead	420,000	434,000	434,000

DEVELOPING BUDGETED VARIABLE OVERHEAD RATES

Webb uses a four-step approach when developing its variable overhead rate:

◆ **Step 1:** *Choose the period to be used for the budget.* Webb uses a 12-month budget period to smooth seasonal effect on activities.

◆ **Step 2:** *Select the cost-allocation base(s) used to allocate variable overhead costs to the output produced.* Webb's operating managers believe that machine-hours are an important driver of variable manufacturing overhead costs. On the basis of an engineering study, Webb estimated it will take 0.40 of a machine-hour per actual unit of output and budgets 57,600 machine-hours to produce the budgeted output of 144,000 jackets in 2007 and decided to use this measure as the cost-allocation base (see the Focus on Values and Behaviours feature on p. 296 for a discussion on the challenges facing managers when they select a cost allocation base).

◆ **Step 3:** *Identify the variable overhead costs associated with each cost-allocation base to produce variable overhead cost pools.* Webb groups all its variable overhead costs (e.g., energy, machine maintenance, engineering support, indirect materials, and indirect manufacturing labour) in one cost pool. Webb's total budgeted variable manufacturing overhead costs for 2007 are $1,728,000.[2]

◆ **Step 4:** *Estimate the budgeted variable overhead rate per unit.* This per unit rate will be used to allocate variable overhead costs to the total output produced. Dividing the total variable manufacturing overhead costs of $1,728,000 by the total budgeted machine hours of 57,600 gives the estimated rate of $30 per standard machine hour to allocate these costs. Webb has also budgeted 0.40 machine hours per jacket which when multiplied by the standard rate gives $12 per jacket as the budgeted variable overhead cost rate per unit of output. This budgeted variable overhead cost rate will be used both in the static budget for 2007 and the monthly performance reports prepared during 2007.

$$\begin{array}{c}\text{Budgeted inputs allowed} \\ \text{per output unit}\end{array} \times \begin{array}{c}\text{Budgeted costs} \\ \text{per input unit}\end{array} = 0.40 \times \$30$$

$$= \$12 \text{ per output unit}$$

A different approach is to adjust the past actual variable overhead cost rate per unit of the allocation base to adjust for expected inflation, for example.

VARIABLE OVERHEAD COST VARIANCES

We now illustrate how the budgeted variable manufacturing overhead rate is used in computing Webb's variable manufacturing overhead cost variances. The following data are for April 2007:

Cost Item/Allocation Base	Actual Results	Flexible Budget Amount (for 10,000 Output Units)	Static Budget Amount (for 12,000 Output Units)
1. Variable manufacturing overhead costs	$130,500	$120,000	$144,000
2. Variable manufacturing overhead costs per machine-hour (1 ÷ 5)	$ 29	$ 30	$ 30
3. Variable manufacturing overhead costs per output unit (1 ÷ 4)	$ 13.05	$ 12	$ 12
4. Output units (jackets)	10,000	10,000	12,000
5. Machine-hours	4,500	4,000	4,800

Static Budget and Flexible Budget Analyses

The Level 1 static-budget variance for variable manufacturing overhead cost is shown in Exhibit 8-1:

$$\begin{array}{c}\text{Variable overhead} \\ \text{static budget variance}\end{array} = \begin{array}{c}\text{Actual} \\ \text{results}\end{array} - \begin{array}{c}\text{Static budget} \\ \text{amount}\end{array}$$

$$= \$130,500 - \$144,000$$

$$= \$13,500 \text{ F}$$

As you learned from Chapter 7, however, a flexible-budget analysis enables Webb to focus attention on understanding the differences between actual costs and actual quantities in contrast to budgeted costs and budgeted quantities for an actual output level of 10,000 jackets.

Additional insight into the ability of Webb's managers to control variable manufacturing overhead can be gained by moving to the Level 2 flexible budget analysis, also shown in Exhibit 8-1. The budgeted amounts in Level 2 recognize that 10,000 output units were produced instead of the budgeted 12,000 output units. The April 2007 flexible budget for variable manufacturing overhead is $120,000 (0.4 × 10,000 × $30).

---

[2]The budgeted variable manufacturing overhead per 10,000 jackets is $120,000 and the budgeted output is 144,000 jackets. Therefore, the budgeted amount is 144,000 ÷ 10,000 × $120,000 = $1,728,000.

EXHIBIT 8-1
Static and Flexible Budget Analysis of Variable Manufacturing Overhead Costs for the Webb Company for April 2007

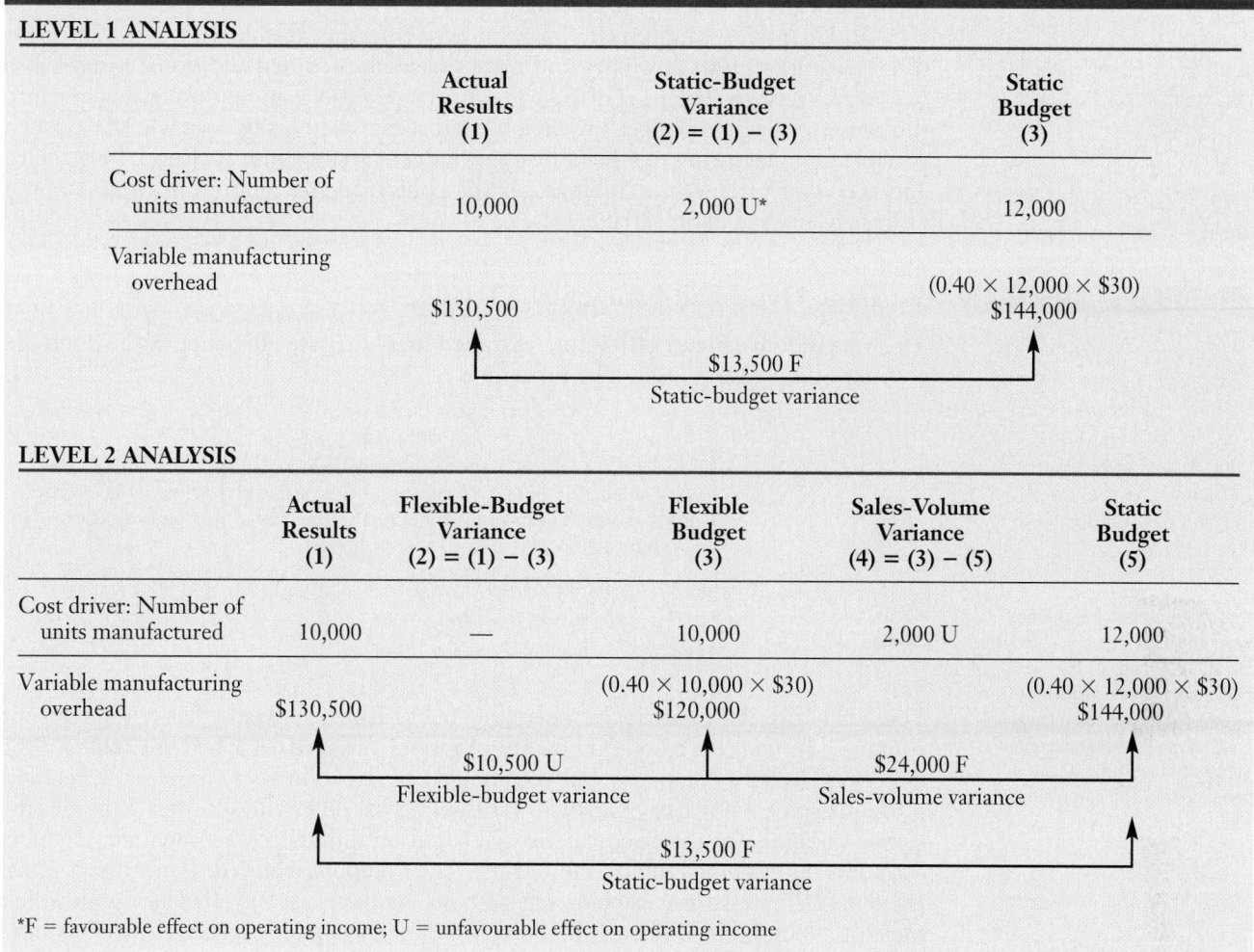

LEVEL 1 ANALYSIS

	Actual Results (1)	Static-Budget Variance (2) = (1) − (3)	Static Budget (3)
Cost driver: Number of units manufactured	10,000	2,000 U*	12,000
Variable manufacturing overhead	$130,500		(0.40 × 12,000 × $30) $144,000

$13,500 F
Static-budget variance

LEVEL 2 ANALYSIS

	Actual Results (1)	Flexible-Budget Variance (2) = (1) − (3)	Flexible Budget (3)	Sales-Volume Variance (4) = (3) − (5)	Static Budget (5)
Cost driver: Number of units manufactured	10,000	—	10,000	2,000 U	12,000
Variable manufacturing overhead	$130,500		(0.40 × 10,000 × $30) $120,000		(0.40 × 12,000 × $30) $144,000

$10,500 U
Flexible-budget variance

$24,000 F
Sales-volume variance

$13,500 F
Static-budget variance

*F = favourable effect on operating income; U = unfavourable effect on operating income

The variable manufacturing overhead sales volume variance arises solely because the actual number of output units sold by Webb differs from the budgeted number of output units sold.

In this chapter, we again use a columnar solution format as a helpful and intuitive approach to compute variances. Examples include Exhibits 8-1, 8-2, 8-3, 8-5 and 8-6.

$$\text{Variable overhead sales volume variance} = \text{Flexible-budget amount} - \text{Static-budget amount}$$
$$= \$120,000 - \$144,000$$
$$= \$24,000 \text{ F}$$

The variable manufacturing overhead flexible-budget variance arises because Webb's actual variable manufacturing overhead cost differs from that budgeted for the actual output units sold:

$$\text{Variable overhead flexible-budget variance} = \text{Actual results} - \text{Flexible-budget amount}$$
$$= \$130,500 - \$120,000$$
$$= \$10,500 \text{ U}$$

This $10,500 unfavourable flexible-budget variance shows that Webb's actual variable manufacturing overhead exceeded the flexible-budget amount by $10,500 for the 10,000 jackets actually produced in April 2007. While this can focus attention on what happened, Webb's managers will want to explain why the variance arose to help them solve any production problems.

In Chapter 7 we illustrated how subdividing the flexible-budget variance for direct-cost items into efficiency and price variances provided additional insight into causes of variance. We now discuss how managers can gain additional insight into the causes of flexible budget variance for indirect cost items by splitting the Level 2 variable manufacturing overhead flexible-budget variance into its Level 3 efficiency and spending variances. Exhibit 8-2 is the columnar presentation of these Level 3 efficiency and spending variances.

Variable Overhead Efficiency Variance

The **variable overhead efficiency variance** measures the efficiency with which the cost allocation base is used. The formula is

$$\begin{pmatrix} \text{Variable overhead} \\ \text{efficiency variance} \end{pmatrix} = \begin{pmatrix} \text{Actual units of} \\ \text{variable overhead} \\ \text{cost-allocation base} \\ \text{used for actual output} \\ \text{units achieved} \end{pmatrix} - \begin{pmatrix} \text{Budgeted units of} \\ \text{variable overhead cost-} \\ \text{allocation base allowed} \\ \text{for actual output units} \\ \text{achieved} \end{pmatrix} \times \begin{pmatrix} \text{Budgeted} \\ \text{variable overhead} \\ \text{cost-allocation rate} \end{pmatrix}$$

$$= [4,500 - (10,000 \times 0.40)] \times \$30$$
$$= (4,500 - 4,000) \times \$30 = 500 \times \$30$$
$$= 15,000 \text{ U}$$

You will notice the similarity between how the variable overhead efficiency variance is computed for indirect costs and how the efficiency variance described in Chapter 7 for direct-cost items is computed. But you should pay attention because the interpretation of the Chapter 7 efficiency variances for direct costs differs. In Chapter 7, input efficiency variances for direct-cost items are based on differences between actual inputs used and the budgeted inputs allowed for actual outputs achieved. For indirect costs, efficiency variances for variable overhead costs are based on the efficiency with which the cost-allocation base is used. Webb's unfavourable variable overhead efficiency variance of $15,000 means that actual machine-hours (the cost-allocation base) were higher than the budgeted machine-hours allowed to manufacture 10,000 jackets. Possible

EXHIBIT 8-2
Columnar Presentation of Variance Analysis: Variable Manufacturing Overhead for the Webb Company

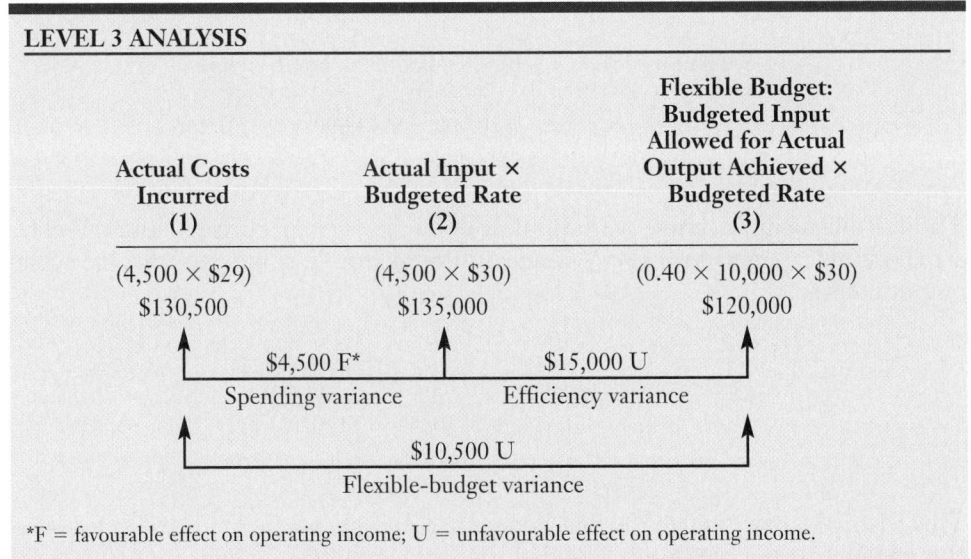

LEVEL 3 ANALYSIS		
Actual Costs Incurred (1)	Actual Input × Budgeted Rate (2)	Flexible Budget: Budgeted Input Allowed for Actual Output Achieved × Budgeted Rate (3)
(4,500 × $29)	(4,500 × $30)	(0.40 × 10,000 × $30)
$130,500	$135,000	$120,000

$4,500 F* Spending variance $15,000 U Efficiency variance

$10,500 U Flexible-budget variance

*F = favourable effect on operating income; U = unfavourable effect on operating income.

causes and management responses to this higher-than-budgeted machine-hour usage include the following:

Possible Causes for Exceeding Budget	Potential Management Responses
1. Workers were less skilled than expected in using machines.	1. Encourage the human resources function to implement better employee-hiring practices and training procedures.
2. Production scheduler inefficiently scheduled jobs, resulting in more machine-hours than budgeted.	2. Improve plant operations by installing production scheduling software.
3. Machines were not maintained in good operating condition.	3. Ensure preventive maintenance is done on all machines.
4. Webb's sales staff promised a distributor a rush delivery, which resulted in more machine-hours used than budgeted.	4. Coordinate production schedules with sales staff and distributors and share information with them.
5. Budgeted machine time standards were set too tight.	5. Commit more resources to develop appropriate standards.

Management's response to this $15,000 unfavourable variance would be guided by which cause(s) best describe(s) the April 2007 results.

The use of cotton thread for sewing jackets illustrates the difference between the efficiency variance for direct-cost inputs and the efficiency variance for variable overhead cost categories. If Webb classifies cotton thread as a direct-cost item, the direct materials efficiency variance will indicate whether more or less cotton thread per jacket is used than was budgeted for the actual output achieved. In contrast, if Webb classifies cotton thread as an indirect-cost item, the variable manufacturing overhead efficiency variance will indicate whether Webb used more or fewer machine-hours (the cost-allocation base for variable manufacturing overhead) than were budgeted for the actual output achieved. Any variation in cotton thread usage other than that budgeted to vary with respect to machine-hours will be shown in the variable manufacturing overhead spending variance.

Let us assume that Webb's managers discovered one reason the machines operated below budgeted efficiency levels in April 2007 was because insufficient maintenance was performed in the prior two months. A former plant manager delayed maintenance in a presumed attempt to meet monthly budget cost targets. As we discussed in Chapter 6, managers should not be focused on meeting short-run budget targets, if it is likely to result in harmful long-run consequences. Webb has since strengthened its internal maintenance procedures so that failure to do monthly maintenance as completely as needed raises a "red flag" that must be immediately explained to management. Underskilled workers were another reason for actual machine-hours exceeding budgeted machine-hours. As a result, Webb initiated steps to improve hiring and training practices.

Variable Overhead Spending Variance

The **variable overhead spending variance** is the difference between actual variable overhead cost per unit of the cost-allocation base and budgeted variable overhead cost per unit of the cost-allocation base, multiplied by actual quantity of variable overhead cost-allocation base used for actual output.

The formula for the variable overhead spending variance is

$$
\begin{aligned}
\text{Variable overhead} \atop \text{spending variance} &= \left(\begin{array}{c} \text{Actual variable} \\ \text{overhead cost} \\ \text{per unit of cost-} \\ \text{allocation base} \end{array} - \begin{array}{c} \text{Budgeted variable} \\ \text{overhead cost per} \\ \text{unit of cost-} \\ \text{allocation base} \end{array} \right) \times \begin{array}{c} \text{Actual quantity of variable} \\ \text{overhead cost-allocation} \\ \text{base used for actual output} \\ \text{units achieved} \end{array} \\
&= (\$29 - \$30) \times 4{,}500 \\
&= -\$1 \times 4{,}500 = \$4{,}500 \text{ F}
\end{aligned}
$$

Variable overhead spending variance. The difference between the actual variable overhead cost per unit of the cost allocation base and budgeted variable overhead cost per unit of the cost-allocation base multiplied by the actual quantity of the variable overhead allocation base used for the actual output units achieved.

Webb operated in April 2007 with a lower-than-budgeted variable overhead cost per machine-hour. Hence, there is a favourable variable overhead spending variance.

The variable overhead spending variance is computed similarly to the price variance described in Chapter 7 for direct-cost items such as direct materials. Do not assume, however, that the causes of these two variances are the same. Webb's managers now want to explain why the actual variable overhead cost per unit of the cost allocation base is lower than the budgeted variable overhead cost per unit of the cost-allocation base. Two main causes could explain a variable overhead spending variance of $4,500 F at Webb:

◆ **Cause A.** The actual prices of individual items included in variable overhead differ from their budgeted prices—for example, the April 2007 purchase prices of energy, indirect materials, or indirect manufacturing labour were less than the budget prices. The price effects could be the result of skillful negotiation on the part of the purchasing manager, oversupply in the market, or lower quality of inputs such as indirect materials. Webb's response would depend on what was discovered to be the cause of the variance. For example, if the concerns are about quality, Webb would seek to put in place new quality management systems.

◆ **Cause B.** The actual usage of individual items included in variable overhead differs from the budgeted usage—for example, the budgeted usage of energy, indirect materials, or indirect manufacturing labour was less than the usage assumed in setting the $30 budgeted variable manufacturing overhead rate per machine-hour. Webb's managers would want to understand the possible causes for the efficiency with which variable overhead costs are used. These causes include skill levels of workers, maintenance of machines, and the efficiency of the manufacturing process. Let us assume Webb's managers discovered that Webb used fewer supervision resources per machine-hour because of manufacturing process improvements, and then they would begin organizing cross-functional teams to see if more process improvements could be achieved.

Cause A has implications for the purchasing area of Webb. Cause B has implications for the production area of Webb. Distinguishing between these two causes for a variable overhead spending variance requires detailed information about the budgeted prices and the budgeted quantities of the individual line items in the variable overhead cost pool.

Below is a summary of the variable manufacturing overhead variances computed in this section:

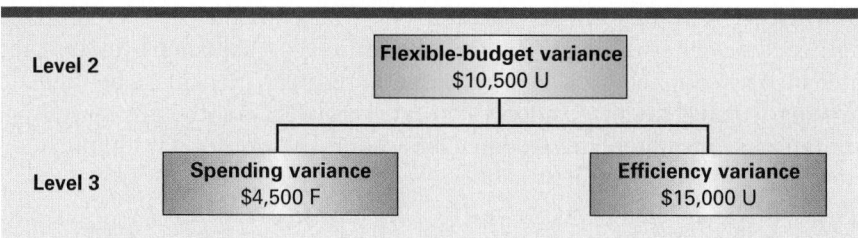

The key cause of Webb's unfavourable flexible budget variance is that the actual use of machine-hours is higher than budgeted.

DEVELOPING BUDGETED FIXED OVERHEAD RATES

Fixed overhead costs are, by definition, a lump sum that does not change in total despite changes in a cost driver. Although total fixed costs are usually included in flexible budgets, they remain the same total amount within the relevant range regardless of the output level chosen to "flex" the variable costs and revenues. The five steps in developing Webb Company's budgeted fixed overhead rate are as follows:

◆ **Step 1:** *Choose the time period used to compute the budget.* As with variable overhead rates, the budget period is typically 12 months. Chapter 4 provides three reasons for using annual overhead rates rather than, say, monthly rates: reducing the influence of seasonality, reducing the effect of the varying number of days in a month, and preventing management time from being tied up in monthly budget rate setting.

◆ **Step 2:** *Select the cost-allocation base to use in allocating fixed overhead costs to output produced.* Webb uses machine-hours as the only cost-allocation base for fixed manufacturing overhead costs. Why? Because Webb's managers believe that, in the long run, fixed manufacturing overhead costs will increase or decrease to the levels needed to support the number of machine-hours. Therefore, in the long run, the number of machine-hours is the only cost driver of fixed manufacturing overhead costs. The number of machine-hours is the denominator in the budgeted fixed overhead rate computation and is called the **denominator level**. In manufacturing settings, the denominator level is called, more specifically, the **production denominator level** or **production denominator volume**. For simplicity, we assume Webb expects to operate at capacity in fiscal year 2007— with a budgeted amount of 57,600 machine-hours for a budgeted output of 144,000 jackets.[3]

> **Denominator level (production denominator level, production denominator volume).** Quantity of the allocation base used to allocate fixed overhead costs to a cost object.

◆ **Step 3:** *Identify the costs in the fixed overhead cost pool(s).* This is the numerator of the budgeted rate computation. For Webb, fixed manufacturing overhead costs include amortization, plant leasing costs, property taxes, plant manager's salary, and some administrative costs, all of which are included in a single cost pool. Webb's budget is $276,000 for April 2007.

◆ **Step 4:** *Estimate the budgeted quantity of the allocation base(s).* This is the denominator of the budgeted rate computation. It is termed the denominator level. Webb uses machine-hours as its allocation base. It budgets to manufacture 12,000 jackets in April 2007. The budgeted machine-hours to manufacture 12,000 jackets is 4,800 (12,000 × 0.40 budgeted machine-hours per output unit).

◆ **Step 5:** *Compute the budgeted fixed overhead rate(s).*

$$\begin{aligned}\text{Budgeted fixed overhead rate} \atop \text{per unit of allocation base} &= \frac{\text{Budgeted fixed overhead costs}}{\text{Budgeted quantity of allocation base units}} \\ &= \$276{,}000 \div 4{,}800 \text{ machine-hours} \\ &= \$57.50 \text{ per machine-hour}\end{aligned}$$

FIXED OVERHEAD COST VARIANCES

The Level 1 static-budget variance for Webb's fixed manufacturing overhead is $9,000 U:

$$\begin{aligned}\text{Fixed overhead} \atop \text{static-budget variance} &= \text{Actual results} - \text{Static-budget amount} \\ &= \$285{,}000 - \$276{,}000 \\ &= \$9{,}000 \text{ U}\end{aligned}$$

> The flexible-budget variance for fixed manufacturing overhead (FMOH) is not subdivided into separate price and efficiency variances.
> The $9,000 unfavourable flexible-budget variance for FMOH arose because Webb incurred more FMOH costs than the lump-sum amount budgeted. That's why it's called a spending variance.

The actual results for fixed manufacturing overhead are shown in Exhibit 7-2 (p. 246). The static budget amount for fixed manufacturing overhead is based on 12,000 output units. Given that it is for a fixed cost, this same $276,000 would be the budgeted amount for all output levels in the relevant range. There is no "flexing" of fixed costs.

[3]Because Webb plans its capacity over multiple periods, anticipated demand in 2007 is less than capacity. Companies vary in the denominator levels they choose; some may choose budgeted output and others may choose capacity. In either case, the basic approach and analysis presented in this chapter is unchanged. Chapter 9 discusses choosing a denominator level and its implications in more detail.

The fixed overhead flexible-budget variance is the same as the fixed overhead static-budget variance. Why? Because there is no "flexing" of fixed costs. For Level 3 analysis (decomposing the flexible-budget variance into its efficiency and spending components), the total flexible-budget variance is attributed to spending variance because this is the only cause for this variance in fixed costs.

The $9,000 unfavourable variance simply means that Webb spent more on fixed manufacturing overhead in April 2007 than it budgeted, and the result will be a decrease in this month's gross margin of $9,000. Reasons for the unfavourable spending variance could be higher plant-leasing costs, higher amortization on plant and equipment, and higher administrative costs such as a higher than budgeted salary paid to the plant manager. Let us assume Webb investigated this variance and found that there was a $9,000 per month unexpected increase in its equipment leasing costs. However, management concluded that the new lease rates were competitive with lease rates available elsewhere. If this were not the case, management would look to lease equipment from other suppliers.

A summary of the Levels 1, 2, and 3 variance analyses for Webb's fixed manufacturing overhead in April 2007 is shown here.

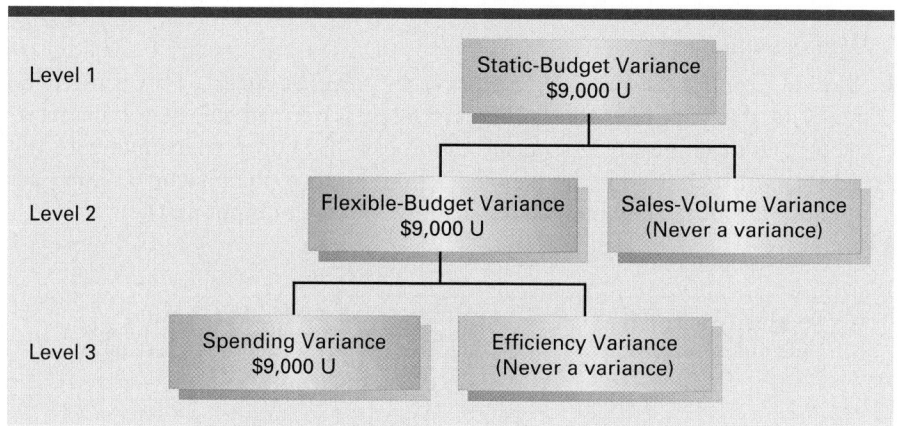

There is never a sales-volume variance in Level 2 for fixed overhead costs. Why? Because budgeted fixed costs are, by definition, unaffected by sales-volume changes. Similarly, there is never an efficiency variance in Level 3 for fixed overhead costs because within the relevant range, differences in output levels do not affect fixed costs. Managers cannot be more or less efficient in dealing with a specified amount of fixed costs (see the Global Surveys of Company Practice box on p. 299).

PRODUCTION-VOLUME VARIANCE

Production-volume variance (denominator-level variance, output-level overhead variance). Difference between budgeted fixed overhead and the fixed overhead allocated. Fixed overhead is allocated based on the budgeted fixed overhead rate times the budgeted quantity of the fixed overhead allocation base for the actual output units achieved.

The variances discussed so far in this chapter are presented in Exhibit 8-3: Panel A for variable costs and the first three columns of panel B for fixed costs. We now discuss a new variance for fixed overhead costs (shown on the right-hand side of Exhibit 8-3, Panel B). The **production-volume variance** is the difference between budgeted fixed overhead and the fixed overhead allocated. Fixed overhead is allocated based on the fixed overhead rate times the quantity of the fixed overhead allocation base for the actual output units achieved. Other terms for this variance include **denominator-level variance** and **output-level overhead variance.**

The formula for the production volume variance, expressed in terms of allocation base units (machine-hours for Webb), is

$$\begin{array}{c} \text{Production-volume} \\ \text{variance} \end{array} = \begin{array}{c} \text{Budgeted} \\ \text{fixed} \\ \text{overhead} \end{array} - \left(\begin{array}{c} \text{Fixed overhead allocated using} \\ \text{budgeted input allowed for} \\ \text{actual output units achieved} \end{array} \times \begin{array}{c} \text{Budgeted fixed} \\ \text{overhead rate} \end{array} \right)$$

$$= \$276{,}000 - (0.40 \times 10{,}000 \times \$57.50)$$
$$= \$276{,}000 - (4{,}000 \times \$57.50)$$
$$= \$276{,}000 - \$230{,}000$$
$$= \$46{,}000 \text{ U}$$

Question: When the production-volume variance is unfavourable, what is the relationship between FMOH allocated and budgeted FMOH?
Answer: FMOH allocated is *less than* FMOH budgeted as in the Web example.

EXHIBIT 8-3
Variance Analysis: Variable and Fixed Manufacturing Overhead for the Webb Company

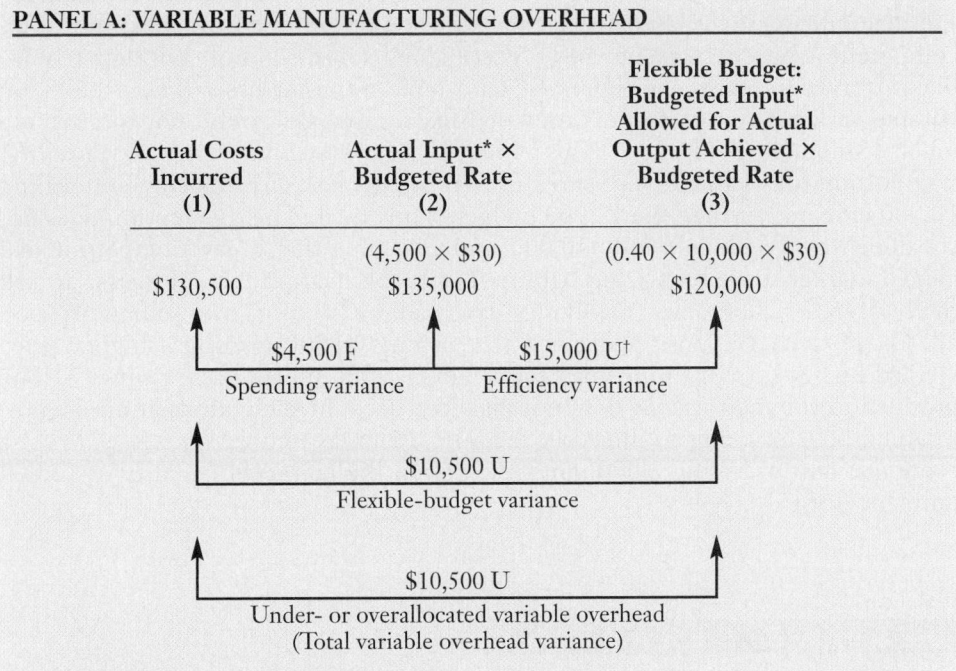

PANEL A: VARIABLE MANUFACTURING OVERHEAD

Actual Costs Incurred (1)	Actual Input* × Budgeted Rate (2)	Flexible Budget: Budgeted Input* Allowed for Actual Output Achieved × Budgeted Rate (3)
	(4,500 × $30)	(0.40 × 10,000 × $30)
$130,500	$135,000	$120,000

$4,500 F — Spending variance
$15,000 U† — Efficiency variance
$10,500 U — Flexible-budget variance
$10,500 U — Under- or overallocated variable overhead (Total variable overhead variance)

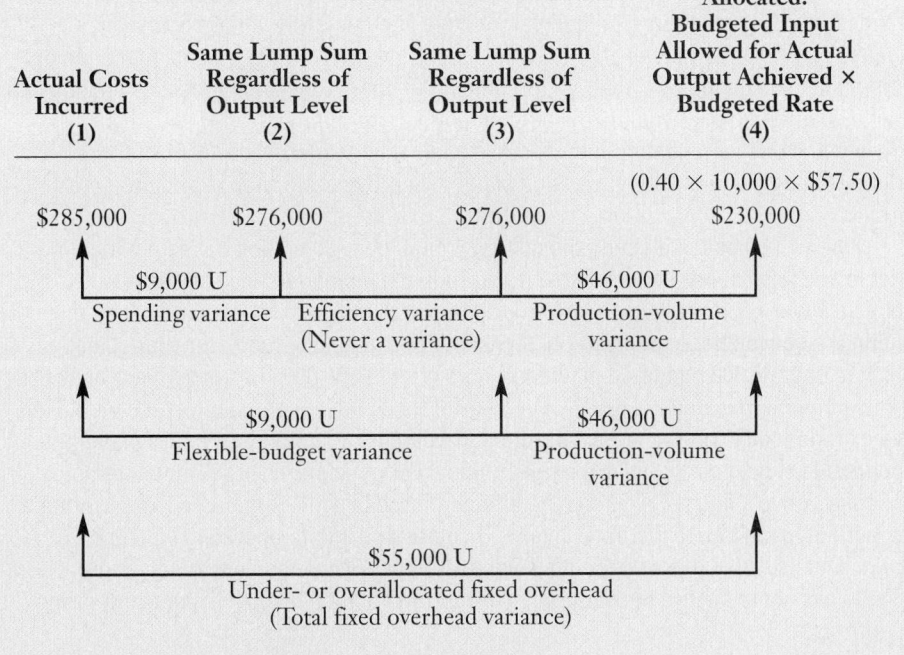

PANEL B: FIXED MANUFACTURING OVERHEAD

Actual Costs Incurred (1)	Same Lump Sum Regardless of Output Level (2)	Same Lump Sum Regardless of Output Level (3)	Allocated: Budgeted Input Allowed for Actual Output Achieved × Budgeted Rate (4)
			(0.40 × 10,000 × $57.50)
$285,000	$276,000	$276,000	$230,000

$9,000 U — Spending variance
Efficiency variance (Never a variance)
$46,000 U — Production-volume variance
$9,000 U — Flexible-budget variance
$46,000 U — Production-volume variance
$55,000 U — Under- or overallocated fixed overhead (Total fixed overhead variance)

*For overhead costs, input refers to units of cost-allocation base.
†F = favourable effect on operating income; U = unfavourable effect on operating income.

The amount used for budgeted fixed overhead will be the same lump sum shown in the static budget and also in any flexible budget within the relevant range. Fixed overhead costs allocated is the sum of the individual fixed overhead costs allocated to each of the products manufactured during the accounting period.

Panel A of Exhibit 8-3 does not have the column 4 shown for Panel B. Why? Because column 4 does not apply to variable overhead costs. The amount of variable overhead is always the same as the flexible-budget amount.

OBJECTIVE 6

Explain why the production-volume variance may not be a good measure of the economic cost of unused capacity

When allocating FMOH for the inventory-costing purpose, we "unitize" FMOH (see Chapter 2, p. 38). In contrast, budgeted FMOH is fixed over a wide range of output levels. The production-volume variance is zero only if FMOH allocated *equals* budgeted FMOH. If so, the actual output level (expressed in terms of the FMOH cost-allocation base) is equal to the denominator level used to compute the budgeted FMOH cost rate.

Interpreting the Production-Volume Variance

The production volume variance arises whenever actual production differs from the denominator level used to calculate the budgeted fixed overhead rate. We compute this rate because inventory costing and some types of contracts require fixed overhead costs to be expressed on a unit-of-output basis. The production volume variance results from "unitizing" fixed costs. Be careful not to attribute much economic significance to this variance; the most common misinterpretation is to assume this variance measures the economic cost of producing and selling 10,000 units rather than the 12,000 budgeted for April. This assumption does not consider why Webb sold only 10,000 units. Assume that a new competitor had gained market share by pricing below what Webb charges its customers. To sell the budgeted 12,000 units, Webb may have had to reduce its own selling price on all 12,000 units. Suppose it decided that selling 10,000 units at a higher price yielded higher operating income than selling 12,000 units at a lower price. The production volume variance does not take into account such information. Hence, it would be misleading to interpret the $46,000 unfavourable amount as Webb's economic cost of selling 2,000 units fewer than the budgeted quantity of 12,000 units for April.

FOCUS ON VALUES AND BEHAVIOURS

The Challenges of Overhead Variances

Management accountants are constantly monitoring all aspects of a company's financial activities, which gives them a unique perspective into overhead variance analysis. Because overhead variances are challenging for managers to understand, management accountants must acquire a deep understanding of operations and processes so they can provide an in-depth examination of the company's performance. Armed with this knowledge, management accountants can explain to managers the reasons for the variances and help them develop action plans to improve performance and promote learning.

When it comes to selecting the quantity of the cost-allocation base for allocating variable and fixed overhead costs to output produced, managers may be tempted to choose a lower capacity level (denominator) to avoid unfavourable variances and the resulting negative effects on operating income. For example, if Webb's management team had used 48,000 budgeted machine-hours (that is, 120,000 jackets per year or 10,000 jackets per month) instead of 57,600 machine-hours as the denominator, Webb would not have experienced an unfavourable production-volume variance. But Webb's management accountants should ask if this is the right choice. For example, is 48,000 machine-hours too conservative a figure? Wouldn't the effect of increasing the budgeted fixed overhead cost per output unit be to increase inventory values and inflate operating income? Wouldn't it mislead managers about available capacity? Management accountants must always act to ensure the accuracy of reported numbers even if it means reporting lower profits.

Managers must always explore the why of a variance before concluding that the label unfavourable or favourable necessarily indicates, respectively, poor or good management performance. Understanding the reasons for a variance also helps managers decide on future courses of action. Should they try to reduce capacity, increase sales, or do nothing? Based on their analysis of the situation, Webb's managers decided to reduce some capacity but continued to maintain some excess capacity to accommodate unexpected surges in demand. Chapter 9 and Chapter 13 examine these issues in more detail.

> Inventoriable costs are all costs of a product that are regarded as assets and expensed as cost of goods sold when the product is sold (see Chapter 2, p. 39).

Throughout this chapter, it is assumed that companies have made a distinction between those costs that are variable and those costs that are fixed. However, some companies have not segregated their costs into these two categories, in particular within the overhead costs. For these companies, the variable manufacturing overhead variances are not determined and all overhead costs are assumed to be fixed. Any interpretation of the variance analysis for these companies is limited due to this limitation in the detail of their costing systems.

INTEGRATED ANALYSIS OF OVERHEAD-COST VARIANCES

Exhibit 8-3 illustrates the four variances explained in this chapter. When all four variances are presented, it is called a four-variance analysis.

OBJECTIVE 7

Explain how variance analysis can provide an integrated overview of overhead-cost variances

Four-Variance Analysis

	Spending Variance	Efficiency Variance	Production-Volume Variance
Variable Manufacturing Overhead	$4,500 F	$15,000 U	(Never a variance)
Fixed Manufacturing Overhead	$9,000 U	(Never a variance)	$46,000 U

Detailed four-variance analyses are more common in large, complex businesses. That's because it is impossible for managers at a company such as Power Corporation of Canada to keep track of all that is happening within their areas of responsibility. The detailed four-variance analyses help managers identify and focus attention on the areas not operating as expected. Managers of small businesses understand their operations better based on personal observations and nonfinancial measures. They find less value in doing the additional measurements (such as distinguishing variable from fixed manufacturing overhead) required for four-variance analyses.

Power Corporation of Canada
www.powercorporation.com

The four variances in this presentation are the two variable manufacturing overhead variances and the two fixed manufacturing overhead variances. Note also that two areas show "Never a variance." Why? The efficiency variance pertains only to variable manufacturing overhead. There can be no efficiency for fixed manufacturing overhead because this amount is a lump sum regardless of the output level within the relevant range during a specified time period. The production-volume variance pertains only to fixed manufacturing overhead. It arises because a lump sum must be allocated to individual output units for inventory costing (and, in some cases, for contract reimbursement).

Three-Variance Analysis

	Spending Variance	Efficiency Variance	Production-Volume Variance
Total Manufacturing Overhead	$4,500 U	$15,000 U	$46,000 U

The two spending variances from the four-variance analysis have been combined in the three-variance analysis. The only loss of information in the three-variance analysis is in the overhead spending variance area—only one spending variance is reported

Combined-variance analysis. Approach to overhead-variance analysis that combines variable-cost and fixed cost variances.

instead of separate variable and fixed overhead spending variances. Three-variance analysis is sometimes called **combined-variance analysis**, because it combines variable- and fixed-cost variances when reporting overhead cost variances.

Two-Variance Analysis

	Flexible-Budget Variance	**Production-Volume Variance**
Total Manufacturing Overhead	$19,500 U	$46,000 U

The spending and efficiency variances from the three-variance analysis have been combined under the two-variance analysis.

One-Variance Analysis

	Total Overhead Variance
Total Manufacturing Overhead	$65,500 U

The single variance of $65,500 U in one-variance analysis is the sum of the flexible-budget variance and the production-volume variance under two-variance analysis. Using figures from Exhibit 8-3, the total overhead variance is the difference between the total actual manufacturing overhead incurred ($130,500 + $285,000 = $415,500) and the manufacturing overhead allocated to the actual output units produced ($120,000 + $230,000 = $350,000). The $65,500 unfavourable total manufacturing overhead variance for the Webb Company in April 2007 is largely the result of the $46,000 unfavourable production-volume variance. Using the four-variance analysis presentation, the next-largest amount (after the $46,000) is the $15,000 unfavourable variable overhead efficiency variance. This variance arises from the additional 500 machine-hours used in April 2007 above the 4,000 machine-hours allowed to manufacture the 10,000 jackets. The two spending variances ($4,500 F and $9,000 U) partially offset each other.

The variances in Webb's four-variance analysis are not necessarily independent of each other. For example, Webb may purchase lower-quality machine fluids (giving rise to a favourable spending variance); this results in a slower operating speed for the machines than was budgeted (giving rise to an unfavourable efficiency variance).

OVERHEAD-COST VARIANCES IN NONMANUFACTURING SETTINGS

Our Webb Company example examines variable and fixed manufacturing overhead costs. Under generally accepted accounting principles, both variable and fixed manufacturing overhead costs are inventoriable costs for financial reporting purposes and therefore will affect cost of goods sold. In contrast, the overhead costs of non-manufacturing areas of the value chain (such as R&D and marketing) are not inventoriable costs but rather are period costs. Under generally accepted accounting principles there is a choice. These costs may be normally amortized noninventoriable costs, which have no effect on cost of goods sold. Alternatively, the costs can be immediately expensed to the period in which they are incurred. Should the overhead costs of nonmanufacturing areas be examined using the variance analysis framework discussed in this chapter? Variable-cost information pertaining to nonmanufacturing as well as manufacturing costs is often used in pricing decisions and decisions about which products or services to push or de-emphasize. Variance analysis of all variable overhead costs is a main consideration when making such decisions. For example, managers in industries such as automobiles, consumer durables, cement, and steel, in which distribution costs are high, may use standard costing to give reliable and timely information on variable distribution overhead spending variances and efficiency variances.

Consider service-sector companies such as airlines, hospitals, hotels, and railroads. The measures of output commonly used in these companies are passenger-miles flown, patient-days provided, room-days, and tonne-kilometres of freight hauled, respectively. Few costs can be traced to these outputs in a cost-effective way. The majority of costs are fixed overhead costs (for example, costs of equipment, buildings, and staff). Using capacity effectively is the key to profitability, and fixed overhead variances can help managers in this task.

Consider the following data for United Airlines for the years 2000 and 2003. Available Seat Miles (ASM) are the actual seats in a plane multiplied by the distance travelled.

Year	Total ASM (Millions) (1)	Revenue per ASM (2)	Cost per ASM (3)	Gross Margin per ASM (4) = (2) − (3)
2000	175,485	$0.1103	$0.1066	$0.0037
2003	136,630	$0.1006	$0.1104	−$0.0098

After September 11, 2001, as air travel declined, United's revenues decreased but a majority of its costs comprising fixed costs of airport facilities, equipment, and personnel did not. United had a large unfavourable production-volume variance as its capacity remained unutilized. As column 1 of the preceding table indicates, United responded by reducing its capacity from 175,485 million ASMs to 136,630 million but, unable to fill even the planes it was left with, revenue per ASM declined (column 2) and cost per ASM increased (column 3). United filed for Chapter 11 bankruptcy

Retail businesses, such as Kmart, also have high capacity-related fixed costs (lease and occupancy costs). Sales declines result in unused capacity and unfavourable fixed-cost variances. Kmart reduced fixed costs by closing some of its stores, but it also had to file for Chapter 11 bankruptcy.

GLOBAL SURVEYS OF COMPANY PRACTICE

Variance Analysis and Control Decisions

There is widespread usage of the variances discussed in Chapters 7 and 8. A survey of United Kingdom companies reported the following percentages:[a]

Variance	Percentage of Companies Computing Variance	Percentage of Companies Viewing the Variance as "Above Average Importance" or "Vitally Important" in Control Decisions
Sales volume	77%	70%
Selling price	75	69
Materials price	94	69
Materials efficiency	80	66
Labour price	63	36
Labour efficiency	73	65
Overhead spending	89	69
Production volume	41	28

In addition, a recent survey of 270 Danish chief management accountants found that 74% consider variance analysis "important" or "very important."[b] Another survey of U.K. and New Zealand manufacturers found that after adopting modern management techniques, including just-in-time and advanced manufacturing technologies, 87% of U.K. and 84% of New Zealand respondents experienced either no change or an increased importance in the role of variance analysis in their control systems.[c]

[a]Drury, C., S. Braund, P. Osborne, and M. Tayles, *A Survey of Management Accounting Practices in UK Manufacturing Companies* (London: Chartered Association of Certified Accountants, 1993).

[b]Mouritsen, J., "Five Aspects of Accounting Departments' Work," *Management Accounting Research* (1996).

[c]Guilding, C., D. Lamminmaki, and C. Drury, "Budgeting and Standard Costing Practices in New Zealand and the United Kingdom," *The International Journal of Accounting* (1998).

and began seeking government guarantees to obtain the loans it needed to bring it out of bankruptcy.

In other service-sector companies such as banking, measures of output are more difficult to identify. Banks provide a variety of services to their customers, such as chequing accounts, loans, credit cards, and retirement or other investment accounts. Most costs of these activities are overhead costs. Technology has made it easier to trace overhead costs to activities. For example, when employees record the time they spend on each activity in an activity database, a computer-generated report of total labour-hours and costs per activity can be provided to managers. Standard costing techniques can then be applied to manage the overhead costs of activities.

Variance analysis of fixed nonmanufacturing overhead costs is also important for companies that work on a full-actual-cost-plus basis—that is, where it is reimbursed for its full actual costs plus an additional percentage of those costs. Here, information on these variances enables more accurate estimates of actual costs to be computed. In many other cases, however, managers do not conduct detailed variance analysis of fixed nonmanufacturing costs. Most believe little information is gained by computing spending or efficiency variances for these fixed nonmanufacturing costs.

DIFFERENT PURPOSES OF MANUFACTURING OVERHEAD COST ANALYSIS

Different types of cost analysis may be appropriate for different purposes. Consider the planning and control purpose and the inventory costing for financial reporting purposes. Panel A of Exhibit 8-4 depicts variable manufacturing overhead for each purpose; panel B depicts fixed manufacturing overhead for each purpose.

Variable Manufacturing Overhead Costs

Webb's variable manufacturing overhead is shown in panel A of Exhibit 8-4 as being variable, with respect to output units (jackets) produced, for both the planning and control purpose (graph 1) and the inventory costing purpose (graph 2). The greater the number of output units manufactured, the higher the budgeted total variable manufacturing overhead costs and the total variable manufacturing overhead costs allocated to output units.

Graph 1 of Exhibit 8-4 presents an overall picture of how total variable overhead might behave. Of course, variable overhead consists of many items, including energy costs, repairs, indirect labour, and so on. Managers help control variable overhead costs by budgeting each line item and then investigating possible causes for any significant variances.

Fixed Manufacturing Overhead Costs

Panel B of Exhibit 8-4 (graph 3) shows that, for the planning and control purpose, fixed overhead costs do not change in the 8,000-to-16,000-unit output range. Consider a monthly leasing cost of $20,000 for a building under a three-year leasing agreement. Managers control this fixed leasing cost at the time the lease is signed. During any month in the leasing period, management can do little to change this $20,000 lump sum payment. Contrast this description of fixed overhead with how these costs are depicted for the inventory costing purpose, graph 4 of panel B. Under generally accepted accounting principles, fixed manufacturing costs are capitalized as part of inventory on a unit-of-output basis. Every output unit that Webb manufactures will increase the fixed overhead allocated to products by $23 ($57.50 per machine-hour $\times$ 0.40 machine-hours per output unit). Managers should not use this unitization of fixed manufacturing overhead costs for their planning and control.

The denominator level in each graph in Exhibit 8-4 is expressed in output units produced. Alternatively, we could also have expressed this denominator in terms of input units. For Webb, machine-hours would be the chosen denominator, as this is the allocation base for both variable and fixed manufacturing overhead costs.

EXHIBIT 8-4
Behaviour of Variable and Fixed Manufacturing Overhead Costs for Planning and Control
and for Inventory Costing

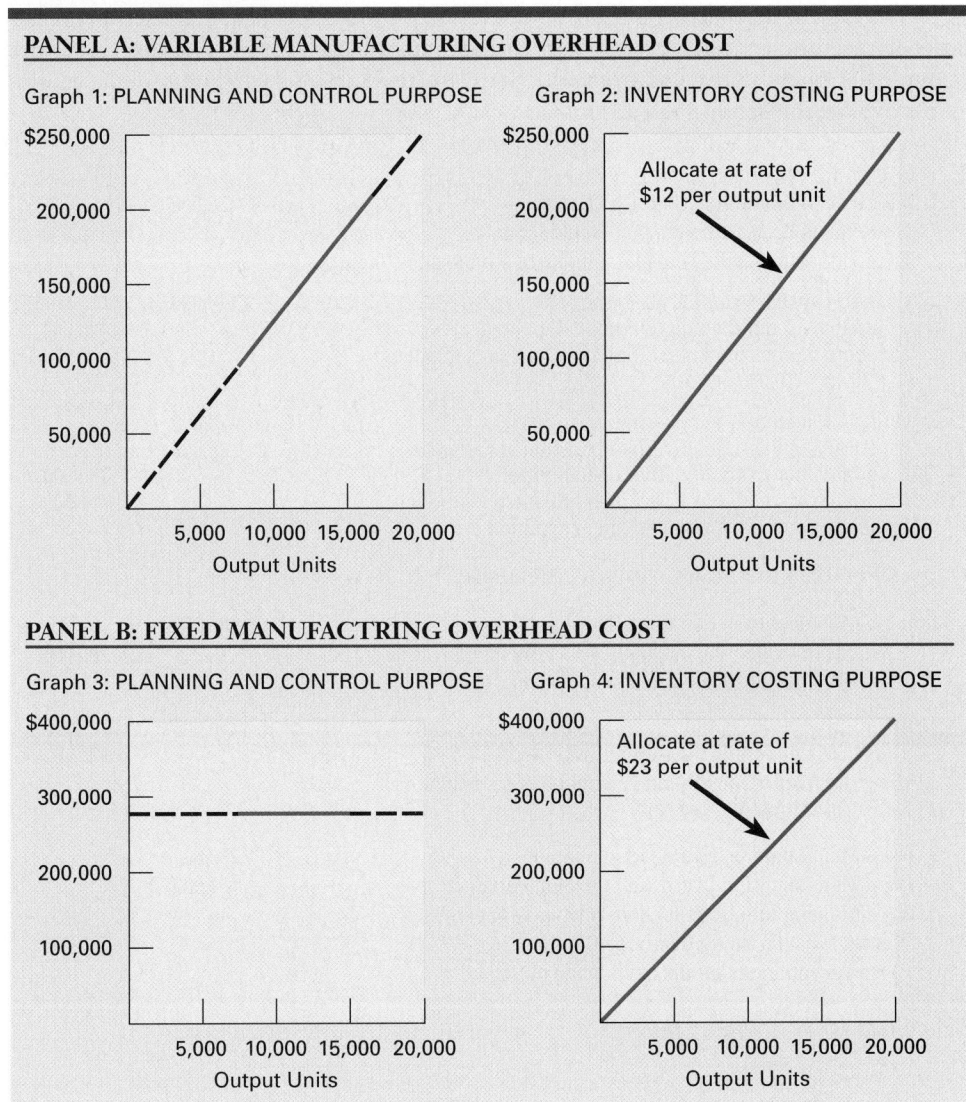

PANEL A: VARIABLE MANUFACTURING OVERHEAD COST

Graph 1: PLANNING AND CONTROL PURPOSE   Graph 2: INVENTORY COSTING PURPOSE

Allocate at rate of $12 per output unit

PANEL B: FIXED MANUFACTRING OVERHEAD COST

Graph 3: PLANNING AND CONTROL PURPOSE   Graph 4: INVENTORY COSTING PURPOSE

Allocate at rate of $23 per output unit

JOURNAL ENTRIES FOR OVERHEAD COSTS AND VARIANCES

Recording Overhead Costs

Previously, in Chapter 4 in the Robinson Company job-costing example, a single manufacturing overhead control account was used. Chapter 8 illustrates separate variable and fixed manufacturing overhead control accounts. Each overhead control account requires its own overhead allocated account.

Consider the following journal entries for the Webb Company. Recall that for April 2007,

	Actual Results	Flexible Budget Amount (10,000 Units)	Allocated Amount
Variable manufacturing overhead	$130,500	$120,000*	$120,000*
Fixed manufacturing overhead	285,000	276,000†	230,000‡

*0.40 × 10,000 × $30 = $120,000.
†$276,000 is the budgeted fixed manufacturing overhead.
‡0.40 × 10,000 × $57.50 = $230,000.

The budgeted variable overhead rate is $30 per machine-hour. The denominator level for fixed manufacturing overhead is 4,800 machine-hours of input with a budgeted rate of $57.50 per machine-hour. Webb uses four-variance analysis.

During the accounting period, actual variable overhead and actual fixed overhead costs are accumulated in separate control accounts. As each unit is manufactured, the budgeted variable and fixed overhead rates are used to record the amounts in the respective overhead allocated accounts.

Entries for variable manufacturing overhead for April 2007 are

1. Variable Manufacturing Overhead Control   130,500
      Accounts Payable Control and other accounts   130,500
      To record actual variable manufacturing overhead costs incurred.

2. Work-in-Process Control   120,000
      Variable Manufacturing Overhead Allocated   120,000
      To record variable manufacturing overhead cost allocated
         (0.40 × 10,000 × $30).

3. Variable Manufacturing Overhead Allocated   120,000
      Variable Manufacturing Overhead Efficiency Variance   15,000
        Variable Manufacturing Overhead Control   130,500
        Variable Manufacturing Overhead Spending Variance   4,500
      To isolate variances for the accounting period.

Entries for fixed manufacturing overhead are

1. Fixed Manufacturing Overhead Control   285,000
      Wages Payable, Accumulated Amortization, etc.   285,000
      To record actual fixed overhead costs incurred.

2. Work-in-Process Control   230,000
      Fixed Manufacturing Overhead Allocated   230,000
      To record fixed manufacturing overhead costs allocated
         (0.40 × 10,000 × $57.50).

3. Fixed Manufacturing Overhead Allocated   230,000
      Fixed Manufacturing Overhead Spending Variance   9,000
      Fixed Manufacturing Production-Volume Variance   46,000
        Fixed Manufacturing Overhead Control   285,000
      To isolate variances for the accounting period.

The end-of-period adjustments for these variances are now discussed.

Overhead Variances and End-of-Period Adjustments

Chapter 4 outlined the adjusted allocation rate approach and the proration approach to handling the end-of-period difference between manufacturing overhead incurred and manufacturing overhead allocated. Consider Webb's variable manufacturing overhead. The budgeted rate was $30 per machine-hour. The actual rate is $29 per machine-hour.

Under the adjusted allocation rate approach, Webb would adjust the job record of every job worked on during the year. This adjustment, in effect, would entail using the actual rate per machine-hour of $29 instead of the budgeted rate of $30. Then, Webb would accordingly recompute the ending inventory and cost of goods sold for the accounting period. This approach has several benefits. Individual job records are restated to show actual costs accurately. Also, ending inventory and cost of goods sold would accurately show actual variable overhead incurred. A similar approach could be used to restate the fixed manufacturing overhead in job records. Providing all accounting records are on compatible computer systems, the adjusted allocation rate approach can often be done in a low-cost, timely manner.

The proration approach is used where managers view the adjusted allocation rate approach as not being cost-effective. At the end of the fiscal year, the fixed manufacturing overhead spending variance is written off to cost of goods sold if it is immaterial in amount, or prorated among Work-in-Process Control, Finished Goods Control, Cost of Goods Sold, and the Production-Volume Variance on the basis of fixed manufacturing overhead allocated to these accounts as described in Chapter 4, pp. 130–133. Note that the proration method, all things being equal, will reduce the cost of goods sold because some of the fixed manufacturing overhead spending variance has been prorated to inventoriable costs, which will increase inventory on the balance sheet. Some companies combine the writeoff and proration methods—that is, they write off the portion of the variance that is due to inefficiency and could have been avoided and prorate the portion of the variance that is unavoidable. Assume that the balance in the Fixed Manufacturing Overhead Spending Variance account as of April 2007 is also the balance at the end of the 2007 and immaterial in amount. The following journal entry records the writeoff to Cost of Goods Sold.

Cost of Goods Sold	9,000	
Fixed Manufacturing Overhead Spending Variance		9,000

We now address the production-volume variance. Assume that the balance in Fixed Manufacturing Overhead Production-Volume Variance as of April 2007 is also the balance at the end of 2007. Also assume that some of the jackets manufactured during 2007 are in work-in-process and finished goods inventory at the end of the year. A strong argument is often made by many management accountants for writing off to Cost of Goods Sold and not prorating an unfavourable production-volume variance. Proponents of this argument contend that the unfavourable production-volume variance of $46,000 measures the cost of resources expended for 2,000 jackets that were not produced ($23 per jacket × 2,000 jackets = $46,000). Prorating these costs would inappropriately result in allocating fixed costs incurred for the 2,000 jackets that were not produced to the jackets that were produced. The jackets produced already bear their representative share of fixed costs of $23 per jacket. Therefore, this argument favours charging the unfavourable production-volume variance against the year's revenues so that fixed costs of unused capacity are not carried in work-in-process and finished goods inventory. There is, however, an alternative view. This view regards the denominator level chosen as a "soft" rather than a "hard" measure of the fixed resources required and needed to produce each jacket. Suppose for example that, either because of the design of the jacket or the functioning of the machines, it took more machine-hours than previously thought to manufacture each jacket. Consequently, Webb could make only 10,000 jackets rather than the planned 12,000 in April. In this case, the $276,000 of budgeted fixed manufacturing overhead costs support the production of the 10,000 jackets manufactured. Under this reasoning, prorating the fixed overhead production-volume variance would appropriately spread fixed manufacturing overhead costs among Work-in-Process Control, Finished Goods Control, and Cost of Goods Sold.

What about a favourable production-volume variance? Suppose Webb manufactured 13,800 jackets in April 2007.

$$\begin{aligned}\text{Production-volume variance} &= \begin{array}{c}\text{Budgeted}\\\text{fixed}\\\text{overhead}\end{array} - \begin{array}{c}\text{Fixed overhead allocated using}\\\text{budgeted cost per output unit}\\\text{allowed for actual output produced}\end{array}\\ &= \$276,000 - (\$23 \text{ per jacket} \times 13,800 \text{ jackets})\\ &= \$276,000 - \$317,400\\ &= \$41,400 \text{ F}\end{aligned}$$

Because actual production exceeded the planned capacity level, clearly the fixed manufacturing overhead costs of $276,000 supported production of, and so should be allocated to, all 13,800 jackets. Prorating the production-volume variance achieves this outcome and reduces the amounts in Work-in-Process Control, Finished Goods Control, and Cost of Goods Sold. Proration is also the most conservative approach in the sense that it results in a lower operating income than if all of the favourable production-volume variance were credited to Cost of Goods Sold.

One more point is relevant to the discussion of whether to prorate the production-volume variance or to write it off to cost of goods sold. If variances are always written off to cost of goods sold, a company could set its standards to either increase (for financial reporting purposes) or decrease (for tax purposes) operating income. For example, Webb could generate a favourable (unfavourable) production-volume variance by setting the denominator level used to allocate fixed overhead costs low (high) and thereby increase (decrease) operating income. The proration method has the effect of approximating the allocation of fixed costs based on actual costs and actual output and so is not susceptible to the manipulation of operating income via the choice of the denominator level.

There is no clear-cut or preferred approach for closing out the production-volume variance. The appropriate accounting procedure is a matter of judgment and depends on the circumstances of each case. Variations of the proration method may be desirable. For example, a company may choose to write off a portion of the production-volume variance and prorate the rest. The goal is to write off that part of the production-volume variance that represents the cost of capacity not used to support the production of output during the period. The rest of the production-volume variance is prorated to Work-in-Process Control, Finished Goods Control, and Cost of Goods Sold.

If Webb were to write off the production-volume variance to Cost of Goods Sold, it would make the following journal entry.

Cost of Goods Sold	46,000	
Fixed Manufacturing Overhead Production-Volume Variance		46,000

The three main options for disposing of variances under this approach are the following:

1. Proration based on the allocated overhead amount (before proration) in the ending balances of Work-in-Process Control, Finished Goods Control, and Cost of Goods Sold

2. Proration based on total ending balances (before proration) in Work-in-Process Control, Finished Goods Control, and Cost of Goods Sold

3. Immediate write-off to Cost of Goods Sold

Webb could use any one of these options when prorating the $10,500 of under-allocated variable manufacturing overhead (and the $55,000 of underallocated fixed manufacturing overhead).

MOH cost items can be controlled on the production floor through personal observation and timely nonfinancial measures of individual items (for example, overtime authorization, idle time, and defect rates). The accounting system transforms these nonfinancial measures into financial measures that inform managers of the materiality (significance) of the variances.

FINANCIAL AND NONFINANCIAL PERFORMANCE MEASURES

The overhead variances discussed in this chapter are examples of financial performance measures. Managers also find that nonfinancial measures provide useful information. Examples of such measures that Webb would likely find useful in planning and controlling its overhead costs are as follows:

There is debate over the relative weights to be given to financial and nonfinancial measures. For example, some experts maintain that nonfinancial measures, such as product quality and customer satisfaction, should be given more emphasis than financial measures. Chapter 13 considers this issue in detail.

1. Actual indirect materials usage in metres per machine-hour, compared with budgeted indirect materials usage in metres per machine-hour

2. Actual energy usage per machine-hour, compared with budgeted energy usage per machine-hour

3. Actual machining time per job, compared with budgeted machining time per job

ACTIVITY-BASED COSTING AND VARIANCE ANALYSIS

Illustrate how the flexible-budget variance approach can be used in activity-based costing

ABC systems classify costs of various activities into a cost hierarchy: output-unit level, batch level, product sustaining, and facility sustaining. The basic principles and concepts for variable and fixed manufacturing overhead costs presented earlier in the chapter can be extended to ABC systems. In this section, we illustrate variance analysis for variable and fixed batch-level setup overhead costs. Batch-level costs are resources sacrificed on activities that are related to a group of units of product(s) or service(s) rather than to each individual unit of product or service.

We will use the example of Lyco Brass Works, which manufactures Jacutaps, a line of decorative brass faucets for Jacuzzis. Lyco manufactures Jacutaps in batches.

To manufacture a batch of Jacutaps, Lyco must set up the machines and moulds. Setup costs are batch-level costs because they are associated with batches rather than individual units of products. Doing setups is a skilled activity. Hence, a separate setup department is responsible for setting up machines and moulds for different types of Jacutaps. Lyco regards setup costs as overhead costs of products.

Setup costs consist of some costs that are variable and some costs that are fixed with respect to the number of setup-hours. Variable costs of setups consist of wages paid to hourly setup labour and indirect support labour, costs of maintenance of setup equipment, and costs of indirect materials and energy used during setups. Fixed setup costs consist of costs of engineers, supervisors, and setup equipment leases.

Information regarding Jacutaps for 2007 follows:

	Static-Budget Amounts	Actual Amounts
1. Units of Jacutaps produced and sold	180,000	151,200
2. Batch size (units/batch)	150	140
3. Number of batches (Line 1 ÷ Line 2)	1,200	1,080
4. Setup-hours per batch	6	6.25
5. Total setup-hours (Line 3 × Line 4)	7,200	6,750
6. Variable overhead cost per setup-hour	$ 20	$ 21
7. Variable setup overhead costs (Line 5 × Line 6)	$144,000	$141,750
8. Total fixed setup overhead costs	$216,000	$220,000

Flexible Budget and Variance Analysis for Variable Setup Overhead Costs

To prepare the flexible budget for variable setup overhead costs, Lyco starts with the actual units of output produced, 151,200 units, and proceeds with the following steps.

◆ **Step 1:** *Using the budgeted batch size, calculate the number of batches that should have been used to produce the actual output.* Lyco should have manufactured the 151,200 units of output in 1,008 batches (151,200 ÷ 150).

◆ **Step 2:** *Using budgeted setup-hours per batch, calculate the number of setup-hours that should have been used.* At the budgeted quantity of 6 setup-hours per batch, 1,008 batches should have required 6,048 setup-hours (1,008 × 6).

◆ **Step 3:** *Using the budgeted variable cost per setup-hour, calculate the flexible budget for variable setup overhead costs.* The flexible-budget amount is 6,048 setup-hours × $20 per setup-hour = $120,960.

$$\begin{array}{l} \text{Flexible-budget} \\ \text{variance for variable} \\ \text{setup overhead costs} \end{array} = \begin{array}{c} \text{Actual} \\ \text{costs} \end{array} - \begin{array}{c} \text{Flexible-} \\ \text{budget costs} \end{array}$$

$$= 6{,}750 \times \$21 - 6{,}048 \times \$20$$
$$= \$141{,}750 - \$120{,}960$$
$$= \$20{,}790 \text{ U}$$

Exhibit 8-5 presents the variances for variable setup overhead costs in columnar form.

The flexible-budget variance for variable setup overhead costs can be subdivided into efficiency and spending variances.

$$\begin{array}{l} \text{Variable setup} \\ \text{overhead efficiency} \\ \text{variance} \end{array} = \left(\begin{array}{c} \text{Actual units of} \\ \text{variable overhead} \\ \text{cost-allocation base} \\ \text{used for actual output} \end{array} - \begin{array}{c} \text{Budgeted units of} \\ \text{variable overhead cost-} \\ \text{allocation base allowed} \\ \text{for actual output} \end{array} \right) \times \begin{array}{c} \text{Budgeted} \\ \text{variable} \\ \text{overhead rate} \end{array}$$

$$= (6{,}750 - 6{,}048) \times \$20$$
$$= 702 \times \$20$$
$$= \$14{,}040 \text{ U}$$

The unfavourable variable setup overhead efficiency variance of $14,040 arises because the actual number of setup-hours (6,750) exceeds the number of setup-hours that Lyco should have used (6,048) for the number of units it produced.

Because setup costs are at the batch level, the budgeted quantity of input allowed for actual output is calculated at the batch level. The quantity of setup-hours allowed is based on the number of batches it should have taken to produce the actual quantity of output. Although both ABC systems and traditional costing systems allocate MOH costs to output units produced, ABC has the advantage that there are better cause-and-effect relationships between the cost-allocation bases chosen and the related cost pools.

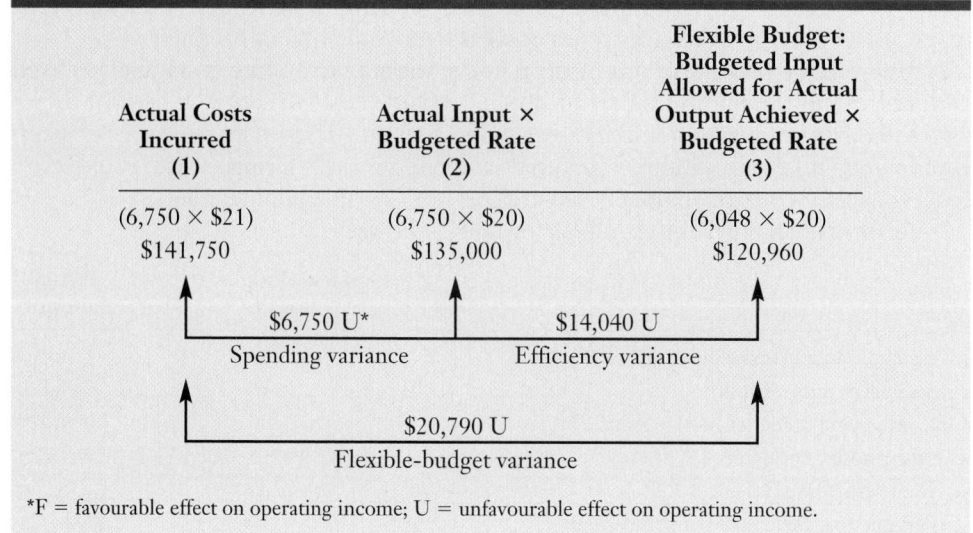

Actual Costs Incurred (1)	Actual Input × Budgeted Rate (2)	Flexible Budget: Budgeted Input Allowed for Actual Output Achieved × Budgeted Rate (3)
(6,750 × $21)	(6,750 × $20)	(6,048 × $20)
$141,750	$135,000	$120,960

$6,750 U* → Spending variance

$14,040 U → Efficiency variance

$20,790 U → Flexible-budget variance

*F = favourable effect on operating income; U = unfavourable effect on operating income.

Two reasons for the unfavourable efficiency variance are (1) smaller actual batch sizes of 140 units instead of budgeted batch sizes of 150 units, which results in Lyco producing the 151,200 units in 1,080 batches instead of 1,008 batches, and (2) higher actual setup-hours per batch of 6.25 hours instead of the budgeted setup-hours per batch of 6 hours.

Explanations for smaller-than-budgeted batch sizes could include (1) quality problems if batch sizes exceed 140 faucets or (2) high costs of carrying inventory. Explanations for longer actual setup-hours per batch could include (1) problems with equipment, (2) demotivated or inexperienced employees, or (3) inappropriate setup-time standards.

$$\begin{matrix} \text{Variable setup} \\ \text{overhead spending} \\ \text{variance} \end{matrix} = \left(\begin{matrix} \text{Actual variable} \\ \text{overhead cost} \\ \text{per unit of cost-} \\ \text{allocation base} \end{matrix} - \begin{matrix} \text{Budgeted variable} \\ \text{overhead cost per} \\ \text{unit of cost-} \\ \text{allocation base} \end{matrix} \right) \times \begin{matrix} \text{Actual quantity of variable} \\ \text{overhead cost-allocation} \\ \text{base used for actual output} \\ \text{units achieved} \end{matrix}$$

$$= (\$21 - \$20) \times 6,750$$
$$= -\$1 \times 6,750 = \$6,750 \text{ U}$$

The unfavourable spending variance indicates that Lyco operated in 2007 with higher-than-budgeted variable overhead cost per setup-hour. Two main reasons that could contribute to the unfavourable spending variance are (1) the actual prices of individual items included in variable overhead, such as setup labour, indirect support labour, or energy, are higher than the budgeted prices, and (2) the actual quantity usage of individual items such as indirect support labour and energy increases more than the increase in setup-hours, due perhaps to setups becoming more complex because of equipment problems. Thus, equipment problems could lead to an unfavourable efficiency variance because setup-hours increase, but they could also lead to an unfavourable spending variance because each setup-hour requires more resources from the setup-cost pool than the budgeted amounts.

Identifying the reasons for the variances is important because it helps managers plan for corrective action. We now consider fixed setup overhead costs.

Flexible Budget and Variance Analysis for Fixed Setup Overhead Costs

For fixed setup overhead costs, the flexible-budget amount equals the static-budget amount of $216,000. Why? Because there is no "flexing" of fixed costs.

$$\begin{array}{rl} \text{Fixed setup overhead} & = \text{Actual} - \text{Flexible-budget} \\ \text{flexible-budget variance} & \quad \text{costs} \quad\quad \text{costs} \\ & = \$220{,}000 - \$216{,}000 \\ & = \$4{,}000 \text{ U} \end{array}$$

The fixed setup overhead spending variance is the same amount as the fixed overhead flexible-budget variance (because fixed overhead costs have no efficiency variance).

$$\begin{array}{rl} \text{Fixed setup overhead} & = \text{Actual} - \text{Flexible-budget} \\ \text{spending variance} & \quad \text{costs} \quad\quad \text{costs} \\ & = \$220{,}000 - \$216{,}000 \\ & = \$4{,}000 \text{ U} \end{array}$$

The unfavourable fixed setup overhead spending variance could be due to lease costs of new setup equipment or higher salaries paid to engineers and supervisors. Lyco may have incurred these costs to alleviate some of the difficulties it was having in setting up machines.

To calculate the production-volume variance, Lyco first computes the budgeted cost-allocation rate for fixed setup overhead costs using the four-step approach described earlier.

◆ **Step 1:** *Choose the time period used to compute the budget.* Lyco uses a period of 12 months (the year 2007).

◆ **Step 2:** *Select the cost-allocation base to use in allocating fixed overhead costs to the cost object(s).* Lyco uses budgeted setup-hours as the cost-allocation base for fixed setup overhead costs. Budgeted setup-hours for 2007 per the static budget are 7,200 hours.

◆ **Step 3:** *Identify the fixed overhead costs associated with the cost-allocation base.* Lyco's fixed setup overhead cost budget for 2007 is $216,000.

◆ **Step 4:** *Compute the rate per unit of the cost-allocation base used to allocate fixed overhead costs to the cost object(s).* Dividing the $216,000 from step 3 by the 7,200 setup-hours from step 2, Lyco estimates a fixed setup overhead cost rate of $30 per setup-hour:

$$\begin{array}{rl} \text{Budgeted fixed setup} & = \dfrac{\text{Budgeted total costs in overhead cost pool}}{\text{Budgeted total quantity of cost-allocation base}} = \dfrac{\$216{,}000}{7{,}200 \text{ setup-hours}} \\ \text{overhead cost rate} & \\ & = \$30 \text{ per setup-hour} \end{array}$$

Exhibit 8-6 presents the variance analysis of fixed setup overhead in columnar form.

$$\begin{array}{rl} \text{Production-volume} & \text{Budgeted fixed} \quad\quad \text{Fixed setup overhead allocated} \\ \text{variance for fixed setup} = & \text{setup overhead} - \text{using budgeted input allowed for} \\ \text{overhead costs} & \quad\quad \text{costs} \quad\quad\quad\quad \text{actual output units produced} \\ & = \$216{,}000 - (1{,}008 \text{ batches} \times 6 \text{ hours per batch}) \times \$30 \\ & = \$216{,}000 - (6{,}048 \times \$30) = \$216{,}000 - \$181{,}440 \\ & = \$34{,}560 \text{ U} \end{array}$$

During 2007, Lyco planned to produce 180,000 units of Jacutaps but actually produced only 151,200 units. The unfavourable production-volume variance measures the amount of extra fixed setup costs that Lyco incurred for setup capacity it planned to use but did not.

One interpretation is that the unfavourable $34,560 production-volume variance represents inefficient utilization of setup capacity. However, Lyco may have earned higher operating income by selling 151,200 units at a higher price than what it would have earned by selling 180,000 units at a lower price. The production-volume variance should be interpreted cautiously because it does not consider such information.

EXHIBIT 8-6

Columnar Presentation of Fixed Setup Overhead Variance Analysis: Lyco Brass Works for 2007

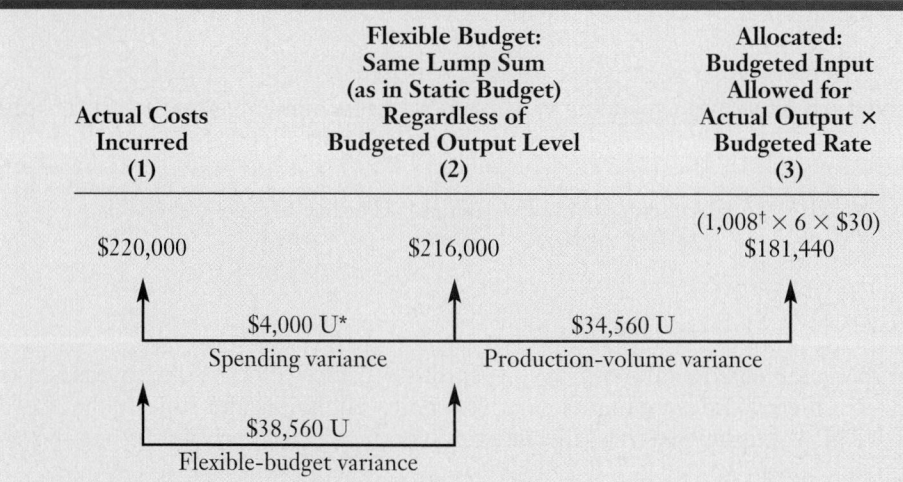

*F = favourable effect on operating income; U = unfavourable effect on operating income.
†1,008 batches = 151,200 units ÷ 150 units per batch

PROBLEM FOR SELF-STUDY

PROBLEM

Maria Lopez is the newly appointed president of Laser Products. She is examining the May 2007 results for the Aerospace Products division. This division manufactures wing parts for satellites. Lopez's current concern is with manufacturing overhead costs at the Aerospace Products division. Both variable and fixed manufacturing overhead costs are allocated to the wing parts based on laser-cutting-hours. The budgeted cost rates are variable manufacturing overhead of $200 per hour and fixed manufacturing overhead of $240 per hour. The budgeted laser-cutting time per wing part is 1.50 hours. Budgeted production and sales for 2007 is 5,000 wing parts. Budgeted fixed manufacturing overhead costs for May 2007 are $1,800,000.

Actual results for 2007 are as follows:

Wing parts produced and sold	4,800 units
Laser-cutting-hours used	8,400 hours
Variable manufacturing overhead costs	$1,478,400
Fixed manufacturing overhead costs	$1,832,200

REQUIRED

1. Compute the spending variance and the efficiency variance for variable manufacturing overhead.
2. Compute the spending variance and the production volume variance for fixed manufacturing overhead.
3. Give two explanations for the variances in requirements 1 and 2.

SOLUTION

1. and 2. See Exhibit 8-7.
3. a. Variable manufacturing overhead spending variance ($201,600 F). One possible reason is that the actual prices of individual items included in variable overhead (such as cutting fluids) are lower than the budgeted prices. A second

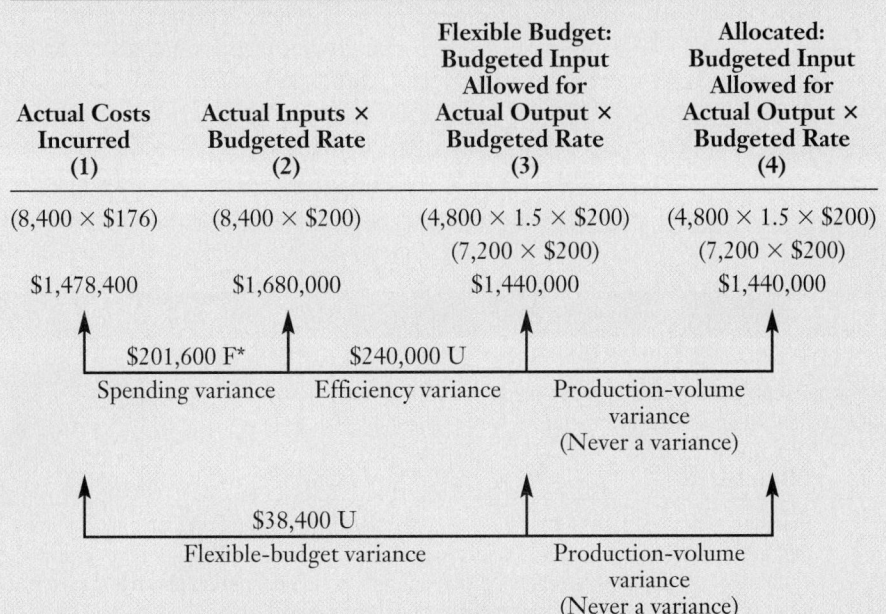

PANEL A: VARIABLE MANUFACTURING OVERHEAD

Actual Costs Incurred (1)	Actual Inputs × Budgeted Rate (2)	Flexible Budget: Budgeted Input Allowed for Actual Output × Budgeted Rate (3)	Allocated: Budgeted Input Allowed for Actual Output × Budgeted Rate (4)
(8,400 × $176)	(8,400 × $200)	(4,800 × 1.5 × $200) (7,200 × $200)	(4,800 × 1.5 × $200) (7,200 × $200)
$1,478,400	$1,680,000	$1,440,000	$1,440,000

↑←——— $201,600 F* ———→↑←——— $240,000 U ———→↑ ↑
Spending variance ———— Efficiency variance ———— Production-volume variance (Never a variance)

↑←———————————— $38,400 U ————————————→↑ ↑
Flexible-budget variance ———— Production-volume variance (Never a variance)

PANEL B: FIXED MANUFACTURING OVERHEAD

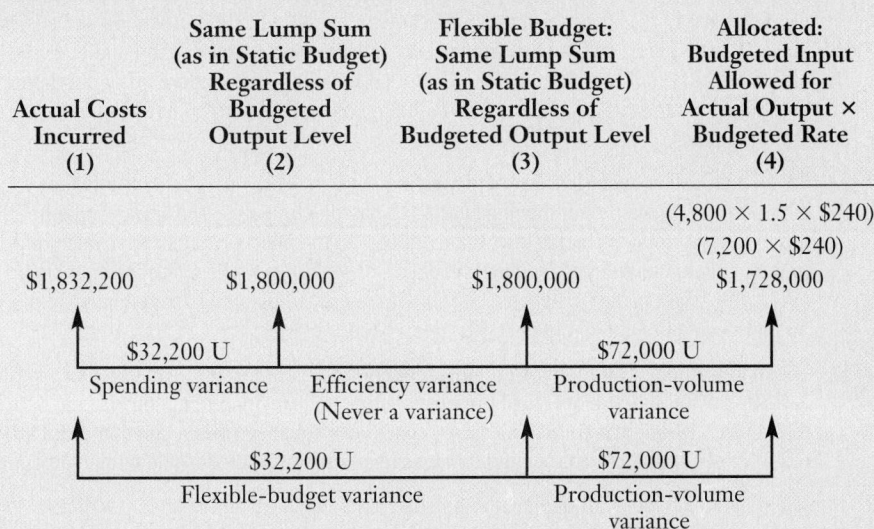

Actual Costs Incurred (1)	Same Lump Sum (as in Static Budget) Regardless of Budgeted Output Level (2)	Flexible Budget: Same Lump Sum (as in Static Budget) Regardless of Budgeted Output Level (3)	Allocated: Budgeted Input Allowed for Actual Output × Budgeted Rate (4)
			(4,800 × 1.5 × $240) (7,200 × $240)
$1,832,200	$1,800,000	$1,800,000	$1,728,000

↑←——— $32,200 U ———→↑ ↑←——— $72,000 U ———→↑
Spending variance ———— Efficiency variance (Never a variance) ———— Production-volume variance

↑←——— $32,200 U ———→↑ ↑←——— $72,000 U ———→↑
Flexible-budget variance ———— Production-volume variance

*F = favourable effect on operating income; U = unfavourable effect on operating income.

possible reason is that the percentage increase in the actual quantity usage of individual items in the variable overhead cost pool is less than the percentage increase in machine-hours compared to the flexible budget.

b. Variable manufacturing overhead efficiency variance ($240,000 U). One possible reason is inadequate maintenance of laser machines, causing them to take more laser time per wing part. A second possible reason is use of less-trained workers with the laser-cutting machines resulting in longer laser time per wing part.

c. Fixed manufacturing overhead spending variance ($32,200 U). One possible reason is that the actual prices of individual items in the fixed-cost pool unexpectedly increased from those budgeted (such as an unexpected increase in machine leasing costs). A second possible reason is misclassification of items as fixed that are in fact variable.

d. Production-volume variance ($72,000 U). Actual production of wing parts is 4,800 units compared with the 5,000 units budgeted. One possible reason is demand factors, such as a decline in the aerospace program that led to a decline in the demand for aircraft parts. A second possible reason is supply factors, such as a production stoppage due to labour problems or machine breakdowns.

DECISION POINTS   SUMMARY

The following decision guidelines use a question-and-answer format to summarize the chapter's main points. Each decision presents a key question. The guideline is the answer to that question.

DECISIONS	GUIDELINES
1. How do managers plan variable overhead costs and fixed overhead costs?	Planning of both variable and fixed overhead costs involves undertaking only activities that add value and then being efficient in that undertaking. The key difference is that for variable-cost planning, ongoing decisions during the budget period play a larger role, whereas for fixed-cost planning, most key decisions must be made before the start of the period.
2. Why do companies use standard costing?	A standard-costing system traces direct costs to a cost object by multiplying the standard prices or rates times the standard inputs allowed for actual output produced and assigns indirect costs based on the standard indirect rates times the standard quantities of the allocation bases allowed for the actual output produced. The standard costs of products are known at the start of the period. To manage costs, managers compare actual and standard costs.
3. What variances can be calculated for variable overhead?	When the flexible budget for variable overhead is developed, an overhead-efficiency variance and an overhead-spending variance can be computed. The variable overhead efficiency variance evaluates the actual quantity of the cost-allocation base used relative to the budgeted quantity of the cost-allocation base. The variable overhead spending variance evaluates the actual cost per unit of the cost-allocation base relative to the budgeted cost per unit of the cost-allocation base.
4. Is the variable overhead efficiency variance identical to the efficiency variance for a direct-cost item?	These two efficiency variances are not identical. The variable overhead efficiency variance indicates whether more or less of the *cost allocation base* per output unit was used relative to the flexible budget amount. The direct-cost item efficiency variance indicates whether more or less of the *input* per output unit was used relative to the flexible budget amount.
5. How is a budgeted fixed overhead cost rate calculated?	The budgeted fixed overhead cost rate is calculated by dividing the budgeted fixed overhead costs by the denominator level of the cost-allocation base.
6. How should you interpret the production-volume variance?	Interpret cautiously the production-volume variance as a measure of the economic cost of unused capacity. One caution: management may have maintained some extra capacity to meet uncertain demand surges that are important to satisfy. Another caution: the production-volume variance focuses only on fixed overhead costs. The production-volume variance does not take into account any decreases in the selling price of output necessary to spur extra demand that would, in turn, make use of any idle capacity.
7. What is the most detailed way for a company to reconcile actual overhead incurred with the amount allocated during a period?	A four-variance analysis presents spending and efficiency variances for variable overhead costs and spending and production-volume variances for fixed overhead costs. By analyzing these four variances together, managers can reconcile the actual overhead costs with the amount of overhead allocated to output produced during a period.
8. Can the flexible-budget variance approach for analyzing overhead costs be used in activity-based costing?	Flexible budgeting in ABC systems gives insight into why actual overhead activity costs differ from budgeted overhead activity costs. Using output and input measures for an activity, a four-variance analysis can be conducted.

This chapter contains definitions of the following important terms:

combined-variance analysis (p. 298)
denominator level (p. 293)
denominator-level variance (p. 294)
non-value-added cost (p. 286)
output-level overhead variance (p. 294)
production denominator level (p. 293)

production denominator volume (p. 293)
production-volume variance (p. 294)
value-added cost (p. 286)
variable overhead efficiency variance (p. 290)
variable overhead spending
   variance (p. 291)

ASSIGNMENT MATERIAL

QUESTIONS

8-1 What are the steps in planning variable overhead costs?

8-2 How does the planning of fixed overhead costs differ from the planning of variable overhead costs?

8-3 How does a standard-costing system differ from an actual-costing system?

8-4 What are the steps in developing a budgeted variable overhead cost allocation rate?

8-5 The spending variance for variable manufacturing overhead is affected by several factors. Explain.

8-6 Assume variable manufacturing overhead is allocated using machine-hours. Give three possible reasons for a $30,000 favourable variable overhead efficiency variance.

8-7 Describe the difference between a direct materials efficiency variance and a variable manufacturing overhead efficiency variance.

8-8 What are the steps in developing a budgeted fixed overhead rate?

8-9 Why is the flexible-budget variance the same amount as the spending variance for fixed manufacturing overhead?

8-10 Explain how four-variance analysis differs from one-, two-, and three-variance analysis.

8-11 Describe one caveat that will affect whether a production-volume variance is a good measure of the economic cost of unused capacity.

8-12 Why is there no efficiency variance for fixed manufacturing overhead costs?

8-13 "Overhead variances should be viewed as interdependent rather than independent." Give an example.

8-14 Explain how the analysis of fixed overhead costs differs for (a) planning and control on the one hand and (b) inventory costing for financial reporting on the other.

8-15 How can the Levels 1 to 3 variance analysis approach be used in control of costs in activity areas?

EXERCISES

8-16 **Variable manufacturing overhead, variance analysis.** Esquire Clothing is a manufacturer of designer suits. The cost of each suit is the sum of three variable costs (direct materials costs, direct manufacturing labour costs, and manufacturing overhead costs) and one fixed-cost category (manufacturing overhead costs). Variable manufacturing overhead cost is allocated to each suit based on budgeted direct manufacturing labour-hours per suit. For June 2007, each suit is budgeted to take 4 labour-hours. Budgeted variable manufacturing overhead costs per labour-hour are $14.40. The budgeted number of suits to be manufactured in June 2007 is 1,040.

Actual variable manufacturing overhead costs in June 2007 were $62,597 for 1,080 suits started and completed. There was no beginning or ending inventory of suits. Actual direct manufacturing labour-hours for June were 4,536.

REQUIRED
1. Compute the static-budget variance, the flexible-budget variance, and the sales-volume variance for variable manufacturing overhead.
2. Comment on the results.

8-17 Fixed manufacturing overhead, variance analysis (continuation of 8-16). Esquire Clothing allocates fixed manufacturing overhead to each suit using budgeted direct manufacturing labour-hours per suit. Data pertaining to fixed manufacturing overhead costs for June 2007 are $74,880, budgeted, and $76,700, actual.

REQUIRED

1. Compute the spending variance and the flexible-budget variance for fixed manufacturing overhead. Comment on these results.
2. Compute the production volume variance for June 2007. What inferences can Esquire Clothing draw from this variance?

8-18 Variable manufacturing overhead variance analysis. The French Bread Company bakes baguettes for distribution to upscale grocery stores. The company has two direct-cost categories, direct materials and direct manufacturing labour. Variable manufacturing overhead is allocated to products based on standard direct manufacturing labour-hours. Baguettes are baked in batches of 100 loaves. Following is some pertinent data for the French Bread Company:

Direct manufacturing labour use	2.00 hours per batch
Variable manufacturing overhead	$12.00 per direct labour-hour

The French Bread Company recorded the following additional data for the year ended December 31, 2007:

Planned (budgeted) output	3,200,000 baguettes
Actual production	2,800,000 baguettes
Direct manufacturing labour	50,400 hours
Actual variable MOH	$816,480

REQUIRED

1. What is the denominator used for allocating manufacturing overhead (i.e., how many direct manufacturing labour-hours is French Bread budgeting for)?
2. Prepare a complete analysis of variable manufacturing overhead (Levels 1 through 3). Use the exhibits in this chapter for reference.
3. Discuss the variances you have calculated. Posit possible explanations for these variances.

8-19 Fixed manufacturing overhead variance analysis (continuation of 8-18). The French Bread Company has two direct-cost categories, direct materials and direct manufacturing labour. Fixed manufacturing overhead is allocated to products on the basis of standard direct manufacturing labours. Baguettes are baked in batches of 100 loaves. Following is some pertinent data for the French Bread Company:

Direct manufacturing labour use	2.00 hours per batch
Fixed manufacturing overhead	$4.00 per direct labour-hour

The French Bread Company recorded the following additional data for the year ended December 31, 2007:

Planned (budgeted) output	3,840,000 baguettes
Actual production	3,360,000 baguettes
Direct manufacturing labour	50,400 hours
Actual fixed MOH	$326,400

REQUIRED

1. Prepare a variance analysis of fixed manufacturing overhead costs.
2. Is fixed overhead under- or overallocated? By how much?
3. Comment on your results. Discuss the various variances and explain what may be driving them.

8-20 Manufacturing overhead, variance analysis. Zyton assembles its CardioX product at its Scottsdale plant. Manufacturing overhead (both variable and fixed) is allocated to each CardioX unit using budgeted assembly time hours. Budgeted assembly time per CardioX product is two hours. The budgeted variable manufacturing overhead cost per assembly time hour is $48. The budgeted number of CardioX units to be assembled in March 2007 is 8,000. Budgeted fixed manufacturing overhead costs are $576,000.

Actual variable manufacturing overhead costs for March 2007 were $732,600 for 7,400 units actually assembled. Actual assembly-time-hours were 16,280. Actual fixed manufacturing overhead costs were $604,104.

1. Conduct a four-variance analysis for Zyton's Scottsdale plant.
2. Comment on the results in requirement 1.
3. How does the planning and control of variable manufacturing overhead costs differ from that of fixed manufacturing overhead costs?

8-21 Spending and efficiency overhead variances, service sector. Home Cooking (HC) operates a home meal delivery service. It has agreements with 20 restaurants to pick up and deliver meals to customers who phone or fax in orders. HC is currently examining its overhead costs for May 2007.

Variable overhead costs for May 2007 were budgeted at $2 per hour of home delivery time. Fixed overhead costs were budgeted at $28,800. The budgeted number of home deliveries in May 2007 was 9,600. Delivery time, the allocation base for variable and fixed overhead costs, is budgeted to be 0.80 hour per delivery.

Actual results for May 2007 were as follows:

Variable overhead	$17,008
Fixed overhead	$33,120
Number of home deliveries	8,952
Hours of delivery time	6,714

Customers are charged $12 per delivery. The delivery driver is paid $7 per delivery. HC receives a 10% commission on the meal costs that the restaurants charge the customers who use HC.

REQUIRED
1. Compute spending and efficiency variances for HC's variable and fixed overhead in May 2007. Comment on the results.
2. How might HC manage its variable overhead costs differently from the way it manages its fixed overhead costs?

Excel Application For students who wish to practise their spreadsheet skills, the following is a step-by-step approach to creating an Excel spreadsheet to work this problem.

Step-by Step
(Program your spreadsheet to perform all necessary calculations. Do not "hard-code" any of your variance calculations.)

1. At the top of a new spreadsheet, create an "Original Data" section for the data provided for Home Cooking, with rows labelled "Output Units (number of deliveries)," "Hours of Delivery Time," "Hours per Delivery," "Variable Overhead Costs," "Variable Overhead Costs per Hour of Delivery Time," and "Fixed Overhead Costs." Create columns for "Actual Results" and "Flexible Budget Amounts." Enter the data provided for HC in this section. You will have to enter calculations for actual hours per delivery, budgeted hours of delivery time, budgeted variable overhead costs per hour of delivery time, and actual variable overhead cost per hour of delivery time.
2. Skip two rows, and create a section, "Variance Calculations," with rows for "Actual Costs Incurred," "Actual Input × Budgeted Rate," "Budgeted Input Allowed for Actual Output × Budgeted Rate," "Spending Variance," "Efficiency Variance," and "Fixed Overhead Spending Variance." Use the data from the Original Data section to calculate actual costs incurred, actual input times budgeted rate, and budgeted input allowed for actual times budgeted rate.
3. For Problem 1, use the data you created in step 2 to calculate spending and efficiency variances for Home Cooking's variable overhead in May 2007. For Problem 2, use the actual and budgeted fixed overhead costs in the Original Data section to calculate the spending variance for Home Cooking's fixed overhead in May 2007.
4. *Verify the accuracy of your spreadsheet.* Go to your Original Data section and change the actual number of deliveries from 8,952 to 9,000. If you programmed your spreadsheet correctly, then the variable manufacturing overhead efficiency variance should change to ($972) favourable.

8-22 Spending and efficiency overhead variances, distribution. Package Postal Service (PPS) operates a parcel delivery service. PPS's costing system has one direct-cost category (delivery driver payments) and two overhead categories—variable delivery overhead and fixed delivery overhead. In 2007 it charged retail companies and mail-order catalogue companies $18 per delivery. Delivery drivers in 2007 were contracted at $6 per delivery. Variable delivery overhead for September 2007 was budgeted at $2.40 per hour of delivery time. Budgeted fixed delivery overhead in September 2007 was $144,000. PPS budgeted 100,000 deliveries for September 2007. Delivery time, the allocation base for variable and fixed overhead costs, is budgeted to be 0.25 hours per delivery.

Actual results for September 2007 were as follows:

Variable delivery overhead	$ 72,000
Fixed delivery overhead	$154,080
Number of deliveries	96,000
Hours of delivery time	28,800

REQUIRED

1. Compute the spending and efficiency variances for PPS's variable delivery overhead costs in September 2007. Compute the spending and production volume variances for PPS's fixed delivery overhead costs in September 2007. Comment on the results.
2. What problems might PPS face in managing (a) its direct costs, (b) its variable delivery overhead costs, and (c) its fixed delivery overhead costs?

8-23 Four-variance analysis, fill in the blanks. Use the given manufacturing overhead data to fill in the blanks.

	Variable	Fixed
Actual costs incurred	$14,280	$7,200
Allocated to products	10,800	5,400
Flexible budget: Budgeted input allowed for actual output achieved × budgeted rate	10,800	6,000
Actual input × budgeted rate	12,000	6,000

Use F for favourable and U for unfavourable:

	Variable	Fixed
1. Spending variance	$ _____	$ _____
2. Efficiency variance	_____	_____
3. Production-volume variance	_____	_____
4. Flexible-budget variance	_____	_____
5. Underallocated (overallocated) manuf. overhead	_____	_____

8-24 Straightforward four-variance overhead analysis. The Lopez Company uses a standard-cost system in its manufacturing plant for auto parts. Its standard cost of an auto part, based on a denominator level of 4,000 output units per year, included six machine-hours of variable manufacturing overhead at $9.60 per hour and six machine-hours of fixed manufacturing overhead at $18 per hour. Actual output achieved was 4,400 units. Variable manufacturing overhead incurred was $294,580. Fixed manufacturing overhead incurred was $447,590. Actual incurred machine-hours were 28,600.

REQUIRED

1. Prepare an analysis of all variable manufacturing overhead and fixed manufacturing overhead variances, using the four-variance analysis.
2. Prepare journal entries using the four-variance analysis.
3. Describe how individual variable manufacturing overhead items are controlled from day to day. Also, describe how individual fixed manufacturing overhead items are controlled.

8-25 Straightforward coverage of manufacturing overhead, standard cost system. The Singapore division of a Canadian telecommunications company uses a standard cost system for its machine-based production of telephone equipment. Data regarding production during June are as follows:

Variable manufacturing overhead costs incurred	$186,120
Variable manufacturing overhead costs allocated (per standard machine-hour allowed for actual output achieved)	$ 14.40
Fixed manufacturing overhead costs incurred	$481,200
Fixed manufacturing overhead budgeted	$468,000
Denominator level in machine-hours	15,600
Standard machine-hours allowed per unit of output	0.30
Units of output	49,200
Actual machine-hours used	15,960
Ending work-in-process inventory	0

REQUIRED

1. Prepare an analysis of all manufacturing overhead variances. Use the four-variance analysis framework illustrated in Exhibit 8-3, p. 295.
2. Prepare journal entries for manufacturing overhead without explanations.
3. Describe how individual variable manufacturing overhead items are controlled from day to day. Also, describe how individual fixed manufacturing overhead items are controlled.

8-26 Total overhead, three-variance analysis. The Atlantic Canada Air Force Base has an extensive repair facility for jet engines. It developed standard costing and flexible budgets to account for this activity. Budgeted variable overhead at a level of 8,000 standard monthly direct labour-hours was $76,800; budgeted total overhead at 10,000 standard direct labour-hours was $237,120. The standard cost allocated to repair output included a total overhead rate of 120% of standard direct labour cost.

Total overhead incurred for October was $298,800. Direct labour costs incurred were $242,928. The direct labour price variance was $11,568 U. The direct labour flexible-budget variance was $17,328 U. The standard labour price was $19.20 per hour. The production-volume variance was $16,800 F.

REQUIRED

1. Compute the direct labour efficiency variance and the spending, efficiency, and production volume variances for overhead. Also, compute the denominator level.
2. Describe how individual variable manufacturing overhead items are controlled from day to day. Also, describe how individual fixed manufacturing overhead items are controlled.

8-27 Four-variance analysis, working backwards. Lookmeup.com is striving to become a Web portal. The site allows surfers to find anything they want to look up—be it a person, a site, a company, or news article—through one interactive and easy-to-use interface. Most of Lookmeup.com's operating overhead is due to Internet connection costs. Lookmeup.com faces both fixed and variable Internet connection charges. Following is the four-variance analysis of Lookmeup.com's operations overhead:

	Spending Variance	Efficiency Variance	Production-Volume Variance
Variable Operating Overhead	$44,400 F	$28,800 F	Never a variance
Fixed Operating Overhead	$16,800 U	Never a variance	$20,400 U

REQUIRED

1. For total operating overhead, compute the following:
   a. Spending variance
   b. Efficiency variance
   c. Production-volume variance
   d. Flexible-budget variance
   e. Total overhead variance
   Arrange your results in a suitable format for presenting three-variance, two-variance, and one-variance analyses.
2. If Lookmeup.com's total actual operating overhead was $420,000, what was the operating overhead allocated to actual output units provided?
3. Can you say whether fixed operating overhead was under- or overallocated? If so, by what amount?
4. Are Lookmeup.com's different variances in the four-variance analysis above necessarily independent? Explain and provide an example.

8-28 Overhead variances, missing information. Blakely Printing prepared its budget at 10,000 machine hours. Blakely reported a $900 unfavourable spending variance for fixed overhead and a $300 unfavourable spending variance for variable overhead. The budgeted variable overhead rate is $6 per machine hour. The input allowed for actual output was 9,900 machine hours. Actual machine hours were 9,800, and actual total overhead costs were $96,000.

REQUIRED

1. Compute variable overhead efficiency variance, flexible-budget variance, and the amount underallocated or overallocated.
2. Calculate fixed overhead production-volume variance, flexible-budget variance, and the amount underallocated or overallocated.

8-29 Variance analysis, graphs. Homer Metal Stamping budgets and allocates overhead costs using machine-hours. Homer's budget for 2007 was 10,000 machine-hours. Following is additional information relating to overhead for 2007:

Budgeted fixed overhead	$ 720,000
Actual fixed overhead	$ 708,000
Budgeted variable overhead	$1,200,000
Actual variable overhead	$1,320,000
Budgeted machine-hours allowed for actual output	9,800
Actual machine-hours used	9,500

REQUIRED
1. Compute the variable overhead spending variance and efficiency variance.
2. Compute the fixed overhead spending variance and production-volume variance.
3. Draw graphs similar to those in Exhibit 8-4, Panel A (variable overhead) and Panel B (fixed overhead) on page 301.

8-30 Comprehensive review of Chapters 7 and 8, static budget. *The Monthly Herald* budgets to produce 300,000 copies of its monthly newspaper for August 2007. It is budgeted to run 15,000,000 print pages in August with 50 print pages per newspaper. Actual production in August 2007 was 320,000 copies with 17,280,000 print pages run. Each paper was only 50 print pages, but quality problems with paper led to many pages being unusable.

Variable costs comprise direct materials, direct labour, and variable indirect costs. Variable and fixed indirect costs are allocated to each copy on the basis of print pages. The driver for all variable costs is the number of print pages. Data pertaining to August 2007 are as follows:

	Budgeted	Actual
Direct materials	$216,000	$269,568
Direct labour costs	54,000	60,134
Variable indirect costs	72,000	76,723
Fixed indirect costs	108,000	116,400

Data pertaining to revenues for *The Monthly Herald* in August 2007 are:

	Budgeted	Actual
Circulation revenue	$168,000	$184,800
Advertising revenue	432,000	473,520

The Monthly Herald sells for $0.60 per copy in 2007. No change from this budgeted price of $0.60 per copy occurred in August 2007. The actual direct labour rate in August 2007 was $34.80 per hour. Actual and budgeted pages produced per direct labour-hour in August 2007 was 10,000 print pages. Copies produced but not sold have no value. Advertising revenue covers payments from all advertising sources.

REQUIRED
1. Present a static-budget variance (Level 1) report for *The Monthly Herald*.
2. Comment on the results in requirement 1.

8-31 Comprehensive review of Chapters 7 and 8, flexible budget (continuation of 8-30).

REQUIRED
1. Prepare a comprehensive set of variances for each of the four categories of cost of *The Monthly Herald*.
2. Comment on the results in requirement 1. What extra insights are available with a flexible-budget analysis over that of a static-budget analysis?

PROBLEMS

8-32 Graphs and overhead variances. The Carvelli Company is a manufacturer of housewares. In its job-costing system, manufacturing overhead (both variable and fixed) is allocated to products based on budgeted machine-hours. The budgeted amounts are taken from Carvelli's standard-costing system. The budget for 2007 included:

Variable manufacturing overhead	$10.80 per machine-hour
Fixed manufacturing overhead	$86,400,000
Denominator level	4,000,000 machine-hours

REQUIRED

1. Prepare four graphs, two for variable manufacturing overhead and two for fixed manufacturing overhead. Each pair of graphs should display how total manufacturing overhead costs of Carvelli will be depicted for the purpose of (a) planning and control and (b) inventory costing.
2. Suppose that 3,500,000 machine-hours were allowed for actual output achieved in 2007, but 3,800,000 machine-hours were used. Actual manufacturing overhead was variable, $43,320,000; fixed, $86,640,000. Compute (a) variable manufacturing overhead spending and efficiency variances and (b) the fixed manufacturing overhead spending and production-volume variances. Use the columnar presentation illustrated in Exhibit 8-2 (p. 290).
3. What is the amount of the under- or overallocated variable manufacturing overhead? Of the under- or overallocated fixed manufacturing overhead? Why are the flexible-budget variance and the under- or overallocated overhead amount always the same for variable manufacturing overhead but rarely the same for fixed manufacturing overhead?
4. Suppose the denominator level was 3,000,000 rather than 4,000,000 machine-hours. What variances in requirement 2 would be affected? Recompute them.

8-33 Journal entries (continuation of 8-32). Refer to requirement 2. Consider variable manufacturing overhead and then fixed manufacturing overhead.

REQUIRED

Prepare the journal entries for (a) the incurrence of overhead, (b) the allocation of overhead, and (c) the isolation and closing of overhead variances to Cost of Goods Sold for the year.

8-34 Variance analysis for an activity area. CellOne is a cellular phone service reseller, contracting with major cellular operators for airtime in bulk and then reselling service to retail customers. Having adopted an ABC system last year, CellOne has defined the following activity areas—contracting, marketing, technical service, and customer service.

The technical service area has one major cost driver—technical support hours. One hour of technical support is budgeted for every 5,000 minutes of airtime sold. For the month ended August 31, 2007, CellOne budgeted to sell 6,850,000 minutes; however, actual minutes sold totalled 7,350,000. During August 2007, 1,500 actual technical support hours were logged. Some additional data follow:

	Actual	Budget
Variable technical service activity costs	$37,800	$39,456
Fixed technical service activity costs	$81,000	$83,844

Budgeted input allowed for actual output achieved totalled 1,470 hours of technical support.

REQUIRED

1. What is the actual variable technical service activity area cost per technical support hour? Budgeted cost per hour?
2. What is the allocated fixed technical service area overhead?
3. Calculate the spending variance, the efficiency variance, and the flexible-budget variance for variable overhead costs. Explain these variances based on the data provided.
4. Has CellOne management under- or overallocated fixed overhead for August 2007? Show how you calculate the under/overallocation.

8-35 Four-variance analysis, find the unknowns. Consider each of the following situations—cases A, B, and C—independently. Data refer to operations of April 2007. For each situation, assume a standard-cost system. Also assume the use of a flexible budget for control of variable and fixed manufacturing overhead based on machine-hours.

	Cases		
	A	B	C
1. Fixed manufacturing overhead incurred	$12,720	—	$14,400
2. Variable manufacturing overhead incurred	8,400	—	—
3. Denominator level in machine-hours	—	—	1,100
4. Standard machine-hours allowed for actual output achieved	500	780	—
Flexible budget data:			
5. Fixed manufacturing overhead	—	$ 8,100	—
6. Variable manufacturing overhead (per standard machine-hour)	—	8.50	5.00
7. Budgeted fixed manufacturing overhead	$12,000	—	$13,200
8. Budgeted variable manufacturing overhead*	—	—	—
9. Total budgeted manufacturing overhead*	—	15,030	—
Additional data:			
10. Standard variable manufacturing overhead rate (per machine-hour)	15	—	—
11. Standard fixed manufacturing overhead allocated	12,000	—	—
12. Production-volume variance	—	500 U	600 F
13. Variable manufacturing overhead spending variance	950 F	0	350 U
14. Variable manufacturing overhead efficiency variance	—	0	100 U
15. Fixed manufacturing overhead spending variance	—	300 F	—
16. Actual machine-hours used	—	—	—

*For standard machine-hours allowed for actual output achieved.

REQUIRED

Fill in the blanks under each case. (*Hint:* Prepare a worksheet similar to that in Exhibit 8-3, p. 295. Fill in the knowns and then solve for the unknowns.)

8-36 **Working backward from given variances.** The Mancusco Company uses a flexible budget and standard costs to aid planning and control of its manufacturing operations. Its normal costing system for manufacturing has two direct-cost categories (direct materials and direct manufacturing labour—both variable) and two indirect-cost categories (variable manufacturing overhead and fixed manufacturing overhead, both allocated using direct manufacturing labour-hours).

At the 40,000 budgeted direct manufacturing labour-hour level for August, budgeted direct manufacturing labour is $960,000, budgeted variable manufacturing overhead is $576,000, and budgeted fixed manufacturing overhead is $768,000. The following actual results are for August:

Direct materials price variance (based on purchases)	$211,200 F
Direct materials efficiency variance	82,800 U
Direct manufacturing labour costs incurred	627,300
Variable manufacturing overhead flexible budget variance	12,420 U
Variable manufacturing overhead efficiency variance	21,600 U
Fixed manufacturing overhead incurred	716,952
Fixed manufacturing overhead spending variance	51,048 F

The standard cost per kilogram of direct materials is $13.80. The standard allowance is three kilograms of direct materials for each unit of product. Thirty thousand units of product were produced during August. There was no beginning inventory of direct materials. There was no beginning or ending work in process. In August, the direct materials price variance was $1.32 per kilogram.

In July, labour troubles caused a major slowdown in the pace of production, resulting in an unfavourable direct manufacturing labour efficiency variance of $54,000. There was no manufacturing labour price variance. These troubles persisted into August. Some workers quit. Their replacements had to be hired at higher rates, which had to be extended to all workers. The actual average wage rate in August exceeded the standard average wage rate by $0.60.

1. Compute the following for August:
   a. Total kilograms of direct materials purchased
   b. Total number of kilograms of excess direct materials used
   c. Variable manufacturing overhead spending variance
   d. Total number of actual hours of direct manufacturing labour-hours used
   e. Total number of standard direct manufacturing labour-hours allowed for the units produced
   f. Production-volume variance

2. Compare and contrast the different methods available to Mancuso to control (i) variable manufacturing overhead and (ii) fixed manufacturing overhead.

8-37 Flexible budgets, four-variance analysis. (CMA, adapted) Nolton Products uses a standard-costing system. It allocates manufacturing overhead (both variable and fixed) to products based on standard direct manufacturing labour-hours (DLH). Nolton develops its manufacturing overhead rate from the current annual budget. The manufacturing overhead budget for 2007 is based on budgeted output of 720,000 units requiring 3,600,000 direct manufacturing labour-hours. The company is able to schedule production uniformly throughout the year.

A total of 66,000 output units requiring 315,000 direct labour-hours were produced during May 2007. Manufacturing overhead (MOH) costs incurred for May amounted to $433,000. The actual costs as compared with the annual budget and 1/12 of the annual budget are shown below.

Annual Manufacturing Overhead Budget 2007

	Total Amount	Per Output Unit	Per DLH Input Unit	Monthly MOH Budget May 2007	Actual MOH Costs for May 2007
Variable MOH:					
Indirect manufacturing labour	$1,080,000	$1.50	$0.300	$ 90,000	$ 90,000
Supplies	1,476,800	2.05	0.410	123,000	133,000
Fixed MOH:					
Supervision	777,600	1.08	0.216	64,800	61,200
Utilities	648,000	0.90	0.180	54,000	64,800
Amortization	1,209,600	1.68	0.336	100,800	84,000
Total	$5,191,200	$7.21	$1.442	$432,600	$433,000

REQUIRED
Calculate the following amounts for Nolton Products for May 2007:

1. Fixed manufacturing overhead costs allocated and flexible budget for variable manufacturing overhead
2. Variable manufacturing overhead spending variance
3. Fixed manufacturing overhead spending variance
4. Variable manufacturing overhead efficiency variance
5. Production-volume variance

Be sure to identify each variance as favourable (F) or unfavourable (U).

8-38 Overhead analysis. Armstrong Corporation uses standard costing. The following information is for 2007:

Static-budget machine-hours	33,000
Fixed overhead budget costs	$ 5,940,000
Fixed overhead actual costs	$ 5,400,000
Variable overhead actual costs	$11,520,000
Variable overhead rate per machine-hour	$ 360
Actual machine-hours used	30,000
Budgeted machine-hours allowed for actual output	35,000

REQUIRED
1. Calculate variable overhead spending variance and efficiency variance.
2. Compute fixed overhead spending variance and production-volume variance.

8-39 Sales-volume variance, production-volume variance. Morano Company prepared its budgeted output and sales at its maximum capacity of 20,000 units for 2007. However, due to efficiency improvements, Morano was able to sell 22,000 units for the year. Other data for 2007 follow:

Budgeted fixed overhead costs	$600,000
Budgeted selling price	$ 120
Budgeted variable cost per unit	$ 48

REQUIRED
1. Calculate the budgeted profit per unit, the operating income based on the budgeted profit per unit, the flexible-budget operating income, and the static-budget operating income.
2. Compute sales-volume variance and production-volume variance. What do each of these variances measure?

8-40 Activity-based costing, variance analysis. Asma Surgical Instruments, Inc., makes a special line of forceps, SFA, in batches. Asma randomly selects forceps from each SFA batch for quality-testing purposes. Quality-testing costs are batch-level costs. A separate quality-testing section is responsible for SFA quality testing.

Quality-testing costs consist of some variable and some fixed costs in relation to the quality-testing hours. The following information is for 2007:

	Static-Budget Amounts	Actual Amounts
Units of SFA produced and sold	21,000	22,000
Batch size (number of units per batch)	500	550
Testing-hours per batch	5.5	5.4
Variable overhead cost per testing-hour	$ 48.00	$ 50.40
Total fixed testing overhead costs	$34,650	$32,659

REQUIRED
1. For variable testing overhead costs, compute the efficiency and spending variances. Comment on the results.
2. For fixed testing overhead costs, compute the spending and the production-volume variances. Comment on the results.

8-41 Comprehensive variance analysis. FlatScreen manufactures flat-panel LCD displays. The displays are sold to major PC manufacturers. Following is some manufacturing overhead data for FlatScreen for the year ended December 31, 2007:

	Actual	Flexible Budget	Allocated Amount
Variable manufacturing overhead	$1,838,592	$1,843,200	$1,843,200
Fixed manufacturing overhead	$8,404,992	$8,354,304	$9,031,680

FlatScreen's budget was based on the assumption that 17,760 units (panels) will be manufactured during 2007. The planned allocation rate was two machine-hours per unit. FlatScreen uses machine-hours as the cost driver. Actual number of machine-hours used during 2007 was 36,480. The budgeted variable manufacturing overhead costs equal $1,704,960.

REQUIRED
Compute the following quantities (you should be able to do so in the prescribed order):
1. Budgeted number of machine-hours planned
2. Budgeted fixed manufacturing overhead costs per machine-hour
3. Budgeted variable manufacturing overhead costs per machine-hour
4. Budgeted number of machine-hours allowed for actual output achieved
5. Actual number of output units
6. Actual number of machine-hours used per panel
7. Allocated amount for fixed manufacturing overhead

8-42 Journal entries (continuation of 8-41).

REQUIRED
1. Prepare appropriate journal entries for variable and fixed manufacturing overhead (you will need to calculate the different variances to accomplish this).
2. Overhead variances may be used to reconcile the cost of goods sold account at the end of the fiscal year. Cost of goods sold (COGS) is then entered on the income statement. Show how COGS is reconciled through journal entries.

8-43 Review of Chapters 7 and 8, three-variance analysis. (CPA, adapted) The Beal Manufacturing Company's job-costing system has two direct-cost categories, direct materials and direct manufacturing labour. Manufacturing overhead (both variable and fixed) is allocated to products based on standard direct manufacturing labour-hours (DLH). At the beginning of 2007, Beal adopted the following standards for its manufacturing costs:

	Input	Cost per Output Unit
Direct materials	3 kilograms at $6 per kilogram	$ 18
Direct manufacturing labour	5 hours at $18 per hour	90
Manufacturing overhead:		
Variable	$7.20 per DLH	36
Fixed	$9.60 per DLH	48
Standard manufacturing cost per output unit		$192

The denominator level for total manufacturing overhead per month in 2007 is 40,000 direct manufacturing labour-hours. Beal's flexible budget for January 2007 was based on this denominator level. The records for January indicate the following:

Direct materials purchased	25,000 kilograms at $6.24 per kilogram
Direct materials used	23,100 kilograms
Direct manufacturing labour	40,100 hours, at $17.52 per hour
Total actual manufacturing overhead (variable and fixed)	$720,000
Actual production	7,800 output units

REQUIRED

1. Prepare a schedule of total standard manufacturing costs for the 7,800 output units in January, 2007.
2. For January 2007, compute the following variances, indicating whether each is favourable (F) or unfavourable (U):
   a. Direct materials price variance, based on purchases
   b. Direct materials efficiency variance
   c. Direct manufacturing labour price variance
   d. Direct manufacturing labour efficiency variance
   e. Total manufacturing overhead spending variance
   f. Variable manufacturing overhead efficiency variance
   g. Production-volume variance

8-44 Variance analysis for ABC. Starport manufactures and launches space stations. The stations are custom-made according to specifications furnished by the ordering party. Starport has adopted an ABC system and has defined activity areas as follows: design, prototyping, testing, fabrication, launching, and assembly. In what follows, we focus on the launching activity area.

Starport launches space station components into orbit from a base located on a remote island in the Pacific Ocean. Components are assembled in orbit according to the custom designs. Starport sells unused capacity in its launch facilities to launch other companies' products into orbit and beyond. The launching activity area has both variable and fixed costs. You are presented with the following data for the year ended December 31, 2007:

	Actual	Budget
Launches	265	250
Launch hours	5,300	5,500
Variable launch activity area costs (millions)	$ 445.20	$ 448.80
Fixed launch activity area costs (millions)	$1,971.60	$2,032.80

REQUIRED

1. Complete the numbers in the following table. The calculations will assist you in answering requirement 2.
2. Prepare an analysis of Starport's 2007 launching activity area costs.
3. Analyze your results. Provide explanations for the variances you calculate.

	Actual Results	Flexible-Budget Amount
1. Output units (launches)	265	?
2. Launch-hours	5,300	?
3. Launch-hours per launch	?	?
4. Variable launch-activity costs	$ 445,200,000	?
5. Variable launch-activity costs per launch-hour	?	?
6. Variable launch-activity costs per launch	?	?
7. Fixed launch-activity costs	$1,971,600,000	?
8. Fixed launch-activity costs per launch-hour	?	?
9. Fixed launch-activity costs per launch	?	?

COLLABORATIVE LEARNING PROBLEMS

8-45 Hospital overhead variances, four-variance analysis. The Sharon Hospital, a large metropolitan health-care complex, has had difficulty controlling its accounts receivable. Costs currently available from the information system are inaccurate and have led to gross errors in reports to government funding agencies that show the hospital is operating at a deficit. The hospital managers are concerned that the poor quality of information could lead to their replacement by others appointed by the government.

With the participation of the billing department, a set of standard costs and standard amounts was developed for 2007. These standard costs can be used in a flexible budget with separate variable-cost and fixed-cost categories. The output unit is defined to be a single bill.

The accountant of Sharon Hospital provides you with the following for April 2007:

Variable overhead costs, allowance per standard hour	$ 12
Fixed overhead flexible budget variance	$ 240 F
Total budgeted overhead costs for the bills prepared	$27,000
Production-volume variance	$ 1,080 F
Variable cost spending variance	$ 2,400 U
Variable cost efficiency variance	$ 2,400 F
Standard hours allowed for the bills prepared	1,800 labour-hours

REQUIRED

Form groups of two or more students to compute the following:

1. Actual hours of input used
2. Fixed overhead budget
3. Fixed overhead allocated
4. Budgeted fixed overhead rate per hour
5. Denominator level in hours

8-46 Standard setting, benchmarking, ethics (continuation of 8-45). Ira Stone, the president of Sharon Hospital, has a meeting with the Medical Economics Group (MEG). MEG is a consulting firm in the health services sector. It reports that Sharon's billing operations are grossly inefficient. Its standard costing per bill is above 90% of the 130 hospitals MEG tracks in its benchmarking database.

Stone suspects the billing group deliberately "padded" its standard costs and standard amounts. Despite large investment in new information systems, the standards for 2007 were not below actual results for 2006. Stone does not want to institute a witch hunt, but he does want to eliminate the fat in Sharon's cost structure.

REQUIRED

1. How might Sharon's billing operations group have "padded" its standard costs and standard amounts? Why might they do this padding?
2. What steps should Stone take to "reduce the fat" in the overhead costs of the billing operations at Sharon Hospital?

Inventory costing is important to businesses because managers must make pricing decisions to not only cover costs but also provide a return. Managers must decide upon issues such as which costs to include and on what level of output capacity to base their overall costs.

The wide range of products produced and the complexity of the production processes complicate Imperial Oil's inventory costing practices, which also affects the cost of goods sold. Given the volatility of the prices of oil and gasoline products, inventory costing is especially important to companies in the oil and gas industry.

LEARNING OBJECTIVES

After studying this chapter, you should be able to

1. Identify the key feature that distinguishes variable costing from absorption costing

2. Prepare income statements using absorption costing and variable costing

3. Explain differences in operating income under absorption costing and variable costing

4. Understand how absorption costing influences performance evaluation decisions

5. Differentiate throughput costing from variable costing and absorption costing

6. Describe the various capacity concepts that can be used in absorption costing

7. Explain how the choice of denominator level affects reported operating income and inventory costs

8. Understand the major factors managers consider in choosing a capacity level to compute the budgeted fixed overhead cost rate

9. Describe how attempts to recover fixed costs of capacity may lead to price increases and lower demand

CHAPTER 9

Income Effects of Alternative Inventory Costing Methods

The reported income number captures the attention of managers in a way few other numbers do. Consider three examples:

1. Planning decisions typically include an analysis of how the considered options affect future reported income.

2. An increase in reported income is the object of many decisions related to cost reduction.

3. Reported income is a key number in the performance evaluation of managers.

The decisions managers make related to valuation of inventories for manufacturing companies are informed primarily by cost accounting information. Inventory values affect not only the current assets on the balance sheet but also gross margin, earnings before interest and taxes, and net income on the income statement. This is because inventory values affect cost of goods sold. In this chapter we examine two such choices:

1. *Inventory costing choices.* The cost accounts provide information enabling managers to choose what costs will be inventoriable and therefore recorded as inventory assets when they are incurred. For internal planning and control

purposes we present three alternatives from which managers may choose: variable costing, absorption costing, and throughput costing.

2. *Denominator-level capacity choices.* The choices here relate to the preselected level of the cost-allocation base used to set budgeted fixed manufacturing cost rates. For internal planning and control purposes, we present four alternatives from which managers may choose: theoretical capacity, practical capacity, normal utilization, and master-budget utilization.

◆ PART ONE: INVENTORY COSTING METHODS

The two most commonly encountered methods of costing inventories are variable costing and absorption costing. Note that only manufacturing costs are included in both inventory valuation and cost of goods sold. We discuss these two valuation methods first and then cover throughput costing.

VARIABLE COSTING AND ABSORPTION COSTING

Variable manufacturing costs often vary with the quantity or volume of output units produced. In contrast, variable nonmanufacturing costs such as sales commissions often vary with the dollar value of revenue from the quantity or volume of units sold.

OBJECTIVE 1

Identify the key feature that distinguishes variable costing from absorption costing

Variable costing (direct costing). Inventory costing method in which only variable manufacturing costs are included as inventoriable costs. All fixed costs and all nonmanufacturing costs are excluded from inventoriable costs; they are costs of the period in which they are incurred.

Absorption costing. Inventory costing method in which all manufacturing costs are included as inventoriable costs. All non-manufacturing costs are classified as costs of the period in which they are incurred.

Variable costing and absorption costing differ in one key respect: whether fixed manufacturing costs (both direct and indirect) are classified as inventoriable costs or as period costs. Recall that *inventoriable costs* for a manufacturing company are costs associated with the acquisition and conversion of materials and all other manufacturing inputs into goods for sale; these costs are first recorded as an asset (inventory) and then subsequently become an expense when the goods are sold.

Variable costing is a method of inventory costing in which only *variable manufacturing* costs are included as inventoriable costs. This method excludes all fixed and all nonmanufacturing costs from inventoriable costs. All fixed costs and all manufacturing costs are classified as period costs and expensed during the specific time period they are incurred. **Absorption costing** is a method of inventory costing in which inventory "absorbs" both variable and fixed manufacturing costs as inventoriable costs but classifies all nonmanufacturing costs as period costs. Throughout Chapter 9, we assume that the chosen denominator level for calculating the variable and fixed manufacturing overhead allocation rates is a production output–related variable—for example, direct labour-hours, direct machine-hours, and units of output produced.

We will illustrate differences between the two costing methods using the Radius Company, which manufactures specialty clothing belts. Radius allocates costs using a normal costing system. That is, its direct costs are traced to products using actual prices multiplied by the actual inputs used, but its indirect (overhead) costs are allocated using budgeted indirect-cost rate(s) multiplied by actual inputs used. The allocation base for all manufacturing costs is units of output produced. The allocation base for all marketing costs is units of output sold. Note that in both methods, only manufacturing costs are included in inventoriable costs.

To summarize: How fixed manufacturing costs are classified is the main difference between variable and absorption costing.

We assume the following for 2007:

◆ The budgeted number equals the actual number of units produced (1,100,000 units).

◆ The budgeted number equals the actual number of units sold (1,000,000 units).

◆ The budgeted equals actual fixed costs.

◆ Work in process is minimal.

◆ There is no beginning inventory on January 1, 2007.

◆ All variable costs are driven by an output unit–related variable. (We assume, for example, batch-level and product-sustaining costs are zero.)

With 2007 production of 1,100,000 units and sales of 1,000,000 units, the ending inventory on December 31, 2007, is 100,000 units.

The per unit and total actual costs for 2007 are as follows:

	Per Unit	Total Costs
Variable costs:		
Direct materials	$ 3.50	$ 3,850,000
Direct manufacturing labour	1.60	1,760,000
Indirect manufacturing costs	0.90	990,000
Manufacturing costs	6.00	6,600,000
Direct marketing costs	0.80	800,000
Indirect marketing costs	1.60	1,600,000
Marketing costs	2.40	2,400,000
Total variable costs	$ 8.40	$ 9,000,000
Fixed costs:		
Direct manufacturing costs	$ 0.30	$ 330,000
Indirect manufacturing costs	1.70	1,870,000
Manufacturing costs	2.00	2,200,000
Direct marketing costs	2.10	2,100,000
Indirect marketing costs	3.40	3,400,000
Marketing costs	5.50	5,500,000
Total fixed costs	$ 7.50	$ 7,700,000

The heart of the difference between variable and absorption costing for financial reporting is accounting for fixed manufacturing costs:

		Direct	Indirect
Same under Both Methods	} Variable	Direct manufacturing cost	Indirect manufacturing cost
Differs under the Two Methods	} Fixed	Direct manufacturing cost	Indirect manufacturing cost

Both methods capitalize all variable manufacturing costs (both direct and indirect). Capitalizing means these costs are first recorded as an asset when incurred. The variable costing method deducts fixed manufacturing costs (both direct and indirect) as a period cost of the period in which they are incurred. An example of a fixed direct manufacturing cost is the annual lease cost of a machine dedicated exclusively to the assembly of a product. The annual lease cost of a building in which multiple products are assembled illustrates a fixed indirect manufacturing cost. Examples of variable direct manufacturing costs are direct materials and direct manufacturing labour.

The absorption method capitalizes both variable and fixed manufacturing costs as an inventoriable cost. These costs become expenses in the form of cost of goods sold when sales occur. Inspect the classification of inventoriable costs under the two methods for Radius as shown below and it is clear that under absorption costing the total unit inventoriable cost is higher than under the variable costing method. Accurately classifying the costs determines both the appropriate inventory valuation and estimates of cost of goods sold expense using each method.

	Variable Costing		Absorption Costing	
Variable manufacturing costs:				
Direct materials	$3.50		$3.50	
Direct manufacturing labour	1.60		1.60	
Indirect manufacturing costs	0.90	6.00	0.90	6.00
Fixed manufacturing costs:				
Direct manufacturing costs	–		0.30	
Indirect manufacturing costs	–	–	1.70	2.00
Total inventoriable costs		$6.00		$8.00

OBJECTIVE 2

Prepare income statements
using absorption costing and
variable costing

Exhibit 9-1 presents the variable costing and absorption costing income statements for the Radius Company in 2007. The absorption costing income statement uses the gross margin format introduced in Chapter 2. The variable costing income statement uses the contribution format introduced in Chapter 3. Why different formats for each method? The contribution format highlights the distinction between variable and fixed costs whereby all fixed costs are period costs and excluded from calculating the variable cost of goods sold. The gross margin format highlights the distinction between manufacturing and nonmanufacturing costs whereby all nonmanufacturing costs are period costs and excluded from calculating the absorption cost of goods sold. Many companies using absorption costing find it unnecessary to design a cost accounting system that distinguishes between variable and fixed costs.

Highlight the fixed manufacturing costs of $2,200,000 in Exhibit 9-1. The income statement under variable costing deducts the $2,200,000 lump sum as a period cost in 2007. In contrast, the income statement under absorption costing regards each finished unit as absorbing $2 of fixed manufacturing costs. Under absorption costing the $2,200,000 is initially capitalized as an inventoriable cost in 2007. Given the preceding data for Radius, $2,000,000 subsequently becomes an expense in 2007, and $200,000 remains an asset—part of ending finished goods inventory, 100,000 units × $2—at December 31, 2007. The variable manufacturing costs are accounted for in the same way in both income statements in Exhibit 9-1.

Never overlook the heart of the matter. The key difference between variable costing and absorption costing is how managers decide to classify fixed manufacturing costs. When inventory levels change, operating income will differ between the two methods because of the difference in accounting for fixed manufacturing overhead. Compare sales of 900,000, 1,000,000, and 1,100,000 units by the Radius Company in 2007. Fixed manufacturing costs would be included in the 2007 expense as follows:

	Fixed Manufacturing Costs Treated as an Expense in 2007
Variable costing, where	
◆ Sales are 900,000, 1,000,000, or 1,100,000 units	$2,200,000
Absorption costing, where	
◆ Sales are 900,000 units, $400,000 (200,000 × $2) held back in inventory	$1,800,000
◆ Sales are 1,000,000 units, $200,000 (100,000 × $2) held back in inventory	$2,000,000
◆ Sales are 1,100,000 units, $0 held back in inventory	$2,200,000

Direct costing (variable costing). Inventory costing method in which all variable manufacturing costs are included as inventoriable costs. All fixed manufacturing costs are excluded from inventoriable costs; they are costs of the period in which they are incurred.

Some companies use the term **direct costing** to describe the inventory costing method we call *variable costing*. This is unfortunate terminology for two reasons: (1) Variable costing excludes all direct costs except those classified as direct variable manufacturing costs. The variable costing method excludes direct fixed manufacturing costs and any direct nonmanufacturing costs (such as marketing) from inventoriable costs. (2) Variable costing includes both direct and some indirect manufacturing costs (variable indirect manufacturing costs).

COMPARISON OF STANDARD VARIABLE COSTING AND STANDARD ABSORPTION COSTING

Our next example explores the implications of accounting for fixed manufacturing costs in more detail. The Stassen Company manufactures and markets telescopes. It uses a standard costing system for both its manufacturing and its marketing costs.[1]

[1]For ease of exposition, we assume that the Stassen Company uses a standard-costing system for all its operating costs—that is, it uses standards for both variable and fixed costs in both its manufacturing and marketing.

EXHIBIT 9-1
Comparison of Variable Costing and Absorption Costing Income Statements for the Year Ended December 31, 2007, for the Radius Company (quantity of units is in thousands, dollar values are reported in thousands)

	A	B	C
1	**PANEL A: VARIABLE COSTING**		
2	Revenues $17 × 1,000 units (in thousands)		$17,000
3	Variable costs:		
4	Beginning inventory	$ –	
5	Variable manufacturing costs: $6 × 1,100 units	6,600	
6	Cost of goods available for sale	6,600	
7	Deduct ending inventory: $6 × 100 units	(600)	
8	Variable cost of goods sold	6,000	
9	Variable marketing costs: $2.40 × 1,000 units sold	2,400	
10	Adjustment for variable cost variances	–	
11	Total variable costs		8,400
12	Contribution margin		8,600
13	Fixed costs:		
14	Fixed manufacturing costs $2 × 1,100	2,200	
15	Fixed marketing costs $5.50 × 1,000 units sold	5,500	
16	Adjustment for cost variances	–	
17	Total fixed costs		7,700
18	Operating income		$ 900
19			
20	**PANEL B: ABSORPTION COSTING**		
21	Revenues $17 × 1,000 units (in thousands)		$17,000
22	Cost of goods sold:		
23	Beginning inventory	$ –	
24	Variable manufacturing costs: $6 × 1,100 units	6,600	
25	Allocated fixed manufacturing costs $2 × 1,100	2,200	
26	Cost of goods available for sale	8,800	
27	Deduct ending inventory: $8 × 100 units	(800)	
28	Adjustment for manufacturing variances	–	
29	Cost of goods sold		8,000
30	Gross margin		$ 9,000
31	Marketing costs:		
32	Variable marketing costs $2.40 × 1,000 units sold	2,400	
33	Fixed marketing costs $5.50 × 1,000 units sold	5,500	
34	Adjustment for marketing variances	–	
35	Total marketing costs		7,900
36	Operating income		$ 1,100

It began business on January 1, 2007, and it is now March 2007. The president asks you to prepare comparative income statements for January 2007 and February 2007. The following simplified data in units are available:

	A	B	C
		January 2007	February 2007
1	**Unit Data**		
2	Beginning inventory	–	200
3	Production	600	650
4	Sales	400	750
5	Ending inventory	200	100

	A	B	C
1	**Other data**		
2	Selling price	$ 99	per unit sold
3	Standard variable unit manufacturing costs	$ 20	per unit produced
4	Standard variable unit marketing costs	$ 19	per unit sold
5	Standard fixed monthly manufacturing costs	$12,800	
6	Standard fixed monthly marketing costs	$10,400	
7	Budgeted denominator level of monthly production	800	output units

The total standard variable manufacturing costs per unit of $20 includes $11 for direct materials. For simplicity, we assume all fixed manufacturing costs are indirect product costs.

We assume work in process is minimal. There were no beginning or ending inventories of materials. On January 1, 2007, there was no beginning inventory of finished goods. To highlight the effect of the production volume variance, we assume there were no price, efficiency, or spending variances for any costs in either January or February of 2007. The standard fixed manufacturing cost per unit is $16 ($12,800 ÷ 800). Thus, the key standard cost data per units of denominator-level capacity are

Variable costs:	
Standard variable manufacturing costs	$20
Standard variable marketing costs	19
Total variable costs	$39
Manufacturing costs:	
Standard variable manufacturing costs	$20
Standard fixed manufacturing costs $12,800 ÷ 800	16
Total manufacturing costs	$36

Stassen expenses all variances to cost of goods sold in the accounting period in which they occur.

Assume that managers at Stassen receive a bonus based on reported monthly income. The following points illustrate how the choice between variable and absorption costing will affect Stassen's reported monthly income and hence the bonuses their managers will receive.

Comparative Income Statements

Exhibit 9-2 contains the comparative income statements under variable costing (Panel A) and absorption costing (Panel B) for the Stassen Company in January 2007 and February 2007. The operating income numbers are

	January 2007	February 2007
(1) Absorption costing	$4,000	$20,200
(2) Variable costing	800	21,800
(3) Difference = (1) – (2)	$3,200	$(1,600)

In Panel A, Variable Costing, all variable-cost line items are at standard cost except the adjustment for variances. This item would include all price, spending, and efficiency variances related to variable cost items (which are zero in our Stassen example).

EXHIBIT 9-2
Stassen Company: Comparison of Variable Costing and Absorption Costing Income
Statements for January 2007 and February 2007

A	B	C
1 **PANEL A: VARIABLE COSTING**		
2	**January 2007**	**February 2007**
3 Revenue $99 × 400; 750 units	$39,600	$74,250
4 Variable costs:		
5 Beginning inventory $20 × 0; 200 units	–	4,000
6 Variable cost of goods manufactured $20 × 600; 650 units	12,000	13,000
7 Cost of goods available for sale	12,000	17,000
8 Ending inventory $20 × 200; 100	(4,000)	(2,000)
9 Variable manufacturing cost of goods sold	8,000	15,000
10 Variable marketing cost $19 × 400; 750 units	7,600	14,250
11 Total standard variable costs	15,600	29,250
12 Contribution margin (standard)	24,000	45,000
13 Adjustment for variable cost variances to COGS	–	–
14 Total variable costs	15,600	29,250
15 Contribution margin	24,000	45,000
16 Fixed costs:		
17 Fixed manufacturing costs	12,800	12,800
18 Fixed marketing costs	10,400	10,400
19 Total standard fixed costs	23,200	23,200
20 Adjustment for fixed cost variances	–	–
21 Total fixed costs	23,200	23,200
22 Operating income	$ 800	$21,800
23		
24 **PANEL B: ABSORPTION COSTING**		
25	**January 2007**	**February 2007**
26 Revenue $99 × 400; 750 units	$39,600	$74,250
27 Cost of goods sold		
28 Beginning inventory $36 × 0; 200 units	–	7,200
29 Variable manufacturing costs $20 × 600; 650 units	12,000	13,000
30 Allocated fixed manufacturing costs $16 × 600; 650 units	9,600	10,400
31 Cost of goods available for sale	21,600	30,600
32 Deduct ending inventory: $36 × 200; 100 units	(7,200)	(3,600)
33 Total standard cost of goods sold	14,400	27,000
34 Gross margin at standard	25,200	47,250
35 Adjustment for manufacturing variances to COGS*	3,200 U	2,400 U
36 Cost of goods sold	17,600	29,400
37 Gross margin	22,000	44,850
38 Marketing costs:		
39 Variable marketing costs $19 × 400; 750	7,600	14,250
40 Fixed marketing costs	10,400	10,400
41 Total standard marketing costs	18,000	24,650
42 Adjustment for marketing variances	–	–
43 Total marketing costs	18,000	24,650
44 Operating income	$ 4,000	$20,200
45		
46 *Production volume variance for January $16 × 200 where the denominator of 800 units exceeds the volume produced and the allocation rate is $12,800 ÷ 800 = $16/unit. Similarly, the production volume variance for February is $16 × 150.		

In Panel B, Absorption Costing, all cost of goods sold line items are at standard cost except the adjustment for variances. This item includes all manufacturing cost variances—price, spending, efficiency, and production-volume variances. Only the production-volume variance is nonzero in our Stassen example.

Keep the following points in mind about absorption costing as you study panel B of Exhibit 9-2:

1. The inventoriable costs are $36 per unit, not $20, because fixed manufacturing costs ($16), as well as variable manufacturing costs ($20), are assigned to each unit of product.

2. The $16 fixed manufacturing cost rate was based on a denominator level of 800 units per month ($12,800 ÷ 800 = $16). Whenever actual *production* (not sales) volume varies from the denominator level of 800 units, a production-volume variance arises. This variance is the difference between actual and denominator-level volumes multiplied by $16, the rate.

3. The production-volume variance, which relates to fixed manufacturing overhead, exists only under absorption costing and not under variable costing because fixed costs are not allocated in the variable costing method. All other variances exist under both absorption costing and variable costing.

4. The absorption costing income statement classifies costs primarily by *business function*, such as manufacturing and marketing. In contrast, the variable costing income statement features *cost behaviour* (variable or fixed) as the basis of classification. Absorption costing income statements need not differentiate between the variable and fixed costs. Exhibit 9-2 does make this differentiation for the Stassen Company to highlight how individual line items are classified differently under variable and absorption costing formats.

OBJECTIVE 3

Explain differences in operating income under absorption costing and variable costing

Explaining Differences in Operating Income

If the inventory level increases during an accounting period, variable costing will generally report less operating income than absorption costing. When the inventory level decreases, variable costing will generally report more operating income than absorption costing. These differences in operating income are due solely to moving fixed manufacturing costs into inventories as inventories increase and out of inventories as they decrease.

The difference between operating income under absorption costing and variable costing can be computed by formula 1, which is illustrated with Exhibit 9-2 data:[2]

Formula 1

$$\begin{pmatrix} \text{Absorption costing} \\ \text{operating} \\ \text{income} \end{pmatrix} - \begin{pmatrix} \text{Variable costing} \\ \text{operating} \\ \text{income} \end{pmatrix} = \begin{pmatrix} \text{Fixed manufacturing} \\ \text{costs in} \\ \text{ending inventory} \end{pmatrix} - \begin{pmatrix} \text{Fixed manufacturing} \\ \text{costs in} \\ \text{beginning inventory} \end{pmatrix}.$$

January 2007 $4,000 − $800 = (200 × $16) − (0 × $16)
$3,200 = $3,200

February 2007 $20,200 − $21,800 = (100 × $16) − (200 × $16)
−$1,600 = −$1,600

Fixed manufacturing costs in ending inventory are a current-period expense under variable costing that absorption costing defers to future periods.

---

[2]This formula assumes that the amounts used for beginning and ending inventory are after proration of manufacturing overhead variances.

Two alternative formulas can be used if we assume that all manufacturing variances are written off as period costs, that no change occurs in work-in-process inventory, and that no change occurs in the budgeted fixed manufacturing overhead rate between accounting periods:

Formula 2

$$\left(\begin{array}{c}\text{Absorption costing}\\\text{operating}\\\text{income}\end{array}\right) - \left(\begin{array}{c}\text{Variable costing}\\\text{operating}\\\text{income}\end{array}\right) = \left(\begin{array}{c}\text{Units}\\\text{produced}\end{array} - \begin{array}{c}\text{Units}\\\text{sold}\end{array}\right) \times \left(\begin{array}{c}\text{Budgeted fixed}\\\text{manufacturing}\\\text{cost rate}\end{array}\right)$$

January 2007
$$\$4,000 - \$800 = (600 - 400) \times \$16$$
$$\$3,200 = \$3,200$$

February 2007
$$\$20,200 - \$21,800 = (650 - 750) \times \$16$$
$$-\$1,600 = -\$1,600$$

Formula 3

$$\left(\begin{array}{c}\text{Absorption costing}\\\text{operating}\\\text{income}\end{array}\right) - \left(\begin{array}{c}\text{Variable costing}\\\text{operating}\\\text{income}\end{array}\right) = \left(\begin{array}{c}\text{Ending}\\\text{inventory}\\\text{in units}\end{array} - \begin{array}{c}\text{Beginning}\\\text{inventory}\\\text{in units}\end{array}\right) \times \left(\begin{array}{c}\text{Budgeted fixed}\\\text{manufacturing}\\\text{cost rate}\end{array}\right).$$

January 2007
$$\$4,000 - \$800 = (200 - 0) \times \$16$$
$$\$3,200 = \$3,200$$

February 2007
$$\$20,200 - \$21,800 = (100 - 200) \times \$16$$
$$-\$1,600 = -\$1,600$$

Effect of Sales and Production on Operating Income

The period-to-period change in operating income under variable costing is driven solely by changes in the unit level of sales, given a constant contribution margin per unit. Consider for Stassen the variable costing operating income in February 2007 versus that in January 2007:

$$\begin{array}{c}\text{Change in}\\\text{operating income}\end{array} = \begin{array}{c}\text{Contribution}\\\text{margin}\end{array} \times \begin{array}{c}\text{Change in unit}\\\text{sales level}\end{array}$$

$$\$21,800 - \$800 = (\$99 - \$39) \times (750 - 400)$$
$$\$21,000 = \$60 \times 350$$
$$\$21,000 = \$21,000$$

Note that under variable costing, Stassen managers cannot increase operating income (and hence their bonuses) by producing for inventory.

Under absorption costing, however, period-to-period change in operating income is driven by variations in *both* the unit level of sales and the unit level of production. Exhibit 9-3 illustrates this point. The exhibit shows how absorption costing operating income for February 2007 changes as the production level in February 2007 changes. This exhibit assumes that all variances (including the production-volume variance) are written off to cost of goods sold at the end of each accounting period. The beginning inventory in February 2007 of 200 units and the February sales of 750 units are unchanged. Exhibit 9-3 shows that production of only 550 units meets February 2007 sales of 750. Operating income at this production level is $18,600. By producing more than 550 units in February 2007, Stassen increases absorption costing operating income. Each unit in February 2007 ending inventory will increase February operating income by $16. For example, if 800 units are produced, ending inventory will be 250 units and operating income will be $22,600. This amount is $4,000 more than what operating income is with zero ending inventory (250 units × $16 = $4,000) on February 28, 2007. Recall that Stassen's managers receive a bonus based on monthly operating income. Absorption costing enables them to increase operating income (and hence their bonuses) by producing for inventory.

EXHIBIT 9-3

Stassen Company: Effect on Absorption Costing Operating Income of Different Production Levels Holding the Unit Sales Level Constant—Data for February 2007 with Sales of 750 units

	February 2007 Production Level				
	550	650	700	800	850
Unit data:					
Beginning inventory	200	200	200	200	200
Production	550	650	700	800	850
Goods available for sale	750	850	900	1,000	1,050
Sales	750	750	750	750	750
Ending inventory	0	100	150	250	300
Income statement:					
Revenues	$74,250	$74,250	$74,250	$74,250	$74,250
Beginning inventory	7,200	7,200	7,200	7,200	7,200
Variable manufacturing costs*	11,000	13,000	14,000	16,000	17,000
Fixed manufacturing costs†	8,800	10,400	11,200	12,800	13,600
Cost of goods available for sale	27,000	30,600	32,400	36,000	37,800
Ending inventory‡	0	3,600	5,400	9,000	10,800
Cost of goods sold (at standard cost)	27,000	27,000	27,000	27,000	27,000
Adjustment for manufacturing variances§	4,000 U	2,400 U	1,600 U	0	800 F
Total cost of goods sold	31,000	29,400	28,600	27,000	26,200
Gross margin	43,250	44,850	45,650	47,250	48,050
Total marketing and administrative costs	24,650	24,650	24,650	24,650	24,650
Operating income	$18,600	$20,200	$21,000	$22,600	$23,400

*$20 per unit.
†Assigned at $16 per unit.
‡$36 per unit.
§(Production in units − 800) × $16. All written off to cost of goods sold at end of the accounting period.

Exhibit 9-3 illustrates how a Stassen manager could increase February 2007 operating income from $18,600 to $22,600 by producing an additional 250 units for inventory. This will increase the costs of doing business without an attendant increase in revenue obtained from additional sales. Managers whose performance evaluation and compensation are based on absorption costing income have incentives to increase production solely to increase reported income. Each additional unit produced absorbs fixed manufacturing costs that would otherwise have been written off as a cost of the period.

PERFORMANCE MEASURES AND ABSORPTION COSTING

Undesirable Buildup of Inventories

Absorption costing is the required inventory valuation method for external reporting in Canada, and to avoid any internal confusion that could arise by using a different valuation method for internal planning and control most companies use one method for both internal and external purposes (see Global Surveys of Company Practice). Using the same method for valuation and performance evaluation helps avoid situations wherein managers take action that enhances their individual evaluation but harms overall corporate performance. This method includes all production costs when valuing inventory that has been sold and better informs the long-run pricing and product mix decisions. In the long run the revenue must cover total costs plus generate profit if a company is to thrive.

Unfortunately, absorption costing can lead managers to increase operating income in the short run by increasing the production schedule independent of customer demand. In practice this is a well-known possibility and can be controlled either

Usage of Variable Costing and Absorption Costing by Companies

Surveys of company practice in the United States, Scandinavia, and Asia report that approximately 20% to 55% of companies use variable costing in their internal accounting system. In addition, up to 30% of companies use both variable costing and absorption costing:

	United States[a]	China[b]	Estonia[c]	Finland[d]	India[e]	Malaysia[f]	Norway[g]
Variable costing used	24%	32%	39%	42%	50%	23%	55%
Absorption costing used	76	68	55	31	48	46	29
Both systems used	—	6	28	2	31	16	—

Surveys to date have not extensively examined the usage of throughput costing.

Many companies using variable costing for internal reporting, short-run decisions, and performance evaluation also use absorption costing for external reporting or tax reporting. Companies that use variable costing for internal accounting make an adjustment at the end of the quarter (for quarterly reporting) or at the end of the fiscal year (for annual reporting) to prorate fixed manufacturing overhead to inventory and cost of goods sold to prepare absorption-costing statements for external reporting. The most common problem reported by companies using variable costing is the difficulty of classifying costs into fixed or variable categories.

[a] Ernst & Young, *2003 Survey of Management Accounting* (New York: Ernst & Young, March 2003).

[b] Firth, M., "The Diffusion of Managerial Accounting Procedures in the People's Republic of China and the Influence of Foreign Partnered Joint Ventures," *Accounting Organizations and Society* (1996).

[c] Haldma, T., and K. Lääts, "Contingencies Influencing the Management Accounting Practices of Estonian Manufacturing Companies," *Management Accounting Research* (2002).

[d] Lukka, K., and M. Granlund, "Cost Accounting in Finland: Current Practice and Trends of Development," *The European Accounting Review* (1996).

[e] Joshi, P., "The International Diffusion of New Management Accounting Practices: The Case of India," *Journal of International Accounting, Auditing & Taxation* (2001).

[f] Chun, L., N. Kassim, and B. Minai, "Are Management Accounting Systems in Malaysia Outmoded?" *Singapore Management Review* (2000).

[g] Bjornenak, T., "Conventional Wisdom and Costing Practices," *Management Accounting Research* (1997).

by monitoring the inventory levels or choosing a variable cost method for internal performance evaluation of the efficiency and effectiveness of manufacturing activities. See Focus on Values and Behaviours (p. 335) to understand some external controls of inventory valuation practices and revenue recognition. The added advantage of variable costing is to reveal the cost-volume-profit relationships that improve the quality of information upon which managers make short-run decisions. Exhibit 9-4 compares the key differences between variable and absorption costing.

The undesirable effects of an increase in production in order to increase operating income in the short run by increasing end-of-period inventory may be sizable, and they can arise in several ways, as the following examples show:

1. A plant manager may switch production to those orders that absorb the highest amount of fixed manufacturing costs, irrespective of the customer demand for these products (called "cherry picking" the production line). Some difficult-to-manufacture items may be delayed, resulting in failure to meet promised customer delivery dates.

2. A plant manager may accept a particular order to increase production even though another plant in the same company is better suited to handle that order.

Question	Variable Costing	Absorption Costing	Comment
Are fixed manufacturing costs inventoried?	No	Yes	Basic theoretical question when these costs should be expensed as period costs.
Is there a production-volume variance?	No	Yes	Choice of denominator level affects measurement of operating income under absorption costing only.
How are the other variances treated?	Same	Same	Highlights that the basic difference is the accounting for fixed manufacturing costs, not the accounting for any variable manufacturing costs.
Are classifications between variable and fixed costs routinely made?	Yes	Not always	Absorption costing can be easily modified to obtain subclassifications for variable and fixed costs, if desired (for example, see Exhibit 9-1, Panel B).
How do changes in unit inventory levels affect operating income?			
Production = sales	Equal	Equal	Differences are attributable to the timing of when fixed manufacturing costs become period costs
Production > sales	Lower*	Higher†	
Production < sales	Higher	Lower	
What are the effects on cost-volume-profit relationships?	Driven by unit sales level	Driven by unit sales level and unit production level	Management control benefit: Effects of changes in production level on operating income are easier to understand under variable costing.

*That is, lower operating income than under absorption costing.
†That is, higher operating income than under variable costing.

3. To meet increased production, a manager may defer maintenance beyond the current accounting period. Although operating income may increase now, future operating income will probably decrease because of increased repairs and less efficient equipment.

Early criticisms of absorption costing concentrated on whether fixed manufacturing overhead qualified as an asset under generally accepted accounting principles. However, current criticisms of absorption costing have increasingly emphasized its potentially undesirable incentives for managers. Indeed, one critic labels absorption costing as "one of the black holes of cost accounting," in part because it may induce managers to make decisions "against the long-run interests" of the company.

Proposals for Revising Performance Evaluation

Critics of absorption costing have made a variety of proposals for revising how managers are evaluated. Their proposals include the following:

1. *Change the accounting system.* As discussed previously and will be shown later in this chapter, both variable and throughput costing reduce the incentives of managers to build up inventory.

2. *Careful budgeting and inventory planning* to reduce management's freedom to build up excess inventory. For example, the budgeted monthly balance sheets have estimates of the dollar amount of inventories. If actual inventories exceed these dollar amounts, top management can investigate the inventory buildups.

3. *Incorporate a carrying charge for inventory* in the internal accounting system. For example, an inventory carrying charge of 1% per month could be assessed for the investment tied up in inventory and for spoilage and obsolescence when evaluating a manager's performance.

Bristol-Myers Squibb's Questionable Inventory Strategy

How many units should be produced? What denominator level should be used to calculate the budgeted fixed manufacturing overhead rate? How should the production-volume variance be disposed of at the end of the fiscal year? The choices that managers and management accountants make affect performance evaluations, compensation, and reported operating income. The challenge facing companies is that the answers to these questions are far from clear-cut, which requires managers and management accountants to exercise considerable judgment.

Management accountants may face pressure from managers to make choices that increase (or sometimes decrease) operating income. Consider the case of Bristol-Myers Squibb (BMS), the New York–based pharmaceutical company. Between 1999 and 2001, the company produced much more product than it sold to consumers. This action increased operating income under absorption costing. But BMS went much further, by offering incentives to wholesalers to build their inventories and then recording deliveries to wholesalers as revenues. This step allowed BMS to meet its quarterly revenue forecasts. Following an investigation, the U.S. Department of Justice and the Securities and Exchange Commission concluded that the loading of inventories onto wholesalers could not be recognized as revenues. BMS was charged with overstating revenues by US$2.5 billion from 1999 through 2001. In a 2004 interview, chief financial officer Andrew Bonfield stated that the company is working to "improve the transparency and quality of its financial disclosures."

The problems at Bristol-Myers Squibb illustrate why management accountants must possess a strong sense of integrity to guide their decisions. They must help managers run their businesses as effectively as possible, not overproducing solely to make numbers look better or to push finished goods onto wholesalers and distributors to meet sales targets. They must also prepare reports that accurately represent what happened, allocating only the appropriate fixed costs to inventory. Commitment to these goals is what companies demand from their management accountants.

Source: Barbara Martinez, "Bristol-Myers Again Restates Results," *The Wall Street Journal,* March 16, 2004.

4. *Change the time period used to evaluate performance.* Critics of absorption costing give examples where managers take actions that maximize quarterly or annual income at the potential expense of long-run income. By evaluating performance over a three-to-five-year period, the incentive to take short-run actions that reduce long-term income is reduced.

Bristol-Myers Squibb
www.bms.com

5. *Include nonfinancial as well as financial variables in the measures used to evaluate performance.* Companies currently are using nonfinancial variables, such as the following, drawn from the Stassen data:

(a) $\dfrac{\text{Ending inventory in units February 2007}}{\text{Beginning inventory in units February 2007}} = \dfrac{200}{100} = 2$

(b) $\dfrac{\text{Units produced in February 2007}}{\text{Units sold in February 2007}} = \dfrac{650}{750} = 0.867$

A good report of manufacturing performance would show not only stable inventory ratios of outputs over time for each product, but also a production to sales volume ratio very close to 1 to indicate all production and inventory was sold during the period it was produced. Of course, these nonfinancial ratios would also be interpreted in light of, for example, fluctuations due to seasonal demand, perishability, and other factors appropriate to a specific manufacturing situation.

THROUGHPUT COSTING

Some critics of existing costing systems maintain that even variable costing promotes an excessive amount of costs being inventoried. They argue that only direct materials are "truly variable" with respect to volume (quantity) of units produced and ideally the quantity of units produced should meet the quantity demanded by customers. Production managers can rarely control direct materials and labour prices, nor fixed manufacturing overhead, but they can control direct materials efficiency variances by matching volumes produced as closely as possible to volumes demanded. To reward efficient and effective production, **throughput costing** (also called **super-variable costing**) treats all costs except variable direct materials as period costs that are expensed when they are incurred. Only variable direct materials costs are inventoriable. Conceptually, this means that the overhead and labour costs are not considered as a source of future benefit for internal planning and control purposes. All other things equal, this method is most conservative and leads to the lowest internally reported operating income in comparison to either variable or absorption costing. As you can see from Exhibit 9-5, each unsold unit reduces the throughput contribution by only $11 but reduces operating income by $39. When innovation cycles are very short, obsolescence can occur almost overnight and the assumption that unsold production is unlikely to produce future benefit may be appropriate. In situations such as this, achieving expected profit targets requires an intense focus on minimizing period costs incurred due to the production of unsold units. This is a more recently designed method of inventory valuation and is not widely adopted.[3]

EXHIBIT 9-5
Throughput Costing for Stassen Company

	A	B	C
1		**January 2007**	**February 2007**
2	**Unit Data Production:**	**600**	**650**
3	**Unit Data Sales:**	**400**	**750**
4	Income Statement:		
5	Revenue $99 × 400; 750	$39,600	$74,250
6	Variable direct materials costs:		
7	Beginning inventory $11 × 0; 200 units	–	2,200
8	Direct materials in goods manufactured $11 × 600; 650	6,600	7,150
9	Cost of goods available for sale	6,600	9,350
10	Ending inventory $11 × 200; 100	(2,200)	(1,100)
11	Direct materials standard cost	4,400	8,250
12	Adjustment for direct materials variances	–	–
13	Total variable direct materials costs	4,400	8,250
14	Throughput contribution*	35,200	66,000
15	Other costs:		
16	Manufacturing ($12,800 + $9) × 600; 650	18,200	18,650
17	Marketing ($10,400 + $19) × 400; 750	18,000	24,650
18	Adjustment for variances	–	–
19	Total other costs	36,200	43,300
20	Operating income	$ (1,000)	$22,700
21			
22	*Throughput contribution is the difference between revenues and variable direct materials costs		

[3]See E. Goldratt, *The Theory of Constraints* (New York: North River Press, 1990); E. Noreen, D. Smith, and J. Mackey, *The Theory of Constraints and Its Implications for Management Accounting* (New York: North River Press, 1995).

Exhibit 9-5 is the throughput costing income statement for the Stassen Company. Compare the operating income amounts reported with those for absorption and variable costing:

	Absorption Costing	Throughput Costing	Variable Costing
January 2007	$ 4,000	$ 800	$ (1,000)
February 2007	20,200	21,800	22,700

Analog Devices, Inc.
www.analog.com

Yield Improvements and the Production-Volume Variance at Analog Devices

Analog Devices, Inc. (ADI) produces integrated circuits and systems used in computers, broadband modems, medical instruments, and consumer electronics. Improving yield—the quantity of good die produced on a silicon wafer divided by the total number of die that could be printed and produced on the wafer—is critical to delivering high-quality products at low cost.

For internal-reporting purposes, ADI uses variable costing. Fixed costs—comprising fixed overhead costs—are allocated to products only for the purposes of external reporting. The denominator level used to allocate standard fixed overhead costs to products is machine capacity assuming efficient operations—for example, machines working six hours per day. However, suppose running the machines only four hours a day is adequate to meet actual demand. The result is an unfavourable production-volume variance because budgeted fixed overhead costs exceed the overhead costs allocated to production.

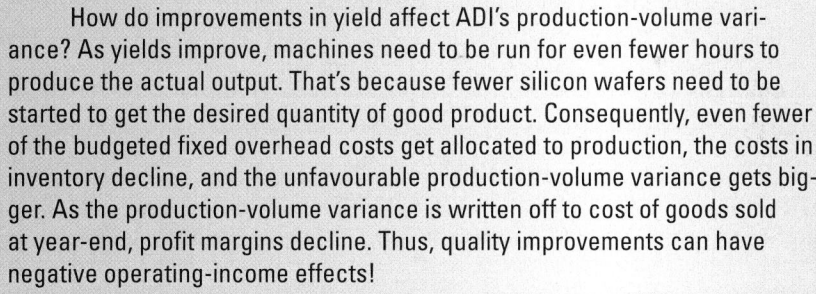

How do improvements in yield affect ADI's production-volume variance? As yields improve, machines need to be run for even fewer hours to produce the actual output. That's because fewer silicon wafers need to be started to get the desired quantity of good product. Consequently, even fewer of the budgeted fixed overhead costs get allocated to production, the costs in inventory decline, and the unfavourable production-volume variance gets bigger. As the production-volume variance is written off to cost of goods sold at year-end, profit margins decline. Thus, quality improvements can have negative operating-income effects!

The performance evaluation of production planners at ADI was weighted more toward satisfying customer orders than reducing inventory levels. Thus, even as yields improved, planners were reluctant to reduce the number of wafer starts until they were sure that the higher yields would continue. They did not want to be in a position in which ADI lacked inventory to meet customer requests. Building up inventory also improved short-run operating income.

Commenting on the tensions and trade-offs, ADI's chairman and president warned, "Unless quality improvement and other more-fundamental performance measures are elevated to the same level of importance as financial measures, when conflicts arise, financial considerations win out." However, believing in the long-run benefits of higher quality, ADI continued to improve yield, and it developed performance measures that gave incentives to production planners and operations managers to not produce more product simply to absorb more fixed overhead costs into inventory. This strategy has proven very successful. ADI is a leading semiconductor company with 2003 revenues of over US$2 billion and 60,000 customers worldwide.

Source: Analog Devices: *The Half-Life System,* Harvard Business School case number 9-190-061, Analog Devices 2003 Annual Report, and discussions with company management.

Only the $11 direct materials cost per unit is inventoriable under throughput costing (compared with $36 for absorption costing and $20 for variable costing). Where production exceeds sales (as in January 2007), throughput costing results in the largest amount of costs being expensed to the current period. Throughput contribution in Exhibit 9-5 is revenues minus all variable direct materials costs.

Advocates of throughput costing maintain there is reduced incentive for building up excess inventories vis-à-vis the case when variable or (especially) absorption costing is used. Reducing inventory levels means less funds are tied up in inventory and hence more funds are available to invest in productive outlets. Moreover, reducing inventory levels typically means reducing inventory spoilage and obsolescence costs.

Variable costing, absorption costing, and throughput costing may be combined with actual, normal, or standard costing. Exhibit 9-6 presents a capsule comparison of a job-costing record under nine alternative inventory costing systems:

Variable Costing	Absorption Costing	Throughput Costing
1. Actual costing	4. Actual costing	7. Actual costing
2. Normal costing	5. Normal costing	8. Normal costing
3. Standard costing	6. Standard costing	9. Standard costing

The data in Exhibit 9-6 represent the debits to job-costing account(s) (that is, the amounts assigned to products) under alternative inventory costing systems.

Variable costing has been a controversial subject among accountants—not so much because there is disagreement about the need for delineating between variable and fixed costs for management planning and control, but because there is a question about using variable costing for *external* reporting. Those favouring variable costing for external reporting maintain that the fixed portion of manufacturing costs is more closely related to the capacity to produce than to the production of specific units. Supporters of absorption costing maintain that inventories should carry a fixed manufacturing cost component. Why? Since both variable and fixed manufacturing costs are necessary to produce goods, both types of costs should be inventoriable, regardless of their having different behaviour patterns.

EXHIBIT 9-6
Capsule Comparison of Alternative Inventory Costing Systems

		Actual Costing	Normal Costing	Standard Costing
Absorption Costing / Variable Costing / Throughput Costing	**Variable Direct Materials Costs**	Actual prices × Actual quantity of inputs used	Actual prices × Actual quantity of inputs used	Standard prices × Standard quantity of inputs allowed for actual output achieved
	Variable Direct Conversion* Costs	Actual prices × Actual quantity of inputs used	Actual prices × Actual quantity of inputs used	Standard prices × Standard quantity of inputs allowed for actual output achieved
	Variable Manufacturing Overhead Costs	Actual variable overhead rate × Actual quantity of cost-allocation bases used	Budgeted variable overhead rates × Actual quantity of cost-allocation bases used	Standard variable overhead rates × Standard quantity of cost-allocation bases allowed for actual output achieved
	Fixed Direct Manufacturing Costs	Actual prices × Actual quantity of inputs used	Actual prices × Actual quantity of inputs used	Standard prices × Standard quantity of inputs allowed for actual output achieved
	Fixed Manufacturing Overhead Costs	Actual fixed overhead rates × Actual quantity of cost-allocation bases used	Budgeted fixed overhead rates × Actual quantity of cost-allocation based used	Standard fixed overhead rates × Standard quantity of cost-allocation bases allowed for actual output achieved

*Conversion costs are all manufacturing costs minus direct materials costs.

Absorption costing (or variants close to it) is the method required to achieve the external regulatory purpose of accounting systems. For example, when companies whose shares are traded on the Toronto Stock Exchange report financial results to the Ontario Securities Commission, generally accepted accounting principles as stated in the *CICA Handbook* must be followed. Thus, all manufacturing costs plus some product overhead must be included as inventoriable costs. Overhead costs must be allocated between those costs related to manufacturing activities (inventoriable costs) and those not related to manufacturing activities. For external reporting to shareholders, companies around the globe tend to follow the generally accepted accounting principle that all manufacturing overhead is inventoriable.

CAPSULE COMPARISON OF INVENTORY COSTING METHODS

Throughput costing is not permitted for the external regulatory purpose of accounting systems if it results in materially different numbers to those reported by absorption costing. Advocates of throughput costing emphasize the internal purposes of management accounting data.

◆ PART TWO: CAPACITY CONCEPTS AND ABSORPTION COSTING

Now we examine how alternative capacity concepts affect fixed manufacturing overhead rates and operating income under absorption costing. Reported cost numbers can be sizably affected by the choice of a denominator level. This can be important in many contexts, such as pricing and contracting based on reported cost numbers.

ALTERNATIVE CAPACITY CONCEPTS

We use an iced tea bottling plant to illustrate several alternative capacity concepts. The Bushells Company produces bottles of iced tea. The variable manufacturing costs of each bottle are $0.35. The fixed monthly manufacturing costs of the bottling plant are $50,000. Bushells uses absorption costing for its monthly internal reporting system and for financial reporting to shareholders. Bushells could use any one of at least four different capacity concepts for computing the fixed manufacturing overhead rate—theoretical capacity, practical capacity, normal capacity utilization, and master-budget capacity utilization. Whichever the denominator-level capacity concept, Bushells defines its denominator in output units (bottles of iced tea).

OBJECTIVE 6

Describe the various capacity concepts that can be used in absorption costing

Theoretical Capacity and Practical Capacity

The term *capacity* means constraint, an upper limit. **Theoretical capacity** is the capacity concept that is based on the production of output at full efficiency all the time. Bushells can produce 2,400 bottles an hour when the bottling lines are operating at full speed. There is a maximum of two eight-hour shifts per day because of a labour union agreement. Thus, the theoretical monthly capacity would be

Theoretical capacity. The capacity concept based on the production of output at maximum efficiency all the time.

$$2,400 \text{ per hour} \times 16 \text{ hours} \times 30 \text{ days} = 1,152,000 \text{ bottles}$$

Theoretical capacity is theoretical in the sense that it does not allow for any plant maintenance, any interruptions because of bottle breakages on the filling lines, or a host of other factors. Although it is a rare plant that is able to operate at theoretical capacity, it can represent a goal or target level of usage.

    Practical capacity is the capacity concept that reduces theoretical capacity for unavoidable operating interruptions such as scheduled maintenance time, shutdowns for holidays and other days, and so on. Assume that the practical hourly production rate is 2,000 bottles an hour and that the plant can operate 25 days a month. The practical monthly capacity is thus

Practical capacity. The capacity concept that reduces theoretical capacity for unavoidable operating interruptions such as scheduled maintenance time, shutdowns for holidays and other days, and so on.

$$2,000 \text{ per hour} \times 16 \text{ hours} \times 25 \text{ days} = 800,000 \text{ bottles}$$

Engineering, economic, and human factors are important to consider when estimating theoretical or practical capacity. Engineers at the Bushells plant can provide input on the technical capabilities of machines for filling bottles. In some cases, however, an increase in capacity may be technically possible but not economically sound. For example, the labour union may actually permit a third shift per day but only at unusually high wage rates that clearly do not make financial sense in the iced tea market. Human safety factors, such as increased injury risk when the line operates at faster speeds, are also important to consider.

Normal Capacity Utilization and Master-Budget Capacity Utilization

Both theoretical capacity and practical capacity measure the capacity in terms of what a plant can supply. In contrast, normal utilization and master budget utilization measure the denominator level in terms of demand for the output of the plant. In many cases, budgeted demand is well below the supply available (productive capacity).

Normal capacity utilization. The capacity concept based on the level of capacity utilization that satisfies average customer demand over a period (say, two or three years) that includes seasonal, cyclical, or other trend factors.

Master-budget capacity utilization. The capacity concept based on the anticipated level of capacity utilization for the coming budget period.

Normal capacity utilization is the capacity concept based on the level of capacity utilization that satisfies average customer demand over a period (say, of two to three years) that includes seasonal, cyclical, or other trend factors. **Master-budget capacity utilization** is the capacity concept based on the anticipated level of capacity utilization for the next budget period. These two denominator levels can differ—for example, when an industry has cyclical periods of high and low demand or when management believes that the budgeted production for the coming period is unrepresentative of "long-term" demand (see Concepts in Action on p. 337).

Consider our Bushells example of iced tea production. The master budget for 2007 is based on production of 400,000 bottles per month. Hence, the master budget denominator level is 400,000 bottles. However, Bushells' senior management believes that over the next one to three years the normal monthly production level will be 500,000 bottles. These people view the 2007 budgeted production level of 400,000 bottles to be "abnormally" low. Why? A major competitor has been sharply reducing its iced tea selling prices and has also been spending enormous amounts on advertising. Bushells expects that the lower prices and advertising blitz will be a short-run phenomenon and that in 2008 the market share it has lost to this competitor will be regained.

A major reason for choosing master-budget capacity utilization over normal capacity utilization is the difficulty of forecasting normal utilization in many industries with long-run cyclical patterns. For example, many Canadian garment and shoe manufacturing companies in the 1990s believed that they were in a downturn of the demand cycle and that there would be an upturn shortly. Unfortunately, the cycle has not yet turned upward in demand. A similar problem occurs when estimating "normal" demand. Some marketing managers are prone to overestimating their ability to regain lost market share. Their estimate of "normal" demand for their product may be based on an overly optimistic outlook ("anticipating roses when all that exist are thorns").

EFFECT ON FINANCIAL STATEMENTS

OBJECTIVE 7

Explain how the choice of denominator level affects reported operating income and inventory costs

Bushells has budgeted fixed manufacturing costs of $50,000 per month. Assume that actual costs are also $50,000. To keep this example simple, we assume all fixed manufacturing costs are indirect. The budgeted fixed manufacturing overhead rates in May 2007 for the four alternative capacity concepts discussed are as follows:

Capacity Concept (1)	Budgeted Fixed Manufacturing Overhead per Month (2)	Budgeted Capacity Level (in Bottles) (3)	Budgeted Manufacturing Overhead Cost Rate (4) = (2) ÷ (3)
Theoretical capacity	$50,000	1,152,000	$0.0434
Practical capacity	50,000	800,000	0.0625
Normal capacity utilization	50,000	500,000	0.1000
Master-budget capacity utilization	50,000	400,000	0.1250

The budgeted fixed manufacturing overhead rate based on master-budget capacity utilization ($0.1250) represents an increase of more than 188% from the rate based on theoretical capacity ($0.0434).

Assume now that Bushells's actual production in May 2007 is 460,000 bottles of iced tea. Actual sales are 420,000 bottles. Also assume no beginning inventory on May 1, 2007, and no price, spending, or efficiency variances in manufacturing for May 2007. The manufacturing plant sells bottles of iced tea to another division for $0.50 per bottle. Its only costs are variable manufacturing costs of $0.35 per bottle and $50,000 per month for fixed manufacturing overhead. Bushells writes off all variances to cost of goods sold each month.

The budgeted manufacturing costs per bottle of iced tea for each capacity concept are the sum of $0.35 in variable manufacturing costs and the budgeted fixed manufacturing overhead costs (shown from the preceding table).

Capacity Concept (1)	Variable Manufacturing Costs (2)	Fixed Manufacturing Overhead Cost Rate (3)	Total Manufacturing Costs (4) = (2) + (3)
Theoretical capacity	$0.3500	$0.0434	$0.3934
Practical capacity	0.3500	0.0625	0.4125
Normal capacity utilization	0.3500	0.1000	0.4500
Master budget capacity utilization	0.3500	0.1250	0.4750

Each capacity concept will result in a different production-volume variance.

$$\text{Production-volume variance} = \left(\begin{array}{c}\text{Denominator} \\ \text{level in} \\ \text{output units}\end{array} - \begin{array}{c}\text{Actual} \\ \text{output units}\end{array}\right) \times \begin{array}{c}\text{Budgeted fixed} \\ \text{manufacturing overhead} \\ \text{rate per output unit}\end{array}$$

$$\text{Theoretical capacity} = (1,152,000 - 460,000) \times \$0.0434$$
$$= \$30,033 \text{ U (rounded up)}$$

$$\text{Practical capacity} = (800,000 - 460,000) \times \$0.0625$$
$$= \$21,250 \text{ U}$$

$$\text{Normal capacity utilization} = (500,000 - 460,000) \times \$0.1000$$
$$= \$4,000 \text{ U}$$

$$\text{Master-budget capacity utilization} = (400,000 - 460,000) \times \$0.1250$$
$$= \$7,500 \text{ F}$$

Exhibit 9-7 shows how the choice of a denominator affects Bushells' operating income for May 2007. Using the master-budget denominator results in assigning the highest amount of fixed manufacturing overhead costs per bottle to the 40,000 bottles in ending inventory. Accordingly, operating income is highest using the master budget capacity utilization denominator. Recall that Bushells had no beginning inventory on May 1, 2007, production in May of 460,000 bottles, and sales in May of 420,000 bottles. Hence, the ending inventory on May 31 is 40,000 bottles. The differences between the operating income for the four denominator-level concepts in Exhibit 9-7 are due to different amounts of fixed manufacturing overhead being inventoried:

Capacity Concept	Fixed Manufacturing Overhead in May 31, 2007, Inventory
Theoretical capacity	40,000 × $0.0434 = $1,736
Practical capacity	40,000 × 0.0625 = 2,500
Normal capacity utilization	40,000 × 0.1000 = 4,000
Master budget capacity utilization	40,000 × 0.1250 = 5,000

Thus, in Exhibit 9-7 the difference in operating income between the master budget capacity utilization concept and the normal capacity utilization concept of $1,000 ($8,000 – $7,000) is due to the difference in fixed manufacturing overhead inventoried ($5,000 – $4,000).

EXHIBIT 9-7
Bushells Company: Income Statement Effects of Alternative Capacity Concepts for May 2007

	Theoretical Capacity	Practical Capacity	Normal Capacity Utilization	Master-Budget Capacity Utilization
Sales, $0.50 × 420,000	$210,000	$210,000	$210,000	$210,000
Cost of goods sold:				
Beginning inventory	0	0	0	0
Variable manufacturing costs*	161,000	161,000	161,000	161,000
Fixed manufacturing overhead costs†	19,964	28,750	46,000	57,500
Cost of goods available for sale	180,964	189,750	207,000	218,500
Ending inventory‡	15,736	16,500	18,000	19,000
Total COGS (at standard costs)	165,228	173,250	189,000	199,500
Adjustment for manufacturing variances§	30,033 U	21,250 U	4,000 U	7,500 F
Total COGS	195,261	194,500	193,000	192,000
Gross margin	14,739	15,500	17,000	18,000
Marketing costs	10,000	10,000	10,000	10,000
Operating income	$ 4,739	$ 5,500	$ 7,000	$ 8,000

*$0.35 × 460,000 = $161,000.
†Fixed manufacturing overhead costs:
$0.0434 × 460,000 = $19,964
$0.0625 × 460,000 = $28,750
$0.1000 × 460,000 = $46,000
$0.1250 × 460,000 = $57,500
‡Ending inventory costs:
($0.3500 + $0.0434) × (460,000 – 420,000) = $15,736
($0.3500 + $0.0625) × (460,000 – 420,000) = $16,500
($0.3500 + $0.1000) × (460,000 – 420,000) = $18,000
($0.3500 + $0.1250) × (460,000 – 420,000) = $19,000
§The only variance for Bushells in May 2007 is the production-volume variance. See text (p. 341) for the computations.

There is no requirement that Canadian companies use the same capacity concept for internal reporting, financial reporting, and income tax purposes. Nevertheless, the costs of record keeping and the desire for simplicity often lead companies to choose the same denominator level for internal reporting and tax purposes. Income tax rulings by Canada Revenue Agency (CRA) effectively prohibit use of the theoretical capacity or practical capacity denominator-level concepts. Both these concepts typically result in companies taking writeoffs of fixed manufacturing overhead as tax deductions more quickly than desired by the CRA. The CRA requires companies to use the master-budget denominator level (along with full proration of variances between inventories and cost of goods sold) for income tax reporting.

CHOOSING A CAPACITY LEVEL

OBJECTIVE 8

Understand the major factors managers consider in choosing a capacity level to compute the budgeted fixed overhead cost rate

Which capacity level should a company use to calculate the budgeted fixed manufacturing cost per bottle? In choosing a capacity level, managers consider several factors, including (a) effect on product costing and capacity management, (b) effect on pricing decisions, (c) effect on performance evaluation, (d) effect on financial statements (see p. 340), (e) regulatory requirements, and (f) difficulties in forecasting chosen capacity-level concepts (see p. 345). We now discuss each factor.

Effect on Product Costing and Capacity Management

Cost data from a normal-costing system or a standard-costing system are often used in pricing or product-mix decisions. As the Bushells example illustrates, the use of theoretical capacity results in an unrealistically small fixed manufacturing overhead cost per bottle because it is based on an idealistic and unattainable level of capacity. Theoretical capacity is rarely used to calculate the budgeted fixed manufacturing cost per bottle because it departs significantly from the real capacity available to a company.

Many companies favour practical capacity as the denominator to calculate the budgeted fixed manufacturing cost per bottle. Practical capacity in the Bushells example represents the maximum number of bottles that Bushells intends to produce per year. If Bushells had consistently planned to produce fewer bottles of iced tea, it would have built a smaller plant and incurred lower costs.

Bushells budgets $0.0625 in fixed manufacturing overhead cost per bottle based on the $50,000 it costs to acquire the capacity to produce 800,000 bottles. This plant capacity is acquired well before Bushells uses the capacity and even before Bushells knows how much of the capacity it will actually use. That is, the budgeted fixed manufacturing cost of $0.0625 per bottle measures the *cost per bottle of supplying the capacity*.

Demand for Bushells' iced tea in 2007 is expected to be 400,000 bottles lower than practical capacity. The cost of *supplying* the capacity needed to make bottles is still $0.0625 per bottle. That's because capacity is acquired in "lumpy" amounts, and it costs $50,000 per year to acquire the capacity to make 800,000 bottles. The capacity and its cost are fixed *in the short run*; the capacity supplied cannot be reduced to match the capacity needed in 2007. As a result, not all of the capacity supplied at $0.0625 per bottle will be needed or used in 2007. Using practical capacity, managers can subdivide the cost of resources supplied into used and unused components.

Using practical capacity fixes the cost of capacity at the cost of supplying the capacity, regardless of the demand for the capacity. Highlighting the cost of capacity acquired but not used directs managers' attention to managing unused capacity, perhaps by designing new products to fill unused capacity, leasing out unused capacity to others, or eliminating unused capacity. In contrast, using either of the capacity levels based on the demand for Bushells' iced tea—master-budget capacity utilization or normal capacity utilization—hides the amount of unused capacity. If Bushells had used the master-budget capacity utilization as the capacity level, it would have calculated the budgeted fixed manufacturing cost per bottle as $0.1250 ($50,000 ÷ 400,000 bottles). This calculation does not use data about practical capacity, so it does not separately identify the cost of unused capacity. Note, however, that the cost of $0.1250 per bottle includes a charge for unused capacity—the $0.0625 fixed manufacturing resource that would be used to produce each bottle at practical capacity plus the cost of unused capacity allocated to each bottle, $0.0625 per bottle.

From the perspective of long-run product costing, which cost of capacity should Bushells use for pricing purposes for benchmarking its product cost structure against competitors: $0.0625 per bottle based on practical capacity or $0.1250 per bottle based on master-budget capacity utilization? Probably, the $0.0625 per bottle based on practical capacity. Why? Because $0.0625 per bottle represents the budgeted cost per bottle of only the capacity used to produce the product and explicitly excludes the cost of any unused capacity. Customers will be willing to pay a price that covers the cost of the capacity actually used but will not want to pay for capacity that is not used to produce the product. Customers expect Bushells to manage its unused capacity or bear the cost of unused capacity, not pass it along to them. Moreover, if Bushells' competitors manage unused capacity more effectively, the cost of capacity in the competitors' cost structures (which guides competitors' pricing decisions) is likely to approach $0.0625 per bottle. In the next section we show how the use of normal capacity utilization or master-budget capacity utilization can result in setting selling prices that are not competitive.

Effect on Pricing Decisions and the Downward Demand Spiral

The easiest way to understand the *downward demand spiral* is via an example. Assume Bushells uses master-budget capacity utilization of 400,000 bottles for product costing in 2007. The resulting manufacturing cost is $0.4750 per bottle. Assume a competitor (Lipton Iced Tea) in December 2006 offers to supply a major

Practical capacity need not be constant over time. For example, improvements to plant layout and increases in labour efficiency can both result in significant increases in practical capacity in the same plant over time.

customer of Bushells (a customer who was expected to purchase 100,000 bottles in 2007 at $0.45 per bottle). The Bushells manager, not wanting to show a loss on the account and wanting to recoup all costs in the long run, declines to match the competitor's price and the account is lost. The lost account means budgeted fixed manufacturing costs of $50,000 will be spread over the remaining master-budget volume.

Suppose yet another customer of Bushells—also accounting for 100,000 bottles of budgeted volume—receives a bid from a competitor priced at $0.50. The Bushells manager compares this bid with his revised unit cost, declines to match the competition, and the account is lost. The planned output would shrink further to 200,000 units. The budgeted fixed manufacturing cost per unit for the remaining 200,000 now would be $0.25 ($50,000 ÷ 200,000 bottles).

The **downward demand spiral** for a company is the continuing reduction in the demand for its products that occurs when prices of competitors' products are not met and (as demand drops further) higher and higher unit costs result in more and more reluctance to meet competitors' prices.

The use of practical capacity as the denominator to calculate the budgeted fixed manufacturing cost per bottle would avoid the recalculation of unit costs when expected demand levels change. That's because the fixed cost rate would be calculated based on the capacity available rather than the capacity used to meet demand. Managers who use reported unit costs in a mechanical way to set prices are less likely to promote a downward demand spiral when they use practical capacity concepts than when they use the normal capacity or master-budget capacity utilization concepts.

Effect on Performance Evaluation

Consider how the choice between normal capacity utilization, master-budget capacity utilization, and practical capacity affects how a marketing manager is evaluated. Normal capacity utilization is often used as a basis for long-term plans. The normal capacity utilization depends on the time span selected and the forecasts made for each year. *However, normal capacity utilization is an average that provides no meaningful feedback to the marketing manager for a particular year.* Using normal capacity utilization as a reference for judging current performance of a marketing manager is an example of misusing a long-run measure for a short-run purpose. The master-budget capacity utilization, rather than normal capacity utilization or practical capacity, is what should be used for evaluating a marketing manager's performance in the current year. That's because the master budget is the principal short-run planning and control tool. Managers feel more obligated to reach the levels specified in the master budget, which should have been carefully set in relation to the maximum opportunities for sales in the current year.

When large differences exist between practical capacity and master-budget capacity utilization, several companies classify part of the large difference as *planned unused capacity*. One reason for this approach is performance evaluation. Consider our Bushells iced-tea example. The managers in charge of capacity planning usually do not make pricing decisions. Top management decided to build an iced-tea plant with 800,000 bottles of practical capacity, focusing on demand over the next five years. But Bushells' marketing managers, who are mid-level managers, make the pricing decisions. These executives believe they should be held accountable only for the manufacturing overhead costs related to their potential customer base in 2007. The master-budget capacity utilization suggests a customer base in 2007 of 400,000 bottles. Using responsibility accounting principles, part of the budgeted total fixed manufacturing costs would be attributed to the fixed capacity costs of meeting 2007 demand. The remaining costs would be separately shown as the capacity cost of meeting long-run demand increases expected to occur beyond 2007.

Downward demand spiral. Progressive reduction in demand for a company's products and services. This arises when a company utilizes fixed cost based on the quantity of sales. As sales decrease, the unitized fixed cost rate increases. Thus an increased fixed manufacturing rate is allocated to each unit of output, leading companies to raise their unit sales price.

Similar issues arise for manufacturing managers who are evaluated on the basis of master-budget capacity utilization and are held responsible for controlling manufacturing overhead costs.

CAPACITY COSTS AND DENOMINATOR-LEVEL ISSUES

Let's consider several more factors that affect the planning and control of capacity costs.

1. Costing systems, such as normal costing or standard costing, do not recognize uncertainty in the way managers recognize it. A *single* amount rather than a range of possible amounts is used as the denominator when calculating budgeted fixed manufacturing cost per unit in absorption costing. Yet, managers face uncertainty about demand—they even face uncertainty about their capability to supply. Bushells' plant has estimated practical capacity of 800,000 bottles. The estimated master-budget capacity utilization for 2007 is 400,000-bottles. These estimates are uncertain. Managers recognize uncertainty in their capacity planning decisions. Bushells built its current plant with an 800,000-bottle practical capacity in part to provide the capability to meet possible demand surges. Even if these demand surges do not occur in a given period, it would be wrong to conclude that all capacity not used in a given period is wasted resources. *The gains from meeting sudden demand surges may well require having unused capacity in some periods.*

2. The fixed manufacturing overhead cost rate is based on a numerator—budgeted fixed manufacturing overhead costs—and a denominator—some measure of capacity or capacity utilization. Our discussion so far has emphasized issues concerning the choice of the denominator. Challenging issues also arise in measuring the numerator. For example, deregulation of the electric utility industry has resulted in many electric utilities becoming unprofitable. This situation has led to write-downs in the values of their plant and equipment. The write-downs reduce the numerator via the amortization used to compute fixed capacity cost per kilowatt-hour of electricity produced.

3. Capacity costs arise in nonmanufacturing parts of the value chain, as well as with the manufacturing costs emphasized in this chapter. Bushells may acquire a fleet of vehicles capable of distributing the practical capacity of its iced-tea plant. When actual production is below the practical capacity, there will be unused capacity cost issues with the distribution function, as well as with the manufacturing function.

   As you saw in Chapter 8, capacity cost issues are prominent in many service-sector companies, such as airlines, hospitals, railroads, and banks, even though these companies carry no inventory and so have no inventory-costing issues. For example, in calculating the fixed overhead cost per patient-day in its obstetrics and gynecology department, a hospital must decide what denominator to use—practical capacity, normal utilization, or master-budget utilization. Its decision may have implications for capacity management, as well as pricing and performance evaluation.

4. To focus on the two main ideas—(a) choosing a denominator in order to (b) calculate a budgeted fixed manufacturing cost rate—our Bushells example assumed that all fixed manufacturing overhead costs had a single cost driver: bottles of iced tea produced. As you saw in Chapter 5, activity-based costing systems have multiple overhead cost pools at the output-unit, batch, product-sustaining, and facility-sustaining levels, each with its own cost driver. In calculating the activity cost rates (for setups and material handling, say), management must choose a capacity level for the quantity of the cost driver (setup-hours or loads moved). Should it use practical capacity, normal capacity utilization, or master-budget capacity utilization? For all the reasons described in the chapter (such as pricing and capacity management), most proponents of activity-based costing argue that practical capacity should be used as the denominator to calculate activity cost rates.

PROBLEM

Suppose that the Bushells Company in our example is computing the operating income for May 2008. This month is identical to May 2007, the results of which are in Exhibit 9-7 (p. 342), except that master-budget capacity utilization for 2008 is 600,000 bottles per month instead of 400,000 bottles. There was no beginning inventory on May 1, 2008, and no variances other than the production-volume variance. Bushells writes off this variance to cost of goods sold each month.

REQUIRED

How would the results in Exhibit 9-7 for Bushells Company be different if the month is May 2008 rather than May 2007? Show your computations.

SOLUTION

The only change in the Exhibit 9-7 results will be for the master-budget capacity utilization level. The budgeted fixed manufacturing overhead cost rate in May 2008 is

$$\frac{\$50,000}{600,000 \text{ bottles}} = \$0.0833 \text{ per bottle}$$

The manufacturing cost per bottle becomes $0.4333 ($0.3500 + $0.0833). In turn, the production volume variance for May 2008 becomes

$$(600,000 - 460,000) \times (\$0.0833) = \$11,662 \text{ U}$$

The income statement for May 2008 is now

Revenues	$210,000
Cost of goods sold:	
Beginning inventory	0
Variable manufacturing costs:	
$0.35 × 460,000	161,000
Fixed manufacturing costs:	
$0.0833 × 460,000	38,318
Cost of goods available for sale	199,318
Ending inventory:	
$0.4333 × (460,000 – 420,000)	17,332
Total cost of goods sold (at standard costs)	181,986
Adjustment for variances	11,662 U
Total cost of goods sold	193,648
Gross margin	16,352
Marketing costs	10,000
Operating income	$ 6,352

The higher denominator level in the 2008 master budget means that lower fixed manufacturing overhead costs are inventoried in May 2008 than in May 2007, given identical sales and production levels.

DECISION POINTS   SUMMARY

The following decision guidelines use a question-and-answer format to summarize the chapter's main points. Each decision presents a key question. The guideline is the answer to that question.

DECISIONS	GUIDELINES
1. How does variable costing differ from absorption costing?	Variable costing and absorption costing differ in only one respect: how to account for fixed manufacturing costs. Under variable costing, fixed manufacturing costs are excluded from

inventoriable costs and are a cost of the period in which they are incurred. Under absorption costing, fixed manufacturing costs are inventoriable and become a part of cost of goods sold in the period when sales occur.

2. What formats do companies use when preparing income statements under variable costing and absorption costing?

The variable costing income statement is based on the contribution-margin format. The absorption costing income statement is based on the gross-margin format.

3. How do level of sales and level of production affect operating income under variable costing and absorption costing?

Under variable costing, operating income is driven by the unit level of sales. Under absorption costing, operating income is driven by the unit level of production, as well as by the unit level of sales.

4. Why might managers build up finished goods inventory if they use absorption costing?

When absorption costing is used, managers can increase current operating income by producing more units for inventory. Producing for inventory absorbs more fixed manufacturing costs into inventory and reduces costs expensed in the period. Critics of absorption costing label this manipulation of income as the major negative consequence of treating fixed manufacturing overhead as an inventoriable cost.

5. How does throughput costing differ from variable costing and absorption costing?

Throughput costing treats all costs except direct materials as costs of the period in which they are incurred. Throughput costing results in a lower amount of manufacturing costs being inventoried than either variable or absorption costing.

6. What are the various capacity levels a company can use to calculate budgeted fixed manufacturing cost rate?

Capacity levels can be measured in terms of what a plant can supply—theoretical capacity or practical capacity. Capacity can also be measured in terms of demand for the output of a plant—normal capacity utilization or master budget capacity utilization.

7. How does the capacity level chosen to calculate the budgeted fixed overhead cost rate affect the production-volume variance?

When the chosen capacity level exceeds the actual production level, there will be an unfavourable production-volume variance; when the chosen capacity level is less than the actual production level, there will be a favourable production-volume variance.

8. What are the major factors managers consider in choosing the capacity level to compute the budgeted fixed overhead cost rate?

The major factors managers consider in choosing the capacity level to compute the budgeted fixed manufacturing cost per unit are (a) effect on product costing and capacity management, (b) effect on pricing decisions, (c) effect on performance evaluation, (d) effect on financial statements, (e) regulatory requirements, and (f) difficulties in forecasting chosen capacity-level concepts.

9. Should a company with high fixed costs and unused capacity raise selling prices to fully recoup its costs?

No, companies with high fixed costs and unused capacity may encounter ongoing and increasingly greater reductions in demand if they continue to raise selling prices to fully recoup variable and fixed costs from a declining sales base. This phenomenon is called the downward demand spiral.

APPENDIX: PRODUCTIVITY MEASUREMENT

Chapter 3 introduced cost-volume-profit analysis. If variable costing is used, the breakeven point (operating income of $0) is computed in the usual manner. There is only one breakeven point in this case, and it is a function of (1) fixed costs, (2) contribution margin per unit, and (3) unit level of sales. Holding (1) and (2) constant, operating income rises as the unit level of sales rises, and vice versa.

The formula for computing the breakeven point with variable costing is a special case of the more general target operating income formula from Chapter 3 (pp. 75–76):

$$QT = \frac{\text{Total fixed costs} + \text{Target operating income}}{\text{Contribution margin per unit}}$$

= Number of units sold to earn the target operating income

Breakeven occurs when the target operating income is $0. In our Stassen illustration for 2007 (see p. 328):

$$QT = \frac{(\$12,800 + \$10,400) + \$0}{\$99 - (\$20 + \$19)} = \frac{\$23,200}{\$60}$$

$$= 387 \text{ units (rounded)}^4$$

If absorption costing is used, the required number of units sold to achieve a specific target operating income is not unique because of the number of variables involved. The following formula highlights the factors that will affect the target operating income under absorption costing:

$$QT = \frac{\begin{matrix}\text{Total} \\ \text{fixed} \\ \text{costs}\end{matrix} + \begin{matrix}\text{Target} \\ \text{operating} \\ \text{income}\end{matrix} + \left[\begin{matrix}\text{Fixed} \\ \text{manufacturing} \\ \text{cost rate}\end{matrix} \times \left(\begin{matrix}\text{Breakeven} \\ \text{sales} \\ \text{in units}\end{matrix} - \begin{matrix}\text{Units} \\ \text{produced}\end{matrix}\right)\right]}{\text{Contribution margin per unit}}$$

This formula has three terms in the numerator compared with two terms in the numerator of the QT variable-costing formula stated earlier. The extra term added to the numerator under absorption costing is as follows:

$$\left[\begin{matrix}\text{Fixed manufacturing} \\ \text{cost rate}\end{matrix} \times \left(\begin{matrix}\text{Breakeven sales} \\ \text{in units}\end{matrix} - \begin{matrix}\text{Units} \\ \text{produced}\end{matrix}\right)\right]$$

This term captures the additional amount of target operating income in the numerator due to absorption costing moving fixed manufacturing costs to inventory from costs of goods sold under variable costing for all units produced that exceed the breakeven sales quantity. The breakeven point is defined as the quantity for which the target operating income is $0. Consider Stassen Company in 2008. One breakeven point under absorption costing for production of 500 units is as follows:

$$QT = \frac{(\$12,800 + \$10,400) + \$0 + [\$16(QT - 500)]}{\$99 - (\$20 + \$19)}$$

$$= \frac{\$23,200 + \$16QT - \$8,000}{\$60}$$

$$\$60QT = \$15,200 + \$16QT$$

$$\$44QT = \$15,200$$

$$QT = 346 \text{ (rounded)}$$

The breakeven point under absorption costing depends on (1) fixed costs, (2) contribution margin per unit, (3) unit level of sales, (4) unit level of production, and overhead cost rate. For Stassen in 2007, a combination of 346 units sold, 500 units produced, and an 800-unit denominator level would result in an operating income of $0.[5] Note, however, that there are many combinations of these five factors that would give an operating income of $0. For example, a combination of 291 units sold, 650 units produced, and an 800-unit denominator level also results in an operating income of $0 under absorption costing.

Suppose in our illustration that actual production in 2008 was equal to the denominator level, 800 units. Also suppose that there were no units sold and no fixed operating costs. All the production would be placed in inventory, and so all the fixed manufacturing overhead would be included in inventory. There would be no production-volume variance. Thus, the company would break even with no sales whatsoever! In contrast, under variable costing the operating loss would be equal to the fixed manufacturing costs of $12,800.

---

[4]Operating income is not $0 because the breakeven number of units is rounded up to 387 from 386.67.

Proof of breakeven point:

Revenues, $99 × 387	$38,313
Variable costs, $39 × 387	15,093
Contribution margin, $60 × 387	23,220
Fixed costs	23,200
Operating income	$ 20

[5]Operating income is not $0 because the breakeven number of units is rounded up to 346 from 345.45.

This chapter contains definitions of the following important terms:

absorption costing (p. 324)	practical capacity (p. 339)
direct costing (p. 326)	super-variable costing (p. 336)
downward demand spiral (p. 344)	theoretical capacity (p. 339)
master-budget capacity utilization (p. 340)	throughput costing (p. 336)
normal capacity utilization (p. 340)	variable costing (p. 324)

ASSIGNMENT MATERIAL

QUESTIONS

9-1 "Differences in operating income between variable and absorption costing are due solely to accounting for fixed costs." Do you agree? Explain.

9-2 Why is the term *direct costing* a misnomer?

9-3 Do companies in either the service sector or the merchandising sector make choices about absorption costing versus variable costing?

9-4 Explain the main conceptual issue under variable and absorption costing regarding the proper timing for the release of fixed manufacturing overhead as expense.

9-5 "Companies that make no variable cost/fixed cost distinctions must use absorption costing and those that do make variable cost/fixed cost distinctions must use variable costing." Do you agree? Explain.

9-6 "The main trouble with variable costing is that it ignores the increasing importance of fixed costs in modern manufacturing." Do you agree? Why?

9-7 Give an example of how, under absorption costing, operating income could fall even though the unit sales level rises.

9-8 What are the factors that affect the breakeven point under variable costing?

9-9 Why might *throughput costing* be also called *super-variable costing?*

9-10 Critics of absorption costing have increasingly emphasized its potential for promoting undesirable incentives for managers. Give an example.

9-11 What are two ways of reducing the negative aspects associated with using absorption costing to evaluate the performance of a plant manager?

9-12 Describe the downward demand spiral and its implications for pricing decisions.

9-13 Will the financial statements of a company always differ when different choices at the start of the period are made regarding the denominator-level capacity concept?

9-14 Which denominator-level concepts emphasize what a plant can supply? Which denominator-level concepts emphasize what customers demand for products produced by a plant?

9-15 Name one reason why many companies prefer the master-budget capacity utilization-level concept rather than the normal capacity utilization-level concept.

EXERCISES

9-16 Variable and absorption costing, explaining operating income differences. Nascar Motors assembles and sells motor vehicles. It uses an actual costing system, in which unit costs are calculated each month. Data relating to April and May of 2007 are

	April	May
Unit data:		
Beginning inventory	0	150
Production	500	400
Sales	350	520
Variable cost data:		
Manufacturing costs per unit produced	$12,000	$12,000
Marketing costs per unit sold	3,000	3,000

Fixed cost data:

Manufacturing costs	$2,000,000	$2,000,000
Marketing costs	600,000	600,000

The selling price per motor vehicle is $28,800.

REQUIRED

1. Present income statements for Nascar Motors in April and May of 2007 under (a) variable costing and (b) absorption costing.
2. Prepare a numerical reconciliation and explanation of the difference between operating income for each month under absorption costing and variable costing.

Excel Application For students who wish to practise their spreadsheet skills, the following is a step-by-step approach to creating an Excel spreadsheet to work this problem.

Step-by-Step

(Program your spreadsheet to perform all necessary calculations. Do not "hard-code" any of your calculations.)

1. At the top of a new spreadsheet, create an "Original Data" section for the unit data, variable cost data, and fixed cost data for April and May in exactly the same format as shown for Nascar Motors on page 349.
2. Skip two rows, and create a section called "Inventoriable Costs," with rows for "Variable Manufacturing Costs," "Fixed Indirect Manufacturing Costs for April," "Fixed Indirect Manufacturing Costs for May," "Total Inventoriable Costs for April," and "Total Inventories Costs for May," and columns for "Variable Costing" and "Absorption Costing." Assume the budgeted denominator level of production for April and May is 500 units, which is the same as actual production in April. Use data from the Original Data section to compute inventoriable costs under both variable and absorption costing. (*Hint:* Under absorption costing, the fixed indirect manufacturing costs allocated to each unit of inventory should reflect total fixed manufacturing costs divided by the actual level of production, whereas inventoriable costs under variable costing should reflect only variable manufacturing costs.)
3. Skip two rows, and create a section called "Problem 1" and a subsection, "Panel A: Variable Costing." Following the format in Panel A, Exhibit 9-2 (p. 329), set up an income statement using the contribution-margin format by creating rows for "Revenues," "Beginning Inventory," "Variable Manufacturing Costs," "Cost of Goods Available for Sale," "Ending Inventory," "Variable Cost of Goods Sold," "Variable Marketing Costs," "Total Variable Costs," "Contribution Margin," "Fixed Manufacturing Costs," "Fixed Marketing Costs," "Total Fixed Costs," and "Operating Income." Create columns for April and May. Complete this income statement using the data you created in steps 1 and 2.
4. Skip two rows, and create another subsection, "Panel B: Absorption Costing." Following the format in Panel B, Exhibit 9-2, set up an income statement using the gross-margin format by creating rows for "Revenues," "Beginning Inventory," "Variable Manufacturing Costs," "Fixed Manufacturing Costs," "Costs of Goods Available for Sale," "Ending Inventory," "Cost of Goods Sold," "Gross Margin," "Variable Marketing Costs," "Fixed Marketing Costs," "Total Marketing Costs," and "Operating Income." Create columns for April and May. Complete this income statement using data you created in steps 1 and 2.
5. *Verify the accuracy of your spreadsheet.* Go to your Original Data section and change fixed manufacturing costs for April and May from $2,000,000 to $2,500,000. If you programmed your spreadsheet correctly, operating income under absorption costing for April should change to $2,480,000.

9-17 Throughput costing (continuation of 9-16). The unit variable manufacturing costs of Nascar Motors are

	April	May
Direct materials	$8,040	$8,040
Direct manufacturing labour	1,500	1,500
Manufacturing overhead	1,800	1,800

REQUIRED

1. Present income statements for Nascar Motors in April and May of 2007 under throughput costing.
2. Contrast the results in requirement 1 with those in requirement 1 of Exercise 9-16.
3. Give one motivation for Nascar Motors to adopt throughput costing.

9-18 Variable and absorption costing, explaining operating income differences. BigScreen Corporation manufactures and sells 50-inch television sets. It uses an actual costing system, in which unit costs are calculated on a monthly basis. Data relating to January, February, and March of 2007 are as follows:

	January	February	March
Unit data:			
Beginning inventory	0	300	300
Production	1,000	800	1,250
Sales	700	800	1,500
Variable cost data:			
Manufacturing costs per unit produced	$ 1,080	$ 1,080	$ 1,080
Marketing costs per unit sold	600	600	600
Fixed cost data:			
Manufacturing costs	$400,000	$400,000	$400,000
Marketing costs	140,000	140,000	140,000

The selling price per unit is $3,000.

REQUIRED
1. Present income statements for BigScreen in January, February, and March of 2007 under (a) variable costing and (b) absorption costing.
2. Explain any differences between (a) and (b) for January, February, and March.

9-19 Throughput costing (continuation of 9-18). The unit variable manufacturing costs of BigScreen Corporation are as follows:

	January	February	March
Direct materials	$ 680	$ 680	$ 680
Direct manufacturing labour	100	100	100
Manufacturing overhead	300	300	300
	$1,080	$1,080	$1,080

REQUIRED
1. Present income statements for BigScreen in January, February, and March of 2007 under throughput costing.
2. Contrast the results in requirement 1 with those in requirement 1 of Exercise 9-18.
3. Give one motivation for BigScreen to adopt throughput costing.

9-20 Absorption and variable costing. (CMA) Osawa, Inc., planned and actually manufactured 200,000 units of its single product in 2007, its first year of operation. Variable manufacturing costs were $24 per unit produced. Variable marketing and administrative costs were $10 per unit sold. Planned and actual fixed manufacturing costs were $600,000. Planned and actual fixed marketing and administrative costs totalled $400,000 in 2007. Osawa sold 120,000 units of product in 2007 at a selling price of $48 per unit.

REQUIRED
1. Osawa's 2007 operating income using absorption costing is (a) $920,000, (b) $418,182, (c) $1,254,000, (d) $1,760,000, (e) none of these.
2. Osawa's 2007 operating income using variable costing is (a) $2,600,000, (b) $1,504,256 (c) $680,000, (d) $2,040,000, (e) none of these.

9-21 Comparison of actual costing methods. The Rehe Company sells its razors at $3.60 per unit. The company uses a first-in, first-out actual costing system. A new fixed manufacturing overhead allocation rate is computed each year by dividing the actual fixed manufacturing overhead cost by the actual production units. The following simplified data are related to its first two years of operation:

	Year 1	Year 2
Unit data:		
Sales	1,000	1,200
Production	1,400	1,000

Cost:		
Variable manufacturing	$ 840	$ 600
Fixed manufacturing	700	700
Variable marketing and administration	1,000	1,200
Fixed marketing and administration	400	400

REQUIRED

1. Prepare income statements based on (a) variable costing and (b) absorption costing for each year.
2. Prepare a reconciliation and explanation of the difference in the operating income for each year resulting from the use of absorption costing and variable costing.
3. Critics have claimed that a widely used accounting system has led to undesirable buildups of inventory levels.

   a. Is variable costing or absorption costing more likely to lead to such buildups? Why?
   b. What can be done to counteract undesirable inventory buildups?

9-22 **Income statements.** (SMA) The Mass Company manufactures and sells a single product. The following data cover the two latest years of operations:

	2006	2007
Unit data:		
Sales	25,000	25,000
Beginning inventory	1,000	1,000
Ending inventory	1,000	5,000
Selling price per unit	$ 48	$ 48
Cost data:		
Standard fixed costs:		
Manufacturing overhead	$120,000	$120,000
Marketing and administrative	$190,000	$190,000
Standard variable costs per unit:		
Direct materials	$ 12.60	
Direct manufacturing labour	$ 9.50	
Manufacturing overhead	$ 4.00	
Marketing and administrative	$ 1.20	

The denominator level is 30,000 output units per year. The Mass Company's accounting records produce variable costing information, and year-end adjustments are made to produce external reports showing absorption costing information. All variances are charged to cost of goods sold.

REQUIRED

1. Prepare two income statements for 2007, one under variable costing and one under absorption costing.
2. Explain briefly why the operating income figures computed in requirement 1 agree or do not agree.
3. Give two advantages and two disadvantages of using variable costing for internal reporting.

PROBLEMS

9-23 **Variable costing versus absorption costing.** The Mavis Company uses an absorption costing system based on standard costs. Total variable manufacturing costs, including direct materials costs, were $3.60 per unit; the standard production rate was ten units per machine-hour. Total budgeted and actual fixed manufacturing overhead costs were $420,000. Fixed manufacturing overhead was allocated at $7 per machine-hour ($420,000 ÷ 60,000 machine-hours of denominator level). The selling price is $6 per unit. Variable marketing and administrative costs, which are driven by units sold, were $1 per unit. Fixed marketing and administrative costs were $120,000. Beginning inventory in 2007 was 30,000 units; ending inventory was 40,000 units. Sales in 2007 were 540,000 units. The same standard unit costs persisted throughout 2006 and 2007. For simplicity, assume that there were no price, spending, or efficiency variances.

REQUIRED

1. Prepare an income statement for 2007 assuming that all under- or overallocated overhead is written off directly at year-end as an adjustment to cost of goods sold.
2. The president has heard about variable costing. She asks you to recast the 2007 statement as it would appear under variable costing. Explain the difference in operating income as calculated in requirements 1 and 2.
3. Graph how fixed manufacturing overhead is accounted for under absorption costing. There will be two lines, one for the budgeted fixed overhead (which is equal to the actual fixed manufacturing overhead in this case) and one for the fixed overhead allocated. Show how the over- or underallocated manufacturing overhead might be indicated on the graph.

9-24 Breakeven under variable and absorption costing (continuation of 9-23).

REQUIRED

1. Compute the breakeven point in units under variable costing.
2. Compute the breakeven point in units under absorption costing.
3. Suppose that production were exactly equal to the denominator level, but no units were sold. Fixed manufacturing costs are unaffected. Assume, however, that all marketing and administrative costs were avoided. Compute operating income under (a) variable costing and (b) absorption costing. Explain the difference between your answers.

9-25 Variable vs. absorption costing. The Zwatch Company manufactures trendy, high-quality, moderately priced watches. As Zwatch's senior financial analyst, you are asked to recommend a method of inventory costing. The CFO will use your recommendation to construct Zwatch's 2007 income statement. The following data are for the year ended December 31, 2007:

Beginning inventory, January 1, 2007	85,000 units
Ending inventory, December 31, 2007	34,500 units
2007 sales	345,400 units
Selling price (to distributor)	$ 26.40 per unit
Variable manufacturing cost per unit, including direct materials	$ 6.12 per unit
Variable operating cost per unit sold	$1.10 per unit sold
Fixed manufacturing overhead	$ 1,440,000
Denominator-level machine-hours	6,000
Standard production rate	50 units per machine-hour
Fixed operating costs	$ 1,080,000

Assume standard unit costs are constant. Also, assume no price, spending, or efficiency variances.

REQUIRED

1. Prepare income statements under variable and absorption costing for the year ended December 31, 2007.
2. What are Zwatch's operating incomes under each costing method (in percentage terms)?
3. Explain the difference in operating income between the two methods.
4. Which costing method would you recommend to the CFO? Why?

9-26 Absorption vs. variable costing. Sonnenheim Bamberger is a German pharmaceutical company that provides a single drug—Mimic™—for the treatment of hair loss in men. Sonnenheim began commercial production of Mimic on January 1, 2007. Patients use three pills per day (365 days a year). Sonnenheim marketing analysts estimate 50,000 patients will use Mimic in 2007. Production in 2007 is 54,750,000 units (pills). However, only 44,800 patients are prescribed Mimic during 2007. Each patient used three pills per day for 365 days a year. The average wholesale selling price (the price Sonnenheim receives from distributors) is $1.44 per pill. Sonnenheim's actual costs are as follows:

Variable costs per unit	
Manufacturing costs *per pill produced*	
Direct materials	$0.06
Direct manufacturing labour	0.04
Manufacturing overhead	0.11
Marketing costs *per pill sold*	0.07
Fixed costs	
Manufacturing costs	$7,358,400
R&D	4,905,600
Marketing	19,622,400

1. What is the number of Mimic pills actually sold in 2007, assuming all patients began using the drug on January 1 and used it through December 31? What is ending inventory on December 31, 2007?
2. Calculate operating income under variable costing and absorption costing for Sonnenheim Bamberger for the year ended December 31, 2007. The allocation bases for fixed manufacturing costs under absorption costing is $0.15 per unit (pill) produced. All variances are written off to cost of goods sold.
3. Explain differences in operating income in requirement 2.

9-27 Throughput costing (continuation of Exercise 9-26). Sonnenheim is concerned with the inventory buildup in 2007. It receives advice from a consultant to use throughput costing.

REQUIRED
1. Calculate operating income under throughput costing for the year ended December 31, 2007.
2. Why might use of throughput costing reduce inventory buildup?

9-28 Capacity management, denominator-level capacity concepts. Each of the following items is identified by a number:

1. Should be used for performance evaluation
2. Measures the denominator level in terms of demand for the output of the plant
3. Represents the expected level of capacity utilization for the next budget period
4. Is based on producing at full efficiency all the time
5. Takes into account seasonal, cyclical, and trend factors
6. Measures the denominator level in terms of what a plant can supply
7. Represents an ideal benchmark
8. Highlights the cost of capacity acquired but not used
9. Hides the cost of capacity acquired but not used
10. Should be used for long-term pricing purposes
11. If used as the denominator-level concept, would avoid the restatement of unit costs when expected demand levels change

REQUIRED
Match each of the items with one or more of the following denominator-level capacity concepts by putting appropriate letter(s) by each number:

a. Theoretical capacity
b. Practical capacity
c. Normal capacity utilization
d. Master-budget capacity utilization

9-29 Denominator-level problem. The Spalding Sails company produces the Spalding 26, a very popular 8-metre recreational yacht. Spalding Sails takes pride in the high quality they build into their affordable yachts. The company has been in business for 35 years. Management has recently adopted absorption costing and is debating which denominator-level concept to use. This Spalding 26 sells for an average price of $18,000. Budgeted fixed manufacturing overhead for 2007 is estimated at $4,560,000. Spalding uses subassembly operators that provide component parts. Assume for simplicity each yacht can be started and completed in a single shift. The following are the denominator-level options that management has been considering:

a. Theoretical capacity—based on 2 shifts, completion of 5 boats per shift, and a 360-day year—$2 \times 5 \times 360 = 3,600$.
b. Practical capacity—theoretical capacity adjusted for unavoidable interruptions, breakdowns, etc.—$2 \times 4 \times 300 = 2,400$.
c. Normal capacity utilization—based on the marketing department's estimate of 1,200 units.
d. Master-budget capacity utilization—the booming stock market and a record number of baby boomers retiring over the coming year has prompted the marketing department to issue a special estimate for 2007 of 1,440 units.

REQUIRED
1. Calculate the budgeted fixed manufacturing overhead cost rates under the four alternative denominator-level concepts.
2. Why compute fixed costs at the individual product level? Why is this done under absorption costing?
3. Why would Spalding Sails prefer to use either theoretical or practical capacity?
4. Under a cost-based pricing system, what is the negative aspect of a master budget denominator level? What may be the positive aspect?

9-30 Alternative denominator-level concepts. Lucky Lager recently purchased a brewing plant from a bankrupt company. It was constructed only two years ago. The plant has budgeted fixed manufacturing overhead of $50 million per year ($4.167 million each month) in 2007. Paul Vautin, the controller of the brewery, must decide on the denominator-level concept to use in its absorption costing system for 2007. The options available to him are

A. Theoretical capacity: 600 barrels an hour for 24 hours a day for 365 days = 5,256,000 barrels
B. Practical capacity: 500 barrels an hour for 20 hours a day for 350 days = 3,500,000 barrels
C. Normal capacity utilization for 2007: 400 barrels an hour for 20 hours a day for 350 days = 2,800,000 barrels
D. Master-budget capacity utilization for 2007 (separate rates computed for each half-year):
   ◆ January to June 2007 budget—320 barrels an hour for 20 hours a day for 175 days = 1,120,000 barrels
   ◆ July to December 2007 budget—480 barrels an hour for 20 hours a day for 175 days = 1,680,000 barrels

Variable standard manufacturing costs per barrel are $51.40 (variable direct materials, $38.40 variable manufacturing labour, $6.00; and variable manufacturing overhead, $7.00). The brewery "sells" its output to the sales division of Lucky Lager at a budgeted price of $82.00 per barrel.

REQUIRED

1. Compute the budgeted fixed manufacturing overhead rate using each of the four denominator-level concepts for (a) beer produced in March 2007 and (b) beer produced in September 2007. Explain why any differences arise.
2. Explain why the theoretical capacity and practical capacity concepts are different.
3. Which denominator-level concept would the plant manager of the brewery prefer when senior management of Lucky Lager is judging plant manager performance during 2007? Explain.

9-31 Operating income effects of alternative denominator-level concepts (continuation of 9-30). In 2007, the brewery of Lucky Lager showed these results:

Unit data in barrels:

Beginning inventory, January 1, 2007	0
Production	2,600,000
Ending inventory, December 31, 2007	200,000

The brewery had actual costs of

Cost data:

Variable manufacturing	$144,456,000
Fixed manufacturing overhead	$48,758,400

The sales division of Lucky Lager purchased 2,400,000 barrels in 2007 at the $82 per barrel rate.

All manufacturing variances are written off to cost of goods sold in the period in which they are incurred.

REQUIRED

1. Compute the operating income of the brewery using the following: (a) theoretical capacity, (b) practical capacity, and (c) normal capacity utilization denominator-level capacity concepts. Explain any differences between (a), (b), and (c).
2. What denominator-level concept would Lucky Lager prefer for income tax reporting? Explain.
3. Explain the ways in which the Canada Revenue Agency might restrict the flexibility of a company like Lucky Lager, which uses absorption costing to reduce its reported taxable income.

9-32 Standard absorption, variable, and throughput costing. (CMA) The Byrd Company is a manufacturer of appliances for both residential and commercial use. The company's accounting and financial reporting system is primarily designed to meet external reporting requirements in accordance with generally accepted accounting principles. For inventory costing purposes, Byrd uses the absorption costing method in conjunction with a standard costing system. Costs are allocated to products on a units-produced basis. The denominator of fixed manufacturing costs is normal capacity utilization in production units. Relevant information on Byrd's steam cooker appliance for the last two years is as follows:

Unit Data	2006	2007
Beginning inventory	900	1,400
Production	2,000	400
Sales	1,500	1,700
Normal capacity utilization	2,000	2,000

The standard costs for this product are the same in 2005, 2006, and 2007.

Financial Data	2006	2007
Selling price per unit	$ 120	$ 120
Standard variable direct manufacturing costs per unit*	48.70	48.70
Standard variable indirect manufacturing costs per unit	15	15
Variable marketing costs per unit sold	1	1
Total budgeted (and actual) fixed manufacturing costs	10,000	10,000
Total fixed marketing costs	3,000	3,000
Net unfavourable variance[†] pertaining to variable manufacturing costs	1,000	1,000

*Standard variable direct materials costs are $28 per unit.
[†]All variances are written off to cost of goods sold in the period incurred.

Currently, Byrd evaluates the performance of its product-line managers and calculates the bonus based on operating income computed on an absorption costing basis. It has been suggested that the use of variable costing for internal reporting purposes would more accurately reflect the performance of each product-line manager.

REQUIRED
1. Calculate the Byrd Company's operating income on its steam cooker appliance line for 2006 and 2007 using (a) absorption costing, (b) variable costing, and (c) throughput costing.
2. Discuss the features of variable costing that allow it to reflect the performance of Byrd's product-line managers more accurately. Be sure to include in your discussion how absorption costing may influence a product-line manager's behaviour differently from the way variable costing would.
3. What are the pros and cons of adopting throughput costing?

9-33 **The All-Fixed Company.** (R. Marple, adapted) It is the end of 2007. The All-Fixed Company began operations in January 2006. The company is so named because it has no variable costs. All its costs are fixed; they do not vary with output.

All-Fixed is located on the bank of a river and has its own hydroelectric plant to supply power, light, and heat. The company manufactures a synthetic fertilizer from air and river water and sells its product at a price that is not expected to change. It has a small staff of employees, all hired on a fixed annual salary. The output of the plant can be increased or decreased by adjusting a few dials on a control panel.

The following are data regarding the operations of the All-Fixed Company:

	2006	2007*
Sales (tonne)	10,000	10,000
Production (tonne)	20,000	—
Selling price per tonne	$ 36	$ 36
Costs (all fixed):		
Manufacturing	$280,000	$280,000
Marketing and administrative	$ 40,000	$ 40,000

*Management adopted the policy, effective January 1, 2007, of producing only as much product as was needed to fill sales orders. During 2007, sales were the same as for 2006 and were filled entirely from inventory at the start of 2007.

REQUIRED
1. Prepare income statements with one column for 2006, one column for 2007, and one column for the two years together, using (a) variable costing and (b) absorption costing.
2. What is the breakeven point under (a) variable costing and (b) absorption costing?

3. What inventory costs would be carried on the balance sheets at December 31, 2006, and 2007, under each method?
4. Assume that the performance of the top manager of the company is evaluated and rewarded largely on the basis of reported operating income. Which costing method would the manager prefer? Why?

9-34 The Semi-Fixed Company. The Semi-Fixed Company began operations in 2006 and differs from the All-Fixed Company (described in Problem 9-33) in only one respect: it has both variable and fixed manufacturing costs. Its variable manufacturing costs are $8.40 per tonne, and its fixed manufacturing costs are $140,000 per year. The denominator level is 20,000 tonnes per year.

REQUIRED
1. Using the same data as in Problem 9-33 except for the change in manufacturing cost behaviour, prepare income statements with adjacent columns for 2006, 2007, and the two years together, under (a) variable costing and (b) absorption costing.
2. Explain the differences in operating income for Semi-Fixed Company and All-Fixed Company.
3. What inventory costs would be carried on the balance sheets at December 31, 2006, and 2007, under each method?
4. Assume that the performance of the top manager of the company is evaluated and rewarded largely based on reported operating income. Which costing method would the manager prefer? Why?

9-35 Comparison of variable costing and absorption costing. Consider the following data:

Hinkle Company
Income Statement for the Year Ended December 31, 2007

	Variable Costing	Absorption Costing
Revenues	$8,400,000	$8,400,000
Costs of goods sold (at standard)	4,392,000	5,490,000
Fixed manufacturing overhead	1,200,000	—
Manufacturing variances (all unfavourable):		
Direct materials price and efficiency	60,000	60,000
Direct manufacturing labour price and efficiency	72,000	72,000
Variable manufacturing overhead spending and efficiency	36,000	36,000
Fixed manufacturing overhead:		
Spending	120,000	120,000
Production volume	—	480,000
Total marketing costs (all fixed)	1,200,000	1,200,000
Total administrative costs (all fixed)	600,000	600,000
Total costs	7,680,000	8,058,000
Operating income	$ 720,000	$ 342,000

The inventories, carried at standard costs, were

	Variable Costing	Absorption Costing
December 31, 2006	$1,584,000	$1,980,000
December 31, 2007	72,000	90,000

REQUIRED
1. Tim Hinkle, president of the Hinkle Company, has asked you to explain why the operating income for 2007 is less than for 2006, even though sales have increased 40% over last year. What will you tell him?
2. At what percentage of denominator level was the plant operating during 2007?
3. Prepare a numerical reconciliation and explanation of the difference between the operating incomes under absorption costing and variable costing.
4. Critics have claimed that a widely used accounting system has led to undesirable buildups of inventory levels.

    a. Is variable costing or absorption costing more likely to lead to such buildups? Why?
    b. What can be done to counteract undesirable inventory buildups?

9-36 Inventory costing and management planning. It is November 30, 2007. Consider the income statement (shown below) for the operations of Industrial Products, Inc., for January through November 2007.

Production in the past three months has been 100 units monthly. Practical capacity is 125 units monthly. To retain a stable nucleus of key employees, management never schedules monthly production at fewer than 40 units.

Maximum available storage space for inventory is regarded as 200 units. The sales outlook for the next four months is 70 units monthly. Inventory is never to be fewer than 50 units.

Industrial Products, Inc.
Income Statement for 11 Months Ended November 30, 2007

	Units	Dollars	
Revenues @ $1,200	1,000		$1,200,000
Cost of goods sold:			
Beginning inventory, December 31, 2006, @ $960	50	$ 48,000	
Manufacturing costs @ $960, including $720 per unit for fixed manufacturing overhead	1,100	1,056,000	
Total standard cost of goods available for sale	1,150	1,104,000	
Ending inventory, November 30, 2007, @ $960	150	144,000	
Standard cost of goods sold*	1,000		960,000
Gross margin			240,000
Marketing, distribution, and customer-service costs:			
Variable, 1,000 units @ $60		60,000	
Fixed, @ $12,000 monthly		132,000	192,000
Operating income			$ 48,000

*There are no variances for the 11-month period considered as a whole.

The company uses a standard absorption costing system. The denominator production level is 1,200 units annually. All variances are disposed of at year-end as an adjustment to cost of goods sold.

REQUIRED
1. The division manager is given an annual bonus that is geared to operating income. Assume that the manager wants to maximize the company's operating income for 2007. How many units should the manager schedule for production in December? Note that you do not have to (nor should you) compute the operating income for 2007 in this or in subsequent parts of this problem.
2. Assume that standard variable costing is in use rather than standard absorption costing. Would variable costing operating income for 2007 be higher, lower, or the same as standard absorption costing income, assuming that production for December is 80 units and sales are 70 units? Why?
3. If standard variable costing were used, what production schedule should the division manager set? Why?
4. Assume that the manager is interested in maximizing his performance over the long run and that performance is being judged based on net income. Assume that the company's income tax rate will be substantially reduced in 2008 and that the year-end writeoffs of variances are acceptable for income tax purposes. Assume that standard absorption costing is used. How many units should be scheduled for production in December? Why?
5. Assume that the total production and total sales for 2006 and 2007, taken together, will be unchanged by the specific decision in requirement 4. Assume also that the standards will be unchanged in 2008. Suppose the decision in requirement 4 is to schedule 50 units instead of an originally scheduled 120 units. By how much will operating income in 2008 be affected by the decision to schedule 50 units in December 2007? (That is, how much operating income is shifted from 2007 to 2008?)

9-37 Some additional requirements for Problem 9-36; absorption costing and production-volume variances.

REQUIRED

1. What operating income will be reported for 2007 as a whole, assuming that the implied cost behaviour patterns will continue in December as they did in January through November (without regard to your answer to requirement 1 in Problem 9-36), and that production for December is 80 units and sales are 70 units?
2. Assume the same conditions as in requirement 1 except that a monthly denominator level of 125 units (practical capacity) was used in setting fixed manufacturing overhead rates for inventory costing throughout 2007. What production volume variance would be reported for 2007?

9-38 Effects of denominator-level concept choice. The Wong Company installed standard costs and a flexible budget on January 1, 2007. The president was pondering how fixed manufacturing overhead should be allocated to products. Machine-hours were chosen as the allocation base. Her remaining uncertainty was the denominator-level concept for machine-hours. She decided to wait for the first month's results before making a final choice of what denominator-level concept should be used from that day forward.

In January 2007, the actual units of output had a standard of 70,000 machine-hours allowed. If the company used practical capacity as the denominator-level concept, the fixed manufacturing overhead spending variance would be $12,000, unfavourable, and the production volume variance would be $43,200, unfavourable. If the company used normal capacity utilization as the denominator-level concept, the production volume variance would be $24,000, favourable. Budgeted fixed manufacturing overhead was $144,000 for the month.

REQUIRED

1. Compute the denominator level, assuming that the normal capacity utilization concept is chosen.
2. Compute the denominator level, assuming that the practical capacity concept is chosen.
3. Suppose you are the executive vice-president. You want to maximize your 2007 bonus, which depends on 2007 operating income. Assume that the production volume variance is charged or credited to income at year-end. Which denominator-level concept would you favour? Why?

9-39 Downward demand spiral and profitability assessment. Iotera, Inc., manufactures compact portable storage solutions for the portable personal computer market. Iotera's products are very popular and have attracted an almost cult-like following, especially among laptop warriors and PDA (personal digital assistant) junkies. Iotera's chief competitor, Sybest, is based in Silicon Valley. Iotera is currently engaged in a vicious price war with Sybest. Unfortunately, Iotera must also contend with rapidly dropping prices for high-tech consumer products.

Iotera, Inc., manufactures three products—Duda, a 1 Gb 3.5" floppy system; Rock, a 5 Gb cartridge-based system; and Funky, a 1 Tb cutting-edge optical mini-disk system. Once the darling of Wall Street, bad times have come to Iotera. Management is now questioning the profitability of each product and would like to discontinue any product whose gross profit margin percentage is less than 10 percent.

Iotera's current cost accounting system is rather simplistic. The single overhead allocation base is direct labour-hours. The allocation rate per hour is calculated by summing variable and fixed overhead costs and dividing by the number of direct labour-hours. Product cost is calculated by multiplying the number of direct labour-hours required to manufacture the product by the overhead rate and adding this amount to the direct labour and direct materials costs.

Budgeted cost data for 2007 for Iotera appear on the next page.

REQUIRED

1. What is the overhead allocation rate per labour-hour? Will Iotera discontinue any product? Iotera would redirect all available capacity freed up from dropping a product to the most profitable product in total dollar terms that is retained. Complete the budgeted cost data table to answer this question.
2. Consider the products Iotera will produce after any decisions in requirement 1. It now considers average selling prices for 2007 as follows: Duda, $52.20; Rock, $262.80; and Funky, $468.00. Compute the profitability of each product using the new selling prices; will Iotera discontinue any product?
3. Consider what products Iotera will produce after any decisions in requirements 1 and 2. Assume that anything produced can be sold, and that total overhead is unchanged at $5,191,690. Due to packaging and warehouse constraints, Iotera's capacity is limited to the production of 200,000 units in 2007 (each product produced constitutes a single unit, regardless of product type).
   a. Recalculate costs and gross margins under this scenario.
   b. Will Iotera consider dropping any additional products?

c. How has the overhead allocation rate changed?

d. What has happened to the profit margins on the remaining products, and how has this affected Iotera's total gross profits?

4. What recommendations would you make to management regarding the current product-costing system and product decision policies?

Budgeted Cost Data for Iotera, Inc., in 2007

Total overhead costs	$5,191,690	
Total labour-hours	60,089	
Allocation rate per labour-hour	?	

	Duda	**Rock**	**Funky**	**Iotera, Inc.**
Product characteristics				
Direct labour-hours per 10 units	1	?	10	
Total units produced	123,190	72,600	?	?
Total labour-hours spent	?	?	4,210	60,089
Product costs				
Direct materials per unit	$19.44	$107.76	$221.52	
Direct labour per unit @ 21.60 per hour	?	?	?	
Allocated overhead per unit	?	?	?	
Total product costs	?	?	?	
Average selling price	$47.76	$190.80	$384.00	
Gross margin per unit	?	?	?	
Total revenues	?	?	?	?
Total costs	?	?	?	?
Operating income	?	?	?	?

9-40 Cost allocation, downward demand spiral. Western Health Maintenance (WHM) operates a chain of ten hospitals in the Los Angeles area. For many years, it has operated a central food-catering facility in Santa Monica, which delivers meals to the ten hospitals. The Santa Monica facility has the capacity to serve 3,650,000 meals a year (10,000 meals a day). In 2007 it budgeted for 2,920,000 meals (8,000 meals a day), based on demand estimates from each hospital controller. The budgeted variable costs per meal in 2007 are $4.56, which includes delivery to the hospital. Budgeted fixed costs for 2007 are $5,256,000.

In July 2007, the new WHM president announces that each hospital is to be a profit centre. In addition, the head of each hospital can purchase services from outside WHM, providing these services meet the WHM quality requirements. The president gives catering as an example. Roy Cheung, the head of the Santa Monica catering facility, is less than pleased. This facility will also become a profit centre (it has been a cost centre for many years) under the reorganization.

Cheung charged each hospital $6.36 per meal in 2007—comprising $4.56 variable cost plus $1.80 allocation of budgeted fixed costs. Several hospitals complained about the cost and the quality of the food. (Cheung sarcastically labels the quality complaints as "recycled mystery-meat stories.") Indeed, the cost rose from $5.88 in 2006 to $6.36 in 2007. Cheung defended the increase, claiming he needed to spread the same fixed costs over a smaller number of patient-days in 2007. WHM experienced negative press on a local TV station in 2006 and early 2007, and local doctors are referring fewer patients to the WHM hospitals.

In October 2007, Cheung started to prepare the 2008 budget, including the new cost to be charged per meal. He estimated that the total annual demand for meals at all ten WHM hospitals will be 2,550,000. Then he learned that three of the ten hospitals will use an outside canteen service, which reduces the 2008 budgeted demand at the Santa Monica facility to 2,000,000 meals. No change in total fixed costs or variable costs per meal is expected in 2008.

REQUIRED

1. How did Cheung compute the budgeted fixed costs per meal in 2007?

2. What alternative cost-per-meal figures might Cheung compute for meals delivered to WHM hospitals in 2008? Which cost figure should Cheung use? Why?

3. What factors should Cheung consider in pricing meals the Santa Monica facility prepares for the WHM hospitals?

9-41 ABC and capacity usage. Zaynab Bibi Company has identified the following activities and cost drivers for its manufacturing overhead. Zaynab calculates activity cost rates based on cost driver capacity.

Activity	Activity Costs	Cost Driver Capacity
Machine setup	$600,000	5,000 setup-hours
Material handling	240,000	100,000 kilograms of material

Zaynab makes only two products: Daska and Kothi. During 2007, Daska required 3,000 machine setup-hours and handling of 40,000 kilograms of materials. Kothi's production required 1,500 setup-hours and handling of 50,000 kilograms of materials.
1. Calculate the total amount of costs allocated to both products from each activity.
2. Compute the cost of unused capacity for each activity.

9-42 ABC and capacity usage. The controller of Harris Corporation has collected the following data for two activities. Harris calculates activity cost rates based on cost driver capacity.

Activity	Cost Driver	Capacity	Cost
Power	Kilowatt hours	50,000 kilowatt hours	$240,000
Quality inspection	Number of inspections	10,000 inspections	360,000

The company makes two products: Tulsa and Okla. For the year just ended, the following consumption of cost driver was reported:

Product	Kilowatt hours	Quality Inspections
Tulsa	10,000	5,000
Okla	35,000	4,000

REQUIRED
1. Compute the total amount of costs allocated to both products from each activity.
2. Calculate the cost of unused capacity for each activity.

9-43 Cost behaviour, activity-based costing, capacity usage. Finn and Sawyer Company employs five individuals for its bill-processing activity. Each of the employees is paid an annual salary of $36,000. The budgeted annual activity output of bill processing is 6,000 bills per employee. All other costs in the bill-processing activity are variable and are budgeted at $27,000 for the year. During the year, 26,000 bills were actually processed.

REQUIRED
1. Calculate the budgeted fixed rate, budgeted variable rate, and the budgeted rate for bill-processing activity.
2. Compute the total capacity available in bill-processing activity in units.
3. Compute the unused capacity in bill-processing activity in units.
4. Calculate the total cost of bill-processing capacity supplied, the cost of used capacity of bill-processing activity, and the cost of unused capacity of bill-processing activity.

9-44 Downward demand spiral. Pismo Company manufactures 1 terabyte optical mini-disk systems. The current year's monthly production and sales are budgeted at 10,000 units. Pismo's variable manufacturing cost per unit is $240, and its monthly fixed manufacturing overhead costs total $1,200,000. Pismo sets the selling price of its product by adding a 100% markup to the full product cost per unit. The full product cost per unit includes variable manufacturing cost per unit plus the fixed manufacturing overhead cost per unit based on fully allocating total fixed manufacturing overhead costs to the units produced.

REQUIRED
1. Compute Pismo Company's budgeting selling price.
2. Due to intense competition, Pismo had to revise its budgeted monthly production and sales downward to 8,000 units. Compute Pismo Company's revised budgeted selling price.
3. Comment on your results in 1 and 2 above.

9-45 Denominator volume, production-volume variance. National Electronics, Inc., acquired plant assets based on forecasts of long-range demand for its products. Its budgeted manufacturing overhead costs for 2007 are $12,600,000. Under each of the four alternative denominator-level capacity concepts, National's capacity is

Denominator-Level Capacity Concept	Denominator Level (in machine-hours)
Theoretical capacity	2,100,000
Practical capacity	1,500,000
Normal capacity utilization	1,312,500
Master-budgeted capacity utilization	1,000,000

REQUIRED

1. Calculate budgeted fixed manufacturing overhead rate per machine-hour for each denominator-level capacity concept.
2. For 2007 actual output, 1,100,000 budgeted machine-hours were allowed. Compute production-volume variance under each of the denominator-level capacity concept assumptions.

9-46 Variable and absorption costing and breakeven points. Shasta Hills, a winery in British Columbia, manufactures a premium white cabernet and sells primarily to distributors. Wine is sold in cases of one dozen bottles. In the year ended December 31, 2007, Shasta Hills sold 242,400 cases at an average selling price of $112.80 per case. The following additional data are for Shasta Hills for the year ended December 31, 2007 (assume constant unit costs and no price, spending, or efficiency variances):

Beginning inventory, January 1, 2007	32,600 cases
Ending inventory, December 31, 2007	24,800 cases
Fixed manufacturing overhead	$4,504,320
Fixed operating costs	$7,882,560
Variable costs per case	
Direct materials	
Grapes	$19.20 per case
Bottles, corks, and crates	$12.00 per case
Direct labour	
Bottling	$7.20 per case
Winemaking	$16.80 per case
Aging	$2.40 per case

On December 31, 2007, the unit costs per case for closing inventory are $55.20 for variable costing and $73.20 for absorption costing.

REQUIRED

1. Calculate cases of production for Shasta Hills in 2007.
2. Find the breakeven point (number of cases) in 2007:
   a. under variable costing
   b. under absorption costing
3. Grape prices are expected to increase 25% in 2008. Assuming all other data remain constant, what is the minimum number of cases Shasta Hills must sell in 2008 to break even? Calculate the breakeven point:
   a. under variable costing
   b. under absorption costing
4. Assume the owners of Shasta Hills want to increase 2008 operating income 10% over 2007 levels. Using the same data as in requirement 3, recalculate the target quantity of cases under variable and absorption costing. Use approximation method re absorption costing.

9-47 Absorption costing, standard costs, management ethics. Industrial Engineering Company (IEC) is a multinational business selling metal products used in the assembly of many cars, trucks, and planes. IEC has more than 50 manufacturing divisions worldwide and is listed on the Toronto Stock Exchange. IEC has consistently reported annual earnings growth rates of 15% or more for each of the past ten years.

Division managers at IEC receive an annual bonus of 30% of their annual salary if the plant operating income increases 15% or more over the previous year's operating income. Division managers who increase operating income more than 10% but less than 15% receive a bonus of 5% of their annual salary. Division managers who do not achieve a 10% increase in operating income receive no bonus. Instead, they receive a visit from the IEC corporate consulting team.

Bob Wood is manager of the Mississauga, Ontario, division, which manufactures crankshafts for sale to automobile manufacturers. Wood has just received a 30% bonus for 2007. Mary Easson, head of the IEC corporate consulting team, is less than impressed by Wood's performance. She suspects him of producing for inventory and collects the following information on the Mississauga division for 2007:

Unit data in crankshafts:		
Beginning inventory		0
Production		480,000
Ending inventory		30,000
Sales		450,000
Selling price per unit	$	79.20
Cost data:		
Standard variable costs per crankshaft:		
Direct materials	$	24.00
Direct manufacturing labour		6.00
Manufacturing overhead		14.40
Variable marketing		4.80
Standard fixed costs:		
Manufacturing overhead		$10,800,000
Marketing		1,200,000

Manufacturing overhead is allocated to each crankshaft based on standard machine-hours. Each crankshaft has a standard machining time of 30 minutes. The denominator level in 2007 was the master-budget capacity utilization for the Mississauga plant, 500,000 crankshafts. A standard absorption costing system is used for each IEC plant. All variances are recorded as a cost of the period in which they are incurred.

All auto companies require suppliers to deliver on a just-in-time basis (that is, just before the crankshafts are required for assembly). The last four months of 2007 saw a reduction in the orders auto companies placed for crankshafts.

The price, spending, and efficiency manufacturing variances for 2007 were $360,000, unfavourable. The total marketing variances were $187,200, favourable (variable $156,000 favourable and fixed $31,200 favourable).

Operating income for the Mississauga division in 2006 was $1,712,412.

REQUIRED
1. Compute the absorption costing operating income for the Mississauga division in 2007.
2. Why might Easson believe that in 2007 Wood engaged in behaviour not in the best interests of IEC? How might Wood respond to any charges Easson might make about producing for inventory?
3. Is the problem Easson raised likely to be eliminated by her talking to Wood about management ethics? Explain.

9-48 Absorption costing, management ethics (continuation of 9-47). Mary Easson decides to undertake a systematic investigation of how the combination of the existing division manager bonus plan and absorption costing may be causing division managers to make decisions not in the best interests of Industrial Engineering Company (IEC). She will first visit the Morristown division of IEC, which manufactures more than 100 different metal products.

REQUIRED
1. Name three types of behaviour that Easson should look for that would suggest problems for IEC with the existing bonus plan and accounting system.
2. What possible changes might Easson consider if her investigation produces widespread evidence of systematic poor decision making by division managers at IEC?

COLLABORATIVE LEARNING PROBLEM

9-49 Absorption, variable, and throughput costing. The Waterloo, Ontario, plant of Maple Leaf Motors assembles the Icarus motor vehicle. The standard unit manufacturing cost per vehicle in 2007 is

Direct materials	$7,200
Direct manufacturing labour	2,160
Variable manufacturing overhead	2,400
Fixed manufacturing overhead	?

The Waterloo plant is highly automated. Maximum productive capacity per month is 4,000 vehicles. Variable manufacturing overhead is allocated to vehicles based on assembly time on the line. The standard assembly time per vehicle is 20 hours. Fixed manufacturing overhead in 2007 is allocated based on the standard assembly time for the budgeted normal capacity utilization of the plant. In 2007, the budgeted normal capacity utilization is 3,000 vehicles per month. The budgeted monthly fixed manufacturing overhead is $9,000,000.

On January 1, 2007, there is zero beginning inventory of Icarus vehicles. The actual unit production and sales figures for the first three months of 2007 are

	January	February	March
Production	3,200	2,400	3,800
Sales	2,000	2,900	3,200

Assume no direct-materials variances, no direct manufacturing labour variances, and no manufacturing overhead spending or efficiency variances in the first three months of 2007.

Pierre Rougeau, a vice-president of Maple Leaf Motors, is the manager of the Waterloo plant. His compensation includes a monthly bonus that is 0.5% of monthly operating income. Operating income is calculated using absorption costing. Maple Leaf Motors reports monthly absorption costing income statements. Each month an adjustment to cost of goods sold is made for the total manufacturing variances occurring in that month.

The Waterloo plant "sells" each Icarus to Maple Leaf's marketing subsidiary at $19,200 per vehicle. No marketing costs are incurred by the Waterloo plant.

INSTRUCTIONS
Form groups of two or more students to complete the following requirements.

REQUIRED
1. Compute (a) the unit fixed manufacturing overhead cost and (b) the unit total manufacturing cost.
2. Compute the monthly operating income for January, February, and March under absorption costing. What bonus is paid each month to Rougeau?
3. How much would the use of variable costing change the bonus paid each month to Rougeau if the same 0.5% figure is applied to variable costing operating income?
4. Explain the differences in the bonuses paid each month to Rougeau in requirements 2 and 3.
5. How much would the use of throughput costing change the bonus paid each month to Rougeau if the same 0.5% figure is applied to throughput costing operating income?
6. Describe different approaches Maple Leaf Motors could use to reduce the dysfunctional aspects associated with absorption costing at its Waterloo plant.

PART THREE

CHAPTER **10**

Determining How Costs Behave

With large-scale production of airplanes at Bombardier, as managers and workers learn through experience, they become more efficient. This "learning-curve effect" results in reducing the variable cost per unit—significant when those variable costs are attached to high-priced goods such as commercial aircraft. The opportunity to significantly reduce costs through practice and training highlights the importance of understanding how different factors affect cost behaviour.

LEARNING OBJECTIVES

After studying this chapter, you should be able to

1. Explain the two assumptions frequently used in cost behaviour estimation

2. Describe linear cost functions and three common ways in which they behave

3. Recognize various approaches to cost estimation

4. Outline six steps in estimating a cost function based on current or past cost relationships

5. Describe three criteria to evaluate and choose cost drivers

6. Explain and give examples of nonlinear cost functions

7. Distinguish between the cumulative average time learning model and incremental unit time learning model

8. Understand data problems encountered in estimating cost functions

This chapter focuses on how to understand cost behaviour—how costs change because of changes in activity levels, quantity or volume produced, and so on. Knowing how costs vary by identifying the drivers or causes of costs and by distinguishing fixed from variable costs is one key to making good management decisions. Many managerial functions, such as planning and control, rely on cost accounting analysts who make excellent predictions of how costs will behave. With respect to planning, managers want to answer questions such as: What price should we charge? Should we make the item or buy it? What effect will a 20% increase in units sold have on operating income? With respect to controlling costs, managers rely heavily on their knowledge of cost behaviour to interpret variances. Defining the factors affecting costs and understanding the relationship among these factors and cost behaviour are among the most important functions of the cost accountant.

GENERAL ISSUES IN ESTIMATING COST FUNCTIONS

Cost functions. Describe how costs change as their cost drivers change.

Linear cost function. Cost function in which the graph of total costs versus a single cost driver forms a straight line within the relevant range.

Slope coefficient. Coefficient term in a cost estimation model that indicates how much total costs change for each unit change in the cost driver within the relevant range.

Basic Assumptions and Examples of Cost Functions

If a cause-and-effect relationship can be established, then cost behaviour can be modelled as a function or result of changes in the causes of the cost. A cost function is a mathematical function describing cost behaviour patterns—how costs change with changes in the cost driver. Cost functions can be plotted by measuring the cost driver or cause (such as the number of batches produced or perhaps the number of machine hours consumed) on the horizontal or the x-axis and the corresponding amount of total costs that result from changes in the cost driver on the vertical or y-axis.

Two assumptions are frequently made when estimating cost functions:

1. Variations in the total costs of a cost object are explained by variations in a single cost driver.

2. **Cost functions** describe how costs change as their cost drivers change. Cost behaviour is adequately modelled by a straight line describing a *linear cost function*. This straight line approximates the relationship between the cost and its cost driver within the relevant range. A **linear cost function** is a cost function where, within the relevant range, the graph of total costs versus a single cost driver forms a straight line.

We use these assumptions throughout much of this chapter. Later sections give examples of nonlinear cost behaviour patterns in which the plot of the relationship between the cost driver and total costs is not a straight line. The last section in the appendix to this chapter describes how changes in two or more cost drivers can explain changes in the level of total costs. We illustrate cost functions in the context of negotiations between Cannon Services and World Wide Communications (WWC) for exclusive use of a telephone line between Toronto and Paris. WWC offers Cannon Services three alternative cost structures.

◆ **Alternative 1:** $5 per minute of phone use. Consistent with the definition in Chapter 2, this is a *strictly variable cost* for Cannon Services. The number of phone minutes used is the cost driver; that is, the number of phone minutes used is the factor whose change causes a change in total costs.

Panel A in Exhibit 10-1 presents the *strictly variable or proportionately variable* cost. Total costs (measured along the vertical y-axis) change in proportion to the number of phone minutes used (measured along the horizontal x-axis) within the relevant range. The *relevant range*, described in Chapter 2, limits the range of the cost driver where the relationship between total costs and the driver is valid. There are no fixed costs. Every additional minute adds $5 to total costs. Panel A of Exhibit 10-1 illustrates the $5 **slope coefficient**, the amount by which total costs change for a unit change in the cost driver within the relevant range.

We can write the cost function in Panel A of Exhibit 10-1 as

$$y = \$5X$$

where X measures the number of phone minutes used and y measures the total costs of the phone minutes based on calculating the result of inserting the appropriate values of X in the cost function. *Throughout the chapter, uppercase letters, such as X, refer to the actual observations or data and lowercase letters, such as y, represent the results of calculations made using the cost function.*

◆ **Alternative 2:** $10,000 per month. Under this alternative, Cannon Services has a fixed cost of $10,000.

Panel B in Exhibit 10-1 presents the *fixed cost*. The total costs will be $10,000 per month regardless of the number of phone minutes used. (We use the same cost driver, the number of phone minutes used, to compare cost behaviour patterns under various alternatives.) The fixed cost of $10,000 in mathematics is referred to as a

EXHIBIT 10-1
Examples of Linear Cost Functions

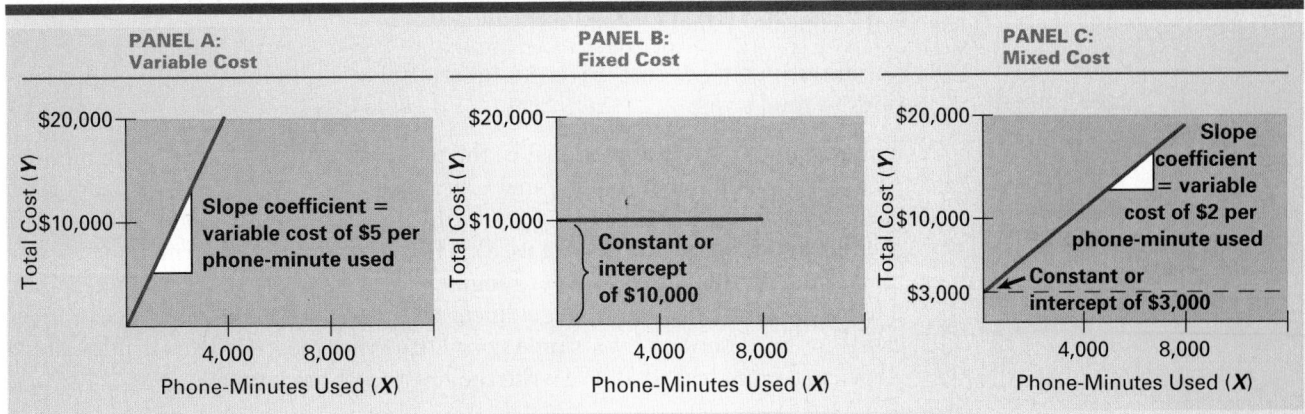

PANEL A: Variable Cost — Slope coefficient = variable cost of $5 per phone-minute used

PANEL B: Fixed Cost — Constant or intercept of $10,000

PANEL C: Mixed Cost — Slope coefficient = variable cost of $2 per phone-minute used; Constant or intercept of $3,000

constant or **intercept**. The intercept is the component of total costs that remains unchanged as the cost driver changes within the relevant range. Under alternative 2, the constant or intercept accounts for all the costs, since there are no variable costs. The slope is zero.

We can write the cost function in Panel B of Exhibit 10-1 as

$$y = \$10,000$$

showing that total costs will be $10,000, regardless of the number of phone minutes used by Cannon Services.

> **Constant (intercept).** The component of total costs that, within the relevant range, does not vary with changes in the level of the cost driver.

◆ **Alternative 3:** $3,000 per month plus $2 per minute of phone use. This is an example of a *mixed* cost. A **mixed cost** (or **semivariable cost**) is a cost that has both fixed and variable elements. Panel C in Exhibit 10-1 presents the mixed cost. It has one component that is fixed regardless of the number of phone minutes used ($3,000 per month) and another component that is variable with respect to the number of phone minutes used ($2 per minute of phone use). In this example, the constant or intercept is $3,000 and the slope coefficient is $2.

> **Mixed cost (semivariable cost).** A cost that has both fixed and variable elements.

We can write the cost function in Panel C of Exhibit 10-1 as

$$y = \$3,000 + \$2X$$

In the case of mixed costs, the total costs in the relevant range increase in part as the number of phone minutes used increases within the relevant range. For example, when 4,000 phone minutes are used, the total costs are [$3,000 + ($2 × 4,000)] = $11,000, but when 8,000 phone minutes are used, the total costs are [$3,000 + ($2 × 8,000)] = $19,000. Although the number of phone minutes used has doubled, the total costs have increased to only 1.73 ($19,000 ÷ $11,000) times the original costs.

Understanding cost behaviour patterns is a crucial input in choosing between the alternatives. Suppose Cannon Services expects to use at least 4,000 phone minutes per month. Its costs for 4,000 phone minutes under the three alternatives would be as follows:

◆ **Alternative 1:** $20,000 ($5 per phone minute × 4,000 phone minutes)
◆ **Alternative 2:** $10,000
◆ **Alternative 3:** $11,000 [$3,000 + ($2 per phone minute × 4,000 phone minutes)].

Alternative 2 is the least costly. Moreover, if Cannon used more than 4,000 phone minutes, alternatives 1 and 3 would be even more costly than alternative 2. Cannon would prefer alternative 2.

Basic Terms

Note two features of the cost functions in the Cannon Services/WWC example. For specificity, consider Panel C.

1. Variations in a *single* cost driver (number of phone minutes used) explain variations in total costs.

2. The cost functions are linear; that is, the plot of total costs versus phone minutes used is a straight line. Because Panel C is a straight line, the only information we need to draw the graph is the constant or intercept term ($3,000) and the slope coefficient ($2 per phone minute used). These two pieces of information describe total costs for the entire relevant range of the number of phone minutes used. That is, within the relevant range, linear cost functions (in the single cost driver case) can be described by a single constant or intercept (called a) and a single slope coefficient (called b). We write the linear cost function as

$$y = a + bX$$

- ◆ **Alternative 1:** $a = \$0$ and $b = \$5$ per phone minute used
- ◆ **Alternative 2:** $a = \$10,000$, $b = \$0$ per phone minute used
- ◆ **Alternative 3:** $a = \$3,000$, $b = \$2$ per phone minute used.

Cost estimation. The measurement of past cost relationships.

The Cannon Services/WWC example illustrates variable, fixed, and mixed cost functions using information about future cost structures proposed to Cannon by WWC. Often, however, cost functions are estimated from past cost data. **Cost estimation** is the attempt to measure *past* causal relationships among cost drivers and total costs. For example, managers could use cost estimation to understand what causes marketing costs to change from year to year (either the quantity of cars sold or the number of new models introduced) and its fixed and variable cost components. Managers are interested in estimating past cost behaviour patterns primarily because these estimates can help them make more accurate **cost predictions**, or forecasts, about future costs. Improved cost predictions help managers make more informed planning and control decisions, such as the marketing costs budget for next year.

Cost prediction. Forecast of future costs.

Chapter 2 outlined three other specifications necessary to classify costs into their variable- and fixed-cost components. We review them briefly here.

Cost estimation underlies many topics in cost accounting. Examples include CVP analysis (Chapter 3), flexible budgets and variances (Chapters 7, 8, and 16), and variable costing (Chapter 9).

- ◆ *Choice of cost object.* A particular cost item could be variable with respect to one cost object and fixed with respect to another. For example, annual van registration and licence costs would be a variable cost when the cost object is the number of vans owned and operated by SuperShuttle, an airport transportation company. But registration and licence costs for a particular van are fixed costs when the cost object is the number of kilometres that the van covered during the year.

- ◆ *Time span.* Whether a cost is variable or fixed with respect to a particular driver depends on the time span considered in the decision situation. The longer the time span, other things being equal, the more likely it is that the cost will be variable. For example, inspection salaries and costs at the Bombardier Company are typically fixed in the short run with respect to hours of inspection activity. But in the long run, Bombardier's total inspection costs will vary with the inspection time required: more inspectors will be hired if more inspection is needed, while some inspectors will be reassigned to other tasks if less inspection is needed.

- ◆ *Relevant range.* Accountants and managers use linear cost functions to approximate the relation of total costs to cost drivers within a relevant range. Exhibit 10-2 plots the relationship over several years between total direct manufacturing labour costs and the number of snowboards produced each year by Ski Authority at its manufacturing plant. Costs are nonlinear outside the relevant range. In this case, nonlinearities occur when the snowboard output is low caused by inefficiencies arising from inexperienced manufacturing labour. Nonlinearities occur at very high levels of production because of greater congestion in the plant and the need for more coordination.

EXHIBIT 10-2
Linearity within Relevant Range

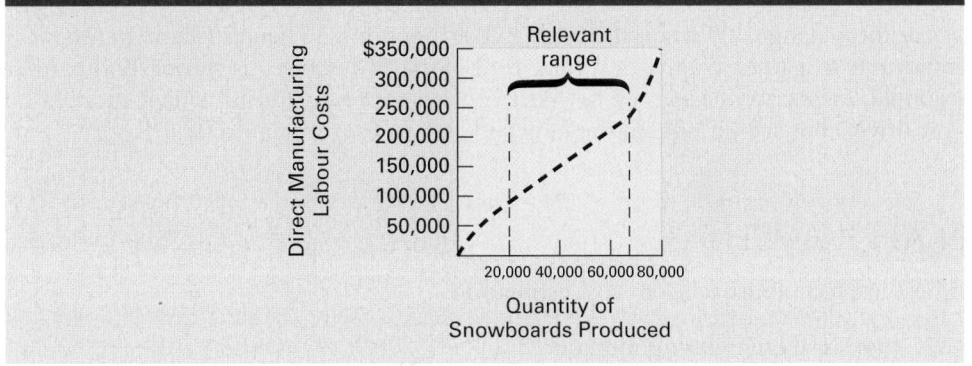

If you've taken a microeconomics course, the cost function in Exhibit 10-2 should look familiar. Below the relevant range, total costs increase at a decreasing rate due to economies of scale. Above the relevant range, diminishing marginal returns cause total costs to increase at an increasing rate.

THE CAUSE-AND-EFFECT CRITERION IN CHOOSING COST DRIVERS

The most important issue in estimating a cost function is to determine whether a cause-and-effect relationship exists between the cost driver and the resulting costs. The cause-and-effect relationship might arise in several ways.

1. It may be due to a physical relationship between costs and the cost driver. An example of a physical relationship occurs when units of production are used as the cost driver of materials costs. To produce more units requires more materials, which results in higher materials costs.

2. Cause and effect can arise from a contractual arrangement, as in the Cannon Services example described earlier, where the number of phone minutes used is the cost driver of the telephone line costs.

3. Cause and effect can be implicitly established by logic and knowledge of operations. An example occurs when the number of component parts is used as a cost driver of design costs. It seems intuitively clear that a complex product design with many component parts that must fit together precisely will incur higher design costs than a simple product with few parts.

Be careful not to interpret a high correlation, or connection, between two variables to mean that either variable causes the other. Simply because one event follows another, it is not logical to conclude that the first event caused the second. A high correlation between two variables, u and v, indicates merely that the two variables move together. It is possible that either u causes v or that v causes u; u and v may interact or both may be caused by a third variable z. Finally, the correlation may be due to chance. No conclusions about cause and effect are warranted, irrespective of how high the correlations are. For example, higher production generally results in higher materials costs and higher labour costs. Materials costs and labour costs are highly correlated, but neither causes the other. Most statistical software packages include the Granger causality test to assess if a causal relationship exists or if the variables are simply correlated.

For many years, church attendance and alcohol consumption were positively correlated. This did not occur because attending church increased people's alcohol consumption or because drinking alcohol promoted piety. Rather, it occurred because of the *increasing population* and its independent effects on both church attendance and alcohol consumption. The lesson: high correlation between two variables does not necessarily mean that a cause-and-effect relationship exists.

Consider another example. Over the past 36 years, with the exception of 1998 through 2001, the New York Stock Exchange Index has almost always increased during the year in which an original National Football League team (such as the Green Bay Packers) has won the Super Bowl, and almost always decreased in the year in which an original American Football League team (such as the New England Patriots) has won.[1] There is, however, no plausible cause-and-effect explanation for this high correlation.

Only a true cause-and-effect relationship, not merely correlation, establishes an economically plausible relationship between costs and their cost drivers. Economic plausibility gives analysts confidence that the estimated relationship will appear again and again in other similar sets of data. Establishing economic plausibility is a vital aspect of cost estimation.

[1]http://money.cnn.com/2003/01/21/markets/superbowl_stock_indicator/

Recall from Chapter 2 that when a cause-and-effect relationship exists between a change in the level of an activity and a change in the level of total costs, the activity measure is referred to as a *cost driver*. We use the terms *level of activity* and *level of cost driver* interchangeably when measuring cost functions. When estimating costs, it is important to gather data over a long time horizon because, as in our Bombardier example, inspection costs may be fixed in the short run (during which there is no cost driver) but are variable in the long run and do have a cost driver.

COST ESTIMATION APPROACHES

There are four approaches to cost estimation:

1. Industrial engineering method

2. Conference method

3. Account analysis method

4. Quantitative analyses of cost relationships

These approaches differ in the costs of conducting the analysis, the assumptions they make, and the evidence they provide about the accuracy of the estimated cost function. They are not mutually exclusive. Many organizations use a combination of these approaches.

Industrial Engineering Method

Industrial engineering method (work measurement method). Approach to cost estimation that first analyzes the relationship between inputs and outputs in physical terms.

Lillian Gilbreth
www.sdsc.edu/ScienceWomen/gilbreth.html

The **industrial engineering method**, also called the **work measurement method**, estimates cost functions by analyzing the relationship between inputs and outputs in physical terms. This method has its roots in studies and techniques developed by Lillian and Frank Gilbreth in the early twentieth century. Consider, for example, Elegant Rugs, a carpet manufacturer that uses inputs of cotton, wool, dyes, direct labour, machine time, and power.

Production output is square metres of carpet. Time-and-motion studies analyze the time and materials required to perform the various operations to produce the carpet. For example, a time-and-motion study may conclude that to produce 20 square metres of carpet requires two bales of cotton and eleven litres of dye. Standards and budgets transform these physical input and output measures into costs. The result is an estimated cost function relating total manufacturing costs to the cost driver, square metres of carpet.

The industrial engineering method can be very time-consuming. Some government contracts mandate its use. Many organizations, however, find it too costly for analyzing their entire cost structure. More frequently, organizations use this approach for direct-cost categories such as materials and labour but not for indirect-cost categories such as manufacturing overhead. Physical relationships between inputs and outputs may be difficult to specify for individual overhead cost items.

Conference Method

Conference method. Approach to cost estimation that develops cost estimates based on analysis and opinions gathered from various departments of an organization.

Co-operative Bank
www.co-operativebank.co.uk

VISA
www.visa.ca

The **conference method** estimates cost functions based on analysis and opinions about costs and their drivers gathered from various departments of an organization (purchasing, process engineering, manufacturing, employee relations, and so on). The Co-operative Bank in the United Kingdom has a cost estimating department that develops cost functions for its retail banking products (current accounts, VISA cards, mortgages, and so on) based on a consensus of estimates from the relevant departments. The bank uses this information to price products, to adjust its product mix to the products that are most profitable, and to monitor and measure cost improvements over time.

The conference method allows cost functions and cost estimates to be developed quickly. The pooling of expert knowledge from each value-chain area gives the conference method credibility. The accuracy of the cost estimates largely depends on the care and detail taken by the people providing the inputs.[2]

Account Analysis Method

The **account analysis method** estimates cost functions by classifying cost accounts in the ledger as variable, fixed, or mixed with respect to the identified cost driver. Typically, managers use qualitative rather than quantitative analysis when making these cost classification decisions. The account analysis approach is widely used.[3]

Consider indirect manufacturing labour costs for a small production area (or cell) at Elegant Rugs, which weaves carpets for homes and offices and uses state-of-the-art automated weaving machines. These costs include maintenance, quality control, and setup costs for the machines. During the most recent 12-week period, Elegant Rugs worked the machines in the cell for a total of 862 hours and incurred total indirect manufacturing labour costs of $12,501. Management wants the cost analyst to use the account analysis method to estimate a linear cost function for indirect manufacturing labour costs with machine-hours as the cost driver.

The cost analyst, based on experience, identifies and separates total indirect manufacturing labour costs ($12,501) into costs that are fixed ($2,157) and costs that are variable ($10,344), given the cost driver is the number of machine-hours worked. Variable costs per machine-hour are $10,344 ÷ 862 = $12. The general cost equation, $y = a + bX$, is:

Indirect manufacturing labour costs = $2,157 + ($12 × number of machine-hours).

The indirect manufacturing labour cost per machine-hour is $12,501 ÷ 862 = $14.50. Management at Elegant Rugs can use the cost function to estimate the indirect manufacturing labour costs of using 950 machine-hours to produce carpet in the next 12-week period. Using the cost function, estimated costs = $2,157 + (950 × 12) = $13,557. The indirect manufacturing labour costs per machine-hour decrease to $13,557 ÷ 950 = $14.27, as fixed costs are spread over a greater number of machine hours.

Organizations differ with respect to the care taken in implementing account analysis. In some organizations, individuals thoroughly knowledgeable about the operations make the cost classification decisions. For example, costs such as machine lubricants and materials-handling labour would usually be classified by manufacturing managers, whereas costs such as advertising brochures and sales salaries would usually be classified by marketing managers. In other organizations, only cursory analysis is conducted, sometimes by individuals with limited knowledge of operations, before cost classification decisions are made. Clearly, the former approach would provide more accurate cost classifications, and hence estimates of the fixed and variable components of the cost, than the latter. Supplementing the account analysis method with the conference method improves its credibility.

Quantitative Analyses of Cost Relationships

Quantitative analyses of cost relationships are formal methods to fit linear cost functions to past data observations. Columns B and C of Exhibit 10-3 (p. 372) break down the $12,501 of total indirect manufacturing labour costs and the 862 total machine-hours for the most recent 12-week period into weekly data. Note that the data are paired. For example, week 12 shows indirect manufacturing labour costs of $963 and 48 machine-hours. The next section uses the data in Exhibit 10-3 to illustrate two different quantitative ways to estimate a cost function: the high-low method and regression analysis. Column D will be used later to illustrate how to evaluate the accuracy of alternative cost drivers for the same cost.

Account analysis method.
Approach to cost estimation that classifies cost accounts in the ledger as variable, fixed, or mixed with respect to the cost driver. Typically, qualitative rather than quantitative analysis is used in making these classification decisions.

The industrial engineering, conference, and account analysis methods require less historical data than most quantitative analyses. Consequently, cost estimation for a new product will usually begin with one or more of these three methods. Quantitative analysis may be used for this product later on, after the company collects the necessary historical data.

[2]The conference method is further described in W. Winchell, *Realistic Cost Estimating for Manufacturing*, 2nd ed. (Dearborn, Mich.: Society for Manufacturing Engineers, 1991).

[3]Survey evidence appears in M. M. Mowen, *Accounting for Costs as Fixed and Variable* (Montvale, N.J.: National Association of Accountants, 1986).

EXHIBIT 10-3
Weekly Indirect Manufacturing Labour Costs, Machine-Hours, and Direct Manufacturing Labour-Hours for Elegant Rugs

	A	B	C	D
1			Indirect	Direct
2		Cost Driver:	Manufacturing	Manufacturing
3	Week	Machine-Hours	Labour Costs	Labour-Hours
4		(X)	(y)	Alternative (X)
5	1	68	$ 1,190	30
6	2	88	1,211	35
7	3	62	1,004	36
8	4	72	917	20
9	5	60	770	47
10	6	96	1,456	45
11	7	78	1,180	44
12	8	46	710	38
13	9	82	1,316	70
14	10	94	1,032	30
15	11	68	752	29
16	12	48	963	38
17	Total	862	$12,501	462

STEPS IN ESTIMATING A COST FUNCTION

OBJECTIVE 4

Outline six steps in estimating a cost function based on current or past cost relationships

There are six steps in estimating a cost function based on an analysis of current or past cost relationships:

◆ **Step 1:** Choose the dependent variable (y, the variable to be predicted, which is some type of cost)
◆ **Step 2:** Identify the cost driver(s) (X[s], the independent variable[s])
◆ **Step 3:** Collect data on y, the dependent variable, and X(s), the cost driver(s)
◆ **Step 4:** Plot the data
◆ **Step 5:** Estimate the cost function
◆ **Step 6:** Evaluate the estimated cost function.

As we discussed earlier in this chapter, choosing a cost driver or independent variable to explain changes in costs is not straightforward. **Independent variables** reliably explain, at least in part, the changes in the dependent variable. Frequently, the cost analyst will cycle through these steps several times trying alternative economically plausible cost drivers to see which cost driver best fits the data. We will take a closer look at quantitative analysis using the Elegant Rugs example.

Independent variable. Reliably explains, at least in part, the changes in the dependent variable.

Dependent variable. The cost variable to be predicted in a cost estimation or prediction model.

◆ **Step 1:** *Choose the dependent variable.* Choice of the **dependent variable** (the cost variable to be predicted) will depend on the purpose for estimating a cost function. In the Elegant Rugs example, the dependent variable is indirect manufacturing labour costs. Therefore all costs that are classified with respect to indirect manufacturing labour must be included in the cost function.
◆ **Step 2:** *Identify the cost driver(s).* The chosen cost driver is the cause that should predict the dependent variable costs. Therefore, the cost driver or level of activity should have an economically plausible relationship with the dependent variable and be accurately measurable. Ideally, all the individual items included in the dependent variable should have the same cost driver(s). Where a single relationship does not exist, the cost analyst should investigate the possibility of estimating

more than one cost function. In the Elegant Rugs example the cost driver is also the cost-allocation base, but this will not always be the case; therefore, the more general term, cost driver, is used to identify independent variables.

Consider several types of fringe benefits paid to employees and their cost drivers:

The chapter focuses on a single independent variable or cost driver. The appendix to this chapter (pp. 390–403) describes how multiple cost drivers can be used to predict a cost.

Fringe Benefit	Cost Driver
Health benefits	Number of employees
Cafeteria meals	Number of employees
Pension benefits	Salaries of employees
Life insurance	Salaries of employees

The costs of health benefits and cafeteria meals can be combined into one cost pool, because they both have the same cost driver, number of employees. Pension benefits and life insurance costs have a different cost driver, salaries of employees, and hence should not be combined with health benefits and cafeteria meals. Instead, they should be combined in a separate cost pool and estimated using salaries of employees receiving the benefits as the cost driver.

◆ **Step 3:** *Collect data on the dependent variable and the cost driver(s).* This step is usually the most difficult one in cost analysis. Cost analysts obtain data from company documents, from interviews with managers, and through special studies. These data may be time series data or cross-sectional data. *Time series data* pertain to the same entity (organization, plant, activity area, and so on) over a sequence of past time periods. Weekly observations of indirect manufacturing labour costs and machine-hours in the Elegant Rugs illustration are an example of time series data. The ideal time series database would contain numerous observations for a firm whose operations have not been affected by economic or technological change. Stable technology ensures that data collected in the estimation period represent the same underlying relationship between the dependent variable and the cost driver(s). Moreover, the time periods (for example, daily, weekly, or monthly) used to measure the dependent variable and the cost driver(s) should be identical. *Cross-sectional data* pertain to different entities for the same time period. For example, studies of personnel costs and loans processed at 50 individual branches of a bank during March would produce cross-sectional data for March. A later section of this chapter describes problems that arise in data collection.

◆ **Step 4:** *Plot the data.* This step is important. The saying "A picture is worth a thousand words" conveys the benefits of plotting the data. The general relation between the dependent variable and the cost driver can readily be observed in a plot of the data. Moreover, the plot highlights extreme observations that analysts should check. Was there an error in recording the data or an unusual event, such as a labour strike, that makes these observations unrepresentative of the normal relationship between the dependent variable and the cost driver? Plotting the data can also provide insight into whether the relation is approximately linear and what the relevant range of the cost function is.

If there were extreme observations, the manager would need to find out if these observations were correct or the result of an error. If correct, managers would include the observations if they were representative and discard them if they were unusual.

Exhibit 10-4 plots the weekly data from columns B and C of Exhibit 10-3. There is strong visual evidence of a positive relation between indirect manufacturing labour costs and machine-hours (that is, when machine-hours go up, so do costs). There do not appear to be any extreme observations in Exhibit 10-4. The relevant range is from 46 to 96 machine-hours per week.

◆ **Step 5:** *Estimate the cost function.* We show how to estimate the cost function for our Elegant Rugs data using the high-low method and regression analysis.

◆ **Step 6:** *Evaluate the estimated cost function.* We describe criteria for evaluating a cost function after illustrating the high-low method and regression analysis.

EXHIBIT 10-4
Plot of Weekly Indirect Manufacturing Labour Costs and Machine-Hours for Elegant Rugs

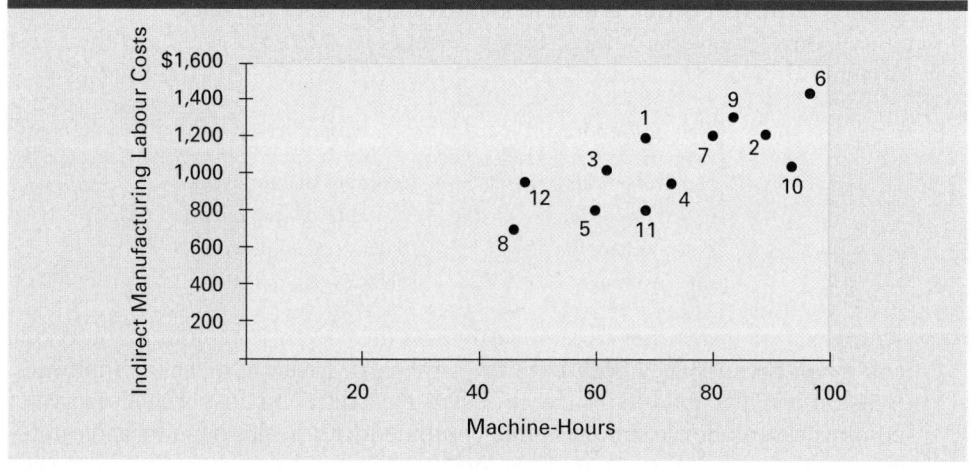

High-Low Method

High-low method. Method used to estimate a cost function that entails using only the highest and lowest observed values of the cost driver within the relevant range.

Managers, at times, use very simple methods to estimate cost functions. An example is the **high-low method**, which entails using only the highest and lowest observed values of the *cost driver* within the relevant range. The line connecting these two points becomes the estimated cost function.

We illustrate the high-low method using data from Exhibit 10-3.

	Indirect Manufactring Labour Costs Δy	**Machine-Hours** ΔX
Highest observation of cost driver (week 6)	$1,456	96
Lowest observation of cost driver (week 8)	710	46
Difference	$ 746	50

The slope coefficient, b, is calculated as:

$$\text{Slope coefficient } b = \frac{\Delta y}{\Delta X}$$

$$= \$746 \div 50 = \$14.92 \text{ per machine-hour}$$

To compute the constant, we can use either the highest or the lowest observation of the cost driver. The two calculations yield the same answer (because the solution technique solves two linear equations with two unknowns, the slope coefficient and the constant).

$$y = a + bX, \quad a = y - bX$$

At the highest observation of the cost driver,

$$\text{Constant } a = \$1,456 - (\$14.92 \times 96) = \$23.68$$

At the lowest observation of the cost driver,

$$\text{Constant } a = \$710 - (\$14.92 \times 46) = \$23.68$$

Therefore, the high-low estimate of the cost function is

$$y = a + bX$$
$$= \$23.68 + (\$14.92 \times \text{machine-hours})$$

The bottom line in Exhibit 10-5 shows the estimated cost function using the high-low method. The estimated cost function is a straight line joining the observations with the highest and lowest values of the cost driver (machine-hours). The

EXHIBIT 10-5
High-Low Method for Weekly Indirect Manufacturing Labour Costs and Machine-Hours for Elegant Rugs

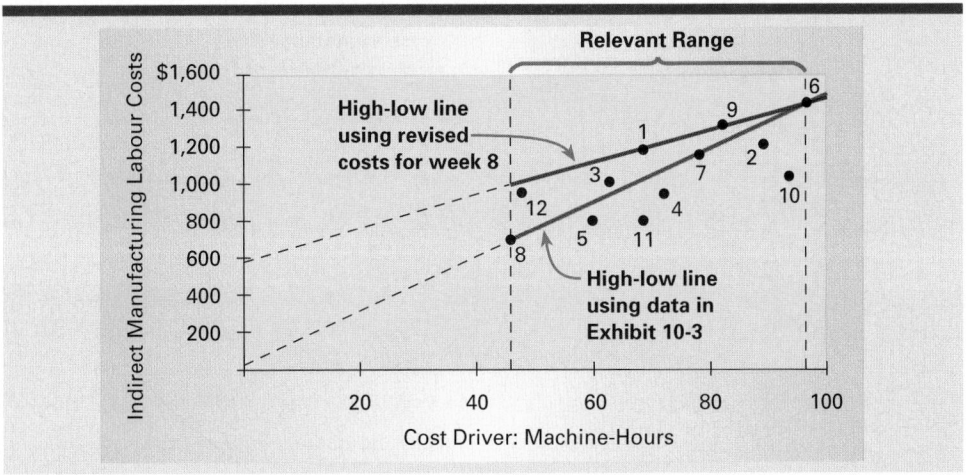

constant, or intercept, term does not serve as an estimate of the fixed costs of Elegant Rugs if no machines were run. Why? Because running no machines and shutting down the plant is outside the relevant range. The intercept term is the constant component of the equation that provides the best (linear) approximation of how a cost behaves within the relevant range.

Suppose indirect manufacturing labour costs in week 6 were $1,280 instead of $1,456 while 96 machine-hours were worked. In this case, the highest observation of the cost driver (machine-hours of 96 in week 6) will not coincide with the next highest observation of the dependent variable (costs of $1,316 in week 9). Given that causality runs from the cost driver to the dependent variable in a cost function, choosing the highest and lowest observation of the cost driver is appropriate. The high-low method would estimate the new cost function still using data from weeks 6 and 8.

There is an obvious danger of relying on only two observations. Suppose that because of certain provisions in the labour contract that guarantee certain minimum payments, indirect manufacturing labour costs in week 8 were $1,000 instead of $710 when only 46 machine-hours were worked. The top line in Exhibit 10-5 shows the revised estimated cost function using the high-low method. It lies above the data. In this case, picking the highest and lowest observations for the machine-hours variable can result in an estimated cost function that poorly describes the underlying (linear) cost relationship between indirect manufacturing labour costs and machine-hours.

Sometimes the high-low method is modified so that the two observations chosen are a representative high and a representative low. The reason is that management wants to avoid having extreme observations (outliers), which arise from abnormal events, affect the cost function. Even with such a modification, this method ignores information from all but two observations when estimating the cost function.

Linear Regression Analysis Method

Unlike the high-low method, regression analysis uses all available data to estimate the cost function. **Linear regression analysis** is a formal statistical analysis that assumes, among other things, a linear relationship exists between the change in the dependent and independent variable(s). Regression analysis is a statistical method that measures the *average* amount of change in the dependent variable that is associated with a unit change in one or more independent variables. In the Elegant Rugs example, the dependent variable is total indirect manufacturing labour costs. The independent variable, or cost driver, is machine-hours. **Simple regression** analysis estimates the relationship between the dependent variable and one independent variable; **multiple regression** analysis estimates the relationship between the dependent variable and multiple independent variables.

We emphasize the interpretation and use of output from computer software programs for regression analysis and so only present detailed computations for deriving the

Linear regression analysis. A formal statistical analysis that assumes, among other things, a linear relationship exists between the change in the dependent and independent variable(s).

Simple regression. Regression model that uses only one independent variable to estimate the dependent variable.

Multiple regression. Regression model that uses more than one independent variable to estimate the dependent variable.

EXHIBIT 10-6
Regression Model for Weekly Indirect Manufacturing Labour Costs and Machine-Hours for Elegant Rugs

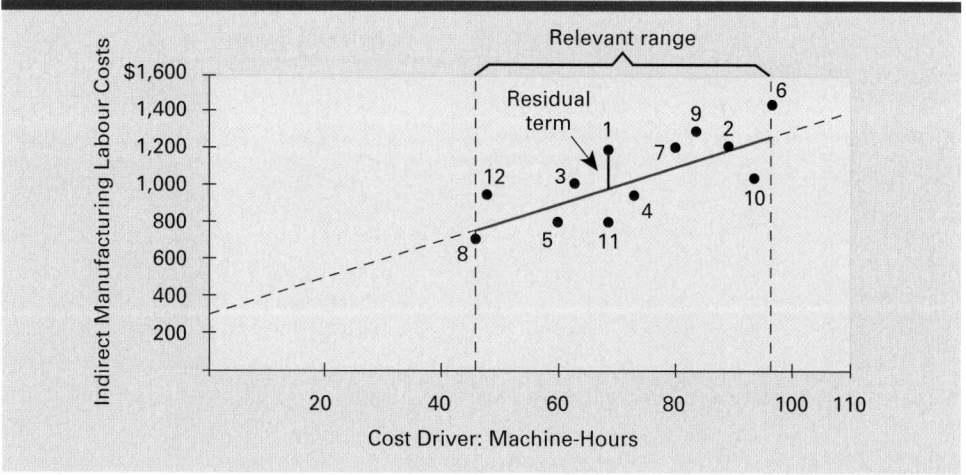

regression line in this chapter's appendix. Commonly available programs (for example, SPSS, SAS, Lotus, and Excel) on mainframes and personal computers calculate all the statistics referred to in this chapter. While we illustrate calculations using Excel, the following discussion emphasizes how managers interpret and use the regression analysis results to make key strategic decisions. Exhibit 10-6 depicts the line developed using regression analysis that best fits the data in columns B and C of Exhibit 10-3.

The estimated cost function is

$$y = \$300.98 + \$10.31X$$

where y is the predicted indirect manufacturing labour costs (dependent variable) for any level of machine-hours (X, independent variable). The constant, or intercept, term of the regression a is $300.98, and the slope coefficient b is $10.31 per machine-hour.

> The regression line is fitted through a set of observations so that it best represents the underlying relationship or pattern in the observations.

How do we derive the regression equation and regression line in Exhibit 10-6? We use the least-squares technique. We draw the regression line to minimize the sum of the squared vertical distances from the data points (the various points on the graph) to the regression line. Vertical differences measure distance between actual cost and the estimated cost for each observation. The difference between actual and predicted cost is called the **residual term** (also called **disturbance term** and **error term**). The smaller the sum of the squared values of the residual terms (sum of ordinary least squares, OLS), the better the fit between predicted costs and actual cost observations. Goodness of fit indicates the strength of the relationship between the cost driver and costs. The regression line in Exhibit 10-6 rises reasonably steeply from left to right. The positive slope of this line indicates that, on average, indirect manufacturing labour costs increase as machine-hours increase.

> **Residual term (disturbance term, error term).** The difference between the actual and the predicted amount of a dependent variable (such as a cost) in a regression model.

The vertical dashed lines in Exhibit 10-6 indicate the relevant range. As discussed previously, the estimated cost function applies only to cost driver levels *within the relevant range*, not to cost driver levels outside the relevant range.

The estimate of the slope coefficient b indicates that the average indirect manufacturing labour costs vary at the rate of $10.31 for every machine-hour within the relevant range. Management can use this equation when budgeting for future indirect manufacturing labour costs. For instance, if 90 machine-hours are budgeted for the upcoming week, the predicted indirect manufacturing labour costs would be

$$y = \$300.98 + (\$10.31 \times 90) = \$1,228.88$$

Compare the regression equation with the high-low equation in the preceding section, which was $23.68 + $14.92 per machine-hour. For 90 machine-hours, the predicted cost based on the high-low equation is $23.68 + ($14.92 × 90) = $1,366.48. Suppose that for three weeks over the next 12-week period, Elegant Rugs runs its machines for 90 hours each week. Assume average indirect manufacturing labour costs for those three weeks are $1,300. Based on the high-low prediction of $1,366.48, Elegant Rugs would conclude it has performed well. But comparing the $1,300 performance with the $1,228.88 prediction of the regression model tells a different story and would probably prompt Elegant Rugs to search for ways to improve its cost performance.

Intelligent application of regression analysis requires knowledge of both operations and cost accounting. Consider the costs to maintain and repair metal-cutting machines at Helix Corporation, a manufacturer of filing cabinets. Helix schedules repairs and maintenance when production is at a low level to avoid having to take machines out of service when they are needed most. A plot and regression analysis of the monthly data will then show high repair costs in months of low production and low repair costs in months of high production. The engineering link between units of production and repair costs, however, is usually clear-cut. Over time there is a cause-and-effect relation: the higher the level of production, the higher the repair costs. To estimate the relation correctly, a thoughtful analyst will recognize that repair costs will tend to lag behind periods of high production and will use *lagged* production as the cost driver. In equation form, if the cost estimate (y) is for time period t_1 then the lagged measure of the cost driver (X) is the value estimated at time period t_0, thus:

$$y_{t=1} = a + bX_{t=0}$$

EVALUATING AND CHOOSING COST DRIVERS

Correctly identifying the cost driver and separating fixed costs from variable costs are important inputs for many management decisions. Suppose management at Elegant Rugs is thinking of introducing a new style of carpet. Sales of 650 square metres of this carpet are expected each week at a price of $12 per square metre. To make this decision, management needs to estimate costs. The key to doing so is identifying the correct cost drivers and cost functions. Consider, in particular, indirect manufacturing labour costs. Management believes that both machine-hours and direct manufacturing labour-hours are plausible cost drivers of indirect manufacturing labour costs. It estimates that 72 machine-hours and 21 direct manufacturing labour-hours would be required to produce the square metres of carpet it needs.

What guidance do the different cost estimation methods provide for choosing among cost drivers (see Focus on Values and Behaviours on the next page)? The industrial engineering method relies on analyzing physical relationships between costs and cost drivers, which are difficult to specify in this case. The conference method and the account analysis method use subjective assessments to choose a cost driver and to estimate the fixed and variable components of the cost function. In these cases, management must go with its best judgment. Management cannot use these methods to test and try alternative cost drivers. The major advantage of quantitative methods is that managers can use these methods to evaluate different cost drivers. We illustrate how using the regression analysis approach.

Suppose Elegant Rugs wants to evaluate whether direct manufacturing labour-hours is a better cost driver than machine-hours for indirect manufacturing labour costs. The cost analyst at Elegant Rugs inputs the data in columns C and D of Exhibit 10-3 into a computer program and estimates the cost function:

$$y = \$744.67 + \$7.72X$$

Exhibit 10-7 shows the plot for indirect manufacturing labour costs and direct manufacturing labour-hours, and the regression line that best fits the data.

Which cost driver should Elegant Rugs choose? We consider three of the most important criteria:

1. *Economic plausibility*. Both cost drivers are economically plausible. However, in the state-of-the-art, highly automated production environment of Elegant Rugs, costs are likely to be more closely related to machine-hours than to direct manufacturing labour-hours.

2. *Goodness of fit*. Compare Exhibits 10-6 and 10-7. The vertical differences between actual and predicted costs are much smaller for machine-hours than for direct

OBJECTIVE 5

Describe three criteria to evaluate and choose cost drivers

As in most applications, the cost function in the Elegant Rugs example is not valid at shutdown ($X = 0$) because that point is outside the relevant range (see Exhibit 10-7). That is, the y-intercept, $744.67, is not the fixed costs at 0 direct manufacturing labour-hours because at shutdown many costs can be avoided (for example, laying off salaried personnel). The $744.67 is an arithmetic result from solving the regression equation to provide the best linear fit of the data.

Boeing's Management Accountants: Embracing Opportunities and Tackling Challenges

Understanding how costs behave is a valuable technical skill. Managers look to management accountants to help them identify cost drivers, estimate cost relationships, and determine the fixed and variable components of costs. To be effective, management accountants must have a clear understanding of the business operations and must be seen as vital members of the management team. They must also be able to convey their findings so that managers who are unfamiliar with the technical details can understand the issues in a way that is helpful when making decisions.

Let's consider an example. Chicago-based Boeing landed the role of lead systems integrator (LSI) for a multiyear, [US]$14.8-billion defense missile-shield contract with the U.S. government. This deal could lead to 20 years and [US]$100 billion worth of work on military combat systems. The contract shifts Boeing toward more software-based programs and more management roles instead of pure military hardware manufacturing. This is a great opportunity for Boeing, but these new opportunities also create many challenges. As LSI, Boeing must hire contractors and collect fees for overseeing projects, which means examining unfamiliar categories of costs. For Boeing's management accountants, helping to determine the underlying cost drivers involved in this strategic shift—from manufacturer to contractor—is critical, as is the ability to help managers estimate new cost relationships and fixed and variable costs.

Determining cost drivers is not simply an analytical skill but one that requires good judgment. A manager may exert pressure on management accountants to favour one cost driver over another—perhaps because it reduces the costs assigned to the manager's pet project or because it makes the manager's performance look better. If management accountants want to ensure that their analysis is sound and that the decisions based on their analysis are value-enhancing, they should never be persuaded by unethical pressures from management.

manufacturing labour-hours—machine-hours has a stronger relationship with indirect manufacturing labour costs.

3. *Slope of regression line*. Again compare Exhibits 10-6 and 10-7. The machine-hours regression line has a relatively steep slope while the direct manufacturing labour hours regression line is relatively flat (small slope). A relatively flat

EXHIBIT 10-7

Regression Model for Weekly Indirect Manufacturing Labour Costs and Direct Manufacturing Labour-Hours for Elegant Rugs

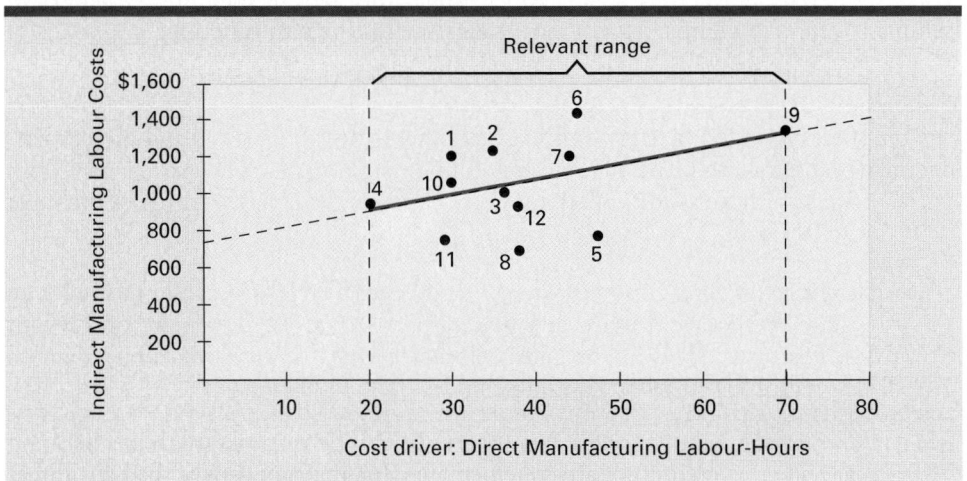

regression line indicates a weak or no relationship between indirect manufacturing labour costs and direct manufacturing labour-hours, since, on average, changes in direct manufacturing labour-hours appear to have a minimal effect on indirect manufacturing labour costs.

Elegant Rugs should choose machine-hours as the cost driver and use the cost function $y = \$300.98 + (\$10.31 \times \text{machine-hours})$ to predict future indirect manufacturing labour costs. Using this model, Elegant Rugs would predict costs of $y = \$300.98 + (\$10.31 \times 72) = \$1,043.30$. Had it used direct manufacturing labour-hours as the cost driver, it would have incorrectly predicted costs of $\$744.67 + (\$7.72 \times 21) = \$906.79$. If Elegant Rugs systematically underestimates costs and chooses incorrect cost drivers for other indirect costs as well, it would conclude that the costs of manufacturing the new style of carpet are quite low and essentially fixed (the regression line is relatively flat). But the actual costs driven by machine-hours would prove to be much higher. Without identifying the correct cost drivers, management would be misled into believing the new style of carpets is more profitable than it actually is.

Incorrectly estimating the cost function will also have repercussions for cost management and cost control. Suppose direct manufacturing labour-hours was used as the cost driver, and actual indirect manufacturing labour costs were $970. Actual costs would then be higher than the predicted costs of $906.79. Management would feel compelled to find ways to cut costs. In fact, based on the preferred machine-hour cost driver, the plant has actual costs lower than the predicted amount ($1,043.30)—a performance that management should seek to replicate, not change.

In the Elegant Rugs example, machine-hours dominated direct manufacturing labour-hours on all three criteria. But what if this were not the case? Then, economic plausibility would be the most important criterion. Statistical techniques can be used to evaluate trade-offs between the other two criteria: goodness of fit and significance of independent variable.

COST DRIVERS AND ACTIVITY-BASED COSTING

Activity-based costing (ABC) systems focus on individual activities in a value-added function of the value chain—such as product design, machine setup, material handling, distribution, and customer service—as the fundamental cost objects: To implement ABC systems, managers must identify a cost driver for each activity (see Chapter 5 for a full discussion). For example, using methods described in this chapter, the manager must decide whether the number of loads moved or the weight of loads moved is the cost driver of material-handling costs (see Concepts in Action on p. 380).

To choose the cost driver and use it to estimate the cost function in our material-handling example, the manager collects data on material-handling costs and the quantities of the two competing cost drivers over a long enough period. Why a long period? Because in the short run, material-handling costs may be fixed and, therefore, will not vary with changes in the level of the cost driver. In the long run, however, there is a clear cause-and-effect relationship between material-handling costs and the cost driver. Suppose number of loads moved is the cost driver of material-handling costs. Increases in the number of loads moved will require more material-handling labour and equipment; decreases will result in equipment being sold and labour being reassigned to other tasks.

ABC systems have a great number and variety of cost drivers and cost pools. That means ABC systems require many cost relationships to be estimated. In estimating the cost function for each cost pool, the manager must pay careful attention to the cost hierarchy. For example, if a cost is a batch-cost such as setup cost, the manager must only consider batch-level cost drivers like number of setup-hours.

A cost hierarchy categorizes costs into different cost pools on the basis of the different types of cost drivers. A common four part cost hierarchy is output unit-level costs, batch-level costs, product-sustaining costs, and facility-sustaining costs (see pp. 161–162).

Managers implementing ABC systems use a variety of methods—industrial engineering, conference, and regression analysis—to estimate slope coefficients. In making these choices, managers trade off level of detail, accuracy, feasibility, and costs of estimating cost functions.

Nonlinear cost function. Cost function in which the graph of total costs in relation to a single cost driver does not form a straight line within the relevant range.

NONLINEARITY AND COST FUNCTIONS

In practice, cost functions are not always linear. A **nonlinear cost function** is a cost function where, within the relevant range, the graph of total costs with a single cost driver does not form a straight line. Exhibit 10-2 (p. 369) graphically illustrated a cost function that is nonlinear over the range from 0 to 80,000 snowboards produced.

Activity-Based Costing: Identifying Cost and Revenue Drivers

Many cost estimation methods presented in this chapter are essential to service- and retail-sector implementations of activity-based costing. To determine the cost of an activity in the banking industry, ABC systems often rely on expert analyses and opinions gathered from operating personnel (the conference method). For example, the Loan Department staff in banks will subjectively estimate the costs of the loan processing activity and the quantity of the related cost driver—the number of loans processed, a batch-level cost driver, as distinguished from the amount of the loans, an output unit-level cost driver—to derive the cost of processing a loan.

ABC systems in government agencies, in contrast, frequently use input-output relationships (the industrial engineering method) to identify cost drivers and the cost of an activity. The City of Indianapolis Department of Transportation uses work-measurement methods to determine the direct and indirect costs associated with its 35 primary activities. Similar processes have helped the U.S. Postal Service determine the cost of each post-office transaction and the U.S. Patent and Trademark Office identify the costs of each patent examination.

Regression analysis is another helpful tool for determining the cost drivers of activities. Consider how fuel service retailers (that is, gas stations with convenience stores) identify the principal cost driver for labour within their operations. Two possible cost drivers are gasoline sales and convenience store sales. Gasoline sales are batch-level activities because payment transactions occur only once for each gasoline purchase, regardless of the volume of gasoline purchased; whereas convenience store sales are output unit-level activities that vary based on the amount of food, drink, and other products sold. Fuel service retailers generally use convenience store sales as the basis for assigning labour costs because multiple regression analyses confirm that convenience store sales, not gasoline sales, are the major cost driver of labour.

Can these cost estimation methods also be used to identify drivers of revenue? For example, how should banks structure their Guaranteed Investment Certificate (GIC) offerings? At one bank, the cost of processing a GIC is fixed regardless of the amount of the certificate, but the revenue is a function of the dollar amount of the certificate. Therefore, a 90-day $500 GIC that is reopened four times a year generates only $5 a year on a 1% interest spread, which is considerably less revenue than the cost of processing the transactions. By applying ABC concepts and using the conference method, the bank found that 30% of its GIC offerings were providing 88% of GIC profits, while another 30% of GICs were serviced at a loss of 7%. As a result of these findings, management worked to enhance revenues through a combination of higher minimum balances, new products, and process redesign.

Source: Based on "The Cooperative Bank," Harvard Business School Case No. N9-195–196; City of Indianapolis: "Activity-Based Costing of City Services (A)," Harvard Business School Case No. N9-196–115; Barton, T., and J. MacArthur, "Activity-Based Costing and Predatory Pricing: The Case of the Petroleum Retail Industry," *Management Accounting Quarterly* (Spring 2003); Carter, T., A. Sedaghat, and T. Williams, "How ABC Changed the Post Office," *Management Accounting* (February 1998); Peckenpaugh, J., "Teaching the ABCs," *Government Executive* (April 2002); and Sweeney, R., and J. Mays, "ABM," *Management Accounting* (March 1997).

OBJECTIVE 6

Explain and give examples of nonlinear cost functions

Consider another example. Economies of scale in advertising may enable an advertising agency to double the number of advertisements for less than double the costs. Even direct materials costs are not always linear variable costs. Consider quantity discounts on direct materials purchases. As shown in Exhibit 10-8, the total direct materials costs rise, but they rise more slowly as the cost driver increases because of quantity discounts. The cost function in Exhibit 10-8 has $b = \$25$ for 1 to 1,000 units purchased; $b = \$15$ for 1,001 to 2,000 units purchased; and $b = \$10$ for 2,000 or more units purchased ($a = \$0$ for all ranges of the units purchased). The cost per unit falls at each price break; that is, the cost per unit decreases with larger orders.

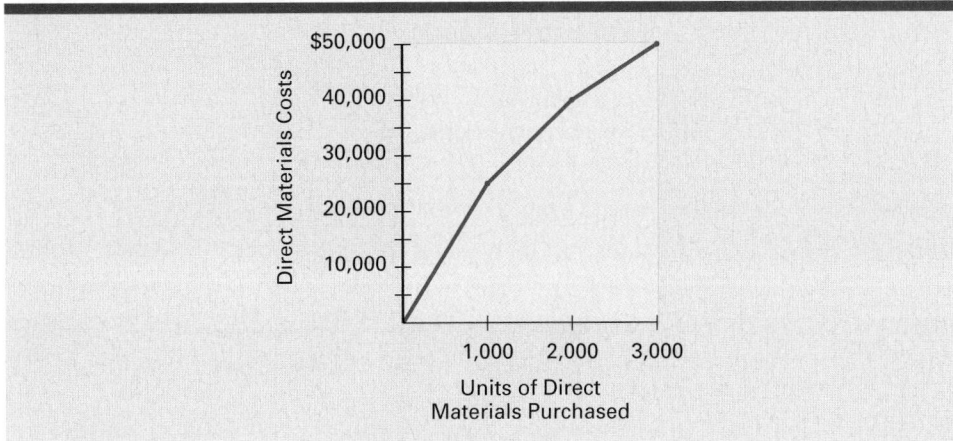

Step cost functions are also examples of nonlinear cost functions. A **step cost function** is a cost function in which the cost is constant over various ranges of the cost driver, but the cost either increases or decreases by discrete amounts (that is, in steps) as the cost driver moves from one range to the next. The graph in Exhibit 10-9 shows a *step variable cost function*, a step cost function in which cost is constant over narrow ranges of the cost driver in each relevant range. Exhibit 10-9 shows the relationship between setup costs and units of production. The pattern is a step cost function because setup costs are incurred only when each production batch is started. This step pattern behaviour also occurs when inputs such as production scheduling, product design labour, and process engineering labour are acquired in discrete quantities but used in fractional quantities. For example, during a one-year period a process engineer may work to improve manufacturing on several product lines. The engineer's actual salary would be divided and allocated to each product line based on the fraction of time spent improving each process. As shown in Exhibit 10-9, management often approximates step variable costs with a variable cost function.

The graph in Exhibit 10-10 shows a *step fixed cost function* for Crofton Steel, a company that operates large heat treatment furnaces to harden steel parts. The main difference relative to Exhibit 10-9 is that the cost in a step fixed cost function is constant over large ranges of the cost driver in each relevant range. The ranges indicate the number of furnaces being used (each furnace costing $300,000). The cost changes from one range to the next higher range when the hours of furnace time demanded require the use of another furnace. The relevant range indicates that the company expects to operate with two furnaces at a cost of $600,000. Management considers the cost of operating furnaces as a fixed cost within the relevant range of operation.

Step cost function. A cost function in which the cost is constant over various ranges of the cost driver, but the cost increases by discrete amounts (that is, in steps) as the cost driver moves from one range to the next.

EXHIBIT 10-9
Step Variable Cost Function

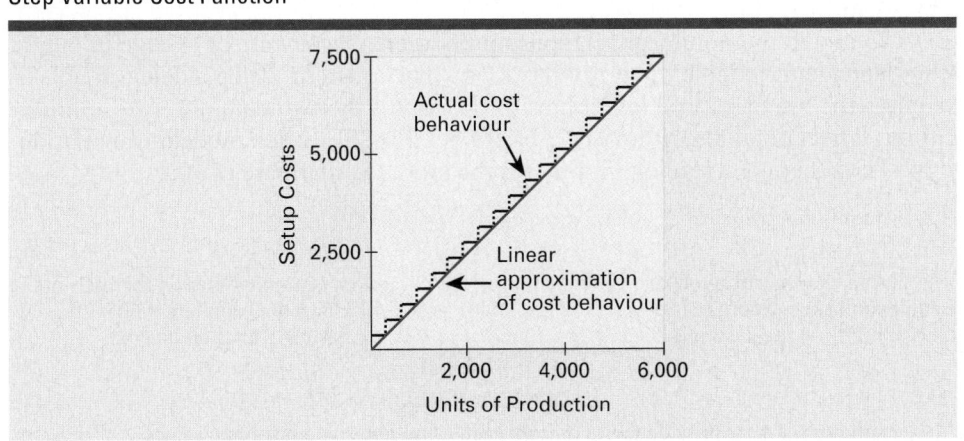

Effective cost management utilizes a particular level of step fixed costs as fully as possible (that is, on a particular step, operate as far to the right side as feasible). For example, in Panel C of Exhibit 10-9, needing 4,000 hours of furnace time will fully utilize two furnaces.

EXHIBIT 10-10
Step Fixed Cost Function

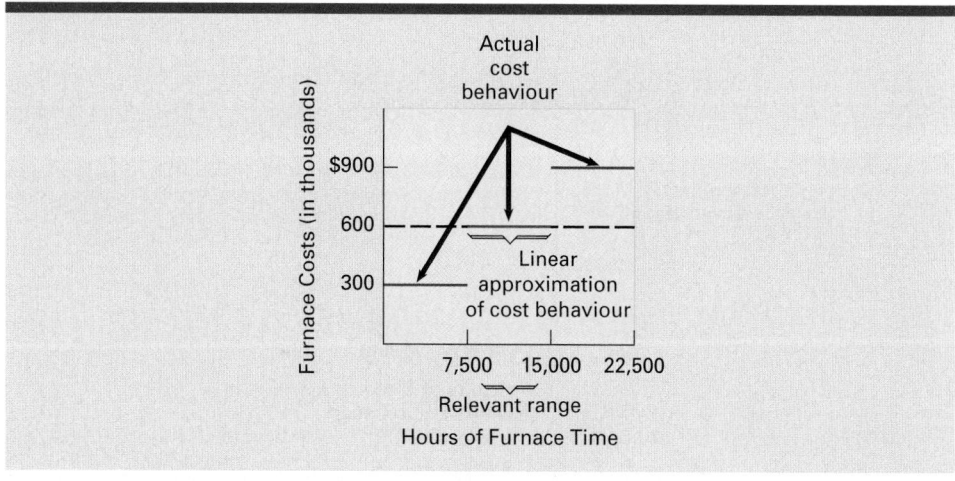

LEARNING CURVES AND NONLINEAR COST FUNCTIONS

The nonlinear or curvilinear relationship of total produced relative to quantity of labour input reflects progress in producing outputs. Progress results from learning through both making and resolving errors so they can be avoided in future, and through practice so that repetitive tasks are finished more quickly. Improved, simpler product design, production processes, and equipment also create progress. In this chapter we will examine only progress arising as people learn both from their mistakes, and through practice to produce more output of appropriate quality in less time. The underlying assumption for this relationship is that direct manufacturing labour-hours (DLH) necessary to complete a unit of production will decrease by a constant percentage each time the production quantity is doubled. This concept was defined mathematically years ago by an engineer at Boeing.

Learning curve. Function that shows how labour-hours per unit decline as units of production increase.

Experience curve. Function that shows how full product costs per unit (including manufacturing, marketing, distribution, and so on) decline as units of output increase.

Learning Curve Calculator
www1.jsc.nasa.gov/bu2/learn.html

Experience Curve Effects
http://en.wikipedia.org/wiki/
Experience_curve_effects

The **learning curve** is a mathematical function illustrating how the ratio of quantity produced increases at a faster rate than the rate at which the time spent in activities of production decreases (Q_t output ÷ Q_t DLH). The **experience curve** describes the same learning effect but it applies to far more than production activities to encompass all activities comprising the value chain. When the rate of change in output produced is greater than the rate of change in the cost of time spent this describes a nonlinear or curvilinear relationship between total production and total DLH. If the rate of change in costs is the same as the rate of change in DLH then it will also be an accurate description or model of the relationship between production and total input costs.

We begin with Exhibit 10-11 which graphs the comparison of two types of nonlinear or learning curve relationships. The top line illustrates how incremental learning affects the nonlinear relationship between quantity produced and quantity of DLH input. The lower line illustrates how cumulative learning affects the nonlinear relationship between quantity produced and quantity of DLH input. In both examples we assume that there is a constant rate of decrease in DLH of 20% each time quantity of output doubles.

To model the nonlinear relationship between a faster rate of change in output (the dependent variable y) relative to input (the cause or independent variable x) requires the use of natural logarithms ($\ln x$), one of the two common types of logarithms. The natural logarithm uses a base e = 2.71828... when modelling a relationship. The other common logarithm uses the more familiar base of 10.[4]

[4]Logarithm is the inverse of exponentiation, e.g. let $x = 100$: $10^2 = 100$

$$2 = \log_{10} 100$$

when using the logarithm of base 10. When using the natural logarithmic function the basis of the calculation of the exponent is e = 2.71828.... If you raise 2.71828 to the exponent 4.605170... ($2.71828^{4.605170}$) the answer is 99.99996... rounded to 100, e.g. let $x = 100$ then $\ln(x)$ is:

$$e^{4.605170} = 100$$

$$4.605170 = \ln(100)$$

Most mathematics texts provide tables of logarithmic and natural logarithmic values.

EXHIBIT 10-11
Plots for Incremental Unit Time Learning Model

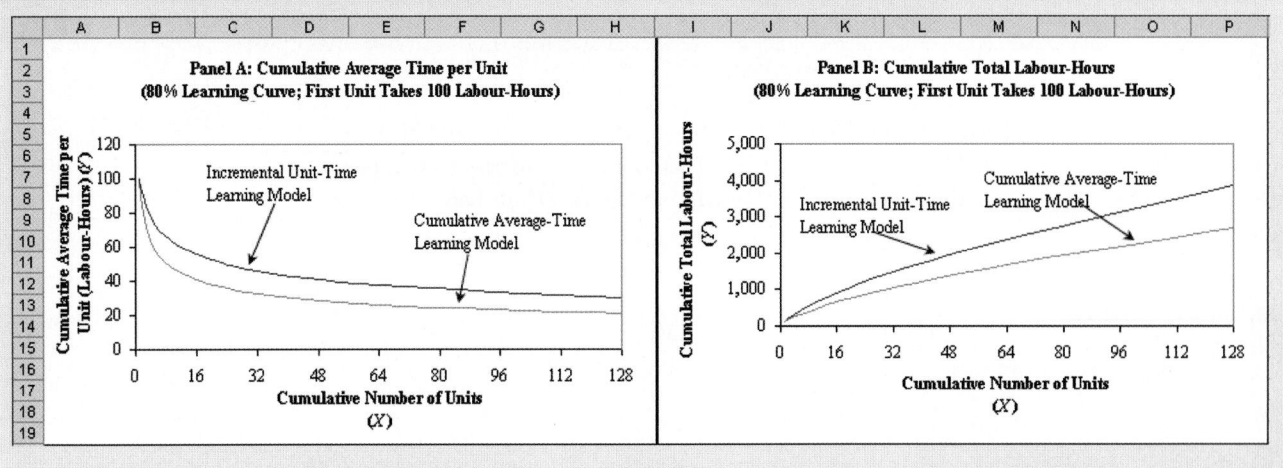

Incremental Unit Time Learning Model

In the **incremental unit time learning model,** the incremental unit time (the time needed to produce the last unit) declines by a constant percentage each time the cumulative quantity of units produced doubles. Exhibit 10-11 illustrates the incremental unit time learning model with an 80% learning curve. We assume that there is a constant rate of decrease in DLH of 20% each time quantity of output doubles.

The incremental unit time model predicts that when quantity of output doubles from 1 to 2 units it will take on average 80 DLH (80% × 100 DLH) to produce the second unit. When output doubles again from 2 to 4 units it will take on average 64 DLH (80% × 80 labour-hours) to produce the fourth unit, and so on. Panel A in Exhibit 10-11 shows the cumulative *average* time per unit when the first unit requires 100 DLH to produce but each subsequent unit takes only 80% of the time required for its predecessor. The mathematical function and calculations are shown in Exhibit 10-12. This model predicts that it will take 180 DLH to produce a total of 2 units; 250.21 DLH to produce a total of 3 units; and 314.21 DLH to produce a total of 4 units. Panel B in Exhibit 10-11 shows the cumulative *total* DLH to produce total quantities of outputs when learning has an incremental effect on DLH required.

Which of these two models is preferable? The one that more accurately approximates the behaviour of manufacturing labour-hour usage as production levels increase is better. The choice can be decided only on a case-by-case basis. Engineers, plant managers, and workers are good sources of information on the amount and type of learning actually occurring as production increases. Plotting this information is helpful in selecting the appropriate model.

The Problem for Self Study on page 388 illustrates the cumulative average time learning model and the incremental unit time learning model in a job-costing situation.

Cumulative Average Time Learning Model

In the **cumulative average time learning model**, the cumulative average time per unit declines by a constant percentage each time the cumulative quantity of units produced doubles. Exhibit 10-13 on page 385 illustrates the cumulative average time learning model with an 80% learning curve. The 80% means that when the quantity of units produced is doubled from X to $2X$, the cumulative average time *per unit* for the $2X$ units is 80% of the cumulative average time *per unit* for the X units. In other words, average time per unit drops by 20%. Panel A in Exhibit 10-11 shows the cumulative average time per unit for this model of the effect of learning on DLH required in the lower curved line. Notice that the total labour time is accumulating at a slower rate (column D in Exhibit 10-13). This is because the effect of learning is modelled differently for the cumulative than the incremental model.

Incremental unit time learning model. Learning curve model in which the incremental unit time (the time needed to produce the last unit) declines by a constant percentage each time the cumulative quantity of units produced doubles.

Question: Does a higher learning percentage (say, 90% rather than 80%) indicate a faster rate of learning? *Answer:* No, a higher learning percentage actually indicates a *slower* rate of learning. For example, consider in Exhibit 10-13 the row for two cumulative units. Under this 80% learning curve, the cumulative average time per unit is 80 labour-hours. If the rate of learning had been 90%, the cumulative average time per unit would have been 90 labour-hours (100 × 0.90).

OBJECTIVE 7

Distinguish between the cumulative average time learning model and incremental unit time learning model

Cumulative average time learning model. Learning curve model in which the cumulative average time per unit declines by a constant percentage each time the cumulative quantity of units produced doubles

EXHIBIT 10-12
Incremental Unit Time Learning Model

	A	B	C	D	E	F
1			**80% Learning Curve**			
2						
3	**Cumulative**	**Individual Unit Time**		**Cumulative**	**Cumulative**	
4	**Number of**	**for Xth Unit $(y)^{-b}$:**		**Total Time:**	**Average Time per**	
5	**Units (X)**	**Labour Hours**		**Labour-Hours**	**Unit: Labour-Hours**	
6	**(1)**	**(2)**		**(3)**	**(4) = (3) ÷ (1)**	
7	1	100.00		100.00	100.00	E9 = D9 ÷ A9
8	2	80.00	= (100 × 0.8)	180.00	90.00	
9	3	70.21		250.21	83.40	
10	4	64.00	= (80 × 0.8)	314.21	78.55	
11	5	59.56		373.77	74.75	
12	6	56.17		429.94	71.66	
13	7	53.45		483.39	69.06	
14	8	51.20	= (64 × 0.8)	534.59	66.82	
15	9	49.29		583.88	64.88	
16	10	47.65		631.53	63.15	
17	11	46.21		677.74	61.61	
18	12	44.93		722.67	60.22	
19	13	43.79		766.46	58.96	
20	14	42.76		809.22	57.80	
21	15	41.82		851.04	56.74	
22	16	40.96	= (51.2 × 0.8)	892.00	55.75	
23						
24	*The mathematical relationship underlying the incremental unit-time learning model is:					
25	$y = aX^{-b}$					
26	where y = Time (labour-hours) taken to produce the last single unit					
27	X = Cumulative number of units produced					
28	a = Time (labour-hours) required to produce the first unit					
29	b = Factor used to calculate incremental unit time to produce units					
30	$= \dfrac{\ln \text{(learning-curve \% in decimal form)}}{\ln 2}$					
31	For an 80% learning curve, $b = \ln 0.8 \div \ln 2 = -0.2231 \div 0.6931 = -0.3219$					
32	When $X = 3$, $a = 100$, $b = -0.3219$					
33	$y = 100 \times 3^{0.3219} = 70.21$ labour hours					
34	The cumulative total time when $X = 3$ is $100 + 80 + 70.21 = 250.21$ labour-hours.					
35	Numbers in the table may not be exact because of rounding.					

The cumulative model uses the average time per unit based on the most recent quantity of units produced. While the first unit took 100 DLH, the first two took on average only 80 DLH to produce each one. Therefore the total time to produce two units is only 160 DLH (2 × 80 DLH). When three units were produced, it took on average 70.21 DLH to produce each one. The total time to produce three units was 210.63 DLH (3 × 71.21 DLH). It took, on average, 64 DLH to produce each of four units for a total of 256 DLH (4 × 64 labour hours) and so on. Panel B of Exhibit 10-11 illustrates the cumulative *total* DLH to produce total quantities of outputs when learning has a cumulative effect on DLH required (100 + 80 + 70.21 + 64 + 51.20). Simply put, people are learning faster using this model than under the incremental unit time model.

Setting Prices, Budgets, and Standards

Predictions of costs should allow for learning. Consider the data in Exhibit 10-13 for the cumulative average time learning model. Suppose the variable costs subject to learning effects consist of direct manufacturing labour ($20 per DLH) and related overhead ($30 per DLH). Management should predict the costs shown in Exhibit 10-14 (p. 386).

Canadian laws prohibit price discrimination—charging different customers different prices for the same product or service—if the intent is to lessen or prevent competition.

EXHIBIT 10-13
Cumulative Average Time Learning Model

	A	B	C	D	E	F
1		80% Learning Curve				
2						
3	Cumulative	Cumulative		Cumulative	Individual Unit	
4	Number	Average Time		Total Time:	Time for Xth	
5	of Units (X)	Per Unit (y)*: Labour Hours		Labour-Hours	Unit: Labour Hours	
6	(1)	(2)		(3) = (1) × (2)	(4)	
7	1	100.00		100.00	100.00	E9=D9−D8=210.63−160.00
8	2	80.00	= (100 × 0.8)	160.00	60.00	
9	3	70.21		210.63	50.63	
10	4	64.00	= (80 × 0.8)	256.00	45.37	
11	5	59.56		297.80	41.80	
12	6	56.17		337.02	39.22	
13	7	53.45		374.15	37.13	
14	8	51.20	= (64 × 0.8)	409.60	35.45	
15	9	49.29		443.61	34.01	
16	10	47.65		476.50	32.89	
17	11	46.21		508.31	31.81	
18	12	44.93		539.16	30.85	
19	13	43.79		569.27	30.11	
20	14	42.76		598.64	29.37	
21	15	41.82		627.30	28.66	
22	16	40.96	= (51.2 × 0.8)	655.36	28.06	
23						
24	*The mathematical relationship underlying the cumulative average time learning model is:					
25	$y = aX^b$					
26	where y = Cumulative average time (labour-hours) per unit					
27	X = Cumulative number of units produced					
28	a = Time (labour-hours) required to produce the first unit					
29	b = Factor used to calculate cumulative average time to produce units					
30	1. The value of b is calculated as					
31	$\dfrac{\ln (\text{learning-curve \% in decimal form})}{\ln 2}$					
32	For an 80% learning curve, $b = \ln 0.8 \div \ln 2 = -0.2231 \div 0.6931 = -0.3219$.					
33	When $X = 3$, $a = 100$, $b = -0.3219$,					
34	$y = 100 \times 3^{-0.3219} = 70.21$ labour hours					
35	2. The cumulative total time when $X = 3$ is $70.21 \times 3 = 210.63$ labour-hours					
36	3. The individual unit times in column 4 are calculated using the data in column D. For example, the individual unit time for the third unit is 50.63 labour-hours (210.63 − 160.00) Numbers in the table may not be exact because of rounding.					

These data show that the effects of the learning curve could have a major influence on decisions. For example, a company might set an extremely low selling price on its product to generate high demand. As the company's production increases to meet this growing demand, costs per unit drop. The company rides the product down the learning curve as it establishes a higher market share. Although the company may have earned little on its first unit sold—it may actually have lost money—the company earns more profit per unit as output increases.

EXHIBIT 10-14
Predicting Costs Using Learning Curves

	A	B	C	D	E	F
1		Cumulative				
2	Cumulative	Average Time	Cumulative	Cumulative Costs		Additions to
3	Number of	per Unit:	Total Time:	at $50 per		Cumulative
4	Units	Labour-Hours[a]	Labour-Hours[a]	Labour-Hour		Costs
5	1	100.00	100.00	$ 5,000	(100.00 × $50)	$ 5,000
6	2	80.00	160.00	8,000	(160.00 × $50)	3,000
7	4	64.00	256.00	12,800	(256.00 × $50)	4,800
8	8	51.20	409.60	20,480	(409.60 × $50)	7,680
9	16	40.96	655.36	32,768	(655.36 × $50)	12,288
10						
11	[a]Based on the cumulative average time learning model. See Exhibit 10-12 (p. 384) for the computation of these amounts.					

Alternatively, subject to legal and other considerations, the company might set a low price on just the final eight units. After all, the labour and related overhead costs per unit are predicted to be only $12,288 for these final eight units ($32,768 – $20,480). The per-unit costs of $1,536 on these final eight units ($12,288 ÷ 8) are much lower than the $5,000 costs per unit of the first unit produced.

Many companies incorporate learning curve effects when evaluating performance. For example, the Nissan Motor Company sets assembly labour efficiency standards for new models of cars after taking into account the learning that will occur as more units are produced.

Both the incremental and cumulative learning curve models assume that labour time will decrease as the quantity of outputs produced increases. Other companies have developed models to explain how quality improves as workers learn to produce new products. Factors such as either organizing people into specialized groups or training people in several phases of the production process and rotating them periodically to perform different tasks also contribute to improving the quality of products.

Analog Devices, Inc.
www.analog.com

DATA COLLECTION AND ADJUSTMENT ISSUES

The ideal database for estimating cost functions quantitatively has two characteristics:

1. It contains numerous reliably measured observations of the cost driver(s) and the dependent variable. Errors in measuring the costs and cost driver(s) are particularly serious. They result in inaccurate estimates of the effect of the cost driver(s) on costs.

2. It considers many values for the cost driver over a wide range. Using only a few values that are grouped closely together considers too small a segment of the relevant range and reduces the confidence in the estimates obtained.

Unfortunately, cost analysts typically do not have the advantage of working with a database having both characteristics. This section outlines some frequently encountered data problems and steps the analyst can take to overcome them.

1. The time period for measuring the dependent variable (for example, indirect manufacturing labour costs) does not properly match the period for measuring the cost driver(s). This problem often arises when accounting records are not kept on an accrual basis. Consider a cost function with machine lubricant costs as the dependent variable and machine-hours as the cost driver. Assume that the lubricant is purchased sporadically and stored for later use. Records maintained on a cash basis will indicate no lubricant consumption in many months and sizable lubricant consumption in other months. This is an obviously inaccurate picture of what is actually

taking place. The analyst should use accrual accounting to measure consumption of machine lubricants to better match costs with the cost driver in this example.

2. Fixed costs are allocated as if they were variable (see Chapter 2, p. 38, for a full discussion of unitized costs). For example, costs such as amortization, insurance, or rent may be allocated to products to calculate costs per unit of output. *The danger is to regard these costs as variable rather than as fixed. They seem to be variable because of the allocation methods used.* To avoid this problem, the analyst should distinguish carefully between fixed and variable costs, and should not treat allocated fixed costs per unit as a variable cost.

3. Data are either not available for all observations or are not uniformly reliable. Missing cost observations often arise from a failure to record a cost or from classifying a cost incorrectly. Data on cost drivers often originate outside the internal accounting system. For example, the accounting department may get data on testing times for medical instruments from the company's manufacturing department and data on the number of items shipped to customers from the distribution department. The reliability of such data varies greatly among organizations. In some systems, data are still recorded manually rather than electronically. Manually recorded data typically have a higher percentage of missing observations and erroneously entered observations than electronically entered data. To minimize this problem, the cost analyst should design data collection reports that regularly and routinely obtain the required data and should follow up immediately whenever data are missing.

4. Extreme values of observations occur from errors in recording costs (for example, a misplaced decimal point); from nonrepresentative time periods (for example, from a period in which a major machine breakdown occurred or from a period in which delay in delivery of materials from an international supplier curtailed production); or from observations being outside the relevant range. Analysts should adjust or eliminate unusual observations before estimating a cost relationship; otherwise, an incorrect estimate will result.

5. There is no homogeneous relationship between the individual cost items in the dependent variable pool and the cost driver. A homogeneous relationship exists when each activity whose costs are included in the dependent variable has the same cost driver. Consider materials procurement overhead costs. This overhead cost account can include a diverse set of activities (for example, new vendor negotiations, materials ordering, incoming inspection, and materials-handling). If each activity has the same cost driver, the homogeneous relationship principle suggests that a single cost function can be estimated for the entire cost pool. Where the cost driver for each activity is different, separate cost functions, each with its own cost driver, would be estimated for each activity.

6. The relationship between cost and the cost driver is not stationary; that is, the underlying process that generated the observations has not remained stable over time. For example, the relationship between manufacturing overhead costs and machine-hours is unlikely to be stationary if the data cover a period in which new technology was introduced. One way to test whether the relationship is stationary in this case is to split the sample into two parts and estimate separate cost relationships for the before- and after-technology-change periods. If the estimated coefficients for the two periods are similar, then the analyst can pool all the data to estimate a single cost relationship. Pooling data provides a larger data set for the estimation, which increases the confidence in the cost predictions being made.

7. Inflation has affected the dependent variable, the cost driver, or both. For example, inflation may cause costs to change even when there is no change in the cost driver. To study the underlying cause-and-effect relationship between the cost driver and costs, the analyst should remove purely inflationary price effects from the data.

In many cases, a cost analyst must expend much effort to reduce the effect of these problems before estimating a cost function based on past data.

PROBLEM

The Helicopter Division of Aerospatiale is examining helicopter assembly costs at its plant in Marseilles, France. It has received an initial order for eight of its new land-surveying helicopters. Aerospatiale can adopt one of two methods of assembling the helicopters:

	A	B	C	D	E
1		**Labour-Intensive Assembly**		**Machine-Intensive Assembly**	
2		**Method**		**Method**	
3	Direct material cost per helicopter	$40,000		$36,000	
4	Direct assembly labour time for first helicopter	2,000	labour-hours	800	labour-hours
5	Learning curve for assembly labour time per helicopter	85%	cumulative average time[a]	90%	incremental unit time[b]
6	Direct assembly labour cost	$ 30	per hour	$ 30	per hour
7	Equipment-related indirect manufacturing cost	$ 12	per direct-assembly labour-hour	$ 45	per direct-assembly labour-hour
8	Materials-handling-related indirect manufacturing cost	50%	of direct material cost	50%	of direct material cost
9					
10	[a]Using the formula (p. 383), for an 85% learning curve, $b = \dfrac{\ln 0.85}{\ln 2} = \dfrac{-0.162519}{0.693147} = -0.234465$				
11	[b]Using the formula (p. 384), for a 90% learning curve, $b = \dfrac{\ln 0.90}{\ln 2} = \dfrac{-0.105361}{0.693147} = -0.152004$				

REQUIRED

1. How many direct-assembly labour-hours are required to assemble the first eight helicopters under (a) the labour-intensive method and (b) the machine-intensive method?
2. What is the total cost of assembling the first eight helicopters under (a) the labour-intensive method and (b) the machine-intensive method?

SOLUTION

1. a. The following calculations show the labour-intensive assembly method based on an 85% cumulative average-time learning model (using Excel):

	A	B	C	D
1		**Cumulative**		**Incremental**
2	**Cumulative**	**Average Time**	**Cumulative**	**Time for**
3	**Number**	**per Unit (y):**	**Total Time:**	**Xth Unit:**
4	**of Units**	**Labour-Hours**	**Labour-Hours**	**Labour-Hours**
5	**(1)**	**(2)**	**(3) = (1) × (2)**	**(4)**
6	1	2,000	2,000	2,000
7	2	1,700 (2,000 × 0.85)	3,400	1,400
8	3	1,546	4,638	1,238
9	4	1,445 (1,700 × 0.85)	5,780	1,142
10	5	1,371	6,855	1,075
11	6	1,314	7,884	1,029
12	7	1,267	8,869	985
13	8	1,228.25 (1,445 × 0.85)	9,826	957

Cumulative average-time per unit for the Xth unit in column 2 is calculated as $y = aX^b$; see Exhibit 10-13 (p. 385).
For example, when $X = 3$, $y = 2,000 \times 3^{-0.234465} = 1,546$ labour-hours.

b. The following calculations show the machine-intensive assembly method based on a 90% incremental unit-time learning model:

	A	B	C	D	E
1		Incremental			Cumulative
2	Cumulative	Unit Time		Cumulative	Average Time
3	Number	for Xth Unit (y):		Total Time:	per Unit:
4	of Units	Labour-Hours		Labour-Hours	Labour-Hours
5	(1)	(2)		(3)	(4) = (3) ÷ (1)
6	1	800		800	800
7	2	720	(800 × 0.9)	1,520	760
8	3	677		2,197	732
9	4	648	(720 × 0.9)	2,845	711
10	5	626		3,471	694
11	6	609		4,080	680
12	7	595		4,675	668
13	8	583	(648 × 0.9)	5,258	657

Individual unit time for the Xth unit in column 2 is calculated as $y = aX^b$; see Exhibit 10-12 (p. 384). For example, when $X = 3$, $y = 800 \times 3^{-0.152004} = 677$ labour-hours.

2. Total costs of assembling the first eight helicopters are:

	A	B	C
1		Labour-Intensive	Machine-Intensive
2		Assembly Method	Assembly Method
3		(using data from part la)	(using data from part lb)
4	Direct materials:		
5	8 helicopters × $40,000, $36,000 per helicopter	$320,000	$288,000
6	Direct assembly labour:		
7	9,826 hours: 5,258 hours × $30/hour	294,780	157,740
8	Indirect manufacturing costs		
9	Equipment related		
10	9,826 hours × $12/hour; 5,258 hours × $45/hour	117,912	236,610
11	Materials-handing-related		
12	0.50 × $320,000; $288,000	160,000	144,000
13	Total assembly costs	$982,692	$826,350

The machine-intensive method's assembly costs are $66,342 lower than the labour-intensive method ($892,692 − $826,350).

The following decision guidelines use a question-and-answer format to summarize the chapter's main points. Each decision presents a key question. The guideline is the answer to that question.

DECISIONS

GUIDELINES

1. What assumptions are usually made when estimating a cost function?

The two assumptions frequently made in cost behaviour estimation are (a) changes in total costs can be explained by changes in the level of a single activity, and (b) cost behaviour can adequately be approximated by a linear function of the activity level within the relevant range.

	DECISIONS	GUIDELINES
2.	What is a linear cost function and what types of cost behaviour can it represent?	A linear cost function is a cost function in which, within the relevant range, the graph of total costs based on the level of a single activity is a straight line. Linear cost functions can be described by a constant, *a*, which represents the estimate of the total cost component (the intercept) that, within the relevant range, does not vary with changes in the level of the activity, and a slope coefficient, *b*, which represents the estimate of the amount by which total costs change for each unit change in the level of the activity within the relevant range. Three types of linear cost functions are variable, fixed, and mixed (or semivariable).
3.	What are the different approaches that can be used to estimate a cost function?	Four methods for estimating cost functions are the industrial engineering method, the conference method, the account analysis method, and quantitative analysis methods (the high-low method and the regression analysis method). If possible, the cost analyst should apply more than one method. Each method is a check on the others.
4.	What are the steps to estimate a cost function based on an analysis of a past cost relationship?	There are six steps to estimate a cost function based on an analysis of past cost relationships: (a) choose the dependent variable; (b) identify the cost driver; (c) collect data on the dependent variable and the cost driver; (d) plot the data; (e) estimate the cost function; and (f) evaluate the estimated cost function. In most situations, working closely with operations managers, the cost analyst will cycle through these steps several times before identifying an acceptable cost function.
5.	How should a company evaluate and choose cost drivers?	Three criteria for evaluating and choosing cost drivers are (a) economic plausibility, (b) goodness of fit, and (c) slope of the regression line (see Appendix).
6.	What is a nonlinear cost function and how does it arise?	A nonlinear cost function is a cost function in which the graph of total costs based on the level of a single activity is not a straight line within the relevant range. Nonlinear costs can arise because of quantity discounts, step cost functions, and learning-curve effects.
7.	What are the different types of learning curve models a company can use?	The learning curve is an example of a nonlinear cost function. Labour-hours per unit decline as units of production increase. In the cumulative average time learning model, the cumulative average time per unit declines by a constant percentage each time the cumulative quantity of units produced doubles. In the incremental unit time learning model, the incremental unit time (the time needed to produce the last unit) declines by a constant percentage each time the cumulative quantity of units produced doubles.
8.	What are the common data problems a company must watch for when estimating costs?	The most difficult task in cost estimation is collecting high-quality, reliably measured data on the costs and the cost driver. Common problems include missing data, extreme values of observations, changes in technology, and distortions resulting from inflation.

APPENDIX: REGRESSION ANALYSIS

To obtain reliable cost functions, managers find it helpful to consult with a technical expert on regression analysis.

	A	B	C	D
1			**Indirect**	**Direct**
2		**Cost Driver:**	**Manufacturing**	**Manufacturing**
3	**Week**	**Machine-Hours**	**Labour Costs**	**Labour-Hours**
4		**(X)**	**(y)**	**Alternative (X)**
5	1	68	$ 1,190	30
6	2	88	1,211	35
7	3	62	1,004	36
8	4	72	917	20
9	5	60	770	47
10	6	96	1,456	45
11	7	78	1,180	44
12	8	46	710	38
13	9	82	1,316	70
14	10	94	1,032	30
15	11	68	752	29
16	12	48	963	38
17	Total	862	$12,501	462

This appendix describes formulas for estimating the regression equation and several commonly used statistics. We use the data for Elegant Rugs presented in Exhibit 10-3 (p. 372), as shown on page 390. The appendix also discusses goodness of fit, significance of independent variables, and specification analysis of estimation assumptions for regression analysis.

Estimating the Regression Line

The least-squares technique for estimating the regression line minimizes the sum of the squares of the vertical deviations (distances) from the data points to the estimated regression line.

The object is to find the values of a and b in the predicting equation $y = a + bX$, where y is the predicted cost value as distinguished from the observed cost value, which we denote by Y. We want to find the numerical values of a and b that minimize $\Sigma(Y - y)^2$. This calculation is accomplished by using two equations, usually called the *normal equations:*

$$\Sigma Y = na + b(\Sigma X)$$
$$\Sigma XY = a(\Sigma X) + b(\Sigma X^2)$$

where n is the number of data points; ΣX and ΣY are respectively the sums of the given X and Y values; ΣX^2 is the sum of squares of the X values; and ΣXY is the sum of the amounts obtained by multiplying each of the given X values by the associated observed Y value.

Exhibit 10-15 shows the calculations required for obtaining the line that best fits the data of indirect manufacturing labour costs and machine-hours for Elegant Rugs. Substituting into the two normal equations simultaneously, we obtain

$$12{,}501 = 12a + 862b$$
$$\text{and} \quad 928{,}716 = 862a + 64{,}900b$$

EXHIBIT 10-15

Computation for Least-Squares Regression between Indirect Manufacturing Labour Costs and Machine-Hours for Elegant Rugs

	A	B	C	D	E	F	G	H	I
1			Indirect						
2		Machine-	Manufacturing				Variance of	Unexplained	Variance of
3		Hours*	Labour Costs*				Y	Variance	X
4	Week	X	Y	X^2	XY	$y = a + bX$	$(Y - \bar{Y})^2$	$(Y - y)^2$	$(X - \bar{X})^2$
5	(1)	(2)	(3)	(4)	(5)	(6)	(7)	(8)	(9)
6	1	68	$1,190	4,624	80,920	$ 1,002.06	$ 21,978	$ 35,321.44	14.69
7	2	88	1,211	7,744	106,568	1,208.26	28,646	7.51	261.36
8	3	62	1,004	3,844	62,248	940.20	1,425	4,070.44	96.69
9	4	72	917	5,184	66,024	1,043.30	15,563	15,951.69	0.03
10	5	60	770	3,600	46,200	919.58	73,848	22,374.18	140.03
11	6	96	1,456	9,216	139,776	1,290.74	171,603	27,310.87	584.03
12	7	78	1,180	6,084	92,040	1,105.16	19,113	5,601.03	38.03
13	8	46	710	2,116	32,660	775.24	110,058	4,256.26	667.36
14	9	82	1,316	6,724	107,912	1,146.40	75,213	28,764.16	103.36
15	10	94	1,032	8,836	97,008	1,270.12	95	56,701.13	491.36
16	11	68	752	4,624	51,136	1,002.06	83,955	62,530.00	14.69
17	12	48	963	2,304	46,224	795.86	6,202	27,935.78	568.03
18		862	$12,501	64,900	928,716	$12,498.98	$607,699	$290,824.49	$2,979.66
19	Means X, Y	71.8333	$ 1,041.75						
20	a=	$300.98							
21	b=	$ 10.31							
22	*Same data as columns B, C of Exhibit 10-3 (p. 372)								

The solution is $a = \$300.98$ and $b = \$10.31$, which can be obtained by direct substitution if the normal equations are re-expressed symbolically as follows:

$$a = \frac{(\Sigma Y)(\Sigma X^2) - (\Sigma X)(\Sigma XY)}{n(\Sigma X^2) - (\Sigma X)(\Sigma X)} \quad \text{and} \quad b = \frac{n(\Sigma XY) - (\Sigma X)(\Sigma Y)}{n(\Sigma X^2) - (\Sigma X)(\Sigma X)}$$

For our illustration, we now have

$$a = \frac{(12,501)(64,900) - (862)(928,716)}{12(64,900) - (862)(862)} = \$300.98$$

$$b = \frac{12(928,716) - (862)(12,501)}{12(64,900) - (862)(862)} = \$10.31$$

Placing the amounts for a and b in the equation of the least-squares line, we have

$$y = \$300.98 + \$10.31X$$

where y is the predicted indirect manufacturing labour costs for any specified number of machine-hours within the relevant range. Generally, these computations are done using software packages such as SPSS, SAS, Lotus, and Excel.

Goodness of Fit

Goodness of fit. Measures how well the predicted values of the cost, y, match the actual cost observations, Y.

Coefficient of determination (r^2). Measures the percentage of variation in a dependent variable explained by one or more independent variables.

Goodness of fit for a simple linear regression (one independent variable X) measures how well y, the predicted values of cost based on the cost driver, X, match actual cost observations, Y. The regression analysis method computes a formal measure of goodness of fit, called the coefficient of determination. The **coefficient of determination, r^2,** measures the percentage of variation in Y (cost, the dependent variable) explained by or associated with variation in X (the cost driver, independent variable). The coefficient of determination (r^2) indicates the proportion of the variance in the dependent variable, Y, calculated as $(\overline{Y})^2 \div n$, that is explained by changes in the independent variable(s) X (where $\overline{Y} = \Sigma Y \div n$). It is more convenient to express the coefficient of determination as 1 minus the proportion of total variance that is *not* explained by the independent variable.

$$r^2 = 1 - \frac{\text{Unexplained variation}}{\text{Total variation}} = 1 - \frac{\Sigma(Y - y)^2}{\Sigma(Y - \overline{Y})^2}$$

From Exhibit 10-16, $\Sigma Y = 12,501$ and $\overline{Y} = 12,501 \div 12 = 1,041.75$. Therefore, to obtain the total variation,

$$\Sigma(Y - \overline{Y})^2 = (1,190 - 1,041.75)^2 + (1,211 - 1,041.75)^2 + \cdots + (963 - 1,041.75)^2$$

$$= 607,699$$

Each value of X generates a prediction, y. For example, in week 1, $y = \$300.98 + (\$10.31 \times 68) = \$1,002.06$. Therefore, to obtain the unexplained variation,

$$\Sigma(Y - y)^2 = (1,190 - 1,002.06)^2 + (1,211 - 1,208.26)^2 + \cdots + (963 - 795.86)^2$$

$$= 35,321 + 8 + \cdots + 27,936 = 290,824$$

$$r^2 = 1 - \frac{290,824}{607,699} = 0.52$$

The calculations indicate that r^2 increases as the predicted values, y, more closely approximate the actual observations, Y. The r^2 of 0.52 indicates that 52% of the variation in y can be explained by the corresponding change in X. If some other independent variable was tested with respect to the same y and its r^2 was equal to 0.26, you could safely say the changes in the second independent variable were only half as good at explaining changes in y as the first. The range of r^2 is from 0 (implying no explanatory power) to 1 (implying that changes in the independent variable or cost driver perfectly explain 100% of the change in the dependent variable cost). When $r^2 = 1$, the predicted cost values exactly equal actual cost values and no random factors disrupt the cause-effect between cost driver and cost. Generally, $r^2 \geq 0.30$ passes the goodness-of-fit test.

Correlation

In attempts to improve the goodness of fit measure, r^2, managers may indiscriminantly include more independent variables producing a *multiple linear regression* model to predict cost. The problem they face is that at least two of the independent variables may be correlated. In essence some part of the explanation of changes in cost are explained twice by the two cost drivers. Consider the situation where one cost driver explains 30% of the change in costs, and adding a second cost driver results in 45% of the change being explained. The second variable may be explaining the same 15% of the change as the first did. This is called multicollinearity (see p. 402).

When specifying a multiple linear regression, managers must measure whether the cost drivers are correlated. If they are correlated, then a different equation to measure r^2 which takes this fact into account must be used. A practical issue that managers must also keep in mind is that if the added variables in the model have no economic plausibility as cost driver(s) then improvements to r^2 become meaningless. Goodness of fit has meaning only if the relationship between costs and the cost drivers is economically plausible.

Correlation. Arises when at least two independent variables in a multiple linear regression explain part of the same change in the dependent variable.

Significance of Independent Variables

A key question that managers ask is do changes in the economically plausible independent variable result in significant changes in the dependent variable, or, alternatively, is the coefficient of the independent variable X, the slope b of the regression line, significant? In statistics this is referred to as a hypothesis. All statistical tests begin with a null hypothesis (H_0). The **null hypothesis** is a statement to be rejected if an analysis of the data fails a specified statistical test. In Chapter 10 our H_0 is usually that the cost driver is a statistically significant explanatory variable with respect to costs. The alternative hypothesis (H_a) is that H_0 is not correct. Statistical **significance** measures the probability that an appropriate analysis of the data permits the conclusion reject the null hypothesis, although some probability of error remains.

If the slope measured by b is significantly different from zero, then managers can have some confidence that as the coefficient changes in the model of the cost driver these changes to b will explain much of the change in cost. Recall, for example, that in the regression of machine-hours on indirect manufacturing labour costs in the Elegant Rugs illustration, b is estimated from a sample of 12 observations.[5] The estimate, b, is subject to random factors, as are all sample statistics. That is, a different sample of 12 data points will give a different estimate of b. The **standard error of the estimated coefficient** indicates how much the estimated value, b, is likely to be affected by random factors.

As the calculated value of the standard error decreases, the effect of random factors on the estimate of b decreases; in other words, the value of b is not due to good or bad luck in drawing a particular sample of 12 data points. In practical terms this could mean that the data points did not arise when key sources of labour were ill, or a machine broke down—both random events that would affect the estimate of the value of b.

Null hypothesis (H_0). A statement to be rejected if an analysis of the data fails a specified statistical test.

Significance. Measures the probability that an appropriate analysis of the data permits the conclusion to reject the null hypothesis, although some probability of error remains.

Standard error of the estimated coefficient. Regression statistic that indicates how much the estimated value is likely to be affected by random factors.

Student t-distribution

The **student t-statistic** of the b coefficient measures how large the value of the estimated coefficient is relative to its standard error. The **critical value** or benchmark t-statistic for inferring that a b coefficient has explanatory power that is significantly different from zero depends on the **degrees of freedom (d.f.)** in a regression and the **confidence level** with which managers want to make statements about the explanatory power of b. Degrees of freedom is the number of data points free to vary in the sample. The number of degrees of freedom is calculated as the sample size n minus the number of coefficients k estimated in the regression ($d.f. = n - k$).

Student t-statistic. A ratio of how large the estimated value of a coefficient is relative to its standard error.

Critical value. A benchmark value for the t-statistic indicating whether or not changes to b have power significantly different from zero (random effect) to explain the corresponding changes in the dependent variable.

Degrees of freedom (d.f.). The number of data points in a sample that are free to vary.

Confidence level. The probability that a statement made by managers about b is correct.

[5]It is not good practice to have fewer than 30 data points. The use of a small sample of data points increases the probability that the estimated value of the coefficient (for example, b) is biased. *Bias* means the estimate is almost always too high or too low relative to the actual value. Graphically, the slope would be too steep or too shallow. If the slope was too steep then the predicted cost would almost always be too high relative to the observed cost. The way the calculation of the variance, s^2, of the sample can correct for bias is by dividing the sum of squared deviations by $n-1$. The standard deviation s is obtained simply by taking the square root of s^2, the variance. In this way the appropriate value of s will be used to calculate the t-statistic.

The confidence level is the probability that a statement made by managers regarding how well changes in b (a cost driver) explain changes in y (cost) is correct. Notice that even at a 99% confidence level there is still a 1% probability the manager is incorrect. This error is known as a type 2 error where a false H_0 has not been rejected. A type 1 error arises when a true H_0 has been rejected.

The student t-distribution is used when the population variance is unknown. There is a different t-distribution for each $d.f.$ and confidence level. As the sample size n approaches infinity, the t-distribution becomes a normal distribution. For a linear regression, the intercept as well as the coefficient for each independent variable should be tested using a t-statistic to ascertain whether or not each is statistically significant. This is a five-stage process of gathering information about the population and the sample, calculating the t-statistic, calculating the $d.f.$, deciding on the confidence level required, and establishing whether or not the calculated t-statistic equals or exceeds the benchmark or critical value for both the degrees of freedom and the chosen confidence level.

Parameters. Parameters describe populations whereas statistics describe samples.

◆ **Step 1:** A population is described using **parameters** whereas a sample from a population is described using statistics. We almost always deal with statistics but the equation of the student t-statistic requires information on both the population mean which is denoted as the parameter μ, the sample mean which is denoted as the statistic $\bar{x}$, and the standard deviation which is denoted as the statistic s as well as the sample size n (number of data points).

◆ **Step 2:** Calculate the t-statistic—use the equation shown below:

$$t = \frac{\bar{x} - \mu}{s / \sqrt{n}} \tag{1}$$

In linear regression the t-statistic is obtained by dividing the coefficient for the variable (either the intercept a or b the coefficient of the independent variable X) by its standard error value. Both the t-statistic and the standard error value are always printed out by the statistical software package.

◆ **Step 3:** Calculate the $d.f.$—the t-statistic has a t-distribution with $n - k$ *degrees of freedom* where n is the number of data points and k is the number of independent variables (cost drivers) in the regression equation. If there is only one independent variable in a simple linear regression model to explain cost with $n = 12$, then $d.f. = 12 - 1 = 11$. If there are 12 data points but two independent variables in a multiple linear regression model to explain cost, then $k = 2$ and $d.f. = 12 - 2 = 10$. Once the $d.f.$ and t-statistic are calculated, how likely is it that our t-statistic is correctly telling us whether the slope b is significantly different from zero? To answer this question, most tables of t-statistics indicate two levels of confidence one can have that there is indeed a significant difference, either 95% or 99%.

◆ **Step 4:** Decide on the *confidence level*—confidence level defines the probability, expressed as a percentage, of making a correct statement. A 95% confidence level means that there is a 95% probability that the statement managers will make about the statistical significance of a or b is correct. This is also known as a 5% level of significance that there is a 5% probability of error ($p = 1 - 0.95 = 0.05$) and there is no statistical significance. The **p values** are always provided to show the level of significance of the coefficient. The t-statistic is statistically significant at a 95% confidence level when $p \leq 0.05$. When $p \leq 0.01$, then there is a 99% probability that the result is statistically significant and a correct statement has been made. **Statistically significant** refers to the results of an appropriate statistical test that permits the conclusion to reject the null hypothesis, although there remains some probability of error, usually either 0.05 (5%) or 0.01 (1%).

p values. Show the level of statistical significance of the coefficient(s) of the independent variable(s).

Statistically significant. Refers to the results of an appropriate statistical test that permits the conclusion to reject the null hypothesis, although there remains some probability of error, usually either 0.05 (5%) or 0.01 (1%).

◆ **Step 5:** Establish if the calculated t-statistic equals or exceeds the *critical value* or benchmark for a given sample size n, $d.f.$, and confidence level. The critical value or benchmark for the t-statistic must be equalled or exceeded by the calculated t-statistic for the result to be statistically significant. The benchmark increases as either the confidence level increases or sample size decreases.

Remember the lower the number of data points in the sample, the higher is the critical value of the t-statistic which demarks statistical significance. If the $d.f. = 11$, the benchmark value t-statistic obtained from equation (1) above is 2.201 for a confidence level of 95% and 3.106 for a confidence level of 99%. A value below 2.201 with a sample size of 12 and one independent variable ($d.f. = n - k = 12-1 = 11$) means the results are not statistically significant and a correct statement cannot be made at a 95% confidence level.

Below is a sample of critical values for t-statistic at 95% confidence level and 99% confidence level:

Table of Critical Values—t-Statistic

Degrees of Freedom	95% Confidence Level	99% Confidence Level
1	12.706	63.657
2	4.303	9.925
3	3.182	5.841
4	2.776	4.604
5	2.571	4.032
6	2.447	3.707
7	2.365	3.499
8	2.306	3.355
9	2.262	3.250
10	2.228	3.169
11	2.201	3.106
12	2.179	3.055
15	2.131	2.947
25	2.060	2.787
40	2.021	2.704
60	2.000	2.660
infinity	1.960	2.576

Source: From Appendix C of Philip C. Abrami, Paul Cholmsky, and Robert Gordon, *Statistical Analysis for the Social Sciences* (Boston, MA: Allyn & Bacon, 2001).

Exhibit 10-16 presents a convenient format for summarizing the regression results for indirect manufacturing labour costs and machine-hours. There are 12 data points and one coefficient for one independent variable X in this simple linear regression, therefore $k = 1$ and $d.f. = 11$. The t-value for the slope coefficient, b, is $\$10.31 \div \$3.12 = 3.30$, which exceeds the critical value of 3.106 for $d.f. = 11$ at the 99% confidence level. Managers can say with 99% confidence that the coefficient of the machine-hours

EXHIBIT 10-16

Simple Regression Results with Indirect Manufacturing Labour Costs as Dependent Variable and Machine-Hours as Independent Variable for Elegant Rugs

	A	B	C	D	E	F
1		Coefficients	Standard Error	t-Statistic		= Coefficient/Standard Error
2		(1)	(2)	(3) = (1) + (2)		= B3/C3
3	Intercept	$300.98	$229.75	1.31 ⟶		= 300.98/229.75
4	Independent Variable: Machine-Hours (X)	$ 10.31	$ 3.12	3.3		
5						
6	Regression Statistics					
7	R Square	0.52				
8	Durbin-Watson Statistic	2.05				

variable is significantly different from zero. The probability is low (less than 1%) that the true value of the machine-hours coefficient lies outside the range $10.31 ± (3.106 × $3.12) or $10.31 ± $9.69, or from $0.62 and $20.00. Therefore, we can conclude that changes in machine-hours do affect indirect manufacturing labour costs.

Similarly, using data from Exhibit 10-16, the t-value for the constant term, a, is $300.98 ÷ $229.76 = 1.31, which is less than the critical value for $d.f.$ = 11 and a confidence level of 95% of 2.20. This indicates that, within the relevant range, the constant term is not significantly different from zero.

Specification Analysis of Estimation Assumptions

Specification analysis is the testing of the assumptions of regression analysis. If the assumptions of (1) linearity within the relevant range, (2) constant variance of residuals, (3) independence of residuals, and (4) normality of residuals hold, the simplest regression procedures give reliable estimates of unknown coefficient values. This section provides a brief overview of specification analysis. When these assumptions are not satisfied, more complex regression procedures are necessary to obtain the best estimates for the values of coefficients.[6]

1. *Linearity within the relevant range.* **Linearity** is a common assumption that a linear relationship exists between the independent variable X and the dependent variable Y within the relevant range. If a linear regression model is used to estimate a fundamentally nonlinear relationship, the coefficient estimates obtained will be inaccurate.

   Where there is only one independent variable, the easiest way to check for linearity is by studying the data on a scatter diagram, a step that often is unwisely skipped. Exhibit 10-6 (p. 376) presented a scatter diagram for the indirect manufacturing labour costs and machine-hours variables of Elegant Rugs shown in Exhibit 10-3 (p. 372). The scatter diagram revealed that linearity appears to be a reasonable assumption for these data.

   The learning curve models discussed on pages 382–386 are examples of non-linear cost functions; costs increase when the level of production increases, but by lesser amounts than would occur with a linear cost function. In this case, the analyst should estimate a nonlinear cost function that explicitly incorporates learning effects.

2. *Constant variance of* **residuals**. The vertical deviation of the *observed* value, Y, from the regression line estimate, y, is called the *residual term, disturbance term*, or *error term, $u = Y - y$.* The goal of regression analysis is to ascertain with some specified level of confidence and $d.f.$ that changes in the independent variable explain changes in the dependent variable in a consistent, predictable way. When this is the case, if the dependent variable is cost then cost can be controlled by controlling the cost driver. If the model, however, is not very good then there will be a large difference between the predicted change in cost based on a change in the cost driver, and the actual change in cost. This difference is the residual.

   The assumption of constant variance implies that the residual terms are unaffected by the level of the independent variable. This means that if the cost driver is doubled, for example, the difference between the predicted and actual cost, the residual, will not double. If the residual value does double then this is a strong indication that there is a relationship between the value of the independent variable and the value of the residuals. If the variance is not constant then a different test of significance called the Durbin-Watson test should be used.

   The assumption also implies that there is a uniform scatter, or dispersion, of the data points about the regression line. The scatter diagram is the easiest way to check for **constant variance**. This assumption holds for Panel A of Exhibit 10-17 but not for Panel B. Constant variance is also known as **homoskedasticity**. Violation of this assumption is called **heteroskedasticity**.

[6]For details see, for example, C. J. Watson, P. Billingsley, D. J. Croft, and D. V. Huntsberger, *Statistics for Management and Economics*, 5th ed. (Needham Heights: Allyn and Bacon, 1993), and W. H. Greene, *Econometric Analysis*, 3rd ed. (Upper Saddle River, N.J.: Prentice Hall, 1996).

EXHIBIT 10-17
Constant Variance of Residuals Assumption

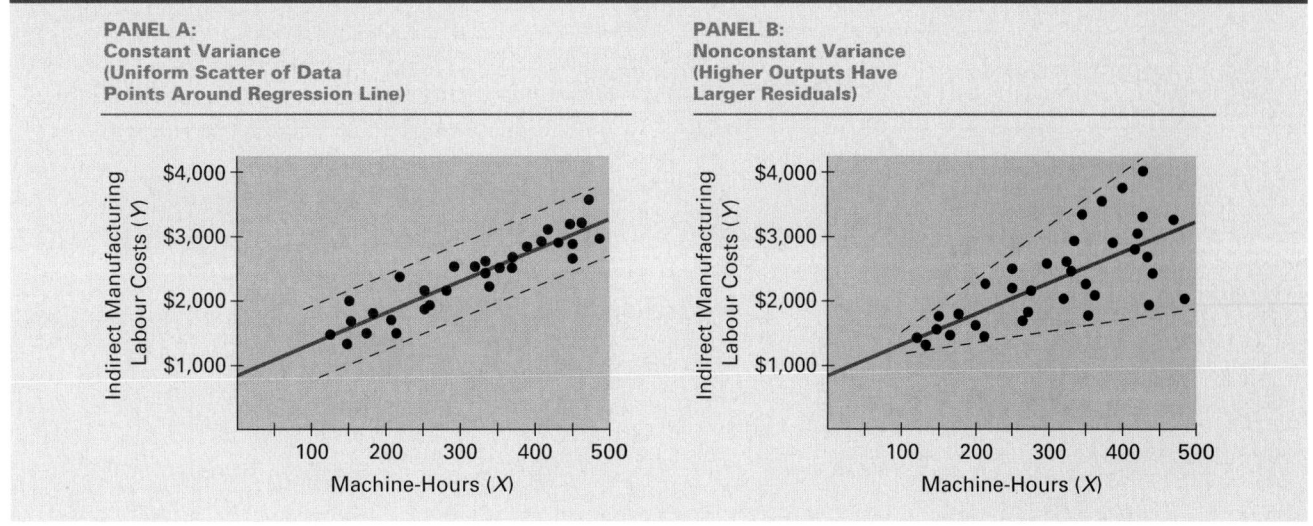

PANEL A:
Constant Variance
(Uniform Scatter of Data
Points Around Regression Line)

PANEL B:
Nonconstant Variance
(Higher Outputs Have
Larger Residuals)

The scatter plots shown in Exhibit 10-17 illustrate two situations for cross-sectional data. This data would be available at the same point in time from, for example, several different factories owned by the same company. In Panel A, the predicted relationship between Indirect Manufacturing Labour Cost (dependent variable Y) and Machine Hours consumed (independent variable or cost driver X) is linear. The dots are the actual observed values of indirect manufacturing labour cost and consumption of machine hours. The actual or observed values should differ from those predicted by the straight line because of random (unpredictable) effects of different factors. These differences, the residuals, are represented visually by the distances between the dots and the straight line. They are scattered randomly around the straight line. Managers can conclude the residuals are homoskedastic.

Panel B, however, indicates a clear pattern of increasing divergence between the observed and predicted relationship. The increasing divergence arises as the quantity of machine hours consumed increases. This means that the changes in the independent variable (quantity of direct materials) are increasingly less able to explain the change in the value of the indirect manufacturing labour costs. Another as-yet-unidentified variable is affecting this relationship and causing a systematic change in the value of the residuals. Managers can infer that the residual values are heteroskedastic and the model is not a good model to explain what causes differences in indirect manufacturing labour costs across the different factories at a single point in time.

Heteroskedasticity does not affect the precision of the regression estimates for the values of a and b. It does, however, reduce the reliability of the estimates of the standard errors. Recall that the standard error is some measure of random factors and is the denominator of the student t-statistic. If this estimate of the denominator is unreliable, so too is the calculation of the t-statistic. An unreliable t-statistic value means managers cannot be as confident about the correctness of their statements about the statistical significance of a and b.

3. *Independence of residuals.* The assumption of the independence of residuals is that the residual term for any one observation is not related to the residual term for any other observation. When data points are selected over some time period it is possible that the value of the data point at the current time depends on the value of the data point at a previous time. If this is the case then the value of the residual at the current time may depend on the value of the residual at a previous time. Conceptually it is important to understand that the dependence or **serial correlation** occurs among the residual values of the same variable. A specific instance of serial correlation, called **autocorrelation**, arises

Autocorrelation (serial correlation). The time dependence of the current value of a data point for a variable on some previous value for the same variable.

EXHIBIT 10-18
Independence of Residuals Assumption

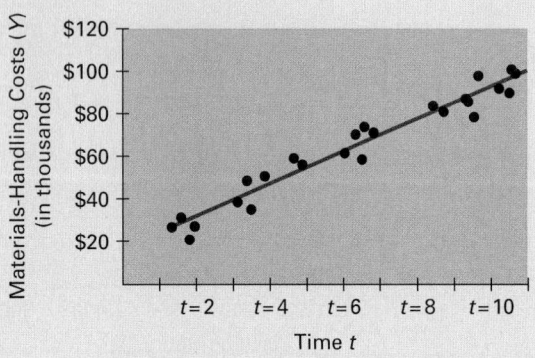

PANEL A:
Independence of Residuals
(No Pattern in Residuals)

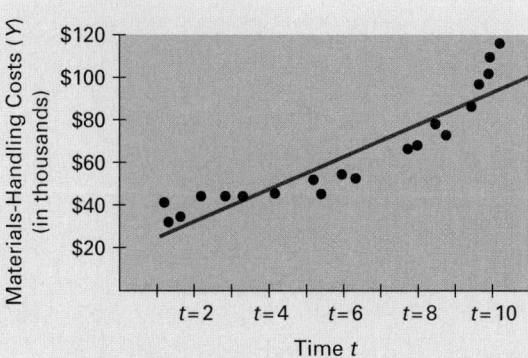

PANEL B:
Autocorrelation in Residuals
(An "S" distribution of the
residuals around the straight
line predicting the value of Y)

when the current value of the residual depends on the value immediately prior to or after it (positive and negative autocorrelation respectively).

Autocorrelation is most frequently observed in time series data, illustrated in Exhibit 10-18. Exhibit 10-18 shows the predicted linear effect of time (independent variable X) on Materials-Handling Costs (dependent variable Y). The dots are data points around the predicted line, which show the change in actual (observed) materials handling costs measured at successive points in time. Panel A illustrates the absence of autocorrelation in the plot of the residuals (the difference between data points on the line (predicted) and actual observations of materials handling costs at a point in time). The actual observations are randomly distributed around the line and fairly close to it. This means changes in materials handling costs can be well explained and predicted using this model because there is no autocorrelation among the residuals.

In Panel B, however, there is a systematic pattern in the plot of the residuals. The residuals form an oscillating pattern around two turning points at time period 4 and time period 9. Throughout the time periods when measures of actual Materials-Handling Costs are taken, there exists some relationship between the current and next value of the residual, positive autocorrelation. This systematic s-shaped oscillation in the plot of the residuals should alert a manager to the presence of autocorrelation. Some as-yet-unidentified factor is systematically affecting the value of the residual terms. The manager cannot be confident that the model can be used to predict future costs.

Autocorrelation among the residual values in a time series of data has an effect similar to heteroskedasticity or nonconstant variance in the residuals of cross-sectional data. The presence of autocorrelation does not affect the precision of the regression estimates of the values of the coefficients of a and b. It does, however, affect the residuals of the coefficients of a and b, which in turn affect the confidence with which inferences can be drawn from the regression estimates. The actual intercept a and slope b are not accurately represented by the predicted values of the dependent variable (Y), the straight line, and in fact the linear model may be completely inappropriate.

The **Durbin-Watson statistic d** can confirm the presence or absence of autocorrelation in the measures of the independent variable (X)[7]. To use d, we

Durbin-Watson
http://hadm.sph.sc.edu/courses/
J716/Dw.html and
www.csus.edu/indiv/j/jensena/
mgmt105/durbin.htm

Durbin-Watson statistic d. Tests for the presence of serial correlation among residuals of a linear regression model using ordinary least squares (OLS).

[7]Formally, the Durbin-Watson statistic is calculated as: $d = \dfrac{\sum_{t=2}^{n}(e_t - e_{t-1})^2}{\sum_{t=1}^{n}(e^2)}$, where d = Durbin-Watson statistic, e = residuals (predicted minus actual value), and t = time period (www.csus.edu/indiv/j/jensena/mgmt105/durbin.htm) accessed June 8, 2005.

must start with a null hypothesis. In this case, H_0 is that no autocorrelation exists among the residuals. The critical values for d range from 0 to 4. When H_0 cannot be rejected $d \approx 2$. Thus we can state our null hypothesis quantitatively as H_0: $d \approx 2$. When lagged values of the independent variable(s) are used to explain changes in the dependent variable (Y) then d is biased toward not rejecting H_0: $d \approx 2$. The table of critical values, below, shows the lower (D-L) and upper (D-U) range of critical values for the case of one (X = 1) and two (X = 2) independent variables for specific numbers of observations at both the 95% and 99% confidence levels.

Durbin-Watson Table of Critical Values

Observations N Confidence		X = 1 D–L	D–U	X = 2 D–L	D–U
15	95%	1.08	1.36	0.95	1.54
	99%	0.81	1.07	0.70	1.25
20	95%	1.20	1.71	1.10	1.54
	99%	0.95	1.15	0.86	1.27
25	95%	1.29	1.45	1.21	1.55
	99%	1.05	1.21	0.98	1.30
30	95%	1.35	1.49	1.28	1.57
	99%	1.13	1.26	1.07	1.34

Source: http://hadm.sph.sc.edu/courses/J716/Dw.html

There are three possible outcomes that must be considered after calculating the d statistic. If, after calculating d, the value ranges between 0 and 1 then positive autocorrelation exists and you must reject H_0. If, after calculating d, the value ranges from (4 – D-L) to 4 then negative autocorrelation exists and again you must reject H_0. For values of d that range either between D-L and D-U or between (4 – D-U) and (4 – D-L) managers can make no statistically conclusive statements about the absence or presence of autocorrelation among the residuals. To use the table below, the calculated value of d when there are 15 observations of a single independent variable (X = 1) must be compared to the critical values in the table for D-L and D-U. If managers are satisfied being 95% confident of their conclusion then the following would be the case:

d (Calculated)	H_0	Critical Value(s)	Reason
0 to 1.08 (D-L)	reject	$d < 2$	positive autocorrelation
1.08 to 1.36 or	inconclusive*	D-U $< d <$ D-L	
2.64 to 2.69	inconclusive	(4–D-U) $< d <$ (4–D-L)	
2.92 to 4	reject	(4–D-L) $< d <$ 4	negative autocorrelation

*inconclusive means managers can neither accept nor reject H_0 with 95% confidence.

For the regression results of Elegant Rugs in Exhibit 10-16, $d = 2.05$. The comparison with critical values in the table above shows there is no statistical basis on which to reject H_0: $d \approx 2$. Therefore, managers of Elegant Rugs can say with 95% confidence (there is still a 5% probability they will be incorrect) there is no autocorrelation among the residuals. The model will provide reliable predictions of future Materials-Handling Costs.

d (Calculated)	H_0	Critical Value(s)	Reason
2.05	accept	$d > 2$	no evidence of autocorrelation

Normality. Means the assumption is that the calculated values of the residuals are distributed normally around the regression line.

4. *Normality of residuals.* The **normality** of residuals assumption means that the calculated values of the residuals are distributed normally around the regression line. This assumption is necessary for making inferences about y, a, and b.

EXHIBIT 10-19
Simple Regression Results with Indirect Manufacturing Labour Costs as Dependent Variable and Direct Manufacturing Labour-Hours as Independent Variable (Cost Driver) for Elegant Rugs

	A	B	C	D	E	F	G	H
1		Coefficients	Standard Error	t-Statistic				
2		(1)	(2)	(3) = (1) ÷ (2)				
3	Intercept	$744.67	$217.61	3.42				
4	Independent Variable: Direct Manufacturing Labour-Hours (X)	$ 7.72	$ 5.40	1.43 ⟶		= Coefficient/Standard Error = B4/C4 = 7.72/5.40		
5								
6	Regression Statistics							
7	R Square	0.17						
8	Durbin-Watson Statistic	2.26						

Using Regression Output to Choose between Cost Functions

Consider the two cost functions we described earlier:

$$y = a + (b \times \text{machine-hours})$$
$$y = a + (b \times \text{direct manufacturing labour-hours})$$

Exhibits 10-6 (p. 376) and 10-7 (p. 378) presented plots of the data for the two regressions. Exhibit 10-16 reported regression results for the cost function using machine-hours as the independent variable. Exhibit 10-19 presents comparable regression results for the cost function using direct manufacturing labour-hours as the independent variable.

Based on the material in this appendix, which regression is better? Exhibit 10-20 compares these two cost functions in a systematic way. For several criteria, the cost function based on machine-hours is preferable to the cost function based on direct manufacturing labour-hours. The economic plausibility criterion is especially important.

Do not always assume that any one cost function will perfectly satisfy all the criteria in Exhibit 10-20. A cost analyst must often make a choice between "imperfect" cost functions, in the sense that the data of any particular cost function will not perfectly meet one or more of the assumptions underlying regression analysis.

EXHIBIT 10-20
Comparison of Alternative Cost Functions for Indirect Manufacturing Labour Costs Estimated with Simple Regression for Elegant Rugs

Criterion	Cost Function 1: Machine-Hours as Independent Variable	Cost Function 2: Direct Manufacturing Labour-Hours as Independent Variable
Economic plausibility	A positive relationship between indirect manufacturing labour costs (technical support labour) and machine-hours is economically plausible in a highly automated plant.	A positive relationship between indirect manufacturing labour costs and direct manufacturing labour-hours is economically plausible, but less so than machine-hours in a highly automated plant on a week-to-week basis.
Goodness of fit	$r^2 = 0.52$ Excellent goodness of fit	$r^2 = 0.17$ Poor goodness of fit
Significance of independent variable(s)	The t-value of 3.30 is significant.	The t-value of 1.43 is not significant.
Specification analysis of estimation assumptions	Plot of the data indicates that assumptions of linearity, constant variance, independence of residuals, and normality of residuals hold, but inferences drawn from only 12 observations are not reliable; Durbin-Watson statistic = 2.05.	Plot of the data indicates that assumptions of linearity, constant variance, independence of residuals, and normality of residuals hold, but inferences drawn from only 12 observations are not reliable; Durbin-Watson statistic = 2.26.

Multiple Regression and Cost Hierarchies

In some cases, a satisfactory estimation of a cost function may be based on only one independent variable, such as machine-hours. In many cases, however, basing the estimation on more than one independent variable is more economically plausible and improves accuracy. The most widely used equations to express relationships between two or more independent variables and a dependent variable are linear in the form:

$$Y = a + b_1X_1 + b_2X_2 \cdots + u$$

where:

Y = cost variable to be predicted

$X_1, X_2, \ldots$ = independent variables on which the prediction is to be based

$a, b_1, b_2, \ldots$ = estimated coefficients of the regression model

u = residual term that includes the net effect of other factors not in the model and measurement errors in the dependent and independent variables

Example: Consider the Elegant Rugs data in Exhibit 10-21. Indirect manufacturing labour costs include sizable costs incurred for setup and changeover costs when production on one carpet batch is stopped and production on another batch is started. Management believes that, in addition to machine-hours (an output-unit-level cost driver), indirect manufacturing labour costs are also affected by the number of different batches of carpets produced during each week (a batch-level driver). Elegant Rugs estimates the relation between two independent variables, machine-hours and number of separate carpet jobs worked on during the week, and indirect manufacturing labour costs.

> Multiple regression analysis is useful for estimating total costs when different levels of the cost hierarchy are involved. This example uses number of machine-hours (an output unit-level cost driver) and number of production batches (a batch-level cost driver).

Exhibit 10-22 on the next page presents results for the following multiple regression model, using data in columns B, C, and E of Exhibit 10-22:

$$y = \$42.58 + \$7.60X_1 + \$37.77X_2$$

where X_1 is the number of machine-hours and X_2 is the number of production batches. It is economically plausible that both machine-hours and production

EXHIBIT 10-21
Weekly Indirect Manufacturing Labour Costs, Machine-Hours, Direct Manufacturing Labour-Hours, and Number of Production Batches for Elegant Rugs

	A	B	C	D	E
1			Number of	Direct	Indirect
2			Production	Manufacturing	Manufacturing
3	Week	Machine-Hours	Batches	Labour-Hours	Labour-Costs
4		(X_1)	(X_2)		(Y)
5	1	68	12	30	$ 1,190
6	2	88	15	35	1,211
7	3	62	13	36	1,004
8	4	72	11	20	917
9	5	60	10	47	770
10	6	96	12	45	1,456
11	7	78	17	44	1,180
12	8	46	7	38	710
13	9	82	14	70	1,316
14	10	94	12	30	1,032
15	11	68	7	29	752
16	12	48	14	38	963
17	Total	862	144	462	$12,501

EXHIBIT 10-22
Multiple Regression Results with Indirect Manufacturing Labour Costs and Two Independent Variables or Cost Drivers (Machine-Hours and Production Batches) for Elegant Rugs

	A	B	C	D	E	F	G
		Coefficients	Standard Error	t-Statistic			
1							
2		(1)	(2)	(3) = (1) ÷ (2)			
3	Intercept	$42.58	$213.91	0.20			
4	Independent variable 1: Machine-hours (X_1)	$ 7.60	$ 2.77	2.74 ⟶	= Coefficient/Standard Error = B4/C4 = 7.60/2.77		
5	Independent variable 2: Number of production batches (X_2)	$37.77	$ 15.25	2.48			
6							
7	**Regression Statistics**						
8	R Square	0.72					
9	Durbin-Watson Statistic	2.49					

batches would help explain variations in indirect manufacturing labour costs at Elegant Rugs. The r^2 of 0.52 for the simple regression using machine-hours (Exhibit 10-17) increases to 0.72 with the multiple regression in Exhibit 10-22. The t-values suggest that the independent variable coefficients of both machine-hours and production batches are significantly different from zero ($t = 2.74$ for the coefficient on machine-hours, and $t = 2.48$ for the coefficient on production batches). The multiple regression model in Exhibit 10-23 satisfies both economic and statistical criteria, and it explains much greater variation in indirect manufacturing labour costs than does the simple regression model using only machine-hours as the independent variable. The information in Exhibit 10-22 indicates that both machine-hours and production batches are important cost drivers of monthly indirect manufacturing labour costs at Elegant Rugs.

In Exhibit 10-22, the slope coefficients—$7.60 for machine-hours and $37.77 for production batches—measure the change in indirect manufacturing labour costs associated with a unit change in an independent variable (assuming that the other independent variable is held constant). For example, indirect manufacturing labour costs increase by $37.77 when one more production batch is added, assuming that the number of machine-hours is held constant.

An alternative approach would create two separate cost pools—one for costs tied to machine-hours and another for costs tied to production batches. Elegant Rugs would then estimate the relationship between the cost driver and overhead costs separately for each cost pool. The difficult task under that approach would be properly dividing overhead costs into the two cost pools.

Multicollinearity

A major concern that arises with multiple regression is multicollinearity. **Multicollinearity** exists when two or more independent variables are highly correlated with each other. The rule of thumb is if the correlation between X_1 and X_2 is ≤ 0.70 then there is no issue of correlated independent variables. If the correlation is > 0.70 then one of the independent variables must be dropped. Multicollinearity increases the standard errors of the coefficients of the individual variables. The result is that there is greater uncertainty about the underlying value of the coefficients of the individual independent variables. That is, variables that are economically and statistically significant will appear insignificant.

The coefficients of correlation between the potential independent variables for Elegant Rugs in Exhibit 10-22 are:

Multicollinearity. Exists when two or more independent variables in a regression model are highly correlated.

Pairwise Combinations	Coefficient of Correlation
Machine-hours and direct manufacturing labour-hours	0.12
Machine-hours and production batches	0.40
Direct manufacturing labour-hours and production batches	0.31

These results indicate that multiple regressions using any pair of the independent variables in Exhibit 10-22 are not likely to encounter multicollinearity problems.

If severe multicollinearity exists, try to obtain new data that does not suffer from multicollinearity problems. Do not drop an independent variable (cost driver) that should be included in a model because it is correlated with another independent variable. Omitting such a variable will cause the estimated coefficient of the independent variable included in the model to be biased away from its true value.

TERMS TO LEARN

This chapter contains definitions of the following important terms:

account analysis method (p. 371)
autocorrelation (p. 397)
coefficient of determination, r^2 (p. 392)
conference method (p. 370)
confidence level (p. 393)
constant (p. 367)
constant variance (p. 396)
correlation (p. 393)
cost estimation (p. 368)
cost function (p. 366)
cost prediction (p. 368)
critical value (p. 393)
cumulative average time learning
    model (p. 383)
degrees of freedom, *d.f.* (p. 393)
dependent variable (p. 372)
disturbance term (p. 376)
Durbin-Watson statistic *d* (p. 398)
error term (p. 376)
experience curve (p. 382)
goodness of fit (p. 392)
heteroskedasticity (p. 396)
high-low method (p. 374)
homoskedasticity (p. 396)
incremental unit time learning model (p. 383)
independent variable (p. 372)
industrial engineering method (p. 370)

intercept (p. 367)
learning curve (p. 382)
linear cost function (p. 366)
linear regression analysis (p. 375)
linearity (p. 396)
mixed cost (p. 367)
multicollinearity (p. 402)
multiple regression (p. 375)
nonlinear cost function (p. 379)
normality (p. 399)
null hypothesis, H_0 (p. 393)
parameter (p. 394)
p value (p. 394)
residual (p. 396)
residual term (p. 376)
semivariable cost (p. 367)
serial correlation (p. 397)
significance (p. 393)
simple regression (p. 375)
slope coefficient (p. 366)
specification analysis (p. 396)
standard error of the estimated
    coefficient (p. 393)
statistically significant (p. 394)
step cost function (p. 381)
student *t*-statistic (p. 393)
work measurement method (p. 370)

ASSIGNMENT MATERIAL

QUESTIONS

10-1 What two assumptions are frequently made when estimating a cost function?

10-2 Describe three alternative linear cost functions.

10-3 What is the difference between a linear and a nonlinear cost function? Give an example of each type of cost function.

10-4 "High correlation between two variables means that one is the cause and the other is the effect." Do you agree? Explain.

10-5 Name four approaches to estimating a cost function.

10-6 Describe the conference method for estimating a cost function. What are two advantages of this method?

10-7 Describe the account analysis method for estimating a cost function.

10-8 List the six steps in estimating a cost function based on an analysis of current or past cost relationships. Which step is typically the most difficult for a cost analyst?

10-9 When using the high-low method, should you base the high and low observations on the dependent variable or on the cost driver?

10-10 Describe three criteria for evaluating cost functions and choosing cost drivers.

10-11 Define learning curve. Outline two models that can be used when incorporating learning into the estimation of cost functions.

10-12 Discuss four frequently encountered problems when collecting cost data on variables included in a cost function.

10-13 What are the four key assumptions examined in specification analysis in the case of simple regression?

10-14 "All the independent variables in a cost function estimated with regression analysis are cost drivers." Do you agree? Explain.

10-15 "Multicollinearity exists when the dependent variable and the independent variable are highly correlated." Do you agree? Explain.

EXERCISES

10-16 Estimating a cost function. The controller of the Ijiri Company wants you to estimate a cost function from the following two observations in a general ledger account called Maintenance:

Month	Machine-Hours	Maintenance Costs Incurred
January	4,000	$3,600
February	7,000	4,680

REQUIRED
1. Estimate the cost function for maintenance.
2. Can the constant in the cost function be used as an estimate of the fixed maintenance cost per month? Explain.

10-17 Identifying variable, fixed, and mixed cost functions. The Pacific Corporation operates car rental agencies at more than 20 airports. Customers can choose from one of three contracts for car rentals of one day or less:
- **Contract 1:** $60 for the day
- **Contract 2:** $36 for the day plus $0.24 per kilometre travelled
- **Contract 3:** $1.20 per kilometre travelled

REQUIRED
1. Present separate plots for each of the three contracts, with costs on the vertical axis and kilometres travelled on the horizontal axis.
2. Describe each contract as a linear cost function of the form $y = a + bX$.
3. Describe each contract as a variable, fixed, or mixed cost function.

10-18 Various cost-behaviour patterns. (CPA, adapted) Select the graph that matches the numbered manufacturing cost data. Indicate by letter which of the graphs best fits each of the situations or items described.

The vertical axes of the graphs represent total dollars of cost, and the horizontal axes represent production output during a calendar year. In each case, the zero point of dollars and production is at the intersection of the two axes. The graphs may be used more than once.
1. Annual amortization of equipment, where the amount of amortization charged is computed by the machine-hours method.
2. Electricity bill—a flat fixed charge, plus a variable cost after a certain number of kilowatt-hours are used, where the quantity of kilowatt-hours used varies proportionately with quantity of production output.

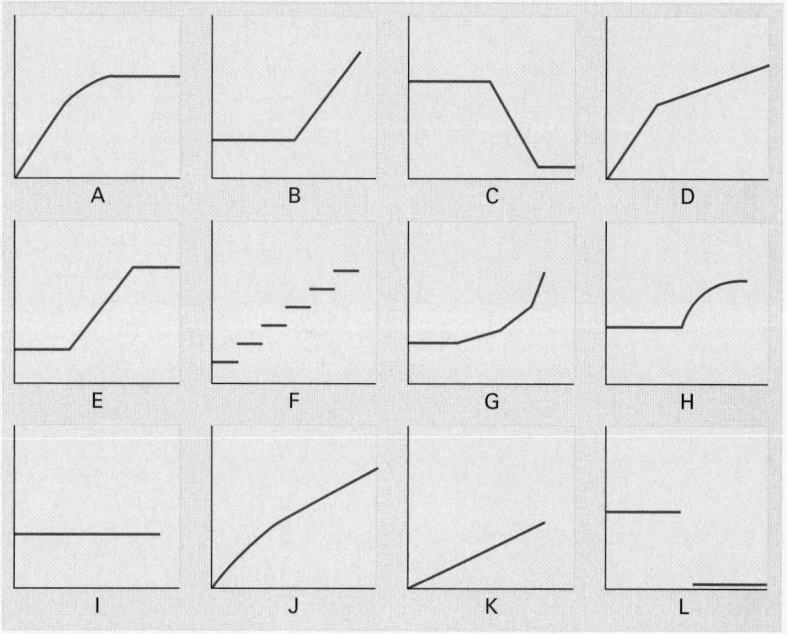

3. City water bill, which is computed as follows:

First 1,000,000 litres or less	$1,000 flat fee
Next 10,000 litres	$0.003 per litre used
Next 10,000 litres	$0.006 per litre used
Next 10,000 litres	$0.009 per litre used
And so on	And so on

The litres of water used vary proportionately with the quantity of production output.

4. Cost of lubricant for machines, where cost per unit decreases with each kilogram of lubricant used (for example, if one kilogram is used, the cost is $10; if two kilograms are used, the cost is $19.98; if three kilograms are used, the cost is $29.94) with a minimum cost per kilogram of $9.20.

5. Annual amortization of equipment, where the amount is computed by the straight-line method. When the amortization rate was established, it was anticipated that the obsolescence factor would be greater than the wear-and-tear factor.

6. Rent on a manufacturing plant donated by the city, where the agreement calls for a fixed fee payment unless 200,000 labour-hours are worked, in which case no rent need be paid.

7. Salaries of repair personnel, where one person is needed for every 1,000 machine-hours or less (that is, 0 to 1,000 hours requires one person, 1,001 to 2,000 hours requires two people, etc.).

8. Cost of direct materials used (assume no quantity discounts).

9. Rent on a manufacturing plant donated by the county, where the agreement calls for rent of $100,000 reduced by $1 for each direct manufacturing labour-hour worked in excess of 200,000 hours, but a minimum rental fee of $20,000 must be paid.

10-19 Matching graphs with descriptions of cost behaviour. (D. Green) On the following page are a number of charts, each indicating some relationship between cost and a cost driver. No attempt has been made to draw these charts to any particular scale; the absolute numbers on each axis may be closely or widely spaced.

Indicate by number which one of the charts best fits each of the situations or items described. Each situation or item is independent of all the others; all factors not stated are assumed to be irrelevant. Some charts will be used more than once; some may not apply to any of the situations. Note that category 14, "No relationship," is not the same as 15, "Some other pattern."

If the horizontal axis represents the production output over the year and the vertical axis represents *total cost or revenue*, indicate the one best pattern or relationship for the following:

1. Direct materials costs
2. Supervisors' salaries
3. A breakeven chart
4. Mixed costs—for example, fixed electrical power demand charge plus variable usage rate

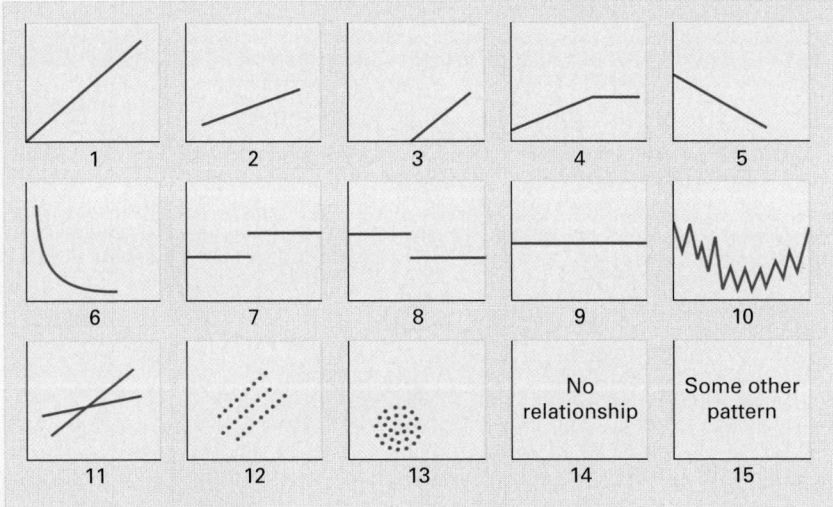

5. Amortization of plant, computed on a straight-line basis
6. Data supporting the use of a variable cost rate, such as manufacturing labour cost of $14 per unit produced
7. Incentive bonus plan that pays managers $0.10 for every unit produced above some level of production
8. Interest charges on money borrowed at a fixed rate of interest to finance the acquisition of a plant, before any payments on principal

10-20 Account analysis method. Lorenzo operates a brushless car wash. Incoming cars are put on an automatic, continuously moving conveyor belt. Cars are washed as the conveyor belt carries the car from the start station to the finish station. After the car moves off the conveyor belt, the car is dried manually. Workers then clean and vacuum the inside of the car. Workers are managed by a single supervisor. Lorenzo serviced 80,000 cars in 2007. Lorenzo reports the following costs for 2007:

Account Description	Costs
Car wash labour	$288,000
Soap, cloth, and supplies	38,400
Water	33,600
Power to move conveyor belt	86,400
Amortization	76,800
Supervision	36,000
Cashier	19,200

REQUIRED
1. Classify each account as variable or fixed with respect to cars washed. Explain.
2. Lorenzo expects to wash 90,000 cars in 2008. Use the cost classification you developed in requirement 1 to estimate Lorenzo's total costs in 2008.
3. Calculate the average cost of washing a car in 2007 and 2008. (Use the expected 90,000 car wash level for 2008.)

10-21 Account analysis method. Gower, Inc., a manufacturer of plastic products, reports the following manufacturing costs and account analysis classification for the year ended December 31, 2007.

Account	Classification	Amount
Direct materials	All variable	$360,000
Direct manufacturing labour	All variable	270,000
Power	All variable	45,000
Supervision labour	20% variable	67,500
Materials-handling labour	50% variable	72,000
Maintenance labour	40% variable	90,000
Amortization	0% variable	114,000
Rent, property taxes, and administration	0% variable	120,000

Gower, Inc., produced 75,000 units of product in 2007. Gower's management is estimating costs for 2008 based on 2007 numbers. The following additional information is available for 2008:

a. Direct materials prices in 2008 are expected to increase by 5% compared with 2007.
b. Under the terms of the labour contract, direct manufacturing labour wage rates are expected to increase by 10% in 2008 compared with 2007.
c. Power rates and wage rates for supervision, materials-handling, and maintenance are not expected to change from 2007 to 2008.
d. Amortization costs are expected to increase by 5%, and rent, property taxes, and administration costs are expected to increase by 7%.
e. Gower, Inc. expects to manufacture and sell 80,000 units in 2008.

REQUIRED

1. Prepare a schedule of variable, fixed, and total manufacturing costs for each account category in 2008. Estimate total manufacturing costs for 2008.
2. Calculate Gower's total manufacturing cost per unit in 2007 and estimated total manufacturing cost per unit in 2008.
3. How can you get better estimates of fixed and variable costs? Why would these better estimates be useful to Gower?

10-22 **Estimating a cost function, high-low method.** Laurie Daley is examining customer service costs in the Southern Region of Capitol Products. Capitol Products has over 200 separate electrical products that are sold with a six-month guarantee of full repair or replacement with a new product. When a product is returned by a customer, a service report is made. This service report includes details of the problem and the time and cost of resolving the problem. Weekly data for the most recent ten-week period are

Week	Customer Service Department Costs	Number of Service Reports
1	$16,614	201
2	24,750	276
3	15,530	122
4	22,142	386
5	17,810	274
6	26,268	436
7	20,198	321
8	25,715	328
9	21,920	243
10	20,198	161

REQUIRED

1. Plot the relationship between customer service costs and number of service reports. Is the relationship economically plausible?
2. Use the high-low method to compute the cost function, relating customer service costs to the number of service reports.
3. What variables, in addition to number of service reports, might be cost drivers of monthly customer service costs of Capitol Products?

10-23 **Linear cost approximation.** Terry Lawler, managing director of the Winnipeg Consulting Group, is examining how overhead costs behave with variations in monthly professional labour-hours billed to clients. Assume the following historical data:

Total Overhead Costs	Professional Labour-Hours Billed to Clients
$408,000	3,000
480,000	4,000
522,000	5,000
572,400	6,000
634,800	7,000
704,400	8,000

REQUIRED

1. Compute the linear cost function, relating total overhead cost to professional labour-hours, using the representative observations of 4,000 and 7,000 hours. Plot the linear

cost function. Does the constant component of the cost function represent the fixed overhead costs of the Winnipeg Consulting Group? Why?

2. What would be the predicted total overhead costs for (a) 5,000 hours and (b) 8,000 hours using the cost function estimated in requirement 1? Plot the predicted costs and actual costs for 5,000 and 8,000 hours.

3. Lawler had a chance to accept a special job that would have boosted professional labour-hours from 4,000 to 5,000 hours. Suppose Lawler, guided by the linear cost function, rejected this job because it would have brought a total increase in contribution margin of $45,600, before deducting the predicted increase in total overhead cost, $51,600. What is the actual total contribution margin forgone?

10-24 **Cost-volume-profit and regression analysis.** Oxbow Corporation manufactures a children's bicycle, model CT8. It currently makes the bicycle frame in-house. During 2007, it manufactured 30,000 frames at a total cost of $1,080,000. Ryan Corporation has offered to supply as many frames as Oxbow wants at a cost of $34.20 per frame. Oxbow anticipates needing 36,000 frames each year for the next few years.

REQUIRED

1. **a.** What is the average cost of manufacturing a bicycle frame in 2007? How does it compare with Ryan's offer?

    b. Can Oxbow use the answer in requirement 1(a) to determine the cost of manufacturing 36,000 bicycle frames? Explain your answer.

2. Oxbow's cost analyst uses annual data from past years to estimate the following regression equation with total manufacturing costs of the bicycle frame as the dependent variable (y) and number of bicycle frames as the independent variable (X)

$$y = \$518,400 + \$18X$$

During the years used to estimate the regression equation, the production of bicycle frames varied from 28,000 to 36,000. Using this equation, estimate how much it would cost Oxbow to manufacture 36,000 bicycle frames. How much more costly or less costly is it than acquiring the frames from Ryan?

3. What other information would you need in order to be confident that the equation in requirement 2 accurately predicts the cost of manufacturing bicycle frames?

10-25 **Regression analysis, service company.** (CMA, adapted) Bob Jones owns a catering company that prepares banquets and parties for both individual and business functions throughout the year. Jones's business is seasonal, with a heavy schedule during the summer months and the year-end holidays and a light schedule at other times. During peak periods there are extra costs.

One of the major events Jones's customers request is a cocktail party. He offers a standard cocktail party and has developed the following cost structure on a per-person basis.

Food and beverages	$18.00
Labour (0.5 hour × $12.00 per hour)	6.00
Overhead (0.5 hour × $16.80 per hour)	8.40
Total costs per person	$32.40

Jones is quite certain about his estimates of the food, beverages, and labour costs but is not as comfortable with the overhead estimate. This estimate was based on the actual data for the past 12 months presented here. These data indicate that overhead expenses vary with the direct labour-hours expended. The $16.80 estimate was determined by dividing total overhead expended for the 12 months by total labour-hours.

Month	Labour-Hours	Overhead Costs
January	2,500	$ 66,000
February	2,700	70,800
March	3,000	72,000
April	4,200	76,800
May	7,500	92,400
June	5,500	85,200
July	6,500	88,800
August	4,500	80,400
September	7,000	90,000

October	4,500	81,600
November	3,100	74,400
December	6,500	87,600
Total	57,500	$966,000

Jones has recently become aware of regression analysis. He estimated the following regression equation with overhead costs as the dependent variable (y) and labour-hours as the independent variable (X):

$$y = \$57{,}925 + \$4.71X$$

REQUIRED

1. Plot the relationship between overhead costs and labour-hours. Draw the regression line and evaluate it using the criteria of economic plausibility, goodness of fit, and slope of the regression line.
2. Using data from the regression analysis, find the variable cost per person for a cocktail party.
3. Bob Jones has been asked to prepare a bid for a 200-person cocktail party to be given next month. Determine the minimum bid price that Jones would be willing to submit to earn a positive contribution margin.

Excel Application For students who wish to practise their spreadsheet skills, the following is a step-by-step approach to creating an Excel spreadsheet to work this problem.

Step-by-Step

1. At the top of a new spreadsheet, create an "Original Data" section for the data provided for Bob Jones Catering. Create columns for "Month," "Labour-Hours," and "Overhead Costs" in the same format as the table of monthly labour hours and overhead costs shown for Bob Jones Catering.
2. Skip two rows, and create a section, "Regression Output."
3. Skip two more rows, and create a section, "Regression Diagram."
4. Estimate the regression equation with overhead costs as the dependent variable and labour hours as the independent variable by carrying out the following steps: (a) click on the tools menu and choose the "Data Analysis" option*; (b) in the "Data Analysis" dialog box, click on "Regression" and click "OK"; (c) click in the "Input y Range" box so the cursor is in the box, then use your mouse to highlight the cells in the "Overhead Costs" column; (d) click in the "Input × Range" box so the cursor is in this box, then use your mouse to highlight the cells in the "Labour-Hours" column; (e) under "Output options" select "Output Range" and click in the "Output Range" box so the cursor is in the box, then use your mouse to highlight a cell in the "Regression Output" section you created in step 4; (f) click "OK" to close the regression dialog box.
5. After completing step 4, you will have a variety of regression statistics in your "Regression Output" section. In this output, there is a column, "Coefficients," and two rows, "Intercept" and "X Variable 1." The number in the intercept row of the coefficients column is your estimate of the intercept; the number in the x variable row of the coefficients column is your estimate of the slope.
6. Use the chart wizard to create a scatterplot of the relationship between overhead costs and labour-hours. Draw the regression line through these points by doing the following: (a) place the pointer on one of the data points on the graph and right click on your mouse and choose "Add Trendline"; (b) in the "Add Trendline" dialog box, choose "Linear" and click "OK."
7. After completing step 6, Excel will draw the regression line you calculated in step 6 through the data points. Use the resulting regression plot to answer question 1, and use the slope coefficient that you calculated in step 6 to answer question 2.

10-26 Regression analysis, activity-based costing, choosing cost drivers. Jill Goldstein has been collecting data over the last year in an effort to understand the cost drivers of distribution costs at Waterloo Corporation, a manufacturer of brass door handles. Distribution costs include the costs of organizing different shipments as well as physically handling and moving packaged units. Goldstein believes that, because the product is heavy, number of units moved will affect distribution costs significantly but she is not certain that this is the case. Goldstein collects the following monthly data for the past 12 months.

---

*If this option is not present, you will need to add it by selecting Add-Ins, then clicking the box next to Analysis Toolpak, then clicking on OK. You can then proceed with the problem.

Month	Distribution Costs	Number of Packaged Units Moved	Number of Shipments Made
January	$ 33,600	51,000	200
February	24,000	43,000	210
March	20,400	28,000	185
April	38,400	67,000	315
May	48,000	73,000	335
June	28,800	54,000	225
July	26,400	37,000	190
August	42,000	72,000	390
September	50,400	71,000	280
October	27,600	56,000	360
November	39,600	52,000	380
December	26,400	45,000	270
Total	$405,600	649,000	3,340

Goldstein estimates the following regression equations:

$$y = \$1,618.45 + (\$0.595 \times \text{Number of packaged units moved})$$
$$y = \$12,500.57 + (\$76.52 \times \text{Number of shipments made})$$

REQUIRED

1. Present plots of the monthly data and the regression lines underlying each of the following cost functions:
   a. Distribution costs = $a + (b \times$ Number of packaged units moved)
   b. Distribution costs = $a + (b \times$ Number of shipments made)
   Which cost driver for support overhead costs would you choose? Explain your answer briefly.

2. Goldstein anticipates moving 40,000 units in 220 shipments next month. Using the cost function you chose in requirement 1, what distribution costs should Goldstein budget?

3. If Goldstein chose the wrong cost function—the cost function other than the one you chose in requirement 1—and 40,000 units were moved in 220 shipments, would you expect actual costs to be lower than, to be greater than, or to closely approximate the predictions made using the "wrong" cost driver and cost function? Explain your answer briefly and discuss any other implications of choosing the "wrong" cost driver and cost function.

10-27 **Learning curve, cumulative average time learning curve.** Global Radar manufactures radar systems. It has just completed the manufacture of its first newly designed system, RS-32. It took 3,000 direct manufacturing labour-hours (DMLH) to produce this one unit. Global believes that a 90% cumulative average time learning model for direct manufacturing labour-hours applies to RS-32. (A 90% learning curve implies $b = -0.1520$) The variable costs of producing RS-32 are as follows:

Direct materials costs	$96,000 per RS-32
Direct manufacturing labour costs	$30 per DMLH
Variable manufacturing overhead costs	$18 per DMLH

REQUIRED

Calculate the total variable costs of producing two, four, and eight units.

10-28 **Learning curve, incremental unit time learning curve.** Assume the same information for Global Radar as in Exercise 10-27 except that Global Radar uses a 90% incremental unit-time learning curve as a basis for forecasting direct manufacturing labour-hours. (A 90% learning curve implies $b = -0.1520$)

REQUIRED

1. Calculate the total variable costs of producing two, three, and four units.
2. If you solved Exercise 10-27, compare your cost predictions in the two exercises for two and four units. Why are the predictions different?

PROBLEMS

10-29 Organizing data, high-low method. Ken Howard, financial analyst at JVR Corporation, a manufacturer of precision parts, is examining the behaviour of quarterly maintenance costs for budgeting purposes. Howard collects data on machine-hours worked and maintenance costs for the past 13 quarters. The data are as follows:

Quarter	Machine-Hours	Maintenance Costs
1	90,000	$282,000
2	110,000	222,000
3	100,000	264,000
4	120,000	240,000
5	85,000	288,000
6	105,000	204,000
7	95,000	258,000
8	115,000	234,000
9	95,000	282,000
10	115,000	228,000
11	105,000	270,000
12	125,000	216,000
13	90,000	300,000

REQUIRED

1. **a.** Present plots of the quarterly data underlying the cost function: Maintenance costs = $a + (b \times$ Machine-hours).
   b. Estimate the cost function for the data represented by the plots in requirement 1(a) using the high-low method.
   c. How well does the cost function fit the data?

2. **a.** Construct a table and present plots of the quarterly data relating machine-hours in a quarter (t, say) to maintenance costs in the following quarter ($t + 1$). That is, plot machine-hours in quarter 1 against maintenance costs in quarter 2, machine-hours in quarter 2 against maintenance costs in quarter 3, and so on.
   b. Estimate the cost function for the data represented by the plots in requirement 2(a) using the high-low method.
   c. How well does the cost function fit the data?

3. Howard anticipates that JVR will operate machines for 95,000 hours in quarter 14. Calculate the predicted maintenance costs in quarter 14 using the cost functions estimated in requirements 1(b) and 2(b). What maintenance costs should Howard budget for quarter 14? Explain your answer briefly.

10-30 High-low versus regression method. (CIMA, heavily adapted) Anna Martinez, the financial manager at the Casa Real restaurant, is working with Jan Brown, the marketing manager, to establish whether there is any relationship between newspaper advertising and sales revenue at the restaurant. They obtain the following monthly data for the past 10 months:

Month	Revenues	Advertising Expense
March	$60,000	$2,400
April	84,000	3,600
May	66,000	1,800
June	78,000	4,200
July	66,000	1,200
August	78,000	2,400
September	54,000	1,800
October	96,000	4,800
November	66,000	3,000
December	72,000	3,000

They estimate the following regression equation:

$y = \$47,402 + (8.723 \times$ Advertising Expense), where y is the monthly revenue

1. Plot the relationship between advertising expense and revenues.
2. Draw the regression line and evaluate it using the criteria of economic plausibility, goodness of fit, and slope of the regression line.
3. Use the high-low method to compute the cost function, relating advertising expense and revenues.
4. Using (a) the regression equation and (b) the high-low equation, what is the increase in revenues for each $1,000 spent on advertising within the relevant range?
5. Should Martinez and Brown use the cost function estimated from the regression method or the high-low method to predict the effect of advertising on revenues? Explain briefly.

10-31 Regression analysis, activity-based costing, choosing cost drivers. Larry Chu, the plant controller at Rohan Plastics, wants to identify cost drivers for support overhead cost.

Indirect support consists of skilled staff responsible for the efficient functioning of all aspects (setup, production, maintenance, and quality control) of the plastic injection-moulding facility. In talking to the support staff, Chu has the impression that they spend a good portion of their time ensuring that the equipment is set up correctly and checking that the first units of production in each batch are of good quality.

Chu has collected the following monthly data for the past 12 months:

Month	Support Overhead	Machine-Hours	Number of Batches
January	$100,800	2,250	309
February	49,200	2,400	128
March	75,600	2,850	249
April	52,800	2,100	159
May	52,800	2,700	216
June	57,600	2,250	174
July	79,200	3,800	264
August	55,200	3,600	162
September	39,600	1,850	147
October	79,200	3,300	219
November	97,200	3,750	303
December	68,400	2,000	106
Total	$807,600	32,850	2,436

Chu estimates the following regression equations:

$$y = \$33,707 + (\$12.27 \times \text{Machine-hours})$$

and $\quad y = \$19,237 + (\$236.76 \times \text{Number of batches})$

where y is the monthly support overhead.

REQUIRED

1. Present plots of the monthly data and the regression lines underlying each of the following cost functions:
   a. Support overhead costs = $a + (b \times \text{machine-hours})$
   b. Support overhead costs = $a + (b \times \text{number of batches})$
   Which cost driver for support overhead costs would you choose?
2. Chu anticipates 2,600 machine-hours and 300 batches will be run next month. Using the cost driver you chose in requirement 1, what support overhead costs should Chu budget?
3. **a.** Chu adds 20% to costs as a first cut for determining target revenues (and hence prices). Costs other than support overhead are expected to equal $150,000 next month. Compare the target revenue numbers obtained if (i) machine-hours and (ii) number of batches is used as the cost driver. Discuss what would happen if Chu picked the "wrong" cost driver—the cost driver other than the one you chose in requirement 1—to set target revenues and prices.
   b. Describe any other implications of choosing the "wrong" cost driver and cost function.

10-32 Cost estimation, cumulative average time learning curve. The Nautilus Company, which is under contract to the Canadian Coast Guard, assembles search and rescue boats. As part of its research program, it completes the assembly of the first of a new model (PT109) of search and rescue boats. The Canadian Coast Guard is impressed with the PT109. It requests that Nautilus submit a proposal on the cost of producing another seven PT109s.

The accounting department at Nautilus reports the following cost information for the first PT109 assembled by Nautilus:

Direct materials	$120,000
Direct manufacturing labour (10,000 labour-hours × $36)	360,000
Tooling cost*	60,000
Variable manufacturing overhead[†]	240,000
Other manufacturing overhead[‡]	90,000
	$870,000

*Tooling can be reused at no extra cost, since all of its cost has been assigned to the first search and rescue boat.
[†]Variable overhead incurred is directly affected by direct manufacturing labour-hours; a rate of $24 per hour is used for purposes of bidding on contracts.
[‡]Other overhead is allocated at a flat rate of 25% of direct manufacturing labour costs for purposes of bidding on contracts.

Nautilus uses an 85% cumulative average time learning curve as a basis for forecasting direct manufacturing labour-hours on its assembling operations. (An 85% learning curve implies $b = -0.2345$.)

REQUIRED

1. Prepare a prediction of the total costs for producing the seven PT109s for the Coast Guard. (Nautilus will keep the first search and rescue boat assembled, costed at $870,000, as a demonstration model for other potential customers.)
2. What is the difference between (a) the predicted total costs for producing the seven PT109s in requirement 1 and (b) the predicted total costs for producing the seven PT109s assuming that there is no learning curve for direct manufacturing labour? (That is, for (b) assume a linear function for direct labour-hours and units produced.)

10-33 **Cost estimation, incremental unit time learning curve**. Assume the same information for the Nautilus Company as that in requirement 1 of Problem 10-32 with one exception, that Nautilus uses an 85% incremental unit time learning curve as a basis for forecasting direct manufacturing labour-hours on its assembling operations. (An 85% learning curve implies $b = -0.2345$.)

REQUIRED

1. Prepare a prediction of the total expected costs for producing the seven PT109s for the Coast Guard.
2. If you solved requirement 1 of Problem 10-32, compare your cost prediction there with the one you made here. Why are the predictions different?

10-34 **Promotion of a new product, simple and multiple regression analysis.** (Chapter Appendix, S. Stickel, adapted) "What does all this mean. All I really want to know is whether I should advertise or not, and where?" said Rick Savalas, the sales manager of Cleanhair Products Inc. Rick has asked for your help to understand the results of regression analyses that have been prepared by his assistants for a new product, Glowbright, that Cleanhair Products recently introduced. The notation used is as follows:

y estimated sales of Glowbright
X_1 dollars incurred on discount coupons placed in magazines
X_2 dollars spent on advertising Glowbright on television

Standard errors of the coefficients (not t-statistics) are in parentheses.

1. $y = \$457,200 + \$4.78\,X_1$ $r^2 = 0.47$
         ($2.08)
2. $y = \$560,400 + \$5.08\,X_2$ $r^2 = 0.53$
         ($2.23)
3. $y = \$902,760 + \$1.04\,X_1 + \$1.09\,X_2\ r^2 = 0.88$
         ($0.95)   ($1.19)

REQUIRED

1. For each of the regressions, perform a statistical test and indicate whether sales are affected by discount coupons and television advertising.
2. Contrast the multiple regression results (equation 3) with the simple regression results (equations 1 and 2) in terms of the statistical tests that you performed in

requirement 1. Suggest a possible explanation for any differences in the results of the statistical tests.

3. Interpret the $4.78, the $5.08, the $1.04, and the $1.09 coefficients in the regression equations. Specifically, explain briefly what the coefficients imply about whether and how Rick should advertise.

10-35 Evaluating alternative simple regression models, not-for-profit. (Chapter Appendix) Kathy Hanks, executive assistant to the president of Eastern University, is concerned about the overhead costs at her university. Cost pressures are severe, so controlling and reducing overhead is very important. Hanks believes overhead costs incurred are generally a function of the number of different academic programs (including different specializations, degrees, and majors) that the university has and the number of enrolled students. Both have grown significantly over the years. She collects the following data:

Year	Overhead Costs (in thousands)	Number of Academic Programs	Enrolled Students
1	$16,200	29	3,400
2	23,040	36	5,000
3	20,160	49	2,600
4	24,120	53	4,700
5	23,400	54	3,900
6	27,720	58	4,900
7	28,440	88	5,700
8	24,120	72	3,900
9	27,360	83	3,500
10	35,640	73	3,700
11	37,440	101	5,600
12	45,720	103	7,600

◆ **Regression 1.** Overhead costs = $a + (b \times$ number of academic programs)

Variable	Coefficient	Standard Error	t-Value
Constant	$8,553.30	$4,002.41	2.14
Independent variable 1: number of academic programs	$ 288.76	$ 56.80	5.08

$r^2 = 0.72$; Durbin-Watson statistic = 2.07.
The adjusted $R^2 = 0.693$

◆ **Regression 2.** Overhead costs = $a + (b \times$ number of enrolled students)

Variable	Coefficient	Standard Error	t-Value
Constant	$7,190.10	$6,081.45	1.18
Independent variable 1: number of enrolled students	$ 4.53	$ 1.29	3.52

$r^2 = 0.55$; Durbin-Watson statistic = 0.82.
The adjusted $R^2 = 0.509$

REQUIRED
1. Plot the relationship between overhead costs and each of the following variables: (a) number of academic programs and (b) number of enrolled students.
2. Compare and evaluate the two simple regression models estimated by Hanks. Use the comparison format employed in Exhibit 10-19 (p. 400).
3. What insights do the analyses provide about controlling and reducing overhead costs at the University?

10-36 Evaluating multiple regression models, not-for-profit (continuation of Problem 10-35). (Chapter Appendix)

REQUIRED
1. Given your findings in Problem 10-35, should Hanks use multiple regression analysis to better understand the cost drivers of overhead costs? Explain your answer.
2. Hanks decides that the simple regression analysis in Problem 10-35 should be extended to a multiple regression analysis. She finds the following result:

◆ **Regression 3.** Overhead costs = $a + (b_1 \times$ number of academic programs$) + (b_2 \times$ number of enrolled students$)$

Variable	Coefficient	Standard Error	t-Value
Constant	$3,335.54	$4,344.06	0.77
Independent variable 1: number of academic programs	$ 214.04	$ 61.84	3.46
Independent variable 2: number of enrolled students	$ 2.24	$ 1.11	2.02

$r^2 = 0.81$; Durbin-Watson statistic = 1.91.

The adjusted $R^2 = 0.766$

The coefficient of correlation between number of academic programs and number of students is 0.60. Use the format in Exhibit 10-22 to evaluate the multiple regression model. (Assume linearity, and constant variance and normality of residuals.) Should Hanks choose the multiple regression model over the two simple regression models of Problem 10-35?

3. How might the president of Eastern University use these regression results to manage overhead costs?

10-37 Purchasing department cost drivers, activity-based costing, simple regression analysis. (Chapter Appendix) Fashion Flair operates a chain of ten retail department stores. Each department store makes its own purchasing decisions. Barry Lee, assistant to the president of Fashion Flair, is interested in better understanding the drivers of purchasing department costs. For many years, Fashion Flair has allocated purchasing department costs to products on the basis of the dollar value of merchandise purchased. An item costing $120 is allocated ten times as much overhead costs associated with the purchasing department as an item costing $12 is allocated.

Lee recently attended a seminar titled "Cost Drivers in the Retail Industry." In a presentation at the seminar, Couture Fabrics, a leading competitor that has implemented activity-based costing, reported the number of purchase orders and the number of suppliers to be the two most important cost drivers of purchasing department costs. The dollar value of merchandise purchased on each purchase order was not found to be a significant cost driver by Couture Fabrics. Lee interviewed several members of the purchasing department at the Fashion Flair store in Victoria. These people told Lee that they believed that Couture Fabrics' conclusions also applied to their purchasing department.

Lee collects the following data for the most recent year for the ten retail department stores of Fashion Flair:

y Department Store	X_1 Purchasing Department Costs (PDC)	X_2 Dollar Value of Merchandise Purchased (MP$)	X_3 Number of Purchase Orders (no. of POs)	Number of Suppliers (no. of Ss)
Saskatoon	$1,827,600	$ 81,978,000	4,357	132
Chicago	1,320,000	40,147,200	2,550	222
Victoria	656,400	145,392,000	1,433	11
Miami	2,458,800	143,479,200	5,944	190
New York	1,267,200	40,206,000	2,793	23
Calgary	634,800	35,824,800	1,327	33
Seattle	1,845,600	123,450,000	7,586	104
St. Louis	2,104,800	46,408,800	3,617	119
Toronto	1,934,400	167,174,400	1,707	208
Vancouver	1,508,400	157,132,800	4,731	201

Lee decides to use simple regression analysis to examine whether one or more of three variables (the last three columns in the table) are cost drivers of purchasing department costs. Summary results for these regressions are as follows:

◆ **Regression 1.** PDC = $a + (b \times$ MP$)$; $n = 10$, $d.f. = 9$

Variable	Coefficient	Standard Error	t-Value
Constant	$1,246,873	$412,127	3.03
Independent variable 1: MP$	0.0031	0.0037	0.84

$r^2 = 0.08$; Durbin-Watson statistic = 2.43. Adjusted $R^2 = -0.03$

◆ **Regression 2.** PDC = a + (b × no. of POs); n = 10, d.f. = 9

Variable	Coefficient	Standard Error	t-Value
Constant	$876,858	$318,502	2.75
Independent variable 1: no. of POs	$ 188.36	$ 77.62	2.43

r^2 = 0.42; Durbin-Watson statistic = 2.016. Adjusted R^2 = 0.352

◆ **Regression 3.** PDC = a + (b × no. of Ss); n = 10, d.f. = 9

Variable	Coefficient	Standard Error	t-Value
Constant	$977,833.99	$297,385.63	3.29
Independent variable 1: no. of Ss	$ 4,649.77	$ 2,036.75	2.28

r^2 = 0.39; Durbin-Watson statistic = 2.056. Adjusted R^2 = 0.3187

REQUIRED

1. Compare and evaluate the three simple regression models estimated by Lee. Graph each one. Also, use the format employed in Exhibit 10-19 (p. 400) to evaluate the information.
2. Do the regression results support the Couture Fabrics presentation about purchasing department cost drivers? Which of these cost drivers would you recommend in designing an activity-based cost system?
3. How might Lee gain additional evidence on drivers of purchasing department costs at each store of Fashion Flair?

10-38 Purchasing department cost drivers, multiple regression analysis (continuation of 10-37). (Chapter Appendix) Barry Lee decides that the simple regression analysis reported in Problem 10-37 could be extended to a multiple regression analysis. He finds the following results for several multiple regressions:

◆ **Regression 4.** PDC = a + (b_1 × no. of POs) + (b_2 × no. of Ss)

Variable	Coefficient	Standard Error	t-Value
Constant	$ 582,460	$ 308,872	1.89
Independent variable 1: no. of POs	$ 147.86	$ 69.23	2.14
Independent variable 2: no. of Ss	$3,542.80	$1,771.74	2.00

r^2 = 0.63; Durbin-Watson statistic = 2.098. Adjusted R^2 = 0.529

◆ **Regression 5.** PDC = a + (b_1 × no. of POs) + (b_2 × no. of Ss) + (b_3 × MP$)

Variable	Coefficient	Standard Error	t-Value
Constant	$ 593,620	$ 372,246	1.59
Independent variable 1: no. of POs	$ 148.86	$ 76.18	1.95
Independent variable 2: no. of Ss	$3,580.87	$1,994.23	1.80
Independent variable 3: MP$	−0.0002	0.0030	−0.07

r^2 = 0.63; Durbin-Watson statistic = 2.09. Adjusted R^2 = 0.45

The coefficients of correlation between pairwise combinations of the variables are

	PDC	MP$	No. of POs
MP$	0.29		
No. of POs	0.65	0.27	
No. of Ss	0.63	0.34	0.29

REQUIRED

1. Evaluate regression 4 using the economic plausibility, goodness of fit, significance of independent variables, and specification analysis criteria. Compare regression 4 with regressions 2 and 3 in Problem 10-37. Which model would you recommend that Lee use? Why?
2. Compare regression 5 with regression 4. Which model would you recommend that Lee use? Why?
3. Lee estimates the following data for the Saskatoon store for next year: dollar value of merchandise purchased, $90,000,000; number of purchase orders, 3,900; number of suppliers,

110. How much should Lee budget for purchasing department costs for the Saskatoon store for next year?

4. What difficulties may arise in multiple regressions that do not arise in simple regressions? Is there evidence of such difficulties in either of the multiple regressions presented in this problem?

5. Give two examples of decisions where the regression results reported here (and in Problem 10-37) could be informative.

10-39 Regression computations, ethics. (Chapter Appendix) Cambridge Engineering manufactures small electric motors. Data on manufacturing labour costs and units produced for the last four quarters are as follows:

Quarter	Manufacturing Labour Costs	Units Produced
1	$211,200	9,000
2	208,800	10,000
3	198,000	9,000
4	246,000	12,000
Total	$864,000	40,000

Peter Smith, the manufacturing manager, is evaluated on how labour costs in a quarter compare with labour costs in the previous four quarters. In the recently concluded Quarter 5, Cambridge Engineering produced 12,000 motors and incurred manufacturing labour costs of $249,600. Smith is very happy with the results. Over the previous four quarters, the average manufacturing labour cost per unit is $21.60 ($864,000 ÷ 40,000 units) resulting in a benchmark for Quarter 5 of $21.60 × 12,000 = $259,200. Just as Smith is thinking about what he might do with the bonus, Allison Hart, the plant controller, knocks on Smith's door.

Allison Hart: I am sorry that we couldn't beat the benchmark over the last four quarters. We certainly gave it our best shot.

Peter Smith: What do you mean we didn't beat the benchmark? Here are the numbers I just calculated. Against a benchmark of $259,200, we achieved $249,600.

Allison Hart: No, that's not how the calculations are done. Some of the labour costs are fixed and others vary with production. My analysis here first separates out the fixed from the variable components. My calculations then show that our Quarter 5 performance was worse than the previous four quarters.

Peter Smith: Please review your calculations. I am sure you can report better numbers than that. This regression approach you are using is subject to estimation error. You should make some adjustment for that. If we don't show senior management that we are succeeding in reducing labour costs, they might shut us down because they do not believe that we can be competitive. I am sure that no one in this plant wants that to happen.

REQUIRED

1. Verify, either by using the actual formulae given in the Appendix, or by using a software program on a computer, that the regression equation is given by

$$y = \$78,000 + (\$13.80 \times \text{Units produced})$$

with an $r^2 = 0.88$. Adjusted $R^2 = 0.819$

2. What is the benchmark for Quarter 5 that Allison Hart had calculated?

3. Why is there a difference between the benchmark calculated by Peter Smith and the benchmark calculated in requirement 2? Which benchmark do you prefer? Explain your answer.

4. Identify the steps that Allison Hart should follow in attempting to resolve the situation created by Peter Smith's comment about adjusting the benchmark.

10-40 Data analysis and ethics. Comdex Electronics makes videocassette recorders (VCRs). Sales of VCRs have been very steady over the past ten years. Helen Gibbs, the manager of the department that makes the head mechanism for the VCR, is keen on introducing robots into the department to improve VCR quality. To obtain funding, Gibbs knows that she will need to justify the investment in terms of labour cost savings. Gibbs estimates average annual labour costs in the department of $1,449,000 over the past ten years. Labour costs over the past three years have averaged $960,000. If robots are introduced, labour costs would decrease to $660,000 per year. Average savings in labour costs of at least $480,000 per year are needed to justify the investment in robots. Gibbs uses the $1,440,000 number in her analysis. She then asks Joan Mistry, the management accountant, to review her calculations before she submits the robot proposal to senior management.

Mistry has a problem with Gibbs's analysis. She feels that by using a long time period of ten years, Gibbs was able to show larger labour cost savings than was justified. Mistry knew that Gibbs would be unhappy with these findings.

Mistry also felt that the robot investment was good for the company. She tried to redo the analysis in a way that might show larger cost savings, even though she knew that the assumptions she was using were not appropriate. Nothing she tried could change the conclusion that the cost savings were not large enough to justify the investment in robots. Gibbs is upset when she sees Mistry's report. She tells Mistry, "Try something else. I am sure you can come up with a set of assumptions under which this investment can be justified. You and I both know this is a good investment for the company to make. Quality is essential if we are to compete."

REQUIRED
1. Calculate the labour cost savings if Gibbs uses average labour costs incurred (a) over the past ten years and (b) over the past three years. Does it make a difference in terms of justifying the robot investment?
2. Why do you think the average labour costs over the past ten years differ significantly from the average labour costs over the past three years?
3. Explain whether Joan Mistry's initial attempts to redo the data analysis to justify the robot investment were ethical.
4. Identify the steps that Joan Mistry should follow in attempting to resolve this situation.

COLLABORATIVE LEARNING PROBLEM

10-41 High-low method, alternative regression functions, accrual accounting adjustments. Trevor Kennedy, the cost analyst at a can manufacturing plant of United Packaging, is seeking to examine the relationship between total engineering support costs reported in the plant records and machine-hours. These costs have two components: (1) labour (which is paid monthly) and (2) materials and parts (which are purchased from an outside vendor every three months). After further discussion with the operating manager, Kennedy discovers that the materials and parts numbers reported in the monthly records are on an "as purchased" basis and not on an "as used" or accrual accounting basis. By examining materials and parts usage records, Kennedy is able to restate the materials and parts costs to an "as used" basis. (No restatement of the labour costs was necessary.) The reported and restated costs are as follows:

Month	Labour: Reported Costs (1)	Materials and Parts: Reported Costs (2)	Materials and Parts: Restated Costs (3)	Total Engineering Support: Reported Costs (4) = (1) + (2)	Total Engineering Support: Restated Costs (5) = (1) + (3)	Machine-Hours (6)
March	$416	$1,016	$218	$1,432	$ 634	30
April	625	0	493	625	1,118	63
May	478	0	322	478	800	49
June	426	1,153	274	1,579	700	38
July	568	0	418	568	986	57
August	740	0	419	740	1,159	73
September	294	985	150	1,279	444	19
October	584	0	437	584	1,021	53
November	517	0	348	517	865	42

The regression results, when total engineering support reported costs (column 4) are used as the dependent variable, are

◆ **Regression 1.** Engineering support reported costs = $a + (b \times$ machine-hours)

Variable	Coefficient	Standard Error	t-Value
Constant	$1,671.41	$366.60	4.56
Independent variable 1: machine-hours	$ (17.08)	$ 7.38	–2.31

$r^2 = 0.43$; Durbin-Watson statistic = 2.48. Adjusted $R^2 = 0.35$

The regression results, when total engineering support restated costs (column 5) are used as the dependent variable, are

◆ **Regression 2.** Engineering support restated costs = a + (b × machine-hours)

Variable	Coefficient	Standard Error	t-Value
Constant	$211.52	$64.46	3.28
Independent variable 1: machine-hours	$ 13.73	$ 1.30	10.59

$r^2 = 0.94$; Durbin-Watson statistic = 1.54. Adjusted $R^2 = 0.933$

INSTRUCTIONS
Form groups of two or more students to complete the following requirements.

REQUIRED
1. Present a plot of the data for the cost function relating the *reported costs* for total engineering support to machine-hours. Present a plot of the data for the cost function relating the *restated costs* for total engineering support to machine-hours. Comment on the plots.
2. Compute estimates of the cost functions ($y = a + bX$) for reported engineering support costs and machine-hours and restated engineering support costs and machine-hours using the high-low method.
3. Contrast and evaluate the cost function estimated with regression using restated data for materials and parts with the cost function estimated with regression using the data reported in the plant records. Use the comparison format employed in Exhibit 10-19 (p. 400).
4. Of all the cost functions estimated in requirements 2 and 3, which one would you choose to best represent the relationship between engineering support costs and machine-hours? Why?
5. Kennedy expects 50 machine-hours to be worked in December. What engineering support costs should Kennedy budget for December?
6. What problems might Kennedy encounter when restating the materials and parts costs recorded to an "as used" or accrual accounting basis?
7. Why is it important for Kennedy to pick the correct cost function? That is, illustrate two potential problems Kennedy could run into, by choosing a cost function other than the one you chose in requirement 4.

Gildan Activewear is a multinational company that produces casual wear offshore and distributes to retailers such as GAP, Hudson's Bay Company, and Old Navy. The company's managers require excellent information to decide what quantities of material to purchase, where to manufacture the products, and whether to expand or close manufacturing facilities.

CHAPTER 11

Decision Making and Relevant Information

LEARNING OBJECTIVES

After studying this chapter, you should be able to

1. Describe a five-step sequence in the decision process

2. Distinguish relevant costs and revenues from irrelevant costs and revenues in any decision situation

3. Understand the difference between quantitative factors and qualitative factors in decisions

4. Identify two potential problems in relevant-cost analysis

5. Describe the opportunity cost concept; explain why it is used in decision making

6. Describe the key concept in choosing which among multiple products to produce when there are capacity constraints

7. Discuss the key issue managers must consider when adding or dropping customers and segments

8. Explain why the book value of equipment is irrelevant in equipment replacement decisions

9. Explain how conflicts can arise between the decision model used by a manager and the performance model used to evaluate the manager

Working with managers to make decisions is one of the main functions of the management accountant and an important thrust of this book. The use of accounting information for decision making has been a consistent theme in earlier chapters. In this chapter, we focus on specific and common decisions such as accepting or rejecting a one-time-only special order, insourcing or outsourcing products or services, and replacing or keeping equipment. We place special stress on the importance of distinguishing between relevant and irrelevant financial information when making these decisions.

Each manager has a method, often called a decision model, for deciding among different courses of action. A *decision model* is a formal method for making a choice, frequently involving quantitative analysis. Accountants serve as technical experts, supplying managers with relevant data to guide their decisions. Quantitative models exist to plan and control a company's activities using both financial and nonfinancial performance evaluation indicators.

Predictions and Models

Consider a strategic decision that Precision Sporting Goods, a manufacturer of golf clubs, faces: Should it reorganize a manufacturing assembly line to reduce manufacturing labour costs? For simplicity, assume that the only alternatives are "do not rearrange" and "rearrange." The rearrangement will eliminate all manual handling of materials. The current manufacturing line uses 20 workers—15 workers operate machines and 5 workers handle materials. Each worker puts in 2,000 hours annually. The rearrangement is predicted to cost $90,000. The predicted production output of 25,000 units for the next year will be unaffected by the decision. Also unaffected by the decision are the predicted selling price per unit of $250, direct materials costs per unit of $50, other manufacturing overhead of $750,000, and marketing costs of $2,000,000. The cost driver is units of production.

To make the decision, management proceeds in a sequence of steps. The first step is to gather more information about manufacturing labour costs. The historical manufacturing labour rate of $14 per hour is the starting point for predicting total manufacturing labour costs under both alternatives. The manufacturing labour rate is expected to increase to $16 per hour following a recently negotiated increase in employee benefits.

The second step is to predict future costs under the two alternatives. Predicted manufacturing labour costs under the "do not rearrange" alternative are 20 workers × 2,000 hours × $16 per hour = $640,000. Predicted manufacturing labour costs under the "rearrange" alternative are 15 workers × 2,000 hours × $16 per hour = $480,000. Predicted costs of rearrangement are $90,000.

As the third step, Precision Sporting Goods' management compares the predicted savings from eliminating materials-handling labour costs (5 workers × 2,000 hours × $16 per hour = $160,000) to the costs of rearrangement of $90,000. It also takes into account other qualitative considerations such as the effect that reducing the number of workers will have on employee morale. After weighing the costs and benefits, management chooses the "rearrange" alternative. Management next implements the decision in the fourth step by rearranging the manufacturing assembly line.

Models and Feedback

As the fifth and final step, management gathers information about the actual results of the plant rearrangement to evaluate performance and to provide feedback. Actual results show that the new manufacturing labour costs are $550,000 (because of, say, lower-than-expected manufacturing labour productivity) rather than the predicted $480,000. This feedback may lead to better implementation, perhaps through a change in supervisory behaviour, employee training, or personnel so that the $480,000 target is achieved in subsequent periods. However, the feedback may convince the decision maker that the prediction method, rather than the implementation, was faulty. Perhaps the prediction method for similar decisions in the future should be modified to allow for worker training or learning time.

Exhibit 11-1 on p. 422 summarizes the five-step decision process that we just described—gathering information, making predictions, choosing an alternative, implementing the decision, and evaluating actual performance to provide feedback. The feedback, in turn, might affect future predictions, the prediction method itself, the decision model, or the implementation.

Shareholders want managers to make decisions that are in the shareholders' best interest.

Norsys Software Corp.
www.norsys.com/netica.html

Canadian Operational Research Society
www.cors.ca/whator/corse.htm

OBJECTIVE 1

Describe a five-step sequence in the decision process

EXHIBIT 11-1
Accounting Information and the Decision Process

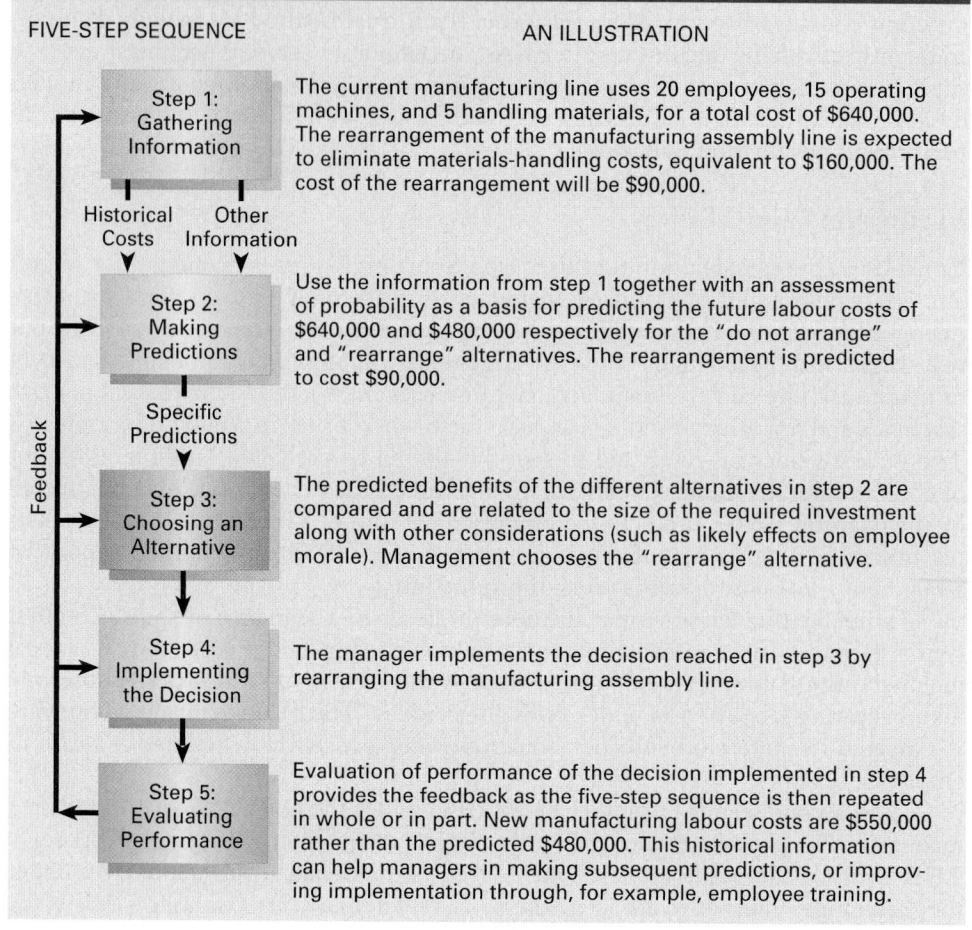

FIVE-STEP SEQUENCE

AN ILLUSTRATION

Step 1: Gathering Information
— Historical Costs — Other Information —

The current manufacturing line uses 20 employees, 15 operating machines, and 5 handling materials, for a total cost of $640,000. The rearrangement of the manufacturing assembly line is expected to eliminate materials-handling costs, equivalent to $160,000. The cost of the rearrangement will be $90,000.

Step 2: Making Predictions
— Specific Predictions —

Use the information from step 1 together with an assessment of probability as a basis for predicting the future labour costs of $640,000 and $480,000 respectively for the "do not arrange" and "rearrange" alternatives. The rearrangement is predicted to cost $90,000.

Step 3: Choosing an Alternative

The predicted benefits of the different alternatives in step 2 are compared and are related to the size of the required investment along with other considerations (such as likely effects on employee morale). Management chooses the "rearrange" alternative.

Step 4: Implementing the Decision

The manager implements the decision reached in step 3 by rearranging the manufacturing assembly line.

Step 5: Evaluating Performance

Evaluation of performance of the decision implemented in step 4 provides the feedback as the five-step sequence is then repeated in whole or in part. New manufacturing labour costs are $550,000 rather than the predicted $480,000. This historical information can help managers in making subsequent predictions, or improving implementation through, for example, employee training.

(Feedback)

THE MEANING OF RELEVANCE

Relevant Costs and Relevant Revenues

The most important decision-making concepts in this chapter are relevant costs and relevant revenues. **Relevant costs** are those *expected future costs* that *differ* between alternative courses of action. The two key aspects to this definition are that the costs must occur in the future and that they must differ between the alternative courses of action. We focus on the future because *every decision deals with the future*—whether it be 20 seconds ahead (the decision to adjust a dial) or 20 years ahead (the decision to plant and harvest pine trees). The function of decision making is to select courses of action intended to improve future outcomes. *Nothing can be done to alter the past.* Future costs *must* differ among the alternatives. If they do not, irrespective of the decision, there will be no difference in costs and therefore no future improvement in cost outcomes. Likewise, **relevant revenues** are those expected future revenues that differ between alternative courses of action.

In Exhibit 11-2, the $640,000 and $480,000 manufacturing labour costs are relevant costs—they are expected future costs that differ between the two alternatives. The past manufacturing labour rate of $14 per hour and total past manufacturing labour costs of $560,000 (2,000 hours × 20 workers × $14 per hour) are not relevant, even though they may play a role in preparing the $640,000 and $480,000 labour cost predictions. *Although they may be a useful basis for making informed judgments for predicting expected future costs, historical costs in themselves are irrelevant to a decision.* Why? Because they deal strictly with the past, not the future, and cannot be changed.

EXHIBIT 11-2
Determining Relevant Revenues and Relevant Costs for Precision Sporting Goods

	All Revenues and Costs		Relevant Revenues and Costs	
	Alternative 1: Do Not Reorganize	Alternative 2: Reorganize	Alternative 1: Do Not Reorganize	Alternative 2: Reorganize
Revenues[a]	$6,250,000	$6,250,000	—	—
Costs:				
Direct materials[b]	1,250,000	1,250,000	—	—
Manufacturing labour	640,000[c]	480,000[d]	$ 640,000[c]	$ 480,000[d]
Manufacturing overhead	750,000	750,000	—	—
Marketing	2,000,000	2,000,000	—	—
Reorganization costs	—	90,000	—	90,000
Total costs	4,640,000	4,570,000	640,000	570,000
Operating income	$1,610,000	$1,680,000	$(640,000)	$(570,000)

$70,000 Difference $70,000 Difference

[a]25,000 units × $250 per unit = $6,250,000   [c]20 workers × 2,000 hours per worker × $16 per hour = $640,000
[b]25,000 units × $50 per unit = $1,250,000   [d]15 workers × 2,000 hours per worker × $16 per hour = $480,000

Exhibit 11-2 presents the quantitative data underlying the choice between the "do not rearrange" and the "rearrange" alternatives. The first two columns present *all data*. The last two columns present only relevant costs or revenues. The revenues, direct materials, manufacturing overhead, and marketing items can be ignored. Why? Because although they are expected future costs, they do not differ among the alternatives. They are thus irrelevant. The data in Exhibit 11-2 indicate that rearranging the production line will increase next year's predicted operating income by $70,000. Note that we reach the same conclusion whether we use all data or include only the relevant data in the analysis. By confining the analysis to only the relevant data, managers can clear away related but irrelevant data that might confuse them.

The difference in total cost between two alternatives is a **differential** or **net relevant cost.** The differential cost between alternatives 1 and 2 in Exhibit 11-2 is $70,000.

Quantitative and Qualitative Relevant Information

We divide the consequences of alternatives into two broad categories: *quantitative* and *qualitative*. **Quantitative factors** are outcomes that are measured in numerical terms. Some quantitative factors are financial—that is, they can be easily expressed in financial terms. Examples include the costs of direct materials, direct manufacturing labour, and marketing. Other quantitative factors are nonfinancial—that is, they can be measured numerically, but they are not expressed in financial terms. Reduction in product development time for a manufacturing company and the percentage of on-time flight arrivals for an airline company are examples of quantitative, nonfinancial factors. **Qualitative factors** are outcomes that cannot be measured in numerical terms. Employee morale is an example.

Cost analysis generally emphasizes quantitative factors that can be expressed in financial terms. Despite the difficulty and sometimes the impossibility of measuring qualitative and nonfinancial quantitative factors in financial terms, these factors remain important. Managers must at times give more weight to either qualitative or nonfinancial quantitative factors than to financial factors. For example, Precision Sporting Goods may find that it can purchase a part from an outside supplier at a

Managers may prefer to focus only on relevant revenues and relevant costs (the last two columns in Exhibit 11-2) because in doing so they reduce their information load by excluding irrelevant data. Too much information decreases rather than increases the quality of a manager's decisions as well as increases the time it takes to make decisions.

Differential cost (net relevant cost). Difference in total cost between two alternatives.

OBJECTIVE 3

Understand the difference between quantitative factors and qualitative factors in decisions

Quantitative factors. Outcomes that are measured in numerical terms.

Qualitative factors. Outcomes that cannot be measured in numerical terms.

price that is lower than what it costs to manufacture the part in-house. The company may still choose to make the part in-house because it feels that the supplier is unlikely to meet the demanding delivery schedule—a quantitative nonfinancial factor—and because purchasing the part from outside may adversely affect employee morale—a qualitative factor. Trading off nonfinancial and financial considerations is seldom easy.

AN ILLUSTRATION OF RELEVANCE: CHOOSING OUTPUT LEVELS

Managers often make decisions that affect output levels. For example, managers must choose whether to introduce a new product or sell more units of an existing product. When changes in output levels occur, managers are interested in the effect they have on the organization and on operating income. Why? Because maximizing organizational objectives (typically, operating income in our illustrations) also increases managers' rewards.

ONE-TIME-ONLY SPECIAL ORDERS

Management sometimes faces the decision of accepting or rejecting one-time-only special orders when there is idle production capacity and when the order has no long-run implications. We assume that all costs can be classified as either variable with respect to a single driver (units of output) or fixed. The following example illustrates how focusing on revenues, variable costs, and contribution margins can provide key information for decisions about the choice of output level. The example also indicates how reliance on unit-cost numbers calculated after allocating fixed costs can mislead managers about the effect that increasing output has on operating income.

Example 1: Surf Gear manufactures quality beach towels at its highly automated plant. The plant has a production capacity of 48,000 towels each month. Current monthly production is 30,000 towels. Retail department stores account for all existing sales. Expected results for the coming month (August) are shown in Exhibit 11-3. (These amounts are predictions based on past costs.) We assume all costs can be classified as either fixed or variable with respect to a single cost driver (units of output).

Exhibit 11-3 presents data in an absorption costing format: In this exhibit, the manufacturing cost of $12 per unit and the marketing cost of $7 per unit include both variable and fixed costs. The sum of all costs (variable and fixed) in a particular business function of the value chain, such as manufacturing costs or marketing costs, are called business function costs. Full product costs, in this case $19 per unit, are the sum of all variable and fixed costs in all business functions of the value chain (R&D, design, production, marketing, distribution, and customer service). For Surf Gear, full costs of the product consist of costs in manufacturing and marketing because these are the only business functions.

As a result of a strike at its existing towel supplier, a luxury hotel chain has offered to buy 5,000 towels from Surf Gear in August at $11 per towel. No subsequent sales to this hotel chain are anticipated. Fixed manufacturing costs are tied to the 48,000-towel production capacity. That is, fixed manufacturing costs relate to the production capacity available, regardless of the capacity used. If Surf Gear accepts the special order, it will use existing idle capacity to produce the 5,000 towels, and fixed manufacturing costs will not change. No marketing costs will be necessary for the 5,000-unit one-time-only special order. Accepting this special order is not expected to affect the selling price or the quantity of towels sold to regular customers. Should Surf Gear accept the hotel chain's offer?

No marketing costs are necessary for the special order, so the manager of Surf Gear will focus only on manufacturing costs. Based on the manufacturing cost per unit of $12—which is greater than the $11-per-unit price offered by the hotel chain—the manager might decide to reject the offer.

EXHIBIT 11-3
Budgeted Income Statement for August, Absorption-Costing Format for Surf Gear[a]

	A	B	C
1		Total	Per Unit
2	Units sold	30,000	
3			
4	Revenues	$ 600,000	$20.00
5	Cost of goods sold (manufacturing costs)		
6	Variable manufacturing costs	225,000	7.50[b]
7	Fixed manufacturing costs	135,000	4.50[c]
8	Total cost of goods sold	360,000	12.00
9	Marketing costs		
10	Variable marketing costs	150,000	5.00
11	Fixed marketing costs	60,000	2.00
12	Total marketing costs	210,000	7.00
13	Full costs of the product	570,000	19.00
14	Operating income	$ 30,000	$ 1.00
15			
16	[a]Surf Gear incurs no R&D, product-design, distribution, or customer-service costs		

17	[b]Variable manufacturing = Direct material + Direct manufacturing + Variable manufacturing
	   cost per unit cost per unit labour cost per unit overhead per unit
	      = $6.00 + $0.50 + $1.00 = $7.50		

18	[c]Fixed manufacturing = Fixed direct manufacturing + Fixed manufacturing
	   cost per unit labour cost per unit overhead per unit
	      = $1.50 + $3.00 = $4.50		

Exhibit 11-4 on p. 426 presents data in a contribution income statement format. The relevant costs are the expected future costs that differ between the alternatives— the variable manufacturing costs of $37,500 ($7.50 per unit × 5,000 units). The fixed manufacturing costs and all marketing costs (including variable marketing costs) are irrelevant in this case; they will not change in total whether or not the special order is accepted. Therefore, the only relevant items here are sales revenues and variable manufacturing costs. Given the $11 relevant revenue per unit (the special-order price) and the $7.50 relevant costs per unit, Surf Gear would gain an additional $17,500 [($11 − $7.50) × 5,000] in operating income per month by accepting the special order. In this example, comparisons based on either total amounts or relevant amounts (Exhibit 11-4) avoid the misleading implication of the absorption cost per unit (Exhibit 11-3).

The additional costs of $7.50 per unit that Surf Gear will incur if it accepts the special order for 5,000 towels are sometimes called incremental costs, outlay costs, or out-of-pocket costs. **Incremental, outlay,** or **out-of-pocket costs** are additional costs to obtain an additional quantity, over and above existing or planned quantities, of a cost object. Surf Gear could avoid these costs if it did not accept the special order. Surf Gear incurs no incremental fixed manufacturing costs if it accepts the special order; those costs will not change whether or not the special order is accepted. Fixed manufacturing costs do not change in Exhibit 11-4 because the analysis assumes that the 5,000-towel special order will use already acquired capacity that will otherwise remain idle for August and the two months following.

The assumption of no long-run implications is crucial in the analysis we present for the one-time-only special order decision. Suppose, for example, that Surf Gear is concerned that the retail department stores (its regular customers) will demand a lower price if it sells towels at $11 a towel to the luxury hotel chain. In this case, the analysis of the luxury hotel chain order must be modified to consider both the short-term benefits from accepting the order and the long-term consequences on Surf Gear's business and profitability.

Incremental costs (outlay costs, out-of-pocket costs). Additional costs to obtain an additional quantity over and above existing or planned quantities of a cost object.

EXHIBIT 11-4
Comparative Income Statements for August, Contribution Income Statement Format for Surf Gear

	A	B	C	D	E
1		Without One-Time-		With One-Time-Only	
2		Only Special Order		Special Order	Difference,
3		30,000 Units		35,000 Units	5,000 Units
4		Per Unit	Total	Total	Total
5	Sales	$20.00	$600,000	$655,000	$55,000
6	Variable costs:				
7	Manufacturing*	7.50	225,000	262,500	37,500
8	Marketing**	5.00	150,000	150,000	—
9	Total variable costs	12.50	375,000	412,500	37,500
10	Contribution margin	7.50	225,000	242,500	17,500
11					
12	Fixed costs:				
13	Manufacturing***	4.50	135,000	135,000	—
14	Marketing	2.00	60,000	60,000	—
15	Total fixed costs	6.50	195,000	195,000	—
16	Operating Income	$ 1.00	$ 30,000	$ 47,500	$17,500
17					
18	*Variable manufacturing costs = direct materials ($6) + direct manufacturing labour ($0.50) + manufacturing overhead ($1) = $7.50				
19	**No variable marketing costs are incurred for the 5,000 one-time-only special order @ $11/towel.				
20	***Fixed manufacturing costs = direct manufacturing labour ($1.50) + manufacturing overhead ($3) = $4.50. Note these are unaffected by the one-time-only special order.				

How Unit Costs Can Mislead

Unit-cost data can often help in the cost analysis. Nevertheless, they can also mislead decision-makers in two major ways:

1. **When irrelevant costs are included.** Consider the $4.50 per unit allocation of fixed direct manufacturing labour and manufacturing overhead costs in the one-time-only special-order decision for Surf Gear (see Exhibit 11-4). This $4.50 per unit cost is irrelevant given the assumptions of our example and therefore should be excluded.

2. **When unit costs at different output levels are compared.** Generally, managers use total fixed costs rather than unit costs. Then, if desired, the total fixed costs can be unitized. Machinery sales personnel, for example, may brag about the low unit costs of using their new machines. However, they sometimes neglect to say that the unit costs are based on outputs far in excess of their prospective customer's current or anticipated production levels. Consider, for example, a new machine that costs $100,000, is capable of producing 100,000 units over its useful life, and has a zero terminal disposal price. The salesperson may represent the machine-related costs per unit to be $1. This amount is incorrect if the company anticipates a total demand of, say, only 50,000 units over the useful life of the machine (unit cost would be $100,000 ÷ 50,000 = $2). Unitizing fixed costs over different production levels can be particularly misleading.

Pitfalls in Relevant-Cost Analysis

One pitfall in relevant-cost analysis is to assume that all variable costs are relevant. In the Surf Gear example, the marketing costs of $5 per unit are variable but not relevant. Why? Because for the special-order decision, Surf Gear incurs no incremental marketing costs.

A second pitfall is to assume that all fixed costs are irrelevant. Consider fixed manufacturing costs. In our example, we assume that the extra production of 5,000 towels per month does not affect fixed manufacturing costs. That is, we assume that the relevant range is at least from 30,000 to 35,000 towels per month. In some cases, however, the extra 5,000 towels might increase fixed manufacturing costs. Assume that Surf Gear would have to run three shifts of 16,000 towels per shift to achieve full capacity of 48,000 towels per month. Increasing the monthly production from 30,000 to 35,000 would require a partial third shift, because two shifts alone could produce only 32,000 towels. This extra shift would probably increase fixed manufacturing costs, thereby making any incremental fixed manufacturing costs relevant for this decision.

The best way to avoid these two pitfalls is to focus first and foremost on the relevance concept. Always require each item included in the analysis *both* (1) to be an expected future revenue or cost and (2) to differ between the alternatives.

Confusing Terminology

Many different terms are used to describe the costs of specific products and services. Exhibit 11-5 presents several different unit-cost numbers using the data from column 1 of Exhibit 11-4. **Business function costs** are the sum of all the costs (variable costs and fixed costs) in a particular business function in the value chain. For example, manufacturing costs are $12 per unit, and marketing costs are $7 per unit. For inventory costing purposes, absorption costs are often used as a synonym for manufacturing costs.

Business function costs. The sum of all the costs in a particular business function.

Full product costs refer to the sum of all the costs in all the business functions in the value chain (R&D, design, production, marketing, distribution, and customer service). Full product costs in Exhibit 11-5 are $19 per unit.

Managers use terms such as *business function costs* and *full product costs* differently. In a given situation, you must understand their exact meanings.

Full product costs. The sum of all the costs in all the business functions: R&D, design, production, marketing, distribution, and customer service.

EXHIBIT 11-5
Variety of Cost Terms for Surf Gear* Using Unit-Cost Data from Exhibit 11-4

	A	B	C	D	E	F
1		Variable	Fixed	Manufacturing		Full
2		Product	Product	(Absorption)	Marketing	Product
3		Costs	Costs	Costs**	Costs**	Costs
4	Variable manufacturing costs	$ 7.50		$ 7.50		$ 7.50
5	Variable marketing costs	5.00			$5.00	5.00
6	Fixed manufacturing costs		$4.50	4.50		4.50
7	Fixed marketing costs	—	2.00	—	2.00	2.00
8		$12.50	$6.50	$12.00	$7.00	$19.00
9						
10	*In this example marketing costs include distribution and customer service costs, and there are no R&D or product design costs.					
11	**Business function costs					

OUTSOURCING AND MAKE/BUY DECISIONS

We now consider a second common and important example of a company's decision to make a part or buy it. As in the previous section, we retain the assumption of idle capacity.

Outsourcing and Idle Facilities

Outsourcing is the process of purchasing goods and services from outside vendors rather than producing the same goods or providing the same services within the organization, which is called **insourcing.** For example, Kodak prefers to manufacture its own films (insourcing) but has IBM do its data processing (outsourcing). Toyota relies on outside vendors to supply some parts and components but chooses to manufacture other parts internally. In making decisions about outsourcing and insourcing, cost is a major factor.

Decisions about whether a producer of goods or services will insource or outsource are also called **make/buy decisions.** Sometimes qualitative factors dictate management's make/buy decision. For example, Dell Computers must buy the Pentium chip for its personal computers from Intel because it does not have the know-how and technology to make the chip itself. Sometimes a company may prefer to make the product in-house to retain control of the product and technology. For example, to safeguard Coca-Cola's formula, the company does not outsource the manufacture of its concentrate. What are the most important factors in the make/buy decision? Surveys of company practices indicate they are quality, dependability of supplies, and cost.

Example 2: The Soho Company manufactures a three-in-one stereo consisting of a CD player, a cassette deck, and a digital radio. Columns 1 and 2 of the following table show the current costs for manufacturing the CD-player unit of the stereo system based on an analysis of various manufacturing activities:

	Total Current Costs of Producing 1,000,000 Units in 2,500 Batches (1)	Current Cost per Unit (2) = (1) ÷ 1,000,000	Expected Total Costs of Producing 1,000,000 Units in 5,000 Batches Next Year (3)	Expected Cost per Unit (4) = (3) ÷ 1,000,000
Direct materials	$ 9,000,000	$ 9.00	$ 9,000,000	$ 9.00
Direct manufacturing labour	2,400,000	2.40	2,400,000	2.40
Variable manufacturing overhead costs of power and utilities	1,600,000	1.60	1,600,000	1.60
Mixed (variable and fixed) manufacturing overhead costs of materials handling and setup	1,750,000	1.75	2,000,000	2.00
Fixed manufacturing overhead costs of plant lease, insurance, and administration	3,000,000	3.00	3,000,000	3.00
Total manufacturing costs	$17,750,000	$17.75	$18,000,000	$18.00

Currently, materials-handling and setup activities occur each time a batch of CD players is made. Soho produces 1,000,000 CD players in 2,500 batches, with 400 units in each batch. The number of batches is the cost driver for these costs. Total materials-handling costs and setup costs equal fixed costs of $500,000 plus variable costs of $500 per batch [$500,000 + (2,500 batches × $500 per batch) = $1,750,000]. Soho is considering whether to produce CD players in smaller batch sizes. Soho

Outsourcing. Process of purchasing goods and services from outside vendors rather than producing the same goods or providing the same services within the firm.

Insourcing. Process of producing goods or providing services within the firm rather than purchasing those same goods or services from outside vendors.

Make/buy decisions. Decisions about whether a producer of goods or services will produce goods or services within the firm or purchase them from outside vendors.

Dell Computers
www.dell.ca

anticipates producing the 1,000,000 CD players next year in 5,000 batches of 200 units per batch. Through continuous improvement, the company expects to reduce variable costs for materials handling and setup to $300 per batch. No other changes in variable cost per unit or fixed costs are anticipated.

Another manufacturer offers to sell Soho 1,000,000 CD players next year for $16 per unit on whatever delivery schedule Soho wants. Assume that financial factors will be the basis of this make-or-buy decision. Should Soho make or buy the CD player?

Columns 3 and 4 of the preceding table indicate the expected total costs and expected cost per unit of producing 1,000,000 CD players next year. Direct material costs, direct manufacturing labour costs, and variable manufacturing overhead costs that vary with units produced are not expected to change because Soho plans to continue to produce 1,000,000 units next year at the same variable cost per unit as this year. Materials-handling and setup costs are expected to increase, even with no change in total production quantity. That's because these costs will vary with the number of batches, not the number of units produced. Soho's managers expect total materials-handling costs and setup costs to be $2,000,000 [$500,000 + (5,000 batches × the cost per batch of $300)]. Soho expects fixed manufacturing overhead costs to remain the same. The expected manufacturing cost per unit for next year is $18. At first glance, it appears that the company should buy CD players because the expected $18-per-unit cost of making the CD player is more than the $16 per unit to buy it. But a make/buy decision is often not obvious. To make a decision, management needs to answer the question: What is the difference in relevant costs between the alternatives?

For the moment, suppose (a) the capacity now used to make the CD players will become idle next year if the CD players are purchased and (b) the $3,000,000 of fixed manufacturing overhead will continue to be incurred next year, regardless of the decision made. Assume the $500,000 in fixed salaries to support materials handling and setup will not be incurred if the manufacture of CD players is completely shut down.

Exhibit 11-6 presents the relevant-cost computations. Note that Soho will *save* $1,000,000 by making CD players rather than buying them from the outside supplier. Making CD players is the preferred alternative. The figures in Exhibit 11-6 are valid only if the released facilities remain idle. If the component part is bought from the outside supplier, the released facilities can potentially be used for other, more profitable purposes. More generally, then, the choice in our example is not fundamentally whether to make or buy; it is how best to use available facilities.

EXHIBIT 11-6
Relevant (Incremental) Items for Make/Buy Decision for CD Players at Soho

	Total Relevant Costs		Relevant Cost Per Unit	
	Make	Buy	Make	Buy
Outside purchase of parts		$16,000,000		$16.00
Direct materials	$ 9,000,000		$ 9.00	
Direct manufacturing labour	2,400,000		2.40	
Direct manufacturing overhead	1,600,000		1.60	
Mixed (variable and fixed) materials handling and setup overhead	2,000,000	—	2.00	—
Total costs*	$15,000,000	$16,000,000	$15.00	$16.00
Difference in favour of making CD players	$1,000,000		$1.00	

*The $3,000,000 of plant-lease, plant-insurance, and plant-administration costs could be included under both alternatives. Conceptually, they do not belong in a listing of relevant costs because these costs are irrelevant to the decision. Practically, some managers prefer to include them in order to list all costs incurred under each alternative.

Note how the key concepts of relevance presented in Exhibit 11-6 apply here:

◆ Current cost data in Example 2 columns 1 and 2 (p. 428) play no role in the analysis in Exhibit 11-6 because for next year's make/buy decision these costs are past costs and, hence, irrelevant. Their usefulness lies in helping predict future costs.

◆ Exhibit 11-6 shows $2,000,000 of future materials-handling and setup costs under the make alternative but not under the buy alternative. Why? Because buying CD players rather than manufacturing them will save $2,000,000 in future variable costs per batch and avoidable fixed costs. The $2,000,000 represents future costs that differ between the alternatives and therefore is relevant to the make-or-buy decision.

◆ Exhibit 11-6 excludes the $3,000,000 of plant-lease, insurance, and administration costs under both alternatives. Why? Because these future costs will not differ between the alternatives; therefore, they are irrelevant.

In this example the incremental cost of making the CD players is the additional total cost of $15,000,000 that Soho will incur if it decides to manufacture rather than outsource the players. The $3,000,000 of fixed manufacturing overhead is not an incremental cost because Soho will incur these costs regardless of whether or not it makes the CD players. Similarly the incremental cost of outsourcing the CD players is the additional total cost of $16,000,000 that Soho will incur from the buy decision. A *differential cost* is the difference in total cost between two alternatives. In Exhibit 11-6, the differential cost ($16,000,000 − $15,000,000) is $1,000,000. Note that *incremental* and *differential cost* are sometimes interchanged in practice. When these terms are used, ensure you know what they mean.

We define *incremental revenue* and *differential revenue* similarly to incremental cost and differential cost. **Incremental revenue** is any additional total revenue from one alternative, whereas **differential revenue** is the difference between the total revenue of two or more alternatives.

Strategic and Qualitative Factors

Strategic and qualitative factors affect outsourcing decisions. For example, Soho may prefer to manufacture CD players in-house to retain control over the design, quality, reliability, and delivery schedules of the CD players it uses in its stereos. Conversely, despite the cost advantages documented in Exhibit 11-6, Soho may prefer to outsource, become a smaller and leaner organization, and focus on areas of its core competencies—the manufacture and sale of stereos. As an example of focus, advertising companies, such as J. Walter Thompson, only do the creative and planning aspects of advertising (their core competencies), and they outsource production activities, such as film, photographs, and illustrations.

Of course, outsourcing is not without its risks. As a company's dependence on its suppliers increases, suppliers could increase prices and let quality and delivery performance slip. To minimize these risks, companies generally enter into long-term contracts with their suppliers that specify costs, quality, and delivery schedules. Intelligent managers will build close partnerships or alliances with a few key suppliers, teaming with suppliers on design and manufacturing decisions and building a culture of and commitment to quality and timely delivery. Toyota goes so far as to send its own engineers to improve suppliers' processes. Companies such as Ford, Hyundai, Panasonic, and Sony have found that suppliers that are allowed to gain expertise and grow have researched and developed innovative new products, met demands for increased quantities, maintained quality and on-time delivery, and lowered costs—actions that the companies themselves would not have had the competencies to achieve. The Concepts in Action box describes how companies are outsourcing services to lower-cost countries, which is also called *offshoring*.

Outsourcing decisions invariably have a long-run horizon in which the financial costs and benefits of outsourcing become more uncertain. Almost always,

Incremental revenue. Added or unexpected revenue arising if a specified, previously unplanned alternative is chosen.

Differential revenue. The difference between the total revenue of two or more alternatives.

The Benefits and Costs of "Offshoring"

Recently, companies and public policy experts have engaged in a significant debate about "offshoring," which is the outsourcing of jobs to other countries. This increasingly prevalent practice involves replacing domestic employees with professionals in other countries at substantially lower labour costs. Typically, companies headquartered in the United States have outsourced jobs to India, China, Russia, Israel, and Ireland.

Offshoring is popular with companies because it yields significant cost savings. Within the high-tech sector, for example, a software developer for IBM in the United States costs US$56 an hour, whereas one in China costs only US$12.50 an hour, including salary and benefits. Similar opportunities for cost savings are found in the customer-service, technical-support, manufacturing, and supply-chain functions. Savings resulting from offshoring increase profits or are passed on to consumers via lower prices. McKinsey & Company, a consulting firm, estimates that in the long run outsourcing could result in as much as a 50% increase in profits for some American businesses.

However, offshoring does not come without costs, and these costs can be significant. A recent study by Hewitt Associates found that many companies fail to account for many of the costs associated with offshoring. Hewitt found, for example, that fewer than half of the companies had considered the effect of higher taxes in the countries where they were offshoring jobs, about 75% had not considered the impact of offshoring on costs in the rest of the supply chain, and only 34% had considered the costs of shutting down domestic facilities.

The economic impact of offshoring has so far been small. For example, even though American spending on offshore IT software and services rose from US$2.5 billion to US$10 billion during the 1998 to 2003 period, offshoring was responsible for fewer than 10% of the overall domestic job losses experienced within that sector. Furthermore, the U.S. Bureau of Labor Statistics predicts that there will be more than one million additional jobs for computer specialists in America before 2012. Nevertheless, outsourcing raises questions about how workers can be retrained and prepared for new high-skilled jobs.

Sources: M. Baily, *Exploding the Myths About Offshoring* (April 2004). Available from McKinsey & Company. http://www.mckinsey.com/knowledge/mgi/reports/Offshoring/exploding_myths.asp; W. Bulkeley, "IBM Documents Give Rare Look at Sensitive Plans on 'Offshoring'," *The Wall Street Journal*, January 19, 2004; D. Legard, "Gartner: Backlash Against Offshoring to Vanish by 2006," Infoword.com, June 15, 2004. http://www.infoworld.com/article/04/06/15/HNoffshorebacklash_1.html; *Offshoring: Is It a Win–Win Game?* (May 2004). Available from McKinsey & Company. http://www.mckinsey.com/knowledge/mgi/reports/offshore.asp; A. Reynolds, "Offshoring Which Jobs?" *Washington Times*, June 6, 2004. http://www.cato.org/dailys/06-13-04.html; "Study Notes Offshoring Downside," CNN/*Money*, March 5, 2004. http://money.cnn.com/2004/03/04/news/economy/outsourcing_costs/; *The Comprehensive Impact of Offshore IT Software and Services Outsourcing on the U.S. Economy and the IT Industry* (March 2004). Available from Global Insight. http://www.globalinsight.com/publicDownload/genericContent/03-30-04_execsum.pdf; "The Great Hollowing-Out Myth," *The Economist*, February 19, 2004. http://www.economist.com/agenda/PrinterFriendly.cfm?Story_ID=2454530

strategic and qualitative factors such as those described here become important determinants of the outsourcing decision. Weighing all these factors requires the exercise of considerable management judgment and care.

OPPORTUNITY COSTS AND OUTSOURCING

For purposes of the introductory example, the calculations in Exhibit 11-6 (p. 429) assumed that the capacity currently used to make CD players will remain idle if Soho purchases the parts from the outside manufacturer. However, the released capacity can be used for other, more profitable purposes. The choice Soho's managers are faced with then is not whether to make or buy but how best to use available production capacity.

OBJECTIVE 5

Describe the opportunity cost concept; explain why it is used in decision making

Example 3: Suppose that if Soho decides to buy CD players for its stereos from the outside supplier, then Soho's best use of the capacity that becomes available is to produce 500,000 Discmans, a portable, stand-alone CD player. From a manufacturing standpoint, Discmans are similar to stereo CD players. With help from operating managers, John Marquez, Soho's management accountant, estimates the following future revenues and costs if Soho decides to manufacture and sell Discmans:

Incremental future revenues		$8,000,000
Incremental future costs		
Direct materials	$3,400,000	
Direct manufacturing labour	1,000,000	
Variable overhead (utilities)	600,000	
Materials handling and setup overhead	500,000	
Total incremental future costs		5,500,000
Incremental future operating income		$2,500,000

Because of capacity constraints, Soho can make either CD players for its stereo unit or Discmans, but not both. Which of the following three alternatives should Soho choose?

1. Make stereo CD players and do not make Discmans
2. Buy stereo CD players and do not make Discmans
3. Buy stereo CD players and make Discmans

Exhibit 11-7, Panel A, summarizes the "total alternatives" approach—the incremental expected future costs and expected future revenues for *all* alternatives. Alternative 3, buying stereo CD players and using the available capacity to make and

You probably will find the total-alternatives approach easier to understand. To use it, merely analyze the cash flows into and out of the company. We suggest you use the total-alternatives approach until you are sufficiently comfortable with the concept of opportunity cost to use the opportunity-cost approach.

EXHIBIT 11-7
Total-Alternatives Approach and Opportunity-Cost Approach to Make/Buy Decisions for Soho Company

	Alternatives for Soho		
Relevant Items	**1. Make Stereo CD Players and Do Not Make Discmans**	**2. Buy Stereo CD Players and Do Not Make Discmans**	**3. Buy Stereo CD Players and Make Discmans**
PANEL A: Total-Alternatives Approach to Make/Buy Decisions			
Total incremental future costs of making/buying stereo CD players (from Exhibit 11-6)	$15,000,000	$16,000,000	$16,000,000
Deduct excess of future revenues over future costs from Discmans	0	0	(2,500,000)
Total relevant costs under total-alternatives approach	$15,000,000	$16,000,000	$13,500,000
PANEL B: Opportunity-Cost Approach to Make/Buy Decisions			
Total incremental future costs of making/buying stereo CD players (from Exhibit 11-6)	$15,000,000	$16,000,000	$16,000,000
Opportunity cost: Profit contribution forgone because capacity will not be used to make Discmans, the next-best alternative	2,500,000	2,500,000	0
Total relevant costs under opportunity-cost approach	$17,500,000	$18,500,000	$16,000,000

Note that the differences in costs across the columns in Panels A and B are the same: The cost of alternative 3 is $1,500,000 less than the cost of alternative 1, and $2,500,000 less than the cost of alternative 2.

sell Discmans, is the preferred alternative. The future incremental costs of buying stereo CD players from an outside supplier ($16,000,000) are more than the future incremental costs of making stereo CD players in-house ($15,000,000). But Soho can use the capacity freed up by buying stereo CD players to gain $2,500,000 in operating income (incremental future revenues of $8,000,000 minus total incremental future costs of $5,500,000) by making and selling Discmans. The *net relevant* costs of buying stereo CD players and making and selling Discmans are $16,000,000 − $2,500,000 = $13,500,000.

Note that the differences in costs across the columns in Panels A and B are the same: The cost of alternative 3 is $1,500,000 less than the cost of alternative 1, and $2,500,000 less than the cost of alternative 2.

Consider alternative 1, make stereo CD players and do not make Discmans, and ask, What are all the costs of making stereo CD players under this alternative? Certainly, Soho will incur $15,000,000 of incremental costs to make stereo CD players. But is this the entire cost? No, because by deciding to use limited manufacturing resources to make stereo CD players, Soho will give up the opportunity to earn $2,500,000 by not using these resources to make Discmans. Therefore, the relevant costs of making stereo CD players are the incremental costs of $15,000,000 plus the opportunity cost of $2,500,000.

Next consider alternative 2, buy stereo CD players and do not make Discmans. The incremental cost of buying stereo CD players will be $16,000,000. Similar to alternative 1, there is also an opportunity cost of $2,500,000 as a result of deciding not to make Discmans.

Finally, consider alternative 3, buy stereo CD players and make Discmans. The incremental cost of buying stereo CD players will be $16,000,000. The opportunity cost is zero. Why? Because by choosing this alternative, Soho will not forgo the profit it can earn from making and selling Discmans.

Panel B leads management to the same conclusion as Panel A: buying stereo CD players and making Discmans is the preferred alternative.

Panels A and B of Exhibit 11-7 describe two consistent approaches to decision making with capacity constraints. The total-alternatives approach in Panel A includes all future incremental costs and revenues. For example, under alternative 3, the additional future operating income from *using capacity to make and sell Discmans* ($2,500,000) is subtracted from the future incremental cost of buying stereo CD players ($16,000,000). The opportunity-cost analysis in Panel B takes the opposite approach. It focuses on stereo CD players. *Whenever capacity is not going to be used to make and sell Discmans*, the future forgone operating income is added as an opportunity cost of making or buying stereo CD players, as in alternatives 1 and 2. (Note that when Discmans are made, as in alternative 3, there is no "opportunity cost of not making Discmans.") Therefore, whereas Panel A *subtracts* $2,500,000 under alternative 3, Panel B *adds* $2,500,000 under alternative 1 and also under alternative 2. Panel B highlights the idea that when capacity is constrained, the relevant revenues and costs of any alternative equal the incremental future revenues and costs *plus* the opportunity cost. However, when more than two alternatives are being considered simultaneously, it is generally easier to use the total-alternatives approach.

Deciding to use a resource in a particular way causes a manager to give up the opportunity to use the resource in alternative ways. The lost opportunity is a cost that the manager must take into account when making a decision. **Opportunity cost** is the contribution to income that is forgone (rejected) by not using a limited resource in its next-best alternative use. Opportunity costs are not incorporated into formal financial accounting records. Why? Because historical record keeping is limited to transactions involving alternatives that were *actually selected*, rather than alternatives that were rejected. Rejected alternatives do not produce transactions and so they are not recorded. If Soho makes stereo CD players, it will not make Discmans, and it will not record any accounting entries for Discmans. Yet the opportunity cost of making stereo CD players, which equals the operating income that Soho forgoes by not making Discmans, is a crucial input into the make/buy decision. Consider again Exhibit 11-7, Panel B. On the basis of only the incremental costs systematically recorded in the accounting system, it is less costly for Soho to make rather than buy stereo CD players. Recognizing the opportunity cost of $2,500,000 leads to the different conclusion that it is preferable to buy stereo CD players.

Opportunity cost. The contribution to income that is forgone (rejected) by not using a limited resource in its best alternative use.

Suppose Soho has sufficient capacity to make Discmans even if it makes stereo CD players. In this case, Soho has a fourth alternative: make stereo CD players and make Discmans. For this alternative, the opportunity cost of making stereo CD players is $0 because Soho does not give up the $2,500,000 operating income from making Discmans even if it chooses to make stereo CD players. The relevant costs are $15,000,000 (incremental costs of $15,000,000 plus opportunity cost of $0). Under these conditions, Soho would prefer to make stereo CD players, rather than buy them, and also make Discmans.

Besides quantitative considerations, the make/buy decision should consider strategic and qualitative factors as well. If Soho decides to buy stereo CD players from an outside supplier, it should consider factors such as the supplier's reputation for quality and timely delivery. Soho would also want to consider the strategic consequences of selling Discmans. For example, will selling Discmans take Soho's focus away from its stereo business?

Carrying Costs of Inventory

The notion of opportunity cost can also be illustrated using Soho. Soho will pay cash for the stereo CD players it buys. Based on the information below, which purchasing alternative is more economical for Soho?

Annual estimated stereo CD player requirements for next year	1,000,000 units
Cost per unit when each purchase is equal to 10,000 units	$ 16.00
Cost per unit when each purchase is equal to or greater than 500,000 units; $16 minus 1% discount	$ 15.84
Cost of a purchase order	$ 500.00

Alternatives under consideration:
  A. Make 100 purchases of 10,000 units each during the next year
  B. Make 2 purchases of 500,000 units each during the next year

Average investment in inventory:
  A. *(10,000 units × $16.00 per unit) ÷ 2 $ 80,000
  B. *(500,000 units × $15.84 per unit) ÷ 2 $3,960,000

Annual rate of return if the cash is invested elsewhere (e.g., bonds or shares) at the same level of risk as the investment in inventory   9.0%

The example assumes that stereo-CD-player purchases will be used up uniformly throughout the year. The average investment in inventory during the year is the cost of inventory when a purchase is received plus the cost of inventory just prior to the delivery of the next purchase (in this example zero) divided by 2.

The following table presents two alternatives:

	Alternative A: Make 100 Purchases of 10,000 Units Each During the Year (1)	Alternative B: Make 2 Purchases of 500,000 Units Each During the Year (2)	Difference (3) = (1) − (2)
Annual purchase-order costs (100 purchase orders × $500/purchase order; 2 purchase orders × $500/purchase order)	$ 50,000	$ 1,000	$ 49,000
Annual purchase costs (1,000,000 units × $16.00/unit; 1,000,000 units × $15.84/unit)	16,000,000	15,840,000	160,000
Annual rate of return that could be earned if investment in inventory were invested elsewhere at the same level of risk (opportunity cost) (0.09 × $80,000; 0.09 × $3,960,000)	7,200	356,400	(349,200)
Relevant costs	$16,057,200	$16,197,400	$(140,200)

The opportunity cost of holding inventory is the income forgone by tying up money in inventory and not investing it elsewhere. The opportunity cost would not be recorded in the accounting system because, once the alternative of investing money elsewhere is rejected, there are no transactions related to this alternative to record. On the basis of the costs recorded in the accounting system (purchase-order costs and purchase costs), Soho would erroneously conclude that making two purchases of 500,000 units each is the least costly alternative. Column 3, however, indicates that, consistent with the trends toward holding smaller inventories, purchasing smaller quantities of 10,000 units 100 times a year is preferred to purchasing 500,000 units twice during the year. Why? Because the lower opportunity cost of holding smaller inventory exceeds the higher purchase and ordering costs. If the opportunity cost of money tied up in inventory were greater than 9% per year, or if other incremental benefits of holding lower inventory were considered—such as lower insurance, materials-handling, storage, obsolescence, and breakage costs—making 100 purchases would be even more economical.

PRODUCT MIX DECISIONS UNDER CAPACITY CONSTRAINTS

Companies with capacity constraints, such as Soho, must also often decide which products to make and in what quantities. When a multiple-product plant operates at full capacity, managers must often make decisions regarding which products to emphasize. These decisions frequently have a short-run focus. For example, General Mills must continually adapt the mix of its different products to short-run fluctuations in materials costs, selling prices, and demand. Throughout this section, we assume that, as short-run changes in product mix occur, the only costs that change are those that are variable with respect to the number of units produced (and sold).

Analysis of individual product contribution margins provides insight into the product mix that maximizes operating income. Consider Power Engines, a company that manufactures engines for a broad range of commercial and consumer products. At its Calgary, Alberta, plant, it assembles two engines—a snowmobile engine and a boat engine. Information on these products is as follows:

OBJECTIVE 6

Describe the key concept in choosing which among multiple products to produce when there are capacity constraints

General Mills
www.generalmills.com

	Snowmobile Engine	Boat Engine
Selling price	$800	$1,000
Variable costs per unit	560	625
Contribution margin per unit	$240	$ 375

At first glance, boat engines appear more profitable than snowmobile engines. The product to be emphasized, however, is not necessarily the product with the higher individual contribution margin per unit. Rather, managers should aim for the *highest contribution margin per unit of the constraining factor*—that is, the scarce, limiting, or critical factor. The constraining factor restricts or limits the production or sale of a given product. (See also Chapter 19 on the theory of constraints.)

Assume that only 600 machine-hours are available daily for assembling engines. Additional capacity cannot be obtained in the short run. Power Engines can sell as many engines as it produces. The constraining factor, then, is machine-hours. It takes two machine-hours to produce one snowmobile engine and five machine-hours to produce one boat engine.

	Snowmobile Engine	Boat Engine
Contribution margin per engine	$240	$375
Machine-hours required to produce one engine	2 machine-hours	5 machine-hours
Contribution margin per machine-hour (240 ÷ 2; 375 ÷ 5)	$120	$75
Total contribution margin for 600 machine-hours ($120 × 600; $75 × 600)	$72,000	$45,000

Producing snowmobile engines contributes more margin per machine-hour, which is the constraining factor in this example. Therefore, choosing to emphasize snowmobile engines is the correct decision. Other constraints in manufacturing settings can be the availability of direct materials, components, or skilled labour, as well as financial and sales considerations. In a retail department store, the constraining factor may be linear metres of display space. The greatest possible contribution margin per unit of the constraining factor yields the maximum operating income.

As you can imagine, in many cases a manufacturer or retailer must meet the challenge of trying to maximize total operating income for a variety of products, each with more than one constraining factor. The problem of formulating the most profitable production schedules and the most profitable product mix is essentially that of maximizing the total contribution margin in the face of many constraints. Optimization techniques, such as the linear programming technique discussed in the appendix to this chapter, help solve these complicated problems.

Finally, there is the question of managing the bottleneck constraint to increase output and, therefore, contribution margin. Can the available machine-hours for assembling engines be increased beyond 600, for example, by reducing idle time? Can the time needed to assemble each snowmobile engine (two machine-hours) and each boat engine (five machine-hours) be reduced, for example, by reducing setup time and processing time of assembly? Can quality be improved so that constrained capacity is used to produce only good units rather than some good and some defective units? Can some of the assembly operations be outsourced to allow more engines to be built? Implementing any of these options will likely require Power Engines to incur incremental costs. Power Engines will implement only those options whose benefits of higher contribution margins exceed the costs. *Instructors and students who, at this point, want to explore these issues in more detail can go to the section in Chapter 19 titled "Theory of Constraints and Throughput Contribution Analysis" (pp. 755–759) and then return to this chapter without any loss of continuity.*

CUSTOMER PROFITABILITY, ACTIVITY-BASED COSTING, AND RELEVANT COSTS

The Allied West example illustrates a keep-or-discontinue decision, but the object of the decision is a *customer* rather than a *product*. The example uses activity-based costing concepts that you are familiar with from Chapter 5.

In addition to making choices among products, companies must often decide about whether they should add some customers and drop others. This section illustrates relevant-revenue and relevant-cost analysis when different cost drivers are identified for different activities in activity-based costing. The cost object in our example is customers. The analysis focuses on customer profitability at Allied West, the west coast sales office of Allied Furniture, a wholesaler of specialized furniture.

Allied West supplies furniture to three local retailers, Vogel, Brenner, and Wisk. Exhibit 11-8 presents representative revenues and costs of Allied West by customers for the year 2007. Additional information on Allied West's costs for different activities at various levels of the cost hierarchy is as follows:

1. Materials-handling labour costs vary with the number of units of furniture shipped to customers.

2. Different areas of the warehouse stock furniture for different customers. Materials-handling equipment in an area and amortization costs on the equipment are identified with individual customer accounts. Any equipment not used remains idle. The equipment has a one-year useful life and zero disposal price.

3. Allied West allocates rent to each customer account based on the amount of warehouse space occupied by the products to be shipped to that customer.

4. Marketing costs vary with the number of sales visits made to customers.

5. Purchase order costs vary with the number of purchase orders received; delivery processing costs vary with the number of shipments made.

6. Allied West allocates fixed general administration costs to customers based on dollar sales made to each customer.

EXHIBIT 11-8
Customer Profitability Analysis for Allied West

	Vogel	Brenner	Wisk	Total
Sales	$500,000	$300,000	$400,000	$1,200,000
Cost of goods sold	370,000	220,000	330,000	920,000
Materials-handling labour	41,000	18,000	33,000	92,000
Materials-handling equipment cost written off as amortization	10,000	6,000	8,000	24,000
Rent	14,000	8,000	14,000	36,000
Marketing support	11,000	9,000	10,000	30,000
Purchase orders and delivery processing	13,000	7,000	12,000	32,000
General administration	20,000	12,000	16,000	48,000
Total operating costs	479,000	280,000	423,000	1,182,000
Operating income	$ 21,000	$ 20,000	$(23,000)	$ 18,000
Allocated corporate costs				24,000
				$ (6,000)

Relevant-Cost Analysis of Discontinuing a Customer

Exhibit 11-8 indicates a loss of $23,000 on sales to Wisk. Allied West's manager believes this loss occurred because Wisk places many low-volume orders with Allied, resulting in high purchase order, delivery processing, materials-handling, and marketing activity. Allied West is considering several possible actions with respect to the Wisk account—reducing its own costs of supporting Wisk by becoming more efficient, cutting back on some of the services it offers Wisk, charging Wisk higher prices, or dropping the Wisk account. The following analysis focuses on the operating income effect of dropping the Wisk account.

The key question is what are the relevant costs and relevant revenues? The following information about the effect of reducing various activities related to the Wisk account is available.

1. Dropping the Wisk account will save cost of goods sold, materials-handling labour, marketing support, purchase order, and delivery processing costs incurred on the Wisk account.

2. Dropping the Wisk account will mean that the warehouse space currently occupied by products for Wisk and the materials-handling equipment used to move them will become idle.

3. Dropping the Wisk account will have no effect on fixed general administration costs.

Exhibit 11-9 on p. 438 presents the relevant-cost computations. Allied West's operating income will be $15,000 lower if it drops the Wisk account, so Allied decides to keep the Wisk account. The last column in Exhibit 11-9 shows that the cost savings from dropping the Wisk account, $385,000, is not enough to offset the loss of $400,000 in revenue. The key reason is that amortization, rent, and general administration costs will not decrease if the Wisk account is dropped.

Now suppose that if Allied drops the Wisk account, it could lease the extra warehouse space to the Sanchez Corporation, which has offered $20,000 per year for it. Then the $20,000 that Allied would receive would be the opportunity cost of continuing to use the warehouse to service Wisk. Allied would gain $5,000 by dropping the Wisk account ($20,000 from lease revenue minus lost operating income of $15,000). Before reaching a final decision, however, Allied must examine whether Wisk can be made more profitable so that supplying products to Wisk earns more

EXHIBIT 11-9
Relevant-Cost Analysis for Allied West Dropping the Wisk Account

	Amount of Total Revenues and Total Costs		Difference: Incremental (Loss in Revenue and Savings in Costs from Dropping Wisk Account)
	Keep Wisk Account	Drop Wisk Account	
Sales	$1,200,000	$800,000	$(400,000)
Cost of goods sold	920,000	590,000	330,000
Materials-handling labour	92,000	59,000	33,000
Materials-handling equipment cost written off as amortization	24,000	24,000	—
Rent	36,000	36,000	—
Marketing support	30,000	20,000	10,000
Purchase orders and delivery processing	32,000	20,000	12,000
General administration	48,000	48,000	—
Total operating costs	1,182,000	797,000	385,000
Operating income	$ 18,000	$ 3,000	$ (15,000)

than the $20,000 from leasing to Sanchez. Allied must also consider qualitative factors such as the effect of the decision on Allied's reputation for developing stable, long-run business relationships.

Relevant-Cost Analysis of Adding a Customer

Suppose that in addition to dropping the Wisk account, Allied is evaluating the profitability of substituting a customer, Loral. Allied is already paying rent of $36,000 for the warehouse and is incurring general administration costs of $48,000. These costs will not change if Loral is added as a customer. Loral is a customer with a profile much like Wisk's. Suppose Allied predicts other revenues and costs of doing business with Loral to be the same as those described under the Wisk column of Exhibit 11-8. Should Allied substitute Loral as a customer? Exhibit 11-10 shows incremental revenues exceed incremental costs by $7,000. Allied would prefer to substitute Loral as a customer for Wisk. One key point is that the cost of acquiring new equipment to support the Loral order (written off as amortization of $8,000 in Exhibit 11-10) is included as a relevant cost. Why? Because this cost can be avoided if Allied decides not to do business with Loral. Note the critical distinction here. Amortization cost is irrelevant in deciding whether to drop Wisk as a customer (because it is a past cost), but the purchase cost of the new equipment that will then be written off as amortization in the future is relevant in deciding whether to add Loral as a new customer.

Relevant-Revenue and Relevant-Cost Analysis of Discontinuing or Adding Branches or Segments

Companies periodically confront decisions about discontinuing or adding branches or business segments. For example, given Allied West's expected loss of $6,000 (see Exhibit 11-8), should it be closed? Assume that closing Allied West will have no effect on total corporate-office costs.

Exhibit 11-11, column 1, presents the relevant-revenue and relevant-cost analysis using data from the Total column in Exhibit 11-8. The revenue losses of

EXHIBIT 11-10
Relevant-Cost Analysis for Dropping the Wisk Account and Adding the Loral Account

	(Loss in Revenues) and Savings in Costs from Dropping Wisk Account (1)	Incremental Revenues and (Incremental Costs) from Adding Loral Account (2)
Revenues	$(400,000)	$400,000
Cost of goods sold	330,000	(330,000)
Furniture-handling labour	33,000	(33,000)
Furniture-handling equipment cost written off as amortization	0	(8,000)
Rent	0	0
Marketing support	10,000	(10,000)
Sales-order and delivery processing	12,000	(12,000)
General administration	0	0
Corporate-office costs	0	0
Total costs	385,000	(393,000)
Effect on operating income (loss)	$ (15,000)	$ 7,000

$1,200,000 will exceed the cost savings of $1,158,000, leading to a decrease in operating income of $42,000. Allied West should not be closed down. The key reasons are that closing Allied West will not save amortization costs of $24,000, which is a past or sunk cost (see p. 441), and actual total corporate costs. Corporate costs allocated to various sales offices will change but not decline in total. The $24,000 no longer allocated to Allied West will be allocated to other sales offices. Therefore, the $24,000 of allocated corporate costs should not be included as expected cost savings from closing Allied West.

EXHIBIT 11-11
Relevant-Revenue and Relevant-Cost Analysis for Closing Allied West and Opening Allied South

	(Loss in Revenues) and Savings in Costs from Closing Allied West (1)	Incremental Revenues and (Incremental Costs) from Opening Allied South (2)
Revenues	$(1,200,000)	$1,200,000
Cost of goods sold	920,000	(920,000)
Furniture-handling labour	92,000	(92,000)
Furniture-handling equipment cost written off as amortization	0	(25,000)
Rent	36,000	(36,000)
Marketing support	30,000	(30,000)
Sales-order and delivery processing	32,000	(32,000)
General administration	48,000	(48,000)
Corporate-office costs	0	0
Total costs	1,158,000	(1,183,000)
Effect on operating income (loss)	$ (42,000)	$ 17,000

Now suppose Allied Furniture has the opportunity to open another sales office, Allied South, whose revenues and costs would be identical to Allied West's costs, including a cost of $25,000 to acquire material-handling equipment with a one-year useful life and zero disposal value. Opening this office will have no effect on total corporate costs. Should Allied Furniture open Allied South? Exhibit 11-11, column 2, indicates that it should do so because opening Allied South will increase operating income by $17,000. As before, the cost of new equipment (written off as amortization) is relevant. But the point here is to ignore allocated corporate costs and focus on actual total corporate-office costs. Total corporate costs will not change if Allied South is opened and, hence, these costs are irrelevant.

IRRELEVANCE OF PAST COSTS AND EQUIPMENT REPLACEMENT DECISIONS

Book value. The original cost minus accumulated amortization of an asset.

The illustrations in this chapter have shown that expected future costs that do not differ among alternatives are irrelevant. Now we return to the idea that all past costs are irrelevant.

Consider an example of equipment replacement. The irrelevant cost illustrated here is the **book value** (original cost minus accumulated amortization) of the existing equipment. Assume that the Tormart Company is considering replacing a metal-cutting machine for aircraft parts with a more technically advanced model. The new machine has an automatic quality-testing capability and is more efficient than the old machine. The new machine, however, has a shorter life. The Tormart Company uses the straight-line amortization method. Sales of aircraft parts ($1.1 million per year) will be unaffected by the replacement decision. Summary data on the existing machine and the replacement machine are as follows:

Original cost	$1,000,000	$600,000
Useful life	5 years	2 years
Current age	3 years	0 years
Remaining useful life	2 years	2 years
Accumulated amortization	$600,000	Not acquired yet
Book value	$400,000	Not acquired yet
Current disposal value (in cash)	$40,000	Not acquired yet
Terminal disposal value (in cash 2 years from now)	$0	$0
Annual operating costs (maintenance, energy, repairs, coolants, and so on)	$800,000	$460,000

To focus on the main concept of relevance, we ignore the time value of money in this illustration.

Exhibit 11-12 presents a cost comparison of the two machines. Some managers would not replace the old machine because it would entail recognizing a $360,000 "loss on disposal" ($400,000 book value minus $40,000 current disposal price); retention would allow spreading the $400,000 book value over the next two years in the form of "amortization expense" (a term more appealing than "loss on disposal").

We can apply our definition of relevance to four commonly encountered items in equipment replacement decisions such as the one facing Tormart Company:

1. *Book value of old machine.* Irrelevant, because it is a past (historical) cost. All past costs are "down the drain." Nothing can change what has already been spent or what has already happened.

2. *Current disposal price of old machine.* Relevant, because it is an expected future cash inflow that differs between alternatives.

3. *Gain or loss on disposal.* This is the algebraic difference between items 1 and 2. It is a meaningless combination blurring the distinction between the irrelevant

Although the book value of old equipment is irrelevant in a keep-or-replace decision, managers may still be concerned about book value for two reasons: (1) if the equipment is replaced, the entire "Loss on Disposal" will appear in the current period's income statement, and (2) it is undesirable to admit a loss.

EXHIBIT 11-12
Cost Comparison—Replacement of Machinery, Including Relevant and Irrelevant Items for the Tormart Company

	Two Years Together		
	Keep	Replace	Difference
Sales	$2,200,000	$2,200,000	—
Operating costs:			
Cash operating costs	1,600,000	920,000	$680,000
Old machine book value:			
Periodic writeoff as amortization	400,000	—	—
or Lump sum writeoff	—	400,000* ⎫	
Current disposal price of old machine	—	(40,000)* ⎬	40,000
New machine cost, written off		⎭	
periodically as amortization	—	600,000	(600,000)
Total operating costs	2,000,000	1,880,000	120,000
Operating income	$ 200,000	$ 320,000	$120,000

*In a formal income statement, these two items would be combined as "loss on disposal of machine" of $360,000.

book value and the relevant disposal price. Each item should be considered separately.

4. *Cost of new machine.* Relevant, because it is an expected future cash outflow that will differ between alternatives.

Exhibit 11-12 should clarify these four assertions. The difference column in Exhibit 11-12 shows that the book value of the old machine is not an element of difference between alternatives and could be completely ignored for decision-making purposes. No matter what the timing of the charge against revenue, the amount charged is still $400,000 regardless of the alternative chosen because it is a past (historical) cost. Note that the advantage of replacing is $120,000 for the two years together.

In either event, the unamortized cost will be written off with the same ultimate effect on operating income. The $400,000 enters into the income statement either as a $400,000 offset against the $40,000 proceeds to obtain the $360,000 loss on disposal in the current year or as $200,000 amortization in each of the next two years. But how it appears in the income statement is irrelevant to the replacement decision. In contrast, the $600,000 cost of the new machine is relevant because it can be avoided by deciding not to replace.

Past costs that are unavoidable because they cannot be changed, no matter what action is taken, are sometimes described as **sunk costs.** In our example, old equipment has a book value of $400,000 and a current disposal price of $40,000. What are the sunk costs in this case? The entire $400,000 is sunk and down the drain because it represents an outlay made in the past that cannot be changed. Thus, past costs and sunk costs are synonyms.

Sunk costs. Past costs that are unavoidable because they cannot be changed no matter what action is taken.

Exhibit 11-13 on p. 442 concentrates on relevant items only. Note that the same answer (the $120,000 net difference) will be obtained even though the book value is completely omitted from the calculations. The only relevant items are the cash operating costs, the disposal price of the old machine, and the cost of the new machine (represented as amortization in Exhibit 11-13).

Decision makers vary in their preference between the formats presented in Exhibits 11-12 and 11-13. Some prefer the format used in Exhibit 11-12, because it illustrates why some items are irrelevant to the decision. Other managers prefer the format used in Exhibit 11-13, because it is concise.

EXHIBIT 11-13

Cost Comparison—Replacement of Machinery, Relevant Items Only for the Tormart Company

	Two Years Together		
	Keep	**Replace**	**Difference**
Cash operating costs	$1,600,000	$ 920,000	$680,000
Current disposal price of old machine	—	(40,000)	40,000
New machine, written off periodically as amortization	—	600,000	(600,000)
Total relevant costs	$1,600,000	$1,480,000	$120,000

DECISIONS AND PERFORMANCE EVALUATION

Consider our equipment replacement example in light of the five-step sequence in Exhibit 11-1.

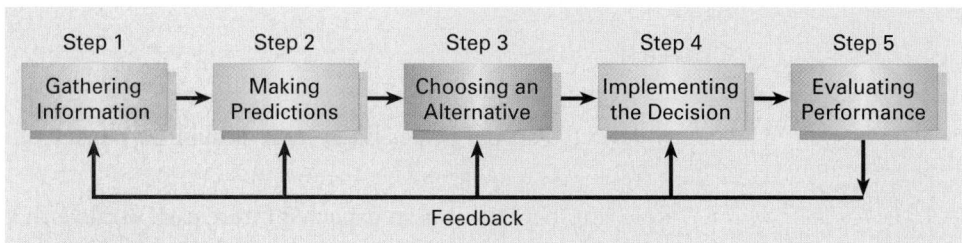

If the decision model (step 3) demands choosing the alternative that will minimize total costs over the life span of the equipment, then the analysis in Exhibits 11-12 and 11-13 dictates replacing rather than keeping. In the real world, however, would the manager replace? The answer depends on the manager's perceptions of whether the decision model is consistent with the performance evaluation model (step 5). The performance evaluation model describes the basis on which the manager's performance is judged.

Managers tend to favour the alternative that makes their performance look best. If the performance evaluation model conflicts with the decision model, the performance evaluation model often prevails in influencing a manager's behaviour. For example, the decision model in Exhibit 11-12, based on a relevant cost analysis over the life of the two machines, favours replacing the machine. But if the manager's promotion or bonus hinges on the first year's operating income performance under accrual accounting, the manager's temptation *not* to replace will be overwhelming. Why? Because the accrual accounting model for measuring performance will show a higher first-year operating income if the old machine is kept than if it is replaced (as the following table shows):

	First-Year Results: Accrual Accounting			
	Keep		**Replace**	
Revenues		$1,100,000		$1,100,000
Operating costs				
Cash operating costs	$800,000		$460,000	
Amortization	200,000		300,000	
Loss on disposal	—		360,000	
Total operating costs		1,000,000		1,120,000
Operating income (loss)		$ 100,000		$ (20,000)

Even if top management's goals are long term (and consistent with the decision model), the subordinate manager's concern is more likely to be short term if his or her evaluation is based on short-run measures such as operating income.

Resolving the conflict between the decision model and the performance evaluation model is frequently a baffling problem in practice. In theory, resolving the difficulty seems obvious—merely design consistent models. Consider our replacement example. Year-by-year effects on operating income of replacement can be budgeted over the planning horizon of two years. The manager would be evaluated on the understanding that the first year would be expected to be poor, the next year much better.

The practical difficulty is that accounting systems rarely track each decision separately. Performance evaluation focuses on responsibility centres for a specific time period, not on projects or individual items of equipment for their entire useful lives. Therefore, the impacts of many different decisions are combined in a single performance report. Top management, through the reporting system, is rarely aware of particular desirable alternatives that were not chosen by subordinate managers.

Consider another conflict between the decision model and the performance evaluation model. Suppose a manager buys a particular machine only to discover that a better machine could have been purchased in its place. The decision model may suggest replacing the existing machine with the better machine, but the manager may be reluctant to do so. Why? Because replacing the machine so soon after its purchase may reflect badly on the manager's capabilities and performance. If the manager's superiors have no knowledge of the better machine, the manager may prefer to keep, rather than replace, the existing machine (see Focus on Values and Behaviours).

FOCUS ON VALUES AND BEHAVIOURS

Beyond the Walls of the Accounting Department

It is not unusual to find management accountants on the manufacturing floor, at the warehouse, in the offices of marketing and sales managers, and in customer-service centres. Why do management accountants spend so much time "in the field"? To properly apply relevant-revenue and relevant-cost concepts to decisions, management accountants must have a good understanding of the business context of decisions. Such an understanding often will lead management accountants to ask questions not considered by others: Is this really a one-time-only special order? What else, if anything, could we do with freed-up capacity if we outsourced a component part? Which resource is constrained and what is the contribution margin per unit of the constrained resource? How would total costs change if we dropped a customer or product line? Managers expect management accountants to articulate clearly why these questions are important. Therefore, management accountants need to build the skill to communicate concepts of relevance and opportunity cost in the simplest possible terms. Management accountants also have the responsibility to make managers aware of qualitative and nonfinancial factors such as the negative effect on employee morale of laying off workers.

Management accountants also need to be alert and informed about conflicts that can arise between models of decision making and performance evaluation. When such conflicts occur, management accountants have the responsibility to explain to managers why the decisions being made are not in the best long-run interests of the company and propose changes in the performance-evaluation model that will minimize these conflicts.

Many companies—such as Cisco Systems, General Electric, and Novartis—design systems that seek to align decision-making models and performance-evaluation models. For example, these companies evaluate the performance of their business-unit managers on the basis of division operating income reduced by an imputed interest cost representing the holding cost of assets, such as inventory and accounts receivable. In this way, the opportunity costs of holding assets that managers include in their decision models are also considered when evaluating the managers' performance, even though these opportunity costs are not recorded in the financial accounting system. As a result, managers in these companies constantly seek ways to increase operating income while reducing investments in assets.

Wally Lewis is manager of the engineering development division of Goldcoast Products. Lewis has just received a proposal signed by all 10 of his engineers to replace the workstations with networked personal computers (networked PCs). Lewis is not enthusiastic about the proposal.

Data on workstations and networked PCs are:

	Workstations	Networked PCs
Original cost	$300,000	$135,000
Useful life	5 years	3 years
Current age	2 years	0 years
Remaining useful life	3 years	3 years
Accumulated amortization	$120,000	Not acquired yet
Current book value	$180,000	Not acquired yet
Current disposal value (in cash)	$95,000	Not acquired yet
Terminal disposal value (in cash 3 years from now)	$0	$0
Annual computer-related cash operating costs	$40,000	$10,000
Annual revenues	$1,000,000	$1,000,000
Annual non–computer-related operating costs	$880,000	$880,000

Lewis's annual bonus includes a component based on division operating income. He has a promotion possibility next year that would make him a group vice-president of Goldcoast Products.

REQUIRED
1. Compare the costs of the workstation and networked PC options. Consider the cumulative results for the three years together, ignoring the time value of money.
2. Why might Lewis be reluctant to purchase the ten networked personal computers?

SOLUTION
1. The following table considers all cost items when comparing future costs of the workstation and networked PC options:

All Items	Three Years Together		
	Workstations	Networked PCs	Difference
Revenues	$3,000,000	$3,000,000	—
Operating costs:			
Non-computer-related operating costs	2,640,000	2,640,000	—
Computer-related cash operating costs	120,000	30,000	$ 90,000
Workstation book value:			
Periodic writeoff as amortization	180,000	—	
or Lump sum writeoff	—	180,000	}
Current disposal price of workstations	—	(95,000)	95,000
Networked PCs, written off periodically as amortization		135,000	(135,000)
Total operating costs	2,940,000	2,890,000	50,000
Operating income	$ 60,000	$ 110,000	$ 50,000

Alternatively, the analysis could focus on only those items in the preceding table that differ across the alternatives.

Relevant Items	Three Years Together		
	Workstations	Networked PCs	Difference
Computer-related cash operating costs	$120,000	$ 30,000	$ 90,000
Current disposal price of workstations	—	(95,000)	95,000
Networked PCs, written off periodically as amortization	—	135,000	(135,000)
Total relevant costs	$120,000	$ 70,000	$ 50,000

The analysis suggests that it is cost-effective to replace the workstations with the networked PCs.

2. The accrual accounting operating incomes for the first year under the "keep workstations" versus the "buy networked PCs" alternatives are as follows:

	Keep Workstations		Buy Networked PCs	
Revenues		$1,000,000		$1,000,000
Operating costs:				
Non-computer-related operating costs	$880,000		$880,000	
Computer-related cash operating costs	40,000		10,000	
Amortization	60,000		45,000	
Loss on disposal of workstations	—		85,000*	
Total operating costs		980,000		1,020,000
Operating income		$ 20,000		$ (20,000)

*$85,000 = book value of mainframe, $180,000 − current disposal price, $95,000.

Lewis would probably react negatively to the expected operating loss of $20,000 if the workstations are replaced as compared to an operating income of $20,000 if the workstations are kept. The decision would eliminate the component of his bonus based on operating income. He might also perceive the $20,000 operating loss as reducing his chances of being promoted to a group vice-president.

DECISION POINTS
SUMMARY

The following question-and-answer format summarizes the chapter's learning objectives. Each decision presents a key question related to a learning objective. The guidelines are the answer to that question.

DECISIONS	GUIDELINES
1. What is the five-step process that can be used to make decisions?	The five-step decision process is (a) obtain information, (b) make predictions, (c) choose an alternative, (d) implement the decision, and (e) evaluate performance to provide feedback.
2. When is a revenue or cost relevant for a particular decision?	To be relevant for a particular decision, a revenue or cost must meet two criteria: (a) it must be an expected future revenue or expected future cost, and (b) it must differ among alternative courses of action.
3. Should both quantitative and qualitative factors be considered in making decisions?	Yes. The outcomes of alternative actions can be quantitative and qualitative. Quantitative outcomes are measured in numerical terms. Some quantitative outcomes can be expressed in financial terms, others cannot. Qualitative factors, such as employee morale, are difficult to measure accurately in numerical terms. Consideration must be given to both quantitative and qualitative factors in making decisions.
4. What potential problems should be avoided in relevant-cost analysis?	Two potential problems to avoid in relevant-cost analysis are (a) making incorrect general assumptions—such as all variable costs are relevant and all fixed costs are irrelevant—and (b) losing sight of grand totals, focusing instead on unit amounts.

DECISIONS	GUIDELINES
5. What is an opportunity cost and why should it be included when making decisions?	Opportunity cost is the contribution to income that is forgone or rejected by not using a limited resource in its next-best alternative use. Opportunity cost is included in decision making because it represents the best alternative way in which an organization could have used its resources had it not made the decision it did.
6. When resources are constrained, how should managers choose which of multiple products to produce and sell?	Under these conditions, managers should select the product that yields the highest contribution margin per unit of the constraining or limiting resource (factor).
7. In deciding to discontinue or add customers, branches, or segments, how should managers take into account allocated overhead costs?	Managers should ignore allocated overhead costs when making decisions about discontinuing and adding customers, branches, and segments. They should focus instead on how total costs differ among alternatives.
8. Is book value of existing equipment relevant in equipment-replacement decisions?	Book value of existing equipment is a past, or historical, cost and, therefore, is irrelevant in equipment-replacement decisions.
9. How can conflicts arise between the decision model and the performance evaluation model used to evaluate the manager?	Top management faces a persistent challenge—that is, making sure that the performance evaluation model of subordinate managers is consistent with the decision model. A common inconsistency is to tell subordinate managers to take a multiple-year view in their decision making but then judge their performance only on the basis of the current year's operating income.

APPENDIX: LINEAR PROGRAMMING

Linear programming (LP) is an optimization technique used to maximize total contribution margin (the objective function), given multiple constraints. LP models typically assume that all costs can be classified as either variable or fixed with respect to a single driver (units of output). LP models also require certain other linear assumptions to hold. When these assumptions fail, other decision models should be considered.[1]

The Power Engines example is an accounting application of linear programming, a technique taught in courses such as operations management, management science, or quantitative analysis for business decisions.

Consider the Power Engines example described earlier in the chapter. Suppose that both the snowmobile and boat engines must be tested on a very expensive machine before they are shipped to customers. The available testing machine time is limited. Production data are as follows:

Department	Available Daily Capacity in Hours	Use of Capacity in Hours per Unit of Product		Daily Maximum Production in Units	
		Snowmobile Engine	Boat Engine	Snowmobile Engine	Boat Engine
Assembly	600 machine-hours	2.0	5.0	300*	120
Testing	120 testing-hours	1.0	0.5	120	240

*For example, 600 machine-hours ÷ 2.0 machine-hours per snowmobile engine = 300, the maximum number of snowmobile engines that the assembly department can make if it works exclusively on snowmobile engines.

Exhibit 11-14 summarizes these and other relevant data. Note that snowmobile engines have a contribution margin of $240 and that boat engines have a contribution margin of $375. Material shortages for boat engines will limit production to 110 boat engines per day. How many engines of each type should be produced daily to maximize operating income?

[1]Other decision models are described in G. Eppen, F. Gould, and C. Schmidt, *Quantitative Concepts for Management* (Englewood Cliffs, N.J.: Prentice-Hall, 1991); and S. Nahmias, *Production and Operations Analysis* (Homewood, Ill.: Irwin, 1993).

Steps in Solving an LP Problem

We use the data in Exhibit 11-14 to illustrate the three steps in solving an LP problem. Throughout this discussion, S equals the number of units of snowmobiles produced and B equals the number of units of boat engines produced.

◆ **Step 1:** *Determine the objective.* The **objective function** of a linear program expresses the objective or goal to be maximized (for example, operating income) or minimized (for example, operating costs). In our example, the objective is to find the combination of products that maximizes total contribution margin in the short run. Fixed costs remain the same regardless of the product mix chosen and are therefore irrelevant. The linear function expressing the objective for the total contribution margin (TCM) is

$$TCM = \$240S + \$375B$$

◆ **Step 2:** *Specify the constraints.* A **constraint** is a mathematical inequality or equality that must be satisfied by the variables in a mathematical model. The following linear inequalities depict the relationships in our example:

Assembly department constraint	$2S + 5B \leq 600$
Testing department constraint	$1S + 0.5B \leq 120$
Material shortage constraint for boat engines	$B \leq 110$
Negative production is impossible	$S \geq 0$ and $B \geq 0$

The coefficients of the constraints are often called *technical coefficients*. For example, in the assembly department, the technical coefficient is two machine-hours for snowmobile engines and five machine-hours for boat engines.

The three solid lines on the graph in Exhibit 11-15 on p. 448 show the existing constraints for assembly and testing and the material shortage constraint.[2]

The feasible alternatives are those combinations of quantities of snowmobile engines and boat engines that satisfy all the constraining factors. The shaded "Area of feasible solutions" in Exhibit 11-15 shows the boundaries of those product combinations that are feasible, or technically possible.

◆ **Step 3:** *Compute the optimal solution.* We present two approaches for finding the optimal solution: the trial-and-error approach and the graphic approach. These approaches are easy to use in our example, because there are only two variables in the objective function and a small number of constraints. An understanding of these two approaches provides insight into LP modelling. In most real-world LP applications, however, managers use computer software packages to calculate the optimal solution.[3]

Objective function. Expresses the objective to be maximized (for example, operating income) or minimized (for example, operating costs) in a decision model (for example, a linear programming model).

◥ S and B in the objective function and the constraints always appear in linear form—for example they never appear as S^2 or B^2 or $\sqrt{S}$ or $\sqrt{B}$, etc. As you can see in Exhibit 11-15, the plots of the objective function and the constraints are linear—they appear as straight lines.

Constraint. A mathematical inequality or equality that must be satisfied by the variables in a mathematical model.

EXHIBIT 11-14
Operating Data for Power Engines

Product	Department Capacity (per Day) in Product Units		Selling Price	Variable Cost per Unit	Contribution Margin per Unit
	Assembly	Testing			
Only snowmobile engines	300	120	$ 800	$560	$240
Only boat engines	120	240	$1,000	$625	$375

[2]As an example of how the lines are plotted in Exhibit 11-15, use equal signs instead of inequality signs and assume for the assembly department that $B = 0$; then $S = 300$ (600 machine-hours ÷ 2 machine-hours per snowmobile engine). Assume that $S = 0$; then $B = 120$ (600 machine-hours ÷ 5 machine-hours per boat engine). Connect those two points with a straight line.

[3]Although the trial-and-error and graphic approaches can be useful for two or possibly three variables, they are impractical when many variables exist. Standard computer software packages rely on the *simplex method*, an interactive step-by-step procedure for determining the optimal solution to an LP problem. It starts with a specific feasible solution and then tests it by substitution to see whether the result can be improved. These substitutions continue until no further improvement is possible and the optimal solution is obtained.

EXHIBIT 11-15
Linear Programming—Graphic Solution for Power Engines

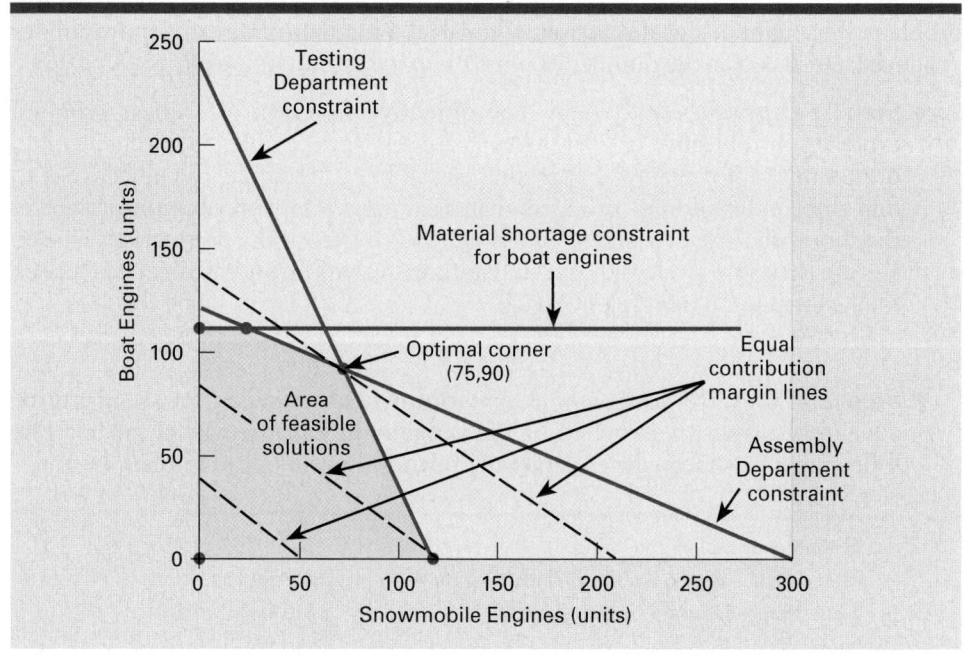

Trial-and-Error Approach The optimal solution can be found by trial and error, by working with coordinates of the corners of the area of feasible solutions. The approach is simple.

First, select any set of corner points and compute the total contribution margin. Five corner points appear in Exhibit 11-15. It is helpful to use simultaneous equations to obtain the exact graph coordinates. To illustrate, the point ($S = 75$, $B = 90$) can be derived by solving the two pertinent constraint inequalities as simultaneous equations:

$$2S + 5B = 600 \qquad (1)$$
$$1S + 0.5B = 120 \qquad (2)$$

Multiplying (2) by 2.0, we get $\qquad 2S + 1B = 240 \qquad (3)$

Subtracting (3) from (1) $\qquad\qquad\qquad 4B = 360$

Therefore $\qquad\qquad\qquad\qquad B = 360 \div 4 = 90$

Substituting for B in (2) $\qquad 1S + 0.5(90) = 120$

$$S = 120 - 45 = 75$$

Given $S = 75$ and $B = 90$, TCM = $240(75) + 375(90) = $51,750.

Second, move from corner point to corner point, computing the total contribution margin at each corner point. The total contribution margin at each corner point is as follows:

Trial	Corner Point (S, B)	Snowmobile Engines (S)	Boat Engines (B)	Total Contribution Margin
1	(0, 0)	0	0	$240(0) + $375(0) = $ 0
2	(0, 110)	0	110	$240(0) + $375(110) = 41,250
3	(25, 110)	25	110	$240(25) + $375(110) = 47,250
4	(75, 90)	75	90	$240(75) + $375(90) = 51,750*
5	(120, 0)	120	0	$240(120) + $375(0) = 28,800

*Indicates the optimal solution.

The optimal product mix is the mix that yields the highest total contribution—75 snowmobile engines and 90 boat engines.

Graphic Approach Consider all possible combinations that will produce an equal total contribution margin of, say, $12,000. That is

$$\$240S + \$375B = \$12,000$$

This set of $12,000 contribution margins is a straight dashed line in Exhibit 11-15 through $(S = 50, B = 0)$ and $(S = 0, B = 32)$. Other equal total contribution margins can be represented by lines parallel to this one. In Exhibit 11-15, we show three dashed lines. The equal total contribution margins increase as the lines get farther from the origin because lines drawn farther from the origin represent more sales of both snowmobile and boat engines.

The optimal line is the one farthest from the origin but still passing through a point in the area of feasible solutions. This line represents the highest contribution margin. The optimal solution is the point at the corner $(S = 75, B = 90)$. This solution will become apparent if you put a ruler on the graph and move it outward from the origin and parallel with the $12,000 line. The idea is to move the ruler as far away from the origin as possible (that is, to increase the total contribution margin) without leaving the area of feasible solutions. In general, the optimal solution in a maximization problem lies at the corner where the dashed line intersects an extreme point of the area of feasible solutions. Moving the ruler out any farther puts it outside the feasible region.

The key to the optimal solution is exchanging a given contribution margin per unit of scarce resource for some other contribution margin per unit of scarce resource. Examine Exhibit 11-15 and consider moving from corner $(S = 25, B = 110)$ to corner $(S = 75, B = 90)$. In the assembly department, each machine-hour devoted to 1 unit of boat engines (B) may be given up (sacrificed or traded) for 2.5 units of snowmobile engines (S) (5 hours required for 1 boat engine ÷ 2 hours required for 1 snowmobile engine). Will this exchange add to profitability? Yes, as shown here:

Total contribution margin at $(S = 25, B = 110)$: $240 × 25 + $375 × 110		$47,250
Added contribution margin from product S by moving to corner $(S = 75, B = 90)$: $(75 - 25) × \$240$	$12,000	
Lost contribution margin from product B by moving to corner $(S = 75, B = 90)$: $(110 - 90) × \$375$	(7,500)	
Net additional contribution margin		4,500
Total contribution margin at $(S = 75, B = 90)$: $240 × 75 + $375 × 90		$51,750

As we move from corner $(S = 25, B = 110)$ to corner $(S = 75, B = 90)$, we are contending with the assembly department constraint. In this department, there is a net advantage of trading 1 unit of B for 2.5 units of S. At corner $(S = 25, B = 110)$, the testing department constraint comes into effect. Should we move to corner $(S = 120, B = 0)$ along the testing department constraint? No. An analysis (not presented) similar to the one here will show that such a move is not worthwhile.

Sensitivity Analysis

What are the implications of uncertainty about the accounting or technical coefficients used in the LP model? Changes in coefficients affect the slope of the objective function (the equal contribution margin lines) or the area of feasible solutions. Consider how a change in the contribution margin of snowmobile engines from $240 to $300 per unit might affect the optimal solution. Assume the contribution margin for boat engines remains unchanged at $375 per unit. The revised objective function will be

$$TCM = \$300S + \$375B$$

Using the trial-and-error approach, calculate the total contribution margin for each of the five corner points described in the table on page 448. The optimal solution is still $(S = 75, B = 90)$.

Now suppose the contribution margin of snowmobile engines is lower than $240 per unit. By repeating the preceding steps, you will find that the optimal

> The Power Engines example illustrates how large changes in contribution margin per unit of product may not affect the optimal product mix if there are no other nearby corner points.

solution will not change so long as the contribution margin of the snowmobile engine does not fall below $150. *Big changes in the contribution margin per unit of snowmobile engines have no effect on the optimal solution.*

What happens if the contribution margin falls below $150? The optimal solution will then shift to the corner ($S = 25$, $B = 110$). Snowmobile engines now generate so little contribution margin per unit that Power Engines will choose to shift its mix in favour of boat engines.

TERMS TO LEARN

This chapter contains definitions of the following important terms:

book value (p. 440)
business function costs (p. 427)
constraint (p. 447)
differential cost (p. 423)
differential revenue (p. 430)
full product costs (p. 427)
incremental costs (p. 425)
incremental revenue (p. 430)
insourcing (p. 428)
make/buy decisions (p. 428)
net relevant cost (p. 423)

objective function (p. 447)
opportunity cost (p. 433)
outlay costs (p. 425)
out-of-pocket costs (p. 425)
outsourcing (p. 428)
qualitative factors (p. 423)
quantitative factors (p. 423)
relevant costs (p. 422)
relevant revenues (p. 422)
sunk costs (p. 441)

ASSIGNMENT MATERIAL

QUESTIONS

11-1 Outline the five-step sequence in a decision process.

11-2 Define *relevant cost*. Why are historical costs irrelevant?

11-3 "All future costs are relevant." Do you agree? Why?

11-4 Distinguish between *quantitative* and *qualitative* factors in decision making.

11-5 Describe two ways in which unit-cost data can mislead a decision maker.

11-6 "Variable costs are always relevant, and fixed costs are always irrelevant." Do you agree? Why?

11-7 "A component part should be purchased whenever the purchase price is less than its total unit manufacturing cost." Do you agree? Why?

11-8 Define *opportunity cost*.

11-9 "Managers should always buy inventory in quantities that result in the lowest purchase cost per unit." Do you agree? Why?

11-10 "Management should always maximize sales of the product with the highest contribution margin per unit." Do you agree? Why?

11-11 "A customer, branch, or business segment that shows negative operating income should be shut down." Do you agree? Explain briefly.

11-12 "Cost written off as amortization is always irrelevant." Do you agree? Why?

11-13 "Managers will always choose the alternative that maximizes operating income or minimizes costs in the decision model." Do you agree? Why?

11-14 Describe the three steps in solving a linear programming problem.

11-15 How might the optimal solution of a linear programming problem be determined?

EXERCISES

11-16 Disposal of assets.

1. A company has an inventory of 1,000 assorted parts for a line of machines that has been discontinued. The inventory cost is $88,000. The parts can be either (a) remachined at total additional costs of $33,000 and then sold for $38,500 or (b) sold as scrap for $2,200. Which action is more profitable? Show your calculations.

2. A truck, costing $110,000 and uninsured, is wrecked its first day in use. It can be either (a) disposed of for $11,000 cash and replaced with a similar truck costing $112,200 or (b) rebuilt for $93,500 and thus be brand-new as far as operating characteristics and looks are concerned. Which action is less costly? Show your calculations.

11-17 The careening personal computer. (W. A. Paton) An employee in the accounting department of a certain business was moving a personal computer from one room to another. As he came alongside an open stairway, he slipped and let the computer get away from him. It went careening down the stairs with a great racket and wound up at the bottom, completely wrecked. Hearing the crash, the office manager came rushing out and turned rather pale when he saw what had happened. "Someone tell me quickly," the manager yelled, "if that is one of our fully amortized items." A check of the accounting records showed that the smashed computer was, indeed, one of those items that had been written off. "Thank God!" said the manager.

REQUIRED

Explain and comment on the point of this anecdote.

11-18 Multiple choice. (CPA) Choose the best answer.

1. The Woody Company manufactures slippers and sells them at $11 a pair. Variable manufacturing costs are $4.95 a pair, and allocated fixed manufacturing costs are $1.65 a pair. The company has enough idle capacity available to accept a one-time-only special order of 20,000 pairs of slippers at $6.60 a pair. Woody will not incur any marketing costs as a result of the special order. What would the effect on operating income be if the special order could be accepted without affecting normal sales? (a) $0, (b) $33,000 increase, (c) $99,000 increase, (d) $132,000 increase.

2. The Reno Company manufactures Part No. 498 for use in its production line. The manufacturing costs per unit for 20,000 units of Part No. 498 are as follows:

Direct materials	$ 6.60
Direct manufacturing labour	33.00
Variable manufacturing overhead	13.20
Fixed manufacturing overhead allocated	17.60
	$70.40

The Tray Company has offered to sell 20,000 units of Part No. 498 to Reno for $66 per unit. Reno will make the decision to buy the part from Tray if there is an overall savings of at least $27,500 for Reno. If Reno accepts Tray's offer, $9.90 per unit of the fixed overhead allocated would be totally eliminated. Furthermore, Reno has determined that the released facilities could be used to save relevant costs in the manufacture of Part No. 575. For Reno to have an overall savings of $27,500, the amount of relevant costs that would have to be saved by using the released facilities in the manufacture of Part No. 575 would be (a) $88,000, (b) $93,500, (c) $137,500, (d) $154,000.

11-19 Special order, activity-based costing. (CMA, adapted) The Award Plus Company manufactures medals for winners of athletic events and other contests. Its manufacturing plant has the capacity to produce 10,000 medals each month; current production and sales are 7,500 medals per month. The company normally charges $165 per medal. Cost information for the current activity level is as follows:

Variable costs that vary with units produced:	
Direct materials	$ 288,750
Direct manufacturing labour	330,000
Variable costs (for setups, materials-handling, quality control, and so on) that vary with number of batches, 150 batches × $550 per batch	82,500
Fixed manufacturing costs	302,500
Fixed marketing costs	192,500
Total costs	$1,196,250

Award Plus has just received a special one-time-only order for 2,500 medals at $110 per medal. Accepting the special order would not affect the company's regular business. Award Plus makes medals for its existing customers in batch sizes of 50 medals (150 batches × 50 medals per batch = 7,500 medals). The special order requires Award Plus to make the medals in 25 batches of 100 each.

REQUIRED
1. Should Award Plus accept this special order? Why? Explain briefly.
2. Suppose plant capacity was only 9,000 medals instead of 10,000 medals each month. The special order must either be taken in full or rejected totally. Should Award Plus accept the special order?
3. As in requirement 1, assume that monthly capacity is 10,000 medals. Award Plus is concerned that if it accepts the special order, its existing customers will immediately demand a price discount of $11 in the month in which the special order is being filled. They would argue that Award Plus's capacity costs are now being spread over more units and that existing customers should get the benefit of these lower costs. Should Award Plus accept the special order under these conditions? Show all calculations.

11-20 Make versus buy, activity-based costing. The Svenson Corporation manufactures cellular modems. It manufactures its own cellular modem circuit boards (CMCB), an important part of the cellular modem. It reports the following cost information about the costs of making CMCBs in 2006 and the expected costs in 2007:

	Current Costs in 2006	Expected Costs in 2007
Variable manufacturing costs:		
Direct materials costs per CMCB	$ 198	$ 187
Direct manufacturing labour costs per CMCB	55	49.50
Variable manufacturing costs per batch for setups, materials-handling, and quality control	1,760	1,650
Fixed manufacturing costs:		
Fixed manufacturing overhead costs that can be avoided if CMCBs are not made	352,000	352,000
Fixed manufacturing overhead costs of plant amortization, insurance, and administration that cannot be avoided even if CMCBs are not made	880,000	880,000

Svenson manufactured 8,000 CMCBs in 2006 in 40 batches of 200 each. In 2007, Svenson anticipates needing 10,000 CMCBs. The CMCBs would be needed in 80 batches of 125 each.

The Minton Corporation has approached Svenson about supplying CMCBs to Svenson in 2007 at $330 per CMCB on whatever delivery schedule Svenson wants.

REQUIRED
1. Calculate the total expected manufacturing (absorption) cost per unit of making CMCBs in 2007.
2. Suppose the capacity currently used to make CMCBs will become idle if Svenson purchases CMCBs from Minton. Should Svenson make CMCBs or buy them from Minton?
3. Now suppose that, if Svenson purchases CMCBs from Minton, its best alternative use of the capacity currently used to make CMCBs is to make and sell special circuit boards (CB3s) to the Essex Corporation. Svenson estimates the following incremental revenues and costs from CB3s:

Total expected incremental future revenues	$2,200,000
Total expected incremental future costs	$2,365,000

Should Svenson make CMCBs or buy them from Minton?

11-21 Which bases to close, relevant-cost analysis, opportunity costs. The Department of National Defence has the difficult decision of deciding which military bases to close down. Military and political factors obviously matter, but cost savings are also an important factor. Consider two naval bases—one in Vancouver, British Columbia, and one in Halifax, Nova Scotia. National Defence has decided that it needs only one of those two bases permanently, so one must be shut down. The decision regarding which base to shut down will be made on cost considerations alone. The following information is available:

a. The Vancouver base was built at a cost of $110 million. The operating costs of the base are $440 million per year. The base is built on land owned by National Defence, so it pays nothing for the use of the property. If the base is closed, the land will be sold to developers for $550 million.

b. The Halifax base was built at a cost of $165 million on land leased by National Defence from private citizens. National Defence can choose to lease the land permanently for an annual lease payment of $3.3 million per year. If it decides to keep the Halifax base open, National Defence plans to invest $66 million in a fixed income note, which at 5% interest will earn the $3.3 million the government needs for the lease payments. The land and buildings will immediately revert to the owner if the base is closed. The operating costs of the base, excluding lease payments, are $330 million per year.

c. If the Vancouver base is closed down, National Defence will have to transfer some personnel to the Halifax facility. As a result, the yearly operating costs at Halifax will increase by $110 million per year. If the Halifax facility is closed down, no extra costs will be incurred to operate the Vancouver facility.

REQUIRED

The British Columbia delegation argues that it is cheaper to close down the Halifax base, for two reasons: (1) it would save $110 million per year in additional costs required to operate the Halifax base and (2) it would save $3.3 million dollars per year in lease payments. (Recall that the Vancouver base requires no cash payments for use of the land because the land is owned by National Defence.) Do you agree with the British Columbia delegation's arguments and conclusions? In your answer, identify and explain all costs that you consider relevant and all costs that you consider irrelevant for the base-closing decision.

11-22 **Inventory decision, opportunity cost.** Lawnox, a manufacturer of lawn mowers, predicts that 240,000 spark plugs will have to be purchased during the next year. The manufacturer estimates that 20,000 spark plugs will be required each month. A supplier quotes a price of $8.80 per spark plug. The supplier also offers a special discount option: if all 240,000 spark plugs are purchased at the start of the year, a discount of 5% off the $8.80 price will be given. Lawnox can invest its cash at 8% per year. It costs Lawnox $220 to place each purchase order.

REQUIRED

1. What is the opportunity cost of interest forgone from purchasing all 240,000 units at the start of the year instead of in 12 monthly purchases of 20,000 units per order?
2. Would this opportunity cost ordinarily be recorded in the accounting system? Why?
3. Should Lawnox purchase 240,000 units at the start of the year or 20,000 units each month?

11-23 **Relevant costs, contribution margin, product emphasis.** The Beach Comber is a takeout food store at a popular beach resort. Susan Sexton, owner of the Beach Comber, is deciding how much shelf space to devote to four different drinks. Pertinent data on these four drinks are as follows:

	Cola	Lemonade	Punch	Natural Orange Juice
Selling price per case	$19.80	$21.12	$29.04	$42.24
Variable costs per case	$14.85	$16.72	$22.11	$33.22
Cases sold per metre of shelf space per day	25	24	4	5

Sexton has a maximum front shelf space of 12 metres to devote to the four drinks. She wants a minimum of 1 metre and a maximum of 6 metres of front shelf space for each drink.

REQUIRED

1. What is the contribution margin per case of each type of drink?
2. A co-worker of Sexton's recommends that she maximize the shelf space devoted to those drinks with the highest contribution margin per case. Evaluate this recommendation.
3. What shelf space allocation for the four drinks would you recommend for the Beach Comber?

11-24 Selection of most profitable product. Body-Builders, Inc., produces two basic types of weightlifting equipment, Model 9 and Model 14. Pertinent data are as follows:

	Per Unit	
	Model 9	**Model 14**
Sales price	$110.00	$77.00
Costs:		
Direct materials	$ 30.80	$14.30
Direct manufacturing labour	16.50	27.50
Variable manufacturing overhead*	27.50	13.75
Fixed manufacturing overhead*	11.00	5.50
Marketing costs (all variable)	15.40	11.00
Total costs	$101.20	$72.05
Operating income	$ 8.80	$ 4.95

*Allocated on the basis of machine-hours.

The weightlifting craze is such that enough of either Model 9 or Model 14 can be sold to keep the plant operating at full capacity. The two products are processed through the same production departments.

REQUIRED

Which product should be produced? If both should be produced, indicate the proportions of each. Briefly explain your answer.

Excel Application For students who wish to practise their spreadsheet skills, the following is a step-by-step approach to creating an Excel spreadsheet to work this problem.

Step-by-Step

1. Open a new spreadsheet. At top, create an "Original Data" section for the data provided by Body-Builders, Inc. Create rows for the per unit data on selling price, costs, and operating income.

(Program your spreadsheet to perform all necessary calculations. Do not "hard-code" any amounts, such as contribution margin per unit, requiring addition, subtraction, multiplication, or division operations.)

2. Skip two rows and create a "Product Mix Analysis" section. Create columns for Model 9 and Model 14 and rows for "Selling Price per Unit, Variable Cost per Unit, Contribution Margin per Unit, Relative Use of Machine-Hours per Unit of Product," and "Contribution Margin per Unit of Machine Time." Use the data from your Original Data section to calculate selling price per unit, variable cost per unit, and contribution margin per unit.

3. In the "Relative output (units of product) per machine-hour" row, enter the *relative* output of units of product per machine-hour for Models 9 and 14, respectively. (*Hint:* Variable and fixed manufacturing overhead are allocated on the basis of machine-hours, and the variable and fixed manufacturing overhead costs per unit for Model 9 are twice as high as for Model 14.)

4. Enter calculations for contribution margin per unit of machine time for Models 9 and 14 by multiplying contribution margin per unit by the relative use of machine-hours per unit of product.

5. *Check the accuracy of your spreadsheet.* Go to your Original Data section and change the selling price of Model 14 from $77 to $75.90 per unit. If you programmed your spreadsheet correctly, contribution margin per unit of machine time for Model 14 should change to $18.70.

11-25 Closing and opening stores. Sanchez Corporation runs two convenience stores in Regina and Saskatoon. Operating income for each store in 2007 follows:

	Regina Store	Saskatoon Store
Revenues	$1,177,000	$946,000
Operating costs		
Cost of goods sold	825,000	726,000
Lease rent (renewable each year)	99,000	82,500
Labour costs (paid hourly)	46,200	46,200
Amortization of equipment	27,500	24,200
Utilities (electricity, heating)	47,300	50,600
Allocated corporate overhead	55,000	44,000
Total operating costs	1,100,000	973,500
Operating income (loss)	$ 77,000	$ (27,500)

The equipment has a remaining useful life of one year and zero disposal price. In a senior management meeting, Maria Lopez, the management accountant at Sanchez Corporation, makes the following comment, "Sanchez can increase its profitability by closing down the Saskatoon store or by adding more stores like it."

REQUIRED

Answer the following questions referring to the preceding data.

1. Calculate Sanchez's operating income if it closes down the Saskatoon store. By closing down the store, Sanchez can reduce overall corporate overhead costs by $47,300. Is Maria Lopez correct?
2. Calculate Sanchez's operating income if it opens another store with revenues and costs identical to the Saskatoon store (including a cost of $24,200 to acquire equipment with a one-year useful life and zero disposal price). Opening this store will increase corporate overhead costs by $4,400. Is Maria Lopez correct?

11-26 Customer profitability, choosing customers. Broadway Printers operates a printing press with a monthly capacity of 2,000 machine-hours. Broadway has two main customers, Taylor Corporation and Kelly Corporation. Data on each customer for January follow:

	Taylor Corporation	Kelly Corporation	Total
Revenues	$132,000	$88,000	$220,000
Variable costs	46,200	52,800	99,000
Fixed costs (allocated on the basis of revenues)	66,000	44,000	110,000
Total operating costs	112,200	96,800	209,000
Operating income	$ 19,800	$(8,800)	$ 11,000
Machine-hours required	1,500 hours	500 hours	2,000 hours

Each of the following requirements refers only to the preceding data; there is *no connection* between the requirements.

REQUIRED

1. Should Broadway drop the Kelly Corporation business? If Broadway drops the Kelly Corporation business, its total fixed costs will decrease by 20%.
2. Kelly Corporation indicates that it wants Broadway to do an *additional* $88,000 worth of printing jobs during February. These jobs are identical to the existing business Broadway did for Kelly in January in terms of variable costs and machine-hours required. Broadway anticipates that the business from Taylor Corporation in February will be the same as that in January. Broadway can choose to accept as much of the Taylor and Kelly business for February as it wants. Assume that total fixed costs for February will be the same as the fixed costs in January. What should Broadway do? What will Broadway's operating income be in February?

11-27 Relevance of equipment costs. The Auto Wash Company has just today paid for and installed a special machine for polishing cars at one of its several outlets. It is the first day of the company's fiscal year. The machine cost $22,000. Its annual operating costs total $16,500, exclusive of amortization. The machine will have a four-year useful life and a zero terminal disposal price.

After the machine has been used for a day, a machine salesperson offers a different machine that promises to do the same job at a yearly operating cost of $9,900, exclusive of amortization. The new machine will cost $26,400 cash, installed. The "old" machine is unique and can be sold outright for only $11,000, minus $2,200 removal cost. The new machine, like the old one, will have a four-year useful life and zero terminal disposal price.

Sales, all in cash, will be $165,000 annually, and other cash costs will be $121,000 annually, regardless of this decision.

For simplicity, ignore income taxes, interest, and present value considerations.

REQUIRED

1. (a) Prepare a statement of cash receipts and disbursements for each of the four years under both alternatives. What is the cumulative difference in cash flow for the four years taken together? (b) Prepare income statements for each of the four years under both alternatives. Assume straight-line amortization. What is the cumulative difference in operating income for the four years taken together? (c) What are the irrelevant items in your presentations in requirements (a) and (b)? Why are they irrelevant?

2. Suppose the cost of the "old" machine was $1.1 million rather than $22,000. Nevertheless, the old machine can be sold outright for only $11,000, minus $2,200 removal cost. Would the net differences in requirements 1 and 2 change? Explain.

3. "To avoid a loss, we should keep the old machine." What is the role of book value in decisions about replacement of machines?

11-28 Equipment upgrade versus replacement. (A. Spero, adapted) The Pacifica Corporation makes steel table lamps. It is considering either upgrading its existing production line or replacing it. The production equipment was purchased two years ago for $660,000. It has an expected useful life of five years, a terminal disposal price of $0, and is amortized on a straight-line basis at the rate of $132,000 per year. It has a current book value of $396,000 and a current disposal price of $99,000. The following table presents expected costs under the upgrade and replace alternatives:

	Upgrade	Replace
Expected one-time-only capital costs	$330,000	$825,000
Variable manufacturing costs per unit	$ 13.20	$ 9.90
Expected production and sales per year	60,000 units	60,000 units
Selling price per unit	$ 27.50	$ 27.50

The expected useful life after the machine is upgraded or replaced is three years, and the expected terminal disposal price is $0. If the machine is upgraded, the $330,000 would be added to the current book value of $396,000 and amortized on a straight-line basis. The new equipment, if purchased, would also be amortized on a straight-line basis.

For simplicity, ignore income taxes, interest, and present value considerations.

REQUIRED

1. Should Pacifica upgrade its production line or replace it?

2. (a) Now suppose the capital expenditure needed to replace the production line is not known. All other data are as given previously. What is the maximum price that Pacifica would be willing to pay for the new line to prefer replacing the existing line over upgrading it? (b) Assume that the capital expenditure needed to replace the production line is $825,000. Now suppose the expected production and sales quantity is not known. For what production and sales quantity would Pacifica prefer to (i) replace the line, (ii) upgrade the line?

3. Consider again the basic information given in this exercise. Suppose John Azinger, the manager of the Pacifica Corporation, is evaluated on operating income. The upcoming year's operating income is crucial to Azinger's bonus. What alternative would Azinger choose?

PROBLEMS

11-29 Multiple choice, comprehensive problem on relevant costs. The following are the Class Company's *unit* costs of manufacturing and marketing a high-style pen at a level of 20,000 units per month:

Manufacturing costs:	
Direct materials	$1.10
Direct manufacturing labour	1.32
Variable manufacturing indirect costs	0.88
Fixed manufacturing indirect costs	0.55
Marketing costs:	
Variable	1.65
Fixed	0.99

REQUIRED

The following situations refer only to the preceding data; there is no connection between the situations. Unless stated otherwise, assume a regular selling price of $6.60 per unit.

Choose the best answer to each of the seven questions. Support each answer with summarized computations.

1. In an inventory of 10,000 units of the high-style pen presented on the balance sheet, the unit cost used is (a) $3.30, (b) $3.85, (c) $5.50, (d) $2.42, (e) $6.49.

2. The pen is usually produced and sold at the rate of 240,000 units per year (an average of 20,000 per month). The selling price is $6.60 per unit, which yields total annual sales of $1,584,000. Total costs are $1,557,600, and operating income is $26,400, or $0.11 per unit. Market research estimates that unit sales could be increased by 10% if prices were cut to $6.38. Assuming the implied cost behaviour patterns are correct, this action, if taken, would
   a. Decrease operating income by a net of $7,920
   b. Decrease operating income by $0.22 per unit ($52,800) but increase operating income by 10% of sales ($158,400) for a net increase of $105,600
   c. Decrease unit fixed costs by 10%, or $0.154, per unit, and thus decrease operating income by $0.066 ($0.22 − $0.154) per unit
   d. Increase unit sales to 264,000 units, which at the $6.38 price would give total sales of $1,684,320; costs at $6.49 per unit for 264,000 units would be $1,713,360; and a loss of $29,040 would result
   e. None of these

3. A cost contract with the government for 5,000 units of the pens calls for the reimbursement of all manufacturing costs plus a fixed fee of $1,100. No variable marketing costs are incurred on the government contract. You are required to compare the following two alternatives:

Sales Each Month to	Alternative A	Alternative B
Regular customers	15,000 units	15,000 units
Government	0 units	5,000 units

Operating income under alternative B is greater than that under alternative A by (a) $1,100, (b) $2,750, (c) $3,850, (d) $330, (e) none of these.

4. Assume the same data with respect to the government contract as in requirement 3 except that the two alternatives to be compared are:

Sales Each Month to	Alternative A	Alternative B
Regular customers	20,000 units	15,000 units
Government	0 units	5,000 units

Operating income under alternative B relative to that under alternative A is (a) $4,400 less, (b) $3,300 greater, (c) $7,150 less, (d) $550 greater, (e) none of these.

5. The company wants to enter a foreign market in which price competition is keen. The company seeks a one-time-only special order for 10,000 units on a minimum-unit-price basis. It expects that shipping costs for this order will amount to only $0.825 per unit, but the fixed costs of obtaining the contract will be $4,400. The company incurs no variable marketing costs other than shipping costs. Domestic business will be unaffected. The selling price to break even is (a) $3.85, (b) $4.565, (c) $4.675, (d) $3.30, (e) $5.50.

6. The company has an inventory of 1,100 units of pens that must be sold immediately at reduced prices. Otherwise, the inventory will be worthless. The unit cost that is relevant for establishing the minimum selling price is (a) $4.95, (b) $4.40, (c) $3.30, (d) $6.49, (e) $1.65.

7. A proposal is received from an outside supplier who will make and ship these high-style pens directly to the Class Company's customers as sales orders are forwarded from Class's sales staff. Class's fixed marketing costs will be unaffected, but its variable marketing costs will be slashed by 20%. Class's plant will be idle, but its fixed manufacturing overhead will continue at 50% of present levels. How much per unit would the company be able to pay the supplier without decreasing operating income? (a) $5.225, (b) $4.345, (c) $3.245, (d) $5.885, (e) none of these.

11-30 Make or buy (continuation of 11-29). Assume that, as in requirement 7 of Problem 11-29, a proposal is received from an outside supplier who will make and ship high-style pens directly to the Class Company's customers as sales orders are forwarded from Class's sales staff. If the supplier's offer is accepted, the present plant facilities will be used to make a new pen whose unit costs will be:

Variable manufacturing costs	$5.50
Fixed manufacturing costs	1.10
Variable marketing costs	2.20
Fixed marketing costs for the new pen	0.55
Total costs	$9.35

Total fixed manufacturing overhead will be unchanged from the original level given at the beginning of Problem 11-29. Fixed marketing costs for the new pens are over and above the fixed marketing costs incurred for marketing the high-style pens at the beginning of Problem 11-29. The reduction of 20% in variable marketing costs carries over to this problem. The new pen will sell for $9.90. The minimum desired operating income on the two pens taken together is $55,000 per year. New pen sales will be 120,000 units.

REQUIRED

What is the maximum purchase cost per unit that the Class Company would be willing to pay for subcontracting the production of the high-style pens?

11-31 **Special-order decision.** The Modern Packing Corporation (MPC) specializes in the manufacture of one-litre plastic bottles. The plastic moulding machines are capable of producing 100 bottles per hour. The firm estimates that the variable cost of producing a plastic bottle is 25 cents. The bottles are sold for 55 cents each.

Management has been approached by a local toy company that would like the firm to produce a moulded plastic toy for them. The toy company is willing to pay $3.30 per unit for the toy. The unit variable cost to manufacture the toy will be $2.64. In addition, MPC would have to incur a cost of $22,000 to construct the mould required exclusively for this order. Because the toy uses more plastic and is of a more intricate shape than a bottle, a moulding machine can produce only 40 units per hour. The customer wants 100,000 units. Assume that MPC has a total capacity of 10,000 machine-hours available during the period in which the toy company wants delivery of the toys. The firm's fixed costs, *excluding* the costs to construct the toy mould, during the same period will be $220,000.

REQUIRED

1. Suppose the demand for its bottles is 750,000 units, and the special toy order has to be either taken in full or rejected totally. Should MPC accept the special toy order? Explain your answer.
2. Suppose the demand for its bottles is 850,000 units, and the special toy order has to be either taken in full or rejected totally. Should MPC accept the special toy order? Explain your answer.
3. Suppose the demand for its bottles is 850,000 units, and MPC can accept any quantity of the special toy order. How many bottles and toys should it manufacture?
4. Suppose the demand for its bottles is 900,000 units, and the special toy order has to be either taken in full or rejected totally. Should MPC accept the special toy order? Explain your answer.
5. Suppose the demand for its bottles is 900,000 units, and MPC can accept any quantity of the special toy order. How many bottles and toys should it manufacture?
6. Suppose the demand for its bottles is 950,000 units, and MPC can accept any quantity of the special toy order. How many bottles and toys should it manufacture?
7. The management has located a firm that has just entered the moulded plastic business. This firm has considerable excess capacity and more efficient moulding machines, and is willing to subcontract the toy job, or any portion of it, for $3.08 per unit. It will construct its own toy mould. Suppose the demand for its bottles is 900,000 units, and MPC can accept any quantity of the special toy order. How many bottles and toys should MPC manufacture? How many toys should it subcontract out?

11-32 **Product mix, relevant costs.** (N. Melumad, adapted) Pendleton Engineering makes cutting tools for metal working operations. It makes two types of tools, R3, a regular cutting tool, and HP6, a high-precision cutting tool. R3 is manufactured on a regular machine but HP6 must be worked on both the regular machine and a high-precision machine. The following information is available:

	R3	HP6
Selling price	$ 120	$ 180
Variable manufacturing costs per unit	$ 72	$ 120
Variable marketing costs per unit	$ 18	$ 42
Budgeted total fixed overhead costs	$350,000	$550,000
Hours required to produce 1 unit on the regular machine	1	0.5

The following additional information is available:

a. Pendleton faces a capacity constraint on the regular machine of 50,000 hours per year.
b. Pendleton has no capacity constraint on the high-precision machine.
c. Of the $550,000 budgeted fixed overhead costs of HP6, $360,000 is for lease payments for the high-precision machine. This cost is charged entirely to HP6 because Pendleton uses the machine exclusively to produce HP6. The leasing agreement for the high-precision machine can be cancelled at any time without penalties.
d. All other fixed overhead costs cannot be changed.

REQUIRED

1. What product mix—that is, how many units of R3 and HP6—will maximize Pendleton's operating income?
2. Suppose Pendleton can increase the annual capacity of the regular machine by 15,000 hours at a cost of $180,000? Should Pendleton increase the capacity of the regular machine by 15,000 machine-hours? By how much will Pendleton's operating income increase?
3. Suppose that the capacity of the regular machine has been increased to 65,000 hours. Pendleton has been approached by Carter Corporation to supply 20,000 units of another cutting tool, S3, for $144 per unit. S3 is exactly like R3 except that its variable manufacturing costs are $84 per unit. What product mix should Pendleton choose to maximize operating income?

11-33 Discontinuing a product line, selling more product. The Northern Furniture Division of Grossman Corporation makes and sells tables and beds. The following revenue and cost information from the division's activity-based costing system is available:

a. On January 1, 2007, the equipment has a book value of $110,000 and zero disposal price. Any equipment not used remains idle.
b. Fixed marketing and distribution costs of a product line can be avoided if the line is discontinued.
c. Fixed general administration costs of the division and corporate-office costs will not change if sales of individual product lines are increased or decreased, or if product lines are added or dropped.

	4,000 Tables	5,000 Beds	Total
Revenues ($137.50 × 4,000; $220 × 5,000)	$550,000	$1,100,000	$1,650,000
Variable direct materials and direct manufacturing labour costs ($82.50 × 4,000; $115.50 × 5,000)	330,000	577,500	907,500
Amortization on equipment used exclusively by each product line	46,200	63,800	110,000
Marketing and distribution costs			
$44,000 (fixed) + $825 per shipment × 40 shipments	77,000		
$66,000 (fixed) + $825 per shipment × 100 shipments		148,500 }	225,500
Fixed general administration costs of the division allocated to product lines based on revenues	121,000	242,000	363,000
Allocated corporate-office costs allocated to product lines on the basis of revenues	55,000	110,000	165,000
Total costs	629,200	1,141,800	1,771,000
Operating income (loss)	$ (79,200)	$ (41,800)	$(121,000)

REQUIRED

1. Should the Furniture Division discontinue the tables product line assuming the released facilities remain idle? Show all calculations.
2. Should the Furniture Division sell 4,000 more tables? Assume that to do so the division would have to acquire equipment costing $46,200 with a one-year useful life and zero terminal disposal value. Assume further that the fixed marketing and distribution costs will not change but that the number of shipments will double. Show all calculations.

11-34 Opportunity cost. (H. Schaefer) The Wolverine Corporation is working at full production capacity producing 10,000 units of a unique product, Rosebo. Manufacturing costs per unit for Rosebo are as follows:

Direct materials	$ 2.20
Direct manufacturing labour	3.30
Manufacturing overhead	5.50
	$11.00

The unit manufacturing overhead cost is based on a variable cost per unit of $2.20 and fixed costs of $33,000 (at full capacity of 10,000 units). The selling costs, all variable, are $4.40 per unit, and the selling price is $22 per unit.

A customer, the Windsor Company, has asked Wolverine to produce 2,000 units of Orangebo, a modification of Rosebo. Orangebo would require the same manufacturing processes as Rosebo. The Windsor Company has offered to pay Wolverine $16.50 for a unit of Orangebo and half the selling costs per unit.

REQUIRED

1. What is the opportunity cost to Wolverine of producing the 2,000 units of Orangebo? (Assume that no overtime is worked.)
2. The Buckeye Corporation has offered to produce 2,000 units of Rosebo for Wolverine so that Wolverine may accept the Orangebo offer. That is, if Wolverine accepts the Buckeye offer, Wolverine would manufacture 8,000 units of Rosebo and 2,000 units of Orangebo and purchase 2,000 units of Rosebo from Buckeye. Buckeye would charge Wolverine $15.40 per unit to manufacture Rosebo. Should Wolverine accept the Buckeye offer? (Support your conclusions with specific analysis.)
3. Suppose Wolverine had been working at less than full capacity, producing 8,000 units of Rosebo at the time the Orangebo offer was made. What is the minimum price Wolverine should accept for Orangebo under these conditions? (Ignore the previous $16.50 unit price.)

11-35 Discontinuing a product line, selling more product, activity-based costing. Home Furnishings makes bookshelves, tables, and beds. The following sales and cost information is available about the profitability of each of these lines:

	Bookshelves	Tables	Beds	Total
Revenues	$825,000	$550,000	$1,100,000	$2,475,000
Direct materials	330,000	242,000	440,000	1,012,000
Direct manufacturing labour	82,500	66,000	88,000	236,500
Setups and materials-handling	49,500	44,000	66,000	159,500
Amortization on tools and fixtures	55,000	52,800	79,200	187,000
Marketing and distribution	82,500	66,000	132,000	280,500
General administration and facilities	165,000	110,000	220,000	495,000
Total costs	764,500	580,800	1,025,200	2,370,500
Operating income (loss)	$ 60,500	$ (30,800)	$ 74,800	$ 104,500

Home Furnishings uses an activity-based cost system to assign costs to products. The following additional information is available:

a. Direct materials and direct manufacturing labour costs vary with the number of units of products manufactured.
b. Setups and materials-handling costs vary with the number of batches made.
c. Tools and fixtures have one-year lives and zero disposal prices.
d. Of the total marketing and distribution costs, $123,750 are fixed costs allocated to product lines based on sales revenue. Fixed marketing and distribution costs allocated to a product line can be avoided if the line is discontinued. The remaining marketing costs vary with the number of shipments made.
e. General administration and facilities costs are fixed costs that will not change if sales of individual product lines are increased or decreased or if product lines are added or dropped. These costs are allocated to product lines based on sales revenues.

REQUIRED

In answering the following requirements, assume that prices of the various products do not change.

1. Should Home Furnishings discontinue the tables product line assuming the released facilities remain idle? Assume Home Furnishings has already acquired the tools and fixtures it needs to manufacture tables.
2. Suppose that if Home Furnishings discontinues the tables product line, the released facilities could be used to sell beds worth an additional $275,000. This would require Home Furnishings to purchase tools and fixtures for $4,400. Assume that there will be no change in either the number of batches in which beds are made or the number of shipments.
   a. Based on your calculations, should Home Furnishings discontinue the tables product line?
   b. What is the opportunity cost of continuing the tables product line?
   c. What other factors should Home Furnishings consider before making a decision?

3. What would be the effect on operating income if Home Furnishings could double its sales of tables? Assume that, at the higher sales, both the number of batches and the number of shipments would be three times and purchases of tools and fixtures would be twice the current levels.

11-36 Considering three alternatives. (CMA) The Auer Company had just completed an order for a special machine from the Jay Company when the Jay Company declared bankruptcy, defaulted on the order, and forfeited the 10% deposit paid on the selling price of $79,750. Auer's manufacturing manager identified the costs already incurred in the production of the special machine for Jay as follows:

Direct materials used		$18,260
Direct manufacturing labour incurred		23,540
Overhead allocated:		
Manufacturing:		
Variable	$11,770	
Fixed	5,885	17,665
Fixed marketing and administration		5,945
Total costs		$65,400

Another company, the Kaytell Corporation, would be interested in buying the special machine if it is reworked to Kaytell's specifications. Auer offered to sell the reworked machine to Kaytell as a special order for a net price (price minus cash discount, if any) of $75,240. Kaytell has agreed to pay the net price when it takes delivery in two months. The additional traceable costs to rework the machine to Kaytell's specifications are as follows:

Direct materials	$ 6,820
Direct manufacturing labour	4,620
	$11,440

A second alternative available to Auer is to convert the special machine to the standard model. The standard model lists for $68,750. The additional incremental costs to convert the special machine to the standard model are

Direct materials	$3,135
Direct manufacturing labour	3,630
	$6,765

A third alternative for the Auer Company is to sell, as a special order, the machine as is (that is, without modification) for a net price of $57,200. However, the potential buyer of the unmodified machine does not want it for 60 days. The buyer offers a $7,700 down payment with final payment upon delivery.

The following additional information is available regarding Auer's operations:

◆ The sales commission rate is 2% on sales of standard models and 3% on special orders. All sales commissions are calculated on net selling price (that is, list price minus cash discount, if any).

◆ Normal credit terms for sales of standard models are 2/10, n/30 (2/10 means a discount of 2% is given if payment is made within 10 days; n/30 means the full amount is due within 30 days). Customers take the discounts except in rare instances. Credit terms for special orders are negotiated with the customer.

◆ The allocation rates for manufacturing overhead and the fixed marketing and administrative costs are

Manufacturing:	
Variable	50% of direct manufacturing labour costs
Fixed	25% of direct manufacturing labour costs
Marketing and administration:	
Fixed	10% of the total of direct materials, direct manufacturing labour costs, and manufacturing overhead costs

- Normal time required for rework is one month.
- A surcharge of 5% of the selling price is placed on all customer requests for minor modifications of standard models.
- Auer normally sells a sufficient number of standard models for the company to operate at a volume in excess of the breakeven point.

Auer does not consider the time value of money in their analyses of special orders whenever the period is less than one year, because the effect is not significant.

REQUIRED

1. Determine the dollar contribution that each of the three alternatives will add to the Auer Company's operating income.
2. If Kaytell makes Auer a counteroffer, what is the lowest price Auer should accept from Kaytell for the reworked machine? Explain your answer.
3. Discuss the influence that fixed manufacturing overhead costs should have on the selling prices Auer quotes for special orders when (a) the firm is operating at or below the breakeven point and (b) the firm's special orders constitute efficient utilization of unused capacity above the breakeven point.

11-37 **Contribution approach, relevant costs.** Air Pacific owns a single jet aircraft and operates between Vancouver and the Hawaiian Islands. Flights leave Vancouver on Mondays and Thursdays and depart from Hawaii on Wednesdays and Saturdays. Air Pacific cannot offer any more flights between Vancouver and Hawaii. Only tourist-class seats are available on its planes. An analyst has collected the following information:

Seating capacity per plane	360 passengers
Average number of passengers per flight	200 passengers
Flights per week	4 flights
Flights per year	208 flights
Average one-way fare	$550
Variable fuel costs	$15,400 per flight
Food and beverage service cost (no charge to passenger)	$22 per passenger
Commission to travel agents paid by Air Pacific (all tickets are booked by travel agents)	8% of fare
Fixed annual lease costs allocated to each flight	$58,300 per flight
Fixed ground services (maintenance, check-in, baggage handling) cost allocated to each flight	$7,700 per flight
Fixed flight crew salaries allocated to each flight	$4,400 per flight

For simplicity, assume that fuel costs are unaffected by the actual number of passengers on a flight.

REQUIRED

1. What is the operating income that Air Pacific makes on each one-way flight between Vancouver and Hawaii?
2. The market research department of Air Pacific indicates that lowering the average one-way fare to $528 will increase the average number of passengers per flight to 212. Should Air Pacific lower its fare?
3. Travel International, a tour operator, approaches Air Pacific on the possibility of chartering (renting out) its jet aircraft twice each month, first to take Travel International's tourists from Vancouver to Hawaii and then to bring the tourists back from Hawaii to Vancouver. If Air Pacific accepts Travel International's offer, Air Pacific will be able to offer only 184 (208 – 24) of its own flights each year. The terms of the charter are as follows: (a) For each one-way flight, Travel International will pay Air Pacific $82,500 to charter the plane and to use its flight crew and ground service staff; (b) Travel International will pay for fuel costs; and (c) Travel International will pay for all food costs. On purely financial considerations, should Air Pacific accept Travel International's offer? What other factors should Air Pacific consider in deciding whether to charter its plane to Travel International?

11-38 **Make or buy, unknown level of volume.** (A. Atkinson) Oxford Engineering manufactures small engines. The engines are sold to manufacturers who install them in such products as lawn mowers. The company currently manufactures all the parts used in these engines but is considering a proposal from an external supplier who wants to supply the starter assembly used in these engines.

The starter assembly is currently manufactured in Division 3 of Oxford Engineering. The costs relating to Division 3 for the past 12 months were as follows:

Direct materials	$220,000
Direct manufacturing labour	165,000
Manufacturing overhead	440,000
Total	$825,000

Over the past year, Division 3 manufactured 165,000 starter assemblies; the average cost for the starter assembly is computed as $5 ($825,000 ÷ 165,000).

Further analysis of manufacturing overhead revealed the following information. Of the total manufacturing overhead reported, only 25% is considered variable. Of the fixed portion, $165,000 is an allocation of general overhead that would remain unchanged for the company as a whole if production of the starter assembly is discontinued. A further $110,000 of the fixed overhead is avoidable if self-manufacture of the starter assembly is discontinued. The balance of the current fixed overhead, $55,000, is the division manager's salary. If self-manufacture of the starter assembly is discontinued, the manager of Division 3 will be transferred to Division 2 at the same salary. This move will allow the company to save the $44,000 salary that would otherwise be paid to attract an outsider to this position.

REQUIRED
1. Tidnish Electronics, a reliable supplier, has offered to supply starter assembly units at $4 per unit. Since this price is less than the current average cost of $5 per unit, the vice-president of manufacturing is eager to accept this offer. Should the outside offer be accepted? (*Hint:* Production output in the coming year may be different from production output in the last year.)
2. How, if at all, would your response to requirement 1 change if the company could use the vacated plant space for storage and, in so doing, avoid $55,000 of outside storage charges currently incurred? Why is this information relevant or irrelevant?

11-39 Make or buy, activity-based costing, opportunity costs. (N. Melumad and S. Reichelstein, adapted) The Ace Bicycle Company produces bicycles. This year's expected production is 10,000 units. Currently, Ace makes the chains for its bicycles. Ace's accountant reports the following costs for making the 10,000 bicycle chains:

Costs	Costs for per Unit	10,000 Units
Direct materials	$4.40	$ 44,000
Direct labour	2.20	22,000
Variable manufacturing overhead (power and utilities)	1.65	16,500
Inspection, setup, materials-handling		2,200
Machine rent		3,300
Allocated fixed costs of plant administration, taxes, and insurance		33,000
Total costs		$121,000

Ace has received an offer from an outside vendor to supply any number of chains Ace requires at $9.02 per chain. The following additional information is available:
a. Inspection, setup, and materials-handling costs vary with the number of batches in which the chains are produced. Ace produces chains in batch sizes of 1,000 units. Ace estimates that it will produce the 10,000 units in ten batches.
b. Ace rents the machine used to make the chains. If Ace buys all its chains from the outside vendor, it does not need to pay rent on this machine.

REQUIRED
1. Assume that, if Ace purchases the chains from the outside supplier, the facility where the chains are currently made will remain idle. Should Ace accept the outside supplier's offer at the anticipated production (and sales) volume of 10,000 units?
2. For this question, assume that if the chains are purchased outside, the facilities where the chains are currently made will be used to upgrade the bicycles by adding mud flaps and reflectors. As a consequence, the selling price on bicycles will be raised by $22. The variable per-unit cost of the upgrade would be $19.80, and additional tooling costs of $17,600 would be incurred. Should Ace make or buy the chains, assuming that 10,000 units are produced (and sold)?
3. The sales manager at Ace is concerned that the estimate of 10,000 units may be high and believes that only 6,200 units will be sold. Production will be cut back,

and this opens up work space, which can be used to add the mud flaps and reflectors whether Ace goes outside for the chains or makes them in-house. At this lower output, Ace will produce the chains in eight batches of 775 units each. Should Ace purchase the chains from the outside vendor?

11-40 Relevant cost of materials. The Hernandez Corporation is bidding on a new construction contract, here called Contract No. 1. If the bid is accepted, work will begin in a few days, on January 1, 2007. Contract No. 1 requires a special cement. Hernandez has already purchased 10,000 kilograms of the special cement for $20,000. The current purchase cost of the cement is $2.40 per kilogram. The company could sell the cement now for $1.60 per kilogram after all selling costs.

Hernandez will also bid on Contract No. 2 one month from now. If Contract No. 1 is not landed, the special cement will be available for Contract No. 2. If Contract No. 1 is landed, Hernandez will need to buy 10,000 kilograms of another grade of cement for $2.50 per kilogram to fulfill Contract No. 2.

If it is not used in either of these two ways, the special cement would be of no use to the company and would be sold a little more than a month from now for $1.50 per kilogram after all selling costs.

The president of Hernandez, Julio Gomez, is puzzled about the appropriate total cost of the special cement to be used in bidding on Contract No. 1. Competition is intense and markups are very thin, so determining the relevant material costs when bidding on Contract No. 1 is crucial.

REQUIRED
1. Suppose Gomez is certain that Hernandez will land Contract No. 2; what (relevant) cost figure should Gomez use for the special cement when bidding on Contract No. 1?
2. This part requires knowledge of the material on decision making under uncertainty in the appendix to Chapter 3. Suppose Gomez estimates a probability of 0.7 that Hernandez will land Contract No. 2. What (relevant) cost figure should Gomez use for the special cement when bidding on Contract No. 1?
3. Suppose Hernandez could sell the special cement now for $2.30 per kilogram after all selling costs (instead of $1.60 per kilogram described in paragraph 1). Suppose Gomez is certain that Hernandez will land Contract No. 2. What (relevant) cost figure should Gomez use for the special cement when preparing a bid on Contract No. 1?

11-41 Optimal production mix. (CMA adapted, Chapter Appendix) Della Simpson, Inc., sells two popular brands of cookies, Della's Delight and Cathy's Chocolate Chip. Both cookies go through the Mixing and Baking Departments, but Della's Delight is also dipped in chocolate in the Coating Department.

Michael Sesnowitz, vice-president for sales, believes that Della Simpson can sell all of its daily production of Cathy's Chocolate Chip and Della's Delight. Both cookies are made in batches of 300 cookies. The batch times (in minutes) for producing each type of cookie and the minutes available per day are as follows:

	Mixing	**Baking**	**Dipping**
Della's Delight (in minutes)	36	12	24
Cathy's Chocolate Chip (in minutes)	18	18	0
Minutes available per day	720	360	384

Revenue and cost data for each type of cookie are

	Della's Delight	**Cathy's Chocolate Chip**
Revenue per batch	$ 630	$ 402
Variable cost per batch	210	102
Monthly fixed costs (allocated to each product)	24,420	19,980

REQUIRED
1. Formulate the decision facing Michael Sesnowitz as an LP model. Use D to represent the quantity of Della's Delight made and sold and C to represent the quantity of Cathy's Chocolate Chip made and sold.
2. Compute the optimal quantities of Della's Delight and Cathy's Chocolate Chip that Della Simpson should make and sell.

11-42 Optimal production plan, computer manufacturer. (Chapter Appendix) Information Technology, Inc., assembles and sells two products: printers and desktop computers.

Customers can purchase either (a) a computer or (b) a computer plus a printer. The printers are *not* sold without the computer. The result is that the quantity of printers sold is equal to or less than the quantity of desktop computers sold. The contribution margins are $240 per printer and $120 per computer.

Each printer requires 7.2 hours' assembly time on production line 1 and 12 hours' assembly time on production line 2. Each computer requires 4.8 hours' assembly time on production line 1 only. (Many of the components of each computer are preassembled by external vendors.) Production line 1 has 28.8* hours of available time per day. Production line 2 has 24 hours of available time per day.

Let X represent units of printers and Y represent units of desktop computers. The production manager must decide on the optimal mix of printers and computers to manufacture.

*Line 1 is actually two parallel lines, each used 14.4 hours per day. To simplify calculations count as one line with 28.8 hours.

REQUIRED

1. Express the production manager's problem in an LP format.
2. Which combination of printers and computers will maximize the operating income of Information Technology? Use both the trial-and-error and the graphic approach.

11-43 Optimal sales mix for a retailer, sensitivity analysis. (Chapter Appendix) Always Open, Inc., operates a chain of food stores open 24 hours a day. Each store has a standard 48,000 square metres of floor space available for merchandise. Merchandise is grouped in two categories: grocery products and dairy products. Always Open requires each store to devote a minimum of 12,000 square metres to grocery products and a minimum of 9,600 square metres to dairy products. Within these restrictions, each store manager can choose the mix of products to carry.

The manager of the Winnipeg store estimates the following weekly contribution margins per square metre: grocery products, $12; dairy products, $3.60.

REQUIRED

1. Formulate the decision facing the store manager as an LP model. Use G to represent square metres of floor space for grocery products and D to represent square metres of floor space for dairy products.
2. Why might Always Open set minimum bounds on the floor space devoted to each line of products?
3. Compute the optimal mix of grocery products and dairy products for the Winnipeg store.
4. Will the optimal mix determined in requirement 3 change if the contribution margins per square metre change to grocery products, $9.60, and dairy products, $6?

11-44 Make versus buy, ethics. (CMA, adapted) Lynn Hardt, a management accountant with the Paibec Corporation, is evaluating whether a component, MTR-85, should continue to be manufactured by Paibec or purchased from Marley Company, an outside supplier. Marley has submitted a bid to manufacture and supply the 32,000 units of MTR-85 that Paibec will need for 2008 at a unit price of $19.03 to be delivered according to Paibec's production specifications and needs. While the contract price of $19.03 is only applicable in 2008, Marley is interested in entering into a long-term arrangement beyond 2008.

Hardt has gathered the following information regarding Paibec's annual cost to manufacture 30,000 units of MTR-85 in 2007.

Direct materials	$214,500
Direct manufacturing labour costs	132,000
Plant space rental costs	92,400
Equipment leasing costs	39,600
Other manufacturing overhead costs	247,500
Total manufacturing costs	$726,000

Hardt has collected the following additional information related to manufacturing MTR-85.

◆ Direct materials used in the production of MTR-85 are expected to increase 8% in 2008.

◆ Paibec's direct manufacturing labour contract calls for a 5% increase in 2008.

◆ Paibec can withdraw from the plant space rental agreement without any penalty. Paibec will have no need for this space if MTR-85 is not manufactured.

◆ The equipment lease can be terminated by paying $6,600.

◆ Forty percent of the other manufacturing overhead is considered variable. Variable overhead changes with the number of units produced. The rate per unit is not expected to change in 2008. The fixed manufacturing overhead costs are not expected to change whether or not MTR-85 is manufactured.

John Porter, plant manager at Paibec Corporation, is concerned that Hardt's analysis may lead to the closing down of the MTR-85 line. Porter indicates to Hardt that the current performance of the plant can be significantly improved on and that the price increases she is assuming are unlikely to occur. Hence, the analysis should be done assuming costs will be considerably below current levels. Hardt knows that Porter is concerned about outsourcing MTR-85 because it will mean that some of his close friends will be laid off. Furthermore, Porter had played a key role in convincing management to produce MTR-85 in-house.

Hardt believes that it is unlikely that the plant will achieve the lower costs Porter describes. She is very confident about the accuracy of the information she has collected, but she is unhappy about laying off employees.

REQUIRED

1. Based on the information Hardt has obtained, should Paibec make MTR-85 or buy it? Show all calculations.
2. What other factors should Paibec consider before making a decision?
3. What should Lynn Hardt do in response to John Porter's comments?

11-45 Ethics and relevant costs. The Pastel Company must reach a make/buy decision with respect to a high-volume, easily made metal tool, RG1. Sean Gray, the cost analyst, estimates the following costs and production information for the 50,000 units of RG1 that are expected to be put into production.

Total direct materials costs	$660,000
Direct manufacturing labour costs (all variable)	$220,000
Manufacturing overhead costs (all fixed)	$440,000
Good units of RG1 manufactured and sold	40,000 units
Units of RG1 scrapped for zero revenue	10,000 units

York Corporation has offered to supply as many units of RG1 as Pastel needs for $23.10 per unit. If Pastel buys RG1 from York instead of manufacturing it in-house, Pastel would be able to save $263,450 of the $440,000 fixed manufacturing overhead costs. (There is no alternative use for the capacity currently used to make RG1.)

Gray shows his analysis to Jim Berry, the controller. Berry does not like what he sees. He asks Gray to review all his assumptions and calculations with the comment, "The yield assumptions you made are very low. I think this plant can achieve much better quality than we have in the past. Better quality will reduce our costs and make them competitive with the outside purchase price." Gray knows that Berry is very concerned about purchasing RG1 from an outside supplier because it will mean that some of his close friends who work on the RG1 line will be laid off. Berry had played a key role in convincing management to produce RG1 in-house.

Gray rechecks his calculations. He believes it is unlikely that the plant can achieve the quality levels it would take for the make alternative to be superior to the buy alternative.

REQUIRED

1. Based on the information Gray obtains, should Pastel make or buy RG1?
2. For what levels of scrap would the make alternative be preferred to purchasing from outside?
3. Evaluate whether Jim Berry's suggestion to Gray to review his estimates is unethical. Will it be unethical for Gray to change his analysis to support the make alternative? What steps should Gray take next?

COLLABORATIVE LEARNING PROBLEM

11-46 Optimal product mix. (CMA, adapted) OmniSport's Plastics Department is currently manufacturing 5,000 pairs of skates annually, making full use of its machine capacity. Presented below are the selling price and costs associated with OmniSport's skates.

Selling price per pair of skates		$117.60
Costs per pair of skates		
Moulded plastic	$ 9.60	
Other direct materials	14.40	
Variable machine operating costs ($19.20 per hour)	28.80	
Manufacturing overhead costs	21.60	
Marketing and administrative costs	18.00[a]	92.40
Operating income per pair of skates		$ 25.20

Note: 5,000 pairs of skates × 1.5 hr/pair of skates = 7,500 hours to complete
[a]$18.00 − $7.20 = $10.80 Selling and administrative costs

OmniSport believes it could sell 8,000 pairs of skates annually if it had sufficient manufacturing capacity. Colcott, Inc., a steady supplier of quality products, has agreed to provide 6,000 pairs of skates per year at a price of $90 per pair delivered to OmniSport's facility.

Jack Petrone, OmniSport's product manager, has suggested that the company can make better use of its Plastics Department by manufacturing snowboard bindings. Petrone believes that OmniSport could expect to sell 12,000 snowboard bindings annually at a price of $72 per binding. Petrone's estimate of the costs to manufacture the bindings is presented next.

Selling price per snowboard binding		$72.00
Costs per snowboard binding		
Moulded plastic	$19.20	
Other direct materials	4.80	
Variable machine operating costs ($19.20 per hour)	9.60[b]	
Manufacturing overhead costs	7.20	
Marketing and administrative costs	16.80[c]	57.60
Operating income per snowboard binding		$14.40

[b]12,000 snowboard bindings $\times$ 0.5 hr/snowboard binding = 6,000 hours, leaving
7,500 hr – 6,000 hr = 1,500 to complete skates at 1.5 hr/pair of skates = 1,000 pairs of skates completed
[c]$16.80 – $7.20 = $9.60 Selling and administrative costs

Other information pertinent to OmniSport's operations is presented below.

◆ An allocated $7.20 fixed overhead cost per unit is included in the marketing and administrative cost for all the purchased and manufactured products. Total fixed and variable marketing and administrative costs for the purchased skates would be $12 per pair.

$12.00 – $7.20 = $4.80 Selling and administrative costs

◆ In the Plastics Department, OmniSport uses machine hours as the allocation base for other manufacturing overhead costs. The fixed manufacturing overhead component of these costs for the current year is the $36,000 of fixed plantwide manufacturing overhead that has been allocated to the Plastics Department.

INSTRUCTIONS
Form groups of two students to complete the following requirement.

REQUIRED
Which product or products should OmniSport manufacture and/or purchase to maximize operating income? Show all calculations.

11-47 Relevant costs, opportunity costs. Larry Miller, the general manager of Basil Software, scheduled a meeting on June 2, 2007, with Nicole Nguyen, sales manager, Andy Ayim, accountant, and Ellen Eisner, software operations manager, to discuss the development and release of Basil Software's new version of its spreadsheet package, Easyspread 2.0. It is only a question of time before other software firms have a package that matches Easyspread 2.0. Nicole Nguyen, the sales manager, could hardly control her enthusiasm for the new product.

Nicole Nguyen: This product is exactly what the market has been waiting for. We should not delay, by even a single day, the introduction of this product. Let's make July 1, 2007, the sales release date.

Ellen Eisner: I don't disagree with Nicole's assessment of the market potential for this product, but I have a problem. The threatened strike by our printers caused us to purchase large quantities of user's manuals for Easyspread 1.0. We don't like to store the manuals separately, so we also got extra diskettes duplicated. The manuals and diskettes were then packaged and shrink-wrapped. We are currently holding 60,000 completed packages, which equals the expected sales for July, August, and September 2007 of Easyspread 1.0. I think we should make October 1, 2007, the expected release date of Easyspread 2.0. This date would enable us to sell all of our inventory of Easyspread 1.0.

Larry Miller: Nicole, do you see any problem with Ellen's suggestion? Our inventory of Easyspread 1.0 seems rather large for us to ignore. If we introduce Easyspread 2.0 on July 1, what would we do with the inventory of Easyspread 1.0 that we currently hold?

Nicole Nguyen: We currently sell Easyspread 1.0 to our wholesalers and distributors for $203.50 each. The additional optimization features in Easyspread 2.0 mean that we should be able to sell Easyspread 2.0 to our distributors for about $203.50. We should not ignore the higher profit margins from Easyspread 2.0. It is true, though, that each time we sell one unit of Easyspread 2.0, we forgo the sale of one unit of Easyspread 1.0. Since the expected demand for Easyspread 2.0 is at least as large as the demand for Easyspread 1.0, we may have to throw away the existing inventory of Easyspread 1.0 once we introduce Easyspread 2.0.

Larry Miller: Andy, you've heard what Nicole and Ellen have to say. I would like you to do a detailed analysis of the alternatives, and let me know within a week what you come up with. We need to make a decision on this one way or another, and we need to do so soon.

When Andy Ayim returned to his office, he pulled out the cost records he had developed for Easyspread 1.0 and Easyspread 2.0. The unit costs for the two products could be summarized as follows:

	Easyspread 1.0	Easyspread 2.0
Manuals, diskettes	$ 22.00	$ 27.50
Development costs	82.50	115.50
Marketing and administration costs	27.50	33.00
Total cost per unit	$132.00	$176.00

The following additional facts are available:
a. Basil contracts with outside vendors to print manuals and duplicate diskettes.
b. Development costs are allocated on the basis of the total costs of developing the software and the anticipated unit sales over the life of the software.
c. Marketing and administration costs are fixed costs in 2007, incurred to support all activities of Basil Software. Marketing and administration costs are allocated to products on the basis of the budgeted revenues from each of the products. The preceding unit costs assume Easyspread 2.0 will be introduced on July 1, 2007.

INSTRUCTIONS
Form groups of three students to complete the following requirements. To answer requirement 2, each student should play the role of one of Larry Miller, Nicole Nguyen, and Ellen Eisner.

REQUIRED
1. Based on financial considerations only, is Basil Software better off introducing Easyspread 2.0 immediately or waiting? Explain your conclusion, clearly identifying relevant and irrelevant costs.
2. What other factors might Nicole Nguyen and Ellen Eisner raise? What factors might Larry Miller consider important?

CHAPTER 12

Pricing Decisions, Product Profitability Decisions, and Cost Management

Manufacturing and selling steel is globally competitive. Steel is a commodity and its price is primarily established in a competitive market according to supply and demand. In the trade disputes that countries bring for adjudication before the World Trade Organization, they commonly allege that competitors are selling their product below market value and materially injuring the domestic industry.

Canadian companies like IPSCO Inc. must understand their costs and the implications for pricing to compete effectively and capture an appropriate market share in an increasingly competitive global market.

LEARNING OBJECTIVES

After studying this chapter, you should be able to

1. Discuss the three major influences on pricing decisions

2. Distinguish between short-run and long-run pricing decisions

3. Price products using the target-costing approach to pricing

4. Apply the concepts of cost incurrence and locked-in costs

5. Price products using the cost-plus approach to pricing

6. Describe two pricing practices in which noncost reasons are important when setting price

7. Understand how life cycle product budgeting and costing assist in pricing decisions

8. Understand the effects of competition laws on pricing

M anagers make pricing decisions about what to charge for the products and services their companies deliver. For brevity, we use the term *pricing decision* in this chapter to include decisions about the profitability of products. These decisions affect the revenues a company earns, which must exceed total costs if profits are to be achieved. Consequently, determining product costs is important for pricing decisions. There is, however, no single way of computing a product cost that is universally relevant for all pricing decisions. Why? Because pricing decisions differ greatly in both their time horizons and their contexts. We emphasize how an understanding of cost behaviour patterns and cost drivers can lead to better pricing decisions and also apply the relevant-revenue and relevant-cost framework described in Chapter 11.

Economic theory indicates that companies acting optimally should produce and sell units until the marginal revenue (the incremental revenue from selling an incremental unit based on the demand for a product) equals the marginal or variable cost (the incremental cost of supplying an incremental unit). The market price is the price that creates a demand for these optimal numbers of units. This chapter describes how managers evaluate demand at different prices, manage their costs to influence supply, and earn a profit.

MAJOR INFLUENCES ON PRICING

OBJECTIVE 1

Discuss the three major influences on pricing decisions

Journal of Economic Theory
www.nyu.edu/jet

Bell
www.bell.ca

Bombardier
www.bombardier.com

Bank of Montreal
www.bmo.ca

Telus
www.telus.ca

There are three major influences on pricing decisions: customers, competitors, and costs.

◆ *Customers.* Managers must always examine pricing problems through the eyes of their customers. A price increase may cause customers to reject a company's product and choose a competing or substitute product because they perceive the substitute provides more value or benefit in use for the price they are willing to pay.

◆ *Competitors.* Competitors' reactions influence pricing decisions. At one extreme, a rival's prices and products may force a business to lower its prices to be competitive. At the other extreme, a business without a rival in a given situation can set higher prices. Managers of a company who know about its rival's technology, plant capacity, and operating policies are able to estimate a rival's costs, which is valuable information in setting competitive prices.

Competition spans international borders. For example, when companies have excess capacity in their domestic markets, they often take an aggressive pricing policy in their export markets. Today, managers often take a global viewpoint, and it is increasingly common for them to consider both domestic and international rivals in making pricing decisions. In the global market, cost and pricing decisions are also affected by fluctuations in the exchange rates of currencies among different countries, as well as tax regimes. These considerations become extremely important for companies manufacturing components in different parts of the world and transferring them to a plant where they are assembled into the final product.

Competitor analysis takes different forms. Many companies, including Bell Canada, Bombardier, Bank of Montreal, and Telus, have established departments to search out information on their competitors' financial performance, patents, technologies, revenue and cost structures, and strategic alliances. Competitors themselves and their customers, suppliers, and former employees are important sources of information. Another form of obtaining information is via reverse engineering—a process of analyzing and tearing apart competitors' products—to incorporate the best features, materials, and technology in a company's own designs.

◆ *Costs.* Companies price products to exceed the costs of making them. The study of cost behaviour patterns gives insight into the income that results from different combinations of price and output quantities sold for a particular product.

Economic theory and surveys of how executives make pricing decisions reveal that companies weigh customers, competitors, and costs differently. Companies selling commodity products such as steel, wheat, and rice have many competitors, each offering identical products. In highly competitive markets one supplier cannot influence the price and must accept the price determined by market forces. The market sets the price, but cost data can help these sellers to decide on the output level that best meets a company's particular profit objective.

In less competitive markets where features can distinguish one product from another (for example, automobiles, cellular phones, flat screen televisions, and laptop computers), managers have some discretion in setting prices. For these differentiated products, the pricing decision depends on three factors. First is how much customers value the product; second is the pricing strategies of competitors; and third is the costs of the product. The price of a product or service is the outcome of the interaction between *demand* for the product or service and its *supply*. Customers influence prices through their effect on demand. Costs influence prices because they affect supply. Competitors offer alternative or substitute products and thereby affect demand and price.

At the extreme are oligopolies where only a few companies produce a product or service, such as the markets for computer chips and petroleum products, and monopolies where there is only a single producer. Monopolists can decide to set prices higher than would be possible in a competitive market; however, if the price is too high, customers will be unwilling to purchase the product. Demand will fall, quantity of sales will decrease, and so will the monopolist's operating income.

PRODUCT COST CATEGORIES AND TIME HORIZON

Chapter 1 described customer satisfaction, continuous improvement, and the dual internal/external focus as important, newly evolving themes in management. Pricing is an area where explicitly these themes come together. For example, charging lower prices for high-quality products is important for customer satisfaction, an external focus. But when prices are lower, costs must be reduced as well. Continuous improvement, an internal focus, is the key to keeping costs down.

OBJECTIVE 2

Distinguish between short-run and long-run pricing decisions

When reducing costs, a company must consider costs in all six value-chain business functions, from R&D to customer service. In computing the costs within these functions that are relevant in a pricing decision, the time horizon of the decision is critical. Most pricing decisions are either short run or long run. Short-run decisions include both pricing for a one-time-only special order with no long-term implications and adjusting product mix and output volume in a competitive market. The time horizon used to compute those costs that differ among the alternatives for short-run decisions is typically six months or less but sometimes as long as a year. Long-run decisions include pricing a product in a major market where price setting has considerable leeway. A time horizon of a year or longer is used when computing relevant costs for these long-run decisions. Many pricing decisions have both short-run and long-run implications. Two key differences affect pricing for the long run versus the short run:

1. Fixed costs that remain unchanged in the short run—for example, the cost of permanently increasing or decreasing capacity—will be relevant only in the long run because they can only be altered over a long time horizon.

2. Profit margins in long-run pricing decisions are often set to earn a reasonable return on investment. Short-run pricing is opportunistic whereby prices are decreased when demand decreases and increased when demand increases.

We next examine short-run pricing decisions.

COSTING AND PRICING FOR THE SHORT RUN

A One-Time-Only Special Order

Consider a one-time-only special order from a customer to supply products for the next four months. Acceptance or rejection of the order will not affect the revenues (units sold or the selling price per unit) from existing sales outlets. The customer is unlikely to place any future sales orders.

Consider a short-run pricing decision facing the management team at Astel Computers. Datatech Corporation has asked Astel to bid on supplying 5,000 Provalue computers over the next three months. After this three-month period, Datatech is unlikely to place any future sales orders with Astel. Datatech will sell Provalue computers under its own brand name in regions and markets where Astel does not sell Provalue. Whether Astel accepts or rejects this order will not affect Astel's revenues—neither the units sold nor the selling price—from existing sales channels.

Relevant Costs for Short-Run Pricing Decisions

Before Astel can bid on Datatech's offer, Astel's managers must first estimate how much it will cost to supply the 5,000 computers. Similar to the Surf Gear example in Chapter 11, the relevant costs Astel's managers must focus on include all direct and indirect costs throughout the value chain that will change in total by accepting the one-time-only special order from Datatech. Astel's managers outline the relevant costs in the following table:

Direct materials ($460 per computer × 5,000 computers)	$2,300,000
Direct manufacturing labour ($64 per computer × 5,000 computers)	320,000
Fixed costs of additional capacity to manufacture Provalue	250,000
Total costs	$2,870,000*

*No additional costs will be required for R&D, design, marketing, distribution, or customer service.

For some decisions, it's erroneous to assume that variable costs are relevant and fixed costs are irrelevant. For example, in the Astel-Datatech special-order decision, the fixed costs of additional capacity to manufacture Provalue are relevant.

The relevant cost per computer is $574 ($2,870,000 ÷ 5,000). Therefore, any selling price above $574 will improve Astel's profitability in the short run. Astel's managers also know that one of its competitors with a highly efficient plant has significant idle capacity and is eager to win the Datatech contract. Armed with all this information, what price should Astel's managers bid for the 5,000-computer order?

Strategic and Other Factors in Short-Run Pricing

In choosing how much to bid, Astel's managers must be strategic. If, based on its market intelligence, Astel believes its competitor will bid between $596 and $610 per computer, Astel could bid $595 per computer and still increase operating income by $105,000 (relevant revenues, $595 × 5,000 = $2,975,000 minus relevant costs, $2,870,000). Management's strategy is to bid as high above $574 as possible while remaining lower than competitors' bids.

Astel's managers also carefully reconsidered the probability Datatech would decide to undercut Astel's selling price in the current markets. If Astel's managers believe this is a significant risk, the relevant costs of the bidding decision should include the contribution margin lost on sales to existing customers. If Astel's managers view the threat to its existing business from accepting the Datatech order to be serious enough, they may decide not to bid for the Datatech business, or they may quote Datatech a price close to the price Astel charges its other customers. After carefully evaluating the situation, Astel's managers conclude that Datatech will not undercut prices to Astel's customers, so Astel makes a bid to supply Provalue computers at a price of $595 each.

Astel's short-run pricing decision focused on identifying a sufficiently low price at which Astel would still make a profit. That's because we assumed (a) Astel has access to extra capacity and (b) a competitor with an efficient plant and idle capacity was likely to make a low bid. However, short-run pricing does not always work this way. Companies may experience strong demand for their products in the short run, but they may have limited capacity. In these cases, companies strategically increase prices in the short run to as much as the market will bear. We observe high short-run prices in the case of new products or new models of older products, such as microprocessors, computer chips, cellular telephones, and software.

COSTING AND PRICING FOR THE LONG RUN

Bechtel Corporation
www.bechtel.com

Many pricing decisions are made for the long run. Buyers—whether a person buying a box of Corn Flakes, a construction company, such as Bechtel Corporation, buying a fleet of tractors, or General Foods Corporation buying audit services—prefer stable prices over an extended time horizon. A stable price reduces the need for continuous monitoring of suppliers' prices. Greater price stability also improves planning and builds long-run buyer-seller relationships.

Calculating Product Costs for Long-Run Pricing Decisions

Obtaining accurate product cost information is essential to a manager making a pricing decision. In industries such as oil and gas and mining, competitive forces set the price for a product, and knowledge of long-run product costs can guide decisions about entering or remaining in the market. In other industries such as specialized machines, appliances, and automobiles, managers have some control over the price charged for a product, and long-run product costs can be used as a base for setting that price.

Consider the Astel Computer Corporation. Astel manufactures two brands of personal computers (PCs)—Deskpoint and Provalue. Deskpoint is Astel's top-of-the-line product sold through computer dealers to large organizations and government accounts. Our analysis focuses on pricing Provalue, a less powerful machine sold through catalogues and mass merchandisers to individual consumers and small organizations.

The manufacturing costs of Provalue are calculated using the activity-based costing (ABC) approach described in Chapters 4 and 5. Astel has three direct manufacturing cost categories (direct materials, direct manufacturing labour, and direct machining costs) and three indirect manufacturing cost pools (ordering and receiving, testing and inspection, and rework) in its accounting system. Astel treats machining costs as a direct cost of Provalue because it is manufactured on machines that are used for no other products. The following table summarizes the activity cost pools, the cost driver for each activity, and the cost per unit of the cost driver that Astel uses to allocate manufacturing overhead costs to products.

Manufacturing Activity	Description of Activity	Cost Driver	Cost per Unit of Cost Driver
1. Ordering and receiving	Placing orders, receiving, and paying for components	Number of orders	$80 per order
2. Testing and inspection	Testing components and final product	Testing-hours	$2 per testing-hour
3. Rework	Correcting and fixing errors and defects	Units reworked	$40 per unit reworked

Astel uses a long-run time horizon to price Provalue. Over this horizon, Astel's management views direct materials costs and direct manufacturing labour costs as variable with respect to the units of Provalue produced, and manufacturing overhead costs as variable with respect to their chosen cost drivers. For example, ordering and receiving costs vary with the number of orders. Staff members responsible for placing orders can be reassigned or laid off in the long run if fewer orders need to be placed. Direct machining costs (rent paid on leased machines) do not vary over this time horizon for the relevant range of production; they are fixed long-run costs.

Astel has no beginning or ending inventory of Provalue in 2007 and manufactures and sells 150,000 units. How does Astel calculate Provalue's manufacturing costs? It uses the following information (summarized in the spreadsheet on the next page), which indicates the resources used to manufacture Provalue in 2007:

1. Direct materials costs per unit of Provalue are $460.

2. Direct manufacturing labour costs per unit of Provalue are $64.

3. Direct fixed costs of machines used exclusively for the manufacture of Provalue are $11,400,000.

4. Number of orders placed to purchase components required for the manufacture of Provalue is 22,500. (We assume for simplicity that Provalue has 450 components supplied by different suppliers and that 50 orders are placed for each component to match Provalue's production schedule.)

5. Number of testing-hours used for Provalue is 4,500,000 (150,000 Provalue units are tested for 30 hours per unit).

6. Number of units of Provalue reworked during the year is 12,000 (8% of the 150,000 units manufactured).

Cost Category (1)	Cost Driver (2)	Details of Cost Driver Quantities (3)		(4)		Total Quantity of Cost Driver (5) = (3) × (4)	Cost per Unit of Cost Driver (6)
				PROVALUE			
				150,000	output units		
Direct Manufacturing Costs							
Direct materials	No. of kits	1	kit per output unit	150,000	output units	150,000	$460
Direct manufacturing labour (DML)	DML hours	3.2	DML hours per output unit	150,000	output units	480,000	$ 20
Direct machining (fixed)	Machine-hours	2	machine-hours per output unit	150,000	output units	300,000	$ 38
Manufacturing Overhead Costs							
Ordering and receiving	No. of orders	50	orders per component	450	components	22,500	$ 80
Testing and inspection	Testing-hours	30	testing-hours per output unit	150,000	output units	4,500,000	$ 2
Rework				8%	defect rate		
	Rework-hours	2.5	rework-hours per defective unit	12,000[a]	defective units	30,000	$ 40
[a]8% defect rate × 150,000 output units = 12,000 defective units							

Exhibit 12-1 indicates that the total cost of manufacturing Provalue is $102 million and the manufacturing cost per unit is $680. Manufacturing, however, is only one business function of the value chain. To set long-run prices that will cover all the costs of doing business and achieve a target profit, Astel's managers must calculate the *full cost* of producing and selling Provalue.

For its nonmanufacturing business functions in the value chain, Astel's managers identify direct costs and choose cost drivers and cost pools for indirect costs that measure cause-and-effect relationships. Astel's managers allocate costs to Provalue based on the quantity of cost-driver units that Provalue uses. Exhibit 12-2 summarizes the operating income for Provalue for 2007 based on an activity-based analysis of costs in all business functions. (For brevity, supporting calculations for nonmanufacturing business functions are not given.) Astel earns $15 million from Provalue, or $100 per unit sold in 2007.

Alternative Long-Run Pricing Approaches

The starting point for pricing decisions can be

1. Market-based

2. Cost-based (also called cost-plus)

The market-based approach to pricing *starts* by asking: Given what our customers want and how our competitors will react to what we do, what price should we charge? The cost-based approach to pricing *starts* by asking: What does it cost us to make this product, and hence what price should we charge that will recoup our costs and produce a desired profit? Both approaches consider customers, competitors, and costs. Only their starting points differ.

Companies may take one of two approaches. Some companies start by antici-pating customer and competitor reactions and then examine costs—the market-based

EXHIBIT 12-1
Manufacturing Costs of Provalue for 2007 Using Activity-Based Costing

	A	B	C
1		Total	
2		Manufacturing	
3		Costs for	Manufacturing
4		150,000 Units	Cost per Unit
5		(1)	(2) = (1) ÷ 150,000
6	Direct manufacturing costs:		
7	Direct materials costs (150,000 units × $460)	$69,000,000	$460
8	Direct manufacturing labour costs (150,000 units × $64)	9,600,000	64
9	Direct machining costs (fixed costs of $11,400,000)	11,400,000	76
10	Direct manufacturing costs	90,000,000	600
11	Manufacturing overhead costs:		
12	Ordering and receiving costs (22,500 orders × $80)	1,800,000	12
13	Testing and inspection costs (4,500,000 hours × $2)	9,000,000	60
14	Rework costs (12,000 units × $100)	1,200,000	8
15	Manufacturing overhead costs	12,000,000	80
16	Total manufacturing costs	$102,000,000	$680

EXHIBIT 12-2
Product Profitability of Provalue for 2007 Using Value-Chain Activity-Based Costing

	A	B	C
1		Total Amounts	
2		for 150,000 Units	Per Unit
3		(1)	(2) = (1) ÷ 150,000
4	Revenue	$150,000,000	$1,000
5	Cost of goods sold[a] (from Exhibit 12-1)	102,000,000	680
6	Operating costs[b]		
7	R&D costs	5,400,000	36
8	Design costs of product and process	6,000,000	40
9	Marketing costs	15,000,000	100
10	Distribution costs	3,600,000	24
11	Customer-service costs	3,000,000	20
12	Operating costs	33,000,000	220
13	Full cost of the product	135,000,000	900
14	Operating income	$ 15,000,000	$ 100
15			
16	[a]Cost of goods sold = Total manufacturing costs because there is no beginning or ending inventory of Provalue in 2007		
17	[b]Numbers for operating-cost line items are assumed without supporting calculations.		

approach. In very *competitive* markets (for example, steel, petroleum products, wheat, and rice) the market-based approach is logical. The items produced or services provided by one company are almost identical to those produced or provided by others, so companies have no influence over the prices customers are willing to pay. In contrast, other companies first look at costs and then consider customers or competitors—the cost-based approach. Companies in *noncompetitive* markets favour this approach because they do not need to respond either to competitors' prices or consumers' reactions. In industries where there is more product differentiation (for example, automobiles, consumer electronics, management consulting, and professional services) firms have more discretion over prices, products, and services. Notice that all companies consider all three factors but their starting points differ. A final decision on price, product, and service is made after evaluating these external influences on pricing along with the costs to produce and sell the product. We will begin by considering the market-based approach.

TARGET COSTING FOR TARGET PRICING

OBJECTIVE 3

Price products using the target-costing approach to pricing

Target price. Estimated price for a product (or service) that potential customers will be willing to pay.

Target operating income per unit. Operating income that a company wants to earn on each unit of a product (or service) sold.

Target cost per unit. Estimated long-run cost per unit of a product (or service) that when sold at the target price enables the company to achieve the targeted income per unit. Derived by subtracting the target operating income per unit from the target price.

Market-based pricing starts with a target price. A **target price** is the estimated price for a product or service that potential customers will pay. This estimate is based on an understanding of customers' perceived value for a product or service and how competitors will price competing products or services. A **target operating income per unit** is the operating income that a company wants to earn on each unit of a product (or service) sold. The target price leads to a *target cost*. A **target cost per unit** is the estimated long-run cost per unit of a product (or service) that, when sold at the target price, enables the company to achieve the target operating income per unit. Target cost per unit is derived by subtracting the target operating income per unit from the target price. Having this understanding of customers and competitors has become important for three reasons:

1. Competition from lower-cost producers has meant that prices cannot be increased.

2. Products are on the market for shorter periods of time, leaving less time and opportunity to recover from pricing mistakes.

3. Customers have become more knowledgeable and demand quality products at reasonable prices.

Understanding Customers' Perceived Value

A company's sales and marketing organization, through close contact and interaction with customers, is usually in the best position to identify customers' needs and their perceived value for a product or service. Companies also conduct market research studies about product features that customers want and the prices they are willing to pay for those features. Increasingly, through statistical analyses of data provided by cards such as Air Miles (often referred to as *data mining*), companies identify the characteristics of their typical customers and how well these match with their intended customer base.

Doing Competitor Analysis

To gauge how competitors might react to a prospective price, a company needs to understand competitors' technologies, products or services, costs, and financial conditions. For example, knowing competitors' technologies and products helps a company (a) to evaluate how distinctive its own products or services will be in the market and (b) to determine the prices it might be able to charge as a result of being distinctive. Where does a company obtain information about its competitors? Usually from customers, suppliers, and employees of competitors, although large companies such as DaimlerChrysler employ people whose sole purpose is to analyze competitors. Another source of information is *reverse engineering*—that is, disassembling and analyzing competitors' products to determine product designs and materials and to become acquainted with the technologies competitors use.

What relevant costs should we include in the target cost calculations? *All* costs, both variable and fixed. Why? Because in the long run, a company's prices and revenues must recover all its costs. If not, the company's best alternative is to shut down. Regarding the shutting-down alternative, all costs, whether fixed or variable, are relevant.

Target cost per unit is often lower than the existing full product cost per unit. To achieve the target cost per unit and the target operating income per unit, the organization must improve its products and processes. Target costing is widely used among different industries around the world.

Implementing Target Pricing and Target Costing

Developing target prices and target costs requires the following five steps:

◆ **Step 1.** Develop a product that satisfies the needs of potential customers.

◆ **Step 2.** Choose a *target price* based on customers' perceived value for the product and the prices competitors charge, and a *target operating income per unit*.

◆ **Step 3.** Derive a *target cost per unit* by subtracting the target operating income per unit from the target price.

◆ **Step 4.** Perform *cost/product analysis*. This step analyzes which aspects of a product or service to target for cost reduction.

◆ **Step 5.** Perform *value engineering* to achieve target costs. **Value engineering** is a systematic evaluation of all aspects of the value-chain business functions, with the objective of reducing costs while satisfying customer needs. Value engineering can result in improvements in product designs, changes in materials specifications, or modifications in process methods.

Value engineering. Systematic evaluation of all aspects of the value-chain business functions, with the objective of reducing costs while satisfying customer needs.

We illustrate the five steps for target pricing and target costing using the Astel Computers example introduced earlier in the chapter.

◆ **Step 1:** *Product planning for Provalue.* Astel is in the process of planning design modifications for Provalue. Astel is very concerned about severe price competition from several competitors.

◆ **Step 2:** *Target price of Provalue.* Astel expects its competitors to lower the prices of PCs that compete against Provalue by 15%. Astel's management believes that it must respond aggressively by reducing Provalue's price by 20%, from $1,000 per unit to $800 per unit. At this lower price, Astel's marketing manager forecasts an increase in annual sales from 150,000 to 200,000 units.

◆ **Step 3:** *Target cost per unit of Provalue.* Astel's management wants a 10% target operating income on sales revenues.

Total target sales revenues	= $800 × 200,000 units = $160,000,000
Total target operating income	= 10% × $160,000,000 = $16,000,000
Target operating income per unit	= $16,000,000 ÷ 200,000 units = $80 per unit
Target cost per unit	= Target price − target operating income per unit
	= $800 − $80 = $720
Total current costs of Provalue	= $135,000,000 (from Exhibit 12-2)
Current cost per unit of Provalue	= $135,000,000 ÷ 150,000 units = $900 per unit

The target cost per unit of $720 is substantially lower than Provalue's existing unit cost of $900. The goal is to find ways to reduce the cost per unit of Provalue by $180, from $900 to $720. The challenge in steps 4 and 5 is to achieve the target cost through cost/product analysis and value engineering.

◆ **Step 4:** *Perform cost/product analysis for Provalue.* Astel's managers consider the following:

◆ The function performed by different component parts such as the motherboard, disc drives, and the graphics and video cards.

◆ The current costs of the different component parts.

♦ The importance that customers place on different product features. For example, Astel's targeted customers place greater emphasis on the reliability of the computer than on video quality.

♦ How different features relate to the functions performed by different component parts. For example, the reliability of the computer can be enhanced by using a simpler motherboard. However, the newly designed computer may not be able to support the top-of-the-line video card, but this is of little concern to Astel because video quality is not as important to Astel's targeted customers.

♦ **Step 5:** *Value engineering for Provalue.* An important element of Astel's value engineering is determining the kind of PC that will meet the needs of potential customers. For example, the existing Provalue design accommodates various upgrades that can make the PC run faster and perform calculations more quickly. It also comes with special audio features. An essential first step in the value engineering process is to determine whether potential customers are willing to pay the price for these features. Customer feedback indicates that customers do not value Provalue's extra features. They want Astel to redesign Provalue into a no-frills PC and sell it at a much lower price. Value engineering at Astel then proceeds with cross-functional teams consisting of marketing managers, product designers, manufacturing engineers, and production supervisors making suggestions for design improvements and process modifications. Cost accountants estimate the savings in costs that would result from the proposed changes.

Value-added cost. A cost that customers perceive as adding value of usefulness to a product or service.

Managers often find the distinction between value-added and non-value-added activities and costs introduced in Chapter 2 useful in value engineering. A **value-added cost** is a cost that customers perceive as adding value, or utility (usefulness), to a product or service. Determining value-added costs requires identifying attributes that customers perceive to be important. For Provalue, these attributes include the PC's features and its price. Activities undertaken within the company (such as the manufacturing line) influence the attributes that customers value. Astel assesses whether each activity adds value or not. Activities and the costs of these activities do not always fall neatly into value-added or non-value-added categories. Some costs fall in the grey area in between, and include both value-added and non-value-added components (see the Concepts in Action box to learn about IKEA's approach to target pricing and target costing).

Value Engineering, Cost Incurrence, and Locked-in Costs

Traditional cost accounting systems do not classify costs as value-added or non-value-added. To obtain this information, management accountants must work closely with production and marketing personnel.

In the Provalue example, direct materials, direct manufacturing labour, and machining costs are value-added costs; ordering and testing costs fall in the grey area (customers perceive some portion of but not all of these costs as necessary for adding value); while rework costs are non-value-added costs. Astel's goal in value engineering would be to reduce and if possible eliminate non-value-added costs such as rework costs by reducing the defect rate. To increase efficiency, Astel's goal in value engineering would be to reduce value-added costs by reducing, for example, direct manufacturing labour costs.

Value engineering seeks to reduce or eliminate non-value-added activities and hence non-value-added costs by reducing the cost drivers of the non-value-added activities. For example, to reduce rework costs, Astel must reduce rework-hours. Value engineering also focuses on achieving greater efficiency in value-added activities to reduce value-added costs. For example, to reduce direct manufacturing labour costs, Astel must reduce the time it takes to make Provalue. But how should Astel reduce rework time and direct manufacturing labour time? We focus on these issues next.

OBJECTIVE 4

Apply the concepts of cost incurrence and locked-in costs

Cost incurrence. Occurs when a resource is sacrificed or used up.

Two key concepts in value engineering and in managing value-added and non-value-added costs are *cost incurrence* and *locked-in costs*. **Cost incurrence** occurs when a resource is sacrificed or used up. Costing systems emphasize cost incurrence. They recognize and record costs only when costs are incurred. Astel's costing system, for example, recognizes the direct materials costs of Provalue as each unit of Provalue is

Extreme Target Pricing and Cost Management at IKEA

For millions of loyal customers throughout the world, Swedish furniture giant IKEA has achieved an almost cult-like status. Known for products with unpronounceable names, flat packaging, and do-it-yourself instructions, IKEA has grown from humble beginnings to become the world's largest furniture retailer with 186 stores in 31 countries. How did this happen? Through aggressive target pricing, coupled with relentless cost management. IKEA's prices typically run 30% to 50% below their competitors' prices.

To achieve such low prices, the process of driving down costs begins with product conceptualization. First, product developers identify gaps in IKEA's current product portfolio. For example, product developers might identify the need to create a new low-price, modern-style couch designed for smaller apartments. Second, product developers and their team survey competitors to determine how much they charge for similar items, and then select a target price that is 30% to 50% less than the competitor's price. With a product concept and price established, product developers then determine what materials will be used and what manufacturer will do the assembly work—all before the new item is even designed. A brief describing the new couch's target cost and basic specifications is submitted for bidding among IKEA's 1,800 suppliers in 55 countries. Suppliers vie to offer the most attractive bid. Subsequently, internal and freelance designers compete to determine the product's final design based on price, function, and materials to be used. This value-engineering process promotes volume-based cost efficiencies throughout the design and production process.

But aggressive cost management does not stop there! All IKEA products are designed to be shipped unassembled in flat packages. The company estimates that shipping costs would be six times greater if all products were shipped assembled. In addition, IKEA stores do not offer many of the amenities their competitors offer, including salespeople, conspicuous price reductions, and free product delivery. Although this perhaps is inconvenient to some potential customers, the relentless focus on lean design, efficiency, and low prices remains a hallmark at IKEA. As founder Ingvar Kamprad once noted, "Waste of resources is a mortal sin at IKEA. Expensive solutions are often a sign of mediocrity, and an idea without a price tag is never acceptable."

Sources: L. Margonelli, "How IKEA Designs Its Sexy Price Tags," *Business 2.0* (October 2002); R. Cooper and W. Chew, "Control Tomorrow's Costs Through Today's Designs," *Harvard Business Review* (January–February 1996); Ingvar Kamprad and IKEA, Harvard Business School case number 9-390-132; O. Burkeman, "The Miracle of Älmhult," *The Guardian* (June 17, 2004).

assembled and sold. But Provalue's direct materials costs per unit are determined much earlier when designers finalize the components that will go into Provalue. Direct materials costs per unit of Provalue are *locked in* (or *designed in*) at the product design stage. **Locked-in costs (designed-in costs)** are those costs that have not yet been incurred but that will be incurred in the future on the basis of decisions that have already been made.

Why is it important to distinguish between when costs are locked in and when costs are incurred? Because it is difficult to alter or reduce costs that have already been locked in. For example, should Astel experience quality problems during manufacturing, its ability to improve quality and reduce scrap may be limited by Provalue's design. Scrap costs are incurred during manufacturing, but could be locked in by a faulty design. Similarly, in the software industry, costs of producing software are often locked in at the design and analysis stage. Costly and difficult-to-fix errors that appear during coding and testing are frequently locked in by bad designs.

Locked-in costs (designed-in costs). Costs that have not yet been incurred but that will be incurred in the future on the basis of decisions that have already been made.

Other examples of how Astel's design decisions affect costs include the following:

1. Design decisions influence direct materials costs through the choices of printed circuit boards and add-on features used in Provalue. Better designs also reduce both product failures in the plant and the time it takes to rework defective products.

2. Designing Provalue so that it is easy to manufacture and easy to assemble decreases direct manufacturing labour costs. For example, designing Provalue so that various parts snap-fit together (rather than having various parts soldered together) saves manufacturing labour time.

3. Designing Provalue with fewer components reduces ordering and materials-handling costs.

4. Simplifying the Provalue design decreases the time required for testing and inspection.

5. Designing Provalue to reduce the need for repairs as well as the time it takes to service and repair Provalue at customer sites reduces customer service costs.

Exhibit 12-3 illustrates how the locked-in cost curve and the cost-incurrence curve might appear in the case of Provalue. (The numbers underlying the graph are assumed.) The bottom curve plots the cumulative costs per unit incurred in different business functions. The top curve plots the cumulative costs locked in. Both curves deal with the same total cumulative costs per unit. The graph emphasizes the wide divergence between the time when costs are locked in and the time when those costs are incurred. In our example, once the product and processes are designed, nearly 87% (say, $780 \div $900) of the unit costs of Provalue are locked in when only about 8% (say, $76 \div $900) of the unit costs are actually incurred. For example, at the end of the design stage, costs such as direct materials, direct manufacturing labour, direct machining, and many manufacturing, marketing, distribution, and customer service overheads are all locked in. To reduce total costs, Astel must act to modify the design before costs get locked in.

EXHIBIT 12-3

Pattern of Cost Incurrence and Locked-in Costs for Provalue

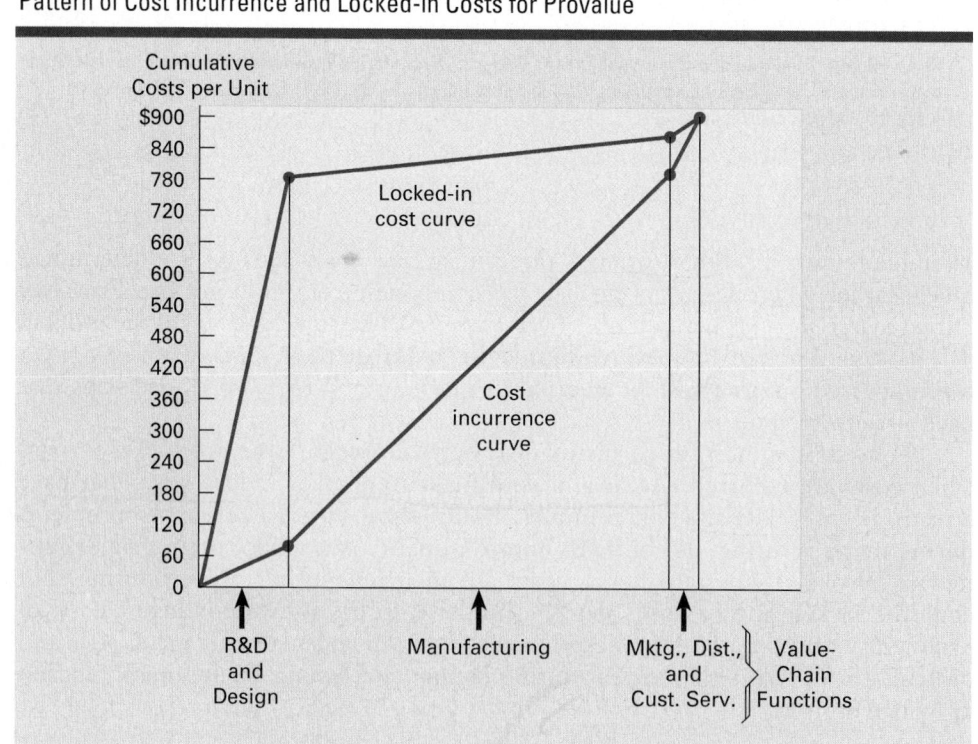

Value-Chain Analysis and Cross-Functional Teams

To help reduce costs, Astel's managers must focus on the design stage. The company organizes a cross-functional value-engineering team consisting of marketing managers, product designers, manufacturing engineers, purchasing managers, suppliers, dealers, and management accountants. The team evaluates the impact of design innovations and modifications on all business functions of the value chain. They choose modifications that have the greatest value to their customers relative to the costs required to provide those features. Here are some of the team's ideas:

◆ Use a simpler, more-reliable motherboard without complex features. Design Provalue so that various parts snap-fit together, rather than solder together, to decrease direct manufacturing labour-hours and the related costs.

◆ Simplify the Provalue design and use fewer components to decrease ordering and receiving costs and also decrease testing and inspection costs.

◆ Design Provalue to be lighter and smaller to reduce distribution and packaging costs.

◆ Design Provalue to reduce repair costs at customer sites to lower customer-service costs.

Companies are always wanting to make improvements and cut costs. For example, because direct material costs are often significant, many manufacturers work closely with their suppliers to achieve the target direct material costs.

FOCUS ON VALUES AND BEHAVIOURS

Pricing Decisions Are Not Arbitrary

Before decision makers at Toyota, IKEA, PALM, and Apple can determine the price of their products, they have a lot to consider. What do our customers want, and what prices are they willing to pay? What are our competitors doing? How can we manage costs to achieve profitability? At each of these companies, management accountants play an important role in helping to answer these questions.

To successfully influence pricing decisions, manage costs, answer the needs of customers, and outdo competitors, management accountants must understand the intricacies of each part of the value chain. At the same time, their colleagues in R&D, manufacturing, and marketing must consider management accountants as integral members of their teams. But why is it important to create a culture of cross-functionality? Consider Toyota Corporation. Toyota's management accountants created "cost sheets" based on their understanding of various processes. These cost sheets helped Toyota's line managers evaluate costs of alternative designs, which contributed to continuous reduction in costs, sales growth, and profitability.

Management accountants must always create a culture of information sharing. They must be able to bring to the attention of manufacturing and marketing managers the cost and profitability of different design alternatives. They need to be comfortable presenting cost information even when design data are incomplete and ambiguous, and they must be ready to refine cost estimates as design details become clearer. If management accountants are unable to perform these tasks, pricing problems will ensue which could benefit competitors and alienate customers.

As we have seen many times before, the role of the management accountant also includes potential ethical obstacles. As it relates to pricing decisions, management accountants must always be careful that their pricing proposals are ethical and legal— no matter how profitable such actions might be in the short run. Consider newspaper reports alleging Medicare fraud. Companies apparently have been charging Medicare, the U.S. government's medical program for senior citizens, higher prices than allowable and for services that were never delivered. In such a situation, it is the management accountant's responsibility to protest illegal or unethical pricing actions. Failure to do so can result in multi-million-dollar fines and significant damage to a company's reputation.

Management accountants use their understanding of the technical and business aspects of the entire value chain to quickly estimate cost savings and to explain the cost implications of alternative design choices to the team. (See also the Focus on Values and Behaviours feature on page 481.) These cost estimates are based on the parts and processes required by the new design.

After going through the cost analysis, Astel's management team feels it has two alternatives: respond less aggressively to its competitors or replace Provalue with a newly designed computer that has fewer complex features and therefore is less costly to make. Astel decides to go with the second alternative.

Do not assume that costs are always locked in at the design stage. In some industries (such as bulk chemical manufacturing, legal, and consulting) costs are locked in and incurred at about the same time. If costs are not locked in early, cost reduction can be achieved right up to the time when costs are incurred. In these cases, costs are lowered through improved operating efficiency and productivity (for example, reducing the time it takes to do a task), rather than better design. Many companies combine value engineering with *kaizen*, or *continuous improvement* methods that seek to improve productivity and eliminate waste during production and delivery of products.

In summary, the target-pricing, target-costing, and value-engineering process has five key aspects:

1. Understanding customer requirements and competitor actions

2. Selecting a target price and determining a target cost

3. Anticipating how costs are locked in before they are incurred

4. Improving product and process designs to achieve target costs and better quality

5. Using cross-functional teams to coordinate actions that need to be taken throughout the value chain

ACHIEVING THE TARGET COST PER UNIT FOR PROVALUE

Astel's value-engineering teams focus their cost-reduction efforts on analyzing the Provalue design. Their goal? To design a high-quality, highly reliable machine with fewer features that meets customers' price expectations and achieves target cost.

Provalue is discontinued. In its place, Astel introduces Provalue II. Provalue II has fewer components than does Provalue and is easier to manufacture and test. The spreadsheet on page 483 compares the direct costs and the manufacturing overhead costs and cost drivers of Provalue and Provalue II. In place of the 150,000 Provalue units manufactured and sold in 2007, Astel expects to make and sell 200,000 Provalue II units in 2008.

Note that value-engineering activities reduce both value-added and non-value-added costs. For example, direct manufacturing labour cost per unit, a value-added cost, is reduced by designing a product that requires fewer direct manufacturing labour-hours (the cost driver for direct manufacturing labour costs). Rework cost per unit, a non-value-added cost, is reduced by simplifying the design to reduce defects during manufacturing and hence rework-hours (the cost driver for rework costs).

Exhibit 12-4 on page 484 presents the target manufacturing costs of Provalue II, assuming no change in the cost per unit of the cost drivers. (The Problem for Self-Study on page 494 considers changes in the cost per unit of the cost drivers.) For comparison, Exhibit 12-4 also reproduces the manufacturing costs per unit of Provalue from Exhibit 12-1. Exhibit 12-4 shows that the new design is expected to reduce the manufacturing cost per unit by $140, to $540 from $680. A similar analysis (not presented) estimates the expected effect of the new design on costs in other value-chain business functions. Exhibit 12-5 on p. 484 shows that the estimated full

	PROVALUE*						PROVALUE II			
			150,000 output units				200,000 output units			
Cost Category (1)	Cost Driver (2)	Details of Cost Driver Quantities (3) / (4)		Total Quantity of Cost Driver (5) = (3) × (4)	Cost per Unit of Cost Driver (6)	Details of Cost Driver Quantities (7) / (8)		Total Quantity of Cost Driver (9) = (7) × (8)	Cost per Unit of Cost Driver (10)
Direct Manufacturing Costs									
Direct materials	No. of kits	1 kit per output unit	150,000 output units	150,000	$460	1 kit per output unit	200,000 output units	200,000	$385
Direct manuf. labour (DML)	DML hours	3.2 DML hours per output unit	150,000 output units	480,000	$ 20	2.65 DML hours per output unit	200,000 output units	530,000	$ 20
Direct machining (fixed)	Machine-hours	2 machine-hours per output unit	150,000 output units	300,000	$ 38	1.5 machine-hours per output unit	200,000 output units	300,000	$ 38
Manufacturing Overhead Costs									
Ordering and receiving	No. of orders	50 orders per component	450 components	22,500	$ 80	50 orders per component	425 components	21,250	$ 80
Testing and inspection	Testing-hours	30 testing-hours per output unit	150,000 output units	4,500,000	$ 2	15 testing-hours per output unit	200,000 output units	3,000,000	$ 2
Rework		8% defect rate				6.5% defect rate			
	Rework-hours	2.5 rework-hours per defective unit	12,000[a] defective units	30,000	$ 40	2.5 rework-hours per defective unit	13,000[b] defective units	32,500	$ 40

[a] 8% defect rate × 150,000 output units = 12,000 defective units

[b] 6.5% defect rate × 200,000 output units = 13,000 defective units

*From spreadsheet on p. 474.

EXHIBIT 12-4
Target Manufacturing Costs of Provalue II for 2008

	A	B	C	D
1		PROVALUE II		PROVALUE
2		Estimated	Estimated	Manufacturing
3		Manufacturing Costs	Manufacturing	Cost per Unit
4		for 200,000 Units	Cost per Unit	(Exhibit 12-1)
5		(1)	(2) = (1) ÷ 200,000	(3)
6	Direct manufacturing costs			
7	Direct material costs (200,000 units × $385 per unit)	$ 77,000,000	$385.00	$460.00
8	Direct manufacturing labour costs (300,000 hours × $20 per hour)	10,600,000	$ 53.00	64.00
9	Direct machining costs (300,000 machine-hours × $38 per machine-hour)	11,400,000	57.00	76.00
10	Direct manufacturing costs	99,000,000	495.00	600.00
11	Manufacturing overhead costs			
12-13	Ordering and receiving costs (21,250 orders × $80 per order)	1,700,000	8.50	12.00
14-15	Testing and inspection costs (3,000,000 hours × $2 per hour)	6,000,000	30.00	60.00
16-17	Rework costs (32,500 rework hours × $40 per hour)	1,300,000	6.50	8.00
18	Manufacturing overhead costs	9,000,000	45.00	80.00
19	Total manufacturing costs	$108,000,000	$540.00	$680.00

EXHIBIT 12-5
Target Product Profitability of Provalue II in 2008

	A	B	C
1		Estimated	Estimated
2		Total Amounts	Total Amount
3		for 200,000 Units	per Unit
4		(1)	(2) = (1) ÷ 200,000
5	Revenues	$160,000,000	$800
6	Cost of goods sold[a] (from Exhibit 12-4)	108,000,000	540
7	Operating costs[b]		
8	R&D costs	4,000,000	20
9	Design costs of product and process	6,000,000	30
10	Marketing costs	18,000,000	90
11	Distribution costs	4,400,000	22
12	Customer-service costs	3,600,000	18
13	Total operating costs	36,000,000	180
14	Full cost of the product	144,000,000	720
15	Operating income	$ 16,000,000	$ 80
16			
17	[a]Cost of goods sold = Total manufacturing costs because there is no beginning or inventory for Provalue II in 2008.		
18	[b]Numbers of operating-cost line items are assumed without supporting calculations		

product cost per unit equals $720—the target cost per unit for Provalue II. Astel's goal is to sell Provalue II at the target price, achieve target cost, and earn the target operating income.[1]

COST-PLUS PRICING

As illustrated in the last section, Astel uses an external market-based approach in its long-run pricing decisions. An alternative approach is to determine a cost-based price. Managers can turn to numerous pricing formulas based on cost. The general formula for setting a price adds a markup to the cost base:

OBJECTIVE 5

Price products using the cost-plus approach to pricing

Cost base	$ X
Markup component	Y
Prospective selling price	$X + Y$

Cost-Plus Target Rate of Return on Investment

Consider a cost-based pricing formula that Astel could use for Provalue II. Assume that Astel's engineers have redesigned Provalue into Provalue II as described earlier and that Astel uses a 12% markup on the full product cost per unit in developing the prospective selling price.

Cost base (full product cost per unit, from Exhibit 12-5)	$720.00
Markup component (12% $\times$ $720)	86.40
Prospective selling price	$806.40

How is the markup percentage of 12% determined? One approach is to choose a markup to earn a *target rate of return on investment*. The **target rate of return on investment** is the target operating income that an organization must earn divided by invested capital. Invested capital can be defined in many ways. In this chapter, we define it as total assets (long-term or fixed assets plus current assets). Companies usually specify the target rate of return required on investments. Suppose Astel's (pretax) target rate of return on investment is 18%. Assume that the capital investment needed for Provalue II is $96 million. The target operating income that Astel must earn from Provalue II can then be calculated as follows:

Target rate of return on investment. The target operating income that an organization must earn divided by invested capital.

Invested capital	$96,000,000
Target rate of return on investment	18%
Total target operating income (18% $\times$ $96,000,000)	$17,280,000
Target operating income per unit of Provalue II ($17,280,000 ÷ 200,000 units)	$ 86.40

The calculation indicates that Astel would like to earn a target operating income of $86.40 on each unit of Provalue II. What markup does this return amount to? Expressed as a percentage of the full product cost per unit of $720, the markup is equal to 12% ($86.40 ÷ $720). Do not confuse the 18% target rate of return on investment with the 12% markup percentage. The 18% target rate of return on investment expresses Astel's expected operating income as a percentage of investment. The 12% markup expresses operating income per unit as a percentage of the full product cost per unit. Astel first calculates the target rate of return on investment, and then determines the markup percentage.

Companies sometimes find it difficult to determine the capital invested to support a product. Computing invested capital requires allocations of investments in equipment and buildings (used for design, production, marketing, distribution, and customer service) to individual products—a difficult and sometimes arbitrary task.

---

[1]For a description of target pricing, target costing, and value engineering in the automobile industry, see R. Cooper, "Nissan Motor Company, Ltd.: Target Costing System," Harvard Business School Case N9–194–040.

Some companies therefore prefer to use alternative cost bases and markup percentages that do not require calculations of invested capital to set price.

Alternative Cost-Plus Methods

We illustrate these alternatives using the Astel example. Exhibit 12-6 separates the cost per unit for each value-chain business function into its variable and fixed components (without providing details of the calculations). The following table illustrates some alternative cost bases and markup percentages.

Cost Base	Estimated Cost per Unit of Provalue II (1)	Markup Percentage (2)	Markup Component for Provalue II (3) = (1) × (2)	Prospective Selling Price for Provalue II (4) = (1) + (3)
Variable manufacturing cost	$483.00	65%	$313.95	$796.95
Variable cost of the product	547.00	45	246.15	793.15
Manufacturing cost	540.00	50	270.00	810.00
Full cost of the product	720.00	12	86.40	806.40

To illustrate the markup calculations, we have assumed (but not derived) the markup percentages in the table. The different cost bases and markup percentages that we use in the table give prospective selling prices that are relatively close to one another. In practice, a company will choose a cost base that it regards as reliable, and a markup percentage on the basis of its experience in pricing products, to recover its costs and earn a desired return on investment. For example, a company may choose a full product cost base if it is unsure about variable and fixed cost distinctions.

The markup percentages in the table vary a great deal, from a high of 65% on variable manufacturing costs to a low of 12% on full product costs. Why? Because the markup based on variable manufacturing costs takes into account the need to earn a profit and to recoup fixed manufacturing costs and other business function costs such as R&D, marketing, and distribution. The greater these costs relative to variable manufacturing costs, the higher the markup percentage. The markup percentage on full product costs is much lower. Why? Because full product costs already include all costs incurred to sell the product. The precise markup percentage also depends on the competitiveness of the product market. Markups and profit margins tend to be lower in more competitive markets.

Surveys indicate that most managers use full product costs (see Global Surveys of Company Practice on page 488)—that is, they include both fixed costs per unit and

EXHIBIT 12-6
Estimated Cost Structure of Provalue II for 2008

Business Function	Estimated Variable Cost per Unit	Estimated Fixed Cost per Unit[a]	Business-Function Cost per Unit
R&D	$ 8	$ 12	$ 20
Design of product/process	10	20	30
Manufacturing	483	57	540
Marketing	25	65	90
Distribution	13	9	22
Customer service	8	10	18
Total	$547	$173	$720
	↑ Per-unit variable cost of the product	↑ Per-unit fixed cost of the product	↑ Per-unit full cost of the product

[a]Based on budgeted annual capacity of 200,000 units.

variable costs per unit in the cost base when making their pricing decisions. The advantages cited for including fixed costs per unit for pricing decisions include the following:

1. *Full product cost recovery.* For long-run pricing decisions, full product costs inform managers of the bare minimum costs they need to recover to continue in business rather than shut down. Using variable costs as a base does not give managers this information. There is then a temptation to engage in excessive long-run price cutting as long as prices give a positive contribution margin. Long-run price cutting, however, may result in long-run revenues being less than long-run (full product) costs, resulting in the company going out of business.

2. *Price stability.* Managers believe that full-cost formula pricing promotes price stability, because it limits the ability of managers to cut prices. Managers prefer price stability because it facilitates planning.

3. *Simplicity.* A full-cost formula for pricing does not require a detailed analysis of cost behaviour patterns to separate costs into fixed and variable components for each product. Calculating variable costs for each product is expensive and prone to errors. For these reasons, many managers believe that full-cost formula pricing meets the cost-benefit test.

Including unit fixed costs when pricing is not without its problems. Allocating fixed costs to products can be somewhat arbitrary. Calculating fixed cost per unit requires an estimate of expected future sales quantities. If actual sales fall short of this estimate, the actual full product cost per unit could exceed price.

Cost-Plus Pricing and Target Pricing

The selling prices computed under cost-plus pricing are *prospective* prices. For example, suppose Astel's initial product design results in a $750 cost for Provalue II. Assuming a 12% markup, Astel sets a prospective price of $840 [$750 + (12% × $750)]. Since the personal computer market is reasonably competitive, customer and competitor reactions to this price may force Astel to reduce the markup percentage and reduce the price to $800. Alternatively, Astel may redesign Provalue II to reduce cost to $720 per unit, as in our example, and achieve a markup of $80 per unit. The eventual design and cost-plus price balance the conflicting tensions among costs, markup, and customer reactions.

The target pricing approach eliminates the need to go back and forth among cost-plus prospective prices, customer reactions, and design and cost modifications. Instead, the target pricing approach first determines product characteristics and price on the basis of customer preferences and competitor responses. The target price then serves to focus and motivate managers to achieve the target cost to earn the target operating income. Sometimes the target cost is not achieved. Managers must then redesign the product, adjust the price, or work with a smaller margin.

Suppliers who provide relatively unique products and services—accountants and management consultants, for example—frequently use cost-plus pricing. Professional service firms set prices on the basis of hourly cost-plus billing rates of partners, managers, and support staff. These prices are, however, reduced in competitive situations. Professional service firms also consider a multiyear client perspective when choosing prices. Chartered accountants, for example, may charge a client a low price initially and higher prices later.

Refined cost driver and cost information play an important role in both cost-plus pricing and target costing and pricing. The identification of cost drivers is critical as managers do value engineering to *cost down* their products—to reduce the cost of a product while still satisfying customer expectations. Service companies such as home repairs, automobile repairs, and architectural firms use a cost-plus pricing method called the *time and materials method.* Individual jobs are priced based on materials and labour time. The price charged for materials equals the cost of materials plus a markup. The price charged for labour represents the cost of labour, allocated overhead, and a markup. Therefore, the price charged for each cost item includes its own markup.

 Suppose the full cost of a product based on sales of 1,000 units is

Variable cost per unit	$30
Fixed cost per unit (avoidable if product is discontinued)	20
Full cost per unit	$50

A manager may be tempted to cut price to, say, $35 because the product still provides a positive contribution margin. However, if sales are only 1,000 units, the $5,000 contribution margin would not recover the $20,000 ($20 per unit × 1,000 units) of fixed costs, and the product would not be profitable. Using full cost per unit measures the costs that must be recovered in the long run if the product is to be profitable.

To attract new clients, public accounting firms often deliberately bid less than their expected full cost on first-time audits, a practice called *low balling*, in anticipation that profits from future audits will more than compensate for the initial shortfall in profit.

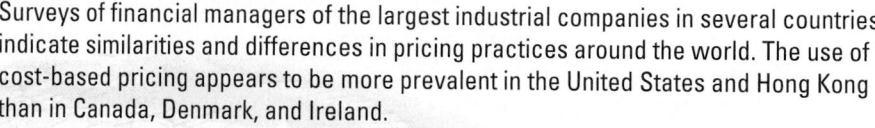

Differences in Pricing Practices and Cost-Management Methods in Various Countries

Surveys of financial managers of the largest industrial companies in several countries indicate similarities and differences in pricing practices around the world. The use of cost-based pricing appears to be more prevalent in the United States and Hong Kong than in Canada, Denmark, and Ireland.

Ranking of pricing method used as a starting point to price products (1 is most important):					
	United States[a]	Canada[b]	Denmark[c]	Hong Kong	Ireland[d]
Market-based	2	1	1	2	1
Cost-based	1	2	2	1	2

Hong Kong and Canadian survey data indicate that when managers are determining the most appropriate pricing method, they consider the following factors: buyer demand, supply and cost of goods and services, the degree of competition, and desired profit.

Among firms using market-based pricing methods, companies in the United States use target costing less frequently than companies in Australia and India.

Use of target costing among firms:			
	United States[e]	Australia[f]	India[g]
Percentage of firms using target costing	26%	38%	35%

When, subject to market considerations, costs are used for pricing decisions, the pattern is consistent—overwhelmingly, companies around the globe prefer to use full costs of the product rather than variable costs.

Ranking of cost methods used in pricing decisions (1 is most important):					
	United States	China[h]	Ireland	New Zealand[i]	United Kingdom
Based on full costs of the product	1	1	1	1	1
Based on variable costs of the product	2	2	2	2	2

[a]Grant Thornton, *Survey of American Manufacturers* (New York: Grant Thornton, 1992).

[b]Ogunmokun, G., L. Chan, and L. Li, "An Exploratory Study of the Pricing Practices of Canadian and Hong Kong Businesses," *International Journal of Management* (1997).

[c]Israelsen, P., M. Anderson, C. Rohde, and P. Sorensen, "Management Accounting in Denmark: Theory and Practice," in Bhimani, A. (ed.) *Management Accounting: European Perspectives* (Oxford: Oxford University Press, 1996).

[d]Clarke, P., "Management Accounting Practices in Large Irish Manufacturing Firms," *Irish Journal of Management* (1997).

[e]Ernst & Young, *2003 Survey of Management Accounting* (New York: Ernst & Young, November 2003).

[f]Crenhall, R., and K. Smith, "Adoption and Benefits of Management Accounting Practices: An Australian Study," *Management Accounting Research* (1998).

[g]Joshi, P., "The International Diffusion of New Management Accounting Practices: The Case of India," *Journal of International Accounting, Auditing & Taxation* (2001).

[h]Firth, M., "The Diffusion of Managerial Accounting Practices in the People's Republic of China and the Influence of Foreign Partnered Joint Ventures," *Accounting, Organizations and Society* (1996).

[i]Lamminmaki, D., and C. Drury, "A Comparison of New Zealand and British Product-Costing Practices," *International Journal of Accounting* (2001).

CONSIDERATIONS OTHER THAN COSTS IN PRICING DECISIONS

Consider the prices airlines charge for a round-trip flight from Toronto to Calgary. A coach-class ticket for the flight is $400 if the passenger stays in Calgary over a Saturday night. It is $1,500 if the passenger returns without staying over a Saturday night. Can this price difference be explained by the difference in the cost to the airlines of these round-trip flights? No, it costs the airline the same amount of money to transport the passenger from Toronto to Calgary and back regardless of whether the passenger stays in Calgary over a Saturday night. How then can we explain this difference in price? We must recognize the potential for price discrimination.

Price discrimination is the practice of charging some customers a higher price than is charged to other customers. How does price discrimination work in our airline example? The demand for airline tickets comes from two main sources: business travellers and pleasure travellers. Business travellers need to travel in order to conduct business on behalf of their companies. They generally travel to their destinations and return home within the same week immediately after completing their work, because time is very important to them. These aspects make business travellers' demand for air travel relatively insensitive to prices. The insensitivity of demand to price changes is called *demand inelasticity*. Airlines can charge business travellers higher fares because the higher fares have little effect on demand and earn higher operating income for the airlines.

Pleasure travellers have a less pressing need to return home during the week—in fact, they generally prefer to spend weekends at their destinations. Since they pay for their tickets themselves, they are much more sensitive to price than the business traveller (demand is more price-elastic). For pleasure travellers, it is profitable for the airlines to keep fares low to stimulate demand. Requiring a Saturday-night stay distinguishes between the two customer segments. The airline company price-discriminates between the two market segments to take advantage of the different sensitivities to prices exhibited by the business and pleasure travellers. Price differences exist even though there is no cost difference in serving the two segments.

In addition to price discrimination, pricing decisions also consider other non-cost considerations such as capacity constraints. **Peak-load pricing** is the practice of charging a higher price for the same product or service when demand approaches physical capacity limits. That is, the prices charged during busy periods (when loads on the system are high) are greater than the prices charged when slack or excess capacity is available. Peak-load pricing can be found in the telephone, telecommunication, hotel, car rental, and electric utility industries. The following are the daily rental rates charged by Discount Car Rental for mid-sized cars rented at Pearson International Airport:

Weekdays (Monday through Thursday)	$42 per day
Weekends (Friday through Sunday)	$38 per day

Discount's incremental costs of renting a car are the same whether the car is rented on a weekday or a weekend. What then explains the difference in prices? We offer two separate, but related, explanations. One explanation is that there is a greater demand for cars during weekdays because of business activity. Faced with capacity limits, Discount raises rental rates to levels that the market will bear.

A second explanation is that the rental rates are a form of price discrimination. During weekdays, the demand for cars comes largely from business travellers who need to rent cars to conduct their business and who are relatively insensitive to prices. Charging higher rental rates during weekdays is profitable because it has little effect on demand. In contrast, the demand for weekend rentals comes largely from nonbusiness or pleasure travellers who are more price-sensitive. Lower rates stimulate demand from these individuals and increase Discount's operating income. Under either explanation, the pricing decision is not driven by cost considerations.

LIFE CYCLE BUDGETING AND COSTING

The **product life cycle** spans the time from initial R&D to the time at which support to customers is withdrawn. For motor vehicles, this time span may range from five to ten years. For some pharmaceutical products, the time span may be fifteen to twenty years. For fashion clothing products and computer games the time span may be less than one year.

Using **life cycle budgeting**, managers estimate the revenues and costs attributable to each product from its initial R&D to its final customer servicing and support in the marketplace. **Life cycle costing** tracks and accumulates the actual costs attributable to each product from start to finish. The terms "cradle-to-grave costing" and "womb-to-tomb costing" convey the sense of fully capturing all costs associated with the product.

Life Cycle Budgeting and Pricing Decisions

Life cycle budgeted costs can provide important information for pricing decisions. For some products, the development period is relatively long, and many costs are incurred before manufacturing. Consider Insight, Inc., a computer software company developing a new accounting package, General Ledger. Assume the following budgeted amounts for General Ledger over a six-year product life cycle:

Years 1 and 2	
R&D costs	$240,000
Design costs	160,000

Years 3 to 6	Total Fixed Costs	Variable Costs per Package
Production costs	$100,000	$25
Marketing costs	70,000	24
Distribution costs	50,000	16
Customer service costs	80,000	30

To be profitable, Insight must generate revenues to cover costs in all six business functions. A product life cycle budget highlights the importance of setting prices and budgeting revenues to recover costs in *all* the value-chain business functions rather than costs in only some of the functions (such as production). The life cycle budget also indicates the costs to be incurred over the life of the product. Exhibit 12-7 presents the life cycle budget for General Ledger.

EXHIBIT 12-7
Budgeted Life Cycle Revenues and Costs for General Ledger Software Package of Insight, Inc.*

	Alternative Selling Price/ Sales Quantity Combinations		
	1	2	3
Selling price per package	$ 400	$ 480	$ 600
Sales quantity in units	5,000	4,000	2,500
Life cycle revenues ($400 × 5,000; $480 × 4,000; $600 × 2,500)	$2,000,000	$1,920,000	$1,500,000
Life cycle costs:			
R&D costs	240,000	240,000	240,000
Design costs of product/process	160,000	160,000	160,000
Production costs:			
$100,000 + ($25 × 5,000); $100,000 + ($25 × 4,000); $100,000 + ($25 × 2,500)	225,000	200,000	162,500
Marketing costs:			
$70,000 + ($24 × 5,000); $70,000 + ($24 × 4,000); $70,000 + ($24 × 2,500)	190,000	166,000	130,000
Distribution costs:			
$50,000 + ($16 × 5,000); $50,000 + ($16 × 4,000); $50,000 + ($16 × 2,500)	130,000	114,000	90,000
Customer service costs:			
$80,000 + ($30 × 5,000); $80,000 + ($30 × 4,000); $80,000 + ($30 × 2,500)	230,000	200,000	155,000
Total life cycle costs	1,175,000	1,080,000	937,500
Life cycle operating income	$ 825,000	$ 840,000	$ 562,500

*This exhibit does not take into consideration the time value of money when computing life cycle revenues or life cycle costs. Chapters 22 and 23 outline how this important factor can be incorporated into such calculations.

Three combinations of the selling price per package and predicted demand are shown. The high nonproduction costs at Insight are readily apparent in Exhibit 12-7. For example, R&D and product design costs constitute more than 30% of total costs for each of the three combinations of selling price and predicted sales quantity. Insight should put a premium on having as accurate a set of revenue and cost predictions for General Ledger as possible, given the high percentage of total life cycle costs incurred before any production begins and before any revenue is received.

Exhibit 12-7 assumes that the selling price per package is the same over the entire life cycle. For strategic reasons, however, Insight may choose to "skim the market" by charging higher prices to customers eager to try General Ledger when it first comes out and lower prices to customers who are willing to wait. The life cycle budget will then express this strategy.

DEVELOPING LIFE CYCLE REPORTS

Most accounting systems emphasize reporting on a calendar basis—monthly, quarterly, and annually. In contrast, product life cycle reporting does not have this calendar-based focus. Consider the life spans of four Insight products shown below:

	Year 1	Year 2	Year 3	Year 4	Year 5	Year 6
General Ledger package						
Law package						
Payroll package						
Engineering package						

Each product spans more than one calendar year.

Developing life cycle reports for each product requires tracking costs and revenues on a product-by-product basis over several calendar periods. For example, the R&D costs included in a product life cycle cost report are often incurred in different calendar years. When R&D costs are tracked over the entire life cycle, the total magnitude of these costs for each individual product can be computed and analyzed.

A product life cycle reporting format offers at least three important benefits:

1. The full set of revenues and costs associated with each product becomes visible. Manufacturing costs are highly visible in most accounting systems. However, the costs associated with upstream areas (for example, R&D) and downstream areas (for example, customer service) are frequently less visible on a product-by-product basis.

2. Differences between products in the percentage of their total costs incurred at early stages in the life cycle are highlighted. The higher this percentage, the more important it is for managers to develop, as early as possible, accurate predictions of the revenues for that product.

3. Interrelationships among business function cost categories are highlighted. For example, companies that cut back their R&D and product design costs may experience major increases in customer service costs in subsequent years. Those costs arise because products fail to meet promised quality-performance levels. A life cycle revenue and cost report prevents such causally related changes among business function costs from being hidden (buried) as they are in annual income statements.

Life cycle costs further reinforce the importance of locked-in costs, target costing, and value engineering in pricing and cost management. For products with long life cycles, a very small fraction of the total life cycle costs are actually incurred at the time when costs are locked in. But locked-in costs will determine how costs will be incurred over several years. Automobile companies combine target costing with life cycle budgeting. For example, DaimlerChrysler, Ford, General Motors, Mercedes, Nissan, and Toyota determine target prices and target costs for their car models on the basis of estimated costs and revenues over a multiyear horizon.

Management of environmental costs provides another example of life cycle budgeting. The enactment of strict environmental laws has introduced tougher environmental standards and increased the penalties and fines for polluting the air and contaminating subsurface soil and groundwater. Environmental costs are often locked in at the product and process design stage itself. To avoid these environmental liabilities, companies design products, processes, and procedures to prevent and reduce pollution over the product's life cycle. The computer manufacturers Compaq and Apple, for example, have recently introduced costly recycling programs to ensure that nickel-cadmium batteries (used to run laptop computers) are disposed of in an environmentally safe way at the end of the product's life.

Customer Life Cycle Costing

Customer life cycle costs. Focuses on the total costs to a customer of acquiring and using a product or service until it is replaced.

A different notion of life cycle costs is **customer life cycle costs.** Customer life cycle costs focus on the total costs to a customer of acquiring and using a product or service until it is replaced. Customer life cycle costs for a car, for example, include the cost of the car itself plus the costs of operating and maintaining the car minus the disposal price of the car. Customer life cycle costs can be an important consideration in the pricing decision. The Ford Motor Company's goal is to design cars that require minimal maintenance for 150,000 kilometres. Ford expects to charge a higher price and/or gain a greater market share by selling these cars.

EFFECTS OF CANADIAN COMPETITION LAW ON PRICING[2]

Pricing practices in most industries are governed by the *Competition Act* (the Act). The purpose of the legislation and its predecessors is to "protect the specific public interest in free competition."[3] This concept is founded on the belief that unrestricted competition improves the performance of industries as a whole and protects the public from unfair pricing practices. Each of the sections discussed below creates criminal offences for contravening the Act.

Under section 50(1)(a) of the Act, a manufacturer cannot price-discriminate between two customers if the intent is to lessen or prevent competition between customers. Four key sections of the price discrimination laws are (1) they apply to manufacturers and not service providers; (2) price discrimination is permissible if differences in prices can be justified by differences in costs; (3) price discrimination is illegal only if the intent is to discriminate between competitors; and (4) it is not an offence to discriminate in pricing, unless doing so is part of a practice of discrimination.[4]

Predatory pricing. Occurs when a company deliberately prices below its costs in an effort to drive out competitors and restrict supply, and then raises prices rather than enlarge demand or meet competition.

To comply with section 50(1)(c) of the Act, pricing must not be predatory. Section 50(1) of the Act states that a business engages in **predatory pricing** when it sells products at unreasonably low prices that either tend to substantially lessen competition or were designed to have that effect.

[2]This section is provided with assistance from Russell Hoffman, LL.B., MBA.

[3]See *Weidman v. Schragge* (1912), 20 CCC 177 at 147, where the Supreme Court of Canada first considered the rationale for regulating trades and industries.

[4]Although a "practice" is not specifically defined, more than one sale is likely required. Further, it should be noted that, in order to contravene this section of the Act, a practice of price discrimination does not have to actually have an adverse effect on competition.

However, it is difficult to state with certainty what the legal thresholds are, as only three cases have ever been decided under this section.[5] In the light of the lack of judicial consideration, and to further clarify matters, the Director of Investigation and Research (the Director) released the *Predatory Pricing Enforcement Guidelines* (the *Guidelines*) on May 21, 1992. In these *Guidelines* the Director defined predatory pricing as "a situation where a dominant firm charges low prices over a long enough period of time so as to drive a competitor from the market or deter others from entering and raises prices to recoup its losses."[6] According to these *Guidelines*, the predator must account for more than 35% of the market and be able to sustain a pricing increase for more than two years after the period of low pricing in order for its actions to be considered predatory pricing.

In determining whether pricing is "unreasonably low," courts draw a distinction between pricing a product above average variable cost and below. It is likely that as long as a product is sold above average variable cost (even if below average total cost), and it cannot be established that the accused would have made a greater total contribution to overhead by raising prices, a court will not find the price "unreasonably low."

In a 1981 case, *R. v. Consumers Glass Co.*,[7] the accused, which sold small plastic lids before 1975, had faced reduced demand for its products. When the accused's competition cut prices by 2% to 3%, it responded by cutting prices by 16% and then a further 5%, which still enabled the accused to cover its average variable costs but not its total costs. The Court held that "it is better for a manufacturer to produce and sell at a loss, than to cease production and suffer the loss of having to bear all the fixed overhead."[8] The Court went on to hold that there was no evidence of predatory pricing, as the accused had lowered its price to retain market share and maximize its contribution to fixed overhead.

In contrast, pricing below average variable costs will only be tolerated by the courts in limited circumstances. In *R. v. Hoffmann-La Roche Ltd.*[9] the Ontario Court of Appeal affirmed the trial judge's decision of an "unreasonably low" price. In this trial it was held that a pharmaceutical firm that chose to combat new competition in the hospital market by giving away Valium was "selling" its products at an unreasonably low price. The year-long Valium giveaways were in response to the new competitor's price reductions of 25% to 50% of the accused's price. The Court stated that in determining the reasonableness or unreasonableness of a particular price it will "take into account all the economic costs, which include the direct production costs as well as any potential future savings or benefits."[10] This includes looking at benefits that derive to related markets, or future markets.

The trial judge then went on to state that the court should look to four general considerations in determining whether the actual price is unreasonably low. First, the difference between the average variable cost and the sale price is important, as the greater the reduction in price, the more likely it is that it will be seen as unreasonable. Second, the length of time during which sales take place at the questionable price is significant; the longer the "deal" continues the more unreasonable the price becomes. Third, the circumstances of the price cut should be considered; defensive price-cutting may be justifiable where offensive price-cutting is not.

Competition Act C-34
laws.justice.gc.ca/en/
C-34

Competition Bureau of Canada
www.competitionbureau.gc.ca

---

[5]Although the Supreme Court of Canada has never considered a case under this section, the most recent of these cases, *R. v. Hoffmann-La Roche Ltd.* (1980), 28 O.R. (2d) 164, was affirmed by the Ontario Court of Appeal in 1981, 125 D.L.R. (3d) 607 (C.A.).

[6]Director of Investigation and Research, "Executive Summary," *Predatory Pricing Enforcement Guidelines* (Ottawa: Consumer and Corporate Affairs Canada, 1992).

[7](1981), 33 O.R. (2d) 228 (H.C.).

[8]Ibid. at 238.

[9]See n. 5 *supra*.

[10]*R. v. Hoffmann-La Roche Ltd.*, p. 199.

Lastly, consideration must be given to any accruals of external or long-term benefits to the seller that result from pricing below costs.[11]

Managers and accountants who are concerned with their conformance to the competition laws would be prudent to have a system that incorporates the following procedures:

1. Collect data in a manner that permits relatively easy compilation of variable costs.

2. Keep detailed records of variable costs for all value-chain business functions and review all proposed prices below variable costs in advance, with a presumption of claims of predatory intent.

Dumping. Under Canadian laws, occurs when a non-Canadian company sells a product in Canada at a price below the market value in the home country and this action materially injures or threatens to materially injure an industry in Canada.

Closely related to predatory pricing is dumping. Under Canadian laws, **dumping** occurs when a non-Canadian company sells goods in Canada at a price below the market value in the home country or receives a government subsidy and this action materially injures or threatens to materially injure an industry in Canada. If dumping is proven, under section 42(I)(c)(ii) of the *Special Import Measures Act* (SIMA), the Canadian International Trade Tribunal (the Tribunal) has the power to impose a countervailing duty on the goods to prevent the recurrence of the material injury.

Cases related to dumping have occurred in the agricultural and automotive industries. In 1990, the Supreme Court of Canada considered an appeal of the Tribunal's decision that the subsidization of corn imports from the United States had caused, was causing, and would likely cause material injury to the production of like goods in Canada. The Supreme Court held that the Tribunal's decision was final in this case and that decisions are generally final unless the Tribunal acts outside the scope of its mandate or its interpretation of the SIMA is patently unreasonable.[12]

Collusive pricing. Companies in an industry conspiring in their pricing and output decisions to achieve a price above the competitive price.

Another violation of the Act is collusive pricing. **Collusive pricing** occurs when companies in an industry conspire in their pricing and output decisions to achieve a price above the competitive price. Section 45 of the Act makes it a criminal offence to conspire, agree, or combine with another person to prevent, lessen, or restrain competition unduly. Collusive pricing violates the Act because an agreement with respect to pricing and output levels prevents competition between the companies in an industry.

PROBLEM FOR SELF-STUDY

Reconsider the Astel Computer example (pp. 482–487). Astel's marketing manager realizes that a further reduction in prices is necessary to sell 200,000 units of Provalue II. To maintain a target profitability of $16 million, or $80 per unit (the same amounts shown in Exhibit 12-5, p. 484), Astel will need to reduce costs of Provalue II by $6 million, or $30 per unit. Astel targets a reduction of $4 million, or $20 per unit, in manufacturing costs, and $2 million, or $10 per unit, in marketing, distribution, and customer-service costs. The cross-functional team assigned to this task proposes the following changes to manufacture a different version of Provalue, called Provalue III:

1. Reduce direct materials and ordering costs by purchasing subassembled components rather than individual components.

2. Reengineer ordering and receiving to reduce ordering and receiving costs per order.

3. Reduce testing time and the labour and power required per hour of testing.

4. Develop new rework procedures to reduce rework costs per hour.

No changes are proposed in direct manufacturing labour costs per unit and in total machining costs. The spreadsheet on page 495 summarizes the cost-driver quantities and the cost per unit of each cost driver for Provalue III compared with Provalue II.

[11]*R. v. Hoffmann-La Roche Ltd.*, pp. 200–204.
[12]See *American Farm Bureau Federation v. Canadian Import Tribunal* (1990), 74 D.L.R. (4th) 449.

								PROVALUE II						PROVALUE III
				200,000 output units					200,000 output units					
Cost Category	Cost Driver	Cost Driver Quantities		Details of Cost Driver Quantities		Total Quantity of Cost Driver	Cost per Unit of Cost Driver	Cost Driver Quantities		Details of Cost Driver Quantities		Total Quantity of Cost Driver	Cost per Unit of Cost Driver
(1)	(2)	(3)		(4)		(5) = (3) × (4)	(6)	(7)		(8)		(9) = (7) × (8)	(10)
Direct Manufacturing Costs													
Direct materials	No. of kits	1	kit per output unit	200,000	output units	200,000	$385	1	kit per output unit	200,000	output units	200,000	$375
Direct manuf. labour (DML)	DML hours	2.65	DML hours per output unit	200,000	output units	530,000	$20	2.65	DML hours per output unit	200,000	output units	530,000	$20
Direct machining (fixed)	Machine-hours	1.5	machine-hours per output unit	200,000	output units	300,000	$38	1.5	machine-hours per output unit	200,000	output units	300,000	$38
Manufacturing Overhead Costs													
Ordering and receiving	No. of orders	50	orders per component	425	components	21,250	$80	50	orders per component	400	components	20,000	$60
Testing and inspection	Testing-hours	15	testing-hours per output unit	200,000	output units	3,000,000	$2	14	testing-hours per output unit	200,000	output units	2,800,000	$1.70
Rework		6.5%		6.5%	defect rate					6.5%	defect rate		
	Rework-hours	2.5	rework-hours per defective unit	13,000[a]	defective units	32,500	$40	2.5	rework-hours per defective unit	13,000[a]	defective units	32,500	$32

[a]6.5% defect rate × 200,000 output units = 13,000 defective units

Will the proposed changes achieve Astel's targeted reduction of $4 million, or $20 per unit, in manufacturing costs for Provalue III? Show your computations.

SOLUTION

Exhibit 12-8 presents the manufacturing costs for Provalue III based on the proposed changes. Manufacturing costs will decline from $108 million, or $540 per unit (Exhibit 12-4), to $104 million, or $520 per unit (Exhibit 12-8), and will achieve the target reduction of $4 million, or $20 per unit.

EXHIBIT 12-8
Target Manufacturing Costs of Provalue III for 2008 Based on Proposed Changes

	A	B	C
		Estimated	Estimated
		Manufacturing Costs	Manufacturing
		for 200,000 Units	Cost per Unit
		(1)	(2) = (1) ÷ 200,000
5	Direct manufacturing costs		
6	Direct material costs (200,000 units × $375 per unit)	$ 75,000,000	$375.00
7	Direct manufacturing labour costs (530,000 hours × $20 per hour)	10,600,000	53.00
8	Direct machining costs (300,000 machine-hours × $38 per machine-hour)	11,400,000	57.00
9	Direct manufacturing costs	97,000,000	485.00
10			
11	Manufacturing overhead costs		
12	Ordering and receiving costs (20,000 orders × $60 per order)	1,200,000	6.00
13	Testing and inspection costs (2,800,000 hours × $1.70 per hour)	4,760,000	23.80
14	Rework costs (32,500 rework hours × $32 per hour)	1,040,000	5.20
15	Manufacturing overhead costs	7,000,000	35.00
16	Total manufacturing costs	$104,000,000	$520.00

DECISION POINTS   SUMMARY

The following question-and-answer format summarizes the chapter's learning objectives. Each decision presents a key question related to a learning objective. The guidelines are the answer to that question.

DECISIONS	GUIDELINES
1. What are the three major influences on pricing decisions?	Customers, competitors, and costs influence prices through their effects on demand and supply—customers and competitors affect demand, and costs affect supply.

2. How do short-run pricing decisions differ from long-run pricing decisions?	Short-run pricing decisions generally focus on a period of less than one year and have no long-run implications. Long-run pricing decisions focus on pricing a product with a time horizon of one year or longer. The time horizon appropriate to a decision on pricing dictates which costs are relevant, how costs can be managed, and the profit that needs to be earned.
3. How do companies price products using target costing?	One approach to long-run pricing is to use a target price. Target price is the estimated price that potential customers are willing to pay for a product or service. Target operating income per unit is subtracted from the target price to determine target cost per unit. Target cost per unit is the estimated long-run cost of a product or service that when sold enables the company to achieve target operating income per unit. The challenge for the organization is to make the necessary cost improvements through value-engineering methods to achieve the target cost.
4. Why is it important to distinguish between cost incurrence and locked-in costs?	Cost incurrence describes when a resource is sacrificed. Locked-in costs are costs not yet incurred but that, based on decisions that have already been made, will be incurred in the future. To reduce costs, techniques such as value engineering are most effective before costs are locked in.
5. How do companies price products using the cost-plus approach?	The cost-plus approach to pricing adds a markup component to a cost base as the starting point for pricing decisions. Many different costs, such as full cost of the product or manufacturing cost, can serve as the cost base in applying the cost-plus formula. Prices are then modified on the basis of customers' reactions and competitors' responses. Therefore, the size of the "plus" is determined by the market.
6. What are price discrimination and peak-load pricing?	Price discrimination is charging some customers a higher price for a given product or service than other customers. Peak-load pricing is charging a higher price for the same product or service when demand approaches physical capacity limits. Under price discrimination and peak-load pricing, prices differ among market segments even though the cost of providing the product or service is approximately the same.
7. What is life cycle budgeting and costing and when should companies use it?	Life cycle budgeting and costing estimate, track, and accumulate the costs (and revenues) attributable to a product from its initial R&D to its final customer servicing and support. Life cycle budgeting and costing are particularly important when (a) nonproduction costs are large, (b) a high percentage of total life cycle costs is incurred before production begins and before any revenues are earned, and (c) a high fraction of the life cycle costs are locked in at the R&D and design stages.
8. How do the legal issues affect pricing?	To comply with laws, a company must not engage in predatory pricing, dumping, or collusive pricing, which lessen competition, put another company at a competitive disadvantage, or harm consumers.

▼ **TERMS TO LEARN**

This chapter contains definitions of the following important terms:

collusive pricing (p. 494)
cost incurrence (p. 478)
customer life cycle costs (p. 492)
designed-in costs (p. 479)
dumping (p. 494)
life cycle budgeting (p. 489)
life cycle costing (p. 490)
locked-in costs (p. 479)
peak-load pricing (p. 489)

predatory pricing (p. 492)
price discrimination (p. 489)
product life cycle (p. 489)
target cost per unit (p. 476)   — TP — TOI
target operating income per unit (p. 476)
target price (p. 476)
target rate of return on investment (p. 485)
value-added cost (p. 478)
value engineering (p. 477)

QUESTIONS

12-1 What are the three major influences on pricing decisions?

12-2 "The relevant costs for pricing decisions are full product costs." Comment.

12-3 Give two examples of pricing decisions with a short-run focus.

12-4 How is activity-based costing useful for pricing decisions?

12-5 Describe two alternative approaches to long-run pricing decisions.

12-6 What is a *target cost per unit?*

12-7 Describe *value engineering* and its role in target costing.

12-8 Give two examples each of a *value-added cost* and a *non-value-added cost.*

12-9 "It is not important for a firm to distinguish between cost incurrence and locked-in costs." Do you agree? Explain.

12-10 What is *cost-plus pricing?*

12-11 Describe three alternative cost-plus methods.

12-12 Give two examples where the difference in the costs of two products or services is much smaller than the difference in their prices.

12-13 What is *life cycle budgeting?*

12-14 What are three benefits of using a product life cycle reporting format?

12-15 Define *predatory pricing, dumping,* and *collusive pricing.*

EXERCISES

12-16 Relevant-cost approach to pricing decisions, special order. The following financial data apply to the videotape production plant of the Dill Company for October 2007:

	Budgeted Manufacturing Costs per Videotape
Direct materials	$1.80
Direct manufacturing labour	0.96
Variable manufacturing overhead	0.84
Fixed manufacturing overhead	1.20
Total manufacturing costs	$4.80

Variable manufacturing overhead varies with respect to units produced. Fixed manufacturing overhead of $1.20 per tape is based on budgeted fixed manufacturing overhead of $180,000 per month and budgeted production of 150,000 tapes per month. The Dill Company sells each tape for $6.

Marketing costs have two components:
◆ Variable marketing costs (sales commissions) of 5% of dollar sales
◆ Fixed monthly costs of $65,000

During October 2007, Lyn Randell, a Dill Company salesperson, asked the president for permission to sell 1,000 tapes at $4.56 per tape to a customer not in its normal marketing channels. The president refused this special order on the grounds that the order would show a loss because the selling price was below the total budgeted manufacturing cost.

REQUIRED

1. What would have been the effect on monthly operating income of accepting the special order?

2. Comment on the president's "below manufacturing costs" reasoning for rejecting the special order.

3. What factors would you recommend that the president consider when deciding whether to accept or reject a special order?

12-17 Relevant-cost approach to short-run pricing decisions. The Tectronics Company is an electronics business with eight product lines. Income data for one of the products (XT-107) for the month just ended (June 2007) are as follows:

Sales, 200,000 units at average price of $120		$24,000,000
Variable costs:		
Direct materials at $42 per unit	$8,400,000	
Direct manufacturing labour at $12 per unit	2,400,000	
Variable manufacturing overhead at $6 per unit	1,200,000	
Sales commissions at 15% of sales	3,600,000	
Other variable costs at $6 per unit	1,200,000	
Total variable costs		16,800,000
Contribution margin		7,200,000
Fixed costs		6,000,000
Operating income		$ 1,200,000

Abrams, Inc., an instruments company, has a problem with its preferred supplier of XT-107 component products. This supplier has had a three-week labour strike and will not be able to supply Abrams with 3,000 units next month. Abrams approaches the sales representative, Sarah Holtz, of the Tectronics Company about providing 3,000 units of XT-107 at a price of $96 per unit. Holtz informs the XT-107 product manager, Jim Vijayan, that she would accept a flat commission of $7,200 rather than the usual 15% if this special order were accepted. Tectronics has the capacity to produce 300,000 units of XT-107 each month, but demand has not exceeded 200,000 units in any month in the last year.

REQUIRED
1. If the 3,000-unit order from Abrams is accepted, what will be the effect on monthly operating income? (Assume the same cost structure as occurred in June 2007.)
2. Vijayan ponders whether to accept the 3,000-unit special order. He is afraid of the precedent that might be set by cutting the price. He says, "The price is below our full cost of $114 per unit. I think we should quote a full price, or Abrams will expect favoured treatment again and again if we continue to do business with them." Do you agree with Vijayan? Explain.

12-18 Short-run pricing, capacity constraints. Boutique Chemicals makes a specialized chemical product, Bolzene, from a specially imported material, Pyrone. To make 1 kilogram of Bolzene requires 1.5 kilograms of Pyrone. Bolzene has a contribution margin of $7.20 per kilogram. Boutique has just received a request to manufacture 3,000 kilograms of Seltium that also requires Pyrone as the material input. Boutique calculates the following costs of making 1 kilogram of Seltium:

Pyrone (2 kilograms × $4.80 per kilogram)	$ 9.60
Direct manufacturing labour	4.80
Variable manufacturing overhead costs	3.60
Fixed manufacturing overhead costs allocated	6.00
Total manufacturing costs	$24.00

Boutique has adequate excess plant capacity to make Seltium.

REQUIRED
1. Suppose Boutique has adequate Pyrone available to make Seltium. What is the minimum price per kilogram that Boutique should charge to manufacture Seltium?
2. Now suppose Pyrone is in short supply. The Pyrone used to make Seltium will reduce the Bolzene that Boutique can make and sell. What is the minimum price per kilogram that Boutique should charge to manufacture Seltium?

12-19 Value-added, non-value-added costs. The Marino Repair Shop repairs and services machine tools. A summary of its costs (by activity) for 2007 is as follows:

a. Materials and labour for servicing machine tools	$ 960,000
b. Rework costs	90,000
c. Expediting costs caused by work delays	72,000
d. Materials-handling costs	60,000
e. Materials procurement and inspection costs	42,000
f. Preventive maintenance of equipment	18,000
g. Breakdown maintenance of equipment	66,000
	$1,308,000

REQUIRED
1. Classify each of the seven costs as value-added, non-value-added, or in the grey area in between.

2. For any costs classified in the grey area, assume 65% of the costs are value-added and 35% are non-value-added. How much of the total costs are value-added and how much are non-value-added?

3. Marino is considering the following changes at the shop: (a) introducing quality improvement programs whose net effect will be to reduce rework and expediting costs by 75% and materials and labour costs by 5%, (b) working with suppliers to reduce materials procurement and inspection costs by 20% and materials-handling costs by 25%, and (c) increasing preventive maintenance costs by 50% to reduce breakdown maintenance costs by 40%. What effect would each of these programs have on value-added costs, non-value-added costs, and total costs as calculated in requirement 2? Comment briefly.

12-20 Target operating income, value-added costs, service company. Carasco Associates is a small structural-design firm that prepares architectural drawings that focus on structural safety for various clients. The architectural plans are then submitted to local government departments for approval. Carasco's income statement for 2007 follows:

Revenues	$816,000
Salaries of professional staff	
(8,000 hours × $60 per hour)	480,000
Travel	21,600
Administration and support	192,000
Total costs	693,600
Operating income	$122,400

An analysis of the percentage of time spent by professional staff on various activities is as follows:

Doing calculations and preparing drawings for clients	75%
Checking calculations and drawings	4%
Correcting drawings	7%
Making changes in response to client requests	6%
Making corrections required by government officials before they give their approval	8%
Total	100%

Further assume that administration and support costs vary with professional labour-hours.

REQUIRED

1. How much of the total costs in 2007 are value-added, non-value-added, or in the grey area in between? Explain your answers briefly. What actions can Carasco take to reduce its costs?

2. If Carasco can eliminate all corrections and proportionately reduce professional labour-hours, how much will Carasco's operating income be?

3. Carasco would like to double operating income in 2008. Carasco can take on as much business as it can get done but it cannot add more professional staff. By how much will Carasco be able to increase its operating income if all corrections are eliminated and the time saved is used to increase revenues proportionately? Assume travel expenses for 2008 will remain at $21,600.

12-21 Target prices, target costs, activity-based costing systems. Snappy Tiles is a small distributor of marble tiles. Snappy identifies its three major activities and cost pools as ordering, receiving and storage, and shipping, and reports the following details for 2007:

Activity	Cost Driver	Quantity of Cost Driver	Cost per Unit of Cost Driver
1. Placing and paying for orders of marble tiles	Number of orders	500	$60 per order
2. Receiving and storage	Number of loads moved	4,000	$36 per load
3. Shipping of marble tiles to retailers	Number of shipments	1,500	$48 per shipment

Snappy buys 250,000 marble tiles at an average cost of $3.60 per tile and sells them to retailers at an average price of $4.80 per tile. Fixed costs are $48,000.

REQUIRED

1. Calculate Snappy's operating income for 2007.

2. For 2008, retailers are demanding a 5% discount off the 2007 price. Snappy's suppliers are only willing to give a 4% discount. Snappy expects to sell the same quantity of marble tiles in 2008 as it did in 2007. If all other costs and cost driver information remain the same, what will Snappy's operating income be in 2008?

3. Suppose further that Snappy decides to make changes in its ordering and receiving and storing practices. By placing long-term orders with its key suppliers, it expects to reduce the number of orders to 200 and the cost per order to $30 per order. By redesigning the layout of the warehouse and reconfiguring the crates in which the marble tiles are moved, Snappy expects to reduce the number of loads moved to 3,125 and the cost per load moved to $33.60. Will Snappy achieve its target operating income of $0.36 per tile in 2008? Show your calculations.

12-22 Cost-plus target return on investment pricing. John Beck is the managing partner of a partnership that has just finished building a 60-room motel. Beck anticipates that he will rent these rooms for 16,000 nights next year (or 16,000 room-nights). All rooms are similar and will rent for the same price. Beck estimates the following operating costs for next year:

Variable operating costs	$3.60 per room-night
Fixed costs:	
Salaries and wages	$210,000
Maintenance of building and pool	44,400
Other operating and administration costs	168,000
Total fixed costs	$422,400

The capital invested in the motel is $1,152,000. The partnership's target return on investment is 25%. Beck expects demand for rooms to be about uniform throughout the year. He plans to price the rooms at full cost plus a markup on full cost to earn the target return on investment. Ignore any income tax effects.

REQUIRED
1. What price should Beck charge for a room-night? What is the markup as a percentage of the full cost of a room-night?
2. Beck's market research indicates that if the price of a room-night determined in requirement 1 were reduced by 10%, the expected number of room-nights Beck could rent would increase by 10%. Should Beck reduce prices by 10%?

12-23 Cost-plus and target pricing. (S. Sridhar, adapted) Waterford, Inc., manufactures and sells 15,000 units of a raft RF17 in 2007. The full cost per unit is $240. Waterford earns a 20% return on an investment of $2,160,000 in 2007. Ignore any income tax effects.

REQUIRED
1. Calculate the selling price of RF17 in 2007. Calculate the markup percentage on the full cost per unit of RF17 in 2007.
2. If the markup percentage on variable costs per unit is 40%, calculate the variable cost per unit of RF17 in 2007.
3. Calculate Waterford's operating income if it sold 13,500 units of RF17 at a price of $276 per unit in 2007. Assume no change in total fixed costs for 2007.
4. In response to competitive pressures, Waterford must reduce the price of RF17 to $252 in 2008 to achieve sales of 15,000 units. Waterford plans to reduce its investment to $1,980,000. If Waterford wants to maintain a 20% return on investment, what is the target cost per unit in 2008?

12-24 Target costs, effect of product-design changes on product costs. Medical Instruments manufactures many products. To compute manufacturing costs, it uses an accounting system with one direct-cost category (direct materials) and three indirect-cost categories:
1. Batch-related setup, production order, and material-handling costs, all of which vary with the number of batches.
2. Manufacturing operations costs that vary with machine-hours.
3. Costs of engineering changes that vary with the number of engineering changes made.
   In response to competitive pressures, product designers at Medical Instruments have employed value-engineering methods to reduce manufacturing costs. Actual information for 2007 and budgeted information for 2008 follow:

	Actuals for 2007	Budgeted for 2008
Total setup, production-order, and material-handling costs	$ 8,640,000	$ 9,000,000
Total number of batches	900	1,000
Total manufacturing operations costs	$14,520,000	$15,000,000
Total quantity of machine-hours worked	220,000	250,000
Total costs of engineering changes	$ 3,168,000	$ 2,400,000
Total number of engineering changes	220	200

The management of Medical Instruments wants to evaluate whether value engineering has succeeded in reducing the target cost per unit of one of its products, HJ6, by 12%. Actual data for 2007 and budgeted data for 2008 for HJ6 follow:

	Actuals for 2007	Budgeted for 2008
Units of HJ6 produced	3,500	4,000
Direct materials cost per unit of HJ6	$ 1,440	$ 1,320
Total number of batches required to produce HJ6	70	80
Total machine-hours required to produce HJ6	21,000	22,000
Number of engineering changes	15	10

REQUIRED
1. Calculate the actual manufacturing cost per unit of HF6 in 2007.
2. Calculate the estimated manufacturing cost per unit of HF6 in 2008.
3. Did Medical Instruments achieve the target cost per unit for HF6?
4. Comment briefly on how Medical Instruments was able to reduce the estimated cost per unit of HF6 in 2008.

12-25 **Considerations other than cost in pricing.** Examples of prices charged by Bell Canada for long-distance telephone calls within Canada at different times of the day and week are as follows:

Peak period (8 a.m. to 6 p.m., Monday through Friday)	Basic rate
Evenings (6 p.m. to 11 p.m., Monday through Friday)	35% savings
Nights and weekends	60% savings

REQUIRED
1. Are there differences in incremental or outlay costs per minute for Bell Canada for telephone calls made during peak hours compared with telephone calls made at other times of the day?
2. Why do you think Bell Canada charges different prices for telephone calls made during peak hours compared with telephone calls made at other times of the day?

12-26 **Life cycle product costing, product emphasis.** Decision Support Systems (DSS) is examining the profitability and pricing policies of its software division. The DSS software division develops software packages for engineers. DSS has collected data on three of its most recent packages:
- **EE-46.** Package for electrical engineers
- **ME-83.** Package for mechanical engineers
- **IE-17.** Package for industrial engineers

Summary details on each package over their two-year "cradle-to-grave" product lives are as follows:

Package	Selling Price	Number of Units Sold	
		Year 1	Year 2
EE-46	$300	2,000	8,000
ME-83	360	2,000	3,000
IE-17	240	5,000	3,000

Assume that no inventory remains on hand at the end of year 2.

DSS is deciding which product lines to emphasize in its software division. In the past two years, the profitability of this division has been mediocre. DSS is particularly concerned with the increase in R&D costs in several of its divisions. An analyst in the software division pointed out that, for one of its most recent packages (IE-17), major efforts had been made to cut back R&D costs.

Last week Nancy Sullivan, the software division manager, attended a seminar on product life cycle management. The topic of life cycle reporting was discussed. Sullivan decides to use this approach in her own division. She collects the following life cycle revenue and cost information for the EE-46, ME-83, and IE-17 packages:

	EE-46		ME-83		IE-17	
	Year 1	Year 2	Year 1	Year 2	Year 1	Year 2
Revenues	$600,000	$2,400,000	$720,000	$1,080,000	$1,200,000	$720,000
Costs:						
R&D	840,000	0	540,000	0	288,000	0
Design of product	222,000	18,000	132,000	12,000	96,000	19,200
Manufacturing	90,000	270,000	126,000	126,000	171,600	78,000
Marketing	168,000	432,000	144,000	180,000	288,000	249,600
Distribution	18,000	72,000	28,800	43,200	72,000	43,200
Customer service	60,000	390,000	54,000	126,000	264,000	465,600

REQUIRED

1. How does a product life cycle income statement differ from an income statement that is fiscal-year–based? What are the benefits of using a product life cycle reporting format?
2. Present a product life cycle income statement for each software package. Which package is the most profitable, and which is the least profitable?
3. How do the three software packages differ in their cost structure (the percentage of total costs in each cost category)?

PROBLEMS

12-27 Pricing of hotel rooms on weekends. Kamal Diamond is the owner of the Galaxy chain of four-star prestige hotels. These hotels are in Chicago, London, Los Angeles, Montreal, New York, Seattle, Tokyo, and Vancouver. Diamond is currently struggling to set weekend rates for the Vancouver hotel (the Vancouver Galaxy). From Sunday through Thursday, the Galaxy has an average occupancy rate of 90%. On Friday and Saturday nights, however, average occupancy declines to less than 30%. Galaxy's major customers are business travellers who stay mainly Sunday through Thursday.

The current room rate at the Galaxy is $180 a night for single occupancy and $216 a night for double occupancy. These rates apply seven nights a week. For many years, Diamond has resisted having rates for Friday and Saturday nights that are different from those for the remainder of the week. Diamond has long believed that price reductions convey a "nonprestige" impression to his guests. The Vancouver Galaxy highly values its reputation for treating its guests as "royalty."

Most room costs at the Galaxy are fixed on a short-stay (per-night) basis. Diamond estimates the variable costs of servicing each room to be $24 a night per single occupancy and $26.40 a night per double occupancy.

Many prestige hotels in Vancouver offer special weekend rate reductions (Friday and/or Saturday) of up to 50% of their Sunday-through-Thursday rates. These weekend rates also include additional items such as a breakfast for two, a bottle of champagne, and discounted theatre tickets.

REQUIRED

1. Would you recommend that Diamond reduce room rates at the Vancouver Galaxy on Friday and Saturday nights? What factors should be considered in his decision?
2. In six months' time, the Grey Cup is to be held in Vancouver. Diamond observes that several four-star prestige hotels have already advertised a Friday-through-Sunday rate for Grey Cup weekend of $360 a night. Should Diamond charge extra for the Grey Cup weekend? Explain.

12-28 Relevant-cost approach to pricing decisions. Stardom, Inc., cans peaches for sale to food distributors. All costs are classified as either manufacturing or marketing. Stardom prepares monthly budgets. The March 2007 budgeted absorption costing income statement is as follows:

Revenues (1,000 crates × $120 a crate)	$120,000	100%
Cost of goods sold	72,000	60
Gross margin	48,000	40
Marketing costs	36,000	30
Operating income	$ 12,000	10%

Normal markup percentage:
$48,000 ÷ $72,000 = 66.7% of absorption cost

Monthly costs are classified as fixed or variable (with respect to the cans produced for manufacturing costs and with respect to the number of crates sold for marketing costs):

	Fixed	Variable
Manufacturing	$24,000	$48,000
Marketing	19,200	16,800

Stardom has the capacity to can 1,500 crates per month. The relevant range in which monthly fixed manufacturing costs will be "fixed" is from 500 to 1,500 crates per month.

REQUIRED
1. Calculate the normal markup percentage based on total variable costs.
2. Assume that a new customer approaches Stardom to buy 200 crates at $66 per crate. The customer does not require additional marketing effort. Additional manufacturing costs of $2,400 (for special packaging) will be required. Stardom believes that this is a one-time-only special order, because the customer is discontinuing business in six weeks' time. Stardom is reluctant to accept this 200-crate special order because the $66 per crate price is below the $72 per crate absorption cost. Do you agree with this reasoning? Explain.
3. Assume that the new customer decides to remain in business. How would this longevity affect Stardom's willingness to accept the $66 per crate offer? Explain.

12-29 Product costs, activity-based costing systems. Executive Power (EP) manufactures and sells computers and computer peripherals to several nationwide retail chains. Johan Farnham is the manager of the printer division. Its two largest selling printers are P-41 and P-63.

The manufacturing cost of each printer is calculated using EP's activity-based costing system. EP has one direct manufacturing cost category (direct materials) and the following five indirect manufacturing cost pools:

Indirect Manufacturing Cost Pool	Allocation Base	Allocation Rate
1. Materials-handling	Number of parts	$1.44 per part
2. Assembly management	Hours of assembly time	$48 per hour of assembly time
3. Machine insertion of parts	Number of machine-inserted parts	$0.84 per machine-inserted part
4. Manual insertion of parts	Number of manually inserted parts	$2.52 per manually inserted part
5. Quality testing	Hours of quality testing time	$30 per testing-hour

Product characteristics of P-41 and P-63 are as follows:

	P-41	P-63
Direct materials costs	$489.00	$350.52
Number of parts	85 parts	46 parts
Hours of assembly time	3.2 hours	1.9 hours
Number of machine-inserted parts	49 parts	31 parts
Number of manually inserted parts	36 parts	15 parts
Hours of quality testing	1.4 hours	1.1 hours

REQUIRED
What is the manufacturing cost of P-41? of P-63?

Excel Application For students who wish to practise their spreadsheet skills, the following is a step-by-step approach to creating an Excel spreadsheet to work this problem.

Step-by-Step
1. Open a new spreadsheet. At the top, create an "Original Data" section for the data provided by Executive Power. Create rows for the indirect manufacturing cost pools of "Materials Handling, Assembly Management, Machine Insertion of Parts, Manual Insertion of Parts, and Quality Testing," and create a column for "Allocation Rate."
2. Skip two rows and enter the data on product characteristics by creating columns for each of the products (P-41) and P-63) and rows for "Direct Materials Costs, Number of Parts, Hours of Assembly Time, Number of Machine-Inserted Parts, Number of Manually Inserted Parts, and Hours of Quality Testing."

(Program your spreadsheet to perform all necessary calculations. Do not "hard-code" any amounts, such as materials-handling cost, requiring addition, subtraction, multiplication, or division operations.)

3. Skip two rows and create a "Manufacturing Cost Calculations" section. Create columns for each of the products (P-41 and P-63) and rows for each of the cost categories including: "Direct Materials, Materials Handling, Assembly Management, Machine Insertion of Parts, Manual Insertion of Parts, and Quality Testing." Enter calculations for these costs using data from the Original Data section.

4. Include calculations for total *indirect* manufacturing product costs (that is, excluding direct materials costs) and total manufacturing product costs on separate rows in this section.

5. *Verify the accuracy of your spreadsheet.* Go to your Original Data section and change the allocation rate for the materials-handling cost pool from $1.44 to $1.80 per part. If you programmed your spreadsheet correctly, total manufacturing product costs for P-41 should change to $969.48.

12-30 **Target cost, activity-based costing systems (continuation of 12-29).** Assume all the information in Problem 12-29. Farnham has just received some bad news. A foreign competitor has introduced products very similar to P-41 and P-63. Given their announced selling prices, Farnham estimates the P-41 clone to have a manufacturing cost of approximately $816 and the P-63 clone to have a manufacturing cost of approximately $468. He calls a meeting of product designers and manufacturing personnel at the printer division. They all agree to have the $816 and $468 figures become target costs for redesigned versions of EP's P-41 and P-63, respectively. Product designers examine alternative ways of designing printers with comparable performance but lower cost. They come up with the following revised designs for P-41 and P-63 (termed P-41 REV and P-63 REV, respectively):

	P-41 REV	**P-63 REV**
Direct materials costs	$457.44	$315.72
Number of parts	71 parts	39 parts
Hours of assembly time	2.1 hours	1.6 hours
Number of machine-inserted parts	59 parts	29 parts
Number of manually inserted parts	12 parts	10 parts
Hours of quality testing	1.2 hours	0.9 hours

REQUIRED

1. What is a target cost per unit?
2. Using the activity-based costing system outlined in Problem 12-29, compute the manufacturing costs of P-41 REV and P-63 REV. How do they compare with the $816 and $468 target costs per unit?
3. Explain the differences between P-41 and P-41 REV and between P-63 and P-63 REV.
4. Assume now that Johan Farnham has achieved major cost reductions in one of the activity areas. As a consequence, the allocation rate in the assembly management activity area will be reduced from $48 to $33.60 per assembly-hour. How will this activity-area cost reduction affect the manufacturing costs of P-41 REV and P-63 REV? Comment on the results.

12-31 **Cost-plus pricing.** (CMA, adapted) Hall Company specializes in packaging bulk drugs. Wyant Memorial Hospital has asked Hall to bid on the packaging of one million doses of medication at full cost plus a return on full cost of no more than 9% after income taxes. Wyant defines cost as including all variable costs of performing the service, a reasonable amount of fixed overhead, and incremental administrative costs. The hospital will supply all packaging materials and ingredients. Wyant has indicated that any bid over $0.084 per dose will be rejected.

Don Greenway, the director of cost accounting, has accumulated the following information prior to the preparation of the bid:

Variable direct manufacturing labour costs	$19.20 per direct manufacturing labour-hour
Variable overhead costs	$7.20 per direct manufacturing labour-hour
Fixed overhead costs	$36.00 per direct manufacturing labour-hour
Incremental administrative costs	$6,000 for the order
Production rate	1,000 doses per direct manufacturing labour-hour

Hall Company is subject to an income tax rate of 40%.

REQUIRED

1. Calculate the minimum price per dose that Hall could bid for the Wyant job without changing Hall's net income.
2. Calculate Hall's bid price per dose using the full cost criterion and the maximum allowable return specified by Wyant.
3. Without considering your answer to requirement 2, assume that the price per dose that Hall calculated using the cost-plus criterion specified by Wyant is greater than the maximum bid of $0.084 per dose allowed by Wyant. Discuss the factors that Hall should consider before deciding whether or not to submit a bid at the maximum price of $0.084 per dose.

12-32 Cost-plus and market-based pricing. Construction Temps, a large labour contractor, supplies contract labour to building construction companies. For 2007, Construction Temps has budgeted to supply 80,000 hours of contract labour. Its variable cost is $14.40 per hour and its fixed costs are $288,000. Roger Mason, the general manager, has proposed a cost-plus approach for pricing labour at full cost plus 20%.

REQUIRED

1. Calculate the price per hour that Construction Temps should charge on the basis of Mason's proposal.
2. Sheila Woods, the marketing manager, has supplied the following information on demand levels at different prices:

Price per Hour	Demand (Hours)
$19.20	120,000
20.40	100,000
21.60	80,000
22.80	70,000
24.00	60,000

Construction Temps can meet any of these demand levels. Fixed costs will remain unchanged for all the preceding demand levels. On the basis of this additional information, what price per hour should Construction Temps charge?
3. Comment on your answers to requirements 1 and 2. Why are they the same or not the same?

12-33 Cost-plus and market-based pricing. (CMA, adapted) Best Test Laboratories evaluates the reaction of materials to extreme increases in temperature. Much of the company's early growth was attributable to government contracts. Recent growth has come from diversification and expansion into commercial markets. Environmental testing at Best Test now includes:

Heat testing	(HTT)	Arctic condition testing	(ACT)
Air turbulence testing	(ATT)	Aquatic testing	(AQT)
Stress testing	(SST)		

Currently, all of the budgeted operating costs are collected in a single overhead pool. All of the estimated testing hours are also collected in a single pool. One rate per test-hour is used for all five types of testing. This hourly rate is marked up by 45% to recover administrative costs, taxes, and profit in the selling price.

Rick Shaw, Best Test's controller, believes that there is enough variation in the test procedures and cost structure to establish separate costing and billing rates. He also believes that the inflexible rate structure currently being used is inadequate in today's competitive environment. After analyzing the following data, he has recommended new rates for Best Test's upcoming fiscal year.

The budgeted total test laboratory costs for the coming year are

Test pool labour (10 employees)	$ 504,000
Supervision	86,400
Equipment amortization	214,152
Heat	204,000
Electricity	148,800

Water		88,800
Setup		69,600
Indirect materials		124,800
Operating supplies		74,400
Total test lab costs		$1,514,952
Total estimated test-hours		106,000

Shaw has determined the resource usage by test type in the following table:

	HTT	ATT	SST	ACT	AQT
Test pool labour employees	3	2	2	1	2
Supervision	40%	15%	15%	15%	15%
Amortization	$57,876	$26,400	$47,076	$38,400	$44,400
Heat	50%	5%	5%	30%	10%
Electricity	30%	10%	10%	40%	10%
Water	—	—	20%	20%	60%
Setup	20%	15%	30%	15%	20%
Indirect materials	15%	15%	30%	20%	20%
Operating supplies	10%	10%	25%	20%	35%
Test-hours	29,680	12,720	27,560	22,260	13,780
Competitors' hourly billing rates	$ 21.00	$ 22.80	$ 18.60	$ 19.20	$ 24.00

REQUIRED

1. Compute the single pool hourly cost and hourly billing rate for Best Test Laboratories.
2. Compute the five separate hourly billing rates for Best Test Laboratories.
3. Discuss what effect the new cost-plus method will have on the pricing structure for each of the five test types. Given the competitors' hourly billing rates, how might Best Test modify its pricing?
4. In general, identify at least three other internal or external factors that influence pricing structure.

12-34 **Life cycle product costing, activity-based costing.** Destin Products makes digital watches. Destin is preparing a product life cycle budget for a new watch, MX3. Development on the new watch with features such as a calculator and a daily diary is to start shortly. Destin expects the watch to have a product life cycle of three years. Estimates about MX3 are as follows:

	Year 1	Year 2	Year 3
Units manufactured and sold	50,000	200,000	150,000
Price per watch	$ 54	$ 48	$ 42
R&D and design costs	$1,080,000	$120,000	—
Manufacturing:			
Variable cost per watch	$ 19.20	$ 18	$ 18
Variable cost per batch	$840	$ 720	$ 720
Watches per batch	400	500	500
Fixed costs	$ 720,000	$720,000	$720,000
Marketing:			
Variable cost per watch	$ 4.32	$ 3.84	$ 3.36
Fixed costs	$ 480,000	$360,000	$360,000
Distribution:			
Variable cost per watch	$ 1.20	$ 1.20	$ 1.20
Variable cost per batch	$ 144	$ 144	$ 120
Watches per batch	200	160	120
Fixed costs	$ 288,000	$288,000	$288,000
Customer service costs per watch	$ 2.40	$ 1.80	$ 1.80

Ignore the time value of money in your answers.

1. Calculate the budgeted life cycle operating income for the new watch.
2. What percentage of the budgeted product life cycle costs will be incurred at the end of the R&D and design stages?
3. An analysis reveals that 80% of the total product life cycle costs of the new watch will be locked in at the end of the R&D and design stages. What implications would this finding have on managing MX3's costs?
4. Destin's Market Research Department estimates that reducing MX3's price by $3.60 each year will increase sales by 10% each year. If sales increase by 10%, Destin plans to increase manufacturing and distribution batch sizes by 10% as well. Assume that all variable costs per watch, variable costs per batch, and fixed costs will remain the same. Should Destin reduce MX3's price by $3.60?

12-35 **Ethics and pricing.** Baker, Inc., manufactures ball bearings. Baker is preparing to submit a bid for a new ball bearings order. Greg Lazarus, controller of the Bearings Division of Baker, Inc., has asked John Decker, the cost analyst, to prepare the bid. Baker determines price on the basis of full product costs plus a markup of 10%. Lazarus tells Decker that he is keen on winning the bid and that the price he calculates should be competitive.

Decker prepares the following costs for the bid:

Direct materials costs	$48,000
Direct manufacturing labour costs	12,000
Design and parts administration overhead costs	4,800
Production order overhead costs	6,000
Setup overhead costs	6,600
Materials-handling overhead costs	7,800
General and administration overhead costs	10,800

All direct costs and 30% of overhead costs are incremental costs of the order.

Lazarus reviews the numbers and says, "As usual, your costs are way too high. You have allocated a lot of overhead costs to this job. You know our fixed overhead is not going to change if we win this order and manufacture the bearings. Ever since we installed this new activity-based costing system, we never seem to be able to come up with reasonable product and job costs. Rework your numbers. You have got to make the costs lower."

On returning to his office, Decker rechecks his numbers. He knows that Lazarus wants this order because the additional revenue from the order would lead to a big bonus for Lazarus and the senior division managers. Decker wonders if he can adjust the costs downward. He knows that if he does not come up with a lower bid, Lazarus will be very upset.

REQUIRED

1. Using Baker's pricing policy and based on Decker's estimates, what price should Baker bid for the ball bearings order?
2. Calculate the incremental costs of the ball bearings order. Why do you think Decker uses full product costs rather than incremental costs in his pricing decisions?
3. Evaluate whether Lazarus's suggestion to Decker to use lower cost numbers is unethical. Will it be unethical for Decker to change his analysis so that a lower price can be bid? What steps should Decker take to resolve this situation?

12-36 **Airline pricing, considerations other than cost in pricing.** Air North is about to introduce a daily round-trip flight from Toronto to Vancouver. Air North offers only one class of seats—Comfort Class, which allows more leg room for passengers—on all its flights. No other airline offers this kind of seat. Air North is in the process of determining how it should price its round-trip tickets. The following information is available:

Seating capacity per plane	360
Maximum demand for seats on any flight	300
Food and beverage service cost for a round trip (no charge to passenger)	$ 48 per passenger
Commission to travel agents paid by Air North on each ticket booked on Air North (assume all of Air North's tickets are booked by travel agents)	8% of fare

Fuel costs for a round-trip flight	$ 28,800	
Fixed annual lease costs allocated to a round-trip flight	$120,000	
Fixed ground services (maintenance, check-in, baggage handling) costs allocated to a round-trip flight	$ 12,000	
Fixed flight crew salaries allocated to a round-trip flight	$ 9,600	

For simplicity, assume that fuel costs are not affected by the actual number of passengers on a flight.

The market research group at Air North segments the market into business and pleasure travellers and provides the following information on the effect of two different prices on the estimated number of seats sold:

	Price Charged	Number of Seats Expected to Be Sold
Business travellers	$ 600	200
	$2,400	190
Pleasure travellers	$ 600	100
	$2,400	20

Assume these prices are the only choices available to Air North. The market research team offers one additional fact. Pleasure travellers start their travel in one week, spend at least one weekend at their destination, and return in some following week. Business travellers usually start and complete their travel within the week. They do not stay over weekends.

REQUIRED

1. If you could charge different prices to business travellers and pleasure travellers, would you? Show all your computations.
2. Explain the key factor (or factors) that drives your answer in requirement 1.
3. How might Air North implement price discrimination? That is, what scheme could the airline devise so that business travellers pay the price the airline would like business travellers to pay, and pleasure travellers pay the price the airline would like pleasure travellers to pay?

12-37 Target prices, target costs, value engineering, cost incurrence, locked-in cost, activity-based costing. Cutler Electronics makes a radiocassette player, CE100, which has 80 components. Cutler sells 7,000 units each month for $84 each. The costs of manufacturing CE100 are $54 per unit, or $378,000 per month. Monthly manufacturing costs incurred are as follows:

Direct materials costs	$218,400
Direct manufacturing labour costs	33,600
Machining costs (fixed)	37,800
Testing costs	42,000
Rework costs	16,800
Ordering costs	4,032
Engineering costs (fixed)	25,368
Total manufacturing costs	$378,000

Cutler's management identifies the activity cost pools, the cost drivers for each activity, and the cost per unit of cost driver for each overhead cost pool as follows:

Manufacturing Activity	Description of Activity	Cost Driver	Cost per Unit of Cost Driver
1. Machining costs	Machining components	Fixed costs	No cost driver
2. Testing costs	Testing components and final product (each unit of CE100 is tested individually)	Testing-hours	$2.40 per testing-hour
3. Rework costs	Correcting and fixing errors and defects	Units of CE100 reworked	$24 per unit
4. Ordering costs	Ordering of components	Number of orders	$25.20 per order
5. Engineering costs	Designing and managing of products and process	Fixed costs	No cost driver

Over a long-run time horizon, Cutler's management views direct materials costs and direct manufacturing labour costs as variable with respect to the units of CE100 manufactured. Each overhead cost described in the preceding table varies, as described, with the chosen cost drivers.

The following additional information describes the existing design:

a. Testing and inspection time per unit is 2.5 hours.

b. Ten percent of the CE100s manufactured are reworked.

c. Cutler places two orders with each component supplier each month. Each component is supplied by a different supplier. It takes one hour to place an order.

To respond to competitive pressures, Cutler must reduce its price to $74.40 per unit and reduce its costs by $9.60 per unit. No additional sales are anticipated at this lower price. However, Cutler stands to lose significant sales if it does not cut its price. Manufacturing has been asked to reduce its costs by $7.20 per unit. Improvements in manufacturing efficiency are expected to yield net savings of $1.80 per radiocassette player, but that is not enough. The chief engineer has proposed a new modular design that reduces the number of components to 50 and also simplifies testing. The newly designed radiocassette player, called "New CE100," will replace CE100.

The expected effects of the new design are as follows:

a. Direct materials costs for New CE100 are expected to be lower by $2.64 per unit.

b. Direct manufacturing labour costs for New CE100 are expected to be lower by $0.60 per unit.

c. Machining time required to manufacture New CE100 is expected to be 20% less. It currently takes one hour to manufacture one unit of CE100.

d. Time required for testing New CE100 is expected to be lower by 20%.

e. Rework is expected to decline to 4% of New CE100s manufactured.

Assume that the cost per unit of the cost driver for CE100 continues to apply to New CE100.

REQUIRED

1. Calculate Cutler's manufacturing cost per unit of New CE100.

2. Will the new design achieve the per-unit cost reduction targets that have been set for the manufacturing costs of New CE 100?

3. The problem describes two strategies to reduce costs: (a) improving manufacturing efficiency and (b) modifying the design. Which strategy has a bigger impact on costs? Why? Explain briefly.

COLLABORATIVE LEARNING PROBLEM

12-38 Target prices, target costs, value engineering. Avery, Inc., manufactures two component parts for the television industry:

◆ **Tvez.** Annual production and sales of 50,000 units at a selling price of $48.72 per unit

◆ **Premia.** Annual production and sales of 25,000 units at a selling price of $72 per unit

Avery includes all R&D and design costs in engineering costs. Assume that Avery has no marketing, distribution, or customer service costs.

The direct and overhead costs incurred by Avery on Tvez and Premia are described as follows:

	Tvez	Premia	Total
Direct materials costs (variable)	$1,020,000	$720,000	$1,740,000
Direct manufacturing labour costs (variable)	360,000	240,000	600,000
Direct machining costs (fixed)	180,000	120,000	300,000
Manufacturing overhead costs:			
Machine setup costs			103,500
Testing costs			585,000
Engineering costs			540,000
Manufacturing overhead costs			1,228,500
Total costs			$3,868,500

Avery's management identifies the following activity cost pools, cost drivers for each activity, and the costs per unit of cost driver for each overhead cost pool:

Manufacturing Activity	Description of Activity	Cost Driver	Cost per Unit of Cost Driver
1. Setup	Preparing machine to manufacture a new batch of products	Setup-hours	$30 per setup-hour
2. Testing	Testing components and final product (Avery tests each unit of Tvez and Premia individually.)	Testing-hours	$2.40 per testing-hour
3. Engineering	Designing products and processes and ensuring their smooth functioning	Complexity of product and process	Costs assigned to products by special study

Over a long-run time horizon, Avery's management views direct materials costs and direct manufacturing labour costs as variable with respect to the units of Tvez and Premia produced. Direct machining costs for each product do not vary over this time horizon and are fixed long-run costs. Overhead costs vary with respect to their chosen cost drivers. For example, setup costs vary with the number of setup-hours. Additional information is as follows:

	Tvez	Premia
1. Production batch sizes	500 units	200 units
2. Setup time per batch	12 hours	18 hours
3. Testing and inspection time per unit of product produced	2.5 hours	4.75 hours
4. Engineering costs incurred on each product	$204,000	$336,000

Avery is facing competitive pressure to reduce the price of Tvez and has set a target price of $41.76, well below its current price of $48.72. The challenge for Avery is to reduce the cost of Tvez. Avery's engineers have proposed a new product design and process improvements for the "New Tvez" to replace Tvez. The new design would improve product quality, and reduce scrap and waste. The reduction in prices will not enable Avery to increase its current sales. (However, if Avery does not reduce prices, it will lose sales.)

The expected effects of the new design relative to Tvez are as follows:
1. Direct materials costs for New Tvez are expected to decrease by $2.40 per unit.
2. Direct manufacturing labour costs for New Tvez are expected to decrease by $0.60 per unit.
3. Time required for testing each unit of New Tvez is expected to be reduced by 0.5 hours.
4. Machining time required to make New Tvez is expected to decrease by 20 minutes. It currently takes one hour to manufacture one unit of Tvez. The machines are dedicated to the production of New Tvez.
5. New Tvez will take seven setup-hours for each setup.
6. Engineering costs are unchanged.

Assume that the batch sizes are the same for New Tvez as for Tvez. If Avery requires additional resources to implement the new design, it can acquire these additional resources in the quantities needed. Further assume the costs per unit of cost driver for the New Tvez are the same as those described for Tvez.

INSTRUCTIONS
Form groups of two students to complete the following requirements.

REQUIRED
1. Develop full product costs per unit for Tvez and Premia, using an activity-based product costing approach.

2. What is the markup on the full product cost per unit for Tvez?
3. What is Avery's target cost per unit for New Tvez if it is to maintain the same markup percentage on the full product cost per unit as it had for Tvez?
4. Will the New Tvez design achieve the cost reduction targets that Avery has set?
5. What price would Avery charge for New Tvez if it used the same markup percentage on the full product cost per unit for New Tvez as it did for Tvez?
6. What price should Avery charge for New Tvez, and what next steps should Avery take regarding New Tvez?

McDonald's, the world's largest fast-food restaurant chain, keeps score along three dimensions: financial, customer satisfaction, and employee satisfaction. By providing managers just these three categories of performance at its corporate-owned stores, the company helps direct their attention to the areas of greatest strategic importance. Managers must focus on all three areas to be sure they are balancing their efforts appropriately.

CHAPTER 13

Strategy, Balanced Scorecard, and Strategic Profitability Analysis

LEARNING OBJECTIVES

After studying this chapter, you should be able to

1. Recognize which of two generic strategies a company is using
2. Understand the process of reengineering
3. Distinguish among the four perspectives of the balanced scorecard
4. Analyze changes in operating income to evaluate strategy
5. Distinguish between engineered and discretionary costs
6. Identify and manage unused capacity

The focus of much of the earlier chapters is on managing operations. In this chapter, we explore the use of management accounting information in the implementation and evaluation of an organization's strategy. Strategy is at the core of any business. It drives the operations of a company and guides managers' short-run and long-run decisions. In this chapter, we describe the balanced scorecard approach to implementing strategy and present ways to analyze operating income for purposes of evaluating strategy. We also show how management accounting information helps strategic initiatives, such as productivity improvement, reengineering, and downsizing. We start, however, by discussing what strategy is.

WHAT IS STRATEGY?

Strategy. The matching of an
organization's capabilities with
opportunities in the marketplace in
order to accomplish its overall
objectives.

Strategy describes how an organization matches its own capabilities with the opportunities in the marketplace to accomplish its overall objectives. In formulating its strategy, an organization must thoroughly understand the industry in which it operates. Industry analysis focuses on five forces: (a) competitors, (b) potential entrants into the market, (c) equivalent products, (d) bargaining power of customers, and (e) bargaining power of input suppliers.[1] The collective effect of these forces shapes an organization's profit potential. In general, profit potential decreases with greater competition, stronger potential entrants, products that are similar, and tougher customers and suppliers.

We illustrate these five forces using the example of Chipset Inc., a manufacturer of linear integrated circuit devices (LICDs) used in modems and communication networks. Chipset produces a single specialized product, CX1. This standard, high-performance microchip can be used in multiple applications that require instant processing of real-time data. CX1 was designed with extensive inputs from key customers.

Competitors   Chipset has many growth opportunities, but it also faces significant competition from many small competitors. Companies in the industry have high fixed costs, therefore persistent pressures are on managers to utilize capacity fully and reduce selling prices. Reducing prices of products is critical for industry growth because it allows LICDs to be incorporated into DSL lines for major corporations such as Earthlink and Verizon. CX1 enjoys a reputation of having slightly superior product features relative to competitive products, but competition is severe along the dimensions of price, timely delivery, and quality. Quality is important because LICD failure disrupts the communication network.

Potential Entrants into the Market   The integrated circuits industry does not attract potential new entrants because current competition keeps profit margins small, and significant capital is needed to set up a new manufacturing facility. Companies that have already been making LICDs are further down the learning curve and hence are likely to have lower costs (see Chapter 10 for a discussion of the learning curve effects on cost). Existing companies also have the advantage of close relationships with customers and suppliers that they have built over the years.

Equivalent Products   Chipset uses a technology that allows its customers to use CX1 flexibly to best meet their needs. The flexible design of CX1, and the fact that it is closely integrated into end-products made by Chipset's customers, reduces the potential for equivalent products or new technologies to replace CX1 during the next few years. This risk is reduced even further if Chipset continuously improves CX1's design and processes to decrease costs.

Bargaining Power of Customers   Customers such as Earthlink and Verizon have bargaining power because each buys large quantities of product. Customers can also obtain microchips from other potential suppliers. Signing a contract to deliver microchips is very important to Chipset. Recognizing this fact, customers negotiate hard to keep prices down.

Bargaining Power of Input Suppliers   Chipset maintains its superior quality in part because it purchases high-quality materials such as silicon wafers, pins for connectivity, and plastic or ceramic packaging from its suppliers. Chipset also employs skilled engineers, technicians, and manufacturing labour. Materials suppliers and employees have some bargaining power to demand higher prices and wages.

[1]M. Porter, *Competitive Strategy* (New York: Free Press, 1980); M. Porter, *Competitive Advantage* (New York: Free Press, 1985); M. Porter, "What Is Strategy?" *Harvard Business Review* (November–December 1996) p. 61–78.

In summary, strong competition and the bargaining powers of customers and suppliers put significant pressure on prices. Chipset can respond to these challenges by adopting one of two basic strategies: differentiating its product or achieving cost leadership.

Product differentiation is an organization's ability to offer products or services that are perceived by its customers as being superior and unique relative to those of its competitors. For example, Samsung has successfully differentiated its products in the electronics industry, as have Merck in the pharmaceutical industry and Coca-Cola in the soft-drinks industry. Through innovative product research and development, and by developing processes that bring products to market rapidly, each of these companies has been able to provide better and differentiated products. This differentiation increases brand loyalty and the prices that customers are willing to pay.

Cost leadership is an organization's ability to achieve low costs relative to competitors through productivity and efficiency improvements, elimination of waste, and tight cost control. Some cost leaders in their respective industries are Home Depot (building products), Samsung (consumer electronics), and Magna International (automotive parts). These companies all provide products and services that are similar to, not differentiated from, those of their competitors, but at a lower cost to the customer. Lower selling prices—rather than unique products or services—provide a competitive advantage for these cost leaders.

What strategy should Chipset follow? CX1 is already somewhat differentiated from competing products. Differentiating CX1 further will be costly but it may allow Chipset to charge a higher price. Conversely, reducing the cost of manufacturing and selling CX1 will allow Chipset to reduce the price of CX1 and spur growth. The CX1 technology allows Chipset's customers to achieve different performance levels by simply altering the number of CX1 units in their products. This solution is more cost effective than designing new customized microchips for different applications. Customers want Chipset to keep the current design of CX1 but to lower its price. Chipset's current engineering talent is also more oriented toward making product and process improvements than in creatively designing brand-new products and technologies. Chipset concludes that it should pursue a cost leadership strategy. Of course, successful cost leadership generally would increase Chipset's market share and help the company to grow.

To be successful, a company must both formulate an effective strategy and implement it vigorously. In the next section, we focus on the balanced scorecard as a tool for implementing strategy.

> **Product differentiation.** An organization's ability to offer products or services that are perceived by its customers as superior and unique relative to those of its competitors.

> **Cost leadership.** An organization's ability to achieve low costs relative to competitors through productivity and efficiency improvements, elimination of waste, and tight cost control.

IMPLEMENTATION OF STRATEGY AND THE BALANCED SCORECARD

Consistent with the score-keeping function, the management accountant has an important role to play by developing measures to assist managers as they track a company's progress in implementing strategy. Many organizations have introduced a *balanced scorecard* approach to manage the implementation of their strategies.

The Balanced Scorecard

The **balanced scorecard** translates an organization's mission and strategy into a comprehensive set of performance measures that provide the framework for implementing its strategy.[2] The balanced scorecard does not focus solely on achieving financial objectives. It also highlights the nonfinancial objectives that an organization must achieve to meet its financial objectives. The scorecard measures an organization's performance from four key perspectives: (1) financial, (2) customer, (3) internal business processes, and (4) learning and growth. A company's strategy influences the measures used in each of these perspectives.

The Balanced Scorecard Institute
www.balancedscorecard.org

> **Balanced scorecard.** The translation of an organization's mission and strategy into a comprehensive set of performance measures that provide the framework for implementing its strategy.

[2]See R.S. Kaplan and D.P. Norton, *The Balanced Scorecard* (Cambridge: Harvard Business School Press, 1996); R.S. Kaplan and D.P. Norton, *The Strategy-Focused Organization: How Balanced Scorecard Companies Thrive in the New Business Environment* (Boston: Harvard Business School Press, 2001); and R.S. Kaplan and D.P. Norton, *Strategy Maps: Converting Intangible Assets into Tangible Outcomes* (Boston: Harvard Business School Press, 2004).

The balanced scorecard gets its name from the attempt to balance financial and nonfinancial performance measures to evaluate both short-run and long-run performance in a single report. Consequently, the balanced scorecard reduces managers' emphasis on short-run financial performance, such as quarterly earnings. Why? Because the nonfinancial and operational indicators measure fundamental changes that a company is making. The financial benefits of these changes may not be captured in short-run earnings, but strong improvements in nonfinancial measures signal the prospect of creating economic value in the future. For example, an increase in customer satisfaction signals higher sales and income in the future. By balancing the mix of financial and nonfinancial measures, the balanced scorecard focuses management's attention on both short-run and long-run performance. The key point, however, is that the balanced scorecard is a tool to improve the company's financial performance by measuring nonfinancial indicators of progress towards strategic financial goals.

Shortly we will illustrate the four perspectives of the balanced scorecard using the Chipset example. To understand the measures Chipset uses to monitor progress under each perspective, it is important to recognize key elements of Chipset's cost leadership strategy—improve quality and reengineer processes. As a result of these initiatives, Chipset plans to reduce costs, downsize, and eliminate capacity in excess of that needed to support future growth. However, it does not want to make deep cuts in personnel that would adversely affect employee morale and hinder future growth.

Quality Improvement and Reengineering at Chipset

One key element of Chipset's strategy to reduce costs is improving quality (that is, reducing defects and improving yields in its manufacturing process). To improve quality, Chipset needs to obtain real-time data about manufacturing process parameters and to implement advanced process control methods. The goal is to ensure that process parameters such as temperature and pressure are maintained within tight ranges. Chipset must also train its front-line workers in quality management techniques to help them identify and resolve defects and problems. Following this training, Chipset needs to empower its workforce to make timely decisions and continuously improve the process.

Another key element of Chipset's strategy to reduce costs is reengineering its order delivery process. **Reengineering** is the fundamental rethinking and redesign of business processes to achieve improvements in critical measures of performance such as cost, quality, service, speed, and customer satisfaction.[3] To illustrate the concept of reengineering, we examine the order delivery system at Chipset Inc. in 2007. Chipset's salespeople work with customers to identify and plan customer needs. A copy of each purchase order received from a customer is sent to manufacturing, where a production scheduler begins the planning for manufacturing the order. Frequently, there is a long waiting time before production begins. After manufacturing is complete, the CX1 chips are sent to the shipping department, which matches the quantities of CX1 to be shipped against customer purchase orders. Often, the completed CX1 chips are held in inventory until a truck is available for shipment to the customer. If the quantity shipped does not match the number of chips requested by the customer, a special shipment is scheduled. The shipping documents are sent to the billing department for issuing of invoices. Special staff in the accounting department follows up with customers for payments.

Chipset discovered that the many transfers across departments (sales, manufacturing, shipping, billing, and accounting) to satisfy a customer order slowed down the process and created delays. A multifunction team from the various departments has reengineered the order delivery process for 2008. Its goal is to make the

[3]See M. Hammer and J. Champy, *Reengineering the Corporation: A Manifesto for Business Revolution* (NY: Harper, 1993); Ruhli, Treichler, and Schmidt, "From Business Reengineering to Management Reengineering—A European Study," *Management International Review* (1995), pp. 361–371; and K Sandberg, "Reengineering Tries a Comeback—This Time for Growth, Not Just for Cost Savings," *Harvard Management Update* (November 2001).

entire organization more customer-focused and reduce delays by eliminating the number of interdepartment transfers. Under the new system, a customer relationship manager is responsible for the entire customer relationship. Chipset has entered into long-term contracts with customers that specify quantities and prices. The customer relationship manager will work closely with the customer and with manufacturing to specify delivery schedules for CX1 one month in advance. The schedule of customer orders will be sent electronically to manufacturing. Completed chips will be shipped directly from the manufacturing plant to customer sites. Each shipment will automatically trigger an invoice that will be sent electronically to the customer.

The experiences of many companies, such as the Royal Bank, Cigna Insurance, Ford Motor, and Siemens AG, indicate that the benefits from reengineering are the most significant when it cuts across functional lines to focus on an entire business process (as in the Chipset example). Reengineering only the shipping or invoicing activity at Chipset rather than the entire order delivery process would not be particularly beneficial. Successful reengineering efforts involve changing roles and responsibilities, eliminating unnecessary activities and tasks, using information technology, and developing employee skills. Chipset's balanced scorecard for 2008 must track Chipset's progress in reengineering the order delivery process from both a nonfinancial and financial perspective.

The Four Perspectives of the Balanced Scorecard

Exhibit 13-1 on page 519 presents Chipset's balanced scorecard. It highlights the four key perspectives of performance—financial, customer, internal business processes, and learning and growth. At the beginning of 2008, Chipset has specified its objectives, measures, initiatives to achieve the objectives, and target performance (the first four columns of Exhibit 13-1). The target performance levels for nonfinancial measures are based on competitor benchmarks. They indicate the performance levels necessary to meet customer needs, compete effectively, and achieve financial goals. The fifth column, which describes actual performance, is completed at the end of 2008. This column shows how well Chipset has performed relative to its target performance.

Competitor benchmarks provide the basis for target performance levels for financial and nonfinancial measures. These benchmarks indicate the performance levels necessary to meet customer needs, compete effectively, and achieve financial goals. Chipset wants to use the balanced scorecard targets to drive the organization to higher levels of performance. Managers therefore set targets to achieve a level of performance distinctly better than its competitors'. Chipset's managers complete the fifth column, reporting actual performance at the end of 2008. This column shows how well Chipset performed relative to target performance.

Financial Perspective   This perspective evaluates the profitability of the strategy. Because cost reduction relative to competitors and growth are Chipset's key strategic initiatives, the financial perspective focuses on how much of operating income and return on capital employed results from reducing costs and selling more units of CX1.

Customer Perspective   This perspective identifies the targeted market segments and measures the company's success in these segments. To monitor its growth objectives, Chipset uses measures such as market share in the communication-networks segment, number of new customers, and customer satisfaction.

Internal Business Process Perspective   This perspective focuses on internal operations that further both the customer perspective by creating value for customers and the financial perspective by increasing shareholder wealth. Chipset determines internal business process improvement targets after benchmarking against key competitors. As we discussed in Chapter 12, there are different sources of competitor cost analyses—published financial statements, prevailing

The BMA Group: Balanced Scorecard and Performance Measurement—Australian Consulting Firm
www.bma.com.au

OBJECTIVE 3

Distinguish among the four perspectives of the balanced scorecard

The strategic goal when setting target performance levels in a balanced scorecard is for the company to become the "best in class" among its competitors.

prices, customers, suppliers, former employees, industry experts, and financial analysts. Chipset also physically takes apart competitors' products to compare them with its own designs. This activity also helps Chipset estimate competitors' costs. The internal business process perspective comprises three principal sub-processes:

♦ **The innovation process:** Creating products, services, and processes that will meet the needs of customers. At Chipset, the key to lowering costs and promoting growth is improving the technology of manufacturing.

♦ **The operations process:** Producing and delivering existing products and services to customers. Chipset's key strategic initiatives are (a) improving manufacturing quality, (b) reducing delivery time to customers, and (c) meeting specified delivery dates.

♦ **Postsales-service process:** Providing service and support to the customer after the sale of a product or service. Chipset monitors how quickly and accurately it is responding to customer-service requests.

Note that each of the four perspectives serves the function of focusing managers' attention on improving a strategic element of the business. All four perspectives are linked to the company's strategic, long-term goals for improvement so that by improving on performance in these four areas managers will improve financial performance.

Learning and Growth Perspective This perspective identifies the capabilities in which the organization must excel to achieve superior internal processes that create value for customers and shareholders. Chipset's learning and growth perspective emphasizes four factors: (1) goal congruence, measured by satisfaction ratings; (2) skill/process development, measured by the percentage of employees trained; (3) workforce empowerment, measured by the percentage of line workers making management decisions; and (4) enhanced information system capabilities, measured by the percentage of processes with real-time feedback.

The arrows in Exhibit 13-1 indicate how gains in the learning and growth perspective lead to improvements in internal business processes which, in turn, lead to higher customer satisfaction and market share and, finally, to superior financial performance. Note how key elements of Chipset's strategy implementation—empowering workers, training, information systems, quality and process improvements, reengineering, and customer focus—filter through the scorecard. These initiatives have been successful from a financial perspective in 2008. Chipset has earned significant operating income from its cost leadership strategy that has also translated into growth.

Aligning the Balanced Scorecard to Strategy

Different strategies call for different scorecards. Suppose that Visilog, another company in the microchip industry, follows a product differentiation strategy by designing custom chips for the communication networks business. Visilog designs its scorecard to fit its strategy. For example, in the financial perspective, Visilog evaluates how much of its operating income comes from charging premium prices for its products. In the customer perspective, Visilog measures the percentage of its revenues from new products (and new customers). In the internal business process perspective, Visilog measures the development of advanced manufacturing capabilities to produce custom chips. In the learning and growth perspective, Visilog measures new-product development time. Of course, Visilog uses some of the measures described in the balanced scorecard in Exhibit 13-1. For example, revenue growth, customer satisfaction ratings, order delivery time, on-time delivery, percentage of front-line workers empowered to manage processes, and employee satisfaction ratings are important measures under the new strategy. The key point, though, is to align the balanced scorecard to company strategy.[4]

---

[4]For simplicity, we have presented the balanced scorecard in the context of companies that have followed either a cost leadership or a product differentiation strategy. Of course, a company may have some products for which cost leadership is critical and other products for which product differentiation is important. The company will then develop separate scorecards to implement the different product strategies. In still other contexts, product differentiation may be of primary importance but some cost leadership must also be achieved. The balanced scorecard measures would then link to this strategy.

EXHIBIT 13-1
The Balanced Scorecard for Chipset Inc. for 2008

Objectives	Measures	Initiatives	Target Performance	Actual Performance
Financial Perspective				
	Operating income from productivity gain	Manage costs and unused capacity	$2,000,000	$2,012,500
Increase shareholder value	Operating income from growth	Build strong customer relationships	$3,000,000	$3,420,000
	Revenue growth		6%	6.48%[a]
Customer Perspective				
Increase market share	Market share in communication-networks segment	Identify future needs of customers	6%	7%
Increase customer satisfaction	Number of new customers	Identify new target-customer segments	1	1[b]
	Customer-satisfaction ratings	Increase customer focus of sales organization	90% of customers give top two ratings	87% of customers give top two ratings
Internal Business Process Perspective				
Improve manufacturing quality and productivity	Yield	Identify root causes of problems and improve quality	78%	79.3%
Reduce delivery time to customers	Order-delivery time	Reengineer order-delivery process	30 days	30 days
Meet specified delivery dates	On-time delivery	Reengineer order-delivery process	92%	90%
Improve postsales service	Service response time	Improve customer-service process	Within 4 hours	Within 3 hours
Improve processes	Number of major improvements in manufacturing and business processes	Organize teams from manufacturing and sales to modify processes	5	5
Improve manufacturing capability	Percentage of processes with advanced controls	Organize R&D/manufacturing teams to implement advanced controls	75%	75%
Learning and Growth Perspective				
Align employee and organization goals	Employee-satisfaction ratings	Employee participation and suggestions program to build teamwork	80% of employees give top two ratings	88% of employees give top two ratings
Develop process skill	Percentage of employees trained in process and quality management	Employee training programs	90%	92%
Empower workforce	Percentage of line workers empowered to manage processes	Have supervisors act as coaches rather than decision makers	85%	90%
Enhance information-system capabilities	Percentage of manufacturing processes with real-time feedback	Improve online and offline data gathering	80%	80%

[a](Revenues in 2008 – Revenues in 2007) ÷ Revenues in 2007 = ($28,750,000 – $27,000,000) ÷ $27,000,000 = 6.48%.

[b]Number of customers increased from seven to eight in 2008.

EXHIBIT 13-2
Frequently Cited Balanced Scorecard Measures

Financial Perspective
Operating income, revenue growth, revenues from new products, gross margin percentage, cost reductions in key areas, economic value added[a] (EVA®), return on investments

Customer Perspective
Market share, customer satisfaction, customer-retention percentage, time taken to fulfill customers' requests, number of customer complaints

Internal Business Process Perspective
Innovation Process: Operating capabilities, number of new products or services, new-product development times, and number of new patents
Operations Process: Yield, defect rates, time taken to deliver product to customers, percentage of on-time deliveries, average time taken to respond to orders, setup time, manufacturing downtime
Postsales Service Process: Time taken to replace or repair defective products, hours of customer training for using the product

Learning and Growth Perspective
Employee education and skill levels, employee-satisfaction ratings, employee turnover rates, information system availability, percentage of processes with advanced controls, percentage of employee suggestions implemented, percentage of compensation based on individual and team incentives

[a]These measures are described in Chapter 24.

Exhibit 13-2 presents some common measures found on company scorecards in the service, retail, and manufacturing sectors.

Implementing a Balanced Scorecard

To successfully implement a balanced scorecard requires commitment and leadership from top management. At Chipset, the team building the balanced scorecard (headed by the vice-president of strategic planning) conducted interviews with senior managers, probed executives about customers, competitors, and technological developments, and sought proposals for balanced scorecard objectives across the four perspectives. The team then met to discuss the responses and build a prioritized list of objectives.

In a meeting with all senior managers, the team sought to achieve consensus on the scorecard objectives and to establish a cause-and-effect linkage across the chosen objectives. Senior management was then divided into four groups, with each group responsible for one of the perspectives. In addition, representatives from the next lower levels of management and key functional managers were included in each group to broaden the base of inputs. The groups identified measures for each objective and the sources of information for each measure. The groups then met to finalize scorecard objectives, measures, targets, and the initiatives to achieve the targets. The final balanced scorecard was communicated and used both to evaluate the performance of managers throughout the company and to ensure widespread engagement and alignment. (See also Focus on Values and Behaviours.)

Features of a Good Balanced Scorecard

A good balanced scorecard design has several features:

1. It tells the story of a company's strategy by articulating a sequence of cause-and-effect relationships. For example, because Chipset's goal is to be a low-cost producer and to emphasize growth, the balanced scorecard describes the specific objectives and measures in the learning and growth perspective

The New Wave of Accounting: Contributing to Strategy

As competition intensifies, organizations increasingly want management accountants involved in the design and implementation of strategy. To be effective members of the strategy team, management accountants must understand the economic environment of their industry as well as their organization's customers and competitors. In response to the changing business landscape, management accountants have begun to develop this understanding.

When implementing strategic measurement systems such as the balanced scorecard, it is important for management accountants to have a broad view. Management accountants are more likely to gain support from managers throughout the value chain if they are able to demonstrate a solid understanding of the external business environment as well as internal business issues such as human resources, operations, and distribution. Without this range of knowledge, it would be difficult for management accountants to work with managers to assemble a scorecard that represents the realities of the business.

By communicating the benefits of strategic measurement systems, management accountants gain credibility and support among managers and other employees whose performance will be held accountable against the metrics in the scorecard. Management accountants need to explain, openly and honestly, any costs and limitations of these measures. At no point should they oversell the measures. Rather, management accountants should educate and train managers and employees in how to use these strategic measurement systems to run their businesses better.

Strategic decisions also entail tough choices—shutting down a division, reallocating resources, or downsizing capacity. Many companies such as AT&T, Boeing, Kodak, General Motors, and Nortel have faced these complicated situations. Management accountants are responsible for presenting the data for these difficult decisions, which makes it crucial that they always present the correct financial details despite pressures they may face to slant the facts one way or another.

that lead to improvements in internal business processes. These, in turn, lead to increased customer satisfaction and market share, as well as higher operating income and shareholder value. Each measure in the scorecard is part of a cause-and-effect chain, a linkage from strategy formulation to financial outcomes.

2. It helps to communicate the strategy to all members of the organization by translating the strategy into a coherent and linked set of understandable and measurable operational targets. Guided by the scorecard, managers and employees take actions and make decisions that aim to achieve the company's strategy. To focus these actions, some companies, such as Mobil and Bank of Montreal, have pushed down and developed scorecards at the division and department levels.

3. In for-profit companies, the balanced scorecard places strong emphasis on financial objectives and measures. Managers sometimes tend to focus too much on innovation, quality, and customer satisfaction as ends in themselves, even if they do not lead to tangible payoffs. A balanced scorecard emphasizes nonfinancial measures as a part of a program to achieve future financial performance. When financial and nonfinancial performance measures are properly linked, many of the nonfinancial measures serve as leading indicators of future financial performance. In the Chipset example,

Not-for-profit organizations have other primary objectives such as number of people served and development goals reached.

The limited number of measures put in place responds to the cognitive limits all individuals have on processing information. The discipline is then imposed on managers to identify those few critical or key elements that, if changed, will improve financial performance over the long run. As managers analyze business functions to sift out strategic from nonstrategic elements they obtain a deeper understanding of the business and its competitive environment. In so doing managers apply the *principle of parsimony* that underlies all science—use as few items as possible to explain a process of change.

the improvements in nonfinancial factors have, in fact, led to improvements in financial factors.

4. The scorecard limits the number of measures used by identifying only the most critical ones. Avoiding a proliferation of measures focuses management's attention on those that are key to the implementation of strategy.

5. The scorecard highlights suboptimal tradeoffs that managers may make when they fail to consider operational and financial measures together. For example, a company for which innovation is a key strategy could achieve superior short-run financial performance by reducing money spent on R&D. A good balanced scorecard would signal that the short-run financial performance may have been achieved by taking actions that hurt future financial performance because a leading indicator of that performance, R&D spending and R&D output, has declined.

Pitfalls When Implementing a Balanced Scorecard

Pitfalls to avoid when implementing a balanced scorecard include the following:

1. Don't assume the cause-and-effect linkages to be precise. They are merely hypotheses (see Chapter 10 for a discussion of causal models). A critical challenge is to identify the strength and speed of the causal linkages among the nonfinancial and financial measures. Hence, an organization must gather evidence of these linkages over time. With experience, organizations should alter their scorecards to include those nonfinancial objectives and measures that are the best leading indicators of subsequent financial performance (a lagging indicator). Committing to evolve the scorecard over time avoids the paralysis associated with trying to design the "perfect" scorecard at the outset.

Balanced scorecard elements and their measures will change over time both as the critical elements of success change and as the understanding of links between measures, process control, and profitability improves.

2. Don't seek improvements across all measures all the time. This approach may be inappropriate because tradeoffs may need to be made across various strategic goals. For example, emphasizing quality and on-time performance beyond a point may not be worthwhile—improving these objectives may be inconsistent with profit maximization.

3. Don't use only objective measures on the scorecard. Chipset's scorecard includes both objective measures (such as operating income from cost leadership, market share, and manufacturing yield) as well as subjective measures (such as customer and employee satisfaction surveys). When using subjective measures, management must trade off the benefits of the richer information these measures provide against the imprecision of and the potential for manipulating these measures.

4. Don't fail to consider both costs and benefits of initiatives such as spending on information technology and research and development before including these objectives in the scorecard. Otherwise management may focus the organization on measures that will not result in overall financial benefits.

Chapter 19 expands on the discussion of how companies use the balanced scorecard to succeed based on quality and timeliness.

5. Don't ignore nonfinancial measures when evaluating managers and employees. Managers tend to focus on what their performance is measured by. Excluding nonfinancial measures when evaluating performance will reduce the significance and importance that managers give to nonfinancial scorecard measures. The Global Surveys of Company Practice indicates that companies implementing the balanced scorecard assign weights to nonfinancial performance measures when evaluating management performance. However, they still assign more than 50% weight to financial results.

Widening the Performance-Measurement Lens Using the Balanced Scorecard

A recent survey of 100 large U.S. companies indicates that 60% use some variation of the balanced scorecard.[a] Frequently, scorecards are used by segments of an organization rather than the entire organization. Moreover, many companies use modifications of the full balanced scorecards, which are more accurately described as partial balanced scorecards. Of these adopters, more than 80% are either using or planning to use the scorecard or variations of it for incentive compensation purposes.

As the following table shows, companies using the scorecard cite the broadening of the performance measures as the most important reason for adopting it.

Reason	Percentage Citing as Highly Important
Combines operational and financial measures	88%
Minimizes reliance on a single measure	67%
Shows if improvement in one area adversely affects another area	35%

Surveys also indicate that the balanced scorecard helps in designing performance measures that communicate strategy and in identifying drivers of key financial performance measures.[b] Despite the broadening of performance measures, companies continue to assign more weight to financial results in performance evaluation.

Performance-Measure Category	Average Relative Weight
Financial perspective	55%
Customer perspective	19%
Internal business process perspective	12%
Learning and growth perspective	14%

The balanced scorecard concept continues to spread across the globe, but, to date, scorecards have not been implemented widely outside the United States. A survey of leading German, Swiss, and Austrian companies found only 26% of companies had adopted balanced scorecards, while another 13% were just beginning implementation.[c] Respondents implementing comprehensive balanced scorecards identified primarily strategic, not financial, benefits to adoption (ranked by response frequency):

◆ Improving alignment of strategic objectives with actions
◆ Clarifying and communicating strategy
◆ Developing a consistent system of objectives in the company
◆ Giving stronger consideration to nonfinancial drivers of performance

Despite the wide range of scorecard-related benefits, surveys also indicate some problems in implementing the balanced scorecard. Among American companies, strategic challenges include (1) difficulty in evaluating the relative importance of different measures, (2) problems in measuring and quantifying important qualitative data, (3) lack of clarity resulting from a large number of measures, and (4) time and expense necessary for designing and maintaining the scorecard. Additionally, some companies in Hong Kong noted that implementation was expensive and time-intensive.[d] These companies also noted that they faced resistance from staff and middle management, and that existing operations and IT systems were not equipped for implementation.

Despite these challenges, surveys indicate that executives continue to find the balanced scorecard effective and useful. In fact, an increasing number of companies in Scandinavia,[e] Finland,[f] Portugal,[g] and Singapore[h] are implementing the balanced scorecard.

[a]Towers Perrin, "CompScan Report: Inside the Balanced Scorecard" (New York: Towers Perrin, January 1996).
[b]Frigo, M., "2001 CMG Survey of Performance Management Trends and Challenges in Performance Management," *Cost Management Update* (Montvale, NJ: Institute of Management Accountants, 2001).
[c]Speckbacher, S., J. Bischof, and T. Pfeiffer, "A Descriptive Analysis of the Implementation of Balanced Scorecards in German-Speaking Countries," *Management Accounting Research* (2003).
[d]"Hong Kong Strikes a Perfect Balance," *Australian CPA* (2003).
[e]Ax, C., and T. Bjornenak, "The Building and Diffusion of Management Accounting Innovations—The Case of the Balanced Scorecard" (Munich: European Accounting Association Congress, 2000).
[f]Malmi, T., "Balanced Scorecard in Finnish Companies: A Research Note," *Management Accounting Research* (2001).

[g]Rodrigues, L., and G. Sousa, "The Use of the Balanced Scorecard in Portugal," *Journal for Management Theory and Practice* (2002).

[h]Chia, A., and H. Hoon, "Adopting and Creating Balanced Scorecards in Singapore-Based Companies," *Singapore Management Review* (2000).

EVALUATING THE SUCCESS OF A STRATEGY

To evaluate how successful it has been in implementing its strategy, Chipset compares the target and actual performance columns of its balanced scorecard in Exhibit 13-1 (p. 519). This comparison indicates that Chipset met most of the targets it had set on the basis of competitor benchmarks. Meeting the targets suggests that the strategic initiatives that Chipset had identified and measured for learning and growth resulted in improvements in internal business processes, customer measures, and financial performance. The financial measures show that Chipset achieved targeted cost savings and growth. The key question is, how does Chipset isolate operating income from specific sources such as cost savings and growth instead of focusing on the change in total operating income?

Some companies might be tempted to gauge the success of their strategies by measuring the change in their operating incomes from one year to the next, but this approach is inadequate. For example, operating income can increase simply because entire markets are expanding, not because a specific strategy has been successful. Also, changes in operating income might be caused by factors outside the strategy. For example, a company such as Chipset that has chosen a cost leadership strategy may find that operating income increases have instead been caused incidentally by, say, some degree of product differentiation. Company managers and accountants need to evaluate the success of a strategy on the basis of whether the sources of operating income increases are the result of implementing the chosen strategy.

To use operating income numbers to evaluate the success of a strategy, a company needs to isolate the operating income due to cost leadership from the operating income due to product differentiation. Of course, successful cost leadership or product differentiation generally increases market share and helps a company to grow. To evaluate the success of a company's strategy, we subdivide changes in operating income into components that can be identified with growth, product differentiation, and cost leadership. Subdividing the change in operating income to evaluate the success of a company's strategy is similar to variance analysis discussed in Chapters 7 and Chapter 8. The focus here, however, is on comparing actual operating performance over two different time periods and explicitly linking that performance to strategic choices. A company is considered successful in implementing its strategy when the amounts of the product differentiation, cost leadership, and growth components align closely with its strategy.

The balanced scorecard methodology can be used in both for-profit and not-for-profit organizations. The Canadian Institute for Health Information analyzes information received from hospitals in Ontario that permits a comparison of each hospital across multiple dimensions of hospital performance. Using a balanced scorecard approach, performance indicators across the four perspectives were identified based on their scientific soundness, relevance, and feasibility. Exhibit 13-3 provides the report of one hospital, which details the specific indicators used and a comparison of this hospital with the other hospitals being analyzed.

STRATEGIC ANALYSIS OF OPERATING INCOME

OBJECTIVE 4

Analyze changes in operating income to evaluate strategy

The following simplified example illustrates how operating-income changes between two years can be divided into components that can describe how successful a company has been with regard to cost leadership, product differentiation, and growth.[5]

[5]For other details, see R. Banker, S. Datar and R. Kaplan, "Productivity Measurement and Management Accounting," *Journal of Accounting, Auditing and Finance* (1989), pp. 528–554; and A. Hayzen and J. Reeve, "Examining the Relationships in Productivity Accounting," *Management Accounting Quarterly* (2000).

Chipset presents the following data for the years 2007 and 2008.

	2007	2008
1. Good units of CX1 produced and sold	1,000,000	1,150,000
2. Defective units of CX1 produced and disposed of at zero net disposal price	500,000	300,000
3. Selling price	$27	$25
4. Direct materials (square centimetres of silicon wafer)	3,000,000	2,900,000
5. Direct materials cost per square centimetre	$1.40	$1.50
6. Manufacturing capacity	1,875,000 units	1,750,000 units
7. Total manufacturing conversion costs	$11,250,000	$10,850,000
8. Manufacturing conversion costs per unit of capacity (Row 7 ÷ Row 6)	$6	$6.20
9. Selling and customer service capacity	60 customers	55 customers
10. Total selling and customer service costs	$4,800,000	$4,400,000
11. Cost per customer of selling and customer service capacity (Row 10 ÷ Row 9)	$80,000	$80,000
12. R&D employees	40	39
13. Total R&D costs	$4,000,000	$3,900,000
14. R&D costs per employee (Row 12 ÷ Row 11)	$100,000	$100,000

Chipset provides the following additional information:

1. Manufacturing conversion costs for each year depend on production capacity defined in terms of the number of units of CX1 that can be produced. Such costs do not vary with the actual quantity of CX1 units produced. Because direct manufacturing labour costs are small (and tied to capacity, not production), Chipset includes these costs and other manufacturing costs as part of manufacturing conversion costs rather than as a separate cost category. To reduce manufacturing conversion costs, management would have to reduce capacity by selling some of the manufacturing equipment and laying off some manufacturing personnel.

> Although difficult, this strategic analysis exemplifies the value added by management accountants as they participate in assessing and provide vital feedback on the effectiveness of implementing strategy.

EXHIBIT 13-3
Hospital Balanced Scorecard

Clinical Utilization and Outcomes

Acute Myocardial Infarction
Use of Selected Diagnostic Technologies ▸
Complications ▸
Readmissions ▸

Asthma
Readmissions ▸

Pneumonia
Complications ▸

Stroke
Length of Stay ▸

Cholecystectomy
Percent Day Surgery ○
Complications ●

Hysterectomy
Length of Stay NR
Complications NR
Readmissions NR

Prostatectomy
Readmissions ▸

Above average performance refers to lower complication rates, lower readmission rates, shorter length of stay, greater use of technology, and higher percentage of day surgery.

Below average performance refers to higher complication rates, higher readmission rates, longer length of stay, less use of technology, and lower percentage of day surgery.

(Continued)

EXHIBIT 13-3 Continued

Financial Performance and Condition

Above average performance refers to higher values for indicators of financial viability, liquidity, capital, and human resources and lower values for indicators of efficiency.

Below average performance refers to lower values for indicators of financial viability, liquidity, capital, and human resources and higher values for indicators of efficiency.

Financial Viability

Total Margin	◗

Efficiency

Unit Cost Performance	◗
Corporate Services	◗
Days in Inventory	◗

Liquidity

Current Ratio	◗
Working Capital	◗

Capital

Equipment Expense	◗

Human Resources

Nursing Care Hours as Percentage of Total Inpatient Nursing Hours	◗
Patient Care Hours as a Percentage of Total Staff Hours	◗

Patient Satisfaction

Above average performance refers to higher scores on each indicator.

Below average performance refers to lower scores on each indicator.

Global Quality	◗
Process Quality	◗
Outcome	◗
Nursing Care	◗
Physician Care	◗
Ancillary Patient Care Staff	◗
Support Services	◗
Housekeeping	◗

System Integration and Change

Above average performance refers to higher scores on each indicator.

Below average performance refers to lower scores on each indicator.

Information Use

Clinical Information Technology	●
Clinical Data-Collection, Dissemination, and Benchmarking	◗
Intensity of Information Use	●

Internal Coordination of Care

Development and Use of Clinical Pathways	●
Coordination of Care	◗

Hospital-Community Integration

Hospital-CCAC Relationships	◗
Hospital-Community Relationships	◗
Continuity of Care	◗
Strategies for Managing ALC Patients	◗

Legend

Above Average Performance	●
Average Performance	◗
Below Average Performance	○
Nonreportable	NR

2. Most of Chipset's marketing costs are costs of selling chips to customers. Selling and customer service costs for each year depend on the number of customers that the selling and customer service functions are designed to support. These costs do not vary with the actual number of customers Chipset sells to in

each year. Chipset had 40 customers in 2007 and 46 customers in 2008. To reduce selling and customer service costs, Chipset management would have to lay off selling and customer service staff.

3. At the start of each year, management uses its discretion to determine the amount of R&D to be done. The amount of R&D is independent of the actual quantity of CX1 produced or the number of customers to whom CX1 is sold.

4. The investment base and asset structure are not materially different in the years 2007 and 2008.

Operating income for each year is as follows:

	2007	2008
Revenues ($27 × 1,000,000; $25 × 1,150,000)	$27,000,000	$28,750,000
Costs		
Direct materials costs ($1.40 × 3,000,000; $1.50 × 2,900,000)	4,200,000	4,350,000
Manufacturing conversion costs ($6 × 1,875,000; $6.20 × 1,750,000)	11,250,000	10,850,000
Selling and customer-service costs ($80,000 × 60; $80,000 × 55)	4,800,000	4,400,000
R&D costs ($100,000 × 40; $100,000 × 39)	4,000,000	3,900,000
Total costs	24,250,000	23,500,000
Operating income	$ 2,750,000	$ 5,250,000
Increase in operating income		$2,500,000

The goal of managers at Chipset is to evaluate how much of this $2,500,000 increase in operating income was caused by the successful implementation of the company's strategy. To do so, they must examine three main analysis components: growth, price recovery, and productivity. Exhibit 13-4 provides a summary of the following analysis of the growth, price-recovery, and productivity effects.

> These calculations resemble those in Chapters 7 and 8. The growth component is analogous to calculating the sales-volume variance; the price-recovery component resembles the calculation of price and spending variances; the productivity component resembles the calculation of the efficiency variances.

The Growth Component

The growth component measures the increase in revenues minus the increase in costs from selling more units of CX1 in 2008 (1,150,000 units) than in 2007 (1,000,000 units), assuming nothing else has changed. That is, the output prices, input prices, efficiencies, and capacities of 2007 are assumed to continue into 2008.

EXHIBIT 13-4
Strategic Analysis of Profitability

	Income Statement Amounts in 2007 (1)	Revenue and Cost Effects of Growth Component in 2008 (2)	Revenue and Cost Effects of Price-Recovery Component in 2008 (3)	Cost Effect of Productivity Component in 2008 (4)	Income Statement Amounts in 2008 (5) = (1) + (2) + (3) + (4)
Revenues	$27,000,000	$4,050,000 F	$2,300,000 U	—	$28,750,000
Costs	24,250,000	630,000 U	720,000 U	$2,100,000 F	23,500,000
Operating income	$ 2,750,000	$3,420,000 F	$3,020,000 U	$2,100,000 F	$ 5,250,000

$2,500,000 F
Change in operating income

Revenue Effect of Growth

$$\begin{array}{c}\text{Revenue effect}\\\text{of growth}\\\text{component}\end{array} = \left(\begin{array}{cc}\text{Actual units of output} & \text{Actual units of output}\\\text{sold in 2008} & - \quad \text{sold in 2007}\end{array}\right) \times \begin{array}{c}\text{Selling price}\\\text{in 2007}\end{array}$$

$$= (1,150,000 - 1,000,000) \times \$27 = \$4,050,000 \text{ F}$$

This component is favourable (F) because it increases operating income. Decreases in operating income are unfavourable (U).

Note that we keep the 2007 price of CX1 unchanged and focus only on the increase in output sold between 2007 and 2008. Why? Because the objective of the revenue effect of the growth component is to isolate the increase in revenues between 2007 and 2008 due solely to the change in the quantity sold, *assuming* the 2007 selling price continues into 2008.

Cost Effect of Growth Of course, to produce the higher output sold in 2008, more inputs would be needed. The cost increase from growth measures the amount by which costs in 2008 would have increased (1) if the relationship between inputs and outputs that existed in 2007 had continued in 2008, and (2) if prices of inputs in 2007 had continued in 2008.

$$\begin{array}{c}\text{Cost effect}\\\text{of growth}\\\text{component}\end{array} = \left(\begin{array}{cc}\text{Actual units of input or capacity}\\\text{that would have been used to}\\\text{produce year 2008 output} & - \quad\begin{array}{c}\text{Actual units of input}\\\text{capacity to produce}\\\text{2007 output}\end{array}\\\text{assuming the same input-output}\\\text{relationship that existed in 2007}\end{array}\right) \times \begin{array}{c}\text{Input}\\\text{prices}\\\text{in 2007}\end{array}$$

We use 2007 input-output relationships and 2007 input prices because the goal is to isolate the increase in costs caused solely by the growth in the units of CX1 sold between 2007 and 2008. As our example assumes that the manufacturing conversion costs, selling and customer-service costs, and R&D costs are fixed, then only the direct materials costs will change with the change in volumes from 2007 to 2008.

To produce 1,150,000 units of CX1 in 2008, as compared to the 1,000,000 units produced in 2007 (15% more), assuming the same rework rate, Chipset would require a proportionate increase in the 3,000,000 square centimetres of direct materials used in 2007. Note that variable direct materials costs are distinguished from fixed costs that include conversion and R&D costs. Fixed costs do not change proportionately as long as the increase in production is within the relevant range, while variable costs will. The quantity of direct materials that would be required equals 3,450,000 square centimetres $\left(3,000,000 \times \frac{1,150,000}{1,000,000}\right)$.

Thus, the cost effects of the growth component are

Direct materials costs	$(3,450,000 - 3,000,000) \times \$1.40$	$= \$630,000$ U
Manufacturing conversion costs	$(1,875,000 - 1,875,000) \times \$6$	$= \quad 0$
Selling and customer-service costs	$(60 - 60) \times \$80,000$	$= \quad 0$
R&D costs	$(40 - 40) \times \$100,000$	$= \quad 0$
Cost effects of growth component		$\underline{\$630,000}$ U

In summary, the net increase in operating income as a result of growth equals

Revenue effect of growth component		$\$4,050,000$ F
Cost effect of growth		
Direct materials costs	630,000 U	
Manufacturing conversion costs	0	
Selling and customer service costs	0	
R&D costs	0	630,000 U
Increase in operating income due to growth component		$\underline{\$3,420,000}$ F

The Price-Recovery Component

The price-recovery component of operating income measures the change in revenues and the change in costs to produce the 1,150,000 units of CX1 manufactured in 2008 as a result of the change in the prices of CX1 and the change in the prices of inputs required to make CX1, assuming that the relationship between inputs and outputs that existed in 2007 continued in 2008.

Revenue Effect of Price Recovery

$$\begin{pmatrix} \text{Revenue effect} \\ \text{of product differentiation} \\ \text{component} \end{pmatrix} = \begin{pmatrix} \text{Selling price} \\ \text{in 2008} \end{pmatrix} - \begin{pmatrix} \text{Selling price} \\ \text{in 2007} \end{pmatrix} \times \begin{pmatrix} \text{Actual units of} \\ \text{output sold} \\ \text{in 2008} \end{pmatrix}$$

$$= (\$25 - \$27) \times 1{,}150{,}000 = \$2{,}300{,}000 \text{ U}$$

Note that the calculation focuses on the decrease in the price of CX1 between 2007 and 2008. Why? Because the objective of the revenue effect of price recovery is to isolate the change in revenues between 2007 and 2008 due solely to the change in selling prices.

Cost Effect of Price Recovery   This calculation focuses on the effect of changes in the prices of inputs. Because of the anticipated change in manufacturing conversion costs, these fixed costs must be considered in order to capture the full cost effect of price recovery.

$$\begin{pmatrix} \text{Cost effect} \\ \text{of product} \\ \text{differentiation} \\ \text{component} \end{pmatrix} = \begin{pmatrix} \text{Input prices} \\ \text{in year 2008} \end{pmatrix} - \begin{pmatrix} \text{Input prices} \\ \text{in year 2007} \end{pmatrix} \times \begin{pmatrix} \text{Actual units of inputs/capacity} \\ \text{that would have been used to} \\ \text{produce year 2008 output} \\ \text{assuming the same input-output} \\ \text{relationship that existed in 2007} \end{pmatrix}$$

Direct materials costs	($1.50 – $1.40) × 3,450,000 = $345,000 U
Manufacturing conversion costs	($6.20 – $6.00) × 1,875,000 = 375,000 U
Selling and customer-service costs	($80,000 – $80,000) × 60 = 0
R&D costs	($100,000 – $100,000) × 40 = 0
Total cost effect of price-recovery component	$720,000 U

Note that the quantity of inputs that would have been needed to produce the output in year 2008 (assuming the relationship between inputs and outputs that existed in 2007 continued in 2008) has already been determined when calculating the cost effects of growth. The calculation focuses on the change in costs caused solely by the change in the prices of inputs between 2007 and 2008.

In summary, the net decrease in operating income attributable to price recovery (measured by the change in output prices relative to the change in input prices) is

Revenue effect of price-recovery		$2,300,000 U
Cost effect of price-recovery		
Direct materials cost	$345,000 U	
Manufacturing conversion costs	375,000 U	
Selling and customer-service costs	0	
R&D costs	0	720,000 U
Decrease in operating income due to price-recovery component		$3,020,000 U

The price-recovery analysis indicates that, even as the prices of its inputs increased, Chipset could not pass these increases on to its customers via higher prices of CX1.

The Productivity Component

The productivity component of operating income compares how costs have decreased as a result of using fewer inputs, a better mix of inputs, and less capacity to produce year 2008 output, assuming year 2008 input prices.

$$\begin{array}{ccc} \text{Productivity/} \\ \text{cost leadership} \\ \text{component} \end{array} = \left(\begin{array}{c} \text{Actual units of} \\ \text{input/capacity to} \\ \text{produce year} \\ \text{2008 input} \end{array} - \begin{array}{c} \text{Actual units of inputs/capacity that} \\ \text{would have been used to produce} \\ \text{year 2008 output assuming the} \\ \text{same input-output relationship that} \\ \text{existed in 2007} \end{array} \right) \times \begin{array}{c} \text{Year} \\ \text{2008} \\ \text{prices} \end{array}$$

Note that the calculations use year 2008 prices and year 2008 output. Why? Because the objective of the productivity component is to isolate the change in costs between 2007 and 2008 caused solely by the change in the quantities, mix, and capacities of inputs.

The actual units of capacity that would have been used to produce year 2008 output, assuming the same input-output relationship that existed in 2007, have already been calculated and explained when computing the growth component (p. 528). The actual units of inputs or capacity to produce year 2008 output is given in the basic data for Chipset on page 527. By using 2008 prices and output, the change in costs between 2007 and 2008 caused solely by change in the quantities, mix, and/or capacity of inputs is isolated.[6]

The productivity component of cost changes is

Direct materials costs	$(2,900,000 - 3,450,000) \times \$1.50$	$= \$825,000$ F
Manufacturing conversion costs	$(1,750,000 - 1,875,000) \times \$6.20$	$= 775,000$ F
Selling and customer-service costs	$(55 - 60) \times \$80,000$	$= 400,000$ F
R&D costs	$(39 - 40) \times \$100,000$	$= 100,000$ F
Increase in operating income due to productivity component		$\$2,100,000$ F

Productivity improvements never occur automatically for fixed costs. The only way to reduce these costs is to reduce capacity (plant, equipment, or human resources).

The productivity component indicates that Chipset was able to increase operating income by improving quality and productivity, eliminating capacity, and reducing costs. The appendix to this chapter examines partial and total factor productivity changes between 2007 and 2008 and describes how the management accountant can obtain a deeper understanding of Chipset's cost leadership strategy.

Exhibit 13-4 (p. 527) summarizes the growth, price recovery, and productivity components of the changes in operating income. At a basic level, companies that have been successful at cost leadership will show large favourable productivity and growth components; companies that have successfully differentiated their products will show large favourable price-recovery and growth components. In Chipset's case productivity contributed $2,100,000 to the increase in operating income and growth contributed $3,420,000. Operating income suffered because Chipset was unable to pass along increases in input prices. Had Chipset been able to differentiate its product, the price effects may have been less unfavourable.

Further Analysis of Growth, Price-Recovery, and Productivity Components

As in all variance and profit analysis, the thoughtful analyst will want to analyze the sources of operating income more closely. For instance, in the Chipset example, growth may have been helped by an increase in industry market size. Therefore, at least a part of the increase in operating income may be attributable to favourable economic conditions in the industry rather than to any successful implementation of strategy. Some of the growth may also have come as a result of a management decision at Chipset to take advantage of its productivity gains by cutting prices. In this case, the increase in operating income from cost leadership equals the productivity

---

[6]The productivity-component calculation uses actual 2008 input prices, whereas its counterpart, the efficiency variance in Chapters 7 and 8, uses budgeted prices. This chapter assumes the forecast year is unfolding as this analysis occurs. Year 2008 prices are used in the productivity calculation because it is real-time information and not a forecast. Chipset wants managers to choose input quantities to minimize costs in 2008 based on currently prevailing prices. If the forecast prices were used, the quantities chosen would be based on outdated, irrelevant prices estimated for use in the 2008 budget. In Chapters 7 and 8 the budgeted price is a forecast that can be changed as the year unfolds to match those prices experienced by the company.

gain plus any increase in operating income from growth in market share attributable to productivity improvements minus any decrease in operating income from a strategic decision to lower prices.

To illustrate these ideas, consider again the Chipset example and the following additional information.

◆ The market growth rate in the industry is 10%. That is, of the 150,000 (1,150,000 − 1,000,000) units of increase in sales of CX1 between 2007 and 2008, 100,000 (10% × 1,000,000) units are due to an increase in industry market size (which Chipset would have benefited from regardless of its productivity gains) and the remaining 50,000 units are due to an increase in market share.

◆ Of the $2 decrease in the selling price of CX1, $1.25 is due to a general decline in the market prices of chips in the industry. The further decrease of $0.75 is the result of a management decision to lower prices to take advantage of its productivity gains, which increased market share by 50,000 units.

Chipset would compute the increase in operating income from cost leadership as follows:

Productivity component	$2,100,000 F
Decrease in price of CX1 ($0.75 × 1,150,000 units)	862,500 U
Growth in market share due to productivity improvement and lower prices	
$3,420,000 (from Exh. 13-4, col. 2) × $\dfrac{50,000 \text{ units}}{150,000 \text{ units}}$	1,140,000 F
Change in operating income due to cost leadership	$2,377,500 F

Further, suppose that the growth in market size was the result of a decrease in industrywide market prices. Then the effect on Chipset's operating income from industrywide effects rather than specific strategic actions is

Change in operating income due to growth in industry market size	
$3,420,000 (Exh. 13-4, Col. 2) × $\dfrac{100,000}{150,000}$	$2,280,000 F
Change in operating income due to decline in industry-wide selling prices	
$1.25 × 1,150,000	1,437,500 U
Effect on operating income of industrywide factors	$ 842,500 F

Lacking a differentiated product, Chipset is unable to pass along increases in input prices to its customers. The effect of product differentiation on operating income is:

Increase in market prices of inputs (cost effect of price recovery)	$720,000 U

The change in operating income between 2007 and 2008 can be summarized as follows:

Change due to cost leadership	$2,377,500 F
Change due to industrywide factors	842,500 F
Change due to product differentiation	720,000 U
Change in operating income	$2,500,000 F

Under different assumptions of how changes in prices affect the quantity of CX1 sold, the analyst will attribute different amounts to the different strategies. The important point, though, is that, consistent with its cost leadership strategy, the productivity gains of $2,100,000 Chipset made in 2008 were key to the operating income increases in 2008. The Problem for Self-Study on page 536 describes the analysis of the growth, price-recovery, and productivity components for a company following a product-differentiation strategy. The Concepts in Action feature on page 532 describes the problems of dot-com companies that emphasized growth but failed to implement coherent strategies of either cost leadership or product differentiation.

Growth-versus-Profitability Choices of Dot-Com Companies

Competitive advantage comes from product differentiation or cost leadership. Successful implementation of these strategies helps a company be profitable and grow. During the dot-com boom in the late 1990s, many dot-com companies pursued a strategy of short-run growth to gain brand recognition and market share, with the goal of later translating such growth into higher prices (via product differentiation) or lower costs (via cost leadership). The most spectacular failures of dot-com companies occurred in companies that followed the "get big fast" model but then failed to differentiate their products or reduce their costs.

One such example is Webvan. At Webvan, customers ordered groceries online. Webvan then delivered these groceries to customers' homes. The benefit to customers was that they avoided the hassle of driving, parking, and standing in line at the supermarket. Webvan's model was to get big fast. *The New York Times* noted that "long before it began to get the bugs out of its initial 100,000-square-foot distribution center in Oakland, California, Webvan began a three-year program to replicate the facility in 26 cities nationwide, at a cost of [US]$35 million each." Webvan also spent large amounts of money on marketing to establish its brand. The operational challenges of an online grocery business are immense. Webvan never generated anywhere near the sales volume it was expecting. The low margins of the retail grocery business, perishable inventory, and large amounts of unused capacity led to heavy losses. In July 2003, Webvan filed for bankruptcy, having spent almost all of the US$1.2 billion of its invested capital.

Webvan did not become profitable because its cost structure was higher than the bricks-and-mortar grocery stores it competed against. Lower costs due to productivity increases or economies of scale did not materialize. Despite brand recognition, Webvan did not have a favourable price-recovery component of operating income because customers were unwilling to pay premium prices for the convenience of online grocery shopping. Without a cost leadership or product differentiation advantage, the growth component of operating income was unfavourable because costs exceeded revenues. The more Webvan sold, the more money it lost, leading to its eventual bankruptcy. Long-run success depends on gaining cost leadership or product differentiation, which Webvan never achieved.

Since Webvan's bankruptcy, new entrants have cautiously entered the online grocery-shopping market. These firms, including Ahold's Peapod and Safeway.com, began operations by minimizing initial investment and costs. Peapod, for example, shares warehousing facilities and operations with local Ahold-owned supermarkets including Giant, Bi-Lo, and Stop and Shop. Like other online grocers, Peapod follows a product-differentiation strategy, charging premium prices for the convenience of online shopping. Additionally, and unlike Webvan, online grocers now have minimum orders, typically US$50. These leaner operations and higher prices have proven successful for these second-generation entrants. Peapod alone had revenues of US$150 million in 2005, and Safeway.com was responsible for increasing profitability of its parent company.

Source: J. Moran, "Online Grocery Services Are on the Rebound," *Hartford Courant* (July 8, 2004); S. Hansel, "An Ambitious Internet Grocer Is Out of Both Cash and Ideas," *The New York Times* (July 10, 2003); S. Kapner, "Early Winner in Online Food; Local and Simple Ways Work for British Grocer," *The New York Times* (July 20, 2003); "Business and Finance," *The Wall Street Journal* (August 9, 1999); and Webvan's 2003 10K filings.

DOWNSIZING AND THE MANAGEMENT OF CAPACITY

As we saw in our discussion of the productivity component, fixed costs are tied to capacity. Unlike variable costs, fixed costs do not change automatically with changes in the level of the cost driver (such as units started into production in the case of manufacturing overhead costs). How then can managers reduce capacity-based fixed costs? The key is in understanding and managing unused capacity. To understand unused capacity, managers find it useful to classify costs into *engineered* and *discretionary* categories.

Engineered costs result specifically from a clear cause-and-effect relationship between output (or cost driver) and the (direct or indirect) resources used to produce that output. In the Chipset example, direct materials costs are an example of direct engineered costs. Manufacturing conversion costs are an example of indirect engineered costs. Consider the year 2008. The output of 1,150,000 units of CX1 and the efficiency with which inputs are converted into outputs result in 1,450,000 units of CX1 started into production. Manufacturing conversion resources needed and used to process 1,450,000 units of CX1 equal $8,990,000 ($6.20 × 1,450,000), assuming that the cost of resources used increases proportionately with the number of units started. Of course, total manufacturing conversion costs are higher ($10,850,000) because they are related to the manufacturing capacity of 1,750,000 units ($6.20 × 1,750,000 = $10,850,000). These costs are fixed in the short run, but, over time, there is a clear cause-and-effect relationship among output, manufacturing capacity required, and manufacturing conversion costs needed. Thus, engineered costs can be either variable or fixed in the short run. Selling and customer-service costs are also examples of engineered costs that are fixed in the short run. There is, however, a clear cause-and-effect relationship between selling and customer-service resources used and the number of customers served.

Discretionary costs have two important features: (1) they arise from periodic (usually yearly) decisions regarding the maximum amount to be incurred and (2) they have no clearly measurable cause-and-effect relationship between output and resources used. There is often a delay between the acquisition of a resource and its eventual use. Examples of discretionary costs include advertising, executive training, R&D, health care, and corporate staff department costs such as legal, human resources, and public relations. The most noteworthy aspect of discretionary costs is that managers are seldom confident that the "correct" amounts are being spent. The founder of Lever Brothers, an international consumer-products company, once noted, "Half the money I spend on advertising is wasted; the trouble is, I don't know which half." In the Chipset example, R&D costs are discretionary costs because there is no measurable cause-and-effect relationship between output of 1,450,000 units produced and R&D resources needed or used.[7]

Relationships between Inputs and Outputs

Engineered costs differ from discretionary costs along two key dimensions: the type of process and the level of uncertainty. Engineered costs pertain to processes that are detailed, physically observable, and repetitive, such as manufacturing or customer service activities. In contrast, discretionary costs are associated with processes that are sometimes called *black boxes*, because they are less precise and not well understood.

Uncertainty refers to the possibility that an actual amount will deviate from an expected amount. The higher the level of uncertainty about the relationship between resources used and outputs, the less likely a cause-and-effect relationship will exist, leading the cost to be classified as a discretionary cost. R&D costs have an uncertain effect on output because other factors such as overall market conditions, competitors' R&D investments, and new product introductions also affect the level of output produced. In contrast, there is a low level of uncertainty about the effect of output on manufacturing conversion resources used because other factors do not affect this relationship.

OBJECTIVE 5

Distinguish between engineered and discretionary costs

Engineered costs. Costs that result from a clear cause-and-effect relationship between output (or cost driver) and the (direct or indirect) resources used to produce that output.

Discretionary costs. Costs that have no clearly measurable cause-and-effect relationship between output and resources used; they arise from periodic decisions regarding the maximum amount of costs to be incurred.

---

[7]Managers also describe some costs as **infrastructure costs,** costs that arise from having property, plant, and equipment and a functioning organization. Examples are amortization, long-run lease rental, and the acquisition of long-run technical capabilities. These costs are generally fixed costs, because they are committed to and acquired before they are used. Infrastructure costs can be engineered or discretionary. For instance, manufacturing overhead costs incurred at Chipset to acquire manufacturing capacity is an infrastructure cost that is an example of an engineered cost. In the long run, there is a clear cause-and-effect relationship between output and lease rental costs needed to produce that output. R&D costs incurred to acquire technical capability is an infrastructure cost that is an example of a discretionary cost. There is no clear cause-and-effect relationship between output and R&D costs incurred.

Infrastructure costs. Costs that arise from having property, plant, and equipment, and a functioning organization.

	Engineered Costs (Examples: Manufacturing, Distribution)	Discretionary Costs (Examples: R&D, Advertising, Public Relations)
Type of process or activity	a. Detailed and physically observable	a. Black box (knowledge of process is sketchy or unavailable)
	b. Repetitive	b. Nonrepetitive or nonroutine
Level of uncertainty (the possibility that actual costs will deviate from expected costs)	Moderate or small (for example, shipping or manufacturing settings)	Large (for example, R&D or advertising settings)

Source: This exhibit is a modification of one suggested by H. Itami.

Uncertainty is greater in the case of discretionary costs such as R&D because, in most cases, R&D resources are committed well before any output is produced. Exhibit 13-5 summarizes these key distinctions between engineered and discretionary costs.

OBJECTIVE 6

Identify and manage unused capacity

Identifying Unused Capacity for Engineered and Discretionary Overhead Costs

How does the distinction between engineered and discretionary costs help a manager to understand and manage unused capacity? Actually, the different types of costs have very different relationships to capacity. Consider first the engineered manufacturing conversion costs. Chipset management indicates that manufacturing capacity can be added or reduced in increments of 125,000 units. Adding capacity, however, takes time. Manufacturing conversion costs are a step function as shown in Exhibit 13-6. Each step represents increments of 125,000 units of capacity at a cost of $775,000. At each step, manufacturing conversion costs are fixed. For example, manufacturing conversion costs are fixed at $9,300,000 if Chipset wants enough capacity to process between 1,375,000 and 1,500,000 units.

EXHIBIT 13-6
Engineered Costs and Unused Capacity at Chipset Inc. in 2008

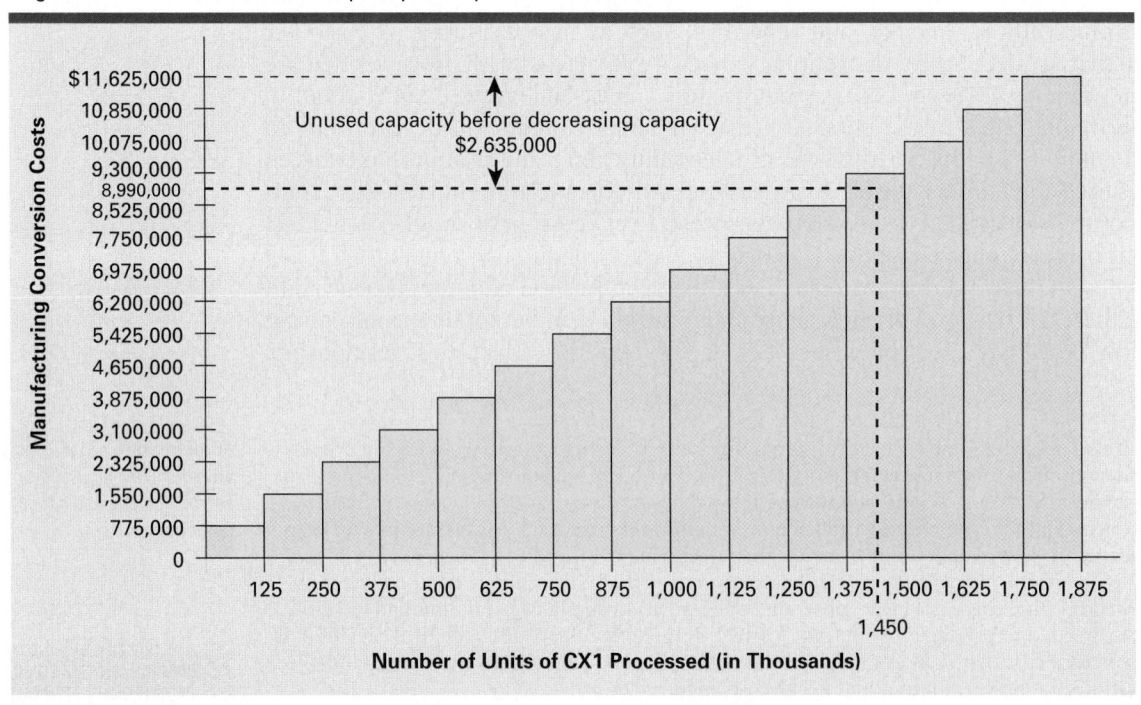

Number of Units of CX1 Processed (in Thousands)

At the start of the year 2008, Chipset has the capacity to process 1,875,000 units. Quality and productivity improvements made during 2008 enable Chipset to produce 1,150,000 units of CX1 by processing 1,450,000 units. Chipset calculates its unused manufacturing capacity as 425,000 (1,875,000 − 1,450,000) units for 2008, which corresponds to manufacturing conversion costs of $2,635,000 ($6.20 × 425,000 units). As shown in Exhibit 13-6, this unused capacity of $2,635,000 can also be calculated as $11,625,000 (manufacturing overhead costs for 1,875,000 units) minus $8,990,000 ($6.20 × 1,450,000, the manufacturing resources used to process 1,450,000 units).

The absence of a cause-and-effect relationship makes identifying unused capacity for discretionary costs much more difficult. Management cannot determine the R&D resources used for the actual output produced to compare R&D capacity against. Consequently, they cannot compute unused capacity as they did in the case of the engineered manufacturing conversion costs.

Managing Unused Capacity

What actions can Chipset management take when it identifies unused capacity? In general, it has two options. It can attempt to eliminate the unused capacity, or it can attempt to use the unused capacity to grow revenues.

In recent years, many companies have tried to *downsize* in an attempt to eliminate their unused capacity. **Downsizing** (also called **rightsizing**) is an integrated approach to configure processes, products, and people to match costs to the activities needed to be performed to operate efficiently and effectively in the present and future. Companies such as Bell Canada, Nortel, General Motors, and IBM have downsized to focus on their core businesses and have instituted organization changes to increase efficiency, reduce costs, and improve quality. Downsizing often means eliminating jobs, which can have an adverse effect on employee morale and the culture of the organization. It is important that downsizing be done in the context of the organization's overall strategy and by retaining individuals with key management, leadership, and technical skills.

Downsizing (rightsizing). An integrated approach to configure processes, products, and people to match costs to the activities needed to be performed to operate efficiently and effectively in the present and future.

Consider Chipset's options with respect to its unused manufacturing capacity. Because it needs to process 1,450,000 units in 2008, it could potentially reduce capacity to 1,500,000 units (recall that manufacturing conversion capacity can be added or reduced only in increments of 125,000 units) resulting in cost savings of $2,325,000 [(1,875,000 − 1,500,000) × $6.20]. Chipset's strategy, however, is not only to cut costs but also to grow its business. So Chipset only reduces its manufacturing capacity by 125,000 units from 1,875,000 units to 1,750,000 units, saving $775,000 ($6.20 × 125,000). It retains some unused capacity for future growth. By avoiding deep cuts in capacity, it also maintains the morale of its skilled and capable workforce. The success of this strategy will depend on Chipset achieving the future growth it has projected.

Chipset makes similar decisions with respect to the engineered selling and customer-service costs. At the start of 2008, Chipset has the capacity to serve 60 customers. Chipset currently has 46 customers, resulting in unused service capacity of 14 customers, which corresponds to $1,120,000 ($80,000 × 14) in selling and customer-service costs. (Recall that it costs $80,000 to support each customer.) Chipset could potentially reduce selling and customer-service capacity by ten customers. However, because the company anticipates adding nine more customers in the near future, it decides only to reduce its selling and customer-service capability from 60 to 55 customers, realizing savings of $400,000 ($80,000 × 5). Chipset's goal is to align its selling and customer-service capabilities of 55 customers with its manufacturing capacity of 1,750,000 units.

Because identifying unused capacity for discretionary costs is difficult, downsizing or otherwise managing this unused capacity is also difficult. Chipset's management uses judgment and discretion to reduce R&D costs by $100,000 in 2008. Its rationale is to cut R&D costs without significantly affecting the output of the R&D activity. Deeper cuts in R&D costs, however, could harm the business by slowing down critically needed product and process improvements. The key is to balance the need for cost reductions without compromising quality, continuous improvement, and future growth.

Following a strategy of product differentiation, Westwood Corporation makes a high-end kitchen range hood, KE8. Westwood presents the following data for the years 2007 and 2008.

	2007	2008
1. Units of KE8 produced and sold	40,000	42,000
2. Selling price	$100	$110
3. Direct materials (square metres)	120,000	123,000
4. Direct materials costs per square metre	$10	$11
5. Manufacturing capacity for KE8	50,000 units	50,000 units
6. Total manufacturing conversion costs	$1,000,000	$1,100,000
7. Manufacturing conversion costs per unit of capacity (Row 6 ÷ Row 5)	$20	$22
8. Selling and customer-service capacity	30 customers	29 customers
9. Total selling and customer-service costs	$720,000	$725,000
10. Cost per customer of selling and customer-service capacity (Row 9 ÷ Row 8)	$24,000	$25,000

Westwood produces no defective units but it wants to reduce direct materials usage per unit of KE8 in 2008. Manufacturing conversion costs in each year depend on production capacity defined in terms of KE8 units that can be produced. Selling and customer-service costs depend on the number of customers that the customer and service functions are designed to support. Westwood has 23 customers in 2007 and 25 customers in 2008. The industry market size for high-end kitchen range hoods increased 5% from 2007 to 2008.

REQUIRED
1. Describe briefly key elements that you would include in Westwood's balanced scorecard.
2. Calculate the growth, price-recovery, and productivity components of changes in operating income between 2007 and 2008.
3. Without doing any more calculations, explain in a few sentences whether Westwood was successful in implementing its strategy.

SOLUTION
1. Key elements that Westwood should include in its balanced scorecard are
   ◆ *Financial perspective.* Operating income growth from charging higher prices on KE8.
   ◆ *Customer perspective.* Market share in high-end kitchen range market, and customer satisfaction.
   ◆ *Internal business perspective.* Manufacturing quality, order delivery time, on-time delivery, and new product features added.
   ◆ *Learning and growth perspective.* Development time for designing new products and improving manufacturing processes.

2. Operating income for each year is as follows:

	2007	2008
Revenues ($100 × 40,000; $110 × 42,000)	$4,000,000	$4,620,000
Costs		
Direct materials costs ($10 × 120,000; $11 × 123,000)	1,200,000	1,353,000
Manufacturing conversion costs ($20 × 50,000; $22 × 50,000)	1,000,000	1,100,000
Selling & cust.-serv. costs ($24,000 × 30; $25,000 × 29)	720,000	725,000
Total costs	2,920,000	3,178,000
Operating income	$1,080,000	$1,442,000
Change in operating income		$362,000 F

The Growth Component

$$\begin{array}{c}\text{Revenue effect} \\ \text{of growth} \\ \text{component}\end{array} = \left(\begin{array}{c}\text{Actual units} \\ \text{of output sold} \\ \text{in 2008}\end{array} - \begin{array}{c}\text{Actual units} \\ \text{of output sold in} \\ 2007\end{array}\right) \times \begin{array}{c}2007 \\ \text{output} \\ \text{price}\end{array}$$

$$= (42,000 - 40,000) \times \$100 = \$200,000 \text{ F}$$

$$\begin{array}{c}\text{Cost effect} \\ \text{of growth} \\ \text{component}\end{array} = \left(\begin{array}{c}\text{Actual units of input/capacity} \\ \text{that would have been used to} \\ \text{produce year 2008 output} \\ \text{assuming the same input-output} \\ \text{relationship that existed in 2007}\end{array} - \begin{array}{c}\text{Actual units of} \\ \text{input/capacity to} \\ \text{produce 2007} \\ \text{output}\end{array}\right) \times \begin{array}{c}\text{Year} \\ 2007 \\ \text{prices}\end{array}$$

Direct materials costs that would be required in 2008 to produce 42,000 units instead of the 40,000 units produced in 2007, assuming the 2007 input-output relationship continued into 2008, equal 126,000 square metres $\left(\frac{120,000}{40,000} \times 42,000\right)$. Manufacturing conversion costs and selling and customer-service costs will not change since adequate capacity exists in 2007 to support year 2008 output and customers.

The cost effects of growth component are

Direct materials costs	$(126,000 - 120,000) \times \$10$ =	$60,000 U
Manuf. conversion costs	$(50,000 - 50,000) \times \$20$ =	0
Selling & cust.-serv. costs	$(30 - 30) \times \$24,000$ =	0
Cost effect of growth component		$60,000 U

In summary, the net increase in operating income as a result of the growth component equals

Revenue effect of growth component	$200,000 F
Cost effect of growth component	60,000 U
Increase in operating income due to growth component	$140,000 F

The Price-Recovery Component

$$\begin{array}{c}\text{Revenue effect of} \\ \text{product differentiation} \\ \text{component}\end{array} = \left(\begin{array}{c}\text{Output price} \\ \text{in 2008}\end{array} - \begin{array}{c}\text{Output price} \\ \text{in 2007}\end{array}\right) \times \begin{array}{c}\text{Actual units of} \\ \text{output sold} \\ \text{in 2008}\end{array}$$

$$= (\$110 - \$100) \times 42,000 = \$420,000 \text{ F}$$

$$\begin{array}{c}\text{Cost effect} \\ \text{of product} \\ \text{differentiation}\end{array} = \left(\begin{array}{c}\text{Input price} \\ \text{in year 2008}\end{array} - \begin{array}{c}\text{Input price} \\ \text{in year 2007}\end{array}\right) \times \begin{array}{c}\text{Actual units of input/capacity that} \\ \text{would have been used to produce} \\ \text{year 2008 output assuming the} \\ \text{same input–output relationship} \\ \text{that existed in 2007}\end{array}$$

Direct materials costs	$(\$11 - \$10) \times 126,000$ =	$126,000 U
Manuf. conversion costs	$(\$22 - \$20) \times 50,000$ =	100,000 U
Selling & cust.-serv. costs	$(\$25,000 - \$24,000) \times 30$ =	30,000 U
Total cost effect of price-recovery component		$256,000 U

In summary, the net increase in operating income as a result of the price-recovery component equals

Revenue effect of price-recovery component	$420,000 F
Cost effect of price-recovery component	256,000 U
Increase in operating income due to price-recovery component	$164,000 F

The Productivity Component

$$
\begin{array}{c}
\text{Productivity/} \\
\text{cost leadership} \\
\text{component}
\end{array}
=
\left(
\begin{array}{c}
\text{Actual units of} \\
\text{input/capacity to} \\
\text{produce year} \\
\text{2008 output}
\end{array}
-
\begin{array}{c}
\text{Actual units of inputs/} \\
\text{capacity that would have been} \\
\text{used to produce year 2008} \\
\text{output assuming the same} \\
\text{input-output relationship} \\
\text{that existed in 2007}
\end{array}
\right)
\times
\begin{array}{c}
\text{Year} \\
\text{2008} \\
\text{prices}
\end{array}
$$

The productivity component of cost changes are

Direct materials costs	$(123,000 - 126,000) \times \$11 =$	$33,000 F
Manuf. conversion costs	$(50,000 - 50,000) \times \$20 =$	0
Selling & cust.-serv. costs	$(29 - 30) \times \$25,000 =$	25,000 F
Increase in operating income due to productivity component		$58,000 F

The change in operating income between 2007 and 2008 can be analyzed as follows:

	Income Statement Amounts in 2007 (1)	Revenue and Cost Effects of Growth Component in 2008 (2)	Revenue and Cost Effects of Price-Recovery Component in 2008 (3)	Cost Effect of Productivity Component in 2008 (4)	Income Statement Amounts in 2008 (5) = (1) + (2) + (3) + (4)
Revenues	$4,000,000	$200,000 F	$420,000 F	—	$4,620,000
Costs	2,920,000	60,000 U	256,000 U	$58,000 F	3,178,000
Operating income	$1,080,000	$140,000 F	$164,000 F	$58,000 F	$1,442,000

$$
\xleftarrow{\hspace{3cm}} \$362,000\ F \xrightarrow{\hspace{3cm}}
$$

Change in operating income

3. The analysis of operating income indicates that Westwood was successful in implementing its product differentiation strategy. The company was able to continue to charge a premium price for KE8. Westwood was also able to earn additional operating income from improving its productivity. The growth in units (from 40,000 to 42,000) was attributable entirely to the 5% increase in market size rather than Westwood's product differentiation strategy.

The following decision guidelines use a question-and-answer format to summarize the chapter's main points. Each decision presents a key question. The guideline is the answer to that question.

DECISIONS	GUIDELINES
1. What are two generic strategies a company can use?	Two generic strategies are product differentiation and cost leadership. Product differentiation is offering products and services that are perceived by customers as being superior and unique. Cost leadership is achieving low costs relative to competitors.
2. What is reengineering?	Reengineering is the rethinking of business processes, such as the order delivery process, to improve critical performance measures such as cost, quality, and customer satisfaction.
3. How can an organization translate its strategy into a set of performance measures?	It can do so by developing a balanced scorecard that provides the framework for a strategic measurement and management system. The balanced scorecard measures performance from four perspectives: (1) financial, (2) customer, (3) internal business processes, and (4) learning and growth.

4. How can a company analyze changes in operating income to evaluate strategy?	To evaluate the success of its strategy, a company can subdivide the change in operating income into growth, price-recovery, and productivity components. The growth component measures the change in revenues and costs from selling greater or fewer units, assuming no changes in prices, efficiencies, or capacities. The price-recovery component measures changes in revenues and costs as a result solely of changes in the prices of outputs and inputs. The productivity component measures the decrease in costs from using fewer inputs and from reducing capacity. A company is considered successful in implementing its strategy when changes in operating income align closely with that strategy.
5. How can a company distinguish between engineered and discretionary costs?	Engineered costs result from a cause-and-effect relationship between output and the resources needed to produce that output. Discretionary costs arise from periodic (usually annual) decisions regarding the maximum amount to be incurred. They are not tied to a cause-and-effect relationship between inputs and outputs.
6. Can a company identify unused capacity and, if so, how can unused capacity be managed?	Identifying unused capacity is easier for engineered costs than for discretionary costs. Downsizing is an approach to managing unused capacity by matching costs to the activities that need to be performed.

APPENDIX: PRODUCTIVITY MEASUREMENT

Productivity measures the relationship between actual inputs used (both quantities and costs) and actual outputs produced. The lower the inputs for a given quantity of outputs or the higher the outputs for a given quantity of inputs, the higher the level of productivity. Measuring productivity improvements over time highlights the specific input-output relationships that contribute to cost leadership.

> **Productivity.** The measurement of the relationship between actual inputs used and actual outputs produced.

Partial Productivity Measures

Partial productivity, the most frequently used productivity measure, compares the quantity of output produced with the quantity of an individual input used. In its most common form, partial productivity is expressed as a ratio:

> **Partial productivity.** The comparison of quantity of output produced with the quantity of an individual input used.

$$\text{Partial productivity} = \frac{\text{Quantity of output produced}}{\text{Quantity of input used}}$$

The higher the ratio, the greater the productivity.

Consider direct materials productivity at Chipset in the year 2008.

$$\begin{aligned}
\text{Direct materials partial productivity} &= \frac{\text{Quantity of CX1 units produced during 2008}}{\text{Direct materials quantity used to produce CX1 in 2008}} \\[2mm]
&= \frac{1,150,000 \text{ units of CX1}}{2,900,000 \text{ cm}^2 \text{ of direct materials}} \\[2mm]
&= 0.40 \text{ units of CX1 per cm}^2 \text{ of direct materials}
\end{aligned}$$

Note that the direct materials partial productivity ignores Chipset's other inputs, manufacturing conversion, selling and customer service, and R&D. Partial productivity measures gain meaning when comparisons are made that examine productivity changes over time, either across several facilities or relative to a benchmark. Exhibit 13-7 on page 540 presents partial productivity measures for Chipset's various inputs for 2007 and 2008 using information from the productivity calculations on page 530. These measures compare the actual inputs used in the year 2008 to produce 1,150,000 units of CX1 with the inputs that would have been used in 2008 had the input-output relationship from 2007 continued in 2008.

Evaluating Changes in Partial Productivities

It is important to distinguish between the partial productivity effects of variable- and fixed-cost components. Why? Because for variable-cost elements, such as direct materials, productivity improvements automatically result in using fewer input

EXHIBIT 13-7
Comparing Chipset's Partial Productivities in 2007 and 2008

Input (1)	Partial Productivity in 2008 (2)	Comparable Partial Productivity Based on 2007 Input–Output Relationships (3)	Percentage Change from 2007 to 2008 (4)
Direct materials	$\dfrac{1,150,000}{2,900,000} = 0.397$	$\dfrac{1,150,000}{3,450,000} = 0.333$	$\dfrac{0.397 - 0.333}{0.333} = 19.2\%$
Manufacturing conversion capacity	$\dfrac{1,150,000}{1,750,000} = 0.657$	$\dfrac{1,150,000}{1,875,000} = 0.613$	$\dfrac{0.657 - 0.613}{0.613} = 7.2\%$
Selling and customer service	$\dfrac{1,150,000}{55} = 20,909$	$\dfrac{1,150,000}{60} = 19,167$	$\dfrac{20,909 - 19,167}{19,167} = 9.1\%$
R&D	$\dfrac{1,150,000}{39} = 29,487$	$\dfrac{1,150,000}{40} = 28,750$	$\dfrac{29,487 - 28,750}{28,750} = 2.6\%$

resources. For example, Chipset's improvements in direct materials productivity in 2008 resulted in 2,900,000 cm² of direct materials being acquired and used rather than the 3,450,000 cm² that would have been required to produce 1,150,000 units of output in 2008 at the 2007 productivity level. On the other hand, for fixed cost elements such as manufacturing conversion costs, using less of the available fixed capacity resources will not lead automatically to lowering the cost of these resources. To improve partial productivity in these cases, management must take actions to release workers or reduce capacity. These actions are often more difficult to implement and, as in Exhibit 13-7, result in lower partial productivity gains for fixed-cost categories than for variable-cost categories.

Consider, for example, manufacturing conversion partial productivity. At the 2007 productivity levels, Chipset would need to start 1,725,000 units of CX1 to produce 1,150,000 units. Chipset has manufacturing capacity of 1,875,000 units. Efficiency improvements in 2008 result in Chipset having to start 1,450,000 units in 2008. Reducing the number of units started into production, however, does not automatically lead to a decrease in manufacturing capacity. Partial productivity increases because Chipset's managers take actions to release workers and reduce manufacturing capacity to 1,750,000 units.

Total Factor Productivity

A major advantage of partial productivity measures is that they focus on a single input. As a result, they are simple to calculate and easily understood by operations personnel. Managers and operators examine these numbers to understand the reasons underlying productivity changes from one period to the next. For example, Chipset's managers will evaluate whether the lower defect rates (that resulted in management's being able to reduce capacity and increase manufacturing conversion partial productivity from 2007 to 2008) were caused by better training of workers, lower absenteeism, lower labour turnover, better incentives, improved methods, or substitution of materials for labour. Isolating the relevant factors is important because it helps Chipset implement and sustain these practices in the future. Chipset can then set targets for gains in manufacturing conversion productivity and monitor planned productivity improvements.

For all their advantages, partial productivity measures also have some serious drawbacks. Because partial productivity focuses on only one input at a time rather than on all inputs simultaneously, it does not allow managers to evaluate the effect of input substitutions on overall productivity. For example, manufacturing conversion partial productivity may increase from one period to the next while direct materials partial productivity may decrease. Partial productivity measures cannot evaluate whether the increase in manufacturing conversion partial productivity offsets the decrease in direct materials partial productivity. Total factor productivity (TFP) or total productivity is a technique for measuring productivity that considers all inputs simultaneously.

Total factor productivity (TFP) is the ratio of the quantity of output produced to the costs of all inputs used, where the inputs are combined on the basis of current period prices.

Total factor productivity (TFP). The ratio of the quantity of output produced to the costs of all inputs used, where the inputs are combined on the basis of current period prices.

$$\text{Total factor productivity} = \frac{\text{Quantity of output produced}}{\text{Costs of all inputs used}}$$

TFP considers all inputs simultaneously and also considers the tradeoffs across inputs based on current input prices. Do not be tempted to think of all productivity measures as physical measures lacking financial content—how many units of output are produced per unit of input. Total factor productivity is intricately tied to minimizing total cost—a financial objective. We next measure changes in TFP at Chipset from 2007 to 2008.

Calculating and Comparing Total Factor Productivity

We first calculate Chipset's TFP in 2008, using 2008 prices and 1,150,000 units of output produced (using information from the first column of the productivity component calculations on p. 530).

$$\begin{aligned}
\frac{\text{Total factor productivity}}{\text{for 2008 using 2008 prices}} &= \frac{\text{Quantity of output produced in 2008}}{\text{Costs of inputs used in 2008 based on 2008 prices}} \\[6pt]
&= \frac{1,150,000}{2,900,000 \times \$1.50 + 1,750,000 \times \$6.20 + 55 \times \$80,000 + 39 \times \$100,000} \\[6pt]
&= \frac{1,150,000}{23,500,000} \\[6pt]
&= 0.048936 \text{ units of output per dollar of input}
\end{aligned}$$

By itself, the 2008 TFP of 0.048936 units of CX1 per dollar of input is not particularly helpful. We need something to compare the 2008 TFP against. One alternative is to compare TFPs of other similar companies in 2008. However, finding similar companies and obtaining accurate comparable data are often difficult. Companies therefore usually compare their own TFP over time. In the Chipset example, we use as a benchmark TFP calculated using the inputs that Chipset would have used in 2007 to produce 1,150,000 units of CX1 at 2008 prices (that is, we use the costs calculated from the second column in the productivity component calculations on p. 530). Why do we use 2008 prices? Because using the current year's (2008) prices in both calculations controls for input price differences and focuses the analysis on the adjustments the manager made in the quantities of inputs in response to changes in prices.

$$\begin{aligned}
\frac{\text{Benchmark}}{\text{TFP}} &= \frac{\text{Quantity of output produced in 2008}}{\substack{\text{Costs of inputs that would have been used} \\ \text{in 2007 to produce 2008 output}}} \\[6pt]
&= \frac{1,150,000}{3,450,000 \times \$1.50 + 1,875,000 \times \$6.20 + 60 \times \$80,000 + 40 \times \$100,000} \\[6pt]
&= \frac{1,150,000}{25,600,000} \\[6pt]
&= 0.044922 \text{ units of output per dollar of inputs}
\end{aligned}$$

Using year 2008 prices, total factor productivity increased 8.94% [(0.048936 − 0.044922) ÷ 0.044922] from 2007 to 2008. Note that the 8.94% increase in TFP equals the $2,100,000 gain (Exhibit 13-4, column 4, p. 527) divided by the

$23,500,000 of actual costs incurred in 2008 (Exhibit 13-4, column 5). Total factor productivity increased because Chipset produced more output per dollar of input in 2008 relative to 2007, measured in both years using 2008 prices. The gain in TFP occurs because Chipset increases the partial productivities of individual inputs and, consistent with its strategy, seeks the least expensive combination of inputs to produce CX1. Note that TFP increases cannot be due to differences in input prices because we used year 2008 prices to evaluate both the inputs that Chipset would have used in 2007 to produce 1,150,000 units of CX1 and the inputs actually used in 2008.

Using Both Partial and Total Factor Productivity Measures

A major advantage of TFP is that it measures the combined productivity of all inputs used to produce output. Therefore, it explicitly considers gains from using fewer physical inputs as well as substitution among inputs. Managers can analyze these numbers to understand the reasons for changes in TFP. For example, Chipset's managers will try to evaluate whether the increase in TFP from 2007 to 2008 was due to better human resource management practices, higher quality of materials, or improved manufacturing methods. Chipset will adopt the most successful practices and use TFP measures to implement and evaluate strategy by setting targets and monitoring trends.

Many companies, such as Monsanto, a manufacturer of fibres, Behlen Manufacturing, a steel fabricator, and Motorola, a microchip manufacturer, use both partial productivity and total factor productivity to evaluate performance. *Partial productivity and TFP measures work best together because the strengths of one are the weaknesses of the other.*

Although TFP measures are comprehensive, operations personnel find financial TFP measures more difficult to understand and less useful than physical partial productivity measures in performing their tasks. Physical measures of manufacturing labour partial productivity, for example, provide direct feedback to workers about output produced per labour-hour worked by focusing on factors within the workers' control. Manufacturing labour partial productivity also has the advantage that it can be easily compared across time periods because it uses physical inputs rather than inputs that are weighted by the prices prevailing in different periods. Workers, therefore, often prefer to tie productivity-based bonuses to gains in manufacturing labour partial productivity. Unfortunately, this situation creates incentives for workers to substitute materials (and capital) for labour, which improves their own productivity measure while possibly decreasing overall productivity of the company as measured by TFP. To overcome the possible incentive problems of partial productivity measures, some companies—for example, TRW and Whirlpool—explicitly adjust bonuses based on manufacturing labour partial productivity for the effects of other factors such as investments in new equipment and higher levels of scrap. That is, they combine partial productivity with TFP-like measures.

▼ TERMS TO LEARN

This chapter contains definitions of the following important terms:

balanced scorecard (p. 515)
cost leadership (p. 515)
discretionary costs (p. 533)
downsizing (p. 535)
engineered costs (p. 533)
infrastructure costs (p. 533)
partial productivity (p. 539)

product differentiation (p. 515)
productivity (p. 539)
reengineering (p. 516)
rightsizing (p. 535)
strategy (p. 514)
total factor productivity
  (TFP) (p. 541)

QUESTIONS

13-1 Define *strategy*.

13-2 Describe the five key forces when analyzing an industry.

13-3 Describe two generic strategies.

13-4 What are the four key perspectives in the balanced scorecard?

13-5 What is reengineering?

13-6 Describe three features of a good balanced scorecard.

13-7 What are three important pitfalls to avoid when implementing a balanced scorecard?

13-8 Describe three key components in doing a strategic analysis of operating income?

13-9 How can an analyst incorporate marketwide factors and the interrelationships between the growth, price-recovery, and productivity components into a strategic analysis of operating income?

13-10 How does an engineered cost differ from a discretionary cost?

13-11 "The distinction between engineered and discretionary costs is irrelevant when identifying unused capacity." Do you agree? Comment briefly.

13-12 What is downsizing?

13-13 What is a partial productivity measure?

13-14 What is total factor productivity?

13-15 "We are already measuring total factor productivity. Measuring partial productivities would be of no value." Do you agree? Comment briefly.

EXERCISES

13-16 Balanced scorecard. La Quinta Corporation manufactures corrugated cardboard boxes. It competes and plans to grow by producing high-quality boxes at a low cost that are delivered to customers in a timely manner. There are many other manufacturers who produce similar boxes. La Quinta believes that continuously improving its manufacturing processes and having satisfied employees are critical to implementing its strategy in 2007.

REQUIRED

1. Is La Quinta's 2007 strategy one of product differentiation or cost leadership? Explain briefly.
2. Indicate two measures you would expect to see under each perspective on La Quinta's balanced scorecard for 2007. Explain your answer briefly.

13-17 Analysis of growth, price-recovery, and productivity components (continuation of 13-16). An analysis of La Quinta's operating income changes between 2006 and 2007 shows the following:

The industry market size for corrugated boxes did not grow in 2007, input prices did not change, and La Quinta reduced the price of its boxes in line with the market.

Operating income for 2006	$1,920,000
Add growth component	72,000
Deduct price-recovery component	(60,000)
Add productivity component	216,000
Operating income for 2007	$2,148,000

REQUIRED

1. Was La Quinta's gain in operating income in 2007 consistent with the strategy you identified in requirement 1 of Exercise 13-16?
2. Explain the productivity component. In general, does it represent savings in only variable costs, only fixed costs, or both variable and fixed costs?

13-18 Strategy, balanced scorecard. Meredith Corporation makes a special-purpose D4H machine used in the textile industry. Meredith has designed the D4H machine for

2007 to be distinct from its competitors. It has been generally regarded as a superior machine. Meredith presents the following data for the years 2006 and 2007.

	2006	2007
1. Units of D4H produced and sold	200	210
2. Selling price	$48,000	$50,400
3. Direct materials (kilograms)	300,000	310,000
4. Direct materials cost per kilogram	$9.60	$10.20
5. Manufacturing capacity in units of D4H	250	250
6. Total manufacturing conversion costs	$2,400,000	$2,430,000
7. Manufacturing conversion costs per unit of capacity	$9,600	$9,720
8. Selling and customer-service capacity	100 customers	95 customers
9. Total selling and customer-service costs	$1,200,000	$1,128,600
10. Selling and customer-service capacity cost per customer	$12,000	$11,880
11. Design staff	12	12
12. Total design costs	$1,440,000	$1,454,400
13. Design costs per employee	$120,000	$121,200

Meredith produces no defective machines, but it wants to reduce direct materials usage per D4H machine in 2007. Manufacturing conversion costs in each year depend on production capacity defined in terms of D4H units that can be produced, not the actual units of D4H produced. Selling and customer-service costs depend on the number of customers that Meredith can support, not the actual number of customers Meredith serves. Meredith has 75 customers in 2006 and 80 customers in 2007. At the start of each year, management uses its discretion to determine the number of design staff for the year. The design staff and costs have no direct relationship with the quantity of D4H produced or the number of customers to whom D4H is sold.

REQUIRED
1. Is Meredith's strategy one of product differentiation or cost leadership? Explain briefly.
2. Describe briefly key elements that you would include in Meredith's balanced scorecard and the reasons for doing so.

13-19 **Strategic analysis of operating income.** Refer to the information in Exercise 13-18.

REQUIRED
1. Calculate the operating income of Meredith Corporation in 2006 and 2007.
2. Calculate the growth, price-recovery, and productivity components of changes in operating income between 2006 and 2007.
3. Comment on your answer in requirement 2. What do these components indicate?

13-20 **Analysis of growth, price-recovery, and productivity components (continuation of 13-19).** Suppose that between 2006 and 2007 the market for Meredith's special-purpose machines grew at 3%, and that industrywide selling prices increased by 2.5%.

REQUIRED
Calculate how much of the change in operating income between 2006 and 2007 is due to industrywide factors, cost leadership, and product differentiation. How successful has Meredith been in implementing its strategy?

13-21 **Identifying and managing unused capacity.** Refer to the Meredith Corporation information in Exercise 13-18.

REQUIRED
1. Where possible, calculate the amount and cost of unused capacity for (a) manufacturing, (b) selling and customer service, and (c) design at the beginning of 2007 based on 2007 production. If you could not calculate the amount and cost of unused capacity, indicate why not.
2. Suppose Meredith can add or reduce its manufacturing capacity in increments of 30 units. What is the maximum amount of costs that Meredith could save by downsizing manufacturing capacity?
3. Meredith, in fact, does not eliminate any of its unused manufacturing capacity. Why might Meredith not downsize?

13-22 **Strategy, balanced scorecard, service company.** Snyder Corporation is a small, information systems consulting firm that specializes in helping companies implement sales management software. The market for Snyder's products is very competitive. To compete, Snyder must deliver quality service at a low cost. Snyder bills clients in terms of units of work performed, which depends on the size and complexity of the sales management system. Snyder presents the following data for the years 2006 and 2007.

	2006	2007
1. Units of work performed	60	70
2. Selling price	$60,000	$57,600
3. Software implementation labour-hours	30,000	32,000
4. Cost per software implementation labour-hour	$72.00	$75.60
5. Software implementation support capacity (in units of work)	90	90
6. Total cost of software implementation support	$432,000	$442,800
7. Software implementation support capacity cost per unit of work	$4,800	$4,920
8. Number of employees doing software development	3	3
9. Total software development costs	$450,000	$468,000
10. Software development costs per employee	$150,000	$156,000

Software implementation labour-hour costs are variable costs. Software implementation support costs for each year depend on the software implementation support capacity (defined in terms of units of work) that Snyder chooses to maintain each year. It does not vary with the actual units of work performed each year. At the start of each year, management uses its discretion to determine the number of software-development employees. The software-development staff and costs have no direct relationship with the number of units of work performed.

REQUIRED
1. Is Snyder Corporation's strategy one of product differentiation or cost leadership?
2. Describe briefly key elements that you would include in Snyder's balanced scorecard and your reasons for doing so.

13-23 Strategic analysis of operating income. Refer to the information in Exercise 13-22.

REQUIRED
1. Calculate the operating income of Snyder Corporation in 2006 and 2007.
2. Calculate the growth, price-recovery, and productivity components of changes in operating income between 2006 and 2007.
3. Comment on your answer in requirement 2. What do these components indicate?

13-24 Analysis of growth, price-recovery, and productivity components (continuation of 13-23). Suppose that during 2007 the market for implementing sales management software increased by 5%, and that Snyder experiences a 1% decline in prices. Assume that any further decreases in selling prices and increases in market share are strategic choices by Snyder's management to implement their cost leadership strategy.

REQUIRED
Calculate how much of the change in operating income between 2006 and 2007 is due to industry market-size factors, cost leadership, and product differentiation. How successful has Snyder been in implementing its strategy?

13-25 Identifying and managing unused capacity. Refer to the Snyder Corporation information in Exercise 13-22.

REQUIRED
1. Where possible, calculate the amount and cost of unused capacity for (a) software implementation support and (b) software development at the beginning of 2007, based on units of work to be performed in 2007. If you could not calculate the amount and cost of unused capacity, indicate why not.
2. Suppose Snyder can add or reduce its software implementation support capacity in increments of 15 units. What is the maximum amount of costs that Snyder could save by downsizing software implementation support capacity?
3. Snyder, in fact, does not eliminate any of its unused software implementation support capacity. Why might Snyder not downsize?

13-26 Balanced scorecard. Following is a random-order listing of perspectives, strategic objectives, and performance measures for the balanced scorecard.

Perspectives	Performance Measures
Internal business process	Percentage of defective product units
Customer	Return on assets
Learning and growth	Number of patents
Financial	Employee turnover rate
	Net income
Strategic Objectives	Customer profitability
Acquire new customers	Percentage of processes with
Increase shareholder value	real-time feedback
Retain customers	Return on sales
Improve manufacturing quality	Average job-related training-hours
Develop profitable customers	per employee
Increase proprietary products	Return on equity
Increase information system capabilities	Percentage of on-time deliveries
Enhance employee skills	by suppliers
On-time delivery by suppliers	Product cost per unit
Increase profit generated by each salesperson	Profit per salesperson
Introduce new products	Percentage of error-free invoices
Minimize invoice error rate	Customer cost per unit
	Earnings per share
	Number of new customers
	Percentage of customers retained

REQUIRED

For each perspective, select those strategic objectives from the list that best relate to it. For each strategic objective, select the most appropriate performance measure(s) from the list.

13-27 Growth, price-recovery, and productivity components. Oceano T-Shirt Company sells a variety of T-shirts. Oceano presents the following data for its first two years of operations, 2006 and 2007. For simplicity, assume that all purchasing and selling costs are included in the average cost per T-shirt and that each customer buys one T-shirt.

	2006	2007
Number of T-shirts purchased	20,000	30,000
Number of T-shirts lost	400	300
Number of T-shirts sold	19,600	29,700
Average selling price	$18.00	$16.80
Average cost per T-shirt	$12.00	$10.80
Administrative capacity in terms of number of customers that can be served	40,000	36,000
Administrative costs	$96,000	$82,080
Administrative cost per customer	$2.40	$2.28

Administrative costs depend on the number of customers that Oceano has created capacity to support, not the actual number of customers served.

REQUIRED
1. Calculate the growth, price-recovery, and productivity components of changes in operating income between 2006 and 2007.
2. Comment on your results in requirement 1.

PROBLEMS

13-28 Balanced scorecard. Caltex Inc. refines gasoline and sells it through its own Caltex Gas Stations. On the basis of market research, Caltex determines that 60% of its customers (medium- to high-income individuals) are willing to pay a higher price for its gas if the gas stations can provide excellent customer service such as a clean facility, a convenience store, friendly employees, quick turnaround, the ability to pay by credit card, and high octane premium fuel. Marketwide prices for inputs and outputs and the market size did not change in 2007. Caltex's balanced scorecard for the year 2007 follows. For brevity, the initiatives taken under each objective are omitted.

Objectives	Measures	Target Performance	Actual Performance
Financial Perspective			
Increase shareholder value	Operating income changes from price recovery	$108,000,000	$114,000,000
	Operating income changes from growth	$78,000,000	$80,400,000
Customer Perspective			
Increase market share	Market share of total gasoline market	10%	9.8%
Internal Business Process Perspective			
Improve gasoline quality	Quality index	94 points	95 points
Improve refinery performance	Refinery reliability index (%)	91%	91%
Ensure gasoline availability	Product availability index (%)	99%	100%
Learning and Growth Perspective			
Increase refinery process capability	Percentage of refinery processes with advanced controls	88%	90%

REQUIRED

1. Was Caltex successful in implementing its strategy in 2007? Explain your answer.
2. Would you have included some measure of employee satisfaction and employee training in the learning and growth perspective? Are these objectives critical to Caltex for implementing its strategy? Why or why not? Explain briefly.
3. Explain how Caltex did not achieve its target market share in the total gasoline market but still exceeded its financial targets. Is "market share of total gasoline market" the correct measure of market share? Explain briefly.
4. Is there a clear cause-and-effect linkage between improvements in the measures in the internal business process perspective and the measures in the customer perspective? That is, would you add other measures to the internal business process perspective or the customer perspective? Why or why not? Explain briefly.
5. Do you agree with Caltex's decision not to include measures of changes in operating income from productivity improvements under the financial perspective of the balanced scorecard? Explain briefly.

13-29 Balanced scorecard. Lee Corporation manufactures various types of colour laser printers in a highly automated facility with high fixed costs. The market for laser printers is competitive. The various colour laser printers on the market are comparable in terms of features and price. Lee believes that satisfying customers with products of high quality at low costs is key to achieving its target profitability. For 2007, Lee plans to achieve higher quality and lower costs by improving yields and reducing defects in its manufacturing operations. Lee will train workers and encourage and empower them to take the necessary actions. Currently, a significant amount of Lee's capacity is used to produce products that are defective and cannot be sold. Lee expects that higher yields will reduce the capacity that Lee needs to use to manufacture products. Lee does not anticipate that improving manufacturing will automatically lead to lower costs because Lee has high fixed costs. Lee plans to lay off workers and sell equipment to reduce some of the unused capacity and use the rest of the capacity to produce and sell more of its current products or improved models of its current products. Selling more products will result in lower fixed costs per unit of product.

Market prices for inputs and outputs and market size did not change in 2007. Lee's balanced scorecard for the just-completed accounting year 2007 follows. For brevity, the initiatives taken under each objective are omitted.

Objectives	Measures	Target Performance	Actual Performance
Financial Perspective			
Increase shareholder value	Operating income changes from productivity	$1,200,000	$480,000
	Operating income changes from growth	$1,800,000	$720,000
Customer Perspective			
Increase market share	Market-share in colour laser printers	5%	4.6%
Internal Business Process Perspective			
Improve manufacturing quality	Yield	82%	85%
Reduce delivery time to customers	Order delivery time	25 days	22 days
Learning and Growth Perspective			
Develop process skills	Percentage of employees trained in process and quality management	90%	92%
Enhance information system capabilities	Percentage of manufacturing processes with real-time feedback	85%	87%

REQUIRED

1. Was Lee successful in implementing its strategy in 2007? Explain.
2. Is Lee Corporation's balanced scorecard useful in helping Lee understand why it did not reach its target market share in 2007? If it is, explain why. If it is not, explain what other measures you might want to add under the customer perspective and why.
3. Would you have included some measure of employee satisfaction in the learning and growth perspective and new-product development in the internal business process perspective? That is, do you think employee satisfaction and development of new products are critical to Lee for implementing its strategy? Why or why not? Explain briefly.
4. What problems, if any, do you see in Lee improving quality and significantly downsizing to eliminate unused capacity?

13-30 Analysis of growth, price-recovery, and productivity components. Halsey and Company sells women's clothing. Halsey's strategy is to offer a wide selection of clothes and excellent customer service, and to charge a premium price. Halsey presents the following data for the years 2006 and 2007. For simplicity, assume that each customer purchases one piece of clothing.

	2006	2007
1. Pieces of clothing purchased and sold	40,000	40,000
2. Average selling price	$72.00	$70.80
3. Average cost per piece of clothing	$48.00	$49.20
4. Selling and customer-service capacity	51,000 customers	43,000 customers
5. Selling and customer-service costs	$428,400	$356,040
6. Selling and customer-service capacity cost per customer	$8.40	$8.28
7. Purchasing and administrative capacity measured by the number of distinct clothing designs purchased	980	850
8. Purchasing and administrative costs	$294,000	$244,800
9. Purchasing and administrative capacity cost per distinct design	$300	$288

Total selling and customer-service costs depend on the number of customers that Halsey has created capacity to support, not the actual number of customers that Halsey serves. Total purchasing and administrative costs depend on purchasing and administrative capacity that Halsey has created (defined in terms of the number of distinct clothing designs that Halsey can purchase and administer). Purchasing and administration costs do not depend on the actual number of clothing pieces purchased. Halsey purchased 930 distinct designs in 2006 and 820 distinct designs in 2007.

Marketwide prices for clothes and the market size were unchanged in 2006 and 2007. At the start of 2007, Halsey planned to increase operating income by 10% over the operating income in 2006.

REQUIRED

1. Is Halsey's strategy one of product differentiation or cost leadership?
2. Calculate Halsey's operating income in 2006 and 2007.
3. Calculate the growth, price-recovery, and productive components of changes in operating income between 2006 and 2007.
4. Does the strategic analysis of operating income indicate Halsey was successful in implementing its strategy in 2007? Explain.

Excel Application For students who wish to practise their spreadsheet skills, the following is a step-by-step approach to creating an Excel spreadsheet to work this problem.

Step-by-Step

1. Open a new spreadsheet. At the top, create an "Original Data" section for the data provided by Halsey Company in exactly the same format as presented on page 548.
   (Program your spreadsheet to perform all necessary calculations. Do not "hard-code" any amounts, such as operating income, requiring addition, subtraction, multiplication, or division operations.)
2. Skip two rows and create an income statement with columns for 2006 and rows for "Revenues, Direct Materials Costs, Selling and Customer-Service Costs, Purchasing and Administrative Costs, Total Costs, and Operating Income." Use the data from your Original Data section to calculate revenues, costs, and operating income for 2007.
3. Skip two rows and create a "Revenue and Cost Effects of Growth" section with a row for "Revenue Effect of Growth," and four rows for each of the different cost categories, "Direct Material Costs, Selling and Customer-Service Costs, Purchasing and Administrative Costs," and a row for the total cost-effect of growth. Using the data from your Original Data section, enter calculations for the revenue effect of growth, the cost effect of growth for each of the different cost categories (direct materials, customer service, and purchasing and administrative), and the total cost effect of growth.
4. Skip two rows and create a "Revenue and Cost Effects of Price Recovery" section in exactly the same format as in step 3. Using the data from your Original Data section, enter calculations for the revenue effect of price recovery, the cost effect of price recovery for each of the different cost categories, and the total cost effect of price recovery.
5. Skip two rows and create a "Cost Effect of Productivity" section in exactly the same format as in steps 3 and 4 without the row for revenues. Using the data from your Original Data section, enter calculations for the cost effect of productivity for each of the different cost categories and the total cost effect of productivity.
6. Skip two rows and create a "Strategic Analysis of Productivity" section in exactly the same format as presented in Exhibit 13-4 (p. 527). Use the data from your income statement and the three components of growth you calculated in steps 3 to 5 to complete this section. Do not hard-code the column for income statement amounts in 2007. This column should simply reflect the sum of the income statement amounts in 2006 and the growth, price-recovery, and productivity components as in Exhibit 13-4 (p. 527). If you programmed your spreadsheet correctly, revenues, costs, and operating income in this column should be the same as the 2007 amounts in your income statement.

13-31 **Analysis of growth, price-recovery, and productivity components.** Winchester Corporation manufactures special ball bearings. In 2007, it plans to grow and increase operating income by capitalizing on its reputation for manufacturing a product that is superior to its competitors'. An analysis of Winchester's operating income changes between 2006 and 2007 shows the following:

Operating income for 2006	$4,140,000
Add growth component	360,000
Add price-recovery component	480,000
Add productivity component	420,000
Operating income for 2007	$5,400,000

Further analysis of these components indicates that the entire growth component is accounted for by an increase in the market size for ball bearings in 2007 and that 90% of the price-recovery component is accounted for by an increase in the market prices of ball bearings in 2007. Input prices did not change from 2006 to 2007.

REQUIRED

1. Is Winchester's 2007 strategy one of product differentiation or cost leadership? Explain briefly.
2. Was Winchester's gain in operating income in 2007 consistent with the strategy you identified in requirement 1? Explain briefly.
3. Assume the effect of the industry-marketing factor is $900,000 F. Illustrate Winchester's performance in chart form and discuss the company's performance based on their strategy of product differentiation, specifically with the increase in O.I. 2006 to 2007.

13-32 Engineered and discretionary overhead costs, unused capacity, repairs and maintenance. Rowland Corporation manufactures gears using turning machines. In 2007, Rowland's turning machines operated for 80,000 hours. Rowland employed four workers in its repairs and maintenance area to fix and repair machines that have broken down or are functioning improperly. In 2007, each repairs and maintenance person was paid a fixed annual salary of $48,000 for 250 days of work at eight hours per day. During 2007, the workers spent 6,000 hours on repairs and maintenance.

REQUIRED

1. Do you think repairs and maintenance costs at Rowland Corporation are engineered costs or discretionary costs? Explain your answer.
2. Assume repairs and maintenance costs are engineered costs. Calculate the cost of unused repairs and maintenance capacity in 2007. Would you recommend that Rowland downsize its repairs and maintenance capacity? Explain your answer briefly.
3. Assume repairs and maintenance costs are discretionary costs. Calculate the cost of unused repairs and maintenance capacity in 2007.

13-33 Engineered and discretionary overhead costs, unused capacity, customer help-desk. Cable Galore, a large cable television operator, had 750,000 subscribers in 2007. Cable Galore employs five customer-help-desk representatives to respond to customer questions and problems. During 2007, each customer-help-desk representative worked eight hours per day for 250 days at a fixed annual salary of $43,200. Cable Galore received 45,000 telephone calls from its customers in 2007. Each call took an average of 10 minutes.

REQUIRED

1. Do you think customer-help-desk costs at Cable Galore are engineered costs or discretionary costs? Explain your answer.
2. Calculate the cost of unused customer-help-desk capacity in 2007 under each of the following two assumptions: (a) customer-help-desk costs are engineered costs and (b) customer-help-desk costs are discretionary costs.
3. Assume that Cable Galore had 900,000 subscribers in 2008 and that the 2007 percentage of telephone calls received to total subscribers continued into 2008. Customer-help-desk capacity in 2008 was the same as it was in 2007. Calculate the cost of unused customer-help-desk capacity in 2008 under each of the following two assumptions: (a) customer-service costs are engineered costs and (b) customer-service costs are discretionary costs.

13-34 Partial productivity measurement. (Chapter Appendix) Berkshire Corporation makes small steel parts. Berkshire management has some ability to substitute direct materials for direct manufacturing labour. If workers cut the steel carefully, Berkshire can manufacture more parts out of a metal sheet, but this will require more direct manufacturing labour-hours. Alternatively, Berkshire can use fewer direct manufacturing labour-hours if it is willing to tolerate a larger quantity of direct materials waste. Berkshire operates in a very competitive market. Its strategy is to produce a quality product at a low cost. Berkshire produces no defective products. It reports the following data for the last two years of operations:

	2006	2007
Output units	375,000	525,000
Direct material used, in kilograms	450,000	610,000
Direct material cost per kilogram	$1.44	$1.50
Direct manufacturing labour-hours used	7,500	9,500
Wages per hour	$24	$30
Manufacturing capacity in output units	600,000	582,000
Manufacturing capacity-related fixed costs	$1,245,600	$1,222,200
Fixed manufacturing costs per unit of capacity	$2.076	$2.10

1. Compute the partial productivity ratios for 2006 and 2007.
2. On the basis of the partial productivity ratios alone, can you conclude whether and by how much productivity improved overall in 2007 relative to 2006? Explain.
3. How might the management of Berkshire Corporation use the partial productivity analysis?

13-35 Total factor productivity (continuation of 13-34). Use the data given for Berkshire Corporation in Problem 13-34.

REQUIRED

1. Compute Berkshire Corporation's total factor productivity in 2007.
2. Compare Berkshire Corporation's total factor productivity performance in 2007 relative to that in 2006.
3. What does total factor productivity tell you that partial productivity measures do not?

13-36 Balanced scorecard, ethics. John Emburey, division manager of the Household Product Division, a maker of kitchen dishwashers, had just seen the balanced scorecard for his division for 2007. He immediately called Patricia Conley, the management accountant for the division, into his office for a meeting. "I think the employee satisfaction and customer satisfaction numbers are way too low. These numbers are based on a random sample of subjective assessments made by individual managers and customer representatives. My own experience indicates that we are doing well on both these dimensions. Until we do a formal survey of employees and customers sometime next year, I think we are doing a disservice to ourselves and this company by reporting such low scores for employee and customer satisfaction. These scores will be an embarrassment for us at the division managers' meeting next month. We need to get these numbers up."

Patricia knew that the employee and customer satisfaction scores were subjective but the procedure she had used was identical to the procedures she had used in the past. She believed the scores represented the unhappiness of employees with the latest work rules and the unhappiness of customers with missed delivery dates. She also knew that these problems would be corrected in time.

REQUIRED

1. Do you think that Household Products Division should include subjective measures of employee satisfaction and customer satisfaction in its balanced scorecard? Explain.
2. What should Patricia Conley do?

COLLABORATIVE LEARNING PROBLEM

13-37 Downsizing. (CMA, adapted) Mayfair Corporation currently subsidizes cafeteria services for its 200 employees. Mayfair is in the process of reviewing the cafeteria services as cost-cutting measures are needed throughout the organization to keep the prices of its products competitive. Two alternatives are being evaluated: downsize the cafeteria staff and offer a reduced menu or contract with an outside vendor.

The current cafeteria operation has four employees with a combined annual salary of $132,000 plus additional employee benefits at 25% of salary. The cafeteria operates 250 days each year, and the costs for utilities and equipment maintenance average $36,000 annually. The daily sales include 100 entrées at $4.80 each, 80 sandwiches or salads at an average price of $3.60 each, plus an additional $240 for beverages and desserts. The cost of all cafeteria supplies is 60% of revenues.

The plan for downsizing the current operation envisions retaining two of the current employees whose combined base annual salaries total $78,000. An entrée would no longer be offered, and prices of the remaining items would be increased slightly. Under this arrangement, Mayfair expects daily sales of 150 sandwiches or salads at a higher average price of $4.32. The additional revenue for beverages and desserts is expected to increase to $276 each day. Because of the elimination of the entrée, the cost of all cafeteria supplies is expected to drop to 50% of revenues. All other conditions of operation would remain the same. Mayfair is willing to continue to subsidize this reduced operation but will not spend more than 20% of the current subsidy.

A proposal has been received from Wilco Foods, an outside vendor who is willing to supply cafeteria services. Wilco has proposed to pay Mayfair $1,200 per month for use of the cafeteria and utilities. Mayfair would be expected to cover equipment repair costs. In addition, Wilco would pay Mayfair 4% of all revenues received above the breakeven point; this payment would be made at the end of the year. All other costs incurred by

Wilco to supply the cafeteria services are variable and equal 75% of revenues. Wilco plans to charge $6.00 for an entrée, and the average price for the sandwich or salad would be $4.80. All other daily sales are expected to average $360. Wilco expects daily sales of 66 entrées and 94 sandwiches or salads.

INSTRUCTIONS

Form groups of two students to complete the following requirements.

REQUIRED

1. Determine whether the plan for downsizing the current cafeteria operation would be acceptable to Mayfair Corporation. Show all calculations.
2. Is the Wilco Foods proposal more advantageous to Mayfair Corporation than the downsizing plan? Show all calculations.

PART FOUR

CHAPTER 14

Cost Allocation

Cost allocations can lead to difficult discussions regarding the determination of a fair share of the costs to be charged to a customer, customer group, division, or company. Bell Canada has had to determine an appropriate share of the costs to be allocated to local calls versus long-distance calls. This decision has become more important given the introduction of competitors for long-distance customers.

LEARNING OBJECTIVES

After studying this chapter, you should be able to

1. Distinguish four purposes for allocating costs to cost objects

2. Describe alternative criteria used to guide decisions related to cost allocations

3. Discuss key decisions faced when collecting costs in indirect-cost pools

4. Distinguish how the single-rate cost-allocation method differs from the dual-rate method

5. Understand how the choice of budgeted versus actual allocation rates changes the risks managers face

6. Distinguish among direct allocation, step-down, and reciprocal methods of allocating support department costs

7. Make decisions that draw on the allocation of common costs using either the stand-alone or incremental methods

8. Explain the importance of explicit agreement between parties when reimbursement is based on costs incurred

Cost allocation is an unavoidable process in most organizations and in nearly every facet of accounting because it is not economically feasible to trace all costs. For facilities-level costs, consider the example of recruiting costs for a return flight from Winnipeg to Calgary, Montreal, and Vancouver. How should a national manufacturer allocate this human resources cost among potential employers in the production department at each location? How should the costs of the accounting, information technology, and legal departments be allocated to each function in the value chain? The answers are seldom clearly right or clearly wrong. Nevertheless, this chapter will provide some insight into the dimensions of the questions of cost allocation, even if the answers seem elusive. Regardless of your profession, you will be faced with many cost-allocation questions in your career.

PURPOSES OF COST ALLOCATION

To motivate managers' liberal use of support services, for example, internal auditing, the decision might be (a) not to allocate the costs of this service to the user departments or (b) to allocate a fixed amount of the service costs to the user departments irrespective of how many internal audit hours they actually consume. In contrast, to motivate managers' prudent use of services, for example, R&D, the decision might be to allocate all service department costs to the user departments.

Indirect costs often comprise a sizable percentage of the costs assigned to cost objects such as products, distribution channels, and customers. Exhibit 14-1 illustrates four possible purposes for allocating indirect costs to such cost objects:

1. To provide information for economic decisions

2. To motivate managers and employees

3. To justify costs or compute reimbursement

4. To measure income and assets for reporting to external parties

The allocation of one particular cost need not satisfy all purposes simultaneously. For example, the salary of an aerospace scientist in a central research department of Boeing or Airbus may be allocated as part of central research costs to satisfy purpose 1 (economic decisions). Under generally accepted accounting principles it must not be allocated to inventory to satisfy purpose 4 (income and asset measurement). It may or may not be allocated to satisfy purpose 2 (motivation). It may or may not be allocated to a government contract to justify a cost to be reimbursed to satisfy purpose 3 (cost reimbursement).

Different costs are appropriate for different purposes. Consider the product costs of the following business functions in the value chain.

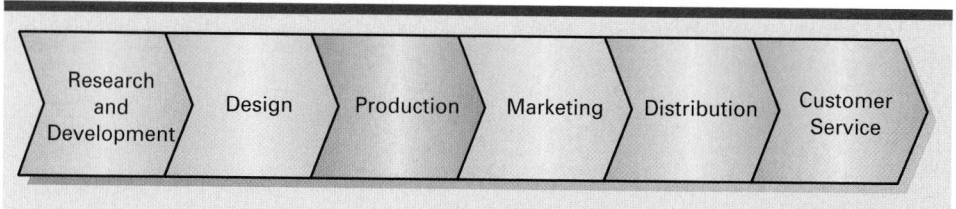

EXHIBIT 14-1
Purposes of Cost Allocation

Purpose	Illustrations
1. To provide information for economic decisions	◆ To decide whether to add a new airline flight
	◆ To decide whether to make a component part of a television set or to purchase it from another manufacturer
	◆ To decide on the selling price for a customized product or service
2. To motivate managers and employees	◆ To encourage the design of products that are simpler to manufacture or less costly to service
	◆ To encourage sales representatives to push high-margin products or services
3. To justify costs or compute reimbursement	◆ To cost products at a "fair" price, often done with government contracts
	◆ To compute reimbursement for a consulting firm that is paid a percentage of the cost savings resulting from the implementation of its recommendations
4. To measure income and assets for meeting external regulatory and legal reporting obligations	◆ To cost inventories for financial reporting to shareholders, bondholders, and so on (under generally accepted accounting principles, inventoriable costs include manufacturing costs but exclude R&D, marketing, distribution, and customer service costs)
	◆ To cost inventories for reporting to tax authorities

The same combination of costs in these six business functions typically will not satisfy each of the four purposes in Exhibit 14-1. For economic decision purposes, the costs in all six functions should be included. For motivation purposes, costs from more than one function are often included to emphasize to managers how costs in different functions are related to each other. For example, some Japanese companies require product designers to incorporate costs farther down the chain than design (such as distribution and customer service, as well as manufacturing) into their product cost estimates. The aim is to focus attention on how different product design options affect the total costs of the organization. For cost reimbursement purposes, the particular contract will often stipulate whether all six of the business functions or only a subset of them are to be reimbursed. For instance, cost reimbursement rules governing government contracts may explicitly exclude marketing costs. For purposes of income and asset measurement for reporting to external parties, inventoriable costs under generally accepted accounting principles include only manufacturing costs (and product design costs in some cases). In Canada, research costs are expensed to the accounting period in which they are incurred, while development costs may be capitalized and charged to future periods.

CRITERIA FOR GUIDING COST-ALLOCATION DECISIONS

The Role of Dominant Criteria

Exhibit 14-2 presents four criteria used to guide decisions related to cost allocations. These decisions include both the number of indirect cost pools and the cost-allocation base for each indirect-cost pool. Managers must first choose the primary purpose for a particular cost allocation and then select the appropriate criterion to implement the allocation. In this chapter we emphasize the superiority of the cause-and-effect and benefits-received criteria, especially when the purpose for cost allocation is related to either economic decisions or motivation.

For government contract purposes the fairness criterion may be more relevant. For example, the Department of National Defence requires facilities to full-cost their services in any proposal to offer unused capacity for sale. Although it would be financially beneficial to sell any unused capacity of a facility as long as the price exceeds the incremental cost, the government does not want to be seen as competing unfairly in the private sector. Thus the price must cover all costs, including allocations of overhead costs (see the Global Surveys of Company Practice box on p. 556).

EXHIBIT 14-2
Criteria for Guiding Cost-Allocation Decisions

1. **Cause and effect.** Using this criterion, managers identify the variable or variables that cause resources to be consumed. For example, managers may use hours of testing as the variable when allocating the costs of a quality testing area to products. Cost allocations based on the cause-and-effect criterion are likely to be the most credible to operating personnel.

2. **Benefits received.** Using this criterion, managers identify the beneficiaries of the outputs of the cost object. The costs of the cost object are allocated among the beneficiaries in proportion to the benefits each receives. For example, consider a corporatewide advertising program that promotes the general image of the corporation rather than any individual product. The costs of this program may be allocated on the basis of division sales; the higher the sales, the higher the division's allocated cost of the advertising program. The rationale behind this allocation is the belief that divisions with higher sales levels apparently benefited from the advertising more than did divisions with lower sales levels and therefore ought to be allocated more of the advertising costs.

3. **Fairness or equity.** This criterion is often cited in government contracts when cost allocations are the basis for establishing a price satisfactory to the government and its supplier. The cost allocation here is viewed as a "reasonable" or "fair" means of establishing a selling price in the minds of the contracting parties. For most allocation decisions, fairness is a lofty objective rather than an operational criterion.

4. **Ability to bear.** This criterion advocates allocating costs in proportion to the cost object's ability to bear them. An example is the allocation of corporate executive salaries on the basis of divisional operating income; the presumption is that the more profitable divisions have a greater ability to absorb corporate headquarters' costs.

 Using the cause-and effect criterion to choose a cost-allocation base means this base is a cost driver of the amount in the indirect cost pool.

The steps in cost allocation are:

Step 1: Determine the purpose of the allocation because the purpose defines what costs will be allocated

Step 2: Decide how to allocate the costs from step 1 by:
  a. Deciding how many indirect-cost pools to form then
  b. Identifying an allocation base (preferably a cost driver) for *each* cost pool.

Why Allocate Corporate and Other Support Costs to Divisions and Departments?

Extensive survey evidence exists on the reasons that managers allocate corporate and other support costs to divisions and departments.

Canadian executives[a] cited the following objectives, ranked in order of importance:

1. To determine costs
2. To evaluate profit centres
3. To fix accountability
4. To allocate costs per usage
5. To promote more effective resource usage
6. To foster cost awareness

These executives encountered the following difficulties in implementing their cost-allocation programs: making the allocations results in losses being reported, friction arises among managers, market prices are unstable, allocations are perceived as arbitrary, usage is hard to monitor, agreement on the allocation method is difficult to obtain, and the allocation process is time-consuming.

A survey[b] of U.S. managers revealed the following purposes, ranked by frequency:

1. To remind profit centre managers that indirect costs exist and that profit centre earnings must be adequate to cover some share of those costs
2. To encourage the use of central services that would otherwise be underutilized
3. To stimulate profit centre managers to put pressure on central managers to control service costs

A similar survey was conducted among Australian[c] and U.K.[d] managers. The two sets of managers gave the same ranking of the following reasons for allocating corporate costs to divisions (in order of importance):

1. To acknowledge that divisions would incur such costs if they were independent units or if the services were not provided centrally
2. To make division managers aware that central costs exist
3. To stimulate divisional managers to put pressure on central support managers to control costs
4. To stimulate divisional managers to economize in usage of central services.

[a]Atkinson, A., *Intrafirm Cost and Resource Allocations: Theory and Practice* (Hamilton: Society of Management Accountants of Canada and Canadian Academic Accounting Association Research Monograph).

[b]Fremgen, J., and S. Liao, *The Allocation of Corporate Indirect Costs* (New York: National Association of Accountants).

[c]Ramadan, S., "The Rationale for Cost Allocation: A Study of U.K. Divisionalised Companies," *Accounting and Business Research* (Winter).

[d]Dean, G., M. Joye, and P. Blayney, *Strategic Management Accounting Survey* (Sydney, Australia: The University of Sydney).

The feasibility of using an individual criterion in Exhibit 14-2 varies according to the context of the cost allocation. Consider using the cause-and-effect criterion for allocating indirect costs to individual products in a multiple-product company. Where the indirect costs are variable and each product is assembled sequentially, the cause-and-effect criterion can guide the choice of a cost-allocation base. In contrast, where the indirect costs are fixed and two or more products are jointly assembled, it is not possible to identify specific cause-and-effect relationships between work on an individual product and the total costs incurred.

Fairness and ability to bear are used less frequently than either cause and effect or benefits received. Fairness is a difficult criterion on which to obtain agreement.[1] Some issues that arise when using the ability-to-bear criterion emerge if you consider a product that consumes a large amount of indirect costs but whose selling price is currently below its direct costs for competitive purposes. This product has no ability to bear any indirect costs of the services it uses. If this proportion of indirect costs is allocated to other products, then the sales price will subsidize the product that is losing money.

When designing and implementing cost allocations, managers must weigh the overall costs and benefits. With rapid advances in technology, the financial costs of collecting and processing timely cost information have rapidly declined. Many companies have either adopted or developed costing systems that use multiple cost-allocation bases where the benefits of improved information for decision making make this task worthwhile.

THE COST-BENEFIT APPROACH

Many companies place great importance on cost-benefit considerations when designing their cost-allocation systems. Companies incur costs not only in gathering data, but also in taking the time necessary to educate management about the chosen system. The more sophisticated the system, in general, the higher these education costs.

The costs of designing and implementing sophisticated cost-allocation systems are highly visible, and most companies work to reduce them. In contrast, the benefits from using a well-designed cost-allocation system—being able to make better-informed make/buy decisions, pricing decisions, cost control decisions, and so on—are difficult to measure and are frequently less visible. Still, designers of cost-allocation systems should consider these benefits as well as costs.

Spurred by rapid reductions in the costs of collecting and processing information, organizations today are moving toward more detailed cost allocation systems. Many companies have now developed manufacturing or distribution overhead costing systems that use more than ten different cost-allocation bases. Also, some businesses have state-of-the-art information technology already in place for operating their plants or distribution networks. Applying this existing technology to the development and operation of a cost-allocation system is less expensive—and thus more inviting—than starting up such a system from scratch.

COST ALLOCATION AND COSTING SYSTEMS

We will use Computer Horizons to illustrate how costs incurred in different parts of an organization can be assigned and then reassigned when costing products, services, customers, or contracts. Computer Horizons has two manufacturing divisions. The Personal Computer Division manufactures its Plum, Plum Laptop, and Super Plum products. The Plum and Plum Laptop are assembled at its St. Louis, Birmingham, and Singapore plants. The Super Plum is assembled at its Vancouver plant. The Peripheral Equipment Division manufactures printers, cables, and other items used with its computer products. It has plants in St. Louis and Toronto.

Exhibit 14-3 presents an overview of the costing system at the St. Louis assembly plant of the Personal Computer Division. This plant assembles the Plum line and the Plum Laptop line. The area within the box in Exhibit 14-3 shows a costing system overview for the Model A version of the Plum. This costing overview is similar to that presented in earlier chapters.

The product costing overviews presented in earlier chapters (and, indeed, in this chapter) are typically only parts of larger costing systems. This larger costing

---

[1]Kaplow and Shavell, for example, in a review of the legal literature observed that "notions of fairness are many and varied. They are analyzed and rationalized by different writers in different ways, and they also typically depend upon the circumstances under consideration. Accordingly, it is not possible to identify a consensus view on these notions . . ." See L. Kaplow and S. Shavell, "Fairness Versus Welfare," *Harvard Law Review*, February 2001.

EXHIBIT 14-3
Cost Tracing and Cost Allocation at the St. Louis Assembly Plant of Computer Horizons

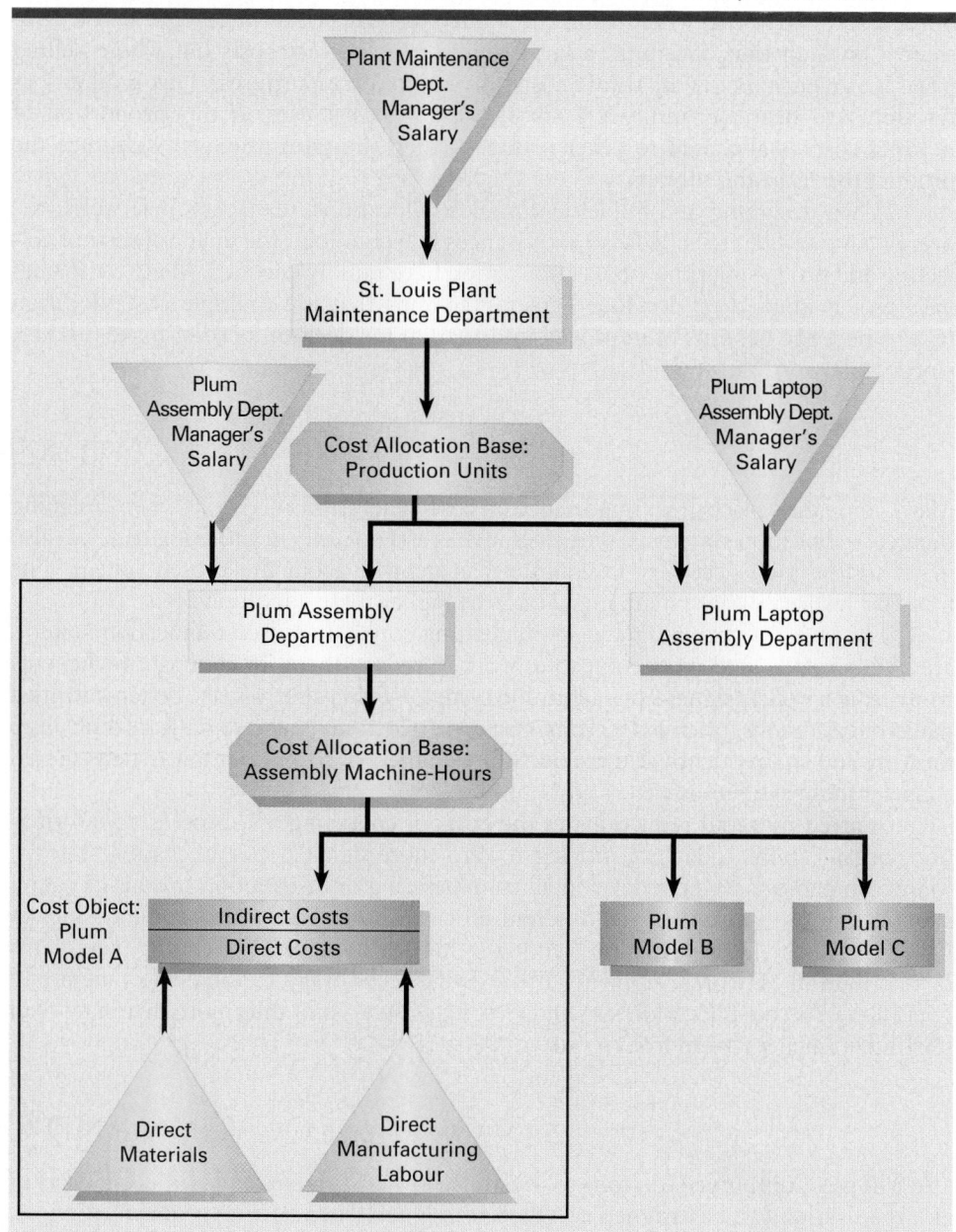

system can be for a plant, a division, or even a whole company with multiple plants and divisions in many countries. Computer Horizons has manufacturing plants located in Canada, the United States, Mexico, Singapore, and the United Kingdom. It has marketing operations in more than 20 countries. Every month it consolidates accounting information from each of its operations to use in its planning and control decisions. A detailed costing overview of this companywide system would be sizably more complex than that in Exhibit 14-3.

The costing system for the St. Louis plant portrayed in Exhibit 14-3 highlights two important points. First, it highlights how there are multiple cost objects in most costing systems. Examples at the St. Louis plant include the Plant Maintenance Department, the Plum Assembly Department, the Plum Laptop Assembly Department, and the separate products in the Plum Assembly Department—for example, Plum Models A, B, and C. Note, however, that Exhibit 14-3 presents only a small subset of the separate cost objects at the St. Louis plant. Other examples include the Procurement Department, the Energy Department, and the various Plum Laptop products (see Concepts in Action box).

Exhibit 14-3 also highlights how an individual cost item can be simultaneously a direct cost of one cost object and an indirect cost of another cost object. Consider the salary of the Plant Maintenance Department manager. This salary is a direct cost traced to the Plant Maintenance Department. Computer Horizons then allocates the costs of this department to the two Assembly Departments at the St. Louis plant using units produced as the allocation base. In turn, the costs of the two Assembly Departments are allocated to individual products, such as the Plum Model A, using assembly machine-hours as the allocation base. Thus, the salary of the Plant Maintenance Department manager is both an indirect cost of each computer assembled at the plant and a direct cost of the Plant Maintenance Department.

Cost Allocations and Inspection Costs at Volkswagen Canada

The reason accountants can assess costs a lot more accurately using ABC is that it allows them to break down overheads and allocate them to the right products. The revelations can be startling. Take an ABC pilot project undertaken in the die-cast engine parts area of the Volkswagen Canada Inc. plant in Barrie, Ontario. Volkswagen was ripe for ABC: it made about 25 engine parts ranging from mass-produced gear housings to highly specialized camshaft-bearing caps. The cost analysis turned up numerous profit laggards. "A lot of them came out negative," says George Waddell, a cost accountant who led the project team. "The whole die-cast operation was profitable then, but that was because maybe five or six of those parts were making a lot of money and covering (for) the ones that were losing money."

How can this happen? Consider one of the not-so-profitable parts: an engine mounting bracket. Random samples of most parts pass through an X-ray machine to check for structural defects that could cause them to break. But a snapped engine-mounting bracket could be a safety hazard. So Volkswagen was X-raying every single bracket to guard against a flawed one slipping through. In fact, X-raying these brackets took up about 80% of machine time. Under the ABC system, when the pool of inspection costs was divided up according to the proportion of X-ray inspections devoted to the various parts, engine brackets carried 80% of the load. Compare that to the old system of costing, where all 25 die-cast engine parts carried a share of inspection costs as one of the overheads. A labour-intensive gear housing that didn't pass through the comprehensive X-ray process got socked with a disproportionate share of overhead. Based on its share of inspections, it should have attracted, say, 5% of these costs—instead of the 50% it might have attracted on the basis of invested labour-hours.

Management is only as good as the information behind it. In Volkswagen's case, knowing the high cost of inspection spurred a decision not to inspect so many brackets. Workers now X-ray 25 from each bin. They only inspect the rest if they find a reject in the sample. ABC analysis has now moved on to Volkswagen's wheel department, where an automated work flow system of looping conveyors has given way to manual trolleys. "The ABC study confirmed that conveyor breakdowns were costing us a lot of downtime," says financial analyst Jim Gurowka. "We found that short spurts get through the system faster than with a continuous conveyor."

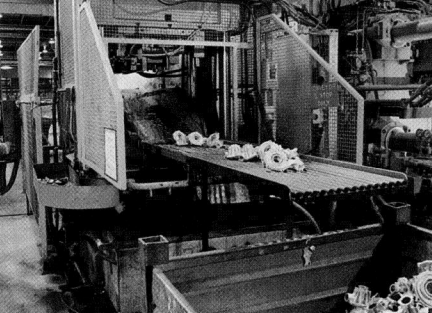

Volkswagen Canada
www.vw.ca

SAS Activity-Based Management
www.sas.com/solutions/abm

INDIRECT-COST POOLS AND COST ALLOCATION

The indirect costs of products assembled at the manufacturing plants of Computer Horizons include (1) costs incurred at corporate headquarters and (2) costs incurred at the manufacturing plants. Exhibit 14-4 illustrates cost pools at both levels.

Choices Related to Indirect Costs

Computer Horizons has several key choices to make when accumulating and subsequently allocating the indirect costs to products of the Personal Computer Division:

◆ Which cost categories from Corporate Headquarters and the other divisions should be included in the indirect costs of the Personal Computer Division? Should all the corporate headquarters cost pools in Exhibit 14-4 be allocated, or should only a subset of them be allocated? For example, some companies exclude corporate public relations from any corporate cost allocations to the divisions; division managers have little say in corporate public relations decisions and would object to allocations as "taxation without representation."

◆ How many cost pools should be used when allocating corporate costs to the Personal Computer Division? A cost pool is a grouping of individual cost items. One extreme is to aggregate all corporate costs into a single cost pool. The other extreme is to have numerous individual corporate cost pools. The concept of homogeneity (described in the following section) is important in making this decision.

◆ Which allocation base should be used for each of the corporate cost pools when allocating corporate costs to the Personal Computer Division? Examples include the following:

Cost Pool	Possible Allocation Bases
Corporate executive salaries	Sales; assets employed; operating income
Treasury Department	Sales; assets employed; estimated time or usage
Legal Department	Estimated time or usage; sales; assets employed
Marketing Department	Sales; number of sales personnel
Payroll Department	Number of employees; payroll dollars
Human Resources Department	Number of employees; payroll dollars; number of new hires

EXHIBIT 14-4

Indirect-Cost Pools (When the Cost Object Is an Individual Product) of Computer Horizons

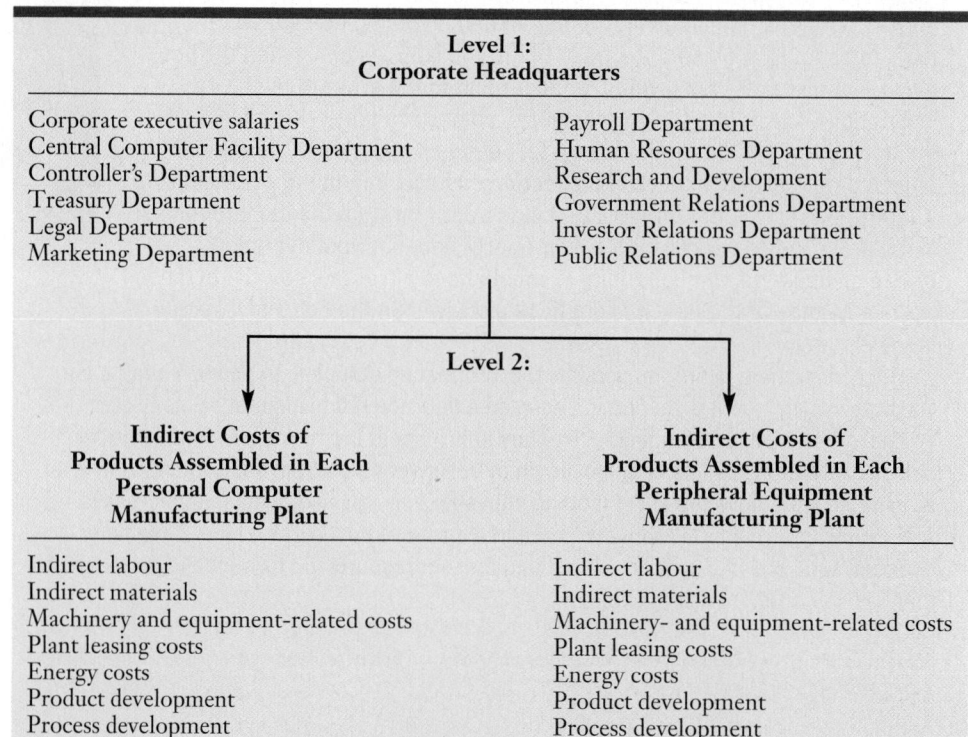

Level 1: **Corporate Headquarters**	
Corporate executive salaries	Payroll Department
Central Computer Facility Department	Human Resources Department
Controller's Department	Research and Development
Treasury Department	Government Relations Department
Legal Department	Investor Relations Department
Marketing Department	Public Relations Department

Level 2:

Indirect Costs of Products Assembled in Each Personal Computer Manufacturing Plant	**Indirect Costs of Products Assembled in Each Peripheral Equipment Manufacturing Plant**
Indirect labour	Indirect labour
Indirect materials	Indirect materials
Machinery and equipment-related costs	Machinery- and equipment-related costs
Plant leasing costs	Plant leasing costs
Energy costs	Energy costs
Product development	Product development
Process development	Process development

♦ Which allocation base should be used when allocating the indirect-cost pools at each manufacturing plant to the products assembled in those plants? Examples include number of parts assembled in each product, direct manufacturing labour-hours, machining-hours, and testing-hours.

These allocation bases for both corporate and plant indirect costs are illustrative only. Managers' choices of allocation bases depend on the purpose served by the cost allocation (see Exhibit 14-1, p. 554), the criteria used to guide the cost allocation (see Exhibit 14-2, p. 555), and the costs of implementing the different allocation bases.

Homogeneity of Cost Pools

A **homogeneous cost pool** is one in which all the activities whose costs are included in the pool have the same or a similar cause-and-effect relationship or benefits-received relationship between the cost allocator and the costs of the activity. Why is homogeneity important? Because using homogeneous indirect cost pools enables more accurate product, service, and customer costs to be obtained. A consequence of using a homogeneous cost pool is that the cost allocations using that pool will be the same as would be made if costs of each individual activity in that pool were allocated separately. The greater the degree of homogeneity, the fewer cost pools required to explain accurately the differences in how products use resources of the organization.

Assume that Computer Horizons wants to use the cause-and-effect criterion to guide cost-allocation decisions. The company should aggregate only those cost pools that have the same cause-and-effect relationship to the cost object. For example, if the number of employees in a division is the cause for incurring both corporate payroll department costs and corporate human resources department costs, the payroll cost pool and the human resources cost pool could be aggregated before determining the combined payroll and human resources cost rate per unit of the allocation base. That is, the combined rate per unit of the allocation base is the same as the sum of the rates if the individual cost pools were allocated separately.

Homogeneous cost pool. A cost pool in which all the activities whose costs are included in the pool have the same or a similar cause-and-effect relationship or benefits-received relationship between the cost allocator and the costs of the activity.

Recognizing More Cost Pools

A variety of factors may prompt managers to consider recognizing multiple cost pools where a single cost pool is currently being used. One factor is the views of line managers and personnel. For example, do they believe important differences exist in how costs are driven or how products use the facilities not currently being recognized using a single cost pool? A second factor is changes made in plant layout, general operations, and so on, such that all products do not use the facility in an equivalent way. A third factor is changes in the diversity of products (or services) produced or in the way those products use the resources in the cost pool. A fourth factor is the changes in information-gathering technology. Improvements in this technology are expanding the ability to develop multiple cost pools.

Allowability of Costs in Cost Pools

A given cost item or amount may be included or excluded from a cost pool depending on the purpose at hand. Consider a consulting firm whose purpose is to price jobs for (1) a commercial client and (2) a government client. When pricing for a commercial client, the consulting firm may include the cost of beer and wine at meals that have a clear business-related rationale. In contrast, when billing the government under a contract, the contract may state that no cost amount for any alcoholic beverage is permitted to enter the cost pools from which costs are allocated to the government.

ALLOCATING COSTS FROM ONE DEPARTMENT TO ANOTHER

In many cases, the costs of a department will include costs allocated from other departments. Three key issues that arise when allocating costs from one department to another are (1) whether to use a single-rate method or a dual-rate method, (2) whether to use budgeted rates or actual rates, and (3) whether to use budgeted quantities or actual quantities. In the following example, nonproduction facilities sustaining costs (see Chapter 5, p. 161) incurred at corporate headquarters are being allocated to the two production departments of the organization.

Single-Rate and Dual-Rate Methods

A **single-rate cost-allocation method** pools all costs in one cost pool and allocates them to cost objects using the same rate per unit of the single allocation base. There is no distinction between costs in the cost pool in terms of cost variability (such as fixed costs versus variable costs). A **dual-rate cost-allocation method** first classifies costs in the cost pool into two pools (typically into a variable-cost pool and a fixed-cost pool). Each pool has a different allocation rate or base.

Consider the Central Computer Department at the corporate headquarters of Computer Horizons (shown in Exhibit 14-4). For simplicity, assume that the only users of this facility are the Personal Computer Division and the Peripheral Equipment Division. The following data apply to the coming budget year:

Fixed costs of operating the facility	$300,000	per year
Total capacity available	1,500	hours
Budgeted long-term usage (quantity) in hours		
Personal Computer Division	800	hours
Peripheral Equipment Division	400	hours
Total	1,200	hours
Budgeted variable costs per hour in the		
1,000- to 1,500-hour relevant range	$200	per hour used

Under the single-rate method, the costs of the Central Computer Department (assuming budgeted usage is the allocation base and budgeted rates are used) would be allocated as follows:

Total cost pool: $300,000 + (1,200 budgeted hours × $200)	$540,000	per year
Budgeted usage	1,200	hours
Budgeted total per hour rate: $540,000 ÷ 1,200 hours	$ 450	per hour used
Allocation rate for Personal Computer Division	$ 450	per hour used
Allocation rate for Peripheral Equipment Division	$ 450	per hour used

The rate of $450 per hour differs sizably from the $200 budgeted variable cost per hour. The $450 rate includes an allocated amount of $250 per hour ($300,000 ÷ 1,200 hours) for the fixed costs of operating the facility. These fixed costs will be incurred whether the computer runs its 1,500-hour capacity, its 1,200-hour budgeted usage, or even, say, only 600 hours' usage.

Using the $450 per hour single-rate method (combined with the budgeted usage allocation base) transforms what is a fixed cost to the Central Computer Department (and to Computer Horizons) into a variable cost to users of that facility. This presents a problem if internal users decide to purchase computer time outside the company. Consider an external vendor that charges less than $450 per hour but more than $200 per hour. A division of Computer Horizons that uses this vendor rather than the Central Computer Department may decrease its own division costs, but the overall costs to Computer Horizons are increased. For example, suppose the Personal Computer Division uses an external vendor that charges $360 per hour when the Central Computer Department has excess capacity. In the short run, Computer Horizons incurs an extra $160 per hour, because this external vendor is used ($360 external purchase price per hour minus the $200 internal variable costs per hour) instead of its own Central Computer Department.

When the dual-rate method is used, allocation bases for each of the fixed and variable cost pools must be chosen. Assume that the budgeted rates are used. The allocation quantities chosen are budgeted rates and usage for fixed costs and budgeted rates with actual usage for variable costs. The total budgeted usage of 1,200 hours comprises 800 hours for the Personal Computer Division and 400 hours for the Peripheral Equipment Division. The costs allocated to the Personal Computer Division would be as follows:

Fixed-cost function (800 hours ÷ 1,200 hours) × $300,000	$200,000 per year
Variable-cost function	$ 200 per hour used

The costs allocated to the Peripheral Equipment Division would be

Fixed-cost function (400 hours ÷ 1,200 hours) × $300,000	$100,000 per hour used
Variable-cost function	$ 200 per hour used

Assume now that during the coming year the Personal Computer Division actually uses 900 hours but the Peripheral Equipment Division uses only 300 hours. The costs allocated to these two divisions would be computed as follows:

Under the Single-Rate Method

Personal Computer Division	900 × $450 = $405,000
Peripheral Equipment Division	300 × $450 = $135,000

Under the Dual-Rate Method

Personal Computer Division	$200,000 + (900 × $200) = $380,000
Peripheral Equipment Division	$100,000 + (300 × $200) = $160,000

Should actual costs of the Central Computer Department differ from the allocated costs, the company would account for over- or underallocated costs using methods described in Chapter 4 (pp. 131–133). One obvious benefit of using the single-rate method is the low cost of implementation. It avoids the expensive analysis necessary to classify the individual cost items of a department into fixed and variable categories. The difficulty is that the single-rate method unitizes fixed costs and a careless manager could perceive this unitized rate as if it were a variable rate. The single-rate method may lead divisions to take actions that appear to be in their own best interests but are not in the best interests of the organization as a whole.

An important benefit of the dual-rate method is that it signals to division managers the different behaviour of variable costs and fixed costs. This important information guides division managers into making decisions that benefit the corporation as well as each division. For example, it would signal that using a third-party computer provider who charges more than $200 per hour results in Computer Horizons being worse off than if it had used its own Central Computer Department, which has a variable cost of $200 per hour.

Budgeted versus Actual Rates

OBJECTIVE 5

Understand how the choice of budgeted versus actual allocation rates changes the risks managers face

The decision on whether to use budgeted cost rates or actual cost rates affects the level of uncertainty user departments face. Budgeted rates let the user departments know in advance the cost rates they will be charged. Users are then better equipped to determine the amount of the service to request and—if the option exists— whether to use the internal department source or outsource to an external vendor. In contrast, when actual rates are used, the user department will not know the rates charged until the end of the period.

Budgeted rates also help motivate the manager of the support department (for example, the Central Computer Department) to improve efficiency. During the budget period, the support department, not the user departments, bears the risk of any unfavourable cost variances. Why? Because the user department does not pay for any costs that exceed the budgeted rates. The manager of the support department would likely view the use of budgeted rates negatively especially when unfavourable cost variances occur because of price increases outside the department's control.

Some organizations recognize that it may not always be best to impose all the risks of variances from budgeted amounts completely on the support department (as when costs are allocated using budgeted rates) or completely on the user departments (as when costs are allocated using actual rates). One corporate response has been to identify uncontrollable factors and relieve the supplier-department manager of responsibility for these variances. Another response has been to have the two departments agree to share the risk (through an explicit formula) of a large, uncontrollable increase in the price of materials used by the support department. The Focus on Values and Behaviours feature describes the role of judgment in cost allocations and the challenges management accountants face.

Budgeted versus Actual Usage Allocation Bases

The choice between actual usage and budgeted usage for allocating department fixed costs also can affect a manager's behaviour. Consider the budget of $300,000 fixed costs at the Central Computer Department of Computer Horizons. Assume that actual and budgeted fixed costs are equal. Assume also that the actual usage by the Personal Computer Division is always equal to the budgeted usage. We now look at the effect on allocating the $300,000 in total fixed costs when actual usage by the Peripheral Equipment Division equals (case 1), is greater than (case 2), and is less than (case 3) the budgeted usage. Recall that the budgeted usage is 800 hours for the Personal Computer Division and 400 hours for the Peripheral Equipment Division. Exhibit 14-5 presents the allocation of total fixed costs of $300,000 to each division for these three cases.

Finance Executives at Boeing: Setting the Wrong Example

Cost allocations invariably require judgment. For example, which method should be used for allocating support-department costs to operating divisions? When working to determine the appropriate method, management accountants should seek to understand the facts, ask tough questions, and propose cost-allocation methods that will help improve decision making within the organization. Because cost allocations to operating divisions will differ according to the method used, division managers may try to convince management accountants to recommend a cost-allocation method that is most favourable to their division. Management accountants must be able to confidently explain how costs will be allocated, why a method was chosen, and how managers should and should not use this information. If management accountants do not resist pressure from managers, they could put the welfare of the company at risk.

As management accountants rise to senior levels in the finance area, their ethical responsibilities increase. Unethical decisions can have even more detrimental consequences. Consider the recent events at Boeing. In October 2002, Darleen Druyun, a senior U.S. Air Force acquisition officer, negotiated a multi-million-dollar NATO aircraft order that Boeing won. She had also been working on a multi-billion-dollar contract to lease and buy Boeing aircraft that would serve as refuelling planes. In November 2002, as Ms. Druyun prepared for retirement from the Air Force, she removed herself from discussions involving Boeing, and in January 2003 she joined Boeing as an executive in its defence business operations.

In December 2003, *The Wall Street Journal* reported, "Actions related to Ms. Druyun's hiring in January 2003 are now the subject of Pentagon and Justice Department probes as well as Congressional scrutiny into the nation's No. 2 defense contractor. Boeing fired both Mr. Sears (Boeing's chief financial officer who had allegedly discussed employment opportunities at Boeing with Ms. Druyun while she still had authority over contracts in which Boeing had an interest) and Ms. Druyun for what it called "unethical" conduct in late November [2002]. Their dealings were a major factor in the resignation a week later of the company's chairman and chief executive, Phil Condit."

Source: A. M. Squeo and J. L. Lunsford, "How Two Officials Got Caught by Pentagon's Revolving Door," *The Wall Street Journal,* December 18, 2003, p. A1.

EXHIBIT 14-5
Effect of Variations in Actual Usage on Departmental Cost Allocations

Case	Actual Usage		Budgeted Usage as Allocation Base		Actual Usage as Allocation Base	
	Personal Computer Division	Peripheral Equipment Division	Personal Computer Division	Peripheral Equipment Division	Personal Computer Division	Peripheral Equipment Division
1	800 hours	400 hours	\$200,000*	\$100,000†	\$200,000*	\$100,000†
2	800 hours	700 hours	\$200,000*	\$100,000†	\$160,000‡	\$140,000‖
3	800 hours	200 hours	\$200,000*	\$100,000†	\$240,000§	\$ 60,000#

$$^* \frac{800}{(800 + 400)} \times \$300,000 \qquad ^\dagger \frac{400}{(800 + 400)} \times \$300,000 \qquad ^\ddagger \frac{800}{(800 + 700)} \times \$300,000$$

$$^\S \frac{800}{(800 + 200)} \times \$300,000 \qquad ^\| \frac{700}{(800 + 700)} \times \$300,000 \qquad ^\# \frac{200}{(800 + 200)} \times \$300,000$$

In case 1, the fixed-cost allocation equals the expected amount. In case 2, the fixed-cost allocation is \$40,000 less to the Personal Computer Division than expected (\$160,000 vs. \$200,000). In case 3, the fixed-cost allocation is \$40,000 more than expected (\$240,000 vs. \$200,000). Consider case 3. Why is there an increase of \$40,000 even though the Personal Computer Division's actual and budgeted usage are exactly equal? Because the fixed costs are spread over fewer hours of usage. Variations in usage in another division will affect the fixed costs allocated to the Personal Computer Division when fixed costs are allocated on the basis of actual usage. When actual usage is the allocation base, user divisions will not know how much cost is allocated to them until the end of the budget period.

When budgeted usage is the allocation base, user divisions will know their allocated costs in advance. This information helps the user divisions with both short-run and long-run planning. The main justification given for the use of budgeted usage to allocate fixed costs relates to long-run planning. Organizations commit to infrastructure costs (such as the fixed costs of a support department) on the basis of a long-run planning horizon; the use of budgeted usage to allocate these fixed costs is consistent with this long-run horizon.

If fixed costs are allocated on the basis of estimated long-run use, some managers may be tempted to underestimate their planned usage. In this way, they will bear a lower fraction of the total costs (assuming all other managers do *not* similarly underestimate). Some organizations offer rewards in the form of salary increases and promotions to managers who make accurate forecasts of long-run usage. Alternatively, some organizations impose cost penalties for underestimating long-run usage. For instance, a higher cost rate may be charged after a division exceeds its budgeted usage.

ALLOCATING COSTS OF SUPPORT DEPARTMENTS

Operating Departments and Support Departments

Many organizations distinguish between operating or core departments and support departments. An **operating** or **core department** (also called a **production department** in manufacturing companies) adds value to a product or service that is observable by a customer. A **support department** (also called a **service department**) provides the services that maintain other internal departments (operating departments and other support departments) in the organization. These are *facilities sustaining costs*. Support departments at Computer Horizons include the Legal Department and the Human Resources Department at corporate headquarters.

Support departments create special accounting problems when they provide reciprocal support to each other as well as support to operating departments. An example of

Operating or core department (production department). A department that adds value to a product or service that is observable by a customer.

Support department (service department). A department that provides the services that maintain other internal departments (operating departments and other support departments) in the organization.

reciprocal support at Computer Horizons would be the Legal Department providing services to the Human Resources Department (such as advice on compliance with labour laws) and the Human Resources Department providing support to the Legal Department (such as advice about the hiring of lawyers and paralegal services). To obtain accurate product, service, and customer costs at Computer Horizons requires inclusion of support department costs as well as operating department costs. This section illustrates alternative ways to recognize support department costs. More accurate support department cost allocations result in more accurate product, service, and customer costs.

Be cautious here for several reasons. First, organizations differ in the departments located at the corporate and division levels therefore their facilities sustaining costs will differ. Some departments located at corporate headquarters of Computer Horizons (for example, R&D) are located at the division level in other organizations. Second, organizations differ in their definitions of *operating department* and *support department*. Always try to ascertain the precise meaning of these terms when analyzing data that include allocations of operating department costs and support department costs. Third, organizations differ in the percentage of total support costs allocated using the methods described in this section. Some companies allocate all support department costs using one of the methods outlined in this section. Other companies only allocate *indirect* support department costs using these methods, with all *direct* support costs traced to the appropriate operating department.

OBJECTIVE 6

Distinguish among direct allocation, step-down, and reciprocal methods of allocating support department costs

Support Department Cost-Allocation Methods

We now examine three methods of allocating the facilities sustaining costs of support departments: *direct, step-down*, and *reciprocal*. To focus on concepts, we use the single-rate method to allocate the costs of each support department. The Problem for Self-Study on page 574 illustrates the use of the dual-rate method for allocating support department costs.

Consider Castleford Engineering, which manufactures engines used in electric power generating plants. Castleford has two support departments and two operating departments in its manufacturing facility:

Support Departments	Operating Departments
Plant maintenance	Machining
Information systems	Assembly

Costs are accumulated in each department for planning and control purposes. For inventory costing, however, the support department costs of Castleford must be allocated to the operating departments. The data for our example are listed in Exhibit 14-6. The percentages in this table can be illustrated by reference to the Plant Maintenance Department. This support department provides a total of 8,000 hours of support work: 20% (1,600 ÷ 8,000) goes to the Information Systems support department; 30% (2,400 ÷ 8,000) to the Machining Department; and 50% (4,000 ÷ 8,000) to the Assembly Department.

Direct allocation method (direct method). Method of support cost allocation that ignores any service rendered by one support department to another; it allocates each support department's total costs directly to the operating departments.

Direct Allocation Method The **direct allocation method** (often called the **direct method**) is the most widely used method of allocating support department costs. This method allocates each support department's costs directly to the operating departments. Exhibit 14-7 illustrates this method using the data in Exhibit 14-6. Note how this method ignores both the 1,600 hours of support time rendered by the Plant Maintenance Department to the Information Systems Department and the 200 hours of support time rendered by Information Systems to Plant Maintenance. The base used to allocate Plant Maintenance is the budgeted total maintenance labour-hours worked in the operating departments: 2,400 + 4,000 = 6,400 hours. This amount excludes the 1,600 hours of support time provided by Plant Maintenance to Information Systems. Similarly, the base used for allocation of Information Systems costs is 1,600 + 200 = 1,800 hours of computer time, which excludes the 200 hours of support time provided by Information Systems to Plant Maintenance.

The benefit of the direct method is its simplicity. There is no need to predict the usage of support department resources by other support departments.

EXHIBIT 14-6
Data for Allocating Support Department Costs at Castleford Engineering for 2007

	A	B	C	D	E	F
1		**SUPPORT**		**OPERATING**		
2		**DEPARTMENTS**		**DEPARTMENTS**		
3		**Plant**	**Information**			
4		**Maintenance**	**Systems**	**Machining**	**Assembly**	**Total**
5	Budgeted manufacturing overhead costs before any interdepartment cost allocations	$600,000	$116,000	$400,000	$200,000	$1,316,000
6	Support work furnished:					
7	By Plant Maintenance					
8	Budgeted labour-hours	—	1,600	2,400	4,000	8,000
9	Percentage	—	20%	30%	50%	100%
10	By Information Systems					
11	Budgeted computer hours	200	—	1,600	200	2,000
12	Percentage	10%	—	80%	10%	100%

EXHIBIT 14-7
Direct Method of Allocating Support Department Costs at Castleford Engineering for 2007

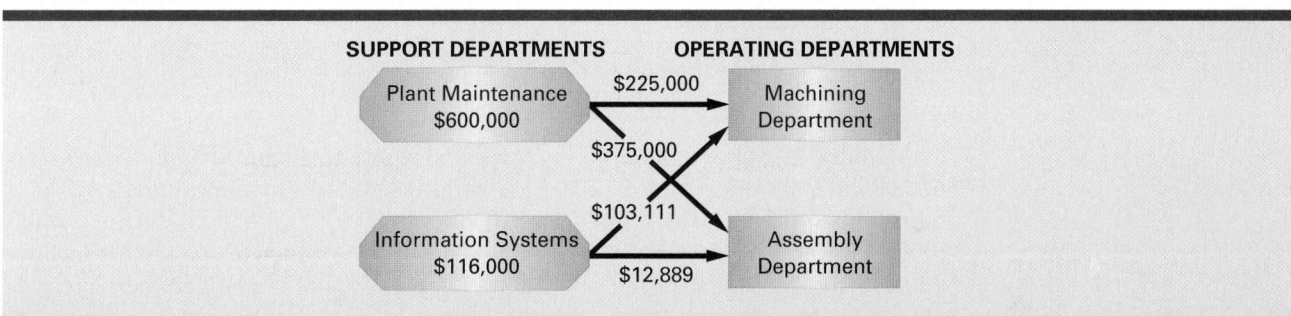

	A	B	C	D	E	F
1		**SUPPORT**		**OPERATING**		
2		**DEPARTMENTS**		**DEPARTMENTS**		
3		**Plant**	**Information**			
4		**Maintenance**	**Systems**	**Machining**	**Assembly**	**Total**
5	Budgeted manufacturing overhead costs before any interdepartment cost allocations	$600,000	$116,000	$400,000	$200,000	$1,316,000
6	Allocation of Plant Maintenance (3/8, 5/8)[a]	(600,000)		225,000	375,000	
7	Allocation of Information Systems (8/9, 1/9)[b]		(116,000)	103,111	12,889	
8	Total budgeted manufacturing overhead of operating departments	$ 0	$ 0	$728,111	$587,889	$1,316,000
9						

10	[a]Base is (2,400 + 4,000) or 6,400 hours; 2,400 ÷ 6,400 = 3/8; 4,000 ÷ 6,400 = 5/8. An equivalent approach is to calculate a budgeted rate for allocating Plant Maintenance Department costs, $600,000 ÷ 6,400 hours = $93.75 per hour. The Machining Department would then be allocated $225,000 ($93.75 per hour × 2,400 hours) and the Assembly Department $375,000 ($93.75 per hour × 4,000 hours)
11	[b]Base is (1,600 + 200), or 1,800 hours; 1,600 ÷ 1,800 = 8/9; 200 ÷ 1,800 = 1/9. An equivalent approach is to calculate a budgeted rate for allocating Information Systems Department Costs, $116,000 ÷ 1,800 hours = $64.444 per hour. The Machining Department would then be allocated $103,111 ($64.444 per hour × 1,600 hours) and the Assembly Department $12,889 ($64.444 per hour × 200 hours). For ease of exposition throughout this section, we will use the fraction of the support department services used by other departments to allocate support department costs to other departments rather than calculate budgeted rates to allocate costs.

Step-Down Allocation Method   Some organizations use the **step-down allocation method** (sometimes called the **step allocation method**, or **sequential allocation method**), which allows for *partial* recognition of the services rendered by support departments to other support departments. This method requires the support departments to be ranked (sequenced) in the order in which the step-down allocation is to proceed. The costs in the first-ranked support department are allocated to the other support departments and to the operating departments. The costs in the second-ranked department are allocated to those support departments not yet allocated and to the operating departments. This procedure is followed until the costs in the last-ranked support department have been allocated to the operating departments. Two ways to determine the sequence to allocate support department costs are as follows:

◆ **Approach A.**   Rank support departments on the percentage of the support department's total support provided to other support departments. The support department with the highest percentage is allocated first. The support department with the lowest percentage is allocated last. In our Castleford Engineering example, the chosen order would be

	Percentage of Total Service Provided to Other Support Departments
1. Plant Maintenance	20%
2. Information Systems	10%

◆ **Approach B.**   Rank support departments on the total dollars of service provided to other support departments. In our Castleford Engineering example, the chosen order would be

	Dollar Amount of Total Service Provided to Other Support Departments
1. Plant Maintenance (0.20 × $600,000)	$120,000
2. Information Systems (0.10 × $116,000)	11,600

Exhibit 14-8 shows the step-down method where the Plant Maintenance costs of $600,000 are allocated first: $120,000 is allocated to Information Systems (20% of $600,000); $180,000 to Machining (30% of $600,000); and $300,000 to Assembly (50% of $600,000). The costs in Information Systems now total $236,000 ($116,000 + $120,000 from the first-round allocation). This $236,000 amount is then allocated between the two operating departments—$209,778 ($\frac{8}{9}$ × $236,000) to Machining and $26,222 ($\frac{1}{9}$ × $236,000) to Assembly.

Under the step-down method, once a support department's costs have been allocated, no subsequent support department costs are allocated or circulated back to it. Thus, once the Plant Maintenance Department costs are allocated, they receive no further allocation from other (lower-ranked) support departments.

Reciprocal Allocation Method   The **reciprocal allocation method** allocates costs by explicitly including the mutual services provided among all support departments. Theoretically, the direct method and the step-down method are less accurate when support departments provide services to one another reciprocally. For example, the Plant Maintenance Department maintains all the computer equipment in the Information Systems Department. Similarly, Information Systems provides database support for Plant Maintenance. The reciprocal allocation method enables us to incorporate interdepartmental relationships *fully* into the support department cost allocations. That is, Plant Maintenance is allocated to Information Systems, and Information Systems is allocated to Plant Maintenance; each is allocated to the operating departments as well. Implementing the reciprocal allocation method requires three steps.[2]

---

[2]The reciprocal allocation method requires iteration. Iteration is a mathematical approach to solving a problem that requires an estimate of the answer to begin solving a system of linear equations. By repeatedly substituting improved estimates, the error term in the equations converges to zero, or the best answer.

EXHIBIT 14-8
Step-Down Method of Allocating Support Department Costs at Castleford Engineering for 2007

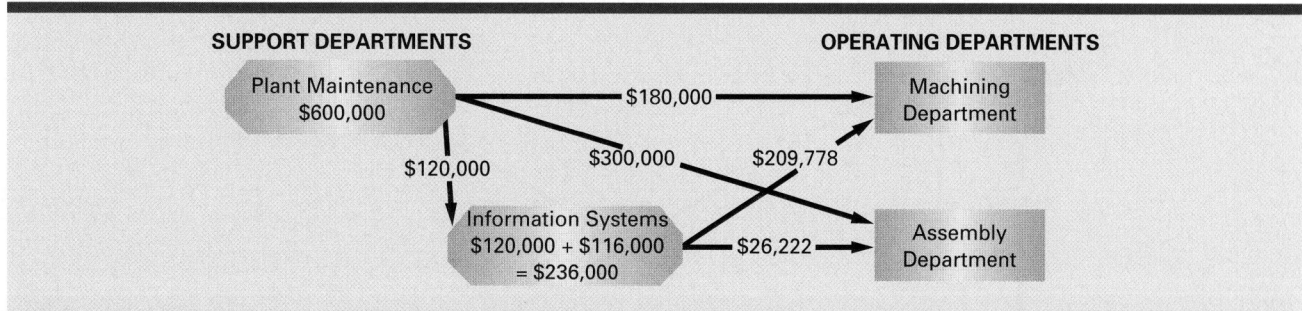

	A	B	C	D	E	F
1		**SUPPORT**		**OPERATING**		
2		**DEPARTMENTS**		**DEPARTMENTS**		
3		**Plant**	**Information**			
4		**Maintenance**	**Systems**	**Machining**	**Assembly**	**Total**
5	Budgeted manufacturing overhead costs before any interdepartment cost allocations	$600,000	$116,000	$400,000	$200,000	$1,316,000
6	Allocation of Plant Maintenance (2/10, 3/10, 5/10)ª	(600,000)	120,000	180,000	300,000	
7			236,000			
8	Allocation of Information Systems (8/9, 1/9)ᵇ		(236,000)	209,778	26,222	
9	Total budgeted manufacturing overhead of operating departments	$ 0	$ 0	$789,778	$526,222	$1,316,000
10						
11	ªBase is (1,600 + 2,400 + 4,000), or 8,000 hours; 1,600 ÷ 8,000 = 2/10; 2,400 ÷ 8,000 = 3/10; 4,000 ÷ 8,000 = 5/10. Instead of using fractions, we could have calculated a budgeted rate for allocating plant maintenance costs to the other departments as described in Exhibit 14-7.					
12	ᵇBase is (1,600 + 200), or 1,800 hours; 1,600 ÷ 1,800 = 8/9; 200 ÷ 1,800 = 1/9.					

◆ **Step 1:** *Express support department costs and reciprocal relationships in linear equation form.* Let PM be the *complete reciprocated costs* of Plant Maintenance and IS be the complete reciprocated costs of Information Systems. We then express the data in Exhibit 14-6 (p. 567) as follows:

$$\text{PM} = \$600{,}000 + 0.1\text{IS (1)}$$
$$\text{IS} = \$116{,}000 + 0.2\text{PM (2)}$$

The 0.1IS term in equation 1 is the percentage of the Information Systems work used by Plant Maintenance. The 0.2PM term in equation 2 is the percentage of the Plant Maintenance work used by Information Systems.

By **complete reciprocated cost** in equations 1 and 2, we mean the actual costs incurred by a support department plus a part of the costs of the other support departments that provide service to it. This complete reciprocated costs figure is sometimes called the **artificial costs** of the support department; it is always larger than the actual costs.

Complete reciprocated cost (artificial costs). The actual cost incurred by the service department plus a part of the costs of the other support departments that provide services to it; always larger than the actual cost.

◆ **Step 2:** *Solve the system of simultaneous equations to obtain the complete reciprocated costs of each support department.* Where there are two support departments, the following substitution approach can be used. Substituting equation 2 into equation 1:

$$\text{PM} = \$600{,}000 + [0.1(\$116{,}000 + 0.2\text{PM})]$$
$$\text{PM} = \$600{,}000 + \$11{,}600 + 0.02\text{PM}$$
$$0.98\text{PM} = \$611{,}600$$
$$\text{PM} = \$624{,}082$$

EXHIBIT 14-9
Reciprocal Method of Allocating Support Department Costs Using Linear Equations at Castleford Engineering for 2007

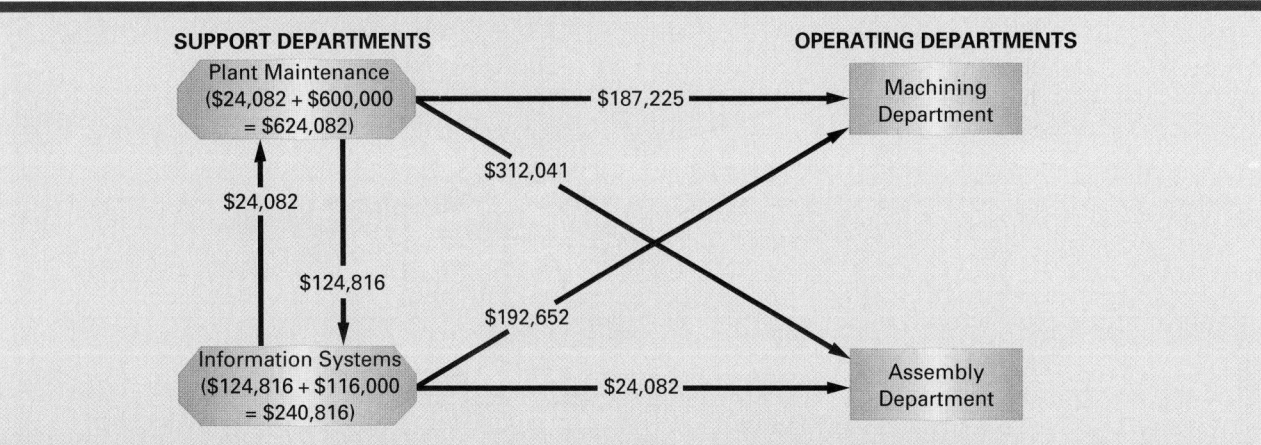

	B	C	D	E	F
A	**SUPPORT**		**OPERATING**		
	DEPARTMENTS		**DEPARTMENTS**		
	Plant	Information			
	Maintenance	**Systems**	**Machining**	**Assembly**	**Total**
5. Budgeted manufacturing overhead costs before any interdepartment cost allocations	$600,000	$116,000	$400,000	$200,000	$1,316,000
6. Allocation of Plant Maintenance (2/10, 3/10, 5/10)[a]	(624,082)	124,816	187,225	312,041	
7. Allocation of Information Systems (1/10, 8/10, 1/10)[b]	24,082	(240,816)	192,652	24,082	
8. Total budgeted manufacturing overhead of operating departments	$ 0	$ 0	$779,877	$536,123	$1,316,000
9.					
10. [a]Base is (1,600 + 2,400 + 4,000), or 8,000 hours; 1,600 ÷ 8,000 = 2/10; 2,400 ÷ 8,000 = 3/10; 4,000 ÷ 8,000 = 5/10					
11. [b]Base is (200 + 1,600 + 200), or 2,000 hours; 200 ÷ 2,000 = 1/10, 1,600 ÷ 2,000 = 8/10; 200 ÷ 2,000 = 1/10.					

Substituting into equation 2:

$$\text{IS} = \$116,000 + 0.2(\$624,082) = \$240,816$$

Where more than two support departments have reciprocal relationships, computer programs can be used to calculate the complete reciprocated costs of each support department.

◆ **Step 3:** *Allocate the complete reciprocated costs of each support department to all other departments (both support and operating departments) on the basis of the usage proportions (based on total units of service provided to all departments).* Consider the Information Systems Department, which has a complete reciprocated cost of $240,816. This amount would be allocated as follows:

To Plant Maintenance ($1/10 \times \$240,816$) =	$ 24,082
To Machining ($8/10 \times \$240,816$)	=	192,652
To Assembly ($1/10 \times \$240,816$)	=	24,082
Total		$240,816

Exhibit 14-9 presents summary data pertaining to the reciprocal method.

One source of confusion to some managers using the reciprocal cost allocation method is why the complete reciprocated costs of the support departments of $864,898 ($624,082 and $240,816 in Exhibit 14-9) exceed their budgeted amount of $716,000 ($600,000 and $116,000 in Exhibit 14-6). The excess of $148,898 ($24,082 for Plant Maintenance and $124,816 for Information Systems) is the total costs that are allocated among support departments. The total costs allocated to the operating departments under the reciprocal allocation method are still only $716,000.

Overview of Methods

Assume that the total budgeted overhead costs of each operating department in the example in Exhibits 14-7 to 14-9 are allocated to individual products on the basis of budgeted machine-hours for the Machining Department (4,000 hours) and budgeted direct labour-hours for the Assembly Department (3,000 hours). The budgeted overhead allocation rates associated with each support department allocation method (rounded to the nearest dollar) are

Support Department Cost Allocation Method	Total Budgeted Costs after Support Overhead Allocation of All Department Costs		Budgeted Overhead Rate per Hour for Product Costing Purposes	
	Machining	Assembly	Machining 4,000 Machine- Hours	Assembly 3,000 Labour- Hours
Direct	$728,111	$587,889	$182	$196
Step-down	789,778	526,222	197	175
Reciprocal	779,877	536,123	195	179

These differences in budgeted overhead rates with alternative support department cost-allocation methods can be important to managers. For example, consider a cost reimbursement contract that uses 100 machine-hours and 15 assembly labour-hours. The support department costs allocated to this contract would be

Direct	$21,140	$182 × 100 + $196 × 15
Step-down	22,325	$197 × 100 + $175 × 15
Reciprocal	22,185	$195 × 100 + $179 × 15

Use of the step-down method would result in the highest cost reimbursement to the contractor. To avoid disputes in cost-reimbursement contracts, managers should always clarify the method that will be used for allocation.

The reciprocal method, while conceptually preferable, is not widely used. The advantage of the direct and step-down methods is that they are relatively simple to compute and understand (see Global Surveys of Company Practice on page 572). However, with the ready availability of computer software to solve sets of simultaneous equations, the extra costs of using the reciprocal method will, in most cases, be minimal. Another advantage is that this method highlights the complete reciprocated costs of support departments and makes clear how these costs differ from either the budgeted or actual costs of the departments. This improved information leads to more informed decisions about what services of a support department to outsource.

For example, assume all of Castleford's support-department costs are variable over the period of a potential outsourcing contract. The third party bids to provide all the Information Technology (IT) services currently provided internally to Castleford. The bid price must be compared to the complete reciprocated costs for this service of $240,816, not the reported departmental cost of $116,000. Why? Because the complete reciprocated costs include the services Plant Maintenance provides to deliver 2,000 hours of computer time to all other departments at Castleford. The hourly rate for the complete reciprocated costs is $120.41 ($240,816 ÷ 2,000 hours). To be competitive, the third party must bid less than either the hourly rate of $120.41 or the total reciprocated cost of $240,816 to improve the company's operating income. In this case the relevant costs of shutting down IT Services are $116,000 plus $124,816 of Plant Maintenance Department costs because these will no longer be incurred to support IT Services, making the total relevant cost savings $240,816. Neither the direct nor step-down methods will provide this relevant information for outsourcing decisions.[3]

[3]Technical issues when using the reciprocal method in outsourcing decisions are discussed in R.S. Kaplan and A.A. Atkinson, *Advanced Management Accounting*, 3rd ed. (Upper Saddle River, N.J.: Prentice Hall, 1998, pp. 73–81).

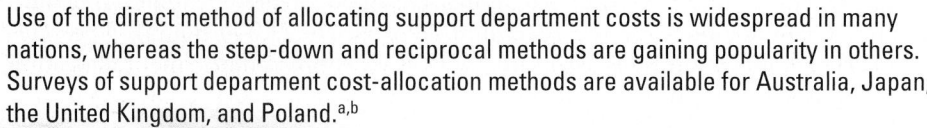

Allocation of Support Department Costs

Use of the direct method of allocating support department costs is widespread in many nations, whereas the step-down and reciprocal methods are gaining popularity in others. Surveys of support department cost-allocation methods are available for Australia, Japan, the United Kingdom, and Poland.[a,b]

Support Department Cost-Allocation Method	Australia	Japan	United Kingdom	Poland
1. Direct method	43%	58%	64%	19%
2. Step-down method	3%	27%	6%	39%
3. Reciprocal method	5%	10%	14%	33%
4. Other method	15%	1%	8%	6%
5. Not allocated	34%	4%	8%	3%

[a]Blaney, P., and I. Yokohama, "Comparative Analysis of Japanese and Australian Cost Accounting and Management Practices" (Working Paper, The University of Sydney, Australia, 1991).

[b]Szychta, A., "The Scope and Application of Management Accounting Methods in Polish Enterprises," *Management Accounting Research* (2002).

The more likely roadblocks to the reciprocal method being widely adopted are (1) many managers find it difficult to understand and (2) the numbers obtained by using the reciprocal method differ little, in some cases, from those obtained by using the direct or step-down method.

ALLOCATING COMMON COSTS

Common cost. The cost of operating a facility, operation, activity area, or like cost object that is shared by two or more users.

Stand-alone cost allocation method. Cost allocation method that allocates the common cost on the basis of each user's percentage of the total of the individual stand-alone costs.

We next consider two methods used to allocate common costs. A **common cost** is a cost of operating a facility, operation, activity, or like cost object that is shared by two or more users. Consider Jason Stevens, a graduating student in Winnipeg who has been invited to an interview with an employer in Halifax. The round-trip Winnipeg–Halifax airfare is $1,200. A week before leaving, Stevens is also invited to an interview with an employer in Montreal. The round-trip Winnipeg–Montreal fare is $800. Stevens decides to combine the two recruiting stops into a Winnipeg–Montreal–Halifax trip that will cost $1,500 in airfare. The $1,500 is a common cost that benefits both employers. Two methods for allocating this common cost between the two potential employers are now discussed: the stand-alone method and the incremental method.

Stand-Alone Cost Allocation Method

The **stand-alone cost allocation method** uses information pertaining to each cost object as a separate operating entity to determine the cost allocation weights. For the airfare common cost of $1,500, information about the separate (stand-alone) return airfares ($1,200 and $800) is used to determine the allocation weights:

$$\text{Halifax employer:} \quad \frac{\$1,200}{\$1,200 + \$800} \times \$1,500 = 0.60 \times \$1,500 = \$900$$

$$\text{Montreal employer:} \quad \frac{\$800}{\$800 + \$1,200} \times \$1,500 = 0.40 \times \$1,500 = \$600$$

Advocates of this method often emphasize an equity or fairness rationale. That is, fairness occurs because each employer bears a proportionate share of total costs in relation to their individual stand-alone costs.

Incremental Cost-Allocation Method

The **incremental cost-allocation method** ranks the individual cost objects and then uses this ranking to allocate costs among those cost objects. The first-ranked cost object is termed the *primary party* and is allocated costs up to its cost as a stand-alone entity. The second-ranked cost object is termed the *incremental party* and is allocated the additional cost that arises from there being two users instead of only the primary user. If there are more than two parties, the nonprimary parties will need to be ranked.

Incremental cost-allocation method. Cost allocation method requiring that one user be viewed as the primary party and the second user be viewed as the incremental party.

Consider Jason Stevens and his $1,500 airfare cost. Assume that the Halifax employer is viewed as the primary party. Stevens's rationale was that he had already committed to go to Halifax. The cost allocations would then be:

Party	Costs Allocated	Costs Remaining to Be Allocated to Other Parties
Halifax (primary)	$1,200	$300 ($1,500 − $1,200)
Montreal (incremental)	300	0

The Halifax employer is allocated the full Winnipeg–Halifax airfare. The nonallocated part of the total airfare is allocated to the Montreal employer. Had the Montreal employer been chosen as the primary party, the cost allocations would have been Montreal, $800 (the stand-alone Winnipeg–Montreal return airfare), and Halifax, $700 ($1,500 − $800). Where there are more than two parties, this method requires them to be ranked and the common costs allocated to those parties in the ranked sequence.

Under the incremental method, the primary party typically receives the highest allocation of the common costs. Not surprisingly, most users in common cost situations propose themselves as the incremental party. In some cases, the incremental party is a newly formed "organization" such as a new product line or a new sales territory. Chances for its short-term survival may be enhanced if it bears a relatively low allocation of common costs.

A caution is appropriate here as regards Stevens's cost-allocation options. His chosen method must be acceptable to each prospective employer. Indeed, some prospective employers may have guidelines that recruiting candidates must follow. For example, the Montreal employer may have a policy that the maximum reimbursable airfare is a seven-day advance booking price in economy class. If this amount is less than the amount that Stevens would receive under (say) the stand-alone method, then the employer's upper-limit guideline would govern how much could be allocated to that interviewer. Stevens should obtain approval before he purchases his ticket as to what cost-allocation method(s) each potential employer views as acceptable.

Disputes over how to allocate common costs are often encountered. The final section of this chapter discusses the role of cost data in contracting. This is also an area where disputes about cost allocation frequently arise.

COST ALLOCATIONS AND CONTRACTS

Many commercial contracts include clauses that require the use of cost accounting information. Examples include

OBJECTIVE 8

Explain the importance of explicit agreement between parties when reimbursement is based on costs incurred

1. A contract between the Department of National Defence and a company designing and assembling a new fighter plane. The price paid for the plane is based on the contractor's costs plus a preset fixed fee.

2. A research contract between a university and a government agency. The university is reimbursed its direct costs plus an overhead rate that is a percentage of direct costs.

3. A contract between an energy-consulting firm and a hospital. The consulting firm receives a fixed fee plus a share of the energy-cost savings arising from the consulting firm's recommendations.

Contract disputes arise with some regularity, often with respect to cost allocation. The areas of dispute between the contracting parties can be reduced by making the "rules of the game" explicit and in writing at the time the contract is signed. Such "rules of the game" include the definition of cost items allowed, the permissible cost-allocation bases, and how differences between budgeted and actual costs are to be handled.

Contracting

There are two main approaches to reimbursing costs as determined by a contract.

1. The *contractor is paid a set price without analysis of actual contract cost data*. This approach is used, for example, where there is competitive bidding, where there is adequate price competition, or where there is an established catalogue with prices quoted for items sold in substantial quantities to the general public.

2. The *contractor is paid after analysis of actual contract cost data*. In some cases, the contract will explicitly state that reimbursement is based on actual allowable costs plus a set fee. This arrangement is a cost-plus contract.

Fairness of Pricing

When uncertainty is high, as in many defence contracts involving new weapons and equipment, contracts are rarely subject to competitive bidding. Why? Because no contractor is willing to assume all the risk. Hence, market-based fixed-price setting fails to attract a contractor, or the resulting price is too outrageously high for the government. So the government assumes a major share of the risks. It negotiates contracts by using costs as a substitute for selling prices as ordinarily set by suppliers in open markets. In this contracting arena, a cost allocation may be difficult to defend on the basis of any cause-and-effect reasoning. Nonetheless, the contracting parties may still view it as a "reasonable" or "fair" means to help establish a selling price. Some costs become "allowable," but others are "unallowable." An **allowable cost** is a cost that the contract parties agree to include in the costs to be reimbursed. Some contracts specify how allowable costs are to be determined. For example, only economy-class airfares may be allowable in a contract. Other contracts identify cost categories that are nonallowable. For example, the costs of lobbying activities and the costs of alcoholic beverages are not allowable costs on some contracts.

Allowable cost. A cost that the parties to a contract agree to include in the costs to be reimbursed.

PROBLEM FOR SELF-STUDY

This problem illustrates how the costs of two corporate support departments are allocated to operating divisions using the dual-rate method. Fixed costs are allocated using budgeted costs and budgeted hours used by other departments. Variable costs are allocated using actual costs and actual hours used by other departments.

Computer Horizons budgets the following amounts for its two central corporate support departments (legal and human resources) in supporting each other and the two manufacturing divisions, the Laptop Division (LTD) and the Work Station Division (WSD):

	A	B	C	D	E	F
		SUPPORT		OPERATING		
1						
2		**Legal**	**Human Resources**			
3		**Department**	**Department**	**LTD**	**WSD**	**Total**
4	**BUDGETED USAGE**					
5	Legal (hours)	—	250	1,500	750	2,500
6	(Percentages)	—	10%	60%	30%	100%
7	Human Resources (hours)	2,500	—	22,500	25,000	50,000
8	(Percentages)	5%	—	45%	50%	100%
9						
10	**ACTUAL USAGE**					
11	Legal (hours)	—	400	400	1,200	2,000
12	(Percentages)	—	20%	20%	60%	100%
13	Human Resources (hours)	2,000	—	26,600	11,400	40,000
14	(Percentages)	5%	—	66.5%	28.5%	100%
15	Budgeted fixed overhead costs before any interdepartment cost allocations	$360,000	$475,000	—	—	$835,000
16	Actual variable overhead costs before any interdepartment cost allocations	$200,000	$600,000	—	—	$800,000

REQUIRED

What amount of support department costs for legal and human resources will be allocated to LTD and WSD using (a) the direct method, (b) the step-down method (allocating the Legal Department costs first), and (c) the reciprocal method using linear equations?

SOLUTION

Exhibit 14-7 presents the computations for allocating the fixed and variable support department costs. A summary of these costs follows:

	Laptop Division (LTD)	Work Station Division (WSD)
(a) Direct Method		
Fixed costs	$465,000	$370,000
Variable costs	470,000	330,000
	$935,000	$700,000
(b) Step-Down Method		
Fixed costs	$458,053	$376,947
Variable costs	488,000	312,000
	$946,053	$688,947
(c) Reciprocal Method		
Fixed costs	$462,513	$372,487
Variable costs	476,364	323,636
	$938,877	$696,123

EXHIBIT 14-10
Alternative Methods of Allocating Corporate Support Department Costs to Operating Divisions of Computer Horizons:
Dual-Rate Method

	A	B	C	D	E	F
		CORPORATE SUPPORT		**OPERATING**		
1						
2		**DEPARTMENTS**		**DIVISIONS**		
3			**Human**			
4		**Legal**	**Resources**			
5	**Allocation Method**	**Department**	**Department**	**LTD**	**WSD**	**Total**
6	**A. DIRECT METHOD**					
7	Fixed Costs	$360,000	$475,000			
8	Legal (1,500 ÷ 2,250; 750 ÷ 2,250)	(360,000)		$240,000	$120,000	
9	Human resources (22,500 ÷ 47,500; 25,000 ÷ 47,500)		(475,000)	225,000	250,000	
10	Corporate support dept. fixed costs allocated to operating divisions	$ 0	$ 0	$465,000	$370,000	$835,000
11	Variable Costs	$200,000	$600,000			
12	Legal (400 ÷ 1,600; 1,200 ÷ 1,600)	(200,000)		$ 50,000	$150,000	
13	Human resources (26,600 ÷ 38,000; 11,400 ÷ 38,000)		(600,000)	420,000	180,000	
14	Corporate support dept. variable costs allocated to operating divisions	$ 0	$ 0	$470,000	$330,000	$800,000
15	**B. STEP-DOWN METHOD**					
16	(Legal Department First)					
17	Fixed Costs	$360,000	$475,000			
18	Legal (250 ÷ 2,500; 1,500 ÷ 2,500; 750 ÷ 2,500)	(360,000)	36,000	$216,000	$108,000	
19	Human resources (22,500 ÷ 47,500; 25,000 ÷ 47,500)		(511,000)	242,053	268,947	
20	Corporate support dept. fixed costs allocated to operating divisions	$ 0	$ 0	$458,053	$376,947	$835,000
21	Variable Costs	$200,000	$600,000			
22	Legal (400 ÷ 2,000; 400 ÷ 2000; 1,200 ÷ 2000)	(200,000)	40,000	$ 40,000	$120,000	
23	Human resources (26,600 ÷ 38,000; 11,400 ÷ 38,000)		(640,000)	448,000	192,000	
24	Corporate support dept. variable costs allocated to operating divisions	$ 0	$ 0	$488,000	$312,000	$800,000
25	**C. RECIPROCAL METHOD**					
26	Fixed Costs	$360,000	$475,000			
27	Legal (250 ÷ 2,500; 1,500 ÷ 2,500; 750 ÷ 2,500)	(385,678)[a]	38,568	$231,407	$115,703	
28	Human resources (2,500 ÷ 50,000; 22,500 ÷ 50,000; 25,000 ÷ 50,000)	25,678	(513,568)[a]	231,106	256,784	
29	Corporate support dept. fixed costs allocated to operating divisions	$ 0	$ 0	$462,513	$372,487	$835,000
30	Variable Costs	$200,000	$600,000			
31	Legal (400 ÷ 2,000; 400 ÷ 2,000; 1,200 ÷ 2,000)	(232,323)[b]	46,465	$ 46,465	$139,393	
32	Human resources (2,000 ÷ 40,000; 26,600 ÷ 40,000; 11,400 ÷ 40,000)	32,323	(646,465)[b]	429,899	184,243	
33	Corporate support dept. variable costs allocated to operating divisions	$ 0	$ 0	$476,364	$323,636	$800,000
34						

35	[a]FIXED COSTS	[b]VARIABLE COSTS
36	Letting LF = Legal Department Fixed Costs, and HRF = Human Resources Department Fixed Costs, the simultaneous equations for the reciprocal method for fixed costs are	Letting LV = Legal Department Variable Costs, and HRV = Human Resources Department Variable Costs, the simultaneous equations for the reciprocal method for variable costs are
37	$LF = \$360,000 + 0.05\ HRF$	$LV = \$200,000 + 0.05\ HRV$
38	$HRF = \$475,000 + 0.10\ LF$	$HRV = \$600,000 + 0.20\ LV$
39	$LF = \$360,000 + 0.05\ (\$475,000 + 0.10\ LF)$	$LV = \$200,000 + 0.05\ (\$600,000 + 0.20\ LV)$
40	$LF = \$385,678$	$LV = \$232,323$
41	$HRF = \$475,000 + 0.10\ (\$385,678) = \$513,568$	$HRV = \$600,000 + 0.20\ (\$232,323) = \$646,465$

The following decision guidelines use a question-and-answer format to summarize the chapter's main points. Each decision presents a key question. The guideline is the answer to that question.

DECISIONS	GUIDELINES
1. What are the four purposes for allocating costs to cost objects?	Four purposes of cost allocation are (a) to provide information for economic decisions, (b) to motivate managers and employees, (c) to justify costs or compute reimbursement, and (d) to measure income and assets for reporting to external parties. Different cost allocations may be appropriate for different purposes.
2. What criteria should managers use to guide cost-allocation decisions?	Managers use the cause-and-effect and the benefits-received criteria to guide most cost-allocation decisions. Other criteria are fairness or equity and ability to bear.
3. What are the key decisions managers must make when collecting costs in indirect-cost pools?	Two key decisions related to indirect-cost pools are the number of indirect-cost pools to form and the individual cost items to be included in each cost pool to make homogeneous cost pools.
4. Should a manager use the single-rate or the dual-rate cost-allocation method?	The single-rate cost-allocation method allocates costs in each cost pool to cost objects using the same rate per unit of the single allocation base. In the dual-rate method, costs are grouped into a variable-cost pool and a fixed-cost pool; each pool uses a different cost-allocation base. If costs can be easily separated into variable and fixed costs, the dual-rate cost-allocation method should be used because it provides better information for making decisions.
5. What factors should a manager consider when deciding whether to use budgeted or actual cost-allocation rates?	When cost allocations are made using budgeted rates, managers of divisions to which costs are allocated face no uncertainty about the rates to be used in that budget period. In contrast, when actual rates are used for cost allocation, managers do not know the rates to be used until the end of the budget period. If actual rates are used, the efficiency of the supplier department affects the costs allocated to the user department.
6. What methods can a manager use to allocate costs of multiple support departments to operating departments?	The three methods are direct, step-down, and reciprocal. The direct method ignores any reciprocal services among support departments and allocates support department costs directly to operating departments. The step-down method allows for partial recognition of services among support departments. The reciprocal method provides full recognition of those services, but it is more complex than the direct or step-down methods.
7. What methods can a manager use to allocate common costs to two or more users?	Common costs are the costs of operating a facility, of an activity, or of a cost object that are shared by two or more users. The stand-alone cost allocation method uses information pertaining to each user of the cost object to determine cost allocation weights. The incremental cost-allocation method ranks individual users of the cost object and allocates common costs first to the primary user and then to the other incremental users.
8. How can contract disputes over reimbursements based on costs be reduced?	Make the cost-assignment rules as explicit as possible (and in writing). These rules should include details such as the allowable cost items, the acceptable cost allocation bases, and how differences between budgeted and actual costs are to be accounted for.

This chapter contains definitions of the following important terms:

allowable cost (p. 574)
artificial costs (p. 569)
common cost (p. 572)
complete reciprocated cost (p. 569)
core department (p. 565)
direct allocation method (p. 566)
direct method (p. 566)
dual-rate cost-allocation method (p. 562)
homogeneous cost pool (p. 561)
incremental cost-allocation method (p. 573)

operating department (p. 565)
production department (p. 565)
reciprocal allocation method (p. 568)
sequential allocation method (p. 568)
service department (p. 565)
single-rate cost-allocation method (p. 562)
stand-alone cost-allocation method (p. 572)
step allocation method (p. 568)
step-down allocation method (p. 568)
support department (p. 565)

ASSIGNMENT MATERIAL

QUESTIONS

14-1 "I am going to focus on the customers of my business and leave cost allocation issues to my accountant." Do you agree with this comment by a division president?

14-2 How can an individual cost item, such as the salary of a plant security guard, be both a direct cost and an indirect cost at the same time?

14-3 A given cost may be allocated for one or more purposes. List four purposes.

14-4 What criteria might be used to guide cost-allocation decisions? Which are the dominant criteria?

14-5 Identify six reasons why Canadian executives allocate costs to divisions and departments.

14-6 How do cost-benefit considerations affect choices by a company about the allocation of indirect costs to products, services, or customers?

14-7 Name three decisions managers face when designing the cost-allocation component of an accounting system.

14-8 Give examples of bases used to allocate corporate cost pools to the operating divisions of an organization.

14-9 Why might a manager prefer that budgeted rather than actual indirect cost-allocation rates be used for costs being allocated to her department from another department?

14-10 "To ensure unbiased cost allocations, fixed indirect costs should be allocated on the basis of estimated long-run use by user department managers." Do you agree? Why?

14-11 Distinguish among the three methods of allocating the costs of service departments to production departments.

14-12 What is the theoretically most defensible method for allocating service department costs?

14-13 Distinguish between two methods of allocating common costs.

14-14 What is one key way to reduce cost-allocation disputes arising with government contracts?

EXERCISES

14-15 Cost allocation in hospitals, alternative allocation criteria. Dave Meltzer went to Lake Tahoe for his annual winter vacation. Unfortunately, he broke his ankle severely while skiing and had to spend two days at the Tahoe General Hospital. Meltzer's insurance company received a $4,800 bill for his two-day stay. One item that caught Meltzer's eye was a $10.62 charge for a roll of cotton. Meltzer was a salesman for Johnson & Johnson and knew that the cost to the hospital of the roll of cotton would be in the $2.20 to $3 range. He asked for a breakdown of how the $10.62 charge was derived. The accounting office of the hospital sent him the following information:

a. Invoiced cost of cotton roll	$ 2.30
b. Processing of paperwork for purchase	0.50
c. Supplies room management fee	0.60
d. Operating-room and patient-room handling charge	1.50
e. Administrative hospital costs	1.00
f. Research-related recoupment	0.50
g. Malpractice insurance costs	1.10
h. Cost of treating uninsured patients	2.62
i. Profit component	0.50
Total	$10.62

Meltzer believes the overhead charge is obscene. He comments, "There was nothing I could do about it. When they come in and dab your stitches, it's not as if you can say, 'Keep your cotton roll. I brought my own.' "

REQUIRED
1. Compute the overhead rate Tahoe General Hospital charged on the cotton roll.
2. What criteria might Tahoe General use to justify allocation of each of the overhead items (b) through (i) in the preceding list? Examine each item separately, and use the allocation criteria listed in Exhibit 14-2 (p. 555) in your answer.
3. What should Meltzer do about the $10.62 charge for the cotton roll?

14-16 Single-rate versus dual-rate cost allocation methods. (W. Crum, adapted) The Ontario Company has a power plant designed and built to serve its three factories. Data for 2007 are as follows:

	Usage in Kilowatt-Hours	
Factory	Budget	Actual
Mississauga	100,000	80,000
Cambridge	60,000	120,000
Burlington	40,000	40,000

Actual fixed costs of the power plant were $1.1 million in 2007; actual variable costs, $2.2 million.

REQUIRED
1. Compute the amount of power costs that would be allocated to Cambridge using a single-rate method for both budgeted and actual usage.
2. Compute the amount of power costs that would be allocated to Cambridge using a dual-rate method for both budgeted and actual usage.

14-17 Single-rate versus dual-rate allocation methods, support department. The power plant that services all manufacturing departments of West Engineering has a budget for the coming year. This budget has been expressed in the following terms on a monthly basis:

Manufacturing Departments	Needed at Practical Capacity Production Level* (Kilowatt-Hours)	Average Expected Monthly Usage (Kilowatt-Hours)
Rockford	10,000	8,000
Peoria	20,000	9,000
Hammond	12,000	7,000
Kankakee	8,000	6,000
Totals	50,000	30,000

*This factor was the most influential in planning the size of the power plant.

The expected monthly costs for operating the department during the budget year are $17,500: $7,000 variable and $10,500 fixed.

REQUIRED
1. Assume that a single cost pool is used for the power plant costs. What dollar amounts will be allocated to each manufacturing department? Use (a) practical capacity and (b) average expected monthly usage as the allocation bases.
2. Assume a dual-rate method; separate cost pools for the variable and fixed costs are used. Variable costs are allocated on the basis of expected monthly usage. Fixed costs are allocated on the basis of practical capacity. What dollar amounts will be allocated to each manufacturing department? Why might you prefer the dual-rate method?

14-18 Cost allocation to divisions. Rembrandt Hotel and Casino is situated in Ontario. The complex includes a 300-room hotel, a casino, and a restaurant. As Rembrandt's new controller, you are asked to recommend the basis used for allocating fixed overhead costs to the three divisions in 2007. You are presented with the following income statement for the year 2007:

	Hotel	Restaurant	Casino
Revenue	$16,625,000	$5,456,000	$12,540,000
Direct costs	10,019,260	3,949,172	4,448,768
Segment margin	$ 6,605,740	$1,506,828	$ 8,091,232

You are also given the following data on the three segments:

	Hotel	Restaurant	Casino
Square metres	80,000	16,000	64,000
# of employees	200	50	250

You may choose to allocate costs based on direct costs, floor space (in square metres), or the number of employees. Total fixed overhead for 2007 was $14,550,000.

REQUIRED

1. Calculate segment margins in percentage terms before allocating fixed overhead costs.
2. Allocate indirect costs to the three divisions using each of the three allocation bases suggested. Calculate segment margins in dollar and percentage terms.
3. Discuss the results. What is your preferred basis for allocating indirect costs to the divisions?
4. Would you recommend shutting any of the three divisions (and possibly reallocating resources to other divisions) as a result of your analysis? If so, which division would you close, and why?

14-19 Single-rate cost allocation method, budgeted versus actual costs and quantities. Fruit Juice, Inc., processes orange juice at its East Miami plant and grapefruit juice at its West Miami plant. It purchases oranges and grapefruit from growers' cooperatives in the Orlando area. It owns its own trucking fleet. Both Miami plants are the same distance from Orlando. The trucking fleet is run as a cost centre. Each Miami plant is billed for the direct costs and the indirect costs of each return trip.

The trucking fleet costs include direct costs (labour costs of drivers, fuel, and toll charges) and indirect costs. Indirect costs include wear and tear on tires and the vehicles, leasing costs, insurance, and state registration fees.

At the start of 2006, the Orange Juice Division budgeted for 150 Orlando to East Miami truck trips, while the Grapefruit Juice Division budgeted for 100 Orlando to West Miami truck trips. On the basis of these 250 budgeted trips, the Trucking Fleet Division budgeted trucking fleet indirect costs of $590,000. The following actual results occurred for 2007:

Trucking fleet indirect costs	$660,000
Trips to East Miami plant	200
Trips to West Miami plant	100

The Trucking Fleet Division uses a single-rate method when allocating indirect trucking costs. The costs charged to each plant equal this rate times the actual number of trips made.

REQUIRED

1. What is the indirect-cost rate per truck trip when (a) budgeted costs and budgeted quantities (trips) are used and (b) actual costs and actual quantities (trips) are used? What dollar amount will be allocated to the Orange Juice Division and the Grapefruit Juice Division for (a) and for (b)?
2. From the viewpoint of the Orange Juice Division, what are the effects of using budgeted costs/quantities rather than actual costs/quantities?

14-20 Dual-rate cost allocation method, budgeted versus actual costs and quantities (continuation of 14-19). Fruit Juice, Inc., decides to examine the effect of using a dual-rate method for allocating indirect trucking costs to each truck trip. At the start of 2007, the budgeted indirect costs were

Variable indirect costs per trip	$ 1,500
Fixed indirect costs	$215,000

The actual results for the 300 round trips made in 2007 were

Variable indirect costs	$465,000
Fixed indirect costs	195,000
	$660,000

Assume all other information to be the same as in Exercise 14-19.

REQUIRED

1. What is the indirect cost per truck trip with a dual-rate method when (a) variable indirect costs are allocated using the budgeted variable indirect rate times actual trips made and (b) fixed indirect costs are allocated using the budgeted fixed indirect cost rate times budgeted trips to be made? What dollar amount will be allocated to the Orange Juice Division and the Grapefruit Juice Division for (a) and for (b)?
2. Compare the results for requirement 1 with that in requirements 1(a) and (b) for Exercise 14-19. From the viewpoint of the Orange Juice Division, what are the effects of using a dual-rate method rather than a single-rate method?

14-21 Direct and step-down allocation. e-books is an online book retailer. The company has four departments. The two revenue-producing departments are corporate sales and consumer sales. The two support departments are administrative (human resources, accounting, and so on) and information systems (IS). Each of the sales departments conducts merchandising and marketing operations independently.

The following data for September 2007 will assist you in allocating costs to the different departments:

	Revenue	# of Employees	Processing Time Used
Corporate Sales	$1,334,200	42	1,920
Consumer Sales	$ 667,100	28	1,600
Administrative	—	14	320
IS	—	21	1,120

Costs incurred in each of the four departments for September 2007 are as follows:

Corporate Sales	$998,770
Consumer Sales	490,360
Administrative	73,200
Information Systems	234,900

The administrative support percentages are based on head count. The information systems support percentages are based on processing time used.

REQUIRED

1. Allocate the support department costs to the revenue-producing departments using the direct method.
2. Develop appropriate overhead allocation rates for the four departments. Rank the support departments on the percentage of services rendered to other support departments (using September departmental costs). Use this ranking and your overhead rates to allocate support costs based on the step-down allocation method.
3. Could you have ranked the support departments differently? If so, how else could you rank the support departments? Had you done so in this problem, would the allocations have changed?

14-22 Reciprocal cost allocation (continuation of 14-21). Consider e-books again. The controller reads a widely used text that states that "the reciprocal method is conceptually the most defensible." He seeks your assistance.

REQUIRED

1. Describe the key features of the reciprocal cost-allocation method.
2. Allocate the support department costs (administrative and information systems) to the two revenue-producing departments using the reciprocal allocation method. Use five decimals to reduce rounding error.
3. Under what conditions is the reciprocal method more accurate than the direct and step-down methods? In the case presented in this problem, which method would you recommend? Why?

14-23 Contracting, cost allocations. Sprout Consulting has been working with Gemini Widgets to improve the widget production process. In the year ended December 31, 2006, Gemini produced and sold 450,000 widgets at $5.70 per widget. Variable costs were $2.90 per widget, and total fixed manufacturing costs were $1,350,000.

As a result of Sprout's analysis, Gemini has been able to produce 12% more widgets in 2007. Gemini has also been able to reduce fixed costs by 25% and variable costs by 10%. The average selling price remained constant from 2006 to 2007.

Sprout's contract was as follows:

◆ a $50,000 fixed fee
◆ 10% of the costs saved on production of up to 450,000 widgets
◆ $0.10 on every widget produced over and above the year 2006 quantity of 450,000 regardless of any cost savings being achieved.

REQUIRED

1. Was Gemini Widgets profitable in 2006? What was Gemini's net income (loss)?
2. Calculate Gemini's budgeted fixed cost per widget in 2006. What did you use for the budgeted denominator level? What was the total cost per widget?
3. Repeat requirements 1 and 2 for 2007. Do not take Sprout's remuneration into account.
4. What is Sprout's total remuneration for this assessment? What is Gemini's operating income after deducting Sprout's remuneration?

14-24 Allocation of common costs. Sam, Sari, and Tony are members of the Toronto Fire Department. They share a penthouse apartment that has a lounge room with the latest 50" TV. Tony owns the apartment, its furniture, and the 50" TV. He can subscribe to a cable television company that has the following packages available:

Package	Rate per Month
A. Basic news	$33
B. Premium movies	26
C. Premium sports	31
D. Basic news and premium movies	51
E. Basic news and premium sports	55
F. Premium movies and premium sports	49
G. Basic news, premium movies, and premium sports	71

Sam is a TV news junkie, has average interest in movies, and zero interest in sports ("They're overpaid jocks"). Sari is a movie buff, likes sports, and avoids the news ("It's all depressing anyway"). Tony is into sports in a big way, has average interest in news, and zero interest in movies ("I always fall asleep before the end"). They all agree that the purchase of the $71 total package is a "win-win-win" situation.

Each works on a different eight-hour shift at the fire station, so conflicts in viewing are minimal.

REQUIRED
1. What criteria might be used to guide the choice about how to allocate the $71 monthly cable fee among Sam, Sari, and Tony?
2. Outline three methods of allocating the $71 among Sam, Sari, and Tony.

14-25 Allocation of travel costs. Joan Ernst, a graduating student at a university in Vancouver, received an invitation to visit a prospective employer in Halifax. A few days later, she received an invitation from a prospective employer in Toronto. She decided to combine her visits, travelling from Vancouver to Halifax, Halifax to Toronto, and Toronto to Vancouver.

Ernst received job offers from both companies. On her return, she decided to accept the offer in Toronto. She was puzzled about how to allocate her travel costs between the two employers. She gathered the following data:

Regular Round-Trip Fares with No Stopovers

Vancouver to Halifax	$1,500
Vancouver to Toronto	$1,200

Ernst paid $1,900 for her three-leg flight (Vancouver to Halifax, Halifax to Toronto, Toronto to Vancouver). In addition, she paid $30 for a limousine from her home to Vancouver Airport and another $30 for a limousine from Vancouver Airport to her home when she returned.

REQUIRED
1. How should Ernst allocate the $1,900 airfare between the employers in Halifax and Toronto? Show the actual amounts you would allocate, and give reasons for your allocations.
2. Repeat requirement 1 for the $60 limousine charges at the Vancouver end of her travels.

14-26 Support department cost allocation; direct and step-down methods. Phoenix Consulting provides outsourcing services and advice to both government and corporate clients. For costing purposes, Phoenix classifies its departments into two support departments (Administrative/Human Resources and Information Systems) and two operating departments (Government Consulting and Corporate Consulting). For the first quarter of 2007, Phoenix incurs the following costs in its four departments:

Administrative/Human Resources (A/HR)	$ 620,000
Information Systems (IS)	$ 2,420,000
Government Consulting (GOVT)	$ 8,776,000
Corporate Consulting (CORP)	$12,472,000

The actual level of support relationships among the four departments for the first quarter of 2007 was

Supplied by	Used by			
	A/HR	IS	GOVT	CORP
A/HR	—	25%	40%	35%
IS	10%	—	30%	60%

The Administrative/Human Resource support percentages are based on head count. The Information Systems support percentages are based on actual hours of computer time used.

REQUIRED

1. Allocate the two support department costs to the two operating departments using the following methods.
   a. Direct method
   b. Step-down method (allocate Administrative/Human Resources first)
   c. Step-down method (allocate Information Systems first)
2. Compare and explain differences in the support department costs allocated to each operating department.
3. Identify three criteria that could determine the sequence for allocating support departments using the step-down method.

14-27 Support department cost allocation, reciprocal method (continuation of 14-26). Assume the same facts as in Exercise 14-26.

REQUIRED

1. Allocate the two support department costs to the two operating departments using the reciprocal method.
2. Compare and explain differences in requirement 1 with those in requirement 1 of Exercise 14-26. Which method do you prefer?

Excel Application For students who wish to practise their spreadsheet skills, the following is a step-by-step approach to creating an Excel spreadsheet to use repeated iterations to work requirement 1 of Exercise 14-26.

Step-by-Step

1. Open up a new spreadsheet. At the top, create an "Original Data" section for the department-cost and support relationship data provided by Phoenix Consulting. Enter the department costs for A/HR, IS, GOVT, and CORP and the level of support relationships (expressed in %) among these departments in exactly the same format as presented above.

(Program your spreadsheet to perform all necessary calculations. Do not "hard-code" any amounts, such as your cost allocation, requiring addition, subtraction, multiplication, or division operations.)

2. Skip two rows and create a section "Cost Allocation—Reciprocal Method" using a similar format to Exhibit 14-9 (p. 570). Create columns for the support departments (A/HR and IS), the operating departments (GOVT and CORP), and for "Totals." Create rows for "Department Costs Before Cost Allocations, 1st Allocation of A/HR Costs, 1st Allocation of IS Costs, 2nd Allocation of A/HR Costs, and 2nd Allocation of IS Costs." You will add more rows as more iterations are needed.

3. Use the department cost data from your Original Data section to fill in the row for Department Costs Before Cost Allocations. Next, use the data on the level of support relationships among the departments from your Original Data section to calculate the 1st and 2nd allocations of A/HR and IS costs. Continue to add rows for further iterations of cost allocations until the costs remaining to be allocated are sufficiently close to zero, at which time allocate any costs remaining in a support department to CORP. When done, include calculations on separate rows for "Total Costs of Operating Departments" and "Total Support Department Costs Allocated to Operating Departments."

4. *Check the accuracy of your spreadsheet:* Go to your Original Data section and change the level of support relationships between the A/HR department and the IS, GOVT, and CORP departments from 25%, 40%, 35% to 25%, 50%, 25%. If you programmed your spreadsheet correctly, total costs (after all cost allocations) in the GOVT department should change to $1,805,641.03.

14-28 Support department cost allocation. (CMA) Computer Information Services is a computer software consulting company. Its three major functional areas are computer programming, information systems consulting, and software training. Carol Birch, a pricing analyst in the Accounting Department, must develop total costs for the functional areas. These costs will guide pricing for new contracts. In computing these costs, Birch is considering two different methods of allocating support department costs—the direct method and the step-down method. Birch assembled the following data on budgeted costs from its two support departments, the Information Systems Department and the Facilities Department.

| | Support Departments | | Operating Departments | | | |
	Information Systems	Facilities	Computer Programming	Consulting	Software Training	Total
Budgeted costs	$51,000	$26,000	$76,000	$111,000	$86,000	$350,000
Information Systems (hours)	—	300	1,200	600	900	3,000
Facilities (thousands of square metres)	200	—	400	600	800	2,000

REQUIRED

1. Allocate the support department costs in Information Systems and Facilities using (a) the direct method and (b) the step-down method (Information Systems first).
2. Explain to Birch any differences between the methods. Which method should she use?

PROBLEMS

14-29 **Allocating costs of support departments; dual rates; direct, step-down, and reciprocal methods.** Magnum T.A., Inc., specializes in the assembly and installation of high-quality security systems for the home and business segments of the market. The four departments at its highly automated state-of-the-art assembly plant are as follows:

Service Departments	Assembly Departments
Engineering Support	Home Security Systems
Information Systems Support	Business Security Systems

The budgeted level of service relationships at the start of the year was

| | Used by | | | |
Supplied by	Engineering Support	Information Systems Support	Home Security Systems	Business Security Systems
Engineering Support	—	0.10	0.40	0.50
Information Systems Support	0.20	—	0.30	0.50

The actual level of service relationships for the year was

| | Used by | | | |
Supplied by	Engineering Support	Information Systems Support	Home Security Systems	Business Security Systems
Engineering Support	—	0.15	0.30	0.55
Information Systems Support	0.25	—	0.15	0.60

Magnum collects fixed costs and variable costs of each department in separate cost pools. The actual costs (in thousands) in each pool for the year were

	Fixed-Cost Pool	Variable-Cost Pool
Engineering Support	$2,800	$8,500
Information Systems Support	8,100	3,750

Fixed costs are allocated on the basis of the budgeted level of service. Variable costs are allocated on the basis of the actual level of service.

The support department costs allocated to each assembly department are allocated to products on the basis of units assembled. The units assembled in each department during the year were

Home Security Systems	7,950 units
Business Security Systems	3,750 units

REQUIRED

1. Allocate the support department costs to the assembly departments using a dual-rate system and (a) the direct method, (b) the step-down method (allocate Information Systems Support first), (c) the step-down method (allocate Engineering Support first), and (d) the reciprocal method. Present results in a format similar to that of Exhibit 14-10 (p. 576).
2. Compare the support department costs allocated to each Home Security Systems unit assembled and each Business Security Systems unit assembled under (a), (b), (c), and (d) in requirement 1.
3. What factors might explain the very limited adoption of the reciprocal method by many organizations?

14-30 Support department cost allocations; single-department cost pools; direct, step-down, and reciprocal methods. The Manes Company has two products. Product 1 is manufactured entirely in Department X. Product 2 is manufactured entirely in Department Y. To produce these two products, the Manes Company has two support departments: A (a materials-handling department) and B (a power-generating department).

An analysis of the work done by Departments A and B in a typical period is as follows:

	Used by			
Supplied by	**A**	**B**	**X**	**Y**
A	—	100	250	150
B	500	—	100	400

The work done in Department A is measured by the direct labour-hours of materials-handling time. The work done in Department B is measured by the kilowatt-hours of power.

The budgeted costs of the support departments for the coming year are

	Department A	**Department B**
Variable indirect labour and indirect materials costs	$ 72,000	$12,000
Supervision	10,000	10,000
Amortization	20,000	20,000
	$102,000	$42,000

The budgeted costs of the operating departments for the coming year are $1,500,000 for Department X and $800,000 for Department Y.

Supervisory costs are salary costs. Amortization in B is the straight-line amortization of power-generation equipment in its nineteenth year of an estimated 25-year useful life; it is old but well-maintained equipment.

REQUIRED

1. What are the allocations of costs of support Departments A and B to operating Departments X and Y using the direct method, two different sequences of the step-down method, and the reciprocal method of reallocation?
2. The power company has offered to supply all the power needed by the Manes Company and to provide all the services of the present Power Department. The cost of this service will be $42 per kilowatt-hour of power. Should Manes accept? Explain.

14-31 Allocating costs of support departments; step-down and direct methods. The Central Valley Company has prepared departmental overhead budgets for normal volume levels before allocations, as follows:

Support departments:		
Building and grounds	$11,000	
Human resources	1,100	
General plant administration	28,699	
Cafeteria (subsidy for operating loss)	1,804	
Storeroom	2,937	
Total support departments		$ 45,540
Operating departments:		
Machining	$38,170	
Assembly	53,790	
Total operating departments		91,960
Total for both departments		$137,500

Management has decided that the most sensible inventory costs are achieved by using individual departmental overhead rates. These rates are developed after appropriate support department costs are allocated to operating departments. Bases for allocation are to be selected from the following:

Department	Direct Manufacturing Labour-Hours	Number of Employees	Square Metres of Floor Space Occupied	Manufacturing Labour-Hours	Total Number of Requisitions
Building and grounds	0	0	0	0	0
Human resources*	0	0	2,200	0	0
General plant administration	0	35	7,700	0	0
Cafeteria	0	10	4,400	1,100	0
Storeroom	0	5	7,700	1,100	0
Machining	5,000	50	33,000	8,800	2,000
Assembly	15,000	100	55,000	18,700	1,000
Total	20,000	200	110,000	29,700	3,000

*Basis used is number of employees.

REQUIRED

1. Using a worksheet, allocate support department costs by the step-down method. Develop overhead rates per direct manufacturing labour-hour for machining and assembly. Allocate the support departments in the order given in this problem. Use the allocation base for each support department you think is most appropriate.
2. Using the direct method, rework requirement 1.
3. Based on the following information about two jobs, determine the total overhead costs for each job by using rates developed in requirements 1 and 2.

	Direct Manufacturing Labour-Hours	
	Machining	Assembly
Job 88	18	2
Job 89	3	17

14-32 Cost allocation and motivation. Environ Petroleum Company is engaged in all phases of exploring, refining, and marketing of oil and petrochemical products. To ensure full compliance with all applicable laws, the company has a legal department staffed by lawyers who have expertise in a variety of legal areas. The top management of Environ wants to motivate all operating managers to seek legal counsel from the in-house lawyers whenever necessary to avoid violation of any laws during the course of its operations.

Currently, users of the Legal Department are allocated cost at a $400 standard hourly rate based on actual usage. The chief financial officer has suggested that department managers would make more use of the Legal Department services, and thus avoid potential legal pitfalls, if the service were provided free of cost to their departments.

REQUIRED

Comment on the proposal of the chief financial officer. Do you have any alternative suggestion(s)?

14-33 Cost allocation to divisions. Lenzig Corporation has three divisions: Fibres, Paper, and Pulp. As Lenzig's new controller, you are reviewing the basis to be used for allocating fixed overhead costs to the three divisions in 2007. The following information is available for 2007:

	Pulp	Paper	Fibres
Revenue	$8,500,000	$17,500,000	$24,000,000
Administrative costs	$1,300,000	$ 1,900,000	$ 3,100,000
Number of employees	300	250	450
Floor space (square metres)	30,000	24,000	66,000
Segment margin	$3,200,000	$ 7,100,000	$ 9,700,000

In the past, Lenzig has allocated fixed overhead costs to the division using segment margin percentages. A review of the fixed overhead costs indicates that they consist of the following:

Human resource management	$1,800,000
Facility	2,700,000
Corporate administration	4,500,000
Total	$9,000,000

After considering the nature of the fixed-cost items, you decide to make the allocations in 2007 using the following bases:

Human resource management	Number of employees
Facility	Floor space
Corporate administration	Divisional administrative costs

REQUIRED

1. Allocate 2007 indirect costs to the three divisions using segment margin percentages.
2. Allocate 2007 indirect costs to the three divisions using the bases you have selected.
3. Discuss the reason(s) why your approach is preferable.

14-34 Cost allocation downward demand spiral. Diversified Inc. is an industrial conglomerate operating in Western Canada. The conglomerate runs 14 companies in a diverse range of businesses from its corporate headquarters in Vancouver. Diversified Inc. also runs a cleaning and maintenance company, Clean Shop Inc., from headquarters in Calgary. Clean Shop provides cleaning and maintenance services to all of Diversified's facilities.

Clean Shop has the capacity to clean and maintain 5,000,000 square metres (m^2) on a daily basis. Total floor space for all of Diversified's facilities as of September 1, 2007, is 2,250,000 m^2 (assume this is average floor space for 2007 in what follows). Bubba Smith, Clean Shop's CEO, prepares the 2008 budget based on growth estimates from corporate headquarters. Bubba estimates an average 2,500,000 m^2 will be cleaned and maintained daily during 2008. Facilities are operational 360 days a year.

For the six months ended June 30, 2007, Clean Shop incurred total costs of $64,800,000. Fixed costs were $16,700,000. Bubba budgets fixed costs of $36,500,000 for 2008. Variable costs are projected to remain at 2007 levels. Bubba figures out what he will charge the subsidiary companies in 2008 (per square metre). He learns that, on average, competitors are charging $0.14 per square metre for similar jobs.

As the year 2007 draws to a close, Johnson Almighty, CEO of Diversified, announces that all of Diversified's units will operate as profit centres beginning January 1, 2008. Toward the end of December, Bubba learns that six of the 14 companies have decided to employ external third-party cleaning and maintenance services. The six companies account for 40% of projected 2008 floor space.

REQUIRED

1. What were Clean Shop's variable costs per square metre in the first half of 2007? What are fixed costs allocated per square metre?
2. Before Almighty's announcement, and assuming Bubba does not plan on margins, how much (per square metre) does Bubba plan to charge the subsidiary companies in 2008? Is this rate competitive? (using estimated square metres in the denominator level)
3. Using the cost-allocation techniques studied in this chapter, what accounting change could Bubba make to come up with a competitive rate?

4. Consider Almighty's announcement. How much must Bubba charge the remaining companies per square metre to break even? How much will Clean Shop lose if Bubba does not change the rate per square metre as calculated in requirement 2? By how much would Bubba have to reduce capacity at Clean Shop to make the business competitive *and* break even? (Assume that any reduction in capacity will bring about a proportional reduction in fixed costs.)

5. Why was 2007 capacity at Clean Shop more than double Diversified's needs? Was Bubba operating in the best interests of Diversified? Explain how surplus capacity at Clean Shop may have affected Diversified's bottom line. What were the underlying accounting practices that allowed such negligence to occur?

14-35 Allocation of central corporate costs to divisions. Dusty Rhodes, the corporate controller of the Richfield Oil Company, is about to make a presentation to the senior corporate executives and the top managers of its four divisions. These divisions are

a. Oil and Gas Upstream (the exploration, production, and transportation of oil and gas)
b. Oil and Gas Downstream (the refining and marketing of oil and gas)
c. Chemical Products
d. Copper Mining

Under the existing internal accounting system, costs incurred at central corporate headquarters are collected in a single pool and allocated to each division on the basis of the actual revenues of each division. The central corporate costs (in millions) for the most recent year are as follows:

Interest on debt	$2,300
Corporate salaries	100
Accounting and control	100
General marketing	100
Legal	100
R&D	200
Public affairs	208
Human resources and payroll	192
	$3,300

"Public affairs" includes the public relations staff, the lobbyists, and the sizable donations Richfield makes to numerous charities and not-for-profit institutions.

Summary data (in millions) related to the four divisions for the most recent year are as follows:

	Oil and Gas Upstream	Oil and Gas Downstream	Chemical Products	Copper Mining	Total
Revenue	$ 7,000	$16,000	$4,000	$3,000	$30,000
Operating costs	$ 3,000	$15,000	$3,800	$3,200	$25,000
Operating income	$ 4,000	$ 1,000	$ 200	$ (200)	$ 5,000
Identifiable assets	$14,000	$ 6,000	$3,000	$2,000	$25,000
Number of employees	9,000	12,000	6,000	3,000	30,000

The top managers of each division share in a divisional income bonus pool. Divisional income is defined as operating income less allocated central corporate costs.

Rhodes is about to propose a change in the method used to allocate central corporate costs. He favours collecting these costs in four separate pools:

◆ **Cost pool 1.** Allocated using identifiable assets of division
Cost Item: Interest on debt
◆ **Cost pool 2.** Allocated using revenue of division
Cost Items: Corporate salaries, accounting and control, general marketing, legal, R&D
◆ **Cost pool 3.** Allocated using operating income (if positive) of division, with only divisions with positive operating income included in the allocation base
Cost Item: Public affairs
◆ **Cost pool 4.** Allocated using number of employees in division
Cost Item: Human resources and payroll

REQUIRED

1. What purposes might be served by the allocation of central corporate costs to each division at Richfield Oil?
2. Compute the divisional income of each of the four divisions when central corporate costs are allocated using revenue of each division.

3. Compute the divisional income of each of the four divisions when central corporate costs are allocated through the four cost pools.

4. What are the strengths and weaknesses of Rhodes's proposal relative to the existing single-pool method?

14-36 Division managers' reactions to the allocation of central corporate costs to divisions (continuation of 14-35). Dusty Rhodes presents his proposal for the use of four separate cost pools to allocate central corporate costs to the divisions. The comments of the top managers of each of the four divisions include the following:

a. By the top manager of the Oil and Gas Upstream Division: "The multiple-pool method of Rhodes's is absurd. We are the only division generating a substantial positive cash flow, and this is ignored in the proposed (and indeed the existing) system. We could pay off any debt very quickly if we were not a cash cow for the rest of the dog divisions in Richfield Oil."

b. By the top manager of the Oil and Gas Downstream Division: "Rhodes's proposal is the first sign that the money we spend in the accounting and control function at corporate headquarters is justified. The proposal is fair and equitable."

c. By the top manager of the Chemical Products Division: "I oppose any cost-allocation method. Last year I was the only major player in the chemical industry to show a positive operating income. We are operating at the bare-bones level. Last year I saved $300,000 by making everyone travel economy class. This policy created a lot of dissatisfaction, but we finally managed to get it accepted. Then at the end of the year we get a charge of $400 million for corporate central costs. What's the point of our division economy drives when they get swamped by allocations of corporate fat?"

d. By the top manager of Copper Mining Division: "I should probably get concerned, but frankly I view it all as bookkeeping entries. If we were in the black, certain aspects would really infuriate me. For instance, why should corporate R&D costs be allocated to the Copper Division? The only research corporate does for us is how to best prepare our division for divestiture."

REQUIRED

How should Rhodes respond to these comments?

14-37 Cost allocation, monthly reports (CMA, revised). Bulldog Inc. is a large manufacturing company that runs its own electrical power plant from the excess steam produced in its manufacturing process. Power is provided to two production departments—Department A and Department B. The capacity of the power plant was originally determined by the expected peak demands of the two production departments. The expected average usage and peak demands are, respectively, 60 percent and 66,000,000 kilowatt hours (kwh) for Department A and 40 percent and 44,000,000 kwh for Department B.

The budgeted monthly costs of producing power, based on normal usage of 100,000,000 kwh, are $30,500,000 in fixed costs and $8,000,000 in variable costs. For November, the actual kwh used was 60,000,000 by Department A and 20,000,000 by Department B. Actual fixed costs were $30,500,000, and actual variable costs were $8,000,000.

Terry Lamb, the controller, prepared the following monthly report:

Bulldog Inc.
Monthly Allocation Report
November 2007

Power plant usage		80,000,000 kwh
Actual costs:		
Fixed		$30,500,000
Variable		8,000,000
Total		$38,500,000
Rate per kwh	($38,500,000 ÷ 80,000,000 kwh)	$ 0.48125
Allocations:		
To Department A	(60,000,000 kwh × $0.48125)	$28,875,000
To Department B	(20,000,000 kwh × $0.48125)	9,625,000
Total allocated		$38,500,000

Lamb fully allocated all power plant costs on the basis of actual kwh used by each production department. This report will be submitted to the two production department operating managers.

REQUIRED

1. Discuss at least two problems with the monthly allocation report prepared by Lamb for November 2007 at Bulldog Inc.
2. Prepare a revised monthly allocation report for November 2006 using a flexible budget approach.
3. Discuss the behavioural implications of Lamb's monthly allocation report for November 2007 on the production managers of Department B at Bulldog Inc.

14-38 **Common costs.** Jason Miller and Eric Jackson would like to lease an office building to open their separate law offices. The building has a total of 1,700 square metres of office space. Miller and Jackson need 1,000 square metres and 700 square metres, respectively. If each rents the space on his own, the rent will be $1 per square metre. If they rent the space together, the rent will decrease to $0.80 per square metre.

REQUIRED

1. Calculate Miller and Jackson's respective share of the rent under the stand-alone cost-allocation method.
2. Do requirement 1 using the incremental cost-allocation method. Assume Miller to be the primary party.
3. What method would you recommend Miller and Jackson use to share the rent?

14-39 **Allocation of central corporate costs to divisions.** Legarde has four geographically dispersed divisions:

| Book Publishing | Broadcasting |
| Print Media | Multimedia |

Under the current allocation system, costs incurred at Legarde corporate headquarters are collected in a single pool and allocated to each division on the basis of its revenues. The central corporate costs for 2007 are

Interest on debt	$ 11,000,000
Human resource management	150,000,000
Corporate administration	50,000,000
Research and development	100,000,000
Advertising	200,000,000
	$511,000,000

Summary data (in millions of dollars) related to the divisions for 2007 are

	Multimedia	Broadcasting	Print Media	Book Publishing
Revenues	$1,400	$4,500	$2,500	$1,600
Direct costs	750	3,500	2,000	1,000
Segment margin	$ 650	$1,000	$ 500	$ 600

The following information on the four divisions is also available:

	Multimedia	Broadcasting	Print Media	Book Publishing
Floor space (square metres)	40,000	160,000	200,000	100,000
Number of employees	1,000	3,000	2,500	1,500
Divisional administrative costs (in millions of dollars)	$150	$400	$250	$200

A review of the central corporate costs for divisions reveals the following:

◆ Out of the total $11 million interest on debt, $6.5 million is for the debt to purchase a building for the Broadcasting division. The remaining $4.5-million interest cost is on the borrowings for the purchase of equipment for the Multimedia division.
◆ No research and development work is done for the Print Media division. The director of research and development estimates that 40% of the work in her responsibility area

is done for the Multimedia division, and the remaining 60% is done equally for the Broadcasting and Book Publishing divisions.

◆ Advertising campaigns sponsored at the central corporate level are to boost the overall corporate image. It is assumed that the benefits to the divisions are in proportion to their revenues.

◆ The resources expended by human resource management on recruiting, training, and so forth for the divisions are approximately in proportion to the number of employees.

◆ To support divisional managers, the corporate management works very closely with them. The divisional administrative costs are a good indicator of the relative size of each division's management team.

◆ Allocate the central corporate costs to divisions that are consistent with cause-and-effect or benefits-received criteria.

14-40 Division cost allocation, R&D, ethics. World Semiconductor (WS) has eight divisions. It has a central R&D group in Waterloo that conducts contract research for each of these eight divisions. At the start of each year, each division estimates the hours of research scientist time at the Waterloo group it will use in the coming year. These estimates are summed for WS as a whole. Each division is charged for budgeted overhead costs incurred at the Waterloo facility on the basis of its relative budgeted percentage use of research scientist time in the coming year. Central R&D bears the risk of any overruns on overhead costs during the year. Each division also pays (in 2007) the Waterloo facility $100 per hour of research scientist time and the actual costs of any materials used on the project.

Toni Goodwin is the controller of the Applied Semiconductor Division (ASD), which is based in Regina, Saskatchewan. She notes that in the first nine months of 2007, ASD was charged $12.597 million for contract research at the Waterloo facility:

Research scientist time	$ 2,564,000
Materials and other direct charges	2,883,000
Overhead cost charge (22% of $32,500,000)	7,150,000
	$12,597,000

The $32,500,000 amount represents WS's budgeted overhead costs for the first nine months of 2007.

It is now time to prepare the 2008 budget. Goodwin estimates that ASD will have a 2008 budget of 30,000 hours of research scientist time at the Waterloo facility. This estimate is based on detailed interviews she has had with operating managers at ASD and on a recent ASD retreat, at which the strategy and operations for 2008 were finalized. Roy Masters, the new president of ASD, is less than pleased with the 30,000 budget number. Goodwin and Masters have the following conversation:

Goodwin: But Roy, you were at the retreat where we all signed off on the 30,000 number.

Masters: I was there, but I think "signed off" is too strong a phrase. By all means use the 30,000 number in our internal planning and budgeting at ASD. However, I want you to tell Waterloo that we are budgeting for only 25,000 hours in 2008.

Goodwin: But . . .

Masters: But nothing, Toni. Everyone plays games in this company. This is the fourth division of World Semiconductor I have worked in. I know for a fact that in all my three prior divisions, we deliberately understated budgeted usage of research scientists to the Waterloo people at the start of each year. Anyway, Waterloo always artificially inflates its estimate of overhead costs for the coming year. They do it every year. Anyone who thinks this is a level playing field is more naive than my dog.

Goodwin: Roy, I have to think about this.

Masters: Don't think too long, Toni. I want the senior managers on my team to be team players. The issue you face, Toni, is whether you want to remain on the team.

REQUIRED
1. Why might Masters want Goodwin to report 25,000 budgeted hours rather than 30,000 budgeted hours to Waterloo?
2. What steps might Waterloo take to reduce WS divisions' understating their budgeted usage of Waterloo research scientist time?
3. What should Goodwin do?

The Hibernia offshore oil field project off the coast of Newfoundland is a joint venture among many companies, including ExxonMobil Canada, Chevron Canada Resources, and Petro-Canada. The costs of this project are shared among the companies investing in this project. Ultimately, the cost of the oil produced and the ultimate costs of processing the oil into a range of products will involve an allocation of these costs to the various products produced.

15

Cost Allocation: Joint Products and Byproducts

LEARNING OBJECTIVES

After studying this chapter, you should be able to

1. Identify the splitoff point(s) in a joint cost situation
2. Distinguish between joint products and byproducts
3. Provide several reasons for allocating joint costs to individual products
4. Allocate joint costs using several different methods
5. Identify the criterion used to support market-based joint cost allocation methods
6. Explain the irrelevance of joint costs in deciding to sell or further process
7. Account for byproducts using two different methods

Prior chapters have emphasized costing for either single-product companies or companies in which individual products are separately produced. We now consider costing for the more complex case where two or more products are simultaneously produced. This chapter examines methods for allocating joint costs to products and services. Some of the topics discussed in this chapter are related to issues already covered in Chapter 14.

Many companies such as ExxonMobil Canada produce two or more products simultaneously using the same processes. A **joint cost** is the cost of a single process that yields multiple products simultaneously. The distillation of coal, for example, gives us coke, gas, and other products. The cost of this distillation process would be called a joint cost. The juncture in the process when one or more products in a joint cost setting become separately identifiable is called the **splitoff point.** An example is the point where coal becomes coke, gas, and other products. **Separable costs** are costs incurred beyond the splitoff point—for example, manufacturing, marketing, and distribution costs—that can be assigned to one or more individual products. At or beyond the splitoff point, decisions relating to sale or further processing of individual products can be made independently of decisions about other products.

Various terms have arisen in conjunction with production processes. A **product** is any output that has a positive sales value (or an output used internally that enables an organization to avoid incurring costs). **Joint products** all have relatively high sales value but are not separately identifiable as individual products until the splitoff point. When a single process yielding two or more products yields only one product with a relatively high sales value, that product is termed a **main product.** A **byproduct** has a low sales value compared with the sales value of the main or joint product(s). **Scrap** has minimal sales value. Some outputs can have a negative revenue when their disposal costs (for example, the costs of handling nonsalable toxic substances) are considered. These disposal costs must be added to the joint production costs that are allocated to the main and joint products. The classification of products as main, joint, byproduct, or scrap can change over time, especially for products (such as tin) whose market price can increase or decrease by, say, 30% or more in any one year.

For example, if logs are processed into standard lumber and wood chips, standard lumber is a main product and wood chips are the byproducts. Why? Because standard lumber has a high total sales value compared to the sales value of wood chips. If the logs are processed into fine grade lumber, standard lumber, and wood chips, then both the fine and standard grade lumber with high sales values are joint products while the wood chips with low sales values are the byproducts.

Exhibit 15-1 shows the relationship between the terms defined in the preceding paragraph. Be careful; these distinctions are not firm in practice. The variety of terminology and accounting practice is bewildering. Always gain an understanding of the terms as used by the particular organization with which you are dealing.

Industries abound in which single processes simultaneously yield two or more products. Exhibit 15-2 presents examples of joint cost situations in diverse industries. In each example in Exhibit 15-2, no individual product can be produced without the accompanying products appearing, although sometimes the proportions can be varied. A poultry farm cannot kill a turkey wing; it has to kill a whole turkey, which yields breasts, thighs, drumsticks, digest, feather meal, and poultry meal in addition to wings. In this example, the focus is on building up costs of individual products as disassembly occurs. This focus contrasts with that of prior chapters that emphasize building up costs of individual products as assembly occurs.

EXHIBIT 15-1

Classification of Products of a Joint Production Process

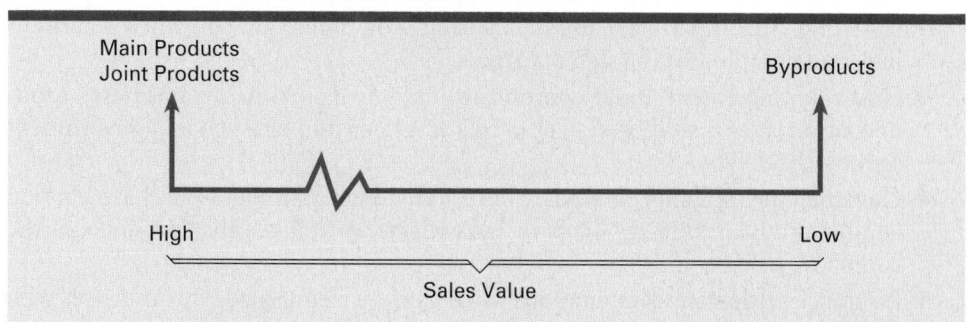

EXHIBIT 15-2
Examples of Joint Cost Situations

Industry	Separable Products at the Splitoff Point
Agriculture and Food Processing	
Cocoa beans	Cocoa butter, cocoa powder, cocoa drink mix, tanning cream
Lambs	Lamb cuts, tripe, hides, bones, fat
Hogs	Bacon, ham, spare ribs, pork roast
Raw milk	Cream, liquid skim
Lumber	Lumber of varying grades and shapes
Turkeys	Breasts, wings, thighs, drumsticks, digest, feather meal, poultry meal
Extractive Industries	
Coal	Coke, gas, benzol, tar, ammonia
Copper ore	Copper, silver, lead, zinc
Petroleum	Crude oil, natural gas, raw LPG
Salt	Hydrogen, chlorine, caustic soda
Chemical Industries	
Raw LPG (liquefied petroleum gas)	Butane, ethane, propane
Crude oil	Gasoline, kerosene, benzene, naphtha
Semiconductor Industry	
Fabrication of silicon-wafer chips	Memory chips of different quality (as to capacity), speed, life expectancy, and temperature tolerance

In some joint cost settings, the number of outputs produced exceed the number of products. This situation can occur where an output, produced as an inherent part of the joint production process, is recycled without any value being added by its production.

For example, the offshore processing of hydrocarbons to yield oil and gas also yields water as an output, which is recycled back into the ocean. Similarly, the processing of mineral ore to yield gold and silver also yields dirt as an output, which is recycled back into the ground. The water and dirt in these examples typically are not classified as products, but they are outputs. No entries are made in the accounting system to record their processing. The physical quantity of these outputs can be large relative to the physical quantity of outputs that are recorded in the accounting system as products. It is only those outputs that have a positive sales value that are typically labelled products.

WHY ALLOCATE JOINT COSTS?

OBJECTIVE 3

Provide several reasons for allocating joint costs to individual products

There are many contexts that require the allocation of joint costs to individual products or services. Examples include

◆ Computation of inventoriable costs and cost of goods sold for external financial statements and reports for income tax authorities.

◆ Computation of inventoriable costs and cost of goods sold for internal financial reporting. Such reports are used in division profitability analysis when determining compensation for division managers.

◆ Cost reimbursement under contracts when only a portion of a business's products or services is sold or delivered to a single customer (such as a government agency).

◆ Customer profitability analysis where individual customers purchase varying combinations of joint products or byproducts as well as other products of the company.

◆ Insurance settlement computations when damage claims made by businesses with joint products, main products, or byproducts are based on cost information.

- Rate regulation when one or more of the jointly produced products or services is subject to price regulation.[1]
- Contract litigation in which costs of joint products are key inputs.

APPROACHES TO ALLOCATING JOINT COSTS

These seven areas mentioned above are illustrative rather than exhaustive. Their wide-ranging natures illustrate why it is important to master methods for allocating joint costs. There are two basic approaches to allocating joint costs:

- **Approach 1:** *Allocate costs using market-based data (for example, revenues).* Three methods that can be used in applying this approach are the:
  1. Sales value at splitoff method
  2. Estimated net realizable value (NRV) method
  3. Constant gross margin percentage NRV method
- **Approach 2:** *Allocate costs using physical measure based data such as weight or volume.*

In prior chapters we emphasized both the cause-and-effect and the benefits-received criteria (see Exhibit 14-2, p. 555) for guiding cost allocation decisions. In joint cost settings, it is not feasible to use the cause-and-effect criterion to guide individual product cost allocations. Joint costs, by definition, cannot be the subject of cause-and-effect analysis at the individual-product level. The cause-and-effect relationship exists only at the joint process level. The benefits-received criterion leads to a preference for methods under approach 1. Revenues, in general, are a better indicator of benefits received than are physical measures such as weight or volume.

In the simplest situation, the joint products are sold at the splitoff point without further processing. We use this case first (termed Example 1) to illustrate two methods, first the sales value at splitoff method and secondly the physical measures method using volume as the metric. Then we consider situations involving further processing beyond the splitoff point (termed Example 2) to illustrate our final two methods, the estimated NRV method and the constant gross margin percent NRV method.

To highlight each joint cost example, we make extensive use of exhibits in this chapter. We use the following notation:

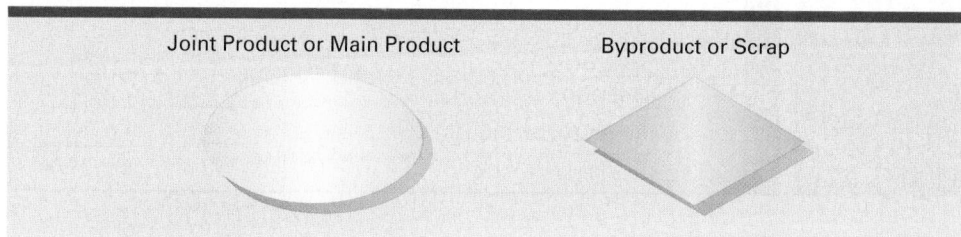

Joint Product or Main Product   Byproduct or Scrap

To enable comparisons across the methods, we report for each method individual gross margin percentages for individual products.

Example 1: Farmers' Dairy purchases raw milk from individual farms and processes it up to the splitoff point, where two products (cream and liquid skim) are obtained. These two products are sold to an independent company, which markets and distributes them to supermarkets and other retail outlets.

Exhibit 15-3 presents an overview of the basic relationships in this example. Summary data for May 2007 are as follows:

- **Raw milk processed:** 4,400 hectolitres (hL) of fluid raw milk with a 10% shrinkage of 400 hL due to evaporation, and spillage to net 4,000 hL of cream and liquid cream for sale. One hectolitre equals 100 litres. After the raw milk is received at Farmers' Dairy's processing plant, it is separated in machines similar to that illustrated on page 596.

[1]See J. Crespi and J. Harris, "Joint Cost Allocation Under the Natural Gas Act: An Historical Review," *Journal of Extractive Industries Accounting*, Vol. 2, No. 2, pp. 133–142. Also see International Accounting Standards Committee Foundation, *IASC Issues Paper: Extractive Industries* (London, United Kingdom: IASB, 2000).

EXHIBIT 15-3
Farmers' Dairy: Example 1 Overview

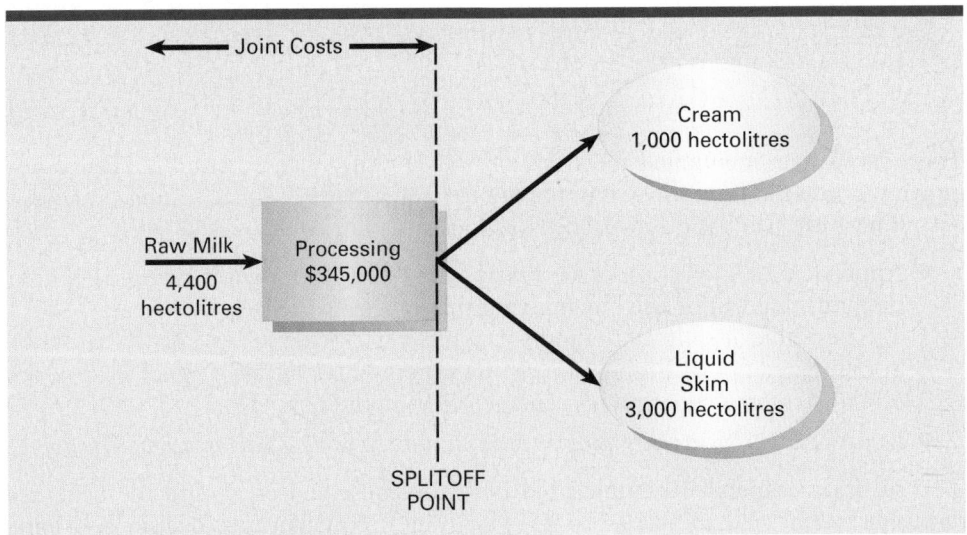

◆ **Inventories:** The inventory amounts are shown in the table below.

◆ Cost of processing 4,400 hL of fluid raw milk and processing it up to the splitoff point to yield 1,000 hL of cream and 3,000 hL of of liquid skim: $345,000

Dairy Farmers of Ontario
www.milk.org/farmto/
processing.html

	A	B	C
1		**Joint Costs**	
2	**Joint costs (costs of 4,400 hectolitres of raw milk and processing to splitoff point)**		**$ 345,000**
3		**Cream**	**Liquid Skim**
4	Beginning Inventory (hectolitres)	0	0
5	Production (hectolitres)	1,000	3,000
6	Sales (hectolitres)	800	900
7	Ending Inventory (hectolitres)	200	2,100
8	Selling price per hectolitre	$155.00	$ 75.00

How much of the joint costs of $345,000 should be allocated to the ending inventory of 200 hL of cream and 2,100 hL of liquid skim? The joint production costs of $345,000 cannot be uniquely identified with or traced to either product. Why? Because the products themselves were not separated before the splitoff point. The joint cost allocation methods we now discuss can be used for costing the inventory of cream and liquid skim as well as determining cost of goods sold.

Sales Value at Splitoff Method

Sales value at splitoff method.
Joint cost allocation method that allocates joint costs on the basis of the relative sales value at the splitoff point of the total production in the accounting period of each product.

The **sales value at splitoff method** allocates joint costs on the basis of the relative sales value at the splitoff point of the total production in the accounting period of each product. In Exhibit 15-4, Panel A on page 597, the sales value at splitoff of the May 2007 production is $155,000 for cream and $225,000 for liquid skim. We then assign a weighting to each product, which is a percentage of total sales value. Using this weighting, we allocate the joint costs to the individual products. This approach uses the sales value of the *entire production of the accounting period* (1,000 hL of cream and 3,000 hL of liquid skim). Why? Because joint costs were incurred on all the units produced, not simply the units sold during the current sales period. Panel B presents the product-line income statement using the sales value at splitoff method.

EXHIBIT 15-4
Farmers' Dairy Product Line Income Statement for May 2007: Joint Costs Allocated Using Sales Value at Splitoff Method

	A	B	C	D
1	**PANEL A: Allocation of Joint Costs Using Sales Value at Splitoff Method**			
2		**Cream**	**Liquid Skim**	**Total**
3	Sales value of total production at splitoff point (1,000 hL × $155/hL; 3,000 hL × $75/hL).	$155,000	$225,000	$380,000
4	Weighting ($155,000 ÷ $380,000; $225,000 ÷ $380,000)	40.789%	59.211%	
5	Joint costs allocated (0.40789 × $345,000; 0.59211 × $345,000)	140,724	204,276	345,000
6	Joint production cost per hectolitre	$140.724	$68.092	
7				
8	**PANEL B: Product-Line Income Statement Using Sales Value at Splitoff Method for May 2007**			
9		**Cream**	**Liquid Skim**	**Total**
10	Revenue (800 hL × $155/hL; 900 hL ×$75.00/hL)	$124,000	$ 67,500	$191,500
11	Cost of goods sold (joint costs) Production costs (0.40789 × $345,000; 0.59211 × $345,000)	140,724	204,276	345,000
12	Deduct ending inventory (200 hL × $140.724/hL; 2,100 hL × $68.092/hL)	(28,145)	(142,993)	(171,138)
13	Cost of goods sold (joint costs)	112,579	61,283	173,862
14	Gross margin	$ 11,421	$ 6,217	$ 17,638
15	Gross margin percentage (Gross margin ÷ Revenue)	9.2%	9.2%	9.2%
16				
17	Suppose Farmers' Dairy has beginning inventory of cream and liquid skim milk in May 2007. Suppose further that when this inventory is sold, Farmers' earns a gross margin different from 9.2%. Then the gross-margin percentage for cream and liquid skim milk will be different from the figures shown. The actual value of the gross-margin percentage depends on the proportion of sales of each product from beginning inventory and the proportion from current period production.			

Use of this method has enabled us to obtain individual product costs and gross margins. Both cream and liquid skim have gross-margin percentages of 9.2%. Note how the sales value at splitoff method follows the benefits-received criterion of cost allocation: Costs are allocated to products in proportion to their revenue-generating power (expected revenue). This method is both straightforward and intuitive. The cost allocation base (total sales value at splitoff) is expressed in terms of a common denominator (amount of revenue) that is systematically recorded in the accounting system. This method, however, requires that selling prices exist for all products at the splitoff point.

> The gross-margin percentages of the individual products are always equal under the sales value at splitoff method when there are no beginning inventories and therefore all products are sold at the splitoff.

Physical Measure Method

The **physical measure method** allocates joint costs on the basis of their relative proportions at the splitoff point, using a common physical measure such as weight or volume of the total production of each product. In Example 1, the $345,000 joint costs produced 1,000 hL of cream and 3,000 hL of liquid skim.

Exhibit 15-5 presents the product-line income statement using this method of joint cost allocation. Panel A illustrates the allocation of joint costs to individual products to calculate cost per hectolitre of cream and liquid skim for ending inventory valuation. This method allocates joint costs on the basis of total hectolitres; therefore, the cost per hectolitre is the same for both products. Panel B presents the product-line income statement using the physical measure method. The gross margin percentages are 44.4% for cream and a *loss* of 15.0% for liquid skim.

> **Physical measure method.** Joint cost allocation method that allocates joint costs on the basis of their relative proportions at the splitoff point, using a common physical measure such as weight or volume of the total production of each product.

EXHIBIT 15-5
Farmers' Dairy Product-Line Income Statement for May 2007: Joint Costs Allocated Using Physical Measure Method

	A	B	C	D
1	**PANEL A: Allocation of Joint Costs Using Physical Measure Method**			
2		**Cream**	**Liquid Skim**	**Total**
3	Physical measure of total production (hectolitres)	1,000	3,000	4,000
4	Weighting (1,000 ÷ 4,000; 3,000 ÷ 4,000)	0.25	0.75	
5	Joint costs allocated (0.25 × $345,000; 0.75 × $345,000)	$ 86,250	$258,750	$345,000
6	Joint production cost per hectolitre	$ 86.25	$ 86.25	
7				
8	**PANEL B: Product-Line Income Statement Using Physical Measure Method for May 2007**			
9				
10		**Cream**	**Liquid Skim**	**Total**
11	Revenues (800 hL × $155/hL; 900 hL × $75/hL)	$124,000	$ 67,500	$191,500
12	Cost of goods sold (joint costs)			
13	Production costs (0.25 × $345,000; 0.75 × $345,000)	86,250	258,750	345,000
14	Deduct ending inventory (200 hL × $86.25/hL; 2,100 hL × $86.25/hL)	(17,250)	(181,125)	(198,375)
15	Cost of goods sold (joint costs)	69,000	77,625	146,625
16	Gross margin	$ 55,000	$ (10,125)	$ 44,875
17	Gross margin percentage (Gross margin ÷ Revenue)	44.4%	−15.0%	23.4%

Under the benefits-received criterion, this method is less desirable than the sales value at splitoff method. Why? Because the physical weights used for allocating joint costs may have no relationship to the revenue-producing power of the individual products. Consider a mine that extracts ore containing gold, silver, and lead. Use of a common physical measure (tonnes) would result in almost all the costs being allocated to the product that weighs the most—lead, which has the lowest revenue-producing power. This costing method is not only inconsistent with the revenue objective, which is to earn revenue from sales of gold and silver, but also distorts the profit per tonne of the three products. The profit per tonne of gold and silver will be overstated while that of lead will show a sizeable loss (see the Concepts in Action box on p. 601).

Another issue arises if the physical measures of output are not straightforward. For example, oil, a liquid, and natural gas, a vapour, are both outputs from production. The physical measure for oil is barrels, but gas is not measured in barrels; therefore, a common measure of equivalent units, such as British Thermal Units (BTU), must be calculated. Most accountants will have to rely on outside technical expertise to complete this calculation. Finally, outputs with zero sales value (such as dirt in gold mining) and byproducts will be excluded from the physical measure used in the denominator.

Example 2: Assume the same situation as in Example 1 except that both cream and liquid skim can be processed further:

- **Cream → buttercream:** 1,000 hL of cream are further processed to yield 800 hL of buttercream at additional processing (separable) costs of $135,000. Buttercream is sold for $385 per hL
- **Liquid skim → condensed milk:** 3,000 hL of liquid skim are further processed to yield 2,000 hL of condensed milk at additional processing costs of $270,000. Condensed milk is sold for $310 per hL.

EXHIBIT 15-6
Farmers' Dairy: Example 2 Overview

PANEL A: Graphical Presentation of Processing for Example 2

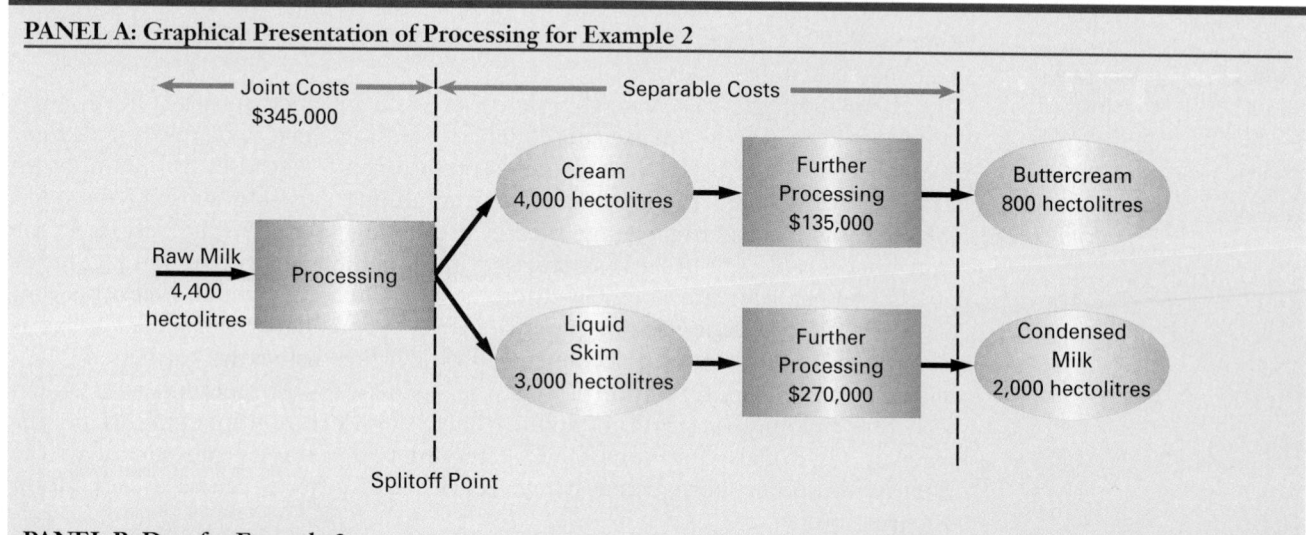

PANEL B: Data for Example 2

	A	B	C	D	E
1		Joint Costs		Buttercream	Condensed Milk
2	Joint costs (costs of 4,400 hL fluid milk and processing to splitoff point)	$345,000			
3	Separable cost of processing 1,000 hL cream into 800 hL of buttercream			$135,000	
4	Separable cost of processing 3,000 hL liquid skim into 2,000 hL condensed milk				$270,000
5					
6		Cream	Liquid Skim	Buttercream	Condensed Milk
7	Beginning inventory (hectolitres)	0	0	0	0
8	Production (hectolitres)	1,000	3,000	800	2,000
9	Transfer for further processing (hectolitres)	1,000	3,000		
10	Sales (hectolitres)			720	1,800
11	Ending inventory (hectolitres)	0	0	80	200
12	Selling price per hectolitre	$ 155.00	$75.00	$ 385.00	$ 310.00

Sales during the accounting period were 720 hL of buttercream and 1,800 hL of condensed milk. Exhibit 15-6 presents an overview of the basic relationships. Panel A illustrates both the basic relationships in the conversion process from raw milk into cream and liquid skim in a joint production process and the separate processing of cream into buttercream as well as liquid skim into condensed milk. Panel B provides the data for Example 2.

Estimated Net Realizable Value (NRV) Method

The **estimated net realizable value (NRV) method** allocates joint costs on the basis of the *relative estimated net realizable value* (expected final sales value in the ordinary course of business minus the expected separable costs of production and marketing of the total production of the period). This method is an alternative when selling prices for one or more products at splitoff do not exist. Using this method for

Estimated net realizable value (NRV) method. Joint cost allocation method that allocates joint costs on the basis of the relative estimated net realizable value (expected final sales value in the ordinary course of business minus the expected separable costs of production and marketing of the total production of the period).

Example 2, Exhibit 15-7, Panel A, illustrates how joint costs are allocated to individual products to calculate the cost per hectolitre of buttercream and condensed milk for ending inventory valuation. Panel B presents the product-line income statement using the NRV method. Gross margin percentages are 19.2% for both buttercream and condensed milk.

Estimating the net realizable value of each product at the splitoff point requires information about the subsequent processing steps to be taken (and their expected separable costs). This is not straightforward because, for example, in petrochemical plants, there are alternatives among possible subsequent steps. Companies will frequently change further processing to exploit fluctuations in the separable costs of each processing stage or in the selling prices of individual products. Under the estimated NRV method, each such change would affect the joint cost allocation percentages. In practice, a set of standard subsequent steps is assumed at the start of the accounting period when using the estimated NRV method. Another consideration is that the estimated NRV method is clear-cut when there is only one splitoff point. When there are multiple splitoff points, however, additional allocations may be required if processes subsequent to the initial splitoff point subsequently converge with each other to create a second joint cost situation.

The sales value at splitoff method is less complex than the estimated NRV method, as it does not require knowledge of the subsequent steps in processing. However, it is not always feasible to use the sales value at splitoff method. Why? Because there may not be any market prices at the splitoff point for one or more individual products. Market prices may not first appear until after processing beyond the splitoff point has occurred.

EXHIBIT 15-7
Joint-Cost Allocation and Product-Line Income Statement Using NRV Method: Farmers' Dairy for May 2007

	A	B	C	D
1	**PANEL A: Allocation of Joint Costs Using Net Realizable Value Method**			
2		**Buttercream**	**Condensed Milk**	**Total**
3	Final sales value of total production during the accounting period (800 hL × $385/hL; 2,000 hL × $310/hL)	$308,000	$620,000	$928,000
4	Deduct separable costs	135,000	270,000	405,000
5	Net realizable value at splitoff point	$173,000	$350,000	$523,000
6	Weighting ($173,000 ÷ $523,000; $350,000 ÷ $523,000)	0.33	0.67	
7	Joint costs allocated (0.33 × $345,000; 0.67 × $345,000)	$113,850	$231,150	$345,000
8	Production cost per hectolitre ([$113,850 + $135,000] ÷ 800 hL [$234,150 + $270,000] ÷ 2,000 hL)	$311.063	$250.575	
9				
10	**PANEL B: Product-Line Income Statement Using Net Realizable Value Method for May 2007**			
11		**Buttercream**	**Condensed Milk**	**Total**
12	Revenue (720 hL × $385/hL; 1,800 hL × $310/hL)	$277,200	$558,000	$835,200
13	Cost of goods sold Joint costs (0.33 × $345,000; 0.67 × $345,000)	113,850	231,150	345,000
14	Separable costs	135,000	270,000	405,000
15	Production costs	248,850	501,150	750,000
16	Deduct ending inventory (80 hL × $311.063; 200 hL × $250.575)	(24,885)	(50,115)	(75,000)
17	Cost of goods sold	223,965	451,035	675,000
18	Gross margin	$ 53,235	$106,965	$160,200
19	Gross margin percentage (Gross margin ÷ Revenue)	19.2%	19.2%	19.2%

Chicken Processing: Costing of Joint Products and Byproducts

Chicken-processing operations provide examples in which joint and byproduct costing issues arise. White breast meat, the highest revenue-generating product, is obtained from the front end of the bird; dark meat from the back end. Other edible products include chicken wings and giblets. There are many inedible products that have a diverse set of uses. For example, poultry feathers are used in bedding and sporting goods.

Poultry companies use individual-product cost information for several purposes. One purpose is in customer-profitability analysis. Customers (such as supermarkets and fast-food restaurants) differ greatly in the mix of products they purchase. Individual-product cost data enable companies to determine differences in individual-customer profitability. A subset of products is placed into frozen storage, which creates a demand for individual-product cost information for inventory valuation.

Companies differ in how they cost individual products. Consider two of the largest U.S. companies: Southern Poultry and Golden State Poultry (disguised names).

Southern Poultry classifies white breast meat as the single main product in its costing system. All other products are classified as byproducts. Selling prices of the many byproducts are used to reduce the chicken-processing costs that are allocated to the main product. White breast meat is often further processed into many individual products (such as trimmed chicken and marinated chicken). The separable cost of this further processing is added to the cost per pound of deboned white breast meat to obtain the cost of further-processed products.

Golden State Poultry classifies any product sold to a retail outlet as a joint product. Such products include breast fillets, half-breasts, thighs, whole legs, and wings. Products not sold to a retail outlet are classified as byproducts. Revenue that will be earned from byproducts is offset against the chicken-processing cost before that cost is allocated among the joint products. Average selling prices of products sold to retail outlets are used to allocate net chicken-processing cost to the individual joint products. Distribution costs of transporting the chicken products from the processing plants to retail outlets are not taken into account when determining weights for joint-cost allocation.

Source: Adapted from conversations with executives of Southern Poultry and Golden State Poultry.

Constant Gross Margin Percentage NRV Method

The **constant gross margin percentage NRV method** allocates joint costs in such a way that the overall gross margin percentage is identical for all the individual products. This method entails three steps:

- ◆ **Step 1.** Compute the overall gross margin percentage.
- ◆ **Step 2.** Use the overall gross margin percentage and deduct the gross margin from the final sales values to obtain the total costs that each product should bear.
- ◆ **Step 3.** Deduct the expected separable costs from the total costs to obtain the joint cost allocation.

Exhibit 15-8, Panel A, illustrates these three steps for allocating the $345,000 joint costs between buttercream and condensed milk in the Farmers' Dairy example to calculate the cost per hectolitre of buttercream and condensed milk for valuation of ending inventory. Panel B presents the product-line income statement for the constant gross margin percentage NRV method.

The tenuous assumption underlying the constant gross margin percentage NRV method is that all the products have the same ratio of cost to sales value.

Constant gross margin percentage NRV method. Joint cost allocation method that allocates joint costs in such a way that the overall gross margin percentage is identical for all the individual products.

The constant gross margin percentage NRV method works in reverse. For each product, the gross margin (based on the overall gross margin percentage) and separable costs are deducted from the final sales value of units produced. The residual amount for each product is its allocation of joint costs.

	A	B	C	D
1	**PANEL A: Allocation of Joint Costs Using Constant Gross Margin Percentage NRV Method**			
2	**Step 1**			
3	Final sales value of total production during the accounting period (800 hL × $385/hL; 2,000 hL × $310)	$928,000		
4	Deduct joint and separable costs ($345,000 + $135,000 + $270,000)	750,000		
5	Gross margin	$178,000		
6	Gross margin percentage (Gross margin ÷ Revenue)	19.181%		
7				
8	**Step 2**	**Buttercream**	**Condensed Milk**	**Total**
9	Final sales value of total production during accounting period (800 hL × $385/hL; 2,000 hL × $310)	$308,000	$620,000	$928,000
10	Deduct gross margin, using constant gross margin percentage (19.181% × $308,000; 19.181% × $620,000)	59,078	118,922	178,000
11	Total production costs	248,922	501,078	750,000
12	**Step 3**			
13	Deduct separable costs	(135,000)	(270,000)	(405,000)
14	Joint costs allocated	$113,922	$231,078	$345,000
15				
16	**PANEL B: Product-Line Income Statement Using Constant Gross Margin Percentage NRV Method for May 2007**			
17		**Buttercream**	**Condensed Milk**	**Total**
18	Revenue (720 hL × $385/hL; 1,800 hL × $310/hL)	$277,200	$558,000	$835,200
19	Cost of goods sold Joint costs (from PANEL A, Step 3)	113,922	231,078	345,000
20	Separable costs	135,000	270,000	405,000
21	Production costs	248,922	501,078	750,000
22	*Deduct ending inventory (80 hL × $311.15/hL; 200 hL × $250.54)	(24,892)	(50,108)	(75,000)
23	Cost of goods sold	224,030	450,970	675,000
24	Gross margin	$ 53,170	$107,030	$160,200
25	Gross margin percentage (Gross margin ÷ revenue)	19.2%	19.2%	19.2%
26				
27	*Total production cost of buttercream ÷ Total production of buttercream	$ 311.153/hL		
28	Total production cost of condensed milk ÷ Total production of condensed milk		$ 250.54/hL	

The constant gross margin percentage NRV method means the gross margin percentage is identical for each product, irrespective of its separable costs. In effect, products with relatively high separable costs are subsidized because they are assigned a lower value of joint costs.

A constant ratio of cost to sales value across products is rarely seen in companies that produce multiple products but have no joint costs.

Comparison of Methods

Which method of allocating joint costs should be chosen? Because the costs are joint in nature, managers cannot use the cause-and-effect criterion in making this choice. Managers cannot be sure what causes what cost when examining joint costs. The benefits-received criterion leads to a preference for the sales value at splitoff point method (or other related revenue or market-based methods). Additional benefits of this method include the following:

1. **No anticipation of subsequent management decisions.** The sales value at splitoff method does not presuppose an exact number of subsequent steps undertaken for further processing.

2. **Availability of meaningful common denominator to compute the weighing factors.** The denominator of the sales value at splitoff method (dollars) is a meaningful one. In contrast, the physical measure method may lack a meaningful common denominator for all the separable products (for example, when some products are liquids and other products are solids).

3. **Simplicity.** The sales value at splitoff method is simple. In contrast, the estimated NRV method can be very complex in operations with multiple products and multiple splitoff points. The total sales value at splitoff is unaffected by any change in the production process after the splitoff point.

OBJECTIVE 5

Identify the criterion used to support market-based joint cost allocation methods

The purpose of the joint cost allocation is important (see the Global Surveys of Company Practice box). Consider rate regulation. Market-based measures are difficult to use in this context. It is circular to use selling prices as a basis for setting prices (rates) and at the same time use selling prices to allocate the costs on which prices (rates) are based. Physical measures represent one joint cost allocation approach available in rate regulation.

Market-based measures are the preferred joint cost allocation, with the net realizable value method the predominant choice. The most common other market-based measure reported in the survey was a variation of the net realizable value method in which the final sales value of each product is used as the allocation base without any deduction for the expected separable costs of production and marketing. This variation

GLOBAL SURVEYS OF COMPANY PRACTICE

Joint-Cost Allocation in the Oil Patch

The petroleum industry is an example of an industry with joint costs. Petroleum mining and processing starts with hydrocarbons being extracted from either onshore or offshore fields. During this process, petroleum companies frequently obtain multiple products from the same field, such as crude oil, natural gas, and raw liquefied petroleum gas (LPG). One survey of European petroleum-producing companies found that 46% allocate joint costs to gas and oil extracted from the same field.[a] Of those companies, 33% use market-based methods, 50% use the physical-measure method, and 17% use other methods.

When LPG is extracted, it is often further processed into butane, ethane, and propane. How are these joint refining costs, which include raw LPG and processing costs, allocated to the separately marketable products produced at the refinery? A survey of American companies focused on joint-cost-allocation methods chosen by refiners for external reporting purposes:[b]

Market-based methods	
Net realizable value	46%
Other	20%
Physical-measure method	
Volume (barrels, gallons, or cubic feet)	27%
Mass (weight or molecular mass)	2%
Other	5%
	100%

Among market-based methods, the NRV method was the predominant choice. The most common other market-based choice was a variation of the NRV method in which the final sales value of each product was used as the allocation base without any deduction for the expected separable costs. This variation illustrates how companies make adjustments to the basic methods described in this chapter, often on the grounds of a perceived cost-benefit basis.

[a] Coopers & Lybrand, *Survey of Accounting Practices in the European Oil and Gas Industry* (Denton, TX: Coopers & Lybrand/University of North Texas, February 1997).

[b] Koester, R., and D. Barnett, "Petroleum Refinery Joint Cost Allocation" (Working Paper, California State University, Dominguez Hills, 1996).

illustrates how companies may make their own adjustment to the basic methods described in this chapter, often on the grounds of a perceived cost-benefit basis.

NO ALLOCATION OF JOINT COSTS

All the preceding methods of allocating joint costs to individual products are subject to criticism. As a result, some companies refrain from joint cost allocation entirely. Instead, they carry all inventories at estimated net realizable value. Income on each product is recognized when production is completed. Industries that use variations of this approach include meat packing, canning, and mining.

Accountants ordinarily criticize carrying inventories at estimated net realizable values. Why? Because income is recognized *before* sales are made. Partly in response to this criticism, some companies using this no-allocation approach carry their inventories at estimated net realizable values minus a normal profit margin.

Exhibit 15-9 presents the product-line income statement with no allocation of joint costs for Example 2. The separable costs are assigned first, which highlights for managers the cause-and-effect relationship between individual products and the costs incurred on them. The joint costs are not allocated to buttercream and condensed milk as individual products.

IRRELEVANCE OF JOINT COSTS FOR DECISION MAKING

No technique for allocating joint product costs should guide management decisions regarding whether a product should be sold at the splitoff point or processed beyond splitoff. When a product is an inevitable result of a joint process, the decision to further process should not be influenced either by the size of the total joint costs or by the portion of the joint costs allocated to particular products. Instead, managers should use the relevant cost concepts introduced in Chapter 11.

Sell or Further Process

The decision to incur additional costs beyond splitoff should be based on the incremental operating income attainable beyond the splitoff point. Example 2 assumed that it was profitable for both cream and liquid skim to be further processed into buttercream and condensed milk, respectively. The incremental analysis for these decisions to further process is as follows:

	Buttercream	Condensed Milk	Total
Incremental revenue (buttercream–cream; liquid skim–condensed milk)	$153,200	$490,500	$643,700
Incremental costs (buttercream–cream; liquid skim–condensed milk)	135,000	270,000	405,000
Incremental operating income	$ 18,200	$220,500	$238,700

EXHIBIT 15-9
Farmers' Dairy Product-Line Income Statement for May 2007: No Allocation of Joint Costs

	A	B	C	D
1		**Buttercream**	**Condensed Milk**	**Total**
2	Produced and sold (buttercream, 720 hL × $385/hL; 1,800 hL × $310/hL)	$277,200	$558,000	$835,200
3	Produced but not sold (buttercream 80 hL × $385/hL; 200 hL × $310/hL)	24,892	50,108	75,000
4	Total sales value of production	302,092	608,108	910,200
5	Separable costs (given)	135,000	270,000	405,000
6	Contribution to joint costs and operating income	$167,092	$338,108	505,200
7	Joint costs (given)			345,000
8	Gross margin			$160,200
9	Gross margin percentage (Gross margin ÷ Revenue)			19.2%

The amount of joint costs incurred up to splitoff ($345,000)—and how it is allocated—is irrelevant in deciding whether to process further cream or liquid skim. Why? Because the joint costs of $345,000 are the same whether or not further processing is done.

Incremental costs are those costs that differ between the alternatives being considered (such as sell or process further). Do not assume that all separable costs in our joint cost allocations for product-costing purposes are always incremental costs. For example, some separable costs may be allocated costs that do not differ between the specific alternatives being considered.

Joint Cost Allocation and Performance Evaluation

The potential conflict between the cost concepts used for decision making and those used for evaluating the performance of managers is a key theme of this book.

If managers make process (and process or sell) decisions using an incremental revenue/incremental cost approach, the resulting budgeted product-line income statement using any of the three methods under the market-based approach (sales value at splitoff, estimated NRV, and constant gross margin percentage NRV) will all show each individual product budgeted to have a positive (or zero) operating income (as long as the incremental costs do not exceed the incremental revenues). In contrast, allocating joint costs using a physical measure can show a manager being responsible for one or more products budgeted to have losses even though the company has higher operating income by producing those products in a joint-product setting (see the Focus on Values and Behaviours box).

Management Accountants: Overcoming the Pitfalls of Allocating Joint Costs

When you think of companies such as the Hershey Company, Oscar Mayer (a subsidiary of Kraft Foods Inc.), and Petro-Canada, perhaps the first thing that comes to mind is a chocolate bar, or a hot dog at a hockey game, or the high cost of gasoline. Chances are you don't think about the accounting challenges the management accountants at these companies face on a daily basis.

But what are the challenges? Consider the process of allocating joint costs to products. Unfortunately, this process is somewhat arbitrary, which means product managers, who are evaluated on product profitability, invariably favour joint-cost allocations that assign the lowest joint costs to their department. However, allocating joint costs in the way that product managers want may not be in the best interests of the company as a whole. Management accountants' decisions should never be influenced by product managers who might be more concerned with their own performance. Therefore, management accountants must diplomatically convey how and why joint costs are allocated and must apply these policies consistently over time.

Challenges with joint-cost allocations can also arise when two separate companies, such as Petro-Canada and British Petroleum, enter into a joint venture to produce crude oil and natural gas from petroleum, with one company processing primarily the crude oil and the other company processing primarily the natural gas. The contract terms often spell out how joint costs—such as labour and manufacturing overhead—are to be allocated. It is the responsibility of the management accountants to ensure that both sides adhere to the terms of the contract when allocating joint costs to the two companies. When circumstances arise that are not specifically covered by the contract clauses, management accountants must have the integrity to make decisions in a fair and unbiased manner.

Consider again our Example 1 (Farmers' Dairy) with the following change. The selling price per hL of liquid skim increases by 20%. This change would not affect the joint costs allocated and the cost of goods computed using the physical measure method (see Exhibit 15-5, p. 598). However, it would affect the revenues of the liquid skim product. The revised product-line income statement for May 2007 using the physical measure method is

	A	B	C	D
1	**PANEL B: Product-Line Income Statement Using Physical Measure Method for May 2007**			
2		**Cream**	**Liquid Skim**	**Total**
3	Revenues (800 hL × $155/hL; 900 hL × $90/hL)	$124,000	$81,000	$205,000
4	Cost of goods sold (joint costs)			
5	Production costs (0.25 × $345,000; 0.75 × $345,000)	86,250	258,750	345,000
6	Deduct ending inventory (200 hL × $86.25/hL; 2,100 hL × $86.25/hL)	(17,250)	(181,125)	(198,375)
7	Cost of goods sold (joint costs)	69,000	77,625	146,625
8	Gross margin	$ 55,000	$ 3,375	$ 58,375
9	Gross margin percentage (Gross margin ÷ Revenue)	44.4%	4.2%	28.5%

Note that the liquid skim product now has a positive gross margin percentage of 4.2% (highly improved from the former *loss* of 15%). On the basis of the initial loss reported using the physical measure method, a manager who is evaluated on the basis of product-by-product gross margin information will be reluctant to process the raw milk into cream and liquid skim to avoid having to explain why liquid skim is being produced at a negative gross margin. This also obscures the opportunity to exploit added profitability from processing further into butter-cream and condensed milk. Under this method, a price change, which is beyond the processing manager's control, is crucial to improving profitability. Use of a market-based joint cost allocation method avoids this situation.

ACCOUNTING FOR BYPRODUCTS

Processes that yield joint products often also yield what are frequently called byproducts—products that have relatively low sales value compared with the sales value of the main or joint product(s). We now discuss accounting for byproducts. To simplify the discussion, consider a two-product example consisting of a main product and a byproduct.

Joint production processes may yield not only joint products and main products but byproducts as well. Although byproducts have low total sales values compared with total sales values of joint or main products, the presence of byproducts in a joint production process can affect the allocation of joint costs. Let's consider a two-product example consisting of a main product and a byproduct.

Example 3: The Westlake Corporation processes timber into fine-grade lumber and wood chips that are used as mulch in gardens and lawns. Information about these products follows:

◆ Fine-grade lumber (the main product)—sells for $505 per thousand board feet (MBF)

◆ Wood chips (the byproduct)—sell for $86 per oven-dried tonne

Data for 2007 are:

	A	B	C	D	E
1		Beginning Inventory	Production	Sales	Ending Inventory
2	Fine grade lumber, million board feet (MMBF)	0	4,000	3,950	50
3	Wood chips, thousands of oven-dried tonnes	0	700	450	250
4		Softwood	Chips		
5	Prices (per MBF, lumber, per tonne, chips)	$505	$ 86		
6		Direct Materials	Conversion	Total	
7	Joint manufacturing costs ($ millions)	$356	$1,068	$1,424	
8	Note: MBF = thousand board feet; MMBF = million board feet				

Joint manufacturing costs for these products were $1,424 million, comprising $356 million for direct materials and $1,068 million for conversion costs. Both products are sold at the splitoff point without further processing, as Exhibit 15-10 shows.

Two byproduct accounting methods will be presented. Method A (the production byproduct method) recognizes byproducts in the financial statements at the time their production is completed. Method B (the sale byproduct method) delays recognition of byproducts until the time of their sale.[2] Recognition of byproducts at the time of production is conceptually correct. Where recognition at the time of sales occurs in practice, it is usually rationalized on the grounds that the dollar amounts of byproducts are immaterial. Exhibit 15-11 presents the income statement of the Westlake Corporation under both methods.

EXHIBIT 15-10
Example 3: Overview of Westlake Corporation

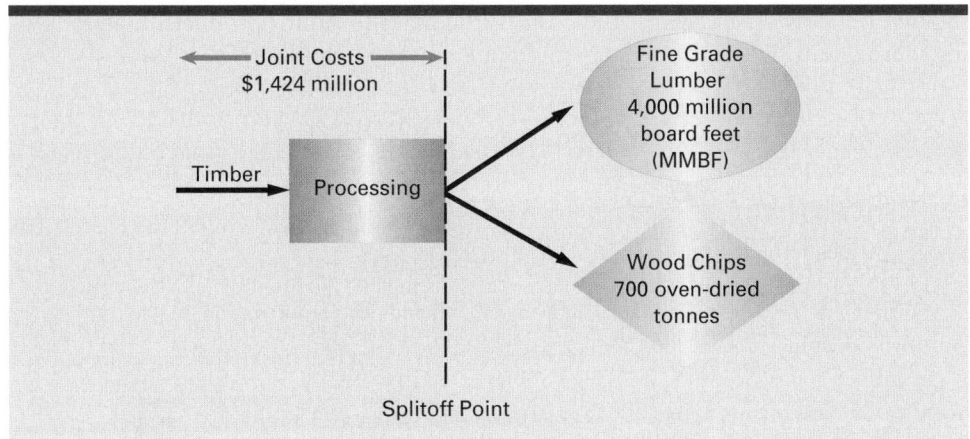

[2]Further discussion on byproduct accounting methods is in C. Cheatham and M. Green, "Teaching Accounting for Byproducts," *Management Accounting News & Views* (Spring 1988): 14–15; and D. Stout and D. Wygal, "Making Byproducts a Main Product of Discussion: A Challenge to Accounting Educators," *Journal of Accounting Education* (1989): 219–233. See also P.D. Marshall and R.F. Dombrowski, "A Small Business Review of Accounting for Primary Products, Byproducts and Scrap," *The National Public Accountant* (February/March 2003): 10–13.

EXHIBIT 15-11
Income Statements of Westlake Corporation for July 2007 Using the Production and Sales
Methods for Byproduct Accounting.

	Production Method	Sales Method
Revenues ($ millions)		
Main product fine grade lumber		
(3,950 MMBF × $505/MMBF)	$1,995	$1,995
Byproduct pulp quality wood chips		
(450 tonnes × $86/tonne)	—	39
Total revenue	1,995	2,034
Cost of goods sold		
Total manufacturing costs	1,424	1,424
Deduct byproduct sales value		
(700 tonnes × $86/tonne)	(60)	$ —
Net manufacturing costs	1,364	1,424
Deduct main product ending inventory	(17)	(18)
Cost of goods sold	1,347	1,406
Gross margin	$ 649	$ 628
Gross margin percentage	32.5%	30.9%
Inventoriable costs (end of the period)		
Main product fine grade lumber	$17.05[a]	$ 17.80[b]
Byproduct pulp quality wood chips	$21.50[c]	$ 0

[a]$1,364 × 50 ÷ 4,000 = $17.05
[b]$1,424 × 50 ÷ 4,000 = $17.80
[c]$86 × 250 = $21.50

Method A: Byproducts Recognized at Time Production Is Completed

This method recognizes the byproduct in the financial statements—the 700 tonnes of wood chips—as it is produced in 2007. The estimated net realizable value from the byproduct is offset against the costs of the main (or joint) products. The following journal entries illustrate this method (all amounts in million $):

1. Work in Process $ 356
       Accounts Payable $ 356
    To record direct materials purchased and used in production.

2. Work in Process $1,068
       Various accounts $1,068
    To record conversion costs in the joint process during 2007; examples include energy, manufacturing supplies, all manufacturing labour, and plant amortization.

3. Byproduct Inventory: Chips $ 60
    Finished goods: Softwood ($1,424 − $60) $1,364
       Work in Process ($356 + 1,068) $1,424
    To record cost of goods completed during 2007.

4a. Cost of Goods Sold $1,347
       Finished Goods: Softwood $1,347
    To record the cost of the main product sold during 2007.

4b. Cash or Accounts Receivable (3,950 × $505) $1,995
       Revenues: Softwood $1,995
    To record the sale of the main product during 2007.

5. Cash or Accounts Receivable (450 × $86) $ 39
       Byproduct Inventory: Chips $ 39
    To record the sale of the byproduct during 2007.

This method reports the byproduct inventories of oven-dried wood chips on the balance sheet at their per-tonne selling price.

One variant of this method would be to report byproduct inventory at its estimated net realizable value reduced by a normal profit margin. When the byproduct inventory is sold in a subsequent period, the income statement would match the selling price with the "net" selling price reported for the byproduct inventory.

Method B: Byproducts Recognized at Time of Sale

This method makes no journal entries until sale of the byproduct occurs. Revenues of the byproduct are reported as a revenue item in the income statement at the time of sale. In the Westlake Corporation example, byproduct revenues in 2007 would be $39 million because only 450,000 tonnes of chips are sold in 2007.

All amounts in million $:

1.	Work in Process	$356	
	Accounts Payable		$356
	To record direct materials purchased and used in production.		
2.	Work in Process	$1,068	
	Various accounts		$1,068
	To record conversion costs in the joint process during 2007; examples include energy, manufacturing supplies, all manufacturing labour, and plant amortization.		
3.	Finished goods: Softwood	$1,424	
	Work in Process ($356 + 1,068)		$1,424
	To record cost of goods completed during 2007.		
4a.	Cost of Goods Sold	$1,406	
	Finished Goods: Softwood		$1,406
	To record the cost of the main product sold during 2007.		
4b.	Cash or Accounts Receivable (3,950 × $505)	$1,995	
	Revenues: Softwood		$1,995
	To record the sale of the main product during 2007.		
5.	Cash or Accounts Receivable (450 × $86)	$39	
	Revenues: Chips		$39
	To record the sale of the byproduct during 2007.		

Method B is rationalized in practice primarily on the grounds that the dollar amounts of byproducts are immaterial. However, this method permits managers to "manage" reported earnings by timing when they sell byproducts. Managers may stockpile byproducts so that they have the flexibility to give revenues a "boost" at opportune times.

PROBLEM FOR SELF-STUDY

Inorganic Chemicals (IC) processes salt into various industrial products. In July 2007, IC incurred joint costs of $100,000 to purchase salt and convert it into two salable products: caustic soda and chlorine. Although there is an active outside market for chlorine, IC processes all 800 tonnes of chlorine it produces into 500 tonnes of PVC (polyvinyl chloride), which is then sold. There were no beginning or ending inventories of salt, caustic soda, chlorine, or PVC in July. Information for July 2007 production and sales follows:

	A	B	C	D
1		Joint Costs		PVC
2	Join costs (costs of salt and processing to splitoff point)	$100,000		
3	Separable cost of processing 800 tonnes chlorine into 500 tonnes PVC			$20,000
4				
5		Caustic Soda	Chlorine	PVC
6	Beginning inventory (tonnes)	0	0	0
7	Production (tonnes)	1,200	800	500
8	Transfer for further processing (tonnes)		800	
9	Sales (tonnes)	1,200	—	500
10	Ending inventory (tonnes)	0	0	0
11	Selling price per tonne in active outside market (for products not actually sold)		$ 75	
12	Selling price per tonne for products sold	$ 50		$ 200

REQUIRED

1. Allocate the joint costs of $100,000 between caustic soda and chlorine under (a) the sales value at splitoff method and (b) the physical measure method.
2. Allocate the joint costs of $100,000 between caustic soda and PVC under the estimated NRV method.
3. What is the gross-margin percentage of (a) caustic soda and (b) PVC under the estimated three allocation methods?
4. Lifetime Swimming Pool Products offers to purchase 800 tonnes of chlorine in August 2007 at $75 per tonne. Assume all other production and sales data are the same for August as they were for July. This sale of chlorine to Lifetime would mean that no PVC would be produced by IC in August. How would accepting this offer affect IC's August 2007 operating income?

SOLUTION

1a. Sales value at splitoff method

	A	B	C	D
1	**Allocation of Joint Costs Using Sales Value at Splitoff Method**	**Caustic Soda**	**Chlorine**	**Total**
2	Sales value of total production at splitoff point (1,200 tonnes × $50 per tonne; 800 tonnes × $75 per tonne)	$60,000	$60,000	$120,000
3	Weighting ($60,000 ÷ $120,000; $60,000 ÷ $120,000)	0.50	0.50	
4	Joint costs allocated (0.50 × $100,000; 0.50 × $100,000)	$50,000	$50,000	$100,000

1b. Physical-measure method

	A	B	C	D
1	**Allocation of Joint Costs Using Physical Measure Method**	**Caustic Soda**	**Chlorine**	**Total**
2	Physical measure of total production (tonnes)	1,200	800	2,000
3	Weighting (1,200 tonnes ÷ 2,000 tonnes; 800 tonnes ÷ 2,000 tonnes)	0.60	0.40	
4	Joint costs allocated (0.60 × $100,000; 0.40 × $100,000)	$60,000	$40,000	$100,000

2. Estimated Net Realizable Value Method

A	B	C	D
1 **Allocation of Joint Costs Using Estimated Net Realizable Value Method**	**Caustic Soda**	**PVC**	**Total**
2 Final sales value of total production during accounting period (1,200 tonnes × $50 per tonne; 500 tonnes × $200 per tonne)	$60,000	$100,000	$160,000
3 Deduct separable costs to complete and sell	0	20,000	20,000
4 Net realizable value at splitoff point	$60,000	$ 80,000	$140,000
5 Weighting ($60,000 ÷ $140,000; $80,000 ÷ $140,000)	$\frac{3}{7}$	$\frac{4}{7}$	
6 Joint costs allocated (caustic, $\frac{3}{7}$ × $100,000; chlorine, $\frac{4}{7}$ × $100,000)	$42,857	$ 57,143	$100,000

3a. Caustic soda

A	B	C	D
1			**Estimated**
2	**Sales Value**	**Physical**	**Net Realizable**
3	**at Splitoff**	**Measure**	**Value**
4 Sales	$60,000	$60,000	$60,000
5 Joint costs	50,000	60,000	42,857
6 Gross margin	$10,000	$ 0	$17,143
7 Gross margin percentage	16.67%	0%	28.57%

3b. PVC

A	B	C	D
1			**Estimated**
2	**Sales Value**	**Physical**	**Net Realizable**
3	**at Splitoff**	**Measure**	**Value**
4 Sales	$100,000	$100,000	$100,000
5 Joint costs	50,000	40,000	57,143
6 Separable costs	20,000	20,000	20,000
7 Gross margin	$ 30,000	$ 40,000	$ 22,857
8 Gross margin percentage	30.00%	40.00%	22.86%

4. Incremental revenue from further processing of chlorine into PVC

(500 tonnes × $200 per tonne) − (800 tonnes × $75 per tonne)	$40,000
Incremental costs of further processing chlorine into PVC	20,000
Incremental operating income from further processing	$20,000

The operating income of Inorganic Chemicals would be reduced by $20,000 if it sold 800 tonnes of chlorine to Lifetime Swimming Pool Products instead of further processing the chlorine into PVC for sale.

DECISION POINTS   SUMMARY

The following decision guidelines use a question-and-answer format to summarize the chapter's main points. Each decision presents a key question. The guideline is the answer to that question.

DECISIONS	GUIDELINES
1. What are a joint cost and a splitoff point?	A joint cost is the cost of a single production process that yields multiple products simultaneously. The splitoff point is the juncture in a joint production process when the products become separately identifiable.

DECISIONS	GUIDELINES
2. How do joint products differ from byproducts?	Joint products have high total sales value at the splitoff point. A byproduct has a low total sales value at the splitoff point compared with the sales value of a joint or main product. Products can change from byproducts to joint products when their total sales values significantly increase or change from joint products to byproducts when their total sales values significantly decrease.
3. Why should joint costs be allocated to individual products?	The purposes of allocating joint costs to products include inventory costing for financial accounting and internal reporting, cost reimbursement, insurance settlements, rate regulation, and product-cost litigation.
4. What methods can be used to allocate joint costs to individual products?	The methods available to allocate joint costs to products are sales value at splitoff, estimated NRV, constant gross margin percentage NRV, and physical measure.
5. Which is the preferred method for allocating joint costs to individual products?	The sales value at splitoff is used when market prices exist at splitoff because using revenues is consistent with the benefits-received criterion, it does not anticipate subsequent management decisions on further processing, and it is simple.
6. Are joint costs relevant in a sell-or-process-further analysis?	No, joint costs and how they are allocated are irrelevant in deciding whether to process further because joint costs are the same whether or not further processing occurs.
7. What methods can be used to account for byproducts?	Byproduct accounting methods differ on whether byproducts are recognized in financial statements at the time of production or at the time of sale. Recognition at the time of production is conceptually correct. Recognition at the time of sale is often used in practice because dollar amounts of byproducts are immaterial.

TERMS TO LEARN

This chapter contains definitions of the following important terms:

byproduct (p. 593)
constant gross margin percentage
   NRV method (p. 601)
estimated net realizable value (NRV)
   method (p. 599)
joint cost (p. 593)
joint products (p. 593)

main product (p. 593)
physical measure method (p. 597)
product (p. 593)
sales value at splitoff method (p. 596)
scrap (p. 593)
separable costs (p. 593)
splitoff point (p. 593)

ASSIGNMENT MATERIAL

QUESTIONS

15-1 Give two examples of industries in which joint costs are found. For each example, what are the individual products at or beyond the splitoff point?

15-2 What is a joint cost?

15-3 Distinguish between a joint product and a byproduct.

15-4 Why might the number of products in a joint cost setting differ from the number of outputs? Give an example.

15-5 Provide three reasons for allocating joint costs to individual products or services.

15-6 Why does the sales value at splitoff method use the sales value of the total production in the accounting period and not just the sales value of the products sold?

15-7 Describe a situation where the sales value at splitoff method cannot be used but the estimated NRV method can be used for joint cost allocation.

15-8 Distinguish between the sales value at splitoff method and the estimated NRV method.

15-9 Give two limitations of the physical measure method of joint cost allocation.

15-10 How might a company simplify its use of the estimated NRV method when the final selling prices can vary sizably in an accounting period and management makes frequent changes to the point at which it sells individual products?

15-11 Why is the constant gross margin percentage NRV method sometimes called a "joint cost and a profit allocation" method?

15-12 "Managers must decide whether a product should be sold at splitoff or processed further. The sales value at splitoff method of joint cost allocation is the best method for generating the information managers need." Do you agree? Why?

15-13 "Managers should consider only additional revenues and separable costs when making decisions about selling now or processing further." Do you agree? Why?

15-14 Describe two major methods to account for byproducts.

15-15 Why might managers with a monthly bonus payment based on attaining a target operating income prefer a byproduct accounting method that recognizes byproducts at the time of sale rather than production?

EXERCISES

15-16 Joint cost allocation, insurance settlement. Chicken Little raises and processes chickens. Each chicken is disassembled into five main parts. Information pertaining to production in July 2007 is as follows:

Parts	Kilograms of Product	Wholesale Selling Price per Kilogram When Production Is Complete
Breasts	100	$1.32
Wings	20	0.48
Thighs	40	0.84
Bones	80	0.24
Feathers	10	0.12

Joint costs of production in July 2007 were $100.

A special shipment of 30 kilograms of breasts and 15 kilograms of wings has been destroyed in a fire. Chicken Little's insurance policy provides for reimbursement for the cost of the items destroyed. The insurance company permits Chicken Little to use a joint cost allocation method. The splitoff point is assumed to be at the end of the production line.

REQUIRED
1. Compute the cost of the special shipment destroyed using (a) the sales value at splitoff method and (b) the physical measure method using kilograms of finished product.
2. Which joint cost allocation method would you recommend that Chicken Little use?

15-17 Joint products and byproducts (continuation of 15-16). Chicken Little is computing the ending inventory values for its July 31, 2007, balance sheet. Ending inventory amounts on July 31 are 15 kilograms of breasts, 6 kilograms of wings, 4 kilograms of thighs, 9 kilograms of bones, and 3 kilograms of feathers.

Chicken Little's management wants to use the sales value at splitoff method. However, they want you to explore the effect on ending inventory values of classifying one or more products as a byproduct rather than a joint or main product.

REQUIRED
1. Assume Chicken Little classifies all five products as joint products. What are the ending inventory values of each product on July 31, 2007?
2. Assume Chicken Little uses a byproduct method that recognizes byproducts in the financial statements at the time production is completed. The total revenues to be received from the sale of byproducts produced that period is offset against the joint cost of production of the joint products. What are the ending inventory values for each joint product and byproduct on July 31, 2007, assuming breasts and thighs are the joint products and wings, bones, and feathers are byproducts.
3. Repeat requirement 2 using the byproduct method that recognizes byproducts in financial statements (as a revenue item) at the time of their sale.
4. Comment on differences in the results in requirements 1, 2, and 3.

15-18 Net realizable value cost allocation method, further process decision. (W. Crum) The Tuscania Company crushes and refines mineral ore into three products in a joint cost operation. Costs and production for 2007 were as follows:

◆ **Department 1,** at initial joint costs of $504,000, produces 20,000 kilograms of Alco, 60,000 kilograms of Devo, 100,000 kilograms of Holo.
◆ **Department 2** processes Alco further at a cost of $120,000.
◆ **Department 3** processes Devo further at a cost of $240,000.

Results for 2007 are

◆ **Alco:** 20,000 kilograms completed; 19,000 kilograms sold for $24 per kilogram; ending inventory, 1,000 kilograms.

◆ **Devo:** 60,000 kilograms completed; 59,000 kilograms sold for $7.20 per kilogram; ending inventory, 1,000 kilograms.

◆ **Holo:** 100,000 kilograms completed; 99,000 kilograms sold for $1.20 per kilogram; ending inventory, 1,000 kilograms; Holo required no further processing.

REQUIRED

1. Use the estimated NRV method to allocate the joint costs of the three products. Compute the total costs and unit costs of ending inventories.

2. Compute the individual gross margin percentages of the three products.

3. Suppose Tuscania receives an offer to sell all its Devo product for a price of $2.40 per kilogram at the splitoff point before going through Department 3, just as it comes off the production line in Department 1. Using last year's figures, would Tuscania be better off by selling Devo that way or processing it through Department 3 and selling it? Show computations to support your answer. Disregard all other factors not mentioned in the problem.

15-19 Process further or sell, joint cost allocation. (R. Capettini) Henley Company produces three joint products, A, B, and C, from a single joint process with a fixed cost of $6,000 and a variable cost of $2.40 per input unit. Each product can be either processed further or, at the splitoff point, it (1) can be sold or (2) must be disposed of at a cost. Out of each input unit, Henley Company produces 1 unit of A, 3 units of B, and 2 units of C. Selling and administrative costs are $16,800.

REQUIRED

1. Given the table below, for each product, should Henley Company process the product further or dispose of it (or sell it) at the splitoff point if Henley Company inputs 5,000 units? Show, for each product, how much better off Henley would be if it followed your advice versus making the alternative decision. Assume that if Henley does not further process a product, it does not incur any of the further processing costs.

Product	Selling Price per Unit at Splitoff Point	Cost per Unit to Dispose of Product at Splitoff Point	Further Processing Costs		Selling Price per Unit after Further Processing
			Fixed	Variable per Unit	
A	—	$0.24	$ 7,200	$1.08	$1.80
B	$0.60	—	1,200	1.20	1.80
C	—	1.08	12,000	1.32	6.48

2. What is Henley Company's gross margin at the 5,000-unit input level?

15-20 Estimated net realizable value method. Illawara, Inc., produces two joint products, cooking oil and soap oil, from a single vegetable oil refining process. In July 2007, the joint costs of this process were $28,800,000. Separable processing costs beyond the splitoff point were cooking oil, $36,000,000, and soap oil, $9,000,000. Cooking oil sells for $60 per drum. Soap oil sells for $30 per drum. Illawara produced and sold 1,000,000 drums of cooking oil and 500,000 drums of soap oil. There are no beginning or ending inventories of cooking oil or soap oil.

REQUIRED
Allocate the $28,800,000 joint costs using the estimated NRV method.

Excel Application For students who wish to practise their spreadsheet skills, the following is a step-by-step approach to creating an Excel spreadsheet to work this problem.

Step-by-Step

1. Open a new spreadsheet. At the top, create an "Original Data" section for the data provided by Illawara, Inc. Create a row for "Joint Costs" and enter the joint costs of the refining process in this row. Skip two rows, create columns for "Cooking Oil" and "Soap Oil," and create rows for "Separate Costs, Selling Price, and Sales Volume" and enter the data for Illawara.

(Program your spreadsheet to perform all necessary calculations. Do not "hard-code" any amounts, such as the weighting for the joint-cost allocation, requiring addition, subtraction, multiplication, or division operations.)

2. Skip two rows, and create a new section, "Joint-Cost Allocation." Create a table in the same format as shown on page 600 with columns for "Cooking Oil, Soap Oil, and Total,

and rows labelled "Final Sales Value of Total Production," "Deduct Separable Costs to Complete and Sell," "NRV at Splitoff Point," "Weighting," and "Joint Costs Allocated."

3. Using the data from your Original Data section, enter the calculations for Final Sales Value of Total Production, Separable Costs to Complete and Sell, and NRV at Splitoff Point for Cooking Oil, Soap Oil, and Total.

4. Use the NRVs at Splitoff Point for Cooking Oil, Soap Oil, and Total from step 3 to calculate the weights on cooking oil and soap oil to be used in the joint-cost allocation. Use these weights to allocate joint costs to cooking oil and soap oil.

5. *Check the accuracy of your spreadsheet:* Go to your Original Data section and change the selling price of cooking oil from $60 per drum to $54 per drum. If your spreadsheet is programmed correctly, joint costs allocated to cooking oil and soap oil should change to $21,600,000 and $7,200,000 respectively.

15-21 Joint cost allocation, process further. The Sinclair Refining Company (SRC) is a 100%-owned subsidiary of Sinclair Oil & Gas. SRC operates a refinery that processes hydrocarbons sold to it by the Sinclair Production Company, another 100%-owned subsidiary of Sinclair Oil & Gas. SRC's refinery has three outputs from its processing of hydrocarbons—crude oil, natural gas liquids, and gas. The first two outputs are liquids, while gas is a vapour. However, gas can be expressed as a liquid equivalent using a standard industry conversion factor. For costing purposes, SRC assumes all three outputs are jointly produced until a single splitoff point where each output separately appears and is then further processed individually.

For August 2007, the following data (in millions) apply:

◆ **Crude oil:** 150 barrels produced and sold at $21.60 per barrel. Separable costs beyond the splitoff point are $210.

◆ **Natural gas liquids:** 50 barrels produced and sold at $18 per barrel. Separable costs beyond the splitoff point are $126.

◆ **Gas:** 800 equivalent barrels produced and sold at $1.56 per equivalent barrel. Separable costs beyond the splitoff point are $252.

SRC paid the Sinclair Production Company $1,680 for hydrocarbons delivered to it from its offshore platform in August 2007. The cost of operating the refinery in August up to the splitoff point was $480, including $120 of gas charges from Deadhorse Utilities, an independent utility company. Deadhorse signed a long-term contract with SRC several years ago when gas prices were much lower than in 2007.

A new federal law has recently been passed that taxes crude oil at 30% of operating income. No new tax is to be paid on natural gas liquid or natural gas. Starting in August 2007, SRC must report a separate product line income statement for crude oil. One challenge facing SRC is how to allocate the joint cost of producing the three separate salable outputs. Assume no beginning or ending inventory.

REQUIRED

1. Draw an exhibit showing the joint cost situation for SRC.
2. Allocate the August 2007 joint cost among the three salable products using (a) the physical measures method and (b) the estimated NRV method. Compute the operating income for each product using each of these methods.
3. Discuss the pros and cons of each method for Sinclair product emphasis decisions.

15-22 Joint cost allocation, physical measures method (continuation of 15-21). Assume that SRC is not able to sell its gas output. The refinery is located in a remote area and a terrorist group has just destroyed major sections of the gas pipeline used to transport the gas to market. The pipeline that carries the crude oil and natural gas liquid is still operational. The Sinclair Production Company must now reinject the gas into the offshore field. The costs of the hydrocarbons to SRC will not be reduced, but Sinclair Production (not SRC) will bear the cost of gas reinjection. No separable costs of gas production beyond the splitoff point will now be incurred.

REQUIRED

1. Assume that the same data for all three outputs for August 2007 apply to the new set of facts. Show the operating income for each salable product using the estimated NRV method of joint cost allocation.
2. Assume the taxation authorities argue that, for crude oil income tax determination, the physical measures method should be used to allocate joint costs and that all outputs (including gas, whether sold or reinjected) should be used in deciding the cost-allocation weights. Do you agree with this argument? Explain your position.

15-23 Alternative methods of joint cost allocation, ending inventories. The Darl Company operates a simple chemical process to reduce a single material into three separate items, here referred to as X, Y, and Z. All three end products are separated simultaneously at a single splitoff point.

Products X and Y are ready for sale immediately upon splitoff without further processing or any other additional costs. Product Z, however, is processed further before being sold. There is no available market price for Z at the splitoff point.

The selling prices quoted below have not changed for three years, and no changes are foreseen for the coming year. During 2007, the selling prices of the items and the total amounts sold were as follows:

◆ **X:** 120 tonnes sold for $1,800 per tonne
◆ **Y:** 340 tonnes sold for $1,200 per tonne
◆ **Z:** 475 tonnes sold for $840 per tonne

The total joint manufacturing costs for the year were $480,000. An additional $240,000 was spent to finish product Z.

There were no beginning inventories of X, Y, or Z. At the end of the year, the following inventories of completed units were on hand: X, 180 tonnes; Y, 60 tonnes; Z, 25 tonnes. There was no beginning or ending work in process.

REQUIRED

1. What will be the cost of inventories of X, Y, and Z for balance sheet purposes and what will be the cost of goods sold for income statement purposes as of December 31, 2007, using (a) the estimated NRV method of joint cost allocation and (b) the constant gross margin percentage NRV method of joint cost allocation?
2. Compare the gross margin percentages for X, Y, and Z using the two methods given in requirement 1.

15-24 Process further or sell, byproduct. (CMA adapted) Newcastle Mining Company (NMC) produces and sells bulk raw coal to other coal companies and exporters. NMC mines and stockpiles the coal; it is then passed through a one-step crushing process before being loaded onto river barges for shipment to customers. The annual output of ten million tonnes, which is expected to remain stable, has an average cost of $24 per tonne with an average selling price of $32.40 per tonne.

Management is currently evaluating the possibility of further processing the coal by sizing and cleaning it in order to expand markets and enhance product revenues. Management has rejected the possibility of constructing a large sizing and cleaning plant because it would require a significant long-term capital investment.

Bill Rolland, controller of NMC, has asked Amy Kimbell, mining engineer, to develop cost and revenue projections for further processing the coal through a variety of contractual arrangements. After extensive discussions with vendors and contractors, Kimbell has prepared the following projections of incremental costs of sizing and cleaning NMC's annual output.

Newcastle Mining Company Sizing and Cleaning Processes

	Incremental Costs
Direct labour	$720,000 per year
Supervisory personnel	120,000 per year
Heavy equipment rental, operating, and maintenance costs	30,000 per month
Contract sizing and cleaning	4.20 per tonne
Outbound rail freight (per 60-tonne rail car)	288 per car

In addition to the preceding cost information, market samples obtained by Kimbell have shown that electrical utilities enter into contracts for sized and cleaned coal similar to that mined by Newcastle at an expected average price of $43.20 per tonne.

Kimbell has learned that 5% of the raw bulk output that enters the sizing and cleaning process will be lost as a primary product. Normally, 75% of this product loss can be salvaged as coal fines. These are small pieces ranging from dust-like particles up to pieces five centimetres in diameter. Coal fines are too small for use by electrical utilities but are frequently sold to steel manufacturers for use in blast furnaces.

Unfortunately, the price for coal fines frequently fluctuates between $16.80 and $28.80 per tonne (F.O.B. shipping point), and the timing of market volume is erratic. Although companies generally sell all their coal fines during a year, it is not unusual to stockpile this product for several months before making any significant sales.

REQUIRED

1. Prepare an analysis to show whether it would be more profitable for Newcastle Mining Company to continue to sell the raw bulk coal or to process it further through sizing and cleaning. (Note: Ignore any value related to the coal fines in your analysis.)

2. a. Taking into consideration any potential value to the coal fines, prepare an analysis to show if the coal fines would affect the results of your analysis prepared in requirement 1.

b. What other factors should be considered in evaluating a sell-or-process-further decision?

15-25 Accounting for a main product and a byproduct. (Cheatham and Green, adapted) Bill Dundee is the owner and operator of Western Bottling, a bulk soft drink producer. A single production process yields two bulk soft drinks, Rainbow Dew (the main product) and Resi-Dew (the byproduct). Both products are fully processed at the splitoff point, and there are no separable costs.

Summary data for September 2007 are as follows:

♦ Cost of soft drink operations = $144,000

♦ Production and sales data:

	Production (in Litres)	Sales (in Litres)	Selling Price per Litre
Main product (Rainbow Dew)	10,000	8,000	$24.00
Byproduct (Resi-Dew)	2,000	1,400	2.40

There were no beginning inventories on September 1, 2007. The following is an overview of operations:

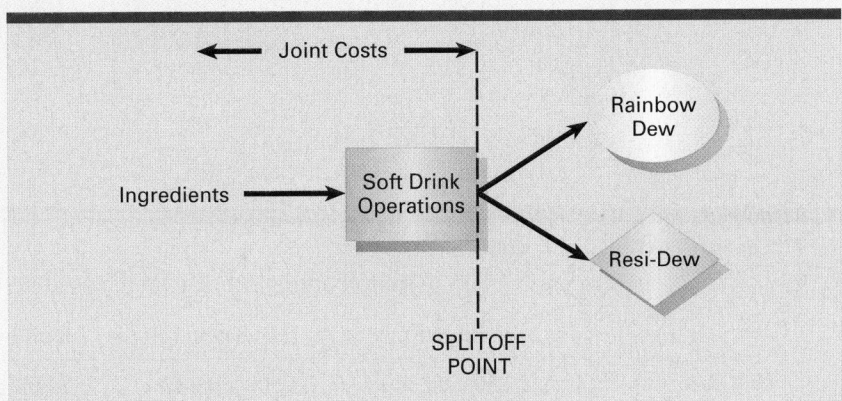

REQUIRED

1. What is the gross margin for Western Bottling under methods A, B, and C of byproduct accounting?

2. What are the inventory amounts reported in the balance sheet on September 30, 2007, for Rainbow Dew and Resi-Dew under each of the two methods of byproduct accounting cited in requirement 1?

3. Which method would you recommend Western Bottling use? Explain.

15-26 Joint costs and byproducts. (W. Crum) The Caldwell Company processes an ore in Department 1, out of which come three products, L, W, and X. Product L is processed further through Department 2. Product W is sold without further processing. Product X is considered a byproduct and is processed further through Department 3. Costs in Department 1 are $960,000 in total; Department 2 costs are $120,000; and Department 3 costs are $60,000. Processing 600,000 kilograms in Department 1 results in 50,000 kilograms of product L, 300,000 kilograms of product W, and 100,000 kilograms of product X.

Product L sells for $12 per kilogram, Product W sells for $2.40 per kilogram, and Product X sells for $3.60 per kilogram. The company wants to make a gross margin of 10% of sales on product X and also allow 25% for marketing costs on product X.

REQUIRED

1. Compute unit costs per kilogram for products L, W, and X, treating X as a byproduct. Use the estimated NRV method for allocating joint costs. Deduct the estimated NRV of the byproduct produced from the joint cost of products L and W.

2. Compute unit costs per kilogram for products L, W, and X, treating all three as joint products and allocating costs by the estimated NRV method.

15-27 Comparison of alternative joint cost allocation methods, further process decision, chocolate products. Roundtree Chocolates manufactures and distributes chocolate products. It purchases cocoa beans and processes them into two intermediate products:

♦ Chocolate powder liquor base

♦ Milk chocolate liquor base

These two intermediary products become separately identifiable at a single splitoff point. Every 500 kilograms of cocoa beans yields 20 four-litre containers of chocolate powder liquor base and 30 four-litre containers of milk chocolate liquor base.

The chocolate powder liquor base is further processed into chocolate powder. Every 20 containers of chocolate powder liquor base yields 200 kilograms of chocolate powder. The milk chocolate liquor base is further processed into milk chocolate. Every 30 containers of milk chocolate liquor base yields 340 kilograms of milk chocolate.

The following is an overview of the manufacturing operations at Roundtree Chocolates:

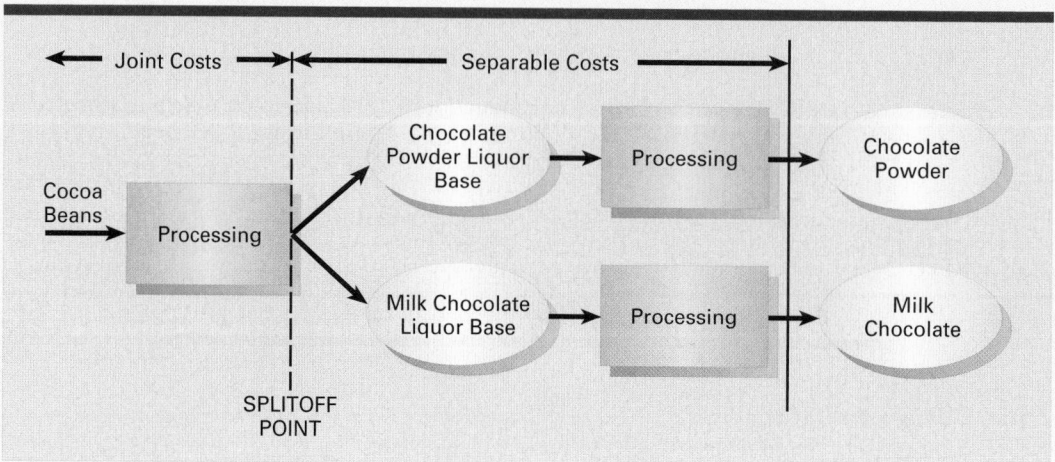

Production and sales data for August 2007 are as follows:
- Cocoa beans processed, 5,000 kilograms
- Costs of processing cocoa beans to splitoff point (including purchase of beans) = $12,000

	Production	Sales	Unit Selling Price
Chocolate powder	2,000 kilograms	2,000 kilograms	$4.80 per kilogram
Milk chocolate	3,400 kilograms	3,400 kilograms	$6.00 per kilogram

The August 2007 separable costs of processing chocolate powder liquor base into chocolate powder are $5,100. The August 2007 separable costs of processing milk chocolate liquor base into milk chocolate are $10,500.

Roundtree fully processes both of its intermediate products into chocolate powder or milk chocolate. There is an active market for these intermediate products. In August 2007, Roundtree could have sold chocolate powder liquor base for $25.20 a container and milk chocolate liquor base for $31.20 a container.

REQUIRED
1. Calculate how the joint costs of $12,000 would be allocated between chocolate powder liquor base and milk chocolate liquor base under each of the following methods: (a) sales value at splitoff, (b) physical measure (containers), (c) estimated NRV, and (d) constant gross margin percentage NRV.
2. What is the gross margin percentage of chocolate powder and milk chocolate under methods (a), (b), (c), and (d) in requirement 1?
3. Could Roundtree Chocolates have increased its operating income by a change in its decision to fully process both of its intermediate products?

15-28 Joint cost allocation, process further or sell. (CMA, adapted) Sonimad Sawmill Inc. (SSI) purchases logs from independent timber contractors and processes the logs into three types of lumber products.

1. Studs for residential building (e.g., walls, ceilings)
2. Decorative pieces (e.g., fireplace mantels, beams for cathedral ceilings)
3. Posts used as support braces (e.g., mine support braces, braces for exterior fences around ranch properties)

These products are the result of a joint sawmill process that involves removal of bark from the logs, cutting the logs into a workable size (ranging from 2.5 to 5 metres long), and then cutting the individual products from the logs, depending on the type of wood (pine, oak, walnut, or maple) and the size (diameter) of the log.

The joint process results in the following costs and output of products for a typical month:

Joint production costs
Direct materials (rough timber logs)	$ 600,000
Debarking (labour and overhead)	60,000
Sizing (labour and overhead)	240,000
Product cutting (labour and overhead)	300,000
Total joint costs	$1,200,000

Product yield and average sales value on a per unit basis from the joint process are as follows:

Product	Monthly Output of Materials at Splitoff Point	Fully Processed Selling Price
Studs	75,000 units	$ 9.60
Decorative pieces	5,000 units	120.00
Posts	20,000 units	24.00

The studs are sold as rough-cut lumber after emerging from the sawmill operation without further processing by SSI. Also, the posts require no further processing beyond the splitoff point. The decorative pieces must be planed and further sized after emerging from the sawmill. This additional processing costs $120,000 per month and normally results in a loss of 10% of the units entering the process. Without this planing and sizing process, there is still an active intermediate market for the unfinished decorative pieces where the selling price averages $72 per unit.

REQUIRED
1. Based on the information given for Sonimad Sawmill Inc., allocate the joint processing costs of $1,200,000 to each of the three product lines using the
   a. sales value at splitoff method.
   b. physical-measure method using volume in units.
   c. estimated net realizable value method.
2. Prepare an analysis for Sonimad Sawmill Inc. to compare processing the decorative pieces further as they currently do with selling them as a rough-cut product immediately at splitoff.
3. Assume Sonimad Sawmill Inc. announced that in six months it will sell the rough-cut product at splitoff due to increasing competitive pressure. Identify at least three types of likely behaviour that will be demonstrated by the skilled labour in the planing and sizing process as a result of this announcement. Include in your discussion how this behaviour could be improved by management.

PROBLEMS

15-29 Alternative methods of joint cost allocation, product-mix decision. Pacific Lumber processes lumber products for sale to lumber wholesalers. Its most popular line is oak products. Oak tree growers sell Pacific Lumber whole trees. These trees are jointly processed up to the splitoff point at which raw select oak, raw white oak, and raw knotty oak become separable products. Each of these raw products is then separately further processed by Pacific Lumber into finished products (select oak, white oak, and knotty oak) that are sold to lumber wholesalers. Data for August 2007 are

a. Joint processing costs (including cost of oak trees) $360,000
b. Separable product at splitoff point
   ◆ Raw select oak   30,000 board feet
   ◆ Raw white oak   50,000 board feet
   ◆ Raw knotty oak   20,000 board feet
c. Final product produced and sold
   ◆ Select oak   25,000 board feet at $19.20 per board foot
   ◆ White oak   40,000 board feet at $10.80 per board foot
   ◆ Knotty oak   15,000 board feet at $8.40 per board foot
d. Separable processing costs
   ◆ For select oak $72,000
   ◆ For white oak $108,000
   ◆ For knotty oak $18,000

There is an active market for raw oak products. Selling prices available in August 2007 were raw select oak ($9.60 per board foot), raw white oak ($4.80 per board foot), and raw knotty oak ($3.60 per board foot).

There were no beginning or ending inventories for August 2007.

REQUIRED

1. Allocate the joint costs to the three products using the
   a. sales value at splitoff method.
   b. physical-measure method.
   c. estimated net realizable value method.
2. Assume that not all final product produced in August 2007 was sold. Ending inventory for August 2007 was select oak (1,000 board feet), white oak (2,000 board feet), and knotty oak (500 board feet). What would be the ending inventory values in the August 30 balance sheet under each product for each of the three methods in requirement 1?
3. Is Pacific Lumber maximizing its total August 2007 operating income by fully processing each raw oak product into its finished product form? Show computations.

15-30 Alternative methods of joint cost allocation, product-mix decisions. The Sunshine Oil Company buys crude vegetable oil. Refining this oil results in four products at the splitoff point: A, B, C, and D. Product C is fully processed at the splitoff point. Products A, B, and D can be individually further refined into Super A, Super B, and Super D. In the most recent month (December), the output at the splitoff point was

Product A	300,000 litres
Product B	100,000 litres
Product C	50,000 litres
Product D	50,000 litres

The joint cost of purchasing the crude vegetable oil and processing it was $120,000.

Sunshine had no beginning or ending inventories. Sales of product C in December were $60,000. Total output of products A, B, and D was further refined and then sold. Data related to December are as follows:

	Separable Processing Costs to Make Super Products	Sales
Super A	$240,000	$360,000
Super B	96,000	120,000
Super D	108,000	144,000

Sunshine had the option of selling products A, B, and D at the splitoff point. This alternative would have yielded the following sales for the December production:

Product A	$60,000
Product B	36,000
Product D	84,000

REQUIRED

1. What is the gross margin percentage for each product sold in December, using the following methods for allocating the $120,000 joint costs: (a) sales value at splitoff, (b) physical measure, and (c) estimated NRV?
2. Could Sunshine have increased its December operating income by making different decisions about the further refining of products A, B, or D? Show the effect on operating income of any changes you recommend.

15-31 Alternative joint-cost-allocation methods, further-process decision. The Wood Spirits Company produces two products, turpentine and methanol (wood alcohol), by a joint process. Joint costs amount to $144,000 per batch of output. Each batch totals 40,000 litres: 25% methanol and 75% turpentine. Both products are processed further without gain or loss in volume. Separable processing costs are methanol, $0.90 per litre; turpentine, $0.60 per litre. Methanol sells for $6.30 per litre. Turpentine sells for $4.20 per litre.

REQUIRED

1. How much joint costs per batch should be allocated to turpentine and to methanol, assuming that joint costs are allocated on a physical-measure (number of litres at splitoff point) basis?
2. If joint costs are to be assigned on an NRV basis, how much joint cost should be assigned to turpentine and to methanol?
3. Prepare product-line income statements per batch for requirements 1 and 2. Assume no beginning or ending inventories.

4. The company has discovered an additional process by which the methanol (wood alcohol) can be made into laboratory ethanol. The selling price of this product would be $18 a litre. Additional processing would increase separate costs $2.70 per litre (in addition to the $0.90 per litre separable cost required to yield methanol). The company would have to pay excise taxes of 20% on the selling price of the product. Assuming no other changes in cost, what is the joint cost applicable to the ethanol (using the NRV method)? Should the company produce the ethanol? Show your computations.

15-32 Joint-costs allocation, relevant costs. (R. Capettini, adapted) Consider the following scenario. Each day a butcher buys a 200-pound pig for $360. The pig can be processed to yield the following three products:

	Selling Price per Pound	Weight (Pounds)
Pork chops	$4.80	30
Ham	$3.60	50
Bacon	$1.44	120
		200

Day 1 The butcher buys a pig. The $360 joint cost of the pig is allocated to individual products based on the relative weights of the products.

	Selling Price	Weight (Pounds)	Revenues	−	Joint Costs Allocated	=	Operating Income
Pork chops	$4.80	30	$144.00	−	$ 54.00	=	$ 90.00
Ham	3.60	50	180.00	−	$ 90.00	=	90.00
Bacon	1.44	120	172.80	−	216.00	=	(43.20)
			$496.80	−	$360.00	=	$136.80

Day 2 The butcher buys an identical pig and throws out the bacon because it has been shown to lose money. She now has 80 pounds of "good output."

	Selling Price	Weight (Pounds)	Revenues	−	Joint Costs Allocated	=	Operating Income
Pork chops	$4.80	30	$144	−	$135.00	=	$ 9.00
Ham	3.60	50	180	−	225.00	=	(45.00)
			$324	−	$360.00	=	$(36.00)

Day 3 The butcher buys an identical pig and throws out the ham and the bacon because they have been shown to lose money. She now has 30 pounds of "good output."

	Selling Price	Weight (Pounds)	Revenues	−	Joint Costs Allocated	=	Operating Income
Pork chops	$4.80	30	$144	−	$360.00	=	$(216.00)
			$144	−	$360.00	=	$(216.00)

Day 4 The butcher buys an identical pig and throws out the whole pig because each product has been shown to lose money. Therefore, she loses $360.

REQUIRED

1. Comment on the preceding series of decisions.
2. How would the joint costs be allocated to all three products using the sales value at splitoff method?
3. Should the operating income numbers from requirement 2 be used to determine if the butcher is better off by selling or not selling individual products? Explain briefly.

15-33 Joint and byproducts, estimated net realizable value method. (CPA) The Harrison Corporation produces three products—Alpha, Beta, and Gamma. Alpha and Gamma are joint products, and Beta is a byproduct of Alpha. No joint costs are to be allocated to the byproduct. The production processes for a given year are as follows:

a. In Department 1, 110,000 kilograms of direct material, Rho, are processed at a total cost of $144,000. After processing in Department 1, 60% of the units are transferred to Department 2, and 40% of the units (now Gamma) are transferred to Department 3.

b. In Department 2, the material is further processed at a total additional cost of $45,600. Seventy percent of the units (now Alpha) are transferred to Department 4, and 30% emerge as Beta, the byproduct, to be sold at $1.44 per kilogram. Separable marketing costs for Beta are $9,720.

c. In Department 4, Alpha is processed at a total additional cost of $28,392. After this processing, Alpha is ready for sale at $6.00 per kilogram.

d. In Department 3, Gamma is processed at a total additional cost of $198,000. In this department, a normal loss of units of Gamma occurs, which equals 10% of the good output of Gamma. The remaining good output of Gamma is then sold for $14.40 per kilogram.

REQUIRED

1. Prepare a schedule showing the allocation of the $144,000 joint costs between Alpha and Gamma using the estimated NRV method. The estimated NRV of Beta should be treated as an addition to the sales value of Alpha.

2. Based on the above numbers, prepare an income statement through gross margin for Alpha using the following facts:

   a. During the year, sales of Alpha were 80% of the kilograms available for sale. There was no beginning inventory.

   b. The estimated NRV of Beta available for sale is to be deducted from the cost of producing Alpha. The ending inventory of Alpha is to be based on the net costs of production.

   c. All other cost and selling price data are listed in (a) to (d).

15-34 Estimated net realizable value method, byproducts. (CMA, adapted) The Princess Corporation grows, processes, packages, and sells three joint apple products: (a) sliced apples that are used in frozen pies, (b) applesauce, and (c) apple juice. The skin of the apple, processed as animal feed, is treated as a byproduct. Princess uses the estimated NRV method to allocate costs of the joint process to its joint products. The byproduct is inventoried at its selling price when produced; the net realizable value of the byproduct is used to reduce the joint production costs before the splitoff point. Details of Princess's production process are presented here:

◆ The apples are washed and the skin is removed in the Cutting Department. The apples are then cored and trimmed for slicing. The three joint products and the byproduct are recognizable after processing in the Cutting Department. Each product is then transferred to a separate department for final processing.

◆ The trimmed apples are forwarded to the Slicing Department, where they are sliced and frozen. Any juice generated during the slicing operation is frozen with the slices.

◆ The pieces of apple trimmed from the fruit are processed into applesauce in the Crushing Department. The juice generated during this operation is used in the applesauce.

◆ The core and any surplus apple pieces generated from the Cutting Department are pulverized into a liquid in the Juicing Department. There is a loss equal to 8% of the weight of the good output produced in this department.

◆ The outside skin is chopped into animal feed and packaged in the Feed Department. It can be kept in cold storage until needed.

A total of 270,000 kilograms of apples entered the Cutting Department during November. The following schedule shows the costs incurred in each department, the proportion by weight transferred to the four final processing departments, and the selling price of each end product.

Processing Data and Costs, November 2007

Departments	Costs Incurred	Proportion of Product by Weight Transferred to Department	Selling Price per Kilogram of Final Product
Cutting	$ 72,000		
Slicing	13,536	33%	$0.96
Crushing	10,260	30	0.66
Juicing	3,600	27	0.48
Feed	840	10	0.12
Total	$100,236	100%	$2.22

REQUIRED

1. The Princess Corporation uses the estimated NRV method to determine inventory cost of its joint products; byproducts are reported on the balance sheet at their

selling price when produced. For the month of November 2007, calculate the following:

 a. The output for apple slices, applesauce, apple juice, and animal feed, in kilograms.
 b. The estimated NRV at the splitoff point for each of the three joint products.
 c. The amount of the cost of the Cutting Department assigned to each of the three joint products and the amount assigned to the byproduct in accordance with corporate policy.
 d. The gross margins in dollars for each of the three joint products.

 2. Comment on the significance to management of the gross margin dollar information by joint product for planning and control purposes, as opposed to inventory costing purposes.

15-35 Joint product/byproduct distinctions, ethics (continuation of 15-34). The Princess Corporation classifies animal feed as a byproduct. The byproduct is inventoried at its selling price when produced; the net realizable value of the product is used to reduce the joint production costs before the splitoff point. Before 2007, Princess classified both apple juice and animal feed as byproducts. These byproducts were not recognized in the accounting system until sold. Revenues from their sale were treated as a revenue item at the time of sale.

  The Princess Corporation uses a "management by objectives" basis to compensate its managers. Every six months, managers are given "stretch" operating-income-to-revenue ratio targets. They receive no bonus if the target is not met and a fixed amount if the target is met or exceeded.

REQUIRED

 1. Assume that Princess managers aim to maximize their bonuses over time. What byproduct method (the pre-2007 method or the 2007 method) would the manager prefer?
 2. How might a controller gain insight into whether the manager of the Apple Products division is "abusing" the accounting system in an effort to maximize his or her bonus?
 3. Describe an accounting system for the Princess Corporation that would reduce "gaming" behaviour by managers with respect to accounting rules for byproducts.

15-36 Byproduct, disposal costs, ethics. Enrique Chemicals, Inc., is a multinational company. One of its subsidiaries is located in a small East European country. The country has only a few environmental protection laws, and even those are not enforced so as "to encourage rapid industrialization." The subsidiary's three major products emerge at splitoff point from a common input. The joint costs are allocated to each product using the sales values at splitoff method. In addition to the three joint products, another product that emerges at splitoff point is a hazardous material. The hazardous material can be dumped into the Gulf at zero cost to the company. Alternatively, it can be processed further and sold as a cleaning liquid.

  The cost accountant responsible for joint-cost allocation presented the following comparative analysis to you, the controller:

	Alternatives	
	Dump into the Gulf	**Process Further**
Revenue	$0	$ 600,000
Costs:		
Further processing	0	360,000
Allocated joint costs	0	300,000
Marketing and distribution	0	60,000
Total costs	0	720,000
Net realizable value	$0	$(120,000)

REQUIRED

 1. Comment on the comparative analysis prepared by the cost accountant purely from a financial perspective. Show any supporting computations.
 2. Assume, regardless of your conclusion in requirement 1, that adopting the process-further alternative would lead to a decrease in the company's operating income. Disposal of the hazardous waste in a manner different than dumping it into the Gulf would also be costly. Discuss the legal and ethical implications of dumping the hazardous material into the Gulf.

COLLABORATIVE LEARNING PROBLEM

15-37 Joint cost allocation, process further or sell byproducts. (CMA) The Goodson Pharmaceutical Company manufactures three joint products from a joint process: Altox, Lorex, and Hycol. Data regarding these products for the fiscal year ended May 31, 2007, are as follows:

	Altox	Lorex	Hycol
Units produced	170,000	500,000	330,000
Selling price per unit at splitoff	$ 4.20	—	$ 2.40
Separable costs	—	$1,680,000	—
Final selling price per unit	—	$ 6.00	—

The joint production cost up to the splitoff point where Altox, Lorex, and Hycol become separable products is $2,160,000 (which includes the $21,000 disposal costs for Dorzine as described below).

The president of Goodson, Arlene Franklin, is reviewing an opportunity to change the way in which these three products are processed and sold. Proposed changes for each product are as follows:

◆ Altox is currently sold at the splitoff point to a manufacturer of vitamins. Altox can also be refined for use as a medication to treat high blood pressure; however, this additional processing would cause a loss of 20,000 units of Altox. The separable costs to further process Altox are estimated to be $300,000 annually. The final product would sell for $6.60 per unit.

◆ Lorex is currently processed further after the splitoff point and sold by Goodson as a cold remedy. The company has received an offer from another pharmaceutical company to purchase Lorex at the splitoff point for $2.70 per unit.

◆ Hycol is an oil produced from the joint process and is currently sold at the splitoff point to a cosmetics manufacturer. Goodson's research department has suggested that the company process this product further and sell it as an ointment to relieve muscle pain. The additional processing would cost $90,000 annually and would result in 25% more units of product. The final product would be sold for $2.16 per unit.

The joint process currently used by Goodson also produces 50,000 units of Dorzine, a hazardous chemical waste product. The company pays $0.42 per unit to dispose of the Dorzine properly. Dietriech Mills, Inc., is interested in using the Dorzine as a solvent; however, Goodson would have to refine the Dorzine at an annual cost of $51,600. Dietriech would purchase all the refined Dorzine produced by Goodson and is willing to pay $0.90 for each unit.

INSTRUCTIONS
Form groups of two or more students to complete the following requirements.

REQUIRED
1. Allocate the $2,160,000 joint production cost to Altox, Lorex, and Hycol using the estimated NRV method.
2. Identify which of the three joint products Goodson should sell at the splitoff point in the future and which of the three main products the company should process further to maximize profits. Support your decisions with appropriate calculations.
3. Assume that Goodson has decided to refine the waste product Dorzine for sale to Dietriech Mills, Inc., and will treat Dorzine as a byproduct of the joint process in the future.
   a. Evaluate whether Goodson made the correct decision regarding Dorzine. Support your answer with appropriate calculations.
   b. Explain whether the decision to treat Dorzine as a byproduct will affect the decisions reached in requirement 2.

The revenues of most large carbonated soft-drink companies—such as Cott, Coca-Cola, Pepsi-Cola, and Schweppes—come from many countries. Revenue analysis that highlights sales mix, sales quantity, market size, and market share is a key input to decisions regarding product and country emphasis.

16
Revenues, Sales Variances, and Customer Profitability Analysis

After studying this chapter, you should be able to

1. Give examples of the bundling of products that give rise to revenue-allocation issues

2. Allocate the revenues of a bundled package to the individual products in that package

3. Provide additional information about the sales-volume variance by calculating the sales-mix and sales-quantity variances

4. Provide additional information about the sales-quantity variance by calculating the market-share and market-size variances

5. Discuss why revenues can differ across customers purchasing the same product

6. Apply the concept of cost hierarchy to customer costing

7. Prepare a customer-profitability report

In prior chapters we highlighted how a detailed understanding of costs is essential when making decisions related to, say, products, services, customers, or departments. We have also highlighted the importance of costs in managing company operations. The other half of the profit equation—revenues—is equally important. Companies that prosper make revenue planning and revenue analysis top priorities for their managers.

This chapter covers three revenue-related topics. Part One on Revenue Allocation examines how challenging revenue-allocation issues arise with the now commonly used practice of selling multiple products or services as a single bundle for a single price. Part Two on Sales Variances highlights how the tools outlined in Chapter 7 can be used to analyze the variances of companies with revenues from multiple products. Part Three on Customer Profitability Analysis explores topics related to customer revenues and customer costs. Having a customer focus is a key theme underlying many planning and control decisions of managers. Part Three highlights several ways management accountants can help managers better focus on their customers. The Appendix shows how the framework outlined in Part Two of this chapter helps analyze cost variances for a company with substitutable inputs.

◆ PART ONE: REVENUE ALLOCATION

REVENUE ALLOCATION AND BUNDLED PRODUCTS

Revenue allocation. The assigning of revenues that are related, but not traceable to, individual products (services, customers, etc.) in an economically feasible (cost-effective) way. A revenue-allocation base is used to make this assignment.

Revenues are inflows of assets (almost always cash or accounts receivable) received for products or services provided to customers. Just as costs can be allocated to specific products, customers, and the like, so can revenues. **Revenue allocation** occurs when revenues that can be related to, but not traced to, individual revenue objects (products, services, divisions, customers, and so on) are assigned to those individual products. Revenue tracing results in a more accurate assignment of revenues to products than does revenue allocation. Just as with cost data, more accurate information is believed to result in better decisions.

The Superhighway Group, a computer software company, will be used to illustrate the issues discussed. Superhighway develops, sells, and supports three software packages:

1. **WordMaster.** Current version is WordMaster 5.0, which was released 36 months ago. WordMaster was the company's initial product.

2. **SpreadMaster.** Current version is SpreadMaster 3.0, which was released 18 months ago.

3. **FinanceMaster.** Current version is FinanceMaster 2.0. This product, the company's most recent, has been its most successful. The 2.0 version was released 6 months ago.

Bundled product. A package of two or more products or services, sold for a single price, whose individual components may be sold as separate items, each with its own stand-alone price.

Superhighway sells these three products individually and also sells them as bundled products. A **bundled product** is a package of two or more products or services, sold for a single price, whose individual components may also be sold as separate items, each with its own stand-alone price. The single price for the bundled product is typically less than the sum of the prices of two or more products if purchased separately. One example is Bell, which bundles its high-speed Internet access with its satellite television and mobile phone service at a price lower than the cost of all three sold separately. Another example is a resort hotel that offers, for a single price, a weekend package that includes services from its lodging (the room), food (the restaurant), and recreational (golfing) divisions. Where individual department or division managers have revenue or profit responsibilities, the issue thus becomes how to allocate the single bundled revenue amount among the individual products in that bundle.

Superhighway encounters revenue-allocation decisions with its bundled product sales (termed "suite sales"). Here, two or more of the software products are sold as a single package. Managers at Superhighway are keenly interested in individual-product profitability figures. There are separate managers for each product who are responsible for the operating income of that product. Moreover, its Software Department engineers are organized on a product-by-product basis and receive a percentage of product profitability as part of their bonus.

REVENUE-ALLOCATION METHODS

How should Superhighway allocate suite revenues to individual products? Information pertaining to its three suite sales and the stand-alone prices of its individual products is shown on the next page.

The two main classes of revenue allocation methods are the stand-alone method and the incremental method. We now discuss each in turn. Both methods are analogous to cost allocation methods discussed in Chapter 14.

Product	Sales Price	Manufacturing Cost per Unit
Stand-alone		
WordMaster	$125	$18
SpreadMaster	150	20
FinanceMaster	225	25
Suite		
Word + Spread	$220	
Word + Finance	280	
Finance + Spread	305	
Word + Finance + Spread	380	

OBJECTIVE 2

Allocate the revenues of a bundled package to the individual products in that package

Stand-Alone Revenue-Allocation Methods

The **stand-alone revenue-allocation method** uses product-specific information pertaining to products in the bundle to determine the weights used to allocate the bundled revenues to those individual products. The term *stand-alone* refers to the product as a separate (nonsuite) item. Consider the Word and Finance suite, which sells for $280. Four stand-alone sources of weights are as follows:

Stand-alone revenue-allocation method. Revenue-allocation method that uses product-specific information pertaining to products in the bundle to determine the weights used to allocate the bundled revenues to those individual products.

1. **Selling prices.** The individual selling prices are $125 for WordMaster and $225 for FinanceMaster. The weights for allocating the $280 between the two products are

$$\text{Word:} \quad \frac{\$125}{\$125 + \$225} \times \$280 = 0.357 \times \$280 = \$100$$

$$\text{Finance:} \quad \frac{\$225}{\$125 + \$225} \times \$280 = 0.643 \times \$280 = \$180$$

2. **Unit manufacturing costs.** This method uses costs of individual products to determine the weights to allocate revenues. Assume unit manufacturing costs are used to determine the weights to allocate and Word and Finance suite revenues of $280:

$$\text{Word:} \quad \frac{\$18}{\$18 + \$25} \times \$280 = 0.419 \times \$280 = \$117$$

$$\text{Finance:} \quad \frac{\$25}{\$18 + \$25} \times \$280 = 0.581 \times \$280 = \$163$$

This method does not recognize differences in the willingness of customers to purchase individual products.

3. **Physical units.** This method gives each product unit in the suite the same weight when allocating suite revenue to individual products. Thus, with two products in the Word plus Finance suite, each product gets 50% of the suite revenues allocated to it.

$$\text{Word:} \quad \frac{1}{1+1} \times \$280 = 0.50 \times \$280 = \$140$$

$$\text{Finance:} \quad \frac{1}{1+1} \times \$280 = 0.50 \times \$280 = \$140$$

It is most appropriate to use physical units when the sales values of the individual products in the bundle are approximately equal. Using physical units for, say, a bundle that includes a washing machine and a box of detergent would be inappropriate because it makes no sense to allocate half of the revenue to the box of detergent.

4. **Stand-alone product revenues.** Stand-alone product revenues will capture the quantity of each product sold as well as their selling prices. Assume that the stand-alone revenues are WordMaster, $28 million; SpreadMaster, $15 million;

and FinanceMaster, $7 million. The weights for the Word and Finances suite would be

$$\text{Word:} \quad \frac{\$28 \text{ million}}{\$28 \text{ million} + \$7 \text{ million}} \times \$280 = 0.80 \times \$280 = \$224$$

$$\text{Finance:} \quad \frac{\$7 \text{ million}}{\$28 \text{ million} + \$7 \text{ million}} \times \$280 = 0.20 \times \$280 = \$56$$

The lower revenue allocation to FinanceMaster is, in part, due to it only being released partway through the year.

These four approaches to determining weights with the stand-alone method yield the following revenue allocations to individual products:

Revenue-Allocation Weights	WordMaster	FinanceMaster
Selling prices	$100	$180
Unit manufacturing costs	117	163
Physical units	140	140
Stand-alone product revenues	224	56

The unit selling price weights are advantageous in that they frequently are the best available external indicator of the benefits companies receive from selling products. Market-based weighting schemes that are closer to the customer better capture a benefits-received notion in a bundled product allocation setting than do cost-based or unit-based weights. Unit-based revenue allocation is typically rationalized on the basis of ease of use or limitations of alternative methods (such as unit selling prices are unstable; or unit manufacturing costs are difficult to calculate at the individual-product level).

Incremental Revenue-Allocation Method

Incremental revenue-allocation method. Revenue-allocation method that ranks the individual products in a bundle and then uses this ranking to allocate the bundled revenues to the individual products.

The **incremental revenue-allocation method** ranks the individual products in a bundle and then uses this ranking to allocate the bundled revenues to these individual products. The first-ranked product is termed the *primary product* in the bundle. The second-ranked product is termed the *first incremental product*, the third-ranked product is the *second incremental product*, and so on.

Who decides on the ranking of products in the incremental revenue-allocation method? One approach is to survey customers on the relative importance of individual products in their decision to purchase the bundled products. A second approach is to use data on recent stand-alone performance of the individual products in the bundle. A third approach is for top management to decide the rankings based on their knowledge or intuition.

Consider again the Word and Finance suite of Superhighway. Assume WordMaster is designated as the primary product. If the suite revenue exceeds the stand-alone revenue of the primary product, the primary product is allocated 100% of its stand-alone revenue. This is the case for the Word and Finance suite. The suite revenue of $280 exceeds the stand-alone revenue of $125 for WordMaster; WordMaster is allocated revenues of $125, with the remaining or residual revenue of $155 ($280 − $125) allocated to FinanceMaster:

▶ Under the incremental revenue-allocation method, all users of the revenue object want to be the first-ranked user. That's because the first-ranked user will be allocated a larger portion of the revenues.

▶ The recalculation when FinanceMaster is the primary product:

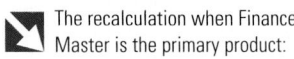

Product	Revenue Allocated	Cumulative Revenue Allocated
FinanceMaster:	$225	$225
WordMaster:	55	280
	$280	

Product	Revenue Allocated	Cumulative Revenue Allocated
WordMaster	$125	$125
FinanceMaster ($280 − $125)	155	$280
Total	$280	

Clearly, the ranking of the individual products in the suite is a key factor in determining the revenues allocated to individual products.

If Superhighway sells equal quantities of WordMaster and FinanceMaster, then the *Shapley value* method allocates to each product the average of the revenues allocated as the primary and first incremental products:

$$\text{WordMaster:} \quad \frac{(\$125 + \$55)}{2} = \$180 \div 2 = \$90$$

$$\text{FinanceMaster:} \quad \frac{(\$225 + \$155)}{2} = \$380 \div 2 = 190$$

$$\text{Total} \qquad\qquad\qquad\qquad\qquad\qquad \$280$$

But what if, in the most recent quarter, Superhighway sells 80,000 units of WordMaster and 20,000 units of FinanceMaster? Because Superhighway sells four times as many units of WordMaster, its managers believe that the sales of the Word + Finance suite are four times more likely to be driven by WordMaster as the primary product. The *weighted Shapley value* method takes this into account by weighting the revenue allocations when WordMaster is the primary product four times as much as when FinanceMaster is the primary product:

$$\text{WordMaster:} \quad \frac{(\$125 \times 4 + \$55 \times 1)}{(4 + 1)} = \frac{\$555}{5} = \$111$$

$$\text{FinanceMaster:} \quad \frac{(\$225 \times 1 + \$155 \times 4)}{(4 + 1)} = \frac{\$845}{5} = 169$$

$$\text{Total} \qquad\qquad\qquad\qquad\qquad\qquad\qquad \$280$$

When there are more than two products in the suite, the incremental revenue-allocation method allocates suite revenues sequentially. Assume WordMaster is the primary product in Superhighway's three-product suite (Word + Finance + Spread). FinanceMaster is the first incremental product, and SpreadMaster is the second incremental product. This suite sells for $380. The allocation of the $380 suite revenues proceeds as follows:

Product	Revenue Allocated	Cumulative Revenue Allocated
WordMaster	$125	$125
FinanceMaster ($280 − $125)	155	$280 (price of Word + Finance suite)
SpreadMaster ($380 − $280)	100	$380 (price of Word + Finance + Spread suite)
Total	$380	

Now suppose WordMaster is the primary product, SpreadMaster is the first incremental product, and FinanceMaster is the second incremental product.

Product	Revenue Allocated	Cumulative Revenue Allocated
WordMaster	$125	$125
SpreadMaster ($220 − $125)	95	$220 (price of Word + Spread suite)
FinanceMaster ($380 − $220)	160	$380 (price of Word + Spread + Finance suite)
Total	$380	

The ranking of the individual products in the suite determines the revenues allocated to them. Product managers at Superhighway likely would differ on how they believe their individual products contribute to sales of the suite products. It is possible that each product manager would claim to be responsible for the primary product in the Word + Finance + Spread suite!

Calculating the Shapley value mitigates this problem because each product is considered as a primary, first-incremental, and second-incremental product. Assuming equal weights on all products, the revenue allocated to each product is an average of the revenues calculated for each product under these different assumptions: FinanceMaster, $180; WordMaster, $87.50; and SpreadMaster, $112.50:

Order			Revenues Allocated to Each Product		
Primary	First Incremental	Second Incremental	FinanceMaster	WordMaster	SpreadMaster
FinanceMaster	WordMaster	SpreadMaster	$225	$ 55 ($280 − $225)	$100 ($380 − $225 − $55)
FinanceMaster	SpreadMaster	WordMaster	$225	$ 75 ($380 − $225 − $80)	$ 80 ($305 − $225)
WordMaster	FinanceMaster	SpreadMaster	$155 ($280 − $125)	$125	$100 ($380 − $125 − $155)
WordMaster	SpreadMaster	FinanceMaster	$160 ($380 − $125 − $95)	$125	$ 95 ($220 − $125)
SpreadMaster	FinanceMaster	WordMaster	$155 ($305 − $150)	$ 75 ($380 − $150 − $155)	$150
SpreadMaster	WordMaster	FinanceMaster	$160 ($380 − $150 − $70)	$ 70 ($220 − $150)	$150
Total:			$1,080	$525	$675
Average Revenue Allocated:			$1,080 ÷ 6 = $180	$525 ÷ 6 = $87.50	$675 ÷ 6 = $112.50

Because the stand-alone revenue-allocation method does not require rankings of individual products in the suite, this method is less likely to cause debates among product managers.

Other Revenue-Allocation Methods

Management's judgment that is not explicitly based on a specific formula is an alternative method of revenue allocation. In one case, the president of a software company decided to issue a set of revenue-allocation weights after the managers of the three products in the bundled suite could not themselves agree on a set of weights. The weights chosen by the president for the three products were 45% for Product A, 45% for Product B, and 10% for Product C. The factors the president considered included stand-alone selling prices (all three were very similar), stand-alone unit sales (A and B were over 10 times more than C), product ratings by independent experts, and consumer awareness. The Product C manager complained that his 10% weighting dramatically short-changed the contribution of Product C to suite revenues. The president responded that its inclusion in the suite greatly increased consumer exposure to Product C with the result that Product C's total revenues would be far larger (even with only 10% of suite revenues) than had it not been included in the suite.

Part One of this chapter has discussed revenue allocation. Part Two discusses sales variances.

PROBLEM

Business Horizons (BH) produces and markets videos for sale to the business community. It hires well-known business speakers to present new developments in their area of expertise in video format. The compensation paid to each speaker is individually negotiated. It always has a component based on the percentage of revenues from the sale of the video, but that percentage is not uniform across speakers. Moreover, some speakers negotiate separate fixed-dollar payments or multiple-video deals.

BH sells most videos as separate items. However, there is a growing trend for videos also to be sold as part of bundled packages. BH offered bundled packages of its three best-selling videos in 2007. Individual and bundled sales of these three videos for 2007 are

Individual Sales

Speaker	Title	Units Sold	Selling Price	Speaker Royalty
Jeannett Smith	Negotiating for Win-Win	25,000	$150	24%
Mark Coyne	Marketing for the Internet	17,000	$120	16%
Laurie Daley	Electronic Commerce	8,000	$130	19%

Bundled Product Sales

Titles in Bundle	Units Sold	Selling Price
Negotiating for Win-Win + Marketing for the Internet	12,000	$210
Negotiating for Win-Win + Electronic Commerce	5,000	$220
Marketing for the Internet + Electronic Commerce	4,000	$190
Negotiating + Marketing + Electronic	11,000	$280

REQUIRED

1. Allocate the bundled product revenues to the individual videos using the stand-alone revenue-allocation method (using selling prices as the weights).
2. Describe (without computations) an alternative method of allocating the bundled product revenues to that in requirement 1.

SOLUTION

1. The weights in the stand-alone method are based on the stand-alone selling prices of the videos in the bundled package. The following table details these weights, which are then used to allocate the revenues of each bundled package to the three individual videos.

	Allocation Formula	Negotiating	Marketing	Electronic
N + M:	($150 ÷ $270) × $210 × 12,000	$1,400,000		
N + E:	($150 ÷ $280) × $220 × 5,000	589,286		
N + M + E:	($150 ÷ $400) × $280 × 11,000	1,155,000		
Total		$3,144,286		
M + N:	($120 ÷ $270) × $210 × 12,000		$1,120,000	
M + E:	($120 ÷ $250) × $190 × 4,000		364,800	
M + N + E:	($120 ÷ $400) × $280 × 11,000		924,000	
Total			$2,408,800	
E + N:	($130 ÷ $280) × $220 × 5,000			$510,714
E + M:	($130 ÷ $250) × $190 × 4,000			395,200
E + N + M:	($130 ÷ $400) × $280 × 11,000			1,001,000
Total				$1,906,914

2. An alternative approach to allocating the bundled product revenues is the incremental revenue-allocation method. Here the individual videos in the bundle are ranked in order of importance, and the revenues are allocated to each product using stand-alone selling prices until all the bundled revenue has been fully allocated. Use of this approach would likely create some friction among the three business speakers. It would be in each speaker's interest to claim to be the primary speaker driving sales of the bundle. The actual 2007 units sold figures would enable Business Horizons to give a market-success-based ranking of individual business speakers if it used the incremental revenue-allocation method.

◆ PART TWO: SALES VARIANCES

SALES-VOLUME VARIANCE COMPONENTS

Part One of this chapter highlighted several issues in obtaining reliable information on the revenues of individual products or services. In Part Two we examine how to calculate variances that use revenue information as a key input. Special attention is paid to companies with multiple products or services and to companies selling the same product or service in multiple distribution channels. Companies such as Cisco, GE, and Hewlett-Packard perform similar analyses because they sell their products through multiple distribution channels, for example, via the Internet, over the telephone, or in retail stores.

Spring Distribution Company sells bottled water. It has two distribution channels: (1) a wholesale distribution channel, in which the wholesaler sells to supermarkets, drugstores, and other stores, and (2) a retail distribution channel for a small number of business customers. Spring classifies all customer-level costs as variable costs and distribution-channel and corporate-sustaining costs as fixed costs. To simplify the sales-variance analysis and calculations, we assume that all these variable costs are variable with respect to units (cases) sold. (This means, for example, that average batch sizes remain the same as the total cases sold vary.) Without this assumption, the analysis would become more complex and would have to be done using the ABC-variance analysis approach described in Chapter 7 (p. 263). The basic insights, however, would not change. Budget data for June 2007 is shown in the table below:

Budget Data for June 2007

	Selling Price per Unit (1)	Variable Cost per Unit (2)	Contribution Margin per Unit (3) = (1) − (2)	Sales Volume in Units (4)	Sales Mix (Based on Units) (5)	Contribution Margin (6) = (3) × (4)
Wholesale channel	$13.37	$12.88	$0.49	712,000	80%[a]	$348,880
Retail channel	14.10	13.12	0.98	178,000	20%	174,440
Total				890,000	100%	$523,320

"Unit" in the column headings refers to a case of 24 bottles
[a]Percentage of unit sales to wholesale channel = 712,000 units ÷ 890,000 total units = 80%.

Actual Data for June 2007

	Selling Price per Unit (1)	Variable Cost per Unit (2)	Contribution Margin per Unit (3) = (1) − (2)	Sales Volume in Units (4)	Sales Mix (Based on Units) (5)	Contribution Margin (6) = (3) × (4)
Wholesale channel	$13.37	$12.88	$0.49	756,000	84%	$370,440
Retail channel	14.10	13.17	0.93	144,000	16%	133,920
Total				900,000	100%	$504,360

The budgeted and actual fixed distribution-channel costs and corporate-sustaining costs are $160,500 and $263,000, respectively.

Recall that the levels of detail introduced in Chapter 7 included the static-budget variance (level 1), the flexible-budget variance (level 2), and the sales-volume variance (level 2). The sales-quantity and sales-mix variances are level 3 variances that subdivide the sales-volume variance.[1]

Static-Budget Variance

The *static-budget variance* is calculated as:

$$\text{Static-budget variance} = \text{Actual results} - \text{Static-budget amount}$$

Our analysis focuses on the difference between actual and budgeted contribution margins (column 6 in the preceding tables). The total static-budget variance is $18,960 U (actual contribution margin of $504,360 − budgeted contribution margin of $523,320). Exhibit 16-1 (columns 1 and 3) uses the columnar format introduced in Chapter 7 to show detailed calculations of the static-budget variance. Managers can gain more insight about the static-budget variance by subdividing it into the flexible-budget variance and the sales-volume variance.

Flexible-Budget and Sales-Volume Variances

The *flexible-budget variance* is calculated as:

$$\text{Flexible-budget variance} = \text{Actual results} - \text{Flexible-budget amount}$$

The *flexible-budget variance* is the difference between an actual result and the corresponding flexible-budget amount based on actual output level in the budget period. The flexible-budget contribution margin is equal to budgeted contribution margin per unit (case) times actual units (cases) sold of each product. Exhibit 16-1,

EXHIBIT 16-1
Flexible-Budget and Sales-Volume Variance Analysis of Spring Distribution for June 2007

	A	B	C	D	E	F	G
1		**Actual Results:**		**Flexible Budget:**		**Static Budget:**	
2		**Actual Units of**		**Actual Units of**		**Budgeted Units of**	
3		**All Products Sold ×**		**All Products Sold ×**		**All Products Sold ×**	
4		**Actual Sales Mix ×**		**Actual Sales Mix ×**		**Budgeted Sales Mix ×**	
5		**Actual Contribution**		**Budgeted Contribution**		**Budgeted Contribution**	
6		**Margin per Unit**		**Margin per Unit**		**Margin per Unit**	
7		**(1)**		**(2)**		**(3)**	
8	Wholesale	900,000 × 0.84 × $0.49 =	$370,440	900,000 × 0.84 × $0.49 =	$370,440	890,000 × 0.80 × $0.49 =	$348,880
9	Retail	900,000 × 0.16 × $0.93 =	133,920	900,000 × 0.16 × $0.98 =	141,120	890,000 × 0.20 × $0.98 =	174,440
10			$504,360		$511,560		$523,320
11			↑	$7,200 U	↑	$11,760 U	↑
12	Level 2			Flexible-budget variance		Sales-volume variance	
13			↑		$ 18,960 U		↑
14	Level 1			Static budget variance			
15							
16	F = favourable effect on operating income; U = unfavourable effect on operating income						

---

[1] The presentation of the variances in this chapter and the appendix draws on teaching notes prepared by J.K. Harris.

column 2, shows the flexible-budget calculations. The flexible budget measures the contribution margin that Spring would have budgeted for the actual quantities of cases sold. The flexible-budget variance is the difference between columns 1 and 2 in Exhibit 16-1. The only difference between columns 1 and 2 is that actual units sold of each product is multiplied by actual contribution margin per unit in column 1 and budgeted contribution margin per unit in column 2. The $7,200 U flexible-budget variance arises because actual contribution margin on retail sales of $0.93 per case is lower than the budgeted amount of $0.98 per case. Spring's management is aware that this difference of $0.05 per case resulted from excessive price discounts, and they have put in place controls to reduce discounts in the future.

The *sales-volume variance* is calculated as:

$$\text{Sales-volume variance} = \left(\begin{array}{c} \text{Actual sales} \\ \text{quantity in units} \end{array} - \begin{array}{c} \text{Static-budget sales} \\ \text{quantity in units} \end{array} \right) \times \begin{array}{c} \text{Budgeted contribution} \\ \text{margin per unit} \end{array}$$

The sales-volume variance shows the effect of the difference between the actual and budgeted quantity of the variable used to "flex" the flexible budget. The sales-volume variance of $11,760 U is the difference between columns 2 and 3 in Exhibit 16-1. Spring's managers can gain substantial insight into the sales-volume variance by subdividing it into the sales-mix variance and the sales-quantity variance.

SALES-MIX AND SALES-QUANTITY VARIANCES

OBJECTIVE 3

Provide additional information about the sales-volume variance by calculating the sales-mix and sales-quantity variances

Exhibit 16-2 shows how both the sales-mix and sales-quantity variances can be calculated using the columnar approach introduced in Chapter 7. Please refer to this exhibit when reading the following discussion of these two variances.

Sales-Mix Variance

Sales-mix variance. The difference between (1) the budgeted amount for the actual sales mix and (2) the budgeted amount if the budgeted sales mix had been unchanged.

The **sales-mix variance** is the difference between two amounts: (1) the budgeted amount for the actual sales mix and (2) the budgeted amount for the budgeted sales mix. The formula for computing the sales-mix variance in terms of the contribution margin for Spring is

$$\text{Sales mix variance} = \begin{array}{c} \text{Actual units of} \\ \text{all products sold} \end{array} \times \left(\begin{array}{c} \text{Actual sales} \\ \text{mix percentage} \end{array} - \begin{array}{c} \text{Budgeted sales} \\ \text{mix percentage} \end{array} \right) \times \begin{array}{c} \text{Budgeted} \\ \text{contribution} \\ \text{margin per unit} \end{array}$$

	Actual Units of All Products Sold	×	(Actual Sales-Mix Percentage	−	Budgeted Sales-Mix Percentage)	×	Budgeted Contribution Margin per Unit	=	Sales-Mix Variance
Wholesale	900,000 units	×	(84.00%	−	80.00%)	×	$0.49 per unit	=	$ 17,640 F
Retail	900,000 units	×	(16.00%	−	20.00%)	×	$0.98 per unit	=	$(35,280) U
Total sales-mix variance									$(17,640) U

A favourable sales-mix variance arises for the wholesale channel because the 84% actual sales-mix percentage exceeds the 80% budgeted sales-mix percentage. In contrast, the retail channel has an unfavourable variance because the 16% actual sales-mix percentage is less than the 20% budgeted sales-mix percentage. The sales-mix variance is unfavourable because actual sales mix shifted toward the less-profitable wholesale channel relative to budgeted sales mix.

The concept underlying the sales-mix variance is best explained in terms of budgeted contribution margin per composite unit of the sales mix. A **composite unit** is a hypothetical unit with weights based on the mix of individual units. For actual sales mix, the composite unit consists of 0.84 units of sales to the wholesale channel and 0.16 units of sales to the retail channel. For budgeted sales mix, the composite

Composite unit. A hypothetical unit with weights based on the mix of individual units.

EXHIBIT 16-2
Sales-Mix and Sales-Quantity Variance Analysis of Spring Distribution for June 2007

	A	B	C	D	E	F	G
1		Flexible Budget:				Static Budget:	
2		Actual Units of		Actual Units of		Budgeted Units of	
3		All Products Sold ×		All Products Sold ×		All Products Sold ×	
4		Actual Sales Mix ×		Budgeted Sales Mix ×		Budgeted Sales Mix ×	
5		Budgeted Contribution		Budgeted Contribution		Budgeted Contribution	
6		Margin per Unit		Margin per Unit		Margin per Unit	
7		(1)		(2)		(3)	
8	Wholesale	900,000 × 0.84 × $0.49 =	$370,440	900,000 × 0.80 × $0.49 =	$352,800	890,000 × 0.80 × $0.49 =	$348,880
9	Retail	900,000 × 0.16 × $0.98 =	141,120	900,000 × 0.20 × $0.98 =	176,400	890,000 × 0.20 × $0.98 =	174,440
10			$511,560		$529,200		$523,320
11			↑	$17,640 U	↑	$5,880 F	↑
12	Level 3			Sales-mix variance		Sales-quantity variance	
13			↑		$ 11,760 U		↑
14	Level 2				Sales-volume variance		

unit consists of 0.80 units of sales to the wholesale channel and 0.20 units of sales to the retail channel. In the following table, budgeted contribution margin per composite unit is computed in column 3 for actual mix and in column 5 for budgeted mix:

	Budgeted Contribution Margin per Unit	Actual Sales-Mix Percentage	Budgeted Contribution Margin per Unit for Actual Mix	Budgeted Sales-Mix Percentage	Budgeted Contribution Margin per Composite Unit for Budgeted Mix
	(1)	(2)	(3) = (1) × (2)	(4)	(5) = (1) × (4)
Wholesale	$0.49	84.00%	$0.4116	80.00%	$0.3920
Retail	0.98	16.00%	0.1568	20.00%	0.1960
			$0.5684		$0.5880

Actual sales mix has a budgeted contribution margin per composite unit of $0.5684. Budgeted sales mix has a budgeted contribution margin per composite unit of $0.5880. Budgeted contribution margin per composite unit can be computed in another way by dividing total budgeted contribution margin of $523,320 by total budgeted units of 890,000 (p. 632): $523,320 ÷ 890,000 units = $0.5880 per unit. The effect of the sales-mix shift for Spring is to decrease budgeted contribution margin per composite unit by $0.0196 ($0.5880 − $0.5684). For the 900,000 units actually sold, this decrease translates to a $17,640 U sales-mix variance ($0.0196 per unit × 900,000 units).

Managers should probe why the $17,640 U sales-mix variance occurred in June 2007. Is the shift in sales mix because, as the analysis in the previous section showed, profitable retail customers proved to be more difficult to find? Is it because of a competitor in the retail channel providing better service at a lower price? Or is it because the initial sales-volume estimates were made without adequate analysis of the potential market?

Sales-Quantity Variance

The **sales-quantity variance** is the difference between two amounts: (1) the budgeted contribution margin based on actual units sold of all products and the

The variances described here—the sales-mix variance, sales-quantity variance, market-share variance, and market-size variance—provide information on why sales differed from expectations, which is especially helpful to marketing managers in planning and controlling their activities

Actual contribution margins per unit are not used in calculating the sales-volume variance or any of the variances that are subdivided from it. That is why Exhibits 16-1 and 16-2 use budgeted contribution margins per unit.

The intuition for the sales-mix variance is that there is a composite unit at the *budgeted mix* and a different composite unit at the *actual mix*. Accordingly, the sales-mix variance (per composite unit) is the difference between the budgeted contribution margins of these two composite units.

Sales-quantity variance. The difference between (1) the budgeted amount based on actual quantities sold of all products and the budgeted mix and (2) the amount in the static budget (which is based on the budgeted quantities to be sold of all products and the budgeted mix).

budgeted mix, and (2) the contribution margin in the static budget (which is based on the budgeted units to be sold of all products and the budgeted mix). The formula for calculating the sales-quantity variance in terms of contribution margin is

$$\text{Sales-quantity variance} = \left(\begin{array}{c}\text{Actual units of} \\ \text{all products sold}\end{array} - \begin{array}{c}\text{Bugeted units of} \\ \text{all products sold}\end{array}\right) \times \begin{array}{c}\text{Budgeted sales-} \\ \text{mix percentage}\end{array} \times \begin{array}{c}\text{Budgeted} \\ \text{contribution} \\ \text{margin per unit}\end{array}$$

	$\left(\begin{array}{c}\textbf{Actual Units of} \\ \textbf{All Products Sold}\end{array}\right.$	$-$	$\left.\begin{array}{c}\textbf{Budgeted Units of} \\ \textbf{All Products Sold}\end{array}\right)$	$\times$	$\begin{array}{c}\textbf{Budgeted Sales-} \\ \textbf{Mix Percentage}\end{array}$	$\times$	$\begin{array}{c}\textbf{Budgeted} \\ \textbf{Contribution} \\ \textbf{Margin per Unit}\end{array}$	$=$	$\begin{array}{c}\textbf{Quantity} \\ \textbf{Variance}\end{array}$
Wholesale	(900,000	–	890,000)	×	80.00%	×	$0.49 per unit	=	$ 3,920 F
Retail	(900,000	–	890,000)	×	20.00%	×	$0.98 per unit	=	1,960 F
Total sales-quantity variance									$ 5,880 F

This variance is favourable when actual units of all products sold exceed budgeted units of all products sold. Spring sold 10,000 more cases than were budgeted, resulting in a $5,880 F sales-quantity variance (also equal to budgeted contribution margin per composite unit for the budgeted sales mix times additional cases sold, $0.5880 × 10,000). Managers would want to probe the reasons for the increase in sales. Did higher sales come as a result of a competitor's distribution problems? Better customer service? Or growth in the overall market? Further insight into the causes of the sales-quantity variance can be gained by analyzing changes in Spring's share of the total industry market and in the size of that market.

MARKET-SHARE AND MARKET-SIZE VARIANCES

OBJECTIVE 4

Provide additional information about the sales-quantity variance by calculating the market-share and market-size variances

Sales depend on overall demand for the industry's products as well as the company's share of the market for bottled water. Assume that Spring derived its total unit sales budget for 2007 from a management estimate of a 25% market share and a total industry sales forecast of 3,560,000 units (0.25 × 3,560,000 units = 890,000 units). For June 2007 actual industry sales were 4,000,000 and Spring's actual market share was 22.5% (900,000 ÷ 4,000,000 = 0.225 or 22.5%). Exhibit 16-3 shows the columnar presentation of the market-share and market-size variances of Spring.

Market-Share Variance

Market-share variance. The difference between (1) the budgeted amount at budgeted mix based on the actual market size in units and the actual market share and (2) the budgeted amount at budgeted mix based on actual market size in units and the budgeted market share.

The **market-share variance** is the difference between two amounts: (1) the budgeted amount based on actual market size in units, *actual market share*, and budgeted contribution margin per composite unit for the budgeted mix, and (2) the budgeted amount based on actual market size in units, *budgeted market share*, and budgeted contribution margin per composite unit for the budgeted mix. The formula for computing the market-share variance in terms of contribution margin for Spring is

$$\text{Market-share variance} = \begin{array}{c}\text{Actual market} \\ \text{size in units}\end{array} \times \left(\begin{array}{c}\text{Actual} \\ \text{market share}\end{array} - \begin{array}{c}\text{Budgeted} \\ \text{market share}\end{array}\right) \times \begin{array}{c}\text{Budgeted contribution} \\ \text{margin per composite} \\ \text{unit for budgeted mix}\end{array}$$

$$= 4,000,000 \text{ units (cases)} \times (0.225 - 0.25) \times \$0.5880 \text{ per unit (case)}$$

$$= \$58,800 \text{ U}$$

EXHIBIT 16-3
Market-Share and Market-Size Variance Analysis of Spring Distribution for June 2007

	A	B	C	D	E	F
1						**Static Budget:**
2		**Actual Market Size ×**		**Actual Market Size ×**		**Budgeted Market Size ×**
3		**Actual Market Share ×**		**Budgeted Market Share ×**		**Budgeted Market Share ×**
4		**Budgeted Average**		**Budgeted Average**		**Budgeted Average**
5		**Contribution Margin**		**Contribution Margin**		**Contribution Margin**
6		**per Unit**		**per Unit**		**per Unit**
7		4,000,000 × 0.225ᵃ × $0.5880ᵇ		4,000,000 × 0.25ᶜ × $0.5880ᵇ		3,560,000 × 0.25ᶜ × $0.5880ᵇ
8		$529,200		$588,000		$523,320
9						
10			$58,800 U		$64,680 F	
11	Level 4		Market-share variance		Market-size variance	
12						
13				$5,880 F		
14	Level 3			Sales-quantity variance		
15						
16	F = favourable effect on operating income U = unfavourable effect on operating income					
17	ᵃActual market share: 900,000 units ÷ 4,000,000 units = 0.225 or 22.5%					
18	ᵇBudgeted average contribution margin per unit: $523,320 ÷ 890,000 units = $0.5880 per unit					
19	ᶜBudgeted market share: 890,000 ÷ 3,560,000 units = 0.25 or 25%					

The budgeted contribution margin per composite unit for the budgeted mix (also known as budgeted average contribution margin per unit) can be calculated using the approach outlined earlier in this chapter.

Market-Size Variance

The **market-size variance** is the difference between two amounts: (1) the budgeted amount based on *actual market size in units*, budgeted market share, and budgeted contribution margin per composite unit for budgeted mix, and (2) the static budget amount based on the *budgeted market size in units*, budgeted market share, and budgeted contribution margin per composite unit for budgeted mix. The formula for computing the market-size variance in terms of contribution margin for Spring is

Market-size variance. The difference between (1) the budgeted amount based on the actual market size in units and the budgeted market share and (2) the static budget amount based on the budgeted market size in units and the budgeted market share.

$$\text{Market-size variance} = \left(\begin{array}{c} \text{Actual market} \\ \text{size in units} \end{array} - \begin{array}{c} \text{Budgeted market} \\ \text{size in units} \end{array} \right) \times \begin{array}{c} \text{Budgeted} \\ \text{market share} \end{array} \times \begin{array}{c} \text{Budgeted contribution} \\ \text{margin per composite} \\ \text{unit for budgeted mix} \end{array}$$

$$= 4{,}000{,}000 \text{ units (cases)} - 3{,}560{,}000) \times 0.25 \times \$0.5880$$

$$= \$64{,}680 \text{ F}$$

The market-size variance is favourable because actual market size, or total consumer demand, increased 440,000 cases or 12.4%* compared to budgeted market size. Managers should probe the reasons for the market-share and market-size variances for June 2007. Was the $58,800 unfavourable market-share variance because of competitors providing better service and offering a lower price? Did Spring's products experience quality-control problems that were the

The concepts of market size and market share are also important to TV networks. A network's advertising revenues increase when the aggregate market (viewers) increases or when the network's share of the market increases. The measures used to calculate market size and market share are debated intensely in the TV industry.

*(4,000,000 − 3,560,000) ÷ 3,560,000 = 0.124 or 12.4%.

EXHIBIT 16-4
Overview of Contribution Margin Variances for Spring Distribution for June 2007

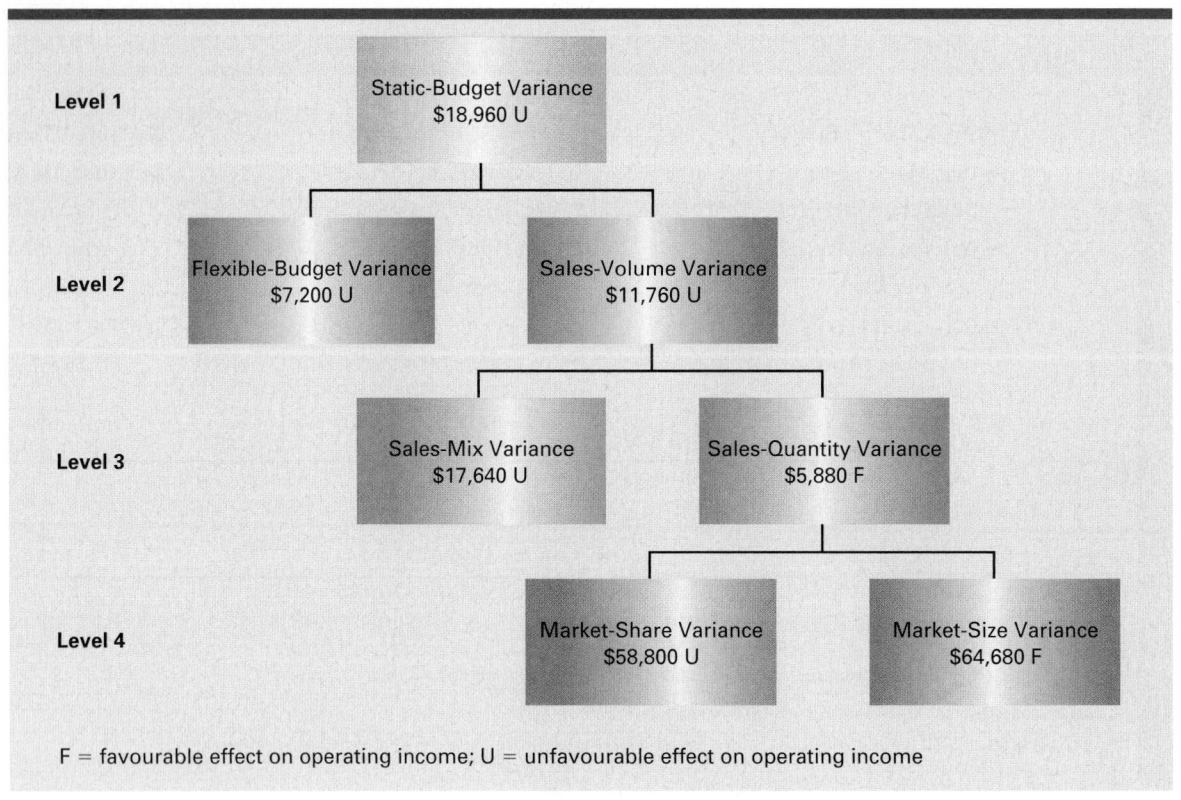

Level 1 — Static-Budget Variance $18,960 U

Level 2 — Flexible-Budget Variance $7,200 U | Sales-Volume Variance $11,760 U

Level 3 — Sales-Mix Variance $17,640 U | Sales-Quantity Variance $5,880 F

Level 4 — Market-Share Variance $58,800 U | Market-Size Variance $64,680 F

F = favourable effect on operating income; U = unfavourable effect on operating income

We calculated market-share and market-size variances (as subdivisions of the *sales-quantity variance*) based on the overall market for bottled water, regardless of whether the water was sold through wholesale or retail channels. If, however, a company has products that it sells in different markets (for example, companies such as GlaxoSmithKline sell both consumer products and pharmaceuticals), the company may decide to calculate market-share and market-size variances for each market separately as an alternative method of subdividing the *sales volume* variance.

subject of negative media coverage? Is the $64,680 F market-size variance because of an increase in market size that can be expected to continue in the future? If yes, Spring has much to gain by attaining or exceeding its budgeted 25% market share.

Some companies place more emphasis on the market-share variance than the market-size variance when evaluating their managers. That's because they believe the market-size variance is influenced by economywide factors and shifts in consumer preferences that are outside the managers' control, whereas the market-share variance measures how well managers performed relative to their peers. Be cautious when computing the market-size variance and the market-share variance. Reliable information on market size and market share is available for some, but not all, industries. The automobile, computer, and television industries are cases in which market-size and market-share statistics are widely available. In other industries, such as management consulting and personal financial planning, information about market size and market share is far less reliable.

Exhibit 16-4 presents an overview of the Level 1 to Level 4 variances. The appendix to this chapter describes mix and quantity variances for production outputs.

The sales-mix variance, sales-quantity variance, market-share variance, and market-size variance can also be calculated in a multiproduct company, in which each individual product has a different contribution margin per unit. The Problem for Self-Study calculates these level 3 and level 4 sales variances in a multiproduct company.

Parts One and Two of this chapter have discussed revenue allocation and sales variances. Part Three discusses customer profitability analysis.

PROBLEM

The Payne Company manufactures two types of vinyl flooring. Budgeted and actual operating data for 2007 are:

	Static Budget			Actual Results		
	Commercial	Residential	Total	Commercial	Residential	Total
Unit sales in rolls	20,000	60,000	80,000	25,200	58,800	84,000
Contribution margin	$10,000,000	$24,000,000	$34,000,000	$11,970,000	$24,696,000	$36,666,000

In late 2006, a marketing research firm estimated industry volume for commercial and residential vinyl flooring for 2007 at 800,000 rolls. Actual industry volume for 2007 was 700,000 rolls.

REQUIRED

1. Compute the sales-mix variance and the sales-quantity variance by type of vinyl flooring and in total. (Compute all variances in terms of contribution margins.)
2. Compute the market-share variance and the market-size variance.
3. What insights do the variances calculated in 1 and 2 provide about Payne Company's performance in 2007?

SOLUTION

1. Actual sales-mix percentage:

$$\text{Commercial} = 25,200 \div 84,000 = 0.30, \text{ or } 30\%$$
$$\text{Residential} = 58,800 \div 84,000 = 0.70, \text{ or } 70\%$$

Budgeted sales-mix percentage:

$$\text{Commercial} = 20,000 \div 80,000 = 0.25, \text{ or } 25\%$$
$$\text{Residential} = 60,000 \div 80,000 = 0.75, \text{ or } 75\%$$

Budgeted contribution margin per unit:

$$\text{Commercial} = \$10,000,000 \div 20,000 \text{ units} = \$500 \text{ per unit}$$
$$\text{Residential} = \$24,000,000 \div 60,000 \text{ units} = \$400 \text{ per unit}$$

	Actual Units of All Products Sold	×	(Actual Sales-Mix Percentage − Budgeted Sales-Mix Percentage)	×	Budgeted Contribution Margin per Unit	=	Sales-Mix Variance
Commercial	84,000 units	×	(0.30 − 0.25)	×	$500 per unit	=	$2,100,000 F
Residential	84,000 units	×	(0.70 − 0.75)	×	$400 per unit	=	1,680,000 U
Total sales-mix variance							$ 420,000 F

	(Actual Units of All Products Sold − Budgeted Units of All Products Sold)	×	Budgeted Sales-Mix Percentage	×	Budgeted Contribution Margin per Unit	=	Sales-Quantity Variance
Commercial	(84,000 units − 80,000 units)	×	0.25	×	$500 per unit	=	$ 500,000 F
Residential	(84,000 units − 80,000 units)	×	0.75	×	$400 per unit	=	1,200,000 F
Total sales-quantity variance							$1,700,000 F

2. Actual market share = 84,000 ÷ 700,000 = 0.12, or 12%
   Budgeted market share = 80,000 ÷ 800,000 = 0.10, or 10%
   Budgeted contribution margin
   per composite unit = $34,000,000 ÷ 80,000 units = $425 per unit
   of budgeted mix

Budgeted contribution margin per composite unit of budgeted mix can also be calculated as:

Commercial: $500 per unit × 0.25 = $125 per unit

Residential: $400 per unit × 0.75 = $300 per unit

$425 per unit

$$\begin{array}{l} \text{Market-share} \\ \text{variance} \end{array} = \begin{array}{c} \text{Actual} \\ \text{market size} \\ \text{in units} \end{array} \times \left(\begin{array}{c} \text{Actual} \\ \text{market} \\ \text{share} \end{array} - \begin{array}{c} \text{Budgeted} \\ \text{market} \\ \text{share} \end{array} \right) \times \begin{array}{c} \text{Budgeted} \\ \text{contribution margin} \\ \text{per composite unit} \\ \text{for budgeted mix} \end{array}$$

= 700,000 units × (0.12 − 0.10) × $425 per unit

= $5,950,000 F

$$\begin{array}{l} \text{Market-share} \\ \text{variance} \end{array} = \left(\begin{array}{c} \text{Actual} \\ \text{market size} \\ \text{in units} \end{array} - \begin{array}{c} \text{Budgeted} \\ \text{market size} \\ \text{in units} \end{array} \right) \times \begin{array}{c} \text{Budgeted} \\ \text{market} \\ \text{share} \end{array} \times \begin{array}{c} \text{Budgeted} \\ \text{contribution margin} \\ \text{per composite unit} \\ \text{for budgeted mix} \end{array}$$

= (700,000 units − 800,000 units) × 0.10 × $425 per unit

= $4,250,000 U

Note that the algebraic sum of the market-share variance and the market-size variance is equal to the sales-quantity variance: $5,950,000 F + $4,250,000 U = $1,700,000 F.

3. Both the sales-mix variance and the sales-quantity variance are favourable. The favourable sales-mix variance occurred because the actual mix comprised more of the higher-margin commercial vinyl flooring. The favourable sales-quantity variance occurred because the actual total quantity of rolls sold exceeded the budgeted amount.

   The company's large favourable market-share variance is due to a 12% actual market share compared with a 10% budgeted market share. The market-size variance is unfavourable because the market size was 100,000 rolls less than the budgeted amount. Payne's performance in 2007 appears to be very good. Although overall market size declined, the company sold more units than budgeted by gaining market share.

◆ PART THREE: CUSTOMER PROFITABILITY ANALYSIS

Customer profitability analysis.
Examines how individual customers, or groupings of customers, differ in their profitability.

Companies that prosper have a strong customer focus in their decisions. Management accountants are giving increased attention to **customer profitability analysis**, which is the reporting and analysis of customer revenues and customer costs. Armed with this information, managers can ensure that customers contributing sizably to the profitability of an organization receive a comparable level of attention from the organization.

CUSTOMER REVENUES AND CUSTOMER COSTS

An analysis of customer differences on both revenues and costs can provide important insight into why differences in customer profitability exist. Consider Spring Distribution Company, which sells bottled water. It has two distribution channels—(a) a retail distribution channel of more than 1,000 business and residential customers, and (b) a wholesale distribution channel that covers sales to supermarkets, drugstores, and other stores. We will focus mainly on customer profitability analysis in Spring's retail distribution channel. The list selling price in this channel is $14.40 per case (unit) while the purchase cost to Spring is $12 per case. If every bottle is sold at its list price in this distribution channel, Spring would earn a gross margin of $2.40 per case.

Customer Revenue Analysis

Let us first consider customer revenues. Data for four of Spring's customers in June 2007 are:

	A	B	C	D	E
1		CUSTOMER			
2		A	B	G	J
3	Cash sold	42,000	33,000	2,900	2,500
4	List selling price	$ 14.40	$ 14.40	$ 14.40	$ 14.40
5	Price discount	$ 0.96	$ 0.24	$ 1.20	$ –
6	Invoice price	$ 13.44	$ 14.16	$ 13.20	$ 14.40
7	Revenues (Row 3 × Row 6)	$564,480	$467,280	$38,280	$36,000

Customer revenue analysis is enhanced by tracking as much detail as possible to explain why customers differ in their revenues. Two variables explain revenue differences across these four customers: (a) the volume of bottles purchased and (b) the magnitude of price discounting. **Price discounting** is the reduction of selling prices below listed levels to encourage an increase in purchases by customers. Companies that record only the invoice price in their information system would not be able to readily track the magnitude of their price discounting (except in the extreme case of a single-product company with a constant list price in the accounting period).[2]

Price discounts are a function of multiple factors, including the volume of product purchased (higher-volume customers receive higher discounts) and the desire to sell to a customer who might help promote sales to other customers. Discounts could also be due to poor negotiating by a salesperson or the unwanted effect of an incentive plan based only on revenues. At no time should price discounts run afoul of the law by way of price discrimination, predatory pricing, or collusive pricing (see pp. 492–494). Price discounts can also be unethical—for example, when discounts are given by pharmaceutical representatives to doctors to encourage them to prescribe a particular drug.

Tracking discounts by customer, and by salesperson, can provide valuable information about ways to improve customer profitability. For example, Spring Distribution may institute a corporate policy to ensure that any volume-based price discounting policy is enforced for customers with decreasing volume as well as those with increasing volume. It may also require its salespeople to obtain approval before giving large discounts to customers not normally qualifying for them. In addition, it could track the future sales of customers that its salespeople argue warrant a sizable price discount due to their predicted "high growth potential." Salespeople who have a poor track record in predicting the future growth of customers may be given additional training in sales forecasting (or may even be encouraged to seek employment elsewhere). For example, Spring should track future sales to customer G to confirm that the $1.20-per-case discount translated into higher future sales.

Customer revenues are one element of customer profitability. The other is customer costs.

Customer Cost Analysis

Chapters 5 and 14 discussed the *cost hierarchy* concept in which costs are categorized into different cost pools on the basis of different types of cost drivers (or cost-allocation bases) or different degrees of difficulty in determining cause-and-effect (or benefits

[2]Further analysis of customer revenues could distinguish between gross revenues and net revenues. This approach would highlight differences across customers in sales returns. Additional discussion of ways to analyze revenue differences across customers is in R.S. Kaplan and R. Cooper, *Cost and Effect* (Boston, Mass.: Harvard Business School Press, 1998), Chapter 10.

Customer-profitability analysis is management accounting's response to the notion that "the customer is priority one" from marketing and management courses. In particular, this section shows how accounting can provide marketing personnel with useful information.

OBJECTIVE 5

Discuss why revenues can differ across customers purchasing the same product

Price discounting. The reduction of selling prices below listed levels to encourage an increase in purchases by customers.

OBJECTIVE 6

Apply the concept of cost hierarchy to customer costing

received) relationships. Spring Distribution has an activity-based costing system that classifies its costs into four categories:

◆ **Customer output unit-level costs**—costs of activities to sell each unit (case) to a customer. An example is product-handling costs of each case sold.

◆ **Customer batch-level costs**—costs of activities that are related to a group of units (cases) sold to a customer. Examples are costs incurred to process orders or to make deliveries.

◆ **Customer-sustaining costs**—costs of activities to support individual customers, regardless of the number of units or batches of product delivered to the customer. Examples are costs of visits to customers or costs of displays at customer sites.

◆ **Distribution-channel costs**—costs of activities related to a particular distribution channel rather than to each unit of product, each batch of product, or specific customers. An example is the salary of the manager of Spring's retail distribution channel.

◆ **Corporate-sustaining costs**—costs of activities that cannot be traced to individual customers or distribution channels. Examples are top-management and general-administration costs.

Spring uses its customer-cost hierarchy to assist managers in decisions made at different levels in this hierarchy. We will now consider decisions made at the individual customer level. Note from these descriptions that four of the five levels of Spring's cost hierarchy closely parallel the cost hierarchy described in Chapter 5, except that Spring focuses on *customers* whereas the cost hierarchy in Chapter 5 focused on *products*. Spring has one additional cost hierarchy category—distribution-channel costs—for the costs it incurs to support its wholesale and retail distribution channels.

Customer-Specific Costs

Spring includes cost of goods sold and selling-related costs for individual customers in this category. Spring is particularly interested in analyzing customer-level indirect costs that are incurred in the first three categories of the customer-cost hierarchy: customer output-unit-level costs, customer batch-level costs, and customer-sustaining costs. Spring believes that it can work with customers to reduce these costs. It believes that customer actions will have less impact on distribution-channel and corporate-sustaining costs. The five activity areas used to collect costs for selling-related costs, cost drivers, and rates are as follows:

Activity Area	Cost Rate and Driver		Cost Hierarchy Category
Product handling	$0.50	per case sold	Customer output-unit-level costs
Order taking	$ 100	per purchase order	Customer batch-level costs
Delivery vehicles	$ 2	per delivery kilometre travelled	Customer batch-level costs
Rush deliveries	$ 300	per expedited delivery	Customer batch-level costs
Visits to customers	$ 80	per sales visit	Customer-sustaining costs

The table below provides information on the quantity of cost driver consumed or used by each customer:

	CUSTOMER			
	A	B	G	J
Number of purchase orders	30	25	15	10
Number of deliveries	60	30	20	15
Kilometres travelled per delivery	5	12	20	6
Number of rush deliveries	1	–	2	–
Number of visits to customers	6	5	4	3

Spring Distribution can use the information underlying Exhibit 16-5 to assist its customers in reducing their consumption of the cost drivers. (See also the Focus on

EXHIBIT 16-5
Customer Profitability Analysis for Four Customers of Spring Distribution for June 2007

A	B	C	D	E
	CUSTOMER			
	A	B	G	J
3 Revenues at list price: $14.40 × 42,000; 33,000; 2,900; 2,500	$604,800	$475,200	$41,760	$36,000
4 Price discount: $0.96 × 42,000; $0.24 × 33,000; $1.20 × 2,900; $0 × 2,500	40,320	7,920	3,480	–
5 Revenues at actual price	564,480	467,280	38,280	36,000
6 Cost of goods sold: $12 × 42,000; 33,000; 2,900; 2,500	504,000	396,000	34,800	30,000
7 Gross margin	60,480	71,280	3,480	6,000
8 Customer-level operating costs				
9 Product handling: $0.50 × 42,000; 33,000; 2,900; 2,500	21,000	16,500	1,450	1,250
10 Order taking: $100 × 30; 25; 15; 10	3,000	2,500	1,500	1,000
11 Delivery vehicles: $2 × (5 × 60); (12 × 30); (20 × 20); (6 × 15)	600	720	800	180
12 Rush deliveries: $300 × 1; 0; 2; 0	300	–	600	–
13 Visits to customers: $80 × 6; 5; 4; 3	480	400	320	240
14 Total customer-level operating costs	25,380	20,120	4,670	2,670
15 Customer-level operating income	$ 35,100	$ 51,160	$(1,190)	$ 3,330

Values and Behaviours feature p. 644). Consider in Exhibit 16-5 a comparison of Customer G, with total purchases (2,900 cases) only 7% the size of Customer A (42,000 cases). Customer G, however, requires one-half the number of purchase orders, two-thirds the number of visits to customers, one-third the number of deliveries, and double the number of rush deliveries. To improve the profitability of Customer G Spring must encourage this customer to request fewer customer visits and rush deliveries as well as larger but fewer purchases.

The ABC system underlying Exhibit 16-5 provides a road-map to facilitate less use of cost drivers by a customer in order to promote cost reduction. Another advantage of ABC is that it highlights a second way cost reduction can be promoted by Spring Distribution. Spring can take actions to reduce the costs in each of its own activity areas. For example, order taking currently is estimated to cost $100 per purchase order. By making its own ordering process more efficient (such as having its customers order electronically), Spring can reduce its costs even if its customers make the same number of orders.

Exhibit 16-6 (p. 645) shows a monthly operating income statement for Spring Distribution. The customer-level operating income of customers A and B in Exhibit 16-5 are shown in columns 8 and 9 of Exhibit 16-6 and information for the remaining customers in Exhibit 16-7 (p. 645). Wholesale customers comprise new data, as do the distribution-channel costs and corporate-sustaining costs. The format of Exhibit 16-6 is based on Spring's cost hierarchy.

All costs incurred to serve customers are not included in customer-level costs and therefore are not allocated to customers in Exhibit 16-6. For example, distribution-channel costs such as the salary of the manager of the retail distribution channel are not included in customer-level costs and are not allocated to customers. Instead, these costs are identified as costs of the distribution channel as a whole. That is because Spring's management believes that changes in the retail channel manager's salary will not affect the behaviour of a specific customer. Distribution-channel costs will be affected only by decisions pertaining to the whole channel, such as a decision to discontinue retail distribution. Another reason Spring does not allocate distribution-channel costs to customers is motivation. Spring's managers contend that salespersons responsible for managing individual customer accounts would lose motivation if their bonuses were affected by the allocation to customers of distribution-channel costs over which they have almost no influence.

So Is the Customer Always Right?

What are some of the most important aspects of a business? The bottom line? Shareholders' perception of a company? The quality of a product or service offered? What about customers? Customers are essential to any business, but unfortunately some customers are not always profitable, which makes customer-profitability analysis a complex issue for management accountants.

Once an organization decides to measure customer profitability, management accountants are responsible for articulating the benefits of such measurements. This can be problematic for management accountants because the sales organizations in most companies are compensated on the basis of revenues, not customer profits. Therefore, the sales force may be reluctant to follow a strategy of serving only profitable customers and taking actions to change the behaviour and buying patterns of those that are unprofitable. Management accountants need to communicate to the sales force why measuring customer profits is critical to the organization. For example, they need to explain what might happen if change does not occur and how customer-profitability analysis can help the company reallocate resources to increase both revenues and profits.

When it comes to customer-profitability analysis, the sales force is not the only part of an organization that may pose challenges for management accountants. Line managers are sometimes surprised by which customers are profitable and which are not because they may assume a company's largest customer is profitable. However, this customer may consume high levels of customer support and actually be unprofitable. For this reason, management accountants must make it a point to team up with line managers when designing the system to calculate customer profitability. Customer-profitability analysis should always be based on a thorough understanding of business processes so that it correctly represents the costs incurred to support different customers.

Consider Fidelity Investments. Fidelity's customer-profitability analysis revealed that some of its customers were unprofitable because of the ways they communicated with the company. Armed with this information, managers made changes to the company's processes. For example, telephone calls from unprofitable customers were placed in a long waiting queue, which was intended to discourage these customers from calling service representatives and to encourage them to instead use less-costly Internet and automated phone-line services. Fidelity's management was concerned that, unhappy with these changes, customers would leave; however, 96% of the targeted customers stayed, switched to lower-cost channels, and became profitable.[a] These short-term successes were shared with other managers, and the company grew more confident about the actions it needed to take. Teamwork, communication, and careful management of the changes were critical to the success of the customer-profitability implementation and the positive results that followed.

[a]See L. Seldon and G. Colvin, "Will This Customer Sink Your Stock?" *Fortune,* September 30, 2003.

Next, consider corporate-sustaining costs such as top-management and general-administration costs. Spring's managers have concluded that there is neither a cause-and-effect nor a benefits-received relationship between any cost-allocation base and corporate-sustaining costs. Consequently, allocation of corporate-sustaining costs serves no useful purpose in decision making, performance evaluation, or motivation. For example, suppose Spring allocated the $263,000 of corporate-sustaining costs to its distribution channels: $173,000 to the wholesale channel and $90,000 to the retail channel. Using information from Exhibit 16-6, the retail channel would then show a loss of $14,080 ($75,920 − $90,000). If this same situation persisted in subsequent months, should Spring shut down the retail distribution channel? No, because if retail distribution were discontinued, corporate-sustaining costs would be unaffected. Allocating corporate-sustaining costs to distribution channels could give the misleading

EXHIBIT 16-6
Income Statement for Spring Distribution in 2007

	A	B	C	D	E	F	G	H	I	J	K	L	M	N
1					**CUSTOMER DISTRIBUTION CHANNELS**									
2				**Wholesale Customers**					**Retail Customers**					
3		Total	Total	A1	A2	A3	•	Total	A^a		B^a		G^a	J^a
4		(1) = (2) + (7)	(2)	(3)	(4)	(5)	(6)	(7)	(8)		(9)		(10)	(11)
5	Revenues (at actual prices)	$12,138,120	$10,107,720	$1,946,000	$1,476,000	•	•	$2,030,400	$564,480		$467,280		•	•
6	Customer-level costs	11,633,760	9,737,280	1,868,000	1,416,000	•	•	1,896,480	529,380	b	416,120	b	•	•
7	Customer-level operating income	504,360	370,440	78,000	60,000	•	•	133,920	$35,100		$ 51,160		•	•
8	Distribution-channel costs	160,500	102,500					58,000						
9	Distribution-channel operating income	343,860	$267,940					$ 75,920						
10	Corporate-sustaining costs	263,000												
11	Operating income	$80,860												
12														
13	^{a}Full details are presented in Exhibit 16-5													
14	^{b}Cost of goods sold + Total customer-level operating costs from Exhibit 16-5													

EXHIBIT 16-7
Customer-Profitability Analysis for Retail Channel Customers: Spring Distribution, June 2007

	A	B	C	D	E	F
1						**Cumulative**
2						**Customer-Level**
3		**Customer-**				**Operating Income**
4		**Level**		**Customer-Level**	**Cumulative**	**as a % of Total**
5		**Operating**	**Customer**	**Operating Income**	**Customer-Level**	**Customer-Level**
6	**Customer**	**Income**	**Revenue**	**Divided by Revenue**	**Operating Income**	**Operating Income**
7	**Code**	**(1)**	**(2)**	**(3) = (1) − (2)**	**(4)**	**(5) = (4) ÷ $133,920**
8	B	$ 51,160	$ 467,280	10.95%	$ 51,160	38.20%
9	A	35,100	564,480	6.22	86,260	64.41
10	C	21,070	255,640	8.24	107,330	80.14
11	D	17,580	277,000	6.35	124,910	93.27
12	F	7,504	123,500	6.08	132,414	98.88
13	J	3,330	36,000	9.25	135,744	101.36
14	E	3,176	193,000	1.65	138,920	103.73
15	G	(1,190)	38,280	−3.11	137,730	102.84
16	H	(1,690)	38,220	−4.42	136,040	101.58
17	I	(2,120)	37,000	−5.73	133,920	100.00
18		$133,920	$2,030,400			

impression that the potential cost savings from discontinuing a distribution channel would be greater than the likely amount.

Consider a distributor of medical supplies to hospitals. It strategically prices each of its services separately. For example, if a hospital wants a rush delivery or special packaging, the distributor charges the hospital an additional price for each particular service. How do customers react? Hospitals that value these services continue to demand them and pay for them while hospitals that do not value these services drop

Customer Profitability at Sprint Nextel

Sprint Nextel, a leading wireless-communications service provider, offers cellular telephone service and wireless-data access to a broad range of businesses, government agencies, and individuals. Sprint Nextel uses cost accounting to price its various wireless service plans and to calculate customer profitability.

The costs of serving different wireless customers vary. Most business customers, for example, require reliable service during peak network usage periods (that is, standard business hours), on-demand two-way messaging, and large amounts of wireless data bandwidth to run PDA and BlackBerry handheld devices. In contrast, many individuals use their wireless phones extensively at night and on weekends and also use features such as text messaging, digital pictures, music ringtones, and video games. Within each segment, each customer differs in its amount of overall usage and geographic location (urban versus rural).

Sprint Nextel considers the costs for each of these services when developing their pricing plans and calculating customer profitability. Therefore, individuals using their phone service sparingly can select a less-expensive plan with limited minutes, for use mostly at night and on weekends, whereas more-demanding individuals and lucrative business customers can choose plans with unlimited telephone minutes, secure wireless data bandwidth access, and guaranteed service reliability . . . for a price. In 2004, Sprint Nextel's base wireless plans ranged from US$15,000 to US$199.99 per month, with additional charges for data services and rural-area roaming. Business and government customers who use Sprint Nextel services extensively are eligible for negotiated volume discounts.

Because of the range in prices, Sprint Nextel analyzes customer profitability to ensure that its prices cover the costs it incurs to provide services to its different customers. Nextel then uses customer-profitability analysis to determine where and how to expand its service network, design new pricing plans, manage costs, and develop strategies to ensure that the company acquires and retains the most profitable customers. The result has been record profitability and a soaring stock price.

Sources: A. Lagocre, "Nextel's Direct Connection to Profits," *Forbes* (February 6, 2004); C. Osborn, "Customer Retention: Can Wireless Data Make 'Em Stay Put?" in *The Future of Wireless: Business Strategies, Broadband Technologies, and Network Operations* (Chicago: International Engineering Consortium, 2004); R. Prentiss and T. Nelson, *Nextel Communications, Inc.* (Raymond James, February 9, 2004); Nextel Communications, Inc., March 11, 2004, 10-K (Reston, VA: Nextel Communications, 2003); Nextel Communications (Multiple pages). Nextel Communications Web site, http://www.nextel.com, accessed July 25, 2004.

them, saving the distributor some costs. This is how the distributor's pricing strategy influences customer behaviour in a way that increases the distributor's revenues or decreases its costs. (See the Concepts in Action feature.)

Some managers and management accountants advocate fully allocating all costs to customers and distribution channels so that (1) the sum of operating incomes of all customers in a distribution channel (segment) equals the operating income of the distribution channel and (2) the sum of the distribution-channel operating incomes equals companywide operating income. These managers and management accountants argue that customers and products must eventually be profitable on a full-cost basis. For some decisions, such as pricing, allocating all costs ensures that long-run prices are set at a level to cover the cost of all resources used to produce and sell products. Nevertheless, the hierarchical format in Exhibit 16-6 distinguishes among various degrees of objectivity when allocating costs, and it dovetails with the different levels at which decisions are made and performance is evaluated. The issue of when and what costs to allocate is another example of the "different costs for different purposes" theme emphasized throughout the book.

Managers find customer profitability analysis useful for several reasons. First, it frequently highlights how vital a small set of customers is to total profitability. Managers need to ensure that the interests of these customers receive high priority. Microsoft uses the phrase "not all revenue dollars are endowed equally in profitability" to stress this key point. Second, when a customer is ranked in the "loss category," managers can focus on ways to make future business with this customer more profitable.

This high percentage contribution by a small number of customers is a common finding in many studies. It highlights the importance of Spring Distribution maintaining good relations with this pivotal set of customers.

Exhibit 16-7 ranks customers on revenue (before price discounts). Three of the four smallest customers (based on revenue) are unprofitable. Moreover, customer E, with revenues of $193,000, is only marginally profitable. Further analysis revealed that a former sales representative gave customer E excessive discounts in an attempt to meet a monthly sales-volume target.

Managers often find the bar chart presentation in Exhibit 16-8 to be the most intuitive way to visualize customer profitability. The highly profitable customers clearly stand out. Moreover, the number of loss-customers and the magnitude of their losses are apparent and focus management attention on how to improve the profitability of these loss-customers.

Assessing Customer Value

The information in Exhibits 16-5 (p. 643) and 16-7 (p. 645) relates to customer profitability in a single accounting period (see the Global Surveys of Company Practice box on p. 648). This is one of several factors that managers should consider in deciding how to allocate resources across customers. These factors include

1. **Short-run and long-run customer profitability.** This factor will be influenced by factors 2 and 3 below as well as by the level of resources likely to be required to retain the accounts.

2. **Customer retention likelihood.** The more likely a customer is to continue doing business with a company, the more valuable the customer. Customers can differ in their loyalty and their willingness to "shop their business" on a frequent basis.

OBJECTIVE 7

Prepare a customer-profitability report

EXHIBIT 16-8
Bar Chart Presentation of Customer Profitability for Spring Distribution

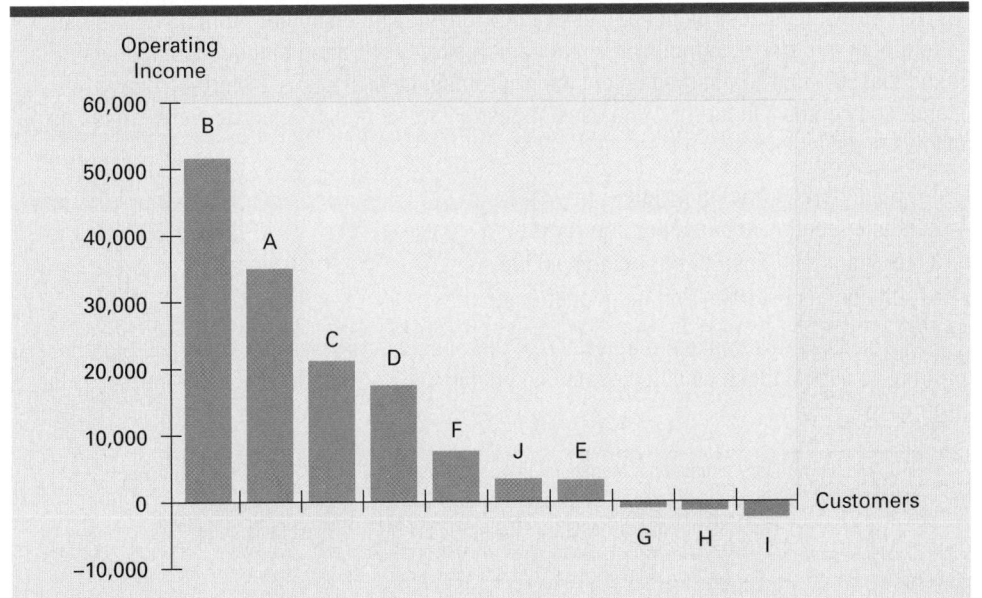

3. **Customer growth potential.** This factor will be influenced by the likely growth of the industry of the customer and the likely growth of the customer (due to, say, its ability to develop new products). This factor will also be influenced by cross-selling opportunities—that is, when a customer of one of the company's products becomes a customer of one or more of the company's other products.

4. **Increases in overall demand from having well-known customers.** Some customers are highly valuable because they have established reputations that make them very useful to mention in sales visits. Other customers are valuable because of their willingness to provide product endorsements.

5. **Ability to learn from a customer.** Customers can be an important source of ideas about new products or ways to improve existing products. Customers willing to provide such input can be especially valuable.

The "80–20 rule" also applies to customers: 80% of a company's profits often come from 20% of its customers. Customer-profitability information can help marketing and customer-service personnel (1) focus on maintaining the best-possible relations with those 20% of customers and (2) transform the other 80% into more-profitable customers.

Managers should be particularly cautious when deciding to drop customers. Short-run profitability reports may provide misleading signals about their long-run profitability. Moreover, as discussed next, not all costs assigned to a customer may be variable with respect to short-run reductions in purchases by customers. It is typically not the case that a policy of dropping any customer currently unprofitable (sometimes called "revenue shedding") will eliminate in the short run all the costs assigned to that customer.

Customer Profitability Analysis Attracts Increasing Attention

A survey of U.S. and Australian managers[a] asked respondents about "the three most important general management priorities that your organization faces today." The top ranked priorities were

1. Customer profitability/satisfaction
2. Cost management/cost control
3. Quality
4. Growth

A growing number of companies are now developing customer profitability systems to reinforce this strategic focus on customers. A survey of United Kingdom companies[b] found that 50% had "embarked on customer profitability analysis . . . A further 12% planned to pursue it in future." The uses of customer profitability analysis were ranked as follows (most important = 1):

1. Guidance for pricing policies
2. Renegotiation of customer contracts
3. Guidance for customer relations policies
4. Influence cost control in respect of customers.

"The 80/20 rule applied (that is, 20% of their customers were generating 80% of the profits)" to 60% of those who had examined cumulative contributions of customers to total profits.

[a]Foster, G., and S. M. Young, "Frontiers of Management Accounting Research," *Journal of Management Accounting Research* (1997).

[b]Innes, J., and F. Mitchell, "A Survey of Activity-Based Costing in the U.K.'s Largest Companies," *Management Accounting Research*.

PROBLEM

Spring Distribution is concerned with the level of its profitability. Its June 2007 operating income of $78,000 is less than 1% of sales ($78,000 ÷ $12,470,000 = 0.63%). Suppose that July 2007 is identical to June 2007 with one exception. In July 2007, Spring conducts an extensive efficiency analysis of its activity areas and is able to reduce their costs to the levels shown below:

Activity Area	Cost Driver Rate
Order taking	$60 per purchase order
Sales visits	$50 per visit
Delivery vehicles	$1.50 per delivery kilometre travelled
Product handling	$0.015 per bottle sold
Expedited deliveries	$200 per expedited delivery

REQUIRED

1. What is the effect of these activity area cost reductions on the July 2007 profitability (customer-specific contribution) of customers A, B, G, and J in Exhibit 16-5 (p. 643)?
2. What are additional ways Spring could seek to improve the profitability of customers A, B, G and J?

SOLUTION

1. The July 2007 activity area cost rate reductions affect only the customer-specific operating costs in Exhibit 16-5. The revised customer-specific contributions to operating income are

	Customer			
	A	B	G	J
Gross margin	$60,480	$71,280	$3,480	$6,000
Customer-specific operating costs				
Order taking[a]	1,800	1,500	900	600
Sales visits[b]	300	250	200	150
Delivery vehicles[c]	450	540	600	135
Product handling[d]	15,120	11,880	1,044	900
Expedited deliveries[e]	200	0	400	0
Total	17,870	14,170	3,144	1,785
Customer-specific contribution	$42,610	$57,110	$ 336	$4,215

[a]$60 × 30; $60 × 25; $60 × 15; $60 × 10
[b]$50 × 6; $50 × 5; $50 × 4; $50 × 3
[c]$1.50 × (5 × 60); $1.50 × (12 × 30); $1.50 × (20 × 20); $1.50 × (6 × 15)
[d]$0.015 × 1,008,000[f]; $0.015 × 792,000[g]; $0.015 × 69,600[h]; $0.015 × 60,000[i]
[e]$200 × 1; $200 × 0; $200 × 2; $200 × 0
[f]42,000 cases × 24 = 1,008,000 bottles
[g]33,000 cases × 24 = 792,000 bottles
[h]2,900 cases × 24 = 69,600 bottles
[i]2,500 cases × 24 = 60,000 bottles

The customer-specific contribution has increased for each customer. The total contribution from these four customers is $104,271 in July 2007 compared to $88,400 in June 2007, an increase of 18%.

2. Spring could seek to improve the profitability of its customers by reducing its cost of goods sold through better negotiating with its supplier. It could also explore the effect of a list price increase, a reduction in price discounts, or encouraging customers to use fewer service units from its five activity areas. The challenge here is to retain, or possibly increase, the customer's willingness to purchase from Spring given the new pricing and cost parameters.

The following decision guidelines use a question-and-answer format to summarize the chapter's main points. Each decision presents a key question. The guideline is the answer to that question.

DECISIONS	GUIDELINES
1. What is product bundling and why does it give rise to revenue-allocation issues?	Bundling occurs when a package of two or more products (or services) is sold for a single price. Revenue allocation of the bundled price is required when managers of the individual products in the bundle are evaluated on product revenues or product operating incomes.
2. What methods can a manager use to allocate revenues of a bundled package to individual products in the package?	Revenues can be allocated for a bundled product using the stand-alone method, the incremental method, or management judgment.
3. What are two explanations for sales-volume variance?	Two explanations are (a) a change in the actual sales mix from the budgeted sales mix (sales-mix variance) and (b) a change in the actual unit sales from the budgeted unit sales (sales-quantity variance).
4. What are two explanations for sales-quantity variance?	Two explanations are (a) a change in the actual share of the market attained compared with the budgeted share (market-share variance) and (b) a change in the actual market size in units compared with the budgeted market size (market-size variance).
5. Why can revenues differ across customers purchasing the same product?	Revenues can differ due to differences in the quantity purchased and discounts given from the list selling price.
6. What is the advantage of using a customer cost hierarchy?	Customer cost hierarchies highlight how some costs can be reliably assigned to individual customers whereas other costs can be reliably assigned only to distribution channels or to corporatewide activities.
7. Why does customer profitability differ across customers?	Different customers place different demands on a company's resources in terms of processing purchase orders, making deliveries, and customer support. Companies should be aware of and devote sufficient resources to maintaining and expanding relationships with key contributors to profitability.

APPENDIX: MIX AND YIELD VARIANCES FOR SUBSTITUTABLE INPUTS

Part Two of this chapter analyzed sales-mix and sales-quantity variances for a company with multiple products. This analysis extended the Chapter 7 coverage of the sales-volume variance. The sales-mix and sales-quantity framework outlined in Part Two can also be applied to the analysis of production-input variances. The prior discussion of these variances in Chapter 7 is easiest to interpret when the inputs into a production process are *nonsubstitutable*, which is often the case. Consider a company assembling voyager satellites for NASA's space program. Once a product design for a satellite is approved, there is a mandate that it be adhered to. The contractor cannot substitute a different combination of doors and door locks, irrespective of price movements of alternative doors and locks. In other cases, however, managers have some leeway in combining inputs. For example, Del Monte can combine material inputs (such as pineapples, cherries, and grapes) in varying proportions for its cans of fruit salad. Within limits, these individual fruits are *substitutable* inputs in making a fruit salad.

This Appendix presents mix and yield variances that highlight the financial implications of mix and yield decisions by managers. These variances divide the efficiency variance that was discussed in Chapter 7. To illustrate mix and yield variances, we examine Delpino Corporation, which makes tomato ketchup. Our example focuses on direct material inputs and substitution among three of these inputs. The same approach can also be used to examine substitutable direct labour inputs.

To produce ketchup of the desired consistency, colour, and taste, Delpino mixes three types of tomatoes grown in three different regions—Latin American tomatoes (Latoms), California tomatoes (Caltoms), and Florida tomatoes (Flotoms).

Delpino's production standards require 1.60 tonnes of tomatoes to produce 1 tonne of ketchup, with 50% of the tomatoes being Latoms, 30% Caltoms, and 20% Flotoms. The direct materials input standards to produce 1 tonne of ketchup are:

0.80 (50% of 1.6) tonne of Latoms at $70 per tonne	$ 56.00
0.48 (30% of 1.6) tonne of Caltoms at $80 per tonne	38.40
0.32 (20% of 1.6) tonne of Flotoms at $90 per tonne	28.80
Total standard cost of 1.6 tonnes of tomatoes	$123.20

Budgeted average cost per tonne of tomatoes is $123.20 ÷ 1.60 tonnes = $77.

Because Delpino uses fresh tomatoes to make ketchup, no inventories of tomatoes are kept. Purchases are made as needed, so all price variances relate to tomatoes purchased and used. Actual results for June 2007 show that a total of 6,500 tonnes of tomatoes were used to produce 4,000 tonnes of ketchup:

3,250	tonnes of Latoms at actual cost of $70 per tonne	$227,500
2,275	tonnes of Caltoms at actual cost of $82 per tonne	186,550
975	tonnes of Flotoms at actual cost of $96 per tonne	93,600
6,500	tonnes of tomatoes	$507,650
	Standard cost of 4,000 tonnes of ketchup at $123.20 per tonne	492,800
	Total variance to be explained	$ 14,850 U

Given the standard ratio of 1.60 tonnes of tomatoes to 1 tonne of ketchup, 6,400 tonnes of tomatoes should be used to produce 4,000 tonnes of ketchup. At the standard mix, the quantities of each type of tomato required are

Latoms	0.50 × 6,400 = 3,200 tonnes
Caltoms	0.30 × 6,400 = 1,920 tonnes
Flotoms	0.20 × 6,400 = 1,280 tonnes

Direct Materials Price and Efficiency Variances

Exhibit 16-9 presents the columnar analysis of the flexible-budget variance for direct materials discussed in Chapter 7. The direct materials price and efficiency variances are calculated separately for each input material and then added together. The variance analysis prompts Delpino to investigate the unfavourable price and efficiency variances—why did they pay more for the tomatoes and use greater quantities than they should have? Were the market prices of tomatoes higher, in general, or could the Purchasing Department have negotiated lower prices? Did the inefficiencies result from inferior tomatoes or from problems in processing?

EXHIBIT 16-9
Direct Materials Price and Efficiency Variances for the Delpino Corporation for June 2007*

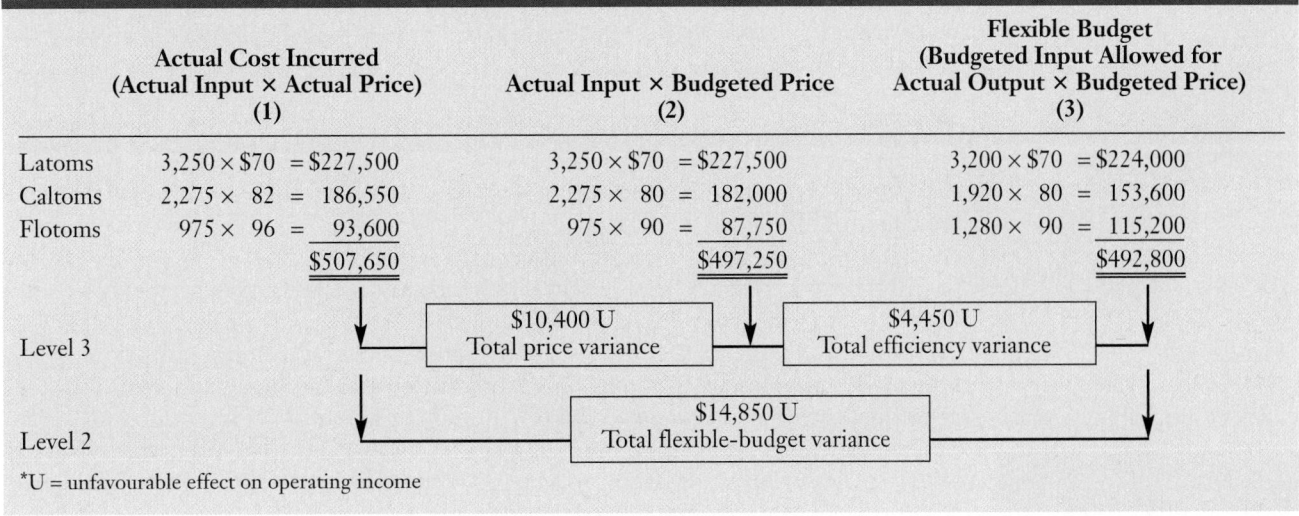

*U = unfavourable effect on operating income

Direct Materials Mix and Direct Materials Yield Variances

Managers sometimes do have discretion to substitute one material for another. For example, the manager of Delpino's ketchup plant has some leeway in combining Latoms, Caltoms, and Flotoms without affecting quality. We will assume that to maintain quality, the mix percentages of each type of tomato can only vary up to 5% from the standard mix. For example, the percentage of Caltoms in the mix can vary between 25% and 35% (30% ± 5%). When inputs are substitutable, direct materials efficiency improvement relative to budgeted costs can come from two sources: (1) using a cheaper mix to produce a given quantity of output and (2) using less input to achieve a given quantity of output. The direct materials yield and mix variances divide the efficiency variance into two variances: the mix variance focuses on how the multiple types of substitutable materials or labour are combined and the yield variance focuses on how much of those inputs are used.

Holding the actual total quantity of all direct materials inputs used constant, the total **direct materials mix variance** is the difference between two amounts: (1) the budgeted cost for the actual mix of the total quantity of direct materials used, and (2) the budgeted cost of the budgeted mix of the actual total quantity of direct materials used. Holding the budgeted input mix constant, the **direct materials yield variance** is the difference between two amounts: (1) the budgeted cost of direct materials based on the actual total quantity of all direct materials inputs used, and (2) the flexible-budget cost of direct materials based on the budgeted total quantity of direct materials inputs for the actual output (see the Concepts in Action feature).

Exhibit 16-10 presents the total direct materials mix and yield variances for the Delpino Corporation.

Direct Materials Mix Variance   Compare columns 1 and 2 in Exhibit 16-10. Both columns calculate cost using the actual total quantity of all inputs used (6,500 tonnes) and budgeted input prices (Latoms, $70; Caltoms, $80; and Flotoms, $90). The *only* difference is that column 1 uses *actual input mix* (Latoms, 50%; Caltoms, 35%; Flotoms, 15%), and column 2 uses *budgeted input mix* (Latoms, 50%; Caltoms, 30%;

Direct materials mix variance. The difference between two amounts: (1) the budgeted cost for the actual mix of the total quantity of direct materials used and (2) the budgeted cost of the budgeted mix of the actual total quantity of direct materials used.

Direct materials yield variance. The difference between (1) the budgeted cost of direct materials based on the actual total quantity of all direct materials inputs used and (2) the flexible-budget cost of direct materials based on the budgeted total quantity of direct materials inputs for the actual output.

Killing a fly with a sledge hammer is effective but not efficient. Killing a fly with a fly swatter is both effective and efficient.

EXHIBIT 16-10
Total Direct Materials Mix and Yield Variances for the Delpino Corporation for June 2007*

	Actual Total Quantity of All Inputs Used × Actual Input Mix Budgeted Price × (1)	Actual Total Quantity of All Inputs Used × Budgeted Input Mix Budgeted Price × (2)	Flexible Budget (Budgeted Total Quantity of All Inputs Allowed for Actual Output Budgeted Input Mix × Budgeted Price) × (3)
Latoms	$6,500 \times 0.50 \times \$70^a = \$227,500$	$6,500 \times 0.50 \times \$70 = \$227,500$	$6,400 \times 0.50 \times \$70 = \$224,000$
Caltoms	$6,500 \times 0.35 \times 80^b = 182,000$	$6,500 \times 0.30 \times 80 = 156,000$	$6,400 \times 0.30 \times 80 = 153,600$
Flotoms	$6,500 \times 0.15 \times 90^c = \underline{87,750}$	$6,500 \times 0.20 \times 90 = \underline{117,000}$	$6,400 \times 0.20 \times 90 = \underline{115,200}$
	$\underline{\$497,250}$	$\underline{\$500,500}$	$\underline{\$492,800}$

Level 4 → | $3,250 F Total mix variance | → | $7,700 U Total yield variance | →

Level 3 → | $4,450 U Total efficiency variance | →

^{a}3,250 ÷ 6,500
^{b}2,275 ÷ 6,500
^{c}975 ÷ 6,500
*F = favourable effect on operating income; U = unfavourable effect on operating income

Tools Against Waste: Variance Analysis at Sandoz

Sandoz US, a subsidiary of Swiss-based Novartis AG, develops generic pharmaceutical substitutes for market-leading therapeutic drugs. To ensure success, Sandoz must develop and deliver its products to wholesalers and retailers at the lowest possible cost. Because the generic drug industry is so competitive, an intricate understanding of product costs is critical. Variance analysis helps managers assess and maintain product profitability.

At its Broomfield, Colorado, manufacturing facility, Sandoz uses standard costs, based on the recipes for each product, to predict the costs associated with producing batches of each generic drug. To monitor and control costs, the plant controller regularly reviews detailed costing information received from the managers on the production floor. The plant controller then uses variance analysis to improve operations. Variance analysis helps support improvements in the manufacturing process, forecast financial results, and set manufacturing standards. Most importantly, it also helps managers find the root cause of process deficiencies. Let's take a closer look at how Sandoz's managers use variance analysis.

Materials cost variances are reviewed on a weekly basis and are analyzed in terms of yield loss. Yield loss is a measure of direct materials efficiency—that is, the difference between the actual quantity of materials used and the expected quantity of materials that should have been used.

Each week, management accountants at Sandoz analyze which products have the top dollar value and the highest volume of yield losses. They forward their findings to production for review, and year-to-date trends are examined by engineers and scientists to determine if changes in processes, materials, and equipment are necessary or if the standards that have been set require modification. Maintaining accurate standards is important because managers use standards to plan direct materials purchases. Inaccuracies about direct materials requirements could lead to direct materials stockouts, cycle time increases, and customer back orders.

But direct materials costs are not the only costs getting attention. Consider direct manufacturing labour costs. Management accountants calculate a standard direct manufacturing labour rate for each manufacturing area (for example, mixing, blending, tableting, and packaging). Managers then review direct manufacturing labour efficiency variances, and management accountants report and track products and work centres with consistently high unfavourable variances. Teams of workers analyze root causes and recommend process and equipment enhancements to improve direct manufacturing labour efficiency and to make standard labour-time adjustments. Accurate labour-time standards are critical because they drive direct manufacturing labour staffing levels.

How has variance analysis and standard costing helped Sandoz? Over the years, the plant has decreased yield and destruction losses, enhancing the company's ability to deliver products that meet customers' expectations and contributing significantly to overall profitability.

Source: Conversations with and documents prepared by Eric Evans and Erich Erchr on March 20, 2004, and May 28, 2004.

and Flotoms, 20%). The difference in costs between the two columns is the total direct materials mix variance, attributable solely to differences in the mix of inputs used. The total direct materials mix variance is the sum of the direct materials mix variances for each input.

Latoms	$(0.50 - 0.50) \times 6,500 \times \$70 = 0.00 \times 6,500 \times \$70$	$= \$$	0	
Caltoms	$(0.35 - 0.30) \times 6,500 \times \$80 = 0.05 \times 6,500 \times \$80$	$=$	26,000 U	
Flotoms	$(0.15 - 0.20) \times 6,500 \times \$90 = (0.05) \times 6,500 \times \$90$	$=$	29,250 F	
Total direct materials mix variance			$\$ \underline{3,250}$ F	

Total Direct Materials Yield Variance   Compare columns 2 and 3 of Exhibit 16-10. Column 2 calculates costs using the budgeted input mix and the budgeted prices. Column 3 calculates the flexible-budget cost based on the budgeted cost of the budgeted total quantity of all inputs used (6,400 tonnes of tomatoes) for the actual output achieved (4,000 tonnes of ketchup) times the budgeted input mix (Latoms, 50%; Caltoms, 30%; Flotoms, 20%). The only difference in the two columns is that column 2 uses the actual total quantity of all inputs used (6,500 tonnes), while column 3 uses the budgeted total quantity of all inputs used (6,400 tonnes). Hence, the difference in costs between the two columns is the total direct materials yield variance, due solely to differences in actual and budgeted total input quantity used. The total direct materials yield variance is the sum of the direct materials yield variances for each input.

$$
\begin{array}{lll}
\text{Latoms} & (6,500 - 6,400) \times 0.50 \times \$70 = 100 \times 0.50 \times \$70 = & \$3,500 \ \text{U} \\
\text{Caltoms} & (6,500 - 6,400) \times 0.30 \times \$80 = 100 \times 0.30 \times \$80 = & 2,400 \ \text{U} \\
\text{Flotoms} & (6,500 - 6,400) \times 0.20 \times \$90 = 100 \times 0.20 \times \$90 = & \underline{1,800} \ \text{U} \\
\text{Total direct materials yield variance} & & \underline{\underline{\$7,700}} \ \text{U}
\end{array}
$$

The total direct materials yield variance is unfavourable because Delpino used 6,500 tonnes of tomatoes rather than the 6,400 tonnes that it should have used to produce 4,000 tonnes of ketchup. Holding the budgeted mix and budgeted prices of tomatoes constant, the budgeted cost per tonne of tomatoes in the budgeted mix is $77 per tonne. The unfavourable yield variance represents the budgeted cost of using 100 more tonnes of tomatoes: $(6,500 - 6,400) \times \$77 = \$7,700$ U.

The direct materials variances computed in Exhibits 16-9 and 16-10 can be summarized as follows:

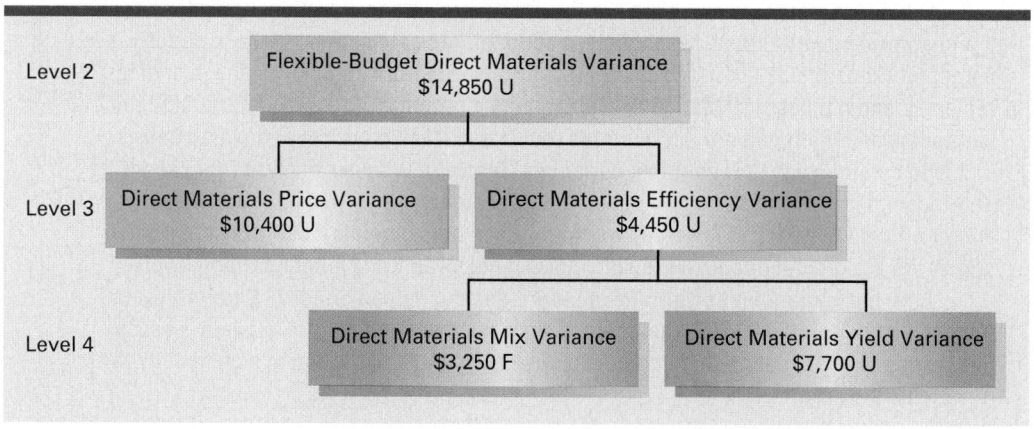

This chapter contains definitions of the following important terms:

QUESTIONS

16-1 Describe how companies are increasingly facing revenue-allocation decisions.

16-2 Distinguish between the stand-alone revenue-allocation method and the incremental revenue-allocation method.

16-3 Identify and discuss arguments individual product managers may put forward to support their preferred revenue allocation method.

16-4 How might a dispute over the allocation of revenues of a bundled product be resolved?

16-5 Show how managers can gain insight into the causes of a sales-volume variance by drilling down into the components of this variance.

16-6 How can the concept of a composite unit be used to explain why an unfavourable total sales-mix variance for revenues occurs?

16-7 Explain why a favourable sales-quantity variance occurs.

16-8 Distinguish between a market-size variance and a market-share variance.

16-9 Why might some companies not compute market-size and market-share variances?

16-10 Why is customer profitability analysis a vitally important topic to managers?

16-11 How can the extent of price discounting be tracked on a customer-by-customer basis?

16-12 "A customer profitability profile highlights those customers that should be dropped to improve profitability." Do you agree?

16-13 Give an example of three types of different levels of costs in a customer cost hierarchy.

16-14 Distinguish between processes where the inputs are nonsubstitutable and where they are substitutable.

16-15 Explain how the direct materials mix and yield variances provide additional information about the direct materials efficiency variance.

EXERCISES

16-16 Revenue allocation, speaking fees. Geoff Carr is a leading public relations expert. He recently convinced three well-known sports personalities to jointly appear on a one-day seminar.

◆ Linda Young is a leading soccer coach. She gave six speeches last year, each at $11,000 per appearance. Young refuses most invitations, preferring to focus on ways to win matches or to relax at home.

◆ Vince Rock is an Olympic gold medallist. Rock gave 50 speeches last year, each at $4,400 per appearance. He loves publicity and rarely says no to invitations.

◆ Juan Malvido is a television sports commentator. Malvido charged $2,200 for each of the 40 appearances he made last year. His television network actively solicits venues at which Malvido talks.

In the past, each speaker has been the only presenter at events at which they appear. Young, Rock, and Malvido will each speak for 2 hours at Carr's one-day seminar.

The first seminar draws 500 people at $220 per head. Carr promised his three speakers he would give them in aggregate 30% of the total revenues. Without discussing it with each speaker, Carr assumes this 30% would be split equally—10% of total revenues to Young, 10% to Rock, and 10% to Malvido.

REQUIRED

1. Describe two alternative ways (other than equal splitting) to allocate the 30% of total revenues among the three speakers.

2. Discuss possible reactions of each speaker to Carr's proposed equal splitting of the 30% of revenues allotted for speaking fees.

16-17 Revenue allocation, bundled products. Pebble Resorts operates a five-star hotel with a world-recognized championship golf course. It has a decentralized management structure. There are three divisions:

◆ Lodging (rooms, conference facilities)

◆ Food (restaurants and in-room service)

◆ Recreation (the golf course, tennis courts, and so on)

Starting next month, Pebble will offer a two-day, two-person "getaway package" deal for $770. This deal includes

◆ Two nights' stay for two in an ocean-view room—separately priced at $704 ($352 per night for two).

◆ Two rounds of golf separately priced at $330 ($165 per round). One person can do two rounds, or two can do one round each.

◆ Candlelight dinner for two at the exclusive Pebble Pacific Restaurant—separately priced at $88 per person.

Samantha Lee, president of the Recreation Division, recently asked the CEO of Pebble Resorts how her division would share in the $770 revenue from the package. The golf course was operating at 100% capacity (and then some). Under the "getaway package" rules, participants who booked one week in advance were guaranteed access to the golf course. Lee noted that every "getaway" booking would displace a $165 booking. She stressed that the high demand reflected the devotion of her team to keeping the golf course rated in the "Best 10 Courses in the World" listings in *Golf Monthly*. As an aside she also noted that the Lodging and Food divisions only had to turn away customers on "peak-season events such as the New Year's period."

REQUIRED

1. Allocate the $770 "getaway package" revenue to the three divisions using
   a. The stand-alone revenue-allocation method
   b. The incremental revenue-allocation method (with recreation first, then lodging, and then food)
   Use unit selling prices as the weights in (a) and (b).
2. What are the pros and cons of (a) and (b) in requirement 1?

16-18 Revenue allocation, bundled products, additional complexities (continuation of 16-17). The individual items in the "getaway package" deal at Pebble Resorts are not fully used by each guest. Assume that 10% of the "getaway package" users in its first month do not use the golfing option, while 5% do not use the food option. The lodging option has a 100% usage rate.

REQUIRED

How should Pebble Resorts recognize this nonuse factor in its revenue sharing of the $770 package across the Lodging, Food, and Recreation divisions?

16-19 Variance analysis of revenues, multiple products. The Penguins play in the North American Ice Hockey League. The Penguins play in the Downtown Arena, which has a capacity of 30,000 seats (10,000 lower-tier seats and 20,000 upper-tier seats). The Downtown Arena charges the Penguins a per-ticket charge for use of their facility. All tickets are sold by the Reservation Network, which charges the Penguins a reservation fee per ticket. The Penguins' budgeted net revenue for each type of ticket in 2007 is computed as follows:

	Lower-Tier Tickets	Upper-Tier Tickets
Selling price	$35.00	$14.00
Downtown Arena fee	11.00	6.60
Reservation Network fee	5.50	3.30
Contribution margin	$18.50	$ 4.10

The budgeted and actual average attendance figures per game in the 2007 season are

	Budgeted Seats Sold	Actual Seats Sold
Lower-tier	8,000	6,600
Upper-tier	12,000	15,400
Total	20,000	22,000

There was no difference between the budgeted and actual net revenue for lower-tier or upper-tier seats.

The manager of the Penguins was delighted that actual attendance was 10% above budgeted attendance per game, especially given the depressed state of the local economy in the past six months.

REQUIRED

1. Compute the sales-volume variance for individual "product" net revenues and total net revenues for the Penguins in 2006.
2. Compute the sales-quantity and sales-mix variances for individual "product" net revenues and total net revenues in 2006.
3. Write a brief analysis of the variances in requirements 1 and 2. Comment on the results.

Excel Application For students who wish to practise their spreadsheet skills, the following is a step-by-step approach to creating an Excel spreadsheet to work this problem.

Step-by-Step

1. Open up a new spreadsheet. At the top, create an "Original Data" section for the data provided by the Penguins in the same format as shown on page 656. Create columns for each type of ticket ("Lower tier" and "Upper tier") and rows for "Selling Price, Downtown Arena Fee, Reservation Network Fee, and Contribution Margin per Ticket." Skip two rows, and create rows for each type of ticket, a "Total" row, and columns for "Budgeted Seats Sold" and "Actual Seats Sold."

(Program your spreadsheet to perform all necessary calculations. Do not "hard-code" any amounts, such as sales-mix variance, requiring addition, subtraction, multiplication, or division operations.)

2. Skip two rows and create a new section, "Problem 1—Sales volume variance calculations." Create rows for "Lower-tier Tickets, Upper-tier Tickets," and "All Tickets." Using the data in your Original Data section, enter calculations for sales-volume variances for each ticket type and total sales-volume variance for all tickets.

3. Skip two rows and create a section, "Problem 2." Create a subsection, "Sales-mix percentages." In this subsection, create rows for each ticket type and columns for "Budgeted" and "Actual." Enter calculations for the budgeted and actual sales-mix percentages for each ticket type.

4. Skip two rows and create another subsection, "Sales-quantity variance calculations." The format for this section should be the same as the one you used in step 2. Using the data from your Original Data section and the sales-mix percentages from step 3, enter calculations for sales-quantity variances for each ticket type and total sales-quantity variance for all tickets.

5. Skip two rows and create another subsection, "Sales-mix variance calculations." The format for this section should be the same as the one you used in step 2. Using the data from your Original Data section and the sales-mix percentages from step 3, enter calculations for sales-mix variances for each ticket type and total sales-mix variance for all tickets.

6. *Check the accuracy of your spreadsheet:* Go to your Original Data section and change the reservation network fee for lower-tier tickets from $5.50 to $6.50. If your spreadsheet is programmed correctly, sales-volume variance should change to $10,560 unfavourable.

16-20 7 Up using variances to read the market. The following is an excerpt from an article that appeared in a recent issue of a trade magazine:

> Remember about 30 years back, when 7 Up began describing itself as the Uncola and ran those great commercials celebrating the "uncola nut"? And remember those cool upside-down 7 Up glasses?

> This, paradoxically, is part of 7 Up's problem. As John Sicher, editor of *Beverage Digest* explains, "7 Up is perceived today as something that appeals to an older generation, not as a hip, with-it brand." Indeed, 7 Up's own research shows that while the soft drink continues to be popular with boomers who grew up on the Uncola campaign, its brand identity is barely a blip on the cultural radar of today's 12- to 24-year-olds, the demographic segment that consumes the most soda. As a result, 7 Up's market share has deteriorated throughout the '90s, even though the share of the citrus-flavoured soda category—which includes 7 Up's primary competitor, Sprite—has increased during the same period.

In the ten years before the article, 7 Up's market share had declined from 3.2% to 2.4%. Five years before the article, 7 Up held a 2.8% market share, compared to Sprite's 4.9%. (Sprite is the category leader in the lemon-lime segment of the soft drink market.) 7 Up's slide has been steady and consistent over the past ten years.

REQUIRED

1. In light of these comments, what variances should 7 Up management have been tracking over the past decade? What story would those variances have told?
2. What factors should you consider in evaluating 7 Up's strategy in the last decade?

16-21 Variance analysis of contribution margin, multiple products; working backward. The Jinwa Corporation sells two brands of wine glasses—Plain and Chic. Jinwa provides the following information for sales in June 2007:

Static budget total contribution margin	$8,400
Budgeted units to be sold of all glasses in June 2007	3,000 units
Budgeted contribution margin per unit of Plain	$2 per unit
Budgeted contribution margin per unit of Chic	$6 per unit
Total sales quantity variance	$1,400 U
Actual sales mix percentage of Plain	68%

All variances are to be computed in contribution margin terms.

REQUIRED

1. Calculate the sales quantity variances for each product for June 2007.
2. Calculate the individual product and total sales mix variances for June 2007. Calculate the individual product and total sales volume variances for June 2007.
3. Briefly describe the conclusions you would draw from the variances.

16-22 Variance analysis of revenues, multiple countries. Cola-King manufactures and sells cola soft drinks in three countries—Canada, Mexico, and the United States. The same product is sold in each market. Budgeted and actual results for 2007 (all in Canadian dollars) are as follows:

	Budget for 2007			**Actual for 2007**		
Country	Selling Price per Carton	Variable Cost per Carton	Units Sold (Cartons in Thousands)	Selling Price per Carton	Variable Cost per Carton	Units Sold (Cartons in Thousands)
Canada	$6.60	$4.00	400,000	$6.82	$4.50	480,000
Mexico	$4.40	$2.80	600,000	$4.68	$2.75	900,000
United States	$7.70	$4.50	1,500,000	$7.48	$4.60	1,620,000

REQUIRED

1. Compute the flexible-budget variance, the sales-volume variance, sales-mix variance, and sales-quantity variance. Show results for each country in your computations.
2. What inferences do you make from the variances computed in requirement 1?

16-23 Customer profitability, service company. Instant Service (IS) is a repair service company specializing in the rapid repair of photocopying machines. Each of its ten clients pays a fixed monthly service fee (based on the type of photocopying machines owned by that client and the number of employees at that site). IS keeps records of the time technicians spend at each client as well as the cost of the equipment used to repair each photocopying machine. IS recently decided to compute the profitability of each customer. The following data (in thousands) pertain to May 2007:

	Customer Revenues	Customer Costs
Avery Group	$265	$182
Duran Systems	185	184
Retail Systems	168	178
Wizard Partners	327	225
Santa Clara College	240	308
Grainger Services	85	74
Software Partners	179	100
Problem Solvers	81	108
Business Systems	142	110
Okie Enterprises	378	231

REQUIRED

1. Compute the operating income of each customer. Prepare exhibits for Instant Service that are similar to Exhibits 16-7 (p. 645) and 16-8 (p. 647). Comment on the results.
2. What options regarding individual customers should Instant Service consider in light of your customer profitability analysis in requirement 1?
3. What problems might Instant Service encounter in accurately estimating the operating cost of each customer?

16-24 Customer profitability, distribution. Figure Four is a distributor of pharmaceutical products. Its activity-based costing system has five activity areas:

Activity Area	Cost Driver and 2007 Rate
1. Order processing	$40 per order
2. Line item ordering	$ 3 per line item
3. Store deliveries	$50 per store delivery
4. Carton deliveries	$ 1 per carton
5. Shelf-stocking	$16 per stocking-hour

Syed Alam, the controller of Figure Four, wants to use this activity-based costing system to examine individual customer profitability within each distribution market. He focuses first on the "mom and pop" single-store distribution market. Two customers are used to exemplify the insights available with the activity-based costing approach. Data pertaining to these two customers in August 2007 are as follows:

	Maple Pharmacy	Oak Hill Pharmacy
Total orders	12	10
Average line items per order	10	18
Total store deliveries	6	10
Average cartons shipped per store delivery	24	20
Average hours of shelf-stocking per store delivery	0	0.5
Average revenue per delivery	$2,640	$1,980
Average cost of goods sold per delivery	$2,310	$1,815

REQUIRED

1. Use the activity-based costing information to compute the operating income of each customer in August 2007. Comment on the results.
2. Alam ranks the individual customers in the "mom and pop" single-store distribution market on the basis of operating income. The cumulative operating income of the top 20% of customers is $55,680. Figure Four reports negative operating income of $21,247 for the bottom 40% of its customers. Make four recommendations that you think Figure Four should consider in light of this new customer profitability information.

16-25 **Direct materials efficiency, mix and yield variances.** (Chapter Appendix, CMA adapted) The Energy Products Company produces a gasoline additive, Gas Gain, that increases engine efficiency and improves gasoline mileage. The actual and budgeted quantities (in litres) of materials required to produce Gas Gain and the budgeted prices of materials in August 2007 are as follows:

Chemical	Actual Quantity	Budgeted Quantity	Budgeted Price
Echol	24,080	25,200	$0.22
Protex	15,480	16,800	0.47
Benz	36,120	33,600	0.17
CT-40	10,320	8,400	0.32

REQUIRED

1. Calculate the total direct materials efficiency variance for August 2007.
2. Calculate the total direct materials mix and yield variances for August 2007.
3. What conclusions would you draw from the variance analysis?

16-26 **Direct materials price, efficiency, mix and yield variances.** (Chapter Appendix) Greenwood, Inc., manufactures apple products such as apple jelly and applesauce. It makes applesauce by blending Tolman, Golden Delicious, and Ribston apples. Budgeted costs to produce 100,000 kilograms of applesauce in November 2007 are as follows:

45,000 kilograms of Tolman apples at $0.32 per kilogram	$14,400
180,000 kilograms of Golden Delicious apples at $0.28 per kilogram	50,400
75,000 kilograms of Ribston apples at $0.24 per kilogram	18,000

Actual costs in November 2007 are	
62,000 kilograms of Tolman apples at $0.30 per kilogram	$18,600
155,000 kilograms of Golden Delicious apples at $0.28 per kilogram	43,400
93,000 kilograms of Ribston apples at $0.22 per kilogram	20,460

REQUIRED

1. Calculate the total direct materials price and efficiency variances for November 2007.
2. Calculate the total direct materials mix and yield variances for November 2007.
3. Comment on your results in requirements 1 and 2.

PROBLEMS

16-27 **Revenue allocation, bundled products.** Athletic Programs (AP) sells exercise videos through television infomercials. It uses a well-known sporting celebrity in each video. Each celebrity receives a share (typically varying between 10% and 25%) of the revenues from sale of that video.

In recent months, AP has started selling its exercise videos in bundled form as well as in individual form. Typically, the bundled products are offered to people who telephone for a specific video after watching an infomercial. Each infomercial is for a specific exercise tape. As a marketing experiment, AP has begun advertising the bundled product at the end of some infomercials in a select set of markets.

Sales in 2007 of three products that have been sold individually, as well as in bundled form, are as follows:

	Average Retail Price	Net Units Sold	Royalty Paid to Celebrity
Individual sales:			
SuperAbs	$42	27,000	15%
SuperArms	$37	53,000	25%
SuperLegs	$27	20,000	18%
Bundled product sales:			
SuperAbs + SuperArms	$62	18,000	?
SuperAbs + SuperLegs	$54	6,000	?
SuperArms + SuperLegs	$44	11,000	?
SuperAbs + SuperArms + SuperLegs	$67	22,000	?

The AP infomercials have received widespread recognition.

REQUIRED
1. What royalty would be paid to the celebrity on each tape for the individual sales in 2007?
2. What royalty would be paid to each celebrity for the bundled product sales in 2007 using
   a. The stand-alone revenue-allocation method (with average retail price as the weight)?
   b. The incremental revenue-allocation method (with SuperArms ranked 1, SuperAbs 2, and SuperLegs 3)?
3. Discuss the relative merits of the two revenue-allocation methods in requirement 2.
4. Assume the incremental revenue-allocation method is used. What alternative approaches could be used to determine the sequence in which the bundled revenue could be allocated to individual products?

16-28 **Variance analysis, sales-mix and sales-quantity variances.** Aussie Infonautics, Inc., produces handheld Windows-compatible organizers. Aussie Infonautics markets three different handheld models. PalmPro is a souped-up version for the executive on the go; PalmCE is a consumer-oriented version; PalmKid is a stripped down version for the young adult market. You are Aussie Infonautics, senior vice-president of marketing. The CEO has discovered that the total contribution margin came in lower than budget, and it is your responsibility to explain to him why actual results are different from the budget. Budgeted and actual operating data for Aussie Infonautics' Inc.'s third quarter (2007) are as follows:

Budgeted Operating Data, Third Quarter 2007

	Selling Price	Variable Costs per Unit	Contribution Margin per Unit	Sales Volume in Units
PalmPro	$384	$182	$202	12,500
PalmCE	274	98	176	37,500
PalmKid	154	65	89	50,000
				100,000

Actual Operating Data, Third Quarter 2007

	Selling Price	Variable Costs per Unit	Contribution Margin per Unit	Sales Volume in Units
PalmPro	$354	$178	$176	11,000
PalmCE	290	92	198	44,000
PalmKid	107	73	34	55,000
				110,000

1. Compute the actual and budgeted contribution margins in dollars and in percentage terms.
2. Calculate the actual and budgeted sales mix for the three products.
3. Calculate the individual product flexible-budget, sales-volume, sales-mix, and sales-quantity variances for the third quarter of 2007.
4. Calculate total sales-volume, sales-mix, and sales-quantity variances for the third quarter of 2007.
5. Given that your CEO is known to have temper tantrums, you want to be well prepared for this meeting. To prepare, write a paragraph or two explaining why actual results were not as good as the budgeted amounts.

16-29 **Market-share and market-size variances (continuation of 16-28).** Aussie Infonautics, Inc.'s senior vice-president of marketing prepared his budget at the beginning of the third quarter assuming a 25% market share. The total handheld organizer market was estimated by Foolinstead Research to reach sales of 400,000 units worldwide in the third quarter. However, actual sales were 500,000 units.

REQUIRED
1. Calculate the market-share and market-size variances for Aussie Infonautics in the third quarter of 2007 (report all variances in terms of contribution margins).
2. Explain what happened based on the market-share and market-size variances.
3. Calculate the actual market size, in units, that would have led to no market-size variance (again using budgeted average contribution margin per unit). Use this market-size figure to find the actual market share that would have led to a zero market-share variance.

16-30 **Variance analysis of contribution margin, multiple products.** Debbie's Delight, Inc., operates a chain of cookie stores. Budgeted and actual operating data of its three Calgary stores for August 2007 are as follows:

Budget for August

	Selling Price per Kilogram	Variable Costs per Kilogram	Contribution Margin per Kilogram	Sales Volume in Kilograms
Chocolate chip	$4.60	$2.50	$2.00	45,000
Oatmeal raisin	5.10	2.70	2.40	25,000
Coconut	5.60	2.90	2.80	10,000
White chocolate	6.10	3.00	3.70	5,000
Macadamia nut	6.60	3.40	3.10	15,000
				100,000

Actual for August

	Selling Price per Kilogram	Variable Costs per Kilogram	Contribution Margin per Kilogram	Sales Volume in Kilograms
Chocolate chip	$4.60	$2.60	$2.00	57,600
Oatmeal raisin	5.30	2.90	2.40	18,000
Coconut	5.60	2.80	2.80	9,600
White chocolate	6.10	3.40	2.70	13,200
Macadamia nut	7.10	4.00	3.10	21,600
				120,000

Debbie's Delight focuses on contribution margin in its variance analysis.

REQUIRED
1. Compute the individual product and total sales volume variances for August 2007.
2. Compute the individual product and total sales quantity variances for August 2007.
3. Compute the individual product and total sales mix variances for August 2007.
4. Comment on your results in requirements 1, 2, and 3.

16-31 **Market-size and market-share variances (continuation of 16-30).** Debbie's Delight assumes a 10% market share of the Calgary market and a budgeted total Calgary market for August 2007 of 1,000,000 sales volume in kilograms. The actual total Calgary market for August 2007 was 960,000 sales volume in kilograms.

Compute the market-size and market-share variances for Debbie's Delight in August 2007. Report all variances in contribution margin terms. Comment on the results.

16-32 Revenue allocation, bundled products. Pétale Parfum (PP) manufactures and sells upscale perfumes. In recent months, PP has started selling its products in bundled form, as well as in individual form. Sales in 2007 of three products that have been sold individually are as follows:

	Retail Price	Units Sold
Stand-alone		
Fraîche	$110	20,000
Désarmer	88	37,500
Innocence	275	20,000
Suite		
Fraîche + Désarmer	165	
Fraîche + Innocence	308	

Each of the products is manufactured by a separate division.

REQUIRED
1. Compute the weights for allocating revenues to each division for each of the bundled products using:
   a. The stand-alone revenue-allocation method based on total revenues of individual products.
   b. The incremental revenue-allocation method, with Innocence ranked 1; Désarmer, 2; and Fraîche, 3, based on retail prices of individual products. According to this ranking, the primary product in a suite has the highest rank, and so on.
2. Recalculate the allocation using the Shapley and the weighted Shapley value methods. What method would you recommend and why?

16-33 Customer profitability, customer cost hierarchy. Ramish Electronics has two retail customers and two wholesale customers. Pertinent information relating to each customer for 2008 follows (all amounts are in thousands of dollars):

	WHOLESALE		RETAIL	
	North America Wholesaler	South America Wholesaler	Big Sam Stereo	World Market
Cost of goods sold	$325,000	$490,000	$112,000	$ 92,000
Delivery costs:				
Regular	300	450	150	80
Expedited	120	200	10	5
Order processing	800	1,000	200	130
Product handling	5,000	6,000	800	900
Sales visits	480	550	240	165
Revenues at list prices	440,000	660,000	143,000	110,000
Discounts from list prices	30,000	50,000	7,000	0

REQUIRED
Ramish's distribution-channel costs are $30 million for wholesale customers and $10 million for retail customers. Its corporate-sustaining costs are $60 million.

1. Calculate customer-level operating income using the format in Exhibit 16-5.
2. Prepare a customer cost hierarchy report using the format in Exhibit 16-6.

16-34 Customer profitability analysis. Zoot's Suits is a ready-to-wear suit manufacturer with headquarters in Toronto. Zoot's has three customers:
◆ April Department Stores, a large department store chain that uses Zoot's to manufacture its own private-label brand
◆ Brothers Stores, a chain of mall-based men's clothing stores
◆ Suitors, a company that sells suits to students on campus through a network of salespersons who travel across the country visiting college and university campuses

Zoot's owner and CEO Al Sims has developed the following activity-based costing system:

Activity Area	Cost Driver	Rate in 2007
1. Order processing	Purchase order	$ 269.50
2. Sales visits	Sales visit	$1,573.00
3. Delivery—regular	Regular delivery	$ 330.00
4. Delivery—rushed	Rushed delivery	$ 935.00
5. Returns processing	Return	$ 203.50

Each suit returned also incurs a $5 stocking fee. In addition, Zoot's credits the customer's account for the full purchase price of all suits returned. Sims wants to evaluate the profitability of each of the three customers in 2007 in order to explore opportunities for increasing the profitability of his company in 2008. Use the following data to answer the questions that follow:

Item	April	Brothers	Suitors
Total number of orders	44	62	212
Total number of sales visits	8	12	22
Regular deliveries	41	48	166
Rush deliveries	3	14	46
Number of returns	4	6	16
Average number of suits per order	400	200	30
List selling price	$200	$200	$200
Average selling price	$140	$160	$170
Average cost	$110	$110	$110
Average number of suits returned	220	160	80

REQUIRED

1. Calculate the operating income per customer. Who is the most profitable customer? Who is the least profitable customer? What contributes to each customer's profitability (or lack thereof)?
2. Provide some recommendations for Al Sims to ponder as he considers his options for increasing the company's profitability in 2007.

16-35 **Customer profitability, distribution.** Spring Distribution has decided to analyze the profitability of another five customers (see pp. 640–648). It buys bottled water at $0.50 per bottle and sells to wholesale customers at a list price of $0.60 per bottle. Data pertaining to five customers are as follows:

	Customer				
	P	Q	R	S	T
Bottles sold	50,000	210,000	1,460,000	764,000	94,000
List selling price	$0.60	$0.60	$0.60	$0.60	$0.60
Actual selling price	$0.59	$0.58	$0.54	$0.57	$0.53
Number of purchase orders	15	25	30	25	30
Number of sales visits	2	4	6	2	3
Number of deliveries	10	30	60	40	20
Kilometres travelled per delivery	14	4	3	8	40
Number of hot-hot runs	0	0	0	0	1

Its five activity areas and their cost drivers are:

Activity Area	Cost Driver and Rate
Order taking	$100 per purchase order
Sales visits	$80 per sales visit
Delivery vehicles	$2 per delivery kilometre travelled
Product handling	$0.02 per bottle sold
Hot-hot runs	$300 per hot-hot run

1. Compute the operating income of each of the five customers now being examined (P, Q, R, S, and T). Comment on the results.
2. What insights are gained by reporting both the list selling price and the actual selling price for each customer?
3. What factors should Spring Distribution consider in deciding whether to drop one or more of customers P, Q, R, S, or T?

16-36 Customer loyalty clubs and profitability analysis. The Sherriton Hotels chain embarked on a new customer loyalty program in 2007. The 2007 year-end data have been collected, and it is now time for you to determine whether the loyalty program should be continued, discontinued, or perhaps altered to improve loyalty and profitability levels at Sherriton.

Sherriton's loyalty program consists of three different customer loyalty levels. All new customers can sign up for the Sherriton Bronze Card—this card provides guests with a complimentary bottle of wine (cost to the chain is $5 per bottle) and $20 in restaurant coupons each night (cost to the chain is $10). Bronze customers also receive a 10% discount off the nightly rate. The program enables the chain to track a member's stays and activities. Once a customer has stayed and paid for 20 nights at any of the chain's locations worldwide, he or she is upgraded to Silver Customer status. Silver benefits include the bottle of wine (cost to the chain is $5 per bottle), $30 in restaurant coupons (cost to the chain is $15), and 20% off every night from the 21st night on. A customer who reaches the 50-night level is upgraded to Gold Customer status. Gold status increases the nightly discount to 30% and replaces the $5 bottle of wine with a bottle of champagne (cost to the chain is $20 per bottle). As well, $40 in restaurant coupons are granted (cost to the chain is $20).

The average full price for one night's stay is $200. The chain incurs variable costs of $65 per night, exclusive of loyalty program costs. Total fixed costs for the chain are $140,580,000. Sherriton operates ten hotels with, on average, 500 rooms each. All hotels are open for business 365 days a year, and approximate average occupancy rates are around 80%. Following are some loyalty program characteristics:

Loyalty Program	Number of Customers	Average Number of Nights per Customer
Gold	2,673	60
Silver	9,174	35
Bronze	88,330	10
No program	240,900	1

Note that a Gold Customer would have received the 10% discount for his or her first 20 stays, received the 20% discount for the next 30 stays, and the 30% discount only for the last ten nights. Assume that all program members signed on to the program the first time they stayed with one of the chain's hotels. Also, assume the restaurants are managed by a 100%-owned subsidiary of Sherriton.

REQUIRED

1. Calculate the program contribution margin for each of the three programs, as well as for the group of customers not subscribing to the loyalty program. Which of the programs is the most profitable? Which is the least profitable? Do not allocate fixed costs to individual rooms or specific loyalty programs.
2. Develop an income statement for Sherriton for the year ended December 31, 2007.
3. What is the average room rate per night? What are average variable costs per night inclusive of the loyalty program?
4. Explain what drives the profitability (or lack thereof) of the most and least profitable loyalty program (again, one of these may be the "no program" option).

16-37 Direct materials price and efficiency variances, direct materials mix and yield variances. (Chapter Appendix) Tropical Fruits, Inc., processes tropical fruit into a fruit salad mix, which it sells to a food-service company. Tropical Fruits has in its budget the following standards for the direct materials inputs to produce a batch of 80 kilograms of tropical fruit salad:

50 kilograms of pineapple at $1.05 per kilogram	$52.50
30 kilograms of watermelon at $0.55 per kilogram	16.50
20 kilograms of strawberries at $0.80 per kilogram	16.00
100	$85.00

Note that 100 kilograms of input quantities are required to produce 80 kilograms of fruit salad. No inventories of direct materials are kept. Purchases are made as needed, so all price variances are related to direct materials used. The actual direct materials inputs used to produce 54,000 kilograms of tropical fruit salad for October were

36,400 kilograms of pineapple at $0.95 per kilogram	$34,580	
18,200 kilograms of watermelon at $0.65 per kilogram	11,830	
15,400 kilograms of strawberries at $0.75 per kilogram	11,550	
70,000	$57,960	

REQUIRED

1. Compute the total direct materials price and efficiency variances in October.
2. Compute the total direct materials mix and yield variances for October.
3. Comment on your results in requirements 1 and 2.
4. How might the management of Tropical Fruits, Inc., use information about the direct materials mix and yield variances?

16-38 Customer profitability, responsibility for environmental cleanup, ethics. Industrial Fluids, Inc. (IF) manufactures and sells fluids used by metal-cutting plants. These fluids enable metal-cutting to be done more accurately and more safely.

IF has more than 1,000 customers. It is currently undertaking a customer profitability analysis. Ariana Papandopolis, a newly hired MBA, is put in charge of the project. One issue in this analysis is IF's liability for its customers' fluid disposal.

Papandopolis discovers that IF may have a responsibility under Canadian environmental legislation for the disposal of toxic waste by its customers. Moreover, she visits ten customer sites and finds dramatic differences in their toxic-waste-handling procedures. She describes one site owned by Acme Metal as an "environmental nightmare about to become a reality." She tells the IF controller that even if they have only one-half of the responsibility for the cleanup at Acme's site, they will still be facing very high damages. He is displeased at the news. Acme Metal has not paid its account to IF for the past three months and has formally announced bankruptcy. He cautions Papandopolis to be careful in her written report. He notes that "IF does not want any smoking guns in its files in the case of subsequent litigation."

REQUIRED

1. As Papandopolis prepares IF's customer profitability analysis, how should she handle any estimates of litigation and cleanup costs that IF may be held responsible for?
2. How should Papandopolis handle the Acme Metal situation when she prepares a profitability report for that customer?

COLLABORATIVE LEARNING PROBLEM

16-39 Customer profitability, credit card operations. The Freedom Card is a credit card that competes with national credit cards such as VISA and MasterCard. Freedom Card is marketed by the Bay Bank. Mario Verdolini is manager of the Freedom Card division. He is seeking to develop a customer-profitability reporting system. He collects the following information on four users of the Freedom Card:

	Customer			
	A	**B**	**C**	**D**
Annual purchases at retail merchants	$80,000	$26,000	$34,000	$8,000
Customer transactions at retail merchants	800	520	272	200
Membership fee paid	$55	$5	$55	$5
Average annual outstanding balance on credit card on which interest is paid to Bay Bank	$6,000	0	$2,000	$100
Inquiries to Bay Bank	6	12	8	2
Credit card replacement due to loss or theft	0	2	1	0

Customer B pays a lower membership fee because his card was issued under a special "lifetime promotion program" in which annual fees are lower as long as the card is used at least once a year. Customer D is a student. Bay Bank charges a lower membership fee to student credit card holders at select universities.

Bay Bank has an activity-based costing system that Verdolini can use in his analysis. The following data apply to 2007:

a. Each customer transaction with a retail merchant costs Bay Bank $0.55 to process.
b. Each customer inquiry to Bay Bank costs $5.

c. Replacing a lost card costs $120.

d. Annual cost to Bay Bank of maintaining a credit card account is $108 (includes sending out monthly statements).

Bay Bank receives 2.0% of the purchase amount from retail merchants when the Freedom Card is used. Bad debts of the Freedom Card in 2007 were 0.5% of the purchase amounts. Thus, Bay Bank nets 1.5% revenue when its credit card holders use the Freedom Card at retail merchants.

Bay Bank had an interest spread of 9% in 2007 on the average outstanding balances on which interest is paid by its credit card holders. An interest spread is the difference between what Bay Bank receives from card holders on outstanding balances and what it pays to obtain the funds so used. Thus, on a $500 average annual outstanding balance in 2007, Bay Bank would receive $45 in interest payment revenues (9% × $500).

INSTRUCTIONS

Form groups of two or more students to complete the following requirements.

REQUIRED

1. Compute the 2007 customer profitability of the four representative credit card users of the Freedom Card.
2. Develop profiles of (a) profitable card holders and (b) unprofitable card holders for Bay Bank.
3. Should Bay Bank charge its card holders for making inquiries (such as outstanding balances) or for replacing lost or stolen cards? At present, no such charges are made.
4. Verdolini has an internal proposal that Bay Bank discontinue a sizable number of the low-volume credit card customers. What factors should he consider in evaluating and responding to this proposal?
5. Verdolini seeks your group's advice on an ethical issue he is facing. A chain of gambling casinos (Lucky Roller) has offered to provide Freedom Card holders with money advances of up to $500 at its casinos. Verdolini observes that from a strict financial perspective, providing money advances to its customers was highly profitable in 2007. Should Freedom Card holders be able to obtain money advances at Lucky Roller gambling casinos?

CHAPTER 17

Process Costing

It is common in resource-based industries for management to have a choice regarding the extent to which the product will be processed. Process costing is needed to assist managers in making these decisions. Highliner Foods must decide whether to sell its fish fresh to local markets or to process the fish into frozen packages that then can be sold to markets around the world. Given that on any day the amount of fish caught is unpredictable, these decisions are ongoing and essential to the operations of Highliner Foods.

LEARNING OBJECTIVES

After studying this chapter, you should be able to

1. Determine when process-costing systems are appropriate
2. Describe five key steps in process costing
3. Calculate and use equivalent units
4. Prepare journal entries for process-costing systems
5. Demonstrate the weighted-average method of process costing
6. Demonstrate the first-in, first-out (FIFO) method of process costing
7. Incorporate standard costs into a process-costing system

A *process-costing system* is a costing system in which the cost of a product or service is obtained by assigning costs to masses of like or similar units. Process-costing systems are used in industries that cost like or similar units of products, which are often mass-produced. In these industries, relatively homogeneous products are processed in a very similar manner and are hence assumed to receive the same amount of direct materials, direct manufacturing labour costs, and manufacturing overhead costs.

PROCESS-COSTING EQUATIONS

OBJECTIVE 1

Determine when process-costing systems are appropriate

Industries using process costing in their manufacturing area include chemical processing, oil refining, pharmaceuticals, plastics, brick and tile manufacturing, semiconductor chips, beverages, and breakfast cereals.

The principal difference between process costing and job costing is the *extent of averaging* used to compute unit costs of products or services. In a job-costing system, individual jobs use different quantities of direct and indirect materials and labour, so it would be incorrect to cost each job at the same average production cost. In contrast, when identical or similar units of products or services are mass-produced, not processed as individual jobs, process costing is used to calculate an average production cost for all units produced (see Global Surveys of Company Practice, p. 670). Unit costs are computed by dividing total costs incurred by the number of units of output from the production process. Some processes such as clothes manufacturing have aspects of both process costing (cost per unit of each operation, such as cutting or sewing, is identical) and job costing (different materials are used in different batches of clothing, say, wool versus cotton). The appendix to this chapter describes costing systems that combine process costing and job costing.

Illustrating Process Costing

The characteristics of the products and services provided by a corporation will determine how the costing system is designed. The objectives of a costing system, as you will recall from Chapter 4, are:

◆ Estimate as accurately as possible the costs of products and services to assist in decisions such as pricing and product mix

◆ Value inventory and cost of goods sold in compliance with external reporting requirements

◆ Manage costs and evaluate actual against expected performance to assist in redesigning the processes comprising the value chain

In this chapter the focus is on applying process-costing techniques to achieve the first two objectives. Job- and process-costing systems are best viewed as the two extremes of a continuum.

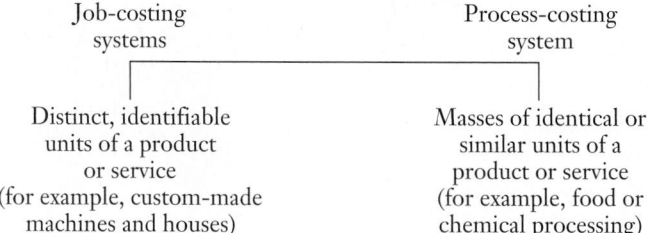

The easiest way to learn process costing is by example. Let us consider the following illustration.

Example: Global Defence, Inc., manufactures thousands of components for missiles and military equipment. We will focus on the production of one of these components, DG-19. The product-costing system for DG-19 has a single direct-cost category (direct materials) and a single indirect-cost category (conversion costs). Each DG-19 unit passes through two departments—the Assembly Department and the Testing Department. Every effort is made to ensure that all DG-19 units are identical and meet a set of demanding performance specifications. Direct materials are added at the beginning of the process in Assembly. Additional direct materials are added at the end of processing in the Testing Department, where final assembly

Global Defence Review 2007
www.global-defence.com

of the DG-19 component occurs. Conversion costs are added evenly during both processes. *Conversion costs* are all manufacturing costs other than direct materials costs. Conversion costs include manufacturing labour, indirect materials, energy, plant amortization, and so on. When the Testing Department finishes work on each DG-19 component, it is immediately transferred to Finished Goods. The following graphic summarizes these facts:

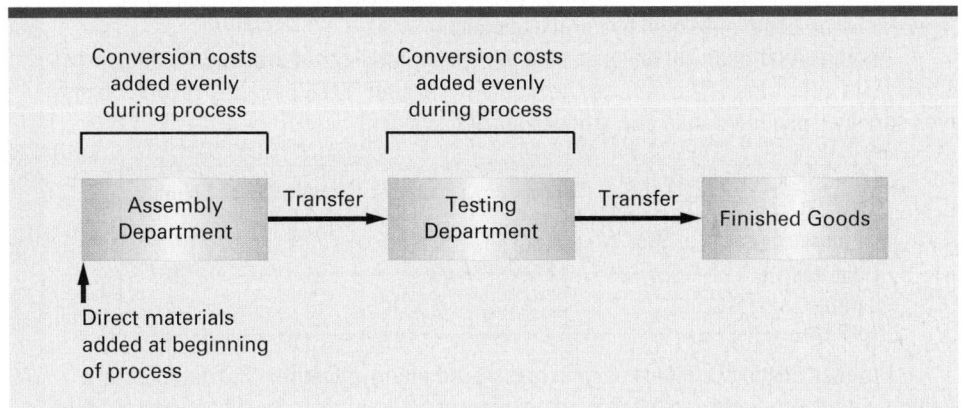

We will use the manufacture of the DG-19 component to illustrate three cases:

- **Case 1**   Process costing with no beginning or ending work-in-process inventory of DG-19—that is, all units are started and fully completed by the end of the accounting period. *This case illustrates the basic averaging of costs idea that is a key feature of process-costing systems.*
- **Case 2**   Process-costing with no beginning work-in-process inventory but an ending work-in-process inventory of DG-19—that is, some units of DG-19 started during the accounting period are incomplete at the end of the period. *This case introduces the concept of equivalent units.*
- **Case 3**   Process costing with both beginning and ending work-in-process inventory of DG-19. *This case describes the effect of weighted-average and first-in, first-out (FIFO) cost-flow assumptions on cost of units completed and cost of work-in-process inventory.*

On January 1, 2007, there was no beginning inventory of DG-19 units. During January 2007, Global Defence started, completed assembly of, and transferred out to the Testing Department, 400 DG-19 units.

Data for the Assembly Department for January 2007 are as follows:

Physical Units for January 2007

Work in process, beginning inventory (January 1)	0 units
Started during January	400 units
Completed and transferred out during January	400 units
Work in process, ending inventory (January 31)	0 units

This physical flow of inventory is the foundation on which to build the cost estimates of Global's products.

Total Costs for January 2007

Direct materials costs added during January	$32,000
Conversion costs added during January	24,000
Total Assembly Department costs added during January	$56,000

Choosing between the weighted-average method and the FIFO method is unnecessary for the first two cases because the beginning work in process inventory is zero. Differences in the weighted-average and FIFO methods of estimating average costs arise only when there is *both* a non-zero beginning work-in-process inventory *and* the manufacturing cost per unit changes from period to period.

Process Costing in Different Industries

Recent surveys indicate that process costing is used extensively at corporations around the world. One survey noted that 52% of Australian companies and 46% of Japanese companies use process costing, making it the most popular product-costing system in both countries.[a] Additional findings from Eastern Europe show that 66% of all Estonian manufacturing companies also use process costing.[b]

Another Australian survey examines the widespread use of process costing across a variety of industries.[c] (The reported percentages exceed 100% because several companies surveyed use more than one product-costing system.)

	Food	Textiles	Metals	Chemicals	Refining
Process costing	96%	91%	92%	75%	100%
Job costing	4	18	25	25	25
Other	—	—	8	12	—

Process costing is widely used in mass-production industries that manufacture homogeneous products, including food, textiles, primary metals, chemicals, and refining. In contrast, job costing is favoured over process costing in industries that produce many distinct products—for example, in printing and publishing, furniture and fixtures, machinery and computers, and electronics.

	Printing and Publishing	Furniture and Fixtures	Machinery and Computers	Electronics
Process costing	20%	38%	43%	55%
Job costing	73	63	65	58
Other	13	—	9	10

Among artisan-based enterprises in Nigeria, 49% of respondents use job costing, whereas only 10% rely on process costing for product-costing purposes.[d]

[a]Wijewardena, H., and A. De Zoysa, "A Comparative Analysis of Management Accounting Practices in Australia and Japan: An Empirical Investigation," *International Journal of Accounting* (1999).

[b]Haldma., T., and K. Lääts, "Contingencies Influencing the Management Accounting Practices in Estonian Manufacturing Companies," *Management Accounting Research* (2002).

[c]Joye, M., and P. Blayney, "Cost and Management Accounting Practices in Australian Manufacturing Companies: Survey Results" (Accounting Research Centre, The University of Sydney, 1991).

[d]Obara, L., and N. Ukpai, "Cost Accounting Practice in the Information Sector of Nigeria: A Survey of Eastern Business Zone" (Tangier, Morocco: African Training and Research Centre in Administration for Development, 2001).

CASE 1: PROCESS COSTING WITH NO BEGINNING OR ENDING WORK-IN-PROCESS INVENTORY

Global Defence records direct materials and conversion costs in the Assembly Department as these costs are incurred. By averaging, the assembly cost per unit of DG-19 would simply be $56,000 ÷ 400 units = $140, itemized as follows:

Direct materials ($32,000 ÷ 400) cost per unit	$ 80
Conversion costs ($24,000 ÷ 400) per unit	60
Assembly Department cost per unit	$140

This case shows that in a process-costing system, unit costs can be averaged by dividing total costs in a given accounting period by total units produced in that period. Because each unit is identical, there is no reason to believe any single unit would cost more to produce than the other units. Therefore, we assume that all units receive the identical amount of direct materials and conversion costs. Organizations that mass-produce standard units can use this simple average costing approach for their processes if there are no incomplete units at the end of each accounting period. This situation frequently occurs in service sector organizations. For example, banks can adopt this process-costing approach to compute the unit cost of 100,000 similar customer deposits made in a month.

CASE 2: PROCESS COSTING WITH NO BEGINNING BUT AN ENDING WORK-IN-PROCESS INVENTORY

OBJECTIVE 2

Describe five key steps in process costing

In February 2007, Global Defence places another 400 units of DG-19 into production. Remember, there is no beginning inventory of partially completed units in the Assembly Department on February 1, 2007, because all units placed into production in January were fully completed by February 1. Customer delays in placing orders for DG-19 prevented the complete assembly of all units started in February. Only 175 units were completed and transferred out to the Testing Department. This means that 225 units remained in the Assembly Department's work-in-process ending inventory as at February 28, 2007.

Data for the Assembly Department for February 2007 are as follows:

	A	B	C	D	E
1		Physical Units	Direct	Conversion	Total
2		(DG-19s)	Materials	Costs	Costs
3	**Flow of Production**	(1)	(2)	(3)	(4) = (2) + (3)
4	Work in process, beginning inventory (February 1)	0			
5	Started during February	400			
7	Completed and transferred out during February	<u>175</u>			
12	Work in process, ending inventory (February 28)	<u>225</u>			
13	Degree of completion of ending work in process		100%	60%	
14	Total costs added during February		$32,000	$18,600	$50,600

The 225 partially assembled units as of February 28, 2007, were fully processed with respect to direct materials. Why? Because all direct materials in the Assembly Department are added at the beginning of the assembly process. Conversion costs are added evenly during the assembly process. How can we estimate the value of the units remaining in the Assembly Department's work in process? The first step is to obtain an estimate of how fully assembled the units are. This means estimating how much of the conversion from raw direct materials to fully assembled units has occurred. Is the conversion 10% complete? Is it 38% complete? The Assembly Department supervisor will provide this information.

Let us assume that the Assembly Department supervisor estimates the units are, on average, 60% converted from raw materials into 100% assembled units. Emphasis is on the word *average*. Some units may be 90% and others may be 10% assembled. In a mass production process, however, it is often impossible and almost always too costly to do a physical inspection to observe the different quantities of units at different stages of full assembly. The physical flow of inventory is the basis for the estimate of average completion for work-in-process inventory. This is a cost-effective method for managers to estimate both production costs of goods available for sale and cost of goods sold as well as the value of ending inventory. It is also feedback on any difference between expected and actual performance (variance). Variance analysis in turn helps managers make the best adjustments to processes in order to reduce costs without reducing quality.

The accuracy of the completion percentages depends on the care and skill of the estimator and the nature of the process. In most situations, for this important estimate the accountant depends upon the expertise of the production engineers, managers, and directors who understand the process. Estimating the degree of completion is usually easier for direct materials than for conversion costs because quantities of materials used can be more accurately measured. The conversion sequence may rely on a chemical process, for example the fermenting of wine or beer. The brewmaster may be unable to measure the specific stage of completion of the chemical process simply by observing the brew. The brewmaster can, however, estimate completion based on the time the direct materials have been fermenting.

Global Defence is assembling separate physical units, but we are assuming it is too costly to count how many incomplete units are at each stage of assembly. Assembly usually consists of a number of basic operations or a specified number of hours, days, weeks, or months. Assembly comprises various steps in stamping, grinding, machining, parts assembly, testing, and so forth. Assume skilled tradespeople undertake these different processes. Then Global Defence must estimate the value of labour conversion costs of goods manufactured. The value of labour conversion depends on what proportion of the total labour needed to complete one unit or one batch has been devoted to units remaining in the Assembly Department's work-in-process inventory.

In some industries, such as semiconductor manufacturing, where millions of units are manufactured and assembled by machine, no exact estimate of the dollars spent in machine-hours for each incomplete unit is possible. In the textile industry, where the unit price is low, thousands of people in a single factory may be working on cutting, sewing, and finishing garments. There are not only vast quantities in process but also vast numbers of people. This makes the task of estimating the stage of completion of each unit too costly. These two examples illustrate why it is often necessary to estimate a single average percentage of completion for all work in process (for example, one-third, one-half, or two-thirds complete). The Focus on Values and Behaviours box describes the challenges management accountants face when making these estimates.

The key point in this example is that a partially assembled unit is not the same as a fully assembled unit. In terms of the accounting cycle illustrated in Exhibit 2-7 (page 43), a fully assembled unit contributes to the cost of goods available for sale (see Panel A). An incomplete unit is work in process and one component of manufacturing costs incurred (see Panel B). One approach to the problem of estimating the two values required for the fully assembled and some partially assembled units is the equivalent unit approach. If Global Defence requires an income statement for the month of February, then it must calculate (1) the cost of fully assembled units in February 2007 in order to estimate cost of goods available for sale and (2) the cost of the partially assembled units still in process at the end of February 2007 in order to estimate manufacturing costs incurred.

We can find the answers to these two questions using a process-costing system and the following five steps:

- ◆ **Step 1.** Summarize the flow of physical units of output.
- ◆ **Step 2.** Compute output in terms of equivalent units.
- ◆ **Step 3.** Compute equivalent unit costs.
- ◆ **Step 4.** Summarize total costs to account for.
- ◆ **Step 5.** Assign these costs to units completed and to units in ending work in process.

Physical Units and Equivalent Units (Steps 1 and 2)

Step 1 tracks the physical units of output. Where did the units come from and how many units are there to account for? Where did they go and how are they accounted for? The physical units column of Exhibit 17-1 on page 674 tracks where the physical units went—175 units completed and transferred out as fully assembled finished goods, and 225 units in the Assembly Department's ending inventory of work in process. This reflects how the original inputs for 400 units have been converted at the end of February.

In step 2, the finished and unfinished output for February must be measured using some common unit that will become the allocation base. Since all physical units of output are not uniformly completed, output in step 2 is stated in *equivalent units*, not in physical units. The total equivalent units converted is the allocation base or denominator for conversion costs. It will be straightforward to estimate an average cost of conversion per unit, the allocation rate. The output was 175 fully assembled units plus 225 partially

Royal Dutch Shell: Making Estimations for All the Wrong Reasons

A key input into process-costing calculations is the degree of completion of inventory, particularly with respect to conversion costs—that is, how much of the total conversion costs needed to complete one unit have been used for units still in process. Process-costing calculations pose many challenges for a company's management accountants because it is difficult to estimate conversion costs accurately. Management accountants must therefore work with department managers to get the best possible information when making these estimates. At the same time, management accountants must recognize the incentives department managers may have to bias estimates in favour of showing higher percentages of completion, resulting in higher inventory valuations and profits. If management accountants want their estimations to be sound, they must act sensitively and thoughtfully but also ask critical, tough-minded questions.

But what happens when management accountants and department managers do not make estimations responsibly? Consider Royal Dutch Shell. Similar to conversion-cost estimations, oil companies must make many engineering and geological estimates and judgments to calculate their proven oil and natural gas reserves, which report beginning inventory. In January 2004, Royal Dutch Shell cut by 20%, or 3.9 billion barrels, its estimates of proven oil and gas reserves. Later on in 2004, *The New York Times* reported:

> Internal corporate documents and interviews with oil executives and industry analysts describe a company that in the go-go period of the 1990s tried to manage its reserve figures much the way other companies managed their earnings—to satisfy investors.
>
> The documents show that worried executives felt compelled to increase the reserves, which throughout the first half of the 1990s were declining because discoveries did not keep pace with production.
>
> According to a confidential internal review . . . senior company executives ignored warnings over several years of the possible inflation of reserves. . . . The review also suggested that there may have been financial incentives for some executives to overstate reserves, although it provided few details. . . . Company officials have said in recent days that there is a minimal connection between increasing reserves and performance-related pay.

As a result of these disclosures, Royal Dutch Shell ousted its chairman, Sir Philip Watts, and another senior executive in March 2004. The U.S. Securities and Exchange Commission is investigating the company's accounting for reserves. Though the role played by the management accountants in this situation is still unclear, the Royal Dutch Shell story serves as a reminder of the importance of acting with integrity.

Source: S. Labaton and J. Gerth, "At Shell, New Accounting and Rosier Oil Outlook," *The New York Times*, March 12, 2004, p. A1.

---

assembled units. The equivalent units are the multipliers that will be used to assign conversion costs to the ending and work-in-process inventories for the Assembly Department.

Equivalent units measure output in terms of the physical quantities of each of the inputs (materials, labour) that have been consumed when producing the units. For example, each equivalent unit of DG-19 comprises the physical quantities of direct materials and the conversion costs inputs necessary to produce output of one fully complete unit of DG-19. In simple terms, given a percentage completion estimate of 10% and 10 unfinished units, how many finished units could Global Defence have completed? If conversion happens uniformly, then the answer is 10 unfinished units that are 10% converted are equivalent to 1 finished unit. The cost allocation base becomes $175 + 1 = 176$ equivalent units.

Equivalent units. Measure of the output in terms of the physical quantities of each of the inputs (factors of production) that have been consumed when producing the units; it is the physical quantities of inputs necessary to produce output of one fully complete unit.

EXHIBIT 17-1
Steps 1 and 2: Summarize Output in Physical Units and Compute Output in Equivalent Units for Assembly Department of Global Defence for February 2007

	A	B	C	D
		(Step 1)	**(Step 2)**	
1				
2			**Equivalent Units**	
3		**Physical**	**Direct**	**Conversion**
4	**Flow of Production**	**Units**	**Materials**	**Costs**
5	Work in process, beginning	0		
6	Started during current period	400		
7	To account for	400		
8	Completed and transferred out during current period	175	175	175
9	Work in process, ending[a]	225		
10	(225 × 100%; 225 × 60%)		225	135
11	Accounted for	400		
12	Work done in current period only		400	310
13				
14	[a]Degree of completion in this department: direct materials, 100%; conversion costs, 60%.			

Process-costing systems separate costs into cost categories according to the timing of when costs are introduced into the process. Only two cost pools are required in the Global Defence example because direct materials are all added at the same time and all conversion costs are assumed to be added to the process at an even rate over time. If, however, direct manufacturing labour was added to the process at *different* times than all other conversion costs, then a third cost pool would be necessary. In this situation we can no longer assume all conversion activities occur at a uniform rate therefore separate estimates of equivalent units will be required for each set of conversion activities.

All 400 units, the 175 fully assembled ones and the 225 partially assembled ones, are complete in terms of direct materials. We assumed all direct materials are added in the Assembly Department at the initial stage of the process. This means the units both finished and unfinished are 100% complete with respect to consuming direct materials. This is why Exhibit 17-1 shows output as 400 *equivalent* units of direct materials.

The 175 fully assembled units are completely processed with respect to conversion costs. The Assembly Supervisor provided an estimate that partially assembled units in ending work in process are 60% complete (on average). Therefore, the conversion activity for the 225 units in the Assembly Department's work in process inventory is equivalent to 60% × 225 = 135 finished units. Now adding the 175 units that are 100% complete to the 135 units that are 60% complete gives a total of 310 equivalent units in the conversion cost allocation base. Hence, Exhibit 17-1 shows output as 310 *equivalent* units of conversion costs. Of course, 175 equivalent units finished will be transferred out to the Testing Department's beginning inventory. The unfinished 135 equivalent units will remain in the Assembly Department's ending work-in-process inventory. This transfer process is an accounting process based on costs. The next step is to calculate the average conversion cost rate and assign the total conversion costs. The cost flow from the Assembly Department to the Testing Department will follow the equivalent units.

Calculation of Product Costs (Steps 3, 4, and 5)

Exhibit 17-2 on page 676 shows step 3: computing equivalent unit costs. In step 3, Global Defence calculates the average cost allocation rates for each cost pool, direct materials inputs, and conversion activities inputs during February. Each cost pool is divided by total equivalent units, resulting in two cost allocation rates per equivalent unit, one for direct materials and one for conversion activities. The total conversion costs are then assigned to each of finished goods and work-in-process inventories by multiplying the average conversion cost rate by quantity of equivalent units in each inventory. We can see the importance of using equivalent units in unit cost calculations by comparing conversion costs for the months of January and February 2007. In both months, the average conversion cost per equivalent unit is the same, $60. But the total equivalent units produced were 400 in January and 310 in February. Consequently the total conversion costs in January of $24,000 are higher than those in February of $18,600.

It is easy to misinterpret what the $18,600 of conversion costs means. Some managers would be tempted to divide the conversion cost pool for February by physical units ($18,600 ÷ 400) to obtain a conversion cost of $46.50 per physical unit. Because they do not understand how the conversion cost was calculated they would erroneously conclude that conversion costs per unit declined from $60 in January to $46.50 in February. This incorrect costing could prompt Global Defence, for example, to inappropriately lower the price of DG-19. A knowledgeable management accountant using Exhibit 17-2 could quickly point out the two different amounts used to calculate physical and equivalent units. The management accountant could then correctly explain to managers how they made this error and avoid the potential decrease in future gross margin.

Step 4 in Exhibit 17-2 summarizes total costs to account for. Because the beginning balance of the work-in-process inventory is zero, total costs to account for consist of the costs added during February: direct materials, $32,000, and conversion costs, $18,600, for a total of $50,600.

Step 5 in Exhibit 17-2 assigns these costs to units completed and transferred out and to units in ending inventory. For example, the 225 physical units in work in process are completely processed with respect to direct materials. Therefore, direct materials costs are 225 equivalent units times $80, which equals $18,000. In contrast, the 225 physical units are 60% complete with respect to conversion costs. Therefore, the conversion costs are 135 equivalent units (60% of 225 physical units) times $60, which equals $8,100. The total cost of ending work in process equals $26,100 ($18,000 + $8,100).

The information Global Defence has calculated for both January and February is summarized below in the same accounting format illustrated in Chapter 2, Panel B of Exhibit 2-7.

> If you remember where the units go in step 1, there is no need to memorize where the costs go in step 5, because the costs attach to the units. In Exhibits 17-1 and 17-2, the costs are attached (1) to units completed and transferred out of Assembly and (2) to units in ending work in process.

Global Defence, Inc., Schedule of Cost of Goods Manufactured Assembly Department for the month ended:	January 31, 2007		February 28, 2007	
Direct materials				
Beginning inventory of direct materials	$ –		$ –	
Purchases of direct materials during the month	32,000		32,000	
Cost of direct materials available for use	32,000		32,000	
Ending inventory of direct materials for the month	–		–	
Direct materials used during the month		$32,000		$32,000
All conversion costs	24,000		18,600	
Total conversion costs		24,000		18,600
Manufacturing costs incurred during the month		56,000		50,600
Beginning work-in-process inventory		–		–
Total manufacturing costs to account for		56,000		50,600
Ending work-in-process inventory		–		(26,100)
Costs of goods manufactured, transferred out to Testing Department		$56,000		$24,500

Journal Entries

Process-costing journal entries are basically like those made in the job-costing system. That is, direct materials and conversion costs are accounted for as in job-costing systems. The main difference is that, in process costing, there is often more

EXHIBIT 17-2
Steps 3, 4, and 5: Compute Equivalent Unit Costs, Summarize Total Costs to Account for, and Assign Costs to Units Completed and to Units in Ending Work in Process, Assembly Department of Global Defence for February 2007

	A	B	C	D	E
1			Total		
2			Production	Direct	Conversion
3			Costs	Materials	Costs
4	Step 3	Cost added during February	$50,600	$32,000	$18,600
5		Divide by equivalent units of work done in current period (Exhibit 17-1)		÷ 400	÷ 310
6		Cost per equivalent unit		$ 80	$ 60
7	Step 4	Total costs to account for	$50,600		
8	Step 5	Assignment of costs:			
9		Work in process ending inventory (225 units)			
10		Direct materials*	$18,000		
11		Conversion costs**	8,100		
12		Total work in process	26,100		
13		Completed and transferred out (175 units)***	24,500		
14		Total costs to account for	$50,600		
15					
16		*225 × $80			
17		**Equivalent units in ending inventory work in process calculated in Step 2 , 135 × $60			
18		***Equivalent units calculated in Step 2, 175 × ($80 + $60)			

than one work-in-process account—in our example, Work in Process—Assembly and Work in Process—Testing. Global Defence purchases direct materials as needed. These materials are delivered directly to the Assembly Department. Using dollar amounts from Exhibit 17-2, summary journal entries for the month of February at Global Defence, Inc., are as follows:

1. Work in Process—Assembly $32,000
     Accounts Payable $32,000
     To record direct materials purchased and
     used in production during February.

2. Work in Process—Assembly $18,600
     [Various accounts] $18,600
     To record Assembly Department conversion costs
     for February; examples include energy,
     manufacturing supplies, all manufacturing
     labour, and plant amortization.

3. Work in Process—Testing $24,500
     Work in Process—Assembly $24,500
     To record cost of goods completed and transferred from
     Assembly to Testing during February.

Exhibit 17-3 shows a general sketch of the flow of costs through the T-accounts. The key T-account, Work in Process—Assembly, shows an ending balance of $26,100.

EXHIBIT 17-3
Flow of Costs in a Process-Costing System, Assembly Department of Global Defence for February 2007

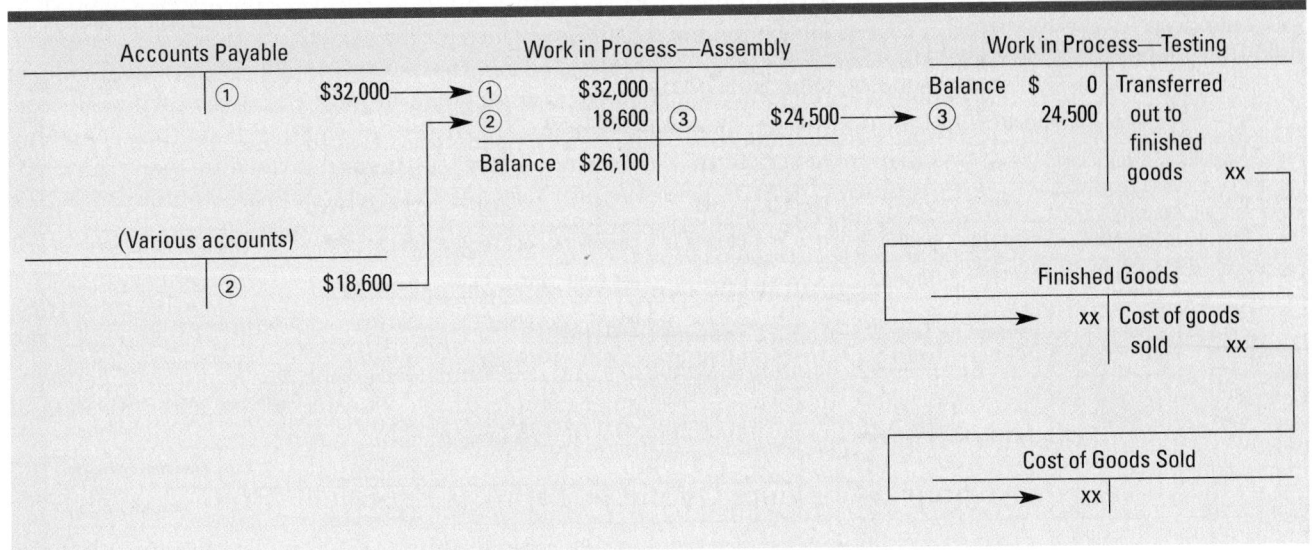

CASE 3: PROCESS COSTING WITH BOTH BEGINNING AND ENDING WORK-IN-PROCESS INVENTORY

At the beginning of March 2007, Global Defence had 225 partially assembled DG-19 units in the Assembly Department. During March 2007, Global Defence placed another 275 units into production. Data for the Assembly Department for March 2007 are:

	A	B	C	D	E
1		Physical Units	Direct	Conversion	Total
2		(DG-19s)	Materials	Costs	Costs
3		(1)	(2)	(3)	(4) = (2) + (3)
4	Work in process, beginning inventory (March 1)	225	$18,000[a]	$ 8,100[a]	$26,100
5	Degree of completion of beginning work in process		100%	60%	
6	Started during March	275			
7	Completed and transferred out during March	400			
8	Work in process, ending inventory (March 31)	100			
9	Degree of completion of ending work in process		100%	50%	
10	Total costs added during March[b]		$19,800	$16,380	$36,180
11					
12	[a]Work in process, beginning inventory (equals work in process, ending inventory for February)				
13	Direct materials: 225 equivalent units × $80 per unit = $18,000				
14	Conversion costs: 135 equivalent units × $60 per unit = $8,100				
15	[b]Direct material conversion costs different than in February per unit				

We now have incomplete units in both beginning and ending work-in-process inventory to account for. Our goal is to use the five steps we described earlier to calculate (1) the cost of units completed and transferred out, and (2) the cost of ending work in process. To assign costs to each of these categories, however, we need to specify assumptions regarding the flow of costs. We next describe the five-step approach to process costing using two alternative cost-flow assumptions—the weighted-average method and the first-in, first-out method. The different assumptions will produce different numbers for cost of units completed and for ending work in process.

OBJECTIVE 5

Demonstrate the weighted-average method of process costing

WEIGHTED-AVERAGE METHOD

The **weighted-average process-costing method** calculates the average equivalent unit cost of the work done to date (regardless of the period in which it was done) and assigns it to equivalent units completed and transferred out and to equivalent units in ending work-in-process inventory. The weighted-average cost is the total of all costs entering the Work in Process account (regardless of whether it is from beginning work in process or from work started during the period) divided by total equivalent units of work done to date. We now describe the five-step procedure introduced in Case 2 using the weighted-average method.

Step 1: Summarize the Flow of Physical Units

The physical units column of Exhibit 17-4 shows where the units came from—225 units from beginning inventory and 275 units started during the current period—and where they went—400 units completed and transferred out and 100 units in ending inventory. These data for March are given on page 677.

Step 2: Compute Output in Terms of Equivalent Units

As we saw in Case 2, even partially assembled units are complete in terms of direct materials because direct materials are introduced at the beginning of the process. For conversion costs, the fully assembled physical units transferred out are, of course, fully completed. The Assembly Department supervisor estimates the partially assembled physical units in March 31 work in process to be 50% complete (on average).

The equivalent units columns in Exhibit 17-4 show the equivalent units of work done to date—equivalent units completed and transferred out and equivalent units in ending work in process (500 equivalent units of direct materials and 450 equivalent units of conversion costs). Notice that the equivalent units of work done to date *also* equal the sum of the equivalent units in beginning inventory (work done in the previous period) and the equivalent units of work done in the current period, because

$$
\begin{array}{l}
\text{Equivalent units} \\
\text{in beginning} \\
\text{work in process}
\end{array}
+
\begin{array}{l}
\text{Equivalent units} \\
\text{of work done in} \\
\text{current period}
\end{array}
=
\begin{array}{l}
\text{Equivalent units completed} \\
\text{and transferred out} \\
\text{in current period}
\end{array}
+
\begin{array}{l}
\text{Equivalent} \\
\text{units in ending} \\
\text{work in process}
\end{array}
$$

EXHIBIT 17-4

Steps 1 and 2: Summarize Output in Physical Units and Compute Output in Equivalent Units Using Weighted-Average Method of Process Costing for Assembly Department of Global Defence for March 2007

	A	B (Step 1)	C (Step 2)	D
			Equivalent Units	
		Physical	Direct	Conversion
	Flow of Production	Units	Materials	Costs
5	Work in process, beginning (given, p. 677)	225		
6	Started during current period (given, p. 677)	275		
7	To account for	500		
8	Completed and transferred out during current period	400	400	400
9	Work in process, ending[a] (given, p. 677)	100		
10	(100 × 100%; 100 × 50%)		100	50
11	Accounted for	500		
12	Work done to date		500	450
13				
14	[a]Degree of completion in this department: direct materials, 100%; conversion costs, 50%.			

The equivalent unit calculation in the weighted-average method is only concerned with total equivalent units of *work done to date* regardless of (a) whether the work was done during the preceding period and is part of beginning work in process or (b) whether it was done during the current period. That is, the weighted-average method *merges* equivalent units in beginning inventory (work done before March) with equivalent units of work done in the current period. Thus, the stage of completion of the current period beginning work in process is *irrelevant* and *not* used in the computation.

Step 3: Compute Equivalent Unit Costs

Exhibit 17-5, step 3, shows the computation of equivalent unit costs separately for direct materials and conversion costs. The weighted-average cost per equivalent unit is obtained by dividing the sum of costs for beginning work in process and costs for work done in the current period by total equivalent units of work done to date. When calculating the weighted-average conversion cost per equivalent unit in Exhibit 17-5, for example, we divide total conversion costs, $24,480 (beginning work in process, $8,100, plus work done in current period, $16,380) by total equivalent units, 450 (equivalent units of conversion costs in beginning work in process and in work done in current period), to get a weighted-average cost of $54.40.

Step 4: Summarize Total Costs to Account For

The total costs to account for in March 2007 are described in the example data: beginning work in process, $26,100 (direct materials, $18,000 and conversion costs, $8,100) plus $36,180 (direct materials costs added during March, $19,800 and conversion costs, $16,380). The total of these costs is $62,280.

Step 5: Assign Costs to Units Completed and to Units in Ending Work in Process

The key point in this step is to cost all work done to date: (1) the cost of units completed and transferred out, and (2) the cost of ending work in process. Step 5 in Exhibit 17-5 takes the equivalent units completed and transferred out and equivalent units in ending

EXHIBIT 17-5

Steps 3, 4, and 5: Compute Cost per Equivalent Unit, Summarize Total Costs to Account for, and Assign Total Costs to, Units Completed and to Units in Ending Work in Process Using Weighted-Average Method of Process Costing for Assembly Department of Global Defence for March 2007

	A	B	C	D	E
1			**Total**		
2			**Production**	**Direct**	**Conversion**
3			**Costs**	**Materials**	**Costs**
4	(Step 3)	Work in process, beginning (given, p. 677)	$26,100	$18,000	$ 8,100
5		Costs added in current period (given, p. 677)	36,180	19,800	16,380
6		Costs incurred to date		$37,800	$24,480
7		Divide by equivalent units of work done to date (Exhibit 17-4)		÷ 500	÷ 450
8		Cost per equivalent unit of work done to date		$ 75.60	$ 54.40
9	(Step 4)	Total costs to account for	$62,280		
10	(Step 5)	Assignment of costs:			
11		Completed and transferred out (400 units)	$52,000	(400[a] × $75.60) + (400[a] × $54.40)	
12		Work in process, ending (100 units)	10,280	(100[b] × $75.60) + (50[b] × $54.40)	
13		Total costs accounted for	$62,280		
14					
15	[a]Equivalent units completed and transferred out from Exhibit 17-4, step 2.				
16	[b]Equivalent units in ending work in process from Exhibit 17-4, step 2.				

work in process calculated in Exhibit 17-4, step 2, and attaches dollar amounts to them. These dollar amounts are the weighted-average costs per equivalent unit for direct materials and conversion costs calculated in step 3. For example, note that the total cost of the 100 physical units in ending work in process consists of:

Direct materials:

   100 equivalent units × weighted-average cost per equivalent unit of $75.60 $7,560

Conversion costs:

   50 equivalent units × weighted-average cost per equivalent unit of $54.40   2,720

   Total costs of ending work in process $10,280

The following table summarizes the total costs to account for and the $62,280 accounted for in Exhibit 17-5. The arrows indicate that costs of units completed and transferred out and in ending work in process are calculated using average total costs obtained after merging costs of beginning work in process and costs added in the current period.

Costs to Account For		Costs Accounted For Calculated at Weighted-Average Cost	
Beginning work in process	$26,100	Completed and transferred out	$52,000
Costs added in current period	36,180	Ending work in process	10,280
Total costs to account for	$62,280	Total costs accounted for	$62,280

Before proceeding, please pause and review Exhibits 17-4 and 17-5 carefully to check your understanding of the weighted-average method. Note that Exhibit 17-4 deals only with physical and equivalent units but not costs. Exhibit 17-5 shows the cost amounts.

The information Global Defence has calculated for the month of March based on the weighted average method of inventory valuation is summarized below in the accounting format illustrated in Exhibit 2-7:

Global Defence, Inc., Schedule of Cost of Goods Manufactured Assembly Department for the Month Ended:	March 31, 2007 Weighted Average	
Direct materials		
Beginning inventory of direct materials	$ –	
Purchases of direct materials during the month	19,800	
Cost of direct materials available for use	19,800	
Ending inventory of direct materials for the month	–	
Direct materials used during the month		$19,800
All conversion costs	16,380	
Total conversion costs		16,380
Manufacturing costs incurred during the month		36,180
Beginning work-in-process inventory		26,100
Total manufacturing costs to account for		62,280
Ending work-in-process inventory		(10,280)
Costs of goods manufactured, transferred out to Testing Department		$52,000

Using dollar amounts from Exhibit 17-5, summary journal entries for the month of March at Global Defence, Inc., are

1. Work in Process—Assembly $19,800
      Accounts Payable $19,800
      To record direct materials purchased and
      used in production during March.

2. Work in Process—Assembly $16,380
      [Various accounts] $16,380
      To record Assembly Department conversion costs
      for March; examples include energy, manufacturing
      supplies, all manufacturing labour, and plant amortization.

3. Work in Process—Testing $52,000
      Work in Process—Assembly $52,000
      To record cost of units completed and transferred
      from Assembly to Testing during March.

The key T-account, Work in Process—Assembly, would show the following:

Work in Process—Assembly			
Beginning inventory, March 1	$26,100	③ Transferred out to Work in	
① Direct materials	19,800	Process—Testing	$52,000
② Conversion costs	16,380		
Ending inventory, March 31	$10,280		

FIRST-IN, FIRST-OUT METHOD

In contrast to the weighted-average method, the **first-in, first-out (FIFO) process-costing method** assigns the cost of the prior accounting period's equivalent units in beginning work-in-process inventory to the first units completed and transferred out, and assigns the cost of equivalent units worked on during the current period first to complete beginning inventory, then to start and complete new units, and finally to units in ending work-in-process inventory. This method assumes that the earliest equivalent units in the Work in Process—Assembly account are completed first.

A distinctive feature of the FIFO process-costing method is that work done on beginning inventory before the current period is kept separate from work done in the current period. Costs incurred in the current period and units produced in the current period are used to calculate costs per equivalent unit of work done in the current period. In contrast, equivalent-unit and cost-per-equivalent-unit calculations in the weighted average method merge the units and costs in beginning inventory with units and costs of work done in the current period.

We now describe the five-step procedure introduced in Case 3 using the FIFO method.

Step 1: Summarize the Flow of Physical Units

Exhibit 17-6, step 1, on page 682, traces the flow of physical units of production. The following observations help explain the physical units calculations:

◆ The first physical units assumed to be completed and transferred out during the period are the 225 units from the beginning work-in-process inventory.

 Of the 275 physical units started, 175 are assumed to be completed. Recall from the March data given on page 677 that 400 physical units were completed during March. The FIFO method assumes that the first 225 of these units were from beginning inventory; thus 175 physical units (400 – 225) must have been started and completed during March.

◆ Ending work-in-process inventory consists of 100 physical units—the 275 physical units started minus the 175 of these physical units completed.

◆ Note that the physical units "to account for" equal the physical units "accounted for" (500 units).

Step 2: Compute Output in Terms of Equivalent Units

Exhibit 17-6 also presents the computations for step 2 under the FIFO method. *The equivalent unit calculations focus on the equivalent units of work done in the current period (March) only.*

 Under the FIFO method, the work done in the current period is assumed to first complete the 225 units in beginning work in process. The equivalent units of work done in March on the beginning work-in-process inventory are computed by multiplying the 225 physical units *by the percentage of work remaining to be done to complete these units:* 0% for direct materials, because the beginning work in process is 100% complete with respect to direct materials, and 40% for conversion costs, because the beginning work in process is 60% complete with respect to conversion costs. The results are 0 (0% × 225) equivalent units of work for direct materials and 90 (40% × 225) equivalent units of work for conversion costs.

 Next, the work done in the current period is assumed to start and complete the next 175 units. The equivalent units of work done on the 175 physical units started and

First-in, first-out (FIFO) process-costing method. Method of process costing that assigns the cost of the earliest equivalent units available (starting with the equivalent units in beginning work-in-process inventory) to units completed and transferred out, and the cost of the most recent equivalent units worked on during the period to ending work-in-process inventory.

EXHIBIT 17-6

Steps 1 and 2: Summarize Output in Physical Units and Compute Output in Equivalent Units Using FIFO Method of Process Costing for Assembly Department of Global Defence for March 2007

	A	B	C	D
1		(Step 1)	(Step 2)	
2			Equivalent Units	
3		Physical	Direct	Conversion
4	**Flow of Production**	Units	Materials	Costs
5	Work in process, beginning (given, p. 677)	225	(Work done before current period)	
6	Started during current period (given, p. 677)	275		
7	To account for	500		
8	Completed and transferred out during current period:			
9	From beginning work in process[a]	225		
10	[225 × (100% − 100%); 225 × (100% − 60%)]		0	90
11	Started and completed	175[b]		
12	(175 × 100%; 175 × 100%)		175	175
13	Work in process, ending[c] (given, p. 677)	100		
14	(100 × 100%; 100 × 50%)		100	50
15	Accounted for	500		
16	Work done in current period only		275	315
17				
18	[a]Degree of completion in this department: direct materials, 100%; conversion costs, 60%.			
19	[b]400 physical units completed and transferred out minus 225 physical units completed and transferred out from beginning work-in-process inventory.			
20	[c]Degree of completion in this department: direct materials, 100%; conversion costs, 50%.			

completed are computed by multiplying 175 units by 100% for both direct materials and conversion costs, because all work on these units is done in the current period.

Finally, the work done in the current period is assumed to start but leave incomplete the final 100 units as ending work in process. The equivalent units of work done on the 100 units of ending work in process are calculated by multiplying 100 physical units by 100% for direct materials (because all direct materials have been added for these units in the current period) and 50% for conversion costs (because 50% of conversion costs work has been done on these units in the current period).

During March 2007, beginning work in process had 0% direct materials and 40% conversion costs added to it. That's because at the start of March, beginning work in process was 100% complete with respect to direct materials and 60% complete with respect to conversion costs. This same concept applies to Exhibits 17-8 and 17-13.

Step 3: Compute Equivalent Unit Costs

Exhibit 17-7 shows the step 3 computation of equivalent units costs *for work done in the current period only* for direct materials and conversion costs. For example, we divide current period conversion costs of $16,380 by current period equivalent units for conversion costs of 315 to obtain cost per equivalent unit of $52.

Step 4: Summarize Total Costs to Account For

The total production costs column in Exhibit 17-7 presents step 4 and summarizes the total costs to account for in March 2007 (beginning work in process and costs added in the current period) of $62,280, as described in the example data (p. 677).

Step 5: Assign Costs to Units Completed and to Units in Ending Work in Process

Finally, Exhibit 17-7 shows the step 5 assignment of costs under the FIFO method. The costs of work done in the current period are first assigned to the additional work done

EXHIBIT 17-7

Steps 3, 4, and 5: Compute Cost per Equivalent Unit, Summarize Total Costs to Account for, and Assign Total Costs to Units Completed and to Units in Ending Work in Process Using FIFO Method of Process Costing for Assembly Department of Global Defence for March 2007

	A	B	C	D	E
			Total		
			Production	Direct	Conversion
			Costs	Materials	Costs
4		Work in process, beginning (given, p. 677)	$26,100	(costs of work done before current period)	
5	(Step 3)	Costs added in current period (given, p. 677)	36,180	$19,800	$16,380
6		Divide by equivalent units of work done in current period (Exhibit 17-6)		÷ 275	÷ 315
7		Cost per equivalent unit of work done in current period		$ 72	$ 52
8	(Step 4)	Total costs to account for	$62,280		
9	(Step 5)	Assignment of costs:			
10		Completed and transferred out (400 units)			
11		Work in process, beginning (225 units)	$26,100		
12		Costs added to beginning work in process in current period	4,680	$(0^a \times \$72) + (90^a \times \$52)$	
13		Total from beginning inventory	30,780		
14		Started and completed (175 units)	21,700	$(175^b \times \$72) + (175^b \times \$52)$	
15		Total costs of units completed and transferred out	52,480		
16		Work in process, ending (100 units):	9,800	$(100^c \times \$72) + (50^c \times \$52)$	
17		Total costs accounted for	$62,280		
18					
19	[a]Equivalent units used to complete beginning work in process from Exhibit 17-6, step 2.				
20	[b]Equivalent units started and completed from Exhibit 17-6, step 2.				
21	[c]Equivalent units in ending work in process from Exhibit 17-6, step 2.				

to complete the beginning work in process, then to the work done on units started and completed during the current period, and finally to the ending work in process. The easiest way to follow step 5 is to take each of the equivalent units calculated in Exhibit 17-6, step 2, and attach dollar amounts to them (using the cost per equivalent unit calculations in step 3). The goal is to determine the total cost of all units completed from beginning inventory and from work started and completed in the current period, and the cost of ending work in process done in the current period.

Notice that the 400 completed units are of two types: 225 units come from beginning inventory, and 175 units are started and completed during March. The FIFO method starts by assigning the costs of the beginning work-in-process inventory of $26,100 to the first units completed and transferred out. This $26,100 is the cost of the 225 equivalent units of direct materials and 135 equivalent units of conversion costs that comprise beginning inventory. The work that generated these costs was done in February, so these units are costed at the February prices of $80 for direct materials and $60 for conversion costs ($225 \times \$80 + 135 \times \$60 = \$26,100$). As we saw in step 2, an additional 90 equivalent units of conversion costs are needed to complete these units in the current period. The current period conversion costs per equivalent unit is $52, so $4,680 (90 \times \$52) of additional costs are needed to complete the beginning inventory. The total production cost for the units in beginning inventory is $26,100 + \$4,680 = \$30,780$. The 175 units started and completed in the current period consist of 175 equivalent units of direct materials and 175 equivalent units of conversion costs. These units are costed at the cost per equivalent unit in the current period (direct materials, $72 and conversion costs, $52) for a total production cost of $21,700.

Under FIFO, the ending work-in-process inventory comes from units that were started but not fully completed during the current period. The total cost of the 100 partially assembled physical units in ending work in process consists of

Direct materials:		
100 equivalent units × cost per equivalent unit in March of $72		$7,200
Conversion costs:		
50 equivalent units × cost per equivalent unit in March of $52		2,600
Total costs of work in process on March 31		$9,800

The following table summarizes the total costs to account for and the costs accounted for of $62,280 in Exhibit 17-7. Notice how under the FIFO method, the layers of beginning work in process and costs added in the current period are kept separate. The arrows indicate where the costs in each layer go (that is, to units completed and transferred out or to ending work in process). Be sure to include the costs of beginning work in process ($26,100) when calculating the costs of units completed from beginning inventory.

Costs to Account For		Costs Accounted For Calculated on a FIFO Basis	
		Completed and transferred out:	
Beginning work in process	$26,100	Beginning work in process	$26,100
Costs added in current period	36,180	Used to complete beginning work in process	4,680
		Started and completed	21,700
		Completed and transferred out	52,480
		Ending work in process	9,800
Total costs to account for	$62,280	Total costs accounted for	$62,280

Before proceeding, please pause and review Exhibits 17-6 and 17-7 carefully to check your understanding of the FIFO method. Note that Exhibit 17-6 deals only with physical and equivalent units but no costs. Exhibit 17-7 shows the cost amounts.

The information Global Defence has calculated for the month of March based on the FIFO method of valuation of inventory is summarized below in the same accounting format as illustrated in Exhibit 2-7 and compared to the amounts obtained using the weighted average method:

Global Defence, Inc., Schedule of Cost of Goods Manufactured Assembly Department for the Month Ended:	March 31, 2007 Weighted Average		March 31, 2007 FIFO	
Direct materials				
Beginning inventory of direct materials	$ –		$ –	
Purchases of direct materials during the month	19,800		19,800	
Cost of direct materials available for use	19,800		19,800	
Ending inventory of direct materials for the month	–		–	
Direct materials used during the month		$19,800		$19,800
All conversion costs	16,380		16,380	
Total conversion costs		16,380		16,380
Manufacturing costs incurred during the month		36,180		36,180
Beginning work-in-process inventory		26,100		26,100
Total manufacturing costs to account for		62,280		62,280
Ending work-in-process inventory		(10,280)		(9,800)
Costs of goods manufactured, transferred out to Testing Department		$52,000		$52,480

The journal entries under the FIFO method parallel the journal entries under the weighted-average method. The only difference is that the entry to record the cost of goods completed and transferred out would be for $52,480 under the FIFO method instead of for $52,000 under the weighted-average method.

Only rarely is an application of pure FIFO ever encountered in process costing. As a result, it should really be called a *modified* or *departmental* FIFO method. Why? Because FIFO is applied within a department to compile the cost of units transferred *out*, but the units transferred *in* during a given period usually are carried at a single average unit cost as a matter of convenience. For example, the average cost of units transferred out of the Assembly Department is $52,480 ÷ 400 units = $131.20 per DG-19 unit. The Assembly Department uses FIFO to distinguish between monthly batches of production. The succeeding department, Testing, however, costs these units (that consist of costs incurred in February and March) at one average unit cost ($131.20 in this illustration). If this averaging were not done, the attempt to track costs on a pure FIFO basis throughout a series of processes would be unduly cumbersome, if not impossible.

COMPARISON OF WEIGHTED-AVERAGE AND FIFO METHOD

The following table summarizes the costs assigned to units completed and those still in process under the weighted-average and FIFO process-costing methods for our example:

	Weighted Average (from Exhibit 17-5)	FIFO (from Exhibit 17-7)	Difference
Cost of units completed and transferred out	$52,000	$52,480	+$480
Work in process, ending	10,280	9,800	−$480
Total costs accounted for	$62,280	$62,280	

The weighted-average ending inventory is higher than the FIFO ending inventory by $480, or 4.9% ($480 ÷ $9,800). This is a significant difference when aggregated over the many thousands of components that Global Defence makes. The weighted-average method in our example also results in lower cost of goods sold and hence higher operating income and higher tax payments than the FIFO method. Differences in equivalent unit costs of beginning inventory and work done during the current period account for the differences in weighted-average and FIFO costs. Recall that the cost per equivalent unit of beginning work in process was greater than the cost per equivalent unit of work done during the period.

For the Assembly Department, FIFO assumes that all the higher-cost prior-period units in beginning work in process are the first to be completed and transferred out while ending work in process consists of only the lower-cost current-period units. The weighted-average method, however, smooths out cost per equivalent unit by assuming that more of the lower-cost units are completed and transferred out, while some of the higher-cost units are placed in ending work in process. Hence, in this example, the weighted-average method results in a lower cost of units completed and transferred out and a higher ending work-in-process inventory relative to FIFO.

Unit costs can differ materially between the weighted-average and FIFO methods when (1) the direct materials or conversion costs per unit vary from period to period and (2) the physical inventory levels of work in process are large in relation to the total number of units transferred out. This means that both gross margin and operating income will differ materially between the two approaches. As companies move towards long term procurement contracts that smooth out the unit cost differences from one time period to another, and towards eliminating inventory, the difference between these two cost estimates will decrease.[1]

---

[1] For example, suppose beginning work-in-process inventory for March was 125 physical units (instead of 225) with a total value of $14,500, and the number of units started during the period is 375. Suppose costs per equivalent unit of work completed in the current period (March) comprised direct materials unit cost of $75 and unit conversion costs of $55. Assume no other changes in the data in the example. Under our new assumptions the cost of units completed and transferred out would be $52,833 under the weighted-average method and $53,000 under the FIFO method. The work-in-process ending inventory would be $10,417 under the weighted-average method and $10,250 under the FIFO method. These differences are $167 and ($167) respectively, far smaller than in the original example.

Managers need feedback about their most recent performance (March in this illustration) in order to plan and improve their future performance. A major advantage of FIFO is that it gives managers information from which they can judge their performance in the current period independently from that in the preceding period. Work done during the current period is vital information for these planning and control purposes.

STANDARD COSTS AND PROCESS COSTING

This section assumes that you have already studied Chapters 7 and 8. If you have not, proceed to the next major section, "Hybrid-Costing Systems," on page 689.

OBJECTIVE 7

Incorporate standard costs into a process-costing system

▼ One reason for using the standard costing method is that it simplifies record keeping.

As we have mentioned, companies that use process-costing systems produce numerous like or similar units of output. Setting standard quantities for inputs is often relatively straightforward in such companies. Standard costs per input unit may then be assigned to the physical standards to develop standard costs.

Weighted-average and FIFO methods become very complicated when used in industries that produce a variety of products. For example, a steel rolling mill uses various steel alloys and produces sheets of various sizes and of various finishes. The items of direct materials are not numerous; neither are the operations performed. But used in various combinations, they yield so great a variety of products that inaccurate costs for each product result if the broad averaging procedure of historical process costing is used. Similarly complex conditions are frequently found, for example, in plants that manufacture rubber products, textiles, ceramics, paints, and packaged food products. As we shall see, standard costing is especially useful in these situations.

The intricacies of weighted-average and FIFO historical costing methods and the conflicts between them are also eliminated by using standard costs.

Computations under Standard Costing

We again use the Assembly Department of Global Defence, Inc., as an example, except this time we assign standard costs to the process. The same standard costs apply in February and March of 2007:

	A	B	C	D	E
		Physical Units	**Direct**	**Conversion**	**Total**
		(DG-19s)	**Materials**	**Costs**	**Costs**
		(1)	(2)	(3)	(4) = (2) + (3)
4	Standard cost per unit		$ 74	$ 54	
5	Work in process, beginning inventory (March 1)	225			
6	Degree of completion of beginning work in process		100%	60%	
7	Beginning work-in-process inventory at standard costs		$16,650[a]	$7,290[a]	$23,940
8	Started during March	275			
9	Completed and transferred out during March	400			
10	Work in process, ending inventory (March 31)	100			
11	Degree of completion of ending work in process		100%	50%	
12	Actual total costs added during March		$19,800	$16,380	$36,180
13					
14	[a]Work in process, beginning inventory at standard costs				
15	Direct materials: 225 equivalent units × $100% completed × $74 per unit = $16,650				
16	Conversion costs: 225 physical units × $60% completed × $54 per unit = $7,290				

Exhibit 17-8 presents steps 1 and 2. These steps are identical to the steps described for the FIFO method in Exhibit 17-6 because, as in FIFO, the standard-costing method also assumes that the earliest equivalent units in beginning work in process are completed first. Work done in the current period for direct materials is 275 equivalent units. Work done in the current period for conversion costs is 315 equivalent units.

EXHIBIT 17-8

Steps 1 and 2: Summarize Output in Physical Units and Compute Output in Equivalent Units Using Standard-Costing Method of Process Costing for Assembly Departmet of Global Defence for March 2007

	A	B	C	D
		(Step 1)	(Step 2)	
2			Equivalent Units	
3		Physical	Direct	Conversion
4	**Flow of Production**	Units	Materials	Costs
5	Work in process, beginning (given)	225		
6	Started during current period (given)	275		
7	To account for:	500		
8	Completed and transferred out during current period:			
9	From beginning work in process[a]	225		
10	225 × (100% − 100%) × (100% − 60%)		–	90
11	Started and completed[b]	175		
12	175 × 100% × 100%		175	175
13	Work in process, ending[c] (given)	100		
14	100 × 100% × 50%		100	50
15	Accounted for:	500		
16	Work done in current period only		275	315
17				
18	[a]Degree of completion in this department: direct materials 100% conversion costs, 60%			
20	[b]400 physical units completed and transferred out minus 225 physical units completed and transferred out from beginning work-in-process inventory			
21	[c]Degree of completion in this department: direct materials, 100% conversion costs, 50%			

Exhibit 17-9 on page 688 describes steps 3, 4, and 5. In step 3, costs per equivalent unit are standard costs: direct materials, $74, and conversion costs, $54. *Therefore, costs per equivalent unit do not have to be computed as they were for the weighted-average and FIFO methods.*

Total costs to account for in Exhibit 17-9, step 4 (that is, the total debits to Work in Process—Assembly), differ from total debits to Work in Process—Assembly under the actual-cost-based weighted-average and FIFO methods. That's because, as in all standard-costing systems, the debits to the Work-in-Process account are at standard costs, rather than actual costs. These standard costs total $61,300 in Exhibit 17-9.

Exhibit 17-9, step 5, assigns total costs to units completed and transferred out and to units in ending work-in-process inventory, as in the FIFO method. Step 5 assigns amounts of standard costs to equivalent units calculated in Exhibit 17-8. These costs are assigned (1) to complete beginning work-in-process inventory, (2) next to start and complete new units, and (3) finally to start new units that are in ending work-in-process inventory. Note how the $61,300 total costs accounted for in step 5 of Exhibit 17-9 equal total costs to account for.

Accounting for Variances

Process-costing systems using standard costs usually accumulate actual costs separately from the inventory accounts. The following is an example. The actual data are recorded in the first two entries. Recall that Global Defence purchases direct materials as needed and that these materials are delivered directly to the Assembly Department. The total variances are recorded in the next two entries. The final entry transfers out the completed goods at standard costs.

1. Assembly Department Direct Materials Control (at actual) $19,800
     Accounts Payable $19,800
   To record direct materials purchased and used in production during March.

EXHIBIT 17-9

Steps 3, 4, and 5: Compute Cost per Equivalent Unit, Summarize Total Costs to Account for, and Assign Total Costs to Units Completed and to Units in Ending Work in Process Using Standard-Costing Method of Process Costing for Assembly Department of Global Defence for March 2007

	A	B	C	D	E	F	G
1			Total				
2			Production	Direct		Conversion	
3			Costs	Materials		Costs	
5	(Step 3)	Standard cost per equivalent unit (given, p. 686)		$ 74		$ 54	
6		Work in process, beginning (given, p. 686)					
7		Direct materials, 225 × $74; Conversion costs, 135 × $54	$23,940	$16,650		$ 7,290	
9		Costs added in current period at standard costs					
10		Direct materials, 275 × $74; Conversion costs, 315 × $54	37,360	$20,350		$17,010	
11	(Step 4)	Total costs to account for	$61,300				
12	(Step 5)	Assignment of costs at standard costs:					
13		Completed and transferred out (400 units)					
14		Work in process, beginning (225 units)	$23,940				
15		Costs added to beginning work in process in current period	4,860	(0ª × $74)	+	(90ª × $54)	
16		Total from beginning inventory	28,800				
17		Started and completed (175 units)	22,400	(175ᵇ × $74)	+	(175ᵇ × $54)	
18		Total costs of units completed and transferred out	51,200				
19		Work in process, ending (100 units):	10,100	(100ᶜ × $74)	+	(50ᶜ × $54)	
20		Total costs account for	$61,300				
21	Summary of variances for current performance:						
22	Costs added in current period at standard costs (see step 3 above)			$20,350		$17,010	
23	Actual costs incurred (given, p. 686)			$19,800		$16,380	
24	Variance			$ 550	F	$ 630	F
25							
26	ªEquivalent units used to complete beginning work in process from Exhibit 17-8, step 2.						
27	ᵇEquivalent units started and completed from Exhibit 17-8, step 2.						
28	ᶜEquivalent units in ending work in process from Exhibit 17-8, step 2.						

This cost control account is debited with actual costs and credited later with standard costs assigned to the units worked on.

2. Assembly Department Conversion Costs Control (at actual) $16,380

    [Various accounts] $16,380

   To record Assembly Department conversion costs for March.

(*Entries 3, 4, and 5 use standard cost dollar amounts from Exhibit 17-9*)

3. Work in Process—Assembly (at standard costs) $20,350

    Direct Materials Variances $ 550

    Assembly Department Direct Materials Control   19,800

   To record actual direct materials used and total direct materials variances.

4. Work in Process—Assembly (at standard costs) $17,010

    Conversion Costs Variances $ 630

    Assembly Department Conversion Costs Control   16,380

   To record actual conversion costs and total conversion costs variances.

5. Work in Process—Testing (at standard costs) $51,200

    Work in Process—Assembly (at standard costs) $51,200

   To record cost of units completed and transferred at standard cost from Assembly to Testing.

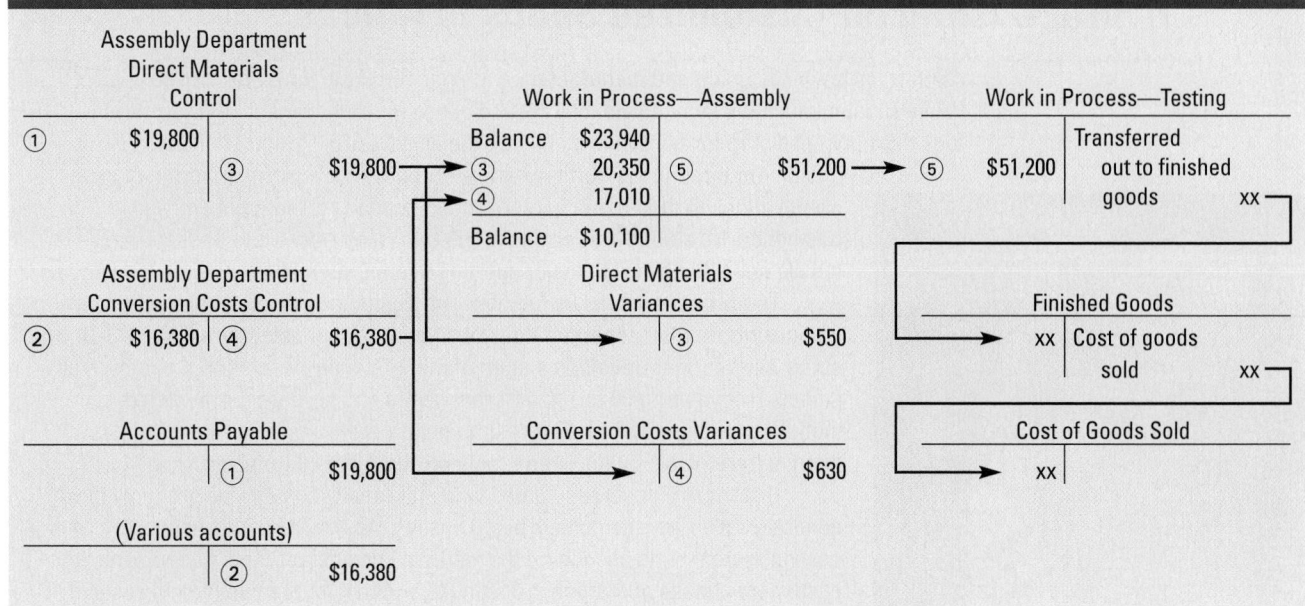

Variances arise under the standard-costing method, as in entries 3 and 4, because the standard costs assigned to products on the basis of work done in the current period do not usually equal the actual costs incurred in the current period. Variances can be measured and analyzed in little or great detail for feedback, control, and decision-making purposes, in the same manner as described in Chapters 7 and 8. Exhibit 17-10 shows how the costs flow through the accounts.

HYBRID-COSTING SYSTEMS

Product-costing systems do not always fall neatly into the categories of job costing or process costing. A **hybrid-costing system** blends characteristics from both job-costing systems and process-costing systems. Job-costing and process-costing systems are best viewed as ends of a continuum:

Hybrid-costing system. A costing system that blends characteristics from both job-costing systems and process-costing systems.

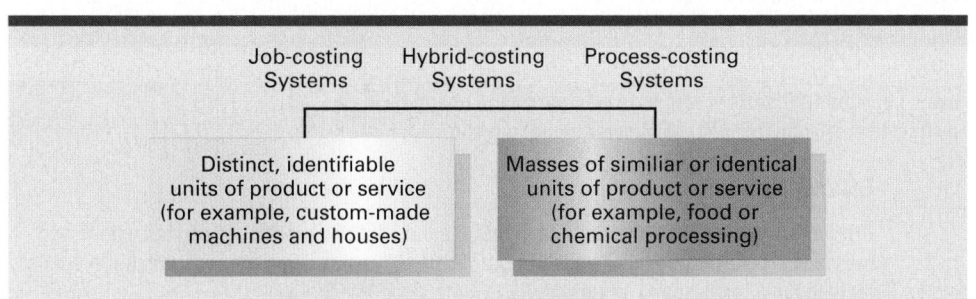

Product-costing systems must often be designed to fit the particular characteristics of different production systems. Many production systems are a hybrid—they have some features of custom-order manufacturing and other features of mass-production manufacturing. Manufacturers of a relatively wide variety of closely related standardized products tend to use a hybrid system. Consider Ford Motor Company. Automobiles may be manufactured in a continuous flow, but each may be customized with a special combination of engine size, transmission, music system, and so on. Companies develop hybrid-costing systems to meet these individual needs. The second chapter appendix presents *operation costing*, a type of hybrid-costing system frequently found in practice (see Concepts in Action box on p. 690).

Hybrid Costing for Customized Shoes at Adidas

Adidas has been designing and manufacturing athletic footwear for more than 80 years. While shoemakers have long individually crafted shoes for professional athletes, Adidas took this concept a step further when it initiated the mi adidas program. Mi adidas allows customers throughout North America, Europe, and Asia the opportunity to create shoes to their exact personal specifications for function, fit, and aesthetics. Mi adidas is available in 100 U.S. retail stores and at specialized mobile units that travel to major sporting events, such as the Boston Marathon.

The process works as follows: The customer goes to a mi adidas station, where a salesperson develops an in-depth customer profile, a 3-D computer scanner develops a scan of the customer's feet, and the customer selects from among 90 to 100 different styles and colours for his or her modularly designed shoe. The resulting data are transferred to an Adidas plant, where small, multiskilled teams produce the customized shoe.

Historically, costs associated with individually customized products have generally fallen into the domain of job costing. Adidas, however, uses a hybrid-costing system—job costing for the material and customizable components that customers choose and process costing to account for the conversion costs of production. The cost of making each pair of shoes is calculated by accumulating all production costs and dividing by the number of shoes made. Even though each pair of shoes is different, the cost of making each pair is the same.

The combination of customization with certain features of mass production is called mass customization. It is the consequence of being able to digitize information that individual customers indicate is important to them. Various products that companies are now able to customize within a mass-production setting (for example, personal computers, blue jeans, bicycles) still require job costing of materials and considerable human intervention. However, as manufacturing systems become flexible, companies are also using process costing to account for the standardized conversion costs.

Sources: "The 'mi adidas' Mass Customization Initiative," IMD case number IMD159; N. Tait, "How 'mi adidas' Provides Personalized Style, Fit," *Apparel* (January 1, 2004); "Adidas America to Introduce Running Customization Shoe at 2002 LaSalle Bank Chicago Marathon," *Chicago Athlete* (October 2, 2002).

DECISION POINTS   SUMMARY

The following decision guidelines use a question-and-answer format to summarize the chapter's main points. Each decision presents a key question. The guideline is the answer to that question.

DECISIONS	GUIDELINES
1. Under what conditions is a process-costing system used?	A process-costing system is used to determine the cost of a product or service when masses of identical or similar units are produced. Industries using process-costing systems include food, textiles, and oil refining.
2. What are the steps in a process-costing system to assign costs to units completed and to units in ending work in process?	The five key steps in a process-costing system are (a) summarize the flow of physical units of output, (b) compute output in terms of equivalent units, (c) compute equivalent-unit costs, (d) summarize total costs to account for, and (e) assign total costs to units completed and to units in ending work in process.
3. What are equivalent units and why is it necessary to calculate them?	Equivalent units are a derived amount of output units that (a) takes the quantity of each input (factor of production) in units completed or in incomplete units in work in process and (b) converts the quantity of input into the amount of completed output units that could be made with that quantity of input. Equivalent-unit calculations are necessary when all physical units of output are not uniformly completed during an accounting period.
4. Are journal entries in process-costing systems similar to journal entries in job-costing systems?	Journal entries in a process-costing system are similar to journal entries in a job-costing system. The main difference is that in a process-costing system, there is a separate Work-in-Process account for each department.

5. What is the weighted-average method of process costing?	The weighted-average method computes unit costs by dividing the total costs to date by the total equivalent units completed to date and assigns this average cost to units completed and to units in ending work-in-process inventory.
6. What is the first-in, first-out method of process costing?	The first-in, first-out (FIFO) method computes unit costs based on costs incurred during the period and equivalent units of work done in the current period. It assigns the costs of the beginning work-in-process inventory to the first units completed and assigns the costs of the equivalent units worked on during the current period first to complete beginning inventory, next to started and completed new units, and finally to units in ending work-in-process inventory.
7. How does the standard-costing method simplify process costing?	Under this method, standard costs serve as the cost per equivalent unit when assigning cost to units completed and to units in ending work-in-process inventory.

APPENDIX I: TRANSFERRED-IN COSTS IN PROCESS COSTING

Many process-costing systems have two or more departments or processes in the production cycle. Ordinarily, as units move from department to department, related costs are also transferred by monthly journal entries. If standard costs are used, the accounting for such transfers is relatively simple. However, if weighted average or FIFO is used, the accounting can become more complex. To illustrate, we now extend our Global Defence, Inc., example to encompass the Testing Department.

Recall that the Assembly Department of Global Defence transfers DG-19 units to its Testing Department. Here the units receive additional direct materials, such as crating and other packing materials to prepare the units for shipment, at the *end* of the process. Conversion costs are added evenly during the Testing Department's process. As the process in Assembly is completed, units are immediately transferred to Testing; as units are completed in Testing, they are immediately transferred to Finished Goods.

The following graphic summarizes these facts:

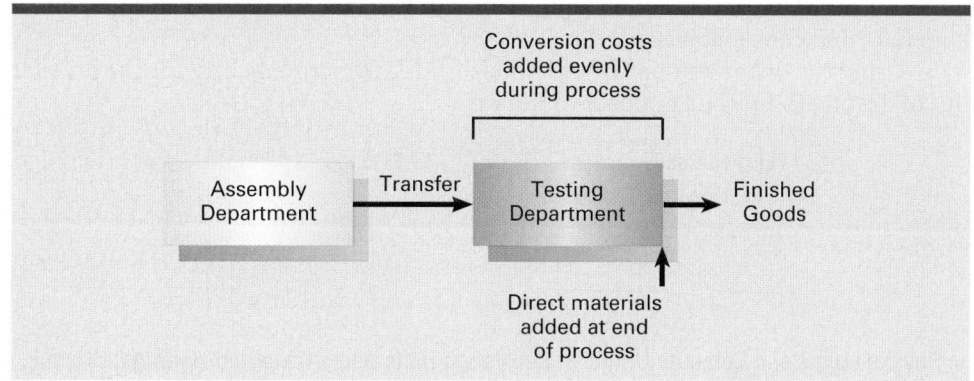

Data for the Testing Department for March 2007 are

	A	B	C	D	E
		Physical Units	Transferred-in	Direct	Conversion
1		(DG-19s)	Costs	Materials	Costs
2					
3	Work in process, beginning inventory (March 1)	240	$33,600	$ 0	$18,000
4	Degree of completion, beginning work in process		100%	0%	62.5%
5	Transferred-in during March	400			
6	Completed and transferred out during March	440			
7	Work in process, ending inventory (March 31)	200			
8	Degree of completion, ending work in process		100%	0%	80%
9	Total costs added during March				
10	Direct materials and conversion costs			$13,200	$48,600
11	Transferred-in (Weighted-average from Exhibit 17-5)[a]		$52,000		
12	Transferred-in (FIFO from Exhibit 17-7)[a]		$52,480		
13					
14	[a] The transferred-in costs during March are different under the weighted-average method (Exhibit 17-5) and the FIFO method (Exhibit 17-7). In our example, beginning work-in-process inventory of $51,600 ($33,600 + $0 + $18,000) is the same under both the weighted-average and FIFO inventory methods because we assume costs per equivalent unit to be the same in both January and February. If costs per equivalent unit had been different in the two months, work-in-process inventory at the end of February (beginning of March) would be costed differently under the weighted-average and FIFO methods. The basic approach to process costing with transferred-in costs, however, would still be the same as what we describe in this section.				

Transferred-in costs (previous department costs). Costs incurred in a previous department that are carried forward as part of the product's cost as it moves to a subsequent department for processing.

Transferred-in costs (or **previous department costs**) are costs incurred in a previous department that are carried forward as part of the product's cost as it moves to a subsequent department for processing. That is, as the units move from one department to the next, their costs move with them. Thus, computations of Testing costs must include transferred-in costs, as well as any additional direct materials costs and conversion costs added in Testing.

Transferred-in costs are treated as if they are a separate direct material added at the beginning of the process. In other words, when successive departments are involved, transferred units from one department become all or a part of the direct materials of the next department; however, they are called transferred-in costs, not direct materials costs.

Transferred-in Costs and the Weighted-Average Method

To examine the weighted-average process-costing method with transferred-in costs, we use the five-step procedure described earlier to assign costs of the Testing Department to units completed and transferred out and to units in ending work in process. Exhibit 17-11 shows steps 1 and 2. The computations are basically the same as the calculations of equivalent units under the weighted-average method for the Assembly Department in Exhibit 17-4, except for the addition of transferred-in costs. The units are fully completed as to transferred-in costs because these costs are simply carried forward from the previous process. Note, however, that direct material costs have a zero degree of completion in both the beginning and ending work in process inventories because, in Testing, direct materials are introduced at the *end* of the process.

Exhibit 17-12 describes steps 3, 4, and 5 for the weighted-average method. Note that beginning work in process and work done in the current period are combined for purposes of computing equivalent unit costs for transferred-in costs, direct materials, and conversion costs.

Using the dollar amount from Exhibit 17-12, the journal entry for the transfer out of Testing to finished goods inventory is

Finished Goods	$120,890	
Work in Process—Testing		$120,890
To transfer units to finished goods.		

EXHIBIT 17-11

Steps 1 and 2: Summarize Output in Physical Units and Compute Output in Equivalent Units Using Weighted-Average Method of Process Costing for Testing Department of Global Defence for March 2007

	A	B	C	D	E
		(Step 1)		**(Step 2)**	
				Equivalent Units	
		Physical	**Transferred-in**	**Direct**	**Conversion**
	Flow of Production	**Units**	**Costs**	**Materials**	**Costs**
5	Work in process, beginning (given, p. 691)	240	(work done before current period)		
6	Transferred-in during current period (given, p. 691)	400			
7	To account for:	640			
8	Completed and transferred out during current period:	440	440	440	440
9	Work in process, ending[a] (given, p. 691)	200			
10	(200 × 100%; 200 × 0%; 200 × 80%)	___	200	0	160
11	Accounted for	640			
12	Work done to date		640	440	600
13					
14	[a]Degree of completion in this department: transferred-in costs, 100%; direct materials, 0%; conversion costs, 80%				

EXHIBIT 17-12

Steps 3, 4, and 5: Compute Cost per Equivalent Unit, Summarize Total Costs to Account for, and Assign Total Costs to Units Completed and to Units in Ending Work in Process Using Weighted-Average Method of Process Costing for Testing Department of Global Defence for March 2007

	A	B	C	D	E	F
1			Total			
2			Production	Transferred-in	Direct	Conversion
3			Costs	Costs	Materials	Costs
4	(Step 3)	Work in process, beginning (given, p. 691)	$ 51,600	$33,600	$ 0	$18,000
5		Costs added in current period (given, p. 691)	113,800	52,000	13,200	48,600
6		Costs incurred to date		$85,600	$13,200	$66,600
7		Divide by equivalent units of work done to date (Exhibit 17-11)		÷ 640	÷ 440	÷ 600
8		Cost per equivalent unit of work done to date		$133.75	$ 30	$ 111
9	(Step 4)	Total costs to account for	$165,400			
10	(Step 5)	Assignment of costs:				
11		Completed and transferred out (440 units)	$120,890	(440* × $133.75) + (440* × $30) + (440* × $111)		
12		Work in process, ending (200 units):	44,510	(200† × $133.75) + (0† × $30) + (160† × $111)		
13		Total costs accounted for	$165,400			
14						
15	*Equivalent units completed and transferred out from Exhibit 17-11, step 2.					
16	†Equivalent units in ending work in process from Exhibit 17-11, step 2.					

Entries to the key T-account, Work in Process—Testing, follow, using information from Exhibit 17-12:

Work in Process—Testing			
Beginning inventory, March 1	$51,600	Transferred out	$120,890
Transferred-in costs	52,000		
Direct materials	13,200		
Conversion costs	48,600		
Ending inventory, March 31	$44,510		

Transferred-in Costs and the FIFO Method

To examine the FIFO process-costing method with transferred-in costs, we again use the five-step procedure. Exhibit 17-13 on page 694 shows steps 1 and 2. Other than considering transferred-in costs, the computations of equivalent units are basically the same as those under the FIFO method for the Assembly Department shown in Exhibit 17-6 (p. 682)

Exhibit 17-14 describes steps 3, 4 and 5. Note that the costs per equivalent unit for the current period in step 3 are only calculated on the basis of costs transferred in and work done in the current period. In steps 4 and 5, the total costs to account for and accounted for of $165,880 under the FIFO method differ from the corresponding amounts under the weighted-average method of $165,400. Why? Because of the different costs of completed units transferred in from the Assembly Department under the two methods ($52,480 under FIFO and $52,000 under weighted average).

Using the dollar amount from Exhibit 17-14, the journal entry for the transfer out to finished goods inventory is

Finished Goods	$122,360	
Work in Process—Testing		$122,360
To transfer units to finished goods.		

EXHIBIT 17-13
Steps 1 and 2: Summarize Output in Physical Units and Compute Output in Equivalent Units Using FIFO Method of Process Costing for Testing Department of Global Defence for March 2007

	A	B	C	D	E
		(Step 1)		(Step 2)	
1					
2				Equivalent Units	
3		Physical	Transferred-in	Direct	Conversion
4	**Flow of Production**	Units	Costs	Materials	Costs
5	Work in process, beginning (given, p. 691)	240	(work done before current period)		
6	Transferred-in during current period (given, p. 691)	400			
7	To account for	640			
8	Completed and transferred out during current period:				
9	From beginning work in process[a]	240			
10	[240 × (100% − 100%); 240 × (100% − 0%); 240 × (100% − 62.5%)]		0	240	90
11	Started and completed	200[b]			
12	(200 × 100%; 200 × 100%; 200 × 100%)		200	200	200
13	Work in process, ending[c] (given, p. 691)	200			
14	(200 × 100%; 200 × 0%; 200 × 80%)		200	0	160
15	Accounted for	640			
16	Work done in current period only		400	440	450
17					
18	[a]Degree of completion in this department: Transferred-in costs, 100%; direct materials, 0%; conversion costs, 62.5%.				
20	[b]400 physical units completed and transferred out minus 240 physical units completed and transferred out from beginning work-in-process inventory.				
21	[c]Degree of completion in this department: transferred-in costs, 100%; direct materials, 0%; conversion costs, 80%.				

Entries to the key T-account, Work in Process—Testing, follow, using information from Exhibit 17-14.

Work in Process—Testing

Beginning inventory, March 1	$51,600	Transferred out	$122,360
Transferred-in costs	52,480		
Direct materials	13,200		
Conversion costs	48,600		
Ending inventory, March 31	$43,520		

Remember that in a series of interdepartmental transfers, each department is regarded as being separate and distinct for accounting purposes. All costs transferred in during a given accounting period are carried at one unit cost figure regardless of whether previous departments used the weighted-average or the FIFO method.

Common Mistakes with Transferred-in Costs

Here are some common pitfalls to avoid when accounting for transferred-in costs:

1. Remember to include transferred-in costs from previous departments in your calculations.

2. In calculating costs to be transferred on a FIFO basis, do not overlook the costs assigned at the beginning of the period to units that were in process but are now included in the units transferred. For example, do not overlook the $51,600 in Exhibit 17-14.

3. Unit costs may fluctuate between periods. Therefore, transferred units may contain batches accumulated at different unit costs. For example, the 400 units transferred in at $52,480 in Exhibit 17-14 using the FIFO method consist of units that have different unit costs for direct materials and conversion costs when these units were worked on in the Assembly Department (see Exhibit 17-7, p. 683). Remember,

EXHIBIT 17-14
Steps 3, 4, and 5: Compute Cost per Equivalent Unit, Summarize Total Costs to Account for, and Assign Total Costs to Units Completed and to Units in Ending Work in Process Using FIFO Method of Process Costing for Testing Department of Global Defence for March 2007

	A	B	C	D	E	F
1			Total			
2			Production	Transferred-in	Direct	Conversion
3			Costs	Costs	Materials	Costs
4		Work in process, beginning (given, p. 693)	$ 51,600	(costs of work done before current period)		
5	(Step 3)	Costs added in current period (given, p. 693)	114,280	$52,480	$13,200	$48,600
6		Divide by equivalent units of work done in current period (Exhibit 17-13)		÷ 400	÷ 400	÷ 450
6		Cost per equivalent unit of work done in current period		$131.20	$ 30	$ 108
7	(Step 4)	Total costs to account for	$165,880			
8	(Step 5)	Assignment of costs:				
9		Completed and transferred out (440 units)				
10		Work in process, beginning (240 units)	$ 51,600			
11		Costs added to beginning work in process in current period	16,920	$(0^a \times \$131.20) + (240^a \times \$30) + (90^a \times \$108)$		
12		Total from beginning inventory	68,520			
13		Started and completed (200 units)	53,840	$(200^b \times \$131.20) + (200^b \times \$30) + (200^b \times \$108)$		
14		Total costs of units completed and transferred out	122,360			
15		Work in process, ending (200 units):	43,520	$(200^c \times \$131.20) + (0^c \times \$30) + (160^c \times \$108)$		
16		Total costs accounted for	$165,880			
17						
18	[a]Equivalent units used to complete beginning work in process from Exhibit 17-13, step 2.					
19	[b]Equivalent units started and completed from Exhibit 17-13, step 2.					
20	[c]Equivalent units in ending work in process from Exhibit 17-13, step 2.					

however, that when these units are transferred in to the Testing Department, they are costed at *one* average unit cost of $131.20 ($52,480 ÷ 400), as in Exhibit 17-14.

4. Units may be measured in different terms in different departments. Consider each department separately. Unit costs could be based on kilograms in the first department and litres in the second, so as units are received by the second department, their measurements must be converted to litres.

APPENDIX II: OPERATION COSTING

This appendix presents key ideas of operation costing and uses an example to illustrate key calculations and journal entries.

Overview of Operation-Costing Systems

An **operation** is a standardized method or technique that is performed repetitively regardless of the distinguishing features of the finished goods. Operations are usually conducted within departments. For instance, a suit maker may have a cutting operation and a hemming operation within a single department. The term operation, however, is often used loosely. It may be a synonym for a department or process. For example, some companies may call their finishing department a finishing process or a finishing operation.

An **operation-costing system** is a hybrid-costing system applied to batches of similar products. Each batch of products is often a variation of a single design and proceeds through a sequence of selected, though not necessarily the same, activities or operations. Within each operation, all product units are treated as being exactly alike, using identical amounts of the operation's resources. Batches are also termed production runs.

Operation. A standardized method or technique that is performed repetitively regardless of the distinguishing features of the finished good.

Operation-costing system. Hybrid-costing system applied to batches of similar products. Each batch of products is often a variation on a single design and proceeds through a sequence of selected (though not necessarily the same) activities or operations. Within each operation all product units use identical amounts of the operation's resources.

Consider a business that makes suits. Management may select a single basic design for every suit that the company manufactures. Depending on specifications, batches of suits vary from each other. One batch may use wool; another batch, cotton. One batch may require special hand stitching; another batch, machine stitching. Other products that are likewise often manufactured in batches are semiconductors, textiles, and shoes.

An operation-costing system uses work orders that specify the needed direct materials and step-by-step operations. Product costs are compiled for each work order. Direct materials that are unique to different work orders are specifically identified with the appropriate work order as in job-costing systems. The conversion cost for each unit passing through a given operation is the same regardless of the work order. Why? Because each unit passing through an operation uses identical amounts of that operation's resources. A single average conversion cost per unit is calculated as in process costing. For each operation, this amount is computed by aggregating conversion costs and dividing them by all units passing through that operation. Our examples assume only two cost categories, direct materials and conversion costs. Of course, operation costing can have more than two cost categories. The costs in each category are identified with work orders using job-costing or process-costing methods as appropriate.

Managers often find operation costing useful in cost management. Why? Because operation costing focuses on the physical processes, or operations, of a given production system. For example, in the manufacturing of clothing, managers are concerned with fabric waste, the number of fabric layers that can be cut at one time, and so on. Operation costing captures the financial impact of the control of physical processes. Feedback from an operation-costing system can therefore provide essential insight into the control of physical processes and the management of operation costs.

Illustration of Operation-Costing System

Consider Baltimore Company, a clothing manufacturer that produces two lines of blazers for department stores. Wool blazers use better-quality materials and undergo more operations than do polyester blazers. Let's look at the following operations in 2007:

	Work Order 423	Work Order 424
Direct materials	Wool	Polyester
	Satin full lining	Rayon partial lining
	Bone buttons	Plastic buttons
Operations		
1. Cutting cloth	Use	Use
2. Checking edges	Use	Do not use
3. Sewing body	Use	Use
4. Checking seams	Use	Do not use
5. Machine sewing of collars and lapels	Do not use	Use
6. Hand sewing of collars and lapels	Use	Do not use

Suppose work order 423 is for 50 wool blazers and work order 424 is for 100 polyester blazers. The following costs are assumed for these two work orders, which were started and completed in March 2007:

	Work Order 423	Work Order 424
Number of blazers	50	100
Direct materials costs	$6,000	$3,000
Conversion costs allocated:		
Operation 1	580	1,160
Operation 2	400	—
Operation 3	1,900	3,800
Operation 4	500	—
Operation 5	—	875
Operation 6	700	—
Total manufacturing costs	$10,080	$8,835

As in process costing, all product units in any work order are assumed to consume identical amounts of conversion costs of a particular operation. Baltimore Company's operation-costing system uses a budgeted rate to calculate the conversion costs of each operation. For example, the costs of operation 1 might be budgeted as follows (amounts assumed):

In the Baltimore Company example, the 20,000 unit denominator level is the sum of wool jackets and polyester jackets that managers expect to be processed in Operation 1. It is appropriate to use this sum of the two types of jackets because each requires the same amount of conversion costs.

$$\begin{matrix} \text{Operation 1 budgeted} \\ \text{conversion cost rate} \\ \text{in 2007} \end{matrix} = \frac{\begin{matrix}\text{Operation 1 budgeted} \\ \text{conversion costs in 2007}\end{matrix}}{\begin{matrix}\text{Operation 1 budgeted} \\ \text{product units in 2007}\end{matrix}}$$

$$= \$232,000 \div 20,000 \text{ units}$$

$$= \$11.60 \text{ per unit}$$

The budgeted conversion costs of operation 1 include labour, power, repairs, supplies, amortization, and other overhead of this operation. If some units have not been completed, so that all units in operation 1 have not received the same amounts of conversion costs, the conversion cost rate is computed by dividing budgeted conversion costs by the *equivalent units* of conversion costs, as in process costing.

As goods are manufactured, conversion costs are allocated to the work orders processed in operation 1 by multiplying the $11.60 conversion costs per unit by the number of product units processed. The conversion costs of operation 1 for 50 wool blazers (work order 423) are $11.60 × 50 = $580, and for 100 polyester blazers (work order 424) are $11.60 × 100 = $1,160. If work order 424 had contained 75 units, its total costs in operation 1 would be $870 ($11.60 × 75). If equivalent units have been used to calculate the conversion cost rate, costs are allocated to work orders by multiplying the conversion cost per equivalent unit by the number of equivalent units in the work order. Direct materials costs of $6,000 for the 50 wool blazers (work order 423) and $3,000 for the 100 polyester blazers (work order 424) are specifically identified with each order as in a job-costing system. Note that operation unit costs are assumed to be the same regardless of the work order but direct materials costs vary across orders as the materials themselves vary.

Journal Entries

Actual conversion costs for operation 1 in March 2007 (assumed to be $24,400, of which $580 are on work order 423 and $1,160 are on work order 424) are entered into a Conversion Costs Control account:

1. Conversion Costs Control $24,400
   Various accounts (such as Wages Payable and Accumulated Amortization) $24,400

Summary journal entries for assigning costs to the polyester blazers (work order 424) follow. Entries for the wool blazers would be similar.

Of the $3,000 of direct materials for work order 424, $2,975 are used in Operation 1. The journal entry for the use of direct materials, which are traced directly to particular batches, for the 100 polyester blazers is as follows:

2. Work in Process, Operation 1 $2,975
   Materials Inventory Control $2,975

The allocation of conversion costs to products in operation costing uses the budgeted rate $11.60 times the 100 units processed, or $1,160.

3. Work in Process, Operation 1 $1,160
   Conversion Costs Allocated $1,160

The transfer of the polyester blazers from operation 1 to operation 3 (recall that the polyester blazers do not go through operation 2) would be journalized as follows:

4. Work in Process, Operation 3 $4,135
   Work in Process, Operation 1 $4,135

After posting, Work in Process, Operation 1 account, appears as follows:

Work in Process, Operation 1

2. Direct materials	$2,975	4. Transferred to Operation 3	4,135
3. Conversion costs allocated	1,160		

The costs of the blazers are transferred through the pertinent operations and then to finished goods in the usual manner. Costs are added throughout the year in the accounts Conversion Costs Control and Conversion Costs Allocated. Any over-allocation or underallocation of conversion costs is disposed of in the same way as overallocated or underallocated manufacturing overhead in a job-costing system.

PROBLEM FOR SELF-STUDY

Allied Chemicals operates a thermo-assembly process as the second of three processes at its plastics plant. Direct materials in thermo-assembly are added at the end of the process. Conversion costs are added evenly during the process. The following data pertain to the Thermo-Assembly Department for 2007.

	A	B	C	D	E
1		Physical	Transferred-in	Direct	Conversion
2		Units	Costs	Materials	Costs
3	Work in process, beginning inventory	50,000			
4	Degree of completion, beginning work in process		100%	0%	80%
5	Transferred in during current period	200,000			
6	Completed and transferred out during current period	210,000			
7	Work in process, ending inventory	?			
8	Degree of completion, ending work in process		100%	0%	40%

REQUIRED
Compute equivalent units under (1) the weighted-average method and (2) the FIFO method.

SOLUTION
1. The weighted-average method uses equivalent units of work done to date to compute cost per equivalent unit. The calculation of equivalent units follows:

	A	B	C	D	E
1		(Step 1)		(Step 2)	
2				Equivalent Units	
3		Physical	Transferred-in	Direct	Conversion
4	Flow of Production	Units	Costs	Materials	Costs
5	Work in process, beginning (given)	50,000			
6	Transferred in during current period (given)	200,000			
7	To account for	250,000			
8	Completed and transferred out during current period:	210,000	210,000	210,000	210,000
9	Work in process, ending[a]	40,000[b]			
10	(40,000 × 100%; 40,000 × 0%; 40,000 × 40%)		40,000	0	16,000
11	Accounted for	250,000			
12	Work done to date		250,000	210,000	226,000
13					
14	[a]Degree of completion in this department: transferred-in costs, 100%; direct materials, 0%; conversion costs, 40%.				
15	[b]250,000 physical units to account for minus 210,000 physical units completed and transferred out.				

2. The FIFO method uses equivalent units of work done in the current period only to compute cost per equivalent unit. The calculations of equivalent units follows:

A	B	C	D	E
	(Step 1)		(Step 2)	
			Equivalent Units	
	Physical	Transferred-in	Direct	Conversion
Flow of Production	Units	Costs	Materials	Costs
Work in process, beginning (given)	50,000			
Transferred in during current period (given)	200,000			
To account for	250,000			
Completed and transferred out during current period:				
From beginning work in process[a]	50,000			
[50,000 × (100% − 100%); 50,000 × (100% − 0%); 50,000 × (100% − 80%)]		0	50,000	10,000
Started and completed	160,000[b]			
(160,000 × 100%; 160,000 × 100%; 160,000 × 100%)		160,000	160,000	160,000
Work in process, ending[c]	40,000[d]			
(40,000 × 100%; 40,000 × 0%; 40,000 × 40%)		40,000	0	16,000
Accounted for	250,000			
Work done in current period only		200,000	210,000	186,000
[a]Degree of completion in this department: transferred-in costs, 100%; direct materials, 0%; conversion costs, 80%.				
[b]210,000 physical units completed and transferred out minus 50,000 physical units completed and transferred out from beginning work-in-process inventory.				
[c]Degree of completion in this department: transferred-in costs, 100%; direct materials, 0%; conversion costs, 40%.				
[d]250,000 physical units to account for minus 210,000 physical units completed and transferred out.				

TERMS TO LEARN

This chapter contains definitions of the following important terms:

equivalent units (p. 673)
first-in, first-out (FIFO) process-costing method (p. 681)
hybrid-costing system (p. 689)
operation (p. 695)

operation-costing system (p. 695)
previous department costs (p. 692)
transferred-in costs (p. 692)
weighted-average process-costing method (p. 677)

ASSIGNMENT MATERIAL

QUESTIONS

17-1 Give three examples of industries that often use process-costing systems.

17-2 In process costing, why are costs often divided into two main classifications?

17-3 Explain equivalent units. Why are equivalent-unit calculations necessary in process costing?

17-4 Name the five key steps in process costing when equivalent units are computed.

17-5 State two conditions under which computing equivalent units will make a material difference to reported inventory amounts.

17-6 Name the three inventory methods commonly associated with process costing.

17-7 Describe the distinctive characteristic of weighted-average computations in assigning costs to units completed and ending work in process.

17-8 Describe the distinctive characteristic of FIFO computations in assigning costs to units completed and ending work in process.

17-9 Why should the FIFO method be called the *modified* or *departmental* FIFO method?

17-10 Identify a major advantage of the FIFO method for purposes of planning and control.

17-11 Identify the main difference between journal entries in process costing and the ones in job costing.

17-12 "Standard cost procedures are particularly applicable to process-costing situations." Do you agree? Why?

17-13 Why should the accountant distinguish between transferred-in costs and additional direct materials costs for a particular department?

17-14 "Transferred-in costs are those incurred in the preceding accounting period." Do you agree? Explain.

17-15 "There's no reason for me to get excited about the choice between the weighted-average and FIFO methods in my process-costing system. I have long-term contracts with my materials suppliers at fixed prices." State the conditions under which you would (a) agree and (b) disagree with this statement, made by a plant controller. Explain.

EXERCISES

17-16 Equivalent units: No beginning inventory. International Electronics manufactures microchips in large quantities. Each microchip undergoes assembly and testing. The total assembly costs during January 2007 were

Direct materials used	$ 740,000
Conversion costs	780,000
Total manufacturing costs	$1,520,000

REQUIRED
1. Assume there was no beginning inventory on January 1, 2007. During January, 10,000 microchips were placed into production and all 10,000 microchips were fully completed at the end of January. What is the unit cost of an assembled microchip in January 2007?
2. Assume that during February 10,000 microchips were placed into production. Further assume the same total assembly costs for January are also incurred in February 2007, but only 9,000 microchips are fully completed at the end of February. All direct materials had been added to the remaining 1,000 microchips. However, on average, these remaining 1,000 microchips were only 50% complete as to conversion costs. (a) What are the equivalent units for direct materials and conversion costs and their respective equivalent unit costs for February? (b) What is the unit cost of an assembled microchip in February 2007?
3. Explain the difference in your answers to requirements 1 and 2.

17-17 Journal entries (continuation of 17-16). Refer to requirement 2 of Exercise 17-16.

REQUIRED
Prepare summary journal entries for the use of direct materials and conversion costs. Also prepare a journal entry to transfer out the cost of goods completed. Show the postings to the Work-in-Process account.

17-18 No beginning inventory, materials introduced in middle of process. Vaasa Chemicals has a mixing department and a refining department. Its process-costing system in the mixing department has two direct materials cost categories (chemical P and chemical Q) and one conversion costs pool. The following data pertain to the mixing department for July 2007:

Production Units:		
Work in process, July 1		0
Units started		55,000
Completed and transferred to refining department		38,500
Costs:		
Chemical P	$275,000	
Chemical Q	77,000	
Conversion costs	$148,500	

Chemical P is introduced at the start of operations in the mixing department, and chemical Q is added when the product is three-fourths completed in the mixing department. Conversion costs are added uniformly during the process. The ending work in process in the mixing department is two-thirds completed.

1. Compute the equivalent units in the mixing department for July 2007 for each cost element.
2. Compute (a) the cost of goods completed and transferred to the refining department during July and (b) the cost of work in process as of July 31, 2007.

17-19 Weighted-average method. The Chatham Company makes chemical compounds in a single processing department. The following information about equivalent units and actual costs for July 2007 is available.

	Direct Materials		Conversion Costs	
	Equivalent Units	Total Costs	Equivalent Units	Total Costs
Work in process, July 1*	22,000	$132,000	15,400	$154,000
Work done during July 2007	33,000	231,000	30,800	331,100
To account for	55,000	$363,000	46,200	$485,100
Completed during July 2007	37,400	?	374,000	?
Work in process, July 31†	17,600	?	88,000	?

*Degree of completion: direct materials, 100%; conversion costs, 70%.
†Degree of completion: direct materials, 100%; conversion costs, 50%.

REQUIRED

1. Calculate the cost per equivalent unit for direct materials and conversion costs.
2. Summarize total costs to account for, and assign these costs to units completed (and transferred out) and to units in ending work in process using the weighted-average method.

17-20 FIFO method. Refer to the information in Exercise 17-19.

REQUIRED

Do Exercise 17-19 using the FIFO method.

Note that you first need to calculate the equivalent units of work done in the current period (for direct materials and conversion costs) to complete beginning work in process, to start and complete new units, and to produce ending work in process.

17-21 Standard-costing method, assigning costs. Refer to the information in Exercise 17-19. Suppose Chatham determines standard costs of $6.10 per (equivalent) unit for direct materials and $10.20 per (equivalent) unit for conversion costs for both beginning work in process and work done in the current period.

REQUIRED

1. Do Exercise 17-19 using the standard-costing method. Note that you first need to calculate the equivalent units of work done in the current period (for direct materials and conversion costs) to complete beginning work in process, to start and complete new units, and to produce ending work in process.
2. Compute the total direct materials and conversion costs variances for July 2007.

17-22 Weighted-average method, equivalent units and unit costs. Consider the following data for the Satellite Assembly Division of Aerospatiale:

	Physical Units (Satellites)	Direct Materials	Conversion Costs
Beginning work in process, (May 1)*	8	$ 5,426,960	$ 1,001,440
Started in May 2007	55		
Completed during May 2007	51		
Ending work in process (May 31)†	12		
Costs added during May 2007		$35,420,000	$15,312,000

*Degree of completion: direct materials, 90%; conversion costs, 40%.
†Degree of completion: direct materials, 60%; conversion costs, 30%.

The Satellite Assembly Division uses the weighted-average method of process costing.

REQUIRED

1. Compute equivalent units for direct materials and conversion costs. Show physical units in the first column of your schedule.
2. Calculate cost per equivalent unit for direct materials and conversion costs.

17-23 Weighted-average method, assigning costs (continuation of 17-22).

REQUIRED

For the data in Exercise 17-22, summarize total costs to account for, and assign these costs to units completed (and transferred out) and to units in ending work in process.

17-24 FIFO method, equivalent units and unit costs. Refer to the information in Exercise 17-22. Suppose the Satellite Assembly Division uses the FIFO method of process costing instead of the weighted-average method.

REQUIRED

1. Compute equivalent units for direct materials and conversion costs. Show physical units in the first column of your schedule.
2. Calculate cost per equivalent unit for direct materials and conversion costs.

17-25 FIFO method, assigning costs (continuation of 17-24).

REQUIRED

For the data in Exercise 17-22, use the FIFO method to summarize total costs to account for, and assign these costs to units completed and transferred out, and to units in ending work in process.

17-26 Standard-costing method, assigning costs. Refer to the information in Exercise 17-22. Suppose the Satellite Assembly Division uses the standard-costing method of process costing. Suppose further that the Satellite Assembly Division determines standard costs of $700,000 per (equivalent) unit for direct materials and $300,000 per (equivalent) unit for conversion costs for both beginning work in process and work done in the current period.

REQUIRED

1. Compute equivalent units for direct materials and conversion costs. Show physical units in the first column of your schedule.
2. Summarize total costs to account for, and assign these costs to units completed and transferred out, and to units in ending work in process.
3. Compute the total direct material and conversion cost variances for May 2006.

17-27 Transferred-in costs, weighted-average method. (Chapter Appendix I) Hideo Chemicals manufactures an industrial solvent in two departments—mixing and cooking. This question focuses on the Cooking Department. During June 2007, 90 tonnes of solvent were completed and transferred out from the Cooking Department. Direct materials are added at one point in time during the process. Conversion costs are added uniformly during the process. Hideo Chemicals uses the weighted-average process costing method. The following information about the actual costs for June 2007 is available.

	Transferred-in Costs		Direct Materials		Conversion Costs	
	Equivalent Tonnes	Total Costs	Equivalent Tonnes	Total Costs	Equivalent Tonnes	Total Costs
Work in process, June 1	40	$44,000	0	$ 0	30	$19,800.00
Work done in June 2007	80	$95,920	90	$39,600	75	$54,697.50
Completed in June 2007	?	?	?	?	?	?
Work in process, June 30	?	?	?	?	?	?

REQUIRED

1. Calculate the equivalent tonnes of solvent completed and transferred out, and in ending work in process for each cost element.
2. Compute cost per equivalent unit for beginning work in process and work done in current period.
3. Summarize total costs to account for, and assign these costs to units completed (and transferred out) and to units in ending work in process using the weighted-average method.

17-28 Transferred-in costs, FIFO method. Refer to the information in Exercise 17-27. Suppose that Hideo uses the FIFO method instead of the weighted-average method in all its departments. The only changes under the FIFO method are that the total transferred-in cost of beginning work in process is $43,120 and that the transferred-in cost of work done in the current period is $94,160.

REQUIRED

Do Exercise 17-27 using the FIFO method.

17-29 Operation costing. (Chapter Appendix II) The Gabriel Corporation produces a standard-sized window in four operations—framing, assembly, staining, and painting. The windows differ in the type of wood (pine, oak) and glass (regular, tempered) used. The framing and assembly operations are common to all windows, but thereafter they are either stained or painted but not both. The total conversion costs for June are

	Framing	Assembly	Staining	Painting
Total conversion costs	$82,500	$115,500	$39,600	$59,400

There is no beginning or ending inventory of windows in June. A total of 3,000 windows are produced in June, half of which are stained and half of which are painted. The conversion cost for each unit passing through a given operation is the same.

Details of two work orders processed in June are as follows:

	Work Order 626	Work Order 750
Number of windows	50	100
Direct materials costs	$5,500	$9,800
Finishing operation	Painting	Staining

REQUIRED
1. Tabulate the conversion costs of each operation, the total units produced, and the conversion cost per unit.
2. Calculate the total costs and the total cost per window of work order 626 and work order 750.

PROBLEMS

17-30 Weighted-average method. Global Defence, Inc., is a manufacturer of military equipment. Its Halifax plant manufactures the Interceptor missile under contract to the Canadian government and friendly countries. All Interceptors go through an identical manufacturing process. Every effort is made to ensure that all Interceptors are identical and meet many demanding performance specifications. The product-costing system at the Halifax plant has a single direct cost category (direct materials) and a single indirect cost category (conversion costs). Each Interceptor passes through two departments—the Assembly Department and the Testing Department. Direct materials are added at the beginning of the process in Assembly. Conversion costs are added evenly throughout the two departments. When the Assembly Department finishes work on each Interceptor, it is immediately transferred to Testing.

Global Defence uses the weighted-average method of process costing. Data for the Assembly Department for October 2007 are

	Physical Units (missiles)	Direct Materials	Conversion Costs
Work in process, October 1*	25	$ 506,000	$ 132,000
Started during October 2007	85		
Completed during October 2007	95		
Work in process, October 31†	15		
Costs added during October 2007		$2,200,000	$1,028,500

*Degree of completion: direct materials, ?%; conversion costs, 60%.
†Degree of completion: direct materials, ?%; conversion costs, 70%.

REQUIRED
1. For each cost element, compute equivalent units of work done in October 2007 in the Assembly Department. Show physical units in the first column.
2. For each cost element, calculate cost per equivalent unit of beginning work in process and of work done in October 2007.
3. Summarize the total Assembly Department costs for October 2007, and assign these costs to units completed (and transferred out) and to units in ending work in process using the weighted-average method.

Excel Application For students who wish to practise their spreadsheet skills, the following is a step-by-step approach to creating an Excel spreadsheet to work this problem.

Step-by-Step
1. Open up a new spreadsheet. At the top, create an "Original Data" section for the Assembly Department data provided by Global Defence. Enter the "Physical Units, Direct Materials, and Conversion Cost" data in exactly the same format as presented above.

(Program your spreadsheet to perform all necessary calculations. Do not "hard-code" any amounts, such as equivalent-unit costs, requiring addition, subtraction, multiplication, or division.)

2. Skip two rows and create a section, "Problem 1," in exactly the same format as in Exhibit 17-4 (p. 678). Create columns for "Physical Units, Equivalent Units of Direct Materials and Equivalent Units of Conversion Costs" and rows for each of the items in Exhibit 17-4 (e.g., first row, "Work in Process, Beginning," and the last row, "Work Done to Date"). Use the data from your Original Data section to complete this section.

3. Skip two rows and create a section, "Problem 2," in the same format as Step 3 of Exhibit 17-5 (p. 679). Create columns for "Total Production Costs," "Direct Materials," and "Conversion Costs."

4. Next, enter a calculation for the "Cost per Equivalent Unit of Work Done to Date" for "Direct Materials" and "Conversion Costs."

5. Skip two rows and create a section, "Problem 3," in the same format as Steps 4 and 5 of Exhibit 17-5 (using columns for "Total Production Costs," "Direct Materials," and "Conversion Costs" created in Step 3).

6. Use the data you created in steps 1 to 4 to complete your "Problem 3" section.

7. *Check the accuracy of your spreadsheet:* Go to your Original Data section and change direct materials costs added for October from $2,200,000 to $2,500,000. If you programmed your spreadsheet correctly, the cost per equivalent unit of work done to date for direct materials in Problem 2 should change to $27,327.27.

17-31 **Journal entries (continuation of 17-30).**

REQUIRED

Prepare a set of summarized journal entries for all October 2007 transactions affecting Work in Process—Assembly. Set up a T-account for Work in Process—Assembly, and post the entries to it.

17-32 **FIFO method (continuation of 17-30 and 17-31).**

REQUIRED

Do Problem 17-30 using the FIFO method of process costing. Explain any difference between the cost of work completed and transferred out and cost of ending work in process in the Assembly Department under the weighted-average method and the FIFO method.

17-33 **Transferred-in costs, weighted average (related to 17-30 to 17-32).** (Chapter Appendix I) Global Defence, Inc., as you know, manufactures the Interceptor missile at its Halifax plant. It has two departments—Assembly Department and Testing Department. This problem focuses on the Testing Department. (Problems 17-30 to 17-32 focused on the Assembly Department.) Direct materials are added at the end of the Testing Department. Conversion costs are added evenly during the Testing Department's process. As work in Assembly is completed, each unit is immediately transferred to Testing. As each unit is completed in Testing, it is immediately transferred to Finished Goods.

Global Defence uses the weighted-average method of process costing. Data for the Testing Department for October 2007 are

	Physical Units (Missiles)	Transferred-in Costs	Direct Materials	Conversion Costs
Work in process, October 1*	35	$1,084,380	$ 0	$ 364,980
Transferred in during October 2007	?			
Completed during October 2007	110			
Work in process, October 31†	20			
Costs added during October 2007		$3,382,000	$3,885,000	$1,581,000

*Degree of completion: transferred-in costs, ?%; direct materials, ?%; conversion costs, 70%.
†Degree of completion: transferred-in costs, ?%; direct materials, ?%; conversion costs, 60%.

REQUIRED

1. What is the percentage of completion for (a) transferred-in costs and direct materials in beginning work-in-process inventory and (b) transferred-in costs and direct materials in ending work-in-process inventory?

2. For each cost element, compute equivalent units of work done in October 2006 in the Testing Department. Show physical units in the first column.

3. For each cost element, calculate the cost per equivalent unit of beginning work in process and of work done in October 2007.

4. Summarize total Testing Department costs for October 2007, and assign these costs to units completed (and transferred out) and to units in ending work in process using the weighted-average method.

5. Prepare journal entries for October transfers from the Assembly Department to the Testing Department and from Testing to Finished Goods.

17-34 Transferred-in costs, FIFO costing (continuation of 17-33).

REQUIRED

Using the FIFO process-costing method, do the requirements of Problem 17-33. The transferred-in costs from the Assembly Department for the beginning work in process on October 1 are $1,078,066. During October, costs transferred in to the Testing Department are $3,358,936.

17-35 Weighted-average method. Star Toys manufactures one type of wooden toy figure. It buys wood as its direct material for the Forming Department of its Fredericton plant. The toys are transferred to the Finishing Department, where they are hand-shaped and metal is added to them.

Star Toys uses the weighted-average method of process costing. Consider the following data for the Forming Department in April 2007:

	Physical Units (Toys)	Direct Materials	Conversion Costs
Work in process, April 1*	350	$ 7,500	$ 2,125
Started during April 2007	2,250		
Completed during April 2007	2,050		
Work in process, April 30†	550		
Costs added during April 2007		$70,000	$42,500

*Degree of completion: direct materials, 100%; conversion costs, 40%.
†Degree of completion: direct materials, 100%; conversion costs, 25%.

REQUIRED

Summarize the total Forming Department costs for April 2007, and assign these costs to units completed (and transferred out) and to units in ending work in process using the weighted-average method.

17-36 Journal entries (continuation of 17-35).

REQUIRED

Prepare a set of summarized journal entries for all April transactions affecting Work in Process—Forming. Set up a T-account for Work in Process—Forming, and post the entries to it.

17-37 FIFO computations (continuation of 17-35 and 17-36).

REQUIRED

Do Problem 17-35, using FIFO and three decimal places for unit costs. Explain any difference between the cost of work completed and transferred out and cost of ending work in process in the Forming Department under the weighted-average method and the FIFO method.

17-38 Transferred-in costs, weighted-average (related to 17-35 through 17-37). (Chapter Appendix I) Star Toys manufactures wooden toy figures at its Fredericton plant. It has two departments—the Forming Department and the Finishing Department. Problems 17-35 to 17-37 focused on the Forming Department. Consider now the Finishing Department, which processes the formed toys through hand-shaping and the addition of metal. For simplicity here, suppose all additional direct materials are added at the end of the process. Conversion costs are added evenly during Finishing operations.

Star Toys uses the weighted-average method of process costing. The following is a summary of the April 2007 operations in the Finishing Department:

	Physical Units (Toys)	Transferred-in Costs	Direct Materials	Conversion Costs
Work in process, April 1*	550	$ 17,750	$ 0	$ 7,250
Transferred in during April 2007	2,050			
Completed during April 2007	2,150			
Work in process, April 30†	450			
Costs added during April 2007		$102,926	$23,100	$38,400

*Degree of completion: transferred-in costs, 100%; direct materials, 0%; conversion costs, 60%.
†Degree of completion: transferred-in costs, 100%; direct materials, 0%; conversion costs, 30%.

REQUIRED

1. Summarize the total Finishing Department costs for April 2007, and assign these costs to units completed (and transferred out) and to units in ending work in process using the weighted-average method. Use three decimals for unit costs.

2. Prepare journal entries for April transfers from the Forming Department to the Finishing Department and from the Finishing Department to Finished Goods.

17-39 Transferred-in costs, FIFO costing (continuation of 17-38).

REQUIRED

1. Using the FIFO process-costing method, do the requirements of Problem 17-38. The transferred-in costs from the Forming Department for the April beginning work in process are $17,520. During April, the costs transferred in are $102,160. All other data are unchanged.

2. Explain any difference between the cost of work completed and transferred out and cost of ending work in process in the Finishing Department under the weighted-average method and the FIFO method.

17-40 Transferred-in costs, weighted-average and FIFO. (Chapter Appendix I) Frito-Lay, Inc., manufactures convenience foods, including potato chips and corn chips. Production of corn chips occurs in four departments: cleaning, mixing, cooking, and drying and packaging. Consider the Drying and Packaging Department, where direct materials (packaging) is added at the end of the process. Conversion costs are added evenly during the process. Suppose the accounting records of a Frito-Lay plant provided the following information for corn chips in its Drying and Packaging Department during a weekly period (week 37):

	Physical Units (Cases)	Transferred-in Costs	Direct Materials	Conversion Costs
Beginning work in process, week 37*	1,300	$29,000	$ 0	$ 9,060
Transferred in during week 37 from Cooking Department	5,050			
Completed during week 37	5,300			
Ending work in process, week 37†	1,050			
Costs added during week 37		$96,000	$25,200	$38,400

*Degree of completion: transferred-in costs, 100%; direct materials, ?%; conversion costs, 80%.
†Degree of completion: transferred-in costs, ?%; direct materials, ?%; conversion costs, 40%.

REQUIRED

1. For each cost element, compute equivalent units of work done in week 37 in the Drying and Packaging Department. Show physical units in the first column.

2. Summarize the total Drying and Packaging Department costs for week 37, and assign these costs to units completed (and transferred out) and to units in ending work in process using the weighted-average method.

3. Assume that the FIFO method is used for the Drying and Packaging Department. The transferred-in costs for work-in-process beginning inventory are $28,920. The transferred-in costs during the week from the Cooking Department are $94,000. All other data are unchanged. Summarize the total Drying and Packaging Department costs for week 37 and assign these costs to units completed (and transferred out) and to units in ending work in process using the FIFO method.

17-41 Standard costing with beginning and ending work in process. The Victoria Corporation uses a standard-costing system for its manufacturing operations. Standard costs for the cooking process are $5.143 per unit for direct materials and $2.571 per unit for conversion costs. All direct materials are introduced at the beginning of the process, but conversion costs are added uniformly during the process. The operating summary for May 2007 included the following data for the cooking process:

> Work-in-process inventories:
> May 1: 3,500 units*
>   (direct materials $18,000; conversion costs $5,400)
> May 31: 5,000 units†
> Units started in May: 20,500
> Units completed and transferred out of cooking in May: 19,000
> Additional actual costs incurred for cooking during May:
>   Direct materials: $125,000
>   Conversion cost: $57,000

*Degree of completion: direct materials, 100%; conversion costs, 60%.
†Degree of completion: direct materials, 100%; conversion costs, 50%.

1. Compute the total standard costs of units transferred out in May and the total standard costs of the May 31 inventory of work in process.
2. Compute the total May variances for direct materials and conversion costs.

17-42 Operation Costing (Chapter Appendix II). Feather Light Shoe Company manufactures two styles of men's shoes: Designer and Regular. Designer style is made from leather, and Regular style uses synthetic materials. Three operations—cutting, sewing, and packing—are common to both styles, but only Designer style passes through a lining operation. The conversion cost rates for 2007 are

	Cutting	Sewing	Lining	Packing
Rate per unit (pair)	$11	$16	$9	$3

Details of two work orders processed in August are

	Work Order 815	Work order 831
Number of units (pairs)	1,000	5,000
Direct materials costs	$30,000	$50,000
Style	Designer	Regular

REQUIRED

Calculate the total costs and the total cost per unit of work order 815 and work order 831.

17-43 Operation costing, equivalent units. (Chapter Appendix II, CMA, adapted) Gregg Industries manufactures a variety of plastic products, including a series of moulded chairs. The three models of moulded chairs, which are all variations of the same design, are Standard (can be stacked), Deluxe (with arms), and Executive (with arms and padding). The company uses batch manufacturing and has an operation-costing system.

Gregg has an extrusion operation and subsequent operations to form, trim, and finish the chairs. Plastic sheets are produced by the extrusion operation, some of which are sold directly to other manufacturers. During the forming operation, the remaining plastic sheets are moulded into chair seats and the legs are added. The Standard model is sold after this operation. During the trim operation, the arms are added to the Deluxe and Executive models and the chair edges are smoothed. Only the Executive model enters the finish operation, where the padding is added. All of the units produced receive the same steps within each operation.

The May production run had a total manufacturing cost of $898,000. The units of production and direct materials costs incurred are as follows:

	Units Produced	Extrusion Materials	Form Materials	Trim Materials	Finish Materials
Plastic sheets	5,500	$ 60,000	$ 0	$ 0	$ 0
Standard model	6,500	72,000	24,000	0	0
Deluxe model	3,500	36,000	12,000	9,000	0
Executive model	2,500	24,000	8,000	6,000	12,000
	18,000	$192,000	$44,000	$15,000	$12,000

Manufacturing costs of production assigned during the month of May were

	Extrusion Operation	Form Operation	Trim Operation	Finish Operation
Direct manufacturing labour	$152,000	$60,000	$30,000	$18,000
Manufacturing overhead	240,000	72,000	39,000	24,000

REQUIRED

1. For each product produced by Gregg Industries during May, determine (a) the unit cost, and (b) the total cost. Be sure to account for all costs incurred during the month, and support your answer with appropriate calculations.
2. Without considering your answer in requirement 1, assume that 1,500 units of the Deluxe model produced during May remained in work in process at the end of the month. These units were 100% complete as to materials costs and 60% complete in the trim operation. Determine the cost of the 1,500 units of the Deluxe model in the work-in-process inventory at the end of May.

17-44 Equivalent unit computations, benchmarking, ethics. Margaret Major is the corporate controller of Leisure Suits. Leisure Suits has 20 plants worldwide that manufacture basic suits for retail stores. Each plant uses a process-costing system. At the end of each month, each plant manager submits a production report and a production cost report. The production report includes the plant manager's estimate of the percentage of completion of the ending work in process as to direct materials and conversion costs. Major uses these estimates to compute the equivalent units of work done in each plant and the cost per equivalent unit of work done for both direct materials and conversion costs in each month. Plants are ranked from 1 to 20 in terms of (a) cost per equivalent unit of direct materials and (b) cost per equivalent unit of conversion costs. Each month Major publishes a report that she calls "Benchmarking for Efficiency Gains at Leisure Suits." The three top-ranked plants on each category receive a bonus and are written up as the best in their class in the company newsletter.

Major has been pleased with the success of her benchmarking program. However, she has heard some disturbing news. She has received some unsigned letters stating that two plant managers have been manipulating their monthly estimates of percentage of completion in an attempt to obtain "best in class" status.

REQUIRED

1. How and why might plant managers "manipulate" their monthly estimates of percentage of completion?
2. Major's first instinct is to contact each plant controller and discuss the problem raised by the unsigned letters. Is that a good idea?
3. Assume that the plant controller's primary reporting responsibility is to the plant manager and that each plant controller receives the phone call from Major mentioned in requirement 2. What is the ethical responsibility of each plant controller (a) to Margaret Major and (b) to Leisure Suits in relation to the equivalent unit information each plant provides for the "Benchmarking for Efficiency" report?
4. How might Major gain some insight into whether the equivalent unit figures provided by particular plants are being manipulated?

COLLABORATIVE LEARNING PROBLEM

17-45 Transferred-in costs, equivalent unit costs, working backwards. Lennox Plastics has two processes—extrusion and thermo-assembly. Consider the June 2007 data for physical units in the thermo-assembly process: beginning work in process, 16,000 units; transferred in from the Extruding Department during June, 10,000; ending work in process, 6,000. Direct materials are added when the process in the Thermo-Assembly Department is 80% complete. Conversion costs are added evenly during the process. Lennox Plastics uses the FIFO method of process costing. The following information is available.

	Transferred-in Costs	Direct Materials	Conversion Costs
Beginning work in process	$90,000	—	$45,000
Percentage completion of beginning work in process	100%	—	60%
Costs added in current period	$58,500	$57,000	$57,200
Cost per equivalent unit of work done in current period	$ 5.85	$ 2.85	$ 4.931

INSTRUCTIONS

Form pairs of students to complete the following requirements.

REQUIRED

1. For each cost category, compute equivalent units of work done in the current period.
2. For each cost category, compute equivalent units of work done to complete beginning work-in-process inventory, to start and complete new units and to produce ending work in process.
3. For each cost category, calculate the percentage of completion of ending work-in-process inventory.
4. Summarize total costs to account for, and assign these costs to units completed (and transferred out) and to units in ending work in process.

PART FIVE

CHAPTER 18

Spoilage, Rework, and Scrap

In the automotive industry, cost control is absolutely essential to profitability. Spoilage, rework, and scrap are areas of cost control that are within the direct influence of management and become a focus for these companies.

Magna International is a global producer of automotive parts and components ranging from modular roofs to complete drive trains and transmissions. To attain this level of success, an ongoing commitment to a careful management of its spoilage, rework, and scrap is necessary.

LEARNING OBJECTIVES

After studying this chapter, you should be able to

1. Distinguish among spoilage, reworked units, and scrap
2. Describe the general accounting procedures for normal and abnormal spoilage
3. Account for spoilage in process costing using the weighted-average method
4. Account for spoilage in process costing using the first-in, first-out (FIFO) method
5. Account for spoilage in process costing using the standard costs method
6. Account for spoilage in job costing
7. Account for reworked units
8. Account for scrap

Managing spoilage, rework, and scrap is a challenge for many companies, regardless of a company's size or the products it manufactures. To control costs, managers are more intensely focused on improving quality and reducing defects. Many managers believe that reducing defects both reduces costs and improves customer satisfaction which makes their company more competitive. Consider these words from a speech by George Fisher when he was chief executive officer of Motorola, an electronics manufacturer:

> We want to improve our quality in everything we do by ten times in two years, by a hundred times in four years, and in six years . . . three and a half defects for every million operations, whether typing, manufacturing, or serving a customer.

The timely recording and prompt attention directing of the costs of defects improves the information that assists managers who make decisions about cost management. Using this information, managers have taken steps to reduce defects and costs by designing better products and processes, investing in production systems such as just-in-time (JIT) and computer-integrated manufacturing (CIM), training and motivating workers, and properly maintaining machines.

This chapter concentrates on three types of costs that arise as a result of defects—spoilage, rework, and scrap—and ways to account for them. The focus is on determining the cost of products and on valuing inventory and cost of goods sold. Chapter 19 discusses other aspects of quality with greater emphasis on cost management and control.

TERMINOLOGY

OBJECTIVE 1

Distinguish among spoilage, reworked units, and scrap

Motorola Canada
www.motorola.ca

Spoilage. Unacceptable units of production that are discarded or sold for net disposal proceeds.

Reworked units. Unacceptable units of production that are subsequently reworked and sold as acceptable finished goods.

Scrap. Residual material remaining after production.

Spoilage, rework, and scrap are often locked in during R&D and product design when the products and production processes are developed.

We start by defining key terms used in the chapter.

Spoilage refers to unacceptable units of production that are discarded or are sold for net disposal proceeds. Partially completed or fully completed units of output may be spoiled. Examples are defective shirts, jeans, shoes, and carpets sold as "seconds," and defective aluminum cans sold to aluminum manufacturers for remelting to produce other aluminum products. **Reworked units** are unacceptable units of production that are subsequently reworked and sold as acceptable finished goods. For example, defective units of products such as pagers, computer disk drives, computers, and telephones can sometimes be repaired and sold as good products. **Scrap** is defined in Chapter 15 as a residual material that results from manufacturing a product. It has low total sales value compared with the total sales value of the product. Examples are short lengths from woodworking operations, edges from plastic moulding operations, and frayed cloth and end cuts from suit-making operations.

Some amount of spoilage, rework, or scrap appears to be an inherent part of many production processes. One example is semiconductor manufacturing, where the products are so complex and delicate that some spoiled units are invariably produced. In this case, the spoiled units cannot be reworked. An example involving spoilage and rework occurs in the manufacture of high-precision machine tools that must be built to very demanding tolerances. In this case, spoiled units can be reworked to meet standards but only at a considerable cost. And in the mining industry, companies process ore that contains varying amounts of valuable metals and rock. Some amount of rock, which is scrap, is inevitable, but its volume can often be decreased. The Global Surveys of Company Practice box on page 711, describes spoilage (rejects), rework and scrap in the U.S. electronics industry. We first focus on spoilage.

DIFFERENT TYPES OF SPOILAGE

OBJECTIVE 2

Describe the general accounting procedures for normal and abnormal spoilage

Normal spoilage. Spoilage that arises under efficient operating conditions; it is an inherent result of the particular production process.

Abnormal spoilage. Spoilage not expected to arise under efficient operating conditions; it is not an inherent part of the chosen production process.

Two key objectives when accounting for spoilage are determining the magnitude of the costs of spoilage and distinguishing between the costs of normal and abnormal spoilage. Managers use this information both to cost products and to control and reduce costs by improving the quality of the product and process.

Normal Spoilage

Normal spoilage is spoilage that arises under efficient operating conditions; it is an inherent result of the particular production process. For a given production process, management must decide the rate of spoilage it is willing to accept as normal. Costs of normal spoilage are typically viewed as a part of the costs of good units manufactured, when good units cannot be made without the simultaneous appearance of spoiled units.

Normal spoilage rates should be computed using the total *good* units completed as the base, not the total *actual* units started. Why? Because total actual units started also include any abnormal spoilage in addition to normal spoilage.

Abnormal Spoilage

Abnormal spoilage is spoilage that is not expected to arise under efficient operating conditions; it is not an inherent part of the chosen production process. Most abnormal spoilage is usually regarded as avoidable and controllable. Line operators and other plant personnel can generally decrease abnormal spoilage by minimizing machine breakdowns, accidents, and the like. Abnormal spoilage costs are written off as losses of the accounting period in which detection of the spoiled units occurs. For the most informative feedback, the Loss from Abnormal Spoilage account should appear in a detailed income statement as a separate line item and not be buried as an indistinguishable part of the cost of goods manufactured.

Rejection in the Electronics Industry

From country to country and from industry to industry, the rates of spoilage and rework vary tremendously. The data in the following table focus on different segments of the U.S. electronics industry. The data reported are median numbers drawn from companies that are members of the American Electronics Association. The spoilage rate is spoilage as a percentage of units inspected. The rework rate is rework as a percentage of units inspected. The scrap rate reports scrap as a percentage of all materials and products purchased. Also reported is the operating-income-to-revenues percentage for each segment of the electronics industry.

Segment of Electronics Industry	Spoilage Rate (% Rejects)	Rework Rate (% Rework)	Scrap Rate (% Scrap)	Operating Income to Revenues
1. Computers and office equipment (includes mainframes, minicomputers, microcomputers, printers, and point-of-sale equipment)	2.6%	6.5%	0.6%	5.3%
2. Electronic components and accessories (includes printed circuit boards and semiconductors)	1.6	2.0	1.6	4.5
3. Specialized production equipment (includes semiconductor production equipment)	7.5	10.0	0.4	5.7
4. Telecommunications equipment (includes telephone, radio, and TV apparatus)	1.0	2.0	1.3	4.7
5. Aerospace, nautical, and military equipment (includes aircraft manufacture and guided missiles)	—	1.5	0.5	6.5
6. Laboratory and measurement devices (includes optical instruments and process-control equipment)	4.9	3.3	0.7	3.9
7. Prepackaged software	1.0	0.8	0.1	4.0

The spoilage rate for specialized production equipment is almost five times greater than the spoilage rate for electronic components and accessories. Electronic components and accessories show a low percentage of rework (in part because rework is not always possible when defects arise). Scrap rates are reasonably small across all industry segments. Operating-income-to-revenues percentage ranges from 3.9% for laboratory and measurement devices to 6.5% for aerospace, nautical, and military equipment. Given these profitability percentages, reductions in spoilage and rework rates can markedly increase the profitability of many companies in the electronics industry.

Source: Adapted from American Electronics Association, *Operating Ratios Survey.* 1993–94 (Santa Clara, CA: American Electronics Association, 1993).

Many companies, such as the Toyota Motor Corporation, adhere to a perfection standard as a part of their emphasis on total quality control. Their ideal goal is zero defects. Hence, all spoilage would be treated as abnormal (see Concepts in Action box on page 713).

Issues about accounting for spoilage arise in both process-costing and job-costing systems. We first present the accounting for spoilage in process-costing systems because it is an extension of the discussion of process costing introduced in Chapter 17.

PROCESS COSTING AND SPOILAGE

A key issue in accounting for spoilage in process-costing systems is how to count spoiled units. As we have already discussed, units of abnormal spoilage should be counted and recorded separately. But what about units of normal spoilage? These units can either be recognized (approach A) or not counted (approach B) when computing output units—actual or equivalent—in a process-costing system. Approach A makes visible the costs associated with spoilage. Approach B spreads the spoilage costs over good units, potentially resulting in less accurate product costs. An **inspection point** is the stage of the production process at which products are examined to determine whether they are acceptable or unacceptable units. Spoilage is typically assumed to occur at the stage of completion where inspection takes place. That's because spoilage is not detected until inspection. In our example, the inspection point is at the end of the process. As a result, the spoiled units are assumed to be 100% complete with respect to direct materials.

Example 1: Chipmakers, Inc., manufactures computer chips for television sets. All direct materials are added at the beginning of the chip-making process. To highlight issues that arise with spoilage, we assume no beginning inventory. In May 2007 the following data are available:

	A	B	C
		Physical	**Direct**
		Units	**Material**
3	Work in process, beginning inventory (May 1)	0	
4	Started during May	10,000	
5	Good units completed and transferred out during May	5,000	
6	Units spoiled (all normal spoilage)	1,000	
7	Work in process, ending inventory (May 31)	4,000	
8	Degree of completion of ending work in process		100%
9	Direct materials costs added in May		$270,000

Exhibit 18-1 calculates and assigns cost per unit of direct materials using approach A and approach B. Approach A shows 10,000 equivalent units of output: 5,000 equivalent units in good units completed (5,000 physical units × 100%), 4,000 units in ending work in process (4,000 physical units × 100%), and 1,000 equivalent units in normal spoilage (1,000 physical units × 100%). Approach B shows 9,000 equivalent units of output: 5,000 equivalent units in good units completed and 4,000 equivalent units in ending work in process. Not counting the equivalent units for normal spoilage in approach B decreases equivalent units, resulting in a higher cost of each good unit. A $30 equivalent-unit cost in approach B (by not counting spoiled units), instead of a $27 equivalent-unit cost in approach A (by counting spoiled units), is assigned to work in process that has not reached the inspection point.

Under approach B, the direct material costs assigned to good units completed and transferred out, which include the costs of normal spoilage, are understated by $12,000—$150,000 instead of $162,000. The 4,000 units in ending work in process contain costs of normal spoilage of $12,000 ($120,000 − $108,000) that do not pertain to the 4,000 units in ending work in process because they have not yet been inspected. That $12,000 belongs with the good units completed and transferred out. The 4,000 units in ending work in process undoubtedly include some units that will be detected as spoiled when they are inspected upon completion in the subsequent accounting period.

In effect, under approach B, these units will bear two charges for spoilage. The ending work in process is being charged for spoilage in the current period, and it will be charged again when inspection occurs as the units are completed. Such

Managing Waste and Environmental Costs at the DuPont Corporation

The DuPont Corporation manufactures a wide range of chemicals and chemical products. DuPont uses the term *waste* to describe the spoilage and scrap it generates. Besides the cost of lost materials, chemical waste is a particular problem because of its impact on the environment. Strict environmental laws require that chemical waste be disposed of in an environmentally safe way, further adding to the cost of generating waste.

DuPont calculates the full costs of waste to include: (1) the costs of materials lost in the chemical process minus their disposal value; (2) the full costs of semi-finished and finished products spoiled; (3) the full costs of disposing of or treating the waste, such as site charges for hazardous waste or costs of scrubbers and biotreatment plants to treat the waste; and (4) the costs of any solvents used to clean plant and equipment as a result of generating waste.

DuPont believes business profits do not have to be gained at the expense of the environment and seeks to reduce the "environmental impact" of all its businesses. DuPont focuses on source reduction (the avoidance of waste altogether, rather than disposal or treatment of waste) as the best way to achieve profitability and environmental performance. DuPont calculates the total cost of waste to highlight to managers the operational and environmental costs of waste, and it rewards managers for reducing waste. This approach motivates individual plants to take actions, such as redesigning products, reconfiguring processes, or investing in capital equipment to reduce waste altogether. For example, DuPont increased its material yield in its US$2-billion Lycra business from 75% in 1990 to more than 90% in 1999.

The company's new process for Terathane® is a good example of how DuPont reduces waste costs. The new process significantly reduces environmental emissions and energy use. Relative to the old technology, the new technology reduced air emissions by 91,000 kilograms, solid waste by 11 million kilograms, aqueous waste by 11 million kilograms, and steam use by more than 68 million kilograms, while generating cost savings of more than US$5 million a year.

Sources: Adapted from Environmental Respect Awards, DuPont Corporation, and based on discussions with Dale Martin, manager, Environmental Effectiveness; C. Holliday, "Sustainable Growth, the DuPont Way," *Harvard Business Review*, September 2001, pp. 129–134.

EXHIBIT 18-1
Effect of Recognizing Equivalent Units in Spoilage for Direct Materials Costs, Chipmakers, Inc., for May 2007

	A	B	C
		Approach A:	**Approach B:**
		Counting Spoiled	**Not Counting Spoiled**
		Units When Computing	**Units When Computing**
		Output in Equivalent	**Output in Equivalent**
		Units	**Units**
6	Costs to account for	$270,000	$270,000
7	Divide by equivalent units of output	÷ 10,000	÷ 9,000
8	Cost per equivalent units of output	$ 27	$ 30
9	Assignment of costs:		
10	Good units completed (5,000 units × $27 per unit; 5,000 units × $30 per unit)	$135,000	$150,000
11	Add normal spoilage (1,000 units × $27 per unit)	27,000	0
12	Total costs of good units completed and transferred out	162,000	150,000
13	Work in process, ending (4,000 units × $27 per unit; 4,000 units × $30 per unit)	108,000	120,000
14	Cost accounted for:	$270,000	$270,000

cost distortions do not occur when spoiled units are recognized in the computation of equivalent units. Approach A has a further advantage. It highlights the cost of normal spoilage to management and thereby focuses management's attention on reducing spoilage. Therefore, we will use approach A to present process costing with spoilage.

The Five-Step Procedure for Process Costing with Spoilage

We illustrate process costing with spoilage using the following example.

Example 2: The Anzio Company manufactures a wooden recycling container in its Processing Department. Direct materials for this product are introduced at the beginning of the production cycle. At the start of production, all direct materials required to make one output unit are bundled together in a single kit. Conversion costs are added evenly during the cycle. Some units of this product are spoiled as a result of defects only detectable at inspection of finished units. Normally, the spoiled units are 10% of the good output. Summary data for July 2007 are as follows:

	A	B	C	D	E
		Physical	Direct	Conversion	Total
		Units	Materials	Costs	Costs
		(1)	(2)	(3)	(4) = (2) + (3)
4	Work in process, beginning inventory (July 1)	1,500	$12,000	$ 9,000	$ 21,000
5	Degree of completion of ending work in process		100%	60%	
6	Started during July	8,500			
7	Good units completed and transferred out during July	7,000			
8	Work in process, ending inventory (July 31)	2,000			
9	Degree of completion of ending work in process		100%	50%	
10	Total costs added during July		$76,500	$89,100	$165,600
11	Normal spoiling as a percentage of good units	10%			
12	Degree of completion of normal spoilage		100%	100%	
13	Degree of completion of abnormal spoilage		100%	100%	

The five-step approach used in Chapter 17 needs only slight modification to accommodate spoilage. The key change is in calculating the number of spoiled units in step 1.

◆ **Step 1:** *Summarize the flow of physical units of output.* Identify both normal and abnormal spoilage.

The number of total spoiled units is computed as follows:

$$\text{Total spoilage} = \left(\begin{array}{c}\text{Units in beginning} \\ \text{work-in-process} \\ \text{inventory}\end{array} + \text{Units started}\right) - \left(\begin{array}{c}\text{Good units} \\ \text{completed and} \\ \text{transferred out}\end{array} + \begin{array}{c}\text{Units in ending} \\ \text{work-in-process} \\ \text{inventory}\end{array}\right)$$

$$= (1,500 + 8,500) - (7,000 + 2,000)$$
$$= 10,000 - 9,000$$
$$= 1,000 \text{ units}$$

Normal spoilage at Anzio's Processing Department is 10% of the 7,000 units of good output, or 700 units. Thus:

$$\text{Abnormal spoilage} = \text{Total spoilage} - \text{Normal spoilage}$$
$$= 1,000 - 700$$
$$= 300 \text{ units}$$

◆ **Step 2:** *Compute output in terms of equivalent units.* Compute equivalent units for spoilage in the same way as for good units. Because Anzio inspects at the completion point, the same amount of work will be done on each spoiled unit and each completed good unit.

◆ **Step 3:** *Compute equivalent unit costs.* The details of this step do not differ from those in Chapter 17. We assume that spoiled units are included in the computation of output units.

◆ **Step 4:** *Summarize total costs to account for.* These are all the costs debited to Work in Process. The details of this step do not differ from those in Chapter 17.

◆ **Step 5:** *Assign these costs to units completed, spoiled units, and units in ending work in process.* This step now includes computation of the cost of spoiled units and the cost of good units.

To proceed through the five steps, we first need to specify the inventory costing method—weighted average, FIFO, or standard costing. We illustrate process costing under each of these inventory methods and show how the computations incorporate normal and abnormal spoilage.

Weighted-Average Method and Spoilage

OBJECTIVE 3

Account for spoilage in process costing using the weighted-average method

Exhibit 18-2, Panel A, on page 716 presents steps 1 and 2 to calculate equivalent units of work done to date and includes calculations of equivalent units of normal and abnormal spoilage. Panel B presents steps 3, 4, and 5 (together called the production cost worksheet). Step 3 presents the equivalent unit cost calculations using the weighted-average method. Note how, for each cost category, the costs of beginning work in process and costs of work done in the current period are totalled and divided by the equivalent units of all work done to date to calculate the weighted-average cost. Step 4 summarizes the total costs to account for. Step 5 assigns costs to completed units, spoiled units, and ending inventory by multiplying the equivalent units calculated in step 2 by the cost per equivalent unit calculated in step 3. Note how the costs of normal spoilage, $13,825, are added to the costs of the related good units. Hence, the cost per good unit completed and transferred out equals the total costs transferred out (including the costs of normal spoilage) divided by the number of good units produced, $152,075 ÷ 7,000 = $21.725. It is not equal to $19.75, the sum of the costs per equivalent unit of direct materials, $8.85, and conversion costs, $10.90. Instead, the cost per good unit is equal to the total cost of direct materials and conversion costs per equivalent unit, $19.75, *plus* a share of the normal spoilage, $1.975 ($13,825 ÷ 7,000) = $21.725. The $5,925 costs of abnormal spoilage are assigned to the Loss from Abnormal Spoilage account and do not appear in the good-unit costs.[1]

In Panel B of Exhibit 18-2, total costs to account for in step 4 represent the debits to the Work-in-Process account. Step 5 represents the credits to the Work-in-Process account with debits (1) to the Loss from Abnormal Spoilage account of $5,925 and (2) to Finished Goods of $152,075 (the cost of units completed and transferred out). Step 5 also shows the ending balance of Work in Process of $28,600.

FIFO Method and Spoilage

OBJECTIVE 4

Account for spoilage in process costing using the first-in, first-out (FIFO) method

In Exhibit 18-3, Panel A, on page 717 presents steps 1 and 2 using the FIFO method that focuses on equivalent units of work done in the current period. Panel B presents steps 3, 4, and 5. Note how the FIFO method keeps the costs of the beginning work-in-process inventory separate and distinct from the costs of work done in the current period when assigning costs. All spoilage costs are assumed to be related to units completed during this period, using the unit costs of the current period.[2] With the exception of accounting for spoilage, the FIFO method is the same as presented in Chapter 17.

---

[1]The actual costs of spoilage (and rework) are often greater than the costs recorded in the accounting system because opportunity costs of disruption of the production line, storage, and lost contribution margins are not recorded in accounting systems. Chapter 19 discusses these opportunity costs from a cost management viewpoint.

[2]If the FIFO method were used in its purest form, normal spoilage costs would be split between the goods started and completed during the current period and those completed from beginning work in process—using the appropriate unit costs of the period in which the units were worked on. The simpler, modified FIFO method, as illustrated in Exhibit 18-3, in effect uses the unit costs of the current period for assigning normal spoilage costs to the goods completed from beginning work in process. This modified FIFO method assumes that all normal spoilage traceable to the beginning work in process was started and completed during the current period.

EXHIBIT 18-2
Weighted-Average Method of Process Costing with Spoilage Forming Department of the Anzio Company for July 2007

	A	B	C	D	E
1		PANEL A: Steps 1 and 2—Summarize Output in Physical Units and Compute Equivalent Units			
2			**(Step 1)**	**(Step 2)**	
3				**Equivalent Units**	
4			**Physical**	**Direct**	**Conversion**
5		**Flow of Production**	**Units**	**Materials**	**Costs**
6		Work in process, beginning (given, p. 714)	1,500		
7		Started during current period (given, p. 714)	8,500		
8		To account for:	10,000		
9		Good unit completed and transferred out during the current period:	7,000	7,000	7,000
10		Normal spoilage[a]	700		
11		(700 × 100%; 700 × 100%)		700	700
12		Abnormal spoilage[b]	300		
13		(300 × 100%; 300 × 100%)		300	300
14		Work in process, ending[c] (given, p. 714)	2,000		
15		(2,000 × 100%; 2000 × 50%)		2,000	1,000
16		Accounted for	10,000		
17		Work done to date		10,000	9,000
18					
19		[a]Normal spoilage is 10% of good units transferred out: 10% × 7,000 = 700 units. Degree of completion of normal spoilage in this			
20		department: direct materials, 100%; conversion costs, 100%.			
21		[b]Abnormal spoilage = Total spoilage − Normal spoilage = 1,000 − 700 = 300 units. Degree of completion of abnormal spoilage			
22		in this department: direct materials, 100%; conversion costs, 100%.			
23		[c]Degree of completion in this department: direct materials, 100%; conversion costs, 50%.			
24					
25		PANEL B: Steps 3, 4, and 5—Compute Cost per Equivalent Unit, Summarize Total Costs to Account For,			
26		and Assign Total Costs to Units Completed, to Spoiled Units, and to Units in Ending Work in Process			
27			**Total**		
28			**Production**	**Direct**	**Conversion**
29			**Costs**	**Materials**	**Costs**
30	(Step 3)	Work in process, beginning (given, p. 714)	$ 21,000	$12,000	$ 9,000
31		Costs added in the current period (given, p. 714)	165,600	76,500	89,100
32		Costs incurred to date		$88,500	$98,100
33		Divide by equivalent units of work done to date		÷10,000	÷9,000
34		Cost per equivalent unit		$ 8.85	$ 10.90
35	(Step 4)	Total costs to account for	$186,600		
36	(Step 5)	Assignment of costs:			
37		Good units completed and transferred out (7,000 units)			
38		Costs before adding normal spoilage	$138,250	(7,000[d] × $8.85) + (7,000[d] × $10.90)	
39		Normal spoilage (700 units)	13,825	(700[d] × $8.85) + (700[d] × $10.90)	
40	(A)	Total costs of good units completed and transferred out	152,075		
41	(B)	Abnormal spoilage (300 units)	5,925	(300[d] × $8.85) + (300[d] × $10.90)	
42	(C)	Work in process, ending (2,000 units):	28,600	(2,000[d] × $8.85) + (1,000[d] × $10.90)	
43	(A + B + C)	Total costs accounted for	$186,600		
44					
45		[d]Equivalent units of direct materials and conversion costs calculated in step 2 in Panel A			

Standard Costs and Spoilage

OBJECTIVE 5

Account for spoilage in process costing using the standard costs method

This section assumes you have studied Chapters 7 and 8 and the standard costs method in Chapter 17. Otherwise, omit this section.

Standard-costing methods can also be used to account for normal and abnormal spoilage. We illustrate how much simpler the calculations of conversion costs become by continuing our Anzio Company example; however, journal entries must be made to account for the variances between standard and actual costs.

Suppose the Anzio Company develops standard costs for the Processing Department. Assume the same standard costs apply to the beginning inventory and to work done in July 2007.

Standard Costs for Processing Department

Direct materials	$ 8.50
Conversion costs	10.50
Total manufacturing cost	$19.00

EXHIBIT 18-3

First-In, First-Out (FIFO) Method of Process Costing with Spoilage Forming Department of the Anzio Company for July 2007

	A	B	C	D
1	**PANEL A: Steps 1 and 2—Summarize Output in Physical Units and Compute Equivalent Units**			
2		**(Step 1)**	**(Step 2)**	
3			**Equivalent Units**	
4		**Physical**	**Direct**	**Conversion**
5	**Flow of Production**	**Units**	**Materials**	**Costs**
6	Work in process, beginning balance (given)	1,500		
7	Started during current period (given)	8,500		
8	To account for:	10,000		
9	Good units completed and transferred out during the current period			
10	From beginning work in process inventory[a]	1,500		
11	1,500 × (100% − 100%); 1,500 × (100% − 60%)		—	600
12	Started and completed[b]	5,500		
13	5,500 × 100%; 5,500 × 100%		5,500	5,500
14	Normal spoilage[c]	700		
15	700 × 100%; 700 × 100%		700	700
16	Abnormal spoilage[d]	300		
17	300 × 100%; 300 × 100%		300	300
18	Work in process, ending balance[e] (given)	2,000		
19	2,000 × 100%; 2,000 × 50%		2,000	1,000
20	Accounted for:	10,000		
21	Work done in current period only		8,500	8,100
22				
23	[a]Degree of completion in this department: direct materials, 100%; conversion costs, 60%.			
24	[b]7,000 physical units completed and transferred out minus 1,500 physical units completed and transferred from beginning			
25	work-in-process inventory.			
26	[c]Normal spoilage is 10% of good units transferred out: 10% × 7,000 = 700 units. Degree of completion of normal spoilage in this			
27	department: direct materials, 100%; conversion costs, 100%.			
28	[d]Abnormal spoilage = Actual spoilage − Normal spoilage = 1,000 − 700 = 300 units. Degree of completion of abnormal spoilage			
29	in this department: direct materials, 100%; conversion costs, 100%.			
30	[e]Degree of completion in this department: direct materials, 100%; conversion costs, 50%.			

EXHIBIT 18-3
(Continued)

			Total Production Costs		Direct Materials		Conversion Costs
31		PANEL B: Steps 3, 4, and 5—Compute Cost per Equivalent Unit, Summarize Total Costs to Account For,					
32		and Assign Total Costs to Units Completed, to Spoiled Units, and to Units in Ending Work in Process					
36	(Step 3)	Work in process, beginning balance (given)	$ 21,000				
37		Costs added in the current period (given)	165,600		$76,500		$89,100
38		Divide by equivalent units of work done in the current period			÷8,500		÷8,100
39		Cost per equivalent unit			$ 9		$ 11
40	(Step 4)	Total costs to account for	$186,600				
41	(Step 5)	Assignment of costs:					
42		Good units completed and transferred out (7,000 units)					
43		Work in process beginning balance (1,500 units)	$ 21,000				
44		Costs added in current period^f	6,600	=	$(0^f \times \$9) + (600^f \times \$11)$		
45		Total from beginning inventory before normal spoilage	27,600				
46		Started and completed before normal spoilage (5,500 units)	110,000	=	$(5,500^f \times \$9) + (5,500^f \times \$11)$		
47		Normal spoilage (700 units)	14,000	=	$(700^f \times \$9) + (700^f \times \$11)$		
48	A	Total costs of good units completed and transferred out	151,600				
49	B	Abnormal spoilage (300 units)	6,000	=	$(300^f \times \$9) + (300^f \times \$11)$		
50	C	Work in process, ending balance (2,000 units)	29,000	=	$(2,000^f \times \$9) + (1,000^f \times \$11)$		
51	A + B + C	Total costs accounted for:	$186,600				
53		^{f}Equivalent units of direct materials and conversion costs calculated in step 2 in Panel A					

Assume the same standard costs per unit also apply to the beginning inventory: 1,500 (1,500 × 100%) equivalent units of direct materials and 900 (1,500 × 60%) equivalent units of conversion costs. Hence, the beginning inventory at standard costs is:

Direct materials, 1,500 units × $8.50/unit	$12,750
Conversion costs, 900 units × $10.50/unit	9,450
Total manufacturing cost	$22,200

Exhibit 18-4, Panel A, presents steps 1 and 2. These steps are the same as for the FIFO methods described in Exhibit 18-3. In step 3, the cost per equivalent unit is simply the standard cost: direct materials, $8.50, and conversion costs, $10.50. Standard costing makes calculating equivalent unit costs unnecessary and so simplifies process costing. The costs to account for in step 4 are at *standard* costs and hence differ from the costs to account for under the weighted-average and FIFO methods, which are at *actual* costs. Step 5 uses standard costs to assign costs to units completed, to normal and abnormal spoilage, and to ending work-in-process inventory. Variances can be measured and analyzed in the manner described in Chapters 7 and 8.

Journal Entries

The information from Panel B in Exhibits 18-2, 18-3, and 18-4 supports the following journal entries:

	Weighted Average		FIFO		STANDARD	
1. Finished Goods	$152,075		$151,600		$146,300	
Work in Process—Processing		$152,075		$151,600		$146,300
To transfer good units completed in July.						
2. Loss from Abnormal Spoilage	$ 5,925		$ 6,000		$ 5,700	
Work in Process—Processing		$ 5,925		$ 6,000		$ 5,700
To recognize abnormal spoilage detected in July.						
3. Work in Process—Processing (at standard costs)					$ 72,250	
Direct Materials Variances					4,250	
Processing Department Direct Materials Control						$ 76,500
4. Work in Process—Processing (at standard costs)					$ 85,050	
Conversion Costs Variance					4,050	
Processing Department Conversion Costs Control						$ 89,100

To record actual direct materials used and total direct materials variances

EXHIBIT 18-4
Use of Standard Cost in Process Costing with Spoilage—Forming Department of the Anzio Company for July 2007

	A	B	C	D
1	**PANEL A: Steps 1 and 2—Summarize Output in Physical Units and Compute Equivalent Units**			
2		**(Step 1)**	**(Step 2)**	
3			**Equivalent Units**	
4		**Physical**	**Direct**	**Conversion**
5	**Flow of Production**	**Units**	**Materials**	**Costs**
6	Work in process, beginning balance (given)	1,500		
7	Started during current period (given)	8,500		
8	To account for:	10,000		
9	Good units completed and transferred out during the current period			
10	From beginning work in process inventory[a]	1,500		
11	$1,500 \times (100\% - 100\%); 1,500 \times (100\% - 60\%)$		–	600
12	Started and completed[b]	5,500		
13	$5,500 \times 100\%; 5,500 \times 100\%$		5,500	5,500
14	Normal spoilage[c]	700		
15	$700 \times 100\%; 700 \times 100\%$		700	700
16	Abnormal spoilage[d]	300		
17	$300 \times 100\%; 300 \times 100\%$		300	300
18	Work in process, ending balance[e] (given)	2,000		
19	$2,000 \times 100\%; 2,200 \times 50\%$		2,000	1,000
20	Accounted for:	10,000		
21	Work done in current period only		8,500	8,100
22				
23	[a]Degree of completion in this department: direct materials, 100%; conversion costs, 60%.			
24	[b]7,000 physical units completed and transferred out minus 1,500 physical units completed and transferred			
25	from beginning work in process inventory.			
26	[c]Normal spoilage is 10% of good units transferred out: $10\% \times 7,000 = 700$ units. Degree of completion of			
27	normal spoilage in this department: direct materials 100%; conversion costs 100%.			
28	[d]Abnormal spoilage = Actual spoilage − Normal spoilage = $1,000 - 700 = 300$ units. Degree of completion			
29	of abnormal spoilage in this department: direct materials 100%; conversion costs, 100%.			
30	[e]Degree of completion in this department: direct materials 100%; conversion costs, 50%.			

EXHIBIT 18-4
(Continued)

			Total Production Costs		Direct Materials		Conversion Costs	
31		**PANEL B: Steps 3, 4, and 5—Compute Cost per Equivalent Unit, Summarize Total Costs to Account For,**						
32		**and Assign Total Costs to Units Completed, to Spoiled Units, and to Units in Ending Work in Process**						
33								
34								
35								
36	(Step 3)	Standard cost per equivalent unit (given)	$ 19.00		$ 8.50		$ 10.50	
37		Work in process, beginning balance (given)	$ 22,200					
38		Costs added in the current period (at standard)	157,300	=	72,250[g]	+	85,050[h]	
39	(Step 4)	Total costs to account for	$179,500					
40		Cost per equivalent unit (at standard)			$ 8.50		$ 10.50	
41	(Step 5)	Assignment of costs:						
42		Good units completed and transferred out (7,000 units)						
43		Work in process beginning balance (1,500 units)	$ 22,200					
44		Costs added in current period[f] (0 × $8.50; 600× $10.50)	6,300	=	$ –	+	$ 6,300	
45		Total from beginning inventory before normal spoilage	28,500					
46		Started and completed before normal spoilage (5,500 units)	104,500	=	46,750	+	57,750	
47		Normal spoilage (700 units)	13,300	=	5,950	+	7,350	
48 A		Total costs of good units completed and transferred out	146,300					
49 B		Abnormal spoilage (300 units)	5,700	=	2,550	+	3,150	
50 C		Work in process, ending balance (2,000 × $8.50; 1,000 × $10.50)	27,500	=	17,000	+	10,500	
51 A + B + C		Total costs accounted for:	$179,500		$ 72,250		$85,050	
52	Summary of variances for current performance							
53	Costs added in current period at standard costs (see step 3 above)				$ 72,250		$85,050	
54	Actual costs incurred (given p. 714)				76,500		89,100	
55	Variance				$ (4,250)	U	$ (4,050)	U
56								
57	[f]Equivalent units of direct materials and conversion costs calculated in step 2 in Panel A							
58	[g]8,500 equivalent units × $8.50							
59	[h]8,100 equivalent units × $10.50							

Allocating Costs of Normal Spoilage

Spoilage might actually occur at various points or stages of the production cycle, but spoilage is typically not detected until one or more specific points of inspection. The cost of spoiled units is assumed to be all costs incurred by spoiled units before inspection. When spoiled goods have a disposal value, the net cost of spoilage is computed by deducting disposal value from the costs of the spoiled goods accumulated to the point of inspection. The unit costs of abnormal and normal spoilage are the same when the two are detected simultaneously. However, situations might arise when abnormal spoilage is detected at a different point from normal spoilage. In such cases, the unit cost of abnormal spoilage would differ from the unit cost of normal spoilage.

Costs of abnormal spoilage are separately accounted for as losses for the period. Recall, however, that normal spoilage costs are added to costs of good units. Accounting for normal spoilage, therefore, raises an additional issue: Should normal spoilage costs be allocated between completed units and ending work-in-process inventory? One approach is to presume that normal spoilage occurs at the inspection point in the production cycle and to allocate its cost over all units that have passed that point. In the Anzio Company example, spoilage is assumed to occur when finished units are inspected, so no cost of normal spoilage is allocated to ending work in process.

Whether the cost of normal spoilage is allocated to the units in ending work-in-process inventory, in addition to completed units, depends strictly on whether they have passed the point of inspection. For example, if the inspection point is presumed to be the halfway stage of the production cycle, work in process that is more than 50% completed is allocated a full measure of normal spoilage costs, calculated on the basis of all costs incurred before the point of inspection. But work in process that is less than 50% completed is not allocated any normal spoilage costs. The appendix to this chapter contains additional discussion concerning various assumptions about spoilage.

Here is another example of how abnormal spoilage may occur other than at inspection points. A foreman at a glass plant discovers a furnace has been contaminated with foreign matter and detects and records abnormal spoilage at this point rather than at the point of completion when the product is inspected.

JOB COSTING AND SPOILAGE

The concepts of normal and abnormal spoilage also apply to job-costing systems. Abnormal spoilage is usually regarded as controllable by the manager. It is separately identified with the goal of eliminating it altogether. Costs of abnormal spoilage are not considered as product manufacturing costs and are written off as costs of the period in which detection occurs. Normal or planned spoilage in job-costing systems, however, are considered part of normal manufacturing costs, although increasingly, managements are tolerating only small amounts of spoilage as normal. The costs are then assigned to individually distinct jobs, a step unnecessary in process costing since masses of similar units are manufactured.

We illustrate the accounting for spoilage in job costing using the following example:

OBJECTIVE 6

Account for spoilage in job costing

Example 3: In the Hull Machine Shop, 5 aircraft parts out of a job lot of 50 aircraft parts are spoiled. Costs assigned up to the point of inspection are $100 per unit. Hull calculates these costs on the basis of its inventory costing assumptions—weighted average, FIFO, or standard costs. We do not, however, emphasize cost-flow assumptions in our presentation here or in subsequent sections. The current disposal price of the spoiled parts is estimated to be $30 per part. When the spoilage is detected, the spoiled goods are inventoried at $30 per unit.

Although not the focus of this example, Hull calculates the $100 cost per part based on its inventory-costing method (weighted average, FIFO, or standard costing).

Normal Spoilage Attributable to a Specific Job When normal spoilage occurs because of the specifications of a specific job, that job bears the cost of the spoilage reduced by the current disposal value of that spoilage. The journal entry to recognize the disposal value of the salvage (items in parentheses indicate subsidiary postings) is as follows:

Materials Control (spoiled goods at current disposal value): 5 × $30	$150	
Work-in-Process Control (specific job): 5 × $30		$150

The effect of this accounting is that the net cost of the normal spoilage, $350 ($500 − $150), becomes a direct cost of the 45 (50 − 5) good units produced.

Because the costs of normally spoiled units attributable to a specific job are in the Work-in-Process account, the cost of both good units and normally spoiled units will be spread over the good units, which increases the cost per unit of the good units. No journal entry is necessary for normal spoilage, except to reduce (credit) the Work-in-Process account for any disposal value of the normal spoilage.

Normal Spoilage Common to All Jobs In some cases, spoilage may be considered a normal characteristic of a given production cycle. The spoilage inherent in the process only coincidentally occurs when a specific job is being worked on. The spoilage then is not attributable, and hence is not charged, to the specific job. Instead, it is costed as manufacturing overhead. The budgeted manufacturing overhead allocation rate includes a provision for normal spoilage cost. Therefore, normal spoilage cost is spread, through overhead allocation, over all jobs rather than loaded on particular jobs only.[3]

Materials Control (spoiled goods at current disposal value): 5 × $30	$150	
Manufacturing Department Overhead Control (normal spoilage): 5 × $70	350	
Work-in-Process Control (specific job): 5 × $100		$500

[3]Note that costs *already assigned to products* are being charged back to Manufacturing Overhead Control, which generally accumulates only *costs incurred*, not both costs incurred and costs already assigned.

Abnormal Spoilage If the spoilage is abnormal, the net loss is highlighted to management by charging the loss to an abnormal loss account:

Materials Control (spoiled goods at current disposal value): 5 × $30	$150	
Loss from Abnormal Spoilage: 5 × $70	350	
Work-in-Process Control (specific job): 5 × $100		$500

REWORKED UNITS

OBJECTIVE 7

Account for reworked units

Reworked units are unacceptable units of production that are subsequently reworked into good units and sold.

Consider the Hull Machine Shop data (Example 3). Assume that the five spoiled parts used in our Hull Machine Shop illustration are reworked. The journal entry for the $500 of total costs (details of costs assumed) assigned to the five spoiled units before considering rework costs are as follows:

Work-in-Process Control	$500	
Materials Control		$200
Wages Payable		200
Manufacturing Overhead Allocated		100

Assume that rework costs equal $190 (direct materials, $40; direct labour, $100; manufacturing overhead, $50).

Normal Rework Attributable to a Specific Job If the rework is normal but occurs because of the requirements of a specific job, the rework costs are charged to that job. The journal entry is as follows:

Work-in-Process Control (specific job)	$190	
Materials Control		$ 40
Wages Payable		100
Manufacturing Overhead Allocated		50

Normal Rework Common to All Jobs When rework is normal and not attributable to any specific job, the costs of rework are charged to manufacturing overhead and spread, through overhead allocation, over all jobs.

Manufacturing Department Overhead Control (rework)	$190	
Materials Control		$ 40
Wages Payable		100
Manufacturing Overhead Allocated		50

Question: Why are both Manufacturing Overhead (MOH) Control and MOH Allocated in the same journal entry? *Answer:* MOH Control is debited because the normal rework is common to all jobs (rather than attributable to a specific job). In such cases, the additional MOH costs incurred to rework the units (such as electricity and materials handling) are spread over all jobs by including an allowance for estimated rework in the budgeted MOH (accounted for by the credit to MOH Allocated).

Abnormal Rework If the rework is abnormal, it is highlighted to management by charging abnormal rework to a separate loss account.

Loss from Abnormal Rework	$190	
Materials Control		$ 40
Wages Payable		100
Manufacturing Overhead Allocated		50

Accounting for rework in process costing only requires abnormal rework to be distinguished from normal rework. Abnormal rework is accounted for as in job costing. Since masses of similar units are manufactured, accounting for normal rework follows the accounting described for normal rework common to all jobs.

Costing rework highlights the resources wasted on activities that would not have to be undertaken if the product were made correctly. It prompts management to seek ways to reduce rework—for example, by designing new products or processes, training workers, or investing in new machines. Calculating rework costs helps management perform cost-benefit analyses for various alternatives.

To emphasize the importance of eliminating rework and to simplify the accounting, some companies expense all rework, including the costs of normal rework, as an expense of the current period.

Scrap is a product that has minimal (frequently zero) sales value compared with the sales value of the main or joint product(s).

OBJECTIVE 8

Account for scrap

There are two major aspects of accounting for scrap:

1. Planning and control, including physical tracking

2. Inventory costing, including when and how to affect operating income

Initial entries to scrap records are most often in physical or nonfinancial terms such as in kilograms or units. In various industries, items such as stamped-out metal sheets are quantified by weighing, counting, or some other expedient means. Scrap records not only help measure efficiency, but also often focus on a tempting source for theft. Scrap reports are prepared as source documents for periodic summaries of the amount of actual scrap compared with budgeted norms or standards. Scrap is either sold or disposed of quickly, or stored in some routine way for later sale, disposal, or reuse (see Concepts in Action box on p. 724).

The tracking of scrap often extends into the financial records. For example, in one survey, 60% of the companies maintained a distinct cost for scrap somewhere in their cost accounting system.[4] The issues here are similar to those discussed in Chapter 15 regarding the accounting for byproducts:

1. When should any value of scrap be recognized in the accounting records: at the time of production of scrap or at the time of sale of scrap?

2. How should revenue from scrap be accounted for?

To illustrate, we extend our Hull Machine Shop example by assuming that the manufacture of aircraft parts generates scrap. We further assume that the normal scrap from a job lot has a total sales value of $45.

Recognizing Scrap at the Time of Sale of Scrap

When scrap is sold, the simplest accounting is to regard scrap sales as a separate line item of other revenues. The journal entry is

| Sale of scrap: | Cash or Accounts Receivable | $45 | |
| | Sales of Scrap | | $45 |

Rework costs are recorded when incurred because they tend to be material in amount. Because scrap is immaterial in amount, it may not be recorded until the time of sale (rather than at the time of production).

Scrap Attributable to a Specific Job Job-costing systems sometimes trace the sales of scrap to the jobs that yielded the scrap. This method is used only when the tracing can be done in an economically feasible way. For example, the Hull Machine Shop and particular customers may reach an agreement that provides for charging specific jobs with all rework or spoilage costs and for crediting these jobs with all scrap sales that arise from them. The journal entry is

Scrap returned to storeroom:	[No journal entry. Memo of quantity received and related job is entered in the inventory record.]		
Sale of scrap:	Cash or Accounts Receivable	$45	
	Work-in-Process Control		$45
	Posting made to specific job record.		

In job costing, the cost of scrap is already in the Work-in-Process account of the job generating the scrap. If the scrap is attributable to that job, the costs are already accounted for and no journal entry is necessary. When the scrap is sold, the Work-in-Process account is decreased (credited) to reduce the cost of the job by the amount of the scrap's disposal value.

Unlike spoilage and rework, there is no cost attached to the scrap, and hence no normal or abnormal scrap. All scrap sales, whatever the amount, are credited to the specific job. Scrap sales reduce the costs of the job.

[4]Price Waterhouse, *Survey of the Cost Management Practices of Selected Midwest Manufacturers* (Cleveland: Price Waterhouse, 1989), p. 10.

Scrap Common to All Jobs   In this case,

Scrap returned to storeroom: [No journal entry. Memo of quantity received and related job is entered in the inventory record.]

This method does not link scrap with any particular physical product. Instead, all products bear regular production costs without any credit for scrap sales except in an indirect manner: The sales of scrap are considered when setting budgeted manufacturing overhead rates. Thus, the budgeted overhead rate is lower than it would be if no credit for scrap sales were allowed in the overhead budget. This accounting for scrap is used in both process-costing and job-costing systems.

CONCEPTS IN ACTION

Managing Waste and Environmental Costs at Toyota

Toyota Motor Corporation, the world's third-largest automotive manufacturer, builds and sells a wide range of vehicles under the Toyota, Lexus, and Scion brands. Toyota has done a wonderful job of reducing waste and environmental costs. Fujio Cho, Toyota's president, defines waste as "anything other than the minimum amount of equipment, materials, parts, space, and workers' time which are absolutely essential to add value to the product." Scrap, generated from wasted materials and parts, poses additional problems because of its impact on the environment. Domestic and international environmental laws dictate that scrap materials be disposed of in an environmentally friendly way; therefore, they add to the cost of generating waste.

Toyota regards environmental preservation and improvement as a top-priority management issue. The company seeks to reduce the environmental burden at every stage of a car's life cycle, from production, distribution, and use to disposal and recycling. Consistent with its corporate culture and the recommendations of the U.S. Environmental Protection Agency and Japanese Ministry of the Environment, Toyota focuses on source reduction (avoidance of waste altogether, rather than disposal and treatment of waste) as the best way to achieve profitability and environmental performance. For example, Toyota reduced the chemical solvents used to clean paint robots by 25%. Toyota and its subsidiary companies have crafted environmental-action guidelines, which include the following:

◆ develop and provide clean products with minimal environmental impact

◆ promote manufacturing that strives for zero landfill waste

◆ expand environmental management systems

◆ participate in public environmental-waste reduction efforts as a responsible corporate citizen

Thus far, the results have been remarkable. Currently, 99% of all scrap metal generated by Toyota plants is recycled; Toyota vehicles are 85% recyclable; hazardous waste has been reduced 40% since 2000; and two U.S. plants do not produce any landfill waste. Overall, these efforts resulted in more than US$38 million of cost savings during 2002. Not satisfied with these results, Toyota plans to further reduce costs by eliminating landfill waste from all plants, by reducing hazardous waste by 95%, and by achieving the highest fuel-efficiency performance in all vehicle classes by the end of 2006.

Sources: J. Newberry, "A Goal of Zero," *Cincinnati Post* (June 30, 2003); Toyota Industries Corporation. *Annual Report 2003.* (Kariya, Japan: Toyota Industries Corporation, 2004); Toyota Motor Corporation. *Environmental & Social Report 2003.* (Toyota-shi, Japan: Toyota Motor Corporation, 2003); Toyota Motor Corporation. "About Toyota: Environmental Commitment—Manufacturing—How Does Toyota Help the Environment." Toyota Motor Corporation Web site, http://www.toyota.com/about/environment/manufacturing/help_environment.html, accessed August 8, 2004; Toyota Motor Corporation. "Toyota Strives to Be a 'Solution to Pollution'—New Report Chronicles the Company's Progress in North America," press release (Long Beach, CA: November 16, 2003).

Recognizing Scrap at the Time of Production of Scrap

Our preceding illustrations assume that scrap returned to the storeroom is sold or disposed of quickly and hence not assigned an inventory cost figure. Scrap, however, sometimes has a significant market value, and the time between storing it and selling or reusing it can be quite long. Under these conditions, the company is justified in inventorying scrap at a conservative estimate of net realizable value so that production costs and related scrap recovery may be recognized in the same accounting period. Some companies tend to delay sales of scrap until the market price is most attractive. Volatile price fluctuations are typical for scrap metal. If scrap inventory becomes significant, it should be inventoried at some "reasonable value"—a difficult task in the face of volatile market prices.

Scrap Attributable to a Specific Job The journal entry in the Hull Machine Shop example is

| Scrap returned to storeroom: | Materials Control | $45 | |
| | Work-in-Process Control | | $45 |

Scrap Common to All Jobs The journal entry in this case is

| Scrap returned to storeroom: | Materials Control | $45 | |
| | Manufacturing Department Overhead Control | | $45 |

Observe that the Materials Control account is debited in place of Cash or Accounts Receivable.

When this scrap is sold, the journal entry is

| Sale of scrap: | Cash or Accounts Receivable | $45 | |
| | Materials Control | | $45 |

Scrap is sometimes reused as direct materials rather than sold as scrap. Then it should be debited to Materials Control as a class of direct materials and carried at its estimated net realizable value. For example, the entries when the scrap generated is common to all jobs are

Scrap returned to storeroom:	Materials Control	$45	
	Manufacturing Department Overhead Control		$45
Reuse of scrap:	Work-in-Process Control	$45	
	Materials Control		$45

The accounting for scrap under process costing follows the accounting for jobs when scrap is common to all jobs since process costing is used to cost the mass manufacture of similar units. The high cost of scrap focuses management's attention on ways to reduce scrap and to use it more profitably. For example, General Motors has redesigned its plastic injection moulding processes to reduce the scrap plastic that must be broken away from its moulded parts. General Motors also regrinds and reuses the plastic scrap as direct materials, saving substantial input costs.

PROBLEM FOR SELF-STUDY

Burlington Textiles has some spoiled goods that had an assigned cost of $40,000 and zero net disposal value.

REQUIRED

Prepare a journal entry for each of the following conditions under (a) process costing (Department A) and (b) job costing:

1. Abnormal spoilage of $40,000

2. Normal spoilage of $40,000 regarded as common to all operations
3. Normal spoilage of $40,000 regarded as attributable to specifications of a particular job

SOLUTION

(a) Process Costing			(b) Job Costing		
1. Loss from Abnormal Spoilage	$40,000		Loss from Abnormal Spoilage	$40,000	
Work in Process—Dept. A		$40,000	Work-in-Process Control (specific job)		$40,000
2. No entry until units are complete and transferred out then the normal spoilage costs are transferred as part of the cost of good units.			Manufacturing Overhead Control	$40,000	
			Work-in-Process Control (specific job)		$40,000
Work in Process—Dept. B	$40,000				
Work in Process—Dept. A		$40,000			
3. Not applicable			No entry. Normal spoilage cost remains in Work-in-Process Control (specific job)		

DECISION POINTS   SUMMARY

The following decision guidelines use a question-and-answer format to summarize the chapter's main points. Each decision presents a key question. The guideline is the answer to that question.

DECISIONS	GUIDELINES
1. What are spoilage, rework, and scrap?	Spoilage is units of production that do not meet the standards required by customers for good units and that are discarded or sold for reduced prices. Rework is unacceptable units that are subsequently repaired and sold as acceptable finished goods. Scrap is material left over when making a product; it has low sales value compared with the sales value of the main product.
2. What are normal and abnormal spoilage and how are they accounted for?	Normal spoilage is inherent in a particular production process and arises even under efficient operating conditions. Abnormal spoilage would not arise under efficient operating conditions. Generally, accounting systems explicitly recognize both types of spoilage when computing the number of output units. Normal spoilage is typically included in the cost of good output units; abnormal spoilage is recorded as a loss for the accounting period in which it is detected.
3. How does the weighted-average method of process costing calculate the costs of good units and spoilage?	The weighted-average method combines costs in beginning inventory with costs of the current period when determining the costs of good units (which include a normal spoilage amount) and the costs of abnormal spoilage.
4. How does the FIFO method of process costing calculate the costs of good units and spoilage?	The FIFO method keeps separate the costs in beginning inventory from the costs of the current period when determining the costs of good units (which include a normal spoilage amount) and the costs of abnormal spoilage.
5. How does the standard-costing method of process costing calculate the costs of good units and spoilage?	The standard-costing method uses standard costs to determine the costs of good units (which include a normal spoilage amount) and the costs of abnormal spoilage.
6. How do job-costing systems account for spoilage?	Normal spoilage specific to a job is assigned to that job, or if common to all jobs, it is allocated as part of manufacturing overhead. Loss from abnormal spoilage is recorded as a cost of the accounting period in which it is detected.

7. How do job-costing systems account for rework?	Completed reworked units should be indistinguishable from nonreworked good units. Normal rework can be assigned to a specific job or, if common to all jobs, as part of manufacturing overhead. Abnormal rework is written off as a cost of the accounting period in which it is detected.
8. How is scrap accounted for?	Scrap is recognized in the accounting records either at the time of its sale or at the time of its production. Sale of scrap, if immaterial, is often recognized as other revenue. If material, the sale of scrap or its net realizable value reduces the cost of a specific job or, if common to all jobs, reduces manufacturing overhead.

APPENDIX: INSPECTION AND SPOILAGE AT INTERMEDIATE STAGES OF COMPLETION IN PROCESS COSTING

Dana Corporation
www.dana.com

Consider how the timing of inspection at various stages of completion affects the amount of normal and abnormal spoilage. Assume that normal spoilage is 10% of the good units passing inspection in the Forging Department of the Dana Corporation, a manufacturer of automobile parts. Direct materials are added at the start of production in the Forging Department. Conversion costs are allocated evenly during the process.

Suppose inspection had occurred at the 20%, 50%, or 100% completion stage. A total of 8,000 units are spoiled in all cases. Note how the number of units of normal spoilage and abnormal spoilage change. Normal spoilage is computed on the number of *good units* that pass the inspection point *in the current period*. The following data are for October 2007.

	Physical Units Inspection at Stage of Completion		
Flow of Production	**at 20%**	**at 50%**	**at 100%**
Work in process, beginning (25%)[a]	11,000	11,000	11,000
Started during October	74,000	74,000	74,000
To account for	85,000	85,000	85,000
Good units completed and transferred out (85,000 − 8,000 spoiled − 16,000 ending)	61,000	61,000	61,000
Normal spoilage	6,600[b]	7,700[c]	6,100[d]
Abnormal spoilage (8,000 − normal spoilage)	1,400	300	1,900
Work in process, ending balance[a]	16,000	16,000	16,000
Accounted for	85,000	85,000	85,000

[a]Degree of completion for conversion costs of this department at the dates of the work-in-process inventories is 75%.
[b]10% × (74,000 units started − 8,000 units spoiled), since only the units started passed the 20% completion inspection point in the current period. Beginning work in process is excluded from this calculation because it is already 25% complete.
[c]10% × (85,000 units − 8,000 units spoiled), since *all* units passed the 50% completion inspection point in the current period.
[d]10% × 61,000 since 61,000 units were fully completed and inspected in the current period.

Exhibit 18-5 on page 728 shows the flow of physical units for October 2007 and illustrates the preceding normal spoilage numbers. Note that 61,000 good units are completed and transferred out (11,000 from beginning work in process and 50,000 started and completed during the period), and 16,000 units are in ending work in process.

To see the number of units passing each inspection point, focus on the vertical lines at the 20%, 50%, and 100% inspection points. Note that the vertical line at 20% cuts two horizontal lines: 50,000 good units started and completed and 16,000 units in ending work in process, for a total of 66,000 good units. (It does not cut the line representing work done on the 11,000 good units completed from beginning work in process because these units were already 25% complete at the start of the period and hence were not inspected this period.) Normal spoilage equals 10% × 66,000 = 6,600 units. Similarly, the vertical line at the 50% point cuts all three horizontal lines, indicating that 11,000 + 50,000 + 16,000 = 77,000 good units pass this point.

Normal spoilage in this case is $10\% \times 77,000 = 7,700$ units. At the 100% point, normal spoilage $= 10\% \times (11,000 + 50,000) = 6,100$ units.

The following diagram shows the computation of equivalent units assuming inspection at the 50% completion stage. The calculations depend on how much direct materials and conversion costs were incurred to get the units to the point of inspection. In the diagram, the spoiled units have a full measure of direct materials and a 50% measure of conversion costs. The computations of equivalent unit costs and the assignments of total costs to units completed and in ending work in process would be similar to those in previous illustrations. Since ending work in process has passed the inspection point in this example, these units would bear normal spoilage costs, just like the units that have been completed and transferred out.

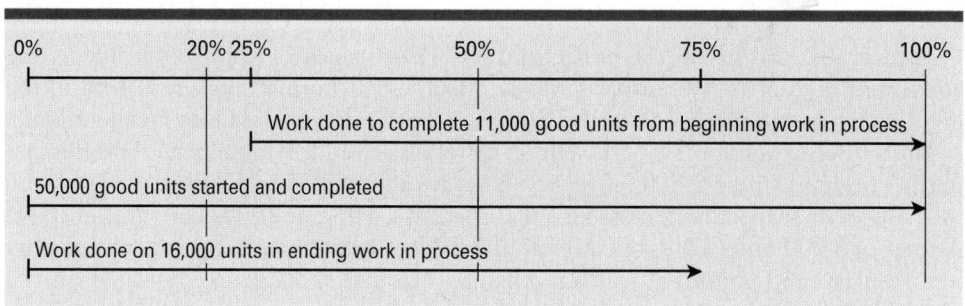

EXHIBIT 18-5

Steps 1 and 2: Computing Equivalent Units with Spoilage Using Weighted-Average Method of Process Costing with Inspection at 50% of Completion for Forging Department of the Dana Corporation for October 2007

| | | | (Step 2) Equivalent Units | |
| | | (Step 1) | | |
Flow of Production	Physical Units	Direct Materials	Conversion Costs
Work in process, beginning[a]	11,000		
Started during current period	74,000		
To account for	85,000		
Good units completed and transferred out	61,000	61,000	61,000
Normal spoilage	7,700		
$(7,700 \times 100\%; 7,700 \times 50\%)$		7,700	3,850
Abnormal spoilage	300		
$(300 \times 100\%; 300 \times 50\%)$		300	150
Work in process, ending[b]	16,000		
$(16,000 \times 100\%; 16,000 \times 75\%)$		16,000	12,000
Accounted for	85,000		
Total work done to date		85,000	77,000

[a]Degree of completion: direct materials, 100%; conversion costs, 25%.
[b]Degree of completion: direct materials, 100%; conversion costs, 75%.

▼ TERMS TO LEARN

This chapter contains definitions of the following important terms:

abnormal spoilage (p. 710)
inspection point (p. 712)
normal spoilage (p. 710)

reworked units (p. 710)
scrap (p. 710)
spoilage (p. 710)

QUESTIONS

18-1 Why is there an unmistakable trend in manufacturing to improve quality?

18-2 Distinguish among spoilage, reworked units, and scrap.

18-3 "Normal spoilage is planned spoilage." Discuss.

18-4 "Costs of abnormal spoilage are losses." Explain.

18-5 "What has been regarded as normal spoilage in the past is not necessarily acceptable as normal spoilage in the present or future." Explain.

18-6 "Units of abnormal spoilage are inferred rather than identified." Explain.

18-7 "In accounting for spoiled goods, we are dealing with cost assignment rather than cost incurrence." Explain.

18-8 "Total input includes abnormal as well as normal spoilage and is therefore irrational as a basis for computing normal spoilage." Do you agree? Why?

18-9 "The point of inspection is the key to the allocation of spoilage costs." Do you agree? Explain.

18-10 "The unit cost of normal spoilage is the same as the unit cost of abnormal spoilage." Do you agree? Explain.

18-11 "In job costing, the costs of normal spoilage that occur while a specific job is being done are charged to the specific job." Do you agree? Explain.

18-12 "The costs of reworking defective units are always charged to the specific jobs where the defects were originally discovered." Do you agree? Explain.

18-13 "Abnormal rework costs should be charged to a loss account, not to manufacturing overhead." Do you agree? Explain.

18-14 When is a company justified in inventorying scrap?

18-15 How do company managements use information about scrap?

EXERCISES

18-16 Weighted-average method, spoilage. Superchip specializes in the manufacture of microchips for aircraft. Direct materials are added at the start of the production process. Conversion costs are added evenly during the process. Some units of this product are spoiled as a result of defects not detectable before inspection of finished goods. Normally, the spoiled units are 15% of the good units transferred out. Spoiled units are disposed of at zero net disposal price.

Superchip uses the weighted-average method of process costing. Summary data for September 2007 are

	Physical Units (Microchips)	Direct Materials	Conversion Costs
Work in process, September 1*	400	$ 76,800	$ 12,240
Started in September 2007	1,700		
Good units completed and transferred out during September 2007	1,400		
Work in process, September 30†	300		
Costs added during September 2007		$453,600	$184,320

*Degree of completion: direct materials, 100%; conversion costs, 30%.

†Degree of completion: direct materials, 100%; conversion costs, 40%.

REQUIRED

1. For each cost element, compute the equivalent units. Show physical units in the first column.

2. For each cost element, calculate the cost per equivalent unit.

3. Summarize the total costs to account for, and assign these costs to units completed and transferred out (to normal spoilage), to abnormal spoilage, and to units in ending work in process.

18-17 FIFO method, spoilage. Refer to the information in Exercise 18-16.

REQUIRED
Do Exercise 18-16 using the FIFO method of process costing.

Excel Application For students who wish to practise their spreadsheet skills, the following is a step-by-step approach to creating an Excel spreadsheet to work this problem.

Step-by-Step
1. Open a new spreadsheet. At the top, create an "Original Data" section for the Assembly Department data provided by Superchip. Enter the data for "Physical Units, Direct Materials," and "Conversion Costs" in exactly the same format as above.

   (Program your spreadsheet to perform all necessary calculations. Do not "hard-code" any amounts—such as equivalent-unit costs—requiring addition, subtraction, multiplication, or division operations.)
2. Skip two rows and create a section, "Problem 1," in the same format as in Panel A of Exhibit 18-3 (p. 717). Create columns for "Physical Units, Equivalent Units of Direct Materials and Equivalent Units of Conversion Costs" and rows for each of the items shown in Exhibit 18-3 (that is, the first row will be "Work in Process, Beginning" and the last row will be "Work Done in Current Period Only"). Use the data from your Original Data section to complete this section.
3. Skip two rows and create a section, "Problem 2," in the same format as Step 3 of Exhibit 18-3, Panel B. Create columns for "Total Production Costs," "Direct Materials, and Conversion Costs."
4. Next, enter a calculation for the "Cost per Equivalent Unit of Work Done in the Current Period" for Direct Materials and Conversion Costs.
5. Skip two rows and create a section, "Problem 3," in the same format as Steps 4 and 5 of Exhibit 18-3, Panel B (using columns for "Total Production Costs," "Direct Materials," and "Conversion Costs" created in Step 3).
6. Use the data you created in steps 1 to 4 to complete your "Problem 3" section.

18-18 Standard costing method, spoilage. Refer to the information in Exercise 18-16. Suppose Superchip determines standard costs of $246 per (equivalent) unit for direct materials and $96 per (equivalent) unit for conversion costs for both beginning work in process and work done in the current period.

REQUIRED
Do Exercise 18-16 using standard costs.

18-19 Spoilage and job costing. (L. Bamber) Bamber Kitchens produces a variety of items in accordance with special job orders from hospitals, plant cafeterias, and university dormitories. An order for 2,500 cases of mixed vegetables costs $7.20 per case: direct materials, $3.60; direct manufacturing labour, $2.40; and manufacturing overhead allocated, $1.20. The manufacturing overhead rate includes a provision for normal spoilage. Consider each requirement independently.

REQUIRED
1. Assume that a labourer dropped 200 cases. Suppose that part of the 200 cases could be sold to a nearby prison for $240 cash. Prepare a journal entry to record this event. Calculate and explain briefly the unit cost of the remaining 2,300 cases.
2. Refer to the original data. Tasters at the company reject 200 of the 2,500 cases. The 200 cases are disposed of for $480. Assume that this rejection rate is considered normal. Prepare a journal entry to record this event, and calculate the unit cost if
   a. The rejection is attributable to exacting specifications of this particular job.
   b. The rejection is characteristic of the production process and is not attributable to this specific job.
   c. Are unit costs the same in requirements 2(a) and 2(b)? Explain your reasoning briefly.
3. Refer to the original data. Tasters rejected 200 cases that had insufficient salt. The product can be placed in a vat, salt added, and reprocessed into jars. This operation, which is considered normal, will cost $240. Prepare a journal entry to record this event, and calculate the unit cost of all the cases if:
   a. This additional cost was incurred because of the exacting specifications of this particular job.
   b. This additional cost occurs regularly because of difficulty in seasoning.
   c. Are unit costs the same in requirements 3(a) and 3(b)? Explain your reasoning briefly.

18-20 Normal and abnormal spoilage in units. The following data, in physical units, describe a grinding process for January:

Work in process, beginning	22,800
Started during current period	180,000
To account for	202,800
Spoiled units	14,400
Good units completed and transferred out	158,400
Work in process, ending	30,000
Accounted for	202,800

Inspection occurs at the 100% completion stage. Normal spoilage is 5% of the good units passing inspection.

REQUIRED
1. Compute the normal and abnormal spoilage in units.
2. Assume that the equivalent unit cost of a spoiled unit is $12. Compute the amount of potential savings if all spoilage were eliminated, assuming that all other costs would be unaffected. Comment on your answer.

18-21 Weighted-average method, spoilage. Anderson Plastics makes plastic rear lamps for cars using an injection moulding process. Spoiled units are detected upon inspection at the end of the process and are disposed of at zero net disposal price. Assume normal spoilage is 15% of the good output produced. Anderson Plastics uses the weighted-average method of process costing. The following information about actual costs for April 2007 is available.

	Direct Materials		Conversion Costs	
	Equivalent Units	Total Costs	Equivalent Units	Total Costs
Work in process, April 1 (15,000 units)	15,000	$144,000	14,000	$168,000
Work done during April 2007	25,000	252,000	28,000	361,200
To account for	40,000	$396,000	42,000	$529,200
Good units completed and transferred out during April 2007	20,000	?	20,000	?
Normal and abnormal spoilage	4,000		4,000	
Work in process, April 30 (20,000 units)	16,000	?	18,000	?

REQUIRED
1. Calculate the cost per equivalent unit of beginning work in process and of work done in the current period for direct materials and conversion costs.
2. Summarize total costs to account for, and assign these costs to units completed (and transferred out), normal spoilage, abnormal spoilage, and ending work in process using the weighted-average method.
3. What is the cost of a good unit completed and transferred out under the weighted-average method?

18-22 FIFO method. Refer to the information in Exercise 18-21.

REQUIRED
Do Exercise 18-21 using the FIFO method.

18-23 Standard-costing method. Refer to the information in Exercise 18-21. Suppose Anderson determines standard costs of $9.84 per (equivalent) unit for direct materials and $12.24 per (equivalent) unit for conversion costs for both beginning work in process and work done in the current period.

REQUIRED
Do Exercise 18-21 using the standard-costing method.

18-24 Equivalent units, equivalent unit costs, spoilage. (CMA, adapted) Consider the following data for November 2007 from the Grey Manufacturing Company, which makes silk pennants and operates a process-costing system. All direct materials are added at the beginning of the process and conversion costs are added evenly during the process. Spoilage is detected upon inspection at the completion of the process. Spoiled units are disposed of at zero net disposal price.

	Physical Units (Pennants)	Direct Materials	Conversion Costs
Work in process, November 1*	1,000	$ 1,560	$ 1,500
Started in November 2007	?		
Good units completed and transferred out during November 2007	9,000		
Normal spoilage	100		
Abnormal spoilage	50		
Work in process, November 30†	2,000		
Costs added during November 2007		$14,616	$33,300

*Degree of completion: direct materials, 100%; conversion costs, 50%.
†Degree of completion: direct materials, 100%; conversion costs, 30%.

REQUIRED
1. Compute the equivalent units of work done in the current period for direct materials and conversion costs. Show physical units in the first column.
2. Calculate the cost per equivalent unit for direct materials and conversion costs.

18-25 **Weighted-average method, assigning costs (continuation of 18-24).**

REQUIRED
For the data in Exercise 18-24, summarize total costs to account for, and assign these costs to units completed (and transferred out), normal spoilage, abnormal spoilage, and to units in ending work in process.

18-26 **FIFO method, spoilage, equivalent units and unit costs.** Refer to the information in Exercise 18-24. Suppose Grey Manufacturing Company uses the FIFO method of process costing instead of the weighted-average method.

REQUIRED
1. Compute equivalent units for direct materials and conversion costs. Show physical units in the first column of your schedule.
2. Calculate cost per equivalent unit for direct materials and conversion costs.

18-27 **FIFO method, assigning costs (continuation of 18-26).**

REQUIRED
For the data in Exercise 18-24, use the FIFO method to summarize total costs to account for, and assign these costs to units completed and transferred out, normal spoilage, abnormal spoilage, and to units in ending work in process.

18-28 **Reworked units, costs of rework.** White Goods assembles washing machines at its Cambridge plant. In February 2007, 60 tumbler units that cost $52.80 each from a new supplier were defective and had to be disposed of at zero disposal price. That new supplier is now bankrupt. White Goods was able to rework all 60 washing machines by substituting new tumbler units purchased from one of its existing suppliers. Each replacement tumbler cost $60.

REQUIRED
1. What alternative approaches are there to account for the materials costs of reworked units?
2. Should White Goods use the $52.80 or $60 amount as the costs of materials reworked? Explain.
3. What other costs might White Goods include in its analysis of the total costs of rework due to the tumbler units purchased from the (now) bankrupt supplier?

18-29 **Scrap, job order costing.** The Mendoza Company has an extensive job-costing facility that uses a variety of metals. Consider each requirement independently.

REQUIRED
1. Job 372 uses a particular metal alloy that is not used for any other job. Assume that scrap is accounted for at the time of sale of scrap. The scrap is sold for $588. Prepare the journal entry.
2. The scrap from Job 372 consists of a metal used by many other jobs. No record is maintained of the scrap generated by individual jobs. Assume that scrap is accounted for at the time of its sale. Scrap totalling $4,800 is sold. Prepare two journal entries that could be used to account for the sale of scrap.
3. Suppose the scrap generated in requirement 2 is returned to the storeroom for future use and a journal entry is made to record the scrap. A month later, the scrap is reused as direct material on a subsequent job. Prepare the journal entries to record these transactions.

PROBLEMS

18-30 Weighted-average method, spoilage. Wang Manufacturing Company uses the weighted-average method of process costing. All direct materials are added at the beginning of the process, and conversion costs are added evenly during the process. Spoiled units are detected upon inspection at the end of the process and are disposed of at zero net disposal value. Summary data for March 2007 are

	Physical Units	Direct Materials	Conversion Costs
Work in process, March 1[a]	30,000	$288,000	$216,000
Started in March 2007	50,000		
Good units completed and transferred out during March 2008	40,000		
Normal spoilage	6,000		
Abnormal spoilage	2,000		
Work in process, March 31[b]	32,000		
Costs added during March 2008		$504,000	$699,840

[a]Degree of completion: direct materials, 100%; conversion costs, 60%.
[b]Degree of completion: direct materials, 100%; conversion costs, 75%.

1. For each cost category, compute equivalent units. Show physical units in the first column of your schedule.
2. For each cost category, calculate cost per equivalent unit.
3. Summarize total costs to account for, and assign these costs to units completed and transferred out (including normal spoilage), to abnormal spoilage, and to units in ending work in process.

18-31 FIFO method, spoilage. Refer to the information in 18-30.

Do Exercise 18-30 using the FIFO method. Note that you first need to calculate the equivalent units of work done in the current period (for direct materials and conversion costs) to complete beginning work in process, to start and complete new units, for normal and abnormal spoilage units, and to produce ending work in process.

18-32 Standard-costing method, spoilage. Refer to the information in Exercise 18-30. Suppose Wang determines standard costs of $9.60 per equivalent unit for direct materials and $12.00 per equivalent unit for conversion costs for both beginning work in process and work done in the current period.

Do Exercise 18-30 using the standard-costing method. Note that you first need to calculate the equivalent units of work done in the current period (for direct materials and conversion costs) to complete beginning work in process, to start and complete new units, for normal and abnormal spoilage units, and to produce ending work in process.

18-33 Weighted-average method, spoilage. The Alston Company operates under a weighted-average method of process costing. It has two departments, Cleaning and Milling. For both departments, conversion costs are added uniformly throughout the processes. Direct materials are added at the beginning of the process in the Cleaning Department, and additional direct materials are added at the end of the milling process. The costs and unit production statistics for May follow. All unfinished work at the end of May is 25% completed as to conversion costs. The beginning inventory (May 1) was 80% completed as to conversion costs as of May 1. All completed work is transferred to the next department.

	Cleaning	Milling
Beginning Inventories		
Cleaning: $1,200 direct materials, $960 conversion costs	$ 2,160	
Milling: $7,740 previous department cost (transferred-in cost) and $2,940 conversion costs		$10,680
Costs Added during Current Period		
Direct materials	$10,800	$ 768
Conversion costs	$ 9,600	$ 5,940

Physical Units

Units in beginning inventory	1,000	3,000
Units started this month	9,000	7,400
Good units completed and transferred out	7,400	6,000
Normal spoilage	740*	300†
Abnormal spoilage	260	100

*Normal spoilage in the Cleaning Department is 10% of good units completed and transferred out.
†Normal spoilage in the Milling Department is 5% of good units completed and transferred out.

ADDITIONAL INFORMATION

1. Spoilage is assumed to occur at the end of each of the two processes when the units are inspected. Spoiled units are disposed of at zero net disposal price.
2. Assume that there is no shrinkage, evaporation, or abnormal spoilage other than that indicated in the information given.
3. Carry unit cost calculations to three decimal places where necessary. Calculate final totals to the nearest dollar.

REQUIRED

Using the weighted-average method, summarize total costs to account for, and assign these costs to units completed (and transferred out), normal spoilage, abnormal spoilage, and to units in ending work in process for the Cleaning Department. (Problem 18-35 explores additional facets of this problem.)

18-34 FIFO method, spoilage. Refer to the information in Problem 18-33.

REQUIRED

Do Problem 18-33 using the FIFO method of process costing. (Problem 18-36 explores additional facets of this problem.)

18-35 Weighted-average method, Milling Department (continuation of 18-33). Refer to the information in Problem 18-33.

REQUIRED

Summarize total costs to account for, and assign these costs to units completed (and transferred out), normal spoilage, abnormal spoilage, and ending work in process for the Milling Department. The cost of goods transferred in during May was $19,536.

18-36 FIFO method, Milling Department (continuation of 18-34). Refer to the information in Problem 18-33.

REQUIRED

Use the FIFO method to summarize total costs to account for, and assign these costs to units completed (and transferred out), normal spoilage, abnormal spoilage, and ending work in process for the Milling Department. The cost of goods transfered in during May was $19,536.

18-37 Job cost spoilage and scrap. (F. Mayne) Canadian Metal Fabricators, Ltd., has a large job, No. 2734, that calls for producing various ore bins, chutes, and metal boxes for enlarging a copper concentrator. The following charges were made to the job in November 2007:

Direct materials	$32,341
Direct manufacturing labour	18,091
Manufacturing overhead	9,046

The contract with the customer called for the total price to be based on a cost-plus approach. The contract defined cost to include direct materials, direct manufacturing labour costs, and manufacturing overhead to be allocated at 50% of direct manufacturing labour costs. The contract also provided that the total costs of all work spoiled were to be removed from the billable cost of the job and that the benefits from scrap sales were to reduce the billable cost of the job.

REQUIRED

1. In accordance with the stated terms of the contract, prepare journal entries for the following two items:
   a. A cutting error was made in production. The up-to-date job cost record for the batch of work involved showed materials of $780, direct manufacturing labour of $600, and allocated overhead of $300. Because fairly large pieces of metal were recoverable, the company believed that the scrap value was $720 and that the materials recovered could be used on other jobs. The spoiled work was sent to the warehouse.

b. Small pieces of metal cuttings and scrap in November 2007 amounted to $1,500, which was the price quoted by a scrap dealer. No journal entries have been made with regard to the scrap until the price was quoted by the scrap dealer. The scrap dealer's offer was immediately accepted.

2. Consider normal and abnormal spoilage. Suppose the contract described above had contained the clause "a normal spoilage allowance of 1% of the job costs will be included in the billable costs of the job."

a. Is this clause specific enough to define exactly how much spoilage is normal and how much is abnormal? Explain. Total spoilage is $960.

b. Repeat requirement 1(a) with this "normal spoilage of 1%" clause in mind. You should be able to provide two slightly different journal entries.

18-38 Job costing, rework. The Bristol Corporation manufactures two brands of motors, SM-5 and RW-8. The costs of manufacturing each SM-5 motor, excluding rework costs, are direct materials, $360; direct manufacturing labour, $72; and manufacturing overhead, $228. Defective units are sent to a separate rework area. Rework costs per SM-5 motor are direct materials, $72; direct manufacturing labour, $54; and manufacturing overhead, $90.

In February 2007, Bristol manufactured 1,000 SM-5 and 500 RW-8 motors, and 80 of the SM-5 motors required rework. Bristol classifies 50 of these motors as normal rework for SM-5 and RW-8, and not specifically attributable to SM-5. None of the RW-8 motors required rework. Bristol allocates manufacturing overhead on the basis of machine-hours required to manufacture SM-5 and RW-8. Each SM-5 and RW-8 motor requires the same number of machine-hours.

REQUIRED

1. Prepare journal entries to record the accounting for rework.
2. What were the total rework costs for SM-5 motors in February 2007?

18-39 Job costing, scrap. The Wong Corporation makes two different types of hubcaps for cars—models HM3 and JB4. Circular pieces of metal are stamped out of steel sheets (leaving the edges as scrap), formed, and finished. The stamping operation is identical for both types of hubcaps. During March, Wong manufactured 20,000 units of HM3 and 10,000 units of JB4. In March, manufacturing costs per unit of HM3 and JB4 before accounting for the scrap are as follows:

	HM3	JB4
Direct materials	$12.00	$18.00
Direct manufacturing labour	3.60	4.80
Materials-related manufacturing overhead (materials-handling, storage, etc.)	2.40	3.60
Other manufacturing overhead	7.20	9.60
Unit manufacturing costs	$25.20	$36.00

Materials-related manufacturing costs are allocated to products at 20% of direct materials costs. Other manufacturing overhead is allocated to products at 200% of direct manufacturing labour costs. Since the same metal sheets are used to make both types of hubcaps, Wong maintains no records of the scrap generated by the individual products. Scrap generated during manufacturing is accounted for at the time it is returned to the storeroom as an offset to materials-related manufacturing overhead. The value of scrap generated during March and returned to the storeroom was $8,400.

REQUIRED

1. Prepare a journal entry to summarize the accounting for scrap during March.
2. Suppose the scrap generated in March was sold in April for $8,400. Prepare a journal entry to account for this transaction.
3. What adjustments, if any, would you make for scrap when calculating the manufacturing cost per unit for HM3 and JB4 in March? Explain.

18-40 Physical units, inspection at various stages of completion. (Chapter Appendix) Normal spoilage is 8% of the good units passing inspection in a forging process. In March, a total of 10,000 units were spoiled. Other data include units started during March, 120,000; work in process, beginning, 14,000 units (23% completed for conversion costs); work in process, ending, 11,000 units (69% completed for conversion costs).

REQUIRED

In columnar form, compute the normal and abnormal spoilage in units, assuming inspection at 15%, 40%, and 100% stages of completion.

18-41 Weighted-average, inspection at 80% completion. (A. Atkinson) (Chapter Appendix) Ottawa Manufacturing produces a plastic toy in a two-stage manufacturing operation.

The company uses a weighted-average process costing system. During June, the following data were recorded for the Finishing Department:

Units of beginning inventory	10,000
Percentage of beginning units completed	25%
Cost of direct materials in beginning work in process	$0
Units started	70,000
Units completed	50,000
Units in ending inventory	20,000
Percentage of ending units completed	95%
Spoiled units	10,000
Costs added during current period:	
Direct materials	$786,240
Direct manufacturing labour	$762,720
Manufacturing overhead	$739,200
Work in process, beginning:	
Conversion costs	$ 50,400
Transferred-in costs	$ 99,480
Cost of units transferred in during current period	$777,000

Conversion costs are incurred evenly throughout the process. Direct materials costs are incurred when production is 90% complete. Inspection occurs when production is 80% complete. Normal spoilage is 10% of all good units that pass inspection. Spoiled units are disposed of at zero net disposal price.

REQUIRED

For June, summarize total costs to account for, and assign these costs to units completed (and transferred out), normal spoilage, abnormal spoilage, and ending work in process.

18-42 **Job costing, spoilage ethics.** (CMA, adapted) The Richport Company manufactures products that often require specification changes or modifications to meet its customers' needs. Still, Richport has been able to establish a normal spoilage rate of 2.5% of normal input. Normal spoilage is recognized during the budgeting process and classified as a component of manufacturing overhead when determining the overhead rate.

Rose Duncan, one of Richport's inspection managers, obtains the following information for Job No. N1192–122 that was recently completed. A total of 122,000 units were started, and 5,000 units were rejected at final inspection yielding 117,000 good units. Duncan noted that 900 of the first units produced were rejected because of a design defect that was considered very unusual; this defect was corrected immediately, and no further units were rejected for this reason. These units were disposed of after incurring an additional cost of $1,440. Duncan was unable to identify a rejection pattern for the remaining 4,100 rejected units. These units can be sold at $8.40 per unit.

The total costs for all 122,000 units of Job No. N1192–122 are presented here. The job has been completed, but the costs have yet to be transferred to finished goods.

Direct materials	$2,635,200
Direct manufacturing labour	2,196,000
Manufacturing overhead	3,513,600
Total manufacturing costs	$8,344,800

REQUIRED

1. Calculate the unit quantities of normal and abnormal spoilage.
2. Prepare the appropriate journal entry (or entries) to properly account for Job No. N1192–122 including spoilage, disposal, and transfer of costs to finished goods control.
3. Richport Company has small profit margins and is anticipating very low operating income for the year. The controller, Thomas Rutherford, tells Martha Gonzales, the management accountant responsible for Job No. N1192–122, the following: "This was an unusual job. I think all 5,000 spoiled units should be considered normal." Martha knows that similar jobs had been done in the past and that the spoilage levels for Job N1192–122 were much greater than in the past. She feels Thomas made these comments because he wants to show higher operating income for the year.
   a. Prepare the journal entry (or entries), similar to the journal entry (or entries) prepared in requirement 2, to account for Job No. N1192–122 if all spoilage were considered normal. By how much will Richport's operating income be affected if all spoilage is considered normal?
   b. What should Martha Gonzales do?

COLLABORATIVE LEARNING PROBLEM

18-43 FIFO method, spoilage, working backward. The Cooking Department of Spicer Inc. uses a process-costing system. Direct materials are added at the beginning of the cooking process. Conversion costs are added evenly during the cooking process. Consider the following data for the Cooking Department of Spicer Inc. for January:

	Physical Units	Direct Materials	Conversion Costs
Work in process, January 1*	10,000	$ 264,000	$ 36,000
Started in January	74,000		
Good units completed and transferred out during January	61,000		
Spoiled units	8,000		
Work in process, January 31†	15,000		
Costs added during January		$1,776,000	$1,130,400
Cost per equivalent unit of work done in January		$ 24	$ 14.40

*Degree of completion: direct materials, 100%; conversion costs, 25%
†Degree of completion: WIP ending; direct materials 100%; conversion cost 80%

Spicer uses the FIFO method of process costing. Inspection occurs when production is 100% completed. Normal spoilage is 11% of good units completed and transferred out during the current period.

INSTRUCTION

Form pairs of students to complete the following requirements.

REQUIRED

1. For each cost category, compute equivalent units of work done in the current period (January).
2. For each cost category, compute equivalent units of work done to complete beginning work-in-process inventory, to start and complete new units, for normal and abnormal spoilage units, and to produce ending work-in-process inventory.
3. For each cost category, calculate the percentage of completion of ending work-in-process inventory.
4. Summarize total costs to account for, and assign these costs to units completed (and transferred out), normal spoilage, abnormal spoilage, and ending work in process.

Defective components can cause dramatic consequences. One flawed component used in computers that control engines caused a space shuttle engine to shut down 1.5 seconds into its ignition sequence. After an extensive investigation, approximately 1,600 components were purged from the controllers.

This defect was discovered during a firing test and did not present an on-board safety threat because the shuttle was empty for this test. Meticulous testing of the entire engine-firing process revealed a flaw that had never before been detected. One result was the creation of new manufacturing standards and testing procedures to avoid future defects of this type.

CHAPTER

19

Cost Management: Quality, Time, and the Theory of Constraints

LEARNING OBJECTIVES

After studying this chapter, you should be able to

1. Explain four cost categories in a cost of quality program

2. Provide examples of nonfinancial quality measures of customer satisfaction and internal performance

3. Apply three methods that companies use to identify quality problems

4. Identify the relevant costs and benefits of quality improvements

5. Describe the benefits of financial and nonfinancial measures of quality

6. Describe customer response time, and explain the reasons for and the cost of lines and delays

7. Apply three main measurements in the theory of constraints

8. Explain four steps in managing bottlenecks

Global competition and increasing customer intolerance for long wait times and poor quality means managers must work hard to remove obstructions to achieving on-time deliveries and satisfactory standards of quality. This chapter examines how management accounting information assists managers to take the initiative in the quality and time areas, and to improve the decisions they must make when faced with many constraints. Chapter 19 expands on the discussion of the balanced scorecard, introduced in Chapter 13. The balanced scorecard is a set of performance measures that provide a framework for implementing an organization's mission and strategy. The focus will be on those measures that relate to using quality, time, and increased throughput to satisfy customers and gain competitive advantage.

This chapter is presented in three parts. Part One is *Quality as a Competitive Tool*, Part Two is *Time as a Competitive Tool*, and Part Three is *Theory of Constraints and Throughput Contribution Analysis*.

PART ONE

QUALITY AS A COMPETITIVE TOOL

Many companies throughout the world—for example, Cisco systems, Motorola, and SNC Lavalin in North America; British Telecom in the United Kingdom; Fujitsu and Toyota in Japan; Crysel in Mexico; and Samsung in Korea—view quality management as one of the most important strategies for success, because it reduces costs and increases customer satisfaction. Several prestigious, high-profile awards—for example, the Malcolm Baldrige Quality Award in North America, the Deming Prize in Japan, and the Premio Nacional de Calidad in Mexico—have been instituted to recognize exceptional quality.

SNC Lavalin
www.snclavalin.com/en/
6_0/6_10.aspx

British Telecom
www.bt.com

International quality standards have emerged. For example, ISO 9001, developed by the International Organization for Standardization, is a set of 20 international standards for quality management and assurance adopted by more than 85 countries. ISO 9001 was created to enable companies to effectively document and certify their quality system elements. Companies such as DuPont and General Electric require suppliers to obtain ISO 9001 certification as a method to reduce their own costs by evaluating, assessing, and working to improve the quality of their suppliers' products. Thus, certification and an emphasis on quality are rapidly becoming conditions for competing in the global market.

Quality improvement programs often result in substantial savings and higher revenues. At Dell Computer, quality initiatives, which have increased customer satisfaction, have also fuelled its 1,912% increase in revenues, 1,884% increase in profits, and 8,015% increase in stock price over the 10 years ending September 2003. Sometimes, the benefit of better quality is preserving revenues, not generating higher revenues. If competitors are improving quality, then a company that does not invest in quality improvement will likely suffer a decline in its market share, revenues, and profits.

As corporations accept increasing responsibility to improve and maintain the environment, they have developed formal monitoring and attention-directing methods to report on environmental quality. For example, Canada is one of 38 industrialized countries to sign the Kyoto Protocol and make the commitment to reduce greenhouse gas emissions from all sources to achieve levels below those recorded in 1990. Both socially and legally, managers must address environmental quality control problems such as air pollution, waste water, oil and chemical spills, hazardous waste, and waste management. The costs of environmental damage (failure costs) can be extremely high to corporations under environmental legislation. Companies can be charged multi-million-dollar fines.

The Standards Council of Canada issues accreditation to companies meeting the ISO14001–2004 standards of environmental management. This ISO standard describes principles and frameworks for (1) environmental management systems to improve the environmental impact of an organization's activities, products, and services and (2) environmental auditing and performance evaluation systems to review and provide feedback on how well an organization has achieved its environmental goals.

The term *quality* refers to a wide variety of factors—fitness for use, the degree to which a product satisfies the needs of a customer, and the degree to which a product conforms to design specification and engineering requirements. We discuss two basic aspects of quality—*quality of design* and **conformance quality.**

Quality of design measures how closely the characteristics of products or services match the needs and wants of customers. Suppose customers of photocopying machines want copiers that combine copying, faxing, scanning, and electronic printing. Photocopying machines that fail to meet these customer needs fail in the quality of their design. Similarly, if customers of a bank want an automated payment system for their monthly bills, not providing this facility would be a quality of design failure.

Conformance quality is the performance of a product or service according to design and production specifications. For example, if a photocopying machine

Conformance quality. The performance of a product or service according to design and production specifications.

mishandles paper or breaks down, it will have failed to satisfy conformance quality. Products not conforming to specifications must be repaired, reworked, or scrapped at an additional cost to the organization. If nonconformance errors are not corrected within the plant and the product breaks down at the customer site, even greater repair costs as well as the loss of customer goodwill—often the highest quality cost of all—may result. In the banking industry, depositing a customer's cheque into the wrong bank account is an example of conformance quality failure. To travel the road from actual performance to customer satisfaction, companies must meet design specifications through conformance quality, but they must also design products to satisfy customers through quality of design.

The following diagram illustrates our framework:

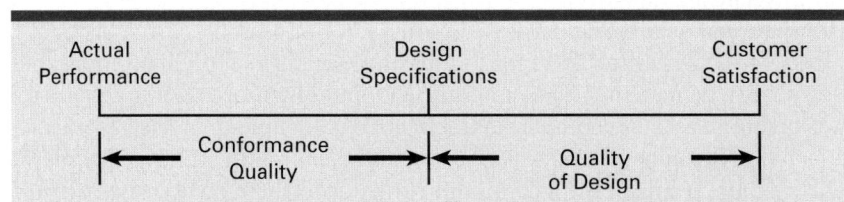

Within this framework are the tasks of managing quality such as identifying quality problems, estimating the costs of quality failures, and estimating the costs of different actions taken to improve quality. We use the Photon Corporation as an example. Photon makes many products. Our presentation focuses on Photon's photocopying machines, which earned an operating income of $24 million on sales of $300 million (20,000 copiers) in 2007.

In Chapter 13, four perspectives from the balanced scorecard were introduced: financial, customer, internal business process, and learning and growth. This discussion begins with financial measures of quality, in particular the costs of conformance quality. This is an internal business process of quality control. The financial costs of poor design quality are primarily the opportunity costs of future lost sales if Photon fails to design a product that meets its customers' demands at a price they are willing to pay. Objective measures of opportunity costs, of something that does not occur, are notoriously difficult, which is why Photon highlights the customer perspective when estimating its opportunity costs.

THE FINANCIAL PERSPECTIVE: COSTS OF QUALITY

The financial perspective of Photon's balanced scorecard includes measures such as revenue growth and operating income—financial measures that are likely to be affected by quality improvement programs. In addition, Photon measures costs of quality. The **costs of quality (COQ)** are costs incurred to prevent or rectify the production of a low-quality product. These costs focus on conformance quality and are incurred in all areas of the value chain. They are classified into four categories:

1. **Prevention costs.** Costs incurred to preclude the production of products that do not conform to specifications

2. **Appraisal costs.** Costs incurred to detect which of the individual units of products do not conform to specifications

3. **Internal failure costs.** Costs incurred to detect a nonconforming product before it is shipped to customers

4. **External failure costs.** Costs incurred to detect a nonconforming product after it is shipped to customers

Exhibit 19-1 presents examples of individual cost of quality items in each of these four categories reported on COQ reports.

EXHIBIT 19-1
Items Pertaining to Cost-of-Quality Reports

Prevention Costs	Appraisal Costs	Internal Failure Costs	External Failure Costs
Design engineering	Inspection	Spoilage	Customer support
Process engineering	Online product manufacturing and process inspection	Rework	Manufacturing/process engineering for external failures
Supplier evaluations		Scrap	
Preventive equipment maintenance	Product testing	Machine repairs	Warranty repair costs
Quality training		Manufacturing/process engineering on internal failures	Liability claims
Testing of new materials			

The items in Exhibit 19-1 are all derived from the business functions comprising the value chain and expand on the internal failure costs of spoilage, rework, and scrap described in Chapters 15 and 18. Photon determines the costs of quality of its photocopying machines using the seven-step activity-based costing approach described in Chapter 5.

◆ **Step 1:** *Identify the chosen cost object(s).* The cost object is the 20,000 photocopying machines that Photon makes. Photon's goal is to calculate the total costs of quality of these machines.

◆ **Step 2:** *Identify the direct costs of quality of the product.* The photocopying machines have no direct costs of quality.

◆ **Step 3:** *Select the cost-allocation bases to use for allocating indirect costs of quality to the product.* Column 1 of Exhibit 19-2, Panel A, on page 742 classifies activities that result in prevention, appraisal, internal failure, and external failure costs and indicates the value-chain business functions in which the costs occur. For example, the inspection activity results in appraisal costs and occurs in the manufacturing function. Photon chooses the number of inspection hours rather than the number of inspections as the cost-allocation base for the inspection activity because inspection-hours has a better cause-and-effect relationship with inspection costs. To avoid details, we do not provide information on the total quantities of each of these cost-allocation bases used in all of Photon's operations and businesses.

◆ **Step 4:** *Identify the indirect costs of quality associated with each cost-allocation base.* These are the total costs (fixed and variable) incurred on each of the costs of quality activities, such as inspections, in all of Photon's operations. To avoid irrelevant details, we do not provide information about these total costs.

◆ **Step 5:** *Compute the rate per unit of each cost-allocation base used to allocate indirect costs of quality to products.* For each activity, the total costs calculated in Step 4 are divided by the total quantity of the cost-allocation base calculated in Step 3 to compute the rate per unit for each cost-allocation base. Column 2 of Exhibit 19-2, Panel A, shows these rates (without supporting calculations).

◆ **Step 6:** *Compute the indirect costs of quality allocated to the product.* Photon first determines the quantities of each of the cost-allocation bases used by the photocopying machines. These quantities are shown in column 3 of Exhibit 19-2, Panel A. For example, Photon determines that photocopying machines use 240,000 inspection-hours. Column 4 of Exhibit 19-2, Panel A, shows the indirect costs of quality of the photocopying machines. For example, photocopying machines use 240,000 inspection-hours. The indirect costs of quality of the photocopying machines, shown in column 4, Panel A, equal the total quantity of the cost-allocation base used by the photocopying machines for each activity (column 3) multiplied by the cost-allocation rate from step 5 (column 2).

◆ **Step 7:** *Determine the total costs of quality by adding all direct and indirect costs of quality assigned to it.* Photon's total cost of quality in the COQ report for

External failure costs. Costs incurred to detect a nonconforming product after it is shipped to customers.

One important management accounting role is preparing cost of quality (COQ) reports for managers (see Exhibit 19-2).

In the Photon example, all the costs of quality are indirect costs of the photocopying machines.

EXHIBIT 19-2
Analysis of Activity-Based Costs of Quality (COQ) for Photocopying Machines at Photon Corporation

	A	B	C	D	E	F	G
1	**PANEL A: COQ REPORT**						**Percentage of**
2		**Cost Allocation**		**Quantity of Cost**		**Total**	**Revenues**
3	**Cost of Quality and Value-Chain Category**	**Rate[a]**		**Allocation Base**		**Costs**	**(5) = (4) ÷**
4	(1)	(2)		(3)		**(4) = (2) × (3)**	**$300,000,000**
5	*Prevention costs*						
6	Design engineering (R & D/Design)	$ 80	per hour	40,000	hours	$ 3,200,000	1.1%
7	Process engineering (R & D/Design)	$ 60	per hour	45,000	hours	2,700,000	0.9
8	Total prevention costs					5,900,000	2.0
9	*Appraisal costs*						
10	Inspection (Manufacturing)	$ 40	per hour	240,000	hours	9,600,000	3.2
11	Total appraisal costs					9,600,000	3.2
12	*Internal failure costs*						
13	Rework (Manufacturing)	$100	per hour	100,000	hours	10,000,000	3.3
14	Total internal failure costs					10,000,000	3.3
15	*External failure costs*						
16	Customer support (Marketing)	$ 50	per hour	12,000	hours	600,000	0.2
17	Transportation (Distribution)	$240	per load	3,000	loads	720,000	0.2
18	Warranty repair (Customer service)	$110	per hour	120,000	hours	13,200,000	4.4
19	Total external failure costs					14,520,000	4.8
20	Total costs of quality					$40,020,000	13.3
21							
22	[a]Amounts assumed.						
23							
24	**PANEL B: OPPORTUNITY COST ANALYSIS**						
25						**Total Estimated**	**Percentage**
26						**Contribution**	**of Revenues**
27	**Cost of Quality Category**					**Margin Lost**	**(3) = (2) ÷**
28	(1)					**(2)**	**$300,000,000**
29	*External failure costs*						
30	Estimated forgone contribution margin						
31	and income on lost sales					$12,000,000[b]	4.0%
32	Total external failure costs					$12,000,000	4.0
33							
34	[b]Calculated as total revenues minus all variable costs (whether output-unit, batch, product-sustaining, or facility-sustaining) on lost sales in 2007. If poor quality causes Photon to lose sales in subsequent years as well, the opportunity costs will be even greater.						

photocopying machines is $40.02 million (bottom of column 4, Panel A), or 13.3% of current revenues (bottom of column 5).

Do not assume, however, that costs reported on COQ reports represent the total costs of quality for a company. COQ reports typically exclude opportunity costs, such as forgone contribution margins and income from lost sales, lost production, or lower prices, that result from poor quality. Why? Because opportunity costs are difficult to estimate and are generally not recorded in financial accounting systems. Nevertheless, opportunity costs can be substantial and important driving forces in quality improvement programs. Exhibit 19-2, Panel B, presents the analysis of the opportunity costs of poor quality at Photon. Photon Corporation's Market Research Department estimates lost sales of 2,000 photocopying machines because of external failures. The forgone contribution and operating income of $12 million measures the financial costs from dissatisfied customers who have returned machines to Photon and from sales lost because of quality problems. Total costs of quality (including opportunity costs) equal $52.02 million (Panel A, $40.02 million + Panel B, $12 million), or 17.34% of current sales. Opportunity costs account for 23% ($12 million ÷ $52.02 million) of Photon's total costs of quality.

Spoilage and rework discussed in Chapter 18 considered only some elements of internal failure costs.

The COQ report and the opportunity cost analysis highlight Photon's high internal and external failure costs. The advantage of the balanced scorecard framework is that Photon does not have to wait for this opportunity cost to arise nor to analyze its financial results to estimate the costs of quality failure. The nonfinancial measures of the customer perspective in the balanced scorecard provide advance warning of the potential costs of internal and external failure.

THE CUSTOMER PERSPECTIVE: NONFINANCIAL MEASURES OF QUALITY AND CUSTOMER SATISFACTION

Even if products and services are defect-free and fully satisfy conformance quality, they will not be effective or sell well unless they also have design quality—that is, unless they satisfy customer needs. Usually management accountants are responsible for maintaining and reporting nonfinancial measures. Similar to companies such as Unilever, Federal Express, and TiVo, Photon measures customer satisfaction trends over time. Measures include:

OBJECTIVE 2

Provide examples of nonfinancial quality measures of customer satisfaction and internal performance

- Market research information on customer preferences and satisfaction with specific features (to measure design quality)
- Market share
- Percentage of customers giving high customer satisfaction ratings
- Defect rate calculated as the number of defective units as a percentage of total units shipped to customers
- Number of customer complaints (companies estimate that for every customer who actually complains, there are 10 to 20 others who have had bad experiences with the product but have not complained)
- Percentage of products that fail soon after delivery
- Customer response time (the difference between scheduled delivery date and date requested by the customer)
- On-time delivery rate (percentage of shipments made on or before the scheduled delivery date)

Federal Express tracks similar measures for customer satisfaction in its overnight delivery business. Management steps in and investigates if these numbers deteriorate over time.

In addition to these routine nonfinancial measures, many companies such as Procter & Gamble conduct surveys to measure customer satisfaction. Surveys serve two objectives. First, they provide a deeper perspective into customer experiences and preferences. Second, they provide a glimpse into features that customers would like future products to have.

THE INTERNAL-BUSINESS-PROCESS PERSPECTIVE: ANALYZING AND IMPROVING QUALITY

Control Charts

Statistical quality control (SQC) or statistical process control (SPC) is a formal means of distinguishing between random variation and nonrandom variation in an operating process. A key tool in SQC is a control chart. A **control chart** is a graph of a series of successive observations of a particular step, procedure, or operation taken at regular time intervals. Each observation is plotted relative to specified ranges that represent the expected distribution. Only those observations outside the specified limits are ordinarily regarded as nonrandom and worth investigating.

Exhibit 19-3 on page 744 presents control charts for the daily defect rates observed at Photon's three production lines. Defect rates in the prior 60 days for each

OBJECTIVE 3

Apply three methods that companies use to identify quality problems

EXHIBIT 19-3
Statistical Quality Control Charts: Daily Defect Rate at the Photon Corporation

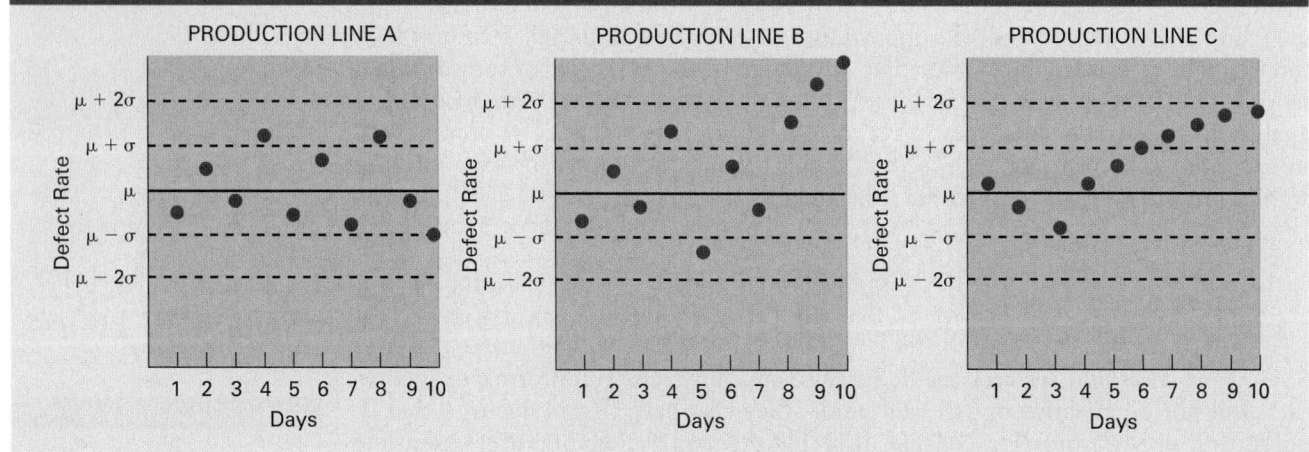

Control chart. Graph of a series of successive observations of a particular step, procedure, or operation taken at regular time intervals. Each observation is plotted relative to specified ranges that represent the expected distribution.

The arithmetic mean is the sum of the observations divided by the number of observations. The standard deviation measures how much the observations differ from the mean. If the observations are clustered around the mean, the standard deviation is small. If the observations are widely dispersed around the mean, the standard deviation is large.

If you have taken a statistics course, you understand the meaning of the 2σ (2 sigma) rule in control charts. If the defect rates are normally distributed and the production process is "in control," then a defect rate of more than 2σ from the mean is due to random variations only about 5% of the time.

Pareto diagram. Diagram that indicates how frequently each type of failure (defect) occurs.

plant were assumed to provide a good basis from which to calculate the distribution of daily defect rates. The arithmetic mean (μ, read "mu") and standard deviation (σ, read "sigma") are the two parameters of the distribution that are used in the control charts in Exhibit 19-3. On the basis of experience, the company decides that any observation outside the $\mu \pm 2\sigma$ range should be investigated.

For production line A in Exhibit 19-3, all observations are within the range of $\pm 2\sigma$ from the mean. Management, then, believes no investigation is necessary. For production line B, the last two observations signal that an out-of-control occurrence is highly likely. Given the $\pm 2\sigma$ rule, both observations would lead to an investigation. Production line C illustrates a process that would not prompt an investigation under the $\pm 2\sigma$ rule but may well be out of control. Note that the last eight observations show a clear direction and that the direction by day 5 is away from the mean. Statistical procedures have been developed using the trend as well as the level of the variable in question to evaluate whether a process is out of control.

Pareto Diagrams

Observations outside control limits serve as inputs to *Pareto diagrams*. A **Pareto diagram** or frequency chart indicates how frequently each type of failure (defect) occurs. Exhibit 19-4 presents a Pareto diagram for Photon's quality problems. Fuzzy and unclear copies are the most frequently recurring problem.

EXHIBIT 19-4
Pareto Diagram for the Photon Corporation

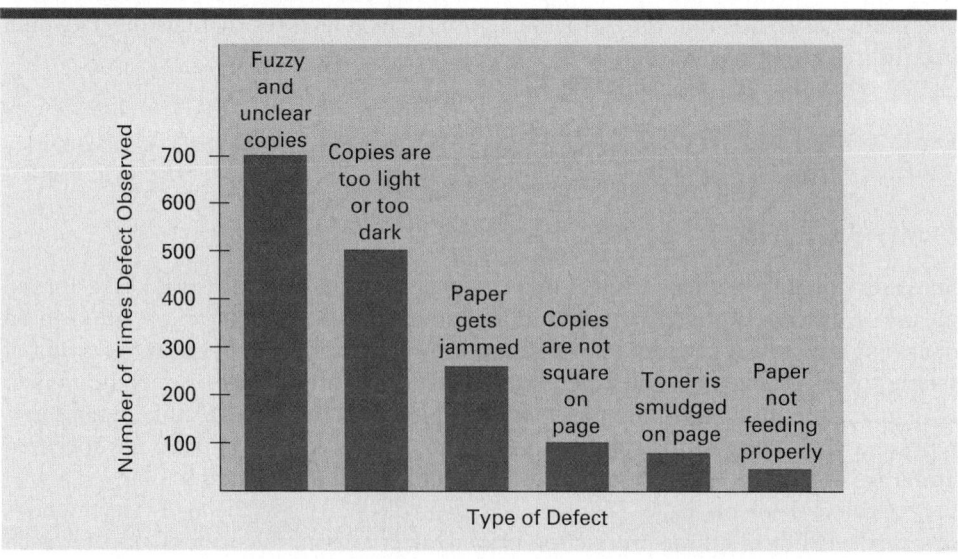

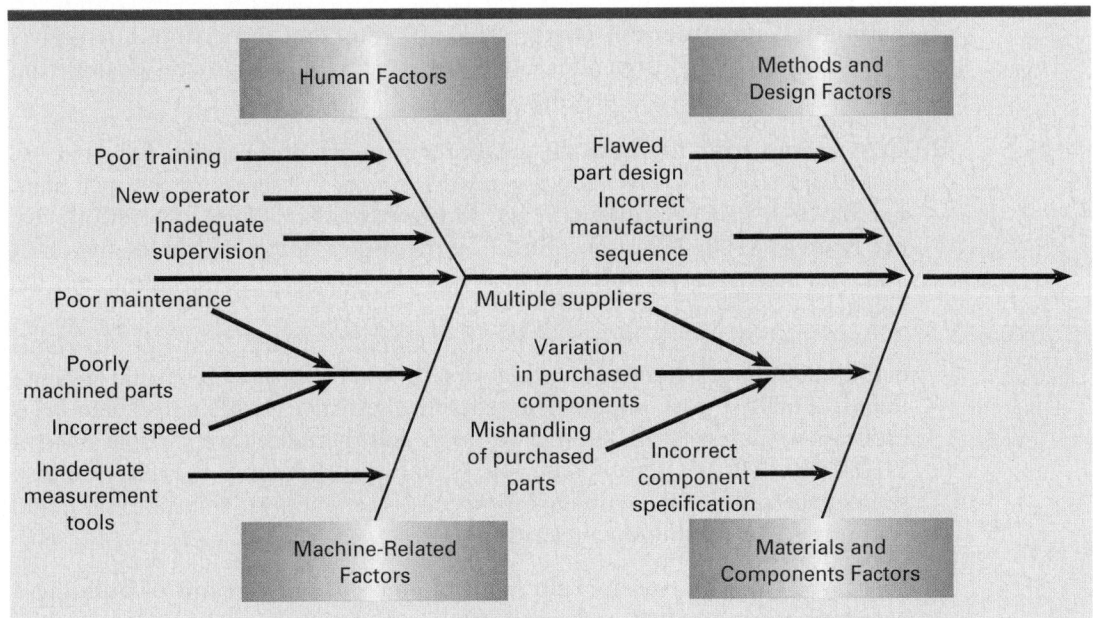

The fuzzy-copy problem results in high rework costs, because, in many cases, Photon discovers the fuzzy image problem only after the copier has been built. Sometimes fuzzy images occur at customer sites, resulting in high warranty and repair costs.

Cause-and-Effect Diagrams

The most frequently occurring problems identified by the Pareto diagram are analyzed using *cause-and-effect diagrams*. A **cause-and-effect diagram** identifies potential causes of failures or defects. As a first step, Photon analyzes the causes of the most frequently occurring failure, fuzzy and unclear copies. Exhibit 19-5 presents the cause-and-effect diagram for this problem. The exhibit identifies four major categories of potential causes of failure—human factors, methods and design factors, machine-related factors, and materials and components factors. As additional arrows are added for each cause, the general appearance of the diagram begins to resemble a fishbone (hence, cause-and-effect diagrams are also called *fishbone diagrams*).[1]

The analysis of quality problems is aided by automated equipment and computers that record the number and types of defects and the operating conditions that existed at the time the defects occurred. Using these inputs, computer programs simultaneously prepare control charts, Pareto diagrams, and cause-and-effect diagrams.

Cause-and-effect diagram (fishbone diagram). Diagram that identifies the potential causes of failures or defects. Four major categories of potential causes of failure are identified: human factors, methods and design factors, machine-related factors, and materials and components factors.

Combinations of methods can help identify quality problems. For example, Photon's managers first used the Pareto diagram to identify the most frequently encountered defect (fuzzy and unclear copies), and then they used the cause-and-effect diagram to identify specific causes of the defect.

RELEVANT COSTS AND BENEFITS OF QUALITY IMPROVEMENT

Careful analysis of the cause-and-effect diagram reveals that the steel frame (or chassis) of the copier is often mishandled as it travels from the suppliers' warehouses to Photon's plant. The frame must satisfy very precise specifications and tolerances; otherwise, various copier components (such as drums, mirrors, and lenses) attached to the frame will be improperly aligned. Mishandling causes the dimensions of the frame to vary from specifications, resulting in fuzzy images.

The team of engineers working to solve the fuzzy-image problem offers two alternative solutions: (1) to improve the inspection of the frame immediately upon delivery or (2) to redesign and strengthen the frame and the containers used to transport them to better withstand mishandling during transportation.

OBJECTIVE 4

Identify the relevant costs and benefits of quality improvements

[1]See P. Clark, "Getting the Most from Cause-and-Effect Diagrams," *Quality Progress* (June 2000).

Should Photon inspect incoming frames more carefully or redesign them and their containers? Exhibit 19-6 shows the costs and benefits of each choice.

1. **Estimated incremental costs:** $400,000 for the inspection alternative; $460,000 for the redesign alternative including $300,000 process engineering and $160,000 design engineering.

2. **Cost savings from less rework, customer support, and repairs.** Exhibit 19-6, lines 9 and 10 show that reducing rework results in savings of $40 per hour. Exhibit 19-2, Panel A, column 2, line 13 (see page 742), shows total rework cost per hour of $100. Why the difference? Because Photon concludes that as it improves quality, it will only save the $40 variable cost per rework-hour, not the $60 fixed cost per rework-hour.

   Exhibit 19-6, line 9, shows the inspection alternative is expected to eliminate 24,000 rework-hours and therefore save variable costs of $960,000 ($40 per hour × 24,000 rework-hours). The redesign alternative (Exhibit 19-6, line 10) is expected to eliminate 32,000 rework-hours and therefore save variable costs of $1,280,000 ($40 per rework-hour × 32,000 rework-hours). Exhibit 19-6 also shows expected variable-cost savings in customer support, transportation, and warranty repair for the two alternatives.

3. **Increased contribution margin from higher sales as a result of building a reputation for quality and performance** (Exhibit 19-6, lines 21 and 22): $1,500,000 for 250 copiers under the inspection alternative and $1,800,000 for 300 copiers under the redesign alternative. This benefit is important because quality improvements cannot always be translated into lower costs. For example, laying off workers (as a result of quality improvements) to reduce costs can adversely affect the morale of employees and limit future quality initiatives. Management should always look for opportunities to generate higher revenues from quality improvements. (The Focus on Values and Behaviours feature illustrates how quality problems can lead to revenue losses.)

EXHIBIT 19-6

Estimated Effect of Quality-Improvement Actions on Costs of Quality for Photocopying Machines at Photon Corporation

	A	B	C	D
		Relevant Costs and Benefits of		
		Further Inspecting		**Redesigning**
	Relevant Items	**Incoming Frames**		**Frames**
	(1)	(2)		(3)
5	Additional inspection and testing costs	$(400,000)		–
6	Additional process engineering costs	–		$ (300,000)
7	Additional design engineering costs	–		(160,000)
8	Savings in rework costs			
9	($40 per hour × 24,000 fewer rework-hours)	960,000		
10	($40 per hour × 32,000 fewer rework-hours)			1,280,000
11	Savings in customer-support costs			
12	($20 per hour × 2,000 fewer customer-support hours)	40,000		
13	($20 per hour × 2,800 fewer customer-support hours)			56,000
14	Savings in transportation costs for repair parts			
15	($180 per load × 500 fewer loads moved)	90,000		
16	($180 per hour × 700 fewer loads moved)			126,000
17	Savings in warranty repair costs			
18	($45 per hour × 20,000 fewer repair-hours)	900,000		
19	($45 per hour × 28,000 fewer repair-hours)			1,260,000
20	Total contribution margin from additional sales			
21	(250 additional copiers × $6,000 per copier)	1,500,000		
22	(300 additional copiers × $6,000 per copier)			1,800,000
23	Net cost savings and additional contribution margin	$3,090,000		$4,062,000
24	Difference in favour of redesigning frame	↑	$972,000	↑

Exhibit 19-6 shows that both the inspection and the redesign alternatives yield net benefits relative to the status quo. However, the net benefits from the redesign alternative are expected to be $972,000 greater.

The costs of a poorly designed frame appear in the form of higher manufacturing, marketing, distribution, and customer service costs, as internal and external failures begin to mount. But these costs are locked in when the frame is designed. Thus, it is not surprising that redesign will yield significant savings.

In the Photon example, lost contribution margin occurs because Photon's repeated external failures damage its reputation for quality, resulting in lost sales. Lost contribution margin can also occur as a result of internal failures. Suppose Photon's manufacturing capacity is fully used. In this case, rework uses up valuable manufacturing capacity and causes the company to forgo contribution margin from producing and selling additional copiers. Suppose Photon could produce and (subsequently) sell an additional 600 copiers by improving quality and reducing rework. The costs of internal failure would then include lost contribution margin of $3,600,000 ($6,000 contribution margin per copier × 600 copiers). This $3,600,000 is the opportunity cost of poor quality.

Photon can use its COQ report to examine interdependencies across the four categories of quality-related costs. In our example, redesigning the frame increases costs of prevention activities (design and process engineering), decreases costs of internal failure (rework), and decreases costs of external failure (warranty repairs).

The Cost of Quality Failure at Firestone

Company and division managers undoubtedly feel pressure to meet quarterly and annual financial performance targets, but these measures should never be pursued without regard to product or service quality. Although quality-control and assurance activities carry significant costs, quality failures are even more costly. As Bridgestone/Firestone, Inc., makers of Firestone tires, learned during a widely publicized recall of 6.5 million tires in 2000, the financial, public-relations, and legal effects of quality failure can be disastrous.

In August 2000, Firestone announced a national recall of its Radial ATX, ATXII, and Wilderness AT tires. Prior to announcing the recall, Firestone had received more than 1,500 claims for property damage, injuries, and even deaths related to tread separation in those tires. Ford Motor Company—Firestone's largest U.S. customer—conducted an analysis that indicated that tires from Firestone's Decatur, Illinois, plant exhibited tendencies to come apart at high speeds, which caused vehicles, especially Ford's popular Explorer sports utility vehicle, to roll over. Although both companies displayed public remorse and began working together in handling the recall, Firestone responded to Ford's study by stating:

> We are confident in the quality of our tires and in the effectiveness of our inspection processes at the Decatur, Illinois, plant and at all of our plants. . . . Like all Bridgestone/Firestone production facilities, the Decatur plant adheres to stringent standards of quality control where every tire is subject to strict inspection by both people and machines at every step of the manufacturing process, from raw material through finished tire. And, every production employee, at each of our plants, receives substantial training before they work on the line. . . . The plant also has received quality awards from our customers, including Ford, General Motors, and Nissan.

In the subsequent weeks, however, the increasing scrutiny of quality practices at Firestone told a different story. In late 1999, when it was found that tread separation among light-truck tires had risen 18.6% during the previous year, Firestone engineers identified tread separation as a "critical performance issue" at their October 2000 quarterly quality meeting. Another study found that the number of warranty claims for ATX and ATXII tires made at the Decatur facility between 1994 and 1996 were three to six times higher than claims for tires made at all other U.S. Firestone plants. And, although overall quality improved after 1996, claim rates remained significantly higher for the Decatur plant than those at all other facilities. These findings—coupled with news that tread separation caused Ford to replace the same, or similar, tires on nearly 50,000 of its vehicles in 16 South American and Asian countries starting in 1999—led most observers to conclude that the rollovers were being caused by Firestone tire defects.

Numerous factors contributed to the quality defects and subsequent lack of action by Firestone, but alert management accountants and financial managers could have called attention to the problem years earlier. A failure to share information among functional units left executives in the dark about how quality defects were harming the company. A Harvard Business School case notes:

> Although the rising cost of claims and lawsuits regarding the Firestone ATX tire was apparently discussed at some quarterly financial meetings beginning in 1997, the matter did not go beyond the finance area which maintained information on claims costs. As [Vice President Gary] Crigger explained: "Claims and lawsuits are not considered to be representative throughout a line. They are considered to be individual cases that occur for a variety of reasons. So they have never been part of [tire] performance evaluation."

This narrow view, a culture in which individuals did not speak up, and inaction cost Firestone dearly. As the recall proceeded, Firestone received thousands of unfavourable news stories, more than 200 lawsuits from angry customers, and high-profile congressional inquiries. On May 22, 2001, Ford announced the further recall of another 13 million tires. Ultimately, Ford ended its relationship with Firestone. Firestone suffered 40% revenue declines in key segments and a US$510 million loss in 2000. It also paid out over US$1 billion in recall-related costs (including new tires, claim settlements, and lawsuits), lost US$10 billion in stock market capitalization, and dismissed most Bridgestone/Firestone corporate executives in the United States and Japan.

Sources: L. S. Payne, "Recall 2000: Bridgestone Corp. (A)," HBS Case No. 9-302-013 (Boston: Harvard Business School Publishing, 2003); S. Govindaraj and B. Jaggi, "Market Overreaction to Product Recall Revisited—The Case of Firestone Tires and the Ford Explorer," *Review of Quantitative Finance and Accounting* (July 2004); D. Welch, "Firestone: Is This Brand Beyond Repair?" *Business Week*, June 11, 2001; "Firestone Decatur Tire Plant Inspection—Defective Tires," Bridgestone America Holdings press release (Nashville, TN: August 13, 2001).

Costs of quality give more insight when managers compare trends over time. In successful quality programs, the costs of quality as a percentage of sales and the costs of internal and external failure as a percentage of total costs of quality should decrease over time. Many companies, for example, Digital Equipment Corporation, Solectron, and Toyota, believe they should eliminate all failure costs and have zero defects.

COSTS OF DESIGN QUALITY

Costs of design quality. Costs incurred to prevent, or arising from, low quality of design.

Our discussion so far has focused on measuring the cost of conformance quality and the methods that companies use to reduce these costs. In addition to conformance quality, companies must also pay attention to quality of design by designing products that satisfy customer needs. The **costs of design quality** refer to costs incurred to prevent, or costs arising from, low quality of design. These costs include the costs of designing a product, and the production, marketing, distribution, and customer-service costs wasted on supporting a poorly designed product. A significant component of these costs is the opportunity cost of sales lost from not producing a product that customers want. Many of these costs are very difficult to measure precisely. For this reason, most companies do not measure the financial costs of design quality.

Nonfinancial Measures of Internal-Business-Process Quality

Prevention costs, appraisal costs, and internal failure costs are examples of financial measures of quality performance inside the company. Most companies monitor both financial and nonfinancial measures of internal quality.

Photon measures internal-business-process quality using the following nonfinancial measures:

◆ Defect rate—the percentage of defective to total units
◆ Average repair time to fix machines at the customer's site
◆ Rework rate—the percentage of reworked to total units
◆ Number of different types of defects analyzed using control charts, Pareto diagrams, and cause-and effect diagrams
◆ Number of design and process changes made

By themselves, nonfinancial measures of quality have limited meaning. They are more informative when management examines trends over time. To prepare this report, the management accountant must review the numbers to ensure that nonfinancial measures are calculated accurately and consistently, and must then present the information to help management evaluate internal quality performance. Management accountants help companies improve quality in multiple ways—they compute the costs of quality, assist in developing cost-effective solutions to quality problems, and provide feedback about quality improvement.

THE LEARNING-AND-GROWTH PERSPECTIVE FOR QUALITY IMPROVEMENTS

Photon's managers have analyzed performance to determine the drivers of internal-business-process quality. Photon measures the following factors in the learning-and-growth perspective in the balanced scorecard:

◆ Employee turnover ratio (number of employees who leave compared with the average total number of employees).
◆ Employee empowerment ratio (number of processes in which employees have the right to make decisions without consulting supervisors compared with the total number of processes).
◆ Employee satisfaction ratio (employees indicating high satisfaction ratings compared with the total employees surveyed).
◆ Employee training rate (percentage of employees trained in different quality-enhancing methods).

These quality-related balanced scorecard measures provide the best information when managers examine trends and relationships (across the learning and growth, the internal business process, and the customer and financial perspectives) over time as they seek to improve performance. To provide information on trends, management accountants must review the nonfinancial measures for accuracy and consistency.

EVALUATING QUALITY PERFORMANCE

Measuring the financial costs of quality and measuring the nonfinancial aspects of quality have distinctly different advantages.

The advantages of the costs of quality (COQ) measures are as follows:

1. COQ focuses attention on how costly poor quality can be.

2. Financial COQ measures are a useful way of comparing different quality improvement programs and setting priorities for achieving maximum cost reduction.

OBJECTIVE 5

Describe the benefits of financial and nonfinancial measures of quality

3. Financial COQ measures serve as a common denominator for evaluating tradeoffs among prevention and failure costs. COQ provides a single, summary measure of quality performance.

The advantages of nonfinancial measures of quality are that they:

1. Are often easy to quantify and easy to understand.

2. Direct attention to physical processes and hence focus attention on the precise problem areas that need improvement.

3. Provide immediate short-run feedback on whether quality improvement efforts have, in fact, succeeded in improving quality.

4. Are useful indicators of long-run performance.

Most organizations use both financial and nonfinancial quality measures to measure quality performance.

♦ PART TWO

TIME AS A COMPETITIVE TOOL

OBJECTIVE 6

Describe customer response time, and explain the reasons for and the cost of lines and delays

Companies increasingly view time as a key variable in competition.[2] Doing things faster helps to increase revenues and decrease costs. For example, a moving company such as United Van Lines will be able to generate more revenues if it can move goods from one place to another faster and on time. Companies such as Wal-Mart also report lower costs from their emphasis on time. They cite, for example, the need to carry less inventory because of their ability to respond rapidly to customer demands.

We focus on *operational measures of time*, which reveal how quickly companies respond to customers' demands for their products and services and the reliability with which these companies meet scheduled delivery dates. Two common operational measures of time are customer response time and on-time performance.

Customer Response Time

Customer response. Amount of time between when a customer places an order for a product or requests a service and when the product or service is delivered to the customer.

Customer response time is the amount of time between when a customer places an order for a product or requests a service and when the product or service is delivered to the customer. A timely response to customer requests is a key competitive factor in many industries. Consider a manufacturer of custom machine tools such as Yamazaki Mazak. Yamazaki's customers value faster delivery because it enables them to produce and sell products made using the new machine tools sooner. Customer response time is critical in many other industries, especially service industries such as banking, car rental, and fast food. Exhibit 19-7 describes components of customer response time.

In the Yamazaki Mazak example, *order receipt time* is the time it takes Mazak's marketing department to describe the customer's exact specifications and to place an order with manufacturing. **Manufacturing lead (or cycle) time** is the time between when the order is ready to start on the production line (ready to be set up) and when it becomes a finished good. Manufacturing lead time includes waiting time plus manufacturing time for the order. An order for machine tools, in the Mazak example, may need to wait and be delayed because the equipment the order requires is busy processing orders that arrived earlier. *Order delivery time* is the time it takes distribution to pick up the order from manufacturing and deliver it to the customer.

Several companies have adopted manufacturing lead time as the base for allocating indirect manufacturing costs to products. The Zytec Corporation (now Artesyn

Customer response time is particularly important in mail-order catalogue companies. These companies often learn that their customers are willing to pay a higher price for faster delivery. Therefore, to compete more effectively with stores (as well as with other mail-order companies), mail-order companies promise delivery of their products in a week or less.

Manufacturing lead time (manufacturing cycle time). Time between when an order is ready to start on the production line (ready to be set up) and when it becomes a finished good.

[2]See G. Stalk and T. Hout, *Competing Against Time* (New York: Free Press, 1990); K. Eisenhardt and S. Brown, "Time Pacing: Competing in Strategic Markets That Won't Stand Still," *Harvard Business Review* (March–April 1998); and T. Willis and A. Jurkus, "Product Development: An Essential Ingredient of Time-Based Competition," *Review of Business* (2001).

EXHIBIT 19-7
Components of Customer-Response Time

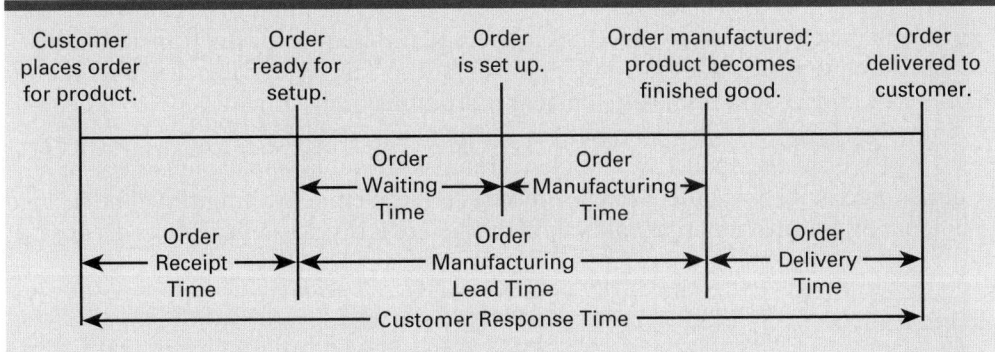

Technologies), a manufacturer of computer equipment, believes that using manufacturing lead time motivates managers to reduce the time taken to manufacture products. In turn, total overhead costs decrease and operating income rises.

On-Time Performance

On-time performance refers to situations in which the product or service is actually delivered at the time it is scheduled to be delivered. Consider Federal Express, which specifies a price per package and a next-day delivery time of 10:30 a.m. for its overnight courier service. Federal Express measures on-time performance by how often it meets its stated delivery time of 10:30 a.m. On-time performance is an important element of customer satisfaction because customers want and expect on-time deliveries. Commercial airlines, for example, gain loyal passengers from consistent on-time service. Note that there is a tradeoff between customer-response time and on-time performance. Simply scheduling longer customer-response times, such as Federal Express scheduling deliveries at 1 p.m. instead of 10:30 a.m., or airlines lengthening scheduled arrival times, eases the achieving of on-time performance (although this tactic could displease customers).

> **On-time performance.** Situations in which the product or service is actually delivered at the time it is scheduled to be delivered.

TIME DRIVERS AND COSTS OF TIME

Managing customer-response time and on-time performance in manufacturing, merchandising, and service companies requires an understanding of the causes of delays and the resulting costs. Delays can occur, for example, in front of a machine in a manufacturing operation, in front of a teller at a bank, or in front of a check-out counter in a store. We focus first on the reasons for delays.

Uncertainty and Bottlenecks as Drivers of Time

A **time driver** is any factor where change in the factor causes a change in the speed with which an activity is undertaken. What are the drivers of time? We consider two of the most important: (1) Uncertainty about when customers will order products or services. For example, the more randomly Mazak receives orders for its machine tools, the more likely that queues will form and delays will occur. (2) Limited capacity and bottlenecks. A **bottleneck** is an operation where the work required to be performed approaches or exceeds the available capacity. For example, a bottleneck is created when products that need to be processed at a particular machine arrive while the machine is busy processing other products.

> **Time driver.** Any factor where a change in the factor causes a change in the speed with which an activity is undertaken.

> **Bottleneck.** An operation where the work required approaches or exceeds the available capacity.

Falcon Works (FW) uses one turning machine to convert steel bars into one specialty component, A22. FW makes this component only after FW's customers order the component. To focus on manufacturing lead time, we assume that FW's order receipt time and order delivery time are minimal.

FW expects it will receive 30 orders, but it could actually receive 10, 20, or 50 orders of A22. Each order is for 1,000 units. Each order will take 100 hours of manufacturing time (8 hours of setup time to clean and prepare the machine, and

92 hours of processing time). The annual capacity of the machine is 4,000 hours. If FW receives the number of orders it expects, the total amount of manufacturing time required on the machine will be 3,000 (100 × 30) hours, which is within the available machine capacity of 4,000 hours. Even though expected capacity utilization is not strained, queues and delays will still occur. Why? Because uncertainty about when FW's customers will place an order may cause the order to be received while the machine is processing another order.

In the single-product case, under certain assumptions about the pattern of customer orders and how orders will be processed,[3] the **average waiting time**, the average amount of time that an order will wait in line before it is set up and processed, equals

Average waiting time. The average amount of time that an order will wait in line before it is set up and processed.

$$\frac{\text{Average number of orders of A22} \times \left(\begin{array}{c}\text{Manufacturing}\\ \text{time for A22}\end{array}\right)^2}{2 \times \left[\begin{array}{c}\text{Annual machine}\\ \text{capacity}\end{array} - \left(\begin{array}{c}\text{Average number}\\ \text{of orders of A22}\end{array} \times \begin{array}{c}\text{Manufacturing}\\ \text{time for A22}\end{array}\right)\right]}$$

$$= \frac{30 \times (100)^2}{2 \times [4,000 - (30 \times 100)]} = \frac{30 \times 10,000}{2 \times (4,000 - 3,000)} = \frac{300,000}{2 \times 1,000} = \frac{300,000}{2,000} = 150 \text{ hours}$$

Our formula describes only the average waiting time. A particular order may happen to arrive when the machine is free, in which case manufacturing will start immediately. In other situations, FW may receive an order while two other orders are waiting to be processed. In this case, the delay will be longer than 150 hours. The average manufacturing lead time for an order of A22 is 250 hours (150 hours of average waiting time + 100 hours of manufacturing time). Note that manufacturing time per order is a squared term in the numerator. It indicates the disproportionately large impact manufacturing time has on waiting time (see the Concepts in Action feature). The longer the manufacturing time, the much greater the chance that the machine will be in use when an order arrives, leading to longer delays. The denominator in this formula measures excess capacity or cushion. The smaller the cushion, the greater the delays because the higher the probability the machine is processing an earlier order. Throughout this section, we use manufacturing lead time to refer to manufacturing lead time for an order.

FW is considering whether to introduce a new product, C33. FW expects to receive ten orders of C33 (each order for 800 units) in the coming year. Each order will take 50 hours of manufacturing time (3 hours of setup time and 47 hours of processing time). The expected demand for A22 will be unaffected whether or not FW introduces C33.

The average waiting time *before* an order is set up and processed is given by the following formula, which is an extension of the formula described earlier for the single-product case.

$$\frac{\left[\begin{array}{c}\text{Average number}\\ \text{of orders of A22}\end{array} \times \left(\begin{array}{c}\text{Manufacturing}\\ \text{time for A22}\end{array}\right)^2\right] + \left[\begin{array}{c}\text{Average number}\\ \text{of orders of C33}\end{array} \times \left(\begin{array}{c}\text{Manufacturing}\\ \text{time for C33}\end{array}\right)^2\right]}{2 \times \left[\begin{array}{c}\text{Annual machine}\\ \text{capacity}\end{array} - \left(\begin{array}{c}\text{Average number}\\ \text{of orders of A22}\end{array} \times \begin{array}{c}\text{Manufacturing}\\ \text{time for A22}\end{array}\right) - \left(\begin{array}{c}\text{Average number}\\ \text{of orders of C33}\end{array} \times \begin{array}{c}\text{Manufacturing}\\ \text{time for C33}\end{array}\right)\right]}$$

$$= \frac{[30 \times (100)^2] + [10 \times (50)^2]}{2 \times [4,000 - (30 \times 100) - (10 \times 50)]} = \frac{(30 \times 10,000) + (10 \times 2,500)}{2 \times (4,000 - 3,000 - 500)}$$

$$= \frac{300,000 + 25,000}{2 \times 500} = \frac{325,000}{1,000} = 325 \text{ hours}$$

[3]The precise technical assumptions are (a) that customer orders for the product follow a Poisson distribution with a mean equal to the expected number of orders (30 in our example) and (b) that orders are processed on a first-in, first-out (FIFO) basis. The Poisson arrival pattern for customer orders has been found to be reasonable in many real-world settings. The FIFO assumption can be modified. Under the modified assumptions, the basic queuing and delay effects will still occur, but the precise formulas will be different.

Overcoming Bottlenecks on the Internet

In 2004, Intel's chief technology officer, Patrick Gelsinger, warned that the World Wide Web was becoming so overloaded with traffic that it might eventually collapse. Could this be true? Although the Internet's digital backbone will not collapse tomorrow, exponential growth in Web usage in recent years already causes many users to suffer from online bottlenecks. These bottlenecks are caused when too many people try to view the same information on a computer server at the same time. They affect all users, but these bottlenecks are most harmful to companies buying and selling their products and services over the Internet.

As companies become increasingly reliant on e-commerce and time-sensitive information sharing, the inability of a company to handle all the traffic on its Web site can become a serious problem. Oracle recently noted that although e-commerce companies generally set a target of 99.99% Web site availability, that still means that a company loses substantial amounts annually because users are unable to conduct their transactions during the 0.01% of bottleneck-related downtime. One study found that more than 40% of online shoppers abandon a transaction if the site they are on is responding too slowly. The costs can be much larger. A 22-hour site outage cost eBay over US$5 million in auction fees. A three-day outage forced ESPN to compensate some of its 260,000 online fantasy baseball players. And site outages caused shares of E-Trade to lose 22% of their market value in one week.

To relieve these bottlenecks and avoid their negative consequences, companies—such as Microsoft, Akamai, EMC, Hitachi, and others—have developed technologies that use remote caching and remote mirroring. Storing, or caching, seldom-updated content on remote servers is one way to reduce network traffic. The Motley Fool Web site, for example, stores its static content on Akamai's third-party global network, which consists of over 2,000 servers. When someone accesses the Motley Fool Web site, the caching system routes each individual request for content to servers that are geographically closer to the user, so the request travels a shorter distance along the Internet for faster page loading and transaction processing.

Remote mirroring allows a company to copy (or "mirror") huge databases in many different geographically remote locations. Using redundant arrays of inexpensive disks (RAID) technology, backup databases are copied via the Internet on computer-storage devices. Each extra copy not only serves as a backup in the event of system crashes, but it also relieves traffic congestion on the Internet. Savris Corp., which manages the Web sites of many companies, uses remote mirroring technology to instantly reroute Web traffic around trouble spots to data sites that have much less traffic and faster response times.

Remote caching and remote mirroring allow companies to efficiently relieve bottleneck constraints, increase capacity, and improve customer-response time. As Internet traffic increases exponentially in the coming years with voice-over IP (VoIP) telephone service and hundreds of millions of new users from developing countries are logging on for the first time, these technologies will be critical to ensuring the stability, operability, and profitability of many of the Internet's most popular sites.

Sources: Risk Management (May 2001); *The Wall Street Journal* (March 20, 2001); *Business Wire* (October 4, 1999); and a poll conducted by www.esearch.com in 1999; " 'Beware of the End of the World (Wide Web),' Says Intel," Fortune.com, September 10, 2004, http://www.forbes.com/execpicks/feeds/general/2004/09/10/generalcomtex_2004_09_10_ir_0000-5884-KEYWORD.Missing.html, accessed September 13, 2004; "Downtime and Lost Revenue," NetSource America, http://www.netsourceamerica.com/welcome.html, accessed June 5, 2006; D. Shand, "Banish Bottlenecks," *Computer World,* April 10, 2000, http://www.computerworld.com/news/ 2000/story/0,11280,44371,00.html, accessed September 17, 2004; T. Wilson, "The Cost of Downtime," http://internetweek.cmp.com/lead/lead073099.htm, accessed June 5, 2006.

Introducing C33 (1) cuts the unused capacity cushion in half (from 1,000 to 500 hours), doubling the average waiting time by halving the denominator; and (2) increases the demands on the process (the numerator) by 25,000 hours, which further increases average waiting time. The total effect of introducing C33 is to increase average waiting time by 117% [(325 − 150) ÷ 150].

Introducing C33 causes average waiting time to more than double from 150 hours to 325 hours. To understand why, think of excess capacity as a cushion for absorbing the shocks of variability and uncertainty in the arrival of customer orders. Introducing C33 causes excess capacity to shrink, increasing the chance that at any point in time, new orders will arrive while existing orders are being manufactured.

With the addition of another product, average manufacturing lead time for A22 is 425 hours (325 hours of average waiting time + 100 hours of manufacturing time), and for C33 it is 375 hours (325 hours of average waiting time + 50 hours of manufacturing time). Note that C33 spends 86.67% (325 ÷ 375) of its manufacturing lead time just waiting for manufacturing to start!

Relevant Revenues and Costs of Time

Should FW introduce product C33? Consider the following information:

Product	Annual Average Number of Orders	Average Selling Price per Order If Average Manufacturing Lead Time per Order Is		Direct Material Cost per Order	Inventory Carrying Cost per Order per Hour
		Less than 300 Hours	More than 300 Hours		
A22	30	$22,000	$21,500	$16,000	$1.00
C33	10	10,000	9,600	8,000	0.50

FW acquires direct materials when it receives an order, rather than waiting until just before manufacturing is scheduled to start because of uncertainty about (1) how long it will take to obtain materials from suppliers and (2) when manufacturing will start.

Note that manufacturing lead times affect both revenues and costs in our example. Revenues are affected because customers are willing to pay a slightly higher price for faster delivery. Direct materials costs and inventory carrying costs are the only costs affected by the decision to introduce C33. Inventory carrying costs usually consist of the opportunity costs of investment tied up in inventory (see Chapter 11) and the relevant costs of storage such as space rental, spoilage, deterioration, and materials-handling. Companies usually calculate inventory carrying costs on a per-order-per-year basis. To simplify computations, we express inventory carrying costs on a per-order-per-hour basis. FW incurs inventory carrying costs for the duration of the wait time and manufacturing time.

Exhibit 19-8 presents relevant revenues and relevant costs that the management accountant would calculate for this decision. The preferred alternative is not to introduce C33. Note that C33 is rejected despite having a positive contribution margin of at least $1,600 ($9,600 − $8,000) per order. Recall, too, that FW's machine has the capacity to process C33 because the machine will, on average, use only 3,500 of the available 4,000 hours. Why is C33 rejected? *The key is to recognize the negative effects of C33 on the existing product A22.* The following table presents the expected loss in revenues and expected increase in costs of using up extra capacity on the turning machine to manufacture C33.

Effect of Increasing Average Manufacturing Lead Time

Product	Expected Loss in Revenues for A22 (1)	Expected Increase in Carrying Costs for All Products (2)	Expected Increase in Carrying Costs of Introducing C33 (3) = (1) + (2)
A22	$15,000[a]	$5,250[b]	$20,250
C33	—	1,875[c]	1,875
Total	$15,000	$7,125	$22,125

[a]($22,000 − $21,500) per order × 30 expected orders = $15,000.
[b](425 − 250) hours per order × $1.00 per hour × 30 expected orders = $5,250.
[c](375 − 0) hours per order × $0.50 per hour × 10 expected orders = $1,875.

Introducing C33 causes the average manufacturing lead time of A22 to increase from 250 hours to 425 hours. This increases inventory carrying costs. Introducing C33 also causes A22's revenues to decrease because it would, on average, take more than 300 hours to manufacture A22. The expected costs of introducing C33 equal $22,125,

EXHIBIT 19-8
Determining Expected Relevant Revenues and Relevant Costs for Falcon Works' Decision to Introduce C33

Relevant Items	Alternative 1: Introduce C33 (1)	Alternative 2: Do Not Introduce C33 (2)	Difference (3) = (1) − (2)
Expected revenues	$741,000[a]	$660,000[b]	$ 81,000
Expected variable costs	560,000[c]	480,000[d]	(80,000)
Expected inventory carrying costs	14,625[e]	7,500[f]	(7,125)
Expected total costs	574,625	487,500	(87,125)
Expected revenues minus expected costs	$166,375	$172,500	$ (6,125)

[a]($21,500 × 30) + ($9,600 × 10) = $741,000; average manufacturing lead time will be more than 300 hours.
[b]($22,000 × 30) = $660,000; average manufacturing lead time will be less than 300 hours.
[c]($16,000 × 30) + ($8,000 × 10) = $560,000.
[d]$16,000 × 30 = $480,000.
[e](Average manufacturing lead time for A22 × Inventory carrying cost per order for A22 × Expected number of orders for A22) + (Average manufacturing lead time for C33 × Inventory carrying cost per order for C33 × Expected number of orders for C33) = (425 × $1.00 × 30) + (375 × $0.50 × 10) = $12,750 + $1,875 = $14,625.
[f]Average manufacturing lead time for A22 × Inventory carrying cost per order for A22 × Expected number of orders for A22 = 250 × $1.00 × 30 = $7,500.

which exceeds C33's expected contribution margin of $16,000 ($1,600 per order × 10 expected orders). FW should choose not to produce C33.

We have described a simple setting to explain the effects of uncertainty and capacity constraints and the relevant revenues and relevant costs of time.[4] How can delays be reduced? Increasing the capacity of the bottleneck resource can reduce lines, delays, and inventories. When demand uncertainty is high, *some* excess capacity is desirable. Companies can increase capacity in several ways. One way, for example, is to reduce the time required for setups and processing by doing these activities more efficiently. Another is to invest in new equipment. Many companies are investing in flexible manufacturing systems that can be programmed to quickly switch from producing one product to producing another. Delays can also be reduced through careful scheduling of orders on machines—for example, by batching similar jobs together for processing.

When there is considerable variability in the arrival of orders at the bottleneck operation, unused capacity acts as a cushion to absorb some of that variability, reducing average waiting time.

◆ PART THREE

THEORY OF CONSTRAINTS AND THROUGHPUT CONTRIBUTION ANALYSIS

The **theory of constraints (TOC)** describes methods to maximize operating income when faced with some bottleneck and some nonbottleneck operations.[5] It defines three measurements:

OBJECTIVE 7

Apply three main measurements in the theory of constraints

[4]Other complexities such as analyzing a network of machines, priority scheduling, and allowing for uncertainty in processing times are beyond the scope of this book. In these cases, the basic queuing and delay effects persist, but the precise formulas are more complex.
[5]See E. Goldratt and J. Cox, *The Goal* (New York: North River Press, 1986); E. Goldratt, *The Theory of Constraints* (New York: North River Press, 1990); E. Noreen, D. Smith, and J. Mackey, *The Theory of Constraints and Its Implications for Management Accounting* (New York: North River Press, 1995); and M. Woeppel, *Manufacturers' Guide to Implementing the Theory of Constraints* (Boca Raton, FL: Lewis Publishing, 2000).

Theory of constraints (TOC).
Describes methods to maximize operating income when faced with some bottleneck and some nonbottleneck operations.

1. **Throughput contribution,** equal to sales revenue minus direct materials costs (see Chapter 9)

2. **Investments (inventory),** equal to the sum of materials costs of direct materials inventory, work-in-process inventory, and finished goods inventory; R&D costs; and costs of equipment and buildings

3. **Operating costs,** equal to all operating costs (other than direct materials) incurred to earn throughput contribution; include salaries and wages, rent, utilities, and amortization

The objective of TOC is to increase throughput contribution while decreasing investments and operating costs. *The theory of constraints considers short-run time horizons and assumes other current operating costs to be fixed costs.* The key steps in managing bottleneck resources are as follows:

OBJECTIVE 8

Explain four steps in managing bottlenecks

◆ **Step 1:** Recognize that the bottleneck resource determines throughput contribution of the plant as a whole.

◆ **Step 2:** Search and find the bottleneck resource by identifying resources with large quantities of inventory waiting to be worked on.

◆ **Step 3:** Keep the bottleneck operation busy and subordinate all nonbottleneck resources to the bottleneck resource. That is, the needs of the bottleneck resource determine the production schedule of nonbottleneck resources.

Step 3 represents a key notion described in Chapter 11: To maximize overall contribution margin, the plant must maximize contribution margin (in this case, throughput contribution) of the constrained or bottleneck resource. For this reason, step 3 suggests that the bottleneck machine always be kept running, not waiting for jobs. To achieve this, companies often maintain a small buffer inventory of jobs waiting for the bottleneck machine. The bottleneck machine sets the pace for all nonbottleneck machines. That is, the output at the nonbottleneck operations is tied or linked to the needs of the bottleneck machine. For example, workers at nonbottleneck machines are not motivated to improve their productivity if the additional output cannot be processed by the bottleneck machine. Producing more nonbottleneck output only creates excess inventory; it does not increase throughput contribution.

◆ **Step 4:** Take actions to increase bottleneck efficiency and capacity—the objective is to increase throughput contribution minus the incremental costs of taking such actions. The management accountant plays a key role in step 4 by calculating throughput contribution, identifying relevant and irrelevant costs, and doing a cost-benefit analysis of alternative actions to increase bottleneck efficiency and capacity.

We illustrate step 4 using the example of Cardinal Industries (CI). CI manufactures car doors in two operations—stamping and pressing. Additional information is as follows:

	Stamping	Pressing
Capacity per hour	20 units	15 units
Annual capacity (6,000 hours of capacity available in each operation; 6,000 hours × 20 units/hour; 15 units/hour)	120,000 units	90,000 units
Annual production and sales	90,000 units	90,000 units
Other fixed operating costs (excluding direct materials)	$720,000	$1,080,000
Other fixed operating costs per unit produced ($720,000 ÷ 90,000 units; $1,080,000 ÷ 90,000 units)	$8 per unit	$12 per unit

Each door sells for $100 and has direct materials costs of $40. Variable costs in other functions of the value chain—R&D, design of products and processes, marketing, distribution, and customer service—are negligible. CI's output is constrained by the capacity of 90,000 units at the pressing operation. What can CI do to relieve the bottleneck constraint at the pressing operation?

a. *Eliminate idle time (time when the pressing machine is neither being set up to process products nor actually processing products) at the bottleneck operation.* CI is considering permanently positioning two workers at the pressing operation. Their sole responsibility would be to unload finished units as soon as one batch of units is processed and to set up the machine to process the next batch. Suppose the annual cost of this action is $48,000 and the effect of this action is to increase bottleneck output by 1,000 units per year. Should CI incur the additional costs? Yes, because CI's relevant throughput contribution increases by $60,000 [1,000 units × (selling price, $100 − direct materials costs, $40)], which exceeds the additional cost of $48,000. All other costs are irrelevant.

b. *Process only those parts or products that increase sales and throughput contribution, not parts or products that remain in finished goods or spare parts inventory.* Manufacturing products that sit in inventory do not increase throughput contribution.

c. *Shift products that do not have to be made on the bottleneck machine to nonbottleneck machines or to outside facilities.* Suppose the Spartan Corporation, an outside contractor, offers to press 1,500 doors at $15 per door from direct materials that CI supplies. Spartan's quoted price is greater than CI's own operating costs in the Pressing Department of $12 per door. Should CI accept the offer? Yes, because pressing is the bottleneck operation. Getting additional doors pressed from outside increases throughput contribution by $90,000 [($100 − $40) × 1,500 doors], while relevant costs increase by $22,500 ($15 × 1,500). The fact that CI's unit cost is less than Spartan's quoted price is irrelevant.

Suppose Gemini Industries, another outside contractor, offers to stamp 2,000 doors from direct materials that CI supplies at $6 per door. Gemini's price is lower than CI's operating cost of $8 per door in the Stamping Department. Should CI accept the offer? Since other operating costs are fixed costs, CI will not save any costs by subcontracting the stamping operations. Total costs will be greater by $12,000 ($6 × 2,000) under the subcontracting alternative. Stamping more doors will not increase throughput contribution, which is constrained by pressing capacity. CI should not accept Gemini's offer.

d. *Reduce setup time and processing time at bottleneck operations (for example, by simplifying the design or reducing the number of parts in the product).* Suppose CI can reduce setup time at the pressing operation by incurring additional costs of $55,000 a year. Suppose further that reducing setup time enables CI to press 2,500 more doors a year. Should CI incur the costs to reduce setup time? Yes, because throughput contribution increases by $150,000 [($100 − $40) × 2,500], which exceeds the additional costs incurred of $55,000. Will CI find it worthwhile to incur costs to reduce machining time at the stamping operation? No. Other operating costs will increase, but throughput contribution will remain unaffected. Throughput contribution increases only by increasing bottleneck output; increasing nonbottleneck output has no effect.

e. *Improve the quality of parts or products manufactured at the bottleneck operation.* Poor quality is often more costly at a bottleneck operation than it is at a non-bottleneck operation. The cost of poor quality at a nonbottleneck operation is the cost of materials wasted. If CI produces 1,000 defective doors at the stamping operation, the cost of poor quality is $40,000 (direct materials cost per unit, $40 × 1,000 doors). No throughput contribution is forgone because stamping has excess capacity. Despite the defective production, stamping can produce and transfer 90,000 doors to the pressing operation. At a bottleneck operation, the cost of poor quality is the cost of materials wasted *plus* the opportunity cost of lost throughput contribution. Bottleneck capacity not wasted in producing defective units could be used to generate additional sales and throughput contribution. If CI produces 1,000 defective units at the pressing operation, the cost of poor quality is $100,000: direct materials cost

> The opportunity cost of lost throughput contribution arising from quality problems at the bottleneck is an internal failure cost.

of $40,000 (direct materials cost per unit, $40 × 1,000 units) plus forgone throughput contribution of $60,000 [($100 − $40) × 1,000 doors].

The high costs of poor quality at the bottleneck operation mean that bottleneck time should not be wasted processing units that are defective. That is, inspection should be done before processing parts at the bottleneck to ensure that only good-quality units are transferred to the bottleneck operation. Also, quality improvement programs should focus on ensuring that bottlenecks produce minimal defects.

If the actions in step 4 are successful, the capacity of the pressing operation will increase and eventually exceed the capacity of the stamping operation. The bottleneck will then shift to the stamping operation. CI should then focus continuous-improvement actions on increasing stamping efficiency and capacity. For example, the contract with Gemini Industries to stamp 2,000 doors at $6 per door from direct materials supplied by CI becomes attractive now. Why? Because throughput contribution increases by ($100 – $40) × 2,000 − $120,000, while costs increase by $12,000 ($6 × 2,000).

The theory of constraints emphasizes the management of bottlenecks as the key to improving the performance of the system as a whole. It focuses on the short-run maximization of throughput contribution—revenues minus materials costs. It is less useful for the long-run management of costs, because it does not model the behaviour of costs or identify individual activities and cost drivers. Instead, it regards operating costs as given and fixed. Activity-based costing (ABC) systems, on the other hand, take a longer-run perspective when more costs can be managed; the focus is on improving processes by eliminating non-value-added activities and reducing the costs of performing value-added activities. ABC systems, therefore, are more useful for long-run pricing, long-run cost control and profit planning, and capacity management. The short-run TOC emphasis on maximizing throughput contribution by managing bottlenecks complements the long-run strategic-cost-management focus of ABC.[6]

Balanced Scorecard and Time-Related Measures

In this section, we use the balanced scorecard to summarize how financial and non-financial measures of time relate to one another. We classify these measures under the four perspectives of the balanced scorecard—financial, customer, internal business processes, and learning and growth. Managers use the balanced scorecard measures to reduce delays and to increase throughput of their bottleneck operations.

Financial measures
Revenue losses or price discounts attributable to delays
Carrying cost of inventories
Throughput contribution minus operating costs

Customer measures
Customer-response time (the time it takes to fulfill a customer order)
On-time performance (delivering a product or service by the scheduled time)

Internal-business-process measures
Average manufacturing time for key products
Idle time at bottleneck operations
Defective units produced at bottleneck operations
Average reduction in setup time and processing time at bottleneck operations

Learning-and-growth measures
Employee satisfaction
Number of employees trained in managing bottleneck operations

[6]For an excellent evaluation of TOC, operations management, cost accounting, and the relationship between TOC and activity-based costing, see A. Atkinson, "*Cost Accounting, the Theory of Constraints, and Costing*" (Issue Paper, CMA Canada, December 2000).

Note the cause-and-effect linkages across these measures. For example, better employee training leads to better management of bottleneck operations, which in turn leads to better customer-response times and higher revenues and throughput contributions. Managers use time-related measures in the balanced scorecard to help them identify actions that improve customer-response times and create long-run competitive advantage.

PROBLEM

The Sloan Corporation is a moving company that transports household goods from one city to another within North America. It measures quality of service in terms of (a) time required to transport goods, (b) on-time delivery (within two days of agreed-upon delivery date), and (c) number of lost or damaged shipments. Sloan is considering investing in a new scheduling and tracking system costing $160,000 per year, which should help it improve performance with respect to items (b) and (c). The following information describes Sloan's current performance and the expected performance if the new system is implemented:

	Current Performance	Expected Future Performance
On-time delivery performance	85%	95%
Variable costs per carton lost or damaged	$60	$60
Fixed cost per carton lost or damaged	$40	$40
Number of cartons lost or damaged per year	3,000 cartons	1,000 cartons

Sloan expects that each percentage point increase in on-time performance will result in revenue increases of $20,000 per year. Sloan's contribution margin percentage is 45%.

REQUIRED
1. Should Sloan acquire the new system?
2. What is the minimum amount of revenue increase that needs to occur for the benefits from the new system to exceed the costs?

SOLUTION
1. Additional costs of the new scheduling and tracking system are $160,000 per year.

Additional annual benefits of the new scheduling and tracking system are

Additional annual sales from improving on-time performance $20,000 (95% − 85% or 10 percentage points)	$200,000
Contribution margin from additional annual revenues 45% × $200,000	$ 90,000
Reduction in costs per year from fewer cartons lost or damaged (only variable costs are relevant) $60 (3,000 − 1,000)	120,000
Total additional benefits	$210,000

Because the expected benefits of $210,000 exceed the costs of $160,000, Sloan should invest in the new system.

2. As long as Sloan earns a contribution margin of $40,000 (to cover incremental costs of $160,000 − relevant variable cost savings of $120,000) from additional annual sales, investing in the new system is beneficial. This contribution margin corresponds to additional sales of $40,000 ÷ 0.45 = $88,889.

The following decision guidelines use a question-and-answer format to summarize the chapter's main points. Each decision presents a key question. The guideline is the answer to that question.

DECISIONS	GUIDELINES
1. What are the four categories of a cost-of-quality program?	Four cost categories in a cost-of-quality program are prevention costs (costs incurred to preclude the production of products that do not conform to specifications), appraisal costs (costs incurred to detect which of the individual units of products do not conform to specifications), internal failure costs (costs incurred by a nonconforming product before it is shipped to customers), and external failure costs (costs incurred by a nonconforming product after it is shipped to customers).
2. What methods can managers use to identify quality problems and improve quality?	Three methods to identify quality problems and to improve quality are (a) control charts, to distinguish random from nonrandom variations in an operating process; (b) Pareto diagrams, which indicate how frequently each type of failure occurs; and (c) cause-and-effect diagrams, which identify potential causes of failure.
3. How do managers identify the relevant costs and benefits of quality improvements?	The relevant costs of quality improvement are the incremental costs to implement the quality program. The relevant benefits are the cost savings and the estimated increase in contribution margin from the higher sales due to quality improvements.
4. What nonfinancial measures of customer satisfaction and internal performance can managers use?	Nonfinancial measures of customer satisfaction include number of customer complaints and on-time delivery rate. Nonfinancial measures of internal quality performance include product defect levels and process yields.
5. Why should managers use both financial and nonfinancial measures of quality?	Financial measures are helpful to evaluate tradeoffs among prevention costs, appraisal costs, and failure costs. Nonfinancial measures identify problem areas that need improvement and serve as indicators of future long-run performance.
6. What is customer-response time? What are the reasons for and the costs of delays?	Customer-response time is the duration between the time a customer places an order for a product or service and the time the product or service is delivered to the customer. Delays occur because of (a) uncertainty about when customers will order products or services and (b) bottlenecks due to limited capacity. Bottlenecks are operations at which the work to be performed approaches or exceeds the available capacity. The costs of delays include lower revenues and increased inventory carrying costs.
7. What three measures do managers need to implement the theory of constraints?	The three measures in the theory of constraints are (a) throughput contribution (equal to revenues minus direct materials cost of the goods sold); (b) investments (equal to the sum of materials costs in direct materials, and work-in-process and finished goods inventories, R&D costs, and costs of equipment and buildings); and (c) operating costs (equal to all operating costs, other than direct materials costs, incurred to earn throughput contribution).
8. What are the steps managers can take to manage bottlenecks?	The four steps in managing bottlenecks are (a) recognize that the bottleneck operation determines throughput contribution, (b) find the bottleneck, (c) keep the bottleneck busy and subordinate all nonbottleneck operations to the bottleneck operation, and (d) increase bottleneck efficiency and capacity.

TERMS TO LEARN

This chapter contains definitions of the following important terms:

appraisal costs (p. 740)
average waiting time (p. 752)
bottleneck (p. 751)
cause-and-effect diagram (p. 745)

conformance quality (p. 739)
control chart (p. 743)
costs of design quality (p. 748)
costs of quality (COQ) (p. 740)

customer response time (p. 750)
external failure costs (p. 741)
fishbone diagram (p. 745)
internal failure costs (p. 740)
manufacturing cycle time (p. 750)
manufacturing lead time (p. 750)
on-time performance (p. 751)

operating costs (p. 756)
Pareto diagram (p. 744)
prevention costs (p. 740)
theory of constraints
   (TOC) (p. 755)
throughput contribution (p. 756)
time driver (p. 751)

▼ ASSIGNMENT MATERIAL

QUESTIONS

19-1 Describe two benefits of improving quality.

19-2 How does conformance quality differ from quality of design? Explain.

19-3 Name two items classified as prevention costs.

19-4 Distinguish between internal failure costs and external failure costs.

19-5 Describe three methods that companies use to identify quality problems.

19-6 "Companies should focus on financial measures of quality because these are the only measures of quality that can be linked to bottom-line performance." Do you agree? Explain.

19-7 Give two examples of nonfinancial measures of customer satisfaction.

19-8 Give two examples of nonfinancial measures of internal performance.

19-9 Distinguish between customer response time and manufacturing lead time.

19-10 "There is no tradeoff between customer response time and on-time performance." Do you agree? Explain.

19-11 Give two reasons why delays occur.

19-12 "Companies should always make and sell all products whose selling prices exceed variable costs." Do you agree? Explain.

19-13 Describe the three main measures used in the theory of constraints.

19-14 Describe the four key steps in managing bottleneck resources.

19-15 Describe three ways to improve the performance of a bottleneck operation.

EXERCISES

19-16 Costs of quality. (CMA, adapted) Bergen Inc. produces telephone equipment at its London plant. In recent years, the company's market share has been eroded by stiff competition from Asian and European competitors. Price and product quality are the two key areas in which companies compete in this market.

Jerry Holman, Bergen's president, decided to devote more resources to the improvement of product quality after learning that his company's products had been ranked fourth in product quality in a 2006 survey of telephone equipment users. He believed that Bergen could no longer afford to ignore the importance of product quality.

Bergen's quality improvement program has now been in operation for two years, and the cost report shown below has recently been issued.

As they were reviewing the report, Sheila Haynes, manager of sales, asked Tony Reese, production manager, what he thought of the quality program. "The work is really moving through the Production Department," replied Reese. "We used to spend time helping the Customer Service Department solve their problems but they are leaving us alone these days."

Semi-Annual Costs of Quality Report, Bergen Inc.
(in Thousands)

	6/30/2007	12/31/2007	6/30/2008	12/31/2008
Prevention costs				
Machine maintenance	$ 258	$ 258	$ 228	$ 192
Training suppliers	6	54	24	18
Design reviews	24	122	120	114
Total prevention costs	288	434	372	324
Appraisal costs				
Incoming inspection	54	64	43	26
Final testing	192	192	168	113
Total appraisal costs	246	256	211	139
Internal failure costs				
Rework	144	127	106	74
Scrap	82	77	50	48
Total internal failure costs	226	204	156	122
External failure costs				
Warranty repairs	83	37	30	28
Customer returns	314	301	139	96
Total external failure costs	397	338	169	124
Total quality costs	$1,157	$1,232	$ 908	$ 709
Total production and sales	$4,944	$5,448	$5,580	$5,412

REQUIRED

1. By analyzing the Cost of Quality Report presented, determine whether Bergen Inc.'s quality improvement program has been successful. List specific evidence to support your answer.
2. Jerry Holman believed that the quality improvement program was essential and that Bergen Inc. could no longer afford to ignore the importance of product quality. Discuss how Bergen could measure the opportunity cost of not implementing the quality improvement program.

19-17 Costs of quality analysis, nonfinancial quality measures. The Hartono Corporation manufactures and sells industrial grinders. The following table presents financial information pertaining to quality in 2007 and 2008 (in thousands):

	2008	2007
Sales	$12,500	$10,000
Line inspection	85	110
Scrap	175	250
Design engineering	240	100
Cost of returned goods	145	60
Product-testing equipment	50	50
Customer support	30	40
Rework costs	135	160
Preventive equipment maintenance	90	35
Product liability claims	100	200
Incoming materials inspection	40	20
Breakdown maintenance	40	90
Product-testing labour	75	220
Training	120	45
Warranty repair	200	300
Supplier evaluations	50	20

REQUIRED

1. Classify the cost items in the table into prevention, appraisal, internal failure, or external failure categories.
2. Calculate the ratio of each COQ category to sales in 2007 and 2008. Comment on the trends in costs of quality between 2007 and 2008.
3. Give two examples of nonfinancial quality measures that Hartono Corporation could monitor as part of a total quality control effort.

Excel Application For students who wish to practise their spreadsheet skills, the following is a step-by-step approach to creating an Excel spreadsheet to work this problem.

Step-by-Step

1. Open a new spreadsheet. Create a row for "Revenues" and columns for "2008" and "2007."

(Program your spreadsheet to perform all necessary calculations. Do not "hard-code" any amounts, such as prevention costs as a percentage of sales, requiring addition, subtraction, multiplication, or division operations.)

2. Skip two rows and create columns for "Cost" and "Cost as a Percentage of Revenues" for 2008. Create two more columns right next to these columns for "Cost" and "Cost as a Percentage of Revenues" for 2007. Create rows for each item of prevention costs (for example, "Preventive Maintenance") and "Total Prevention Costs"; each item of appraisal costs and "Total Appraisal Costs"; each item of internal failure costs and "Total Internal Failure Costs"; and each item of external failure costs and "Total External Failure Costs." Finally, create a row for "Total Costs of Quality."

3. Enter calculations for total cost of a Percentage of Revenues of each Cost of Quality category (for example, total prevention costs) and Total Costs of Quality in 2007 and 2008.

4. Skip two rows and create a section, "COQ Trend Analysis," with rows for "Prevention Costs, Appraisal Costs, Internal Failure Costs, External Failure Costs, and Total Costs of Quality" and columns for "Percent of Sales in 2008" and "Percent of Sales in 2007." Fill in this section using the data you created in steps 2 and 3.

5. Create a bar chart to compare each of the categories and total costs of quality in 2008 and 2007 by highlighting the "Percent of Sales in 2008" and "Percent of Sales in 2007" columns and clicking the chart wizard icon. Choose "Column" under chart type. Format as necessary and click on "Finish."

6. *Verify the accuracy of your spreadsheet:* Change revenues in 2008 from $12,500 to $9,500. If you programmed your spreadsheet correctly, total prevention costs as a percentage of revenues for 2008 should change to 5.3%.

19-18 Costs of quality analysis, nonfinancial quality measures. Ontario Industries manufactures two types of refrigerators, Olivia and Solta. Information on each refrigerator is as follows:

	Olivia	Solta
Units manufactured and sold	10,000 units	5,000 units
Selling price	$2,400	$1,800
Variable costs per unit	$1,440	$960
Hours spent on design	6,000	1,000
Testing and inspection hours per unit	1	0.5
Percentage of units reworked in plant	5%	10%
Rework costs per refrigerator	$600	$480
Percentage of units repaired at customer site	4%	8%
Repair costs per refrigerator	$720	$540
Estimated lost sales from poor quality	—	300 units

The labour rates per hour for various activities are as follows:

Design	$90 per hour
Testing and inspection	$48 per hour

REQUIRED

1. Calculate the costs of quality for Olivia and Solta classified into prevention, appraisal, internal failure, and external failure categories.

2. For each type of refrigerator, calculate the ratio of each COQ item as a percentage of sales. Compare and comment on the costs of quality for Olivia and Solta.

3. Give two examples of nonfinancial quality measures that Ontario Industries could monitor as part of a total quality control effort.

19-19 Nonfinancial measures of quality and time. (CMA, adapted) Eastern Switching Co. (ESC) produces telecommunications equipment. Charles Laurant, ESC's president, believes that product quality is the key to gaining competitive advantage. Laurant implemented a total quality management (TQM) program with an emphasis on customer satisfaction. The following information is available for the first year (2008) of the TQM program compared to the previous year.

	2007	2008
Total number of units produced and sold	12,000	13,200
Units delivered before scheduled delivery date	8,500	9,900
Number of defective units shipped	480	396
Number of customer complaints other than for defective units	500	517
Average time from when customer places order for a unit to when unit is delivered to the customer	30 days	25 days
Number of units reworked during production	600	627
Manufacturing lead time	20 days	16 days
Direct and indirect manufacturing labour hours	108,000	132,000

REQUIRED

1. For each of the years 2007 and 2008, calculate
   a. Percentage of defective units shipped
   b. Customer complaints as a percentage of units shipped
   c. On-time delivery rate
   d. Percentage of units reworked during production
2. On the basis of your calculations in requirement 1, has ESC's performance on quality and timeliness improved?
3. Philip Larkin, a member of ESC's Board of Directors, comments that regardless of the effect that the program has had on quality, the output per labour-hour has declined between 2007 and 2008. Larkin believes that lower output per labour-hour will lead to an increase in costs and lower operating income.
   a. How did Larkin conclude that output per labour-hour declined in 2007 relative to 2008?
   b. Why might output per labour-hour decline in 2008?
   c. Do you think that a lower output per labour-hour will decrease operating income in 2008? Explain briefly.

19-20 Quality improvement, relevant costs, and relevant revenues. The Photon Corporation manufactures and sells 20,000 copiers each year. The variable and fixed costs of reworking and repairing copiers are as follows:

	Variable Costs	Fixed Costs	Total Costs
Rework costs per hour	$ 48	$72	$120
Repair costs			
Customer support costs per/hour	24	36	60
Transportation costs per load	216	72	288
Warranty repair costs per hour	54	78	132

Photon's engineers are currently working to solve the problem of copies being too light or too dark. They propose changing the lens of the copier. The new lens will cost $60 more than the old lens. Each copier uses one lens. Photon uses a one-year time horizon for this decision, since it plans to introduce a new copier at the end of the year. Photon believes that even as it improves quality, it will not be able to save any of the fixed costs of rework or repair.

By changing the lens, Photon expects that it will (1) save 12,000 hours of rework, (2) save 800 hours of customer support, (3) move 200 fewer loads, (4) save 8,000 hours of repair, and (5) sell 100 additional copiers for a total contribution of $720,000.

REQUIRED

1. What are the additional costs of choosing the new lens?
2. What are the additional financial benefits of choosing the new lens?
3. Should Photon change to the new lens? Show your calculations.

19-21 Customer-response time, on-time delivery. Pizzafest Inc. makes and delivers pizzas to homes and offices in the Vancouver area. Fast, on-time delivery is one of Pizzafest's key strategies. Pizzafest provides the following information for the year 2007 about its customer-response time—the amount of time between when a customer calls to place an order and when the pizza is delivered to the customer.

	January–June	July–December
1. Pizzas delivered in 30 minutes or less	120,000	180,000
2. Pizzas delivered in between 31 and 45 minutes	240,000	312,000
3. Pizzas delivered in between 46 and 60 minutes	96,000	84,000
4. Pizzas delivered in between 61 and 75 minutes	24,000	24,000
Total pizzas delivered	480,000	600,000

REQUIRED

1. For January–June 2007 and July–December 2007, calculate the percentage of pizzas delivered in each of the four time intervals (less than 30 minutes, 31 to 45 minutes, 46 to 60 minutes, and 61 to 75 minutes). On the basis of these calculations, has customer-response time improved in July–December 2007 compared with January–June 2007?

2. When customers call Pizzafest, they often ask how long it will take for the pizza to be delivered to their home or office. If Pizzafest quotes a long time interval, customers will often not place the order. If Pizzafest quotes too short a time interval and the pizza is not delivered on time, customers get upset and Pizzafest will lose repeat business. Based on the January–June 2007 data, what maximum customer-response time should Pizzafest quote to its customers if (a) it wants to have an on-time delivery performance of at least 75%? (b) it wants to have an on-time delivery performance of at least 95%?

3. If Pizzafest had quoted the maximum customer-response times you calculated in requirements 2(a) and 2(b), would it have met its on-time delivery performance targets of 75% and 95% respectively for the period July–December 2007?

4. Pizzafest is considering giving an on-time guarantee for January–June 2008. If the pizza is not delivered within 60 minutes of placing the order, the customer gets the pizza free. Pizzafest estimates that it will make additional sales of 20,000 pizzas as a result of giving this guarantee. It estimates that it will fail to deliver a total of 15,000 pizzas on time. The average price of a pizza is $15.60, and the variable cost of a pizza is $8.40.
   a. What is the effect on Pizzafest's operating income of making this offer?
   b. What other factors should Pizzafest consider before making this offer?
   c. What actions can Pizzafest take to reduce customer-response time?

19-22 **Waiting time, banks.** Regal Bank has a small branch in Orillia, Ontario. The counter is staffed by one teller. The counter is open for five hours (300 minutes) each day (the operational capacity). It takes six minutes to serve a customer (service time). The Orillia branch expects to receive 42 customers each day. (Note that the number of customers corresponds to the number of orders in the chapter discussion.)

REQUIRED

1. Using the formula on page 752, calculate how long, on average, a customer will wait in line before being served.

2. How long, on average, will a customer wait in line if the branch expects 50 customers each day and the average time to serve each is 5 minutes?

3. The bank is considering ways to reduce waiting time. How long will customers have to wait, on average, if the time to serve a customer is reduced to 4.5 minutes and the bank expects to serve 50 customers each day?

19-23 **Waiting time, relevant costs, and relevant revenues.** The Orillia branch of Regal Bank is thinking of offering additional services to its customers. Its counter is open for five hours (300 minutes) each day (the operational capacity). If it introduces the new services, the bank expects to serve an average of 60 customers each day instead of the 42 customers it currently averages. It will take 4.5 minutes to serve each customer (service time) regardless of whether the new services are offered. (Note that the number of customers corresponds to the number of orders in the chapter discussion.)

REQUIRED

1. Using the formula on page 752, calculate how long, on average, a customer will wait in line before being served.

2. Regal Bank's policy is that the average waiting time in the line should not exceed five minutes. The bank cannot reduce the time to serve a customer below 4.5 minutes

without significantly affecting quality. To reduce average waiting time for the 60 customers it expects to serve each day, the bank decides to keep the counter open for 391.5 minutes each day. Verify that by keeping the counter open for a longer time, the bank will be able to achieve its goal of an average waiting time of 4.5 minutes or less.

3. The bank expects to generate, on average, $36 in additional operating income each day as a result of offering the new services. The teller is paid $12 per hour and is employed in increments of an hour (that is, the teller can be employed for five, six, seven hours, and so on, but not for a fraction of an hour). If the bank wants average waiting time to be no more than 4.5 minutes, should the bank offer the new services?

19-24 Theory of constraints, throughput contribution, relevant costs. The Mayfield Corporation manufactures filing cabinets in two operations—machining and finishing. Additional information is as follows:

	Machining	Finishing
Annual capacity	100,000 units	80,000 units
Annual production	80,000 units	80,000 units
Fixed operating costs (excluding direct materials)	$768,000	$480,000
Fixed operating costs per unit produced ($768,000 ÷ 80,000; $480,000 ÷ 80,000)	$9.60 per unit	$6.00 per unit

Each cabinet sells for $86.40 and has direct materials costs of $38.40 incurred at the start of the machining operation. Mayfield has no other variable costs. Mayfield can sell whatever output it produces. The following requirements refer only to the preceding data; there is no connection between the situations.

REQUIRED

1. Mayfield is considering using some modern jigs and tools in the finishing operation that would increase annual finishing output by 1,000 units. The annual cost of these jigs and tools is $36,000. Should Mayfield acquire these tools?
2. The production manager of the Machining Department has submitted a proposal to do faster setups that would increase the annual capacity of the Machining Department by 10,000 units and cost $6,000 per year. Should Mayfield implement the change?

19-25 Theory of constraints, throughput contribution, relevant costs. Refer to the information in Exercise 19-24 in answering the following requirements; there is no connection between the situations.

REQUIRED

1. An outside contractor offers to do the finishing operation for 12,000 units at $12 per unit, double the $6 per unit that it costs Mayfield to do the finishing in-house. Should Mayfield accept the subcontractor's offer?
2. The Hunt Corporation offers to machine 4,000 units at $4.80 per unit, half the $9.60 per unit that it costs Mayfield to do the machining in-house. Should Mayfield accept the subcontractor's offer?

19-26 Theory of constraints, throughput contribution, quality. Refer to the information in Exercise 19-24 in answering the following requirements; there is no connection between the situations.

REQUIRED

1. Mayfield produces 2,000 defective units at the machining operation. What is the cost to Mayfield of the defective items produced? Explain your answer briefly.
2. Mayfield produces 2,000 defective units at the finishing operation. What is the cost to Mayfield of the defective items produced? Explain your answer briefly.

PROBLEMS

19-27 Quality improvement, relevant costs, and relevant revenues. The Thomas Corporation sells 300,000 V262 valves to the automobile and truck industry. Thomas has a capacity of 110,000 machine-hours and can produce 3 valves per machine-hour. V262's contribution margin per unit is $9.60. Thomas sells only 300,000 valves because 30,000 valves (10% of the good valves) need to be reworked. It takes one machine-hour to rework 3 valves so that 10,000 hours of capacity are lost in the rework process. Thomas's rework costs are $252,000. Rework costs consist of

Direct materials and direct rework labour (variable costs)	$3.60 per unit
Fixed costs of equipment, rent, and overhead allocation	$4.80 per unit

Thomas's process designers have come up with a modification that would maintain the speed of the process and would ensure 100% quality and no rework. The new process would cost $378,000 per year. The following additional information is available:

- The demand for Thomas's V262 valves is 370,000 per year.
- The Jackson Corporation has asked Thomas to supply 22,000 T971 valves if Thomas implements the new design. The contribution margin per T971 valve is $12. Thomas can make two T971 valves per machine-hour on the existing machine with 100% quality and no rework.

REQUIRED

1. Suppose Thomas's designers implemented the new design. Should Thomas accept Jackson's order for 22,000 T971 valves? Explain.
2. Should Thomas implement the new design?
3. What nonfinancial and qualitative factors should Thomas consider in deciding whether to implement the new design?

19-28 Quality improvement, relevant costs, and relevant revenues. The Tan Corporation makes multicolour plastic lamps in two operations, moulding and welding. The moulding operation has a capacity of 200,000 units per year; welding has a capacity of 300,000 units per year. Annual costs of quality information recorded by Tan is as follows:

- Design of product and process costs $288,000
- Inspection and testing costs 204,000
- Scrap costs (all in the moulding department) 900,000

The demand for lamps is very strong. Tan will be able to sell whatever output quantities it can produce at $48 per lamp.

Tan can start only 200,000 units into production in the Moulding Department because of capacity constraints on the moulding machines. If a defective unit is produced at the moulding operation, it must be scrapped, and the scrap yields no revenue. Of the 200,000 units started at the moulding operation, 30,000 units (15%) are scrapped. Scrap costs, based on total (fixed and variable) manufacturing costs incurred up to the moulding operation, equal $30 per unit as follows:

Direct materials (variable)	$19.20 per unit
Direct manufacturing labour, setup labour, and materials-handling labour (variable)	3.60 per unit
Equipment, rent, and other allocated overhead including inspection and testing costs on scrapped parts (fixed)	7.20 per unit
	$30 per unit

The good units from the Moulding Department are sent to the Welding Department. Variable manufacturing costs at the Welding Department are $3.00 per unit. There is no scrap in the Welding Department. Therefore, Tan's total sales quantity equals the Moulding Department's output. Tan incurs no other variable costs.

Tan's designers have determined that adding a different type of material to the existing direct materials would reduce scrap to zero, but it would increase the variable costs per unit in the Moulding Department by $3.60. Recall that only 200,000 units can be started each year.

REQUIRED

1. What is the additional direct materials cost of implementing the new method?
2. What is the additional benefit to Tan from using the new material and improving quality?
3. Should Tan use the new material?
4. What other nonfinancial and qualitative factors should Tan consider in making a decision?

19-29 Statistical quality control, airline operations. Peoples Skyway operates daily round-trip flights on the London–Vancouver route using a fleet of three 747s, the *Spirit of Birmingham*, the *Spirit of Glasgow*, and the *Spirit of Manchester*. The budgeted quantity of fuel for each round-trip flight is the mean (average) fuel usage. Over the past 12 months, the average fuel usage per round trip is 120 litre-units with a standard deviation of 12 litre-units. A litre-unit is 1,000 litres.

Cilla Black, the operations manager of Peoples Skyway, uses a statistical quality control (SQC) approach in deciding whether to investigate fuel usage per round-trip flight. She investigates those flights with fuel usage greater than two standard deviations from the mean.

In October, Black receives the following report for round-trip fuel usage by the three planes operating on the London–Vancouver route:

Flight	Spirit of Birmingham (Litre-Units)	Spirit of Glasgow (Litre-Units)	Spirit of Manchester (Litre-Units)
1	124.8	123.6	116.4
2	112.8	112.8	124.8
3	116.4	115.2	133.2
4	121.2	128.4	124.8
5	126.0	110.4	146.4
6	128.4	135.6	141.6
7	133.2	118.8	151.2
8	134.2	127.2	136.8
9	138.0	121.2	140.4
10	142.8	111.6	147.6

REQUIRED

1. Using the $\pm 2\sigma$ rule, what variance investigation decisions would be made?
2. Present SQC charts for round-trip fuel usage for each of the three 747s in October. What inferences can you draw from them?
3. Some managers propose that Peoples Skyway present its SQC charts in monetary terms rather than in physical quantity terms (litre-units). What are the advantages and disadvantages of using monetary fuel costs rather than litre-units in the SQC charts?

19-30 **Compensation linked with profitability, on-time delivery, and external quality performance measures; balanced scorecard.** Pacific-Dunlop supplies tires to major automotive companies. It has two tire plants in North America, in Detroit and Los Angeles. The quarterly bonus plan for each plant manager has three components:

a. **Profitability performance.** Add 2% of operating income.
b. **On-time delivery performance.** Add $12,000 if on-time delivery performance to the ten most important customers is 98% or better. If on-time performance is below 98%, add nothing.
c. **Product quality performance.** Deduct 50% of cost of sales returns from the ten most important customers.

Quarterly data for 2007 on the Detroit and Los Angeles plants are as follows:

	January–March	April–June	July–September	October–December
Detroit				
Operating income	$ 960,000	$1,020,000	$ 840,000	$1,080,000
On-time delivery*	98.4%	98.6%	97.1%	97.9%
Cost of sales returns*	$ 21,600	$ 31,200	$ 12,000	$ 30,000
Los Angeles				
Operating income	$1,920,000	$1,800,000	$2,160,000	$2,280,000
On-time delivery*	95.6%	97.1%	97.9%	98.4%
Cost of sales returns*	$ 42,000	$ 40,800	$ 33,600	$ 26,400

*For the ten most important customers.

REQUIRED

1. Compute the bonuses paid in each quarter of 2007 to the plant managers of the Detroit and Los Angeles plants.
2. Discuss the three components of the bonus plan as measures of profitability, on-time delivery, and product quality.
3. Why would you want to evaluate plant managers on the basis of both operating income and on-time delivery?
4. Give one example of what might happen if on-time delivery were dropped as a performance evaluation measure.

19-31 Waiting times, manufacturing lead times. The SRG Corporation uses an injection mould-ing machine to make a plastic product, Z39. SRG makes products only after receiving firm orders from its customers. SRG estimates that it will receive 50 orders for Z39 (each order is for 1,000 units) during the coming year. Each order of Z39 will take 96 hours of machine time (4.8 hours to clean and prepare the machine, called setup, and 91.2 hours to process the order). The annual capacity of the machine is 6,000 hours.

REQUIRED

1. What percentage of the total available machine capacity does SRG expect to use during the coming year?
2. Calculate the average amount of time that an order for Z39 will wait in line before it is processed and the average manufacturing lead time per order for Z39.
3. SRG is considering introducing a new product, Y28. SRG estimates that, on average, it will receive 25 orders of Y28 (each order for 200 units) in the coming year. Each order of Y28 will take 24 hours of machine time (2.4 hours to clean and prepare the machine, and 21.6 hours to process the order). The average demand for Z39 will be unaffected by the introduction of Y28. Calculate the average waiting time for an order received and the average manufacturing lead time per order for each product, if SRG introduces Y28.
4. If SRG introduces Y28, on average what fraction of the total manufacturing lead time will each order of Y28 spend just waiting to be processed?
5. Briefly describe why delays occur in the processing of Z39 and Y28.

19-32 Waiting times, relevant revenues and relevant costs (continuation of 19-31). SRG is still deciding whether or not it should introduce and sell Y28. The following table provides infor-mation on selling prices, variable costs, and inventory carrying costs for Z39 and Y28. SRG will incur additional variable costs and inventory carrying costs for Y28 only if it introduces Y28. Fixed costs equal to 40% of variable costs are allocated to all products produced and sold during the year.

Product	Annual Average Number of Orders	Average Selling Price per Order If Average Manufacturing Lead Time Per Order Is		Variable Costs per Order	Inventory Carrying Costs per Order per Hour
		Fewer than 384 Hours	More than 384 Hours		
Z39	50	$32,400	$31,800	$18,000	$0.75
Y28	25	10,080	9,600	6,000	0.25

REQUIRED

1. Should SRG manufacture and sell Y28? Show all your computations.
2. What is the cutoff price per order above which SRG should manufacture and sell Y28 and below which SRG should choose not to manufacture and sell Y28?

19-33 Manufacturing lead times, relevant revenues, and relevant costs. The Brandt Corporation makes wire harnesses for the aircraft industry. Brandt is uncertain about when and how many customer orders will be received. Brandt makes harnesses only after receiving firm orders from its customers. Brandt has recently purchased a new machine to make wire harnesses, one for Boeing airplanes (B7) and the other for Airbus Industries airplanes (A3). The annual capacity of the new machine is 7,200 hours. The following information is available for next year:

Customer	Annual Average Number of Orders	Manufacturing Time Required	Average Selling Price per Order If Average Manufacturing Lead Time Is		Variable Costs per Order	Inventory Carrying Costs per Order per Hour
			Fewer than 240 Hours	More than 240 Hours		
B7	125	48 hours	$18,000	$17,280	$12,000	$0.50
A3	10	60 hours	16,200	15,552	10,800	0.45

REQUIRED

1. Calculate the average manufacturing lead times per order (a) if Brandt manufactures only B7 and (b) if Brandt manufactures both B7 and A3.

2. Even though A3 has a positive contribution margin, Brandt's managers are evaluating whether Brandt should (a) make and sell only B7 or (b) make and sell both B7 and A3. Which alternative will maximize Brandt's operating income? Show all calculations.
3. What other factors should Brandt consider in choosing between the alternatives in requirement 2?

19-34 Theory of constraints, throughput contribution, relevant costs. Columbia Industries manufactures electronic testing equipment. Columbia also installs the equipment at the customer's site and ensures that it functions smoothly. Additional information on the Manufacturing and Installation Departments is as follows (capacities are expressed in terms of the number of units of electronic testing equipment):

	Equipment Manufactured	Equipment Installed
Annual capacity	400 units per year	300 units per year
Equipment manufactured and installed	300 units per year	300 units per year

Columbia manufactures only 300 units per year because the Installation Department has only enough capacity to install 300 units. The equipment sells for $48,000 per unit (installed) and has direct materials costs of $18,000. All costs other than direct materials costs are fixed. The following requirements refer only to the preceding data; there is no connection between the situations.

REQUIRED
1. Columbia's engineers have found a way to reduce equipment manufacturing time. The new method would cost an additional $60 per unit and would allow Colorado to manufacture 20 additional units a year. Should Columbia implement the new method?
2. Columbia's designers have proposed a change in the direct materials that would increase direct materials costs by $2,400 per unit. This change would enable Columbia to install 320 units of equipment each year. If Columbia makes the change, it will implement the new design on all equipment sold. Should Columbia use the new design?
3. A new installation technique has been developed that will enable Columbia's engineers to install 10 additional units of equipment a year. The new method will increase installation costs by $60,000 each year. Should Columbia implement the new technique?
4. Columbia is considering how to motivate workers to improve their productivity (output per hour). One proposal is to evaluate and compensate workers in the Manufacturing and Installation Departments on the basis of their productivities. Do you think the new proposal is a good idea? Explain briefly.

19-35 Theory of constraints, throughput contribution, quality, relevant costs. Aardee Industries manufactures pharmaceutical products in two departments—Mixing and Tablet-Making. Additional information on the two departments follows. Each tablet contains 0.5 gram of direct materials.

	Mixing	Tablet-Making
Capacity per hour	150 grams	200 tablets
Monthly capacity (2,000 hours available in each of mixing and tablet-making)	300,000 grams	400,000 tablets
Monthly production	200,000 grams	390,000 tablets
Fixed operating costs (excluding direct materials)	$ 19,200	$ 46,800
Fixed operating costs per unit ($19,200 ÷ 200,000; $46,800 ÷ 390,000)	$ 0.096 per gram	$ 0.12 per tablet

The Mixing Department makes 200,000 grams of direct materials mixture (enough to make 400,000 tablets) because the Tablet-Making Department has only enough capacity to process 400,000 tablets. All direct materials costs are incurred in the Mixing Department. Aardee incurs $187,200 in direct materials costs. The Tablet-Making Department manufactures only 390,000 tablets from the 200,000 grams of mixture processed; 2.5% of the direct materials mixture is lost in the tablet-making process. Each tablet sells for $1.20. All costs other than direct materials costs are fixed costs. The following requirements refer only to the preceding data; there is no connection between the situations.

REQUIRED
1. An outside contractor makes the following offer: if Aardee will supply the contractor with 10,000 grams of mixture, the contractor will manufacture 19,500 tablets for Aardee

(allowing for the normal 2.5% loss during the tablet-making process) at $0.144 per tablet. Should Aardee accept the contractor's offer?

2. Another firm offers to prepare 20,000 grams of mixture a month from direct materials Aardee supplies. The company will charge $0.084 per gram of mixture. Should Aardee accept the company's offer?

3. Aardee's engineers have devised a method that would improve quality in the tablet-making operation. They estimate that the 10,000 tablets currently being lost would be saved. The modification would cost $8,400 a month. Should Aardee implement the new method?

4. Suppose that Aardee also loses 10,000 grams of mixture in its mixing operation. These losses can be reduced to zero if the company is willing to spend $10,800 per month in quality improvement methods. Should Aardee adopt the quality improvement method?

5. What are the benefits of improving quality at the mixing operation compared with the benefits of improving quality at the tablet-making operation?

19-36 Quality improvement, Pareto charts, fishbone diagrams. The Murray Corporation manufactures, sells, and installs photocopying machines. Murray has placed heavy emphasis on reducing defects and failures in its production operations. Murray wants to apply the same total quality management (TQM) principles to managing its accounts receivables.

REQUIRED

1. On the basis of your knowledge and experience, what would you classify as failures in accounts receivables?
2. Give examples of prevention activities that could reduce failures in accounts receivables.
3. Draw a Pareto diagram of the types of failures in accounts receivables and a fishbone diagram of possible causes of one type of failure in accounts receivables.

19-37 Ethics and quality. Information from a quality report for 2007 prepared by Lindsey Lavoie, assistant controller of Citocell, a manufacturer of electric motors, follows:

Revenues	$12,000,000
On-line inspection	108,000
Warranty liability	312,000
Product testing	252,000
Scrap	276,000
Design engineering	240,000
Percentage of customer complaints	5%
On-time delivery	90%

Tadao Inaba, the plant manager of Citocell, is eligible for a bonus if the total cost of quality as a percentage of revenues is less than 10%, percentage of customer complaints is less than 4%, and on-time delivery exceeds 92%. Inaba is unhappy because, when preparing her report, Lavoie actually contacted customers to inquire if they had any complaints and if deliveries had been made on time. Inaba would have preferred Lavoie to be less proactive and wait for customers to complain. Inaba's concern with Lavoie's approach is that it introduces subjectivity into the numbers and also fails to capture the seriousness of customers' concerns. "When you wait for a customer to complain, you know they are complaining because it is something important. When you do customer surveys, customers mention whatever is on their mind, even if it is not terribly important."

John Roche, the controller, asks Lavoie to see him. He tells her about Inaba's concerns. "I think Tadao has a point. See what you can do." Lavoie is very confident that the customer complaints are genuine and that customers are concerned about late deliveries. She believes it is important for Citocell to be proactive and obtain systematic and quick customer feedback, and then to use this information to make future improvements. She is also well aware that Citocell had not done customer surveys in the past, and that but for her surveys, Inaba would probably be eligible for the bonus. She is confused about how to handle Roche's request.

REQUIRED

1. Calculate the ratio of each cost of quality category (prevention, appraisal, internal failure, and external failure) to revenues in 2007. Are the total costs of quality as a percentage of revenues less than 10%?
2. Is John Roche's suggestion to Lavoie to reconsider her numbers unethical? Would it be unethical for Lavoie to modify her analysis? What steps should Lavoie take to resolve this situation?

COLLABORATIVE LEARNING PROBLEM

19-38 Quality improvement, relevant costs, and relevant revenues. The Wellesley Corporation makes printed cloth in two operations, weaving and printing. Direct materials costs are Wellesley's only variable costs. The demand for Wellesley's cloth is very strong. Wellesley can sell whatever output quantities it produces at $1,500 per roll to a distributor who then markets, distributes, and provides customer service for the product.

	Weaving	Printing
Monthly capacity	10,000 rolls	15,000 rolls
Monthly production	9,500 rolls	8,550 rolls
Direct material variable costs per roll of cloth processed at each operation	$ 600	$ 120
Fixed operating costs	$3,420,000	$513,000
Fixed operating costs per roll ($3,420,000 ÷ 9,500; $513,000 ÷ 8,550)	$ 360 per roll	$ 60 per roll

Monthly costs of quality information recorded by Wellesley are as follows:
- Product and process design costs $ 360,000
- Scrap costs in Weaving Department   471,000
- Scrap costs in Printing Department   1,060,200

Wellesley can start only 10,000 rolls of cloth in the Weaving Department because of capacity constraints at the weaving machines. If the weaving operation produces defective cloth, the cloth must be scrapped and yields zero net revenue. Of the 10,000 rolls of cloth started at the weaving operation, 500 rolls (5%) are scrapped. Scrap costs per roll, based on total (fixed and variable) manufacturing costs per roll incurred up to the end of the weaving operation, equal $942 per roll as follows:

Direct materials costs per roll (variable)	$600
Fixed operating costs per roll ($3,420,000 ÷ 10,000 rolls)	342
Total manufacturing costs per roll in Weaving Department	$942

The good rolls from the Weaving Department (called grey cloth) are sent to the Printing Department. Of the 9,500 good rolls started at the printing operation, 950 rolls (10%) are scrapped and yield zero net revenue. Scrap costs based on total (fixed and variable) manufacturing costs per unit incurred up to the end of the printing operation equal $1,116 per roll calculated as follows:

Total manufacturing costs per roll in Weaving Department		$942
Printing Department manufacturing costs:		
Direct materials costs per roll (variable)	$120	
Fixed operating costs per roll ($513,000 ÷ 9,500 rolls)	54	
Total manufacturing costs per roll in Printing Department		174
Total manufacturing costs per roll		$1,116

The Wellesley Corporation's total monthly sales of printed cloth equals the Printing Department's output. The following requirements refer only to the preceding data; there is no connection between the situations.

INSTRUCTIONS
Form groups of three students to complete the following requirements.

REQUIRED
1. The Printing Department is considering buying 5,000 rolls of grey cloth from an outside supplier at $1,080 per roll. The Printing Department manager is concerned that the cost of purchasing the grey cloth is much higher than Wellesley's cost of manufacturing the grey cloth. The quality of the grey cloth acquired from outside is very similar to that manufactured in-house. The Printing Department expects that 10% of the rolls obtained from the outside supplier will be scrapped. Should the Printing Department buy the grey cloth from the outside supplier?

2. How much does Wellesley lose if a defective roll is produced in the Printing Department?
3. What is the expected loss to Wellesley if a defective roll is produced in the Weaving Department? Use the expected monetary value criterion described in the appendix to Chapter 3.
4. Wellesley's engineers have developed a method that would lower the Printing Department's scrap rate to 6% at the printing operation. Implementing the new method would cost $420,000 per month. Should Wellesley implement the change?
5. The design engineering team has proposed a modification that would lower the Weaving Department's scrap rate to 3%. The modification would cost the company $210,000 per month. Should Wellesley implement the change?
6. From your answers to requirements 1 to 5, what general conclusions can you draw about implementing TQM programs?

Customers are demanding lower lead time between their orders and receipt of the finished product. Therefore, manufacturers are demanding more frequent deliveries with shorter purchase order lead times from their suppliers. To better service the companies who use their automotive products, Challenger Freight invested in information systems. The technology improved coordination and response times that helped Challenger Freight and its customers to reduce inventory levels.

CHAPTER 20

Inventory Management, Just-in-Time, and Backflush Costing

LEARNING OBJECTIVES

After studying this chapter, you should be able to

1. Identify five categories of costs associated with goods for sale

2. Balance ordering costs and carrying costs using the economic order quantity (EOQ) decision model

3. Identify and reduce conflicts that can arise between EOQ decision models and models used for performance evaluation

4. Use a supply-chain approach to inventory management

5. Differentiate materials requirements planning (MRP) systems from just-in-time (JIT) systems for manufacturing

6. Identify the major features of a just-in-time production system

7. Use backflush costing

8. Describe different ways backflush costing can simplify traditional job-costing systems

Inventory management is a pivotal part of profit planning for manufacturing and merchandising companies. Materials costs often account for more than 50% of total costs in manufacturing companies and more than 70% of total costs in retail companies. Unused material is unsold product and the carrying costs to retain material in various inventories can represent up to 35% of annual manufacturing costs. Accounting information has a key role in inventory management. We first consider retail organizations and then manufacturing companies.

INVENTORY MANAGEMENT IN RETAIL ORGANIZATIONS

Inventory management is the planning, coordinating, and control activities related to the flow of inventory into, through, and from the organization. Consider retailers where the cost of goods sold constitutes the largest single cost item. The following breakdown of operations for two major retailers is illustrative:

	Loblaw Companies	Sobeys Inc.
Sales	100.0%	100.0%
Cost of sales and other expenses	91.9%	95.9%
Depreciation and amortization	1.8%	1.4%
Interest and taxes	2.6%	1.1%
Net income	3.7%	1.6%

With a high level of perishable inventory and low net income percentage, managers in the grocery retail industry must make accurate decisions regarding the purchasing and managing of goods for sale or incur avoidable costs of spoilage.

Costs Associated with Goods for Sale

The following cost categories are important when managing inventories and goods for sale:

1. *Purchasing costs.* **Purchasing costs** consist of the costs of goods acquired from suppliers including incoming freight or transportation costs. These costs usually make up the largest single cost category of goods for sale. Discounts for different purchase order sizes and supplier credit terms affect purchasing costs.

2. *Ordering costs.* **Ordering costs** consist of the costs of preparing and issuing a purchase order. Related to the number of purchase orders processed are special processing, receiving, inspection, and payment costs.

3. *Carrying costs.* **Carrying costs** arise when a business holds inventories of goods for sale. These costs include the opportunity cost of the investment tied up in inventory (see Chapter 11) and the costs associated with storage, such as storage space rental and insurance, obsolescence, and spoilage.

4. *Stockout costs.* A **stockout** occurs when a company runs out of an item for which there is customer demand. A company may respond to the shortfall or stockout by expediting an order from a supplier. Expediting costs of a stockout include the additional ordering costs plus any associated transportation costs. Alternatively, the company may lose a sale due to the stockout. In this case, stockout costs include the lost contribution margin on the sale plus any contribution margin lost on future sales hurt by customer ill-will caused by the stockout.

5. *Quality costs.* The *quality* of a product or service is its conformance with a pre-announced or prespecified standard. As described in Chapter 19, four categories of costs of quality are often distinguished: (a) prevention costs, (b) appraisal costs, (c) internal failure costs, and (d) external failure costs.

The descriptions of the cost categories indicate that some of the relevant costs for making inventory decisions and managing goods for sale are not available in existing accounting systems. Opportunity costs, which are not typically recorded in accounting systems, are an important component in several of these cost categories.

Information technology, such as the scheduling, inventory control, and costing system of Seradex and bar code and radio-frequency identification (RFID) on items, increases reliability and timeliness of inventory data that reduce costs in these five categories. For example, bar-coding technology allows a scanner to capture purchases and sales of individual units. This creates an instantaneous record of inventory movements and helps in the management of purchasing, carrying, and stockout costs. In the sections that follow, we consider how to calculate relevant costs for different inventory-related decisions in merchandising companies.

Economic order quantity (EOQ). Decision model that calculates the optimal quantity of inventory to order. Simplest model incorporates only ordering costs and carrying costs.

Purchase order lead time. Amount of time between the placement of an order and its delivery.

Economic Order Quantity Decision Model

The first major decision in managing goods for sale is deciding how much of a given product to order. The **economic order quantity (EOQ)** decision model calculates the optimal quantity of inventory to order. The simplest version of this model incorporates only ordering costs and carrying costs into the calculation. It assumes the following:

1. The same fixed quantity is ordered at each reorder point.

2. Demand, ordering costs, and carrying costs are certain. The **purchase order lead time**—the time between the placement of an order and its delivery—is also certain.

3. Purchasing costs per unit are unaffected by the quantity ordered. This assumption makes purchasing costs irrelevant to determining EOQ, because purchasing costs of all units acquired will be the same, whatever the order size in which the units are ordered.

4. No stockouts occur. One justification for this assumption is that the costs of a stockout are prohibitively high. We assume that to avoid these potential costs, management always maintains adequate inventory so that no stockout can occur.

5. In deciding the size of the purchase order, management considers the costs of quality only to the extent that these costs affect ordering costs or carrying costs.

Given these assumptions, EOQ analysis ignores purchasing costs, stockout costs, and quality costs. To determine EOQ, we minimize the relevant ordering and carrying costs (those ordering and carrying costs that are affected by the quantity of inventory ordered):

Total relevant costs = Total relevant ordering costs + Total relevant carrying costs

Example: Video Galore sells packages of blank videotapes to its customers; it also rents out tapes of movies and sporting events. It purchases packages of videotapes from Sontek at $14 a package. Sontek pays all incoming freight. No incoming inspection is necessary, as Sontek has a superb reputation for delivering quality merchandise. Annual demand is 13,000 packages, at a rate of 250 packages per week. Video Galore requires a 15% annual return on investment. The purchase order lead time is two weeks. The following cost data are available:

Relevant ordering costs per purchase order		$200.00
Relevant carrying costs per package per year:		
Required annual return on investment, 15% × $14	$2.10	
Relevant insurance, materials-handling, breakage, etc. per year	3.10	5.20

> You may be familiar with calculating EOQ, reorder point, and safety stock from finance or production courses. In those courses, costs for the formulas are assumed. Here you will see that management accountants help (1) decide what costs to include in the formulas and (2) estimate the amounts of the costs.

> Carrying costs are higher than you may think. In many companies, average annual carrying costs exceed 30% of purchasing costs. In the Video Galore example, annual carrying costs are 37% ($5.20 ÷ $14.00) of purchasing costs.

What is the economic order quantity of packages of videotapes? The formula underlying the EOQ model is

$$EOQ = \sqrt{\frac{2DP}{C}}$$

where:

EOQ = Economic order quantity
D = Demand in units for a specified time period (one year in this example)
P = Relevant ordering costs per purchase order
C = Relevant carrying costs of one unit in stock for the time period used for D (one year in this example)

The formula indicates that EOQ increases with demand and ordering costs and decreases with carrying costs.

We can use this formula to determine the EOQ for Video Galore as follows:

$$EOQ = \sqrt{\frac{2 \times 13{,}000 \times \$200}{\$5.20}} = \sqrt{1{,}000{,}000} = 1{,}000 \text{ packages}$$

Therefore, Video Galore should order 1,000 tape packages each time to minimize total ordering and carrying costs.

The total annual relevant costs (TRC) for any order quantity Q can be calculated using the following formula:

$$TRC = \begin{array}{c}\text{Total annual relevant}\\\text{ordering costs}\end{array} + \begin{array}{c}\text{Total annual relevant}\\\text{carrying costs}\end{array}$$

$$= \begin{array}{c}\text{Number of}\\\text{purchase orders}\\\text{per year}\end{array} \times \begin{array}{c}\text{Relevant}\\\text{ordering costs per}\\\text{purchase order}\end{array} + \begin{array}{c}\text{Average inventory}\\\text{in units}\end{array} \times \begin{array}{c}\text{Annual relevant}\\\text{carrying costs of 1}\\\text{unit for a year}\end{array}$$

$$= \left(\frac{D}{Q}\right) \times P + \left(\frac{Q}{2}\right) \times C = \frac{DP}{Q} + \frac{QC}{2}$$

(Note that in this formula, Q can be any order quantity, not just the EOQ.)

When $Q = 1{,}000$ units,

$$TRC = \frac{13{,}000 \times \$200}{1{,}000} + \frac{1{,}000 \times \$5.20}{2}$$

$$= \$2{,}600 + \$2{,}600 = \$5{,}200$$

The number of deliveries each time period (in our example, one year) is:

$$\frac{D}{EOQ} = \frac{13{,}000}{1{,}000} = 13 \text{ deliveries}$$

Exhibit 20-1 shows a graph analysis of the total annual relevant costs of ordering (DP/Q) and carrying inventory $(QC/2)$ under various order sizes (Q), and illustrates the tradeoff between the two types of costs. The larger the order quantity, the higher the annual relevant carrying costs, but the lower the annual relevant ordering costs. *The total annual relevant costs are at a minimum where total relevant ordering costs and total relevant carrying costs are equal* (in the Video Galore example, each equals $2,600).

EXHIBIT 20-1
Ordering Costs and Carrying Costs for Video Galore

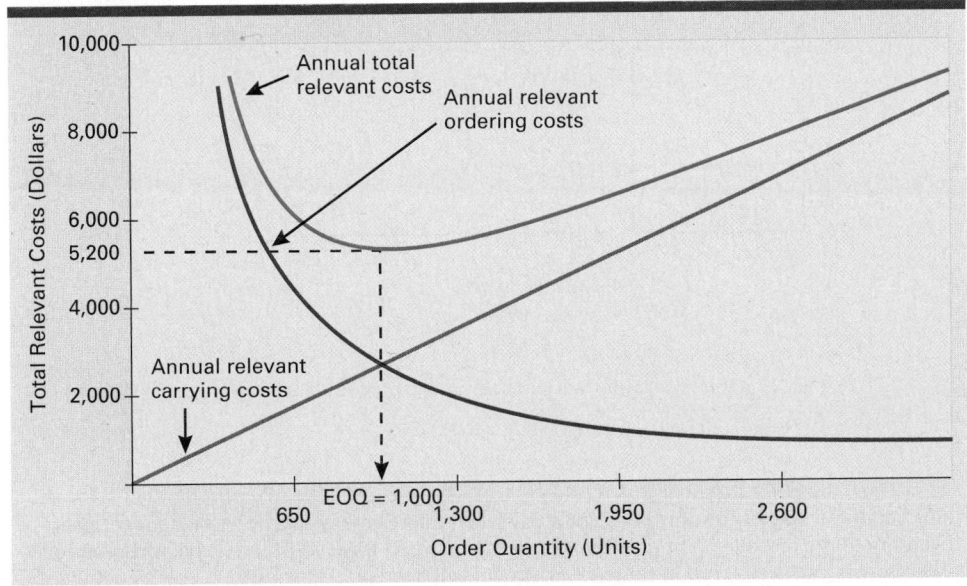

The intuition for the reorder point is that we need to reorder when inventory on hand falls to the level at which it equals the amount needed for sales that will occur during the purchase-order lead time.

Reorder point. The quantity level of the inventory on hand that triggers a new order.

When to Order, Assuming Certainty

The second major decision in dealing with cost of goods for sale is when to order. The **reorder point** is the quantity level of the inventory on hand that triggers a new order. The reorder point is simplest to compute when both demand and lead time are certain:

$$\text{Reorder point} = \frac{\text{Number of units sold}}{\text{per unit of time}} \times \text{Purchase order lead time}$$

Consider our Video Galore example. We choose a week as the unit of time:

Economic order quantity	1,000 packages
Number of units sold per week	250 packages
Purchase order lead time	2 weeks

Thus:

$$\text{Reorder point} = \frac{\text{Number of units sold}}{\text{per unit of time}} \times \text{Purchase order lead time}$$

$$= 250 \times 2 = 500 \text{ packages}$$

So, Video Galore will order 1,000 packages of tapes each time its inventory stock falls to 500 packages.

The graph in Exhibit 20-2 presents the behaviour of the inventory level of tape packages, assuming demand occurs uniformly throughout each week.[1] If the purchase order lead time is two weeks, a new order will be placed when the inventory level reaches 500 tape packages so that the 1,000 packages ordered are received at the time inventory reaches zero.

Safety Stock

So far, we have assumed that demand and purchase order lead time are certain. When retailers are uncertain about the demand, the lead time, or the quantity that suppliers can provide, they often hold safety stock. **Safety stock** is inventory held at all times regardless of inventory ordered using EOQ. It is used as a buffer against unexpected increases in demand or lead time and unavailability of stock from suppliers.

Safety stock. Inventory held at all times regardless of inventory ordered using EOQ. It is a buffer against unexpected increases in demand or lead time and unexpected unavailability of stock from suppliers.

EXHIBIT 20-2
Inventory Level of Tape Packages for Video Galore*

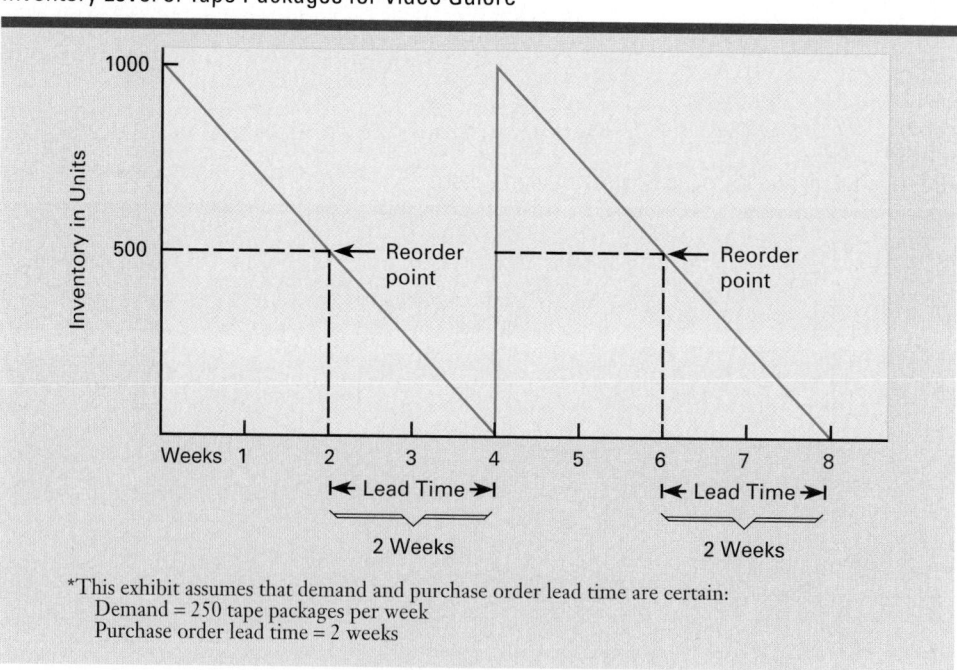

*This exhibit assumes that demand and purchase order lead time are certain:
Demand = 250 tape packages per week
Purchase order lead time = 2 weeks

[1]This handy but special formula does not apply when the receipt of the order fails to increase inventory to the reorder-point quantity (for example, when the lead time is three weeks and the order is a one-week supply). In these cases, orders will overlap.

In our Video Galore example, expected demand is 250 packages per week, but the company's managers feel that a maximum demand of 400 packages per week may occur. If Video Galore's managers decide that the costs of stockout are prohibitive, they may decide to hold safety stock of 300 packages. This amount is the maximum excess demand of 150 packages per week for the two weeks of purchase order lead time. The computation of safety stock hinges on demand forecasts. Managers will have some notion—usually based on experience—of the range of weekly demand.

A frequency distribution based on prior daily or weekly levels of demand provides data for computing the associated costs of maintaining safety stock. Assume that one of seven different levels of demand will occur over the two-week purchase order lead time at Video Galore.

Total Demand for Two Weeks	Units						
	200	300	400	500	600	700	800
Probability (sums to 1.00)	0.06	0.09	0.20	0.30	0.20	0.09	0.06

We see that 500 is the most likely level of demand for two weeks, because it is assigned the highest probability of occurrence. We also see that there is a 0.35 probability that demand will be between 600, 700, and 800 packages (0.20 + 0.09 + 0.06 = 0.35).

If a customer calls Video Galore to buy videotapes, and the store has none in stock, it can "rush" them to the customer at a cost to Video Galore of $4 per package. The relevant stockout costs in this case are $4 per package. The optimal safety stock level is the quantity of safety stock that minimizes the sum of the relevant annual stockout and carrying costs. Recall that the relevant carrying costs for Video Galore are $5.20 per unit per year.

Exhibit 20-3 presents the total annual relevant stockout and carrying costs when the reorder point is 500 units. We need only consider safety stock levels of 0, 100, 200,

In the Video Galore example, stockout costs include only the cost of rush orders, because rush orders are assumed to fully satisfy customer demand. However, stockouts can result in opportunity costs—lost contribution margin on lost current sales and lost future sales.

When calculating safety stock, the tradeoff is between stockout costs and carrying costs. Columns G and H in Exhibit 20-3 illustrate this tradeoff.

EXHIBIT 20-3
Computation of Safety Stock for Video Galore When Reorder Point is 500 Units

	A	B	C	D	E	F	G	H	I
1	Safety	Demand							
2	Stock	Levels			Relevant	Number	Expected	Relevant	Relevant
3	Level	Resulting	Stockout	Probability	Stockout	of Orders	Stockout	Carrying	Total
4	in Units	in Stockouts	in Units[a]	of Stockout	Costs[b]	per Year[c]	Costs[d]	Costs[e]	Costs
5	(1)	(2)	(3) = (2) − 500 − (1)	(4)	(5) = (3) × $4	(6)	(7) = (4) × (5) × (6)	(8) = (1) × $5.20	(9) = (7) + (8)
6	0	600	100	0.20	$ 400	13	$1,040		
7		700	200	0.09	800	13	936		
8		800	300	0.06	1,200	13	936		
9							$2,912	$ 0	$2,912
10	100	700	100	0.09	400	13	$ 468		
11		800	200	0.06	800	13	624		
12							$1,092	$ 520	$1,612
13	200	800	100	0.06	400	13	$ 312	$1,040	$1,352
14	300	—	—	—	—	—	$ 0[f]	$1,560	$1,560
15									
16	[a]Demand level resulting in stockouts − Inventory available during lead time (excluding safety stock), 500 units − safety stock.								
17	[b]Stockout in units × Relevant stockout costs of $400 per unit.								
18	[c]Annual demand, 13,000 ÷ 1,000 EOQ = 13 orders per year.								
19	[d]Probability of stockout × Relevant stockout costs × Number of orders per year.								
20	[e]Safety stock × Annual relevant carrying costs of $5.20 per unit (assumes that safety stock is on hand at all times and that there is no overstocking caused by decreases in expected usage).								
22	[f]At a safety stock level of 300 units, no stockouts will occur and, hence, expected stockout costs = $0.								

and 300 units, since demand will exceed the 500 units of stock available at reordering by 0 if demand is 500, by 100 if demand is 600, by 200 if demand is 700, and by 300 if demand is 800. The total annual relevant stockout and carrying costs would be minimized at $1,352, when a safety stock of 200 packages is maintained. Think of the 200 units of safety stock as extra stock that Video Galore maintains. For example, Video Galore's total inventory of tapes at the time of reordering its EOQ of 1,000 units would be 700 units (the reorder point of 500 units plus the safety stock of 200 units).

CHALLENGES IN ESTIMATING INVENTORY-RELATED COSTS AND THEIR EFFECTS

 Finance courses explain how to calculate the cost of capital.

Considerations in Obtaining Estimates of Relevant Costs

Obtaining accurate estimates of the cost parameters used in the EOQ decision model is a challenging task. For example, the relevant annual carrying costs of inventory consist of *incremental* or *outlay costs* plus the *opportunity cost of capital.*

What are the relevant incremental costs of carrying inventory? Only those costs that vary with the quantity of inventory held—for example, insurance, property taxes, costs of obsolescence, and costs of breakage, shrinkage, warehouse rent, and salaries paid to warehouse workers. Salaries paid to clerks, storekeepers, and materials-handlers, however, are irrelevant if they are unaffected by changes in inventory levels. But, if as inventories decrease these salary costs also decrease as the clerks, storekeepers, and materials-handlers are transferred to other activities or laid off, then these salaries are relevant incremental costs of carrying inventory. Similarly, the costs of storage space owned that cannot be used for other profitable purposes as inventories decrease are irrelevant. But if the space has other profitable uses, or if rental cost is tied to the amount of space occupied, storage costs are relevant incremental costs of carrying inventory.

What is the relevant opportunity cost of capital? It is the return forgone by investing capital in inventory rather than elsewhere. It is calculated as the required rate of return multiplied by those costs per unit that vary with the number of units purchased and that are incurred at the time the units are received. (Examples of these costs per unit are purchase price, incoming freight, and incoming inspection.)

Opportunity costs are not calculated on investments, say, in buildings, if these investments are unaffected by changes in inventory levels. In the case of stockouts, calculating the relevant opportunity costs requires an estimate of the lost contribution margin on that sale as well as on future sales hurt by customer ill-will resulting from the stockout.

Relevant ordering costs are only those ordering costs that change with the number of orders placed (for example, costs of preparing and issuing purchase orders and receiving and inspecting materials).

Cost of a Prediction Error

Our discussion suggests that predicting relevant costs requires care and is difficult. Managers understand that their projections will seldom be flawless. This leads to the question: What is the cost of an incorrect prediction when actual relevant costs are different from the relevant predicted costs used for decision making?

Continuing our example, suppose Video Galore's relevant ordering costs per purchase order are $100 instead of the predicted $200. We can calculate the cost of this prediction error with a three-step approach.

◆ **Step 1:** *Compute the monetary outcome from the best action that could have been taken, given the actual amount of the cost input.* The appropriate inputs are $D = 13,000$ units, $P = \$100$, and $C = \$5.20$. The economic order quantity size is:

$$EOQ = \sqrt{\frac{2DP}{C}}$$

$$= \sqrt{\frac{2 \times 13,000 \times \$100}{\$5.20}} = \sqrt{500,000}$$

$$= 707 \text{ packages (rounded)}$$

The total annual relevant cost when EOQ = 707 is:

$$\text{TRC} = \frac{DP}{Q} + \frac{QC}{2}$$

$$= \frac{13,000 \times \$100}{707} + \frac{707 \times \$5.20}{2}$$

$$= \$1,839 + \$1,838 = \$3,677$$

◆ **Step 2:** *Compute the monetary outcome from the best action on the basis of the incorrect amount of the predicted cost input.* The planned action when the relevant ordering costs per purchase order are predicted to be $200 is to purchase 1,000 packages in each order. The total annual relevant costs using this order quantity when $D = 13,000$ units, $P = \$100$, and $C = \$5.20$ are:

$$\text{TRC} = \frac{13,000 \times \$100}{1,000} + \frac{1,000 \times \$5.20}{2}$$

$$= \$1,300 + \$2,600 = \$3,900$$

◆ **Step 3:** *Compute the difference between the monetary outcomes from steps 1 and 2.*

	Monetary Outcome
Step 1	$3,677
Step 2	3,900
Difference	$ (223)

The cost of the prediction error is only $223, or just over 6% of the relevant total costs of $3,677. Why? Because the total annual relevant costs curve in Exhibit 20-1 (p. 777) is relatively flat over the range of order quantities from 650 to 1,300. *An important feature of the EOQ model is that the total relevant costs are rarely sensitive to minor variations in cost predictions. The square root in the EOQ model reduces the sensitivity of the decision to errors in predicting its inputs.*

In the following section we consider a planning-and-control and performance-evaluation issue that frequently arises when managing inventory.

Goal-Congruence Issues

Goal-congruence issues can arise when there is an inconsistency between the decision model and the model used to evaluate the performance of the person implementing the decision. For example, the absence of recorded opportunity costs in conventional accounting systems raises the possibility of a conflict between the EOQ model's optimal order quantity and the order quantity that the purchasing manager, evaluated on conventional accounting numbers, regards as optimal.

If annual carrying costs are excluded when evaluating the performance of managers, the managers may favour purchasing a larger order quantity than the EOQ decision model indicates is optimal. Companies such as Coca-Cola and Wal-Mart resolve this conflict by designing the performance evaluation system so that the carrying costs, including a required return on investment, are charged to the appropriate manager.

The opportunity cost of the investment tied up in inventory can be reduced by reducing inventory levels. We now discuss just-in-time purchasing, an approach that has led to dramatic reductions in inventories being held by some companies.

OBJECTIVE 3

Identify and reduce conflicts that can arise between EOQ decision models and models used for performance evaluation

JUST-IN-TIME PURCHASING

Just-in-time (JIT) purchasing is the purchase of goods or materials such that a delivery immediately precedes demand or use. JIT purchasing requires organizations to restructure their relationships with suppliers and place smaller and more frequent purchase orders. JIT purchasing can be implemented in both the retail and manufacturing sectors of the economy. Consider JIT purchasing for Hewlett-Packard's (HP's) manufacture of its computer work-station product line. HP has long-term agreements with suppliers who provide the major components for this product line. Each supplier is required to deliver components such that HP's final

Just-in-time (JIT) purchasing. The purchase of goods or materials such that delivery immediately precedes demand or use.

assembly plants meet their own production schedules and yet have minimal inventories on hand of the various components. Delivery to the production floor rather than to a store warehouse is the norm under JIT purchasing. A supplier who does not deliver components on time, or delivers components that fail to meet agreed-upon quality standards, can cause a failure by the HP assembly plant to meet its own scheduled deliveries for computers. Companies adopting JIT purchasing do not have large amounts of material inventories on hand that can enable a production line to continue operating even when some deliveries do not occur on time or where defective materials are delivered. HP shares its planned production schedule with each supplier. JIT purchasing for HP requires a high level of information sharing with suppliers who commit to deliver components in narrow time-windows. We now explore the relationship between JIT purchasing and the EOQ decision model already discussed in this chapter.

http://inventorymanagement
software.ca

JIT Purchasing and EOQ Model Parameters

Companies moving toward JIT purchasing argue that the cost of carrying inventories (parameter C in the EOQ model) has been dramatically underestimated in the past. This cost includes storage costs, spoilage, obsolescence, and opportunity costs such as investment tied up in inventory. The cost of placing a purchase order (parameter P in the EOQ model) is also being reevaluated. Three factors are causing sizable reductions in P:

◆ Companies increasingly are establishing long-run purchasing arrangements in which price and quality dimensions that apply over an extended period are agreed to by both parties. Individual purchase orders occur without any additional negotiation over price or quality in this period.

◆ Companies are using electronic links, such as the Internet, to place purchase orders. Electronic commerce is one of the fastest growing areas of the Internet. The cost of placing some orders on the Internet is estimated to be less than one-tenth (even less than one-hundredth) the cost of placing orders by telephone or by mail.

◆ Companies are increasing the use of purchase cards (similar to consumer credit cards like VISA and MasterCard). Purchasing personnel are given total dollar limits or individual transaction dollar limits. As long as personnel stay within these limits, the traditional labour-intensive procurement approval mechanisms are not required.

Both increases in the carrying cost (C) and decreases in the ordering cost per purchase order (P) result in smaller EOQ amounts.

Exhibit 20-4 analyzes the sensitivity of Video Galore's EOQ to illustrate the economics of smaller and more frequent purchase orders. The analysis presented in Exhibit 20-4 supports JIT purchasing—that is, having a smaller EOQ and placing more frequent orders—as relevant carrying costs increase and relevant ordering costs per purchase order decrease.

EXHIBIT 20-4
Sensitivity of EOQ to Variations in Relevant Ordering and Carrying Costs for Video Galore

	A	B	C	D	E
1	**Relevant Carrying**	**Annual Demand (D) = 13,000 units**			
2	**Costs per Package**	**Relevant Ordering Costs per Purchase Order (P)**			
3	**per Year (C)**	**$200**	**$150**	**$100**	**$30**
4	$ 5.20	EOQ = 1,000	EOQ = 866	EOQ = 707	EOQ = 387
5	7.00	862	746	609	334
6	10.00	721	624	510	279
7	15.00	589	510	416	228

Relevant Benefits and Relevant Costs of JIT Purchasing

The JIT purchasing model is not guided solely by the EOQ model. As discussed earlier (pp. 776–777), the EOQ model is designed to emphasize only the tradeoff between carrying and ordering costs. Inventory management extends beyond ordering and carrying costs to include purchasing costs, stockout costs, and quality costs. The quality of materials and goods and timely deliveries are important motivations for using JIT purchasing, and stockout costs are an important concern. We add these features as we move from the EOQ decision model to present the JIT purchasing model.

Video Galore has recently established an Internet business-to-business purchase-order link with Sontek. Video Galore triggers a purchase order for videotapes by a single computer entry. Payments are made electronically for batches of deliveries, rather than for each individual delivery. These changes reduce the ordering cost from $200 to only $2 per purchase order! Video Galore will use the Internet purchase-order link whether or not it shifts to JIT purchasing. Video Galore is negotiating to have Sontek deliver 100 packages of videotapes 130 times per year (5 times every 2 weeks), instead of delivering 1,000 packages 13 times per year, as shown in Exhibit 20-1. Sontek is willing to make these frequent deliveries, but it would add $0.02 to the price per videotape. Video Galore's required rate of return on investment remains at 15%. Assume the annual relevant carrying cost of insurance, materials handling, shrinkage, breakage, and the like remains at $3.10 per package per year.

Suppose that Video Galore incurs no stockout costs under its current purchasing policy because demand and purchase order lead times over each four-week period are certain. Video Galore's major concern is that lower inventory levels from implementing JIT purchasing will lead to more stockouts because demand variations and delays in supplying tapes are more likely to occur in the short time intervals between supplies under JIT purchasing. Sontek assures Video Galore that its new manufacturing processes enable it to respond rapidly to changing demand patterns. Consequently, stockouts may not be a serious problem. Video Galore expects to incur stockout costs on 150 tape packages each year under a JIT purchasing policy. In the event of a stockout, Video Galore will have to rush-order tape packages at a cost of $4 per package. Should Video Galore implement JIT purchasing?

Exhibit 20-5 compares (1) the incremental costs Video Galore incurs when it purchases videotapes from Sontek under its current purchasing policy with (2) the incremental costs Video Galore would incur if Sontek supplied videotapes under a JIT policy. The difference in the two incremental costs is the relevant savings of JIT purchasing. In other methods of comparing the two purchasing policies, the analysis would include only the relevant costs—those costs that differ between the two alternatives. Exhibit 20-5 shows a net cost savings of $1,246 per year from shifting to a JIT purchasing policy.

Supplier Evaluation and Relevant Costs of Quality and Timely Deliveries

The timely delivery of quality products is particularly crucial in JIT purchasing environments. Defective materials and late deliveries often bring the whole plant to a halt, resulting in forgone contribution margin on lost sales. Companies that implement JIT purchasing choose their suppliers carefully and pay special attention to developing long-run supplier partnerships. Some suppliers are very cooperative with a business's attempts to adopt JIT purchasing. For example, Frito-Lay, which has a large market share in potato chips and other snack foods, makes more frequent deliveries to retail outlets than many of its competitors. The company's corporate strategy emphasizes service to retailers and consistency, freshness, and quality of the delivered product.

What are the relevant costs when choosing suppliers? Consider again our Video Galore example. The Denton Corporation also supplies videotapes. It offers to supply all of Video Galore's videotape needs at a price of $13.80 per package (less than Sontek's price of $14.02) under the same JIT delivery terms as those that

EXHIBIT 20-5
Annual Relevant Costs of Current Purchasing Policy and JIT Purchasing Policy for Video Galore

	A	B	C
		Relevant Costs Under	
1		Current	JIT
2		Purchasing	Purchasing
3		Policy	Policy
4	**Relevant Item**		
5	Purchasing costs		
6	$14 per unit × 13,000 units per year	$182,000	
7	$14.02 per unit × 13,000 units per year		$182,260
8	Ordering costs		
9	$2 per order × 13 orders per year	26	
10	$2 per order × 130 orders per year		260
11	Opportunity carrying costs, required return on investment		
12	0.15 per year × $14 cost per unit × 500[a] units of average inventory per year	1,050	
13	0.15 per year × $14.02 cost per unit × 50[b] units of average inventory per year		105
14	Other carrying costs (insurance, materials handling, breakage, and so on)		
15	$3.10 per unit per year × 500[a] units of average inventory per year	1,550	
16	$3.10 per unit per year × 50[b] units of average inventory per year		155
17	Stockout costs		
18	No stockouts	0	
19	$4 per unit × 150 units per year		600
20	Total annual relevant costs	$184,626	$183,380
21	Annual difference in favour of JIT purchasing	$1,246	
22			
23	[a]Order quantity ÷ 2 = 1,000 ÷ 2 = 500		
24	[b]Order quantity ÷ 2 = 100 ÷ 2 = 50		

Sontek offers. Denton proposes an electronic hookup identical to Sontek's that would make Video Galore's ordering costs $2.00 per purchase order. Video Galore's relevant outlay carrying costs of insurance, materials-handling, breakage, and so on per package per year is $3.10 if it purchases videotapes from Sontek and $1,874 if it purchases from Denton. Should Video Galore buy from Denton? Not before considering the relevant costs of quality and also the relevant costs of failing to deliver on time.

Video Galore has used Sontek in the past and knows that Sontek fully deserves its reputation for delivering quality merchandise on time. In fact Video Galore does not even inspect the tape packages that Sontek supplies, therefore incurring zero inspection costs. Denton, however, does not enjoy as sterling a reputation for quality. Video Galore anticipates the following negative aspects of using Denton:

◆ Video Galore would incur additional inspection costs of $0.05 per package.
◆ Average stockouts of 360 tape packages each year would occur, largely resulting from late deliveries. Denton cannot rush-order tape packages to Video Galore on short notice, causing an additional cost of $4 per package
◆ Customers would likely return 2.5% of all packages sold owing to poor quality of the tapes. Video Galore estimates its additional costs to handle each returned package is $10.

When evaluating and choosing suppliers, quality and on-time delivery become increasingly important as the emphasis shifts away from minimizing purchasing costs to minimizing costs across the entire value chain.

EXHIBIT 20-6
Annual Relevant Costs of Purchasing from Sontek and Denton

	A	B	C
		Relevant Costs of Purchasing from	
1		Sontek	Denton
2	**Relevant Item**		
3	Purchasing costs		
4	$14.02 per unit × 13,000 units per year	$182,260	
5	$ 13.80 per unit × 13,000 units per year		$179,400
6	Ordering costs		
7	$2.00 per order × 130 orders per year	260	
8	$2.00 per order × 130 orders per year		260
9	Inspection costs		
10	No inspection necessary	–	
11	$0.05 per unit × 13,000 units per year		650
12	Opportunity carrying costs, required return on investment		
13	0.15 per year × $14.02 × 50[a] units of average inventory per year	105	
14	0.15 per year × $13.80 × 50[a] units of average inventory per year		104
15	Other carrying costs (insurance, materials handling, breakage, etc.)		
16	$3.10 per unit per year × 50[a] units of average inventory per year	155	
17	$3.00 per unit per year × 50[a] units of average inventory per year		150
18	Stockout costs		
19	$4 per unit × 150 units per year	600	
20	$4 per unit × 360 units per year		1,440
21	Customer returns costs		
22	No customer returns	–	
23	$10 per unit returned × 2.5% units returned × 13,000 units		3,250
24	Total annual relevant costs	$183,380	$185,254
25	Annual difference in favour of Sontek	$1,874	
26	[a]Order quantity ÷ 2 = 100 ÷ 2 = 50		

Exhibit 20-6 presents the relevant costs of purchasing from Sontek and from Denton. Even though Denton is offering a lower price per package, the total relevant costs of purchasing goods from Sontek are lower by $1,874 per year. Selling high-quality merchandise also has nonfinancial and qualitative benefits. For example, offering Sontek's high-quality tapes enhances Video Galore's reputation and increases customer goodwill, which may lead to higher future profitability.

INVENTORY MANAGEMENT AND SUPPLY-CHAIN ANALYSIS

The level of inventories held by retailers is influenced by demand patterns of their customers and supply relationships with their distributors, manufacturers, and suppliers, and so on. The term *supply chain* describes the flow of goods, services, and information from cradle to grave (womb to tomb), regardless of whether those activities occur in the same organizations or other organizations. Chapter 1 introduced this concept using the example of a supply chain in the beverage industry. One point well documented in supply-chain analysis is that there are significant total gains to companies in this supply chain from coordinating their activities and sharing information.

Procter & Gamble's (P&G) experience with their Pampers product illustrates the gains from supply chain coordination. Retailers selling Pampers encounter some variability in weekly demand, despite babies consuming diapers at a relatively steady

OBJECTIVE 4

Use a supply-chain approach to inventory management

rate. However, there was pronounced variability in retailers' orders to the manufacturer (P&G), and even more variability in orders by P&G to its own suppliers. Trade promotions worsened the situation because retailers took advantage of lower prices to increase their inventory for future sales. One result was that high levels of inventory are often held at various stages in the supply chain.

P&G responded by sharing information as well as planning and coordinating activities throughout its supply chain. The retailers shared their daily sales information about Pampers with P&G, their distributors, and their suppliers. This updated sales information reduced the level of uncertainty that manufacturers and the manufacturers' suppliers had about retail demand for Pampers. This reduction in demand uncertainty led to fewer stockouts at the retail level, reduced manufacture of Pampers not subsequently demanded by retailers, a reduction in expedited manufacturing orders, and lower inventories being held by each company in the supply chain. The benefits of supply-chain coordination at P&G have been so great that retailers such as Wal-Mart have contracted with P&G to manage Wal-Mart's retail inventories on a just-in-time basis. This practice is called *supplier- or vendor-managed inventory*. Supply-chain management, however, is not without its challenges (see Global Surveys of Company Practice).

A supply chain is one way for manufacturers to start managing their own inventory better. Of course, the need to produce high-quality products at competitive cost levels leads managers at manufacturing companies to also seek out additional ways to manage their inventories. Numerous systems have been developed to help managers plan and implement production and inventory activities. We now consider two widely used types of systems—materials requirements planning (MRP) and just-in-time (JIT) production.

INVENTORY MANAGEMENT AND MRP

Materials requirements planning (MRP) is a push-through system that manufactures finished goods for inventory on the basis of demand forecasts. MRP uses (a) demand forecasts for the final products; (b) a bill of materials outlining the materials, components, and subassemblies for each final product; and (c) the quantities of materials, components, finished products, and product inventories to predetermine the necessary outputs at each stage of production. Taking into account the lead time required to purchase materials and to manufacture components and finished products, a master production schedule specifies the quantity and timing of each item to be produced. Once scheduled production starts, the output of each department is pushed through the production line whether it is needed or not. The result is often an accumulation of inventory at workstations that receive work they are not yet ready to process.

Inventory management is a key challenge in an MRP system. The management accountant can play several important roles in meeting this challenge. A key role is maintaining accurate and timely information pertaining to materials, work in process, and finished goods inventories. A major cause of unsuccessful attempts to implement MRP systems has been the problem of collecting and updating inventory records. Calculating the full cost of carrying finished goods inventory motivates other actions. For example, instead of storing product at multiple (and geographically dispersed) warehouses, National Semiconductor contracted with Federal Express to airfreight its microchips from a central location in Singapore to customer sites worldwide. The change enabled National to move products from plant to customer in 4 days rather than 45, and to reduce distribution costs from 2.6% to 1.9% of revenues. These benefits subsequently led National to outsource all its logistics to Federal Express, including shipments among its own plants in the United States, Scotland, and Malaysia.

A second role of the management accountant is providing estimates of the setup costs for each production run at a plant, the downtime costs, and carrying costs of inventory. Costs of setting up a production run are analogous to ordering costs in the EOQ model. When the costs of setting up machines or sections of the production line are high (for example, as with a blast furnace in an integrated steel mill), processing larger batches of materials and incurring larger inventory carrying costs is the optimal approach, because it reduces the number of setups that must be made. When setup costs are small, processing smaller batches is optimal because it reduces carrying costs. Similarly, when the costs of downtime are high, there can be sizable benefits from maintaining continuous production.

Challenges in Securing the Benefits of Supply-Chain Management

Supply-chain studies of inventory management reported in the business press frequently cite a wide range of benefits to both manufacturers and retailers. These benefits include fewer stockouts, reduced manufacture of items not subsequently demanded at the retail level, a reduction in rushed manufacturing orders, and lower inventory levels. One recent survey found that 78% of global managers identified the supply-chain function as "very important" or "somewhat important" to their organization's business strategy.[a]

Despite this critical role, many challenges plague effective supply-chain management. Principal among these challenges is receiving and sharing accurate, timely, and relevant information. When asked to rate the accuracy and timeliness of their supply chain's performance information, North American, European, and Asian companies responded as follows:

	North America	Europe	Asia
Exceeds expectations	1.5%	0.0%	9.7%
Meets expectations	43.9%	57.5%	67.7%
Below expectations	48.5%	32.5%	19.4%
Far below expectations	6.1%	10.0%	3.2%

Another survey of 220 retailers and manufacturers highlights some key issues that companies must address to benefit from adopting a supply-chain approach to inventory management.[b] Manufacturers gave the following rankings (in terms of importance) about the information they would like to receive from retailers stocking their products:

1. Retail sales forecasts for the products
2. Sales information on the products (such as daily sales at each retail outlet)
3. Pricing and advertising strategies of the retailer
4. Inventory levels at each retail outlet

A second issue is reducing the obstacles to manufacturers and retailers achieving the benefits of a supply-chain approach. Respondents cited the following obstacles:

1. Communication obstacles—including the unwillingness of some parties to share information
2. Trust obstacles—including the concern that all parties will not meet their agreed-upon commitments
3. Information systems obstacles—including problems because of the information systems of different parties not being technically compatible
4. Limited resources—including problems related to the people and financial resources given to support a supply-chain initiative not being adequate

Adopting a supply-chain approach requires diverse organizations to cooperate and communicate on a broad set of issues. Respondents emphasized this challenge was not always successfully met. Not surprisingly, not all supply-chain initiatives have delivered the initially met projected financial and operating benefits.

---

[a]ITtoolbox/Oracle, "2004 ITtoolbox Supply Chain Survey" (Scottsdale, Arizona, 2004).

[b]Research Incorporated, "Synchronizing the Supply Chain Through Collaborative Design" (Alpharetta, Georgia, 1998).

A key feature of MRP is its push-through approach. We now consider JIT production, which has a demand-pull approach.

INVENTORY MANAGEMENT AND JIT PRODUCTION

Just-in-time (JIT) production (lean production). Production system in which each component on a production line is produced immediately as needed by the next step in the production line.

Just-in-time (JIT) production (also called **lean production**) is a "demand-pull" system in which each component in a production line is produced immediately as the next step in the production line needs the component. The goals are to eliminate non-value-added spoilage and scrap, reduce carrying costs, and improve customer satisfaction. In a JIT production line, manufacturing activity at any particular workstation is prompted by the need for that station's output at the following station. Demand triggers each step of the production process, starting with customer demand for a finished product at the end of the process and working all the way back to the demand for direct materials at the beginning of the process. In this way, demand pulls an order through the production line. The demand-pull feature of JIT production systems achieves close coordination among workstations. It smooths the flow of goods, despite low quantities of inventory. JIT production systems aim to simultaneously (a) meet customer demand in a timely way, (b) with high-quality products, and (c) at the lowest possible total cost. JIT is most financially feasible when availability and prices of resource inputs are relatively constant and production cycles are well controlled.

Companies implementing JIT production systems manage inventories by eliminating (or at least minimizing) them. There are five main features in a JIT production system:

Manufacturing cells. Grouping of all the different types of equipment used to manufacture a given product.

1. Production is organized in **manufacturing cells**, a grouping of all the different types of equipment used to make a given product. Materials move from one machine to another where various operations are performed in sequence. Materials handling costs are minimized.

2. Workers are hired and trained to be multiskilled and capable of performing a variety of operations and tasks including minor repairs and routine maintenance of equipment. This training adds greatly to the flexibility of the plant.

3. Defects are aggressively eliminated (TQM). Because of the tight links between stages in the production line, and the minimal inventories at each stage, defects arising at one stage quickly affect other stages in the line. JIT creates an urgency for solving problems immediately and eliminating the root causes of defects as quickly as possible. TQM is an essential component of any JIT production system.

4. *Setup time*, which is the time required to get equipment, tools, and materials ready to start the production of a component or product, is reduced. Simultaneously *manufacturing lead time*, which is the amount of time from when an order is ready to start on the production line (ready to be set up) to when it becomes a finished good, is reduced. Reducing setup time makes production in smaller batches economical, which in turn reduces inventory levels. Reducing manufacturing lead time enables a company to respond faster to changes in customer demand (see Concepts in Action).

5. Suppliers are selected on the basis of their ability to deliver quality materials in a timely manner. Most companies implementing *JIT production* also implement the *JIT purchasing* methods described earlier in this chapter. JIT plants expect JIT suppliers to provide high-quality goods and make frequent deliveries of the exact quantities specified on a timely basis. Suppliers often deliver materials directly to the plant floor to be immediately placed into production.

After the Encore: Just-in-Time Live Concert CDs

Each year, hundreds of thousands of rock music fans flock to Dave Matthews Band concerts. Although many of them stop by the merchandise stand to pick up a T-shirt or poster after the show ends, soon they will have another option . . . buying a multiple-CD set that contains a professional recording of the entire concert they just saw! Just-in-time production, enabled by recent advances in digital audio and CD-burning technology, now allows fans to relive the live concert experience, as soon as 10 minutes after the final chord is played!

Live concert recordings have long been hampered by production and distribution difficulties. Traditionally, fans could only hear these recordings via unofficial "bootleg" cassettes or CDs. Although some musical acts—ranging from John Mayer to U2—have at times allowed fans to tape their shows, amateur recording devices produced poor sound quality and copies that fans could acquire only through informal trading networks. Artists and record labels also received no compensation for their copyrighted work. Occasionally, artists would release official live albums between studio releases. But due to the remastering and album-production process, these recordings took months, if not years, to reach fans. Further, live albums typically sold few copies, and retail outlets that profit from volume-driven merchandise turnover were somewhat reluctant to carry them.

Enter instant concert recordings. Clear Channel Entertainment's *Instant Live* subsidiary, for example, employs a process consisting of microphones, recording and audio mixing hardware and software, and an army of high-speed CD burners to produce concert recordings during the show. As soon as each song is complete, *Instant Live* engineers burn that track onto hundreds of CDs. At the end of the show, they only have to burn one last song on each CD. Once completed, the CD sets are packaged and rushed to merchandise stands throughout the venue for instant sale. And sell they have! During *Instant Live*'s initial testing, up to 20% of concertgoers bought these CDs, to the tune of US$15 to US$30 each. The artists got US$6 to US$8 from each CD sold, with the remaining money split between the record label, the concert venue, and the recording company. With a captive audience, Berklee College of Music professor Don Jordan notes, "It is almost an impulse buy. You had a great feeling coming out of it and . . . you can put it on again any time you want."

There are, of course, some limitations to this technology. With such a quick turnaround time, engineers cannot edit or remaster any aspect of the show. Therefore, any mistake during the show remains on the final CD. Also, although just-in-time live recordings work successfully in smaller venues, the logistics for arenas, amphitheatres, and stadiums are much more difficult. Dozens of additional employees and hundreds of costly, top-of-the-line CD burners are needed to meet the demands of larger crowds.

Despite these concerns, the benefits of this new technology include sound-quality assurance, near-immediate production turnaround, and low finished-goods carrying costs. Further, these recordings can also be distributed through retailers and artist Web sites. In 2001, Pearl Jam sold all 72 shows of its 2000 world tour through retail outlets, while the Vermont-based group Phish made every 2003 show available on its Web site for download, selling more than 150,000 recordings and grossing US$1.2 million. With such an opportunity, it's no wonder that artists ranging from Incubus to Jimmy Buffett—and Dave Matthews Band—are planning to augment their existing CD sales with just-in-time recordings.

Sources: S. Chartland, "How to Take the Concert Home," *The New York Times*, May 3, 2004; S. Humphries, "Get Your Official `Bootleg' Here," *Christian Science Monitor*, November 21, 2003; S. Knopper, "Live Discs a Hit with Fans," *Rolling Stone*, November 7, 2003; S. Galupo, "Death of the Live Concert Album?" *Washington Times*, July 9, 2004.

Financial Benefits of JIT and Relevant Costs

Early advocates say the benefit of JIT production is lower carrying costs of inventory. But there are other benefits to lower inventories, such as intensifying emphasis on improved quality (by eliminating scrap, rework, and spoilage), and reduced manufacturing lead times. Management accounting provides the information required for managers to calculate the relevant benefits and costs of reduced inventories in JIT systems.

Consider the Emco Corporation, a manufacturer of brass fittings. Emco is considering implementing a JIT production system. Suppose that to implement JIT production, Emco must incur $100,000 in annual tooling costs to reduce setup times. Suppose further that JIT will reduce average inventory by $500,000. Also, relevant costs of insurance, space, materials-handling, and setup will decline by $30,000 per year. The company's required rate of return on inventory investments is 10% per year. Should Emco implement JIT? On the basis of the numbers provided, we would be tempted to say no. Why? Because annual relevant cost savings in carrying costs amount to $80,000 [(10% of $500,000) + $30,000], which is less than the additional annual tooling costs of $100,000.

Our analysis, however, has not considered other benefits of lower inventories in JIT production. For example, Emco estimates that implementing JIT will reduce rework on 500 units each year, resulting in savings of $50 per unit. Also, better quality and faster delivery will allow Emco to charge $2 more per unit on the 20,000 units that it sells each year. The annual relevant quality and delivery benefits from JIT and lower inventory levels equal $65,000 (rework savings, $50 × 500 + additional contribution margin, $2 × 20,000). Total annual relevant benefits and cost savings equal $145,000 ($80,000 + $65,000), which exceeds annual JIT implementation costs of $100,000. Therefore, Emco should implement a JIT production system. The Focus on Values and Behaviours feature on p. 791 describes some of the challenges management accountants face in valuing inventory and implementing JIT. Next is a discussion of planning and control systems in JIT production.

Enterprise Resource Planning (ERP) Systems[2]

The success of a JIT system hinges on the speed of information flows from customers to manufacturers to suppliers. Information flows is a problem for large companies that have fragmented information systems (for sales, manufacturing, and purchasing) spread over dozens of unlinked computer systems. The Enterprise Resource Planning (ERP) system comprises a single database that collects data and feeds it into applications supporting all of a company's business activities. For example, using an ERP system, a salesperson can generate a contract for a customer in Germany, verify the customer's credit limits, and place a production order. The system schedules manufacturing in, say, Brazil, requisitions materials from inventory, orders components from suppliers, and schedules shipment. It also credits sales commissions to the salesperson and records all the costing and financial accounting information.

ERP systems give low-level managers, workers, customers, and suppliers access to operating information. This benefit, coupled with tight coordination across business functions, enables ERP systems to rapidly shift manufacturing and distribution plans in response to changes in supply and demand. Companies believe that an ERP system is essential to support JIT initiatives because of the effect it has on lead times. Using an ERP system, Autodesk, a maker of computer-aided design software, reduced order lead times from 2 weeks to 1 day; Fujitsu

[2]For an excellent discussion, see T. H. Davenport, "Putting the Enterprise into the Enterprise System," *Harvard Business Review*, July–August 1998; also see A. Cagilo, "Enterprise Resource Planning Systems and Accountants: Towards Hybridization?" *European Accounting Review*, May 2003.

reduced lead times from 18 to 1.5 days. ERP systems also help in forecasting demand and doing materials requirements planning as part of their operations and logistics modules.

Although the tight coupling of systems throughout a business streamlines administrative and financial processes and saves costs, it can also make the system large and unwieldy. Because of their complexity, suppliers of ERP systems such as SAP, Baan, Peoplesoft, and Oracle provide software packages that are standard but that can be customized, although at considerable cost. Without some customization, unique and distinctive features that confer strategic advantage will not be available. The challenge when implementing ERP systems is to strike the right balance between systems that are common across all of a company's business and geographical locations and systems that for strategic reasons are designed to be unique.

Challenges of Inventory Valuation and JIT Implementation

Many companies have high inventory levels. Trouble erupts when companies seeking increases in income overstate inventories. El Paso Corporation, a leading provider of natural gas in North America, reported "that an outside investigation had found that some employees might have deliberately overstated oil and gas reserves and that it would need to restate five years of results . . . and take a [US]$1 billion charge [to earnings] . . . The company said certain employees . . . provided reserve estimates that they knew, or should have known, were incorrect when they were reported." A recent survey by *CFO Magazine* found that since 2001, one-fifth of financial executives said they felt more pressure to use accounting methods to "make results appear more favourable" and that 47% have felt pressure from superiors to use aggressive accounting techniques. Recognizing the incentives managers may have to overstate inventory valuations, management accountants must pay careful attention to and correctly record both the physical quantity of inventories and values ascribed to them.

However, in other companies, such as Apple Computer, Volkswagen, Chrysler, Carrier, and IBM, inventory overstatement is not a danger because they use JIT systems and hold very little inventory. Moving to a JIT system brings on different challenges for management accountants.

To successfully implement JIT, management accountants must be comfortable working in a changing and ambiguous environment. They must also be able to balance the demands of different managers. For example, marketing managers may seek greater levels of customization and customer responsiveness that production and purchasing managers find burdensome. Management accountants must be able to recognize the diverse views and needs of a company, evaluate the economics of different options, communicate clearly, and work toward achieving a consensus.

Several of the rewards of moving to a JIT system—more-reliable deliveries to customers and greater customer responsiveness—may be difficult to quantify in the short run. Management accountants must therefore motivate their teams to focus on long-term successes. At Cessna, for example, it wasn't until its third year of using lean manufacturing for its single-engine aircraft and business jets that the company began to see productivity gains in the 40% to 60% range.

Source: T. Damos, "CFO Pressure Cooker," *Fortune*, June 28, 2004. H. Timmons, "El Paso Says Reserves May Have Been Falsified," *The New York Times*, May 4, 2004, p. C14.

Performance Measures and Control in JIT Production

To manage and reduce inventories, the management accountant must also design performance measures to evaluate and control JIT production. Examples of information the management accountant may use are

- Personal observation by production line workers and team leaders
- Financial performance measures such as the inventory turnover ratio (cost of goods sold ÷ average inventory), which is expected to increase
- Nonfinancial performance measures of time, inventory, and quality, such as manufacturing lead time, units produced per hour, and days inventory is on hand
- Manufacturing lead time is expected to decrease
- Units produced per hour, expected to increase
- $\dfrac{\text{Total setup time for machines}}{\text{Total manufacturing time}}$, expected to decrease
- $\dfrac{\text{Number of units requiring rework or scrap}}{\text{Total number of units started and completed}}$, expected to decrease

Personal observation and nonfinancial performance measures are the dominant methods of control. Why? Because they are the most timely, intuitive, and easy-to-comprehend measures of plant performance. Rapid, meaningful feedback is critical because the lack of buffer inventories in a demand-pull system creates added urgency to detect and solve problems quickly.

JIT's Effect on Costing Systems

In reducing the need for materials handling, warehousing, and incoming inspection, JIT systems reduce overhead costs. JIT systems also facilitate the direct tracing of some costs that were formerly classified as overhead. For example, the use of manufacturing cells makes it easy to trace materials handling and machine operating costs to specific products or product families made in specific cells. These costs then become direct costs of those products. Also, the use of multiskilled workers in these cells allows the costs of setup, minor maintenance, and quality inspection to become easily traced direct costs.

The next section discusses *backflush costing*, which is a job-costing system that dovetails with JIT production and is less costly to operate than most traditional costing systems described in Chapters 4, 7, 8, and 9.

BACKFLUSH COSTING

OBJECTIVE 7

Use backflush costing

A unique production system such as JIT leads to its own unique costing system. Organizing manufacturing in cells, reducing defects and manufacturing lead time, and ensuring timely delivery of materials enables purchasing, production, and sales to occur in quick succession with minimal inventories. The absence of inventories makes choices about cost flow assumptions (such as weighted average or first-in, first-out) or inventory costing methods (such as absorption or variable costing) unimportant—all manufacturing costs of a period flow directly into cost of goods sold. The rapid conversion of direct materials to finished goods that are immediately sold simplifies job costing.

Sequential tracking (synchronous tracking). Product costing method in which the accounting system entries occur in the same order as actual purchases and production.

Simplified Normal or Standard Costing

Traditional and standard costing systems (discussed in Chapters 4, 7, and 8) use **sequential tracking** (also called *synchronous tracking*), which is any product costing method in which the accounting system entries occur in the same order as actual purchases and production. These traditional systems track costs sequentially as products pass from direct materials, to work in process, to finished goods, and finally to sales, as shown here. Some have called this the "just in case" system.

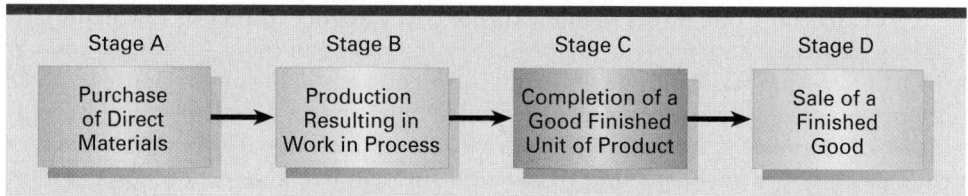

Stage A	Stage B	Stage C	Stage D
Purchase of Direct Materials	→ Production Resulting in Work in Process	→ Completion of a Good Finished Unit of Product	→ Sale of a Finished Good

A sequential tracking costing system would have four trigger points, corresponding to separate journal entries being made at Stages A, B, C, and D. The term **trigger point** refers to a stage in the cycle going from purchase of direct materials (Stage A) to sale of finished goods (Stage D) at which journal entries are made in the accounting system.

An alternative approach to sequential tracking is backflush costing. **Backflush costing** is a costing system that omits recording some or all journal entries relating to the cycle from purchase of direct materials to the sale of finished goods. It is a single-step costing process initiated by the production of a finished good. The manufacturer simply labels the finished product with either a bar code or RFID and scans the unit. This initiates a computer program that attributes quantities of direct materials to appropriate inventories. The program, using either standard or normal costs, will also assign material and conversion costs as well as allocate indirect costs to the finished unit. Some programs both inform the distributor that the product is ready for pickup and delivery to the customer and inform the customer of the status of their order(s) as well as calculate variances using data from other information systems such as payroll and purchasing. Scrap, rework, and spoilage costs can be entered when appropriate to provide accurate unit costing. Where journal entries for one or more stages in the cycle are omitted, the journal entries for a subsequent stage use normal or standard costs to work backward to flush out the costs in the cycle for which journal entries were not made.

The following three examples illustrate backflush costing. To underscore basic concepts, we assume no direct materials variances in any of the examples. The three examples differ in the number and placement of trigger points at which journal entries are made in the accounting system:

	Number of Journal Entry Trigger Points	Location in Cycle Where Journal Entries Made
Example 1	3	Stage A. Purchase of direct materials (called "raw materials")
		Stage C. Completion of unspoiled good finished units of product
		Stage D. Sale of finished goods.
Example 2	2	Stage A. Purchase of direct materials (called "raw materials")
		Stage D. Sale of finished goods.
Example 3	2	Stage C. Completion of unspoiled good finished units of product
		Stage D. Sale of finished goods.

In all three examples, there are no journal entries in the accounting system for work in process (Stage B). These three examples of backflush costing are typically used where the amounts of work in process are small. With just-in-time production, sizable reductions in work in process have occurred.

Example 1: Trigger Points Are Purchase of Direct Materials (Stage A), Completion of Good Finished Units of Product (Stage C), and Sale of Finished Goods (Stage D)

This example uses three trigger points to illustrate how backflushing can eliminate the need for a separate Work-in-Process account. A hypothetical company, Silicon Valley Computer (SVC), produces keyboards for personal computers. For April, there were no beginning inventories of raw materials. Moreover, there is zero beginning and ending work in process.

Trigger point. A stage in the cycle going from purchase of direct materials (Stage A) to sale of finished goods (Stage D) at which journal entries are made in the accounting system.

OBJECTIVE 8

Describe different ways backflush costing can simplify traditional job-costing systems

Backflush costing. Costing system that delays recording changes in the status of a product being produced until unspoiled good finished units appear; it then uses normal or standard costs to work backward to flush out manufacturing costs for the units produced.

SVC has only one direct manufacturing cost category (direct or raw materials) and one indirect manufacturing cost category (conversion costs). All labour costs at the manufacturing facility are included in conversion costs. From its bill of materials (description of the types and quantities of materials) and an operations list (description of operations to be undergone), SVC determines the April standard direct materials costs per keyboard unit of $19 and the standard conversion costs of $12. SVC has two inventory accounts:

Type	Account Title
Combined direct materials and any direct materials in work in process	Inventory: Raw and In-Process Control
Finished goods	Finished Goods Control

Trigger point 1 occurs when materials are purchased. These costs are charged to Inventory: Raw and In-Process Control.

Actual conversion costs are recorded as incurred under backflush costing, just as in other costing systems, and charged to Conversion Costs Control. Conversion costs are allocated to products at trigger point 2—the transfer of units to Finished Goods. This example assumes that under- or overallocated conversion costs are written off to cost of goods sold monthly.

SVC takes the following steps when assigning costs to units sold and to inventories:

◆ **Step 1:** *Record the direct materials purchased during the accounting period.* Assume April purchases of $1,950,000:

Entry (a)	Inventory: Raw and In-Process Control	$1,950,000	
	Accounts Payable Control		$1,950,000

◆ **Step 2:** *Record the incurrence of conversion costs during the accounting period.* Assume that conversion costs are $1,260,000:

Entry (b)	Conversion Costs Control	$1,260,000	
	[Various accounts (such as Accounts Payable Control and Wages Payable)]		$1,260,000

◆ **Step 3:** *Determine the number of finished units manufactured during the accounting period.* Assume that 100,000 keyboard units were manufactured in April.

◆ **Step 4:** *Compute the budgeted or standard costs of each finished unit.* The standard cost is $31 ($19 direct materials + $12 conversion costs) per unit.

◆ **Step 5:** *Record the cost of finished goods completed during the accounting period.* In this case, 100,000 units × $31 = $3,100,000. This step gives backflush costing its name. Up to this point in the operations, the costs have not been recorded sequentially with the flow of product along its production route. Instead, the output trigger reaches back and pulls the standard costs of direct materials from Inventory: Raw and In-Process and the standard conversion costs for manufacturing the finished goods.

Entry (c)	Finished Goods Control	$3,100,000	
	Inventory: Raw and In-Process Control		$1,900,000
	Conversion Costs Allocated		1,200,000

◆ **Step 6:** *Record the cost of goods sold during the accounting period.* Assume that 99,000 units were sold in April (99,000 units × $31 = $3,069,000).

Entry (d)	Cost of Goods Sold	$3,069,000	
	Finished Goods Control		$3,069,000

◆ **Step 7:** *Record under- or overallocated conversion costs.* Actual conversion costs may be under- or overallocated in any given accounting period. Chapter 4 discussed various ways to account for under- or overallocated manufacturing overhead costs. Many companies write off underallocations or overallocations to cost of goods sold only at year-end; other companies, like SVC, do so monthly. Companies that use backflush costing typically have low inventories, so proration of under- or overallocated costs between finished goods and cost of goods sold is less often necessary. The journal entry for the $60,000 difference between actual conversion costs incurred and standard conversion costs allocated would be

Entry (e)	Conversion Costs Allocated	$1,200,000	
	Cost of Goods Sold	60,000	
	Conversion Costs Control		$1,260,000

The April ending inventory balances are

Inventory: Raw and In-Process	$50,000	
Finished Goods, 1,000 units × $31	31,000	
Total inventories	$81,000	

Exhibit 20-7, Panel A, on page 796 summarizes the journal entries for this example. Exhibit 20-8 (p. 797) provides an overview of this version of backflush costing. The elimination of the typical Work-in-Process account reduces the amount of detail in the accounting system.

Units on the production line may still be tracked in physical terms, but there is "no attaching of costs" to specific work orders as they flow along the production cycle. In fact, there are no work orders or labour time tickets in the accounting system. Champion International uses a method similar to Example 1 in its specialty papers plant.

The use of three triggers to make journal entries in Example 1 will result in SVC's backflush costing system reporting costs similar to sequential tracking when SVC has minimal work-in-process inventory. In Example 1, any inventories of raw materials or finished goods are recognized in SVC's backflush costing system when they first appear (as would be done in a costing system using sequential tracking).

Accounting for Variances The accounting for variances between actual costs incurred and standard costs allowed and the disposition of variances is basically the same under all standard costing systems. The procedures are described in Chapters 7 and 8. In Example 1, suppose the direct materials purchased had an unfavourable price variance of $42,000. Entry (a) would then be

Inventory: Raw and In-Process Control	$1,950,000	
Raw Materials Price Variance	42,000	
Accounts Payable Control		$1,992,000

Direct materials are often a large proportion of total manufacturing costs, sometimes over 60%. Consequently, many companies will at least measure the direct materials efficiency variance in total by physically comparing what remains in direct materials inventory against what should be remaining, given the output of finished goods for the accounting period. In our example, suppose that such a comparison showed an unfavourable materials efficiency variance of $90,000. The journal entry would be:

Raw Materials Efficiency Variance	$90,000	
Inventory: Raw and In-Process Control		$90,000

The under- or overallocated manufacturing overhead costs may be split into various overhead variances (spending variance, efficiency variance, and production volume variance) as explained in Chapters 7 and 8.

Example 2: Trigger Points Are Purchases of Direct Materials (Stage A) and Sale of Finished Goods (Stage D)

This example, also based on SVC and using the same data, presents a backflush costing system that, relative to Example 1, is a more dramatic departure from a sequential tracking inventory costing system. The first trigger point in this example

EXHIBIT 20-7
Journal Entries in Backflush Costing

PANEL A, EXAMPLE 1: THREE TRIGGER POINTS—PURCHASE OF DIRECT MATERIALS, COMPLETION OF UNSPOILED GOOD FINISHED UNITS, AND SALE OF FINISHED GOODS

Transactions

(a) Purchase of direct materials[a]	Inventory: Raw and In-Process Control	$1,950,000	
	Accounts Payable Control		$1,950,000
(b) Incur conversion costs	Conversion Costs Control	1,260,000	
	Various Accounts		1,260,000
(c) Completion of good finished units[a]	Finished Goods Control	3,100,000	
	Inventory: Raw and In-Process Control		1,900,000
	Conversion Costs Allocated		1,200,000
(d) Sale of finished goods[a]	Cost of Goods Sold	3,069,000	
	Finished Goods Control		3,069,000
(e) Underallocated or overallocated conversion costs	Conversion Costs Allocated	1,200,000	
	Cost of Goods Sold	60,000	
	Conversion Costs Control		1,260,000

PANEL B, EXAMPLE 2: TWO TRIGGER POINTS—PURCHASE OF DIRECT MATERIALS AND SALE OF FINISHED GOODS

Transactions

(a) Purchase of direct materials[a]	Inventory Control	$1,950,000	
	Accounts Payable Control		$1,950,000
(b) Incur conversion costs	Conversion Costs Control	1,260,000	
	Various Accounts		1,260,000
(c) Completion of good finished units	No entry		
(d) Sale of finished goods[a]	Cost of Goods Sold	3,069,000	
	Inventory Control		1,881,000
	Conversion Costs Allocated		1,188,000
(e) Underallocated or overallocated conversion costs	Conversion Costs Allocated	1,188,000	
	Cost of Goods Sold	72,000	
	Conversion Costs Control		1,260,000

PANEL C, EXAMPLE 3: TWO TRIGGER POINTS—COMPLETION OF UNSPOILED GOOD FINISHED UNITS AND SALE OF FINISHED GOODS

Transactions

(a) Purchase of direct materials	No entry		
(b) Incur conversion costs	Conversion Costs Control	$1,260,000	
	Various Accounts		$1,260,000
(c) Completion of good finished units[a]	Finished Goods Control	3,100,000	
	Accounts Payable Control		1,900,000
	Conversion Costs Allocated		1,200,000
(d) Sale of finished goods[a]	Cost of Goods Sold	3,069,000	
	Finished Goods Control		3,069,000
(e) Underallocated or overallocated conversion costs	Conversion Costs Allocated	1,200,000	
	Cost of Goods Sold	60,000	
	Conversion Costs Control		1,260,000

[a]A trigger point.

is the same as the first trigger point in Example 1 (the purchase of direct materials), but the second trigger point is the sale—not the completed manufacture—of finished units. Toyota's cost accounting at its Kentucky plant is similar to this type of costing system. There are two justifications for this accounting system:

◆ To remove the incentive for managers to produce for inventory. If the value of finished goods inventory includes conversion costs, managers can bolster operating income by producing more units than are sold. Having trigger point 2

EXHIBIT 20-8
General-Ledger Overview of Backflush Costing

PANEL A, EXAMPLE 1: THREE TRIGGER POINTS—PURCHASE OF DIRECT MATERIALS, COMPLETION OF UNSPOILED GOOD FINISHED UNITS, AND SALE OF FINISHED GOODS

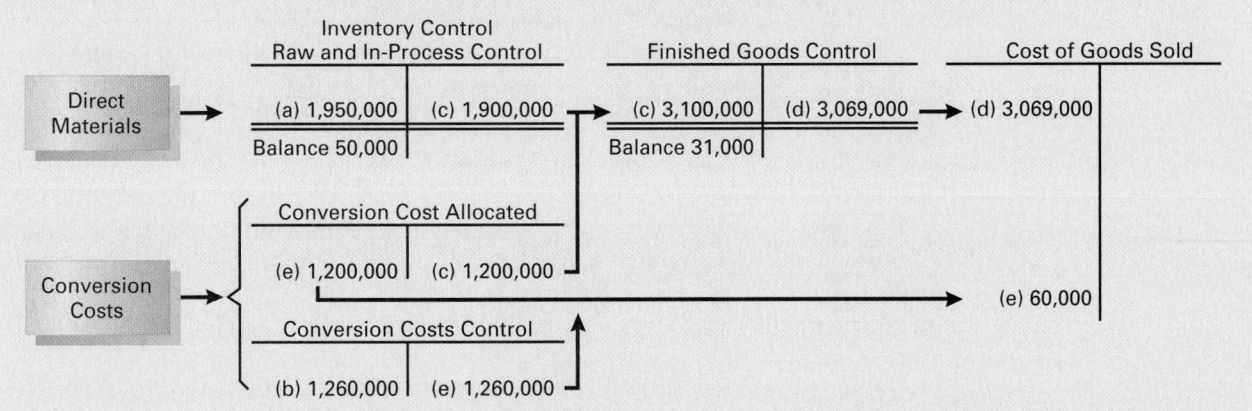

PANEL B, EXAMPLE 2: TWO TRIGGER POINTS—PURCHASE OF DIRECT MATERIALS AND SALE OF FINISHED GOODS

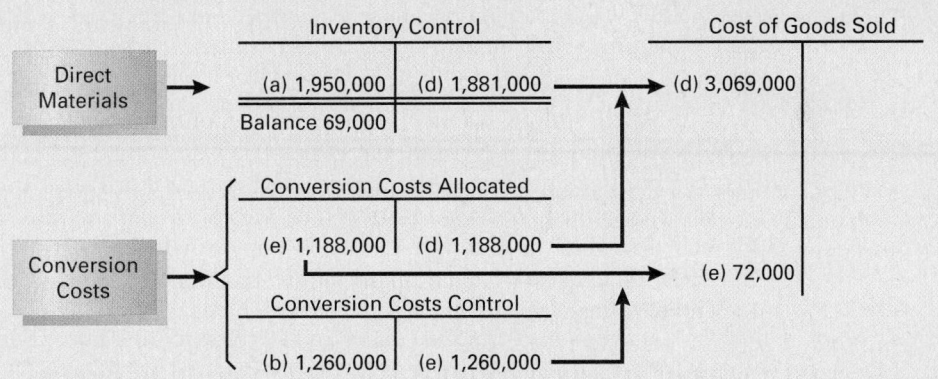

PANEL C, EXAMPLE 3: TWO TRIGGER POINTS—COMPLETION OF UNSPOILED GOOD FINISHED UNITS AND SALE OF FINISHED GOODS

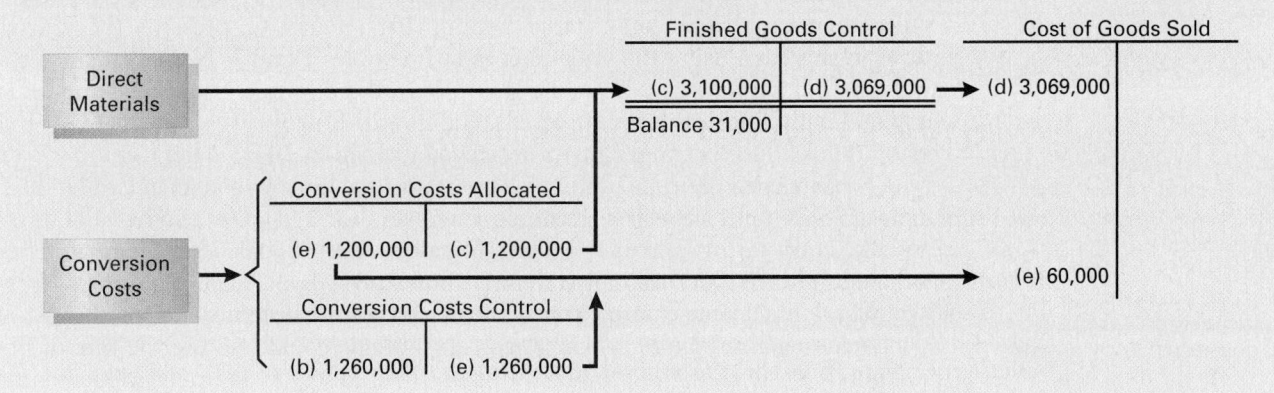

as the sale instead of the completion of production, however, reduces the attractiveness of producing for inventory by recording conversion costs as period costs instead of capitalizing them as inventoriable costs.

◆ To increase managers' focus on selling units.

This variation of backflush costing treats all conversion costs as period costs.

The inventory account in this example is confined solely to direct materials (whether they are in storerooms, in process, or in finished goods). There is only one inventory account:

Type	Account Title
Combined direct materials inventory and any direct materials in work in process and finished goods	Inventory Control

Exhibit 20-7, Panel B, presents the journal entries in this case. Entry (a) is prompted by the same trigger point 1 as in Example 1, the purchase of direct materials. Entry (b) for the conversion costs incurred is recorded in an identical manner as in Example 1. Trigger point 2 is the sale of good finished units (not their production, as in Example 1), so there is no entry corresponding to entry (c) of Example 1. The cost of finished units is computed only when finished units are sold (which corresponds to entry (d) of Example 1): 99,000 units sold × $31 = $3,069,000, consisting of direct materials (99,000 × $19 = $1,881,000) and conversion costs allocated (99,000 × $12 = $1,188,000).

No conversion costs are inventoried. That is, compared to Example 1, Example 2 does not attach $12,000 ($12 per unit × 1,000 units) of conversion costs to finished goods inventory. Hence, Example 2 allocates $12,000 less in conversion costs than Example 1. Of the $1,260,000 in conversion costs, $1,188,000 is allocated at standard cost to the units sold. The remaining $72,000 ($1,260,000 − $1,188,000) of conversion costs is underallocated. Entry (e) in Exhibit 20-7, Panel B, presents the journal entry if SVC, like many companies, writes off these underallocated costs monthly as additions to cost of goods sold.

The April ending balance of Inventory Control is $69,000 ($50,000 direct materials still on hand + $19,000 direct materials embodied in the 1,000 units manufactured but not sold during the period). Exhibit 20-8 provides an overview of this version of backflush costing. Entries are keyed to Exhibit 20-7, Panel B. The approach described in Example 2 closely approximates the costs computed using sequential tracking when a company holds minimal work in process and finished goods inventories.

Example 3: Trigger Points Are Completion of Good Finished Units of Product (Stage C) and Sale of Finished Goods (Stage D)

This example presents an extreme and simpler version of backflush costing. It has only one trigger point for making journal entries to inventory. The trigger point is SVC's completion of finished units. Exhibit 20-7, Panel C, presents the journal entries in this case, using the same data as in Examples 1 and 2. Note that since the purchase of direct materials is not a trigger point, there is no entry corresponding to entry (a)—purchases of direct materials. Exhibit 20-8 provides an overview of this version of backflush costing. Entries are keyed to Exhibit 20-7, Panel C.

Compare entry (c) in Exhibit 20-7, Panel C, with entries (a) and (c) in Exhibit 20-7, Panel A. The simpler version in Example 3 ignores the $1,950,000 purchases of direct materials (entry (a) of Example 1). At the end of April, $50,000 of direct materials purchased has not yet been placed into production ($1,950,000 − $1,900,000 = $50,000), nor has it been entered into the inventory costing system.

Extending Example 3, backflush costing systems could also use the sale of finished goods (instead of the production of finished goods) as the only trigger point. This version of backflush costing would be most suitable for a JIT production system with minimal direct materials, work-in-process, and finished goods inventories. Why? Because this backflush costing system would maintain no inventory accounts.

Special Considerations in Backflush Costing

The accounting illustrated in Examples 1, 2, and 3 does not strictly adhere to generally accepted accounting principles of external reporting. For example, work in process (an asset) exists but is not recognized in the accounting system. Advocates of backflush costing, however, cite the materiality concept in support of these versions

Example 3 does not record accounts payable for direct materials until the products being manufactured are completely through the production process! As a result, this version of backflush costing is feasible only if there is a very short lag between receipt of direct materials and completion of the finished goods.

Question: Are the only journal entries in backflush costing the ones for the trigger points? *Answer:* No, in addition to the trigger-point entries, journal entries must be made for conversion costs incurred and for disposing of underallocated or overallocated conversion costs.

of backflushing. They claim that if inventories are low or their total costs are not subject to significant change from one accounting period to the next, operating income and inventory costs developed in a backflush costing system will not differ materially from the results generated by a system that adheres to generally accepted accounting principles.

Suppose material differences in operating income and inventories do exist between the results of a backflush costing system and those of a conventional standard costing system. An adjustment can be recorded to make the backflush numbers satisfy external reporting requirements. For example, the backflush entries in Example 2 would result in expensing all conversion costs as a part of Cost of Goods Sold ($1,188,000 at standard costs + $72,000 writeoff of underallocated conversion costs = $1,260,000). But suppose conversion costs were regarded as sufficiently material in amount to be included in Inventory Control. Then entry (d), closing the Conversion Costs accounts, would change as shown below:

Original entry (d)	Conversion Costs Allocated	$1,188,000	
	Cost of Goods Sold	72,000	
	Conversion Costs Control		$1,260,000
Revised entry (d)	Conversion Costs Allocated	$1,188,000	
	Inventory Control (1,000 units × $12)	12,000	
	Cost of Goods Sold	60,000	
	Conversion Costs Control		$1,260,000

Criticisms of backflush costing focus mainly on the absence of audit trails—the ability of the accounting system to pinpoint the uses of resources at each step of the production process. The absence of large amounts of materials and work-in-process inventory means that managers can keep track of operations by personal observations, computer monitoring, and nonfinancial measures.

What are the implications of JIT and backflush costing systems for activity-based costing (ABC) systems? Simplifying the production process, as in a JIT system, makes more of the costs direct and so reduces the extent of overhead cost allocations. Simplified ABC systems are often adequate for companies implementing JIT. But even these simpler ABC systems can enhance backflush costing. Costs from ABC systems give relatively more accurate budgeted conversion costs per unit for different products, which are then used in the backflush costing system. The activity-based cost data are also useful for product costing, decision making, and cost management.

PROBLEMS FOR SELF-STUDY

PROBLEM 1
Lee Company has a Singapore plant that manufactures MP3 players. One component is an XT chip. Expected demand is for 5,200 of these chips in March 2007. Lee estimates the ordering cost per purchase order to be $250. The monthly carrying cost for one unit of XT in stock is $5.

REQUIRED
1. Compute the EOQ for the XT chip.
2. Compute the number of deliveries of XT in March 2007.

SOLUTION

1. $\text{EOQ} = \sqrt{\dfrac{2 \times 5,200 \times \$250}{\$5}}$

    = 721 chips (rounded)

2. Number of deliveries $= \dfrac{5,200}{721}$

        = 8 (rounded)

PROBLEM 2

Littlefield Company uses a backflush costing system with three trigger points:

◆ Purchase of direct materials
◆ Completion of good finished units of product
◆ Sale of finished goods

There are no beginning inventories. Information for April 2007 are:

Direct materials purchased	$880,000	Conversion costs allocated	$ 400,000
Direct materials used	$850,000	Costs transferred to finished goods	$1,250,000
Conversion costs incurred	$422,000	Cost of goods sold	$1,190,000

REQUIRED

1. Prepare journal entries for April (without disposing of underallocated or over-allocated conversion costs). Assume there are no direct materials variances.
2. Under an ideal JIT production system, how would the amounts in your journal entries differ from the journal entries in requirement 1?

SOLUTION

1. Journal entries for April are:

Entry (a)	Inventory: Materials and In-Process Control	$ 880,000	
	Accounts Payable Control		$ 880,000
	(direct materials purchased)		
Entry (b)	Conversion Costs Control	$ 422,000	
	Various accounts (such as Wages Payable Control)		$ 422,000
	(conversion costs incurred)		
Entry (c)	Finished Goods Control	$1,250,000	
	Inventory: Materials and In-Process Control		$ 850,000
	Conversion Costs Allocated		400,000
	(standard cost of finished goods completed)		
Entry (d)	Cost of Goods Sold	$1,190,000	
	Finished Goods Control		$1,190,000
	(standard costs of finished goods sold)		

2. Under an ideal JIT production system, if the manufacturing lead time per unit is very short, there could be zero inventories at the end of each day. Entry (c) would be $1,190,000 finished goods production [to match finished goods sold in entry (d)], not $1,250,000. If the Marketing Department could only sell goods costing $1,190,000, the JIT production system would call for direct materials purchases and conversion costs of lower than $880,000 and $422,000, respectively, in entries (a) and (b).

The following decision guidelines use a question-and-answer format to summarize the chapter's main points. Each decision presents a key question. The guideline is the answer to that question.

DECISIONS	GUIDELINES
1. What are the five categories of costs associated with goods for sale?	These categories are purchasing costs (costs of goods acquired from suppliers, including freight and transportation costs), ordering costs (costs of preparing a purchase order and receiving goods), carrying costs (costs of holding inventory of goods for sale), stockout costs (costs arising when a customer demands a unit of product and that unit is not on hand), and quality costs (prevention, appraisal, internal failure, and external failure costs).
2. How do managers use the EOQ model?	The economic order quantity (EOQ) decision model calculates the optimal quantity of inventory to order by balancing ordering and carrying costs. The larger the order quantity, the

higher the annual carrying costs and the lower the annual ordering costs. The EOQ model includes both costs recorded in the financial accounting system and opportunity costs not recorded in the financial accounting system.

3. How can companies reduce the conflict between the EOQ decision model and the models used for performance evaluation?

The opportunity cost of investment tied up in inventory is a key input in the EOQ decision model. Some companies include opportunity costs when evaluating managers so that the EOQ decision model is consistent with the performance evaluation model.

4. What is a supply chain, and what is the benefit of supply-chain analysis?

Supply-chain analysis describes the flow of goods, services, and information from the initial sources of materials and services to the delivery of products to consumers, regardless of whether those activities occur in the same organization or in other organizations. Utilizing a supply-chain approach allows companies to coordinate their activities and reduce inventories throughout the supply chain.

5. How do materials requirement planning (MRP) systems differ from just-in-time (JIT) production systems?

Materials requirement planning (MRP) systems use a "push-through" approach that manufactures finished goods for inventory on the basis of demand forecasts. Just-in-time (JIT) production systems use a "demand-pull" approach in which goods are only manufactured to satisfy customer orders.

6. What are the features of a JIT production system?

Five features of a JIT production system are (a) organizing production in manufacturing cells, (b) hiring and training multiskilled workers, (c) emphasizing total quality management, (d) reducing manufacturing lead time and setup time, and (e) building strong supplier relationships.

7. What is backflush costing?

Backflush costing delays recording some of the journal entries relating to the cycle from purchase of direct materials to the sale of finished goods.

8. How does backflush costing simplify job costing?

Traditional job-costing systems use sequential tracking, in which recording of the journal entries occurs in the same order as actual purchases and progress in production. Most backflush costing systems do not record journal entries for the work-in-process stage of production. Some backflush costing systems also do not record entries for either the purchase of direct materials or the completion of finished goods.

▼ TERMS TO LEARN

This chapter contains definitions of the following important terms:

backflush costing (p. 793)
carrying costs (p. 775)
economic order quantity (EOQ) (p. 776)
inventory management (p. 775)
just-in-time (JIT) production (p. 788)
just-in-time (JIT) purchasing (p. 781)
lean production (p. 788)
manufacturing cells (p. 788)
materials requirements
  planning (MRP) (p. 786)

ordering costs (p. 775)
purchase order lead time (p. 776)
purchasing costs (p. 775)
reorder point (p. 778)
safety stock (p. 778)
sequential tracking (p. 792)
stockout costs (p. 775)
synchronous tracking (p. 792)
trigger point (p. 793)

▼ ASSIGNMENT MATERIAL

QUESTIONS

20-1 Why do better decisions regarding the purchasing and managing of goods for sale frequently cause dramatic percentage increases in net income?

20-2 Name five cost categories that are important in managing goods for sale in a retail organization.

20-3 What assumptions are made when using the simplest version of the economic order quantity (EOQ) decision model?

20-4 Give examples of costs included in annual carrying costs of inventory when using the EOQ decision model.

20-5 Give three examples of opportunity costs that typically are not recorded in accounting systems, although they are relevant to the EOQ model.

20-6 What are the steps in computing the cost of a prediction error when using the EOQ decision model?

20-7 Why might goal-congruence issues arise when an EOQ model is used to guide decisions on how much to order?

20-8 Describe just-in-time (JIT) purchasing and its benefits.

20-9 What are three factors causing reductions in the cost to place purchase orders of materials?

20-10 Describe how the Internet can be used to reduce the costs of placing purchase orders.

20-11 What is supply-chain analysis and how can it benefit manufacturers and retailers?

20-12 What are some obstacles to companies adopting a supply-chain approach?

20-13 What are the main features in a JIT production system?

20-14 Distinguish job-costing systems using sequential tracking from backflush costing.

20-15 Describe three different versions of backflush costing.

EXERCISES

20-16 Economic order quantity for retailer. Football World (FW) operates a megastore featuring sports merchandise. It uses an EOQ decision model to make inventory decisions. It is now considering inventory decisions for its Toronto Argos' jerseys product line. This is a highly popular item. Data for 2007 are

Expected annual demand for jerseys	12,000
Ordering costs per purchase order	$270
Carrying costs per year	$ 12 per jersey

Each jersey costs FW $48 and sells for $90. The $12 carrying cost per jersey comprises the required annual return on investments of $5.76 (12% × $48 purchase price) plus $6.24 relevant insurance, handling costs, and theft-related costs. The purchasing lead time is one week. FW is open 365 days a year.

REQUIRED
1. Calculate the EOQ.
2. Calculate the number of orders that will be placed each year.
3. Calculate the reorder point.

20-17 Economic order quantity, effect of parameter changes (continuation of 20-16). Athletic Products (AP) manufactures the Argos' jerseys that Football World (FW) sells to its customers. AP has recently installed computer software that enables its customers to conduct "one-stop" purchasing using state-of-the-art Web site technology developed by Cisco Systems. FW's ordering cost per purchase order will be $24 using this new technology.

REQUIRED
1. Calculate the EOQ for the Argos' jerseys using the revised ordering cost of $24 per purchase order. Assume all other data from Exercise 20-16 are the same. Comment on the result.
2. Suppose AP proposes to "assist" FW. AP will allow FW's customers to directly order from the AP Web site. AP would directly ship to these customers. AP would pay $12 to FW for every Argos' jersey purchased by one of FW's customers. How would this offer affect inventory management at FW? Should FW accept AP's proposal? Explain.

20-18 EOQ for a retailer. The Cloth Centre buys fabrics and sells them to a wide range of industrial and consumer users. One of the products it carries is denim cloth, used in the manufacture of jeans and carrying bags. The supplier for the denim cloth pays all incoming freight. No incoming inspection of the denim is necessary, because the supplier has a track record of delivering high-quality merchandise. The purchasing officer of the Cloth Centre has collected the following information:

Annual demand for denim cloth	24,000 metres
Ordering costs per purchase order	$192
Carrying costs per year	20% of purchase cost
Safety stock requirements	None
Cost of denim cloth	$9.60 per metre

The purchasing lead time is two weeks. The Cloth Centre is open 250 days a year (50 weeks for five days a week).

REQUIRED
1. Calculate the EOQ for denim cloth.
2. Calculate the number of orders that will be placed each year.
3. Calculate the reorder point for denim cloth.

20-19 EOQ for manufacturer. Beaumont Corporation makes air conditioners. It purchases 14,400 units of a particular type of compressor part, CU29, each year at a cost of $60 per unit. Beaumont requires a 12% annual return on investment. In addition, relevant carrying costs (for insurance, materials-handling, breakage, and so on) are $2.40 per unit per year. Relevant costs per purchase order are $144.

REQUIRED
1. Calculate Beaumont's EOQ for CU29.
2. Calculate Beaumont's total ordering and carrying costs using EOQ.
3. Assume that demand is uniform throughout the year and is known with certainty. The purchasing lead time is half a month. Calculate Beaumont's reorder point for CU29.

Excel Application For students who wish to practise their spreadsheet skills, the following is a step-by-step approach to creating an Excel spreadsheet to work this problem.

Step-by-Step
1. Open a new spreadsheet. At the top, create an "Original Data" section for the data provided by Beaumont Corporation, with rows for "Annual Demand, Purchase Cost per Unit, Required Return on Investment (%), and Relevant Ordering Costs per Purchase Order."

(Program your spreadsheet to perform all necessary calculations. Do not "hard-code" any amounts, such as economic order quantity, requiring addition, subtraction, multiplication, or division operations.)

2. Skip two rows, create a "Relevant Carrying Cost per Unit per Year" section in a format similar to the top of page 785. Create rows and enter calculations for "Required Annual Return on Investment," "Relevant Insurance, Materials Handling, and Breakage Costs per Year," and "Total Carrying Costs per Unit per Year."
3. Skip two rows, create a "Problem 1" section, with rows for each of the inputs into the EOQ formula: D, P, and C. Include a calculation for the "Economic Order Quantity" on a separate row.
4. Skip two rows, create a "Problem 2" section. Create rows and enter calculations for "Annual Relevant Ordering Costs," "Annual Relevant Carrying Costs," and "Relevant Total Costs."
5. Skip two rows, create a "Problem 3" section. Create rows and enter calculations for "Monthly Demand," "Purchasing Lead Time (in months)," and the "Reorder Point."
6. *Check the accuracy of your spreadsheet:* Go to your Original Data section and change the required return on investment from 12% to 15%. If you programmed your spreadsheet correctly, total carrying cost per unit per year should *increase* to $11.40, and your economic order quantity should *decrease* to 603 units.

20-20 Sensitivity of EOQ to changes in relevant ordering and carrying costs. Alyia Company's annual demand for Model X253 is 12,000 units. Alyia is unsure about the relevant carrying cost per unit per year and the relevant ordering cost per purchase order. This table presents six possible combinations of carrying and ordering costs.

Relevant Carrying Cost per Unit per Year	Relevant Ordering Cost per Purchase Order
$12	$360
$12	$240
$18	$360
$18	$240
$24	$360
$24	$240

REQUIRED
1. Determine EOQ for Alyia for each of the relevant ordering and carrying-cost alternatives.
2. How does your answer to requirement 1 give insight into the impact on EOQ of changes in relevant ordering and carrying costs?

20-21 Economic order quantity for retailer, ordering and carrying costs. Office Emporium (OE) is deciding the purchase order quantity for a new modem product. Annual demand is 24,000 units. Ordering costs per purchase order are $144. Carrying costs per modem unit are $12 per year. OE uses an economic-order-quantity model in its purchasing decisions. OE is open 360 days a year.

REQUIRED

1. Calculate OE's EOQ for modems.
2. Calculate OE's total ordering and carrying costs.
3. Assume that demand is known with certainty and the purchasing lead time is five days. Calculate OE's reorder point for modems.

20-22 **Purchase order size for retailer, EOQ, just-in-time purchasing.** The 24-Hour Mart operates a chain of supermarkets. Its best-selling soft drink is Fruitslice. Demand (D) in April for Fruitslice at its Regina supermarket is estimated to be 7,200 cases (24 cans in each case). In March, the Regina supermarket estimated the ordering costs per purchase order (P) for Fruitslice to be $36. The carrying costs (C) of each case of Fruitslice in inventory for a month were estimated to be $1.20. At the end of March, the Regina 24-Hour Mart reestimated its carrying costs to be $1.80 per case per month to take into account an increase in warehouse-related costs.

During March, 24-Hour Mart restructured its relationship with suppliers. It reduced the number of suppliers from 600 to 180. Long-term contracts were signed only with those suppliers that agreed to make product quality checks before shipping. Each purchase order would be made by linking into the suppliers' computer network. The Regina 24-Hour Mart estimated that these changes would reduce the ordering costs per purchase order to $6. The 24-Hour Mart is open 30 days in April.

REQUIRED

1. Calculate the economic order quantity in April for Fruitslice. Use the EOQ model, and assume in turn that
   a. $D = 7,200$; $P = \$36$; $C = \$1.20$
   b. $D = 7,200$; $P = \$36$; $C = \$1.80$
   c. $D = 7,200$; $P = \$6$; $C = \$1.80$

2. How does your answer to requirement 1 give insight into the retailer's movement toward JIT purchasing policies?

20-23 **JIT production, relevant benefits, relevant costs.** The Evans Corporation manufactures cordless telephones. Evans is planning to implement a JIT production system, which requires annual tooling costs of $180,000. Evans estimates that the following annual benefits would arise from JIT production.

a. Average inventory will decline by $840,000, from $1,080,000 to $240,000.
b. Insurance, space, materials-handling, and setup costs, which currently total $240,000, would decline by 30%.
c. The emphasis on quality inherent in JIT systems would reduce rework costs by 20%. Evans currently incurs $420,000 on rework.
d. Better quality would enable Evans to raise the prices of its products by $3.60 per unit. Evans sells 36,000 units each year.

Evans's required rate of return on inventory investment is 12% per year.

REQUIRED

1. Calculate the net benefit or cost to the Evans Corporation from implementing a JIT production system.
2. What other nonfinancial and qualitative factors should Evans consider before deciding on whether it should implement a JIT system?

20-24 **Backflush costing and JIT production.** Road Warrior Corp. assembles hand-held computers that have scaled-down capabilities of laptop computers. Each hand-held computer takes 6 hours to assemble. Road Warrior uses a just-in-time production system and a backflush costing system with three trigger points:

◆ Purchase of direct (raw) materials
◆ Completion of good finished units of product
◆ Sale of finished goods

There are no beginning inventories of materials or finished goods. The following data are for August 2007:

Direct (raw) materials purchased	$3,304,800
Direct (raw) materials used	3,280,320
Conversion cost incurred	868,320
Conversion costs allocated	900,480

Road Warrior records direct materials purchased and conversion costs incurred at actual costs. When finished goods are sold, the backflush costing system "pulls through" standard direct materials costs ($122.40 per unit) and standard conversion costs ($33.60 per unit).

It produced 26,800 finished goods units in August 2007 and sold 26,400 units. The actual direct materials cost per unit in August 2007 was $122.40 while the actual conversion cost per unit was $32.40.

REQUIRED

1. Prepare summary journal entries for August 2007 (without disposing of underallocated or overallocated conversion costs).
2. Post the entries in requirement 1 to T-accounts for applicable Inventory: Raw and In-Process, Conversion Costs Control, Conversion Costs Allocated, and Cost of Goods Sold.
3. Under an ideal JIT production system, how would the amounts in your journal entries differ from those in requirement 1?

20-25 Backflush costing, two trigger points, materials purchase and sale (continuation of 20-24). Assume the same facts as in Exercise 20-24, except for the following change. Road Warrior Corp. now uses a backflush costing system with the following two trigger points:

◆ Purchase of direct (raw) materials
◆ Sale of finished goods

The Inventory Control account here will include direct materials purchased but not yet in production, materials in work in process, and materials in finished goods but not sold. No conversion costs are inventoried. Any underallocated or overallocated conversion costs are written off monthly to Cost of Goods Sold.

REQUIRED

1. Prepare summary journal entries for August, including the disposition of underallocated or overallocated conversion costs.
2. Post the entries in requirement 1 to T-accounts for Inventory Control, Conversion Costs Control, Conversion Costs Allocated, and Cost of Goods Sold.

20-26 Backflush costing, two trigger points, production completion and sale (continuation of 20-24). Assume the same facts as in Exercise 20-24 except now Road Warrior uses only two trigger points, the completion of a good finished unit of product and the sale of finished goods. Any under- or overallocated conversion costs are written off monthly to cost of goods sold.

REQUIRED

1. Prepare summary journal entries for August, including the disposition of under or overallocated conversion costs.
2. Post the entries in requirement 1 to T-accounts for Finished Goods Control, Conversion Cost Control, Conversion Costs Allocated, and Costs of Goods Sold.

PROBLEMS

20-27 Effect of different order quantities on ordering costs and carrying costs, EOQ. Koala Blue retails a broad line of Australian merchandise at its London store. It sells 26,000 Ken Done linen bedroom packages (two sheets and two pillowcases) each year. Koala Blue pays Ken Done Merchandise, Inc., $124.80 per package. Its ordering costs per purchase order are $86.40. The carrying costs per package are $12.48 per year.

Liv Carrol, manager of the London store, seeks your advice on how ordering costs and carrying costs vary with different order quantities. Ken Done Merchandise, Inc., guarantees the $124.80 purchase cost per package for the 26,000 units budgeted to be purchased in the coming year.

REQUIRED

1. Compute the annual ordering costs, the annual carrying costs, and their sum for purchase order quantities of 300, 500, 600, 700, and 900, using the formulas described in this chapter. What is the economic order quantity? Comment on your results.
2. Assume that Ken Done Merchandise, Inc., introduces a computerized ordering network for its customers. Liv Carrol estimates that Koala Blue's ordering costs will be reduced to $48 per purchase order. How will this reduction in ordering costs affect the EOQ for Koala Blue on its linen bedroom packages?

20-28 EOQ, uncertainty, safety stock, reorder point. (CMA, adapted) The Starr Company distributes a wide range of electrical products. One of its best-selling items is a standard electric motor. The management of the Starr Company uses the EOQ decision model to determine the optimal number of motors to order. Management now wants to determine how much safety stock to hold.

The Starr Company estimates annual demand (300 working days) to be 30,000 electric motors. Using the EOQ decision model, the company orders 3,000 motors at a time. The lead time for an order is five days. The annual carrying costs of one motor in safety stock are $12. Management has also estimated that the stockout costs are $24 for each motor they are short.

The Starr Company has analyzed the demand during 200 past reorder periods. The records indicate the following patterns:

Demand During Lead Time	Number of Times Quantity Was Demanded
440	6
460	12
480	16
500	130
520	20
540	10
560	6
	200

REQUIRED

1. Determine the level of safety stock for electric motors that the Starr Company should maintain in order to minimize expected stockout costs and carrying costs. When computing carrying costs, assume that the safety stock is on hand at all times and that there is no overstocking caused by decreases in expected demand. (Consider safety stock levels of 0, 20, 40, and 60 units.)
2. What would be the Starr Company's new reorder point?
3. What factors should the Starr Company have considered in estimating the stockout costs?

20-29 **EOQ, cost of prediction error.** Ralph Menard is the owner of a truck repair shop. He uses an EOQ model for each of his truck parts. He initially predicts the annual demand for heavy-duty tires to be 2,000. Each tire has a purchase price of $60. The incremental ordering costs per purchase order are $48. The incremental carrying costs per year are $4.80 per unit plus 10% of the supplier's purchase price.

REQUIRED

1. Calculate the EOQ for heavy-duty tires, along with the sum of annual relevant ordering costs and carrying costs.
2. Suppose Menard is correct in all his predictions except the purchase price. (He ignored a new law that abolished tariff duties on imported heavy-duty tires, which led to lower prices from foreign competitors.) If he had been a faultless predictor, he would have foreseen that the purchase price would drop to $36 at the beginning of the year and would be unchanged throughout the year. What is the cost of the prediction error?

20-30 **JIT purchasing, relevant benefits, relevant costs.** (CMA, adapted) The Margro Corporation is an automotive supplier that uses automatic turning machines to manufacture precision parts from steel bars. Margro's inventory of raw steel averages $720,000. John Oates, president of Margro, and Helen Gorman, Margro's controller, are concerned about the costs of carrying inventory. The steel supplier is willing to supply steel in smaller lots at no additional charge. Helen Gorman identified the following effects of adopting a JIT inventory program to virtually eliminate steel inventory:

◆ Without scheduling any overtime, lost sales due to stockouts would increase by 35,000 units per year. However, by incurring overtime premiums of $48,000 per year, the increase in lost sales could be reduced to 20,000 units. This would be the maximum amount of overtime that would be feasible for Margro.

◆ Two warehouses currently used for steel bar storage would no longer be needed. Margro rents one warehouse from another company under a cancellable leasing arrangement at an annual cost of $72,000. The other warehouse is owned by Margro and contains 12,000 square metres. Three-quarters of the space in the owned warehouse could be rented for $1.80 per square metre per year.

◆ Insurance and property tax costs totalling $16,800 per year would be eliminated.

Margro's projected operating results for the 2007 calendar year follow. Long-term capital investments by Margro are expected to produce a rate of return of 20%.

Margro Corporation Budgeted Income Statement
For the Year Ending December 31, 2007
(in thousands)

Revenues (900,000 units)		$12,960
Cost of goods sold:		
Variable costs	$4,860	
Fixed costs	1,740	
Total costs of goods sold:		6,600
Gross margin		6,360
Marketing and distribution costs:		
Variable costs	$1,080	
Fixed costs	1,800	
Total marketing and distribution costs		2,880
Operating income		$ 3,480

REQUIRED

1. Calculate the estimated dollar savings (loss) for the Margro Corporation that would result in 2007 from the adoption of the JIT inventory control method.
2. Identify and explain other factors that Margro should consider before deciding whether to install a JIT system.

20-31 Backflush costing and JIT production. The Ronowski Company produces telephones. For June, there were no beginning inventories of raw materials and no beginning and ending work in process. Ronowski uses a JIT production system and backflush costing with three trigger points for making entries in its accounting system:

◆ Purchase of direct (raw) materials
◆ Completion of good finished units of product
◆ Sale of finished goods

Ronowski's June standard cost per unit of telephone product is direct materials, $31.20; conversion costs, $18. There are three inventory accounts:

◆ Inventory: Raw and In-Process Control
◆ Finished Goods Control

The following data apply to June manufacturing:

Raw materials purchased	$6,360,000
Conversion costs incurred	$3,696,000
Number of finished units manufactured	200,000
Number of finished units sold	192,000

REQUIRED

1. Prepare summary journal entries for June (without disposing of under- or overallocated conversion costs). Assume no direct materials variances.
2. Post the entries in requirement 1 to T-accounts for applicable Inventory Control, Conversion Costs Control, Conversion Costs Allocated, and Cost of Goods Sold.

20-32 Backflush, two trigger points, materials purchase and sale. Assume the same facts as in Problem 20-31. Assume that the second trigger point for the Ronowski Company is the sale—rather than the production—of finished units. Also, the inventory account is confined solely to direct materials, whether they would be in a storeroom, in work in process, or in finished goods.

No conversion costs are inventoried. They are allocated at standard cost to the units sold. Any under- or overallocated conversion costs are written off monthly to Cost of Goods Sold.

REQUIRED

1. Prepare summary journal entries for June, including the disposition of under- or overallocated conversion costs. Assume no direct materials variances.
2. Post the entries in requirement 1 to T-accounts for applicable Inventory Control, Conversion Costs Control, Conversion Costs Allocated, and Cost of Goods Sold. Explain the composition of the ending balance of Inventory Control.
3. Suppose conversion costs were sufficiently material in amount to be included in Inventory Control. Using a backflush system, show how your journal entries would be changed in requirement 1. Explain briefly.

20-33 Backflush, two trigger points, production completion and sale (continuation of 21-31). Assume the same facts as in Problem 20-31 except now there are trigger points at the completion of good finished units of product (which are debited to Finished Goods Control at standard costs) and at the sale of finished goods. Any underallocated or overallocated conversion costs are written off monthly to Cost of Goods Sold.

REQUIRED

1. Prepare summary journal entries for June, including the disposition of under- or overallocated conversion costs. Assume no direct materials variances.
2. Post the entries in requirement 1 to T-accounts for applicable Inventory Control, Conversion Costs Control, Conversion Costs Allocated, and Cost of Goods Sold. Explain the composition of the ending balance of Inventory Control.
3. If you did Problem 20-31, compare and explain any differences between the results here and those in Problem 20-31.

20-34 **Relevant benefits and costs of JIT purchasing.** Hardesty Medical Instruments is considering JIT implementation in 2007. Hardesty's annual demand for product XJ-200, a surgical scalpel, is 20,000 units. If Hardesty implements JIT, the purchase price of the scalpel is expected to increase from $12 to $12.06 because of frequent deliveries by Morrison Manufacturing, Inc. Morrison enjoys a sterling reputation for quality and reliability. Ordering costs will remain at $6 per order. However, the annual number of orders placed will be 200 instead of the current 20. As a result of frequent ordering, Hardesty's order size will decrease proportionally. Hardesty's required rate of return on investment is 20%. Other carrying costs (insurance, materials handling, and so on) will remain at $5.40 per unit. Currently, Hardesty has no stockout costs. Lower inventory levels from implementing JIT will lead to $3.60 per unit stockout costs on 100 units during the year.

REQUIRED

1. Calculate the estimated dollar savings (loss) for Hardesty Medical Instruments from the adoption of JIT purchasing using the format of Exhibit 20-5 (p. 784).
2. Under what conditions would it be beneficial for Hardesty to have Morrison manage all inventories in the supply chain?

20-35 **Supplier evaluation and relevant costs of quality and timely deliveries (continuation of 20-34)** Hardesty Medical Instruments installed a JIT purchasing system in 2007 and selected Morrison Manufacturing, Inc., as its supplier. Herriott Manufacturing Corporation also manufactures XJ-200. It offers to supply all of Hardesty's XJ-200 needs at a price of $11.70 per unit (less than Morrison's price of $12.06) under the same JIT delivery terms that Morrison offers. Hardesty's relevant carrying costs of insurance, material handling, and so on, would be $5.28 per unit per year if it purchases from Herriott. Due to the lower quality of Herriott's product, Hardesty anticipates the following negative consequences of purchasing from Herriott:

◆ Hardesty would incur inspection costs of $0.096 per unit.

◆ Average stockouts of 800 units per year would occur from late deliveries, requiring rush orders at a cost of $3.60 per unit.

◆ Customers would likely return 10% of all units sold due to poor quality of the product. Hardesty estimates its additional costs to handle each returned unit are $7.20.

REQUIRED

Calculate the relevant costs of purchasing (1) from Morrison and (2) from Herriott using the format of Exhibit 20-6 (p. 785). From whom should Hardesty buy XJ-200?

20-36 **Supplier evaluation and relevant costs of quality and timely deliveries.** Copeland Sporting Goods is evaluating two suppliers of footballs, Big Red and Quality Sports. Pertinent information about each potential supplier follows:

Relevant Item	Big Red	Quality Sports
Purchase price per unit (case)	$ 60.00	$ 61.20
Ordering costs per order	$ 7.20	$ 7.20
Inspection costs per unit	$ 0.02	$ 0.00
Insurance, material handling, and so on per unit per year	$ 4.00	$ 4.50
Annual demand	12,000 units	12,000 units
Average quantity of inventory held during the year	100 units	100 units
Required return on investment	15%	15%
Stockout costs per unit	$ 24	$ 12
Stockouts per year	350 units	60 units
Customer returns	300 units	25 units
Customer-return costs per unit	$ 30	$ 30

Calculate the relevant costs of purchasing (1) from Big Red and (2) from Quality Sports using the format of Exhibit 20-6 (p. 785) From whom should Copeland buy footballs?

20-37 Backflush costing and JIT production. The Acton Corporation manufactures electrical meters. For August, there were no beginning inventories of direct (raw) materials and no beginning and ending work in process. Acton uses a JIT production system and backflush costing with two trigger points for making entries in the accounting system:

◆ Purchase of direct materials debited to Inventory: Raw and In-Process Control

◆ Completion of good finished units of product debited to Finished Goods Control at standard costs

    Acton's August standard costs per unit are direct materials, $30; conversion costs, $24. The following data apply to August manufacturing:

Direct (raw) materials purchased	$660,000
Conversion costs incurred	$528,000
Number of finished units manufactured	21,000
Number of finished units sold	20,000

REQUIRED
1. Prepare summary journal entries for August (without disposing of under- or overallocated conversion costs). Assume no direct materials variances.
2. Post the entries in requirement 1 to T-accounts for applicable Inventory Control, Conversion Costs Control, Conversion Costs Allocated, and Cost of Goods Sold.

20-38 Backflush, two trigger points, materials purchase and sale. Assume the same facts as in Problem 20-37. Assume that the second trigger point for the Acton Corporation is the sale—rather than the production—of finished units. Also, the Inventory Control account is confined solely to direct materials, whether these materials are in a storeroom, in work in process, or in finished goods. No conversion costs are inventoried. They are allocated at standard cost to the units sold. Any under- or overallocated conversion costs are written off monthly to Cost of Goods Sold.

REQUIRED
1. Prepare summary journal entries for August, including the disposition of under- or overallocated conversion costs. Assume no direct materials variances.
2. Post the entries in requirement 1 to T-accounts for applicable Inventory Control, Conversion Costs Control, Conversion Costs Allocated, and Cost of Goods Sold.

20-39 Backflush, two trigger points, production completion and sale (continuation of 20-37). Assume the same facts as in Problem 20-37 except now there are only two trigger points, the completion of good finished units of product and the sale of finished goods.

REQUIRED
1. Prepare summary journal entries for August, including the disposition of under- or overallocated conversion costs. Assume no direct materials variances.
2. Post the entries in requirement 1 to T-accounts for applicable Inventory Control, Conversion Costs Control, Conversion Costs Allocated, and Cost of Goods Sold.

20-40 Supply-chain analysis, company viewpoints. Manufacturing companies participating in a supply-chain initiative linking manufacturers and retailers recently made the following comments on the benefits of the initiative:

◆ "Receiving better information has allowed us to forecast and reduce inventory levels ..."

◆ "You only produce what you need and that keeps the product and floor cost down."

◆ "There is more accuracy with the retailer's needs so that we can fine tune our production scheduling."

◆ "The inventory levels are lower and we have less waste by not overstocking the warehouses."

    Manufacturing companies highlighted the following information from retailers as most valuable to them:

◆ "We would like to see [the retailers] forward planning expectation of their sales."

◆ "We could use retail store level data on a daily basis and better scanner information."

◆ "Better forecasts, decisions about shelving and shelf allocations by retailers would help."

◆ "I wish we had access to each retailer's sales forecasts and the advertisements that they will be running next."

1. What are the major benefits from adopting a supply-chain approach? Use the comments on page 809 as a prompt to a more detailed discussion. Explain how these benefits can lead to increased operating income.
2. What are the key obstacles to a manufacturer adopting a supply-chain approach?

20-41 Backflush costing, income manipulation, ethics. Shira Honig, the chief financial officer of Silicon Valley Computer, is an enthusiastic advocate of just-in-time production. The SVC Keyboard Division that produces keyboards for personal computers has made dramatic improvements in its operations by a highly successful JIT implementation. The Keyboard Division president now wants to adopt backflush costing.

Honig discusses the backflush costing proposal with Ralph Strong, the controller of SVC. Strong is totally opposed to backflush costing. He argues that it will open up "Pandora's box" as regards allowing division managers to manipulate reported division operating income. A member of Strong's group outlines the three possible variations of backflush costing shown in Exhibits 20-7 and 20-8. Strong notes that none of these three methods track work in process. He asserts that this omission would allow managers to "artificially change" reported operating income by manipulating work-in-process levels. He is especially scathing about the backflush costing where no entries are made until a sale occurs. He comments:

> Suppose the Division has already met its target operating income and wants to shift some of this year's income to next year. Under backflush costing with sale of finished goods as the trigger point, the Division will have an incentive to not make sales this year of goods produced this year. This is a bizarre incentive. I rest my case about why we should stay with a job-costing system using sequential tracking.

Strong concludes that as long as reported accounting numbers are central to SVC's performance and bonus reviews, backflush costing should never be adopted.

REQUIRED
1. What factors should SVC consider in deciding whether to adopt a version of backflush costing?
2. Are Strong's concerns about income manipulation sufficiently important for SVC to not adopt backflush costing?
3. What other ways has SVC to motivate managers to not "artificially change" reported income?

COLLABORATIVE LEARNING PROBLEM

20-42 Backflushing. The following conversation occurred between Brian Richardson, plant manager at Glendale Engineering, and Charles Cheng, plant controller. Glendale manufactures automotive component parts such as gears and crankshafts for automobile manufacturers. Richardson has been very enthusiastic about implementing JIT and about simplifying and streamlining the production and other business processes.

> **Richardson:** Charles, I would like to substantially simplify our accounting in the new JIT environment. Can't we just record one accounting entry at the time we ship products to our customers? I don't want to have our staff spending time tracking inventory from one stage to the next, when we have as little inventory as we do.
>
> **Cheng:** Brian, I think you are right about simplifying the accounting, but we still have a fair amount of raw material and finished goods inventory that varies from period to period depending on the demand for specific products. Doing away with all inventory accounting may be a problem.
>
> **Richardson:** Well, you know my desire to simplify, simplify, simplify. I know that there are some costs of oversimplifying, but I believe that, in the long run, simplification pays big dividends. Why don't you and your staff study the issues involved, and I will put it on the agenda for our next senior plant management meeting.

INSTRUCTIONS
Form groups of two or more students to complete the following requirements.

REQUIRED
1. What backflush costing method would you recommend that Cheng adopt? Remember Richardson's desire to simplify the accounting as much as possible. Develop support for your recommendation.

2. Think about the three examples of backflush costing described in this chapter. These examples differ with respect to the number and types of trigger points used. Suppose your goal of implementing backflush costing is to simplify the accounting, but only if it closely matches the sequential tracking approach. Which backflush costing method would you propose if:

   a. Glendale had no raw materials or work-in-process inventories but did have finished goods inventory?

   b. Glendale had no work-in-process or finished goods inventories but did have raw materials inventory?

   c. Glendale had no raw materials, work-in-process, or finished goods inventories?

3. Backflush costing has its critics. In an article in *Management Accounting*, titled "Beware the New Accounting Myths," R. Calvasina, E. Calvasina, and G. Calvasina state:

   The periodic (backflush) system has never been reflective of the reporting needs of a manufacturing system. In the highly standardized operating environments of the present JIT era, the appropriate system to be used is a perpetual accounting system based on an up-to-date, realistic set of standard costs. For management accountants to backflush on an actual cost basis is to return to the days of the outdoor privy.

   Comment on this statement.

PART SIX

Capital budgeting for projects such as the Confederation Bridge linking Prince Edward Island to New Brunswick reflects a company's long-term strategic plans. Construction took almost four years at a cost of $1 billion. Throughout construction over 5,000 people were employed, but at its peak almost 2,100 construction and 415 staff workers were employed.

The project was a joint venture of Stantec and Jean Muller International (a member of Groupe Egis). Stantec, founded in 1954, is a world-class Canadian engineering company that provides professional design and consulting services in planning, engineering, architecture, interior design, landscape architecture, surveying, and project management. Multi-year projects of this type require careful planning and control.

CHAPTER 21

Capital Budgeting and Cost Analysis

LEARNING OBJECTIVES

After studying this chapter, you should be able to

1. Differentiate between project-by-project orientation of capital budgeting and period-by-period orientation of accrual accounting

2. Explain the time value of money and opportunity costs

3. Identify the six stages of capital budgeting for a project and its predicted outcomes

4. Use and evaluate the two main discounted cash flow (DCF) methods, the net present value (NPV) method, and the internal rate-of-return (IRR) method

5. Use and evaluate how the two main discounted cash flow methods (NPV and IRR) differ

6. Identify relevant cash inflows and outflows for capital budgeting decisions that use DCF methods

7. Use and evaluate the payback method

8. Use and evaluate the accrual accounting rate-of-return (AARR) method

9. Identify investment projects affecting different functions in the value chain and reduce conflict between project approval and performance evaluation measures.

Organizations are often required to make decisions whose consequences are felt over many future years. Such decisions frequently involve large investments of money and have uncertain actual outcomes that have long-lasting effects on the organization. For example, Placer Dome must decide if it will spend $800 million to develop a new gold-mining property. Air Canada must decide whether it should invest billions of dollars in new Boeing 777 and 787 airplanes to renew its fleet. The investments and the financial outcomes from those investments (realized over a number of years) are collectively referred to as **investment projects** or **investment programs**. Poor long-term investment decisions can affect the future stability of an organization, because it is rare that organizations recover money tied up in bad investments. Managers need a long-range planning tool or process to analyze and control investments with long-term consequences.

Capital budgeting is the process of making those long-term planning decisions for investments. Income determination and the planning and control of routine operations focus primarily on the current time period. Capital budgeting is a decision-making and control tool that focuses primarily on projects or programs whose effects span multiple time periods.

Investment projects (investment programs). Investments and financial outcomes from those investments (realized over a number of years).

Capital budgeting. The process of making long-term planning decisions for investments.

TWO FOCUSES OF COST ANALYSIS

Recall a central theme of this book: different costs for different purposes. Capital budgeting decisions focus on the project, which spans multiple time periods. There is a great danger in basing capital budgeting decisions on the current accounting period's income statement, ignoring the future implications of investing in a project. Investment in a project might depress the current period's reported income, but it may still be a worthwhile investment because of the high future cash inflows that it is expected to generate.

Exhibit 21-1 illustrates two different dimensions of cost analysis: (1) the project dimension and (2) the time dimension. Each project is represented in Exhibit 21-1 as a distinct horizontal rectangle. The life of each project is longer than one accounting period. Capital budgeting focusses on the entire life of the project in order to consider *all* cash inflows or cash savings from the investment. The white area in Exhibit 21-1 illustrates the accounting-period focus on income determination and routine planning and control. This cross-section emphasizes the company's performance for the 2010 accounting period. Accounting income is of particular interest to the manager because bonuses are frequently based on reported income. Income reported in an accounting period is also important to a company because of its impact on the company's share price. Excessive focus on short-run accounting income, however, can cause a company to forgo long-term profitability. Successful managers balance short-term accounting-period considerations and longer-term project considerations in their decision process.

The accounting system that corresponds to the project dimension in Exhibit 21-1 is termed *life cycle costing*. This system, described in Chapter 12, accumulates revenues and costs on a project-by-project basis. For example, a life cycle costing statement for a new car project at the Ford Motor Company could encompass a four-year period and would accumulate costs for all business functions in the value chain, from R&D to customer service. This accumulation expands the accrual accounting system, which measures income on a period-by-period basis, to a system that computes income over the entire project covering many accounting periods.

Any system that focuses on the life span of a project must cover several years and thus must consider the time value of money. The *time value of money* takes into

OBJECTIVE 1

Differentiate between project-by-project orientation of capital budgeting and period-by-period orientation of accrual accounting

OBJECTIVE 2

Explain the time value of money and opportunity costs

EXHIBIT 21-1
The Project and Time Dimensions of Capital Budgeting

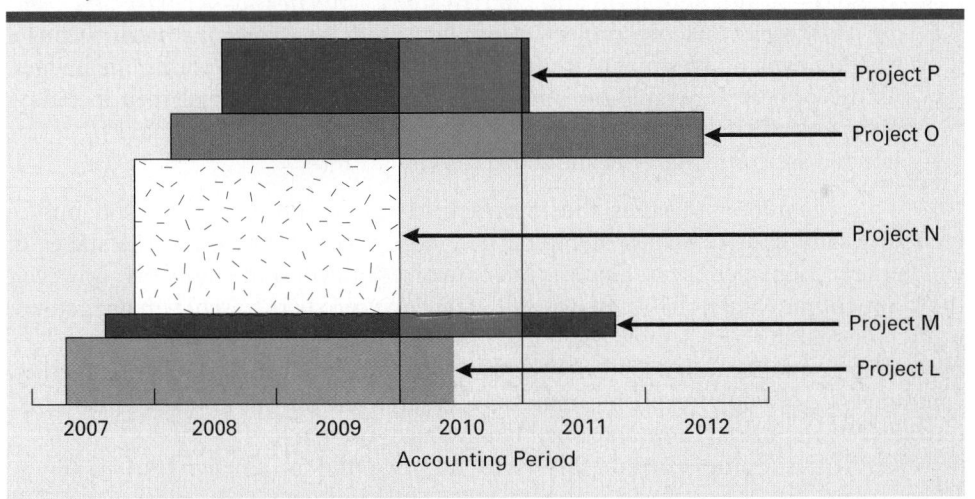

account the fact that a dollar (or any other monetary unit) received today is worth more than a dollar received tomorrow. The reason is that $1 received today can be invested to start earning a return of 10% per year (say) so that it grows to $1.10 at the end of the year. The time value of money is the opportunity cost (the return of $0.10 forgone) from not having the money today.

Capital budgeting focuses on projects that can be accounted for using life cycle costing and that must be evaluated taking into consideration the time value of money.

STAGES OF CAPITAL BUDGETING

We describe six stages in capital budgeting.

◆ **Stage 1—Identification stage.** *Distinguish which types of capital expenditure projects are necessary to accomplish organization objectives and strategies.* Capital expenditure initiatives are closely tied to the strategies of an organization or an organizational subunit. For example, an organization's strategy could be either to increase revenues by targeting new products, customers, markets, or to reduce costs by improving design, productivity, and efficiency. Identifying which types of capital investment projects to invest in is largely the responsibility of line management.

◆ **Stage 2—Search stage.** *Explore several alternative capital expenditure investments that will achieve organization objectives and strategies.* Employee teams from all parts of the value chain evaluate alternative technologies, machines, and project specifications. Some alternatives are rejected early. Others are evaluated more thoroughly in the information-acquisition stage.

◆ **Stage 3—Information-acquisition stage.** *Analyze the predicted costs and predicted consequences of alternative capital investments.* These consequences can be quantitative and qualitative. Capital budgeting emphasizes financial quantitative factors, but nonfinancial quantitative and qualitative factors are also very important. Management accountants help identify these factors.

◆ **Stage 4—Selection stage.** *Choose projects for implementation.* Organizations choose those projects whose predicted outcomes (benefits) exceed predicted costs by the greatest amount. The formal analysis includes only predicted outcomes quantified in financial terms. Managers reevaluate the conclusions reached using formal analysis, by applying managerial judgment to take into account nonfinancial and qualitative considerations. Evaluating costs and benefits is often the responsibility of the management accountant.

◆ **Stage 5—Financing stage.** *Obtain project funding.* Sources of financing include internally (within the organization) generated cash flow from operations and externally generated cash flow from capital markets (equity and debt instruments). Financing is often the responsibility of the treasury function of an organization.

◆ **Stage 6—Implementation and control stage.** *Initiate selected projects and monitor performance.* As the project is implemented, the company must evaluate whether capital investments are being made as scheduled and within the budget. As the project generates cash inflows, monitoring and control may include a postinvestment audit, in which the predictions made at the time the project was selected are compared with the actual results.

This chapter emphasizes the information-acquisition, selection, and implementation and control stages of capital budgeting because these are the stages in which the management accountant is most involved. Beyond the numbers, however, the ability of individual managers to "sell" their own projects to senior management is often pivotal in the acceptance or rejection of projects.

We use information from Lifetime Care Hospital to illustrate capital budgeting. Lifetime Care is a not-for-profit organization that is not subject to taxes. Chapter 22 introduces tax considerations in capital budgeting.

One of Lifetime Care's goals is to improve the productivity of its X-ray Department. To achieve this goal, the manager of Lifetime Care *identifies* a need to purchase a new state-of-the-art X-ray machine to replace an existing machine. The *search* stage yields several alternative models, but the hospital's technical staff focuses on one machine, XCAM8, as being particularly suitable. They next begin to *acquire information* for a more detailed evaluation. Quantitative financial information for the formal analysis follows:

Revenue will remain unchanged regardless of whether the new X-ray machine is acquired or not. Lifetime Care charges a fixed rate for a particular diagnosis, regardless of the number of X-rays taken. The only relevant financial benefit in evaluating Lifetime's decision to purchase the X-ray machine is the cash savings in operating costs. The existing X-ray machine can operate for another five years and will have a disposal price of zero at the end of five years. The initial investment will be $379,100, which is calculated as follows:

Cost of new machine	$372,890
Investment in working capital (supplies and spare parts for the new machine)	$ 10,000
Cash flow from disposal of the old machine (after tax)	$ (3,790)
Net initial investment for the new machine	$379,100

> Most investment projects or programs require an increase in working capital—a cash outlay (usually at the beginning of the project) that will be recovered at the end of the project.

The manager expects the new machine to have a five-year useful life and a disposal price of zero at the end of five years. The new machine is faster and easier to operate and has the ability to X-ray a larger area and will reduce the average number of X-rays taken per patient. This will decrease labour, power, and utilities costs. The manager expects the investment to result in annual cash inflows of $100,000. These cash flows will generally occur throughout the year; however, to simplify computations, we assume that operating cash flows occur at the end of each year. The cash inflows are expected to come from cash savings in operating costs of $100,000 for each of the first four years and $90,000 in year five plus recovery of working capital investment of $10,000 in year five.

Managers at Lifetime Care also identify the following nonfinancial quantitative and qualitative benefits of investing in the new X-ray equipment:

1. **Quality:** Higher-quality X-rays will lead to improved diagnoses and better patient treatment.

2. **Safety:** The greater efficiency of the new machine would mean that X-ray technicians and patients are exposed to fewer of the possibly harmful effects of X-ray radiation.

These nonfinancial benefits are not considered in the formal financial analysis.

In the *selection* stage, managers must decide whether Lifetime Care should purchase the new X-ray machine. They start with financial information. This chapter discusses the following methods that they can use:

◆ Discounted cash flow methods: net present value (NPV) and internal rate-of-return (IRR)

◆ Payback method

◆ Accrual accounting rate-of-return method

DISCOUNTED CASH FLOW METHODS

Discounted cash flow (DCF) measures the cash inflows and outflows of a project as if they occurred at a single point in time so that they can be compared in an appropriate way. The discounted cash flow methods recognize that the use of money has an opportunity cost—return forgone. Because the DCF methods explicitly and routinely weight cash flows by the time value of money, they are usually the best (most comprehensive) methods to use for long-run decisions.

DCF focuses on *cash* inflows and outflows rather than on *operating income* as used in conventional accrual accounting. Cash is invested now with the expectation of receiving a greater amount of cash in the future. Try to avoid injecting accrual

OBJECTIVE 4

Use and evaluate the two main discounted cash flow (DCF) methods, the net present value (NPV) method, and the internal rate-of-return (IRR) method concepts of accounting into DCF analysis. For example, amortization is deducted as an accrual expense when calculating operating income under accrual accounting. It is not deducted in DCF analysis because such expense entails no cash outflow.

The compound interest tables and formulas used in DCF analysis are included in Appendix A. (Appendix A will be used frequently in Chapters 21 and 22.)

There are two main DCF methods:

1. Net present value (NPV)

2. Internal rate of return (IRR)

NPV is calculated using the **required rate of return (RRR)**, which is the minimum acceptable rate of return on an investment. It is the return that the organization could expect to receive elsewhere for an investment of comparable risk. This rate is also called the **discount rate**, **hurdle rate**, or **(opportunity) cost of capital**. When working with IRR, the RRR is used as a point of comparison. Chapter 22 discusses issues encountered in estimating this rate.

Assume that the required rate of return, or discount rate, for the Lifetime Care X-ray machine project is 8%.

Net Present Value Method

The **net present value (NPV) method** calculates the expected net monetary gain or loss from a project by discounting all expected future cash inflows and outflows to the present point in time, using the required rate of return. Only projects with a positive net present value are acceptable. Why? Because the return from these projects exceeds the cost of capital (the return available by investing the capital elsewhere). Managers prefer projects with higher NPVs to projects with lower NPVs, if all other things are equal. Using the NPV method entails the following steps:

◆ **Step 1:** *Sketch the relevant cash inflows and outflows.* The right side of Exhibit 21-2 shows how these cash flows are portrayed. Outflows appear in parentheses. The sketch helps the decision maker organize the data in a systematic way. Note that Exhibit 21-2 includes the outflow for the new machine at year 0, the time of the acquisition. The NPV method focuses only on cash flows. NPV analysis is indifferent to where the cash flows come from (operations, purchase or sale of equipment, or investment or recovery of working capital) and to the accrual accounting treatments of individual cash flow items (for example, amortization costs on equipment purchases).

◆ **Step 2:** *Choose the correct compound interest table from Appendix A.* In our example, we can discount each year's cash flow separately using Table 2 (Appendix A), or we can compute the present value of an annuity using Table 4 (Appendix A). If we use Table 2, we find the discount factors for periods 1–5 under the 8% column. Approach 1 in Exhibit 21-2 presents the five discount factors. Because the investment produces an annuity, a series of equal cash flows at equal intervals, we may use Table 4. We find the discount factor for five periods under the 8% column. Approach 2 in Exhibit 21-2 shows that this discount factor is 3.993 (3.993 is the sum of the five discount factors used in approach 1). To obtain the present value figures, multiply the discount factors by the appropriate cash amounts in the sketch in Exhibit 21-2.

◆ **Step 3:** *Sum the present value figures to determine the net present value.* If the sum is zero or positive, the NPV model indicates that the project should be accepted. That is, its expected rate of return equals or exceeds the required rate of return. If the total is negative, the project is undesirable. Its expected rate of return is below the required rate of return.

Exhibit 21-2 indicates an NPV of $20,200 at the required rate of return of 8%; the expected return from the project exceeds the 8% required rate of return. Therefore, the project is desirable. The cash flows from the project are adequate to (1) recover the net initial investment in the project and (2) earn a return greater than 8% on the investment tied up in the project from period to period. Had the NPV been negative, the project would have been undesirable on the basis of financial considerations.

	A	B	C	D	E	F	G	H	I
1			Net initial investment	$379,100					
2			Useful life	5 years					
3			Annual cash inflow	$100,000					
4			Required rate of return	8%					
5									
6		**Present Value**	**Present Value of**	**Sketch of Relevant Cash Flows at End of Each Year**					
7		**of Cash Flow**	**$1 Discounted at 8%**	**0**	**1**	**2**	**3**	**4**	**5**
8	**Approach 1: Discounting Each Year's Cash Flow Separately**[a]								
9	Net initial investment	$(379,100) ⟵	1.000 ⟵	$(379,100)					
10		92,600 ⟵	0.926 ⟵		$100,000				
11		85,700 ⟵	0.857 ⟵			$100,000			
12	Annual cash inflow	79,400 ⟵	0.794 ⟵				$100,000		
13		73,500 ⟵	0.735 ⟵					$100,000	
14		68,100 ⟵	0.681 ⟵						$100,000
15	NPV if new machine purchased	$ 20,200							
16									
17	**Approach 2: Using Annuity Table**[b]								
18	Net initial investment	$(379,100) ⟵	1.000 ⟵	$(379,100)					
19					$100,000	$100,000	$100,000	$100,000	$100,000
20									
21	Annual cash inflow	399,300 ⟵	3.993 ⟵						
22	NPV if new machine purchased	$ 20,200							
23									
24	*Note:* Parentheses denote relevant cash outflows throughout all exhibits in Chapter 21.								
25	[a]Present values from Table 2, Appendix A at the end of the book. For example, $0.857 = 1 \div (1.08)^2$.								
26	[b]Annuity present value from Table 4, Appendix A. The annuity table value of 3.993 is the sum of the individual discount rates 0.926 + 0.857 + 0.794 + 0.735 + 0.681, subject to rounding.								

Of course, the manager of the hospital must also weigh nonfinancial factors. Consider the reduction in the average number of individual X-rays taken per patient with the new machine. This reduction is a qualitative benefit of the new machine given the health risks to patients and technicians. Other qualitative benefits of the new machine are the better diagnoses and treatments that patients receive. Had the NPV been negative, the manager would need to judge whether the nonfinancial benefits outweigh the negative NPV.

It is important that you not proceed until you thoroughly understand Exhibit 21-2. Compare approach 1 with approach 2 in Exhibit 21-2 to see how Table 4 in Appendix A merely aggregates the present value factors of Table 2. That is, the fundamental table is Table 2; Table 4 reduces calculations when there is an annuity—a series of equal cash flows at equal intervals. The DCF approach answers the question of whether or not a project will break even or generate positive cash flow over its lifetime but does not answer the question of what the return on the investment will be. This question is answered by using the internal rate-of-return method.

> If you use a calculator or computer to calculate the NPV, you will often obtain a slightly different answer for two reasons. The first is that the tables in Appendix A assume cash inflow occurs at the end of each year, whereas many programs for calculators and computers assume the inflow occurs at the beginning of each year. The second reason is rounding—the tables use only 3 decimal places in contrast to 8 or more used in calculators and computers.

Internal Rate-of-Return Method

The **internal rate of return (IRR)** is the discount rate at which the present value of expected cash inflows from a project equals the present value of expected cash outflows of the project. That is, the IRR is the discount rate that makes NPV = $0. IRR is sometimes called the *time-adjusted rate of return*. As in the NPV method, the sources of cash flows and the accrual accounting treatment of individual cash flows are irrelevant to the IRR calculations. We illustrate the computation of the IRR using the X-ray machine project of Lifetime Care. Exhibit 21-3 on page 818 presents the cash flows

> **Internal rate of return (IRR) (time-adjusted rate of return).** Discount rate at which the present value of expected cash inflows from a project equals the present value of expected cash outflows of the project. The IRR is the discount rate that makes NPV = $0.

EXHIBIT 21-3
Internal Rate-of-Return Method: Lifetime Care Hospital's New X-Ray Machine[a]

	A	B	C	D	E	F	G	H	I
1			Net initial investment	$379,100					
2			Useful life	5 years					
3			Annual cash inflow	$100,000					
4			Annual Discount rate	10%					
5									
6		**Present Value**	**Present Value of**	**Sketch of Relevant Cash Flows at End of Each Year**					
7		**of Cash Flow**	**$1 Discounted at 10%**	**0**	**1**	**2**	**3**	**4**	**5**
8	**Approach 1: Discounting Each Year's Cash Flow Separately[b]**								
9	Net initial investment	$(379,100) ◄	1.000 ◄	$(379,100)					
10		90,900 ◄	0.909 ◄		$100,000				
11		82,600 ◄	0.826 ◄			$100,000			
12	Annual cash inflow	75,100 ◄	0.751 ◄				$100,000		
13		68,300 ◄	0.683 ◄					$100,000	
14		62,100 ◄	0.621 ◄						$100,000
15	NPV if new machine purchased[c] (the zero difference proves that the internal rate of return is 10%)	$ 0							
16									
17	**Approach 2: Using Annuity Table**								
18	Net initial investment	$(379,100) ◄	1.000 ◄	$(379,100)					
19					$100,000	$100,000	$100,000	$100,000	$100,000
20									
21	Annual cash inflow	379,100 ◄	3.791[d] ◄						
22	NPV if new machine purchased	$ 0							
23									
24	*Note:* Parentheses denote relevant cash outflows throughout all exhibits in Chapter 21.								
25	[a]The internal rate of return is computed by methods explained on pp. 818–819.								
26	[b]Present values from Table 2, Appendix A at the end of the book.								
27	[c]Sum is $(100) due to rounding. We round to $0.								
28	[d]Annuity present value from Table 4, Appendix A. The annuity table value of 3.791 is the sum of the individual discount rates 0.909 + 0.826 + 0.751 + 0.683 + 0.621, subject to rounding.								

and shows the calculation of the NPV using a 10% discount rate. At a 10% discount rate, the NPV of the project is zero. Therefore, the IRR for the project is 10%. All qualitative and nonfinancial considerations being equal, managers will choose projects with the IRR exceeding the required rate of return by the greatest amount.

How do we determine the 10% discount rate that yields NPV = $0? In most cases, analysts solving capital budgeting problems have a calculator or computer programmed to provide the internal rate of return. Without a calculator or computer program, a trial-and-error approach can provide the answer.

◆ **Step 1:** Try a discount rate and calculate the NPV of the project using that discount rate.

◆ **Step 2:** If the NPV is less than zero, try a lower discount rate. (A lower discount rate will increase the NPV; remember, we are trying to find a discount rate for which NPV = $0.) If the NPV is greater than zero, try a higher discount rate to lower the NPV. Keep adjusting the discount rate until NPV = $0. In the Lifetime Care example, a discount rate of 8% yields NPV of + $20,200 (see Exhibit 21-2). A discount rate of 12% yields NPV of −$18,600 (3.605, the present value annuity factor from Table 4, × $100,000 − $379,100). Therefore, the discount rate that makes NPV = $0 must lie between 8% and 12%. We happen to try 10% and get NPV = $0. Hence, the IRR is 10%.

The step-by-step computations of an internal rate of return are easier when the cash inflows are equal, as in our example. Information from Exhibit 21-3 can be expressed in the following equation:

$$\$379,100 = \text{Present value of annuity of } \$100,000 \text{ at } x\% \text{ for 5 years}$$

Or, using Table 4 (Appendix A), what factor F will satisfy the following equation?

$$\$379,100 = \$100,000F$$
$$F = 3.791$$

On the five-period line of Table 4, find the percentage column that is closest to 3.791. It is exactly 10%. If the factor F falls between the factors in two columns, straight-line interpolation is used to approximate the IRR. (For an illustration of interpolation, see requirement 1 of the Problem for Self-Study on page 833.)

A project is accepted only if the internal rate of return exceeds the required rate of return (the opportunity cost of capital). In the Lifetime Care example, the X-ray machine has an IRR of 10%, which is greater than the required rate of return of 8%. On the basis of financial factors, Lifetime Care should invest in the new machine. If the IRR exceeds the RRR, then the project has a positive NPV when project cash flows are discounted at the RRR. If the IRR equals the RRR, NPV = $0. If the IRR is less than the RRR, NPV is negative. Obviously, managers prefer projects with higher IRRs to projects with lower IRRs, if all other things are equal. The IRR of 10% means that the cash inflows from the project are adequate to (1) recover the net initial investment in the project and (2) earn a return of exactly 10% on investment tied up in the project over its useful life.

Despite the limitations of the IRR method, surveys report its widespread use, probably not only because managers find the IRR method easier to understand, but also because in most instances their decisions would be unaffected by using IRR or NPV. In some cases, however, as when comparing two projects with unequal lives or unequal investments, the two methods will not indicate the same decision.

Comparison of Net Present Value and Internal Rate-of-Return Method

This text emphasizes the NPV method, which has the important advantage that the end result of the computations is dollars, not a percentage. We can therefore add the NPVs of individual independent projects to estimate the effect of accepting a combination of projects. In contrast, the IRRs of individual projects cannot be added or averaged to derive the IRR of the combination of projects.

A second advantage of the NPV method is that we can use it in situations where the required rate of return varies over the life of the project. For example, suppose in the X-ray machine example Lifetime Care has a required rate of return of 8% in years 1, 2, and 3 and 12% in years 4 and 5. The total present value of the cash inflows is as follows:

Year (1)	Cash Inflows (2)	Required Rate of Return (3)	Present Value of $1 Discounted at Required Rate (4)	Total Present Value of Cash Inflows (5) = (4) × (2)
1	$100,000	8%	0.926	$ 92,600
2	100,000	8	0.857	85,700
3	100,000	8	0.794	79,400
4	100,000	12	0.636	63,600
5	100,000	12	0.567	56,700
				$378,000

Given the net initial investment of $379,100, NPV calculations indicate that the project is unattractive: it has a negative NPV of −$1,100 ($378,000 − $379,100). However, it is not possible to use the IRR method to infer that the project should be rejected. The existence of different required rates of return in different years (8% for years 1, 2, and 3 versus 12% for years 4 and 5) means there is not a single RRR that the IRR (a single figure) must exceed for the project to be acceptable.

SENSITIVITY ANALYSIS

To highlight the basic differences between the NPV and IRR methods, we have assumed that the expected values of cash flows will occur for certain. Obviously, managers know that their predictions are imperfect and thus uncertain. To examine how a result will change if the predicted financial outcomes are not achieved or if an underlying assumption changes, managers can use sensitivity analysis, a what-if technique first introduced in Chapter 3.

Sensitivity analysis can take various forms. For example, suppose Lifetime Care management believes forecasted savings are uncertain and difficult to predict. Management could then ask: What is the minimum annual cash savings that will cause us to invest in the new X-ray machine (that is, for NPV = $0)? For the data in Exhibit 21-2, let ACI = annual cash inflows and let NPV = $0. The net initial investment is $379,100, and the present-value factor at the 8% required rate of return for a five-year annuity of $1 is 3.993. Then:

$$NPV = \$0$$
$$3.993A - \$379,100 = \$0$$
$$3.993A = \$379,100$$
$$A = \$94,941$$

Thus, at the discount rate of 8%, annual cash inflows can decrease to $94,941 (a decline of $100,000 − $94,941 = $5,059) before NPV falls below zero. If management believes it can attain annual cash savings of at least $94,941, it could justify investing in the new X-ray machine on financial grounds alone.

Computer spreadsheets enable managers to conduct systematic, efficient sensitivity analysis. Exhibit 21-4 shows how the net present value of the X-ray machine project is affected by variations in (1) the annual cash inflows and (2) the required rate of return. NPVs can also vary with the useful life of a project. Sensitivity analysis helps a manager focus on those decisions that are most sensitive, and it eases the manager's mind about those decisions that are not so sensitive. For the X-ray machine project, Exhibit 21-4 shows that variations in either the annual cash inflows or the required rate of return have sizable effects on NPV.

The rapid changes in technology make estimating the useful life of a project one of the most challenging aspects of analyzing investment projects.

RELEVANT CASH FLOWS IN DISCOUNTED CASH FLOW ANALYSIS

OBJECTIVE 6

Identify relevant cash inflows and outflows for capital budgeting decisions that use DCF methods

The key point of discounted cash flow methods is to focus exclusively on differences in expected future cash flows that result from implementing a project. All cash flows are treated the same, whether they arise from operations, purchase or sale of equipment,

EXHIBIT 21-4

Net Present Value Calculations for Lifetime Care Hospital Under Different Assumptions of Annual Cash Flows and Required Rates of Return[a]

	A	B	C	D	E	F
1	Required	Annual Cash Flow				
2	Rate of Return	$80,000	$90,000	$100,000	$110,000	$120,000
3	6%	$(42,140)	$ (20)	$42,100	$84,220	$126,340
4	8%	$(59,660)	$(19,730)	$20,200	$60,130	$100,060
5	10%	$(75,820)	$(37,910)	$ 0	$37,910	$ 75,820
6						
7	[a]All calculated amounts assume the project's useful life is five years.					

or investment in or recovery of working capital. The opportunity cost and the time value of money are tied to the cash flowing in or out of the organization, not to the source of the cash.

One of the biggest challenges in DCF analysis is determining those cash flows that are relevant to making the decision. Relevant cash flows are expected future cash flows that differ between the alternatives. At Lifetime Care, the alternatives are either to continue to use the old X-ray machine or to replace it with the new machine. The relevant cash flows are the *differences* in cash flows between continuing to use the old machine and purchasing the new one. *When reading this section, focus on identifying future expected cash flows of each alternative and differences in cash flows between alternatives.*

Capital investment projects (for example, purchasing a new machine) typically have five major categories of cash flows: (1) initial investment in machine and working capital, (2) cash flow from current disposal of the old machine, (3) recurring operating cash flows, (4) cash flow from terminal disposal of machine and recovery of working capital, and (5) income tax impacts on cash flows. We discuss the first four categories here, using Lifetime Care's purchase decision of the X-ray machine as an illustration. Income tax effects are described in Chapter 22.

1. **Initial investment.** Two components of investment cash flows are (a) the cash outflow to purchase the machine and (b) the working capital cash outflows.
   a. *Initial machine investment.* These outflows, made for purchasing plant, equipment, and machines, occur in the early periods of the project's life and include cash outflows for transporting and installing the item. In the Lifetime Care example, the $372,890 cost (including transportation and installation costs) of the X-ray machine is an outflow in year 0. These cash flows are relevant to the capital budgeting decision because they will be incurred only if Lifetime decides to purchase the new machine.
   b. *Initial working capital investment.* Investments in plant, equipment, and machines and in the sales promotions for product lines are invariably accompanied by incremental investments in working capital. These investments take the form of current assets, such as receivables and inventories (supplies and spare parts for the new machine in the Lifetime Care example), minus current liabilities, such as accounts payable. Working capital investments are similar to machine investments. In each case, available cash is tied up.

      The Lifetime Care example assumes a $10,000 incremental investment in working capital (supplies and spare parts inventory) if the new machine is acquired. The incremental working capital investment is the difference between the working capital required to operate the new machine (say $15,000) and the working capital required to operate the old machine (say $5,000). The $10,000 additional investment in working capital is a cash outflow in year 0.

2. **Current disposal price of old machine.** Any cash received from disposal of the old machine is a relevant cash inflow (in year 0) because it is an expected future cash flow that differs between the alternatives of investing and not investing in the new project. If Lifetime Care invests in the new X-ray machine, it will be able to dispose of its old machine for $3,790. These proceeds are included as cash inflow in year 0.

   Recall from Chapter 11 that the book value (original cost minus accumulated amortization) of the old equipment is irrelevant. It is a past cost. Nothing can change what has already been spent or what has already happened.

   The net initial investment for the new X-ray machine, $379,100, is the initial machine investment plus the initial working capital investment minus current disposal price of the old machine: $372,890 + $10,000 − $3,790 = $379,100.

3. **Recurring operating cash flows.** This category includes all recurring operating cash flows that differ among the alternatives. Organizations make capital investments to generate cash inflows in the future. These inflows may result from producing and selling additional goods or services, or, as in the Lifetime Care example, from savings in operating cash costs. Recurring operating cash

flows can be net outflows in some periods. For example, oil production may require large expenditures every five years (say) to improve oil extraction rates. Focus on operating cash flows, not on accrued revenues and costs.

To underscore this point, consider the following additional facts about the Lifetime Care X-ray machine example:

◆ Total X-Ray Department overhead costs will not change whether the new machine is purchased or the old machine is kept. The X-Ray Department overhead costs are allocated to individual X-ray machines—Lifetime has several—on the basis of the labour costs for operating each machine. Because the new X-ray machine will have lower labour costs, overhead allocated to it will be $30,000 less than the amount allocated to the machine it is replacing.

◆ Amortization on the new X-ray machine using the straight-line method is $74,578 [(original cost, $372,890—expected terminal disposal price, $0) ÷ useful life, 5 years].

The savings in operating cash flows (labour and materials) of $100,000 in each of the first four years and $90,000 in the fifth year are clearly relevant because they are expected future cash flows that will differ between the alternatives of investing and not investing in the new machine. But what about the decrease in allocated overhead costs of $30,000? What about amortization of $74,578?

a. *Overhead costs.* The key question is do total overhead cash flows decrease as a result of acquiring the new machine? In our example, they do not. Total X-Ray Department overhead costs remain the same whether or not the new machine is acquired. They are fixed costs such as insurance. What changes is the overhead allocated to individual machines. The overhead costs allocated to the new machine are $30,000 less but this additional $30,000 will simply be assigned to *other* machines in the department. No cash flow savings in total overhead occur. Therefore, the $30,000 should not be included as part of recurring operating cash inflows.

b. *Amortization.* Amortization is irrelevant because it is a noncash allocation of costs, whereas DCF is based on inflows and outflows of *cash*. In DCF methods, the initial cost of equipment is regarded as a *lump sum* outflow of cash at year 0. Deducting amortization from operating cash inflows would be counting the lump sum amount twice. What we will examine in the following chapter is the cash flow effect of tax regulations on capital budgeting.

4. **Terminal disposal price of investment.** The disposal of the investment at the date of termination of a project generally increases cash inflow in the year of disposal. Errors in forecasting the terminal disposal price are seldom critical on long-duration projects, because the present value of amounts to be received in the distant future is usually small. Two components of the terminal disposal price of an investment are (a) the terminal disposal price of the machine and (b) the recovery of working capital.

a. *Terminal disposal price of machine.* At the end of the useful life of the project, the initial machine investment may not be recovered at all, or it may be only partially recovered in the amount of the terminal disposal price.

The relevant cash inflow is the difference in expected terminal disposal prices at the end of five years under the two alternatives—the terminal disposal price of the new machine (zero in the case of Lifetime Care) minus the terminal disposal price of the old machine (also zero in the Lifetime Care example).[1]

---

[1] The Lifetime Care example assumes that both the new and the old machine have a future useful life of five years. If instead the old machine had a useful life of only four years, management could choose to evaluate the investment decision over a four-year horizon. In this case, Lifetime's management would need to predict the terminal disposal price of the new machine at the end of four years.

	A	B	C	D	E	F	G	H
1					Sketch of Relevant Cash Flows			
2								
3		End of Year:	0	1	2	3	4	5
4	1a	Initial machine investment	$(372,890)					
5	b	Initial working capital investment	(10,000)					
6	2	Current disposal price of old machine	3,790					
7		Net initial investment	$(379,100)					
8	3	Recurring operating cash flows		$100,000	$100,000	$100,000	$100,000	$ 90,000
9	4a	Terminal disposal price of new machine						–
10	b	Recovery of working capital						10,000
11		Total relevant cash inflows and outflows						
12		as shown in Exhibits 21-2 and 21-3	$(379,100)	$100,000	$100,000	$100,000	$100,000	$100,000

b. *Recovery of working capital.* The initial investment in working capital is usually fully recouped when the project is terminated. At that time, inventories and receivables necessary to support the project are no longer needed. The relevant cash inflow is the difference in the expected working capital recovered under the two alternatives. If the new X-ray machine is purchased, Lifetime Care will recover $15,000 of working capital in year 5. If the new machine is not acquired, Lifetime will recover $5,000 of working capital in year 5, at the end of the useful life of the old machine. The relevant cash inflow in year 5 if Lifetime invests in the new machine is $10,000 ($15,000 – $5,000).

Some capital investments *reduce* working capital. Assume that a computer-integrated manufacturing (CIM) project with a seven-year life will reduce inventories and hence working capital by $20 million from, say, $50 million to $30 million. This reduction will be represented as a $20-million cash inflow for the project at year 0. At the end of seven years, the recovery of working capital will show a relevant cash *outflow* of $20 million. Why? Because the company recovers only $30 million of working capital under CIM rather than the $50 million of working capital it would have recovered had it not implemented CIM.

Exhibit 21-5 above presents the relevant cash inflows and outflows for Lifetime Care's decision to purchase the new machine as described in items 1–4 in the preceding list. The total relevant cash flows for each year are the same as the relevant cash flows used in Exhibits 21-2 and 21-3 to illustrate the NPV and IRR methods.

PAYBACK METHOD

Uniform Cash Flows

We now consider a third method for analyzing the financial aspects of projects. The **payback method** measures the time it will take to recoup, in the form of net cash inflows, the net initial investment in a project. Like NPV and IRR, the payback method does not distinguish the sources of cash inflows (operations, disposal of equipment, or recovery of working capital). In the Lifetime Care example, the X-ray machine costs $379,100, has a five-year expected useful

OBJECTIVE 7

Use and evaluate the payback method

life, and generates a $100,000 uniform cash inflow each year. The payback calculations[2] are as follows:

$$\text{Payback} = \frac{\text{Net initial investment}}{\text{Uniform increase in annual cash flows}}$$

$$= \frac{\$379,100}{100,000} = 3.791 \text{ years}$$

Under the payback method, organizations often choose a cutoff period for a project. The greater the risks of a project, the smaller the cutoff period. Why? Because faced with higher risks, managers would like to more quickly recover the investments they have made. For example, a software development company may use a payback period of one to two years for investment decisions. Projects with a payback period less than the cutoff period are acceptable. Those with a payback period greater than the cutoff period are rejected. If Lifetime's cutoff period under the payback method is three years, Lifetime will reject the new machine. If Lifetime uses a cutoff period of four years, Lifetime will consider the new machine to be acceptable.

The payback method highlights liquidity, which is often an important factor in capital budgeting decisions. Managers prefer projects with shorter paybacks (more liquid) to projects with longer paybacks, if all other things are equal. Projects with shorter payback periods give the organization more flexibility because funds for other projects become available sooner. Also, managers are less confident about cash flow predictions that stretch far into the future. The shorter the payback, the more confident managers can feel that their forecasts are on target.

The major strength of the payback method is that it is easy to understand. Like the DCF methods described previously, the payback method is not affected by accrual accounting conventions such as amortization. Advocates of the payback method argue that it is a handy measure when (1) estimates of profitability are not crucial and preliminary screening of many proposals is necessary and (2) the predicted cash flows in later years of the project are highly uncertain.

Two major weaknesses of the payback method are (1) it neglects the time value of money and (2) it neglects to consider project cash flows after the net initial investment is recovered. Consider an alternative to the $379,100 X-ray machine mentioned earlier. Assume that another X-ray machine, with a three-year useful life and zero terminal disposal price, requires only a $300,000 net initial investment and will also result in cash inflows of $100,000 per year. First, compare the two payback periods:

$$\text{Payback period for machine 1:} = \frac{\$379,100}{100,000} = 3.791 \text{ years}$$

$$\text{Payback period for machine 2:} = \frac{\$300,000}{100,000} = 3.000 \text{ years}$$

Companies often use both the payback and DCF method to select positive NPV projects with an acceptably short payback period.

The payback criterion would favour buying the $300,000 machine, because it has a shorter payback. In fact, if the cutoff period is three years, then Lifetime Care would not acquire machine 1, because it fails to meet the payback criterion. Consider next the NPV of the two investment options using Lifetime Care's 8% required rate of return for the X-ray machine investment. At a discount rate of 8%, the NPV of machine 2 is −$42,300 (2.577, the present value annuity factor for three years at 8% from Table 4 × $100,000 = $257,700 − the net initial investment of $300,000). Machine 1, as we know, has a positive NPV of $20,200 (from Exhibit 21-2). The NPV criterion suggests that Lifetime Care should

---

[2]Cash savings from the new X-ray machine occur *throughout* the year, but for simplicity in calculating NPV and IRR, we assume they occur at the *end* of each year. A literal interpretation of this assumption would imply a payback of four years because Lifetime Care will only recover its investment when cash inflows occur at the end of the fourth year. The calculations shown in this chapter, however, better approximate Lifetime Care's payback on the basis of uniform cash flows throughout the year.

acquire machine 1. Machine 2, with a negative NPV, would fail to meet the NPV criterion. The payback method gives a different answer from the NPV method because the payback method (1) does not consider cash flows after the payback period and (2) does not discount cash flows.

An added problem with the payback method is that choosing too short a cutoff period for project acceptance may promote the selection of only short-lived projects. The organization will tend to reject long-term, positive-NPV projects.

Nonuniform Cash Flows

The payback formula on the preceding page is designed for uniform annual cash inflows. When annual cash inflows are not uniform, the payback computation takes a cumulative form. The years' net cash inflows are accumulated until the amount of the net initial investment has been recovered. Assume that Venture Law Group is considering the purchase of videoconferencing equipment for $150,000. The equipment is expected to provide total cash savings of $380,000 over the next five years, due to reduced travel costs and more-effective use of associates' time. The cash savings occur uniformly throughout each year, but nonuniformly across years. Payback occurs during the third year:

Year	Cash Savings	Cumulative Cash Savings	Net Initial Investment Yet to Be Recovered at the End of the Year
0	—	—	$150,000
1	$50,000	$ 50,000	100,000
2	60,000	110,000	40,000
3	80,000	190,000	—
4	90,000	280,000	—
5	100,000	380,000	—

Straight-line interpolation within the third year, which has cash savings of $80,000, reveals that the final $40,000 needed to recover the $150,000 investment (that is, $150,000 − $110,000 recovered by the end of year 2) will be achieved halfway through year 3 (in which $80,000 of cash savings occur):

$$\text{Payback} = 2 \text{ years} + \left(\frac{\$40,000}{\$80,000} \times 1 \text{ year}\right) = 2.5 \text{ years}$$

The videoconferencing example has a single cash outflow of $150,000 at year 0. Where a project has multiple cash outflows occurring at different points in time, these outflows are added to derive a total cash outflow figure for the project. No adjustment is made for the time value of money when adding these cash outflows in computing the payback period.

ACCRUAL ACCOUNTING RATE-OF-RETURN METHOD

We now consider a fourth method for analyzing the financial aspects of capital-budgeting projects. The **accrual accounting rate of return (AARR)** is an accounting measure of income divided by an accounting measure of investment. It is also called **accounting rate of return** or *return on investment (ROI)*. Note that NPV, IRR, and payback are all based on cash flows whereas AARR is based on accrual accounting. We illustrate AARR for the Lifetime Care example using the project's net initial investment as the denominator:

$$\text{AARR} = \frac{\text{Increase in expected average annual operating income}}{\text{Net initial investment}}$$

If Lifetime Care purchases the new X-ray machine, the increase in expected average annual savings in operating costs will be $98,000: This amount is the total operating savings of $490,000 ($100,000 for four years and $90,000 in year 5) ÷ 5.

OBJECTIVE 8

Use and evaluate the accrual accounting rate-of-return (AARR) method

Accrual accounting rate of return (AARR) (accounting rate of return, return on investment, ROI). Accounting measure of income divided by an accounting measure of investment.

In practice there are variations on this formula. Some companies use "increase in expected average annual operating income" in the numerator and/or "average investment per year" in the denominator.

The new machine has a zero terminal disposal price. Straight-line amortization on the new machine is $372,890 ÷ 5 = $74,578. The net initial investment is $379,100. The accrual accounting rate of return is equal to

$$AARR = \frac{\$98,000 - \$74,578}{\$379,100} = \frac{\$23,422}{\$379,100} = 6.18\%$$

GLOBAL SURVEYS OF COMPANY PRACTICE

Comparison of Capital Budgeting Methods

What methods do companies around the world use for analyzing capital investment decisions? The percentages in the following table indicate how frequently particular capital budgeting methods are used in eight countries. The reported percentages exceed 100% because many companies surveyed use more than one method.

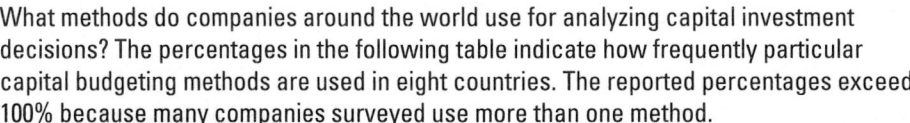

	United States[a]	Australia[b]	Canada[c]	Cyprus[d]	Japan	Poland[e]	Scotland[f]	United Kingdom[g]
Payback	35%	61%	50%	37%	52%	40%	78%	70%
IRR	45%	37%	62%	9%	4%	25%	58%	81%
NPV	50%	45%	41%	11%	6%	30%	48%	80%
AARR	5%	24%	17%	4%	36%	—	31%	56%
Other	8%	7%	8%	49%	5%	50%	—	31%

Some observations about these surveys:

1. Companies in the United States, Australia, Canada, Poland, Scotland, and the United Kingdom tend to use more than one method to evaluate capital investments. (The sum of the capital budgeting percentages in the columns for each of these countries ranges from approximately 150% to 300%.)
2. Japanese and Cypriot companies tend to use one method. (The sum of the capital budgeting percentages for Japan and Cyprus are approximately 100%.)
3. The payback method is popular in all countries. Japanese companies use the payback method as their primary method of analysis in their capital budgeting decisions. Companies in the United States, Australia, Canada, Poland, Scotland, and the United Kingdom use discounted cash flow (DCF) methods (IRR and NPV) extensively.
4. In addition to Canada and the United Kingdom, IRR is the most-used capital-budgeting method in Singapore and Thailand.[h,i]
5. The AARR method lags behind DCF methods in all surveyed countries except Japan, where it is preferred over IRR and NPV.

[a]Ryan, P., and G. Ryan, "Capital Budgeting Practices of the Fortune 1000: How Have Things Changed?" *Journal of Business and Management* (2002).

[b]Blayney, P., and I. Yokohama, "Comparative Analysis of Japanese and Australian Cost Accounting and Management Practices" (Working Paper, The University of Sydney, Australia, 1991).

[c]Jog, V., and A. Srivastava, "Corporate Financial Decision Making in Canada," *Revue Canadienne des Sciences de l'Administration* (1994).

[d]Lazaridis, I., "Capital Budgeting Practices: A Survey of Firms in Cyprus," *Journal of Small Business Management* (2004).

[e]Szychta, A., "The Scope and Application of Management Accounting Methods in Polish Enterprises," *Management Accounting Research* (2002).

[f]Sangster, A., "Capital Investment Appraisal Techniques: A Survey of Current Usage," *Journal of Business, Finance & Accounting* (April 1993).

[g]Arnold, G., and P. Hatzopoulos, "The Theory-Practice Gap in Capital Budgeting: Evidence from the United Kingdom," *Journal of Business, Finance & Accounting* (2000).

[h]Kester, G., and T. Chong, "Capital Budgeting Practices of Listed Firms in Singapore," *Singapore Management Review* (1998).

[i]Arsiraphongphisit, O., G. Kester, and T. Skully, "Financial Policies and Practices of Listed Firms in Thailand: Capital Structure, Capital Budgeting, Cost of Capital, and Dividends," *Journal of Business Administration* (2000).

The AARR method focuses on how investment decisions affect operating income numbers routinely reported by organizations. The AARR of 6.18% indicates the rate at which a dollar of investment generates operating income.

While there is no uniform method of calculating AARR, the interpretation in any situation is that the greater the positive difference between the AARR of a project and the AARR hurdle rate, the more preferable is the project. This method is similar to the IRR method because it provides the answer to the question "what is the rate of return on this project," but the AARR uses operating income rather than cash flow. Because cash flow and time value of money are central to investment project decisions, both the IRR and NPV methods are preferred over the AARR method.[3] On the other hand, AARR calculations use numbers reported in the financial statements and provide managers with forecasts of operating income on the statement of earnings if a project is accepted. In contrast to the payback method, AARR includes income earned throughout the lifetime of a project whereas the payback method only includes cash flows up to the point of payback. The Global Surveys of Company Practice box on p. 826 indicates that companies report a combination of these methods.

COMPLEXITIES IN CAPITAL BUDGETING APPLICATIONS

In this section, we consider some challenging aspects of predicting outcomes in the information-acquisition stage and of choosing projects in the selection stage.

Predicting the Full Set of Benefits and Costs

The factors that companies consider in making CIM decisions are far broader than costs alone. For example, the reasons for introducing CIM technology—faster response time, higher product quality, and greater flexibility in meeting changes in customer preferences—are often to increase revenues and contribution margins. Ignoring the revenue effects underestimates the financial benefits of CIM investments. As we describe below, however, the revenue benefits of technology investments are often difficult to quantify in financial terms. Nevertheless, competitive and revenue advantages are important managerial considerations when introducing CIM.

Exhibit 21-6 on page 828 presents examples of the broader set of factors that companies in the United States, Australia, Japan, and the United Kingdom weigh in evaluating CIM technology. The benefits include

1. **Faster response to market changes.** An automated plant can, for example, make major design modifications (such as switching from a two-door to a four-door car) relatively quickly. To quantify this benefit requires some notion of consumer demand changes that may occur many years in the future and of the manufacturing technology choices made by competitors.

2. **Increased worker knowledge of automation.** If workers have a positive experience with CIM, the company can implement other automation projects more quickly and more successfully. Quantifying this benefit requires a prediction of the company's subsequent automation plans. Survey evidence emphasizes the importance of linking CIM decisions to a company's overall competitive strategies.

Predicting the full set of costs also presents problems. Three classes of costs are difficult to measure and are often underestimated:

1. Costs associated with a reduced competitive position in the industry. If other companies in the industry are investing in CIM, a company not investing in CIM

---

[3]Note that if amortization is calculated as economic amortization (the decline in the present value of future cash flows) under the AARR method, and if operating income and investment are adjusted each year for this amortization, the AARR each year will equal the project's IRR. In practice, however, the book amortization and investment value used in AARR computations are not calculated in this way.

EXHIBIT 21-6

Factors Considered in Making Capital Budgeting Decisions for CIM Projects

Examples of Financial Outcomes	Examples of Nonfinancial and Qualitative Outcomes
Lower direct labour costs	Reduction in manufacturing cycle time
Lower hourly support labour costs	Increase in manufacturing flexibility
Less scrap and rework	Increase in business risk due to higher fixed cost structure
Lower inventory costs	Improved product delivery and service
Increase in software and related costs	Reduction in product development time
Costs of retraining personnel	Faster response to market changes
	Increased learning by workers about automation
	Improved competitive position in the industry

will probably suffer a decline in market share because of its inferior quality and slower delivery performance. Several companies in the machine tool industry that continued to use a conventional manufacturing approach experienced rapid drops in market share after their competitors introduced CIM.

2. Costs of retraining the operating and maintenance personnel to handle the automated facilities.

3. Costs of developing and maintaining the software and maintenance programs to operate the automated manufacturing activities.

Recognizing the Full Time Horizon of the Project

The time horizon of CIM projects can stretch well beyond ten years. Many of the costs are incurred and are highly visible in the early years of adopting CIM. In contrast, important benefits may not be realized until many years after the adoption of CIM. A long time horizon should be considered when evaluating CIM investments.

Difficulties in predicting the full set of benefits and costs and long time horizons also arise in other investment decisions—for example, R&D projects and oil exploration.

Performance Evaluation and the Selection of Projects

OBJECTIVE 9

Identify investment projects affecting different functions in the value chain and reduce conflict between project approval and performance evaluation measures.

The use of the accrual accounting rate of return for evaluating performance can often deter a manager from using DCF methods for capital budgeting decisions. Consider Peter Costner, the manager of the X-Ray Department at Lifetime Care Hospital. The NPV method for capital budgeting indicates that Peter should purchase the new X-ray machine, since it has a positive NPV of $20,200.

Suppose top management of Lifetime Care uses the AARR for judging the X-Ray Department's performance. Peter Costner may consider not purchasing the new X-ray machine if the AARR of 6.18% on the investment reduces his overall AARR and so negatively affects his department's performance. The AARR on the new X-ray machine is low because the investment increases the denominator and, as a result of amortization, also reduces the numerator (operating income) in the AARR computation.

Obviously, there is an inconsistency between citing DCF methods as being best for capital budgeting decisions and then using a different method to evaluate subsequent performance. As long as such practice continues, managers will be tempted to make capital budgeting choices on the basis of accrual accounting rates of return, even though such choices are not in the best interests of the organization. Such temptations become more pronounced if managers are frequently transferred (or promoted), or if annual operating income is important in their evaluations and their compensation plans. Why? Because the manager's performance is being evaluated over short time horizons. The manager has no motivation to use a DCF model to take into account cash flows that will occur in the distant future. Those cash flows will not influence the manager's performance evaluation.

MANAGING THE PROJECT

This section discusses implementation and control of investment projects that improve performance in various functions in the value chain. Two different aspects of management control are discussed—management control of the investment activity itself and management control of the project as a whole.

Management Control of the Investment Activity

Some initial investments such as purchasing X-ray or videoconferencing equipment are relatively easy to implement. Other initial investments such as building shopping malls or new manufacturing plants are more complex and take more time. In the latter case, monitoring and controlling the investment schedules and budgets is critical to the success of the overall project.

Management Control of the Project—Postinvestment Audit

A postinvestment audit compares the predictions of investment costs and outcomes made at the time a project was selected to the actual results. It provides management with feedback about the investment's performance. Suppose, for example, that actual outcomes (operating cash savings from the new X-ray machine in the Lifetime Care example) are much lower than predicted outcomes. Management must then investigate whether this occurred because the original estimates were overly optimistic or because there were problems in implementing the project. Both types of problems are a concern.

Optimistic estimates are a concern because they may result in the acceptance of a project that would otherwise have been rejected. To discourage optimistic estimates, companies such as DuPont maintain records comparing actual performance to the estimates made by individual managers when seeking approval for capital investments. DuPont believes that postinvestment audits discourage managers from making unrealistic forecasts. Problems in implementing a project are an obvious concern because the returns from the project will not meet expectations. Postinvestment audits can point to areas requiring corrective action.

Care should be exercised when performing a postinvestment audit. It should be done only after project outcomes have stabilized. Doing the audit early may give a misleading picture. Obtaining actual data to compare against estimates is often not easy. For example, actual labour cost savings from the new X-ray machine may not be comparable to the estimated savings, because the actual number and types of X-rays taken may be different from the quantities assumed during the capital budgeting process. The Focus on Values and Behaviours feature on page 830 describes how the incentive systems at Enron and the absence of postinvestment audits led managers to overstate project cash inflows and to accept projects that should never have been undertaken. Implementation problems, such as not achieving budgeted revenues or exceeding budgeted costs, are a concern because the returns from the project will then be inadequate. Postinvestment audits can point to areas of implementation that need improvement (such as better quality-control processes). Other benefits, such as the impact on patient treatment, may be difficult to quantify.

Postinvestment audits of capital projects require information on the costs and benefits attributable to the project. It can be costly, however, to untangle those cash flows from the company's overall cash flows.

Long-Term Contracts and Performance Evaluation at Enron

A basic tenet in finance is that when managers make positive NPV decisions and communicate these decisions to financial markets, the stock prices of their companies rise in response. So when Enron entered into a long-term contract to sell gas to the Chicago-based Peoples Gas, Light & Coke Co., Enron's stock price rose to represent the financial market's assessment of the deal. Stock prices change in anticipation of future cash flows. In contrast, accounting income numbers generally measure performance achieved—revenues, expenses, and cash flows that have already occurred during the past year.

Enron, however, recorded the present value of the future cash flows from the contract as income in the year the contract was signed. Enron also compensated managers who brought in these deals on the basis of the NPV of the contract, which required highly subjective judgments based on future prices of natural gas that were very difficult to predict when a contract was signed. Enron's chief risk officer was responsible for challenging and validating these future prices. Enron also sought external verification of price estimates whenever possible. Nevertheless, the absence of established public market prices and postcontract audits created incentives for managers to assume high prices of natural gas in the future, report higher operating income, and claim higher rewards.

Pressure is part of every business, but employees at Enron were under severe scrutiny. Its performance management system ranked all employees within a business group from the best to the worst performers. Employees in the bottom 20% were warned about their performance and were terminated if they showed no significant improvement. This pressure to perform coupled with the opportunity to report higher operating income created a strong temptation to inflate estimates of future cash flows. Enron's culture and lack of values and controls encouraged unethical behaviour. At the time of Enron's collapse in 2001, many managers had been rewarded for anticipated future performance that did not materialize. The important message here for management accountants: Be aware of control-system weaknesses when making capital investment decisions and act with the highest integrity.

Source: M. Salter, L. Levesque, and M. Ciampa, "The Rise and Fall of Enron," Harvard Business School working paper, 2002.

STRATEGIC CONSIDERATIONS IN CAPITAL BUDGETING

Some strategic investments are made to avoid putting a company at a competitive disadvantage. For example, cellular telephone companies such as Motorola, Nokia, and Samsung have added features providing customers Internet access and e-mail capabilities; companies not providing these features will suffer a decline in market share. The benefit of capital investments in this case isn't higher revenues but the prevention of a decline in revenues and profits. Such benefits may be difficult to quantify.

A company's strategy is the source of its strategic capital budgeting decisions. Strategic decisions by WestJet, such as expansion to fly to U.S. and European destinations, required capital investments to be made in several countries (see also the Concepts in Action feature, p. 831). The strategic decision by Barnes & Noble to support book sales over the Internet required capital investments creating barnesandnoble.com and an Internet infrastructure. Bell Canada Enterprise's decision to enter the media industry resulted in a big investment to acquire both *The Globe and Mail* and CTV.

Capital investment decisions that are strategic in nature require managers to consider a broad range of factors that may be difficult to estimate. Consider some of the difficulties of justifying investments in computer-integrated manufacturing (CIM) technology made by companies such as Mitsubishi, Sony, and Audi.

Globalizing Capital Budgeting at AES Corporation

AES Corporation, a Fortune 500 company, is a leading global electricity producer with more than US$30 billion in assets stretched across 30 countries and five continents. Despite impressive international growth throughout the company's 20-year history, the global economic downturn that began in late 2000 devastated AES. The devaluation of key South American currencies, adverse changes in energy regulatory environments, and declines in energy prices weakened AES's cash flow and ability to service debt. As a result, AES stock collapsed and its market capitalization fell nearly 95%, from US$28 billion in December 2000 to US$1.6 billion just two years later.

In response, the AES board of directors asked Rob Venerus, director of the company's new Corporate Analysis & Planning Group, to develop a new methodology for evaluating capital budgeting projects. Historically, capital budgeting at AES was fairly straightforward. Early in the company's history, a relatively simple model was developed, and a 12% discount rate was applied to all projects, regardless of geographic location. This model remained unchanged through the years, despite rapid expansion into new international markets that required advanced financial-analysis methods. For example, when AES entered countries such as Brazil and Argentina, the model failed to properly adjust the required rate of return to account for higher risk, such as regulatory and currency risk. Another factor that created fundamental difficulties for applying this model overseas was an ever-increasing complexity in the financing of international operations.

To overhaul the capital budgeting process so that managers could evaluate each international investment as a distinct opportunity with unique risks, Venerus knew he would have to calculate a cost of capital for each of the many diverse AES businesses. These businesses included power plant construction, energy generation, and power distribution. As a starting point, he considered 15 representative projects from various countries and derived a weighted average cost of capital (WACC) for each project. This involved measuring all of the constituent parts for the projects: the cost of debt, the target capital structure, the local-country tax rates, and an appropriate cost of equity.

During this process Venerus knew he had to find a way to capture the country-specific risks in foreign markets. He developed an approach with two parts. First, he calculated a cost of debt and a cost of equity for each of the 15 projects using U.S. market data. Second, he added the difference between the yield on local government bonds and the yield on corresponding U.S. Treasury bonds to both the cost of debt and the cost of equity. Venerus and his team believed that this difference, or "sovereign spread," approximated the incremental borrowing costs (and market risk) in the local country.

These efforts provided AES with a more sophisticated way to think about capital budgeting risk and its cost of capital around the world. As a global company with operations in countries that were significantly different from the United States, this framework helped AES more accurately evaluate capital projects and protect against overleveraging its assets, which almost imploded the company in 2002. Although subsequent changes to the model's calculations and methodology were made, this process helped AES regain its financial footing through the reevaluation and restructuring of existing capital projects while ensuring that the company only selected new capital projects that met these revised criteria. So far, the company has been successful! By 2004, AES was projecting long-term financial stability and double-digit earnings per share growth through 2008.

Sources: Based on "Globalizing the Cost of Capital and Capital Budgeting at AES," Harvard Business School Case No. 9-204-109, AES Corporation 2003 annual report, and discussions with the case writer and company management.

In CIM, computers give instructions that quickly and automatically set up and run equipment to manufacture many different products. Quantifying these benefits requires some notion of consumer-demand changes that may occur many years in the future. CIM technology also increases worker knowledge of and experience with automation; however, the benefit of this knowledge and experience is difficult to measure. Managers need to develop judgment and intuition to make these decisions.

Customer Value and Capital Budgeting

Consider Potato Supreme, which makes potato products for sale to retail outlets. It is currently analyzing two of its customers: Shine Stores and Always Open. Potato Supreme predicts the following cash flow from operations, net of income taxes (in thousands), from each customer account for the next five years:

	2007	2008	2009	2010	2011
Shine Stores	$1,450	$1,305	$1,175	$1,058	$ 950
Always Open	690	1,160	1,900	2,950	4,160

Which customer is more valuable to Potato Supreme? Looking at only the first year, 2007, Shine Stores provides more than double the cash flow compared to Always Open ($1,450 versus $690). A different picture emerges, however, when looking over the entire five-year horizon. Using Potato Supreme's 10% RRR, the NPV of the Always Open customer is $7,610, compared to $4,591 for Shine Stores (computations not shown). Note how NPV captures in its estimate of customer value the future growth of Always Open. Potato Supreme uses this information to allocate more resources and salespersons to service the Always Open account. Potato Supreme can also use NPV calculations to examine the effects of alternative ways of increasing customer loyalty and retention, such as introducing frequent-purchaser cards.

A comparison of year-to-year changes in customer NPV estimates highlights whether managers have been successful in maintaining long-run profitable relationships with their customers. Suppose the NPV of Potato Supreme's customer base declines 15% in one year. Management can then examine the reasons for the decline, such as aggressive pricing by competitors, and devise new-product development and marketing strategies for the future.

Capital One, a financial-services company, uses NPV to estimate the value of different credit-card customers. Cellular telephone companies such as Cellular One and Verizon attempt to sign up customers for multiple years of service. The objective is to prevent "customer churn," customers switching frequently from one company to another. The higher the probability of customer churn, the lower the NPV of the customer to the telecommunications company.

Investment in Research and Development

Companies such as QLT, Inc., in the Canadian pharmaceutical industry, and Research In Motion (RIM), a Canadian company that is the global leader in designing, manufacturing, and marketing innovative wireless mobile communications such as the BlackBerry™, regard R&D projects as important strategic investments. R&D payoffs are not only more uncertain than other investment projects, but often will occur far into the future. Most companies engaged in these types of investment projects stage their R&D so they have the choice to increase or decrease their investment at different points in time based on its success. This option feature of R&D investments—called real options—is an important aspect of R&D investments and increases the NPV of these investments. That's because a company can limit its losses when things are going badly and take advantage of new opportunities when things are going well.

PROBLEM

Let us revisit the Lifetime Care X-ray machine project. Assume that the expected annual cash inflows are $130,000 instead of $100,000. All other facts are unchanged: a $379,100 net initial investment, a five-year useful life, a zero terminal disposal price, and an 8% required rate of return. Year 5 cash inflows include $10,000 recovery of working capital. When calculating breakeven time, assume that the investment in the X-ray machine will occur immediately after management approves the project. Compute the following:

1. Discounted cash flow
   a. Net present value
   b. Internal rate of return

2. Payback period

3. Accrual accounting rate of return on net initial investment

4. Nonuniform cash flows

Assume (for calculation purposes) that cash outflows and cash inflows occur at the end of each period.

SOLUTION

1. a. NPV = ($130,000 × 3.993) − $379,100

      = $519,090 − $379,100 = $139,990

   b. There are several approaches to computing the IRR. One is to use a calculator with an IRR function; this gives an IRR of 21.16%. An alternative approach is to use Table 4 in Appendix A:

$$\$379,100 = \$130,000F$$

$$F = \frac{\$379,100}{130,000} = 2.916$$

On the five-period line of Table 4, the column closest to 2.916 is 22%. To obtain a more accurate number, straight-line interpolation can be used:

	Present Value	Factors
20%	2.991	2.991
IRR	—	2.916
22%	2.864	—
Difference	0.127	0.075

$$\text{IRR} = 20\% + \frac{0.075}{0.127}(2\%) = 21.18\%$$ (difference due to rounding of PV factor to 3 decimals)

2. Payback = $$\frac{\text{Net initial investment}}{\text{Uniform increase in annual cash flows}}$$

   = $379,100 ÷ $130,000 = 2.92 years

3.   AARR = $$\frac{\text{Increase in expected average annual operating income}}{\text{Net initial investment}}$$

Increase in expected average annual operating savings = [($130,000 × 4) + $120,000] ÷ 5

= $128,000

Average annual amortization = $372,890 ÷ 5 = $74,578

Increase in expected average annual operating income = $128,000 − $74,578

= $53,422

$$\text{AARR} = \frac{\$53,422}{\$379,100} = 14.09\%$$

4. Nonuniform cash flow computations are as follows:

Year	PV Discount Factor at 8% (1)	Investment Cash Outflows (2)	PV of Investment Cash Outflows* (3) = (1) × (2)	Cumulative PV of Investment Cash Outflows* (4)	Cash Inflows (5)	PV of Cash Inflows* (6) = (1) × (5)	Cumulative PV of Cash Inflows* (7)
0	1.000	$379,100	$379,100	$379,100			
1	0.926				$130,000	$120,380	$120,380
2	0.857				130,000	111,410	231,790
3	0.794				130,000	103,220	335,010
4	0.735				130,000	95,550	430,560
5	0.681				130,000	88,530	519,090

*At year 0.

$$\text{BET} = 3 \text{ years} + \frac{(\$379,100 - \$335,010)}{95,550}$$

$$= 3 \text{ years} + \frac{44,090}{95,550}$$

$$= 3.46 \text{ years}$$

DECISION POINTS   SUMMARY

The following decision guidelines use a question-and-answer format to summarize the chapter's main points. Each decision presents a key question. The guideline is the answer to that question.

DECISIONS	GUIDELINES
1. Over what time horizon is capital budgeting done?	Capital budgeting is a long-term planning process for proposed capital projects. The life of a project is usually longer than one year, so capital budgeting decisions consider revenues and costs over long periods. In contrast, accrual accounting measures income on a year-by-year basis.
2. What does the term "time value of money" recognize?	The term recognizes that money received earlier is worth more because of the returns that can be generated sooner.
3. What are the six stages of capital budgeting?	The six stages are (a) the identification stage, (b) the search stage, (c) the information-acquisition stage, (d) the selection stage, (e) the financing stage, and (f) the implementation and control stage.
4. What are the two main discounted cash flow (DCF) methods? What are their advantages?	The two main DCF methods are the net present value (NPV) method and the internal rate-of-return (IRR) method. The NPV method calculates the expected net monetary gain or loss from a project by discounting to the present all expected future cash inflows and outflows, using the required rate of return. A project is acceptable in financial terms if it has a positive NPV. The IRR method computes the rate of return (also called the discount rate) at which the present value of expected cash inflows from a project equals the present value of expected cash outflows from a project. A project is acceptable in financial terms if its IRR exceeds the required rate of return. DCF is the best approach to capital budgeting. It explicitly includes all project cash flows and recognizes the time value of money.
5. What are two advantages of the net present value (NPV) method over the internal-rate-of-return (IRR) method?	The NPV method computes a result in dollars not percentages and can be used where the required rates of return vary over the life of the project.

6. What are the relevant cash inflows and outflows for capital budgeting decisions? How should accrual accounting concepts be considered?	Relevant cash inflows and outflows in DCF analysis are the differences in expected future cash flows as a result of making the investment. Only cash inflows and outflows matter; accrual accounting concepts are irrelevant for DCF methods.
7. What is the payback method? What are its limitations?	The payback method measures the time it will take to recoup, in the form of cash inflows, the total cash amount invested in a project. The payback method neglects both the cash flows after the payback period and the time value of money.
8. What is the accrual accounting rate-of-return (AARR) method? What is its limitation?	The accrual accounting rate of return (AARR) is after-tax operating income divided by a measure of investment. AARR considers profitability but does not consider time value of money.
9. What conflicts can arise between using discounted cash flow methods for capital budgeting decisions and accrual accounting for performance evaluation? How can these conflicts be reduced?	Using accrual accounting to evaluate the performance of a manager or division may create conflicts with using DCF methods for capital budgeting. Frequently, the decision made using a DCF method will not report good "operating income" results in the project's early years under accrual accounting. For this reason, managers are tempted not to use DCF methods even though the decisions based on them would be the best for the company over the long run. This conflict can be reduced by evaluating managers on a project-by-project basis, looking at their ability to achieve the amounts and timing of forecasted cash flows.

▼ TERMS TO LEARN

This chapter contains definitions of the following important terms:

accounting rate of return (p. 825)
accrual accounting rate of
  return (AARR) (p. 825)
capital budgeting (p. 812)
cost of capital (p. 816)
discount rate (p. 816)
discounted cash flow (DCF) (p. 815)
hurdle rate (p. 816)
internal rate of return (IRR) (p. 817)

investment programs (p. 812)
investment projects (p.812)
net present value (NPV) method (p. 816)
opportunity cost of capital (p. 816)
payback method (p. 823)
required rate of return (RRR) (p. 816)
return on investment (ROI) (p. 825)
time-adjusted rate of return (p. 817)

▼ ASSIGNMENT MATERIAL

QUESTIONS

21-1 "Capital budgeting has the same focus as accrual accounting." Do you agree? Explain.

21-2 List and briefly describe each of the six stages in capital budgeting.

21-3 What is the essence of the discounted cash flow method?

21-4 "Only quantitative outcomes are relevant in capital budgeting analyses." Do you agree? Explain.

21-5 How can sensitivity analysis be incorporated in DCF analysis?

21-6 What is the payback method? What are its main strengths and weaknesses?

21-7 Describe the accrual accounting rate-of-return method. What are its main strengths and weaknesses?

21-8 "The trouble with discounted cash flow techniques is that they ignore amortization costs." Do you agree? Explain.

21-9 "Let's be more practical. DCF is not the gospel. Managers should not become so enchanted with DCF that strategic considerations are overlooked." Do you agree? Explain.

21-10 "The net present value method is the preferred method for capital budgeting decisions. Therefore, managers will always use it." Do you agree? Explain.

21-11 "All overhead costs are relevant in NPV analysis." Do you agree? Explain.

21-12 "Managers' control of job projects generally focuses on four critical success factors." Identify those factors.

21-13 Bill Watts, president of Western Publications, accepts a capital-budgeting project advocated by Division X. This is the division in which the president spent his first 10 years with the company. On the same day, the president rejects a capital-budgeting project proposal from Division Y. The manager of Division Y is incensed. She believes that the Division Y project has an internal rate of return at least 10 percentage points above that of the Division X project. She comments, "What is the point of all our detailed DCF analysis? If Watts is panting over a project, he can arrange to have the proponents of that project massage the numbers so that it looks like a winner." What advice would you give the manager of Division Y?

EXERCISES

Throughout the assignment material, ignore the effects of income taxes.

21-14 Exercises in compound interest. To be sure that you understand how to use the tables in Appendix A at the end of this book, solve the following exercises. Ignore income tax considerations. (The correct answers, rounded to the nearest dollar, appear on pp. 845–846.)

REQUIRED

1. You have just won $5,000. How much money will you have at the end of ten years if you invest it at 5% compounded annually? at 12%? (Interpolate the value.)

2. Ten years from now, the unpaid principal of the mortgage on your house will be $89,550. How much do you have to invest today at 5% interest compounded annually to accumulate the $95,650 in ten years? (Interpolate the value.)

3. If the unpaid mortgage on your house in ten years will be $95,650, how much money do you have to invest annually at 8% to have exactly this amount on hand at the end of the tenth year?

4. You plan to save $6,000 of your earnings at the end of each year for the next ten years. How much money will you have at the end of the tenth year if you invest your savings compounded at 12% per year?

5. You have just turned 65, and an endowment insurance policy has paid you a lump sum of $240,000. If you invest the sum at 4%, how much money can you withdraw from your account in equal amounts each year so that at the end of ten years (age 75) there will be nothing left?

6. You have estimated that for the first ten years after you retire you will need an annual cash inflow of $60,000. How much money must you invest at 8% at your retirement age to obtain this annual cash inflow? at 18%?

7. The following table shows two schedules of prospective operating cash inflows, each of which requires the same net initial investment of $12,000 now:

	Annual Cash Inflows	
Year	**Plan A**	**Plan B**
1	$ 1,000	$ 5,000
2	2,000	4,000
3	3,000	3,000
4	4,000	2,000
5	5,000	1,000
Total	$15,000	$15,000

The required rate of return is 8% compounded annually. All cash inflows occur at the end of each year. In terms of net present value, which plan is more desirable? Show your computations.

21-15 Comparison of approaches to capital budgeting. The Building Distributors Group is thinking of buying, at a cost of $264,000, some new packaging equipment that is expected to save $60,000 in cash operating costs per year. Its estimated useful life is ten years, and it will have zero terminal disposal price. The required rate of return is 14%.

REQUIRED

1. Compute the payback period.
2. Compute the net present value.
3. Compute the internal rate of return.
4. Compute the accrual accounting rate of return based on net initial investment. Assume straight-line amortization.

21-16 Comparison of approaches to capital budgeting. City Hospital, a nontaxable institution, estimates that it can save $33,600 a year in cash operating costs for the next ten years if it buys a special-purpose machine at a cost of $132,000. A zero terminal disposal price is expected. City Hospital's required rate of return is 12%.

REQUIRED

1. Compute the payback period.
2. Compute the net present value.
3. Compute the internal rate of return.
4. Compute the accrual accounting rate of return based on net initial investment. Assume straight-line amortization.

21-17 **Capital budgeting with uneven cash flows.** Eastern Cola is considering the purchase of a special-purpose bottling machine for $33,600. It is expected to have a useful life of seven years with a zero terminal disposal price. The plant manager estimates the following savings in cash operating costs:

Year	Amount
1	$12,000
2	9,600
3	7,200
4	6,000
5	4,800
6	3,600
7	3,600
Total	$46,800

Eastern Cola uses a required rate of return of 14% in its capital budgeting decisions.

REQUIRED

1. Compute the payback period.
2. Compute the net present value.
3. Compute the internal rate of return.
4. Compute the accrual accounting rate of return based on net initial investment. Assume straight-line amortization. Use the average annual savings in cash operating costs when computing the numerator of the accrual accounting rate of return.

21-18 **Net present value, internal rate of return, sensitivity analysis.** The Johnson Corporation is planning to buy equipment costing $144,000 to improve its materials-handling system. The equipment is expected to save $48,000 in cash operating costs per year. Its estimated useful life is six years, and it will have zero terminal disposal price. The required rate of return is 12%.

REQUIRED

1. Compute the net present value. Compute the internal rate of return.
2. What is the minimum annual cash savings that will make the equipment desirable on a net present value basis?
3. When might a manager calculate the minimum annual cash savings described in requirement 2 rather than use the $48,000 savings in cash operating costs per year to calculate the net present value or internal rate of return?

21-19 **Comparison of projects, no income taxes.** (CMA, adapted) Fox Valley Healthcare Inc. is a not-for-profit organization that operates eight nursing homes and ten assisted-living facilities. The company has grown considerably over the last three years and expects to continue to expand in the years ahead, particularly in the area of assisted-living facilities for seniors.

Jim Ruffalo, president of Fox Valley, has developed a plan to add a new building for top management and the administrative staff. He has selected a building contractor, Vukacek Construction Co., and has reached agreement on the building and its construction. Vukacek is ready to start as soon as the contract is signed and will complete the work in two years.

The building contractor has offered Fox Valley a choice of three payment plans:

◆ **Plan I** Payment of $240,000 on the signing of the contract and $3,600,000 at the time of completion.
◆ **Plan II** Payment of $1,200,000 on the signing of the contract and $1,200,000 at the end of each of the two succeeding years. The end of the second year is the completion date.
◆ **Plan III** Payment of $120,000 on the signing of the contract and $1,200,000 at the end of each of the three succeeding years.

Ruffalo is not sure which payment plan he should accept. He has asked the treasurer, Lisa Monroe, for her assessment and advice. Fox Valley will finance the construction with a long-term loan and has a borrowing rate of 10%.

REQUIRED

1. Using the net present value method, calculate the comparative cost of each of the three payment plans being considered by Fox Valley Healthcare Inc.
2. Which payment plan should the treasurer recommend? Explain.
3. Discuss the financial factors, other than the cost of the plan, that should be considered in selecting an appropriate payment plan.

21-20 Payback and NPV methods, no income taxes. (CMA, adapted) Cording Manufacturing is a small company that is currently analyzing capital expenditure proposals for the purchase of equipment. The capital budget is limited to $600,000, which Cording believes is the maximum capital it can raise.

Richard King, an outside financial advisor, is preparing an analysis of four projects that Walter Minden, Cording's president, is considering. King has projected the future cash flows for each potential purchase. The information concerning the four projects is given below.

	Project A	Project B	Project C	Project D
Projected cash outflow				
Net initial investment	$240,000	$228,000	$300,000	$252,000
Projected cash inflows				
Year 1	$ 60,000	$ 48,000	$ 90,000	$ 90,000
2	60,000	60,000	90,000	90,000
3	60,000	84,000	72,000	72,000
4	60,000	90,000	96,000	48,000
5	60,000	90,000	120,000	24,000

REQUIRED

1. Since Cording Manufacturing's cash is limited, Walter Minden thinks that the payback method of calculating investments would be the best method for choosing capital-budgeting projects.
   a. Explain what the payback method measures and how it is used. Include in your explanation several benefits and limitations of the payback method.
   b. Calculate the payback period for each of the four projects. Ignore income tax considerations.
2. King would like to compare the projects using the net present value method. The required rate of return for Cording is 10%. All cash flows occur at the end of the year. Calculate the net present value for each project. Ignore income tax considerations.
3. Which projects, if any, would you recommend funding? Briefly state your reasons why.

21-21 Equipment replacement, net present value, relevant costs, payback. Monterey Corporation is a distributor of electronic measurement instruments. It is considering replacing one of its distribution trucks that it had purchased for $64,800 two years ago. The truck has a current book value of $45,600 and a remaining useful life of four years. Its current disposal price is $31,200; in four years its terminal disposal price is expected to be $7,200. The annual cash operating costs of the truck are expected to be $42,000 for each of the next three years and $48,000 in year 4.

Monterey is considering the purchase of a new truck for $67,200. Annual cash operating costs for the new truck are expected to be $30,000. The new truck has a useful life of four years and a terminal disposal price of $9,600.

Monterey Corporation amortizes all its trucks using straight-line amortization calculated on the difference between the initial cost and the terminal disposal price divided by the estimated useful life. Monterey uses a rate of return of 12% in its capital budgeting decisions.

REQUIRED

1. Using a net present value criterion, should Monterey Corporation purchase the new truck?
2. Compute the payback period for Monterey Corporation if it purchases the new truck.

21-22 DCF, accrual accounting rate of return, working capital, evaluation of performance. The Hammerlink Company has been offered a special-purpose metal-cutting machine for $132,000. The machine is expected to have a useful life of eight years with a terminal disposal price of $36,000. Savings in cash operating costs are expected to be $30,000 per year. However, additional working capital is needed to keep the machine running efficiently and without stoppages. Working capital includes such items as filters, lubricants, bearings, abrasives, flexible exhaust pipes, and belts. These items must continually be replaced so that an investment of $9,600 must be maintained in them at all times, but this investment is fully recoverable (will be "cashed in") at the end of the useful life. Hammerlink's required rate of return is 12%.

REQUIRED
1. **a.** Compute the net present value.
   b. Compute the internal rate of return.
2. Compute the accrual accounting rate of return based on the net initial investment. Assume straight-line amortization.
3. You have the authority to make the purchase decision. Why might you be reluctant to base your decision on the DCF model?

PROBLEMS

21-23 DCF, sensitivity analysis, no income taxes. (CMA adapted) Bristol Engineering Inc. manufactures electronic components for the automotive and computer industries and produces a variety of small electronic appliances that are distributed through wholesalers. The company's Research and Development Department has developed an electronic device that management believes could be modified and marketed as an electronic game.

The following information for the new product was developed from the best estimates of the marketing and production managers.

Annual sales volume	1,000,000 units
Selling price	$12 per unit
Cash variable costs	$4.80 per unit
Cash fixed costs	$2,400,000 per year
Investment required	$14,400,000
Project life	5 years

At the end of the five-year useful life there will be a zero terminal disposal price.

Bristol Engineering uses discounted cash-flow analysis in its decision making. Its required rate of return on this project is 14%.

The toy and game industry is a new market for Bristol Engineering, and management is concerned about the reliability of the estimates. The controller has proposed applying sensitivity analysis to selected factors, and is investigating some alternatives. Ignore income taxes in your calculations.

REQUIRED
1. What is the net present value of this investment proposal?
2. What is the effect on the net present value of the following three changes in assumptions? Treat each item independently of the others.
   a. 10% reduction in the selling price.
   b. 10% reduction in annual sales in units.
   c. 10% reduction in the variable cost per unit.
3. Discuss how management would use the data developed in requirements 1 and 2 in its consideration of the proposed capital investment.

21-24 NPV and customer profitability, no income taxes. Christen Granite sells granite counter tops to the construction industry. Christen Granite has three customers: Homebuilders, a small construction company that builds private luxury homes; Kitchen Constructors, a company that designs and builds kitchens for hospitals and hotels; and Subdivision Erectors, a construction company that builds large subdivisions in major metro suburbs. Following are Christen Granite's revenue and cost data by customer for the year ended December 31, 2007.

	Homebuilders	Kitchen Constructors	Subdivision Erectors
Revenues	$54,000	$390,000	$1,032,000
Cost of goods sold	26,400	216,000	660,000
Operating costs	12,000	90,000	282,000

Operating costs include order processing, sales visits, delivery, and special delivery costs. Christen estimates that revenue and costs will increase as follows on an annual basis:

	Homebuilders	Kitchen Constructors	Subdivision Erectors
Revenues	5%	15%	8%
Cost of goods sold	4%	4%	4%
Operating costs	4%	4%	4%

Christen Granite's required rate of return is 10%. Assume that (a) all transactions occur at end-of-period, (b) all revenues are cash inflows, and (c) all costs are cash outflows. Ignore income tax considerations in your analysis.

REQUIRED

1. Calculate operating income per customer for 2007 and for each year of the 2008–2012 period.
2. Christen estimates the value of each customer by calculating the customer's projected NPV over the next five years (2008–2012). Use the operating incomes calculated above to compute the value of all three customers.
3. Recently, Kitchen Construction (KC), Christen's most valuable customer, has been threatening to leave. Lawson Tops, Christen's fiercest competitor, has offered KC a greater discount. KC demands a 20% discount from Christen if the latter wants to keep its business. Should Christen grant KC the 20% discount? What is the five-year value of KC after incorporating the 20% discount? What other factors should Christen consider before making a final decision?
4. What are the possible adverse effects of caving in to KC's pressure?

21-25 Equipment replacement, relevant costs, sensitivity analysis. A toy manufacturer that specializes in making fad items has just developed a $60,000 moulding machine for producing a special toy. The machine has been used to produce only one unit so far. The company will amortize the $60,000 initial machine investment evenly over four years, after which production of the toy will be stopped. The company's expected annual costs will be direct materials, $12,000; direct manufacturing labour, $24,000; and variable manufacturing overhead, $18,000. Variable manufacturing overhead varies with direct manufacturing labour costs. Fixed manufacturing overhead, exclusive of amortization, is $9,000 annually, and fixed marketing and administrative costs are $14,400 annually.

Suddenly a machine salesperson appears. He has a new machine that is ideally suited for producing this toy. His automatic machine is distinctly superior. It reduces the cost of direct materials by 10% and produces twice as many units per hour. It will cost $52,800 and will have a zero terminal disposal price at the end of four years.

Production and sales of 25,000 units per year (sales of $120,000) will be the same whether the company uses the old machine or the new machine. The current disposal price of the toy company's moulding machine is $6,000. Its terminal disposal price in four years will be $3,120.

REQUIRED

1. Assume that the required rate of return is 16%. Using the net present value method, show whether the new machine should be purchased. What is the role of the book value of the old machine in the analysis?
2. What is the payback period for the new machine?
3. As the manager who developed the $60,000 old moulding machine, you are trying to justify not buying the new $52,800 machine. You question the accuracy of the expected cash operating savings. By how much must these cash savings fall before the point of indifference—the point where the net present value of investing in the new machine—reaches zero?

21-26 Payback, net present value, relevant costs, sensitivity analysis. The city of Edmonton has been operating a cafeteria for its employees, but it is considering converting it to a completely automated set of vending machines. If the change is made, the old equipment would be sold now for whatever cash it might bring.

The vending machines would be purchased immediately for cash. A catering firm would take complete responsibility for servicing and replenishing the vending machines and would pay the city a predetermined percentage of the gross vending receipts.

The present cafeteria equipment has ten years of remaining useful life. The new vending machines have a ten-year useful life. The following data are available (in thousands):

Cafeteria cash revenues per year	$144
Cafeteria cash costs per year	$149
Present cafeteria equipment:	
Net book value	$101
Annual amortization cost	$ 7
Current disposal price	$ 5
Terminal disposal price (10 years from now)	$ 0
New vending machines:	
Initial machine investment	$ 77
Terminal disposal price	$ 6
Expected annual gross receipts	$ 96
City's percentage share of receipts	10%
Expected annual cash costs (negligible)	
Present values at 14%:	
$1 due in 10 years	$0.27
Annuity of $1 a year for 10 years	$5.22

The city of Edmonton has a 14% required rate of return.

REQUIRED

Compute the following for the vending machine investment:
1. Expected increase in net annual operating cash inflows as a result of investing in the vending machines
2. Payback period
3. Net present value
4. Point of indifference (zero NPV) in terms of annual gross vending machine receipts

21-27 Relevant costs, replacement decisions, performance evaluation. Ibrahim Asafi, the general manager of the Coronado Company, is contemplating replacing the existing assembly-line equipment in the Assembly Department with automated assembly equipment. Production output and revenues will be unaffected by the replacement decision. Transactions related to the capital investment are cash transactions that would occur today.

	Existing Assembly Equipment	New Automated Assembly Equipment
Original cost	$1,320,000	$1,440,000
Useful life	11 years	5 years
Current age	6 years	0 years
Useful life remaining	5 years	5 years
Accumulated amortization	$ 720,000	$ 0
Book value	$ 636,000	Not acquired yet
Current disposal price (in cash)	$ 240,000	Not acquired yet
Terminal disposal price (in cash, in 5 years)	$ 0	$ 0
Average working capital needed	$ 144,000	$ 84,000

Current annual Assembly Department costs are as follows:

Direct materials	$720,000
Direct manufacturing labour	480,000
Amortization	120,000
Maintenance and repairs	180,000
Other operating costs	60,000
Supervision (allocated as 10% of direct manufacturing labour costs)	48,000
Allocated rent (based on space used)	48,000
Allocated corporate overhead (based on direct manufacturing labour costs)	144,000
Total	$1,800,000

ADDITIONAL INFORMATION

a. Coronado uses straight-line amortization calculated on the difference between the initial equipment investment and the terminal disposal price of the equipment.

b. The new equipment will produce output more swiftly. Therefore, the average working capital investment, if the new equipment is purchased, will decrease.

c. Of the total direct materials costs, $144,000 is waste and scrap. The new equipment is expected to reduce scrap costs to $24,000.

d. The new equipment is expected to reduce direct manufacturing labour costs by $180,000 each year.

e. Maintenance and repairs on the old equipment have been excessive. If the new equipment is acquired, maintenance and repair costs are expected to decrease to $120,000.

f. Coronado collects all supervision costs for all manufacturing departments in the plant into one cost pool. These costs are then allocated to departments on the basis of direct manufacturing labour costs. The Assembly Department has only one supervisor currently. The supervisor will continue in her current position if the new equipment is purchased.

g. The new equipment will reduce the space required for assembly operations by 20%, reducing allocated rent by $9,600. The Coronado Company has no alternative uses for this extra space.

h. Corporate overhead costs are allocated to each department at 30% of direct manufacturing labour costs of each department.

Asafi estimates a required rate of return of 12% for this project.

REQUIRED

1. On the basis of the net present value method, should Asafi replace the existing assembly equipment?

2. Suppose that next year is the last year Coronado will offer the attractive bonus plan currently in place. Asafi's bonus hinges on short-run accrual accounting income for that year. Will Asafi be inclined to replace the Assembly Department equipment? Provide quantitative support for your answer.

3. What nonfinancial and qualitative factors should Asafi consider in coming to a decision?

21-28 Special order, relevant costs, capital budgeting. (A. Spero, adapted) Toys, Inc., sells neon-coated Nightglow cars to several local toy stores. It has the capacity to make 250,000 of these units per year, but during the year ending December 31, 2007, it made and sold 130,000 cars to its existing customers. It makes these cars by dipping its highly unsuccessful Gander model plastic toy cars into a vat of neon paint. It originally purchased 780,000 of the Ganders but has been unable to sell them as Ganders. These plastic cars originally cost $24 per unit, and 650,000 of them remain in inventory.

Toys' accountant has prepared the following cost sheet per Nightglow car:

Selling price per car			$70.80
Manufacturing costs per car:			
Direct materials:			
Plastic cars	$24.00		
Neon paint	7.20		
Boxes	3.60	34.80	
Direct manufacturing labour		9.60	
Vat amortization		12.00	
Allocated plant manager's salary		6.00	
Manufacturing costs per car			62.40
Gross margin per car			8.40
Marketing costs per car ($2.40 of which is variable)			7.20
Operating margin per car			$ 1.20

On December 31, 2007, the Tiny Tot chain asked Toys, Inc., to provide 100,000 Nightglow cars at a special price of $60 per car. Toys, Inc., will not need to incur any marketing cost for the Tiny Tot sale.

Toys, Inc., expected to sell the Nightglow cars to its existing customers for the next four years at the current level of demand of 130,000 units per year and none thereafter. At the end of four years, Toys, Inc., will dispose of the vat and whatever cars remain at zero net disposal price. If Toys accepts the Tiny Tot order, it is certain that its other customers will refuse to pay the current price of $70.80 and will demand a discount. Toys estimates a required rate of return of 16%.

1. Should Toys accept the special order if it must also offer the same price of $60 to its existing customers for the next four years?
2. Suppose Toys is uncertain about the discount the existing customers would demand. Determine the price that Toys, Inc., would have to offer its existing customers for the next four years to be indifferent between accepting and rejecting Tiny Tot's special order.

21-29 Relevant costs, outsourcing, capital budgeting. The Strubel Company currently makes as many units of Part No. 789 as it needs. David Lin, general manager of the Strubel Company, has received a bid from the Gabriella Company for making Part No. 789. Current plans call for Gabriella to supply 1,000 units of Part No. 789 per year at $60 a unit. Gabriella can begin supplying on January 1, 2007, and continue for five years, after which time Strubel will not need the part. Gabriella can accommodate any change in Strubel's demand for the part and will supply it for $60 a unit, regardless of quantity.

Jack Tyson, the controller of the Strubel Company, reports the following costs for manufacturing 1,000 units of Part No. 789:

Direct materials	$26,400
Direct manufacturing labour	13,200
Variable manufacturing overhead	8,400
Amortization on machine	12,000
Product and process engineering	4,800
Rent	2,400
Allocation of general plant overhead costs	6,000
Total costs	$73,200

The following additional information is available:
a. Part No. 789 is made on a machine used exclusively for the manufacture of Part No. 789. The machine was acquired on January 1, 2006, at a cost of $72,000. The machine has a useful life of six years and zero terminal disposal price. Amortization is calculated on the straight-line method.
b. The machine could be sold today for $18,000.
c. Product and process engineering costs are incurred to ensure that the manufacturing process for Part No. 789 works smoothly. Although these costs are fixed in the short run, with respect to units of Part No. 789 produced, they can be saved in the long run if this part is no longer produced. If Part No. 789 is outsourced, product and process engineering costs of $4,800 will be incurred for 2007 but not thereafter.
d. Rent costs of $2,400 are allocated to products on the basis of the floor space used for manufacturing the product. If Part No. 789 is discontinued, the space currently used to manufacture it would become available. The company could then use the space for storage purposes and save $1,200 currently paid for outside storage.
e. General plant overhead costs are allocated to each department on the basis of direct manufacturing labour dollars. These costs will not change in total. But no general plant overhead will be allocated to Part No. 789 if the part is outsourced.

Assume that Strubel requires a 12% rate of return for this project.

REQUIRED
1. Should David Lin outsource Part No. 789? Prepare a quantitative analysis.
2. Describe any sensitivity analysis that seems advisable, but you need not perform any sensitivity calculations.
3. What other factors should Lin consider in making a decision?
4. Lin is particularly concerned about his bonus for 2007. The bonus is based on Strubel's accounting income. What decision will Lin make if he wants to maximize his bonus in 2007?

21-30 Capital budgeting, computer-integrated manufacturing, sensitivity. The Dynamo Corporation is planning to replace one of its production lines, which has a remaining useful life of ten years, book value of $10.8 million, a current disposal price of $6 million, and a negligible terminal disposal value ten years from now. The average investment in working capital is $7.2 million.

Dynamo plans to replace the production line with a computer-integrated manufacturing (CIM) system at a cost of $54 million. Jeremy Burns, the production manager, estimates the following annual cash flow effects of implementing CIM:
a. Cost of maintaining software programs and CIM equipment, $1.8 million
b. Reduction in lease payments due to reduced floor space requirements, $1.2 million
c. Fewer product defects and reduced rework, $5.4 million

In addition, Burns estimates the average investment in working capital will decrease to $2.4 million. The estimated disposal price of the CIM equipment is $16.8 million at the end of ten years. Dynamo uses a required rate of return of 14%.

REQUIRED

1. Compute the net present value of the CIM proposal. On the basis of this criterion, should Dynamo adopt CIM?
2. Burns argues that the higher quality and faster production resulting from CIM will also increase Dynamo's revenues. He estimates additional cash revenues net of cash-operating costs from CIM of $3.6 million per year. Compute the net present value of the CIM proposal under this assumption.
3. Management is uncertain if the cash flows from additional revenues will occur. Compute the minimum annual cash flow from additional revenues that will cause Dynamo to invest in CIM on the basis of the net present value criterion.
4. Discuss the effects of reducing the investment horizon for CIM to five years, Dynamo's usual time period for making investment decisions. Assume disposal prices at the end of five years of the CIM line, $24 million; old production line, $4.8 million. Also assume additional cash revenues net of cash operating costs from CIM of $3.6 million per year.

21-31 **Ethics, capital budgeting.** (CMA, adapted) The Evans Company must expand its manufacturing capabilities to meet the growing demand for its products. The first alternative is to expand its current manufacturing facility, which is located next to a vacant lot in the heart of the city. The second alternative is to convert a warehouse, already owned by Evans, located 20 kilometres outside the city. Evans's controller, George Watson, assigns Kenisha Kincaid, assistant controller, to use net present value computations to evaluate both proposals.

Kincaid obtains the following information. The investment in plant and equipment to expand the current manufacturing facility is $22.8 million, while a $26.40-million investment is required to convert the warehouse. At either site, Evans needs to invest $3.6 million in working capital. Cash revenues from products made in the new facility are expected to equal $15.6 million each year. If the warehouse is converted, cash operating costs are expected to be $12 million per year. Expanding the current facility will result in some efficiencies: annual cash operating costs, if the current facility is expanded, will be $1.2 million lower than the cash operating costs if the warehouse is converted. Evans uses a ten-year period and a 14% required rate of return to evaluate manufacturing investments. The estimated terminal disposal price of the new facility (including recovery of working capital of $3.6 million) at the end of ten years is estimated to be $9.6 million—regardless of where the plant is located. Evans amortizes the investment in plant and equipment using straight-line amortization over ten years on the difference between the initial investment and terminal disposal price.

Watson is upset at Kincaid's conclusions. He returns the proposal to her with the comment, "You must have made an error. The warehouse proposal should look better and have a positive net present value. Work on the projections and estimates."

Kincaid suspects that Watson is anxious to have the warehouse proposal selected because the choice of this location would eliminate his long commute into the city. Feeling some pressure, she checks her calculations but finds no errors. Kincaid reviews her projections and estimates. These too are quite reasonable. Even so, she replaces some of her original estimates with new estimates that are more favourable to the warehouse proposal, although these new estimates are less likely to occur. The revised proposal still has a negative net present value. Kincaid is confused about what she should do.

REQUIRED

1. Calculate the net present value of the proposals to expand the current manufacturing facility and to convert the warehouse. Which project should Evans choose on the basis of the NPV calculations?
2. Was George Watson's conduct unethical when he gave Kenisha Kincaid specific instructions on revising the proposal?
3. Was Kenisha Kincaid's revised proposal for the warehouse conversion unethical?
4. Identify the steps Kenisha Kincaid should take to resolve this situation.

COLLABORATIVE LEARNING PROBLEM

21-32 **Relevant costs, capital budgeting.** (N. Melumad, S. Reichelstein, adapted) The Special Products Division (SPD) of Plastics Unlimited makes specially designed night goggles. Its main production machine broke down on January 1, 2008, and was no longer usable. SPD's manager requested $384,000 to acquire a new machine. Corporate management responded by requesting an analysis of the acquisition as well as an analysis of closing down SPD. SPD's 2007 income statement is as follows:

Special Products Division Income Statement for 2007

Sales (60,000 units)			$1,440,000
Deduct: Costs:			
Variable production costs		$924,000	
Fixed production costs:*			
Machine amortization	$36,000		
Patent amortization	30,000		
Machine maintenance	24,000		
Building space	24,000		
Manager's salary	66,000		
Other fixed costs	18,000		
Total fixed production costs		198,000	
Variable marketing costs		156,000	
Total costs			1,278,000
Operating income			$ 162,000

*That do not vary with units produced and sold.

The externally reported book values of the division assets as of December 31, 2007, are

Cash	$228,000
Machine	72,000
Patent	150,000
Total	$450,000

All of SPD's transactions are cash transactions, and the division maintains no inventories. The contribution margin is expected to remain the same over the next five years if SPD continues to produce and sell goggles.

To make the goggles, the company had to acquire a patent three years ago for $240,000. The patent is being amortized (that is, written off on the income statement) evenly over its lifetime. If the company were to shut down SPD, the patent could be sold for $282,000 to an external buyer.

SPD purchased the existing machine three years ago for $180,000. It is amortized on a straight-line basis over five years. The current disposal price of the broken machine is $4,800.

The new machine has a useful life of five years and an expected disposal price of $60,000. It would be amortized under the straight-line method. Maintenance of the new machine would require $30,000 per year. Machine maintenance costs would not be incurred if SPD is closed down.

SPD uses 1,000 square metres of building space and is charged $24 per square metre by corporate management. If SPD is eliminated, the space can be rented externally for $36 per square metre.

Plastics Unlimited needs an assistant manager in another larger department. If SPD closes, its manager will take the assistant manager position at an annual salary of $72,000. If SPD continues operations, Plastics Unlimited will have to fill the assistant manager position with an outsider at an annual salary of $78,000.

Other fixed costs consist of miscellaneous items such as insurance and indirect labour that would remain at the same levels if SPD continues to produce the goggles and would not be incurred if SPD is closed down.

The firm uses a required rate of return of 16%. Ignore income taxes.

INSTRUCTIONS
Form groups of three students to complete the following requirements.

REQUIRED
1. On the basis of the net present value criterion, should Plastics Unlimited purchase the new machine or close down SPD?
2. Suppose the manager making the decision is compensated on the basis of operating income earned by all divisions of Plastics Unlimited after gain or loss on disposal of assets. The manager will retire at the end of 2008. Which decision would the manager favour? Explain.

ANSWERS TO EXERCISES IN COMPOUND INTEREST
(EXERCISE 21-14)
The general approach to these exercises centres on a key question: Which of the four tables in Appendix A should be used? No computations should be made until after this basic question has been answered with confidence.

1. **From Table 1.** The $5,000 is the present value P of your winnings. Their future value S in ten years will be:

$$S = P(1 + r)^n$$

The conversion factor, $(1 + r)^n$, is on line 10 of Table 1.

Substituting at 5%: $S = 5{,}000 \times 1.629 = \$8{,}145$

Substituting at 12%: $S = 5{,}000 \times 3.106 = \$15{,}530$

2. **From Table 2.** The $95,650 is an *amount of future worth*. You want the present value of that amount, which is $P = S \div (1 + r)^n$.

The conversion factor, $1 \div (1 + r)^n$, is on line 10 of Table 2. Substituting

$$P = \$95{,}650 \times 0.614 = \$58{,}729.10$$

3. **From Table 3.** The $95,650 is *future worth*. You are seeking the uniform amount (annuity) to set aside annually. Note that $1 invested each year for ten years at 8% has a future worth F of $14.487 after ten years, from line 10 of Table 3.

$$S_n = \text{Annual deposit} \times F$$
$$\$95{,}650 = \text{Annual deposit} \times 14.487$$
$$\text{Annual deposit} = \frac{\$95{,}650}{14.487} = \$6{,}602.47$$

4. **From Table 3.** You are seeking the *amount of future worth* of an annuity of $6,000 per year. Note that $1 invested each year for ten years at 12% has a future worth F of $17.549 after ten years.

$$S_n = \$6{,}000F \quad \text{where } F \text{ is the conversion factor}$$
$$= \$6{,}000 \times 17.549 = \$105{,}294$$

5. **From Table 4.** When you reach age 65, you will get $240,000, a present value at that time. You must find the annuity that will exactly exhaust the invested principal in ten years. To pay yourself $1 each year for ten years when the interest rate is 4% requires you to have $8.111 today, from line 10 of Table 4.

$$P_n = \text{Annual withdrawal} \times F$$
$$\$240{,}000 = \text{Annual withdrawal} \times 8.111$$
$$\text{Annual withdrawal} = \frac{\$240{,}000}{8.111} = \$29{,}589.45$$

6. **From Table 4.** You need to find the present value of an annuity for ten years. At 6%:

$$P_n = \text{Annual withdrawal} \times F$$
$$= \$60{,}000 \times 6.710$$
$$= \$402{,}600$$

At 18%:

$$P_n = \$60{,}000 \times 4.494$$
$$= \$269{,}640, \text{ a much lower figure}$$

7. Plan B is preferable. The net present value of plan B exceeds that of plan A by $224 ($591 − $367):

Year	PV Factor at 8%	Plan A Cash Inflows	Plan A PV of Cash Inflows	Plan B Cash Inflows	Plan B PV of Cash Inflows
0	1.000	$(12,000)	$(12,000)	$(12,000)	$(12,000)
1	0.926[a]	1,000	926	5,000	4,630
2	0.857[b]	2,000	1,714	4,000	3,428
3	0.794	3,000	2,382	3,000	2,382
4	0.735	4,000	2,940	2,000	1,470
5	0.681	5,000	3,405	1,000	681
			$ (633)		$ 591

Even though plan B and plan A have the same total cash inflows over the five years, plan B is preferred to plan A because it has greater cash inflows occurring earlier.

[a] $1 \div (1.08)^1 = 0.926$

[b] $1 \div (1.08)^2 = 0.857$

Investment projects such as a major year-round destination resort require managers to consider several dimensions of the decision including tourism trends, economic cycles, the environment, and, ultimately, discounted cash flows. One of the key considerations is the effect on cash of tax paid when investments are made in projects of this type.

Intrawest Corporation has developed year-round destination resorts such as Whistler-Blackcomb in British Columbia and Mont Tremblant in Quebec, pictured above, at costs exceeding $200 million.

CHAPTER 22

Capital Budgeting: A Closer Look

LEARNING OBJECTIVES

After studying this chapter, you should be able to

1. Analyze the impact of income taxes on operating cash flows

2. Analyze the effect of income taxes on capital cash flows and compute the after-tax net present values of projects

3. Explain the after-tax effect on cash of tradeins and disposals of assets

4. Distinguish between the total-project approach and the differential approach in capital budgeting decisions

5. Distinguish between the real rate of return and the nominal rate of return

6. Describe two internally consistent ways to account for inflation in capital budgeting

7. Describe alternative approaches used to recognize the degree of risk in capital budgeting projects

8. Explain the excess present value index and its usefulness in capital budgeting

9. Explain why the internal rate-of-return and the net present value decision rules may rank projects differently

The Income War Tax Act became legislation in 1917 and this was the first time in Canada's history that the federal government was given the legal right to tax income. In 1942, automatic deduction at source began. In 1946 the Income Tax Appeal Board was born and by 1983 it became the Tax Court of Canada although it was 1993 before this court achieved sole jurisdiction over income tax appeals processes. Today Canadian federal and most provincial governments also impose sales taxes and value-added taxes (GST and PST), corporate surtax (a percentage of tax paid), land transfer tax, and large corporations tax. Our discussion, however, will be confined to the effect of capital cost allowance (CCA) on cash paid in corporate income tax. Tax and inflation are considered external factors affecting corporate decisions to undertake investment projects because no single corporation can initiate or change either the rate of taxation or the rate of inflation. This chapter examines how managers analyze the financial effects of income taxes and changing prices in capital budgeting. We discuss risk and uncertainty in capital budgeting, capital budgeting in not-for-profit organizations, and issues in implementing the net present value and the internal rate-of-return decision methods.

INCOME TAXES AND CAPITAL BUDGETING

General Characteristics

Income taxes are cash disbursements and therefore an important cash flow consideration. Income taxes almost always influence the amount and/or the timing of cash flows. Their basic role in capital budgeting is no different from that of any other cash disbursement. Payment of income tax tends to narrow the cash differences between projects.

The Canadian federal and provincial governments raise money through corporate income taxes. Income tax rates differ considerably, and thus, overall corporate income tax rates can vary widely.

Income tax rates also depend on the amount of pretax income. Larger income is taxed at higher rates. In capital budgeting, the relevant rate is the **marginal income tax rate**, that is, the tax rate paid on additional amounts of pretax income. Suppose corporations pay income taxes of 15% on the first $50,000 of pretax income and 30% on pretax income over $50,000. What is the *marginal income tax rate* of a company with $75,000 of pretax income? It is 30%, because 30% of any *additional* income over $50,000 will be paid in taxes. In contrast, the company's *average income tax rate* is only 20% (i.e., 15% × $50,000 + 30% × $25,000 = $15,000 ÷ $75,000 of pretax income). When we assess tax effects of capital budgeting decisions, we will always use the *marginal* tax rate. Why? Because that is the rate applied to the additional cash flows generated by a proposed project.

Organizations that pay income taxes report their net income to the public using the CICA standards as they must in order to obtain a clean audit opinion. These standards allow managers to choose among amortization methods and when necessary change from one method to another. The amortization expense deducted would affect taxable income, something the Canadian Revenue Agency (CRA) does not permit. This is why governments have created laws that, for purposes of paying tax, require corporations to deduct capital cost allowance (CCA) when calculating their taxable income. Legally, the taxable income reported to CRA on a confidential basis differs from mandatory public disclosure under CICA standards. This means that the tax expense on the statement of income, an accrual, will differ from the cash tax paid to the government. The difference between the accrual and the cash flow amounts accumulates as future tax liabilities, which will eventually be paid. This means that the CCA that affects cash flow in the form of corporate income tax paid each year is relevant to assessing investment projects. Amortization, however, is not. In this chapter we are concerned with effects on the cash outflows for taxes. Therefore, we focus on the *tax reporting* rules, not those for public financial reporting.

TAX IMPACT ON OPERATING CASH FLOWS

OBJECTIVE 1

Analyze the impact of income taxes on operating cash flows

Recognizing the impact of income taxes on operating cash flows is straightforward. If a capital proposal results in a reduction in costs, for example, an annual cost saving of $60,000, then the company's taxable income will increase by $60,000 all other things being equal. If the company has a marginal tax rate of 40%, then the company's income taxes will increase by $24,000 ($60,000 × 0.40). A net annual after-tax savings of $36,000 results ($60,000 − $24,000). This means the after-tax savings can be calculated quickly as $60,000 × (1 minus the tax rate) or $60,000 × 0.60 = $36,000.

If operating expenses increase by $250,000, then the taxable income will decrease by $250,000. If the company has a 40% marginal tax rate, then the tax saving will be $100,000 ($250,000 × 0.40). An after-tax cost increase of $150,000 results [$250,000 × (1 − 0.40)]. Thus, to incorporate the impact of income taxes on operating cash flows poses no real difficulty. The difficulty occurs in the recognition of the tax effects of investment expenditures in capital equipment.

In financial reporting, the expenditure on capital equipment results in the recording of the asset and the related amortization expense over the asset's useful economic life. Amortization rates and policies are determined by the company's management and vary from company to company even for the same asset.

To apply a consistent set of regulations and to provide a means to implement government initiatives, the federal government has implemented its own system of **capital cost allowance (CCA)**. The *Income Tax Act* (ITA) does not permit a company to deduct amortization expense in determining taxable income but rather a company is allowed to deduct CCA. If you like, CCA is the legally required income tax counterpart to annual amortization expense in financial reporting.

Capital cost allowance (CCA).
The legally mandatory income tax counterpart to annual amortization expense in financial reporting.

Capital Cost Allowance—Declining Balance Classes

The ITA assigns all capital purchases to a CCA class. (The appendix to this chapter provides a list of some of the more commonly used CCA classes.) For example, a desk would qualify as a Class 8 asset that includes all furniture and fixtures. Class 8 has a predetermined rate of 20% declining balance capital cost allowance. Exhibit 22-1 on page 850 depicts the calculation of CCA for a desk that costs $10,000.

A number of years ago, a company could deduct a full year's worth of CCA on any asset acquired during the year, as long as the company had been in business the entire year. Thus, companies with a December 31 year-end would buy assets on or about December 31 and claim a full year's deduction even though the asset had not really been used to generate the income. To minimize this problem, the government implemented the so-called "half-year rule."

The **half-year rule** assumes that all net additions are purchased in the middle of the year, and thus only one-half of the stated CCA rate is allowed in the first year. Thus in year 1 of the example in Exhibit 22-1, the CCA is $1,000 or 1/2 times 20% multiplied by the $10,000 capital expenditure. This leaves a balance of $9,000 ($10,000 − $1,000), which is known as the **unamortized capital cost (UCC)**.

Half-year rule. The assumption, in calculating capital cost allowance, that all net additions to a company's assets are purchased in the middle of the year, so that only half the applicable capital cost allowance rate is allowed in the first year.

In year 2 and all succeeding years, the rate of 20% is applied to the UCC of the previous year. This results in a declining amount of capital cost allowance for each year. Even after the 25 years shown in Exhibit 22-1, a UCC of $42 remains and will require 15 more years to get to a zero balance (which in practice can only be obtained by rounding to the nearest dollar).

Unamortized capital cost (UCC). The result of subtracting the capital cost allowance from the capital expenditure or its amortized balance.

The CCA of each year is deducted in the calculation of a company's taxable income. Thus, the CCA is not a cash flow. Rather we must multiply the CCA of each year by the company's marginal tax rate to calculate the actual tax savings in each year. In Chapter 21, we recognized the time value of money. Thus, to determine the present value of the tax savings, we would need to multiply the tax savings of each year by the present value factor from Appendix A for each year at the company's required rate of return (say 10%).

This, as you could well imagine, would be a long and laborious task to perform for each capital proposal. An efficient way to calculate the present value of the tax savings is to use the following **tax shield formula**:

Tax shield formula. A formula for calculating the tax savings from deducting capital cost allowance.

$$\text{Present value of tax savings} = \left(\text{Investment} \times \text{marginal tax rate} \right) \left(\frac{\text{CCA rate}}{\text{CCA rate} + \text{required rate of return}} \right) \frac{(2 + \text{required rate of return})}{2 \, (1 + \text{required rate of return})}$$

In the case of the $10,000 desk, the present value of the tax savings from deducting CCA, commonly referred to as the tax shield, is $2,548, computed as follows assuming a 10% required rate of return:

$$\text{Tax shield} = (\$10,000 \times 40\%) \left(\frac{20\%}{20\% + 10\%} \right) \left(\frac{2 + 10\%}{2(1 + 10\%)} \right)$$

$$= \$4,000 \times 0.667 \times 0.955$$

$$= \$2,668 \times 0.955$$

$$= \$2,548$$

EXHIBIT 22-1
Capital Cost Allowance Illustration

CCA—Class 8
Rate is 20% Declining Balance
(rounded to the nearest dollar)

Year 1 (day 1) addition	$10,000	Year 13 UCC	618
CCA year 1 (10%)	1,000	CCA year 14 (20%)	124
Year end UCC	9,000	Year 14 UCC	494
CCA year 2 (20%)	1,800	CCA year 15 (20%)	99
Year 2 UCC	7,200	Year 15 UCC	395
CCA year 3 (20%)	1,440	CCA year 16 (20%)	79
Year 3 UCC	5,760	Year 16 UCC	316
CCA year 4 (20%)	1,152	CCA year 17 (20%)	63
Year 4 UCC	4,608	Year 17 UCC	253
CCA year 5 (20%)	922	CCA year 18 (20%)	51
Year 5 UCC	3,686	Year 18 UCC	202
CCA year 6 (20%)	737	CCA year 19 (20%)	40
Year 6 UCC	2,949	Year 19 UCC	162
CCA year 7 (20%)	590	CCA year 20 (20%)	32
Year 7 UCC	2,359	Year 20 UCC	130
CCA year 8 (20%)	472	CCA year 21 (20%)	26
Year 8 UCC	1,887	Year 21 UCC	104
CCA year 9 (20%)	377	CCA year 22 (20%)	21
Year 9 UCC	1,510	Year 22 UCC	83
CCA year 10 (20%)	302	CCA year 23 (20%)	17
Year 10 UCC	1,208	Year 23 UCC	66
CCA year 11 (20%)	242	CCA year 24 (20%)	13
Year 11 UCC	966	Year 24 UCC	53
CCA year 12 (20%)	193	CCA year 25 (20%)	11
Year 12 UCC	773	Year 25 UCC	$42
CCA year 12 (20%)	155		

Therefore, the net after-tax cost of the desk is $7,452, or $10,000 less $2,548.

A detailed proof of the tax shield formula is not necessary for our purposes, but some explanation will be useful. The first component of the formula, investment times the marginal tax rate, computes the total tax savings over the life of the asset from the CCA deduction. The $4,000, however, does not incorporate any time value of money considerations.

The second component, the CCA rate divided by the sum of the CCA rate plus the required rate of return, calculates the present values of all the annual tax savings assuming the half-year rule did not exist. This is important to note when residual values are discussed later in the chapter.

The third component incorporates an adjustment for the half-year rule. For example, in the above scenario, the tax shield was reduced to 95.5% of the benefit that existed before the introduction of the half-year rule.

Capital Cost Allowance—Other Classes

Most CCA classes use the declining balance method. However, occasionally the straight-line method is used in which the CCA is the same for each year, except for the first and last years, which have one-half of the CCA due to the half-year rule. It is also important to note that CCA applies only to tangible assets. The income tax statutes for intangible assets such as patents, copyrights, and trademarks differ as does the terminology. The statutory deduction is based on 75% of the acquisition cost of the intangible asset. This is termed the **eligible capital property**. Intangible assets, by definition, have an indefinite useful life, and the annual deduction is called the **cumulative eligible capital amount (CECA)**, calculated at 7% on a declining-balance basis. The balance remaining after deducting CECA is called the **cumulative eligible capital (CEC)** pool.

Tradeins and Disposals of Capital Assets

When a capital asset is traded in on another asset or is sold, we do not need to concern ourselves with the net tax book value of the asset.

Assume that a company's Class 8 UCC for all of its furniture and fixtures is $50,000, as shown in Exhibit 22-2, at the end of year 3. Let us also assume that included in the $50,000 is the remaining UCC on the desk of $5,760.

If in year 4 the desk was traded in on a new desk, where the price of the new desk is $12,000, and $4,000 was allowed as a tradein, the Class 8 UCC would increase by $8,000. Note that the CCA system works on a pool basis, in that we are not concerned with the UCC of the specific desk being sold. Rather we are only concerned with the net cash flows. The UCC of the class that existed before the disposal is only reduced by the amount of the cash received. Thus, the actual amount of the UCC of the specific asset is irrelevant to the decision. In this example, the net capital expenditure of $8,000 is the relevant cash flow.

Continuing with the example in Exhibit 22-2, the CCA for year 4 is $10,800. This is a combination of the CCA at the rate of 20% on the opening UCC of $50,000 ($10,000) and the CCA at the half-year rule rate of 10% on the net addition of $8,000 ($800).

Thus, as shown in Exhibit 22-3 on page 852, the net after-tax present value of the cost of the new desk is $5,964. This amount recognizes the fact that the tax shield of $2,036 on the net addition of $8,000 must recognize the half-year rule.

If in the above scenario a new desk had not been purchased, but rather the old desk was sold for $4,000, the CCA would be 20% of $46,000 or $9,200. Note the half-year rule does not apply to net disposals, that is where the amount of disposals exceeds the amount of additions during a given year.

From Exhibit 22-3, note that the sale of $4,000 reduces the future CCA and results in a lost tax shield of $1,067. Thus, the net after-tax present value of the sale is $2,933.

Simplifying Assumptions

It is useful to note that a number of simplifying assumptions have been made when using the tax shield formula:

1. We have assumed that the company's marginal tax rate will remain the same (at 40% in the above examples). Further, the above examples also assume that the company will have a taxable income each year.

Eligible capital property. 75% of the acquisition cost of an intangible asset, and the basis for the annual deduction permitted by the income tax act.

Cumulative eligible capital amount (CECA). The statutory annual deduction permitted on intangible assets; the equivalent of CCA for tangible assets.

Cumulative eligible capital (CEC). The balance remaining after deducting CECA; the equivalent of UCC for tangible assets.

Department of Justice, Canada
http://laws.justice.gc.ca/en/
I-3.3/C.R.C.-c.945/135982.html

> **OBJECTIVE 3**
>
> Explain the after-tax effect on cash of tradeins and disposals of assets

EXHIBIT 22-2
Tradein of a Capital Asset

CCA—Class 8	
Ending UCC—year 3	$50,000
Purchase	12,000
Less: Tradein	(4,000)
Net change in UCC	8,000
Revised UCC	58,000
Year 4—CCA	
20% × $50,000	10,000
10% × $8,000	800
Total CCA	10,800
UCC—year 4	$47,200

EXHIBIT 22-3
Net Capital Cash Flow of Tradeins and Disposals

Tradein:	Purchase price	$12,000
	Tradein	(4,000)
	Net cash payment	8,000
	Tax shield[a]	2,036
	NPV cash outflow	$ 5,964
Disposal:	Sales price	4,000
	Lost tax shield[b]	1,067
	NPV cash inflow	$ 2,933

[a]Includes the half-year adjustment:

$$(\$8{,}000 \times 40\%) \times \left(\frac{20\%}{20\%+10\%}\right) \times \left(\frac{2+10\%}{2(1+10\%)}\right)$$

[b]Excludes the half-year adjustment

$$(\$4{,}000 \times 40\%) \times \left(\frac{20\%}{20\%+10\%}\right)$$

2. Although it is uncommon, governments can change the CCA rates that we have assumed to be constant.

3. We have also assumed that all CCA tax savings occur at the year-end. In reality, companies make monthly instalments. However, the additional cost of attempting to be more precise is not warranted, given the degree of uncertainty that already exists in the estimation of the cash flows.

INCOME TAX COMPLICATIONS

In the foregoing illustrations, we deliberately avoided many possible income tax complications. As all taxpaying citizens know, income taxes are affected by many intricacies, including progressive tax rates, loss carrybacks and carryforwards, varying provincial income taxes, capital gains, distinctions between capital assets and other assets, offsets of losses against related gains, exchanges of property of like kind, exempt income, and so forth.

CONFUSION ABOUT AMORTIZATION

Keep in mind that changes in the tax law occur each year. Always check the current tax law before calculating the tax consequences of a decision.

The meanings of amortization and book value are widely misunderstood. Pause and consider their role in decisions. Suppose a bank has some printing equipment with a book value of $30,000, an expected terminal disposal value of zero, a current disposal value of $12,000, and a remaining useful life of three years. For simplicity, assume that straight-line amortization of $10,000 yearly will be taken.

In particular, note that the inputs to the decision model are the predicted income tax effects on cash. The book loss of $18,000 or the amortization of $10,000 may be necessary for making *predictions*. By themselves, however, they are not inputs to DCF decision models.

The following points summarize the role of amortization regarding the replacement of equipment:

1. **Initial investment.** The amount paid for (and hence amortization on) old equipment is irrelevant except for its effect on tax cash flows. In contrast, the amount paid for new equipment is relevant, because it is an expected future cost that will not be incurred if replacement is rejected.

2. **Do not double-count.** The investment in equipment is a one-time outlay at time zero, so it should not be double-counted as an outlay in the form of amortization. Amortization by itself is irrelevant; it is not a cash outlay.

3. **Relation to income tax cash flows.** Relevant quantities were defined in Chapter 4 as expected future data that will differ among alternatives. Given this definition, book values and past amortization are irrelevant in all capital budgeting decision models. The relevant item is the *income tax cash effect*, not the book value or the amortization.

ALTERNATIVE APPROACHES TO CAPITAL BUDGETING

We turn now to a fuller discussion of how income taxes can affect cash inflows and outflows and also how they influence managers' decisions. We focus on the information-acquisition and selection stages of capital budgeting, highlight the effect of income taxes, and use the net present value method for the formal financial analysis.

OBJECTIVE 4

Distinguish between the total-project approach and the differential approach in capital budgeting decisions

Example: Potato Supreme produces potato products for sale to supermarkets and other retail outlets. It is considering replacing an old packaging machine (purchased three years ago) with a new, more efficient packaging machine that has recently been introduced. The new machine is less labour-intensive and has lower operating costs than the old machine. For simplicity, we assume that

1. All cash outflows or inflows occur at the end of the year (even though cash operating costs generally occur throughout the year).

2. The tax effects of cash inflows and outflows occur at the same time that the inflows and outflows occur.

3. The income tax rate is 30% each year.

4. The equipment is one of several assets that qualify as CCA Class 8, with a CCA rate of up to 20% declining balance. Potato Supreme takes the maximum rate each year.

5. Both the old and the new machine have the same working capital requirements.

6. Potato Supreme is a profitable company.

Summary data for the two machines are as follows:

	Old Machine	New Machine
Original cost	$ 87,500	$200,000
Accumulated amortization	$ 37,500	—
Current book value	$ 50,000	—
Current disposal price	$ 26,000	—
Proceeds of disposition, 4 years from now	$ 6,000	$ 20,000
Annual cash operating costs	$250,000	$150,000
Remaining useful life	4 years	4 years
After-tax required rate of return	10%	10%
Capital cost allowance rate	20% (declining balance)	20% (declining balance)

Potato Supreme uses the net present value method to evaluate whether it should replace the old with the new packaging machine immediately or in four years' time. As in the Lifetime Care example of Chapter 21, the key point in net present value analysis is to identify the relevant cash flows. To emphasize the ideas of relevance, Chapter 21 used the **differential approach**, which analyzes only relevant cash flows—those future cash outflows and inflows that differ between alternatives. The differential approach is generally faster when there are only two alternatives.

When the number of alternatives is more than two, the differential approach becomes unwieldy. Why? Because it forces the analyst into difficult calculations of differences among multiple alternatives. Companies then use the *total-project approach*.

Differential approach. Approach to decision making and capital budgeting that analyzes only those future cash outflows and inflows that differ among alternatives.

Total-project approach. Approach to decision making that incorporates all relevant revenues and relevant costs under each alternative. In capital budgeting decisions, calculates the present value of all future cash inflows and outflows under each alternative separately.

The **total-project approach** calculates the present value of *all* future cash inflows and outflows under each alternative separately. It does not require the identification of cash flows that differ among alternatives. The total-project approach has two steps:

◆ **Step 1.** Calculate the present value of all cash inflows and outflows under the status quo alternative.

◆ **Step 2.** Separately calculate the present value of all cash inflows and outflows under another alternative.

We use the Potato Supreme example to illustrate the two steps of the total-project approach. We then use the differential approach to show that both approaches give the same net present value. The following categories of cash flows are considered in both approaches:

a. Initial machine investment

b. Tax shield on the initial investment

c. Cash flow from current disposal of old machine

d. Lost tax shield from current disposal of machine

e. Recurring after-tax cash operating flows

f. Cash flow from proceeds of disposition of old machine. Other assets remain in this asset class.

g. Lost tax shield from terminal disposal of machine

Total-Project Approach

◆ **Step 1:** *Calculate the present value of total cash flows of replacing the old packaging machine in four years' time.* Under this alternative, cash flow categories that specifically pertain to the new machine are not relevant. But the purchase price is relevant when calculating item g, the lost tax shield. If the purchase price of new equipment exceeds proceeds of disposition of the old equipment, **net addition**, the half-year rule applies.

Net addition. The difference between the purchase price of the new equipment and the proceeds of disposition of the old equipment. When the purchase price exceeds the proceeds of disposition, the half-year rule applies when calculating the lost tax shield; otherwise, the half-year rule does not apply.

a. *Initial machine investment.* No new investment is necessary if Potato Supreme keeps the old packaging machine. Exhibit 22-4, item a, shows an initial machine investment of $0 in year 0.

b. *Tax shield on initial investment.* As there is no new investment, there is then no additional tax shield.

c. *Cash flow from current disposal of old machine.* Since the old machine is kept and not disposed of, Exhibit 22-4, item c, shows after-tax cash flow from current disposal of old machine of $0 in year 0.

d. *Lost tax shield from current disposal of machine.* As the old machine is not sold, no tax shield adjustments are required.

e. *Recurring after-tax cash operating flows.*

Recurring cash operating flows (costs) for the old machine	$(250,000)
Deduct: Income tax savings at 30% of $250,000	75,000
Recurring after-tax cash operating flows	$(175,000)

After-tax cash operating flows of $(175,000) in years 1 to 4 appear as relevant cash outflows in Exhibit 22-4, item e. Our example assumes that Potato Supreme's income tax rate is 30% each year. When future tax rates are uncertain, analysts must predict the tax rate applicable for each year of a project.

f. *Cash flow from proceeds of disposition of old machine. Other assets remain in this asset class.*

Proceeds of disposition at end of year 4	$6,000

The cash flow of $6,000 from the proceeds of disposition of the old machine appears as a cash inflow in year 4 of Exhibit 22-4, item f.

g. *Lost tax shield.* The proceeds of disposition of $6,000 would reduce the CCA pool by $6,000, and thus reduce the future cash savings from capital cost allowance deductions by $1,145.

EXHIBIT 22-4

Total-Project Approach for Potato Supreme: After-Tax Analysis of Replacing Old Machine in Four Years' Time

	Total Present Value	Present Value Discount Factors at 10%	Sketch of Relevant After-Tax Cash Flows				
End of Year:			0	1	2	3	4
Explanations for the after-tax cash flow amounts are given on pp. 854–855.							
a. Initial machine investment	$ 0	◄ 1.000 ◄	$0				
c. After-tax cash flow from immediate proceeds of disposition	0	◄ 1.000 ◄	0				
e. Recurring after-tax cash operating flows	(554,750)	◄ 3.170 ◄⋯⋯⋯	$(175,000)	$(175,000)	$(175,000)	$(175,000)	
f. Cash flow from proceeds of disposition in four years' time	4,098	◄ 0.683 ◄⋯⋯⋯⋯⋯⋯⋯⋯⋯					6,000
g. Lost tax shield from the disposal in four years' time	(783)	◄ 0.683 ◄⋯⋯⋯⋯⋯⋯⋯⋯⋯					($1,146)
Total present value of all cash flows if Potato Supreme replaces the old machine in four years' time	$(551,435)						

Note: Parentheses denote relevant cash outflows throughout all exhibits in this chapter.

$$(\$6,000 \times 0.30) \times \frac{0.20}{(0.20 + 0.10)} \times \frac{2 + 0.10}{2(1 + 0.10)}$$
$$= \$1,800 \times 2 \div 3 \times 0.955 = \$1,146$$

Exhibit 22-4 presents all after-tax cash flows that would arise if Potato Supreme continued to use the old packaging machine. Each cash flow is multiplied by its corresponding present value discount factor to give its present value. The total present value is $(551,435).

◆ **Step 2:** *Calculate the present value of total cash flows of immediately replacing the old packaging machine.*

a. *Initial machine investment.* The original cost of the new packaging machine is $200,000. This amount appears as a cash outflow in year 0 in Exhibit 22-5, item a (p. 856).

b. *Tax shield.* The original cost of $200,000 will generate a cash savings from capital cost allowance of $38,160. This amount is determined by using the tax shield formula.

$$(\$200,000 \times 0.30) \times \frac{0.20}{(0.20 + 0.10)} \times \frac{2 + 0.10}{2(1 + 0.10)}$$
$$= \$60,000 \times \frac{2}{3} \times \frac{2.1}{2.2}$$
$$= \$40,000 \times 0.955 = \$38,200$$

Recall that the tax shield formula calculates the present value of the cash flows.

c. *Cash flow from immediate proceeds of disposition.*

Immediate proceeds of disposition $26,000

Review what is included in the present value analysis. It is the immediate *cash inflow* from the proceeds of disposition of the asset. The book value of the old machine and the loss on disposal do not themselves affect cash flow. The book value, however, enters into the calculation of the loss on disposal of the asset, which in turn affects the accounting net income.

EXHIBIT 22-5
Total-Project Approach for Potato Supreme: After-Tax Analysis of Immediately Purchasing the New Machine

	Total Present Value	Present Value Discount Factors at 10%	Sketch of Relevant After-Tax Cash Flows				
End of Year:			0	1	2	3	4
Explanations for the after-tax cash flow amounts are given on pp. 855 and 856.							
a. Initial machine investment	$(200,000) ← 1.000 ←		$(200,000)				
b. Tax shield	38,200 ← 1.000 ←		$ 38,200				
	$(161,800)						
c. Cash flow from immediate proceeds of disposition of old machine	26,000 ← 1.000 ←		$ 26,000				
d. Lost tax shield from immediate disposal of old machine	$ (4,966) ← 1.000 ←		$ (4,966)				
Net investment	$(140,766)						
e. Recurring after-tax cash operating flows	(332,850) ← 3.170 ←----------------			$(105,000)	$(105,000)	$(105,000)	$(105,000)
f. Cash flow from proceeds of disposition of the new machine in four years' time	13,660 ← 0.683 ←---						$20,000
g. Lost tax shield from disposal of the new machine in four years' time	(2,732) ← 0.683 ←---						(4.000)
Total present value of all cash flows if Potato Supreme immediately replaces the old machine	$(462,688)						

d. *Lost tax shield from immediate disposal of old machine.* The current disposal of $26,000 would reduce the cash savings from future capital cost allowance by $4,966.

$$(\$26,000 \times 0.30) \times \frac{0.20}{0.20 + 0.10} \times \frac{2 + 0.10}{2(1 + 0.10)}$$

$$= \$7,800 \times \frac{2}{3} \times 0.955$$

$$= \$4,966$$

In this case, the half-year rule applies to the calculation of the tax shield formula because the net addition is a positive number ($200,000 − $26,000).

e. *Recurring after-tax cash operating flows.*

Recurring cash operating flows (costs) for the new machine	$(150,000)
Deduct: Income tax savings (30% × $150,000)	45,000
Recurring after-tax cash operating flows	$(105,000)

The after-tax cash operating flows of $(105,000) in years 1 to 4 appear as relevant cash outflows in Exhibit 22-5, item e.

f. *Cash flow from proceeds of disposition of new machine. Other assets remain in this asset class.*

Proceeds from disposition of new machine	$20,000

g. *Lost tax shield from disposition of new machine in four years' time.* Assume no future replacement for the new machine. Therefore, the net addition ($0 − $20,000) will be negative and the half-year rule will not apply. The proceeds of disposition

EXHIBIT 22-6

Differential Approach for Potato Supreme: After-Tax Analysis of Replacing Old Machine

	Total Present Value	Present Value Discount Factors at 10%	Sketch of Relevant After-Tax Cash Flows				
End of Year:			**0**	**1**	**2**	**3**	**4**
Explanations for the after-tax inflow amounts are given on pp. 856 and 857.							
a. Initial machine investment	$(200,000) ← 1.000 ←		$(200,000)				
c. Cash flow from immediate proceeds of disposition of old machine	26,000 ← 1.000 ←		26,000				
Net initial investment	(174,000)		(174,000)				
b. net of d. Tax shield (Exhibit 22-5)	33,234 ← 1.000 ←		33,234				
	(140,766)						
e. Recurring after-tax cash operating flows	221,900	3.170		$70,000	$70,000	$70,000	$70,000
f. Cash flow from proceeds of disposition of old machine in four years' time	(4,098) ← 0.683 ◄-----						$ (6,000)
g. Lost tax shield from disposal of old machine in four years' time	783 ← 0.683 ◄-----						$ 1,146
	(3,315)						
f. Cash flow from proceeds of disposition of new machine in four years' time = ($551,435 − $462,688) = $88,747	13,660 ← 0.683 ◄-----						$20,000
g. Lost tax shield from disposal of new machine in four years' time	(2,732) ← 0.683 ◄-----						$ (4,000)
	10,928						
Net present value if old machine is replaced immediately	$ 88,747						

of $20,000 would reduce the future cash savings from CCA at the maximum rate of 20% by $2,732.

$$(\$20,000 \times 0.30) \times \frac{0.20}{(0.20 + 0.10)}$$

$$= \$6,000 \times \frac{2}{3} = \$4,000$$

Exhibit 22-5 summarizes the relevant after-tax cash flows that would occur if Potato Supreme replaced its old machine immediately. Present values are derived by multiplying cash flows by the corresponding present value discount factors. The total present value of cash flows equals $(462,688). Recall from Exhibit 22-4 that the present value of after-tax cash flows of replacing the old machine in four years' time is $(551,435). The decision to replace the old machine with the new machine immediately has a positive net present value of $88,747 ($551,435 − $462,688) and is therefore preferred.

Differential Approach

Unlike the two-step total-project approach, the differential approach is a one-step method that includes only those cash inflows and outflows that *differ* between the two alternatives. The differential approach compares the cash outflows arising from replacing the old machine with the *savings* in future cash outflows resulting from using the new machine rather than the old machine. We will now examine the differences in cash flows between the keep and replace alternatives in the Potato Supreme example using the categories of cash flows that we described earlier.

a. *Initial machine investment* of $200,000 for the new machine (see Exhibit 22-5) appears as a cash outflow in year 0 in Exhibit 22-6, item a.

c. *Cash flow from immediate proceeds of disposition of old machine* of $26,000 (see Exhibit 22-5) appears as a cash inflow in year 0 in Exhibit 22-6, item c. The initial machine investment, $200,000, minus the cash flow from current disposal of the old machine, $26,000, is the net initial investment of $174,000, shown as a cash outflow in year 0 in Exhibit 22-6.

b. net of d. *Tax shield.* The net initial investment of $174,000 would increase the CCA pool by this amount and thus would generate cash savings from CCA from now to infinity. The cash savings would be $33,199, a figure determined by using the tax shield formula:

$$(\$174,000 \times 0.30) \times \frac{0.20}{(0.20 + 0.10)} \times \frac{(2 + 0.10)}{2(1 + 0.10)}$$

$$= \$52,200 \times \frac{2}{3} \times 0.955$$

$$= \$33,234$$

e. *Recurring after-tax cash operating flows.* Replacing the old machine results in lower after-tax cash operating costs, as follows:

Recurring after-tax cash operating costs if old machine kept (Exhibit 22-4, item e)	$175,000
Deduct: Recurring after-tax cash operating costs if machine replaced (Exhibit 22-5, item e)	105,000
Savings in recurring after-tax cash operating costs if machine replaced	$ 70,000

Exhibit 22-6, item e, shows this $70,000 increase in recurring after-tax cash operating flows in years 1–4.

f. net of g. *Cash flow from proceeds of disposition of each machine in four years' time, net of the lost tax shield of each respective disposal.* The immediate disposition of the old machine results in no disposition of this machine in four years' time. This opportunity cost for the old machine based on Exhibit 22-4 is $3,315 ($4,098 − $793) for the old machine. The opportunity cost for the new machine based on Exhibit 22-5 is $10,928 ($13,550 − $2,732).

In Exhibit 22-5, the terminal disposal of the new machine for $20,000 will result in a lost tax shield of $2,732, the net of which is $10,928.

Both the total-project approach (Exhibits 22-4 and 22-5) and the differential approach (Exhibit 22-6) result in a net present value of $88,747 in favour of immediately replacing the old packaging machine with the new one. When comparing alternatives, these two approaches will always give the same net present value.

CAPITAL BUDGETING AND INFLATION

OBJECTIVE 5

Distinguish between the real rate of return and the nominal rate of return

Inflation. The decline in the general purchasing power of the monetary unit.

Inflation can be defined as the decline in the general purchasing power of the monetary unit (for example, the dollar in Canada or the yen in Japan). An inflation rate of 10% in one year means that what you could buy with $100 (say) at the start of the year will cost you $110 [$100 + (10% × $100)] at the end of the year. Prices increase as more money chases fewer goods. Some countries—for example, Brazil, Israel, Mexico, and Russia—have experienced annual inflation rates of 15% to more than 100%. Even an annual inflation rate of 5% over, say, a five-year period can result in sizable declines in the general purchasing power of the monetary unit over that time.

Why is it important to account for inflation in capital budgeting? Because declines in the general purchasing power of the monetary unit (say, dollars) will inflate future cash flows above what they would have been had there been no inflation. These inflated cash flows will cause the project to look better than it is, unless the analyst recognizes that the inflated cash flows are measured in dollars that have lesser value than the dollars that were initially invested. We now examine how inflation can be explicitly recognized in capital budgeting analysis.

Real and Nominal Rates of Return

When analyzing inflation, distinguish between the real rate of return and the nominal rate of return:

- ◆ **Real rate of return** is the rate of return required to cover only investment risk.
- ◆ **Nominal rate of return** is the rate of return required to cover investment risk and the anticipated decline, due to inflation, in the general purchasing power of the cash that the investment generates. The rates of return (or interest) earned on the financial markets are nominal rates, because they compensate investors for both risk and inflation.

We next describe the relationship between real and nominal rates of return. Assume that the real rate of return for investments in high-risk cellular data transmission equipment at Network Communications is 20% and that the expected inflation rate is 10%. The nominal rate of return[1] is:

$$\text{Nominal rate} = (1 + \text{Real rate})(1 + \text{Inflation rate}) - 1$$
$$= (1 + 0.20)(1 + 0.10) - 1$$
$$= [(1.20)(1.10)] - 1 = 1.32 - 1 = 0.32$$

The nominal rate of return is also related to the real rate of return and the inflation rate as follows:

Real rate of return	0.20
Inflation rate	0.10
Combination (0.20×0.10)	0.02
Nominal rate of return	0.32

Note that the nominal rate is slightly higher than the real rate (0.20) plus the inflation rate (0.10). Why? Because the nominal rate recognizes that inflation also decreases the purchasing power of the real rate of return earned during the year.

Net Present Value Method and Inflation

The watchwords when incorporating inflation into the net present value (NPV) method is *internal consistency.* There are two internally consistent approaches:

- ◆ *Nominal approach.* Predict cash inflows and outflows in nominal monetary units and use a nominal rate as the required rate of return.
- ◆ *Real approach.* Predict cash inflows and outflows in real monetary units *and* use a real rate as the required rate of return.

Consider an investment that is expected to generate sales of 100 units and a net cash inflow of $1,000 ($10 per unit) each year for two years *absent inflation.* If inflation of 10% is expected each year, net cash inflows from the sale of each unit would be $11 ($10 × 1.10) in year 1 and $12.10 [$11 × 1.10 or $10 × (1.10)^2] in year 2 resulting in net cash inflows of $1,100 in year 1 and $1,210 in year 2. The net cash inflows of $1,100 and $1,210 are nominal cash inflows because they include the impact of inflation. *These are the cash flows recorded by the accounting system.* The cash inflows of $1,000 each year are real cash flows because they exclude inflationary effects. Note that the real cash flows equal the nominal cash flows discounted for inflation, $1,000 = $1,100 ÷ 1.10 = $1,210 ÷ (1.10)^2. Many managers find the nominal approach easier to understand and use, because they observe nominal cash flows in their accounting systems and the nominal rates of return on financial markets.

Let's revisit Network Communications, which is deciding whether to invest in equipment to make and sell a cellular data transmission product. The equipment would cost $750,000 immediately. It is expected to have a four-year useful life with a zero terminal disposal price. An annual inflation rate of 10% is expected over this

---

Real rate of return. The rate of return required to cover only investment risk.

Nominal rate of return. Rate of return required to cover investment risk and the anticipated decline due to inflation in the general purchasing power of the cash that the investment generates.

OBJECTIVE 6

Describe two internally consistent ways to account for inflation in capital budgeting

---

[1]The real rate of return can be expressed in terms of the nominal rate of return as follows:

$$\text{Real rate} = \frac{(1 + \text{Nominal rate})}{(1 + \text{Inflation rate})} - 1 = \frac{(1 + 0.32)}{(1 + 0.10)} - 1 = 0.20$$

four-year period. Network Communications requires an after-tax real rate of return of 20% from this project or an after-tax nominal rate of return of 32%.

The following table presents the predicted amounts of real (assuming no inflation) and nominal (after considering cumulative inflation) net cash inflows from the equipment over the next four years (excluding the $750,000 investment in the equipment and before any income tax payments):

Year	Before-Tax Cash Inflows in Real Dollars (1)	Cumulative Inflation Rate Factor* (2)	Before-Tax Cash Inflows in Nominal Dollars (3) = (1) × (2)
1	$500,000	$(1.10)^1 = 1.1000$	$550,000
2	600,000	$(1.10)^2 = 1.2100$	726,000
3	600,000	$(1.10)^3 = 1.3310$	798,600
4	300,000	$(1.10)^4 = 1.4641$	439,230

*1.10 = 1.00 + 0.10 inflation rate.

The income tax rate is 40%. For tax purposes, the equipment will be amortized using a capital cost allowance rate of 30%, declining balance method.

EXHIBIT 22-7

Nominal Approach to Inflation for Network Communications: Predict Cash Inflows and Outflows in Nominal Dollars and Use a Nominal Discount Rate*

	Total Present Value	Present Value Discount Factors at 32%†	Sketch of Relevant After-Tax Cash Flows

End of Year: 0 1 2 3 4

1. Initial equipment investment:

Year	Investment: Outflows
0	$(750,000)

$(750,000) ◄—1,000000 ◄— $(750,000)

2. Cash savings from tax shield $ 127,631‡ ◄—1,000000 ◄— $ 127,631

3. Recurring after-tax cash operating flows: $(622,369)

Year (1)	Recurring Nominal Cash Operating Inflows (2)	Income Tax Outflows (3) = 0.40 × (2)	Recurring Nominal After-Tax Cash Operating Inflows (4) = (2) − (3)
1	$550,000	$220,000	$330,000
2	726,000	290,400	435,600
3	798,600	319,440	479,160
4	439,230	175,692	263,538

250,000 ◄—0.757576 ◄··············$330,000
250,000 ◄—0.573921 ◄······························$435,600
208,333 ◄—0.434789 ◄···$479,160
86,805 ◄—0.329385 ◄···$263,538
795,138

Net present value $ 172,769

*The nominal discount rate of 32% is made up of the real rate of interest of 20% and the inflation rate of 10%: $[(1 + 0.20)(1 + 0.10)] − 1 = 0.32$.
†Present value discount factors are shown to six decimal digits to emphasize that the approaches to inflation in Exhibits 22-7 and 22-8 are equivalent. The formula on Table 2 of Appendix A is used to compute the present value discount factor.

$$‡\$(750,000 \times 0.40) \frac{0.30}{0.30 + 0.32} \times \frac{2 + 0.32}{2(1 + 0.32)}$$

$= \$300,000 \times 0.484 \times 0.879$

$= \$127,631$.

Exhibit 22-7 presents the capital budgeting approach for predicting cash flows in nominal dollars and using a nominal discount rate.[2] The calculations in Exhibit 22-7 exactly follow the calculations used in the Potato Supreme example for initial machine investment, tax shields, and recurring after-tax cash operating flows.

Exhibit 22-8 presents the approach of predicting cash flows in real terms and using a real discount rate. The calculations for item 3, recurring after-tax cash operating flows, are basically the same as before except that the cash inflows are measured in real terms and discounted at real rates.

Both approaches show that the project has a net present value of $172,769 and should therefore be accepted. Why do the two approaches give the same answer? Because, for example, in going from the real approach to the nominal approach, the cash flows are multiplied by and the discount rates are divided by the same cumulative inflation factor.[3]

> Under the nominal approach, first express all amounts in terms of *future-year dollars* (using cumulative inflation rate factors), then discount the resulting amounts to their present value using *nominal discount-rate factors*.

EXHIBIT 22-8

Real Approach to Inflation for Network Communications: Predict Cash Inflows and Outflows in Real Dollars and Use a Real Discount Rate

	Total Present Value	Present Value Discount Factors at 20%*	Sketch of Relevant After-Tax Cash Flows				
End of Year:			0	1	2	3	4
1. Initial equipment investment:							

Year	Investment Outflows
0	$(750,000)

2. Cash savings from tax shield[†]

3. Recurring after-tax cash operating flows:

$(750,000) ← 1.000000 ← $(750,000)
127,631[‡] ← 1.000000 ← 127,631
$(622,369)

Year (1)	Recurring Real Cash Operating Inflows (2)	Income Tax Outflows (3) = 0.40 × (2)	Recurring Real After-Tax Cash Operating Inflows (4) = (2) − (3)					
1	$500,000	$200,000	$300,000	250,000 ← 0.833333 ← $300,000				
2	600,000	240,000	360,000	250,000 ← 0.694444 ← $360,000				
3	600,000	240,000	360,000	208,333 ← 0.578704 ← $360,000				
4	300,000	120,000	180,000	86,805 ← 0.482253 ← $180,000				

795,138

Net present value $ 172,769

*Present value factors are shown to six decimal digits and the present value calculations rounded to emphasize that the approaches to inflation in Exhibits 22-7 and 22-8 are equivalent. The formula on Table 2 of Appendix A is used to compute the present value discount factor.
†The computation of these inflation factors is explained in footnote 3 below.
‡The tax shield formula has used the nominal rate of 32% for demonstration purposes. It is common for companies to use a nominal rate, even though capital cost allowance amounts are not inflated.

[2]The present value discount factors in the example are calculated using six decimal digits to eliminate doubt about the equivalence of the two approaches. In practice, the present value discount factors (to three decimal digits) can be obtained using Table 2 (present value of $1) of Appendix A at the end of the text. The Problem for Self-Study at the end of this chapter uses Table 2.

[3]For example, recurring after-tax *real* cash operating flow in year 2 of $360,000 in Exhibit 22-8 is multiplied by $(1.10)^2$ to give $435,600 in after-tax *nominal* cash operating flows in year 2 in Exhibit 22-7. The *real* discount rate of 0.694444 in year 2 in Exhibit 22-8 is divided by $(1.10)^2$ to give the nominal discount rate of 0.573921 in year 2 in Exhibit 22-7.

The most frequently encountered error when accounting for inflation in capital budgeting is stating cash inflows and outflows in real monetary units and using a nominal discount rate. This error understates the discounted present value of cash flows that occur in the future and therefore creates a bias against the acceptance of many worthwhile capital investment projects.

PROJECT RISK AND REQUIRED RATE OF RETURN

OBJECTIVE 7

Describe alternative approaches used to recognize the degree of risk in capital budgeting projects

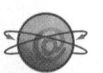

Ontario Power Generation—
Operations
www.opg.com/ops/H_hydro_
overview.asp

The *required rate of return* (RRR), which we discussed in Chapter 21, is a critical variable in discounted cash flow analysis. It is the rate of return that the organization forgoes by investing in a particular project rather than in an alternative project of comparable risk. *Risk* here refers to the business risk of the project, *independent* of the specific manner in which the project is financed—whether with debt or with equity. Here is a safe generalization: The higher the risk, the higher the required rate of return and the faster management would want to recover the net initial investment. Why? Because higher risk means a greater chance that the project may lose money. Management would only be willing to take this added risk if it was compensated with a higher expected return.

The RRR used in discounted cash flow analysis should be internally consistent with the approach applied to predict cash inflows and outflows. The options include various combinations of (1) the real rate and the nominal rate and (2) the pretax and the after-tax rate. The differences among these rates can be sizable, given estimates of inflation that may exceed 10% and corporate tax rates of 30% or more.

Organizations typically use at least one of the following approaches in dealing with the risk factor of projects (see Global Surveys of Company Practice on p. 863):

1. **Varying the required payback time.** Companies such as Nissan that use payback as a project selection criterion vary the required payback to reflect differences in project risk. The higher the risk, the shorter the required payback time. When faced with higher risk, companies also evaluate how to minimize their downside risk if the project is prematurely abandoned before the full cash inflows can be realized. A reason for abandoning a project prematurely arises (as it did for Ontario Power Generation) when government policies regarding environmental protection change and current projects in operation, such as a coal-fired electricity-generating plant, cannot be refurbished (see the Concepts in Action feature on p. 867).[4]

2. **Adjusting the required rate of return.** Companies such as DuPont and Shell Oil use a higher required rate of return when the risk is higher. Estimating a precise risk factor for each project is difficult. Some organizations simplify the task by having three or four general-risk categories (for example, very high, high, average, and low). Each project under consideration is assigned to a specific category. Management uses a predetermined discount rate, assigned to each category, as the required rate of return for projects in that category.

3. **Adjusting the estimated future cash inflows.** Some companies, such as Dow Chemical, reduce the estimated future cash inflows of riskier projects. For example, they may systematically reduce the predicted cash inflows of very-high-risk projects by 30%, high-risk projects by 20%, and average-risk projects by 10%, and make no change to the projected cash inflows of low-risk projects. This approach is called the *certainty equivalent approach*. Since the cash flows for higher-risk projects have already been adjusted downward for their increased riskiness, the RRR used to evaluate those projects is the same as the RRR for low-risk projects. Note how this approach contrasts with adjusting the required rate of return. In that approach, the cash flows are not adjusted for risk, but the RRR is. In the certainty equivalent approach, the cash flows are adjusted for risk, but the RRR is not. Both adjusting the cash flows for risk and then using risk-adjusted RRRs would double-count the risk adjustment.

[4]See J. Grinyer and N. Daing, "The Use of Abandonment Values in Capital Budgeting—A Research Note," *Management Accounting Research* 4 (1993).

Risk Adjustment Methods in Capital Budgeting

How do companies around the globe adjust for risk when evaluating capital investments? The percentages in the following table indicate how frequently particular risk adjustment methods are used in capital budgeting in four countries. The reported percentages exceed 100% because some companies use more than one risk adjustment method. Dashes indicate information was not disclosed in survey.

	Canada*	United States[†]	Australia[‡]	United Kingdom[§]	Taiwan[‖]	Poland[#]
Sensitivity analysis	59%	29%	57%	63%	—	10%
Increase the required rate of return	31%	18%	—	42%	61%	13%
Shorten payback period	24%	17%	—	34%	72%	25%
Estimate probability distribution of future cash flows	18%	12%	11%	15%	—	13%
Compare optimistic and pessimistic forecasts	—	—	63%	—	—	—
Make subjective, nonquantitative assessment	29%	54%	37%	22%	69%	4%
Make no adjustments	10%	37%	—	—	—	—

The surveys indicate that the specific methods managers use vary among countries. A common feature, however, is that managers appear to favour simpler methods (for example, sensitivity analysis, shortening the payback period, increasing the required rate of return, and subjective, nonquantitative assessments) rather than more sophisticated techniques (for example, estimating the probability distribution of future cash flows).

Adapted from: *Jog, V., and A. Srivastava, "Corporate Financial Decision Making in Canada," *Canadian Journal of Administrative Sciences* (1994); [†]Sullivan, C., and K. Smith, "Capital Investment Justification for U.S. Factory Automation Projects," *Journal of the Midwest Finance Association*; [‡]Freeman, M., and G. Hobbes, "Capital Budgeting: Theory versus Practice," *Australian Accountant*; [§]Ho, S., and R. Pike, "Risk Analysis in Capital Budgeting Contexts: Simple or Sophisticated?" *Accounting and Business Research*; [‖]Ho, S., and L. Yang, "Managerial Risk Taking and Handling in Corporate Investment: An Exploratory Study in Taiwan," *Proceedings of the Second International Conference on Asian-Pacific Financial Markets*; [#]Zarzecki, D., and T. Wisniewski, "Investment Appraisal Practice in Poland" (Working Paper, Szcecin University, Szcecin, Poland).

4. **Sensitivity (what-if) analysis.** Companies such as Consumers Energy Company use this approach to examine the consequences of changing key assumptions underlying a capital budgeting project (see the Concepts in Action box on p. 865).

CMS Energy
www.cmsenergy.com/AboutCMS

5. **Estimating the probability distribution of future cash inflows and outflows for each project.** Companies such as Niagara Mohawk use the approach to uncertainty that was discussed in the appendix to Chapter 3. The approach gives due weight to all possible cash flow outcomes to arrive at an expected cash flow and then discounts this amount at the risk-adjusted required rate of return for the investment. Estimating these probability distributions is difficult, but a practical guideline is to limit the number of outcomes under consideration to a small, manageable set. Consider another benefit of estimating the probability distribution of future cash inflows and outflows. Suppose a project has a 60% likelihood of very high cash inflows and a 40% likelihood of minimal cash inflows in its early years. This 40% probability may prompt managers to establish lines of credit with a bank. If the low outcome occurs, these lines of credit would enable the company to avoid a short-run cash flow crisis.

APPLICABILITY TO NOT-FOR-PROFIT ORGANIZATIONS

Discounted cash flow analysis applies to both profit-seeking and not-for-profit organizations. Almost all organizations must decide which investments in long-term assets will accomplish various tasks at the least cost.

Studies of the capital budgeting practices of government agencies at various levels (federal, provincial, and local) and in several countries report that, as in the profit-oriented sector, the following prevails:

1. Urgency is an important factor when allocating funds. For example, capital budgeting for roads is often motivated by physical deficiencies in an existing highway rather than a systematic analysis of alternative road construction projects.

2. Project estimates are sometimes systematically biased. For example, studies report overestimates of the benefits, underestimates of the costs, and underestimates of the time it takes to construct dams and other irrigation infrastructures.

3. There is a tendency to cut capital-budget projects first when there is a strong push to balance a budget or reduce a deficit. Consider the effect of efforts to contain health-care costs in Canada. As a result of these changes and the increased emphasis on controlling hospital charges through competition and regulation, hospitals are increasingly using analytical capital budgeting methods (such as discounted cash flow methods) and are also more carefully auditing the benefits of capital expenditures.

IMPLEMENTING THE NET PRESENT VALUE DECISION RULE

OBJECTIVE 8

Explain the excess present value index and its usefulness in capital budgeting

Excess present value index.
Capital budgeting measure in which the total present value of future net cash inflows of a project is divided by the total present value of the net initial investment.

Executives in both profit-seeking and not-for-profit organizations must frequently work within an overall capital budget limit. This section discusses problems in using the net present value method when there is a restriction on the total funds available for capital spending.

The **excess present value index** (sometimes called the *profitability index*) is the total present value of future net cash inflows of a project divided by the total present value of the net initial investment. The following table illustrates this index for two software graphics packages—Superdraw and Masterdraw—that Business Systems is evaluating:

Project	Present Value at 10% RRR (1)	Net Initial Investment (2)	Excess Present Value Index (3) = (1) ÷ (2)	Net Present Value (4) = (1) − (2)
Superdraw	$1,400,000	$1,000,000	140%	$400,000
Masterdraw	3,900,000	3,000,000	130%	900,000

The excess present value index or profitability index measures the cash flow return per dollar invested. The index is viewed as particularly helpful in choosing between projects when investment funds are limited. Why? Because profitability indexes can identify the projects that will generate the most money from the limited capital available.

Suppose that the developers of each package require that Business Systems market only one software graphics package, so accepting one software package automatically means rejecting the other—that is, the packages are mutually exclusive. Which package should Business Systems choose?

Using the profitability index, Superdraw will be preferred over Masterdraw, because it has a profitability index of 140%, which is higher than the 130% for Masterdraw. But the profitability index analysis assumes that all other things, such as risk and alternative use of funds, are equal. For example, it assumes that choosing between Superdraw and Masterdraw has no effect on the other projects that Business Systems plans to implement. If "all other things" are not "equal," which is often the case, the profitability index may not result in the optimal choice of investment projects.

Continuing the Business Systems example, assume that Business Systems has a total capital budget limit of $5,000,000 for the coming year. It is considering investing in Superdraw or Masterdraw and in any one or more of eight other projects

EXHIBIT 22-9
Allocation of $5,000,000 Capital Budget: Comparison of Two Alternatives for Business Systems

	Alternative 1				Alternative 2		
Project	Net Initial Investment	Excess Present Value Index	Total Present Value at 10%	Project	Net Initial Investment	Excess Present Value Index	Total Present Value at 10%
C	$ 600,000	167%	$1,002,000	C	$ 600,000	167%	$1,002,000
Superdraw	1,000,000	140%	1,400,000				
D	400,000	132%	528,000	D	400,000	132%	528,000
				Masterdraw	3,000,000	130%	3,900,000
F	1,000,000	115%	1,150,000	F	1,000,000	115%	1,150,000
					$5,000,000*		$6,580,000‡
E	800,000	114%	912,000	E	$ 800,000	114%	Reject
B	1,200,000	112%	1,344,000	B	1,200,000	112%	Reject
	$5,000,000*		$6,336,000†				
H	$ 550,000	105%	Reject	H	550,000	105%	Reject
G	450,000	101%	Reject	G	450,000	101%	Reject
I	1,000,000	90%	Reject	I	1,000,000	90%	Reject

*Total budget constraint.
†Net present value = $6,336,000 − $5,000,000 = $1,336,000.
‡Net present value = $6,580,000 − 5,000,000 = $1,580,000.

Risk Analysis in Capital Budgeting Decisions at Consumers Energy Company

Consumers Energy Company (CEC) owns pipelines to distribute natural gas to its customers. About 1,609 of the 32,186 kilometres of Consumers Energy's main pipelines are made of cast iron. Most of CEC's pipelines are made of cathodically protected coated and wrapped steel or of plastic. Gas leaks from cast-iron pipes are almost ten times more than from the other materials. An important capital budgeting decision for CEC is how much of the cast-iron pipes it should replace and when. The benefits of replacing the pipes are lower repairs and maintenance costs and fewer claims following gas leaks, but the precise benefits are far from certain.

To incorporate uncertainty, Consumers Energy estimates a range of values for key parameters—the number of times the pipeline might leak, the quantity of gas that may leak, the dollar claims that may have to be paid, and the repairs and maintenance costs that may be incurred—under each replacement alternative. CEC uses sensitivity analysis to identify the parameters and parameter values that most affect the decision and those that do not. It then develops probability distributions for the key parameters on the basis of structured interviews with experts in different subject areas. CEC calculates net present values for the different alternatives by discounting the expected returns by a risk-adjusted required rate of return. CEC computes net present values on an after-tax basis, using nominal cash flows and nominal discount rates to consistently consider the effects of inflation.

CEC's analysis indicated that the optimal program was to replace the worst cast-iron pipes first and all cast-iron pipes over a 40-year period. In the absence of this detailed and thorough risk-based analysis, CEC's managers would have favoured replacing the cast-iron pipes sooner.

Source: Adapted from Elenbars, K. L., and D. O'Neill, "Formal Decision Analysis Process Guides Maintenance Budgeting," *Pipeline Industry,* October 1994.

(coded B, C, . . . , H, I). Exhibit 22-9 on page 865 presents two alternative combinations of these projects. Note that the project portfolio in alternative 2 is superior to that in alternative 1, despite the greater cash flow return per dollar invested in Superdraw than in Masterdraw. Why? Because the $2,000,000 incremental investment in Masterdraw increases net present value (NPV) by $500,000. The $2,000,000 would otherwise be invested in projects E and B, which have a lower combined NPV of $256,000:

	Present Value	Net Initial Investment	Increase in Net Present Value
Masterdraw	$3,900,000	$3,000,000	
Superdraw	1,400,000	1,000,000	
Increment	$2,500,000	$2,000,000	$500,000
Project E	$ 912,000	$ 800,000	
Project B	1,344,000	1,200,000	
Total	$2,256,000	$2,000,000	$256,000

Note that other than Superdraw, alternative 2 includes projects with the highest excess present value indexes and excludes those with the lowest excess present value indexes. The excess present value index is a useful guide for identifying and choosing projects that will offer the best return on limited capital and that will thereby maximize net present value. But managers cannot base decisions involving mutually exclusive investments of different sizes solely on the excess present value index. The net present value method is the best general guide.

IMPLEMENTING THE INTERNAL RATE-OF-RETURN DECISION RULE

OBJECTIVE 9

Explain why the internal rate-of-return and the net present value decision rules may rank projects differently

The NPV method always indicates the project (or set of projects) that maximizes the NPV of future cash flows. However, surveys of practice report widespread use of the internal rate-of-return (IRR) method. Why? Probably because managers find this method easier to understand and because, in most instances, their decisions would be unaffected by using one method or the other. In some cases, however, the two methods will not indicate the same decision.

Where mutually exclusive projects have unequal lives or unequal investments, the IRR method can rank projects differently from the NPV method. Consider Exhibit 22-10.[5] The ranking by the IRR method favours project X, while the ranking by the NPV method favours project Z. The projects ranked in Exhibit 22-10 differ in both life (5, 10, and 15 years) and net initial investment ($286,400, $419,200, and $509,200).

EXHIBIT 22-10
Ranking of Projects Using Internal Rate of Return and Net Present Value

Project	Life	Net Initial Investment	Annual Cash Flow from Operations, Net of Income Taxes	IRR Method		NPV Method		
				IRR	Ranking	PV of Annual Cash Flow from Operations, Net of Income Taxes	NPV	Ranking
X	5	$286,400	$100,000	22%	1	$379,100	$ 92,700	3
Y	10	419,200	100,000	20	2	614,500	195,300	2
Z	15	509,200	100,000	18	3	760,600	251,400	1

[5]Exhibit 22-10 concentrates on differences in project lives. Similar conflicting results can occur when the terminal dates are the same but the sizes of the net initial investments differ.

Managers using the IRR method implicitly assume that the reinvestment rate is equal to the indicated rate of return for the shortest-lived project. Managers using the NPV method implicitly assume that the funds obtainable from competing projects can be reinvested at the company's required rate of return. The NPV method is generally regarded as conceptually superior. Students should refer to corporate finance texts for more details on these issues, and on the problems of ranking projects with unequal lives or unequal investments.

Capital Budgeting for Pollution Prevention

In response to concerns about the environment, governments have passed many laws to restrict companies' impacts on the environment. Many companies have viewed these laws as imposing costs on them, but attitudes are changing. Companies are increasingly shifting their focus away from pollution control (dealing with the control of environmentally harmful substances) to pollution prevention (minimizing the creation of pollution in the first place, through increased efficiency in the use of materials, energy, water, and other resources). Intelligent use of capital budgeting methods is a key part of this effort.

Suppose a company invests in new manufacturing equipment that allows it to use a less costly and nontoxic direct material. Annual cost savings directly associated with the use of the new equipment include savings in direct material costs and toxic waste disposal. If the capital budgeting analysis ended at this point, however, the investment might show a negative NPV, and the company would, on purely financial grounds, reject the project.

But companies such as DuPont consider other financial benefits. These benefits include cost savings in pollution control activities such as monitoring and testing, permit requirements, and legal compliance reporting. These costs are "hidden" in that they are included in general overhead accounts but typically not identified with specific manufacturing processes. There can also be "hidden" impacts on a company's revenues. For example, the periodic training of employees in pollution control activities adds to costs, and, when there is no idle time, results in lost revenues as a result of having to shut down the plant for a few hours each time a training session is conducted.

Another form of cost savings is the reduction or elimination of various fines or penalties that a company might experience because of noncompliance or accidents. Estimating these costs is more difficult and is generally based on statistical analysis of historical data for the particular company or industry, probability calculations, and professional judgment. Many companies believe an uncertain monetary estimate is probably better than ignoring the potential environmental liability altogether.

Finally, there are more-intangible financial benefits, such as higher revenues from being a more environmentally responsible company. Home Depot buys its lumber products only from a list of "preferred vendors" that it knows to conduct environmentally responsible practices.

Source: D. Jacque Grinnell and Herbert G. Hunt, "Capital Budgeting for Pollution Prevention," *Journal of Cost Management*; Environmental Protection Agency, "Valuing Potential Environmental Liabilities for Managerial Decision Making"; conversations with consulting firm SmithObrien and company managements.

APPENDIX: CCA CLASSES AND RATES

Canada Revenue Agency
www.cra-arc.gc.ca/E/pub/
tp/it285r2/it285r2-e.html

CCA Classes
www.cra-arc.gc.ca/tax/
business/topics/solepartner/
reporting/capital/classes-e.html

Companies may claim up to the percentages shown of the UCC in any year for the specified class of tangible assets (see the table below). The legislation regarding CCA only allows this annual deduction if the asset can be classified under the act; otherwise no deduction is permitted. In establishing the initial value of the asset, if the company has or is entitled to receive financial assistance to acquire the asset, then the dollar value of this assistance may reduce the asset's initial value. In addition, if during the useful life of the asset its value is reappraised downwards, then the UCC must also decrease.

Class	Maximum CCA	Tangible Assets in Pool
1	4%	Buildings or other structures, including component parts acquired after 1987
3	5%	Buildings or other structures, including component parts acquired before 1988
8	20%	Miscellaneous tangible capital property and machinery or equipment not included in another class
9	25%	Electrical generating equipment, radar and radio equipment acquired before 1976
10	30%	Automotive equipment and general-purpose electronic data processing equipment with its systems software
12	100%	Tools or utensils costing less than $200, videotape, certified feature films, computer software
29		Property used in manufacturing or processing acquired before 1988 (2 years straight-line)
39		Property used in manufacturing or processing acquired after 1987 (1988–40%; 1989–35%; 1990–30%; after 1990–25%)

PROBLEM FOR SELF-STUDY

This is a comprehensive review problem. It illustrates both income tax factors and capital budgeting with inflation.

PROBLEM
Stone Aggregates (SA) operates 92 plants producing a crushed stone that is used in many construction projects. Transportation is a major cost item. A scale clerk weighs the products and, on a delivery ticket, records details of the product shipped: its weight, its freight charges, and whether or not it is taxed.

SA is considering a proposal to use computerized delivery ticket–writing equipment at each of its 92 plants. One plant has used the equipment as a pilot site for the past 12 months, generating cash operating cost savings (before taxes) of $300,000 by improving productivity and by reducing plant operating costs and excess shipments to customers. The cost analyst estimates that if the equipment had been in use at all of the company's plants for the past year, net cost savings would have been $25 million (expressed in today's dollars).

The cost of the equipment for all 92 plants is $45 million, which would be payable immediately. This equipment has an expected useful life of four years and a terminal disposal price of $10 million (expressed in today's dollars). The equipment qualifies for a capital cost allowance rate of 25% declining balance. Stone Aggregates expects a 30% income tax rate in each of the next four years.

REQUIRED
1. Does the proposal for the computerized delivery ticket-writing equipment meet SA's 16% after-tax required rate-of-return criterion? This rate of return includes an 8% inflation component. (The real rate of return is 7.4%; recall that nominal rate of return = $[(1 + 0.074)(1 + 0.08)] - 1 = 0.16$.) This 8%

inflation prediction applies to both the cost savings and the terminal disposal price of the equipment. Compute the NPV using nominal dollars and a nominal required rate of return.

2. What other factors would you recommend that SA consider when evaluating the computerized delivery ticket-writing equipment?

SOLUTION

1. Exhibit 22-11 shows the NPV computations. To illustrate an alternative presentation found in practice, the format of Exhibit 22-11 differs from that of Exhibits 22-4, 22-5, and 22-6 (pp. 855, 856, and 857). The proposal for computerized delivery ticket–writing equipment has an NPV of $29,560 million, indicating that—on the basis of financial factors—it is an attractive investment.

2. The analysis in Exhibit 22-11 assumes that net cash savings are $25 million each year. However, operating and implementation costs in the year of changeover to new computerized equipment are often 200% higher than in subsequent years. Consequently, net cash savings may be lower in the first year.

EXHIBIT 22-11
Net Present Value Analysis of Computerized Delivery Ticket-Writing System for Stone Aggregates (in Thousands; n.d. = Nominal Dollars)

	A	B	C	D	E	F
		Total	End of	End of	End of	End of
		Present Value	Year 1	Year 2	Year 3	Year 4
3	**Recurring After-Tax Cash Operating Flows**					
4	1. Recurring cash operating savings (real dollars)	$ –	$25,000	$25,000	$25,000	$25,000
5	2. Cumulative inflation factor (from Table 1, Appendix A for 8%)	–	1.080	1.166	1.260	1.360
6	3. Cash operating savings (n.d.): 1 × 2		$27,000	$29,150	$31,500	$34,000
7	4. Tax payments: 30% × 3		8,100	8,745	9,450	10,200
8	5. Recurring after-tax cash operating savings (n.d.): 3 – 4		$18,900	$20,405	$22,050	$23,800
9	6. Present value discount factor (16% nominal)		0.862	0.743	0.641	0.552
10	7. P.V. of recurring after-tax cash operating savings (n.d.): 5 × 6	$ 58,726	$16,292	$15,161	$14,134	$13,138
11						
12	**Initial Equipment Investment**					
13	New equipment	$(45,000)				
14	Tax shield	7,664*				
15	After tax cash flow effect of equipment investment	(37,336)				
16	Terminal disposal	10,000				
17	Lost tax shield	(1,829)[†]				
18	After tax cash flow effect of terminal disposal	(8,171)				
19	Net present value	$ 29,560				
20						
21	*Tax shield = ($45,000 × 0.30) × $\dfrac{0.25}{0.25 + 0.16}$ × $\dfrac{(2 + 0.16)}{2(1 + 0.16)}$ = $7,664					
22	†Lost tax shield = ($10,000 × 0.30) × $\dfrac{0.25}{0.25 + 0.16}$ = $1,829					
23	(Half-year rule does not apply to disposals.)					

The following decision guidelines use a question-and-answer format to summarize the chapter's main points. Each decision presents a key question. The guideline is the answer to that question.

DECISIONS	GUIDELINES
1. How are operating cash flows affected by income taxes?	Operating cash flows are multiplied by a rate of 1 minus the tax rate to obtain the after-tax operating cash flows.
2. What is capital cost allowance (CCA)?	CCA is the ITA equivalent of amortization. It is the only legally allowable deduction permitted when a corporation calculates the net taxable income on which income taxes will be based.
3. Is an accounting gain on the sale of a capital asset relevant to an assessment of the relevant cash flows related to a new capital project?	No. Accounting gains and losses on the sale of capital assets have no cash flow implications. They are relevant in computing accounting income but are not relevant to an assessment of the cash flows.
4. What is the essential difference between the total-project approach and the differential approach to capital budgeting decisions?	The essential difference is that the total-project approach compares the sum of all of the cash flows between two projects while the differential approach examines the differences in cash flows for each type of cash flow that varies between two projects.
5. What is included in the nominal rate of return that is not in the real rate of return?	The nominal rate of return includes the anticipated rate of inflation due to changes in the general purchasing power of the cash flows.
6. To recognize the impact of inflation, what must be done when using the nominal approach?	In using the nominal approach, the nominal rate of return must be used and applied to cash flows that have been inflated by recognizing the anticipated rates of inflation.
7. Why is it important to recognize risk when evaluating capital budgeting projects?	Risk is an important consideration because riskier projects should require a higher rate of return to compensate for the additional risk.
8. What is the excess present value index?	The excess present value index is the total present value of future net cash inflows of a project divided by the present value of the net initial investment.
9. Under what condition can the internal rate-of-return (IRR) and the net present value (NPV) methods rank projects differently?	Different rankings of projects can arise when mutually exclusive projects have unequal lives or unequal investments.

TERMS TO LEARN

This chapter contains definitions of the following important terms:

capital cost allowance (CCA) (p. 849)
cumulative eligible capital (CEC) (p. 851)
cumulative eligible capital
    amount (CECA) (p. 851)
differential approach (p. 853)
eligible capital property (p. 851)
excess present value index (p. 864)
half-year rule (p. 849)

inflation (p. 858)
marginal income tax rate (p. 848)
net addition (p. 854)
nominal rate of return (p. 859)
real rate of return (p. 859)
tax shield formula (p. 849)
total-project approach (p. 854)
unamortized capital cost (UCC) (p. 849)

ASSIGNMENT MATERIAL

QUESTIONS

22-1 Describe three types of cash flows affected by income taxes.

22-2 "It doesn't matter what accounting amortization method is used. The total dollar tax bills are the same." Do you agree? Explain.

22-3 Give examples of four categories of cash flows considered in capital budgeting analyses.

22-4 Distinguish between the total-project approach and the differential approach to choosing between two capital budgeting projects.

22-5 "Accounting amortization is an irrelevant factor in deciding whether to replace an existing delivery vehicle with a more energy-efficient vehicle." Do you agree? Explain.

22-6 "Income taxes only play a role in capital budgeting because of capital cost allowance tax savings." Do you agree? Explain.

22-7 What are the two basic types of capital cost allowance classes?

22-8 Distinguish between the *nominal* rate of return and the *real* rate of return.

22-9 What are the two internally consistent approaches to incorporating inflation into DCF analysis?

22-10 What approaches might be used to recognize risk in capital budgeting?

22-11 "In practice there is no single rate that a given company can use as a guide for sifting among all projects." Do you agree? Explain.

22-12 "Discounted cash flow techniques are relevant only to profit-seeking organizations." Do you agree? Explain.

22-13 "The excess present value index or profitability index is a useful guide when allocating limited funds among projects." Do you agree? Explain.

22-14 "The net present value method and the internal rate-of-return method always rank different projects identically." Do you agree? Explain.

EXERCISES

22-15 New equipment purchase. Presentation Graphics prepares slides and other aids for individuals making presentations. It estimates it can save $42,000 a year in cash operating costs for the next five years if it buys a special-purpose colour-slide workstation at a cost of $90,000. The workstation qualifies for a capital cost allowance rate of 25%, declining balance, and will have a zero terminal disposal price at the end of year 5. Presentation Graphics has a 12% after-tax required rate of return. Its income tax rate is 40% each year for the next five years.

REQUIRED
Compute (a) net present value, (b) payback period, and (c) internal rate of return.

22-16 Multiple choice. (CPA, adapted) The Apex Company is evaluating a capital budgeting proposal for the current year. The relevant data are as follows:

Year	Present Value of an Annuity of $1 in Arrears at 15%
1	$0.870
2	1.626
3	2.284
4	2.856
5	3.353
6	3.785

The initial equipment investment would be $36,000. Apex would amortize the equipment for accounting purposes on a straight-line basis over six years with a zero terminal disposal price. The before-tax annual cash inflow arising from this investment is $12,000. The income tax rate is 40%, and income tax is paid the same year as incurred. The capital investment qualifies for a capital cost allowance rate of 20%, declining balance. The after-tax required rate of return is 15%. Choose the best answer for each question and show your computations.

1. What is the after-tax accrual accounting rate of return on Apex's initial equipment investment? (a) 10%, (b) 16⅔%, (c) 26⅔%, (d) 33⅓%.

2. What is the after-tax payback period (in years) for Apex's capital budgeting proposal? (a) 5, (b) 2.6, (c) 3, (d) 2.

3. What is the net present value of Apex's capital budgeting proposal? (a) $(7,290), (b) $(1,056), (c) $7,850, (d) $11,760.

4. How much would Apex have had to invest five years ago at 15% compounded annually to have $36,000 now?

(a) $12,960, (b) $17,892, (c) $20,592, (d) cannot be determined from the information given.

22-17 Automated materials-handling capital project, income taxes, sensitivity analysis.
Ontime Distributors operates a large distribution network for health-related products. It is considering an automated materials-handling (AMH) proposal for its major warehouse

to reduce storage space, labour costs, and product damage. The before-tax net cash operating savings from the automation are estimated to be $3.0 million a year. The AMH equipment will cost $7.2 million, payable immediately. The equipment has a useful life of four years and a zero terminal disposal price. The lease on the warehouse expires in four years and is not expected to be renewed. The company has an income tax rate of 40% and an after-tax required rate of return of 12%. Under existing tax laws, the $7.2-million equipment cost qualifies for a capital cost allowance rate of 30%, declining balance.

REQUIRED

1. Compute (a) the net present value and (b) the payback period on the automated materials-handling project.
2. Calculate the minimum annual before-tax net cash operating savings that will make the AMH equipment desirable from a net present value standpoint.
3. What other factors should Ontime Distributors consider in its decision?

22-18 Total project versus differential approach, income taxes. A manufacturer of automobile parts acquired a special-purpose shaping machine for automatically producing a particular part. The machine has been used for one year. It will have no useful economic life after three more years. It cost $105,600, has a current disposal price of $34,800, and has a terminal disposal price of $7,200.

A new machine has become available and is far more efficient than the present machine. It would cost $75,600, would cut annual cash operating costs from $72,000 to $48,000, and would have zero terminal disposal price at the end of its useful life of three years. The applicable income tax rate is 30%. The after-tax required rate of return is 14%.

These machines qualify for a capital cost allowance rate of 20%, declining balance.

REQUIRED

Using the net present value method, show whether the new machine should be purchased (a) under a total project approach and (b) under a differential approach.

22-19 Selling plant, income taxes. (CMA, adapted) Waterford Specialties Corporation, a clothing manufacturer, has a plant that will become idle on December 31, 2006. John Landry, corporate controller, has been asked to look at three options regarding the disposal of the plant.

◆ **Option 1.** The plant, which has been fully amortized for financial reporting, can be sold immediately for $10.8 million.
◆ **Option 2.** The plant can be leased to Auburn Mills, one of Waterford's suppliers, for four years. Under the terms of the lease, Auburn would pay Waterford $240,000 per month in rent and would grant Waterford a special 10% discount off the normal price of $2.40 per metre on 2.37 million metres of fabric purchased by another Waterford plant. Auburn would cover all the plant's ownership costs including property taxes. Waterford expects to sell this plant for $2.4 million at the end of the four-year lease.
◆ **Option 3.** The plant could be used for four years to make souvenir jackets for the 2010 Olympics. Fixed overhead, before any equipment upgrades, is estimated to be $240,000 annually for the four-year period. The jackets are expected to sell for $50.40 each. Unit variable costs are expected to be as follows: direct materials, $24.96; direct manufacturing, marketing, and distribution labour, $7.68; variable manufacturing, marketing, and distribution overhead, $6.96.

The following production and sales of jackets are expected: 2007, 200,000 units; 2008, 300,000 units; 2009, 400,000 units; 2010, 100,000 units. To manufacture the souvenir jackets, some of the plant equipment would have to be upgraded at an immediate cost of $1.8 million to be amortized for financial reporting purposes using straight-line amortization over the four years it will be in use. Because of the modernization of the equipment, Waterford could sell the plant for $3.6 million at the end of four years. The equipment qualifies for a 25% declining balance capital cost allowance rate.

Waterford treats all cash flows as if they occur at the end of the year and uses an after-tax cost of capital of 12%. Waterford is subject to a 40% tax rate.

REQUIRED

1. Would you use the total project approach or the differential approach to choose among the three options? Why?
2. Calculate the net present value of each of the options available to Waterford and determine which option Waterford should select using the net present value criterion.
3. What nonfinancial and qualitative factors should Waterford consider before making its choice?

22-20 Project risk, required rate of return. Esso Petroleum is considering two investment projects. The first project, viewed as a high-risk investment, is drilling equipment for oil exploration activities. Esso expects the drilling equipment to cost $1.2 million and result in operating cash flows before taxes of $444,000 per year for five years. The equipment has a five-year life and a terminal disposal price of zero.

    The second project, viewed as a low-risk investment, is production equipment that will improve the yield in Esso's refinery. Esso expects the production equipment to cost $960,000 and result in operating cash flows before taxes of $360,000 per year for four years. The equipment has a four-year life and a terminal disposal price of zero. Esso's income tax rate is 30%. The production and drilling equipment capital cost allowance rate is 25%, declining balance.

REQUIRED

1. Which project has the higher net present value if Esso uses an after-tax required rate of return (RRR) of 12% for both projects?
2. A manager at Esso objects to the calculations in requirement 1 arguing that riskier investments should have a higher RRR. Suppose Esso requires an 18% after-tax RRR for high-risk investments and a 12% after-tax RRR for low-risk investments. Which project has the higher net present value?
3. Which project do you favour? Why?

22-21 Income taxes, inflation. James Delusio, plant manager of Peoria Metal Works, is considering an investment in special tools of $240,000 on December 31, 2007. The tools have an estimated useful life of four years and a $24,000 terminal disposal price. The tools will enable Peoria to manufacture drill bits to very high tolerances without incurring any incremental costs, and to earn additional cash flows of $2.40 per unit in 2008, $2.54 in 2009, $2.70 in 2010, and $2.86 in 2011. Peoria expects to sell 35,000 units each year for the next four years. Peoria is subject to a 40% tax rate. The after-tax required rate of return is 18%. The tools qualify for a capital cost allowance rate of 35%, declining balance.

REQUIRED

1. Compute the net present value of the project.
2. Delusio feels that inflation will persist for the next four years at the rate of 6% per year. However, the 18% minimum desired rate of return already includes a return required to cover the effects of anticipated inflation. Repeat requirement 1, to take inflationary effects into consideration.
3. Could you have taken inflation into account in a way different from what you did in requirement 2? Broadly describe how without actually performing any calculations.

22-22 Inflation and not-for-profit institution, no tax aspects. Eastern University is considering the purchase of a photocopying machine for $4,200 on December 31, 2007. It has a useful life of five years, has a zero terminal disposal price, and is amortized on a straight-line basis. The cash operating savings are expected to be $1,200 annually, measured in December 31, 2007, dollars. The discount factor is 18.8%, which includes the effects of anticipated inflation of 10%. The university pays no taxes. The present values of $1 discounted at 18.8% received at the end of 1, 2, 3, 4, and 5 periods are 0.842, 0.709, 0.596, 0.502, and 0.423.

REQUIRED

1. A university official computed the net present value of the project using an 18.8% discount rate without adjusting the cash operating savings for inflation. What net present value figure did he compute? Is this approach correct? If not, how would you redo the analysis?
2. (a) What is the real rate of return required by Eastern University for investing in the photocopying machine? (b) Calculate the net present value using the real rate of return approach to incorporating inflation.
3. Compare your analyses in requirements 1 and 2. Present generalizations that seem applicable about the analysis of inflation in capital budgeting.

22-23 Excess present value index. The Bristol Company is a design engineering firm that specializes in designing different types of application-specific chips for the semiconductor industry. It is considering buying new design equipment and has identified two mutually exclusive options, Design Pro and Easychip. It is also considering other capital investments (coded C and D). The following table describes the financial characteristics of these projects:

Project	Present Value of Cash Inflows at 14% Required Rate of Return	Net Initial Investment
Design Pro	$ 900,000	$600,000
Easychip	1,260,000	900,000
Project C	702,000	540,000
Project D	384,000	240,000

REQUIRED

1. For each project, calculate (a) the net present value and (b) the excess present value index. On the basis of the excess present value index only, should Bristol choose Design Pro or Easychip?
2. Supposing Bristol must choose one of Design Pro or Easychip, and supposing Bristol has a capital investment budget of $1,140,000, which projects should Bristol choose?
3. Comment on your answers to requirements 1 and 2.

22-24 Comparison of projects with unequal lives. The manager of the Robin Hood Company is considering two investment projects that are mutually exclusive. The after-tax required rate of return of this company is 10%, and the anticipated cash flows are as follows:

| | | Cash Inflows | | | |
Project No.	Investment Required Now	Year 1	Year 2	Year 3	Year 4
1	$12,000	$14,400	$0	$0	$ 0
2	12,000	0	0	0	21,000

REQUIRED

1. Compute the internal rate of return of both projects. Which project is preferable?
2. Compute the net present value of both projects. Which project is preferable?
3. Comment briefly on the results in requirements 1 and 2. Be specific in your comparisons.

PROBLEMS

22-25 Equipment replacement, income taxes. (CMA, adapted) VacuTech manufactures testing instruments for microcircuits. These instruments sell for $4,200 each. VacuTech incurs cash operating costs of $2,940 to manufacture these instruments. On January 1, 2005, VacuTech bought a vacuum pump for $480,000. VacuTech is considering the purchase of a new, more efficient pump on January 1, 2009 (4 years later). The new pump costs $744,000. The pump qualifies for a capital cost allowance rate of 25%, declining balance. The new pump is expected to have a terminal disposal price of $96,000 at the end of four years. At current rates of production, the new pump's greater efficiency will result in annual cash savings of $150,000.

The old pump will be fully amortized for accounting purposes by December 31, 2008, but it can still be used for another four years. It has a current disposal price of $60,000. If it is used for another four years, the pump's terminal disposal price will be zero.

VacuTech is able to sell all the testing instruments it produces. Because of the increased speed of the new pump, output is expected to increase by 30 units in 2009, 50 units in 2010 and 2011, and 70 units in 2012. Over and above the annual cash savings at current production levels, VacuTech's cash manufacturing costs will decrease by $180 per unit on all *additional* units produced.

VacuTech is subject to a 40% tax rate. VacuTech's after-tax required rate of return is 16%.

REQUIRED

1. Determine whether VacuTech should purchase the new pump by calculating the net present value at January 1, 2009, of the estimated after-tax cash flows that would result from the acquisition.
2. Describe the nonfinancial and qualitative factors that VacuTech should consider before making the pump replacement decision.

22-26 Replacement of a machine, income taxes, sensitivity. (CMA, adapted) The WRL Company operates a snack food centre at the Hartsfield Airport. On January 2, 2005, WRL purchased a special cookie-cutting machine, which has been used for three years. WRL is considering purchasing a newer, more efficient machine. If purchased, the new machine would be acquired today on January 2, 2008. WRL expects to sell 300,000 cookies in each of the next four years. The selling price of each cookie is expected to average $0.60.

WRL has two options: (1) continue to operate the old machine or (2) sell the old machine and purchase the new machine. The seller of the new machine offered no tradein.

The following information has been assembled to help management decide which option is more desirable:

	Old Machine	New Machine
Initial machine investment	$96,000	$144,000
Terminal disposal price at the end of useful life assumed for amortization purposes	$12,000	$24,000
Useful life from date of acquisition	7 years	4 years
Expected annual cash operating costs:		
Variable cost per cookie	$0.24	$0.168
Total fixed costs	$18,000	$16,800
Amortization method used for accounting purposes	Straight-line	Straight-line
Estimated disposal prices of machines:		
January 2, 2008	$48,000	$144,000
December 31, 2011	$8,400	$24,000
Capital cost allowance rate (declining balance)	25%	25%

WRL has a 40% income tax rate and an after-tax required rate of return of 16%.

REQUIRED

1. Use the net present value method to determine whether WRL should retain the old machine or acquire the new machine.
2. How much more or less would the recurring after-tax variable cash operating savings have to be for WRL to exactly earn the 16% after-tax required rate of return? Assume all other data about the investment does not change.
3. Assume that the financial differences between the net present values of the two options are so slight that WRL is indifferent between the two proposals. Identify and discuss the non-financial and qualitative factors that WRL should consider.

22-27 Capital budgeting, make versus buy, income taxes, relevant costs. (CMA, adapted) The Jonfran Company manufactures three different models of paper shredders. Each has a waste container. Jonfran estimates the following number of waste containers needed over the next five years: 2007, 50,000; 2008, 50,000; 2009, 52,000; 2010, 55,000; 2011, 55,000.

The equipment used to manufacture waste containers must be replaced because it has broken. The old equipment has a current disposal price of $1,800. The new equipment would cost $1,152,000. The equipment would go into service on January 1, 2007, and would have a five-year useful life. Under the prevailing tax laws, capital cost allowance is calculated on the double-declining-balance method at a rate of 25%. The terminal disposal at the end of five years is estimated at $14,400.

Jonfran's current manufacturing costs for waste containers are as follows:

Direct materials		$12.00
Direct manufacturing labour		9.60
Variable manufacturing overhead		4.80
Fixed manufacturing overhead:		
Supervision	$2.40	
Amortization on old equipment	3.60	
General administrative overhead	7.20	13.20
Total manufacturing cost per unit		$39.60

An outside supplier has offered to supply all the containers that Jonfran needs over the next five years at a fixed price of $34.80 per container. If the supplier's offer is accepted, Jonfran would not need to replace the equipment.

If the waste containers are purchased outside, the salary and benefits of one supervisor, included in the fixed overhead at $54,000, would be eliminated. There would, however, be no change in general administrative overhead. Jonfran has no alternative use for the extra space that would become available if the containers were purchased from outside. Working capital requirements are approximately the same whether the containers are made or purchased.

Jonfran has a 40% income tax rate. Its after-tax required rate of return on new equipment is 12%.

REQUIRED

1. Use a net present value analysis to determine whether Jonfran should purchase the waste containers from the outside supplier or purchase the new equipment.
2. What nonfinancial and qualitative factors should Jonfran consider before coming to a decision?

22-28 Capital budgeting, inventory changes. (M. Wolfson, J. Harris, adapted) Total Fitness is a small company that makes products for physical fitness. The company is considering whether to add a new line of running shoes to be sold to retail stores. To produce these shoes, special machines costing a total of $131,040 must be acquired. The machines have a useful life of four years, with a combined terminal disposal price of $21,600. The new line of shoes would be dropped at the end of four years. The estimates for the new product line are as follows:

Year	Units Produced	Units Sold	Variable Selling Price	Manufacturing Costs per Unit
1	7,000	6,000	$30.00	$14.40
2	6,500	6,200	30.00	15.60
3	6,500	7,700	28.80	16.80
4	3,000	3,100	26.40	18.00
	23,000	23,000		

Variable marketing, distribution, and customer service costs are estimated at $3.60 per unit and are not expected to change over the four-year period. The selling price data and all cost estimates are expressed in nominal dollars. Accounts receivable and current liabilities are expected to be minimal.

For tax purposes, the machines qualify for a capital cost allowance rate of 25%, declining balance. Manufacturing costs are deductible for tax purposes in the year when the related goods are sold. The company uses the first-in, first-out inventory method for its tax return. Marketing, distribution, and customer service costs are deductible for tax purposes in the year when they are incurred. Assume a 40% tax rate. Also, assume that all operating cash flows and income tax payments occur at the end of the year. The after-tax nominal required rate of return is 16%.

Absorption costing must be used for tax purposes. Amortization is allocated on the basis of the estimates of the units produced each year.

REQUIRED

1. Prepare a schedule of relevant cash flows, including income taxes, for each year.
2. Compute the net present value of adding the new line of running shoes.

22-29 Capital budgeting, inflation, taxation. (J. Fellingham, adapted) Sapna Patel is manager of the customer service division of an electrical appliance store. Sapna is considering buying a repairing machine that costs $12,000 on December 31, 2007. The machine will last five years. Sapna estimates that the incremental pretax cash savings from using the machine will be $3,600 annually. The $3,600 is measured at current prices and will be received at the end of each year. For tax purposes, the machinery qualifies for a capital cost allowance rate of 25%, declining balance. Sapna requires a 10% after-tax real rate of return (that is, the rate of return is 10% when all cash flows are denominated in December 31, 2007, dollars). Use the 10% after-tax real rate of return when answering all four requirements.

REQUIRED

Treat each of the following cases independently.

1. Sapna lives in a world without income taxes and without inflation. What is the net present value of the machine in this world?
2. Sapna lives in a world without inflation, but there is an income tax rate of 40%. What is the net present value of the machine in this world?
3. There are no income taxes, but the annual inflation rate is 20%. What is the net present value of the machine? The cash savings each year will be increased by a factor equal to the cumulative inflation rate.
4. The annual inflation rate is 20%, and the income tax rate is 40%. What is the net present value of the machine?

22-30 Mining, income taxes, inflation, sensitivity analysis. (CMA, adapted) VanDyk Enterprises has been operating a large gold mine for many years. The company wants to acquire equipment that will allow it to extract gold ore from a currently inaccessible area of this mine. Rich Salzman, VanDyk's controller, has gathered the following data to analyze the investment.

The initial cost of acquiring and installing the equipment is $3.6 million. The useful life of the specialized equipment is five years with no salvage value at the end of this period. VanDyk uses the straight-line amortization method for this equipment for financial reporting purposes.

Using the equipment, VanDyk estimates that an additional 300 pounds of gold (16 ounces per pound) will be extracted annually for the next five years. Salzman plans to use an estimated market price of $420 per ounce of gold in his analysis based on expert information. The price of gold is determined by many factors and represents a significant risk factor in this analysis.

The out-of-pocket variable costs to extract, sort, and pack the gold is $120 per ounce. Allocated fixed overhead costs are $48 per ounce.

Two skilled technicians will be hired to operate the new equipment. The total salary and fringe benefit costs for these two employees will be $132,000 annually over the next five years. Periodic maintenance on the equipment is expected to cost $60,000 per year in out-of-pocket costs.

When analyzing projects of this kind, VanDyk uses a 12% after-tax required rate of return and a 40% tax rate. The equipment qualifies for a 30% declining balance capital cost allowance rate.

REQUIRED

1. Determine the payback period.
2. Calculate the after-tax net present value for VanDyk's proposed acquisition of the extraction equipment.
3. Determine the revenue per ounce of gold at which VanDyk's acquisition of the extraction equipment will break even from a net present value perspective where VanDyk earns the 12% after-tax required rate of return.
4. Salzman feels that inflation will occur and persist for the next five years at the rate of 2% per year. Assume all the data given in the problem are already in nominal dollars and that the 12% minimum desired rate of return already includes an element attributable to anticipated inflation. Repeat requirement 2, to take inflationary effects into consideration.

22-31 Robotics capital project, inflation, income taxes. Rustbelt, Inc., purchases second-hand pipeline equipment and "rehabilitates" it for resale. Rustbelt has experienced many industrial accidents involving workers at the spot-welding activity and is looking to invest in robots. The investment will cost $12 million payable immediately and will reduce labour costs, worker insurance costs, and materials usage costs by a total of $8.4 million (in January 1, 2007, dollars) a year. The robots require an addition to annual cash operating costs of $3.6 million (in January 1, 2007, dollars) a year. Hence, the net cash operating savings from using the robots will be $4.8 million annually (in January 1, 2007, dollars). Rustbelt believes that using the robots will eliminate industrial accidents involving workers at the spot-welding activity.

The robots have a four-year useful life with a terminal disposal price of $1.2 million (in January 1, 2007, dollars). The robots qualify for a 25% declining balance capital cost allowance rate. Rustbelt anticipates inflation in its operating costs and in the terminal disposal price of the robots of 20% per year. It uses a 10% after-tax required rate of return for investments expressed in real dollars. Rustbelt's income tax rate is 40%.

REQUIRED

1. What is the nominal after-tax required rate of return of Rustbelt for investments expressed in nominal dollars?
2. What is the net present value of the $12-million investment in robots? Use the approach of predicting cash inflows and outflows in nominal dollars and using a nominal discount rate.
3. What are the advantages of the approach to capital budgeting for inflation in requirement 2 relative to the approach of predicting real cash inflows and outflows and using a real discount rate?
4. What factors other than the net present value figure in requirement 2 should Rustbelt consider in deciding whether or not to invest in robots?

22-32 Ranking projects. (Adapted from NAA Research Report No. 35, pp. 83–85) Assume that six projects, A to F in the table that follows, have been submitted for inclusion in the coming year's budget for capital expenditures:

Project Cash Flows

	Year	A	B	C	D	E	F
Investment	0	$(120,000)	$(120,000)	$(240,000)	$(240,000)	$(240,000)	$(60,000)
	1	0	24,000	84,000	0	6,000	27,600
	2	12,000	24,000	84,000	0	18,000	24,000
	3	24,000	24,000	84,000	0	36,000	12,000
	4	24,000	24,000	84,000	0	60,000	12,000
	5	24,000	24,000	84,000	0	60,000	
Per year	6–9	24,000	24,000		240,000	60,000	
	10	24,000	24,000			60,000	
Per year	11–15	24,000					
Internal rate of return		14%	?	?	?	12.6%	12.0%

REQUIRED

1. Compute the internal rates of return (to the nearest half-percent) for projects B, C, and D. Rank all projects in descending order in terms of the internal rate of return. Show your computations.
2. On the basis of your answer in requirement 1, state which projects you would select, assuming a 10% required rate of return (a) if $600,000 is the limit to be spent, (b) if $660,000 is the limit, and (c) if $780,000 is the limit.
3. Assuming a 16% required rate of return and using the net present value method, compute the net present values and rank all the projects. Which project is more desirable, C or D? Compare your answer with your ranking in requirement 1.
4. What factors other than those considered in requirements 1 to 3 would influence your project rankings? Be specific.

22-33 Ranking of capital budgeting projects, alternative selection methods, capital rationing. (CMA, adapted) Brendan Rogers, division president of Wildwood Manufacturing, is preparing the 2008 capital budget for submission to corporate headquarters at AmiBrands, Inc. AmiBrands has not yet told Rogers what the total amount of funds available for capital projects at Wildwood will be, but the after-tax required rate of return is 12%.

Each project is considered to have the same degree of risk. Projects A and D are mutually exclusive. If project A is chosen, project D cannot be chosen. If project D is chosen, project A cannot be chosen.

When analyzing projects, Wildwood assumes that any budgeted amount not spent on the identified projects will be invested at the after-tax required rate of return, and funds released at the end of a project can be reinvested at the hurdle rate. Further information about each of these projects is presented in the following schedule:

Wildwood Manufacturing Proposed Capital Projects

	Project A	Project B	Project C	Project D	Project E	Project F
Capital investment	$127,200	$240,000	$168,000	$192,000	$172,800	$156,000
Net present value at 12%	$ 83,620	$ 28,528	$(12,274)	$ 89,249	$ 7,232	$ 83,416
Excess present value index (profitability index)	1.66	1.12	0.93	1.46	1.04	1.53
Internal rate of return	35%	15%	9%	22%	14%	26%
Payback period	2.2 years	4.5 years	3.9 years	4.3 years	2.9 years	3.3 years
Economic life	6 years	8 years	5 years	8 years	6 years	8 years

REQUIRED

1. Assume that Wildwood Manufacturing has no budget restrictions for capital expenditures and wants to maximize its value to AmiBrands. Identify the capital investment projects that Wildwood should include in the capital budget it submits to AmiBrands, Inc. Explain the basis for your selection.
2. Ignore your response to requirement 1. Assume that AmiBrands, Inc., has specified that Wildwood Manufacturing will have a restricted budget for capital expenditures, and that Wildwood should select the projects that maximize the company's value. Identify the capital investment projects Wildwood should include in its capital expenditures budget, and explain the basis for your selections, if the budget is (a) $540,000 and (b) $600,000.

22-34 Ethics, discounted cash flow analysis. Jaikumar Griffey, manager of the Household Products Division of the Dudley Company, is trying to decide whether to launch a new model of food blender, BF97. Griffey is particularly excited about this proposal, because it calls for producing the product in the company's old plant at Beaverton, Griffey's home town. During the last recession, Dudley had to shut down this plant and lay off its workers, many of whom had grown up with Griffey and were his friends. Griffey had been very upset when the plant was closed down. If BF97 were produced in the new plant, most of the laid-off workers would be rehired.

Griffey asks Andrew Chen, the management accountant of the Household Products Division, to analyze the BF97 proposal. Through the years the company has found that its products have a useful life of six years, after which the product is dropped and replaced by another new product. Chen gathers the following data.

a. BF97 will require new special-purpose equipment costing $1,080,000. The useful life of the equipment is six years, with a $360,000 estimated terminal disposal price at that time. The equipment qualifies for a capital cost allowance rate of 25%, declining balance.

b. The old plant has a book value of $300,000 and is being amortized for accounting purposes on a straight-line basis at $30,000 annually. The plant is currently being leased to another company. This lease has six years remaining at an annual rental of $54,000. The lease contains a cancellation clause whereby the landlord can obtain immediate possession of the premises upon payment of $36,000 cash (fully deductible for income tax purposes).

c. Certain nonrecurring market research studies and sales promotion activities will amount to a cost of $360,000 at the end of year 1. The entire amount is deductible in full for income tax purposes in the year of expenditure.

d. Additions to working capital will require $240,000 at the outset and an additional $240,000 at the end of two years. This total is fully recoverable at the end of six years.

e. Net cash inflow from operations before amortization and income taxes is expected to be $480,000 in years 1 and 2, $720,000 in years 3 to 5, and $120,000 in year 6.

The after-tax required rate of return is 12%. The income tax rate is 36%.

REQUIRED

1. Use a net present value analysis to determine whether Chen should recommend launching BF97.

2. Chen learns that the new special-purpose equipment required to make BF97 may only be available at a cost of $1.38 million. All other data remain unchanged. He revises his analysis and presents it to Griffey. Griffey is very unhappy with what he sees. He tells Chen, "Try different assumptions and redo your analysis. I have no doubt that this project should be worth pursuing on financial grounds." Chen is aware of Griffey's interest in supporting his home-town community. There is also the possibility that Griffey may be hired as a consultant by the new plant management after he retires next year. Why is Griffey unhappy with Chen's revised analysis? How should Chen respond to Griffey's suggestions? Identify the specific steps that Chen should take to resolve this situation.

22-35 Introduction of new product, income taxes. (W. Bruns) In December 2007, R.E. Torgler was trying to decide whether to add a new line of injection moulded plastic products to those already manufactured and distributed by Reto S.A. To do so, the company would have to buy new injection moulding equipment; none of the existing equipment could be adapted to perform the necessary operation, and Torgler was anxious to retain control of manufacturing. Actually, new injection moulding equipment had been postponed because the product concept was judged to need additional development. But now the product seemed ready.

Sales of the new product were forecast at SFr. 2,400,000 per year, from which a sales commission of 15% would be paid to Reto's sales agents. Actual sales were made in several different currencies but, for simplicity here, all money measurements are stated in their Swiss franc equivalent.

Direct manufacturing costs were budgeted at SFr. 720,000 for materials and SFr. 1,080,000 for labour, leaving an annual cash flow before tax of SFr. 240,000. The new equipment would cost SFr. 720,000 delivered and installed, and was expected to have a useful life of 10 years, with a zero terminal disposal value.

Reto was able to borrow money at 8%.

REQUIRED

1. Ignoring the effect of taxes, what is the internal rate of return (IRR) on the proposed investment. Assume the new equipment would be installed by January 1, 2008, and begin producing on that date.

2. The cost of the equipment can be deducted from annual cash flows before they are subjected to tax. Assuming that the equipment will last 10 years, and that an equal

amount of the cost of SFr. 720,000 will be deducted each year, and that the tax rate is expected to be 45%, what is the IRR on an after-tax basis?

3. Torgler has stated that Reto should be willing to purchase this machine as long as it yielded a return of 12% after taxation. Should he make the investment? Show your calculations.

4. Actually, to stimulate industrial development, the tax rules allow for depreciation deductions up to one-third of the cost of any such investment to be deducted from reported earnings in the first year after the investment, and up to one-fifth of the remainder of the undepreciated investment amount can be deduced in the second year. Thereafter, annual deductions are computed on a straight-line basis such that no more than the original cost of the equipment is depreciated over its useful life. How, if at all, does this affect the attractiveness of the investment?

5. Reto has learned that investment in working capital (receivables and inventories, less payables) amounts to approximately 15% of revenues. Will the additional SFr. 360,000 investment for the new line decrease the rate of return on investment to less than the 12% criterion Torgler has been using?

6. In late December 2007, Reto purchased the equipment, and the operating results turned out as forecast. A year later, Torgler learned that the manufacturer of the new equipment had introduced new models that were more automated. The new equipment cost SFr. 1,200,000 and would permit labour savings of SFr. 240,000 per year, thus doubling the net operating cash flow on the product. As a result of the technological advance, Torgler expected the one-year-old machine could be sold for only SFr. 240,000 despite the fact that its book value was SFr. 480,000. If Reto buys the new machine and depreciates it using allowed tax depreciation over 10 years, would the investment meet the 12% after-tax criterion? Show your calculations.

7. If the one-year-old machine has a zero disposal price, would replacing it with the new machine still be desirable? Show your calculations.

8. Torgler was loath to throw away a nearly new machine and thought he might be better off to keep it one more year and then replace it. Would he be better off? How would you go about addressing this issue? Explain.

9. During 2008, the rate of inflation remained low, and it was expected that it would average about 4% for the year. Torgler wondered how Reto's analysis should reflect this rate of inflation, which he expected might continue for several years. Should an assumed inflation rate change his decision? Explain.

COLLABORATIVE LEARNING PROBLEM

22-36 **Equipment replacement, income taxes, unequal project lives, ethics.** (CMA, adapted) Instant Dinners, Inc. (IDI) makes microwaveable frozen foods. The company is considering purchasing an automated materials-movement system (AMMS) for its Western Plant. Bill Rolland, IDI's chief financial officer, has asked Lealand Forrest, assistant controller, to prepare a net present value analysis for the proposal.

Rolland was instrumental in convincing the board of directors to open the Western Plant. Now, unless significant improvements in cost control and production efficiency are achieved, the Western Plant may be sold. Rolland is anxious to have the Western Plant continue to operate to maintain his credibility with the board and also to help Western's production manager, a longtime friend of Rolland.

The AMMS would replace a number of forklift trucks, eliminate the need for a number of materials-handlers, and increase the output capacity of the Western plant.

Rolland has given Forrest the following information regarding the AMMS investment for the net present value analysis:

Projected useful life	10 years
Purchase/installation	$5,280,000
Increased working capital needed	1,200,000
Increased annual operating costs (excluding amortization) over current costs	240,000
Reduction in annual manufacturing costs over current costs	480,000
Reduction in annual maintenance costs over current costs	360,000
Increase in cash flow from higher sales revenue	840,000
Estimated disposal price at end of useful life	1,020,000
Estimated recovery of working capital at end of useful life	1,200,000

IDI uses straight-line amortization for financial reporting purposes for all its equipment assuming a zero terminal disposal price. The forklift trucks have a net book value of $576,000 with a remaining useful life of eight years and a zero terminal disposal price. If IDI purchases AMMS now, it can sell the forklift trucks for $120,000. To make the ten-year project life of AMMS comparable to that of the forklift alternative, Forrest estimates that if IDI does not buy the AMMS, the company will lease new forklift trucks for the Western Plant for years 9 and 10 at a cost of $96,000 each year.

IDI has a 40% tax rate and requires a 12% after-tax rate of return on this project. Assume that tax effects and cash flows from equipment acquisition and disposal occur at the time of the transaction and that tax effects and cash flows from operations occur at the end of each year. The equipment qualifies for a 30% declining balance capital cost allowance rate.

Rolland was pleased with Forrest's initial analysis. After the initial analysis was completed, Forrest discovered that the estimated terminal disposal price of the AMMS should be $120,000, not $1,020,000, and that the useful life of the system was expected to be eight years, not ten years. Forrest prepared a revised, second analysis based on this new information. On seeing the second analysis, Rolland told Forrest to discard the revised analysis and not to discuss it with anyone at IDI or with the board of directors.

INSTRUCTIONS
Form groups of three students to complete the following requirements.

REQUIRED
1. What is the net present value of the decision to replace forklifts with the AMMS based on the *original estimates* Rolland gave to Forrest?
2. Using net present value analysis, determine whether IDI should purchase and install the AMMS on the basis of the *revised estimates* that Forrest obtained.
3. Explain how Forrest, a management accountant, should evaluate Rolland's directives to conceal the revised analysis.
4. Identify the specific steps Forrest should take to resolve this situation.

PART SEVEN

CHAPTER 23

Management Control Systems, Transfer Pricing, and Multinational Considerations

Choosing transfer prices is an important aspect of transactions between internal divisions based in different countries. Transfer prices are the prices at which assets, both tangible and intangible, as well as services are traded by related parties such as corporate subsidiaries across international borders. Internally, corporations also transfer goods and services among their value-added functions within the same country. When establishing transfer prices, managers must consider tax laws as well as internal factors such as goal congruence, incentives, and autonomy. Transfer prices affect the profits reported in each division and are therefore of interest to both division managers who may receive bonuses based on the division's financial performance and tax officials in the different countries who must ensure their government receives its fair share of taxes.

LEARNING OBJECTIVES

After studying this chapter, you should be able to

1. Describe a management control system and its three key properties

2. Describe the benefits and costs of decentralization

3. Explain transfer prices and criteria used to evaluate them

4. Calculate transfer prices using three methods

5. Illustrate how market-based transfer prices generally promote goal-congruence in perfectly competitive markets

6. Recognize why a transfer price based on full cost plus a markup may lead to suboptimal decisions

7. Understand the range over which two divisions generally negotiate the transfer price when there is excess capacity

8. Present a general guideline for determining a minimum transfer price in transfer-pricing situations

9. Recognize income tax considerations in multinational transfer pricing

Which company has the better management control system: Magna International or BCE, Suncor or Barrick? Beyond the technical aspects, it is essential to consider how management control systems influence the behaviour of the people who use them. Accounting information is the backbone of any management control system. For example, how does cost and budget information help in planning and coordinating the actions of multiple divisions within these companies? This chapter develops the link between strategy, organizational structure, management control systems, and accounting information. It examines the benefits and costs of centralized and decentralized organizational structures and looks at the pricing of products or services transferred between subunits of the same organization.

A **management control system** is a means of gathering and using information to aid and coordinate the process of making planning and control decisions throughout the organization and to guide employee behaviour. Some companies design their management control system around the concept of the balanced scorecard (see Chapter 13 for details). The goal of the system is to improve the collective decisions within an organization.

Consider British Petroleum (BP)'s management control system, which contains both financial and nonfinancial information in each of the four perspectives of the balanced scorecard:

1. **Financial perspective**—for example, stock price, net income, return on investment, cash flow from operations, and cost per litre of gasoline.

2. **Customer perspective**—for example, customer satisfaction, time taken to respond to customer requests for products, customers' repeat purchases, and market share in key market segments.

3. **Internal-business-process perspective**—for example, on-time delivery of gasoline from refineries to retail stations, gasoline quality, refinery downtime, number of days lost due to accidents and environmental problems, speed of service at retail stations, friendliness of employees, and stocking of convenience stores.

4. **Learning-and-growth perspective**—for example, employee satisfaction, absenteeism, information systems capabilities, and number of processes with real-time feedback.

The target performance levels are based on competitor benchmarks, which indicate the performance levels necessary to meet customer needs, compete effectively, and achieve financial goals. Well-designed management control systems use information both from within the company, such as net income and employee satisfaction, and from outside the company, such as share price and customer satisfaction.

Management control systems comprise both formal and informal components. The formal management control system of an organization includes those explicit rules, procedures, performance measures, and incentive plans that guide the behaviour of its managers and employees. The formal control system itself consists of several systems. For example, the management accounting system is a formal accounting system that provides information on costs, revenues, and income. Examples of other formal control systems are human resource systems (providing information on compensation, benefits, recruiting, training, absenteeism, and accidents) and quality systems (providing information on scrap, defects, rework, and late deliveries to customers).

The informal part of the management control system includes such aspects as shared values, loyalties, and mutual commitments among members of the organization and the unwritten norms about acceptable behaviour for promotion that also influence employee behaviour. Examples of slogans that reinforce values and loyalties are "At Ford, Quality Is Job 1," and "At Home Depot, low prices are just the beginning."

> ### OBJECTIVE 1
> Describe a management control system and its three key properties

Management control system. Means of gathering and using information to aid and coordinate the process of making planning and control decisions throughout the organization and to guide employee behaviour.

Management accountants must have the interpersonal and analytical skills necessary to evaluate and implement management control systems, as well as the ability to interpret outputs of these systems. The behavioural issues in this chapter and throughout this book are very important to accountants' careers.

EVALUATING MANAGEMENT CONTROL SYSTEMS

To be effective, management control systems should be closely aligned to an organization's strategies and goals. Two examples of strategies at BP are providing innovative products and services to increase market share in key customer segments (perhaps by targeting customers who are willing to pay more for faster service, better facilities, and well-stocked convenience stores) and reducing costs and targeting price-sensitive customers. Suppose BP decides, wisely or unwisely, to provide innovative products and services. The management control system must then reinforce this goal, and BP should tie managers' rewards to achieving the targeted measures.

BP's balanced scorecard–based management control system can help managers determine if their strategy is working. For example, if BP achieves its targets in the learning-and-growth and internal-business-process perspectives, it is implementing its strategy well. However, if after achieving these targets BP does not see improvements in the customer and financial perspectives, it means its strategy is not working. BP's managers would then have to consider different ways of pursuing the strategy of providing innovative products and services (perhaps by improving the facilities and service at its gas stations), or they could consider changing the strategy to become a low-cost, low-price gasoline supplier.

A second important feature of management control systems is that they should be designed to fit the organization's structure and the decision-making responsibility of individual managers. Different levels of management at BP need different kinds of information to perform their tasks. For example, top management needs share-price information to evaluate how much shareholder value the company has created. Share price, however, is less important for line managers supervising individual refineries. They are more concerned with obtaining information about on-time delivery of gasoline, equipment downtime, product quality, number of days lost to accidents and environmental problems, cost per litre of gasoline, and employee satisfaction.

Now consider the marketing manager at BP. The company's management control system should provide this manager with information about service at the gas stations, customer satisfaction, and market share—information that helps the manager in the planning and control of operations. The marketing manager requires very different information from that required by the refinery manager. But, in both cases, the management control system provides information to aid each manager's decision making and to align his or her actions.

Effective management control systems motivate managers and employees. **Motivation** is the desire to attain a selected goal (the goal-congruence aspect) combined with the resulting drive or pursuit toward that goal (the effort aspect).

Goal-congruence exists when individuals and groups work toward the organization goals that top management desires—that is, managers working in their own best interest take actions that further the overall goals of top management. Suppose the goal of BP's top management is to maximize operating income. If the management control system evaluates the refinery manager *only* on the basis of costs, the manager may be tempted to make decisions that minimize cost but overlook product quality or timely delivery to retail stations, which will likely not maximize operating income of the company as a whole. In this case, the management control system will not achieve goal congruence.

Effort is defined as exertion toward a goal. Effort goes beyond physical exertion, such as a worker producing at a faster rate, to include all conscientious actions (physical and mental). Management control systems motivate employees to exert effort toward attaining organization goals through a variety of incentives tied to the achievement of those goals. These incentives can be monetary (cash, shares, use of a company car, and membership of a club) or nonmonetary (power, self-esteem, and pride in working for a successful company).

To summarize, the primary criterion for evaluating a management control system is how well the information provided promotes the attainment of top management's goals in a cost-effective manner. One way to evaluate if this criterion has been met is to assess how well the management control system fits the organizational structure and the decision-making responsibility of individual managers, as well as how well it motivates individuals within the organization.

Motivation. The desire to attain a selected goal (the goal-congruence aspect) combined with the resulting drive or pursuit toward that goal (the effort aspect).

Goal-congruence. Exists when individuals and groups work toward the organization goals that top management desires at the same time as they work towards their own goals.

Effort. Exertion toward a goal.

ORGANIZATIONAL STRUCTURE AND DECENTRALIZATION

Decentralization. The freedom of managers at lower levels (subunits) of the organization to make decisions.

As we have just seen, management control systems must fit an organization's structure. Many organizations have decentralized structures that give rise to an additional set of management control issues.

Top management makes decisions about decentralization that affect day-to-day operations at all levels of the organization. The essence of **decentralization** is the freedom for managers at lower levels of the organization to make decisions.

As we discuss the issues of decentralization, we use the term *subunit* to refer to any part of an organization. In practice, a subunit may be a large division (the Exploration Division or the Refining Division of BP) or a small group (the two-person advertising department of a local clothing boutique).

Total decentralization *means minimum constraints and maximum freedom for managers to make decisions at the lowest levels of an organization.* Total centralization *means maximum constraints and minimum freedom for managers at the lowest levels.* Most companies' structures fall somewhere in between these two extremes.

Benefits of Decentralization

OBJECTIVE 2

Describe the benefits and costs of decentralization

How should top managers decide how much decentralization is optimal? Conceptually, they try to choose the degree of decentralization that maximizes the excess of benefits over costs. From a practical standpoint, top managers can seldom quantify either the benefits or the costs. Still, the cost-benefit approach helps them focus on the central issues.

Advocates of decentralizing decision-making and granting responsibilities to managers of subunits claim the following benefits:

1. *Creates greater responsiveness to local needs.* Information is the key to intelligent decisions. Compared with executives, subunit managers are better informed about their customers, competitors, suppliers, and employees, as well as about factors that affect the performance of their jobs such as ways to decrease costs and improve quality in response to customer demand.

2. *Leads to quicker decision making.* An organization that gives lower-level managers the responsibility for making decisions can make decisions quickly, creating a competitive advantage over organizations that are slower, because they send the decision-making responsibility upward through layer after layer of management. Interlake, a manufacturer of materials-handling equipment, notes this important benefit of increased decentralization: "We have distributed decision-making powers more broadly to the cutting edge of product and market opportunity." Interlake's materials-handling equipment must often be customized to fit individual customers' needs. Delegating decision making to the sales force allows Interlake to respond quickly to changing customer requirements.

3. *Increases motivation.* Subunit managers are usually more highly motivated when they can exercise greater individual initiative. Johnson & Johnson, a highly decentralized company, maintains that "Decentralization = Creativity = Productivity."

4. *Aids management development and learning.* Giving managers more responsibility promotes the development of an experienced pool of management talent—a pool that the organization can draw from to fill higher-level management positions. The organization also learns who, among its employees, are not management material. Tektronix, an electronics instruments company, expressed this benefit as follows: "Decentralized units provide a training ground for general managers, and a visible field of combat where product champions may fight for their ideas."

5. *Sharpens the focus of managers.* In a decentralized setting, the manager of a small subunit has a concentrated focus. A small subunit is more flexible and nimble than a larger subunit and better able to adapt itself quickly to a fast-opening market opportunity. Also, top management, relieved of the burden of day-to-day operating decisions, can spend more time and energy on strategic planning for the entire organization.

Costs of Decentralization

Advocates of more centralized decision making point out the following costs of decentralizing decision making:

1. *Leads to suboptimal decision making.* **Suboptimal** (also called either **goal-incongruent** or **dysfunctional**) **decision making** arises when a decision's

Suboptimal decision making (goal-incongruent, dysfunctional decision making). Decisions in which the benefit to one subunit is more than offset by the costs or loss of benefits to the organization as a whole.

benefit to one subunit is more than offset by the costs or loss of benefits to the organization as a whole. This cost arises because top management has given up some control over decision making.

Suboptimal decision making may occur when (1) there is a lack of harmony or congruence among the overall organization goals, the subunit goals, and the individual goals of decision makers, (2) subunit managers lack the necessary skills, or (3) subunit managers lack the necessary guidance to evaluate the effects of their decisions on other parts of the organization. Suboptimal decision making is most likely to occur when the subunits in the organization are highly interdependent, such as when the end product of one subunit is the direct material of another subunit.

2. *Results in duplication of activities.* Several individual subunits of the organization may undertake the same activity separately. For example, there may be a duplication of staff functions (accounting, employee relations, and legal) if an organization is highly decentralized. Centralizing these functions, which are crucial to effective management but non-value-added for a customer, helps to reduce their costs through internal operational redesign or downsizing.

3. *Decreases loyalty toward the organization as a whole.* Individual subunit managers may regard the managers of other subunits in the same organization as external parties. Consequently, managers may be unwilling to share significant information or to assist when another subunit faces an emergency.

4. *Increases costs of gathering information.* Managers may spend too much time negotiating the prices for internal products or services transferred among subunits.

Comparison of Benefits and Costs

To choose an appropriate organization structure, top managers must compare the benefits and costs of decentralization, often on a function-by-function basis. For example, the controller's function may be highly decentralized for many attention-directing and problem-solving purposes (such as preparing operating budgets and performance reports) but highly centralized for other purposes (such as processing accounts receivables and developing income tax strategies). Decentralizing budgeting and cost reporting enables the subunit managers, for example, to influence information provided to the subunit to focus only on information relevant for subunits decision making. The balanced scorecard system of management control also aligns and coordinates actions of decentralized subunits. Centralizing income tax strategies, on the other hand, allows the organization to trade off profits in some subunits with losses in others to evaluate the impact on the organization as a whole.

Surveys of North American and European companies report that the decisions made most frequently at the decentralized level and least frequently at the corporate level are related to sources of supplies, products to manufacture, and product advertising. Decisions related to the type and source of long-term financing are made least frequently at the decentralized level and most frequently at the corporate level.[1] Decentralized companies are generally large and unregulated, face great uncertainties in their environments, require detailed local knowledge for performing various jobs, and have few interdependencies among divisions.

Decentralization in Multinational Companies

Because language, customs, cultures, business practices, rules, laws, and regulations vary significantly across countries, multinational corporations are often decentralized. This enables managers to make decisions that exploit their knowledge of local business and political conditions and to deal with uncertainties in their individual environments. Philips, a Dutch conglomerate, delegates marketing and pricing decisions for its television business in the Indian and Singaporean markets to managers in each country. Decentralized multinational corporations often rotate

---

[1]*Evaluating the Performance of International Operations* (New York: Business International, 1989), p. 4; and *Managing the Global Finance Function* (London: Business International, 1992), p. 31.

managers between foreign locations and the home office to improve their abilities to operate in different local environments.

Important drawbacks exist when a decentralization strategy is inappropriately implemented, especially in multinational companies. One of the most important is the lack of control. Barings PLC, a British investment banking firm, went bankrupt and had to be sold when one of its traders in Singapore caused the firm to lose over £1 billion on unauthorized trades. Multinational corporations that implement decentralized decision making usually also design their management control systems to measure and monitor division performance. Information and communications technology eases the flow of data for reporting and control.

CHOICES ABOUT RESPONSIBILITY CENTRES

To measure the performance of subunits in centralized or decentralized organizations, the management control system uses one or a mix of the four types of responsibility centres presented in Chapter 6:

◆ *Cost centre*. Manager accountable for costs only
◆ *Revenue centre*. Manager accountable for revenues only
◆ *Profit centre*. Manager accountable for revenues and costs
◆ *Investment centre*. Manager accountable for investments, revenues, and costs

Centralization or decentralization is not mentioned in these descriptions. Why? Because each of these responsibility units can be found in either of the extremes of centralized and decentralized organizations.

A common misconception is that the term *profit centre* (and, in some cases, *investment centre*) is a synonym for a decentralized subunit and that *cost centre* is a synonym for a centralized subunit. *Profit centres can be coupled with a highly centralized organization, and cost centres can be coupled with a highly decentralized organization.* For example, managers in a division organized as a profit centre may have little leeway in making decisions. They may need to obtain approval from corporate headquarters for every expenditure over, say, $10,000 and may be forced to accept central staff "advice." In another company, divisions may be organized as cost centres, but their managers may have great latitude on capital expenditures and on where to purchase materials and services. In short, the labels "profit centre" and "cost centre" are independent of the degree of decentralization in an organization.

TRANSFER PRICING

In decentralized organizations, individual subunits of an organization act as separate units. In these settings, the management control system often uses transfer prices to both coordinate actions and evaluate performance of the subunits.

An **intermediate product** is a product transferred from one subunit to another subunit of the same organization. This product may be processed further and sold to an external customer. A **transfer price** is the price one subunit (segment, department, division, and so on) of an organization charges for a product or service supplied to another subunit of the same organization. The transfer price creates revenue for the selling subunit and a purchase cost for the buying subunit, affecting operating income numbers for both subunits. The operating incomes can be used to evaluate the performance of each subunit and to motivate managers.

Alternative Transfer-Pricing Methods

First we will discuss transfer of goods and services among divisions in the same country. There are three general methods for determining transfer prices:

1. *Market-based transfer prices.* Upper management may choose to use the price of a similar product or service publicly listed in, say, a trade journal. Also, upper management may select, for the internal price, the external price that a subunit charges to outside customers.

OBJECTIVE 3

Explain transfer prices and criteria used to evaluate them

Intermediate product. Product transferred from one subunit to another subunit of the organization. This product may be processed further and sold to an external customer.

Transfer price. Price one subunit (segment, department, division, etc.) of an organization charges for a product or service supplied to another subunit of the same organization.

2. *Cost-based transfer prices.* Upper management may choose a transfer price based on the costs of producing the product in question. Examples include variable manufacturing costs, manufacturing (absorption) costs, and full product costs. "Full product costs" include all production costs as well as costs from other business functions (R&D, design, marketing, distribution, and customer service). The costs used in cost-based transfer prices can be actual costs or budgeted costs.

3. *Negotiated transfer prices.* In some cases, the subunits of a company are free to negotiate the transfer price between themselves and then to decide whether to buy and sell internally or deal with outside parties. Subunits may use information about costs and market prices in these negotiations, but there is no requirement that the chosen transfer price bear any specific relationship to either cost or market price data. Negotiated transfer prices are often employed when market prices are volatile and change occurs constantly. The negotiated transfer price is the outcome of a bargaining process between the selling and the buying divisions.

Ideally, the chosen transfer-pricing method should lead each subunit manager to make optimal decisions for the organization as a whole. As in all management control systems, transfer prices should help achieve an organization's strategies and goals, and fit its structure. In particular, it should promote *goal-congruence* and a sustained high level of *management effort.* Sellers should be motivated to hold down costs of supplying a product or service, and buyers should be motivated to acquire and use inputs efficiently. If top management favours a high degree of decentralization, transfer prices should also promote a high level of subunit *autonomy* in decision making. **Autonomy** is the degree of freedom to make decisions.

Autonomy. The degree of freedom to make decisions.

AN ILLUSTRATION OF TRANSFER PRICING

In dealing with transfer-pricing issues, top management must address two questions. One is a policy question: Should divisions be permitted to buy from external suppliers when the same goods are available internally? The other is an operational question: What will the transfer price be? Answering this question involves deciding (1) which of the three transfer-pricing methods will be used and (2) how disputes are to be resolved (negotiations, arbitration, or top-management directives).

We continue with an example of internal transfer pricing policies, Northern Petroleum of Calgary, Alberta, which operates its Transportation and Refining Divisions as profit centres (see the Concepts in Action feature on p. 889). The Transportation Division manages the operation of a pipeline that transports crude oil from the Calgary area to the Refining Division in Sarnia, Ontario. The Refining Division processes crude oil into gasoline. (For simplicity, assume that gasoline is the only salable product the refinery makes and that it takes two barrels of crude oil to yield one barrel of gasoline.)

Variable costs in each division are assumed to be variable with respect to a single cost driver in each division: barrels of crude oil produced by the Production Division, barrels of crude oil transported by the Transportation Division, and barrels of gasoline produced by the Refining Division. The fixed costs per unit are based on the budgeted annual output of crude oil to be produced and transported and the amount of gasoline to be produced. Northern Petroleum reports all costs and revenues of its non-Canadian operations in Canadian dollars using the prevailing exchange rate.

◆ The Production Division can sell crude oil to outside parties in the Calgary area at $12 per barrel.

◆ The Transportation Division "buys" crude oil from the Production Division, transports it to Sarnia, and then "sells" it to the Refining Division. The pipeline from Calgary to Sarnia has the capacity to carry 40,000 barrels of crude oil per day.

◆ The Refining Division has been underutilizing its capacity, operating at 30,000 barrels of crude oil a day, using oil delivered by both the Transportation Division (an average of 10,000 barrels per day) and other external suppliers who also deliver to the Sarnia Refinery (an average of 20,000 barrels per day, at $21 per barrel).

◆ The Refining Division sells the gasoline it produces at $58 per barrel.

Exhibit 23-1 on page 890 summarizes Northern Petroleum's variable and fixed costs per unit of the cost driver in each division, the external market prices of buying and selling crude oil, and the external market prices of selling gasoline. Consider the division operating income resulting from three transfer pricing methods applied to a series of transactions involving 100 barrels of crude oil produced by Northern's Production Division.

Transfer-Pricing Decisions at Multree Homes

Multree Homes of Nevada manufactures prefabricated houses. As the company grew, the window-making department underwent several changes as it began selling to external markets. Inherent in the decision to serve outside customers was the evolution of effective transfer-pricing and performance management policies.

Initially functioning as a cost centre, the department's performance was measured by order-filling and on-time delivery ratios in addition to cost variance analysis. This variation of responsibility had a negative impact causing the department to be perceived as a cost creator rather than a value contributor.

All cost centres in Multree that provided goods and services internally were prevented from marketing or purchasing their products externally. Current market rates plus a 20% markup on actual costs were used as the standard. In window-making this resulted in an effective transfer price of US$132 (US$110 actual cost plus 20% markup). The favourable sales price variance gave the appearance that window-making was contributing an extra US$2,000 toward profit. It was able to pass its cost variances on to other departments, which were forced to pay more per window than budgeted, leaving them to report an unfavourable cost variance. Complaints arose suggesting that this transfer-pricing policy favoured some departments at the expense of others and forced internal competition and bitterness that could destabilize the company in the long term.

As a corrective measure, the transfer-pricing policy was adjusted so that the 20% markup was added above budgeted rather than actual costs. This change solved the problem of unfair cost variances but also added complexity to department performance measures without any real improvement in decision making. Ultimately, the window-making and other rival departments agreed that the additional accounting costs inherent in the transfer-pricing policy were not justified as they created no new value and did not motivate management behaviour changes with respect to cost, control, quality improvement, or meeting of production quotas. The window department manager felt a loss of impact and control as managers were not involved in setting the transfer price.

The company then switched window-making back to a cost centre in which standard absorptive manufacturing costs were used as the transfer price between departments. In this way the accounting system and manager responsibility and motivation were in line and non-value-added accounting and management activities were eliminated.

However, the issue of the window-making department selling externally while maintaining its priority to supply internally still existed. The department suggested it could exist as a hybrid cost and profit centre in which the internal transfer price would be set at standard absorptive manufacturing costs (US$120 per window—US$100 variable costs and US$20 fixed costs) and any surplus would be sold externally at US$200 each. Profit from external sales could be used to offset any unfavourable cost variances and the external market price of US$200 could be lowered to the breakeven value of US$175 (US$125 variable costs plus US$50 fixed costs) if necessary.

Allowing the window-making department to sell externally provided the assembly department strength to argue a case for buying externally. Under good management accounting practices, the correct transfer price is always the currently accepted market value. Under these circumstances, the window department would sell externally at US$200/window (achieving greatest profit) and the assembly department would buy externally at US$190/window (achieving lowest cost). With the window department functioning as a true profit centre, assembly was free to buy externally or to negotiate a price internally, just as it would with any other supplier. However, under this system the negotiations become extensive and time-consuming.

Management's final decision was to lift all rewards on internal transfers, citing that internal transfers should only occur when they positively affect the company's cash flows. A performance management system based on profit maximization and cost minimization separate from internal transfer policy provided the best solution for Multree, as it allowed internal transfer prices to be set and utilized without interfering with other value-adding management activities.

Source: Thomas, M., "The Multree Homes Transfer Pricing Evolution," *Management Accounting Quarterly* (Spring 2001).

EXHIBIT 23-1
Operating Data for Northern Petroleum

	A	B	C	D	E	F	G	H
1								
2				**Transportation Division**				
3				Variable cost per barrel of crude oil	$1			
4	Contact price per barrel of crude oil supplied in Calgary	= $12 →		Fixed cost per barrel of crude oil	3			
5				Full cost per barrel of crude oil	$4			
6								
7								
8				Barrels of crude oil transferred				
9								
10								
11				**Refining Division**				
12				Variable cost per barrel of gasoline	$ 8		Market price per barrel of gasoline sold = to external parties	
13	Market price per barrel of crude oil supplied to Sarnia refinery	= $21 →		Fixed cost per barrel of gasoline	6	→		$58
14				Full cost per barrel of gasoline	$14			
15								

◆ **Method A**. Market-based transfer prices
◆ **Method B**. Cost-based transfer prices at 110% of full costs, where full costs are the cost of the transferred-in product plus the division's own variable and fixed costs
◆ **Method C**. Negotiated transfer prices

The transfer prices per barrel of crude oil under each method are as follows.

◆ **Method A: Market-Based Transfer Prices**

From Production Division to Transportation Division = $12
From Transportation Division to Refining Division = $21

◆ **Method B: Cost-Based Transfer Prices at 110% of Full Costs**

Full cost of crude oil plus the Transportation Division's = 1.10($12 + $1 + $3)
　　full costs　　　　　　　　　　　　　　　　　　= $17.60

◆ **Method C: Transfer Prices Negotiated by Divisions to Be between Market-Based and Cost-Based Transfer Prices**

Negotiated transfer price of $19.25 per barrel of crude oil (a price within the range of the market-based and cost-based transfer prices).

Exhibit 23-2 presents division operating incomes per 100 barrels of crude oil reported under each transfer pricing method. Transfer prices create income for the "selling" division and corresponding costs for the "buying" division that cancel out when divisional results are consolidated. The exhibit assumes that the different transfer pricing methods have no effect on the decisions made and actions taken by the division managers. Northern Petroleum's total operating income from producing, transporting, and refining the 100 barrels of crude oil is therefore the same, $600, regardless of internal transfer prices used:

Operating = Revenues − Cost of crude − Transportation − Refining
　income　　　　　　　　　oil　　　　　costs　　　　costs
　= ($58 × 50 barrels of gasoline) − [($12 + $4) × 100 barrels of crude oil]
　　−($14 × 50 barrels of gasoline)
　= $2,900 − ($1,200 + $400) − $700 = $600

EXHIBIT 23-2

Division Operating Income of Northern Petroleum for 100 Barrels of Crude Oil under Alternative Transfer Pricing Methods

	A	B	C	D	E	F	G
1	**Production and Sales Data**						
2	Barrels of crude transferred =	100					
3	Barrels of gasoline sold =	50					
4		**Internal Transfers**			**Internal Transfers at**		**Internal Transfers at**
5		**at Market Price of**			**110% of Full Cost =**		**Negotiated Price of**
6		**$21**			**$17.60**		**$19.25**
7		**per Barrel**			**per Barrel**		**per Barrel**
8	**Transportation Division**						
9	Revenue: 100 × $21; $17.60, $19.25	$2,100			$1,760		$1,925
10	Costs						
11	Crude oil						
12	$12 × 100 barrels of crude oil	1,200			1,200		1,200
13	Division variable costs						
14	$1 × 100 barrels of crude oil	100			100		100
15	Division fixed costs						
16	$3 × 100 barrels of crude oil	300			300		300
17	Total division costs	1,600			1,600		1,600
18	Division operating income	$ 500			$ 160		$ 325
19							
20	**Refining Division**						
21	Revenues: $58 × 50	$2,900			$2,900		$2,900
22	Costs						
23	Transferred-in costs: 100 × $21; $17.60; $19.25	2,100			1,760		1,925
24	Division variable costs						
25	$8 × 50 barrels of gasoline	400			400		400
26	Division fixed costs						
27	$6 × 50 barrels of gasoline	300			300		300
28	Total division costs	2,800			2,460		2,625
29	Division operating income	$ 100			$ 440		$ 275
30							
31	Total operating income for Northern Petroleum	$ 600			$ 600		$ 600

When operating income is constant, we can focus on the effects of different transfer pricing methods on division operating incomes. These incomes differ under the three methods. Analyzing the high and low operating incomes for each division, this exhibit readily shows that the operating income of the Transportation Division benefits most when the market-based method is used ($500 − $160 = $340), whereas the Refining Division benefits most when the full cost method is used ($440 − $100 = $340). This means that each division would choose a different transfer pricing method if its sole criterion were to maximize its own division operating income: the Transportation Division would favour market pricing, and the Refining Division would choose 110% of full costs. Clearly this is why managers whose compensation or promotion directly depends on operating division income take considerable interest in the setting of transfer prices.

Exhibit 23-2 maintains companywide operating income at $600 and illustrates how the choice of a transfer pricing method divides the companywide operating income pie among individual divisions. The transfer price methods do not change the size of the total pie but rather how it is divided between the two divisions. If Northern Petroleum failed to obtain a long-term contract for the crude oil transported to its refinery, then the revenues and operating income would also fluctuate for each division and for the company as a whole, although the proportions or operating income for each division under each transfer pricing method would not fluctuate. The more volatile the market price, the more difficult it would be for Northern Petroleum to predict its future revenues upon which to base its strategic and operating plans. Subsequent sections of this chapter illustrate that the choice of a transfer pricing method can also affect the decisions that individual division managers make and hence the size of the operating income pie itself. We consider this effect as we expand our discussion of market-based, cost-based, and negotiated transfer prices.

MARKET-BASED TRANSFER PRICES

OBJECTIVE 5

Illustrate how market-based transfer prices generally promote goal-congruence in perfectly competitive markets

Perfectly competitive market.
Exists when there is a homogeneous product with equivalent buying and selling prices and no individual buyers or sellers can affect those prices by their own actions.

In perfectly competitive markets, the minimum price the selling division is willing to accept from the buying division is the market price, because the selling division can always sell its output in the external market at that price. The maximum price the buying division is willing to pay to the selling division is the market price, because the buying division can always buy its input in the external market at that price.

Be aware of the conflict distress prices can cause. Because the selling division receives very low revenues from distress prices, managers may decide to produce other products that would not be in the company's best interest in the long run. Alternatively, if the transfer price is based on the long-run average market price, the buying division will prefer to buy externally. If top management *requires* buying internally (at the long-run average market price), autonomy is violated.

Perfectly Competitive Market Case

Transferring products or services at market prices generally leads to optimal decisions when three conditions are satisfied: (1) the intermediate market is perfectly competitive, (2) interdependencies of subunits are minimal, and (3) there are no additional costs or benefits to the corporation as a whole in using the market instead of transacting internally. A **perfectly competitive market** exists when there is a homogeneous product with equivalent buying and selling prices and no individual buyers or sellers can affect those prices by their own actions. By using market-based transfer prices in perfectly competitive markets, a company can meet the criteria of goal-congruence, management effort, optimal subunit performance, and (if desired) subunit autonomy.

Reconsider the Northern Petroleum example, assuming that there is a perfectly competitive market for crude oil in the Calgary area, and that the market price is $21 per barrel. As a result, the Transportation Division can sell and the Refining Division can buy as much crude oil as each wants at $21 per barrel. Northern, however, would like its managers to buy or sell crude oil internally. Think about the decisions that Northern's division managers would make if each had the option to sell or buy crude oil externally. If the transfer price between Northern's Transportation and Refining Divisions is set below $21, the manager of the Transportation Division will be motivated to sell all production to outside buyers at $21 per barrel. If the transfer price is set above $21, the manager of the Refining Division will be motivated to purchase all its crude oil requirements from outside suppliers. A current market value transfer price of $21.00 could motivate both the Transportation and Refining Division to buy and sell internally.

Suppose each division manager is motivated to maximize his or her own division operating income. The Transportation Division will sell (either internally or externally) as much crude oil as it can profitably sell, and the Refining Division will buy (either internally or externally) as much crude oil as it can profitably transport. At a transfer price of $21.00, the actions that maximize division operating income are also the actions that maximize operating income of Northern Petroleum as a whole. Market prices also serve to evaluate the economic performance and profitability of each division individually.

Distress Prices

When supply outstrips demand, market prices may drop well below their historical average. If the drop in prices is expected to be temporary, these low market prices are sometimes called "distress prices." Deciding whether a current market price is a distress price is often difficult. The market prices of several agricultural commodities, such as wheat and oats, have stayed for many years at what observers initially believed were temporary distress levels.

Which transfer pricing method should be used for judging performance if distress prices prevail? Some companies use the distress prices themselves, but others use long-run average prices, or "normal" market prices. In the short run, the manager of the supplier division should meet the distress price as long as it exceeds the incremental costs of supplying the product or service; if not, the supplying division should stop producing and the buying division should buy the product or service from an outside supplier. These actions would increase overall companywide operating income. If the long-run average market price is used, forcing the manager to buy internally at a price above the current market price will hurt the buying division's short-run performance and understate its profitability. If, however, prices remain low in the long run, the manager of the supplying division must decide whether to dispose of some manufacturing facilities or shut down and have the buying division purchase the product from outside.

COST-BASED TRANSFER PRICES

Cost-based transfer prices are helpful when market prices are unavailable, inappropriate, or too costly to obtain. For example, the product may be specialized or unique, price lists may not be widely available, or the internal product may be different from the products available externally in terms of quality and service.

OBJECTIVE 6

Recognize why a transfer price based on full cost plus a markup may lead to suboptimal decisions

Full-Cost Bases

In practice, many companies use transfer prices based on full costs. These prices, however, can lead to suboptimal decisions. Assume that Northern Petroleum makes internal transfers at 110% of full cost. The Sarnia Refining Division purchases, on average, 20,000 barrels of crude oil per day from a local Sarnia supplier, who delivers the crude oil to the refinery. Purchase and delivery cost $21 per barrel. To reduce crude oil costs, the Refining Division has located an independent producer in Calgary who is willing to sell 20,000 barrels of crude oil per day at $16 per barrel, delivered to Northern's pipeline in Calgary. Given Northern's organization structure, the Transportation Division would purchase the 20,000 barrels of crude oil in Calgary, transport it to Sarnia, and then sell it to the Refining Division. The pipeline has excess capacity and can ship the 20,000 barrels at its variable costs of $1 per barrel. Will Northern Petroleum incur lower costs by purchasing crude oil from the independent producer in Calgary or by purchasing crude oil from the Sarnia supplier? Will the Refining Division show lower crude oil purchasing costs by using oil from the Calgary producer or by using its current Sarnia supplier?

The following analysis shows that operating income of Northern Petroleum as a whole would be maximized by purchasing oil from the independent Calgary producer. The analysis compares the incremental costs in all divisions under the two alternatives:

◆ **Alternative 1.** Buy 20,000 barrels from the Sarnia supplier at $21 per barrel. Total costs to Horizon Petroleum = 20,000 × $21 = $420,000.

◆ **Alternative 2.** Buy 20,000 barrels in Calgary at $16 per barrel and transport it to Sarnia at $1 per barrel variable costs. Total costs to Northern Petroleum = 20,000 × ($16 + $1) = $340,000.

There is a reduction in total costs to Northern Petroleum of $80,000 by using the independent producer in Calgary ($420,000 − $340,000).

In turn, suppose the Transportation Division's transfer price to the Refining Division is 110% of full cost. The Refining Division will see its reported division costs increase if the crude oil is purchased from the independent producer in Calgary:

$$\text{Transfer price} = 1.10 \times \left(\begin{array}{c} \text{Purchase price} \\ \text{from Calgary} \\ \text{producer} \end{array} + \begin{array}{c} \text{Unit variable cost} \\ \text{of Transportation} \\ \text{Division} \end{array} + \begin{array}{c} \text{Unit fixed cost} \\ \text{of Transportation} \\ \text{Division} \end{array} \right)$$

$$= 1.10 \times (\$16 + \$1 + \$3) = 1.10 \times \$20 = \$22$$

- ◆ **Alternative 1.** Buy 20,000 barrels from the Sarnia supplier at $21 per barrel. Total costs to Refining Division = 20,000 × $21 = $420,000.
- ◆ **Alternative 2.** Buy 20,000 barrels from the Transportation Division of Northern Petroleum that are purchased from the independent producer in Calgary. Total costs to Refining Division = 20,000 × $22 = $440,000.

As a profit centre, the Refining Division can maximize its short-run division operating income by purchasing from the Sarnia supplier ($420,000 versus $440,000).

The transfer-pricing method has led the Refining Division to regard the fixed cost (and the 10% markup) of the Transportation Division as a variable cost. Why? Because the Refining Division looks at each barrel that it obtains from the Transportation Division as a variable cost of $22—if 10 barrels are transferred, it costs the Refining Division $220; if 100 barrels are transferred, it costs $2,200. From the point of view of Northern Petroleum as a whole, its variable costs per barrel are $17 ($16 to purchase the oil from the independent producer and $1 to transport it to Sarnia). The remaining $5.00 ($22 − $17) per barrel are fixed costs and markups of the Transportation Division. Buying crude oil in Sarnia costs Northern Petroleum $21 per barrel. For the company, it is cheaper to buy from Calgary. But the Refining Division sees the problem differently. From its standpoint, it prefers buying from the Sarnia supplier at a cost of $420,000 (20,000 barrels × $21 per barrel) because buying from Calgary costs the division $440,000 (20,000 barrels × $22). Goal-incongruence is induced by the transfer price based on full cost plus a markup.

Should Northern's top management interfere and force the Refining Division to buy from the Transportation Division? Top management interference would undercut the philosophy of decentralization, so Northern's top management would probably view the decision by the Refining Division to purchase crude oil from external suppliers as an inevitable cost of decentralization and not interfere. Of course, some interference may occasionally be necessary to prevent costly blunders. But recurring interference and constraints would simply transform Northern from a decentralized company into a centralized company.

Constant cost-based transfer prices create an incentive for managers of selling divisions to decrease their costs.

What transfer price will promote goal-congruence for both the Transportation Division and the Refining Division? The minimum transfer price is $17 per barrel; a transfer price below $17 does not provide the Transportation Division with an incentive to purchase crude oil from the independent producer in Calgary while a transfer price above $17 generates contribution margin to cover fixed costs. The maximum transfer price is $21 per barrel; a transfer price above $21 will cause the Refining Division to purchase crude oil from the external market rather than from the Transportation Division. A transfer price between the minimum and maximum transfer prices of $17 and $21 respectively will promote goal-congruence—both divisions will increase their own reported division operating income by purchasing crude oil from the independent producer in Calgary. In particular, a transfer price based on the full costs of $20 without a markup will achieve goal-congruence. The Transportation Division will show no operating income and will be evaluated as a cost centre. Surveys indicate that managers prefer to use full-cost transfer pricing because it yields relevant costs for long-run decisions and because it facilitates pricing on the basis of full product costs.

Using full-cost transfer prices that include an allocation of fixed overhead costs raises other issues. How are indirect costs allocated to products? Have the correct activities, cost pools, and cost drivers been identified? Are the chosen overhead rates actual or budgeted rates? The issues here are similar to the issues that arise in allocating fixed costs (Chapter 14). Full-cost-based transfer prices calculated using activity-based cost drivers can provide more refined allocation bases for allocating costs to products. Using budgeted costs and budgeted rates lets both divisions know the transfer price in advance. Some companies calculate budgeted rates based on practical capacity rather than master-budget capacity utilization levels (Chapter 9). Using budgeted rates and practical capacity overcomes the problem of inefficiencies in actual costs and costs of unused capacity being passed along from the selling to the buying division. That is because transfer prices are based on budgeted (efficient) costs, not what the actual cost or capacity utilization is. Also variations in the quantity of units produced by the selling division do not affect the transfer price.

Variable Cost Bases

Transferring 20,000 barrels of crude oil from the Transportation Division to the Refining Division at the variable cost of $17 per barrel achieves goal congruence, as shown in the preceding section. The Refining Division would buy from the Transportation Division because the Transportation Division's variable cost (which is also the relevant incremental cost for Northern Petroleum as a whole) is less than the $21 price charged by outside suppliers. At the $17 per barrel transfer price, the Transportation Division would record an operating loss and the Refining Division would show large profits because it would be charged only for the variable costs of the Transportation Division. One approach to addressing this problem is to have the Refining Division make a lump-sum transfer payment to cover fixed costs and generate some operating income for the Transportation Division while the Transportation Division continues to make transfers at variable cost. The fixed payment is the price the Refining Division pays for using the capacity of the Transportation Division. The income earned by each division can then be used to evaluate the performance of each division and its manager.

Prorating the Difference between Minimum and Maximum Transfer Prices

An alternative cost-based approach is for Northern Petroleum to choose a transfer price that splits the $4 difference between the maximum transfer price the Refining Division is willing to pay and the minimum transfer price the Transportation Division wants on some equitable basis. Suppose Northern Petroleum allocates the $4 difference on the basis of the budgeted variable costs incurred by the Transportation Division and the Refining Division for a given quantity of crude oil. Using the data in Exhibit 23-2 (p. 891), the variable costs are as follows:

Transportation Division to transport 100 barrels of crude oil	$100
Refining Division to refine 100 barrels of crude oil	400
	$500

The Transportation Division gets to keep $\frac{\$100}{\$500} \times \$4 = \$0.80$, and the Refining Division gets to keep $\frac{\$400}{\$500} \times \$4 = \$3.20$ of the $4 difference. That is, the transfer price between the Transportation Division and the Refining Division would be $17.80 per barrel of crude oil ($16 purchase cost + $1 variable costs + $0.80 that the Transportation Division gets to keep). Essentially, this approach is a budgeted variable cost plus transfer price; the "plus" indicates the setting of a transfer price above variable costs.

To decide on the $0.80 and $3.20 allocation of the $4 contribution to total corporate operating income per barrel, the divisions must share information about their variable costs. In effect, each division does not operate (at least for this transaction) in a totally decentralized manner. Because most organizations are hybrids of centralization and decentralization anyway, this approach deserves serious consideration when transfers are significant. Note, however, that each division has an incentive to overstate its variable costs in order to receive a more favourable transfer price.

> Transfer pricing allocates operating income across divisions, which can mean division managers view one another as competitors, and this limits their willingness to share information and expertise.

Dual Pricing

There is seldom a *single* transfer price that simultaneously meets the criteria of goal-congruence, management effort, and subunit autonomy. Some companies turn to **dual pricing,** using two separate transfer pricing methods to price each interdivision transaction. An example of dual pricing arises when the selling division receives a full cost plus markup-based price and the buying division pays the market price for the internally transferred products. Assume that Northern Petroleum purchases crude oil from the independent producer in Calgary at $16 per barrel. One way of

> **Dual pricing.** Approach to transfer pricing using two separate transfer pricing methods to price each interdivision transaction.

recording the journal entry for the transfer between the Transportation Division and the Refining Division is

1. Credit the Transportation Division (the selling division) with the 110%-of-full-cost transfer price of $22 per barrel of crude oil.

2. Debit the Refining Division (the buying division) with the market-based transfer price of $21 per barrel of crude oil.

3. Debit a corporate cost account for the $1 ($22 − $21) difference between the two transfer prices for the cost of crude oil borne by corporate rather than the Refining Division.

The dual-price method promotes goal-congruence because it makes the Refining Division no worse off if it purchases the crude oil from the Transportation Division rather than from the outside supplier. In either case, the Refining Division's cost is $21 per barrel of crude oil. This dual-price system essentially gives the Transportation Division a corporate subsidy. The results of dual pricing? The operating income for Northern Petroleum as a whole is less than the sum of the operating incomes of the divisions.

Dual pricing is not widely used in practice even though it reduces the goal-congruence problems associated with a pure cost-plus-based transfer pricing method. One concern of top management is that the manager of the supplying division does not have sufficient incentive to control costs with a dual-price system. A second concern is that the dual-price system confuses division managers about the level of decentralization top management seeks. Above all, dual pricing tends to insulate managers from the frictions of the marketplace. Managers should know as much as possible about their subunits' buying and selling markets, and dual pricing reduces the incentive to gain this knowledge.

NEGOTIATED TRANSFER PRICES

Negotiated transfer prices arise as the outcome of a bargaining process between selling and buying divisions. Consider again the choice of a transfer price between the Transportation and Refining Divisions of Northern Petroleum. The Transportation Division has excess capacity that it can use to transport oil from Calgary to Sarnia. The Transportation Division will only be willing to "sell" oil to the Refining Division if the transfer price equals or exceeds $17 per barrel of crude oil (its variable costs). The Refining Division will only be willing to "buy" crude oil from the Transportation Division if the cost equals or is below $21 per barrel (the price at which the Refining Division can buy crude oil in Sarnia).

Given the Transportation Division's unused capacity, Northern Petroleum as a whole maximizes operating income if the Refining Division purchases from the Transportation Division rather than from the Sarnia market (incremental costs of $17 per barrel versus incremental costs of $21 per barrel). Both divisions would be interested in transacting with each other if the transfer price is set between $17 and $21. For example, a transfer price of $19.25 per barrel will increase the Transportation Division's operating income by $19.25 − $17 = $2.75 per barrel. It will increase the Refining Division's operating income by $21 − $19.25 = $1.75 per barrel because Refining can now "buy" the oil for $19.25 inside rather than for $21 outside.

The key question is where between the $17 and $21 the transfer price will be. The answer depends on the bargaining strengths of the two divisions. The Transportation Division has more information about the price less incremental marketing costs of supplying crude oil to outside refineries while the Refining Division has more information about its other available sources of oil. Negotiations become particularly sensitive if Northern evaluates each division's performance on the basis of divisional operating income. The price negotiated by the two divisions will, in general, have no specific relationship to either costs or market price. But cost and price information are often useful starting points in the negotiation process. Exhibit 23-3 on page 898 compares the three methods of transfer pricing discussed. The full-cost based transfer price is the most used and negotiated prices are the least frequently used transfer-pricing method worldwide (see the Global Surveys of Company Practice box on p. 897).

Domestic and Multinational Transfer-Pricing Practices

Transfer pricing remains an important accounting priority for managers around the world. A recent survey of managers in 22 countries, including the United States, Australia, Canada, and Japan, found that 86% of all respondents believed transfer pricing was important to their group's operations.[a]

What transfer-pricing methods are used around the world? The following tables indicate how extensively particular transfer-pricing methods are used in different countries.

A. Domestic Transfer-Pricing Methods

Methods	United States[b]	Australia[c]	Canada[d]	Japan[b]	New Zealand[e]	United Kingdom[f]
Market-based	26%	13%	34%	34%	18%	26%
Cost-based:						
Variable cost	3	—	6	2	10	10
Absorption or full cost	49	—	37	44	61	38
Other	1	—	3	—	—	1
Total	53%	65%	46%	46%	71%	49%
Negotiated	17%	11%	18%	19%	11%	24%
Other	4%	11%	2%	1%	—	1%
	100%	100%	100%	100%	100%	100%

B. Multinational Transfer-Pricing Methods

Methods	United States[b]	Australia	Canada[d]	Japan[b]	New Zealand	United Kingdom
Market-based	35%	—	37%	37%	—	—
Cost-based:						
Variable cost	0	—	5	3	—	—
Absorption or full cost	42	—	26	38	—	—
Other	1	—	2	—	—	—
Total	43%	—	33%	41%	—	—
Negotiated	14%	—	26%	22%	—	—
Other	8%	—	4%	—	—	—
	100%	—	100%	100%	—	—

Note: Dashes indicate information was not disclosed in survey.

The surveys indicate that for domestic transfer pricing, managers in all countries use cost-based transfer prices more frequently than market-based transfer prices. For multinational transfer pricing, managers use cost-based methods only slightly more often than market-based methods. Many companies have market-based transfer prices in some divisions and cost-based transfer prices in others.

Survey evidence indicates that managers consider the following factors important when making domestic transfer-pricing decisions (in order of importance): (1) maximizing consolidated after-tax profits, (2) performance evaluation, and (3) management motivation. Factors cited as important for multinational transfer-pricing decisions include (in order of importance): (1) income tax rate and other tax differences among countries, (2) total income of the company, and (3) income- or dividend-repatriation restrictions.[b,g]

[a]Ernst & Young, *Transfer Pricing 2003 Global Survey* (New York: Ernst & Young, November 2003).

[b]Tang, R., *Transfer Pricing Systems Management: Practical Issues and Cases* (Montvale, NJ: Institute of Management Accountants, 2001).

[c]Joye, M., and P. Blayney, "Cost and Management Accounting Practices in Australian Manufacturing Companies: Survey Results" (Accounting Research Centre, The University of Sydney, 1991).

[d]Tang, R., "Canadian Transfer Pricing in the 1990s," *Management Accounting* (1992).

[e]Hoque, Z., and M. Alam, "Organization Size, Business Objectives, Managerial Autonomy, Industry Conditions, and Management's Choice of Transfer Pricing Methods: A Contextual Analysis of New Zealand Companies" (Working Paper, Victoria University of Wellington, New Zealand, 1998).

[f]Drury, C., S. Braund, P. Osborne, and M. Tayles, *A Survey of Management Accounting Practices in UK Manufacturing Companies* (London: Chartered Association of Certified Accountants, 1993).

[g]Elliot, J., "International Transfer Pricing: A Survey of U.K. and Non-U.K. Groups," *Management Accounting* (1998).

A General Guideline for Transfer-Pricing Situations

OBJECTIVE 8

Present a general guideline for determining a minimum transfer price in transfer-pricing situations

Is there an all-pervasive rule for transfer pricing that leads toward optimal decisions for the organization as a whole? No. Why? Because the three criteria of goal-congruence, management effort, and subunit autonomy must all be considered simultaneously. The following general guideline, however, has proven to be a helpful first step in setting a minimum transfer price in many specific situations:

$$\begin{array}{l} \text{Minimum} \\ \text{transfer price} \end{array} = \begin{array}{l} \text{Additional } incremental \text{ or } outlay \text{ } costs \text{ per} \\ \text{unit incurred up to the point of transfer} \end{array} + \begin{array}{l} Opportunity \text{ } costs \text{ per unit} \\ \text{to the supplying division} \end{array}$$

The term *incremental* or *outlay costs* in this context represents the additional costs that are directly associated with the production and transfer of the products or services. *Opportunity costs* are defined here as the maximum contribution forgone by the supplying division if the products or services are transferred internally. For example, if the supplying division is operating at capacity, the opportunity cost of transferring a unit internally rather than selling it externally is equal to the market price minus variable costs. We distinguish incremental costs from opportunity costs because the accounting system typically records incremental costs but not opportunity costs. We illustrate the general guideline in some specific situations using data from the Production and Transportation Divisions of Northern Petroleum.

1. **A perfectly competitive market for the intermediate product exists, and the selling division has no unused capacity.** If the market for crude oil in

EXHIBIT 23-3

Comparison of Different Transfer-Pricing Methods

Criteria	Market-Based	Cost-Based	Negotiated
Achieves goal-congruence	Yes, when markets are competitive	Often but not always	Yes
Useful for evaluating subunit performance	Yes, when markets are competitive	Difficult unless transfer price exceeds full cost and even then is somewhat arbitrary	Yes, but transfer prices are affected by bargaining strengths of the buying and selling divisions
Motivates management effort	Yes	Yes, when based on budgeted costs; less incentive to control costs if transfers are based on actual costs	Yes
Preserves subunit autonomy	Yes, when markets are competitive	No, because it is rule based	Yes, because it is based on negotiations between subunits
Other factors	Market may not exist, or markets may be imperfect or in distress	Useful for determining full cost of products and services; easy to implement	Bargaining and negotiations take time and may need to be reviewed repeatedly as conditions change

Calgary is perfectly competitive, the Transportation Division can sell all the crude oil it transports to the external market at $21 per barrel, and it will have no unused capacity. The Transportation Division's incremental cost (as shown in Exhibit 23-1, p. 890) is either $13 per barrel (purchase cost of $12 per barrel plus variable transportation cost of $1 per barrel) for oil purchased under the long-term contract or $17 per barrel (purchase cost of $16 plus variable transportation cost of $1) for oil purchased at current market prices from the Calgary producer. The Transportation Division's opportunity cost per barrel of transferring the oil internally is the contribution margin per barrel forgone by not selling the crude oil in the external market: $8 for oil purchased under the long-term contract (market price, $21, minus variable cost, $13) and $4 for oil purchased from the Calgary producer (market price, $21, minus variable cost, $17). In either case,

$$\text{Minimum transfer price per barrel} = \frac{\text{Incremental costs}}{\text{per barrel}} + \frac{\text{Opportunity costs}}{\text{per barrel}}$$

$$= \$13 + \$8 = \$21 = \text{Market price per barrel}$$

Market-based transfer prices are ideal in perfectly competitive markets when there is no idle capacity.

2. **An intermediate market exists that is not perfectly competitive, and the selling division has unused capacity.** In markets that are not perfectly competitive, capacity utilization can only be increased by decreasing prices. Unused capacity exists because decreasing prices is often not worthwhile—it decreases operating income. If the Transportation Division has unused capacity, its opportunity cost of transferring the oil internally is zero because the division does not forgo any external sales or contribution margin from internal transfers. In this case:

$$\text{Minimum transfer price per barrel} = \frac{\text{Incremental cost}}{\text{per barrel}} = \begin{array}{l}\text{Either \$13 per barrel purchased under the} \\ \text{long-term contract, or \$17 per barrel for} \\ \text{oil purchased from the Calgary producer}\end{array}$$

Any transfer price above incremental cost but below $21—the price at which the Refining Division can buy crude oil in Sarnia—motivates the Transportation Division to transport crude oil to the Refining Division and the Refining Division to buy crude oil from the Transportation Division. In this situation, the company could either use a cost-based transfer price or allow the two divisions to negotiate a transfer price between themselves.

In general, though, in markets that are not perfectly competitive, the potential to influence demand and operating income through prices makes measuring opportunity costs more complicated. The transfer price depends on constantly changing levels of supply and demand. There is not just one transfer price; rather, a transfer pricing schedule yields the transfer price for various quantities supplied and demanded, depending on the incremental costs and opportunity costs of the units transferred. Consider the following situation: Suppose the Refining Division receives an order to supply specially processed gasoline. The Refining Division will only profit from this order if the Transportation Division can supply crude oil at a price not exceeding $19 per barrel. Suppose the incremental cost to purchase and supply crude oil is $17 per barrel. In this case, the transfer price that would benefit both divisions must be greater than $17 but less than $19 (rather than $21).

3. **No market exists for the intermediate product.** This would occur, for example, in the Northern Petroleum case if oil from the production well flows directly into the pipeline and cannot be sold to outside parties. Here, the opportunity cost of supplying crude oil internally is zero because the inability to sell crude oil externally means no contribution margin is forgone. At the Transportation Division of Northern Petroleum, the minimum transfer price under the general guideline would be the incremental costs per barrel of either $13 or $17. As in the previous case, any transfer price between the incremental cost and $21 will achieve goal congruence. Knowledge of the incremental cost per barrel of crude oil would be helpful to the Refining Division for many decisions, such as short-run pricing.

In transfer-pricing situations, opportunity cost is the profit the selling division (SD) forgoes by selling internally rather than externally. Assume the SD has no idle capacity for a particular product and can sell all it produces at $4 per unit. Incremental cost is $1 per unit. If the SD sells internally, the opportunity cost is $3 per unit ($4 revenue per unit − $1 incremental cost per unit). In contrast, if the SD has unused capacity with no alternative use, no profit is forgone by selling internally (opportunity cost is $0).

CMA Management Magazine
www.managementmag.com/
index.cfm/ci_id/1321/la_id/1/print/
true.htm
www.managementmag.com/
index.cfm/ci_id/2281/la_id/1

CAmagazine, March, 2005
www.camagazine.com/
index.cfm/ci_id/24841/la_id/1.htm

Related parties. Two subunits of the same corporation.

Arm's length transaction. Sales between a corporation and a nonrelated party.

Comparable uncontrolled price method (CUP). The CRA compares the transfer price to arm's length prices for similar transactions to ensure it falls in the two mid-quartiles of the price range.

Resale price method (RPM). The CRA compares the transfer price to arm's length prices for similar finished goods to ensure it falls in the two mid-quartiles of the price range.

Cost plus method (CPM). The CRA compares the overall financial profitability of the related parties.

Profit split method (PSM). The CRA evaluates the relative value added of the contribution made by the value-added functions of each related party.

Transactional net margin method (TNMM). The basis for evaluation is the corporate ROA.

Tax haven. Country having no tax treaty with Canada with which it shares information.

International financial centre. Country having a tax treaty with Canada and a much lower corporate income tax rate.

Now we will consider factors affecting transfer prices among corporate subunits in different countries. Sales between corporate subunits are called sales between **related parties**, in contrast to external sales between a subunit and a nonrelated party termed **arm's length transactions**. The transfer prices have tax implications and therefore affect the government revenues of each country involved. Tax factors include income taxes, payroll taxes, customs duties, tariffs, sales taxes, value-added taxes, environment-related taxes, and other government levies. We focus on income tax factors as a key consideration in transfer pricing decisions.

The Income Tax Act of Canada (section 247) sets out the laws regarding transfer pricing. The most recent rules were introduced in 1998 after legislative changes in the U.S. and the publication of transfer price guidelines by the Organisation for Economic Co-operation and Development (OECD). The Canada Revenue Agency (CRA) intends to achieve harmonization with OECD and U.S. laws to reduce the costs of tax compliance for multinational corporations. The most important laws limit how companies set transfer prices to one of five methods. Traditional transaction methods include the **comparable uncontrolled price (CUP)**, **resale price method (RPM)**, and **cost plus method (CPM)**. The CUP is analogous to the internal market-based price. The related-party transfer price reported by a corporation is compared to prices for similar transactions among arm's length (nonrelated) parties and must fall within the middle two quartiles of this range of prices. The CRA has confidential comparable tables in its ever-growing database that it uses to make these comparisons.

The RPM requires a company calculate the arm's length resale price and distributors of finished goods typically use this method when the cost of distribution is low relative to the value of the finished goods (i.e., almost non-value-added). Again the CRA compares the estimated transfer price to a range of prices for similar arm's length transactions and usually accepts transfer prices in the two mid-quartiles of this range. The CPM has already been described and highlights the effect of the transfer price on the pre-tax income of each subunit. This method permits corporations the greatest discretion and most readily justified transfer price to the CRA because of the quality of information provided by management accounting and control systems.

The transactional profit methods of setting a transfer price are the **profit split method (PSM)** and **transactional net margin method (TNMM)**. The PSM requires understanding the value added by the functions performed by each related party and the resulting allocation of profit and loss to each subunit. This is illustrated below in the example of GlaxoSmithKline. The fifth method, TNMM, is based on the return on assets (ROA) of the corporation as a whole and provides maximum discretion for establishing a transfer price.

Establishing the arm's length price for value-added services such as marketing or intangible contributions such as research and development knowledge is difficult. The role of the management accountant has increased in importance as has the role of the internal data on pricing already produced by the management accounting and control system because companies must produce contemporaneous documentation for every transfer price transaction or be subject to an automatic financial penalty for failing to do so. Companies are obligated to comply with Canada's tax laws and this audit trail that justifies in detail the transfer price used provides the CRA with evidence companies have made reasonable effort to do what they should to establish the price is arm's length. The CRA auditors may still disagree with and adjust the transfer price despite the documentation provided but no penalty will be imposed for failing to make a reasonable effort to establish an arm's length transfer price.

Corporations may choose a tax minimization strategy by establishing a legitimate subsidiary in a tax haven (e.g., Andorra, Liechtenstein, Monaco). **Tax havens** have no tax agreements with Canada and share no information, which will increase the costs of any tax audit for the company. A second strategy is to establish a legitimate subsidiary in an **international financial centre** with very low income tax rates (e.g., Barbados, Ireland). These centres have tax treaties with Canada. Consider an example of a Canadian company that manufactures and sells products from Ireland. Tax and other incentives offered there result in the Irish division paying lower taxes on its income in

Ireland. Therefore, the company has an incentive to set the transfer price for transfers into Canada as high as possible. Why? To maximize income reported in Ireland where tax rates are lower and reduce income reported in Canada that is taxed at rates as high as 40%. Nevertheless, to make sound transfer pricing decisions, managers must remember that penalties for noncompliance with transfer pricing tax laws can be substantial.

In 2004 GlaxoSmithKline, a multinational pharmaceutical company, was penalized US$5.2 billion on understated U.S. pretax income earned between 1989 and 1996. At issue was how much of the value added for an immensely profitable new drug arose from the marketing efforts of the U.S. or the research and development efforts of the U.K., and how these costs should be allocated (*The Economist*, January 29, 2004).

In Canada the CRA has indicated it will aggressively challenge transfer prices based on costs allocated proportionally to revenues of the related parties, management services to Canadian companies at cost plus, and any dual product prices. While the CRA has published transfer-pricing guidelines (IC87–2R), when disputes arise, the final decision on the transfer price is often negotiated among the tax authorities involved in the dispute. This resolution process is not only costly but can take as long as two years, and any penalties imposed are retroactive and accumulate interest during the process. To avoid costly disputes, companies may choose a third strategy—to request an advance pricing arrangement with all involved tax authorities.

Consider the Northern Petroleum data in Exhibit 23-2 (p. 891). Assume that Northern operates a Transportation Division in Mexico that pays Mexican income taxes at 30% of operating income and that both the Transportation and Refining Divisions based in Canada pay income taxes at 20% of operating income. Northern Petroleum would minimize its total income tax payments with the 110%-of-full-costs transfer pricing method, as shown in the following table:

	Operating Income for 100 Barrels of Crude Oil			Income Tax on 100 Barrels of Crude Oil		
Transfer-Pricing Method	Transportation Division (Mexico) (1)	Refining Division (Canada) (2)	Total (3) = (1) + (2)	Transportation Division (Mexico) (4) = 0.30 × (1)	Refining Division (Canada) (5) = 0.20 × (2)	Total (6) = (4) + (5)
Market price	$500	$100	$600	$150.00	$20	$170.00
110% of full costs	160	440	600	48.00	88	136.00
Negotiated price	325	275	600	97.50	55	152.50

Tax considerations raise additional issues that may conflict with other objectives of transfer pricing. Suppose that the market for crude oil in Calgary is perfectly competitive. In this case, the market-based transfer price achieves goal-congruence and provides effort incentives. It also helps Northern to evaluate the economic profitability of the Transportation Division. But it is costly from an income tax standpoint.

Northern Petroleum would favour using 110% of full costs for tax reporting. Tax laws in Canada and Mexico constrain this option. In particular, the Mexican tax authorities are fully aware of Northern Petroleum's incentives to minimize income taxes by reducing the income reported in Mexico (see also the Concepts in Action feature, p. 902). They would challenge any attempts to shift income to the Transportation and Refining Divisions through a low transfer price.

The perfectly competitive market for crude oil in Mexico would probably force Northern Petroleum to use the market price for transfers from the Production Division to the Transportation Division. Northern Petroleum might successfully argue that the transfer price should be set below the market price because the Production Division incurs no marketing and distribution costs when "selling" crude oil to the Transportation Division. Northern Petroleum could obtain advanced approval of the transfer pricing arrangements from the appropriate tax authorities.

To meet multiple transfer-pricing objectives, a company may choose to keep one set of accounting records for tax reporting and a second set for internal management reporting. The difficulty here is that tax authorities may interpret two sets of books as suggestive of the company manipulating its reported taxable income to avoid tax payments.

U.S. Internal Revenue Service, Japanese National Tax Agency, and Transfer-Pricing Games

Tax authorities and government officials around the world pay close attention to taxes paid by multinational companies operating within their boundaries. At the heart of the issue are the transfer prices that companies use to transfer products from one country to another. The U.S. Internal Revenue Service (IRS) and the Japanese National Tax Agency (NTA) have been among the most active agencies pursuing international transfer pricing disputes.

For example, in 1993, the IRS investigated and concluded that Nissan Motor Company had understated U.S. taxes by setting transfer prices on passenger cars and trucks imported from Japan at "unrealistically" high levels. Nissan argued that it had maintained low margins in the United States to increase long-run market share in a very competitive market. Eventually, Nissan agreed to pay the IRS US$170 million, but the company suffered no loss. That's because the Japanese NTA refunded Nissan the full amount of the IRS payment.

Conversely, in May 1994, Japan's NTA alleged that Coca-Cola Corporation had underreported its taxable income in Japan by charging "excessive" transfer prices to its local subsidiary for materials and concentrate imported from the parent company and by levying "excessive" royalty payments on its Japanese subsidiary for use of its brand name and sales and marketing expertise. The NTA pointed out that the royalties paid by Coca-Cola's Japanese subsidiary were higher than those paid by other companies in the same industry. It also said that the Japanese subsidiary paid royalties even for products it had developed on its own. The NTA imposed taxes and penalties of US$150 million. Coca-Cola filed a complaint with the IRS, charging that the levying of the Japanese tax resulted in the same income being taxed twice, because Coca-Cola had already paid tax on this income in the United States. This complaint led to negotiations between Japanese and U.S. tax authorities to decide which country gets to tax Coca-Cola Japanese income. In a 1998 compromise settlement, Japan's NTA reduced its tax levy against Coca-Cola from US$150 million to US$50 million.

In 2000, Japan's NTA and the IRS had to settle another dispute regarding transfer prices. This time Coca-Cola's Japanese subsidiary had to record an additional US$450 million in taxable income from 1993 through 1999, which meant that it owed approximately US$170 million in back taxes and penalties. To avoid double taxation, the IRS refunded Coca-Cola the tax it had already paid to the United States.

Historically, disputes arose between governments over what constituted a "fair" transfer price because of the absence of an easily observable market price for the transferred product. In 2003, the United States and Japan signed a new tax treaty that, among other things, stipulates that future transfer-pricing disputes be addressed in accordance with the Organisation for Economic Co-operation and Development's *Transfer Pricing Guidelines*, which advocates the use of a more-transparent "arm's length" transfer-pricing protocol.

Although this development has eased disputes between the United States and Japan, the IRS and NTA remain actively engaged in transfer-pricing conflicts with other nations. In 2004, the IRS fined U.K.-based pharmaceutical manufacturer GlaxoSmithKline US$5.2 billion in back taxes and interest, stemming from a transfer pricing dispute regarding profits from 1989 through 1996. Meanwhile, the Japanese NTA brought action against Honda Motor Company in 2004 for understating technology royalties paid to the company from 1997 through 2002 by its Brazilian subsidiary. The NTA is seeking over US$100 million in back taxes. Both cases remain under review.

Sources: Adapted from C. Pass, "Transfer Pricing in Multinational Companies," *Management Accounting* (September 1994); "Coca-Cola Gets 10 Billion Yen Reprieve in Back Taxes," *Yomiuri Shimbun* (February 24, 1998); *Financial Times* (September 3, 1999); *Daily Yomiuri* (February 24, 1998, and April 30, 2000); Morrison & Foster, LLP, *New United States–Japan Tax Treaty Enters into Force: New Withholding Rates Take Effect on July 1, 2004*, April 2004; S. Vollmer and C. Serres, "IRS Fines GlaxoSmithKline $5.2 Billion in Audit of North Carolina Drug Giant," *News & Observer* (Raleigh, NC), January 8, 2004; "Honda's $525.4 Billion Transfer Pricing Adjustment," *Transfer Pricing Times* (July 20, 2004).

Transfer-Pricing Pressures

Transfer pricing requires one subunit manager to earn revenues and another subunit manager to incur costs. Managers are frequently evaluated on the basis of subunit profits. Little wonder, then, that subunit managers care deeply about how transfer prices are set. It is natural for subunit managers to argue for transfer prices that make their own performance look good. Management accountants must ensure that the transfer prices set are in the best interests of the company as a whole. This requires management accountants to understand business issues and the external market environment within which the businesses function. They must also never cave in to pressure from managers that will make a subunit's performance look good while hurting the corporation as a whole.

Transfer prices also have tax implications, particularly when products are transferred across country borders. Setting transfer prices is almost always a matter of judgment. At no time, however, should management accountants choose transfer prices that do not adhere to the tax codes of different countries. The time and cost to resolve transfer pricing disputes can be very high.

Consider Motorola, the electronics products manufacturer. In 2004, the U.S. Internal Revenue Service (IRS) notified the company that it was disputing the way Motorola calculated earnings from 1996 to 2000, resulting in an additional tax liability of US$500 million. The underlying issue was related to transfer pricing involving Motorola's 67 tax entities around the world. The IRS claimed too much profit was left in the company's tax entities abroad and that not enough income was recognized in the United States, resulting in lower tax payments. Company officials vigorously defended their accounting practices and now must convince the IRS that its practices are within the law.

Source: R. Crockett, "Motorola's Taxing Dispute," *Business Week Online*, August 12, 2004, http://www.businessweek.com/bwdaily/dnflash/aug2004/nj20040812_8175_db016.htm, accessed September 17, 2004.

Additional factors that arise in multinational transfer pricing include tariffs and customs duties levied on imports of products into a country. The issues here are similar to the income tax considerations discussed earlier—companies will have incentives to lower transfer prices for products imported into a country to reduce the tariffs and customs duties that those products will attract.

In addition to the various motivations for choosing transfer prices described so far, multinational transfer prices are sometimes influenced by restrictions that some countries place on the payment of income or dividends to parties outside their national borders. By increasing the prices of goods or services transferred into divisions in these countries, companies can increase the funds paid out of these countries without appearing to violate income or dividend restrictions (see Focus on Values and Behaviours, above).

PROBLEM FOR SELF-STUDY

PROBLEM

The Pillercat Corporation is a highly decentralized company. Each division manager has full authority for sourcing decisions and selling decisions. The Machining Division of Pillercat has been the major supplier of the 2,000 crankshafts that the Tractor Division needs each year.

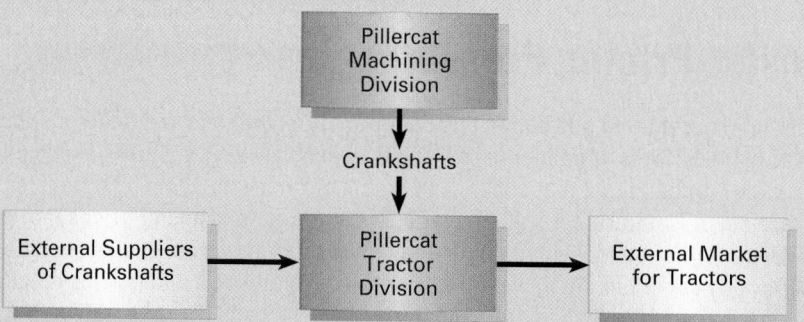

The Tractor Division, however, has just announced that it plans to purchase all its crankshafts in the forthcoming year from two external suppliers at $200 per crankshaft. The Machining Division of Pillercat recently increased its price for the forthcoming year to $220 per unit (from $200 per unit in the current year).

Juan Gomez, manager of the Machining Division, feels that the 10% price increase is fully justified. It results from a higher amortization charge on some new specialized equipment used to manufacture crankshafts and an increase in labour costs. Gomez wants the president of Pillercat Corporation to direct the Tractor Division to buy all its crankshafts from the Machining Division at the price of $220. The additional incremental costs per unit that Pillercat incurs to produce each crankshaft is the Machining Division's variable costs of $190. Fixed cost per crankshaft in the Machining Division equals $20.

	A	B
1	Number of crankshafts purchased by Tractor Division	2,000
2	External supplier's market price per crankshaft	$ 200
3	Variable cost per crankshaft in Machining Division	$ 190
4	Fixed cost per crankshaft in Machining Division	$ 20

REQUIRED

1. Compute the advantage or disadvantage (in terms of monthly operating income) to the Pillercat Corporation as a whole if the Tractor Division buys crankshafts internally from the Machining Division under each of the following cases.

   a. The Machining Division has no alternative use for the facilities used to manufacture crankshafts.

   b. The Machining Division can use the facilities for other production operations, which will result in monthly cash operating savings of $29,000.

   c. The Machining Division has no alternative use for the facilities, and the external supplier drops its price to $185 per crankshaft.

2. As the president of Pillercat, how would you respond to Juan Gomez's request to order the Tractor Division to purchase all of its crankshafts from the Machining Division? Would your response differ according to the scenarios described in parts (a), (b), and (c) of requirement 1? Why?

SOLUTION

1. Computations for the Tractor Division buying crankshafts internally for cases (a), (b), and (c) are:

A	B	C	D
		Case	
	a	b	c
3 Number of crankshafts purchased by Tractor Division	2,000	2,000	2,000
4 External supplier's market price per crankshaft	$ 200	$ 200	$ 185
5 Incremental cost per crankshaft in Machining Division	$ 190	$ 190	$ 190
6 Opportunity costs of the Machining Division supplying	–	$ 29,000	–
7 crankshafts to the Tractor Division			
8			
9 Total purchase costs if buying from an external supplier			
10 (2,000 shafts × $200, $200, $185 per shaft)	$400,000	$400,000	$370,000
11 Incremental costs of buying from the Machining Division			
12 (2,000 shafts × $190 per shaft)	380,000	380,000	380,000
13 Total opportunity costs of the Machining Division	–	29,000	–
14 Total relevant costs	380,000	$409,000	380,000
15 Annual operating income advantage (disadvantage) to			
16 Pillercat of buying from the Machining Division	$ 20,000	$ (9,000)	$ (10,000)
17			

The general guideline introduced on page 898 as a first step in setting a transfer price highlights the alternatives:

	A	B	C	D	E	F	G
		Incremental Cost		Opportunity Cost			External
		per unit Incurred to		per Unit to the		Transfer	Market
3	Case	Point of Transfer	+	Supplying Division	=	price	Price
4	a	$190	+	$ 0	=	$190.00	$200
5	b	$190	+	$14.50[a]	=	$204.50	$200
6	c	$190	+	$ 0	=	$190.00	$185
7							
8	[a] Opportunity per unit = Total opportunity costs ÷ Number of crankshafts = $29,000 ÷ 2,000 = $14.50						

The Tractor Division will maximize monthly operating income of Pillercat Corporation as a whole by purchasing from the Machining Division in case (a) and by purchasing from the external supplier in cases (b) and (c).

2. Pillercat Corporation is a highly decentralized company. If no forced transfer were made, the Tractor Division would use an external supplier, resulting in an optimal decision for the company as a whole in cases (b) and (c) of requirement 1 but not in case (a).

Suppose that in case 1(a), the Machining Division refuses to meet the price of $200. This decision means that the company will be $20,000 worse off in the short run. Should top management interfere and force a transfer at $200? This interference would undercut the philosophy of decentralization. Many top managements would not interfere because they would view the $20,000 as an inevitable cost of a suboptimal decision that occasionally occurs under decentralization. But how high must this cost be before the temptation to interfere would be irresistible? $30,000? $40,000?

Any top management interference with lower-level decision making weakens decentralization. Of course, such interference may occasionally be necessary to prevent costly blunders. But recurring interference and constraints simply transform a decentralized organization into a centralized organization.

The following decision guidelines use a question-and-answer format to summarize the chapter's main points. Each decision presents a key question. The guideline is the answer to that question.

DECISIONS	GUIDELINES
1. What is a management control system and how should it be designed?	A management control system is a means of gathering and using information to aid and coordinate the planning and control decisions throughout the organization, and to guide the behaviour of managers and employees. Effective management control systems are (a) closely aligned to the organization's strategy, (b) fit the organization's structure, and (c) motivate managers and employees to give effort to achieve the organization's goals.
2. What are the benefits and costs of decentralization?	The benefits of decentralization include (a) greater responsiveness to local needs, (b) gains from faster decision making, (c) increased motivation of subunit managers, (d) greater management development and learning, and (e) sharpened focus of subunit managers. The costs of decentralization include (a) suboptimal decision making (loss of control), (b) duplication of activities, (c) decreased loyalty toward the organization as a whole, and (d) increased costs of information gathering.
3. What is a transfer price, and what is it intended to achieve?	A transfer price is the price one subunit charges for a product or service supplied to another subunit of the same organization. Transfer prices seek to achieve (a) goal congruence, (b) management effort, (c) subunit performance evaluation, and (d) subunit autonomy (if desired).
4. What methods can be used to calculate transfer prices?	Transfer prices can be (a) market based, (b) cost based, or (c) negotiated. Different transfer-pricing methods produce different revenues and costs for individual subunits, and hence, different operating incomes for them.
5. What transfer price should be used if the market for the product to be transferred is perfectly competitive?	In perfectly competitive markets, there is no idle capacity, and division managers can buy and sell as much as they want at the market price. Setting the transfer price at the market price motivates division managers to transact internally and to take exactly the same actions as they would if they were transacting in the external market.
6. What problems can arise when full cost plus a markup is used as a transfer price?	A transfer price based on full cost plus a markup may lead to suboptimal decisions because it leads the buying division to regard the fixed costs and the markup of the selling division as variable costs. The buying division may then purchase products from an outside vendor expecting savings in variable costs that, in fact, will not occur.
7. What is the range over which two divisions will negotiate a transfer price when there is unused capacity?	When there is unused capacity, the transfer-price range for negotiations generally lies between the minimum price at which the selling division is willing to sell (its variable cost per unit) and the maximum price the buying division is willing to pay (the price at which the product is available from outside suppliers).
8. What is the general guideline for determining a minimum transfer price?	The general guideline states that the minimum transfer price equals the incremental cost per unit incurred up to the point of transfer plus the opportunity cost per unit to the supplying division resulting from transferring products or services internally.
9. What are the income tax considerations when determining transfer prices?	Transfer prices can reduce income tax payments by recognizing more income in low-tax-rate countries and less income in high-tax-rate countries. However, tax regulations of different countries restrict the transfer prices that companies can choose.

▼

TERMS TO LEARN

This chapter contains definitions of the following important terms:

arm's length transaction (p. 900)
autonomy (p. 888)
comparable uncontrolled price
     method (CUP) (p. 900)
cost plus method (CPM) (p. 900)
decentralization (p. 884)
dual pricing (p. 895)
dysfunctional decision making (p. 885)

effort (p. 884)
goal-congruence (p. 884)
goal-incongruent decision making (p. 885)
intermediate product (p. 887)
international financial centre (p. 900)
management control system (p. 883)
motivation (p. 884)
perfectly competitive market (p. 892)

profit split method (PSM) (p. 900)
related parties (p. 900)
resale price method (RPM) (p. 900)
suboptimal decision making (p. 885)

tax haven (p. 900)
transactional net margin method
(TNMM) (p. 900)
transfer price (p. 887)

▼ ASSIGNMENT MATERIAL

QUESTIONS

23-1 What is a management control system?

23-2 Describe three criteria you would use to evaluate whether a management control system is effective.

23-3 What is the relationship among motivation, goal-congruence, and effort?

23-4 Name three benefits and two costs of decentralization.

23-5 "Organizations typically adopt a consistent decentralization or centralization philosophy across all their business functions." Do you agree? Explain.

23-6 "Transfer pricing is confined to profit centres." Do you agree? Why?

23-7 What are the three general methods for determining transfer prices?

23-8 What properties should transfer pricing systems have?

23-9 "All transfer pricing methods give the same division operating income." Do you agree? Explain.

23-10 Under what conditions is a market-based transfer price optimal?

23-11 What is one potential limitation of full-cost-based transfer prices?

23-12 Give two reasons why a dual-price approach to transfer pricing is not widely used.

23-13 "Cost and price information play no role in negotiated transfer prices." Do you agree? Explain.

23-14 "Under the general transfer-pricing guideline, the minimum transfer price will vary depending on whether the supplying division has idle capacity or not." Do you agree? Explain.

23-15 Why should managers consider income tax issues when choosing a transfer-pricing method?

EXERCISES

23-16 Decentralization, responsibility centres. Quinn Corporation manufactures and sells lighting products. Quinn's sales and marketing divisions are organized along product lines—wall sconces, recessed lights, track lights, and so on. The manufacturing division produces lighting products for all the divisions.

During the planning process, each sales and marketing division specifies the quantity of each style of lights to be manufactured. Senior management then assigns the task of manufacturing the lights to different plants in the manufacturing division. Because manufacturing capacity is limited, some production is also outsourced. Senior management determines the manufacturing schedule on the basis of detailed studies that have been done to measure the time and cost of manufacturing different types of lighting products. Manufacturing managers are evaluated based on achieving target output within budgeted costs.

REQUIRED

1. Are the manufacturing plants in the Manufacturing Division cost centres or profit centres? Explain.

2. Quinn Corporation is considering decentralizing its marketing and manufacturing decisions by letting manufacturing and marketing managers directly negotiate the prices for manufacturing various products.
   a. How should Quinn evaluate manufacturing plant managers under this proposal?
   b. Would you recommend that Quinn Corporation decentralize its marketing and manufacturing decisions? Explain.

23-17 Decentralization, goal-congruence, responsibility centres. Hexton Chemicals consists of seven operating divisions that each operate independently. The operating divisions are supported by a number of support divisions such as R&D, labour relations, and environmental management. The environmental management group consists of 20 environmental engineers. These engineers must seek out business from the operating divisions—that is, the projects they work on must be mutually agreed to and paid for by one of the operating divisions. Under Hexton's rules, the environmental group is required to charge the operating divisions for environmental services at cost.

1. Is the environmental management organization centralized or decentralized?
2. What type of responsibility centre is the environmental management group?
3. What benefits and problems do you see in structuring the environmental management group the way Hexton has? Does it lead to goal-congruence and motivation?

23-18 Effect of alternative transfer pricing methods on division operating income. (CMA, adapted) Ajax Corporation has two divisions. The Mining Division makes toldine, which is then transferred to the Metals Division. The toldine is further processed by the Metals Division and is sold to customers at a price of $180 per unit. The Mining Division is currently required by Ajax to transfer its total yearly output of 400,000 units of toldine to the Metals Division at 110% of full manufacturing cost. Unlimited quantities of toldine can be purchased and sold on the outside market at $108 per unit. To sell the toldine it produces at $108 per unit on the outside market, the Mining Division would have to incur variable marketing and distribution costs of $6 per unit. Similarly, if the Metals Division purchased toldine from the outside market, it would have to incur variable purchasing costs of $3.60 per unit.

The following table gives the manufacturing costs per unit in the Mining and Metals Divisions for the year 2007:

	Mining Division	Metals Division
Direct materials	$14.40	$ 7.20
Direct manufacturing labour costs	19.20	24.00
Manufacturing overhead costs	38.40*	30.00†
Manufacturing costs per unit	$72.00	$61.20

*Manufacturing overhead costs in the Mining Division are 25% fixed and 75% variable.
†Manufacturing overhead costs in the Metals Division are 60% fixed and 40% variable.

REQUIRED

1. Calculate the operating incomes for the Mining and Metals Divisions for the 400,000 units of toldine transferred under each of the following transfer-pricing methods: (a) market price and (b) 110% of full manufacturing costs.
2. Suppose Ajax rewards each division manager with a bonus, calculated as 1% of division operating income (if positive). What is the amount of bonus that will be paid to each division manager under each of the transfer-pricing methods in requirement 1? Which transfer-pricing method will each division manager prefer to use?
3. What arguments would Brian Jones, manager of the Mining Division, make to support the transfer-pricing method that he prefers?

23-19 Decentralization, general guideline, goal congruence. (CMA, adapted) Nogo Motors, Inc., operates as a decentralized multidivision company. The Igo Division of Nogo Motors, Inc., purchases most of its airbags from the Airbag Division. The Airbag Division's incremental costs for manufacturing the airbags are $132 per unit. The Airbag Division is currently working at 80% of capacity. The current market price of the airbags is $168 per unit.

REQUIRED

1. Using the general guideline presented in the chapter, what is the minimum price at which the Airbag Division would sell airbags to the Igo Division?
2. Suppose that Nogo Motors, Inc., requires that whenever divisions with idle capacity sell products internally, they must do so at incremental costs. Evaluate this transfer-pricing policy using the criteria of goal-congruence, evaluating division performance, motivating management effort, and preserving division autonomy.
3. If the two divisions were to negotiate a transfer price, what is the range of possible transfer prices? Evaluate this negotiated transfer-pricing policy using the criteria of goal-congruence, evaluating division performance, motivating management effort, and preserving division autonomy.
4. Do you prefer the transfer-pricing policy in requirement 2 or requirement 3? Explain your answer briefly.

23-20 General guideline, transfer price range. The Shamrock Company manufactures and sells television sets. The Assembly Division assembles the television sets. It buys the screens for the television sets from the Screen Division. The Screen Division is operating at capacity. The incremental cost of manufacturing the screens is $84 per unit. The Screen Division can sell as many screens as it wants in the outside market at a price of $132 per screen. If it sells screens in the outside market, the Screen Division will incur variable sales and distribution cost of $4.80 per unit. Similarly, if the Assembly Division purchases screens from the outside market, it will incur variable purchasing costs of $2.40 per unit.

REQUIRED

1. Using the general guideline presented in the chapter, what is the minimum transfer price at which the Screen Division will sell screens to the Assembly Division?
2. Suppose division managers act autonomously to maximize their division's operating income either by transacting internally or buying and selling in the market. If the two division managers were to negotiate a transfer price, what is the range of acceptable transfer prices?

23-21 Multinational transfer pricing, global tax minimization. The Mornay Company manufactures telecommunications equipment at its Winnipeg factory. The company has marketing divisions throughout the world. A Mornay marketing division in Vienna, Austria, imports 1,000 units of a piece of equipment called Product 4A36 from Canada. The following information is available:

Canadian income tax rate on the Canadian division's operating income	40%
Austrian income tax rate on the Austrian division's operating income	44%
Austrian import duty	10%
Variable manufacturing cost per unit of Product 4A36	$420
Full manufacturing cost per unit of Product 4A36	$600
Selling price (net of marketing and distribution costs) in Austria	$900

Suppose the Canadian and Austrian tax authorities only allow transfer prices that are between the full manufacturing cost per unit and a market price of $780 based on comparable imports into Austria. The Austrian import duty is charged on the price at which the product is transferred into Austria. Any import duty paid to the Austrian authorities is a deductible expense for calculating Austrian income taxes due.

REQUIRED

1. Calculate the after-tax operating income earned by the Canadian and Austrian divisions from transferring 1,000 units of Product 4A36 at (a) full manufacturing cost per unit and (b) market price of comparable imports. (Income taxes are not included in the computation of the cost-based transfer prices.)
2. Which transfer price should the Mornay Company select to minimize the total of company import duties and income taxes? Recall that the transfer price must be between the full manufacturing cost per unit of $600 and the market price of $780 based on comparable imports into Austria. Explain your reasoning.

23-22 Multinational transfer pricing, goal-congruence (continuation of 23-21). Suppose that the Canadian division could sell as many units of Product 4A36 as it makes at $720 based on per unit in the Canadian market, net of all marketing and distribution costs.

REQUIRED

1. From the viewpoint of the Mornay Company as a whole, would after-tax operating income be maximized if it sold the 1,000 units of Product 4A36 in Canada or in Austria?
2. Suppose each division manager acts autonomously to maximize his or her division's after-tax operating income. Will the transfer price calculated in requirement 2 of Exercise 23-21 result in the Canadian division manager taking the actions determined to be optimal in requirement 1 of this exercise? Explain.
3. What is the minimum transfer price that the Canadian division manager would agree to? Does this transfer price result in the Mornay Company as a whole paying more import duty and taxes than the answer to requirement 2 of Exercise 23-21? If so, by how much?

23-23 Transfer pricing methods, goal-congruence. British Columbia Lumber has a Raw Lumber Division and a Finished Lumber Division. The variable costs are:
◆ Raw Lumber Division: $120 per 100 board-feet of raw lumber (a board-foot is about 2,360 cubic centimetres).
◆ Finished Lumber Division: $150 per 100 board-feet of finished lumber
Assume that there is no board-feet loss in processing raw lumber into finished lumber. Raw lumber can be sold at $240 per 100 board-feet. Finished lumber can be sold at $330 per 100 board-feet.

REQUIRED

1. Should British Columbia Lumber process raw lumber into its finished form?
2. Assume that internal transfers are made at 110% of variable costs. Will each division maximize its division operating income contribution by adopting the action that is in the best interests of British Columbia Lumber?

3. Assume that internal transfers are made at market prices. Will each division maximize its division operating income contribution by adopting the action that is in the best interests of British Columbia Lumber?

23-24 Multinational transfer pricing, effect of alternative transfer pricing methods, global income tax minimization. User Friendly Computer, Inc., with headquarters in Regina, manufactures and sells desktop computers. User Friendly has three divisions, each of which is located in a different country:

a. China Division—manufactures memory devices and keyboards
b. South Korea Division—assembles desktop computers, using internally manufactured parts and memory devices and keyboards from the China Division
c. Canadian Division—packages and distributes desktop computers

Each division is run as a profit centre. The costs for the work done in each division that are associated with a single desktop computer unit are as follows:

China Division:	Variable costs	= 1,200 yuan
	Fixed costs	= 2,160 yuan
South Korea Division:	Variable costs	= 288,000 won
	Fixed costs	= 384,000 won
Canadian Division:	Variable costs	= $120
	Fixed costs	= $240

Chinese income tax rate on China Division's operating income	40%
South Korean income tax rate on South Korea Division's operating income	20%
Canadian income tax rate on Canadian Division's operating income	30%

Each desktop computer is sold to retail outlets in Canada for $3,840. Assume that the current foreign exchange rates are:

$$8 \text{ yuan} = \$1 \text{ Cdn.}$$
$$800 \text{ won} = \$1 \text{ Cdn.}$$

Both the China and the South Korea Division sell part of their production under a private label. The China Division sells the comparable memory/keyboard package used in each User Friendly desktop computer to a Chinese manufacturer for 4,320 yuan. The South Korea division sells the comparable desktop computer to a South Korean distributor for 1,248,000 won.

REQUIRED

1. Calculate the after-tax operating income per unit earned by each division under each of the following transfer pricing methods: (a) market price, (b) 200% of full costs, and (c) 300% of variable costs. (Income taxes are not included in the computation of the cost-based transfer prices.)
2. Which transfer pricing method(s) will maximize the net income per unit of User Friendly Computer, Inc.?

Excel Application For students who wish to practise their spreadsheet skills, the following is a step-by-step approach to creating an Excel spreadsheet to work this problem.

Step-by-Step

1. Open a new spreadsheet. At the top, create an "Original Data" section for the data provided by User Friendly Computer. Create rows for the exchange-rate data labelled "Yuan per Dollar" and "Won per Dollar." Skip two rows. Under the heading "China Division," create rows for "Price per Unit, Variable Cost per Unit, Fixed Cost per Unit, and Income Tax Rate." Create two more sets of the same rows under the headings "South Korea Division" and "Canadian Division." Enter price and cost data in the division country's currency.

(Program your spreadsheet to perform all necessary calculations. Do not "hard-code" any amounts, such as net income per unit, requiring addition, subtraction, multiplication, or division operations.)

2. Skip two rows, and create a "Problem 1" section in a similar format to Exhibit 23-2 (p. 891). Create columns for each of the three transfer-pricing methods. Under the heading "China Division," create rows for "Division Revenues per Unit, Division Variable Cost per Unit, Division Fixed Cost per Unit, Division Operating Income per Unit, Income Tax, and Division Net Income per Unit." Under the headings "South Korea Division" and "Canadian Division," create rows for "Division Revenues per Unit, Transferred-In Cost per

Unit, Division Variable Cost per Unit, Division Fixed Cost per Unit, Division Operating Income per Unit, Income Tax, and Division Net Income per Unit." When entering calculations in this section, use the exchange rate data from your Original Data section to convert to Cdn. dollars.

3. Skip two rows, and create a "Problem 2" section. Create columns for each of the three transfer-pricing methods. Create rows for "China Division, South Korea Division, Cdn. Division," and "User Friendly Computer." Enter the division net income under each of the transfer-pricing methods that you calculated in step 2 in this section. In the User Friendly Computer row, enter total net income under each of the transfer-pricing methods.

4. Check the accuracy of your spreadsheet: Go to your Original Data section and change the income tax rate for the South Korea Division from 20% to 35%. If you programmed your spreadsheet correctly, total net income for User Friendly Computer under the market price method should change to $1,533.

23-25 Transfer-pricing dispute. The Allison-Chambers Corporation, manufacturer of tractors and other heavy farm equipment, is organized along decentralized lines, with each manufacturing division operating as a separate profit centre. Each division manager has been delegated full authority on all decisions involving the sale of that division's output both to outsiders and to other divisions of Allison-Chambers. Division C has in the past always purchased its requirement of a particular tractor-engine component from Division A. However, when informed that Division A is increasing its selling price to $180, Division C's manager decides to purchase the engine component from outside suppliers.

Division C can purchase the component for $162 on the open market. Division A insists that, because of the recent installation of some highly specialized equipment and the resulting high amortization charges, it will not be able to earn an adequate return on its investment unless it raises its price. Division A's manager appeals to top management of Allison-Chambers for support in the dispute with Division C and supplies the following operating data:

C's annual purchases of tractor-engine component	1,000 units
A's variable costs per unit of tractor-engine component	$144
A's fixed costs per unit of tractor-engine component	$ 24

REQUIRED

1. Assume that there are no alternative uses for internal facilities. Determine whether the company as a whole will benefit if Division C purchases the component from outside suppliers for $162 per unit.
2. Assume that internal facilities of Division A would not otherwise be idle. By not producing the 1,000 units for Division C, Division A's equipment and other facilities would be used for other production operations that would result in annual cash operating savings of $21,600. Should Division C purchase from outside suppliers?
3. Assume that there are no alternative uses for Division A's internal facilities and that the price from outsiders drops $24. Should Division C purchase from outside suppliers?

23-26 Transfer pricing problem (continuation of 23-25). Refer to Exercise 23-25. Assume that Division A can sell the 1,000 units to other customers at $186 per unit with variable marketing costs of $6 per unit.

REQUIRED

Determine whether Allison-Chambers will benefit if Division C purchases the 1,000 components from outside suppliers at $162 per unit.

PROBLEMS

23-27 Effect of alternative transfer-pricing methods on division operating income. Oceanic Products is a tuna fishing company based in St. John's. It has three divisions:

a. Tuna Harvesting—operates a fleet of 20 trawling vessels.
b. Tuna Processing—processes the raw tuna into tuna fillets.
c. Tuna Marketing—packages tuna fillets in two-kilogram packets that are sold to wholesale distributors at $14.40 each.

The Tuna Processing Division has a yield of 500 kilograms of processed tuna fillets from 1,000 kilograms of raw tuna provided by the Tuna Harvesting Division. The Tuna Marketing Division has a yield of 300 two-kilogram packets from every 500 kilograms of processed tuna fillets provided by the Tuna Processing Division.

(The weight of the packaging material is included in the two-kilogram weight.) Cost data for each division are as follows:

Tuna Harvesting Division

Variable costs per kilogram of raw tuna	$0.24
Fixed costs per kilogram of raw tuna	$0.48

Tuna Processing Division

Variable costs per kilogram of processed tuna	$0.96
Fixed costs per kilogram of processed tuna	$0.72

Tuna Marketing Division

Variable costs per two-kilogram packet	$0.36
Fixed costs per two-kilogram packet	$0.84

Fixed costs per unit are based on the estimated quantity of raw tuna, processed tuna, and two-kilogram packets to be produced during the current fishing season.

Oceanic Products has chosen to process internally all raw tuna brought in by the Tuna Harvesting Division. Other tuna processors in St. John's purchase raw tuna from boat operators at $1.20 per kilogram. Oceanic Products has also chosen to process internally all tuna fillets into the two-kilogram packets sold by the Tuna Marketing Division. Several fish marketing companies in St. John's purchase tuna fillets at $6 per kilogram.

REQUIRED

1. Compute the overall operating income to Oceanic Products of harvesting 1,000 kilograms of raw tuna, processing it into tuna fillets, and then selling it in two-kilogram packets.
2. Compute the transfer prices that will be used for internal transfers (i) from the Tuna Harvesting Division to the Tuna Processing Division and (ii) from the Tuna Processing Division to the Tuna Marketing Division under each of the following transfer-pricing methods:
   a. 200% of variable costs. Variable costs are the costs of the transferred-in product (if any) plus the division's own variable costs.
   b. 150% of full costs. Full costs are the costs of the transferred-in product (if any) plus the division's own variable and fixed costs.
   c. Market price.
3. Oceanic rewards each division manager with a bonus, calculated as 10% of division operating income (if positive). What is the amount of the bonus that will be paid to each division manager under each of the three transfer-pricing methods in requirement 2? Which transfer-pricing method will each division manager prefer to use?

23-28 Goal-congruence problems with cost-plus transfer-pricing methods, dual-price method (continuation of 23-27). Assume that Oceanic Products uses a transfer price of 150% of full cost. Pat Forgione, the company president, attends a seminar on the virtues of decentralization. Forgione decides to implement decentralization at Oceanic Products. A memorandum is sent to all division managers: "Starting immediately, each division of Oceanic Products is free to make its own decisions regarding the purchase of its direct materials and the sale of its finished product."

REQUIRED

1. Give two examples of goal-congruence problems that may arise if Oceanic continues to use the 150%-of-full-costs transfer-pricing method and a policy of decentralization is adopted.
2. Forgione is investigating whether a dual transfer-pricing policy will reduce goal-congruence problems at Oceanic Products. Transfers out of each selling division will be made at 150% of full cost; transfers into each buying division will be made at market price. Using this dual transfer-pricing policy, compute the operating income of each division for a harvest of 1,000 kilograms of raw tuna that is further processed and marketed by Oceanic Products.
3. Compute the sum of the division operating incomes in requirement 2. Why might this sum not equal the overall corporate operating income from the harvesting of 1,000 kilograms of raw tuna and its further processing and marketing?
4. What problems may arise if Oceanic Products uses the dual transfer-pricing system described in requirement 2?

23-29 Pertinent transfer price. Europa, Inc., has two divisions, A and B, that manufacture expensive bicycles. Division A produces the bicycle frame, and Division B assembles the rest of the bicycle onto the frame. There is a market for both the subassembly and the final product.

Each division has been designated as a profit centre. The transfer price for the subassembly has been set at the long-run average market price. The following data are available to each division:

Estimated selling price for final product	$360
Long-run average selling price for intermediate product	240
Incremental costs for completion in Division B	180
Incremental costs in Division A	144

The manager of Division B has made the following calculation:

Selling price for final product		$360
Transferred-in costs (market)	$240	
Incremental costs for completion	180	420
Contribution (loss) on product		$ (60)

REQUIRED

1. Should transfers be made to Division B if there is no excess capacity in Division A? Is the market price the correct transfer price?
2. Assume that Division A's maximum capacity for this product is 1,000 units per month and sales to the intermediate market are now 800 units. Should 200 units be transferred to Division B? At what transfer price? Assume that for a variety of reasons, Division A will maintain the $240 selling price indefinitely; that is, Division A is not considering lowering the price to outsiders even if idle capacity exists.
3. Suppose Division A quoted a transfer price of $180 for up to 200 units. What would be the contribution to the company as a whole if the transfer were made? As manager of Division B, would you be inclined to buy at $180?

23-30 Pricing in imperfect markets (continuation of 23-29). Refer to Problem 23-29.

REQUIRED

1. Suppose the manager of Division A has the option of (a) cutting the external price to $234 with the certainty that sales will rise to 1,000 units or (b) maintaining the outside price of $240 for the 800 units and transferring the 200 units to Division B at some price that would produce the same operating income for Division A. What transfer price would produce the same operating income for Division A? Does that price coincide with that recommended by the general guideline in the chapter so that the desirable decision for the company as a whole would result?
2. Suppose that if the selling price for the intermediate product is dropped to $234, outside sales can be increased to 900 units. Division B wants to acquire as many as 200 units if the transfer price is acceptable. For simplicity, assume that there is no outside market for the final 100 units of Division A's capacity.
   a. Using the general guideline, what is (are) the minimum transfer price(s) that should lead to the correct economic decision? Ignore performance evaluation considerations.
   b. Compare the total contributions under the alternatives to show why the transfer price(s) recommended lead(s) to the optimal economic decision.

23-31 Multinational transfer pricing, global tax minimization. Industrial Diamonds, Inc., based in Vancouver, has two divisions:
a. Philippine Mining Division. Operates a mine in the Philippines containing a rich body of raw diamonds.
b. Canadian Processing Division. Processes the raw diamonds into polished diamonds used in industrial applications.

The costs of the Philippine Mining Division are
◆ Variable costs, 3,000 pesos per kilogram of raw industrial diamonds
◆ Fixed costs, 6,000 pesos per kilogram of raw industrial diamonds

Industrial Diamonds has a corporate policy of further processing diamonds in Vancouver. Several diamond-polishing companies in the Philippines buy raw diamonds from other local mining companies at 12,000 pesos per kilogram. Assume that the current foreign exchange rate is 25 pesos = $1 Cdn.

The costs of the Canadian Processing Division are:
◆ Variable costs, $240 per kilogram of polished industrial diamonds
◆ Fixed costs, $720 per kilogram of polished industrial diamonds

Assume that it takes two kilograms of raw industrial diamonds to yield one kilogram of polished industrial diamonds. Polished diamonds sell for $4,800 per kilogram.

1. Compute the transfer price (in $Cdn) for one kilogram of raw industrial diamonds transferred from the Philippine Mining Division to the Canadian Processing Division under two methods: (a) 300% of full costs and (b) market price.
2. Assume a world of no income taxes. One thousand kilograms of raw industrial diamonds are mined by the Philippine Division and then processed and sold by the Canadian Processing Division. Compute the operating income (in $Cdn) for each division of Industrial Diamonds, Inc., under each transfer-pricing method in requirement 1.
3. Assume that the corporate income tax rate is 20% in the Philippines and 35% in Canada. Compute the after-tax operating income (in $Cdn) for each division under each transfer pricing method in requirement 1. (Income taxes are not included in the computation of the cost-based transfer price. Industrial Diamonds does not pay Canadian taxes on income already taxed in the Philippines.)
4. Which transfer-pricing method in requirement 1 will maximize the total after-tax operating income of Industrial Diamonds?
5. What factors, in addition to global tax minimization, might Industrial Diamonds consider in choosing a transfer-pricing method for transfers between its two divisions?

23-32 Multinational transfer pricing and taxation. (Richard Lambert, adapted) Anita Corporation, headquartered in Canada, manufactures state-of-the-art milling machines. It has two marketing subsidiaries, one in Brazil and one in Switzerland, that sell its products. Anita is building one new machine, at a cost of $600,000. There is no market for the equipment in Canada. The equipment can be sold in Brazil for $1,200,000, but the Brazilian subsidiary would incur transportation and modification costs of $240,000. Alternatively, the equipment can be sold in Switzerland for $1,140,000, but the Swiss subsidiary would incur transportation and modification costs of $300,000. The Canadian company can sell the equipment to either its Brazilian subsidiary or its Swiss subsidiary but not to both. The Anita Corporation and its subsidiaries operate in a very decentralized manner. Managers in each company have considerable autonomy, with each manager interested in maximizing company income.

1. From the viewpoint of Anita and its subsidiaries taken together, should the Anita Corporation manufacture the equipment? If it does, where should it sell the equipment to maximize total operating income? What would the operating income for Anita and its subsidiaries be from the sale? Ignore any income tax effects.
2. What range of transfer prices will result in achieving the actions determined to be optimal in requirement 1? Explain your answer.
3. The effective income tax rates for this transaction are as follows: 40% in Canada, 60% in Brazil, and 15% in Switzerland. The tax authorities in the three countries are uncertain about the cost of the intermediate product and will allow any transfer price between $600,000 and $840,000. If Anita and its subsidiaries want to maximize after-tax operating income, (a) should the equipment be manufactured and (b) where and at what price should it be transferred?
4. Now suppose managers act autonomously to maximize their own company's after-tax operating income. The tax authorities will allow transfer prices only between $600,000 and $840,000. Which subsidiary will get the product and at what price? Is your answer the same as your answer in requirement 3? Explain why or why not.

23-33 Transfer pricing, goal-congruence. The Sather Corporation manufactures and sells 10,000 boom boxes. It buys the cassette deck for the boom box from the Cassette Deck Division. The Cassette Deck Division is operating at capacity and producing 12,000 cassette decks. The demand for cassette decks is strong. Any cassette deck not sold to the Assembly Division can be sold in the outside market for $42 per unit. The Cassette Deck Division currently sells 10,000 cassette decks to the Assembly Division and 2,000 cassette decks in the outside market. The incremental cost of manufacturing the cassette deck is $30 per unit.

A crucial component for producing high-quality cassette decks is the (cassette) head mechanism. The Cassette Deck Division manufactures the head mechanism for its cassette decks. Many outside suppliers have offered to supply cassette decks to Sather. To ensure quality, Sather requires that any outside supplier wanting to supply cassette decks to Sather must purchase the head mechanism from the Cassette Deck Division. The Cassette Deck Division's incremental cost of manufacturing the head mechanism is $14.40 per unit. The Cassette Deck Division will charge $21.60 per unit for the head mechanism. The Cassette Deck Division has excess manufacturing capacity for manufacturing the head mechanism. That is, even if the Cassette Deck Division manufactures the head mechanism for outside suppliers, it will still be able to manufacture and sell 12,000 cassette decks for sale in the outside market at $42 per unit.

Johnson Corporation, an outside supplier, is currently negotiating to supply 10,000 cassette decks to the Assembly Division for a price in the range of $44.40 to $51.60. If Johnson gets the business it will buy the head mechanism from the Cassette Deck Division for $21.60 per unit.

REQUIRED

1. From the standpoint of Sather Corporation as a whole, should the Assembly Division accept Johnson Corporation's offer at (a) a price of $44.40 per cassette deck? (b) a price of $51.60 per cassette deck? Show all calculations.
2. What transfer price for cassette decks will result in the Cassette Deck Division and the Assembly Division taking actions that are optimal for Sather Corporation as a whole? Explain your answer.

23-34 **Utilization of capacity.** (J. Patell, adapted) The California Instrument Company (CIC) consists of the Semiconductor Division and the Process-Control Division, each of which operates as an independent profit centre. The Semiconductor Division employs craftsmen who produce two different electronic components, the new high-performance Super-chip and an older product called Okay-chip. These two products have the following cost characteristics:

	Super-chip	Okay-chip
Direct materials	$ 2.40	$1.20
Direct manufacturing labour		
2 hours × $16.80; 0.5 hours × $16.80	33.60	8.40

Annual overhead in the Semiconductor Division totals $400,000, all fixed. Owing to the high skill level necessary for the craftsmen, the semiconductor division's capacity is set at 50,000 hours per year.

One customer orders a maximum of 15,000 Super-chips per year, at a price of $72 per chip. If CIC cannot meet this entire demand, the customer curtails its own production. The rest of the Semiconductor's Division's capacity is devoted to the Okay-chip, for which there is unlimited demand at $14.40 per chip.

The Process-Control Division provides only one product, a process-control unit, with the following cost structure:

Direct materials (circuit board)	$72
Direct manufacturing labour (5 hours × $12)	60

Fixed overhead costs of the Process-Control Division are $96,000 per year. The current market price of the control unit is $158.40 per unit.

A joint research project has just revealed that a single Super-chip could be substituted for the circuit board currently used to make the process-control unit. Using Super-chip would require an extra hour of labour per control unit for a new total of 6 hours per control unit.

REQUIRED

1. Calculate the contribution margin per hour of selling Super-chip and Okay-chip. If no transfers of Super-chip were made to the Process-Control Division, how many Super-chips and Okay-chips should the Semiconductor Division sell?
2. The Process-Control Division expects to sell 5,000 control units this year. From the viewpoint of California Instruments as a whole, should 5,000 Super-chips be transferred to the Process-Control Division to replace circuit boards? Show all calculations.
3. If demand for the control unit is sure to be 5,000 units, but its *price* is uncertain, what should the transfer price of Super-chip be to ensure that the division managers' actions maximize operating income for CIC as a whole? (All other data are unchanged.)
4. If demand for the control unit is sure to be 12,000 units, but its *price* is uncertain, what should the transfer price of Super-chip be to ensure that the division managers' actions maximize operating income for CIC as a whole? (All other data are unchanged.)

23-35 **Ethics, transfer pricing.** The Belmont Division of Durham Industries manufactures component R47, which it transfers to the Alston Division at 200% of variable costs. The variable costs of R47 are $16.80 per unit. Joe Lasker, the management accountant of the Belmont Division, calls Hal Tanner, his assistant, into his office. Lasker says, "I am not sure about the fixed and variable cost distinctions you are making. I think the variable costs are higher than $16.80 per unit."

Tanner knows that showing higher variable costs will increase the Belmont Division's profits and lead to higher bonuses for the division employees. However,

Tanner is uncomfortable about making any changes because he has used the same method to classify costs as either fixed or variable over the last few years. But Tanner knows that fixed and variable cost distinctions are not always clear cut.

REQUIRED

1. Calculate Belmont Division's contribution margin from transferring 10,000 units of R47 in 2007 if (a) variable costs are $16.80 per unit, and (b) variable costs are $19.20 per unit.
2. Evaluate whether Lasker's suggestion to Tanner regarding variable costs is ethical. Would it be ethical for Tanner to revise the variable cost per unit? What steps should Tanner take to resolve this situation?

COLLABORATIVE LEARNING PROBLEM

23-36 Goal-congruence, taxes, different market conditions. The Saskatchewan Corporation makes water pumps. The Engine Division makes the engines and supplies them to the Assembly Division where the pumps are assembled. Saskatchewan is a successful and profitable corporation that attributes much of its success to its decentralized operating style. Each division manager is compensated on the basis of division operating income.

The Assembly Division currently acquires all its engines from the Engine Division. The Assembly Division manager could purchase similar engines in the market for $480.

The Engine Division is currently operating at 80% of its capacity of 4,000 units and has the following particulars:

Direct materials ($150 per unit × 3,200 units)	$480,000
Direct manufacturing labour ($60 per unit × 3,200 units)	192,000
Variable manufacturing overhead costs ($30 per unit × 3,200 units)	96,000
Fixed manufacturing overhead costs	624,000

All the Engine Division's 3,200 units are currently transferred to the Assembly Division. No engines are sold in the outside market.

The Engine Division has just received an order for 2,000 units at $450 per engine that would utilize half the capacity of the plant. The order has either to be taken in full or rejected totally. The order is for a slightly different engine than what the Engine Division currently makes but takes the same amount of manufacturing time. To produce the new engine would require direct materials per unit of $120, direct manufacturing labour per unit of $48, and variable manufacturing overhead costs per unit of $30.

INSTRUCTIONS

Form groups of two or three students to complete the following requirements.

REQUIRED

1. From the viewpoint of the Saskatchewan Corporation as a whole, should the Engine Division accept the order for the 2,000 units?
2. What range of transfer prices result in achieving the actions determined to be optimal in requirement 1, if division managers act in a decentralized manner?
3. The manager of the Assembly Division has proposed a transfer price for the engines equal to the full cost of the engines including an allocation of overhead costs. The Engine Division allocates overhead costs to engines on the basis of the total capacity of the plant used to manufacture the engines.
   a. Calculate the transfer price for the engines transferred to the Assembly Division under this arrangement.
   b. Do you think that the transfer price calculated in requirement 3(a) will result in achieving the actions determined to be optimal in requirement 1, if division managers act in a decentralized manner?
   c. Comment in general on one advantage and one disadvantage of using full costs of the producing division as the basis for setting transfer prices.
4. Now consider the effect of income taxes.
   a. Suppose the Assembly Division is located in a country that imposes a 10% tax on income earned within its boundaries, while the Engine Division is located in a country that imposes no tax on income earned within its boundaries. What transfer price would be chosen by the Saskatchewan Corporation to minimize tax payments for the corporation as a whole? Assume that only transfer prices that are greater than or equal to full manufacturing costs and less than or equal to the market price of "substantially similar" engines are acceptable to the taxing authorities.

b. Suppose that the Saskatchewan Corporation announces the transfer price computed in requirement 4(a) to price all transfers between the Engine and Assembly Divisions. Each division manager then acts autonomously to maximize division operating income. Will division managers acting in a decentralized manner achieve the actions determined to be optimal in requirement 1?

5. Consider your responses to requirements 1 to 4 and assume the Engine Division will continue to have opportunities for outside business as described in requirement 1. What transfer-pricing policy would you recommend Saskatchewan use and why? Would you continue to evaluate division performance on the basis of division operating incomes?

Hotels, such as the Sheraton in Tasmania, aim to maximize return on investment by increasing the income earned on each dollar of revenue and by increasing revenue per dollar of investment. Hotel managers' performance measures generally include both financial performance measures such as return on investment and nonfinancial performance measures such as occupancy levels.

CHAPTER 24

Performance Measurement, Compensation, and Multinational Considerations

LEARNING OBJECTIVES

After studying this chapter, you should be able to

1. Select financial and nonfinancial performance measures for use in a balanced scorecard

2. Design an accounting-based performance measure

3. Analyze profitability using the DuPont method of measuring return on investment (ROI)

4. Use the residual-income (RI) measure and recognize its advantages

5. Describe the economic value added (EVA®) method

6. Distinguish between current cost and historical cost asset-measurement methods

7. Indicate the difficulties that arise when comparing the performance of divisions operating in different countries

8. Recognize the role of salaries and incentives in compensation arrangements

9. Describe the four levers of control and why they are necessary

We have discussed performance measurement in many of the earlier chapters, each time within a specific accounting context. Chapter 11, for example, described situations where the correct decision based on a relevant cost analysis (e.g., buying new equipment) may not be implemented because the performance measurement system induced the manager to act differently. This chapter discusses the design, implementation, and uses of performance measures more generally.

Performance measures are a central component of a management control system. Making good planning and control decisions requires information about how different subunits of the organization have performed. To be effective, management control systems must also motivate managers and employees to strive to achieve organization goals. Performance evaluation and rewards are key elements for motivating employees.

Performance measurement of an organization's subunits should be a prerequisite for allocating resources within that organization. When a subunit undertakes new activities, it forecasts revenues, costs, and investments. Periodic comparisons of the actual revenues, costs, and investments with the budgeted amounts can help guide top management's decisions about future allocations.

Performance measurement of managers is used in decisions about their salaries, bonuses, future assignments, and career advancement. Moreover, the very act of measuring their performance can motivate managers to strive for the goals used in their evaluation.

This chapter examines issues in designing performance measures for different levels of an organization and for managers at these different levels. We discuss both financial and nonfinancial performance measures.

FINANCIAL AND NONFINANCIAL PERFORMANCE MEASURES

Chapters 13 and 23 noted how the information used in a management control system can be financial or nonfinancial. Many common performance measures such as operating income rely on internal financial and accounting information. Increasingly, companies are supplementing internal financial measures with measures based on external financial information (for example, share prices), internal nonfinancial information (such as manufacturing lead time), and external nonfinancial information (such as customer satisfaction). In addition, companies are benchmarking their financial and nonfinancial measures against other companies that are regarded as the "best performers." To compete effectively in the global market, companies need to perform at or near the "best of the breed."

An increasing number of organizations present both financial and nonfinancial performance measures for various organization subunits in a single report called the *balanced scorecard* (see Chapter 13). Different companies stress various elements in their scorecards, but most scorecards include:

1. **Financial perspective**—share price, net income, return on sales, return on investment, economic value added

2. **Customer perspective**—market share in different geographic locations, customer satisfaction, average number of repeat visits

3. **Internal-business-process perspective**—Customer-service time for making reservations, for check-in, and in restaurants; cleanliness of hotel and room, quality of room service; time taken to clean rooms; quality of restaurant experience; number of new services provided to customers (fax, wireless Internet, video games); time taken to plan and build new hotels

4. **Learning-and-growth perspective**—employee education and skill levels, employee satisfaction, employee turnover, hours of employee training, and information-system availability.[1]

As in all balanced scorecard implementations, the goal is to make improvements in the learning-and-growth perspective that will lead to improvements in the internal-business-process perspective that, in turn, will result in improvements in the customer and financial perspectives. Some performance measures, such as the number of new patents developed, have a long-run time horizon. Other measures, such as direct materials efficiency variances, overhead spending variances, and yield, have a short-run time horizon. We focus on the most widely used performance measures covering an intermediate to long-run time horizon. These are internal financial measures based on accounting numbers routinely maintained by organizations.

---

[1] See R. Kaplan and D. Norton, *The Balanced Scorecard* (Boston: Harvard Business School Press, 1996); S. Hronec, *Vital Signs* (New York: American Management Association, 1993); R. S. Kaplan and D. P. Norton, *The Strategy-Focused Organization: How Balanced Scorecard Companies Thrive in the New Business Environment* (Boston: Harvard Business School Press, 2001); and R. S. Kaplan and D. P. Norton, *Strategy Maps: Converting Intangible Assets into Tangible Outcomes* (Boston: Harvard Business School Press, 2004).

DESIGNING AN ACCOUNTING-BASED PERFORMANCE MEASURE

OBJECTIVE 2

Design an accounting-based performance measure

Designing an accounting-based performance measure requires the following steps:

◆ **Step 1:** *Choosing the variable(s) congruent with top management's financial goal(s).* Does operating income, net income, return on assets, or revenues, for example, best measure a subunit's financial performance?

◆ **Step 2:** *Choose the time horizons of each performance measure.* For example, should performance measures, such as return on assets, be calculated for one year or for a multi-year horizon?

◆ **Step 3:** *Choosing definitions of the items included in the variables in step 1.* For example, should assets be defined as total assets or net assets (total assets minus total liabilities)?

◆ **Step 4:** *Choosing measures for the items included in the variables in step 1.* For example, should assets be measured at historical cost, current cost, or present value?

◆ **Step 5:** *Choosing a target against which to gauge performance.* For example, should all subunits have as a target the same required rate of return on assets?

◆ **Step 6:** *Choosing the timing of feedback.* For example, should manufacturing performance reports be sent to top management daily, weekly, or monthly?

These six steps need not be done sequentially. The issues considered in each step are interdependent, and a decision maker will often proceed through these steps several times before deciding on an accounting-based performance measure. The answers to the questions raised at each step depend on top management's beliefs about how well proposed measures achieve both cost effectiveness and goal-congruence, how well they provide incentives for employee effort, and if they preserve an appropriate level of subunit autonomy as discussed in Chapter 23.

DIFFERENT PERFORMANCE MEASURES

This section presents step 1 by describing four measures commonly used to evaluate the economic performance of organization subunits. Good performance measures promote goal-congruence with the organization's objectives and facilitate comparisons across different subunits. We illustrate these measures using the example of Hospitality Inns.

Hospitality Inns owns and operates three motels, located in Saskatoon, Saskatchewan; Brandon, Manitoba; and Hull, Quebec. Exhibit 24-1 summarizes data for each of the three motels for the most recent year (2006). At present, Hospitality Inns does not allocate to the three separate motels the total long-term debt of the company. Exhibit 24-1 indicates that the Hull motel generates the highest operating income, $510,000. The Brandon motel generates $300,000; the Saskatoon motel, $240,000. But is this comparison appropriate? Is the Hull motel the most "successful"? Actually, the comparison of operating income ignores potential differences in the *size* of the investments in the different motels. **Investment** refers to the resources or assets used to generate income. The question then is not how large operating income is per se, but how large it is given the resources that were used to earn it.

Investment. Resources or assets used to generate income.

Three approaches include investment in performance measures: return on investment (ROI), residual income (RI), and economic value added (EVA®). A fourth approach measures return on sales (ROS).

OBJECTIVE 3

Analyze profitability using the DuPont method of measuring return on investment (ROI)

Return on Investment

Return on investment (ROI) is an accounting measure of income divided by an accounting measure of investment.

Return on investment (ROI). An accounting measure of income divided by an accounting measure of investment.

$$\text{Return on investment (ROI)} = \frac{\text{Income}}{\text{Investment}}$$

ROI is the most popular approach to incorporating the investment base into a performance measure. ROI appeals conceptually because it blends all the major

EXHIBIT 24-1
Annual Financial Data for Hospitality Inns for 2006

	A	B	C	D	E
1		Saskatoon	Brandon	Hull	Total
2		(1)	(2)	(3)	(4) = (1) + (2) + (3)
3	Motel revenues	$1,200,000	$1,400,000	$3,185,000	$5,785,000
4	Motel variable costs	310,000	375,000	995,000	1,680,000
5	Motel fixed costs	650,000	725,000	1,680,000	3,055,000
6	Motel operating income	240,000	300,000	510,000	1,050,000
7	Interest costs on long-term debt at 10%				450,000
8	Income before income taxes				600,000
9	Income tax at 30%				180,000
10	Net income				$ 420,000
11	Net book values at the end of 2006:				
12	Current assets	$ 400,000	$ 500,000	$ 600,000	$1,500,000
13	Long-term assets	600,000	1,500,000	2,400,000	4,500,000
14	Total assets	$1,000,000	$2,000,000	$3,000,000	$6,000,000
15	Current liabilities	$ 50,000	$ 150,000	$ 300,000	$ 500,000
16	Long-term debt	—	—	—	4,500,000
17	Shareholders' equity	—	—	—	1,000,000
18	Total liabilities and shareholders' equity				$6,000,000

ingredients of profitability (revenues, costs, and investment) into a single number. ROI can be compared with the rate of return on opportunities elsewhere, inside or outside the company. Like any single performance measure, however, ROI should be used cautiously and in conjunction with other performance measures.

ROI is also called the accounting rate of return or the accrual accounting rate of return (see Chapter 21). Managers usually use the term ROI in the context of evaluating the performance of a division or subunit, and accrual accounting rate of return when evaluating a project. Companies vary in the way they define both the numerator and the denominator of the ROI. For example, some firms use operating income for the numerator. Other firms use net income. Some firms use total assets in the denominator. Others use total assets minus current liabilities.

Hospitality Inns can increase ROI by increasing revenues or decreasing costs (both these actions increase the numerator), or by decreasing investments (decreases the denominator). ROI can often provide more insight into performance when it is divided into the following components:

$$\frac{\text{Revenues}}{\text{Investment}} \times \frac{\text{Income}}{\text{Revenues}} = \frac{\text{Income}}{\text{Investment}}$$

This approach is widely known as the *DuPont method of profitability analysis.* The DuPont approach recognizes that there are two basic ingredients in profit making: using assets to generate more revenue and increasing income per dollar of revenue. An improvement in either ingredient without changing the other increases return on investment.

Consider the ROI of each of the three Hospitality motels in Exhibit 24-1. For our calculations, we are using the operating income of each motel for the numerator and total assets of each motel for the denominator.

Motel	Operating Income	÷	Total Assets	=	ROI
Saskatoon	$240,000	÷	$1,000,000	=	24%
Brandon	$300,000	÷	$2,000,000	=	15%
Hull	$510,000	÷	$3,000,000	=	17%

Using these ROI figures, the Saskatoon motel appears to make the best use of its total assets.

Assume that the top management at Hospitality Inns adopts a 30% target ROI for the Saskatoon motel. How can this return be attained? The DuPont method illustrates the present situation and three alternatives:

	Operating Income (1)	Revenue (2)	Total Assets (3)	Operating Income Revenue (4) = (1) ÷ (2)	×	Revenue Total Assets (5) = (2) ÷ (3)	=	Operating Income Total Assets (6) = (1) ÷ (3)
Current Situation	$240,000	$1,200,000	$1,000,000	0.20	×	1.2	=	24%
Alternatives								
A. Decrease assets (e.g., receivables). Revenue and operating income per dollar of revenue remain constant	$240,000	$1,200,000	$ 800,000	0.20	×	1.5	=	30%
B. Increase revenues (e.g., sell more rooms). Assets and operating income per dollar of revenue remain constant.	$300,000	$1,500,000	$1,000,000	0.20	×	1.5	=	30%
C. Decrease costs (e.g. efficient maintenance) to increase operating income per dollar of revenue; assets remain constant.	$300,000	$1,200,000	$1,000,000	0.25	×	1.2	=	30%

ROI tells managers how much income each dollar of investment generates. Here is the intuition for the two ROI components: (1) Income ÷ Revenues (*return on sales*) tells how much of each revenue dollar becomes income; the goal is to get higher income per revenue dollar. (2) Revenues ÷ Investment (*investment turnover*) tells how many revenue dollars are generated by each dollar of investment; the goal is to make each investment dollar "work harder" to generate more revenues.

Other alternatives, such as increasing the selling price per room, could increase both the revenue per dollar of total assets and the operating income per dollar of revenue.

ROI highlights the benefits that managers can obtain by reducing their investments in current or fixed assets. Some managers are conscious of the need to boost revenues or to control costs but pay less attention to reducing their investment base. Reducing investments means decreasing idle cash, managing credit judiciously, determining proper inventory levels, and spending carefully on fixed assets.

Residual Income

Residual income is income minus a required dollar return on the investment.[2]

$$\text{Residual income} = \text{Income} - (\text{Required rate of return} \times \text{Investment})$$

The required rate of return multiplied by investment is also called the *imputed cost* of the investment. **Imputed costs** are costs recognized in particular situations that are not regularly recognized by accrual accounting procedures. An imputed cost is not recognized in accounting records because it is not an incremental cost but instead represents the return forgone by Hospitality Inns as a result of tying up cash in various investments of similar risk. Assume that each motel faces similar risks. Hospitality Inns defines residual income for each motel as motel operating income minus a required rate of return of 12% of the total assets of the motel:

Motel	Operating Income	−	Required Rate of Return	×	Investment	=	Residual Income
Saskatoon	$240,000	−	12%	×	$(1,000,000)	=	$120,000
Brandon	$300,000	−	12%	×	$(2,000,000)	=	$ 60,000
Hull	$510,000	−	12%	×	$(3,000,000)	=	$150,000

[2]Just as in the case of ROI, companies using RI vary in the way they define income (for example, operating income or net income) and investment (for example, total assets or total assets minus current liabilities).

Given the 12% required rate of return, the Hull motel is performing best in terms of residual income.

Some firms favour the residual-income approach because managers will concentrate on maximizing an absolute amount (dollars of residual income) rather than a percentage (return on investment). The objective of maximizing residual income assumes that as long as a division earns a rate in excess of the required return for investments, that division should expand.

The objective of maximizing ROI may induce managers of highly profitable divisions to reject projects that, from the viewpoint of the organization as a whole, should be accepted. To illustrate, assume that Hospitality's required rate of return on investment is 12%. Assume also that an expansion of the Saskatoon motel will increase its operating income by $160,000 and increase its total assets by $800,000. The ROI for the expansion is 20% ($160,000 ÷ $800,000), which makes it attractive to Hospitality Inns as a whole. By making this expansion, however, the Saskatoon manager will see the motel's ROI decrease:

$$\text{Preexpansion ROI} = \frac{\$240,000}{1,000,000} = 24\%$$

$$\text{Postexpansion ROI} = \frac{(\$240,000 + \$160,000)}{(\$1,000,000 + \$800,000)} = \frac{\$400,000}{1,800,000} = 22.2\%$$

The annual bonus paid to the Saskatoon manager may decrease if ROI is a key component in the bonus calculation and the expansion option is selected. In contrast, if the annual bonus is a function of residual income, the Saskatoon manager will view the expansion favourably:

Preexpansion residual income = $240,000 − (12% × $1,000,000) = $120,000
Postexpansion residual income = $400,000 − (12% × $1,800,000) = $184,000

Goal-congruence is more likely to be promoted by using residual income rather than ROI as a measure of the division manager's performance.

Economic Value Added (EVA®)

Economic value added (EVA®)[3] is a specific type of residual income calculation that has recently attracted considerable attention. **Economic value added (EVA®)** equals after-tax operating income *minus* the (after-tax) weighted-average cost of capital *multiplied* by total assets minus current liabilities.[4]

EVA® substitutes the following numbers in the residual-income calculations: (1) income equal to after-tax operating income, (2) a required rate of return equal to the weighted-average cost of capital, and (3) investment equal to total assets minus current liabilities. We use the Hospitality Inns data in Exhibit 24-1 to illustrate EVA®.

$$\begin{matrix} \text{Economic} \\ \text{value added} \\ \text{(EVA®)} \end{matrix} = \begin{matrix} \text{After-tax} \\ \text{operating income} \end{matrix} - \left[\begin{matrix} \text{Weighted-average} \\ \text{cost of capital} \end{matrix} \times \left(\begin{matrix} \text{Total} \\ \text{assets} \end{matrix} - \begin{matrix} \text{Current} \\ \text{liabilities} \end{matrix} \right) \right]$$

---

[3]O'Byrne and D. Young, *EVA and Value-Based Management: A Practical Guide to Implementation* (New York: McGraw-Hill, 2000); J. Stein, J. Shiely, and I. Ross, *The EVA Challenge: Implementing Value Added Change in an Organization* (New York: John Wiley and Sons, 2001).

[4]When implementing EVA®, companies make several adjustments to the operating income and asset numbers reported under generally accepted accounting principles (GAAP). For example, when calculating EVA®, costs such as R&D, restructuring costs, and leases that have long-run benefits are recorded as assets (which are then amortized), rather than as current operating costs. The goal of these adjustments is to obtain a better representation of the economic assets, particularly intangible assets, used to earn income. Of course, the specific adjustments applicable to a company will depend on its individual circumstances.

Question: What required rate of return should management use to calculate residual income? *Answer:* The company's weighted-average cost of capital. Conceptually, it would be better to use the cost of capital based on each subunit's risk level. For example, an oil-exploration division would warrant a higher required rate of return than an oil-refining division because the risk of failing to find oil is far higher than the risks of refining oil already being produced. Generally, the cost of capital based on each subunit's risk level is not externally available.

Managers vary in their judgment of how best to define income (for example, operating income or net income) and investment (for example, total assets employed or total assets employed minus current liabilities).

Generally, RI is more likely than ROI to induce goal-congruence. This preference for RI over ROI parallels the preference for net present value over internal rate of return when managers produce a capital budget.

OBJECTIVE 5

Describe the economic value added (EVA®) method

Economic value added (EVA®).
After-tax operating income minus the (after-tax) weighted average cost of capital multiplied by total assets minus current liabilities.

The key calculation is the weighted-average cost of capital (WACC), which equals *after-tax* average cost of all the long-term funds used by Hospitality Inns. The company has two sources of long-term funds—long-term debt with a market and book value of $4.5 million issued at an interest rate of 10%, and equity capital that has a market value of $3 million (and a book value of $1 million).[5] Since interest costs are tax-deductible, the after-tax cost of debt financing equals $0.10 \times (1 - \text{tax rate}) = 0.10 \times (1 - 0.30) = 0.10 \times 0.70 = 0.07$, or 7%. The cost of equity capital is the opportunity cost to investors of not investing their capital in another investment that is similar in risk to Hospitality Inns. Suppose that Hospitality's cost of equity capital is 15%.[6] The WACC computation, which uses market values of debt and equity, is as follows:

$$\text{WACC} = \frac{(0.07 \times \$4,500,000) + (0.15 \times \$3,000,000)}{\$4,500,000 + \$3,000,000}$$

$$= \frac{(\$315,000 + \$450,000)}{\$7,500,000} = \frac{\$765,000}{\$7,500,000}$$

$$= 0.102 \text{ or } 10.2\%$$

The company applies the same WACC to all its motels, since each motel faces similar risks.

Total assets minus current liabilities (see Exhibit 24-1, p. 921) can also be computed as:

$$\text{Total assets} - \text{Current liabilities} = \text{Long-term assets} + \text{Current assets} - \text{Current liabilities}$$
$$= \text{Long-term assets} + \text{Working capital}$$

where working capital = current assets − current liabilities. After-tax motel operating income is:

$$\frac{\text{Motel operating}}{\text{income}} \times (1 - \text{Tax rate}) = \frac{\text{Motel operating}}{\text{income}} \times (1 - 0.30) = \frac{\text{Motel operating}}{\text{income}} \times 0.70$$

EVA® calculations for Hospitality Inns are as follows:

Motel	After-Tax Operating Income −	Weighted Average Cost of Capital ×	Total Assets	Current − Liabilities =	EVA®
Saskatoon	$240,000 × 0.70 −	[10.2%	× ($1,000,000 − $ 50,000)] =		$71,100
Brandon	$300,000 × 0.70 −	[10.2%	× ($2,000,000 − $150,000)] =		$21,300
Hull	$510,000 × 0.70 −	[10.2%	× ($3,000,000 − $300,000)] =		$81,600

EVA® Information
www.sternstewart.com

The Hull motel has the highest EVA®. EVA®, like residual income, charges managers for the cost of their investments in long-term assets and working capital. Value is created only if after-tax operating income exceeds the cost of investing the capital. To improve EVA®, managers must earn more operating income with the same capital, use less capital, or invest capital in high-return projects. After implementing EVA®, CSX, a railroad company, began running trains with three locomotives instead of four by scheduling arrivals just in time for unloading, rather than having trains arrive at their destination several hours in advance. The result? Higher profits because of lower fuel costs, and less capital invested in locomotives. Chief executive officers of companies such as AT&T, Briggs & Stratton, Coca-Cola, CSX, Equifax, FMC, and Quaker Oats credit the EVA® concept with motivating decisions that have increased shareholder value.

[5]The market value of Hospitality Inns' equity exceeds book value because book value, based on historical cost, does not measure the current value of the company's assets and because various intangible assets, such as the company's brand name, are not shown at current value in the balance sheet under GAAP.

[6]For details on calculating cost of equity capital adjusted for risk, see J. Van Horne, *Financial Management and Policy*, 12th ed. (Upper Saddle River, NJ: Prentice Hall, 2002).

Return on Sales

The income-to-revenue (sales) ratio—often called **return on sales (ROS)**—is a frequently used financial performance measure. ROS is one component of ROI in the DuPont method of profitability analysis. To calculate the ROS of each of Hospitality's motels, we use operating income divided by revenues. The ROS for each motel is

Return on sales (ROS). Income-to-revenue sales ratio.

Motel	Operating Income	÷	Revenues	=	ROS
Saskatoon	$240,000	÷	$1,200,000	=	20.00%
Brandon	$300,000	÷	$1,400,000	=	21.43%
Hull	$510,000	÷	$3,185,000	=	16.01%

The Brandon hotel has the highest ROS, whereas its performance is rated worse than the other hotels using performance measures such as ROI, RI, and EVA®.

The following table summarizes the performance and ranking of each motel under each of the four performance measures:

Motel	ROI	Rank	Residual Income	Rank	EVA®	Rank	ROS	Rank
Saskatoon	24%	1	$120,000	2	$71,100	2	20.00%	1
Brandon	15%	3	$ 60,000	3	$21,300	3	21.43%	2
Hull	17%	2	$150,000	1	$81,600	1	16.01%	3

The residual-income and EVA® rankings differ from the ROI and ROS rankings. Consider the ROI and residual-income rankings for the Saskatoon and Hull motels. The Hull motel has a smaller ROI. Although its operating income is only slightly more than twice that of the Saskatoon motel ($510,000 versus $240,000), its total assets are three times as large ($3 million versus $1 million). The return on assets invested in the Hull motel is not as high as the return on assets invested in the Saskatoon motel. The Hull motel has a higher residual income because it earns a higher operating income after covering the 12% required return on investment. The Brandon motel has the highest ROS but the lowest ROI. Why? Because although it earns very high income per dollar of revenue, it generates very low revenues per dollar of assets invested. Is any one method superior to the others? No, because each evaluates a slightly different aspect of performance. For example, in markets where revenue growth is limited, return on sales is the most meaningful indicator of a subunit's performance.

ROS measures how effectively costs are managed; ROI measures which investment yields the highest return. To evaluate overall aggregate performance, ROI or residual-income-based measures are more appropriate, since they consider both income earned and investments made. Residual-income and EVA® measures overcome some of the goal-congruence problems that ROI measures might introduce. Some managers favour EVA® because it explicitly considers tax effects, while pretax residual-income measures do not. Other managers favour pretax residual-income because it is easier to compute and because it often leads to the same conclusions as EVA®. The Global Surveys of Company Practice feature (p. 926) indicates that, generally, companies use multiple financial measures to evaluate performance.

CHOOSING THE TIME HORIZON OF THE PERFORMANCE MEASURES: STEP 2

Another consideration in designing accounting-based performance measures is choosing the time horizon of the performance measures. The ROI, RI, EVA®, and ROS calculations represent the results for a single time period, a year in our example. Managers could take actions that cause short-run increases in these measures but are in conflict with the long-run interests of the organization. For example, managers may curtail R&D and plant maintenance in the last three months of a fiscal year to achieve a target level of annual operating income. For this reason, many companies evaluate subunits on the basis of ROI, RI, EVA®, and ROS over multiple years.

Key Financial Performance Measures Used Around the Globe

Multiple global surveys indicate extensive use of financial performance measures. The percentage of the largest U.S. companies that view specific financial performance measures as most important are income in comparison with budget, 49%; return on investment (ROI), 29%; economic value added (EVA®), 14%; return on sales (ROS), 3%; and other measures, 5%.[a] Similar to many U.S. companies, Australian, Indian, and Dutch corporations also focus on ROI and income.[b,c,d] In contrast, 82% of Japanese companies use return on sales (ROS), whereas only 37% use ROI in measuring financial performance.[e] Some researchers argue that Japanese managers favour ROS because it is easier to calculate, lessens the emphasis on short-term profitability, and is a market-oriented measure that provides more-useful insights for making pricing and target costing decisions. The following table presents the key financial performance measures (in order of importance) used by companies in seven different countries.

Country	Key Financial Performance Measures
United States	Income, ROI, EVA®
Australia	ROI, income
Germany[f]	Revenue, contribution margin (on a per-unit basis)
India	ROI, income
Japan	ROS, ROI
Netherlands	ROI, cash flow, income
Singapore[g]	ROI

[a]Tang, R., "Canadian Transfer Pricing in the 1990s," *Management Accounting* (1992).

[b]Crenhall, R., and K. Smith, "Adoption and Benefits of Management Accounting Practices: An Australian Study," *Management Accounting Research* (1998).

[c]Joshi, P., "The International Diffusion of New Management Accounting Practices: The Case of India," *Journal of International Accounting, Auditing & Taxation* (2001).

[d]Groot, T., "Managing Costs in The Netherlands: Past Theory and Current Practice," in Bhimani, A. (ed.) *Management Accounting: European Perspectives* (Oxford: Oxford University Press, 1996).

[e]Wijewardena, H., and A. De Zoysa, "A Comparative Analysis of Management Accounting Practices in Australia and Japan: An Empirical Investigation," *International Journal of Accounting* (1999).

[f]Scherrer, G., "Management Accounting: A German Perspective," in Bhimani, A. (ed.) *Management Accounting: European Perspectives* (Oxford: Oxford University Press, 1996).

[g]Ghosh, B., and Y. Chan, "Management Accounting in Singapore—Well in Place?" *Managerial Auditing Journal* (1997).

Another reason for evaluating subunits over a multi-year time horizon is that the benefits of actions taken in the current period may not show up in short-run performance measures such as the current year's ROI or RI. For example, the investment in a new hotel may adversely affect ROI and RI in the short run but benefit ROIs and RIs in the long run.

A multi-year analysis highlights another advantage of the RI measure. The net present value of all the cash flows over the life of an investment equals the net present value of RIs.[7] This means that if managers use net present value analysis to make investment decisions (as prescribed in Chapter 21), using multi-year RI to evaluate managers' performances achieves goal-congruence.

Another way that companies motivate managers to take a long-run perspective is by compensating them on changes in the market price of the company's shares (in addition to using multi-year accounting-based performance measures). Why does this approach help to extend managers' time horizons? Because share prices more rapidly incorporate the expected future period effects of current decisions.

ALTERNATIVE DEFINITIONS OF INVESTMENT

We use the different definitions of investment that companies use to illustrate step 2 when designing accounting-based performance measures. Definitions include the following:

1. *Total assets available.* Includes all business assets, regardless of their particular purpose.

2. *Total assets employed.* Defined as total assets available minus idle assets and minus assets purchased for future expansion. For example, if the Hull motel in Exhibit 24-1 (p. 921) has unused land set aside for potential expansion, the total assets employed by the motel would exclude the cost of that land.

3. *Working capital (current assets minus current liabilities) plus long-term assets.* This definition excludes that portion of current assets financed by short-term creditors.

4. *Shareholders' equity.* Use of this definition for each individual motel in Exhibit 24-1 requires allocation of the long-term liabilities of Hospitality Inns to the three motels, which would then be deducted from the total assets of each motel.

Most companies that employ ROI, residual income, or EVA® for performance measurement use either total assets available or working capital plus long-term assets as the definition of investment. However, when top management directs a division manager to carry extra assets, total assets employed can be more informative than total assets available. The most common rationale for using working capital plus long-term assets is that the division manager often influences decisions on the short-term debt of the division.

---

[7]We are grateful to S. Reichelstein for pointing this out. To see this equivalence, suppose the $400,000 investment in the Saskatoon hotel increases operating income by $70,000 per year as follows: Increase in operating cash flows of $150,000 each year for five years minus amortization of $80,000 per year ($400,000 ÷ 5), assuming straight-line amortization and zero terminal disposal price. Amortization reduces the investment amount by $80,000 each year. Assuming a required rate of return of 12%, net present values of cash flows and residual incomes are as follows:

Year	0	1	2	3	4	5	Net Present Value
(1) Cash flow	−$400,000	$150,000	$150,000	$150,000	$150,000	$150,000	
(2) Present value of $1 discounted at 12%	1	0.89286	0.79719	0.71178	0.63552	0.56743	
(3) Present value: (1) × (2)	−$400,000	$133,929	$119,578	$106,767	$ 95,328	$ 85,115	$140,717
(4) Operating income		$ 70,000	$ 70,000	$ 70,000	$ 70,000	$ 70,000	
(5) Assets at start of year		$400,000	$320,000	$240,000	$160,000	$ 80,000	
(6) Capital charge: (5) × 12%		$ 48,000	$ 38,400	$ 28,800	$ 19,200	$ 9,600	
(7) Residual income: (4) − (6)		$ 22,000	$ 31,600	$ 41,200	$ 50,800	$ 60,400	
(8) Present value of RI: (7) × (2)		$ 19,643	$ 25,191	$ 29,325	$ 32,284	$ 34,273	$140,716

CHOOSING MEASUREMENT ALTERNATIVES FOR PERFORMANCE MEASURES: STEPS 3 AND 4

Current cost. Asset measure based on the cost of purchasing an asset today identical to the one currently held. It is the cost of purchasing the services provided by that asset if an identical asset cannot currently be purchased.

Distinguish step 3 from step 4. Step 3 requires managers to define the components of the performance measure chosen in step 1. For example, managers may define "investment" as total assets employed minus current liabilities. After choosing the definition in step 3, managers choose the basis for measuring dollar values in the definition in step 4 (for example, historical cost or current cost).

To illustrate step 3 in the design of accounting-based performance measures, consider different ways to measure assets included in the investment calculations. Should they be measured at historical cost, present value, current cost, or current disposal price? Should gross book value or net book value be used for depreciable assets? We now examine these issues.

Current Cost

Current cost is the cost of purchasing an asset today identical to the one currently held. It is the cost of purchasing the services provided by that asset if an identical asset cannot currently be purchased. Of course, measuring assets at current costs will result in different ROIs compared to the ROIs calculated based on historical costs.

We illustrate the current-cost ROI calculations using the Hospitality Inns example (see Exhibit 24-1) and then compare current- and historical-cost-based ROIs. Assume the following information about the long-term assets of each motel:

	Saskatoon	Brandon	Hull
Age of facility (at end of 2006)	8 years	4 years	2 years
Gross book value of long-term assets	$1,400,000	$2,100,000	$2,800,000
Accumulated amortization (straight line)	800,000	600,000	400,000
Net book value (at end of 2006)	$ 600,000	$1,500,000	$2,400,000
Amortization expense for 2006	$ 100,000	$ 150,000	$ 200,000

Hospitality Inns assumes a 14-year estimated useful life, assumes no terminal disposal price for the physical facilities, and calculates amortization on a straight-line basis.

An index of construction costs for the eight-year period that Hospitality Inns has been operating (year 0 = 100) is as follows:

Year	1	2	3	4	5	6	7	8
Construction cost index	110	122	136	144	152	160	174	180

Earlier in this chapter, we computed an ROI of 24% for Saskatoon, 15% for Brandon, and 17% for Hull (see p. 921). One possible explanation of the high ROI for Saskatoon is that this motel's long-term assets are expressed in terms of year 0 construction price levels (eight years ago) and that the long-term assets for the Brandon and Hull motels are expressed in terms of the higher, more recent construction price levels, which depress ROIs for these motels.

Exhibit 24-2 illustrates a step-by-step approach for incorporating current-cost estimates for long-term assets and amortization into the ROI calculation. The aim is to approximate what it would cost today to obtain assets that would produce the same expected operating income as the subunits currently earn. (Similar adjustments to represent current costs of capital employed and amortization can also be made in the residual income and EVA calculations.) The current-cost adjustment dramatically reduces the ROI of the Saskatoon motel.

	Historical Cost ROI	Current Cost ROI
Saskatoon	24%	10.82%
Brandon	15%	11.05%
Hull	17%	14.70%

Adjusting for current costs negates differences in the investment base caused solely by differences in construction price levels. Consequently, compared to historical-cost ROI, current-cost ROI is a better measure of the current economic returns from the investment. For example, current-cost ROI indicates that taking into account current construction price levels, investing in a new motel in Saskatoon will result in an ROI closer to 10.8% than to 24%. If Hospitality Inns were to invest in a new motel today, investing in one like the Hull motel offers the best ROI.

Step 1: Restate long-term assets from gross book value at historical cost to gross book value at current cost as of the end of 2006:

Motel	Gross Book Value of Long-Term Assets at Historical Cost	×	Construction Cost Index in 2006	÷	Construction Cost Index in Construction Year	=	Gross Book Value of Long-Term Assets at Current Cost at End of 2006
Saskatoon	$1,400,000	×	(180	÷	100)	=	$2,520,000
Brandon	$2,100,000	×	(180	÷	144)	=	$2,625,000
Hull	$2,800,000	×	(180	÷	160)	=	$3,150,000

Step 2: Derive net book value of long-term assets at current cost as of the end of 2006. (Assume estimated useful life of each motel is 14 years.)

Motel	Gross Book Value of Long-Term Assets at Current Cost at End of 2006	×	(Estimated Remaining Useful Life	÷	Estimated Total Useful Life)	=	Net Book Value of Long-Term Assets at Current Cost at End of 2006
Saskatoon	$2,520,000	×	(6	÷	14)	=	$1,080,000
Brandon	$2,625,000	×	(10	÷	14)	=	$1,875,000
Hull	$3,150,000	×	(12	÷	14)	=	$2,700,000

Step 3: Calculate the current cost of total assets at the end of year 8. (Assume the current assets of each motel are expressed in year 8 dollars.)

Motel	Current Assets at end of 2006 (from Exhibit 24-1)	+	Long-Term Assets Derived in Step 2 (above)	=	Current Cost of Total Assets at End of 2006
Saskatoon	$400,000	+	$1,080,000	=	$1,480,000
Brandon	$500,000	+	$1,875,000	=	$2,375,000
Hull	$600,000	+	$2,700,000	=	$3,300,000

Step 4: Calculate current-cost amortization expense in 2006 dollars.

Motel	Gross Book Value of Long-Term Assets at Current Cost at End of 2006	÷	Estimated Total Useful Life	=	Current Cost of Amortization Expense in 2006 Dollars
Saskatoon	$2,520,000	÷	14	=	$180,000
Brandon	$2,625,000	÷	14	=	$187,500
Hull	$3,150,000	÷	14	=	$225,000

Step 5: Calculate year 8 operating income using year 8 current cost amortization.

Motel	Historical Cost Operating Income	−	Current Cost of Amortization Expense in 2006 Dollars	−	Historical Cost Amortization Expense	=	Operating Income for 2006 Using Current Cost Amortization Expense in 2006 Dollars
Saskatoon	$240,000	−	($180,000	−	$100,000)	=	$160,000
Brandon	$300,000	−	($187,500	−	$150,000)	=	$262,500
Hull	$510,000	−	($225,000	−	$200,000)	=	$485,000

Step 6: Calculate ROI using current cost estimates for long-term assets and amortization expense.

Motel	Operating Income for 2006 Using Current Cost Amortization Expense in 2006 Dollars	÷	Current Cost of Total Assets at End of 2006	=	ROI Using Current Cost Estimate
Saskatoon	$160,000	÷	$1,480,000	=	10.82%
Brandon	$262,500	÷	$2,375,000	=	11.05%
Hull	$485,000	÷	$3,300,000	=	14.70%

A drawback of the current-cost method is that obtaining current-cost estimates for some assets can be difficult.[8] Why? Because the estimate requires a company to consider technological advances when determining the current cost of assets needed to earn today's operating income.

Long-Term Assets: Gross or Net Book Value?

Because historical-cost investment measures are used often in practice, there has been much discussion about the relative merits of using gross book value (original cost) or net book value (original cost minus accumulated amortization). Using the data in Exhibit 24-1 and page 928, the ROI calculations using net book values and gross book values of plant and equipment are as follows:

	Operating Income (from Exhibit 24-1)	Net Book Value of Total Assets (from Exhibit 24-1)	Accumulated Amortization (from p. 928)	Gross Book Value of Total Assets	2006 ROI Using Net Book Value of Total Assets	2006 ROI Using Gross Book Value of Total Assets
	(1)	(2)	(3)	(4) = (2) + (3)	(5) = (1) ÷ (2)	(6) = (1) ÷ (4)
Saskatoon	$240,000	$1,000,000	$800,000	$1,800,000	24%	13.33%
Brandon	$300,000	$2,000,000	$600,000	$2,600,000	15%	11.54%
Hull	$510,000	$3,000,000	$400,000	$3,400,000	17%	15.00%

> When using net book value, the declining denominator increases ROI as an asset ages, all other things equal. Evaluating managers based on assets at net book value rather than gross book value increases incentives for retaining old property, plant, and equipment.

Using the gross book value, the ROI of the older Saskatoon motel (13.33%) is lower than that of the newer Hull motel (15%). Those who favour using gross book value claim that it enables more accurate comparisons across subunits. For example, using gross book value calculations, the return on the original plant and equipment investment is higher for the newer Hull motel than for the older Saskatoon motel. This probably reflects the decline in earning power of the Saskatoon motel. In contrast, using the net book value masks this decline in earning power, because the constantly decreasing base results in a higher ROI (24%); this higher rate may mislead decision makers into thinking that the earning power of the Saskatoon motel has not decreased.

The proponents of using net book value as a base maintain that it is less confusing because (1) it is consistent with the total assets shown on the conventional balance sheet and (2) it is consistent with net income computations that include deductions for amortization. Surveys of company practice report net book value to be the dominant asset measure used by companies in their internal performance evaluations.

CHOOSING TARGETED LEVELS OF PERFORMANCE AND TIMING OF FEEDBACK: STEP 5

> Because older assets valued at historical cost inflate ROI (particularly if investment is defined as net book value rather than gross book value), top management may set higher target ROIs for divisions with older assets.

We next consider step 5, target setting for accounting-based measures against which to compare actual performance. Recall that historical-cost-based accounting measures are often inadequate for evaluating economic returns on new investments and sometimes create disincentives for new expansion. Despite these problems, historical-cost ROIs *can* be used to evaluate current performance by adjusting target ROIs. Consider our Hospitality Inns example. The key is to recognize that the motels were built at different times, which in turn means they were built at different levels of the construction cost index. Top management could adjust the target historical-cost ROIs accordingly, perhaps setting Saskatoon's ROI at 26%, Brandon's at 18%, and Hull's at 19%.

Nevertheless, the alternative of comparing actual to target performance is frequently overlooked in the literature. Critics of historical cost have indicated how high rates of return on old assets may erroneously induce a manager not to replace assets. Regardless, the manager's mandate is often "Go forth and attain the budgeted results." The budget, then, should be carefully negotiated with full knowledge of historical-cost accounting pitfalls. *The desirability of tailoring a budget to a particular subunit and a particular accounting system cannot be overemphasized.* For example, many problems of asset valuation and income measurement (whether based on historical cost or

---

[8]When a specific cost index (such as the construction cost index) is not available, companies use a general index (such as the consumer price index) to approximate current costs.

current cost) can be satisfactorily solved if top management gets everybody to focus on what is attainable in the forthcoming budget period—regardless of whether the financial measures are based on historical costs or some other measure, such as current costs.

Top management often sets continuous improvement targets. Consider companies implementing EVA®. These companies have generally found it cost-effective to use historical-cost net assets rather than estimates of market or replacement values. Why? Because top management evaluates operations on year-to-year changes in EVA®, not on absolute measures of EVA®. Evaluating performance on the basis of *improvements* in EVA® makes the initial method of calculating EVA® less important.

CHOOSING THE TIMING OF FEEDBACK: STEP 6

The final step in designing accounting-based performance measures is the timing of feedback. Timing of feedback depends largely on how critical the information is for the success of the organization, the specific level of management that is receiving the feedback, and on the sophistication of the organization's information technology. For example, motel managers responsible for room sales will want information on the number of rooms sold each day on a daily or, at most, weekly basis. Why? Because a large percentage of motel costs are fixed costs, so that achieving high room sales and taking quick action to reverse any declining sales trends are critical to the financial success of each motel. Supplying managers with daily information about room sales would be much easier if Hospitality Inns had a computerized room reservation and check-in system. Senior management, on the other hand, in their oversight role may look at information about daily room sales only on a monthly basis. In some instances (for example, because of concern about the low sales to total assets ratio of the Brandon motel), they may want the information weekly.

For example, managers who are responsible for day-to-day operations usually require more frequent feedback than top management.

PERFORMANCE MEASUREMENT IN MULTINATIONAL COMPANIES

Comparing the performance of divisions of a multinational company operating in different countries creates additional difficulties:[9]

OBJECTIVE 7

Indicate the difficulties that arise when comparing the performance of divisions operating in different countries

♦ The economic, legal, political, social, and cultural environments differ significantly across countries.

♦ Governments in some countries limit selling prices of and impose controls on a company's products. For example, developing countries in Asia, Latin America, and Eastern Europe impose tariffs and duties to restrict the import of certain goods. Beginning in 2005, the General Agreement on Tariffs and Trade (GATT) seeks to reduce and eliminate tariffs and duties imposed.

♦ Availability of materials and skilled labour, as well as costs of materials, labour, and infrastructure (power, transportation, and communication) may also differ significantly across countries.

♦ Divisions operating in different countries keep score of their performance in different currencies. Issues of inflation and fluctuations in foreign currency exchange rates then become important.

We focus on the last of these issues next.

Calculating the Foreign Division's ROI in the Foreign Currency

Suppose Hospitality Inns invests in a motel in Mexico City. The investment consists mainly of the costs of buildings and furnishings. The following information is available:

♦ The exchange rate at the time of Hospitality's investment on December 31, 2006, is 3 pesos = $1.

♦ During 2007, the Mexican peso suffers a steady and steep decline in its value.

♦ The exchange rate on December 31, 2007, is 6 pesos = $1.

♦ The average exchange rate during 2007 is $[(3 + 6) \div 2] = 4.5$ pesos = $1.

[9]M. Z. Iqbal, T. Melcher, and A. Elmallah, *International Accounting—A Global Perspective* (Cincinatti: Southwestern ITP, 2002).

- The investment (total assets) in the Mexico City motel = 9,000,000 pesos.
- The operating income of the Mexico City motel in 2007 = 1,800,000 pesos.

What is the historical-cost-based ROI for the Mexico City motel in 2007?

Some specific questions arise. Should we calculate the ROI in pesos or in dollars? If we calculate the ROI in dollars, what exchange rate should we use? How does the ROI of Hospitality Inns Mexico City (HIMC) compare with the ROI of Hospitality Inns Hull (HIH), which is also a relatively new motel of roughly the same size? Hospitality Inns may be interested in this information for making future investment decisions.

$$\text{HIMC's ROI (calculated using pesos)} = \frac{\text{Operating income}}{\text{Total assets}} = \frac{1,800,000 \text{ pesos}}{9,000,000 \text{ pesos}} = 20\%$$

HIMC's ROI of 20% is higher than HIH's ROI of 17% (computed on p. 921). Does this mean that HIMC outperformed HIH on the ROI criterion? Not necessarily. Why? Because HIMC operates in a very different economic environment than does HIH.

The peso has declined steeply in value relative to the dollar in 2007. Research studies show that the peso's decline is correlated with correspondingly higher inflation in Mexico relative to Canada.[10] A consequence of the higher inflation in Mexico is that HIMC will charge higher prices for its motel rooms, which will increase HIMC's operating income and lead to a higher ROI. Inflation clouds the real economic returns on an asset and makes ROI calculated on historical cost of assets unrealistically high. Why? Because had there been no inflation, HIMC's room rates and hence operating income would have been much lower. Differences in inflation rates between the two countries make a direct comparison of HIMC's peso-denominated ROI with HIH's dollar-denominated ROI misleading.

Calculating the Foreign Division's ROI in Canadian Dollars

One way to achieve a more meaningful comparison of historical-cost-based ROIs is to restate HIMC's performance in dollars. But what exchange rate(s) should be used to make the comparison meaningful? Assume operating income was earned evenly throughout 2007. We use the average exchange rate of 4.5 pesos = $1 to convert the operating income from pesos to dollars: 1,800,000 pesos ÷ 4.5 = $400,000. The effect of dividing the operating income in pesos by the higher pesos-to-dollars exchange rate is that any increase in operating income in pesos as a result of inflation is undone when converting back to dollars.

At what rate should we convert HIMC's total assets of 9,000,000 pesos? At the exchange rate prevailing when the assets were acquired on December 31, 2006, namely 3 pesos = $1. Why? Because HIMC's book value of assets is recorded at the December 31, 2006, cost, and is not revalued as a result of inflation in Mexico in 2007. Since the book value of assets is unaffected by subsequent inflation, so should the exchange rate used to convert it into dollars. Using exchange rates after December 31, 2006, would be incorrect, because these rates incorporate the higher inflation in Mexico in 2007. Total assets would be converted to 9,000,000 pesos ÷ 3 = $3,000,000. Then:

$$\text{HIMC's ROI (calculated using dollars)} = \frac{\text{Operating income}}{\text{Total assets}} = \frac{\$400,000}{\$3,000,000} = 13.33\%$$

These adjustments make the historical-cost-based ROIs of the two motels comparable because they negate the effects of any differences in inflation rates between the two countries. HIMC's ROI of 13.33% is less than HIH's ROI of 17%.

Residual income calculated in pesos suffers from the same problems as ROI calculated using pesos. Instead, calculating HIMC's residual income in dollars adjusts for changes in exchange rates and facilitates comparisons with Hospitality's other motels:

$$\text{HIMC's residual income} = \$400,000 - (12\% \times \$3,000,000)$$
$$= \$400,000 - \$360,000 = \$40,000$$

[10]W. Beaver and M. Wolfson, "Foreign Currency Translation Gains and Losses: What Effect Do They Have and What Do They Mean?" *Financial Analysts Journal* (March–April 1984); F.D.S. Choi, "Resolving the Inflation/Currency Translation Dilemma," *Management International Review*, Vol. 34, Special Issue, 1994; H. Louis, "The Value Relevance of the Foreign Translation Adjustment," *The Accounting Review* (October 2003).

which is also less than HIH's residual income of $150,000. In interpreting HIMC's and HIH's ROI and residual income, note that they are historical-cost-based calculations. They do, however, pertain to relatively new motels.

DISTINCTION BETWEEN MANAGERS AND ORGANIZATIONAL UNITS[11]

As noted before in this and several earlier chapters, the performance evaluation of a manager should be distinguished from the performance evaluation of an organization subunit, such as a division of a company. For example, historical-cost-based ROIs for a particular division can be used to evaluate a manager's performance relative to a budget or over time, even though historical-cost ROIs may be unsatisfactory for evaluating economic returns earned by the subunit. But using historical-cost ROIs to compare the performance of managers of different subunits can be misleading. In the Hospitality Inns example, Hospitality Inns Hull's (HIH's) ROI of 17% exceeds Hospitality Inns Mexico City's (HIMC's) ROI of 13.33% after adjusting for the higher inflation in Mexico. The ROIs may give some indication of the economic returns from each motel but do not mean that the manager of HIH performed better than the manager of HIMC. Why? Because among other factors, HIMC's ROI may have been adversely affected relative to HIH's ROI because of externalities beyond the HIMC manager's control such as legal, political, and government regulations as well as economic conditions in Mexico.

Consider another example. Companies often put the most skillful division manager in charge of the weakest division in an attempt to change its fortunes. Such an effort may take years to bear fruit. Furthermore, the manager's efforts may result merely in bringing the division up to a minimum acceptable ROI. The division may continue to be a poor profit performer in comparison with other divisions, but it would be a mistake to conclude from the poor performance of the division that the manager is necessarily performing poorly.

This section focuses on developing basic principles for evaluating the performance of a division manager of an individual subunit. The concepts we discuss apply, however, to all organization levels. Later sections consider specific examples at the individual-activity level and the total-organization level. For specificity, we use the residual income (RI) performance measure throughout.

The Basic Tradeoff: Creating Incentives versus Imposing Risk

The performance evaluation of managers and employees often affects their compensation. Compensation arrangements run the range from a flat salary with no direct performance-based bonus (as in the case of government officials) to rewards based only on performance (as in the case of employees of real estate agencies). Most often, however, a manager's total compensation includes some combination of salary and a performance-based bonus. An important consideration in designing compensation arrangements is the tradeoff between creating incentives and imposing risk. We illustrate this tradeoff in the context of our Hospitality Inns example.

Sally Fonda owns the Hospitality Inns chain of motels. Roger Brett manages the Hospitality Inns Saskatoon (HIS) motel. Assume that Fonda uses RI to measure performance. To achieve good results as measured by RI, Fonda would like Brett to control costs, provide prompt and courteous service, and reduce receivables. But even if Brett did all those things, good results are by no means guaranteed. HIS's RI is affected by many factors outside Fonda's and Brett's control, such as a recession in the Saskatoon economy, or weather that might negatively affect HIS. Alternatively, noncontrollable factors might have a positive influence on HIS's RI. Noncontrollable factors make HIS's profitability uncertain and risky.

Fonda is an entrepreneur (the owner) who does not mind bearing risk, but Brett does not like being subject to risk; that is why he chose to be an employee rather than an owner. One way of insuring Brett against risk is to pay Brett a flat salary, regardless of the actual amount of residual income attained. All the risk would then be borne by

People who decide to become entrepreneurs (owners) are generally more risk-tolerant than those who decide to work for others (managers). It is more cost efficient for owners to bear risk than managers, because managers demand a premium (extra compensation) for bearing risk. The objective of many compensation plans is to provide managers with incentives to work hard while minimizing the risk placed on them.

---

[11]The presentations here draw (in part) on teaching notes prepared by S. Huddart, N. Melumad, and S. Reichelstein.

Fonda. There is a problem here, however, because the effort that Brett puts in is difficult to monitor. The absence of performance-based compensation provides Brett with no incentive to work harder or undertake extra physical and mental effort beyond the minimum necessary to retain his job or to uphold his own personal values.

Moral hazard[12] describes contexts in which an employee prefers to exert less effort (or report distorted information) than the effort (or information) desired by the owner because the employee's effort (or information) cannot be accurately monitored and enforced. In some repetitive jobs—for example, in electronics assembly—a supervisor can monitor the workers' actions, and the moral hazard problem may not arise. However, the manager's job is often to gather information and exercise judgment on the basis of the information obtained, and monitoring a manager's effort is thus considerably more difficult.

Paying no salary and rewarding Brett *only* on the basis of some performance measure—RI, in our example—raises different concerns. Brett would now be motivated to strive to increase RI because his rewards would increase with increases in RI. But compensating Brett on RI also subjects Brett to risk. Why? Because HIS's RI depends not only on Brett's effort, but also on external factors such as inflation or other changes in the economy over which Brett has no control. More succinctly, Brett's management effort may be overwhelmed by good or bad luck associated with these changes in externalities.

To compensate Brett (who does not like being subject to risk) for taking on uncontrollable risk, Fonda must pay Brett some extra compensation within the structure of the RI-based arrangement. Thus, using performance-based incentives will cost Fonda more money, *on average*, than paying Brett a flat salary. Why "on average"? Because Fonda's compensation payment to Brett will vary with RI outcomes. When averaged over these outcomes, the RI-based compensation will cost Fonda more than would paying Brett a flat salary. The motivation for having some salary and some performance-based bonus in compensation arrangements is to balance the benefits of incentives against the extra costs of imposing uncontrollable risk on the manager.

Intensity of Incentives and Financial and Nonfinancial Measurements

What dictates the intensity of the incentives? That is, how large should the incentive component be relative to salary? A key question is: How well does the performance measure capture the manager's ability to influence the desired results?

Measures of performance that are superior change significantly with the manager's performance and not very much with changes in factors that are beyond the manager's control. Consequently, superior performance measures motivate the manager but limit the manager's exposure to uncontrollable risk and hence reduce the cost of providing incentives to get the manager to accept the incentive program. On the other hand, measures of performance are inferior if they fail to capture the manager's performance and fail to induce managers to improve. When owners have superior performance measures available to them, they place greater reliance on incentive compensation.

Suppose Brett has no authority to determine investments. Further suppose revenue is determined largely by external factors such as the local economy. Brett's actions influence only costs. Using RI as a performance measure in these circumstances subjects Brett's bonus to excessive risk, because two components of the performance measure (investments and revenues) are unrelated to his actions. The management accountant might suggest that, to create stronger incentives, Fonda consider using a different performance measure for Brett—perhaps HIS's costs—that more closely captures Brett's effort. Note that in this case, RI may be a perfectly good measure of the economic viability of HIS, but it is not a good measure of Brett's performance.

---

[12]The term *moral hazard* originated in insurance contracts to represent situations where insurance coverage, which relieves the owner of assets of part of the risks of loss and/or damage, caused insured parties to take less care of their properties than they would if they bore the full costs of replacement and/or repair. One response to moral hazard in insurance contracts is the system of deductibles (that is, the insured pays for damages below a specified amount). You are familiar with the concept if you have worked in teams to obtain marks for your output. The presence of a team spreads the risk of a low mark among the team's members.

The salary component of compensation dominates when performance measures sensitive to a manager's effort are unavailable (as in the case of some corporate staff and government officials). This is not to say, however, that incentives are completely absent; promotions and salary increases do depend on some overall measure of performance, but the incentives are less direct. Employers give stronger incentives when superior measures of performance are available to them and when monitoring the employee's effort is very difficult (real estate agencies, for example, reward employees mainly on commissions on houses sold).

In evaluating Brett, Fonda uses measures from multiple perspectives of the balanced scorecard because nonfinancial measures on the balanced scorecard—employee satisfaction and the time taken for check-in, cleaning rooms, and providing room service—are more sensitive to Brett's actions. Financial measures such as RI are less sensitive to Brett's actions because they are affected by external factors such as local economic conditions that are beyond Brett's control.

Another reason for using nonfinancial measures in the balanced scorecard is that these measures follow Hospitality Inns' strategy and are drivers of future performance. Evaluating managers on these nonfinancial measures motivates them to take actions that will sustain long-run performance. Therefore, evaluating performance in all four perspectives of the balanced scorecard promotes both short- and long-run actions. Surveys show that division managers' compensation plans include a mix of salary, bonus, and long-term compensation tied to earnings and share price of the company. The goal is to balance division and companywide, as well as short-term and long-term incentives.

Benchmarks and Relative Performance Evaluation

Owners can use benchmarks to evaluate performance. Benchmarks representing best practice may be available inside or outside the overall organization. In our Hospitality Inns example, benchmarks could be other similar motels, either within or outside the Hospitality Inns chain. Suppose Brett has authority over revenues, costs, and investments. In evaluating Brett's performance, Fonda would want to use as a benchmark a motel of a similar size that is influenced by the same uncontrollable factors—for example, location, demographic trends, and economic conditions—that affect HIS. *Differences* in performances of the two motels occur only because of differences in the two managers' performances, not because of random factors. Thus, benchmarking, also called *relative performance evaluation,* "filters out" the effects of the common noncontrollable factors.

Can the performance of two managers responsible for running similar operations within a company be benchmarked against one another? Yes, but one problem is that the use of these benchmarks may reduce incentives for these managers to help one another. That is, a manager's performance-evaluation measure improves either by doing a better job or by making the other manager look bad. Failing to work together as a team is not in the best interests of the organization as a whole. In this case, using benchmarks for performance evaluation can lead to goal-incongruence.

If managers are evaluated on a single performance measure, they will treat other critical success factors as secondary to that single measure. For example, managers might curtail advertising and maintenance to increase the current year's ROI. This is why performance evaluation needs to be based on a variety of critical success factors such as in the balanced scorecard.

When possible, owners use performance-evaluation measures that are tightly linked to managers' efforts. Managers are evaluated based on things they can affect, even if they are not completely controllable. For example, salespersons often earn commissions based on the amount of sales revenues they generate. Salespersons can affect the amount of sales they generate by working harder, but they cannot control other factors (such as the economy and competitors' products) that also affect the amount of their sales.

PERFORMANCE MEASURES AT THE INDIVIDUAL ACTIVITY LEVEL

This section focuses on incentive issues that arise in the context of individual activities. The principles described here, however, can be applied at all levels of the organization.

Performing Multiple Tasks

Most employees perform more than one task as part of their jobs. Marketing representatives sell products, provide customer support, and gather market information. Other jobs have multiple aspects to them. Manufacturing workers, for example, are responsible for both the quantity and the quality of their products. Employers want employees to allocate their time and effort intelligently among various tasks or aspects of their jobs.

Consider, for example, mechanics at an auto repair shop. Their jobs have at least two distinct and important aspects. The first aspect is the repair work. Performing more repair work would generate more revenues for the shop. The second aspect is customer satisfaction. The higher the quality of the job, the more likely the customer will be pleased. If the employer wants an employee to focus on both these aspects, then the employer must measure and compensate performance on both.

Suppose the employer can easily measure the quantity of auto repairs but not their quality. If the employer rewards workers on a piece-rate system—which pays workers only on the basis of the number of repairs actually performed—mechanics will likely increase the number of repairs they make at the expense of quality. Sears experienced this problem when it introduced by-the-job rates for their mechanics. Sears's management responded by taking the following steps to motivate workers to balance both quantity and quality: (1) Management dropped the piece-rate system and paid mechanics an hourly salary, a step that reduced emphasis on the quantity of repair. Mechanics' promotions and pay increases were determined on the basis of management's assessment of each mechanic's overall performance regarding quantity and quality of repairs. (2) Management began evaluating employees, in part, using data such as customer satisfaction surveys, the number of dissatisfied customers, or the number of customer complaints. (3) Management also employed independent staff to randomly monitor whether the repairs performed were of high quality.

Note that nonfinancial measures (such as customer satisfaction measures) play a central role in motivating mechanics to emphasize both quantity and quality. The goal is to measure both aspects of the mechanics' jobs and to balance incentives so that both aspects are properly emphasized.

Team-Based Compensation Arrangements

Team-based incentive compensation encourages employees to work together to achieve common goals. Individual-based incentive compensation rewards employees for their own performance, consistent with responsibility accounting. A mix of both types of incentives encourages employees to maximize their own performance while working together in the best interest of the company as a whole.

Many manufacturing, marketing, and design problems require employees with multiple skills, experiences, and judgments to pool their talents. In these situations, a team of employees achieves better results than employees acting on their own.[13] Companies give incentives and bonuses to individuals on the basis of team performance. Team incentives encourage cooperation, with individuals helping one another as they strive toward a common goal. The blend of knowledge and skills needed to change methods and improve efficiency puts a team in a better position than a lone individual to respond to incentives.[14] TRW, Whirlpool, and Monsanto in the United States, Novartis (a Swiss pharmaceutical company), and Nissan Motors in Japan are examples of companies that use some form of team-based incentives.

Whether team-based compensation is desirable depends, to a great extent, on the culture and management style of a particular organization. One criticism of teams is that individual incentives to excel are dampened, harming overall performance. This problem becomes more acute when effort cannot be monitored. Unproductive team members contribute less than the effort expected (shirk); nevertheless, they share equally in the team's reward. Shirking is a pervasive problem and you have probably experienced shirking at least once when you have worked with teams of students to obtain shared marks for output.

EXECUTIVE PERFORMANCE MEASURES AND COMPENSATION

OBJECTIVE 8

Recognize the role of salaries and incentives in compensation arrangements

The principles of performance evaluation described in the previous sections also apply to executive compensation plans at the total-organization level. Executive compensation plans are based on both financial and nonfinancial performance measures and consist of a mix of (1) base salary; (2) annual incentives (for example, cash bonus based on yearly net income); (3) long-term incentives (for example, stock options based on achieving a specified return by the end of a five-year period); and (4) fringe benefits (for example, life insurance, an office with a view, or a personal secretary).[15]

Designers of executive compensation plans emphasize three factors: achievement of organization goals, administrative ease, and the likelihood that affected managers will perceive the plan as fair.

[13]J. Katzenbach and D. Smith, *The Wisdom of Teams* (Boston: The Harvard Business School Press, 1993).

[14]*Teams That Click: The Results-Driven Manager Series* (Boston: Harvard Business School Press, 2004)

[15]*The Wall Street Journal*/Mercer Human Resource Consulting, *2003 CEO Compensation Survey and Trends* (May, 2004).

Well-designed plans use a compensation mix that carefully balances risk and short- and long-term incentives. For example, evaluating performance on the basis of annual ROI would sharpen an executive's short-term focus. Using ROI and stock option plans over, say, five years would motivate the executive to take a long-term view as well. Stock options are covered in detail in finance courses; however, they are not difficult to understand. Stock options give executives and employees the right to buy company shares at a specified price (called the exercise price) within a specified period. Suppose that on September 16, 2004, BP gave its CEO the option to buy 200,000 shares of the company at any time before June 30, 2012, at the September 16, 2004, market price of $49 per share. Let's say BP's share price rises to $69 per share on March 24, 2010; these options are "in the money." If the CEO exercises share options on all 200,000 shares, the CEO would earn $20 ($69 − $49) per share on 200,000 shares, or $4 million. If BP's share price remains below $49 during the entire period, these shares will be "out of the money" and the CEO will simply forgo the right to buy the shares. By linking CEO compensation to increases in the company's share price, the stock option plan motivates the CEO to improve the company's long-run performance and share price (see the Concepts in Action feature on p. 938). Accounting rules in force at the time this book was written require Canadian companies to recognize stock option expense in their income statements according to standards published by the CICA. The International Accounting Standards Board requires the same disclosure. Accounting regulators in the United States are currently debating whether to require all companies to recognize stock option expense in their income statements, replacing the note disclosure currently required of the effect on net income and earnings per share had the company recognized a compensation expense equal to the estimated fair market value of the options on the grant date.[16]

The Ontario Securities Commission (OSC) and the U.S. Securities and Exchange Commission (SEC) requires detailed disclosures of the compensation arrangements of top-level executives. Investors use this information to evaluate the relationship between compensation and performance across companies generally, across companies of similar sizes, and across companies operating in similar industries.

Strategy and Levers of Control[17]

OBJECTIVE 9

Describe the four levers of control and why they are necessary

Given the management accounting focus of this book, this chapter has emphasized the role of quantitative financial and nonfinancial performance evaluation measures that companies use to implement their strategies. These measures—such as ROI, RI, EVA®, ROS, customer satisfaction, and employee satisfaction—monitor critical performance factors that help managers monitor progress toward attaining the company's strategic goals. Because these measures help diagnose whether a company is performing to expectations, they are collectively called **diagnostic control systems**. Companies motivate managers to achieve these goals by holding managers accountable for and by rewarding them for meeting these goals. Recently, however, it has become clear that sometimes one consequence of the pressure to perform is that managers materially misstate financial measures to obscure actual performance (e.g., Enron, WorldCom, and Tyco; see also the Focus on Values and Behaviours feature on p. 939). Avoiding unethical and illegal behaviour requires that companies balance the push for performance resulting from diagnostic control systems, the first of four levers of control, with three other levers: *boundary systems*, *belief systems*, and *interactive control systems*.

Boundary systems describe standards of behaviour and codes of conduct expected of all employees, especially actions that are off-limits. Ethical behaviour on the

Diagnostic control systems. A set of measures to help diagnose if a company is performing to expectations.

Boundary systems. Describe the standards of behaviour and codes of conduct for all employees.

---

[16]If the exercise price is less than the market price of the shares on the date the options are granted, the company must recognize compensation cost equal to the difference between the two prices. This difference is less than the fair market value of the options. The company can choose either to recognize the full fair market value as a cost or disclose in a note to the financial statements the effect on net income and earnings per share.

[17]For a more-detailed discussion see R. Simons, "Control in an Age of Empowerment," *Harvard Business Review* (March-April 1995).

CEO Compensation and Company Performance

Over the years, CEO compensation has been a hot-button issue for many publicly traded companies, their shareholders, the general public, and governments. The recent wave of corporate scandals has only intensified the scrutiny placed on the large salaries, stock-option grants, and other executive perks given to corporate heads. The following table summarizes the 2003 compensation packages for the highest-paid CEOs of *Fortune 500* companies:

CEO	Company	Return to Shareholders in 2003	Total Compensation ($US)	Salary & Bonus	Value of Stock Options Granted in 2003	Value of Restricted Stock Granted in 2003	Other
Larry Culp, Jr.	Danaher	39.8%	$53,000,000	6%	41%	52%	1%
Chuck Cawley	MBNA	32.9%	$52,100,000	14%	32%	53%	1%
John Chambers	Cisco Systems	85.0%	$47,700,000	0%	100%	0%	0%
James Cayne	Bear Stearns	36.1%	$42,400,000	26%	20%	25%	29%
Larry Glasscock	Anthem	19.2%	$32,900,000	10%	24%	0%	66%

These packages are generally characterized by substantial stock-option grants, which are directly linked to a company's stock-price performance. CEOs with stock-option-heavy packages, such as John Chambers of Cisco, earn very high compensation if their companies perform well. In contrast, the following table outlines the 2003 compensation packages for the lowest-paid *Fortune 500* CEOs:

CEO	Company	Return to Shareholders in 2003	Total Compensation ($US)	Salary & Bonus	Value of Stock Options Granted in 2003	Value of Restricted Stock Granted in 2003	Other
Richard Kinder	Kinder Morgan	50.3%	$ 1	100%	0%	0%	0%
Warren Buffett	Berkshire Hathaway	15.8%	$308,000	32%	0%	0%	68%
Charles Jenkins, Jr.	Publix Supermarkets	N/A	$564,000	96%	0%	0%	4%
Donald Anderson	TransMontaigne	39.0%	$595,000	70%	0%	29%	1%
Glenn Tilton	UAL	13.4%	$777,000	96%	0%	0%	4%

The lowest-paid *Fortune 500* CEOs are characterized by the absence of stock options in their compensation arrangements, though Richard Kinder owns 19.5% of Kinder Morgan stock and Warren Buffett has a net worth of over US$36 billion, mostly in Berkshire Hathaway stock. These compensation packages lack a strong, direct link to company performance.

This raises an interesting question: Does a company's performance differ depending on how a CEO is compensated? Most shareholders, analysts, and boards of directors believe that linking compensation to performance motivates CEOs, attracts talent, and is seen as fair. But changes are coming. As a result of external pressures and strengthened demand for results, boards of directors and their compensation committees are making modifications in the structure of CEO compensation packages. Many companies, such as General Electric and Microsoft, are moving away from granting stock options, rebalancing the long-term incentive mix, and reining in overall pay while strengthening the link between pay and performance.

Sources: Adapted from M. Boyle, "When Will They Stop?" *Fortune* (May 3, 2004) and *The Wall Street Journal*/Mercer Human Resource Consulting, 2003 CEO Compensation Survey and Trends (New York: Mercer Human Resource Consulting, May 2004).

part of managers is paramount. In particular, numbers that subunit managers report should be free of overstated assets, understated liabilities, fictitious revenues, and understated costs. In Canada, the Canadian Securities Administrators (CSA) withdrew their proposed guidelines, Multilateral Instrument 52–111, covering corporate governance and internal control regulations for any company listed on a Canadian stock exchange. The CSA reasoned that most large Canadian companies were already compliant with the **Sarbanes-Oxley Act,** which became law in the U.S. in 2002, because these companies are listed on both U.S. and Canadian stock exchanges. Currently, the CICA has proposed it will adopt the International Accounting Standards Board standards. For these reasons and others, the CSA will amend its Multilateral Instrument 52–109 to include internal control regulations.

Sarbanes-Oxley Act. U.S. law requiring appropriate governance and internal control processes as specified in the Act.

Most large Canadian companies are already listed on U.S. stock exchanges and, because they have already taken the steps needed to comply with Sarbanes-Oxley, will not have to incur additional costs. Costs of compliance have been reported on average to be approximately US$4.3 million, but have been reported as high as US$40 million.[18] The broad scope of Canadian legislation on corporate governance includes the requirement that the CEO accept full responsibility for any material misstatement of financial information. Under Sarbanes-Oxley, companies must publish their codes of ethics and of conduct as part of the material audited for their annual report.'

FOCUS ON VALUES AND BEHAVIOURS

The Courage to Say No

Managers often face intense performance pressures. Sometimes these pressures cause them to search for ways—sometimes unethical and illegal—to book profit that makes their performance look better and helps them earn higher rewards. Management and financial accountants must never participate in these illegal actions, as the case of Betty Vinson illustrates.

Vinson joined WorldCom as a staff accountant in 1996 and was soon promoted to a senior accounting position responsible for compiling quarterly results. As the telecommunications industry revenues dried up in 2000, WorldCom faced immense pressure to reduce expenses and remain profitable. When expense reduction failed, CFO Scott Sullivan and Controller David Myers asked Vinson and her accounting colleagues to draw down US$828 million from a reserve account instead of recording expenses. Convinced the transaction was wrong, she nonetheless participated when told it was a one-time solution. From late 2000 to early 2002, Vinson was continually pressured into making illegal transfers, including re-entering "line costs" as capital expenditures rather than operating leases, in clear violation of SEC rules.

Though Vinson resolved to resign, she faced personal financial pressures as the provider of income and health insurance for her family. Vinson remained at WorldCom and continued the fraudulent accounting practices. In 2002, Vinson decided she had had enough. Unfortunately, it was too late. The SEC had already begun an inquiry into WorldCom's accounting practices and on June 26, 2002, announced that it had found US$3.8 billion in fraudulent accounting entries at WorldCom.

Vinson cooperated with federal regulators and prosecutors and initially believed she would not be prosecuted. But U.S. attorneys had other ideas: Because Vinson had made her own decisions about the capital expenditure accounts into which line costs were transferred, she bore responsibility for WorldCom's accounting fraud. Vinson was named as an unindicted co-conspirator. She pleaded guilty to two criminal counts of conspiracy and securities fraud in October 2002. Vinson is awaiting final sentencing and could serve a maximum term of up to 15 years in prison.

Source: Pulliam, S., "Over the Line: A Staffer Ordered to Commit Fraud Balked, Then Caved," *The Wall Street Journal*, June 23, 2003, p. A1

[18]"SOX Causes Jump in Audit Costs, but Benefits Seen," www.accountingweb.com/
cgi-bin/item.cgi?id=100788&d=815&h=817&f=816&dateformat=%B%20e,%20Y,
accessed June 6, 2006.

Dofasco Inc.
www.dofasco.com/bins/index.asp

TransCanada Corporation
www.transcanada.com/
company/djsi2005.html

Enbridge Inc.
www.enbridge.com/
csrReport2005/environmental
Performance/

Conference Board of Canada
www.conferenceboard.
ca/GCSR/CR_AT/codes_
principles.htm

The Sullivan Foundation
www.thesullivanfoundation.org/
gsp/

Dow Jones Sustainability World Index (DJSI World). A measure of environmental performance comparing companies and ranking companies worldwide.

Sullivan Principles. Support economic, social, and political justice by companies where they do business.

Belief systems. Articulate the mission, purpose, and core values of a company.

Intrinsic motivation. The desire to achieve self-satisfaction from good performance, regardless of external rewards.

Codes of business conduct signal appropriate and inappropriate individual behaviour. The following is a portion of Caterpillar Tractor's "Code of Worldwide Business Conduct and Operating Principles":

> The law is a floor. Ethical business conduct should normally exist at a level well above the minimum required by law. Caterpillar employees shall not accept costly entertainment or gifts (excepting mementos and novelties of nominal value) from dealers, suppliers and others with whom we do business. And we won't tolerate circumstances that produce, or reasonably appear to produce, conflict between personal interests of an employee and interests of the company.

Division managers often cite enormous pressure from top management "to make the budget" as excuses or rationalizations for not adhering to ethical accounting policies and procedures. A healthy amount of motivational pressure is desirable, as long as the "tone from the top" and the code of conduct simultaneously communicate the absolute need for all managers to behave ethically at all times. Managers should train employees to behave ethically and promptly and severely reprimand unethical conduct, regardless of the benefits that might accrue to the company from unethical actions. Some companies, such as Lockheed-Martin, emphasize ethical behaviour by routinely evaluating employees against a business code of ethics.

Many organizations also set explicit boundaries precluding actions that harm the environment. Environmental violations (such as water and air pollution) carry heavy fines and are prison offences under Canadian laws and those of other countries. But in many companies, environmental responsibilities extend beyond legal requirements. There are also many international indices of environmental performance, such as the **Dow Jones Sustainability World Index (DJSI World).** Some companies, such as Dofasco (a Canadian steel company), TransCanada Corporation (a Canadian natural gas transportation company), and Unilever Group (a U.S. manufacturer of consumer products), believe that a high ranking on this index is sufficiently important to positively affect share price, and they announce their rankings on the Internet and in formal press releases.

Socially responsible companies, such as Starbucks, also report specific performance measures to affirm their commitment to human rights and fair pricing. German, Swiss, Dutch, and Scandinavian companies also report on social responsibility disclosures such as employee welfare and community development activities. There exist many sets of global principles, such as the **Sullivan Principles,** that can be used to compare corporate performance in the area of social responsibility. Comparative charts and lists can be found at the Web links shown in the margin.

Belief systems articulate the mission, purpose, and core values of a company. They describe the accepted norms and patterns of behaviour expected of all managers and employees with respect to each other, shareholders, customers, and communities. Johnson & Johnson describes its values and norms in its credo statement:

> We believe our first responsibility is to the doctors, nurses and patients, to mothers and fathers and all others who use our products and services . . . . Everything we do must be of high quality.
>
> We are responsible to our employees . . . . We must respect their dignity and recognize their merit. They must have a sense of security in their jobs . . . . We must be mindful of ways to help our employees fulfill their family responsibilities and provide opportunity for development and advancement . . . . Our actions must be just and ethical.
>
> We are responsible to the communities in which we live . . . . We must support good works and charities and bear our fair share of taxes . . . . We must encourage better health and education.
>
> Our final responsibility is to our stockholders. Business must make a sound profit . . . . We must experiment with new ideas . . . develop innovative programs and pay for mistakes.

Johnson & Johnson's credo is intended to inspire managers and employees to do their best. Values and culture generate organization commitment, pride, and belonging and are an important source of intrinsic motivation. **Intrinsic motivation** is the desire to achieve self-satisfaction from good performance regardless of external rewards such as bonuses or promotion. Intrinsic motivation comes from being given greater responsibility, doing interesting and creative work, having pride in doing that work, establishing commitment to the organization, and developing personal bonds with co-workers. High intrinsic motivation enhances performance because managers and workers have a sense of achievement, feel satisfied with their jobs, and see opportunities for personal growth.

Interactive control systems are formal information systems that managers use to focus organization attention and learning on key strategic issues. An excessive focus on diagnostic control systems and critical performance variables can cause an organization to ignore emerging threats and opportunities—changes in technology, customer preferences, regulations, and industry competition that can undercut a business.

Interactive control systems. Formal information systems to focus managers' attention and learning on key strategic issues.

Interactive control systems track strategic uncertainties that businesses face, such as the emergence of digital imaging in the case of Kodak and Fujifilm, airline deregulation in the case of American Airlines and Southwest Airlines, and the shift in customer preferences for mini- and microcomputers in the case of IBM. The result is ongoing discussion and debate about assumptions and action plans. New strategies emerge from the dialogue and debate surrounding the interactive process. Interactive control systems force busy managers to step back from the actions needed to manage the business today and to shift their focus forward to positioning the organization for the opportunities and threats of tomorrow.

Measuring and rewarding managers for achieving critical performance variables is an important driver of corporate performance. But these diagnostic control systems must be counterbalanced by the other levers of control—boundary systems, belief systems, and interactive control systems—to ensure that proper business ethics, inspirational values, and attention to future threats and opportunities are not sacrificed to achieve business results.

PROBLEM FOR SELF-STUDY

PROBLEM
Budgeted data of the baseball manufacturing division of Home Run Sports for February 2007 are as follows:

Current assets	$ 400,000
Long-term assets	600,000
Total assets	$1,000,000
Production output	200,000 baseballs per month
Target ROI (operating income ÷ total assets)	30%
Fixed costs	$ 400,000 per month
Variable costs	$ 4 per baseball

REQUIRED
1. Compute the minimum unit selling price necessary to achieve the 30% target ROI, assuming ROI is based on total assets.
2. Using the selling price from requirement 1, separate the target ROI into its two components using the DuPont method.
3. Pamela Stephenson, division manager, receives 5% of the monthly residual income of the baseball manufacturing division as a bonus. Compute her bonus for February 2007, using the selling price from requirement 1. Home Run Sports uses a 12% required rate of return on total division assets when computing division residual income.

SOLUTION
1.
$$\text{Target operating income} = 30\% \text{ of } \$1,000,000$$
$$= \$300,000$$
$$\text{Let } P = \text{Selling price}$$
$$\text{Sales} - \text{Variable costs} - \text{Fixed costs} = \text{Operating income}$$
$$200,000P - (200,000 \times \$4) - \$400,000 = \$300,000$$
$$200,000P = \$300,000 + \$800,000 + \$400,000 = \$1,500,000$$
$$P = \$7.50$$

Proof:	Sales, 200,000 × $7.50	$1,500,000
	Variable costs, 200,000 × $4	800,000
	Contribution margin	700,000
	Fixed costs	400,000
	Operating income	$300,000

2. $\dfrac{\text{Revenues}}{\text{Investment}} \times \dfrac{\text{Income}}{\text{Revenues}} = \dfrac{\text{Income}}{\text{Investment}}$

$\dfrac{\$1,500,000}{\$1,000,000} \times \dfrac{\$300,000}{\$1,500,000} = \dfrac{\$300,000}{\$1,000,000}$

$\quad 1.5 \quad \times \quad 0.2 \quad = 0.30 \text{ or } 30\%$

3. Residual income = Operating income − Required return on investment

$\qquad = \$300,000 - (0.12 \times \$1,000,000)$

$\qquad = \$300,000 - \$120,000$

$\qquad = \$180,000$

Stephenson's bonus is $9,000 (5% of $180,000).

DECISION POINTS SUMMARY

The following decision guidelines use a question-and-answer format to summarize the chapter's main points. Each decision presents a key question. The guideline is the answer to that question.

DECISIONS	GUIDELINES
1. What financial and nonfinancial measures do companies use?	Financial measures such as return on investment and residual income measure aspects of both manager performance and organization-subunit performance. In many cases, financial measures are supplemented with nonfinancial measures of performance, such as customer satisfaction ratings, number of defects, and productivity.
2. What are the steps in designing an accounting-based performance measure?	The steps are (a) choose performance measures that align with top management's financial goal(s), (b) choose the time horizon of each performance measure, (c) choose a definition of the components in each performance measure, (d) choose a measurement alternative for each performance measure, (e) choose a target level of performance, and (f) choose the timing of feedback.
3. How does the DuPont method analyze return on investment?	The DuPont method describes return on investment (ROI) as the product of two components: income divided by revenues (return on sales) and revenues divided by investment (investment turnover). ROI can be increased in three ways: by increasing revenues, by decreasing costs, and by decreasing investment.
4. What is residual income and what are its advantages?	Residual income (RI) is income minus a dollar amount for required return on investment. RI is designed to overcome some of the limitations of ROI. For example, RI is more likely than ROI to promote goal-congruence. ROI may induce managers of highly profitable divisions to reject projects that, from the perspective of the organization as a whole, should be accepted.
5. What is the economic value added method?	Economic value added (EVA®) is a variation of the RI calculation. It equals the after-tax operating income minus the product of after-tax weighted-average cost of capital and total assets minus current liabilities.
6. What is the current cost of an asset?	The current cost of an asset is the cost now of purchasing an asset identical to the one currently held. Historical-cost measurement methods consider the original cost of the asset net of accumulated amortization.
7. What difficulties arise when comparing the performance of divisions in different countries?	Comparing the performance of divisions operating in different countries is difficult because of legal, political, social, economic, and currency differences. ROI calculations for subunits operating in different countries need to be adjusted for differences in inflation between the two countries and changes in exchange rates.
8. How do salaries and incentives work together in compensation arrangements?	Organizations create incentives by rewarding managers on the basis of performance. But managers may face risks because random factors beyond the managers' control may also affect performance. Owners choose a mix of salary and incentive compensation to trade off the incentive benefit against the cost of imposing risk.

9. What are the levers of control and why does a company need to implement them?

The four levers of control are diagnostic control systems, boundary systems, belief systems, and interactive control systems. Implementing the four levers of control helps a company simultaneously strive for performance, behave ethically, inspire employees, and respond to strategic threats and opportunities.

TERMS TO LEARN

This chapter contains definitions of the following important terms:

belief systems (p. 940)
boundary systems (p. 937)
current cost (p. 928)
diagnostic control systems (p. 937)
Dow Jones Sustainability World Index (DJSI World) (p. 940)
economic value added (EVA®) (p. 923)
imputed costs (p. 922)
interactive control systems (p. 941)

intrinsic motivation (p. 940)
investment (p. 920)
moral hazard (p. 934)
residual income (p. 922)
return on investment (ROI) (p. 920)
return on sales (ROS) (p. 925)
Sarbanes-Oxley Act (p. 939)
Sullivan Principles (p. 940)

ASSIGNMENT MATERIAL

QUESTIONS

24-1 Give two examples of financial performance measures and two examples of nonfinancial performance measures.

24-2 What are the five steps in designing an accounting-based performance measure?

24-3 What factors affecting ROI does the DuPont method highlight?

24-4 "Residual income is not identical to ROI although both measures incorporate income and investment into their computations." Do you agree? Explain.

24-5 Describe economic value added.

24-6 Give three definitions of investment used in practice when computing ROI.

24-7 Distinguish between measuring assets based on present value, current cost, and historical cost.

24-8 What special problems arise when evaluating performance in multinational companies?

24-9 Why is it important to distinguish between the performance of a manager and the performance of the organization subunit for which the manager is responsible? Give examples.

24-10 Describe moral hazard.

24-11 "Managers should be rewarded only on the basis of their performance measures. They should be paid no salary." Do you agree? Explain.

24-12 Explain the management accountant's role in helping organizations design stronger incentive systems for their employees.

24-13 Explain the role of benchmarking in evaluating managers.

24-14 Explain the incentive problems that can arise when employees have to perform multiple tasks as part of their jobs.

24-15 List four components of executive compensation plans.

EXERCISES

24-16 **Return on investment; comparisons of three companies.** (CMA, adapted) Return on investment is often expressed as follows:

$$\frac{\text{Income}}{\text{Investment}} = \frac{\text{Revenues}}{\text{Investment}} \times \frac{\text{Income}}{\text{Revenues}}$$

1. What advantages are there in the breakdown of the computation into two separate components?
2. Fill in the following blanks:

	Companies in Same Industry		
	A	B	C
Revenue	$1,200,000	$600,000	?
Income	$ 120,000	$ 60,000	?
Investment	$ 600,000	?	$6,000,000
Income as a percentage of revenue	?	?	0.5%
Investment turnover	?	?	2
Return on investment	?	1%	?

After filling in the blanks, comment on the relative performance of these companies as thoroughly as the data permit.

Excel Application For students who wish to practise their spreadsheet skills, the following is a step-by-step approach to creating an Excel spreadsheet to work this problem.

Step-by-Step

1. Open a new spreadsheet. At the top, create a table in the same format as provided for this problem, with columns for companies A, B, and C and rows for "Revenues, Income, Investment, Income as a Percentage of Revenue, Investment Turnover, and ROI." Enter the data provided in the table (leave cells blank when a "?" appears in the table). (Program your spreadsheet to perform all necessary calculations. Do not "hard-code" any amounts, such as ROI for Company A, requiring addition, subtraction, multiplication, or division operations.)
2. Enter calculations for each of the missing items. For example, to calculate revenues for Company C, enter a calculation that multiplies Company C's investment by Company C's investment turnover.
3. Verify the accuracy of your spreadsheet: Change investment for Company A from $600,000 to $480,000. If you programmed your spreadsheet correctly, ROI for Company A should change to 25%.

24-17 Analysis of return on invested assets, comparison of three divisions. Quality Products, Inc., is a soft drink and food products company. It has three divisions: soft drinks, snack foods, and family restaurants. Results for the past three years are as follows (in millions):

	Soft Drink Division	Snack Foods Division	Restaurant Division	Quality Products, Inc.
Operating Revenues				
2005	$3,360	$2,400	$1,260	$7,020
2006	3,600	2,880	1,500	7,980
2007	4,320	3,120	1,836	9,276
Operating Income				
2005	144	432	126	702
2006	192	480	137	809
2007	288	504	120	912
Total Assets				
2005	1,440	1,488	960	3,888
2006	1,500	1,680	1,200	4,380
2007	1,680	1,716	1,560	4,956

REQUIRED
Use the DuPont method to explain changes in the operating income to total assets ratio over the 2005 to 2007 period for each division. Comment on the results.

24-18 ROI and RI. (D. Kleespie) The Gaul Company produces and distributes a wide variety of recreational products. One of its divisions, the Goscinny Division, manufactures and sells "menhirs," which are very popular with cross-country skiers. The demand for these menhirs is relatively insensitive to price changes. The Goscinny Division is considered to be an investment centre and in recent years has averaged a return on investment of 20%. The following data are available for the Goscinny Division and its product:

Total annual fixed costs	$1,200,000
Variable costs per menhir	$ 360
Average number of menhirs sold each year	10,000
Average operating assets invested in the division	$1,920,000

REQUIRED
1. What is the minimum selling price per unit that the Goscinny Division could charge in order for Mary Obelix, the division manager, to get a favourable performance rating? Management considers an ROI below 20% to be unfavourable.
2. Assume that the Gaul Company judges the performance of its investment centre managers on the basis of residual income rather than ROI, as was assumed in requirement 1. The company's required rate of return is considered to be 15%. What is the minimum selling price per unit that the Goscinny Division should charge for Obelix to receive a favourable performance rating?

24-19 Pricing and return on investment. Hardy, Inc., assembles motorcycles and uses long-run (defined as three to five years) average demand to set the budgeted production level and costs for pricing. Prices are then adjusted only for large changes in assembly wage rates or direct materials prices. You are given the following data:

Direct materials, assembly wages, and other variable costs	$ 1,584 per unit
Fixed costs	$ 360,000,000 per year
Target return on investment	20%
Normal utilization of capacity (average output)	1,000,000 units
Investment (total assets)	$1,080,000,000

REQUIRED
1. What operating income percentage on revenues is needed to attain the target return on investment of 20%? What is the selling price per unit?
2. Using the selling price per unit calculated in requirement 1, what rate of return on investment will be earned if Hardy assembles and sells 1,500,000 units? 500,000 units?
3. The company has a management bonus plan based on yearly division performance. Assume that Hardy assembled and sold 1,000,000, 1,500,000, and 500,000 units in three successive years. Each of three people served as division manager for one year before being killed in an automobile accident. As the principal heir of the third manager, comment on the bonus plan.

24-20 Financial and nonfinancial performance measures, goal-congruence. (CMA, adapted) Summit Equipment specializes in the manufacture of medical equipment, a field that has become increasingly competitive. Approximately two years ago, Ben Harrington, president of Summit, decided to revise the bonus plan (based, at the time, entirely on operating income) to encourage division managers to focus on areas that were important to customers and that added value without increasing cost. In addition to a profitability incentive, the revised plan also includes incentives for reduced rework costs, reduced sales returns, and on-time deliveries. Bonuses are calculated and awarded semiannually on the following basis. A base bonus is calculated at 2% of operating income. The bonus amount is then adjusted by the following amounts:

a. i. Reduced by excess of rework costs over 2% of operating income.
  ii. No adjustment if rework costs are less than or equal to 2% of operating income.
b. Increased by $6,000 if over 98% of deliveries are on time, by $2,400 if 96–98% of deliveries are on time, and by $0 if on-time deliveries are below 96%.
c. i. Increased by $3,600 if sales returns are less than or equal to 1.5% of sales.
  ii. Decreased by 50% of excess of sales returns over 1.5% of sales.

Note: If the calculation of the bonus results in a negative amount for a particular period, the manager simply receives no bonus, and the negative amount is not carried forward to the next period.

Results for Summit's Charter and Mesa Divisions for the year 2007, the first year under the new bonus plan, follow. In the previous year, 2006, under the old bonus plan, the Charter Division manager earned a bonus of $32,472 and the Mesa Division manager a bonus of $26,928.

	Charter Division		Mesa Division	
	January 1, 2007 to June 30, 2007	**July 1, 2007 to December 31, 2007**	**January 1, 2007 to June 30, 2007**	**July 1, 2007 to December 31, 2007**
Sales	$5,040,000	$5,280,000	$3,420,000	$3,480,000
Operating income	$ 554,400	$ 528,000	$ 410,400	$ 487,200
On-time delivery	95.4%	97.3%	98.2%	94.6%
Rework costs	$ 13,800	$ 13,200	$ 7,200	$ 9,600
Sales returns	$ 100,800	$ 84,000	$ 53,700	$ 51,000

REQUIRED

1. Why did Harrington need to introduce these new performance measures? That is, why does Harrington need to use these performance measures over and above the operating income numbers for the period?
2. Calculate the bonus earned by each manager for each six-month period and for the year 2007.
3. What effect did the change in the bonus plan have on each manager's behaviour? Did the new bonus plan achieve what Harrington desired? What changes, if any, would you make to the new bonus plan?

24-21 **ROI, RI, EVA®.** (D. Solomons, adapted) Consider the following data for the two geographical divisions of the Potomac Electric Company that operate as profit centres:

	Atlantic Division	**Pacific Division**
Total assets	$1,200,000	$6,000,000
Current liabilities	300,000	1,800,000
Operating income	240,000	900,000

REQUIRED

1. Calculate the return on investment (ROI) using operating income as the measure of income and using total assets as the measure of investment.
2. Potomac Electric has used residual income as a measure of management success, the variable it wants a manager to maximize. Using this criterion, what is the residual income for each division using operating income and total assets if the required rate of return on investment is 12%?
3. Potomac Electric has two sources of funds: long-term debt with a market value of $4,200,000 and an interest rate of 10%, and equity capital with a market value of $4,200,000 at a cost of equity of 14%. Potomac's income tax rate is 40%. Potomac applies the same weighted-average cost of capital to both divisions, since each division faces similar risks. Calculate the economic value added for each division. Which of the measures calculated in requirements 1, 2, and 3 would you recommend Potomac Electric use? Why? Explain briefly.

24-22 **RI, EVA®.** The Burlingame Transport Company operates two divisions, a Truck Rental Division that rents to individuals, and a Transportation Division that transports goods from one city to another. Results reported for the last year are as follows:

	Truck Rental Division	**Transportation Division**
Total assets	$780,000	$1,140,000
Current liabilities	144,000	240,000
Operating income before tax	90,000	192,000

REQUIRED

1. Calculate the residual income for each division using operating income before tax and investment equal to total assets minus current liabilities. The required rate of return on investments is 12%.
2. The company has two sources of funds: long-term debt with a market value of $1,080,000 at an interest rate of 10% and equity capital with a market value of $720,000 at a cost of equity of 15%. Burlingame's income tax rate is 40%. Burlingame applies the same weighted-average cost of capital to both divisions, since each division faces similar risks. Calculate the economic value added (EVA®) for each division.

3. Using your answers to requirements 1 and 2, what would you conclude about the performance of each division? Explain briefly.

24-23 Various measures of profitability. When the Coronet Company formed three divisions a year ago, the president told the division managers that an annual bonus would be paid to the most profitable division. However, absolute division operating income as conventionally computed would not be used. Instead, the ranking would be affected by the relative investments in the three divisions. Options available include ROI and residual income. Investment can be measured using gross book value or net book value. Each manager has now written a memorandum claiming entitlement to the bonus. The following data are available:

Division	Gross Book Value of Division Assets	Division Operating Income
Mastex	$480,000	$57,000
Banjo	456,000	55,200
Randal	300,000	36,960

All the assets are fixed assets that were purchased ten years ago and have ten years of useful life remaining. A zero terminal disposal price is predicted. Coronet's required rate of return on investment used for computing residual income is 10% of investment.

REQUIRED

Which method for computing profitability did each manager choose? Make your description specific and brief. Show supporting computations. Where applicable, assume straight-line amortization.

24-24 ROI, RI, measurement of assets. (CMA, adapted) Ashton Corporation recently announced a bonus plan to be awarded to the manager of the most profitable division. The three division managers are to choose whether ROI or RI will be used to measure profitability. In addition, they must decide whether investment will be measured using gross book value or net book value of assets. Ashton defines income as operating income and investment as total assets. The following information is available for the year just ended:

Division	Gross Book Value of Assets	Accumulated Amortization	Operating Income
Bristol	$960,000	$516,000	$113,640
Darden	912,000	492,000	110,040
Gregory	600,000	336,000	73,680

Ashton uses a required rate of return of 10% on investment to calculate RI.

REQUIRED

Each division manager has selected a method of bonus calculation that ranks his or her division Number 1. Identify the method for calculating profitability that each manager selected, supporting your answer with appropriate calculations.

24-25 Multinational performance measurement. The Sandvik Corporation manufactures electric motors in Canada and Sweden. The Canadian and Swedish operations are organized as decentralized divisions. The following information is available for 2007:

	Canadian Division	Swedish Division
Operating income	$1,440,000	7,862,400 kronor
Total assets	$9,600,000	50,400,000 kronor

Assume that the exchange rate at the time of Sandvik's investment in Sweden on December 31, 2006, was 6 kronor = $1. During 2007, the Swedish krona declined steadily in value so that the exchange rate on December 31, 2007, is 7 kronor = $1. The average exchange rate during 2007 is $[(6 + 7) \div 2] = 6.5$ kronor = $1.

REQUIRED

1. Calculate the Canadian Division's return on investment for 2007.
2. Calculate the Swedish Division's return on investment for 2007 in kronor.
3. Senior management at Sandvik wants to know which division earned a better return on investment in 2007. What would you tell them? Explain your answer.

24-26 Multinational performance measurement, ROI, RI. Loren Press operates two printing presses that operate as separate divisions, one located in Dundas, Ontario, and the other in Lyon, France. The following information is available for 2005. The required rate of return on investments is 15%.

	Dundas Division	Lyon Division
Operating income	$ 918,000	648,000 Euros
Total assets	$5,400,000	3,600,000 Euros

Both investments were made on December 31, 2004. The exchange rate at the time of Loren's investment in France on December 31, 2004, was 0.60 Euros = $1. During 2005, the Euro declined steadily in value, reaching an exchange rate on December 31, 2005, of 0.75 Euros = $1. The average exchange rate during 2005 is [(0.60 + 0.75) ÷ 2] = 0.675 Euros = $1.

REQUIRED

1. **a.** Calculate the Dundas Division's return on investment for 2005.
   b. Calculate the Lyon Division's return on investment for 2005 in French francs.
   c. Which division earned a better return on investment in 2005? Explain.
2. Senior management wants to compare the performance of the two divisions using residual income. Which division do you think had the better residual-income performance? Explain your answer.
3. On the basis of your answers to requirements 1 and 2, which division is performing better? If you had to promote one of the division managers to vice-president, which would you choose? Explain.

24-27 Risk-sharing, incentives, benchmarking, multiple tasks. The Dexter Division of AMCO sells car batteries. AMCO's corporate management gives Dexter management considerable operating and investment autonomy in running the division. AMCO is considering how it should compensate Jim Marks, the general manager of the Dexter Division. Proposal 1 calls for paying Marks a fixed salary. Proposal 2 calls for paying Marks no salary and compensating him only on the basis of the division's ROI (calculated on the basis of operating income before any bonus payments). Proposal 3 calls for paying Marks some salary and some bonus based on ROI. Assume that Marks does not like bearing risk.

REQUIRED

1. **a.** Evaluate each of the three proposals, specifying the advantages and disadvantages of each.
   b. Suppose that AMCO competes against Tiara Industries in the car battery business. Tiara is roughly the same size and operates in a business environment that is very similar to Dexter's. The senior management of AMCO is considering evaluating Marks on the basis of Dexter's ROI minus Tiara's ROI. Marks complains that this approach is unfair because the performance of another firm, over which he has no control, is included in his performance evaluation measure. Is Marks's complaint valid? Why or why not?
2. Now suppose that Marks has no authority for making capital investment decisions. Corporate management makes these decisions. Is return on investment a good performance measure to use to evaluate Marks? Is return on investment a good measure to evaluate the economic viability of the Dexter Division? Explain.
3. Dexter's salespersons are responsible for selling and providing customer service and support. Sales are easy to measure. Although customer service is very important to Dexter in the long run, it has not yet implemented customer service measures. Marks wants to compensate his sales force only on the basis of sales commissions paid for each unit of product sold. He cites two advantages to this plan: (a) it creates very strong incentives for the sales force to work hard and (b) the company pays salespersons only when the company itself is earning revenues and has cash. Do you like his plan? Why or why not?

PROBLEMS

24-28 ROI performance measures based on historical cost and current cost. Mineral Waters Ltd. operates three divisions that process and bottle sparkling mineral water. The historical-cost accounting system reports the following data for 2007:

	Calistoga Division	Alpine Springs Division	Rocky Mountains Division
Revenues	$600,000	$ 840,000	$1,320,000
Operating costs (excluding amortization)	360,000	456,000	720,000
Plant amortization	84,000	120,000	144,000
Operating income	$156,000	$ 264,000	$ 456,000
Current assets	$240,000	$ 300,000	$ 360,000
Fixed assets—plant	168,000	1,080,000	1,584,000
Total assets	$408,000	$1,380,000	$1,944,000

Mineral Waters estimates the useful life of each plant to be twelve years with a zero terminal disposal price. The straight-line amortization method is used. At the end of 2007, the Calistoga plant is ten years old, Alpine Springs plant is three years old, and Rocky Mountains plant is one year old.

An index of construction costs of plants for mineral water production for the ten-year period that Mineral Waters has been operating (1997 year-end = 100) is:

1997	2004	2006	2007
100	136	160	170

Given the high turnover of current assets, management believes that the historical-cost and current-cost measures of current assets are approximately the same.

REQUIRED

1. Compute the ROI (operating income to total assets) ratio of each division using historical-cost measures. Comment on the results.
2. Use the approach in Exhibit 24-2 (p. 929) to compute the ROI of each division, incorporating current-cost estimates as of 2007 for amortization and fixed assets. Comment on the results.
3. What advantages might arise from using current-cost asset measures as compared with historical-cost measures for evaluating the performance of the managers of the three divisions?

24-29 **Evaluating managers, ROI, value-chain analysis of cost structure.** User Friendly Computer is one of the largest personal computer companies in the world. The board of directors was recently (March 2007) informed that User Friendly's president, Brian Karmo, was resigning to "pursue other interests." An executive search firm recommends that the board consider appointing Peter Diamond (current president of Computer Power) or Norma Provan (current president of Peach Computer). You collect the following financial information on Computer Power and Peach Computer for 2005 and 2006 (in millions):

	Computer Power		Peach Computer	
	2005	2006	2005	2006
Total assets	$432.0	$408.0	$192.0	$288.0
Revenues	$400.0	$320.0	$200.0	$350.0
Costs:				
R&D	36.0	16.8	18.0	43.5
Design	15.0	8.4	3.6	11.6
Production	102.0	112.0	82.8	98.6
Marketing	75.0	92.4	36.0	66.7
Distribution	27.0	22.4	18.0	23.2
Customer service	45.0	28.0	21.6	46.4
Total costs	300.0	280.0	180.0	290.0
Operating income	$100.0	$ 40.0	$ 20.0	$ 60.0

In early 2007, a computer magazine gave Peach Computer's main product five stars (its highest rating on a five-point scale). Computer Power's main product was given three stars, down from five stars a year ago because of customer service problems. The computer magazine also ran an article on new product introductions in the personal computer industry. Peach Computer received high marks for new products in 2006. Computer

Power's performance was called "mediocre." One "unnamed insider" of Computer Power commented: "Our new product cupboard is empty."

REQUIRED

1. Use the DuPont method to analyze the ROI of Computer Power and Peach Computer in 2005 and 2006. Comment on the results.
2. Compute the percentage of costs in each of the six business-function cost categories for Computer Power and Peach Computer in 2005 and 2006. Comment on the results.
3. Rank Diamond and Provan as potential candidates for president of User Friendly Computer.

24-30 **ROI, RI, ROS, management incentives.** (CMA, adapted) The Jump-Start Division (JSD) of Mason Industries manufactures go-carts and other recreational vehicles. JSD is considering building a new plant in 2007. The investment will cost $3.0 million. The expected revenues and costs for the new plant in 2007 are:

Revenues	$2,880,000
Variable costs	960,000
Fixed costs	1,344,000
Operating income	$ 576,000

JSD's ROI in 2006 is 24% and its return on sales (ROS) is 20%. ROI is defined as operating income divided by total assets. The bonuses of Maureen Grieco, the division manager of JSD, and other JSD managers are based on division ROI.

REQUIRED

1. If Mason Industries uses ROI to evaluate division managers, explain why JSD would be reluctant to build the new plant. Show all calculations.
2. Suppose Mason Industries uses RI as the basis for awarding bonuses to JSD's managers. Suppose further that the required rate of return on investment is 15%. Would JSD be more willing to build the new plant? Explain.
3. Calculate the ROS for the new plant. What are the advantages and disadvantages of using this measure to determine the bonuses paid to JSD's managers?

24-31 **Division manager's compensation, risk sharing, incentives (continuation of 24–30).** The management of Mason Industries is considering the following alternative compensation arrangements for Maureen Grieco, the division manager of JSD:

◆ Make Grieco's compensation a fixed salary without any bonuses. Mason's management believes that one advantage of this arrangement is that Grieco will be less inclined to reject future investments just because of their impact on ROI or RI.

◆ Make all of Grieco's compensation depend on the division's RI. The benefit of this arrangement is that it creates incentives for Grieco to aggressively seek and accept all proposals that increase JSD's RI.

◆ Evaluate Grieco's performance using benchmarking by comparing JSD's RI against the RI achieved by managers of other companies that also manufacture and sell go-carts and recreational vehicles and have comparable levels of investment. Mason's management believes that the advantage of benchmarking is that it focuses attention on Grieco's performance relative to peers rather than on the division's absolute performance.

REQUIRED

1. Assume Grieco is risk adverse and does not like bearing risk. Using concepts of performance evaluation described in this chapter, evaluate each of the three proposals that Mason's management is considering. Indicate the positive and negative features of each proposal.
2. What compensation arrangement would you recommend? Explain briefly.

24-32 **Relevant costs, performance evaluation, goal-congruence.** Pike Enterprises has three operating divisions. The managers of these divisions are evaluated on their divisional operating income, a figure that includes an allocation of corporate overhead proportional to the revenues of each division. The operating income statement (in thousands) for the first quarter of 2007 is as follows:

	Andorian Division	Orion Division	Tribble Division	Total
Revenues	$2,400	$1,440	$1,920	$5,760
Cost of goods sold	1,260	648	768	2,676
Gross margin	1,140	792	1,152	3,084
Division overhead	300	150	192	642
Corporate overhead	480	288	384	1,152
Division operating income	$ 360	$ 354	$ 576	$1,290

The manager of the Andorian Division is unhappy that his profitability is about the same as the Orion Division's and is much less than the Tribble Division's, even though his revenues are much higher than either of these other two divisions. The manager knows that he is carrying one line of products with very low profitability. He was going to replace this line of business as soon as more profitable product opportunities became available, but he has kept it because the line is marginally profitable and uses facilities that would otherwise be idle. That manager now realizes, however, that the sales from this product line are attracting a fair amount of corporate overhead because of the allocation procedure, and maybe the line is already unprofitable for him. This low-margin line of products had the following characteristics for the most recent quarter (in thousands):

Revenues	$960
Cost of goods sold	720
Avoidable division overhead	120

REQUIRED

1. Prepare the operating income statement for Pike Enterprises for the second quarter of 2007. Assume that revenues and operating results are identical to those of the first quarter except that the manager of the Andorian Division has dropped the low-margin product line from his product group.
2. Is Pike Enterprises better off from this action?
3. Is the Andorian Division manager better off from this action?
4. Suggest changes for Pike's system of division reporting and evaluation that will motivate division managers to make decisions that are in the best interests of Pike Enterprises as a whole. Discuss any potential disadvantages of your proposal.

24-33 Historical cost and current cost ROI measures. Nobillo Corporation owns and manages convenience stores. The following information on three stores is collected for the year 2007:

	City Plaza	South Station	Central Park
Operating income	$108,000	$144,000	$ 72,000
Historical cost of investment	$360,000	$600,000	$288,000
Current cost of investment	$720,000	$840,000	$540,000
Age of store	10 years	5 years	8 years

REQUIRED

1. Compute the ROI for each store where investment is measured at (a) historical cost and (b) current cost.
2. How would you judge the performance of each store?

24-34 ROI, RI, investment decisions. The Media Group has three major divisions:

a. Newspapers—owns leading newspapers on four continents
b. Television—owns major television networks on three continents
c. Film studios—owns one of the five largest film studios in the world

Summary financial data for 2006 and 2007 are as follows (in millions):

	Operating Income		Revenues		Total Assets	
	2006	2007	2006	2007	2006	2007
Newspapers	$1,080	$1,320	$5,400	$5,520	$5,280	$5,880
Television	156	192	7,200	7,680	3,240	3,600
Film studios	264	240	1,920	1,980	3,000	3,120

The manager of each division has an annual bonus plan based on division return on investment (ROI). ROI is defined as operating income divided by total assets. Senior executives from divisions reporting increases in ROI from the prior year are automatically eligible for a bonus. Senior executives of divisions reporting a decline in the division ROI have to provide persuasive explanations for the decline to be eligible for a limited bonus.

Ken Kearney, manager of the Newspapers Division, is considering a proposal to invest $240 million in high-speed printing presses with colour-print options. The estimated increment to 2008 operating income would be $36 million. The Media Group has a 12% required rate of return for investments in all three divisions.

REQUIRED

1. Use the DuPont method to explain differences among the three divisions in their 2007 division ROI. Use 2007 total assets as the investment base.

2. Why might Kearney be less than enthusiastic about the high-speed printing press investment proposal?
3. Rupert Prince, chairman of the Media Group, receives a proposal to base senior executive compensation at each division on division residual income. Compute the residual income of each division in 2007.
4. Would adoption of a residual income measure reduce Kearney's reluctance to adopt the high-speed printing press investment proposal?

24-35 **Division managers' compensation (continuation of 24-34).** Rupert Prince seeks your advice on revising the existing bonus plan for division managers of the Media Group. Assume division managers do not like bearing risk. He is considering three ideas:
◆ Make all of each division manager's compensation depend on division ROI.
◆ Make all of each division manager's compensation depend on companywide ROI.
◆ Use benchmarking, and compensate each division manager on the basis of his or her own division's ROI minus the average ROI of the other two divisions.

REQUIRED
Evaluate each of the three ideas Prince has put forth using performance evaluation concepts described in this chapter. Indicate the positive and negative features of each proposal.

24-36 **Ethics, manager's performance evaluation.** (A. Spero, adapted) Hamilton Semiconductors manufactures specialized chips that sell for $24 each. Hamilton's manufacturing costs consist of variable costs of $2.40 per chip and fixed costs of $10,800,000. Hamilton also incurs $480,000 in fixed marketing costs each year.

Hamilton calculates operating income using absorption costing—that is, Hamilton calculates manufacturing costs per unit by dividing total manufacturing costs by actual production. Hamilton costs all units in inventory at this rate and expenses the costs in the income statement only when the units in inventory are sold. The next year, 2007, appears to be a difficult year for Hamilton. It expects to sell only 500,000 units. The demand for these chips fluctuates considerably so Hamilton usually holds minimal inventory.

REQUIRED
1. Calculate Hamilton's operating income in 2007 if Hamilton manufactures (a) 500,000 units and (b) 600,000 units.
2. Would it be unethical for Randy Jones, the general manager of Hamilton Semiconductors, to produce more units than can be sold in order to show better operating results? Jones's compensation has a bonus component based on operating income. Explain your answer.
3. Would it be unethical for Jones to ask distributors to buy more product than they need? Hamilton follows the industry practice of booking sales when products are shipped to distributors. Explain your answer.

COLLABORATIVE LEARNING PROBLEM
24-37 **ROI, RI division manager's compensation, nonfinancial measures.** Key information for the Peoria Division (PD) of Barrington Industries for 2007 follows:

Revenues	$18,000,000
Operating income	2,160,000
Total assets	12,000,000

PD's managers are evaluated and rewarded on the basis of ROI defined as operating income divided by total assets. Barrington Industries expects its divisions to increase ROI each year.

The year 2008 appears to be a difficult year for PD. PD had planned new investments to improve quality but, in view of poor economic conditions, has postponed the investment. ROI for 2008 was certain to decrease had PD made the investment.

Management is now considering ways to meet its target ROI of 20% for next year. It anticipates revenues to be steady at $18,000,000 in 2008.

INSTRUCTIONS
Form groups of two or more students to complete the following requirements.
1. Calculate PD's return on sales (ROS) and ROI for 2007.
2. a. By how much would PD have to cut costs in 2008 to achieve its target ROI of 20% in 2008, assuming no change in total assets between 2007 and 2008?

b. By how much would PD have to decrease total assets in 2008 to achieve its target ROI of 20% in 2008, assuming no change in operating income between 2007 and 2008?

3. Calculate PD's RI in 2007 assuming a required rate of return on investment of 15%.

4. PD wants to increase RI by 50% in 2008. Assuming it could cut costs by $54,000 in 2008, by how much would PD have to decrease total assets in 2008?

5. Barrington Industries is concerned that the focus on cost cutting and asset sales will have an adverse long-run effect on PD's customers. Yet Barrington wants PD to meet its financial goals. What other measurements, if any, do you recommend that Barrington use? Explain briefly.

A

Notes on Compound Interest and Interest Tables

Interest is the cost of using money. It is the rental charge for funds, just as renting a building and equipment entails a rental charge. When the funds are used for a period of time, it is necessary to recognize interest as a cost of using the borrowed ("rented") funds. This requirement applies even if the funds represent ownership capital and if interest does not entail an outlay of cash. Why must interest be considered? Because the selection of one alternative automatically commits a given amount of funds that could otherwise be invested in some other alternative.

Interest is generally important, even when short-term projects are under consideration. Interest looms correspondingly larger when long-run plans are studied. The rate of interest has significant enough impact to influence decisions regarding borrowing and investing funds. For example, $100,000 invested now and compounded annually for 10 years at 8% will accumulate to $215,900; at 20%, the $100,000 will accumulate to $619,200.

INTEREST TABLES

Many computer programs and pocket calculators are available that handle computations involving the time value of money. You may also turn to the following four basic tables to compute interest.

Table 1—Future Amount of $1

Table 1 shows how much $1 invested now will accumulate in a given number of periods at a given compounded interest rate per period. Consider investing $1,000 now for three years at 8% compound interest. A tabular presentation of how this $1,000 would accumulate to $1,259.70 follows:

Year	Interest per Year	Cumulative Interest Called Compound Interest	Total at End of Year
0	$ —	$ —	$1,000.00
1	80.00	80.00	1,080.00
2	86.40	166.40	1,166.40
3	93.30	259.70	1,259.70

This tabular presentation is a series of computations that could appear as follows:

$$S_1 = \$1,000(1.08)^1$$
$$S_2 = \$1,000(1.08)^2$$
$$S_3 = \$1,000(1.08)^3$$

The formula for the "amount of 1," often called the "future value of \$1" or "future amount of \$1," can be written

$$S = P(1 + r)^n$$
$$S = \$1,000(1 + 0.08)^3 = \$1,259.70$$

S is the future value amount; P is the present value, \$1,000 in this case; r is the rate of interest; and n is the number of time periods.

Fortunately, tables make key computations readily available. A facility in selecting the *proper* table will minimize computations. Check the accuracy of the preceding answer using Table 1.

Table 2—Present Value of \$1

In the previous example, if \$1,000 compounded at 8% per year will accumulate to \$1,259.70 in 3 years, then \$1,000 must be the present value of \$1,259.70 due at the end of 3 years. The formula for the present value can be derived by reversing the process of *accumulation* (finding the future amount) that we just finished.

If $$S = P(1 + r)^n$$

then $$P = \frac{S}{(1 + r)^n}$$

$$P = \frac{\$1,259.70}{(1.08)^3} = \$1,000$$

Use Table 2 to check this calculation.

When accumulating, we advance or roll forward in time. The difference between our original amount and our accumulated amount is called *compound interest*. When discounting, we retreat or roll back in time. The difference between the future amount and the present value is called *compound discount*. Note the following formulas (where $P = \$1,000$):

$$\text{Compound interest} = P[(1 + r)^n - 1] = \$259.70$$

$$\text{Compound discount} = S\left[1 - \frac{1}{(1 + r)^n}\right] = \$259.70$$

Table 3—Amount of Annuity of \$1

An (ordinary) *annuity* is a series of equal payments (receipts) to be paid (or received) at the *end* of successive periods of equal length. Assume that \$1,000 is invested at the end of each of 3 years at 8%:

$$0 \qquad 1 \qquad 2 \qquad 3$$

End of Year	Amount		
1st payment	\$1,000.00 ➤ \$1,080.00 ➤		\$1,166.40, which is \$1,000(1.08)²
2nd payment	\$1,000.00 ➤		1,080.00, which is \$1,000(1.08)¹
3rd payment			1,000.00
Accumulation (future amount)			\$3,246.40

The preceding arithmetic may be expressed algebraically as the amount of an ordinary annuity of $1,000 for 3 years = $1,000(1 + r)^2 + $1,000(1 + r)^1 + $1,000.

We can develop the general formula for S_n, the amount of an ordinary annuity of $1, by using the example above as a basis:

1. $\quad\quad\quad\quad\quad\quad\quad\quad\quad\quad S_n = 1 + (1 + r)^1 + (1 + r)^2$

2. Substitute: $\quad\quad\quad\quad\quad\quad\quad S_n = 1 + (1.08)^1 + (1.08)^2$

3. Multiply (2) by $(1 + r)$: $\quad\quad (1.08)S_n = (1.08)^1 + (1.08)^2 + (1.08)^3$

4. Subtract (2) from (3): $\quad\quad 1.08S_n - S_n = (1.08)^3 - 1$
   Note that all terms on the right-hand side are removed except $(1.08)^3$ in equation (3) and 1 in equation (2).

5. Factor (4): $\quad\quad\quad\quad\quad\quad S_n(1.08 - 1) = (1.08)^3 - 1$

6. Divide (5) by $(1.08 - 1)$: $\quad S_n = \dfrac{(1.08)^3 - 1)}{1.08 - 1} = \dfrac{(1.08)^3 - 1}{.08}$

7. The general formula for the amount of an ordinary annuity of $1 becomes: $\quad S_n = \dfrac{(1 + r)^n - 1}{r}$ or $\dfrac{\text{Compound interest}}{\text{Rate}}$

This formula is the basis for Table 3. Look at Table 3 or use the formula itself to check the calculations.

Table 4—Present Value of an Ordinary Annuity of $1

Using the same example as for Table 3, we can show how the formula of P_n, *the present value of an ordinary annuity*, is developed.

| | 0 | 1 | 2 | 3 |

End of Year

1st payment	$\dfrac{1,000}{(1.08)^1} = \$\ 925.93$ $\longleftarrow$ $\$1,000$
2nd payment	$\dfrac{1,000}{(1.08)^2} = \$\ 857.34$ $\longleftarrow$ $\$1,000$
3rd payment	$\dfrac{1,000}{(1.08)^3} = \underline{\$\ 793.83}$ $\longleftarrow$ $\$1,000$
Total present value	$\underline{\underline{\$2,577.10}}$

For the general case, the present value of an ordinary annuity of $1 may be expressed:

1. $\quad\quad\quad\quad\quad\quad\quad\quad P_n = \dfrac{1}{1 + r} + \dfrac{1}{(1 + r)^2} + \dfrac{1}{(1 + r)^3}$

2. Substitute $\quad\quad\quad\quad\quad P_n = \dfrac{1}{1.08} + \dfrac{1}{(1.08)^2} + \dfrac{1}{(1.08)^3}$

3. Multiply by $\dfrac{1}{1.08}$: $\quad P_n\dfrac{1}{1.08} = \dfrac{1}{(1.08)^2} + \dfrac{1}{(1.08)^3} + \dfrac{1}{(1.08)^4}$

4. Subtract (3) from (2): $\quad P_n - P_n\dfrac{1}{1.08} = \dfrac{1}{1.08} - \dfrac{1}{(1.08)^4}$

5. Factor: $\quad\quad\quad\quad\quad P_n\left(1 - \dfrac{1}{(1.08)}\right) = \dfrac{1}{1.08}\left[1 - \dfrac{1}{(1.08)^3}\right]$

6. or $\quad\quad\quad\quad\quad\quad P_n\left(\dfrac{.08}{1.08}\right) = \dfrac{1}{1.08}\left[1 - \dfrac{1}{(1.08)^3}\right]$

7. Multiply by $\dfrac{1.08}{0.08}$: $P_n = \dfrac{1}{0.08}\left[1 - \dfrac{1}{(1.08)^3}\right]$

The general formula for the present value of an annuity of $1.00 is:

$$P_n = \frac{1}{r}\left[1 - \frac{1}{(1+r)^n}\right] = \frac{\text{Compound discount}}{\text{Rate}}$$

Solving,

$$P_n = \frac{0.2062}{0.08} = 2.577$$

The formula is the basis for Table 4. Check the answer in the table. The present value tables, Tables 2 and 4, are used most frequently in capital budgeting.

The tables for annuities are not essential. With Tables 1 and 2, compound interest and compound discount can readily be computed. It is simply a matter of dividing either of these by the rate to get values equivalent to those shown in Tables 3 and 4.

TABLE 1
Compound Amount of $1.00 (The Future Value of $1.00).
$S = P(1 + r)^n$. In this table $P = 1.00.

Periods	2%	4%	6%	8%	10%	12%	14%	16%	18%	20%	22%	24%	26%	28%	30%	32%	40%	Periods
1	1.020	1.040	1.060	1.080	1.100	1.120	1.140	1.160	1.180	1.200	1.220	1.240	1.260	1.280	1.300	1.320	1.400	1
2	1.040	1.082	1.124	1.166	1.210	1.254	1.300	1.346	1.392	1.440	1.488	1.538	1.588	1.638	1.690	1.742	1.960	2
3	1.061	1.125	1.191	1.260	1.331	1.405	1.482	1.561	1.643	1.728	1.816	1.907	2.000	2.097	2.197	2.300	2.744	3
4	1.082	1.170	1.262	1.360	1.464	1.574	1.689	1.811	1.939	2.074	2.215	2.364	2.520	2.684	2.856	3.036	3.842	4
5	1.104	1.217	1.338	1.469	1.611	1.762	1.925	2.100	2.288	2.488	2.703	2.932	3.176	3.436	3.713	4.007	5.378	5
6	1.126	1.265	1.419	1.587	1.772	1.974	2.195	2.436	2.700	2.986	3.297	3.635	4.002	4.398	4.827	5.290	7.530	6
7	1.149	1.316	1.504	1.714	1.949	2.211	2.502	2.826	3.185	3.583	4.023	4.508	5.042	5.629	6.275	6.983	10.541	7
8	1.172	1.369	1.594	1.851	2.144	2.476	2.853	3.278	3.759	4.300	4.908	5.590	6.353	7.206	8.157	9.217	14.758	8
9	1.195	1.423	1.689	1.999	2.358	2.773	3.252	3.803	4.435	5.160	5.987	6.931	8.005	9.223	10.604	12.166	20.661	9
10	1.219	1.480	1.791	2.159	2.594	3.106	3.707	4.411	5.234	6.192	7.305	8.594	10.086	11.806	13.786	16.060	28.925	10
11	1.243	1.539	1.898	2.332	2.853	3.479	4.226	5.117	6.176	7.430	8.912	10.657	12.708	15.112	17.922	21.199	40.496	11
12	1.268	1.601	2.012	2.518	3.138	3.896	4.818	5.936	7.288	8.916	10.872	13.215	16.012	19.343	23.298	27.983	56.694	12
13	1.294	1.665	2.133	2.720	3.452	4.363	5.492	6.886	8.599	10.699	13.264	16.386	20.175	24.759	30.288	36.937	79.371	13
14	1.319	1.732	2.261	2.937	3.797	4.887	6.261	7.988	10.147	12.839	16.182	20.319	25.421	31.691	39.374	48.757	111.120	14
15	1.346	1.801	2.397	3.172	4.177	5.474	7.138	9.266	11.974	15.407	19.742	25.196	32.030	40.565	51.186	64.359	155.568	15
16	1.373	1.873	2.540	3.426	4.595	6.130	8.137	10.748	14.129	18.488	24.086	31.243	40.358	51.923	66.542	84.954	217.795	16
17	1.400	1.948	2.693	3.700	5.054	6.866	9.276	12.468	16.672	22.186	29.384	38.741	50.851	66.461	86.504	112.139	304.913	17
18	1.428	2.026	2.854	3.996	5.560	7.690	10.575	14.463	19.673	26.623	35.849	48.039	64.072	85.071	112.455	148.024	426.879	18
19	1.457	2.107	3.026	4.316	6.116	8.613	12.056	16.777	23.214	31.948	43.736	59.568	80.731	108.890	146.192	195.391	597.630	19
20	1.486	2.191	3.207	4.661	6.727	9.646	13.743	19.461	27.393	38.338	53.358	73.864	101.721	139.380	190.050	257.916	836.683	20
21	1.516	2.279	3.400	5.034	7.400	10.804	15.668	22.574	32.324	46.005	65.096	91.592	128.169	178.406	247.065	340.449	1171.356	21
22	1.546	2.370	3.604	5.437	8.140	12.100	17.861	26.186	38.142	55.206	79.418	113.574	161.492	228.360	321.184	449.393	1639.898	22
23	1.577	2.465	3.820	5.871	8.954	13.552	20.362	30.376	45.008	66.247	96.889	140.831	203.480	292.300	417.539	593.199	2295.857	23
24	1.608	2.563	4.049	6.341	9.850	15.179	23.212	35.236	53.109	79.497	118.205	174.631	256.385	374.144	542.801	783.023	3214.200	24
25	1.641	2.666	4.292	6.848	10.835	17.000	26.462	40.874	62.669	95.396	144.210	216.542	323.045	478.905	705.641	1033.590	4499.880	25
26	1.673	2.772	4.549	7.396	11.918	19.040	30.167	47.414	73.949	114.475	175.936	268.512	407.037	612.998	917.333	1364.339	6299.831	26
27	1.707	2.883	4.822	7.988	13.110	21.325	34.390	55.000	87.260	137.371	214.642	332.955	512.867	784.638	1192.533	1800.927	8819.764	27
28	1.741	2.999	5.112	8.627	14.421	23.884	39.204	63.800	102.967	164.845	261.864	412.864	646.212	1004.336	1550.293	2377.224	12347.670	28
29	1.776	3.119	5.418	9.317	15.863	26.750	44.693	74.009	121.501	197.814	319.474	511.952	814.228	1285.550	2015.381	3137.935	17286.737	29
30	1.811	3.243	5.743	10.063	17.449	29.960	50.950	85.850	143.371	237.376	389.758	634.820	1025.927	1645.505	2619.996	4142.075	24201.432	30
35	2.000	3.946	7.686	14.785	28.102	52.800	98.100	180.314	327.997	590.668	1053.402	1861.054	3258.135	5653.911	9727.860	16599.217	130161.112	35
40	2.208	4.801	10.286	21.725	45.259	93.051	188.884	378.721	750.378	1469.772	2847.038	5455.913	10347.175	19426.689	36118.865	66520.767	700037.697	40

TABLE 2 (*Place a clip on this page for easy reference.*)
Present Value of $1.00.

$$P = \frac{S}{(1+r)^n}.$$ In this table $S = \$1.00$.

Periods	2%	4%	6%	8%	10%	12%	14%	16%	18%	20%	22%	24%	26%	28%	30%	32%	40%	Periods
1	0.980	0.962	0.943	0.926	0.909	0.893	0.877	0.862	0.847	0.833	0.820	0.806	0.794	0.781	0.769	0.758	0.714	1
2	0.961	0.925	0.890	0.857	0.826	0.797	0.769	0.743	0.718	0.694	0.672	0.650	0.630	0.610	0.592	0.574	0.510	2
3	0.942	0.889	0.840	0.794	0.751	0.712	0.675	0.641	0.609	0.579	0.551	0.524	0.500	0.477	0.455	0.435	0.364	3
4	0.924	0.855	0.792	0.735	0.683	0.636	0.592	0.552	0.516	0.482	0.451	0.423	0.397	0.373	0.350	0.329	0.260	4
5	0.906	0.822	0.747	0.681	0.621	0.567	0.519	0.476	0.437	0.402	0.370	0.341	0.315	0.291	0.269	0.250	0.186	5
6	0.888	0.790	0.705	0.630	0.564	0.507	0.456	0.410	0.370	0.335	0.303	0.275	0.250	0.227	0.207	0.189	0.133	6
7	0.871	0.760	0.665	0.583	0.513	0.452	0.400	0.354	0.314	0.279	0.249	0.222	0.198	0.178	0.159	0.143	0.095	7
8	0.853	0.731	0.627	0.540	0.467	0.404	0.351	0.305	0.266	0.233	0.204	0.179	0.157	0.139	0.123	0.108	0.068	8
9	0.837	0.703	0.592	0.500	0.424	0.361	0.308	0.263	0.225	0.194	0.167	0.144	0.125	0.108	0.094	0.082	0.048	9
10	0.820	0.676	0.558	0.463	0.386	0.322	0.270	0.227	0.191	0.162	0.137	0.116	0.099	0.085	0.073	0.062	0.035	10
11	0.804	0.650	0.527	0.429	0.350	0.287	0.237	0.195	0.162	0.135	0.112	0.094	0.079	0.066	0.056	0.047	0.025	11
12	0.788	0.625	0.497	0.397	0.319	0.257	0.208	0.168	0.137	0.112	0.092	0.076	0.062	0.052	0.043	0.036	0.018	12
13	0.773	0.601	0.469	0.368	0.290	0.229	0.182	0.145	0.116	0.093	0.075	0.061	0.050	0.040	0.033	0.027	0.013	13
14	0.758	0.577	0.442	0.340	0.263	0.205	0.160	0.125	0.099	0.078	0.062	0.049	0.039	0.032	0.025	0.021	0.009	14
15	0.743	0.555	0.417	0.315	0.239	0.183	0.140	0.108	0.084	0.065	0.051	0.040	0.031	0.025	0.020	0.016	0.006	15
16	0.728	0.534	0.394	0.292	0.218	0.163	0.123	0.093	0.071	0.054	0.042	0.032	0.025	0.019	0.015	0.012	0.005	16
17	0.714	0.513	0.371	0.270	0.198	0.146	0.108	0.080	0.060	0.045	0.034	0.026	0.020	0.015	0.012	0.009	0.003	17
18	0.700	0.494	0.350	0.250	0.180	0.130	0.095	0.069	0.051	0.038	0.028	0.021	0.016	0.012	0.009	0.007	0.002	18
19	0.686	0.475	0.331	0.232	0.164	0.116	0.083	0.060	0.043	0.031	0.023	0.017	0.012	0.009	0.007	0.005	0.002	19
20	0.673	0.456	0.312	0.215	0.149	0.104	0.073	0.051	0.037	0.026	0.019	0.014	0.010	0.007	0.005	0.004	0.001	20
21	0.660	0.439	0.294	0.199	0.135	0.093	0.064	0.044	0.031	0.022	0.015	0.011	0.008	0.006	0.004	0.003	0.001	21
22	0.647	0.422	0.278	0.184	0.123	0.083	0.056	0.038	0.026	0.018	0.013	0.009	0.006	0.004	0.003	0.002	0.001	22
23	0.634	0.406	0.262	0.170	0.112	0.074	0.049	0.033	0.022	0.015	0.010	0.007	0.005	0.003	0.002	0.002	0.000	23
24	0.622	0.390	0.247	0.158	0.102	0.066	0.043	0.028	0.019	0.013	0.008	0.006	0.004	0.003	0.002	0.001	0.000	24
25	0.610	0.375	0.233	0.146	0.092	0.059	0.038	0.024	0.016	0.010	0.007	0.005	0.003	0.002	0.001	0.001	0.000	25
26	0.598	0.361	0.220	0.135	0.084	0.053	0.033	0.021	0.014	0.009	0.006	0.004	0.002	0.002	0.001	0.001	0.000	26
27	0.586	0.347	0.207	0.125	0.076	0.047	0.029	0.018	0.011	0.007	0.005	0.003	0.002	0.001	0.001	0.001	0.000	27
28	0.574	0.333	0.196	0.116	0.069	0.042	0.026	0.016	0.010	0.006	0.004	0.002	0.002	0.001	0.001	0.000	0.000	28
29	0.563	0.321	0.185	0.107	0.063	0.037	0.022	0.014	0.008	0.005	0.003	0.002	0.001	0.001	0.000	0.000	0.000	29
30	0.552	0.308	0.174	0.099	0.057	0.033	0.020	0.012	0.007	0.004	0.003	0.002	0.001	0.001	0.000	0.000	0.000	30
35	0.500	0.253	0.130	0.068	0.036	0.019	0.010	0.006	0.003	0.002	0.001	0.001	0.000	0.000	0.000	0.000	0.000	35
40	0.453	0.208	0.097	0.046	0.022	0.011	0.005	0.003	0.001	0.001	0.000	0.000	0.000	0.000	0.000	0.000	0.000	40

TABLE 3
Compound Amount of Annuity of $1.00 in Arrears* (Future Value of Annuity).

$$S_n = \frac{(1+r)^n - 1}{r}$$

Periods	2%	4%	6%	8%	10%	12%	14%	16%	18%	20%	22%	24%	26%	28%	30%	32%	40%	Periods
1	1.000	1.000	1.000	1.000	1.000	1.000	1.000	1.000	1.000	1.000	1.000	1.000	1.000	1.000	1.000	1.000	1.000	1
2	2.020	2.040	2.060	2.080	2.100	2.120	2.140	2.160	2.180	2.200	2.220	2.240	2.260	2.280	2.300	2.320	2.400	2
3	3.060	3.122	3.184	3.246	3.310	3.374	3.440	3.506	3.572	3.640	3.708	3.778	3.848	3.918	3.990	4.062	4.360	3
4	4.122	4.246	4.375	4.506	4.641	4.779	4.921	5.066	5.215	5.368	5.524	5.684	5.848	6.016	6.187	6.362	7.104	4
5	5.204	5.416	5.637	5.867	6.105	6.353	6.610	6.877	7.154	7.442	7.740	8.048	8.368	8.700	9.043	9.398	10.946	5
6	6.308	6.633	6.975	7.336	7.716	8.115	8.536	8.977	9.442	9.930	10.442	10.980	11.544	12.136	12.756	13.406	16.324	6
7	7.434	7.898	8.394	8.923	9.487	10.089	10.730	11.414	12.142	12.916	13.740	14.615	15.546	16.534	17.583	18.696	23.853	7
8	8.583	9.214	9.897	10.637	11.436	12.300	13.233	14.240	15.327	16.499	17.762	19.123	20.588	22.163	23.858	25.678	34.395	8
9	9.755	10.583	11.491	12.488	13.579	14.776	16.085	17.519	19.086	20.799	22.670	24.712	26.940	29.369	32.015	34.895	49.153	9
10	10.950	12.006	13.181	14.487	15.937	17.549	19.337	21.321	23.521	25.959	28.657	31.643	34.945	38.593	42.619	47.062	69.814	10
11	12.169	13.486	14.972	16.645	18.531	20.655	23.045	25.733	28.755	32.150	35.962	40.238	45.031	50.398	56.405	63.122	98.739	11
12	13.412	15.026	16.870	18.977	21.384	24.133	27.271	30.850	34.931	39.581	44.874	50.895	57.739	65.510	74.327	84.320	139.235	12
13	14.680	16.627	18.882	21.495	24.523	28.029	32.089	36.786	42.219	48.497	55.746	64.110	73.751	84.853	97.625	112.303	195.929	13
14	15.974	18.292	21.015	24.215	27.975	32.393	37.581	43.672	50.818	59.196	69.010	80.496	93.926	109.612	127.913	149.240	275.300	14
15	17.293	20.024	23.276	27.152	31.772	37.280	43.842	51.660	60.965	72.035	85.192	100.815	119.347	141.303	167.286	197.997	386.420	15
16	18.639	21.825	25.673	30.324	35.950	42.753	50.980	60.925	72.939	87.442	104.935	126.011	151.377	181.868	218.472	262.356	541.988	16
17	20.012	23.698	28.213	33.750	40.545	48.884	59.118	71.673	87.068	105.931	129.020	157.253	191.735	233.791	285.014	347.309	759.784	17
18	21.412	25.645	30.906	37.450	45.599	55.750	68.394	84.141	103.740	128.117	158.405	195.994	242.585	300.252	371.518	459.449	1064.697	18
19	22.841	27.671	33.760	41.446	51.159	63.440	78.969	98.603	123.414	154.740	194.254	244.033	306.658	385.323	483.973	607.472	1491.576	19
20	24.297	29.778	36.786	45.762	57.275	72.052	91.025	115.380	146.628	186.688	237.989	303.601	387.389	494.213	630.165	802.863	2089.206	20
21	25.783	31.969	39.993	50.423	64.002	81.699	104.768	134.841	174.021	225.026	291.347	377.465	489.110	633.593	820.215	1060.779	2925.889	21
22	27.299	34.248	43.392	55.457	71.403	92.503	120.436	157.415	206.345	271.031	356.443	469.056	617.278	811.999	1067.280	1401.229	4097.245	22
23	28.845	36.618	46.996	60.893	79.543	104.603	138.297	183.601	244.487	326.237	435.861	582.630	778.771	1040.358	1388.464	1850.622	5737.142	23
24	30.422	39.083	50.816	66.765	88.497	118.155	158.659	213.978	289.494	392.484	532.750	723.461	982.251	1332.659	1806.003	2443.821	8032.999	24
25	32.030	41.646	54.865	73.106	98.347	133.334	181.871	249.214	342.603	471.981	650.955	898.092	1238.636	1706.803	2348.803	3226.844	11247.199	25
26	33.671	44.312	59.156	79.954	109.182	150.334	208.333	290.088	405.272	567.377	795.165	1114.634	1561.682	2185.708	3054.444	4260.434	15747.079	26
27	35.344	47.084	63.706	87.351	121.100	169.374	238.499	337.502	479.221	681.853	971.102	1383.146	1968.719	2798.706	3971.778	5624.772	22046.910	27
28	37.051	49.968	68.528	95.339	134.210	190.699	272.889	392.503	586.481	819.223	1185.744	1716.101	2481.586	3583.344	5164.311	7425.699	30866.674	28
29	38.792	52.966	73.640	103.966	148.631	214.583	312.094	456.303	669.447	984.068	1447.608	2128.965	3127.798	4587.680	6714.604	9802.923	43214.343	29
30	40.568	56.085	79.058	113.283	164.494	241.333	356.787	530.312	790.948	1181.882	1767.081	2640.916	3942.026	5873.231	8729.985	12940.859	60501.081	30
35	49.994	73.652	111.435	172.317	271.024	431.663	693.573	1120.713	1816.652	2948.341	4783.645	7750.225	12527.442	20188.966	32422.868	51869.427	325400.279	35
40	60.402	95.026	154.762	259.057	442.593	767.091	1342.025	2360.757	4163.213	7343.858	12936.535	22728.803	39792.982	69377.460	120392.883	207874.272	1750091.741	40

*Payments (or receipts) at the end of each period.

TABLE 4 (*Place a clip on this page for easy reference.*)
Present Value of Annuity $1.00 in Arrears.*

$$P_n = \frac{1}{r}\left[1 - \frac{1}{(1+r)^n}\right]$$

Periods	2%	4%	6%	8%	10%	12%	14%	16%	18%	20%	22%	24%	26%	28%	30%	32%	40%	Periods
1	0.980	0.962	0.943	0.926	0.909	0.893	0.877	0.862	0.847	0.833	0.820	0.806	0.794	0.781	0.769	0.758	0.714	1
2	1.942	1.886	1.833	1.783	1.736	1.690	1.647	1.605	1.566	1.528	1.492	1.457	1.424	1.392	1.361	1.331	1.224	2
3	2.884	2.775	2.673	2.577	2.487	2.402	2.322	2.246	2.174	2.106	2.042	1.981	1.923	1.868	1.816	1.766	1.589	3
4	3.808	3.630	3.465	3.312	3.170	3.037	2.914	2.798	2.690	2.589	2.494	2.404	2.320	2.241	2.166	2.096	1.849	4
5	4.713	4.452	4.212	3.993	3.791	3.605	3.433	3.274	3.127	2.991	2.864	2.745	2.635	2.532	2.436	2.345	2.035	5
6	5.601	5.242	4.917	4.623	4.355	4.111	3.889	3.685	3.498	3.326	3.167	3.020	2.885	2.759	2.643	2.534	2.168	6
7	6.472	6.002	5.582	5.206	4.868	4.564	4.288	4.039	3.812	3.605	3.416	3.242	3.083	2.937	2.802	2.677	2.263	7
8	7.325	6.733	6.210	5.747	5.335	4.968	4.639	4.344	4.078	3.837	3.619	3.421	3.241	3.076	2.925	2.786	2.331	8
9	8.162	7.435	6.802	6.247	5.759	5.328	4.946	4.607	4.303	4.031	3.786	3.566	3.366	3.184	3.019	2.868	2.379	9
10	8.983	8.111	7.360	6.710	6.145	5.650	5.216	4.833	4.494	4.192	3.923	3.682	3.465	3.269	3.092	2.930	2.414	10
11	9.787	8.760	7.887	7.139	6.495	5.938	5.453	5.029	4.656	4.327	4.035	3.776	3.543	3.335	3.147	2.978	2.438	11
12	10.575	9.385	8.384	7.536	6.814	6.194	5.660	5.197	4.793	4.439	4.127	3.851	3.606	3.387	3.190	3.013	2.456	12
13	11.348	9.986	8.853	7.904	7.103	6.424	5.842	5.342	4.910	4.533	4.203	3.912	3.656	3.427	3.223	3.040	2.469	13
14	12.106	10.563	9.295	8.244	7.367	6.628	6.002	5.468	5.008	4.611	4.265	3.962	3.695	3.459	3.249	3.061	2.478	14
15	12.849	11.118	9.712	8.559	7.606	6.811	6.142	5.575	5.092	4.675	4.315	4.001	3.726	3.483	3.268	3.076	2.484	15
16	13.578	11.652	10.106	8.851	7.824	6.974	6.265	5.668	5.162	4.730	4.357	4.033	3.751	3.503	3.283	3.088	2.489	16
17	14.292	12.166	10.477	9.122	8.022	7.120	6.373	5.749	5.222	4.775	4.391	4.059	3.771	3.518	3.295	3.097	2.492	17
18	14.992	12.659	10.828	9.372	8.201	7.250	6.467	5.818	5.273	4.812	4.419	4.080	3.786	3.529	3.304	3.104	2.494	18
19	15.678	13.134	11.158	9.604	8.365	7.366	6.550	5.877	5.316	4.843	4.442	4.097	3.799	3.539	3.311	3.109	2.496	19
20	16.351	13.590	11.470	9.818	8.514	7.469	6.623	5.929	5.353	4.870	4.460	4.110	3.808	3.546	3.316	3.113	2.497	20
21	17.011	14.029	11.764	10.017	8.649	7.562	6.687	5.973	5.384	4.891	4.476	4.121	3.816	3.551	3.320	3.116	2.498	21
22	17.658	14.451	12.042	10.201	8.772	7.645	6.743	6.011	5.410	4.909	4.488	4.130	3.822	3.556	3.323	3.118	2.498	22
23	18.292	14.857	12.303	10.371	8.883	7.718	6.792	6.044	5.432	4.925	4.499	4.137	3.827	3.559	3.325	3.120	2.499	23
24	18.914	15.247	12.550	10.529	8.985	7.784	6.835	6.073	5.451	4.937	4.507	4.143	3.831	3.562	3.327	3.121	2.499	24
25	19.523	15.622	12.783	10.675	9.077	7.843	6.873	6.097	5.467	4.948	4.514	4.147	3.834	3.564	3.329	3.122	2.499	25
26	20.121	15.983	13.003	10.810	9.161	7.896	6.906	6.118	5.480	4.956	4.520	4.151	3.837	3.566	3.330	3.123	2.500	26
27	20.707	16.330	13.211	10.935	9.237	7.943	6.935	6.136	5.492	4.964	4.524	4.154	3.839	3.567	3.331	3.123	2.500	27
28	21.281	16.663	13.406	11.051	9.307	7.984	6.961	6.152	5.502	4.970	4.528	4.157	3.840	3.568	3.331	3.124	2.500	28
29	21.844	16.984	13.591	11.158	9.370	8.022	6.983	6.166	5.510	4.975	4.531	4.159	3.841	3.569	3.332	3.124	2.500	29
30	22.396	17.292	13.765	11.258	9.427	8.055	7.003	6.177	5.517	4.979	4.534	4.160	3.842	3.569	3.332	3.124	2.500	30
35	24.999	18.665	14.498	11.655	9.644	8.176	7.070	6.215	5.539	4.992	4.541	4.164	3.845	3.571	3.333	3.125	2.500	35
40	27.355	19.793	15.046	11.925	9.779	8.244	7.105	6.233	5.548	4.997	4.544	4.166	3.846	3.571	3.333	3.125	2.500	40

*Payments (or receipts) at the end of each period.

B

Cost Accounting in Professional Examinations

This appendix describes the role of cost accounting in professional examinations. We use professional examinations in Canada, the United States, Australia, Japan, and the United Kingdom to illustrate the role.[1] A conscientious reader who has solved a representative sample of the problems at the end of the chapters will be well prepared for the professional examination questions dealing with cost accounting. This appendix aims to provide perspective, instill confidence, and encourage readers to take the examinations.

CANADIAN PROFESSIONAL EXAMINATIONS

Three professional accounting designations are available in Canada:

Designation	Sponsoring Organization
Certified Management Accountant (CMA)	Society of Management Accountants (SMA)
Certified General Accountant (CGA)	Certified General Accountants' Association (CGA)
Chartered Accountant (CA)	Canadian Institute of Chartered Accountants (CICA)

The CMA represents over 27,000 certified management accountants employed throughout Canadian business, industry, and government.

The CMA Entrance Examination is a two-day examination, divided into three broad categories:

1. Management accounting area   50%–60%
2. Financial accounting area   20%–30%
3. Management studies   15%–25%

Objective questions comprise 100% of the first examination and the second exam is a single complex case. Topics covered on recent examinations in the management accounting area include relevant costing, transfer pricing, capital budgeting, performance measures, activity-based costing, cost allocation, and productivity.

The Society of Management Accountants publishes *CMA: The Management Accounting Magazine* monthly. This magazine includes details of courses that assist students in preparing for the CMA examination.

---

[1] We appreciate help from Bill Langdon (Canada), Tom Craven (United States), John Goodwin (Australia), Michi Sakurai (Japan), and Louise Drysdale and Andrea Jeffries (U.K.).

CPA and CMA Designations

Many American readers may eventually take the Certified Public Accountant (CPA) examination or the Certified Management Accountant (CMA) examination. Certification is important to professional accountants for many reasons, such as the following:

1. Recognition of achievement and technical competence by fellow accountants and by users of accounting services
2. Increased self-confidence in one's professional abilities
3. Membership in professional organizations offering programs of career-long education
4. Enhancement of career opportunities
5. Personal satisfaction

The CPA certificate is issued by individual states; it is necessary for obtaining a state's licence to practise as a Certified Public Accountant. A prominent feature of public accounting is the use of independent (external) auditors to give assurance about the reliability of the financial statements supplied by managers. These auditors are called Certified Public Accountants in the United States and Chartered Accountants in many other English-speaking nations. The major U.S. professional association in the private sector that regulates the quality of external auditing is the American Institute of Certified Public Accountants (AICPA).

The CMA designation is offered by the Institute of Management Accountants (IMA). The IMA is the largest association of management accountants in the world.[2] The major objective of the CMA certification is to enhance the development of the management accounting profession. In particular, focus is placed on the modern role of the management accountant as an active contributor to and a participant in management. The CMA designation is gaining increased stature in the business community as a credential parallel to the CPA designation.

The CMA examination consists of 4 parts taken during 2 days (16 hours):

◆ Part 1: Economics, finance, and management
◆ Part 2: Financial accounting and reporting
◆ Part 3: Management reporting, analysis, and behavioural issues
◆ Part 4: Decision analysis and information systems

Questions regarding ethical issues will appear on any part of the examination. A person who has successfully completed the U.S. CPA examination is exempt from Part 2.

Cost/management accounting questions are prominent in the CMA examination. The CPA examination also includes such questions, although they are less extensive than questions regarding financial accounting, auditing, and business law. On the average, cost/managerial accounting represents 35% to 40% of the CMA examination and 5% of the CPA examination. This book includes many questions and problems used in past CMA and CPA examinations. Careful study of appropriate topics in this book will give candidates sufficient background for succeeding in the cost accounting portions of the professional examinations.

The IMA publishes *Management Accounting* monthly. Each issue includes advertisements for courses that help students prepare for the CMA examination.[3]

---

[2]The IMA has a wide range of activities driven by many committees. For example, the Management Accounting Practices Committee issues statements on both financial accounting and management accounting. The IMA also has an extensive continuing-education program.

[3]Other U.S. professional associations also require detailed knowledge of cost accounting. For example, the Certified Cost Estimator/Analyst (CCEA) program is administered by the Society of Cost Estimating and Analysis, 101 South Whiting Street, Suite 313, Alexandria, VA 22304. The society's primary purpose is to improve the effectiveness of cost estimation and price analysis. Special attention is given to contract cost estimation.

The Australian Society of Certified Practising Accountants is the largest body representing accountants in Australia. Their professional designation is termed a CPA (Certified Practising Accountant). The basic entry requirement for Associate membership of the Society is an approved Bachelors degree. Associates of the Society can advance to CPA status by passing the CPA program and having the required amount of relevant work experience. There are two compulsory core segments in the program. Core I covers the practical application of the more common accounting standards and ethics, while more technical standards (such as foreign currency translation) are covered in the Core II segment. Candidates are then required to take three segments from seven elective subjects. These subjects are (1) external reporting, (2) insolvency and reconstruction, (3) management accounting, (4) management of information systems, (5) auditing, (6) treasury, and (7) taxation. Personal financial planning and superannuation is a new elective subject that will soon be added to the electives.

The management accounting segment topics include:

1. Management accounting in the contemporary business environment
2. Accounting for strategic management
3. Long-term project planning and management
4. Costing for decision making
5. Performance measurement and reward systems

The Australian Accountant, published each month (except January), includes advertisements for courses that help students prepare for the CPA examination.

The Institute of Chartered Accountants in Australia (ICAA) has membership requirements that include passing four core modules (Taxation, Accounting I, Accounting II, and Ethics) and one elective module (one of which is Advanced Management Accounting). Management related topics are in both the Accounting II and Advanced Management Accounting modules. These include:

◆ purpose and perspective (including strategic and operational management; organizations, goals, ethics; operational environments; cost concepts);

◆ strategic management accounting (including strategic applications, project evaluation and capital budgeting);

◆ operational management accounting (including decision analysis, financial planning and management, product and service costing, control and performance evaluation).

There are two major management accounting organizations—Japanese Industrial Management and Accounting Association and Enterprise Management Association. The JIMAA is the oldest, largest, and most authoritative accounting organization of its kind in Japan. It directs a School of Cost Control and a School of Corporate Tax Accounting. There are two courses in the School of Cost Control—Preparatory Course and Cost Control Course. These courses are taught by university professors and executives from member corporations. The Enterprise Management Association is the Japanese chapter of the U.S.-based Institute of Management Accountants.

The Chartered Institute of Management Accountants (CIMA) is the largest professional management accounting body in the United Kingdom. CIMA provides a wide range of services to members in commerce, education, government, and the accounting profession.

The syllabus for the CIMA examination consists of four stages:

1. Preparation for business and accounting (including "foundation costing")
2. The tools of management accounting (including "operational cost accounting")
3. The rules of a profession (including "management accounting applications")
4. The application of knowledge to business management and finance (including "strategic management accounting" and "management accounting control systems")

Management Accounting, published monthly by CIMA, includes details of courses assisting students in preparing for their examinations.

Management accounting topics are also covered by several other professional bodies. The syllabus for the examinations of the Chartered Association of Certified Accountants (ACCA) has three stages: I (Foundation), II (Certificate), and III (Professional). Skills examined in III include information for control and decision making, management and strategy, and financial strategy. Other accounting bodies include the Institute of Chartered Accountants in England and Wales (ICAEW) and the Institute for Chartered Accountants of Scotland (ICAS). Both institutes have requirements that cover proficiency in "general management" topics as well as professional accounting topics.

NAME INDEX

Note: The names of the companies or people for which weblinks are provided are printed in **boldface**, as well as the page number on which the weblink appears.

Proctor & Gamble, 214, 743, 785–786
Publix Supermarkets, 938

Q
QLT Inc., 3, 8, 832
Quaker Oats, 924

R
Research In Motion (RIM), 3, **11**, 832
Rogers Cable, 16
Rogers Communications Inc., 1
Royal Air Force, 120
Royal Bank, 517
Royal Dutch/Shell, 673
Royal Navy, 120

S
Safeway.com, 532
Samsung, 515, 739, 830
Sandoz US, 251–254, 653
Schweppes, 625
Sears, 936
Sears Appliance Services, 47, 48
Sears Canada Inc., 40
SEC. *See* U.S. Securities and Exchange
    Commission
Seradex, 775
Shell Oil, 862
Sheraton Hotel, 918
Siemens Nixdorf, 517
Siemens VDO, 13
Singapore Airlines, 30
Sleeman, 7
SMAC Ontario, 19
Snapple Beverage, 199
SNC Lavalin, 739
Sobeys Inc., 775
Society of Management Accountants
    of Canada (SMAC), 17

Solectron, 748
Sony Corporation, 4, 5, 70, 430, 830
Southwest Airlines, 941
Standards Council of Canada, 739
Stantec, 812
Starbucks, 258, 940
Stern Stewart, 924
Stop and Shop, 532
Sullivan, Scott, 81, 939
The Sullivan Foundation, 940
Suncor, 882

T
Tektronix, 885
Telus, 470
Tilton, Glenn, 938
Tim Horton's, 217
TiVo, 743
Toronto Stock Exchange, 339
Torys LLP, 114
Toyota Motor Corporation, 4, 6, 428, 430,
    481, 492, 711, 724, 739, 748, 827
TransCanada Corporation, 940
TransMontaigne, 938
TRW, 936
Tyco International, 812, 937

U
UAL, 938
Unibroue, 7
Unilever Group, 743, 940
United Airlines, 299
United Van Lines, 750
U.S. Air Force, 120
U.S. Bureau of Labor Statistics, 431
U.S. Department of Defense (DoD), 32, 120
U.S. Department of Justice, 335, 564
U.S. Environmental Protection Agency, 724
U.S. Internal Revenue Service, 902, 903

U.S. Marine Corps, 120
U.S. Navy, 120
U.S. Postal Service, 380
U.S. Securities and Exchange Commission,
    335, 673, 937, 939

V
Venerus, Rob, 831
Verizon, 514, 832
Vinson, Betty, 939
VISA, 370, 782
Volkswagen, 791
Volkswagen Canada Inc., 559

W
Waddell, George, 559
Wal-Mart, 6, 750, 781
Wal-Mart Canada Corp., 10–11
Walker Mowers, 286
Wall Street Journal, 564
Watts, Philip, 673
Webvan, 532
Welch, Jack, 199
WestJet, 3, 7, 70, 830
Whirlpool Corporation, 936
Whistler-Blackcomb, 847
World Trade Organization, 469
World Wide Benchmarking
    Resource Guide, 266
WorldCom, 16, 69, 81, 937, 939
WS Industries, 172

Y
Yamazaki Mazak, 750, 751
YBM, 16
Yoplait Company, 13

Z
Zytec Corporation, 75

SUBJECT INDEX

Note: Key terms and the pages on which they are defined are printed in **boldface**.

foreign exchange rates, 218
four-variance analysis, 297–298
full-cost transfer prices, 893–894
full product cost recovery, 487
full product costs, 427

G

general ledger, 123
generally accepted accounting principles
    (GAAP), 2, 14
global perspectives
    absorption costing, 333
    activity-based costing (ABC), varying
      interest in, 170
    balanced scorecard, 523
    budget practices, 200–201
    capital budgeting, 826, 863
    cost allocation, 556
    cost-allocation bases for manufacturing
      overhead, 115
    cost-management methods, 488
    customer profitability analysis, 648
    electronics industry, rejection in, 711
    fixed costs, reduction of, 81
    management accountants, 12
    pricing practices, 488
    process-costing systems, 670
    risk adjustment methods, 863
    standard costs, 252
    supply-chain management, 787
    support department cost allocation, 572
    transfer-pricing practices, domestic and
      multinational, 897
    variable costing, 333
    variable costs *versus* fixed costs, 36
    variance analysis and control
      decisions, 299
goal-congruence, 884, 888
goal-congruence issues, 781
goal-incongruent decision making, 885
goodness of fit, 392
government
    contracting with government
      agencies, 50
    overcharging, 32
graph method, 74–75
graphic approach, 449
gross book value, 930
gross margin, 85
    versus contribution margin, 85–86
    manufacturing-sector companies, 86
    merchandising-sector companies, 85–86
gross margin percentage, 86
growth component of operating income,
    527–528
guidelines. *See* management accounting
    guidelines

H

half-year rule, 849, 855
heteroskedasticity, 396
high-low method, 374–375
homogeneous cost pools, 158, 561
homoskedasticity, 396
human aspects of budgeting, 217–218
hurdle rate, 816
hybrid-costing system, 689

I

idle time, 48
imputed costs, 922
incentives
    versus imposition of risk, 919–934
    intensity of, 934–935
income
    net income, 71
    operating income. *See* operating income
    target net income,and income taxes,
      76–77
    target operating income, 75–76
income statements
    absorption costing, 326–330
    budgeted income statement,
      211–211, 224
    contribution income statement, 72
    variable costing, 326–330
Income Tax Act, 849, 900
income tax cash effect, 853
income taxes
    amortization, 852–853
    average income tax rate, 848
    and capital budgeting, 848–857
    capital cost allowance. *See* capital cost
      allowance
    as cash flow consideration, 848
    as CFO responsibility, 14
    comparable uncontrolled price (CUP)
      method, 900
    complications, 852
    cost plus method (CPM), 900
    differential approach, 853, 857
    international financial centre, 900
    investment cash flows, impact on,
      849–852
    marginal income tax rate, 848
    multinational transfer pricing, 900–903
    operating cash flows, impact on, 848
    profit split (PSM) method, 900
    resale price method (RPM), 900
    target net income and, 76–77
    tax havens, 900
    tax minimization strategy, 900
    total-project approach, 853–857
    transactional net margin method
      (TNMM), 900
income-to-revenue (sales) ratio, 925
Income War Tax Act, 847
incremental cost-allocation method, 573
incremental costs, 425, 898
incremental revenue, 430
**incremental revenue-allocation method,
    628**–630
**incremental unit time learning model,
    383**–385
independence of residuals, 397, 398
independent variables, 372, 375, 390, 393
indirect-cost pools, 158–163
indirect-cost rate, 116, 121
indirect costs of a cost object, 12, 31
    adjusted allocation rate approach, 131
    budgeted indirect costs, 130–133
    cost allocation, 560–561
    design of operations, 33
    versus direct costs, 32
    end-of-period indirect costs, 130–133

examples, 38
factors affecting classifications, 32–33
information-gathering technology, 32
job costing, 115–116
materiality of cost, 32
overabsorbed indirect costs, 130
overallocated indirect costs, 130
overapplied indirect costs, 130
problems of, 31
proration approach, 131–133
and refined costing systems, 157
simultaneous classifications, 38
underabsorbed indirect costs, 130
underallocated indirect costs, 130
underapplied indirect costs, 130
write-off to cost of goods sold
    approach, 133
indirect labour costs, 47
indirect manufacturing costs, 40
industrial engineering method, 370
industry analysis, 514–515
inflation, 858
    and capital budgeting, 858–862
    effects on data, 387
    internal consistency, 859
    and net present value, 859–861
    nominal approach, 859–861
    nominal rate of return, 859
    real approach, 859–861
    real rate of return, 859
infobarn, 2
information
    and decision process, 421
    qualitative relevant information, 423
    quantitative relevant information, 423
    relevance, 422–424
    in responsibility accounting, 217
information-gathering technology, 32
information technology
    advancements, 157
    inventory data and, 775
    and standard costing, 262
infrastructure costs, 533
initial investment, 852
innovation, 7
innovation process, 518
input-efficiency variances, 249
input-price variances, 249
input quantities, 250–251
input suppliers, 514
inputs, 533
insourcing, 428
inspection costs, 559
inspection point, 712
interactive control systems, 941
intercept, 367
intermediate product, 887
internal audit, 14
internal-business-process perspective,
    517–518, 743–745, 749, 919
internal failure costs, 740
internal rate-of-return decision rule,
    866–868
internal rate of return (IRR), 817–819
international financial centre, 900
international perspective. *See* global
    perspectives

Photo Credits

Page 1, *Career Insider Accounting*, www.careerinsider.ca; Page 8, Federal Express Corporation; Page 29, Courtesy of DaimlerChrysler; Page 69, Photo Courtesy of Ford Canada; Page 82, Gail Albert Halaban/Corbis/SABA Press Photos, Inc.; Page 111, Barrett & MacKay Photography Inc.; Page 120, U.S. Air Force; Page 152, Ed Kashi/CORBIS; Page 173, Ariel Skelley/Corbis/Stock Market; Page 196, CP PHOTO/Adrian Wyld; Page 210, Rusty Jarrett/Getty Images, Inc.; Page 243, © Teri Stratford. All rights reserved; Page 255, Charles O'Rear/CORBIS; Page 285, Photo courtesy of Inco Limited; Page 323, Photo courtesy of Imperial Oil; Page 337, Brownie Harries/Corbis/Stock Market; Page 365, Image provided courtesy of Bombardier Inc.; Page 380, AP Wide World Photos; Page 420, Courtesy of Gildan; Page 469, © Glow Images/Alamy Images; Page 479, Michael Newman/PhotoEdit; Page 513, Frank Siteman/PhotoEdit; Page 532, Peapod, Inc.; Page 553, Courtesy of Bell Canada; Page 559, Courtesy Volkswagon Canada; Page 592, Photo courtesy of Hibernia, www.hibernia.ca; Page 596, © PHOTOTAKE/Alamy Images; Page 601, Peter Frischmuth/Argus/Peter Arnold, Inc.; Page 625, Courtesy the Watt Group, Toronto, Canada; Page 646, Jeff Greenberg/PhotoEdit; Page 653, Bill Aron/Photo Edit; Page 667, © High Liner Foods Inc; Page 690, Adidas—Salomon AG; Page 709, Thierry Dosogne/Iconica/Getty Images; Page 713, DuPont; Page 724, Lucas Schifres/Corbis/Stock Market; Page 738, NASA; Page 753, Jochen Tack/DAS FOTOARCHIV/Peter Arnold, Inc.; Page 774, Courtesy Challenger Motor Freight; Page 789, Harry How/Getty Images; Page 812, Strait Crossing Bridge Limited; Page 831, Mason Morfit/Getty Images, Inc.—Taxi; Page 847, CP Photo/Jonathan Hayward; Page 865, Courtesy Consumers Power Company; Page 867, AP/Wide World Photos; Page 882, Page 882, Superstock; Page 902, Bruce Hands/Getty Images, Inc.—Stone Allstock; Page 918, Superstock; Page 938, Laura Ranch/AP Wide World Photos.